ADIRONDACK COMMUNITY COLLEGE

W9-DII-440

The Oxford Dictionary of
Difficult Words

The Oxford Dictionary of
Difficult Words

Edited by Archie Hobson

OXFORD
UNIVERSITY PRESS
2001

OXFORD
UNIVERSITY PRESS

New York Oxford
Athens   Auckland   Bangkok   Bogotá
Buenos Aires   Kolkata   Cape Town   Chennai   Dar es Salaam
Delhi   Florence   Hong Kong   Istanbul   Karachi
Kuala   Lumpur   Madrid   Melbourne
Mexico City   Mumbai   Nairobi   Paris   São Paulo   Shanghai   Singapore
Taipei   Tokyo   Toronto   Warsaw

and associated companies in
Berlin   Ibadan

The Oxford Dictionary of Difficult Words is based on the New Oxford
American Dictionary, published in the United States in 2001.
© Oxford University Press 2001

Published by Oxford University Press, Inc., 198 Madison Avenue,
New York, New York 10016
www.oup-usa.org
www.askoxford.com

Oxford is a registered trademark of Oxford University Press.

All rights reserved. No part of this publication may be reproduced, stored in a retrieval system, or
transmitted in any form or by any means, electronic, mechanical, photocopying, recording, or
otherwise, without the prior permission of Oxford University Press.

Library of Congress Cataloging in Publication Data

Data available
ISBN 0-19-514673-5

This book includes some words that are, or are asserted to be, proprietary names or trademarks.
Their inclusion does not imply that they have acquired for legal purposes a nonproprietary or general
significance, nor is any other judgment implied concerning their legal status. In cases where the
editor has some evidence that a word is used as a proprietary name or trademark, this is indicated by
the designation trademark, but no judgment concerning the legal status of such words is made or
implied thereby.

10 9 8 7 6 5 4 3 2 1
Printed in the United States of America on acid-free paper

Contents

Preface

Everyday words we know as well as we know our own names, and we use them as naturally as breathing. But what about those thousands of other words that we can't quite commit to memory—but that come up all the time in reading, in meetings, or in the classroom? Words like lucubrate ('discourse learnedly in writing'), demesne ('land attached to a manor'), and cynosure ('a person or thing that is the center of attention or admiration') hover on the margins of our vocabularies. We run across such words from time to time, and when we do we may not know quite what they mean, or we simply draw a blank.

The *Oxford Dictionary of Difficult Words* presents the words we really need to know, without the added burden of those we never look up. The definitions are concise and clear, and are enhanced by sentences and phrases that show the word, or a certain sense of it, used in context. Usage notes are there to help make your use of words more precise and powerful.

This dictionary will help you understand words outside your everyday "working" vocabulary, words that are too learned, specialized, or highbrow for day-to-day usage. Abundant cross references help distinguish words that are related ('deism' and 'theism') or opposite ('esoteric' and 'exoteric'). The *Oxford Dictionary of Difficult Words* is a handy reference that can be carried with you to enhance your reading and learning experience wherever you go.

How to Use the
Oxford Dictionary of Difficult Words

The "entry map" below explains the different parts of an entry.

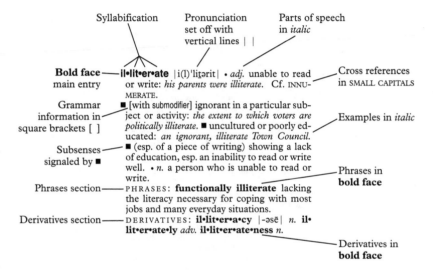

Syllabification

Pronunciation set off with vertical lines | |

Parts of speech in *italic*

Bold face main entry

Grammar information in square brackets [ ]

Subsenses signaled by ■

Phrases section

Derivatives section

il•lit•er•ate |i(l)ˈlit̬ərit| • *adj.* unable to read or write: *his parents were illiterate.* Cf. INNU-MERATE.
■ [with submodifier] ignorant in a particular subject or activity: *the extent to which voters are politically illiterate.* ■ uncultured or poorly educated: *an ignorant, illiterate Town Council.* ■ (esp. of a piece of writing) showing a lack of education, esp. an inability to read or write well. • *n.* a person who is unable to read or write.
PHRASES: **functionally illiterate** lacking the literacy necessary for coping with most jobs and many everyday situations.
DERIVATIVES: **il•lit•er•a•cy** |-əsē| *n.* **il•lit•er•ate•ly** *adv.* **il•lit•er•ate•ness** *n.*

Cross references in SMALL CAPITALS

Examples in *italic*

Phrases in **bold face**

Derivatives in **bold face**

Main entries and other boldface forms

Main entries appear in boldface type, as do inflected forms, idioms and phrases, and derivatives. The words PHRASES and DERIVATIVES introduce those elements. Main entries and derivatives of two or more syllables show syllabification with centered dots.

Parts of speech

Each new part of speech is introduced by a small centered dot.

Senses and subsenses

The main sense of each word follows the part of speech and any grammatical information (e.g., [trans.] before a verb definition). If there are two or more main senses for a word, these are numbered in boldface. Closely related subsenses of each main sense are introduced by a solid black box. In the entry for **illiterate** above, the main sense of "unable to read or write" is followed by several related senses, including "ignorant in a particular subject or activity" and "uncultured or poorly educated."

Example sentences

Example sentences are shown in italic typeface; certain common expressions appear in bold italic typeface within examples (e.g., "immunity from" in the example *the rebels were given **immunity from** prosecution*).

Cross references

Cross references to main entries appear in small capitals. For example, in the entry **illiterate** seen previously, a cross reference is given in small capitals to the entry for INNUMERATE.

Usage notes

Usage notes appear in boxes after the entry to which they refer:

> **lat•ter** | ˈlætər | • *adj.* [attrib.] **1** situated or occurring nearer to the end of something than to the beginning: *the latter half of 1989.*
> ■ belonging to the final stages of something, esp. of a person's life: *heart disease dogged his latter years.* ■ recent: *the project has had low cash flows in latter years.* **2** (**the latter**) denoting the second or second mentioned of two people or things: *the Russians could advance into either Germany or Austria—they chose the latter option.*
>
> USAGE: **Latter** means 'the second-mentioned of two.' Its use to mean 'the last-mentioned of three or more' is common, but is considered incorrect by some because **latter** means 'later' rather than 'latest.' *Last* or *last-mentioned* is preferred where three or more things are involved.

Appendix

A handy appendix at the back of the book features a list of prefixes, suffixes, and combining forms with a brief gloss of each form's meaning and examples of words in which it appears.

Staff

Managing Editor: Elizabeth J. Jewell

Senior Editor: Archie Hobson

Editors: Suzanne Stone Burke
Orin Hargraves
Christine Lindberg
Ramona Michaelis
Susan Norton

Pronunciation Editors: John Bollard
Linda Costa
Sharon Goldstein
Ellen Johnson
Rima McKinzey

Editorial Assistant: Karen Fisher

Proofreaders: Meredith Brosnan
Alan Hartley
Adrienne Makowski
Susan Sigalas

Data Entry: Teresa Ouellette
Kimberly Roberts

Key to the Pronunciations

This dictionary uses a simple respelling system to show how entries are pronounced, using the following symbols:

æ	*as in*	**hat** |hæt|, **fashion** |'fæsHən|, **carry** |'kærē|
ā	*as in*	**day** |dā|, **rate** |rāt|, **maid** |mād|, **prey** |prā|
ä	*as in*	**lot** |lät|, **father** |'fäTHər|, **barnyard** |'bärn͵yärd|
b	*as in*	**big** |big|
CH	*as in*	**church** |CHərCH|, **picture** |'pikCHər|
d	*as in*	**dog** |dôg|, **bed** |bed|
e	*as in*	**men** |men|, **bet** |bet|, **ferry** |'ferē|
ē	*as in*	**feet** |fēt|, **receive** |ri'sēv|
er	*as in*	**air** |er|, **care** |ker|
ə	*as in*	**about** |ə'bowt|, **soda** |'sōdə|, **mother** |'məTHər|, person |'pərsən|
f	*as in*	**free** |frē|, **graph** |græf|, **tough** |təf|
g	*as in*	**get** |get|, **exist** |ig'zist|, **egg** |eg|
h	*as in*	**her** |hər|, **behave** |bi'hāv|
i	*as in*	**guild** |gild|, **women** |'wimin|
ī	*as in*	**time** |tīm|, **fight** |fīt|, **guide** |gīd|, **hire** |hīr|
ir	*as in*	**ear** |ir|, **beer** |bir|, **pierce** |pirs|
j	*as in*	**judge** |jəj|, **carriage** |'kærij|
k	*as in*	**kettle** |'ketl̩|, **cut** |kət|
l	*as in*	**lap** |læp|, **cellar** |'selər|, **cradle** |'krādl|
m	*as in*	**main** |mān|, **dam** |dæm|
n	*as in*	**honor** |'änər|, **maiden** |'mādn|
NG	*as in*	**sing** |siNG|, **anger** |'æNGgər|
ō	*as in*	**go** |gō|, **promote** |prə'mōt|
ô	*as in*	**law** |lô|, **thought** |THôt|, **lore** |lôr|
oi	*as in*	**boy** |boi|, **noisy** |'noizē|
o͞o	*as in*	**wood** |wŏŏd|, **football** |'fŏŏt͵bôl|, **sure** |SHŏŏr|
o͞o	*as in*	**food** |fo͞od|, **music** |'myo͞ozik|
ow	*as in*	**mouse** |mows|, **coward** |'kowərd|
p	*as in*	**put** |pŏŏt|, **cap** |kæp|
r	*as in*	**run** |rən|, **fur** |fər|, **spirit** |'spirit|

s	*as in*	**sit** | sit|, **lesson** |'lesən|
SH	*as in*	**shut** | SHət|, **social** | 'sōSHəl|, **action** | 'ækSHən|
t	*as in*	**top** | täp|, **seat** | sēt|
ṯ	*as in*	**butter** | 'bəṯər|, **forty** | 'fôrṯē|, **bottle** | 'bäṯl|
TH	*as in*	**thin** |THin|, **truth** |tro͞oTH|
T̲H̲	*as in*	**then** |T̲H̲en|, **father** |'fäT̲H̲ər|
v	*as in*	**never** |'nevər|, **very** |'verē|
w	*as in*	**wait** |wāt|, **quick** |kwik|
(h)w	*as in*	**when** |(h)wen|, **which** |(h)wiCH|
y	*as in*	**yet** |yet|, **accuse** |ə'kyo͞oz|
z	*as in*	**zipper** |'zipər|, **musician** |myo͞o'ziSHən|
ZH	*as in*	**measure** |'mezHər|, **vision** |'vizHən|

Foreign Sounds

KH	*as in*	**Bach** | bäKH|
N	*as in*	**en route** |äN 'ro͞ot|, **Rodin** |rō'dæN|
œ	*as in*	**hors d'oeuvre** |ôr 'dœvrə|, **Goethe** | 'gœtə|
Y	*as in*	**Lully** |lY'lē|, **Utrecht** | 'Y͵treKHt|

Cutbacks

A hyphen will replace a section of a pronunciation when that section would be repeated redundantly. Cutbacks will occur primarily in three areas:

a) where the headword has a variant pronunciation:

quasiparticle \| ͵kwāzī'pärṯəkəl, ͵kwäzē-\|

b) in derivative blocks:

dangle \| 'dæNGgəl\|
dangler \|-glər\|
dangly \|-glē\|

Note: Cutbacks always refer back to the headword pronunciation, not the preceding derivative.

c) at irregular plurals:

parenthesis \|pə'renTHəsis\|
parentheses \|-͵sēz\|

Stress marks

Stress marks are placed before the affected syllable. The primary stress mark is a short vertical line above the letters ['] and signifies greater pronunciation emphasis should be placed on that syllable. The secondary stress mark is a short vertical line below the letters [͵] and signifies a weaker pronunciation emphasis.

Additional information

- Some pronunciations show a letter within parenthesis to indicate this as a variant pronunciation. For example, some people say the d in sandwich, others do not.

- Variant pronunciations, separated by semicolons, are generally listed with the more common pronunciation first.

- A hyphen sometimes serves to separate syllables where the pronunciation would otherwise be confusing.

- Generally, only the first of two identical headwords will have a pronunciation given.

- Where a derivative adds a common suffix to the headword, the derivative may not have a pronunciation. A pronunciation will not be shown for suffixes such as "-less," "-ness," "-ly," each time they appear in derivatives.

Aa

ab•a•cus |ˈæbəkəs| • *n.* (pl. **abacuses**) **1** an oblong frame with rows of wires or grooves along which beads (originally *calculi*) are slid, used for calculating. **2** (in architecture) the flat slab on top of a capital, supporting the architrave (the main horizontal beam).

a•base |əˈbās| • *v.* [trans.] behave in a way so as to belittle or degrade (someone): *I watched my colleagues **abasing themselves** before the board of trustees.*
DERIVATIVES: **a•base•ment** *n.*

a•bash |əˈbasH| • *v.* [trans.] [usu. as adj.] (**abashed**) cause to feel embarrassed, disconcerted, or ashamed: *she was not abashed at being caught.*
DERIVATIVES: **a•bash•ment** *n.*

a•bate |əˈbāt| • *v.* [intrans.] (of something perceived as hostile, threatening, or negative) become less intense or widespread: *the storm suddenly abated.* ■ [trans.] cause to become smaller or less intense: *nothing abated his crusading zeal.* ■ [trans.] (in law) lessen, reduce, or remove (a nuisance): *this action would not have been sufficient to abate the odor nuisance.*

ab•at•toir |ˈæbəˌtwär| • *n.* a slaughterhouse.

ab•bre•vi•ate |əˈbrēvēˌāt| • *v.* [trans.] (usu. **be abbreviated**) shorten (a word, phrase, or text): *the business of artists and repertory, commonly abbreviated A&R* | [as adj.] (**abbreviated**) *an abbreviated version of the earlier work.* Cf. ABRIDGE.

ab•di•cate |ˈæbdiˌkāt| • *v.* [intrans.] (of a monarch) renounce one's throne: *in 1918 Kaiser Wilhelm abdicated as German emperor* | [trans.] *Ferdinand abdicated the throne in favor of the emperor's brother.* ■ [trans.] fail to fulfill or undertake (a responsibility or duty): *the government was accused of abdicating its responsibility* | [intrans.] *faced with possible controversy, the editors abdicated and ran an unrelated story.*
DERIVATIVES: **ab•di•ca•tion** |-ˈkāSHən| *n.*

ab•do•men |ˈæbdəmən; æbˈdōmən| • *n.* the part of the body of a vertebrate containing the digestive organs; the belly. In humans and other mammals it is contained between the diaphragm and the pelvis. ■ Zoology the posterior part of an arthropod's body, esp. the segments of an insect's body behind the thorax.
DERIVATIVES: **ab•dom•i•nal** |æbˈdämənl| *adj.*

ab•duct |æbˈdəkt| • *v.* [trans.] **1** take (someone) away illegally by force or deception; kidnap: *the executive who disappeared may have been abducted.* **2** (of a muscle) move (a limb or part) away from the midline of the body or from another part.
DERIVATIVES: **ab•duc•tion** *n.* **ab•duc•tor** *n.*

a•beam |əˈbēm| • *adv.* on a line at right angles to a ship's or an aircraft's length.

■ (**abeam of**) opposite the middle of (a ship or aircraft): *she was lying almost abeam of us.*

a•be•ce•dar•i•an |ˌābēsēˈderēən| • *adj.* **1** arranged alphabetically: *in abecedarian sequence.* **2** rudimentary; elementary: *had only an abecedarian understanding of the technology.* • *n.* a person who is just learning; a novice.

ab•er•rant |ˈæbərənt; əˈber-| • *adj.* departing from an accepted standard: *aberrant behavior.* ■ diverging from the normal type: *aberrant chromosomes.*
DERIVATIVES: **ab•er•rance** *n.* **ab•er•ran•cy** |-ənsē| *n.* **ab•er•rant•ly** *adv.*

ab•er•ra•tion |ˌæbəˈrāSHən| • *n.* a departure from what is normal, usual, or expected, typically one that is unwelcome. ■ a person whose beliefs or behavior are unusual or unacceptable. ■ a departure from someone's usual moral character or mental ability, typically for the worse. ■ (in biology) a characteristic that deviates from the normal type. ■ the failure of light rays to converge at one focus because of a defect in a lens or mirror. ■ the apparent displacement of a celestial object from its true position, caused by the relative motion of the observer and the object.
DERIVATIVES: **ab•er•ra•tion•al** |-SHəl| *adj.*

a•bet |əˈbet| • *v.* (**abetted, abetting**) [trans.] encourage or assist (someone) to do something wrong, in particular, to commit a crime or other offense: *he was found guilty of **aiding and abetting** others.*
DERIVATIVES: **a•bet•ment** *n.* **a•bet•tor** |əˈbetər| (also **a•bet•ter**) *n.*

a•bey•ance |əˈbāəns| • *n.* a state of temporary disuse or suspension: *matters were **held in abeyance** pending further inquiries.* ■ (in legal use) the position of being without, or waiting for, an owner or claimant: *the estate is in abeyance.*
DERIVATIVES: **a•bey•ant** |əˈbāənt| *adj.*

ab•hor |æbˈhôr| • *v.* (**abhorred, abhorring**) [trans.] regard with disgust and hatred.
DERIVATIVES: **ab•hor•rer** *n.*

ab•hor•rent |æbˈhôrənt; -ˈhär-| • *adj.* inspiring disgust and loathing; repugnant: *snakes are abhorrent to many.*

a•bide |əˈbīd| • *v.* **1** [intrans.] (**abide by**) accept or act in accordance with (a rule, decision, or recommendation): *I said I would abide by their decision.* **2** [trans.] (**can/could not abide**) be unable to tolerate (someone or something): *if there is one thing I cannot abide it is a lack of discipline.* **3** [intrans.] (of a feeling or a memory) continue without fading or being lost. ■ live; dwell.

ab in•i•ti•o |ˌæb əˈnisHēˌō| • *adv.* from the beginning (used chiefly in formal or legal contexts): *the agreement should be declared void ab initio.* • *adj.* [attrib.] starting from the beginning: *he was instructing ab initio pilots.*

a•bi•ot•ic |ˌābīˈätik| • adj. physical rather than biological; not derived from living organisms.
■ devoid of life; sterile. Cf. BIOTA.

ab•ject |ˈæbˌjekt; æbˈjekt| • adj. **1** [attrib.] (of a situation or condition) extremely bad, unpleasant, and degrading: *abject poverty.*
■ (of an unhappy state of mind) experienced to the maximum degree: *his letter plunged her into abject misery.* ■ (of a failure) absolute and humiliating. **2** (of a person or their behavior) completely without pride or dignity; self-abasing: *an abject apology.*
DERIVATIVES: **ab•jec•tion** |æbˈjekSHən| n. **ab•ject•ly** adv. **ab•ject•ness** n.

ab•jure |æbˈjoŏr| • v. [trans.] solemnly renounce (a belief, cause, or claim): *to abjure the Catholic faith.*
DERIVATIVES: **ab•ju•ra•tion** |ˌæbjəˈrāSHən| n.

ab•la•tion |əˈblāSHən| • n. **1** the surgical removal of body tissue. **2** the removal of snow and ice by melting or evaporation, typically from a glacier or iceberg.
■ the erosion of rock, typically by wind action.
DERIVATIVES: **ab•late** |əˈblāt| v.

ab•la•tive |ˈæblətiv| • adj. [attrib.] **1** relating to or denoting a case (esp. in Latin) of nouns and pronouns (and words in grammatical agreement with them) indicating separation or an agent, instrument, or location. **2** (of surgical treatment) involving ablation. **3** of, relating to, or subject to ablation through melting or vaporization: *the spacecraft's ablative heat shield.* • n. a word in the ablative case.
■ (**the ablative**) the ablative case.

ab•laut |ˈæblowt| • n. a change of vowel in related words or forms, e.g., in Germanic strong verbs (e.g., in *sing, sang, sung*).

ab•lu•tion |əˈblooSHən| • n. (usu. **ablutions**) the act of washing oneself (often used for humorously formal effect). *the women performed their ablutions.*
■ a ceremonial act of washing parts of the body or sacred containers.
DERIVATIVES: **ab•lute** v. **ab•lu•tion•ar•y** |-ˌnerē| adj.

ab•ne•gate |ˈæbniˌgāt| • v. [trans.] renounce or reject (something desired, expected, or valuable): *attempts to abnegate personal responsibility.*
DERIVATIVES: **ab•ne•ga•tor** |-ˌgātər| n.

ab•ne•ga•tion |ˌæbniˈgāSHən| • n. the act of renouncing or rejecting something: *abnegation of political power.*
■ (also **self-abnegation**) self-denial.

ab•nor•mal |æbˈnôrməl| • adj. deviating from what is normal or usual, typically in a way that is undesirable or worrying: *the patient's abnormal behavior.*
DERIVATIVES: **ab•nor•mal•ly** adv.

a•bol•ish |əˈbäliSH| • v. [trans.] formally put an end to (a system, practice, or institution): *the monarchy was abolished in 1959.*
DERIVATIVES: **a•bol•ish•er** n. **a•bol•ish•ment** n. **a•bo•li•tion** n.

ab•o•li•tion•ist |ˌæbəˈliSHənist| • n. a person who favors the abolition of a practice or institution, esp. capital punishment or (in US history, usu. **Abolutionist**) slavery.
DERIVATIVES: **ab•o•li•tion•ism** n.

a•bom•i•na•ble |əˈbäm(ə)nəbəl| • adj. causing moral revulsion: *the Gestapo's abominable cruelty.*
■ informal very unpleasant: *a cup of abominable soup.*
DERIVATIVES: **a•bom•i•na•bly** |-blē| adv.

a•bom•i•nate |əˈbäməˌnāt| • v. [trans.] regard with intense aversion; detest; loathe.
DERIVATIVES: **a•bom•i•na•tor** |-ˌnātər| n.

a•bom•i•na•tion |əˌbäməˈnāSHən| • n. a thing that causes disgust or hatred: *the Pharisees regarded Gentiles as an abomination to God* | *concrete abominations masquerading as hotels.*
■ a feeling of hatred: *their abomination of indulgence.*

ab•o•rig•i•nal |ˌæbəˈrijənl| • adj. (of peoples, animals, and plants) inhabiting or existing in a land from the earliest times or from before the arrival of colonists; indigenous.
■ (**Aboriginal**) of or relating to the Australian Aboriginals or their languages. • n. an aboriginal inhabitant of a place.
■ (**Aboriginal**) a person belonging to one of the indigenous peoples of Australia. any of the numerous Australian Aboriginal languages.

USAGE: **Aboriginals** (rather than **Aborigines**) is now the preferred plural form when referring to Australian Aboriginal peoples.

a•bor•ti•fa•cient |əˌbôrtəˈfāSHənt| • adj. (chiefly of a drug) causing abortion. • n. an abortifacient drug.

a•bor•tive |əˈbôrtiv| • adj. **1** failing to produce the intended result: *Pat made two abortive attempts at suicide.* **2** (of an organ or organism) rudimentary; arrested in development: *abortive medusae.*
■ (of a virus infection) failing to produce symptoms. ■ acting to counter the development of a disease. **3** [attrib.] causing or resulting in abortion: *abortive techniques.*
DERIVATIVES: **a•bor•tive•ly** adv.

ab o•vo |æb ōvō; äb| • adv. from the very beginning.

a•brade |əˈbrād| • v. [trans.] scrape or wear away by friction or erosion: *a landscape slowly abraded by a fine, stinging dust.*
DERIVATIVES: **a•brad•er** n. **a•bra•sion** n.

a•bra•sive |əˈbrāsiv; -ziv| • adj. (of a substance or material) capable of polishing or cleaning a hard surface by rubbing or grinding.
■ tending to rub or graze the skin: *the trees were abrasive to the touch.* ■ (of sounds or music) rough to the ear; harsh: *fast abrasive rhthyms.*
■ (of a person or manner) showing little concern for the feelings of others; harsh: *her abrasive and arrogant personal style won her few friends.* • n. a substance used for grinding, polishing, or cleaning a hard surface.

a•bridge |əˈbrij| • v. [trans.] (usu. **be abridged**) **1** shorten (a book, movie, speech, or other text) without substantially compro-

mising the sense: *the 900-page novel has been abridged* | [as adj.] (**abridged**) *an abridged text of the speech.* **2** curtail (rights or privileges): *even the right to free speech can be abridged.*
DERIVATIVES: **a•bridg•er** *n.* **a•bridg•ment** (also **a•bridge•ment**) *n.*

ab•ro•gate |ˈæbrəˌgāt| • *v.* [trans.] repeal or do away with (a law, right, or formal agreement): *a proposal to abrogate the right to strike.*
DERIVATIVES: **ab•ro•ga•tion** |ˌæbrəˈgā-sHən| *n.*

ab•rup•tion |əˈbrəpsHən| • *n.* the sudden breaking away of a portion from a mass.
■ (also **placental abruption**) separation of the placenta from the wall of the uterus, esp. when it occurs prematurely during pregnancy.

ab•scess |ˈæbˌses| • *n.* a swollen area within body tissue, caused by infection, containing an accumulation of pus.

ab•scis•sion |æbˈsizHən| • *n.* **1** a cutting off or violent separation. **2** the natural detachment of parts of a plant, typically dead leaves and ripe fruit.
DERIVATIVES: **ab•scind** *v.* **ab•scise** |-ˈsīz| *v.*

ab•scond |æbˈskänd| • *v.* [intrans.] leave hurriedly and secretly, typically to avoid detection of or arrest for an unlawful action such as theft: *she absconded with the remaining thousand dollars.*
■ (of someone on bail) fail to surrender oneself for custody at the appointed time. ■ (of a person kept in detention or under supervision) escape: *176 detainees absconded.*
DERIVATIVES: **ab•scond•er** *n.*

ab•sinthe |ˈæbˌsinTH| (also **absinth**) • *n.* **1** the shrub wormwood (*Artemisium absinthium*).
■ an essence made from this. **2** a potent green aniseed-flavored liqueur that turns milky when water is added. Prepared from wormwood, it is now largely banned because of its toxicity.

ab•so•lute |ˈæbsəˌlo͞ot; ˌæbsəˈlo͞ot| • *adj.* **1** not qualified or diminished in any way; total: *absolute secrecy* | *the attention he gave you was absolute.*
■ used for general emphasis when expressing an opinion: *the policy is absolute folly.* ■ (of powers or rights) not subject to any limitation; unconditional: *no one dared challenge her absolute authority* | *human right to life is absolute.* ■ (of a ruler) having unrestricted power: *he proclaimed himself absolute monarch.* ■ (of a legal decree) final: *the decree of nullity was made absolute.* ■ (in law, of title to ownership or a lease) guaranteed. **2** viewed or existing independently and not in relation to other things; not relative or comparative: *absolute moral standards.*
■ (of a grammatical construction) syntactically independent of the rest of the sentence, as in *dinner being over, we left the table.* ■ (of a transitive verb) used without an expressed object (e.g., *guns kill*). ■ (of an adjective) used without an expressed noun (e.g., *the brave*). • *n.* (in philosophy) a value or principle that

is regarded as universally valid or that may be viewed without relation to other things: *good and evil are presented as absolutes.*
■ (**the absolute**) that which exists without being dependent on anything else. ■ (**the absolute**) Theology ultimate reality; God.
DERIVATIVES: **ab•so•lute•ness** *n.*

ab•so•lute mu•sic • *n.* instrumental music composed solely as music and not intended to represent or illustrate literature, painting, or any extraneous idea.

ab•so•lu•tion |ˌæbsəˈlo͞osHən| • *n.* formal release from guilt, obligation, or punishment.
■ an ecclesiastical declaration of forgiveness of sins: *the priest administered absolution.*

ab•so•lut•ism |ˈæbsələˌtizəm| • *n.* the acceptance of or belief in absolute principles in political, philosophical, ethical, or theological matters.
DERIVATIVES: **ab•so•lut•ist** *n.* & *adj.*

ab•so•lut•ize |ˈæbsələˌtīz| • *v.* [trans.] make (or treat as) absolute.
DERIVATIVES: **ab•so•lut•i•za•tion** |ˌæbsəˌlo͞oti'zāsHən| *n.*

ab•solve |əbˈzälv; -ˈzôlv; -ˈsälv; -ˈsôlv| • *v.* [trans.] set or declare (someone) free from blame, guilt, or responsibility: *the pardon absolved them of any crimes.*
■ (in Christian theology) give absolution for (a sin).

ab•sorb |əbˈzôrb; -ˈsôrb| • *v.* [trans.] **1** take in or soak up (energy, or a liquid or other substance) by chemical or physical action, typically gradually: *buildings can be designed to absorb and retain heat* | *steroids are absorbed into the bloodstream.* Cf. ADSORB.
■ take in and assimilate (information, ideas, or experience): *she absorbed the information in silence.* ■ take control of (a smaller or less powerful entity), making it a part of oneself by assimilation: *the family firm was absorbed into a larger group.* ■ use or take up (time or resources): *arms spending absorbs roughly 2 percent of the national income.* ■ take up and reduce the effect or intensity of (sound or an impact). **2** engross the attention of (someone): *the work absorbed him and continued to make him happy.*
DERIVATIVES: **ab•sorb•er** *n.* **ab•sorp•tion** *n.*

ab•squat•u•late |ˌæbˈskwäCHəˌlāt| • *v.* leave abruptly: *the overthrown dictator absquatulated to the US.*
DERIVATIVES: **ab•squat•u•la•tion** |æb ˌskwäCHə'lāsHən| *n.*

ab•stain |əbˈstān; æb-| • *v.* [intrans.] **1** restrain oneself from doing or enjoying something: *abstaining from chocolate.*
■ refrain from drinking alcohol. **2** formally decline to vote either for or against a proposal or motion.
DERIVATIVES: **ab•stain•er** *n.* **ab•sten•tion** *n.*

ab•ste•mi•ous |æbˈstēmēəs; əb-| • *adj.* not self-indulgent, esp. when eating and drinking.
DERIVATIVES: **ab•ste•mi•ous•ly** *adv.* **ab•ste•mi•ous•ness** *n.* **ab•sten•tion** *n.*

ab•sti•nence |'æbstənəns| • *n.* the fact or practice of restraining oneself from indulging in something, typically alcohol: *six years of abstinence.*
DERIVATIVES: **ab•sti•nent** *adj.* **ab•sti•nent•ly** *adv.*

ab•stract • *adj.* |əb'strækt; 'æb,strækt| existing in thought or as an idea but not having a physical or concrete existence: *abstract concepts such as love or beauty.*
■ dealing with ideas rather than events. ■ not based on a particular instance; theoretical. ■ (of a word, esp. a noun) denoting an idea, quality, or state rather than a concrete object: *abstract words like truth or equality.* ■ (in the arts) characterized by lack of, or freedom from, representational qualities. • *v.* |æb'strækt| [trans.] **1** consider (something) theoretically or separately from something else: *to abstract religion from its historical context can be misleading.*
■ [intrans.] form a general idea in this way: *to attempt to form a general policy by abstracting from particulars.* **2** extract or remove (something): *applications to abstract more water from streams.*
■ used euphemistically to say that someone has stolen something: *his pockets contained all he had been able to abstract from the apartment.* ■ (**abstract oneself**) withdraw: *as our relationship developed you seemed to abstract yourself.* **3** make a written summary of (an article or book). • *n.* |'æb,strækt| **1** a summary or statement of the contents of a book, article, or formal speech: *the abstracts must be as concise as possible.* **2** an abstract work of art: *a big unframed abstract.* **3** (**the abstract**) that which is abstract; the theoretical consideration of something: *the abstract must be made concrete by examples.*
PHRASES: **in the abstract** in a general way; without reference to specific instances.
DERIVATIVES: **ab•stract•ly** *adv.* **ab•stract•er** |-tər| *n.*

ab•struse |əb'strōōs; æb'strōōs| • *adj.* difficult to understand; obscure. Cf. ARCANE, RECONDITE.
DERIVATIVES: **ab•struse•ly** |əb'strōōslē; æb'strōōslē| *adv.* **ab•struse•ness** |əb'strōōsnəs; æb'strōōsnəs| *n.*

ab•surd•ism |əb'sərd,izəm; -'zərd-| • *n.* **1** the belief that human beings exist in a purposeless, chaotic universe. **2** expression of such a belief in the arts. **3** an instance of such expression.
DERIVATIVES: **ab•surd•ist** *adj. & n.*

a•bu•li•a |ə'bōōlēə| (also **aboulia**) • *n.* an absence of willpower or an inability to act decisively, as a symptom of mental illness.

a•buse • *v.* |ə'byōōz| [trans.] **1** use (something) to bad effect or for a bad purpose; misuse.
■ make excessive and habitual use of (alcohol or drugs, esp. illegal ones). **2** treat (a person or an animal) with cruelty or violence, esp. regularly or repeatedly.
■ assault (someone, esp. a woman or child) sexually. [as adj.] (**abused**) *abused children.*

■ use or treat in such a way as to cause damage or harm: *he had been abusing his body for years.* ■ speak in an insulting and offensive way to or about (someone). • *n.* |ə'byōōs| **1** the improper use of something: *alcohol abuse* | *an abuse of public funds.*
■ unjust or corrupt practice: *protection against fraud and abuse* | *human rights abuses.* **2** cruel and violent treatment of a person or animal: *a black eye and other signs of physical abuse.*
■ violent treatment involving sexual assault, esp. on a repeated basis: *young people who have suffered sexual abuse.* ■ insulting and offensive language: *waving his fists and hurling abuse at the other driver.*

a•bu•sive |ə'byōōsiv; -ziv| • *adj.* **1** extremely offensive and insulting: *the starting pitcher was ejected for using abusive language* | *he became quite abusive and swore at her.* **2** engaging in or characterized by habitual violence and cruelty: *abusive parents* | *an abusive relationship.* **3** involving injustice or illegality: *the abusive and predatory practices of businesses.*
DERIVATIVES: **a•bu•sive•ly** *adv.* **a•bu•sive•ness** *n.*

a•but |ə'bət| • *v.* (**abutted, abutting**) [trans.] (of an area of land or a building) be next to or have a common boundary with: *gardens abutting Madison Avenue* | [intrans.] *a park abutting on an area of wasteland.* Cf. ADJOIN, ADJACENT.
■ touch or lean upon: *masonry may crumble where a roof abuts it.*

a•bys•mal |ə'bizməl| • *adj.* **1** extremely bad; appalling: *the quality of her work is abysmal.* **2** very deep.
DERIVATIVES: **a•bys•mal•ly** *adv.*

a•byss |ə'bis| • *n.* a deep or seemingly bottomless chasm: *a rope led down into the dark abyss* | *I was stagnating in an abyss of boredom.*
■ a wide or profound difference between people; a gulf: *the abyss between the two nations.* ■ the regions of hell conceived of as a bottomless pit: *Satan's dark abyss.* ■ (**the abyss**) a catastrophic situation seen as likely to occur: *teetering on the edge of the abyss of a political wipeout.*

a•byss•al |ə'bisəl| • *adj.* relating to or denoting the depths or bed of the ocean, esp. at depths between about 10,000 and 20,000 feet.
■ relating to or occurring at great depth in the earth's crust: *abyssal rocks.*

ac•a•deme |,ækə'dēm; 'ækə,dēm| • *n.* the academic environment or community; academia.

ac•a•de•mi•cian |,ækədə'miSHən; ə,kædə-| • *n.* a teacher or scholar; an intellectual; a member of an academy.

a•cad•e•my |ə'kædəmē| • *n.* (pl. **-ies**) **1** a place of study or training in a special field: *a police academy.*
■ any place of study. ■ a secondary school, typically a private one: *he had passed all his finals at Greenville Academy.* ■ (**the Academy**) the teaching school founded by Plato. ■ Plato's followers or philosophical system. **2** a society or institution of distinguished scholars,

artists, or scientists, that aims to promote and maintain standards in its particular field: *the National Academy of Sciences.*
■ (**Académie française** or **French Academy**) an official body, established in the 1630s, whose primary role has been to "protect" the French language against perceived threats to its purity. ■ the community of scholars; academe: *a writing and publishing world outside the academy.*
A•ca•di•an |ə'kādēən| • *adj.* of or relating to historical Acadia (later, Nova Scotia) or its people. • *n.* a native or inhabitant of Acadia.
■ a French-speaking descendant of the early French settlers in Acadia. ■ a descendant of the deported Acadians who settled in Louisiana in the 18th century; a CAJUN.
a cap•pel•la |ˌä kə'pelə| • *adj.* & *adv.* (with reference to choral music) without instrumental accompaniment: [as adj.] *an a cappella Mass* | [as adv.] *the trio usually performs a cappella.*
ac•cede |æk'sēd| • *v.* [intrans.] **1** assent or agree to a demand, request, or treaty: *the authorities did not accede to the strikers' demands.* **2** assume an office or position: *he acceded to the post of director in September* | *Elizabeth I acceded to the throne in 1558.*
■ become a member of a community or organization.
ac•cel•er•an•do |äkˌselə'rändō; ˌä,CHelə-| • *adj.* & *adv.* (in music) with a gradual increase of speed (used chiefly as a direction). • *n.* (pl. accelerandos or accelerandi |-dē|) a passage to be performed with such an acceleration.
ac•cent • *n.* |'ækˌsent| **1** a distinctive mode of pronunciation of a language, esp. one associated with a particular nation, locality, or social class: *spoke English with a strong German accent.*
■ the mode of pronunciation used by native speakers of a language: *she never mastered the French accent.* **2** a distinct emphasis given to a syllable or word in speech by stress or pitch.
■ a mark on a letter or word to indicate pitch, stress, or vowel quality. ■ (in music) an emphasis on a particular note or chord. **3** [in sing.] a special or particular emphasis: *the accent is on participation.*
■ a feature that gives a distinctive visual emphasis to something: *blue woodwork and accents of red.* • *v.* |'ækˌsent; æk'sent| [trans.] emphasize (a particular feature): *fabrics that accent the background colors in the room.*
■ play (a musical note, a beat of the bar, etc.) with an accent.
DERIVATIVES: **ac•cen•tu•al** |æk'senCHəw-əl| *adj.*
ac•cen•tu•ate |æk'senCHəˌwāt| • *v.* [trans.] make more noticeable or prominent.
ac•cept |æk'sept| • *v.* [trans.] **1** (in law) give an affirmative answer to (an offer or proposal), thus entering into a contract: *I accepted their salary offer.* **2** agree to pay (a draft or bill of exchange at maturity) by signing it.

DERIVATIVES: **ac•cept•ance** *n.* **ac•cept•er** *n.*
ac•cess |'ækˌ ses| • *n.* **1** a means of approaching or entering a place: *the staircase gives access to the top floor* | *wheelchair access* | *the building has a side access.*
■ the right or opportunity to use or benefit from something: *do you have access to a computer?* | *awards to help people gain access to training.* ■ the right or opportunity to approach or see someone: *we were denied access to our grandson.* ■ the action or process of obtaining or retrieving information stored in a computer's memory. ■ the condition of being able to be reached or obtained: *a campaign to improve access for the disabled.* ■ [as adj.] denoting noncommercial broadcasting produced by local independent groups, rather than by professionals: *public-access television.* **2** [in sing.] an attack or outburst of an emotion: *I was suddenly overcome with an access of rage.* • *v.* [trans.] (usu. **be accessed**) **1** (in computing) obtain, examine, or retrieve (data or a file). **2** approach or enter (a place): *single rooms have private baths accessed via the balcony.*

USAGE: Although the verb **access** is standard and common in computing and related terminology, the word is primarily a noun. Outside computing contexts its use as a verb in the sense of 'approach or enter a place' is often regarded as nonstandard (*you must use a password to access the account*). Even weaker is its use in an abstract sense (*access the American dream*). It is usually clear enough to say 'enter' or 'gain access to.'

ac•ces•si•ble |æk'sesəbəl| • *adj.* **1** (of a place) able to be reached or entered: *the town is accessible by bus* | *a building made accessible to disabled people.*
■ (of an object, service, or facility) able to be easily obtained or used: *making learning opportunities more accessible to adults.* ■ easily understood: *this Latin grammar is lucid and accessible.* **2** (of a person, typically one in a position of authority or importance) friendly and easy to talk to.
DERIVATIVES: **ac•ces•si•bil•i•ty** |-ˌsesə'bilitē| *n.* **ac•ces•si•bly** |-blē| *adv.*
ac•ces•sion |æk'seSHən| • *n.* **1** the attainment or acquisition of a position of rank or power, typically that of monarch or president: *Elizabeth's accession to the throne.*
■ the action or process of formally joining or being accepted by an association, institution, or group: *the accession of Alaska into the Union.* **2** a new item added to an existing collection of books, paintings, or artifacts.
■ an amount added to an existing quantity of something: *did not anticipate any further accession of wealth from the estate.* **3** the formal acceptance of a treaty or agreement: *accession to the Treaty of Paris.* • *v.* [trans.] (usu. **be accessioned**) record (a new item) as an addition to a library, museum, or other collection.
ac•ces•so•ry |æk'ses(ə)rē| • *n.* (pl. **-ies**) **1** a thing that can be added to something else in

order to make it more useful, versatile, or attractive: *a range of bathroom accessories.*
■ a small article or item of clothing carried or worn to complement a garment or outfit. **2** (in legal use) someone who gives assistance to the perpetrator of a crime, without directly committing it: *she was charged as an accessory to murder.* • *adj.* [attrib.] contributing to or aiding an activity or process in a minor way; subsidiary or supplementary.

ac•cip•i•ter |æk'sipitər| • *n.* a hawk of a group distinguished by short, broad wings and relatively long legs.

ac•claim |ə'klām| • *v.* [trans.] (usu. **be acclaimed**) praise enthusiastically and publicly: *the conference was acclaimed as a considerable success* | [with obj. and complement] *he was acclaimed a great painter.* • *n.* enthusiastic and public praise: *she has won acclaim for her commitment to democracy.*

ac•cla•ma•tion |ˌæklə'māsHən| • *n.* loud and enthusiastic approval, typically to welcome or honor someone or something.

ac•cli•mate |'æklə,māt| • *v.* [intrans.] (usu. **be acclimated**) become accustomed to a new climate or to new conditions: *it will take a few days to get acclimated to the altitude.* ((also **acclimatize**)
■ respond physiologically or behaviorally to a change in a single environmental factor: *trees may acclimate to high CO_2 levels by reducing the number of stomata.*
DERIVATIVES: **ac•cli•ma•tion** |ˌæklə'māsHən| *n.*

ac•cli•ma•tize |ə'klīmə,tīz| • *v.* [intrans.] acclimate: *they acclimatized themselves before ascending Everest.*
■ (in biology) respond physiologically or behaviorally to changes in a complex of environmental factors. Compare with ACCLIMATE.
■ [trans.] inure (a plant) to cold.
DERIVATIVES: **ac•cli•ma•ti•za•tion** |əˌklīməti'zāsHən| *n.*

ac•cliv•i•ty |ə'klivitē| • *n.* (pl. **-ies**) an upward slope. Cf. DECLIVITY.
DERIVATIVES: **ac•cliv•i•tous** |-itəs| *adj.*

ac•co•lade |'ækə,lād; -läd| • *n.* **1** an award or privilege granted as a special honor or as an acknowledgment of merit: *the ultimate accolade of a visit by the president.*
■ an expression of praise or admiration. **2** a touch on a person's shoulders with a sword at the bestowing of a knighthood.

ac•com•mo•da•tion•ist |əˌkämə'dāsHənist| • *n.* a person who seeks compromise with an opposing point of view, typically a political one.
DERIVATIVES: **ac•com•mo•da•tion•ism** *n.*

ac•com•plice |ə'kämplis| • *n.* a person who helps another commit a crime.

ac•cord |ə'kôrd| • *v.* **1** [trans.] give or grant someone (power, status, or recognition): *the powers accorded to the head of state* | [with two objs.] *the young man had accorded her little notice.* **2** [intrans.] (**accord with**) (of a concept or fact) be harmonious or consistent with. • *n.* an official agreement or treaty.

■ agreement or harmony: *the government and the rebels are in accord on one point.*

ac•cost |ə'kôst; ə'käst| • *v.* [trans.] approach and address (someone) boldly or aggressively: *reporters accosted him in the street.*
■ approach (someone) with hostility or harmful intent.
■ approach and address (someone) with sexual intent.

ac•couche•ment |äkŌŌSH'mäɴ; ə'kŌŌSHmənt| • *n.* the action of giving birth to a baby.

ac•count•ant |ə'kownt(ə)nt| • *n.* a person whose job is to keep or inspect financial accounts. The profession is called **accountancy**, the process **accounting**.

ac•cou•ter |ə'kŌŌtər| (also **accoutre**) • *v.* (**accoutered**, **accoutering**; **accoutred**, **accoutring**) [trans.] (usu. **be accoutered**) clothe or equip, typically in something noticeable or impressive.

ac•cou•ter•ment |ə'kŌŌtərmənt; -trə-| (also **accoutrement**) • *n.* (usu. **accouterments**) additional items of dress or equipment, or other items carried or worn by a person or used for a particular activity.
■ a soldier's outfit other than weapons and garments.

ac•credit |ə'kredit| • *v.* (**accredited**, **accrediting**) [trans.] (usu. **be accredited**) **1** give credit (to someone) for: *he was accredited with being one of the world's fastest sprinters.*
■ attribute (an action, saying, or quality) to: *the discovery of distillation is usually accredited to the Arabs.* **2** (of an official body) give authority or sanction to (someone or something) when recognized standards have been met: *schools that do not meet the standards will not be accredited.* **3** give official authorization for (someone, typically a diplomat or journalist) to be in a particular place or to hold a particular post: *ambassadors accredited to Baghdad.*
DERIVATIVES: **ac•cred•i•ta•tion** |əˌkredə'tāsHən| *n.*

ac•cre•tion |ə'krēsHən| • *n.* the process of growth or increase, typically by the gradual accumulation of additional layers or matter: *the accretion of sediments in coastal mangroves.*
■ a thing formed or added by such growth or increase: *about one-third of California was built up by accretions.* ■ (in astronomy) the coming together and cohesion of matter under the influence of gravitation to form larger bodies.
DERIVATIVES: **ac•crete** *v.* **ac•cre•tive** |ə'krētiv| *adj.*

ac•crue |ə'krŌŌ| • *v.* (**accrues, accrued, accruing**) [intrans.] (of sums of money or benefits) be received by someone in regular or increasing amounts over time: *financial benefits will accrue from restructuring* | [as adj.] (**accrued**) *the accrued interest.*
■ [trans.] accumulate or receive (such payments or benefits). ■ [trans.] make provision for (a charge) at the end of a financial period for work that has been done but not yet invoiced.
DERIVATIVES: **ac•cru•al** |ə'krŌŌəl| *n.*

ac·cul·tur·ate |əˈkəlCHəˌrāt| • v. assimilate or cause to assimilate a different culture, typically the dominant one: [intrans.] *acculturated to the United States* | [trans.] *the next weeks were spent acculturating the field staff* | [as adj.] (**acculturated**) *an acculturated American*.
DERIVATIVES: **ac·cul·tur·a·tion** |əˌkəlCHəˈrāSHən| *n.* **ac·cul·tur·a·tive** |-rātiv; -ˌrakhtiv| *adj.*

ac·cum·bent • *adj.* reclining; recumbent. • *n.* a person who reclines.

ac·cu·sa·tive |əˈkyo͞ozətiv| • *adj.* relating to or denoting a grammatical case of nouns, pronouns, and adjectives (esp. in classical languages) that expresses the object of an action or the goal of motion. Cf. OBJECTIVE. • *n.* a word in the accusative case.
■ (**the accusative**) the accusative case.

a·ce·di·a |əˈsēdēə| • *n.* (also **accidie**) spiritual or mental sloth; apathy; one of the 'seven deadly sins'.

a·cer·bic |əˈsərbik| • *adj.* ((also **acerb**) 1 (esp. of a comment or style of speaking) sharp and forthright. 2 tasting sour or bitter.
DERIVATIVES: **a·cer·bi·cal·ly** |-ik(ə)lē| *adv.* **a·cer·bi·ty** |-bitē| *n.*

a·ce·ta·min·o·phen |əˌsētəˈminəfən| • *n.* an analgesic drug used to treat headaches, arthritis, etc., and also to reduce fever, often as an alternative to aspirin.

a·cet·y·lene |əˈsetlən; -ˌēn| • (also **ethyne**) *n.* a colorless pungent-smelling hydrocarbon gas, which burns with a bright flame, used in welding (with an *acetylene torch*) and formerly in lighting.

A·chae·an |əˈkēən| • *adj.* of or relating to Achaea in ancient Greece. • *n.* an inhabitant of Achaea.
■ (esp. in Homeric contexts) Greek. • *n.* an inhabitant of Achaea.
■ (esp. in Homeric contexts) a Greek.

A·cha·tes |əˈkātēz| (in classical legend) a companion of Aeneas. His loyalty to his friend was so exemplary as to become proverbial, hence the term *fidus Achates* ('faithful Achates').

Ach·er·on |ˈækəˌrän; -rən| (in Greek mythology) one of the rivers of Hades.
■ literary item for hell.

Achil·les heel • *n.* a weakness or vulnerable point. The **achilles tendon** connects calf muscles to the heel.

a·cid·u·lous |əˈsijələs| • *adj.* sharp-tasting or sour.
■ (of a person's remarks or tone) bitter or cutting.

ac·knowl·edge |ækˈnälij| • *v.* 1 accept or admit the existence or truth of: [trans.] *the plight of the refugees was acknowledged by the authorities* | [with clause] *the government acknowledged that the tax was unfair* | [with direct speech] *"That's true," she acknowledged.* 2 [trans.] (of a body of opinion) recognize the fact or importance or quality of: *the art world has begun to acknowledge his genius.*
■ express or display gratitude for or appreciation of: *he received a letter acknowledging his services.* ■ accept the validity or legitimacy of:

Henry acknowledged Richard as his heir. 3 [trans.] show that one has noticed or recognized (someone) by making a gesture or greeting: *she refused to acknowledge my presence.*
■ confirm (receipt of something).
DERIVATIVES: **ac·knowl·edge·able** *adj.* **ac·knowl·edg·ment** (also **ac·knowl·edge·ment**) *n.*

ac·me |ˈækmē| • *n.* [in sing.] the point at which someone or something is best, perfect, or most successful: *at the acme of her career.*

ac·o·lyte |ˈækəˌlīt| • *n.* a person assisting the celebrant in a religious service or procession.
■ an assistant or follower.

a·cous·tic |əˈko͞ostik| • *adj.* [attrib.] 1 relating to sound or the sense of hearing: *the acoustic range of dogs.*
■ (of building materials) used for soundproofing or modifying sound: *acoustic tiles.* ■ (of an explosive mine or other weapon) designed to be set off by sound waves. 2 (of music or musical instruments) not having electrical amplification: *acoustic guitar.*
■ (of a person or group) playing such instruments. • *n.* 1 (usu. **acoustics**) the properties or qualities of a room or building that determine how sound is transmitted in it: *Symphony Hall has perfect acoustics.*
■ (**acoustic**) the acoustic properties or ambience of a sound recording or of a recording studio. 2 (**acoustics**) [treated as sing.] the branch of physics concerned with the properties of sound. 3 a musical instrument without electrical amplification, typically a guitar.
DERIVATIVES: **a·cous·ti·cal** *adj.* **a·cous·ti·cal·ly** |-ik(ə)lē| *adv.*

ac·qui·esce |ˌækwēˈes| • *v.* [intrans.] accept something reluctantly but without protest: *pressed for time, we acquiesced in their decision.*
DERIVATIVES: **ac·qui·es·cence** |-ˈesəns| *n.*

ac·quis·i·tive |əˈkwizitiv| • *adj.* excessively interested in acquiring money or material things.
DERIVATIVES: **ac·quis·i·tive·ly** *adv.* **ac·quis·i·tive·ness** *n.*

ac·quit |əˈkwit| • *v.* (**acquitted, acquitting**) 1 [trans.] (usu. **be acquitted**) free (someone) from a criminal charge by a verdict of not guilty: *she was acquitted on all counts* | *the jury acquitted him of murder.* 2 (**acquit oneself**) conduct oneself or perform in a specified way: *the Israeli windsurfers acquitted themselves well at the 1994 championship.*
■ (**acquit oneself of**) discharge (a duty or responsibility): *they acquitted themselves of their charge with vigilance.*

ac·quit·tal |əˈkwitl| • *n.* a judgment that a person is not guilty of a crime with which he or she has been charged: *the trial resulted in an acquittal.*

ac·rid |ˈækrid| • *adj.* having an irritatingly strong and unpleasant taste or smell: *acrid fumes.*

■ angry and bitter: *an acrid farewell.*
DERIVATIVES: **a•crid•i•ty** |ə'kriditē| *n.* **ac•rid•ly** *adv.*

ac•ri•mo•ny |'ækrə,mōnē| • *n.* bitterness or ill feeling: *a quagmire of lawsuits, acrimony, and finger-pointing.*
DERIVATIVES: **ac•ri•mo•ni•ous** *adj.* **ac•ri•mo•ni•ous•ly** *adv.*

ac•ro•meg•a•ly |,ækrō'megəlē| • *n.* abnormal growth of the hands, feet, and face, caused by overproduction of growth hormone by the pituitary gland.
DERIVATIVES: **ac•ro•me•gal•ic** |-mə'gælik| *adj.*

ac•ro•nym |'ækrə,nim| • *n.* a word formed from the initial letters of other words (e.g., *radar, NATO, laser*).

ac•ro•pho•bi•a |,ækrə'fōbēə| • *n.* extreme or irrational fear of heights.
DERIVATIVES: **ac•ro•pho•bic** |-'fōbik| *adj.* & *n.*

a•cros•tic |ə'krôstik; ə'kräs-| • *n.* a poem, word puzzle, or other composition in which certain letters (typically, the first) in each line form a word or words.

a•cryl•ic |ə'krilik| • *adj.* (of synthetic resins and textile fibers) made from polymers of acrylic acid or acrylates. ■ of, relating to, or denoting paints based on acrylic resin as a medium: *acrylic colors | an acrylic painting.* • *n.* **1** an acrylic textile fiber: *a sweater in four-ply acrylic.* **2** (often **acrylics**) an acrylic paint. ■ a painting executed in acrylics: *a show of her acrylics.*

ac•tion•a•ble |'ækshənəbəl| • *adj.* (in legal use) giving sufficient reason to take legal action: *slanderous remarks are actionable.*

ac•tion paint•ing • *n.* a technique and style of abstract painting in which paint is randomly splashed, thrown, or poured on the canvas.

ac•tiv•ism |'æktə,vizəm| • *n.* the policy or action of using vigorous campaigning to bring about political or social change.
DERIVATIVES: **ac•tiv•ist** *n.*

act of God • *n.* an instance of uncontrollable natural forces in operation (often used in insurance claims). Cf. FORCE MAJEURE.

ac•tu•al•i•ty |,ækchū'wælitē| • *n.* (pl. **-ies**) actual existence, typically as contrasted with what was intended, expected, or believed: *the building looked as impressive in actuality as it did in magazines.* ■ (**actualities**) existing conditions or facts: *the grim actualities of prison life.*

ac•tu•al•ize |'ækchəwə,līz| • *v.* [trans.] make a reality of: *he had actualized his dream and achieved the world record.*
DERIVATIVES: **ac•tu•al•i•za•tion** |,ækchəwəli'zāshən| *n.*

ac•tu•ar•y |'ækchə,werē| • *n.* (pl. **-ies**) a person who compiles and analyzes statistics and uses them to calculate insurance risks and premiums.
DERIVATIVES: **ac•tu•ar•i•al** |,ækchə'werēəl| *adj.* **ac•tu•ar•i•al•ly** |,ækchə'werēəlē| (also **actuarily**) *adv.*

ac•tu•ate |'ækchə,wāt| • *v.* **1** [trans.] cause (a machine or device) to operate; activate: *the pendulum actuates an electrical switch.* **2** (usu. **be actuated**) cause (someone) to act in a particular way; motivate: *the defendants were actuated by malice.*
DERIVATIVES: **a•tu•a•tion** |,ækchə'wāshən| *n.* **ac•tu•a•tor** |-'wāṯər| *n.*

a•cu•i•ty |ə'kyōōiṯē| • *n.* sharpness or keenness of thought, vision, or hearing: *visual acuity.*

a•cu•men |ə'kyōōmən; 'ækyə-| • *n.* the ability to make good judgments and quick decisions, typically in a particular domain: *business acumen.*

a•cute |ə'kyōōt| • *adj.* **1** (of a bad, difficult, or unwelcome situation or phenomenon) present or experienced to a severe or intense degree: *an acute housing shortage.* Cf. CRITICAL. ■ (of a disease or its symptoms) of short duration but typically severe: *acute appendicitis.* Often contrasted with CHRONIC. ■ denoting or designed for patients with such conditions: *acute patients.* **2** having or showing a perceptive understanding or insight: shrewd: *an acute awareness of changing fashions.* ■ (of a physical sense or faculty) highly developed; keen: *an acute sense of smell.* **3** (of an angle) less than 90°. ■ having a sharp end; pointed. ■ (of a sound) high; shrill. • *n.* short for *acute accent*, placed over certain letters (esp. vowels) in some languages to indicate a feature such as altered sound quality.
DERIVATIVES: **a•cute•ly** *adv.* **a•cute•ness** *n.*

ad•age |'ædij| • *n.* a proverb or short statement expressing a general truth.

a•da•gio |ə'däjēō; ə'däzH-| • *adj.* & *adv.* (esp. as a musical direction) in slow tempo. • *n.* (also **Adagio**) (pl. **-os**) a movement or composition marked to be played adagio.

ad•a•mant |'ædəmənt| • *adj.* refusing to be persuaded or to change one's mind: *he is adamant that he is not going to resign.* • *n.* a legendary rock or mineral to which many, often contradictory, properties were attributed, formerly associated with diamond or lodestone.
DERIVATIVES: **ad•a•mance** *n.* **ad•a•man•cy** |-mənsē| *n.* **ad•a•mant•ly** *adv.*

ad•a•man•tine |,ædə'mæn,tīn; -tin-; -,tēn| • *adj.* unbreakable and unshakeable: *her adamantine will.*

a•dapt |ə'dæpt| • *v.* [trans.] make (something) suitable for a new use or purpose; modify: [with obj. and infinitive] *hospitals have had to be adapted for modern medical practice | the policies can be adapted to suit individual needs and requirements.* | [as adj.] (**adapted**) *these plants are well adapted to low light.* ■ [intrans.] become adjusted to new conditions: *they were slow to adapt to change* ■ alter (a text) to make it suitable for filming, broadcasting, or the stage: *the miniseries was adapted from Wouk's novel.*
DERIVATIVES: **a•dap•tive** |-tiv| *adj.*

USAGE: Avoid confusing **adapt** with **adopt**. Trouble sometimes arises because in *adapting* to new conditions an animal or plant can be said to *adopt* something, e.g., a new color or behavior pattern.

ad•ap•ta•tion |ˌædæpˈtāSHən; ˌædəp-| • n. the action or process of adapting or being adapted: *the adaptation of teaching strategy to meet students' needs.*
■ a movie, television drama, or stage play that has been adapted from a written work, typically a novel: *filming her adaptation of a beloved children's book.* ■ a change by which an organism or species becomes better suited to its environment.

ad•den•dum |əˈdendəm| • n. (pl. **addenda** |-də|) an item of additional material, typically omissions, added at the end of a book or other publication.

ad•dict•ed |əˈdiktid| • adj. physically and mentally dependent on a particular substance, and unable to stop taking it without incurring adverse effects: *she became **addicted to** alcohol and diet pills.*
■ enthusiastically devoted to a particular thing or activity: *he's **addicted to** computers.*

ad•duce |əˈd(y)o͞os| • v. [trans.] cite as evidence: *a number of factors are adduced to explain the situation.*
DERIVATIVES: **ad•duc•i•ble** adj.

ad•duc•tor |əˈdəktər| (also **adductor muscle**) • n. a muscle whose contraction moves a limb or other part of the body toward the midline of the body or toward another part.

a•dept • adj. |əˈdept| very skilled or proficient at something: *he is **adept** at cutting through red tape* | *an adept negotiator.* • n. |ˈædept; əˈdept| a person who is skilled or proficient at something: *they are **adepts** at kung fu and karate.*
DERIVATIVES: **a•dept•ly** adv. **a•dept•ness** n.

ad•here |ædˈhir| • v. [intrans.] (**adhere to**) stick fast to (a surface or substance): *paint won't adhere well to a greasy surface.*
■ believe in and follow the practices of: *the people adhere to Islam.* ■ represent truthfully and in detail: *the account adhered firmly to fact.*

ad•her•ent |ædˈhirənt; -ˈher-| • n. someone who supports a particular party, person, or set of ideas: *he was a strong **adherent of** monetarism.* • adj. sticking fast to an object or surface: *the eggs have thick sticky shells to which debris is often adherent.*
DERIVATIVES: **ad•her•ence** n.

ad•he•sive |ædˈhēsiv; -ziv| • adj. able to stick fast (adhere) to a surface or object; sticky: *an adhesive label.* • n. a substance used for sticking objects or materials together; glue.
DERIVATIVES: **ad•he•sive•ly** adv. **ad•he•sive•ness** n.

ad hoc |ˈæd ˈhäk; ˈhōk| • adj. & adv. formed, arranged, or done for a particular purpose only: [as adj.] *an ad hoc committee was formed to supplement the work of three standing committees* | *the discussions were on an ad hoc basis* | [as adv.] *the group was constituted ad hoc.*

ad in•fi•ni•tum |ˌæd infəˈnītəm| • adv. again and again in the same way; for ever: *registration is for seven years and may be renewed ad infinitum.*

ad•i•pose |ˈædəˌpōs| • adj. (esp. of body tissue) used for the storage of fat.
DERIVATIVES: **ad•i•pos•i•ty** |ˌædəˈpäsite| n.

ad•ja•cent |əˈjāsənt| • adj. **1** next to or adjoining something else: *adjacent rooms* | *the area **adjacent to** the fire station.* **2** (of geometric angles) having a common vertex and a common side.
DERIVATIVES: **ad•ja•cen•cy** n.

ad•join |əˈjoin| • v. [trans.] be next to and joined with (a building, room, or piece of land): *the dining room adjoins a small library* | [as adj.] (**adjoining**) *walked into an adjoining room.*

ad•journ |əˈjərn| • v. [trans.] break off (a meeting, legal case, or game) with the intention of resuming it later: *the meeting was adjourned until December 4.*
■ [no obj., with adverbial] (of people who are together) go somewhere else, typically for refreshment: *they **adjourned to** a local bar.* ■ put off or postpone (a resolution or sentence): *the motion was adjourned.*
DERIVATIVES: **ad•journ•ment** n.

ad•judge |əˈjəj| • v. [with obj. and complement] (usu. **be adjudged**) consider or declare to be true or the case: *she was adjudged guilty* | [with obj. and infinitive] *most of us adjudged him to be offensive.*
■ (**adjudge something to**) (in legal use) award something judicially to someone: *the court adjudged legal damages to the injured people.* ■ [with obj. and infinitive] (in legal use) condemn (someone) to pay a penalty: *the defaulter was adjudged to pay the whole amount.*
DERIVATIVES: **ad•judg•ment** (also **ad•judge•ment**) n.

ad•ju•di•cate |əˈjo͞odiˌkāt| • v. [intrans.] make a formal judgment or decision about a problem or disputed matter: *the committee adjudicates on all betting disputes* | [trans.] *the case was adjudicated in the Superior Court.*
■ act as a judge in a competition. ■ [with obj. and complement] pronounce or declare judicially: *he was adjudicated bankrupt.*
DERIVATIVES: **ad•ju•di•ca•tion** |əˌjo͞odiˈkāSHən| n. **ad•ju•di•ca•tive** |-ˌkātiv| adj. **ad•ju•di•ca•tor** |-ˌkātər| n.

ad•junct |ˈæjəNGkt| • n. **1** a thing added to something else as a supplementary rather than an essential part: *computer technology is an adjunct to learning.*
■ a person who is another's assistant or subordinate. **2** a word or phrase used to amplify or modify the meaning of another word or words in a sentence. • adj. [attrib.] connected or added to something, typically in an auxiliary way: *alternative or adjunct therapies.*
■ (of academic personnel) attached to the staff of a university in a temporary or assistant capacity: *an adjunct professor.*
DERIVATIVES: **ad•junc•tive** |əˈjəNG(k)tiv| adj.

ad•jure |ə'jŏŏr| • *v.* [with obj. and infinitive] urge or request (someone) solemnly or earnestly to do something: *I adjure you to tell me the truth.*
DERIVATIVES: **ad•ju•ra•tion** |,æjə'rāSHən| *n.* **ad•jur•a•to•ry** |-ə,tôrē| *adj.*

ad•ju•tant |'æjətənt| • *n.* a military officer who acts as an administrative assistant to a senior officer.
■ a person's assistant or deputy.
DERIVATIVES: **ad•ju•tan•cy** *n.*

ad•ju•vant |'æjəvənt| • *adj.* (of medical therapy) applied after initial treatment for cancer, esp. to suppress secondary tumor formation.
• *n.* a substance that enhances the body's immune response to an antigen.

ad lib |'æd 'lib| • *v.* (**ad libbed, ad libbing**) [intrans.] speak or perform in public without previously preparing one's words: *Charles had to ad lib because he had forgotten his script* | [trans.] *she ad libbed half the speech.* ■ perform music without following a written score; improvise. • *n.* something spoken or performed in such a way: *he came up with an apt ad lib.* • *adv.* & *adj.* **1** spoken or performed without previous preparation: *an ad lib commentary* [as adv.] *speaking ad lib.* **2** as much and as often as desired: [as adv.] *the price includes meals and drinks ad lib* | [as adj.] *the pigs are fed on an ad lib system.* **3** (in musical directions) in an improvised manner with freedom to vary tempo and instrumentation.

ad li•tem |æd 'lītəm| • *adj.* (esp. of a guardian) appointed to act in a lawsuit on behalf of a child or other person who is not considered capable of representing himself or herself.

ad•mi•ral•ty |'ædmərəltē| • *n.* (pl. **-ies**) **1** the rank or office of an admiral. **2** the jurisdiction of courts of law over cases concerning ships or the sea and other navigable waters.

ad•mis•si•ble |əd'misəbəl| • *adj.* **1** acceptable or valid, esp. as evidence in a court of law: *under certain conditions, hearsay may be admissible.* **2** having the right to be admitted to a place: *foreigners were admissible only as temporary workers.*
DERIVATIVES: **ad•mis•si•bil•i•ty** |-,misə'bilitē| *n.*

ad•mix•ture |æd'miksCHər| • *n.* a mixture: *he felt that his work was an admixture of aggression and creativity.*
■ something mixed with something else, typically as a minor ingredient: *green with an admixture of black.* ■ the action of adding such an ingredient.

ad•mon•ish |əd'mäniSH| • *v.* [trans.] warn or reprimand someone firmly: *she admonished me for appearing at breakfast unshaven* | [with obj. and direct speech] *"You mustn't say that, " Ruth admonished her.*
■ [with obj. and infinitive] advise or urge (someone) earnestly: *she admonished him to drink no more than one glass of wine.* ■ warn (someone) of something to be avoided: *he admonished the people against the evil of such practices.*
DERIVATIVES: **ad•mon•ish•ment** *n.*

ad•mon•i•to•ry |əd'mänə,tôrē| • *adj.* giving or conveying a warning or reprimand; admonishing: *the sergeant lifted an admonitory finger.*
DERIVATIVES: **ad•mo•ni•tion** |,ædmə'niSHən| *n.*

ad nau•se•am |æd 'nôzēəm| • *adv.* referring to something that has been done or repeated so often that it has become annoying or tiresome: *the inherent risks of nuclear power have been debated ad nauseam.*

A•do•nai |,ädō'nī; -'noi| • *n.* a Hebrew name for God.

A•don•is |ə'dänis| (in Greek mythology) a beautiful youth loved by both Aphrodite and Persephone.
■ [as n.] (**an Adonis**) an extremely handsome young man.

a•dopt |ə'däpt| • *v.* [trans.] legally take another's child and bring it up as one's own: *there are many people eager to adopt a baby.*
■ take up or start to use or follow (an idea, method, or course of action): *this approach has been adopted by many big banks.* ■ take on or assume (an attitude or position): *he adopted a patronizing tone* | *adopt a knees-bent position.* ■ (**adopt someone as**) choose someone to receive special recognition: *at least 23 people adopted as "prisoners of conscience" remain in jail.* ■ formally approve or accept (a report or suggestion): *the committee voted to adopt the proposal.* ■ choose (a textbook) as standard or required for a course of study. ■ choose (an animal) to become a house pet: *we're looking to adopt a mature dog.* ■ (of a local authority or group) accept responsibility for the maintenance of (something, e.g., a road).
DERIVATIVES: **a•dopt•a•ble** *adj.* **a•dopt•ee** |-'tē| *n.* **a•dopt•er** *n.* **a•dop•tion** *n.*

USAGE: See **usage** at ADAPT.

a•dop•tive |ə'däptiv| • *adj.* [attrib.] as a result of the adoption of another's child: *adoptive parents.*
■ having a specified relation by adoption: *adoptive brother* | *adoptive family.*
■ denoting a country or city to which a person has moved and in which they have chosen to reside permanently: *Paris soon became her adoptive home.*
DERIVATIVES: **a•dop•tive•ly** *adv.*

a•dorn |ə'dôrn| • *v.* [trans.] make more beautiful or attractive: *pictures and prints adorned his walls.*
DERIVATIVES: **a•dorn•er** *n.* **a•dorn•ment** *n.*

ad rem |'æd 'rem| • *adv.* & *adj.* relevant to what is being done or discussed at the time.

ad•re•nal |ə'drēnl| • *adj.* of, relating to, or denoting a pair of ductless glands situated above the kidneys. Each consists of a core region (**adrenal medulla**) secreting epinephrine and norepinephrine, and an outer region (**adrenal cortex**) secreting corticosteroids. • *n.* (usu. **adrenals**) an adrenal gland.

a•dren•al•ine |ə'drenl-in| (also **adrenalin**) • *n.* another term for EPINEPHRINE: *performing live really gets your adrenaline going.*

■ (**Adrenalin**) trademark the hormone epinephrine extracted from animals or prepared synthetically for medicinal purposes.

a•droit |ə'droit| • adj. clever or skillful in using the hands or mind: *he was adroit at tax avoidance | an adroit woodworker.*
DERIVATIVES: **a•droit•ly** adv. **a•droit•ness** n.

ad•sorb |æd'zôrb; -'sôrb| • v. [trans.] (of a solid) hold (molecules of a gas or liquid or solute) as a thin film on the outside surface or on internal surfaces within the material: *charcoal will not adsorb nitrates | the dye is adsorbed onto the fiber.* Cf. ABSORB.
DERIVATIVES: **ad•sorb•a•ble** adj. **ad•sorp•tion** n. **ad•sorp•tive** adj.

ad•u•late |'æjə,lāt| • v. [trans.] praise (someone) excessively or obsequiously.
DERIVATIVES: **ad•u•la•tion** n. **ad•u•la•tor** |-,lāt̮ər| n. **ad•u•la•to•ry** |-lə,tôrē| adj.

a•dul•ter•ate • v. |ə'dəltə,rāt| [trans.] render (something) poorer in quality by adding another substance, typically an inferior one: *the meat was adulterated with bread crumbs.*
DERIVATIVES: **a•dul•ter•a•tion** |ə,dəltə 'rāSHən| n. **a•dul•ter•a•tor** |-,rāt̮ər| n.

a•dul•ter•y |ə'dəlt(ə)rē| • n. voluntary sexual intercourse between a married person and a person who is not his or her spouse: *she was committing adultery with a much younger man.*
DERIVATIVES: **a•dul•ter•er** n. **a•dul•ter•ous** adj.

ad•um•brate |'ædəm,brāt; ə'dəm-| • v. [trans.] report or represent in outline.
■ indicate faintly: *the walls were adumbrated by the meager light.* ■ foreshadow or symbolize: *what qualities in Christ are adumbrated by the vine?* ■ overshadow.
DERIVATIVES: **ad•um•bra•tion** |,ædəm 'brāSHən| n. **ad•um•bra•tive** |ə'dəmbrət̮iv; 'ædəm,brā-| adj.

ad va•lo•rem |,æd və'lôrəm| • adv. & adj. (of the levying of tax or customs duties) in proportion to the estimated value of the goods or transaction concerned.

ad•vec•tion |æd'vekSHən| • n. the transfer of heat or matter by the flow of a fluid, esp. horizontally in the atmosphere or the sea. Cf. CONVECTION.
DERIVATIVES: **ad•vect** |-'vekt| v. **ad•vec•tive** |-tiv| adj.

ad•vent |'æd,vent| • n. [in sing.] the arrival of a notable person, thing, or event: *the advent of television.*
■ (**Advent**) the first season of the Christian church year, leading up to Christmas and including the four preceding Sundays. ■ (**Advent**) the coming or second coming of Christ.

Ad•vent•ist |'æd,ventist| • n. a member of any of various Christian sects emphasizing belief in the imminent second coming of Christ.
DERIVATIVES: **Ad•vent•ism** |-,tizəm| n.

ad•ven•ti•tious |,ædven'tiSHəs| • adj. happening or carried on according to chance rather than design or inherent nature: *my adventures were always adventitious, always thrust on me.*
■ coming from outside; not native: *the adventitious population.* ■ (in biology) formed accidentally or in an unusual anatomical position: *propagation of sour cherries by adventitious shoots.* ■ (of a root) growing directly from the stem or other upper part of a plant.
DERIVATIVES: **ad•ven•ti•tious•ly** adv.

ad•ven•tur•ism |əd'venCHə,rizəm| • n. the willingness to take risks in business or politics (esp. in the context of foreign policy); actions, tactics, or attitudes regarded as daring or reckless.
DERIVATIVES: **ad•ven•tur•ist** n. & adj.

ad•ver•sar•i•al |,ædvər'serēəl| • adj. involving or characterized by conflict or opposition: *industry and government had an adversarial relationship.*
■ opposed; hostile. ■ (of a trial or legal procedure) in which the parties in a dispute have the responsibility for finding and presenting evidence.
DERIVATIVES: **ad•ver•sar•i•al•ly** adv.

ad•verse |æd'vərs; 'ædvərs| • adj. preventing success or development; harmful; unfavorable: *taxes are having an adverse effect on production | adverse weather conditions.*
DERIVATIVES: **ad•verse•ly** adv.

USAGE: **Adverse** means 'hostile, unfavorable, opposed,' and is usually applied to situations, conditions, or events, not people, e.g., *The dry weather has had an adverse effect on the garden.* **Averse** is related in origin and also has the sense of 'opposed,' but is usually employed to describe a person's attitude, e.g., *I would not be averse to making the repairs myself.*

ad•ver•si•ty |æd'vərsit̮ē| • n. (pl. **-ies**) adverse fortune; difficulties: *resilience in the face of adversity | she overcame many adversities.*

ad•vo•cate • n. |'ædvəkit| a person who publicly supports or recommends a particular cause or policy: *he was an untiring advocate of economic reform.*
■ a person who pleads on someone else's behalf: *care managers can become advocates for their clients.* ■ a pleader in a court of law; a lawyer: *Marshall was a skilled advocate but a mediocre judge.* • v. |-,kāt| [trans.] publicly recommend or support: *they advocated strict adherence to Islam.*
DERIVATIVES: **ad•vo•ca•tion** |,ædvə 'kāSHən| n. **ad•vo•ca•tor** |-,kāt̮ər| n.

ae•gis |'ējis| • n. [in sing.] a particular person or organization's protection, backing, or support: *negotiations were conducted under the aegis of the UN.*
■ (in classical art and mythology) an attribute of Zeus and Athena (or their Roman counterparts Jupiter and Minerva) usually represented as a goatskin shield.

ae•o•li•an |ē'ōlēən| • adj. **1** (also **eolian**) relating to or arising from the action of the wind: *fluvial and aeolian sediments.* **2** of or relating to Aeolus, Greek god of the winds.
■ characterized by a sighing or moaning sound

as if produced by the wind: *there is a pure aeolian quality, a music as of storms telling their secret.*

aer•ate | 'erāt | • *v.* [trans.] introduce air into (a material): *aerate the lawn with a garden fork.* DERIVATIVES: **aer•a•tion** |-'āsHən| *n.* **aer•a•tor** |-ā‚tər| *n.*

aer•i•al | 'erēəl | • *adj.* [attrib.] existing, happening, or operating in the air: *an aerial battle* | *an aerial tramway.*

■ coming or carried out from the air, esp. using aircraft: *aerial bombardment of civilian targets* | *aerial photography.* ■ (of part of a plant) growing above ground. ■ (of a bird) spending much of its time in flight. ■ of or in the atmosphere; atmospheric. ■ insubstantial and hard to grasp or define; ethereal: *the church may draw fine and aerial distinctions.* DERIVATIVES: **aer•i•al•ly** *adv.*

aer•ie | 'erē; 'ērē | (also **eyrie**) • *n.* a large nest of a bird of prey, esp. an eagle, typically built high in a tree or on a cliff.

aer•o•bic |ə'rōbik; e'rō-| • *adj.* (in biology) relating to, involving, or requiring free oxygen: *simple aerobic bacteria.* Cf. ANEROBIC.

■ relating to or denoting exercise that improves or is intended to improve the efficiency of the body's cardiovascular system in absorbing and transporting oxygen. DERIVATIVES: **aer•o•bi•cal•ly** *adv.*

aer•o•bics |ə'rōbiks; e'rō-| • *plural n.* [often treated as sing.] vigorous exercises designed to strengthen the heart and lungs.

aer•o•dy•nam•ics |‚erōdī'næmiks| • *plural n.* [treated as sing.] the study of the properties of moving air, and esp. of the interaction between the air and solid bodies moving through it.

■ the properties of a solid object regarding the manner in which air flows around it. ■ [treated as pl.] these properties insofar as they result in maximum efficiency of motion. DERIVATIVES: **aer•o•dy•nam•i•cist** |-sist| *n.*

aer•o•sol | 'erə‚sôl; -‚säl| • *n.* a substance enclosed under pressure and able to be released as a fine spray, typically by means of a propellant gas.

■ a container holding such a substance. ■ a colloidal suspension of particles dispersed in air or gas.

aes•thete | 'es‚THēt | (also **esthete**) • *n.* a person who has or affects to have a special appreciation of art and beauty.

aes•thet•ic |es'THeṯik| (also **esthetic**) • *adj.* concerned with or relating to beauty or the appreciation of beauty: *the pictures give great aesthetic pleasure.*

■ giving or designed to give pleasure through beauty; of pleasing appearance. • *n.* [in sing.] a set of principles underlying and guiding the work of a particular artist or artistic movement: *the Cubist aesthetic.* DERIVATIVES: **aes•thet•i•cal•ly** |-ik(ə)lē| *adv.*

aes•the•ti•cian |‚esTHə'tisHən| (also **esthetician**) • *n.* 1 a person who is knowledgeable about the nature and appreciation of beauty,

esp. in art. 2 someone who gives beauty treatments, as in a beauty parlor; a beautician.

aes•ti•val • *adj.* variant spelling of ESTIVAL.

aes•ti•vate • *v.* variant spelling of ESTIVATE.

af•fa•ble | 'æfəbəl | • *adj.* friendly, good-natured, or easy to talk to: *an affable and agreeable companion.* DERIVATIVES: **af•fa•bil•i•ty** |-'bilitē| *n.* **af•fa•bly** |-blē| *adv.*

af•fect[1] |ə'fekt| • *v.* [trans.] have an effect on; make a difference to: *the dampness began to affect my health* | [with clause] *your attitude will affect how successful you are.*

■ touch the feelings of (someone); move emotionally: [as adj.] (**affecting**) *a highly affecting account of her experiences in prison.* ■ (of an illness) attack or infect: *people who are affected by AIDS.* DERIVATIVES: **af•fect•ing•ly** *adv.*

> USAGE: **Affect** and **effect** are both verbs and nouns, but only **effect** is common as a noun, usually meaning 'a result, consequence, impression, etc.,' e.g., *My father's warnings had no effect on my adventurousness.* (The noun **affect** is restricted almost entirely to psychology.) As verbs, they are used differently. **Affect** means 'to produce an effect upon,' e.g., *Smoking during pregnancy can affect the baby's development.* The verb **affect**, except when used in contexts involving the feelings, often serves as a vague substitute for more exact verbs; use sparingly. **Effect** means 'to bring about,' e.g., *The negotiators effected an agreement.*

af•fect[2] • *v.* [trans.] pretend to have or feel (something): *as usual I affected a supreme unconcern* | [with infinitive] *a book that affects to loathe the modern world.*

■ use, wear, or assume (something) pretentiously or so as to make an impression on others: *an American who had affected a British accent.*

af•fect[3] | 'æfekt; ə'fekt| • *n.* (in psychology) emotion or desire, esp. as influencing behavior or action. DERIVATIVES: **af•fect•less** *adj.* **af•fect•less•ness** *n.*

af•fec•ta•tion |‚æfek'tāsHən| • *n.* behavior, speech, or writing that is artificial and designed to impress: *she called the room her boudoir, which he thought an affectation.*

■ a studied display of real or pretended feeling: *an affectation of calm.*

af•fect•ed |ə'fektid| • *adj.* 1 influenced or touched by an external factor: *apply moist heat to the affected area.* 2 artificial, pretentious, and designed to impress: *the gesture appeared thoroughly affected.* 3 [predic.] disposed or inclined in a specified way: *you might become differently affected toward him.* DERIVATIVES: **af•fect•ed•ly** *adv.* (in sense 2).

af•fec•tive |ə'fektiv| • *adj.* relating to moods, feelings, and attitudes: *affective disorders.* DERIVATIVES: **af•fec•tive•ly** *adv.* **af•fec•tiv•i•ty** |‚æfek'tivitē| *n.*

af•fi•ance |ə'fīəns| • *v.* (**be affianced**) be

engaged to marry: *Ann Elliott was affianced to Col. Lewis Morris.*

af•fi•da•vit |ˌæfi'dāvit| • *n.* a written statement confirmed by oath or affirmation, for use as evidence in a court of law.

af•fil•i•ate • *v.* |ə'filē,āt| [trans.] (usu. **be affiliated with**) officially attach or connect (a subsidiary group or a person) to an organization: *the college is affiliated with the University of Wisconsin.* | [as adj.] (**affiliated**) *affiliated union members.* ■ [intrans.] officially join or become attached to an organization: *the membership of the National Writers Union voted to affiliate with the United Auto Workers.* • *n.* |-it| a person or organization officially attached to a larger body: *the company established links with British affiliates.*
DERIVATIVES: **af•fil•i•a•tion** *n.* **af•fil•i•a•tive** |-ətiv; -,ātiv| *adj.*

af•fin•i•ty |ə'finitē| • *n.* (pl. **-ies**) (often **affinity between/for/with**) a spontaneous or natural liking or sympathy for someone or something: *he has an affinity for the music of Berlioz.* ■ a similarity of characteristics suggesting a relationship, esp. a resemblance in structure between animals, plants, or languages: *a building with no affinity to contemporary architectural styles.* ■ relationship, esp. by marriage as opposed to blood ties.

af•firm |ə'fərm| • *v.* state as a fact; assert strongly and publicly: [trans.] *he affirmed the country's commitment to peace* | [with clause] *we affirm that God's grace is available to all.* | [with direct speech] *"Pessimism," she affirmed, "is the most rational view."* ■ [trans.] declare one's support for; uphold or defend: *the referendum affirmed the republic's right to secede.* ■ [trans.] Law accept or confirm the validity of (a judgment or agreement); ratify. ■ [intrans.] (in law) make a formal declaration rather than taking an oath. ■ (of a court) uphold (a decision)on appeal.
DERIVATIVES: **af•firm•er** *n.*

af•firm•a•tion |ˌæfər'māsHən| • *n.* the action or process of affirming or being affirmed: *an affirmation of basic human values* | *he nodded in affirmation.* ■ a formal declaration by a person who declines to take an oath (as in court) for reasons of conscience.

af•firm•a•tive |ə'fərmətiv| • *adj.* agreeing with a statement or to a request: *I muttered something affirmative.* ■ (of a vote) expressing approval or agreement. ■ supportive, hopeful, or encouraging: *the music's natural buoyancy and affirmative character.* ■ active or obligatory: *they have an affirmative duty to stop crime in their buildings.* ■ stating that a fact is so; making an assertion. Contrasted with *interrogative* and *negative.* • *n.* a statement of agreement with an assertion or request: *he accepted her reply as an affirmative.* ■ (**the affirmative**) a position of agreement or confirmation: *his answer veered toward the affirmative* | *took the affirmative in the first debate.* ■ a word or particle used in making

assertions. ■ a statement asserting that something is true of the subject of a proposition. • *exclam.* expressing agreement with a statement or request; yes.
DERIVATIVES: **af•firm•a•tive•ly** *adv.*

affirm•ative ac•tion • *n.* treatment benefiting those who tend to suffer from discrimination, esp. in relation to employment or education.

af•fix • *v.* |ə'fiks| [trans.] stick, attach, or fasten (something) to something else: *he licked the stamp and affixed it to the envelope.* • *n.* |'æ,fiks| an additional element placed at the beginning (a prefix) or end (a suffix) of a root, stem, or word, or in the body (an infix) of a word, to modify its meaning.
DERIVATIVES: **af•fix•a•tion** |ˌæfik'sāsHən| *n.*

af•fla•tus |ə'flātəs| • *n.* a divine creative impulse or inspiration: *the afflatus of youth.*

af•flict |ə'flikt| • *v.* [trans.] (of a problem or illness) cause pain or suffering to; affect or trouble: *serious ills afflict the industry* | *his younger child was afflicted with a skin disease.* | [as plural n.] (**the afflicted**) *he comforted the afflicted.* ■ (in astrology, of a celestial body) be in a stressful aspect with (another celestial body or a point on the ecliptic): *Jupiter is afflicted by Mars in opposition.*
DERIVATIVES: **af•flic•tive** |-tiv| *adj.*

af•flic•tion |ə'fliksHən| • *n.* something that causes pain or suffering: *a crippling affliction of the nervous system.* ■ pain or suffering: *poor people in great affliction.* ■ (in astrology) an instance of one celestial body afflicting another.

af•flu•ent |'æflōōənt; ə'flōō-| • *adj.* **1** (esp. of a group or area) having a great deal of money; wealthy: *the affluent societies of the western world* | [as plural n.] (**the affluent**) *only the affluent could afford to travel abroad.* **2** (of water) flowing freely or in great quantity. Cf. EFFLUENT. • *n.* a tributary stream.
DERIVATIVES: **af•flu•ence** *n.* **af•flu•ent•ly** *adv.*

af•flux |'æfləks| • *n.* a flow of something, esp. water or air.

af•front |ə'frənt| • *n.* an action or remark that causes outrage or offense: *he took his son's desertion as a personal affront* | *this kind of privilege is an affront to democracy.* • *v.* [trans.] (usu. **be affronted**) offend the modesty or values of: *she was affronted by his familiarity.*

a•fi•cio•na•do |ə,fisH(ē)ə'nädō; ə,fisyə-| • *n.* (pl. **-os**) a person who is very knowledgeable and enthusiastic about an activity, subject, or pastime.

Af•ri•can A•mer•i•can • *n.* a black American. • *adj.* of or relating to black Americans.

USAGE: **African American** is the currently accepted term in the US, having first become common in the late 1980s. See also **usage** at BLACK.

a•gape |ä'gä,pā; 'ägə-| • *n.* Christian love, esp. as distinct from erotic love (Eros) or emotional affection. ■ a communal meal in token of Christian fellowship, as held by early Christians in commemoration of the Last Supper.

age•ism |ˈāj,izəm| (also **agism**) • *n.* prejudice or discrimination on the basis of a person's age, esp. against older persons.

DERIVATIVES: **age•ist** (also **ag•ist**) *adj. & n.*

a•gen•cy |ˈājənsē| • *n.* **1** [often with adj.] a business or organization established to provide a particular service, typically one that involves organizing transactions between two other parties: *an advertising agency* | *aid agencies.*
■ a department or body providing a specific service for a government or similar organization: *the Environmental Protection Agency.* ■ the function or position of an agent. ■ the body of law concerning the rights and duties of agents and their principals. **2** action or intervention, esp. such as to produce a particular effect: *canals carved **by the agency of** running water* | *a belief in various forms of supernatural agency.*
■ a thing or person that acts to produce a particular result: *the movies could be an agency molding the values of the public.*

a•gen•da |əˈjendə| • *n.* a list of items of business to be considered and discussed at a meeting: *the question of nuclear weapons had been removed from the agenda.*
■ a list or program of things to be done or problems to be addressed: *he vowed to put jobs at the top of his agenda* | *the government had its own agenda.*

USAGE: Although **agenda** ('things to be done') is the plural of *agendum* in Latin, in standard modern English it is a normal singular noun with a normal plural form (**agendas**).

a•gent pro•vo•ca•teur |äˌzHän(t) prəˌvôkəˈtər| • *n.* (pl. **agents provocateurs** |äˌzHän(t)(s) prəˌvôkəˈtər(z)| pronunc. same) a person, typically working secretly with the police, who induces others to break the law so that they can be convicted.

ag•glom•er•ate • *v.* |əˈgläməˌrāt| collect or form into a mass or group: [trans.] *companies agglomerate series of outlets* | [intrans.] *these small particles soon agglomerate together.* • *n.* |-rit| a mass or collection of things.
■ a volcanic rock consisting of large fragments bonded together. • *adj.* |-rit| collected or formed into a mass.

DERIVATIVES: **ag•glom•er•a•tion** |əˌgläm-əˈrāsHən| *n.* **ag•glom•er•a•tive** |-ˌrātiv; -rətiv| *adj.*

ag•glu•ti•nate |əˈglo͞otnˌāt| • *v.* firmly stick or be stuck together to form a mass: [as adj.] (**agglutinated**) *rhinoceros horns are agglutinated masses of hair.*

DERIVATIVES: **ag•glu•ti•na•tion** |əˌglo͞otn-ˈāsHən| *n.*

ag•gran•dize |əˈgranˌdīz| • *v.* [trans.] increase the power, status, or wealth of: *an action intended to aggrandize the Nazi regime.*
■ enhance the reputation of (someone) beyond what is justified by the facts: *he hoped to aggrandize himself by dying a hero's death.*

DERIVATIVES: **ag•gran•dize•ment** |-ˌdīzmənt; -diz-| *n.* **ag•gran•diz•er** *n.*

ag•gra•vate |ˈagrəˌvāt| • *v.* [trans.] **1** make (a problem, injury, or offense) worse or more serious: *military action would only aggravate the situation.* **2** annoy or exasperate (someone), esp. persistently: [as adj.] (**aggravating**) *she found him thoroughly aggravating and unprofessional.*

DERIVATIVES: **ag•gra•vat•ing•ly** *adv.* **ag•gra•va•tion** |ˌagrəˈvāsHən| *n.*

USAGE: **Aggravate** in the sense 'annoy or exasperate' dates back to the 17th century and has been so used by respected writers ever since. Writers seeking precision, however, would do well to preserve the word's historical meaning of 'to make heavier,' in the sense of 'weighing down' or 'piling on,' and not use **aggravate** as simply another word for *irritate*. The same goes for **aggravation** when *irritation* would serve. See also **usage** at EXASPERATE.

ag•gre•gate • *n.* |ˈagrəgit| **1** a whole formed by combining several (typically disparate) elements: *the council was an aggregate of three regional assemblies.* **2** a material or structure formed from a mass of fragments or particles loosely compacted together.
■ pieces of broken or crushed stone or gravel used to make concrete, or more generally in building and construction work. • *adj.* [attrib.] formed or calculated by the combination of many separate units or items; total: *aggregate profits.*
■ (of a group of plant species) comprising several very similar species formerly regarded as a single species. ■ denoting the total supply or demand for goods and services in an economy at a particular time: *aggregate demand* | *aggregate supply.* • *v.* |-ˌgāt| form or group into a class or cluster: [trans.] *the statistics aggregate men having several kinds of occupation* | [intrans.] *the butterflies aggregate in dense groups.*

DERIVATIVES: **ag•gre•ga•tion** |-ˈgāsHən| *n.* **ag•gre•ga•tive** |-ˌgātiv| *adj.*

ag•grieved |əˈgrēvd| • *adj.* feeling resentment at having been unfairly treated: *they were aggrieved at the outcome* | *his brother is the aggrieved party.*

DERIVATIVES: **ag•griev•ed•ly** |-vidlē| *adv.*

a•ghast |əˈgast| • *adj.* [predic.] filled with horror or shock: *when the news came out they were aghast* | *aghast at an act of cruelty.*

ag•ile |ˈajəl| • *adj.* able to move quickly and easily: *Ruth was as agile as a monkey* | *his vague manner concealed an agile mind.*

DERIVATIVES: **ag•ile•ly** |ˈajə(l)lē| *adv.* **a•gil•i•ty** |əˈjilitē| *n.*

ag•i•tate |ˈaji,tāt| • *v.* [trans.] make (someone) troubled or nervous: *the thought of questioning Toby agitated him* | [as adj.] (**agitated**) *red and agitated with the effort of arguing.*
■ [intrans.] campaign to arouse public concern about an issue in the hope of prompting action: *they agitated for a reversal of the decision.* ■ stir or disturb (something, esp. a liquid) briskly: *agitate the water to disperse the oil.*

DERIVATIVES: **ag•i•tat•ed•ly** *adv.* **ag•i•ta• tion** *n.*

ag•it•prop |ˈæʒit͵präp| • *n.* political (originally communist) propaganda, esp. in art or literature: [as adj.] *agitprop painters.*

ag•nate |ˈæg͵nāt| • *n.* a person descended from the same male ancestor as another specified or implied person, esp. through the male line. • *adj.* descended from the same male ancestor as a specified or implied subject, esp. through the male line. Cf. COGNATE.
■ of the same clan or nation.
DERIVATIVES: **ag•nat•ic** |ægˈnætik| *adj.* **ag•na•tion** |ægˈnāSHən| *n.*

ag•nos•tic |ægˈnästik| • *n.* a person who believes that nothing is known or can be known of the existence or nature of God or of anything beyond material phenomena; a person who claims neither faith nor disbelief in God. Cf. ATHEISM.
■ a person who professes no belief or position on a given topic: [as adj.] *I'm agnostic on estate taxes.* • *adj.* of or relating to agnostics or agnosticism.
DERIVATIVES: **ag•nos•ti•cism** |-tə͵sizəm| *n.*

ag•o•nist |ˈægənist| • *n.* (in literature, etc.) another term for PROTAGONIST.
DERIVATIVES: **ag•o•nism** |-͵nizəm| *n.* **ag• o•nis•tic** *adj.*

ag•o•ra•pho•bi•a |͵ægərəˈfōbēə| • *n.* extreme or irrational fear of crowded spaces or public places.
DERIVATIVES: **ag•o•ra•pho•bic** |-ˈfōbik| *adj. & n.* **ag•o•ra•phobe** |ˈægərə͵fōb| *n.*

a•grar•i•an |əˈgrerēən| • *adj.* of or relating to cultivated land or the cultivation of land.
■ relating to landed property. • *n.* a person who advocates a redistribution of landed property.

ag•ri•busi•ness |ˈægrə͵biznis| • *n.* **1** agriculture conducted on commercial principles, esp. using advanced technology.
■ an organization engaged in this. **2** the group of industries dealing with agricultural produce and services required in farming.
DERIVATIVES: **ag•ri•busi•ness•man** |͵ægrə'biznismən| *n.* (pl. **-men**) .

a•gron•o•my |əˈgränəmē| • *n.* the science of soil management and crop production.
DERIVATIVES: **ag•ro•nom•ic** |͵ægrəˈnämik| *adj.* **ag•ro•nom•i•cal** |͵ægrəˈnämikəl| *adj.* **ag•ro•nom•i•cal•ly** |͵ægrəˈnämik(ə)lē| *adv.* **a•gron•o•mist** |-mist| *n.*

a•him•sa |əˈhim͵sä| • *n.* (in the Hindu, Buddhist, and Jain tradition) the principle of non-violence toward all living things.

aide-de-camp |ˈäd də ˈkæmp| • *n.* (pl. **aides-de-camp** |ˈädz| pronunc. same) a military officer acting as a confidential assistant to a senior officer.

aide-me•moire |ˈäd mem'wär| • *n.* (pl. **aides-memoires** |ˈädz| or **aides-memoire** pronunc. same) an aid to the memory, esp. a book or document.
■ an informal diplomatic message.

a•kim•bo |əˈkimbō| • *adv.* with hands on the hips and elbows turned outward: *she stood with* **arms akimbo**, *frowning at the small boy.*
■ (of other limbs) flung out widely or haphazardly.

a•kin |əˈkin| • *adj.* of similar character: *something akin to gratitude overwhelmed her* | *genius and madness are akin.*
■ related by blood: *he was akin to the royal family.*

a•lac•ri•ty |əˈlækritē| • *n.* brisk and cheerful readiness: *she accepted the invitation with alacrity.*

al•a•me•da |͵æləˈmädə| • *n.* (in Spain and Spanish-speaking regions) a public walkway or promenade shaded with trees.

al•ba•tross |ˈælbə͵trôs; -͵träs| • *n.* (pl. **albatrosses**) a very large oceanic bird with long narrow wings. Albatrosses are found mainly in the southern oceans, with three kinds in the North Pacific.
■ a source of frustration or guilt; an encumbrance (in allusion to Coleridge's *The Rime of the Ancient Mariner*): *an albatross of a marriage.*

al•be•it |ôlˈbē-it; æl-| • *conj.* although: *he was making progress, albeit rather slowly.*

al•bes•cent |ælˈbesənt| • *adj.* growing or shading into white: *the albescent waves on the horizon.*

al•bi•no |ælˈbīnō| • *n.* (pl. **-os**) a person or animal having a congenital absence of pigment in the skin and hair (which are thus white) and the eyes (which are thus typically pink).
■ an abnormally white animal or plant. [as modifier] *an albino tiger.*
DERIVATIVES: **al•bi•nism** |ˈælbə͵nizəm| *n.*

Al•bi•on |ˈælbēən| • *n.* a poetic or literary term for Britain or England (often used in referring to ancient or historical times).

al•ca•ic |ælˈkāik| • *adj.* written in or denoting a verse meter occurring in four-line stanzas. • *n.* (usu. **alcaics**) alcaic verse.

al•che•my |ˈælkəmē| • *n.* the medieval forerunner of chemistry, based on the supposed transformation of matter. It was concerned particularly with attempts to convert base metals into gold or to find a universal ELIXIR.
■ a process by which paradoxical results are achieved or incompatible elements combined with no obvious rational explanation: *his conducting managed by some alchemy to give a sense of fire and ice.*
DERIVATIVES: **al•chem•ic** |ælˈkemik| *adj.* **al•chem•i•cal** |ælˈkemikəl| *adj.* **al•che•mist** |-mist| *n.* **al•che•mize** |-͵mīz| *v.*

al den•te |äl ˈdentä; æl| • *adj. & adv.* (of food, typically pasta) cooked so as to be still firm when bitten.

a•le•a•to•ry |ˈālēə͵tôrē; ˈæl-| • *adj.* depending on the throw of a die or on chance; random.
■ relating to music or other forms of art involving elements of random choice by a performer or artist.

a•lex•i•a |əˈleksēə| • *n.* the inability to see words or to read, caused by a defect of the brain. Also called *word blindness.* Cf. DYSLEXIA.

al•fres•co |æl'freskō; äl | • *adv.* & *adj.* in the open air: [as adj.] *an alfresco luncheon.*

al•ga |'ælgə| • *n.* (usu. in pl. **algae** |-jē|) a simple nonflowering plant of a large assemblage that includes mainly aquatic kinds such as seaweeds and many single-celled forms. Some of the latter are responsible for a green coating on tree trunks and a green scum or bloom in ponds.
•Divisions Chlorophyta (**green algae**), Heterokontophyta (**brown algae**), and Rhodophyta (**red algae**); some (or all) are frequently placed in the kingdom Protista.
DERIVATIVES: **al•gal** |-gəl| *adj.*

algid • *n.* cold or chilly.

Al•gon•qui•an |æl'gäNGk(w)ēən| (also **Algonkian**) • *adj.* denoting, belonging to, or relating to a family of North American Indian languages formerly spoken across a vast area from the Atlantic seaboard to the Great Lakes and the Great Plains. • *n.* **1** this family of languages. **2** a speaker of any of these languages.

Algonquian forms one of the largest groups of American Indian languages, including Ojibwa, Cree, Blackfoot, Cheyenne, Fox, Menomini, and Delaware, which were or are spoken mainly in the area that now includes the eastern United States and Canada.

Al•gon•quin |æl'gäNGk(w)ən| (also **Algonkin**) • *n.* **1** a member of an American Indian people living in Canada along the Ottawa River and its tributaries and westward to the north of Lake Superior. **2** the dialect of Ojibwa spoken by this people. • *adj.* of or relating to this people or their language.

USAGE: The use of **Algonquin** to refer generically to the Algonquian peoples or their languages is incorrect.

al•go•rithm |'ælgə,riTHəm| • *n.* a process or set of rules to be followed in calculations or other problem-solving operations, esp. by a computer: *a basic algorithm for division.*
DERIVATIVES: **al•go•rith•mic** |,ælgə 'riTHmik| *adj.* **al•go•rith•mi•cal•ly** |,ælgə 'riTHmik(ə)lē| *adv.*

a•li•as |'ālēəs| • *adv.* used to indicate that a named person is also known or more familiar under another specified name: *Eric Blair, alias George Orwell.*
■ indicating another term or synonym: *the catfish—alias bullhead—is a mighty tasty fry-up.* • *n.* a false or assumed identity: *a spy operating under several aliases.*
■ (in computing) an alternative name or label that refers to a file, command, address, or other item, and can be used to locate or access it. • *v.* [trans.] (usu. **be aliased**) misidentify (a signal frequency), introducing distortion or error.

al•i•bi |'ælə,bī| • *n.* (pl. **alibis**) a claim or piece of evidence that one was elsewhere when an act, typically a criminal one, is alleged to have taken place: *she has an alibi for the whole of yesterday evening* | [as adj.] *an alibi defense.*
■ an excuse or pretext: *a handy alibi for failure and inadequacy.* • *v.* (**alibis, alibied, alibiing**) [trans.] offer an excuse or defense for (someone), esp. by providing an account of their whereabouts at the time of an alleged act: *her friend agreed to alibi her.*
■ [intrans.] make excuses: *not once do I recall him whining or alibiing.*

al•ien |'ālyən; 'ālēən| • *adj.* belonging to a foreign country or nation.
■ unfamiliar and disturbing or distasteful: *bossing anyone around was alien to him* | *they found the world of night school education a little alien.* ■ [attrib.] relating to or denoting beings supposedly from other worlds; extraterrestrial: *an alien spacecraft.* ■ (of a plant or animal species) introduced from another country and later naturalized. • *n.* a foreigner, esp. one who is not a naturalized citizen of the country where they are living: *an illegal alien.*
■ a hypothetical or fictional being from another world. ■ a plant or animal species originally introduced from another country and later naturalized.
DERIVATIVES: **al•ien•ness** *n.*

al•ien•ate |'ālēə,nāt; 'ālyə-| • *v.* [trans.] **1** cause (someone) to feel isolated or estranged: *an urban environment that alienates its inhabitants* | [as adj.] (**alienated**) *an alienated, angst-ridden 22-year-old.*
■ cause (someone) to become unsympathetic or hostile: *the association does not wish to alienate its members.* **2** transfer ownership of (property rights) to another person or group.

al•ien•a•tion |,ālēə'nāsHən; ,ālyə-| • *n.* the state or experience of being isolated from a group or an activity to which one should belong or in which one should be involved: *unemployment may generate political alienation.*
■ loss or lack of sympathy; estrangement: *public alienation from bureaucracy.* ■ (in Marxist theory) a condition of workers in a capitalist economy, resulting from a lack of identity with the products of their labor and a sense of being controlled or exploited. ■ a state of depersonalization or loss of identity in which the self seems unreal, thought to be caused by difficulties in relating to society and the resulting prolonged inhibition of emotion. ■ a type of faulty recognition in which familiar situations or persons appear unfamiliar. Cf. DÉJÀ VU. ■ (also **alienation effect**) an effect, sought by some dramatists, whereby the audience remains objective and does not identify with the actors. ■ the transfer of the ownership of property rights.

al•i•mo•ny |'ælə,mōnē| • *n.* a husband's or wife's court-ordered provision for a spouse after separation or divorce; maintenance: *paying both alimony and child support.*

al•ka•loid |'ælkə,loid| • *n.* Chemistry any of a class of nitrogenous organic compounds of plant origin that have pronounced physiological actions on humans. They include many drugs (morphine, quinine) and poisons (atropine, strychnine).

al•lay |ə'lā| • *v.* [trans.] diminish or put at rest (fear, suspicion, or worry): *the report attempted to educate the public and allay fears.*

■ relieve or alleviate (pain or hunger): *some stale figs partly allayed our hunger.*

al•lée |ä'lā| • *n.* an alley in a formal garden or park, bordered by trees or bushes.

al•lege |ə'lej| • *v.* claim or assert that someone has done something illegal or wrong, typically without proof that this is the case: [with clause] *he **alleged that** he had been assaulted* | [with obj. and infinitive] *the offenses are alleged to have been committed outside the woman's home* | *he is **alleged to have** assaulted five men.*
■ (usu. **be alleged**) suppose or affirm to be the case: *the first artifact ever alleged to be from Earhart's aircraft.*
DERIVATIVES: **al•le•ga•tion** *n.*

al•le•giance |ə'lējəns| • *n.* loyalty or commitment of a subordinate to a superior or of an individual to a group or cause: *those wishing to receive citizenship must **swear allegiance to** the republic* | *a complex pattern of cross-party allegiances.*

al•le•go•ry |'ælə,gôrē| • *n.* (pl. **-ies**) a story, poem, or picture that can be interpreted to reveal a hidden meaning, typically a moral or political one: *Pilgrim's Progress is an allegory of the spiritual journey.*
■ the genre to which such works belong. ■ a symbol.
DERIVATIVES: **al•le•go•ri•cal** *adj.* **al•le•go•rist** |-ist| *n.*

al•le•gro |ə'legrō| • *adj. & adv.* (esp. as a musical direction) at a brisk tempo. • *n.* (pl. **-os**) a passage or movement in an allegro tempo.

al•lele |ə'lēl| • *n.* (in genetics) one of two or more alternative forms of a gene that arise by mutation and are found at the same place on a chromosome. Also called **allelomorph.**
DERIVATIVES: **al•lel•ic** |ə'lēlik; ə'lel-| *adj.*

al•ler•gen |'ælərjən| • *n.* a substance that causes an allergic reaction.
DERIVATIVES: **al•ler•gen•ic** |,ælər'jenik| *adj.* **al•ler•ge•nic•i•ty** |,ælərjə'nisi̯tē| *n.*

al•le•vi•ate |ə'lēvē,āt| • *v.* [trans.] make (suffering, deficiency, or a problem) less severe: *he couldn't prevent her pain, only alleviate it* | *measures to alleviate unemployment.*
DERIVATIVES: **al•le•vi•a•tion** |ə,lēvē'āsHən| *n.* **al•le•vi•a•tor** |-,ātər| *n.*

al•lit•er•a•tion |ə,litə'rāsHən| • *n.* the occurrence of the same letter or sound at the beginning of adjacent or closely connected words. *"I put it in a pot on the porch," I pronounced, unmindful of the alliteration.* | *alliterations are clustered in Anglo-Saxon poems.* Cf. ASSONANCE.
DERIVATIVES: **al•lit•er•ate** *v.* **al•lit•er•a•tive** *adj.*

al•lo•cate |'ælə,kāt| • *v.* [trans.] divide up and distribute (something) in a planned manner: *the authorities **allocated** 50,000 places **to** refugees* | [with two objs.] *students are allocated accommodation on a yearly basis.*
DERIVATIVES: **al•lo•ca•ble** |-kəbəl| *adj.* **al•lo•ca•tor** |-,kātər| *n.* **al•lo•ca•tion** *n.*

al•lo•cu•tion |,ælə'kyōōsHən| • *n.* a formal speech giving advice or a warning.

al•lop•a•thy |ə'läpəTHē| • *n.* the treatment of disease by conventional means, i.e., with drugs having effects opposite to the symptoms. Cf. HOMEOPATHY.
DERIVATIVES: **al•lo•path•ic** |,ælə'pæTHik| *adj.* **al•lop•a•thist** |-THist| *n.*

al•lot |ə'lät| • *v.* (**allotted, allotting**) [trans.] give or apportion (something) to someone as a share or task: *equal time was allotted to each* | [with two objs.] *I was allotted a little room in the servants' block.* Cf. ALLOCATE.

al•loy • *n.* |'æ,loi| a metal made by combining two or more metallic elements, esp. to give greater strength or resistance to corrosion: *an alloy of nickel, bronze, and zinc* | *flat pieces of alloy* | [as adj.] *alloy wheels.*
■ an inferior metal mixed with a precious one. • *v.* |'æ,loi; ə'loi| [trans.] mix (metals) to make an alloy: *alloying tin with copper to make bronze.*
■ debase (something) by adding something inferior.

al•lude |ə'lōōd| • *v.* [intrans.] (**allude to**) suggest or call attention to indirectly; hint at: *she had a way of alluding to Jean but never saying her name.*
■ mention without discussing at length: *we will allude briefly to the main points.* ■ (of an artist or a work of art) recall (an earlier work or style) in such a way as to suggest a relationship with it: *the photographs allude to Italian Baroque painting.*

al•lure |ə'loŏr| • *n.* the quality of being powerfully and mysteriously attractive or fascinating: *people for whom gold holds no allure.* • *v.* [trans.] powerfully attract or charm; tempt: [as adj.] (**alluring**) *the town offers alluring shops and restaurants.*
DERIVATIVES: **al•lure•ment** *n.* **al•lur•ing•ly** *adv.*

al•lu•sion |ə'lōōzHən| • *n.* an expression designed to call something to mind without mentioning it explicitly; an indirect or passing reference: ***an allusion to** Shakespeare* | *a classical allusion.*
■ the practice of making such references, esp. as an artistic device.

al•lu•vi•al |ə'lōōvēəl| • *adj.* relating to or derived from clay, silt, or sand left by flood water in a river valley or delta (alluvium): *rich alluvial soils.*

al•ma ma•ter |'älmə 'mätər; 'ælmə| • *n.* (**one's Alma Mater**) the school, college, or university that one once attended.
■ the anthem of a school, college, or university.

al•o•pe•ci•a |,ælə'pēsH(ē)ə| • *n.* the partial or complete absence of hair from areas of the body where it normally grows; baldness.

al•pha |'ælfə| • *n.* the first letter of the Greek alphabet (A, α), transliterated as "a."
■ [as adj.] denoting the first of a series of items or categories. ■ (of animals in a group) the socially dominant individual: *he rose to be alpha male of his troop at the very early age of 16.*
PHRASES: **alpha and omega** the beginning and the end (esp. used by Christians as a title for Jesus). ■ the essence or most important features: *collective bargaining is seen as the alpha and omega of trade unionism.*

al•pha•nu•mer•ic |,ælfən(y)ōō'merik| • *adj.*

consisting of or using both letters and numerals: *alphanumeric data* | *an alphanumeric keyboard.* • *n.* a character that is either a letter or a number.

DERIVATIVES: **al•pha•nu•mer•i•cal** *adj.*

al•ter•ca•tion | ˌôltər'kāsHən | • *n.* a noisy argument or disagreement, esp. in public: *I had an altercation with the ticket collector.*

al•ter e•go • *n.* a person's secondary or alternative personality.

■ an intimate and trusted friend.

al•ti•tude | 'ælti,t(y)ōōd | • *n.* the height of an object or point in relation to sea level or ground level: *flight data including airspeed and altitude flying at altitudes over 15,000 feet.*

■ great height: *the mechanism can freeze at altitude.* ■ the apparent height of a celestial object above the horizon, measured in angular distance. ■ (in geometry) the length of the perpendicular line from a vertex to the opposite side of a figure.

DERIVATIVES: **al•ti•tu•di•nal** | ˌælti't(y)ōōdn-əl | *adj.*

al•tru•ism | 'æltrə,wizəm | • *n.* the belief in or practice of disinterested and selfless concern for the well-being of others: *some may choose to work with vulnerable elderly people out of altruism.*

■ behavior of an animal that benefits another at its own expense.

DERIVATIVES: **al•tru•ist** *n.* **al•tru•is•tic** | ˌæltrə'wistik | *adj.* **al•tru•is•ti•cal•ly** | ˌæltrə 'wistik(ə)lē | *adv.*

a•mal•gam | ə'mælgəm | • *n.* a mixture or blend: *a curious amalgam of the traditional and the modern.*

■ an alloy of mercury with another metal, esp. one used for dental fillings.

a•mal•ga•mate | ə'mælgə,māt | • *v.* combine or unite to form one organization or structure: [trans.] *he* **amalgamated** *his company* **with** *another* | [intrans.] *numerous small railroad companies amalgamated* | [as adj.] (**amalgamated**) *his true genius lies in synthesis, in an amalgamated vision.*

■ (in chemistry) alloy (a metal) with mercury: [as adj.] (**amalgamated**) *amalgamated zinc.*

DERIVATIVES: **a•mal•ga•ma•tion** *n.*

a•man•u•en•sis | ə,mænyə'wensis | • *n.* (pl. **amanuenses** | -,sēz |) a literary or artistic assistant, in particular one who takes dictation or copies manuscripts.

am•a•ranth | 'æmə,rænTH | • *n.* **1** any plant of the genus *Amaranthus,* some grown for food, usually having small green, red, or purple tinted flowers. **2** an imaginary flower that never fades. **3** a purple color.

DERIVATIVES: **am•a•ran•thine** | ˌæmə 'rænTHin; -,THīn | *adj.*

a•mass | ə'mæs | • *v.* [trans.] gather together or accumulate (a large amount or number of valuable material or things) over a period of time: *starting from nothing he had amassed a huge fortune.*

■ [intrans.] (of people) gather together in a crowd or group: *the soldiers were amassing from all parts of Spain.*

DERIVATIVES: **a•mass•er** *n.*

am•a•to•ry | 'æmə,tôrē | • *adj.* [attrib.] relating to or induced by sexual love or desire: *his amatory exploits.*

Am•a•zon | 'æmə,zän; 'æməzən | • *n.* a member of a legendary race of female warriors believed by the ancient Greeks to exist in Scythia (near the Black Sea in modern Russia) or elsewhere on the edge of the known world.

■ (also **amazon**) a tall and strong or athletic woman.

DERIVATIVES: **Am•a•zo•ni•an** | ˌæmə'zōnēən | *adj.*

am•bi•dex•trous | ˌæmbi'dekst(ə)rəs | • *adj.* (of a person) able to use the right and left hands equally well: *few of us are naturally ambidextrous.*

■ (of an implement) designed to be used by left-handed and right-handed people with equal ease.

DERIVATIVES: **am•bi•dex•ter•i•ty** | -deks 'teritē | *n.* **am•bi•dex•trous•ly** *adv.*

am•bi•ence | 'æmbēəns | (also **ambiance**) • *n.* [usu. in sing.] the character and atmosphere of a place: *the relaxed ambience of the cocktail lounge is popular with guests.*

am•bi•ent | 'æmbēənt | • *adj.* [attrib.] of or relating to the immediate surroundings of something: *the liquid is stored at below ambient temperature.*

am•big•u•ous | æm'bigyəwəs | • *adj.* (esp. of language) open to more than one interpretation; having a double meaning: *the question is rather ambiguous* | *ambiguous phrases.* | *an ambiguous expression.*

■ unclear or inexact because a choice between alternatives has not been made: *this whole society is morally ambiguous* | *the election result was ambiguous.*

DERIVATIVES: **am•big•u•i•ty** *n.* **am•big•u•ous•ly** *adv.*

am•bit | 'æmbit | • *n.* [in sing.] the scope, extent, or bounds of something: *within the ambit of federal law.*

am•biv•a•lent | æm'bivələnt | • *adj.* having mixed feelings or contradictory ideas about something or someone: *some loved her, some hated her, few were ambivalent about her* | *an ambivalent attitude toward terrorism.*

DERIVATIVES: **am•biv•a•lence** *n.* **am•biv•a•lent•ly** *adv.*

am•bro•sia | æm'brōZH(ē)ə | • *n.* (in Greek & Roman Mythology) the food of the gods: *the tea was ambrosia after the slop I'd been drinking.*

■ something very pleasing to taste or smell: *the tea was ambrosia after the slop I'd been drinking.* ■ a dessert made with oranges and shredded coconut.

DERIVATIVES: **am•bro•sial** *adj.*

am•bu•la•to•ry | 'æmbyələ,tôrē | • *adj.* relating to or adapted for walking.

■ able to walk; not bedridden: *ambulatory patients.* ■ relating to patients who are able to walk: *an ambulatory care facility.* ■ movable; mobile: *an ambulatory ophthalmic service.* • *n.* (pl. **-ies**) a place for walking, esp. an aisle or cloister in a church or monastery.

am•bus•cade | 'æmbə,skād; ˌæmbə'skād | • *n.* an ambush. • *v.* [trans.] attack from an ambush.

■ [intrans.] lie in ambush: [as adj.] (**ambuscaded**) *ambuscaded thousands swarmed up over the embankment.*

a•mel•io•rate |ə'mēlyə,rāt| • v. [trans.] make (something bad or unsatisfactory) better: *the reform did much to ameliorate living standards.*
DERIVATIVES: **a•mel•io•ra•tion** |ə,mēlyə'rāsHən| n. **a•mel•io•ra•tive** |-rətiv; -,rātiv| adj. **a•mel•io•ra•tor** |-,rātər| n.

a•me•na•ble |ə'mēnəbəl; ə'men-| • adj. (of a person) open and responsive to suggestion; easily persuaded or controlled: *parents who have had easy babies and amenable children.*
■ [predic.] (**amenable to**) (of a thing) capable of being acted upon in a particular way; susceptible: *patients with cardiac failure not amenable to treatment.*
DERIVATIVES: **a•me•na•bil•i•ty** |ə,mēnə'bilitē; ə,men-| n. **a•me•na•bly** |-blē| adv.

a•mend |ə'mend| • v. [trans.] make minor changes in (typically, a text) in order to make it fairer, more accurate, or more up-to-date: *the rule was amended to apply only to nonmembers.*
■ modify formally, as a legal document or legislative bill: *did she amend her original will later on?* | *pressuring Panama to amend its banking laws.* ■ make better; improve: *if you can amend people's attitudes.* ■ archaic put right: *a few things had gone wrong, but these had been amended.*
DERIVATIVES: **a•mend•a•ble** adj. **a•mend•er** n.

a•men•i•ty |ə'menitē; ə'mē-| • n. (pl. **-ies**) (usu. **amenities**) a desirable or useful feature or facility of a building or place: *heating is regarded as a basic amenity.* | *this resort has all the amenities.*
■ the pleasantness of a place or a person: *the exertion of amenity toward fellow workers.*

Am•er•a•sian |,æmər'āzHən| • adj. having one American and one Asian parent. • n. a person with one American and one Asian parent.

A•mer•i•can In•di•an • n. a member of any of the indigenous peoples of North, Central, and South America, esp. those of North America. • adj. of or relating to any of these groups.

USAGE: The term **American Indian** has been steadily replaced, esp. in official contexts, by the more recent term **Native American** (first recorded in the 1950s and becoming prominent in the 1970s). The latter is preferred by some as being a more accurate description (the word *Indian* recalling Columbus's assumption that, on reaching America, he had reached the east coast of India). **American Indian** is still widespread in general use, however, partly because it is not normally regarded as offensive by American Indians themselves.

a•mi•a•ble |'āmēəbəl| • adj. having or displaying a friendly and pleasant manner: *an amiable, unassuming fellow.*
■ having pleasing qualities; congenial; agreeable: *an amiable movie about a nerdy student's romantic fantasies.*

DERIVATIVES: **a•mi•a•bil•i•ty** |,āmēə'bilitē| n. **a•mi•a•bly** |-blē| adv. **a•mi•a•ble•ness** n.

am•i•ca•ble |'æmikəbəl| • adj. (of relations between people) having a spirit of friendliness; without serious disagreement or rancor: *there will be an amicable settlement of the dispute.*
DERIVATIVES: **am•i•ca•bil•i•ty** |,æmikə'bilitē| n. **am•i•ca•bly** |-blē| adv.

a•miss |ə'mis| • adj. [predic.] not quite right; inappropriate or out of place: *there was something amiss about his calculations.*
• adv. wrongly or inappropriately: *how terrible was the danger of her loving amiss.* | *don't take this amiss, it's all good-humored teasing.*

am•i•ty |'æmitē| • n. a friendly relationship: *international amity and goodwill.*

am•ne•sia |æm'nēzHə| • n. a partial or total loss of memory.
DERIVATIVES: **am•ne•si•ac** |æm'nēzē,æk; -zHē,æk| n. & adj. **am•ne•sic** |-zik; -sik| adj. & n. **am•nes•tic** |æm'nestik| adj.

am•nes•ty |'æmnistē| • n. (pl. **-ies**) an official pardon for people who have been convicted, esp. of political offenses: *an amnesty for political prisoners* | *the new law granted amnesty to those who illegally left the country.* Cf. CLEMENCY.
■ an undertaking by the authorities to take no action against specified offenses or offenders often during a fixed period: *a month-long weapons amnesty.* ■ a general pardon: *rebel soldiers still in the field were offered amnesty.* • v. (**-ies, -ied**) [trans.] grant an official pardon to: *the guerrillas would be amnestied and allowed to return to civilian life.*

am•ni•on |'æmnē,än; -ən| • n. (pl. **amnions** or **amnia** |-nēə|) the innermost membrane that encloses the embryo of a mammal, bird, or reptile.
DERIVATIVES: **am•ni•ot•ic** |,æmnē'ätik| adj: *the amniotic fluid is contained within the amniotic cavity.*

amniotic • adj. of or relating to the amnion.

a•mok |ə'mək; ə'mäk| (also **amuck**) • adv. (in phrase **run amok**) behave uncontrollably and disruptively: *stone-throwing anarchists running amok* | *her feelings seemed to be running amok.*

a•mor•al |ā'môrəl| • adj. lacking a moral sense; unconcerned with the rightness or wrongness of something: *an amoral attitude toward sex.*
DERIVATIVES: **a•mo•ral•i•ty** |,āmə'rælitē| n. **a•mor•al•ism** |-,lizəm| n. **a•mor•al•ist** |-list| n.

USAGE: **Amoral** is distinct in meaning from **immoral**: **immoral** means 'not conforming to accepted standards of morality'; **amoral** is a more neutral, impartial word (following the pattern of *apolitical, asexual*). **Amoral**, then, may refer to a judge's ruling that is concerned only with narrow legal or financial issues, as well as to a 'social deviant' lacking a sense of right and wrong. **Nonmoral**, meaning 'not to be judged from a moral standpoint', is used esp. of natural phenomena or processes: *We accept evolution as nonmoral.*

am•o•rist |ˈæmərist| • *n.* a person who is in love or who writes about love.

am•o•rous |ˈæmərəs| • *adj.* showing, feeling, or relating to sexual desire: *she rejected his amorous advances* | *her mood was amorous.*
DERIVATIVES: **am•o•rous•ly** *adv.* **am•o•rous•ness** *n.*

a•mor•phous |əˈmôrfəs| • *adj.* without a clearly defined shape or form: *amorphous blue forms and straight black lines.*
■ vague; ill-organized; unclassifiable: *who can interpret his amorphous statements.* ■ (of a group of people or an organization) lacking a clear structure or focus: *an amorphous and leaderless legislature.* ■ (of a solid) noncrystalline; having neither definite form nor apparent structure.
DERIVATIVES: **a•mor•phous•ly** *adv.* **a•mor•phous•ness** *n.*

am•or•tize |ˈæmərˌtīz| • *v.* [trans.] reduce or extinguish (a debt) by money regularly put aside: *loan fees can be amortized over the life of the mortgage.*
■ gradually write off the initial cost of (an asset): *they want to amortize the tooling costs quickly.* Cf. DEPRECIATE.
DERIVATIVES: **am•or•ti•za•tion** |ˌæmərti ˈzāsHən; əˌmôrti-| *n.*

a•mour |əˈmoŏr; äˈmoŏr| • *n.* a secret or illicit love affair or lover: *she used to conduct her amours with great discretion.*

a•mour pro•pre |äˌmoŏr ˈprôpr(ə)| • *n.* a sense of one's own worth; self-respect: *few indications in him of ordinary* amour propre *or common vanity.*

am•per•sand |ˈæmpərˌsænd| • *n.* the sign & (standing for *and*, as in *Smith & Co.*, or the Latin *et*, as in *&c.*).

am•phet•a•mine |æmˈfetəˌmēn; -min| • *n.* a synthetic, addictive, mood-altering drug, used illegally as a stimulant: *the amphetamine put him on a high for an hour* | *he was jailed for three months for possessing amphetamines.*

am•phib•i•an |æmˈfibēən| • *n.* a cold-blooded vertebrate animal of a class (Amphibia) that comprises the frogs, toads, newts, and salamanders. They are distinguished by having an aquatic gill-breathing larval stage followed (typically) by a terrestrial lung-breathing adult stage.
■ a seaplane, tank, or other vehicle that can operate on land and on water. • *adj.* of or relating to this class of animals: *reptile and amphibian biology.*

am•pho•ra |ˈæmfərə| • *n.* (pl. **amphorae** |-ˌrē| or **amphoras**) a tall ancient Greek or Roman jar with two handles and a narrow neck.

am•ple |ˈæmpəl| • *adj.* (**ampler**, **amplest**) enough or more than enough; plentiful: *there is ample time for discussion* | *an ample supply of consumer goods.*
■ large and accommodating: *he leaned back in his ample chair.* ■ used euphemistically to convey that someone is overweight: *she stood with her hands on her ample hips.*
DERIVATIVES: **am•ple•ness** *n.* **am•ply** |-p(ə)lē| *adv.*

am•pli•fy |ˈæmpləˌfī| • *v.* (**-ies, -ied**) [trans.] (often **be amplified**) increase the volume of (sound), esp. using an amplifier: *the accompanying chords were amplified to a painful level* | [as adj.] (**amplified**) *amplied pop music was playing.*
■ increase the amplitude of (an electrical signal or other oscillation). ■ cause to become more marked or intense: *urban policy initiatives amplified social polarization.* ■ make multiple copies of (a gene or DNA sequence). ■ enlarge upon or add detail to (a story or statement): *the notes amplify information contained in the statement.*
DERIVATIVES: **am•pli•fi•ca•tion** |ˌæmpləfi ˈkāsHən| *n.*

am•pul•la |æmˈpoŏlə; -ˈpələ| • *n.* (pl. **ampullae** |-lē|) a roughly spherical flask with two handles, used in ancient Rome.
■ a flask for sacred uses such as holding holy oil. ■ (in anatomy & zoology) a cavity, or the dilated end of a duct, shaped like a Roman ampulla.

am•u•let |ˈæmyəlit| • *n.* an ornament or small piece of jewelry thought to give protection against evil, danger, or disease.

An•a•bap•tism |ˌænəˈbæpˌtizəm| • *n.* the doctrine that baptism should be administered only to believing adults, held by a radical Protestant sect that emerged during the 1520s and 1530s.
DERIVATIVES: **An•a•bap•tist** *n.* & *adj.*

a•nach•ro•nism |əˈnækrəˌnizəm| • *n.* a thing belonging or appropriate to a period other than that in which it exists, esp. a thing that is conspicuously old-fashioned: *everything was as it would have appeared in centuries past apart from one anachronism, a bright yellow construction crane.*
■ an act of attributing a custom, event, or object to a period to which it does not belong: *the text is full of anachronisms suggesting later additions.*
DERIVATIVES: **a•nach•ro•nis•tic** |əˌnækrə ˈnistik| *adj.* **a•nach•ro•nis•ti•cal•ly** |əˈ ˌnækrəˈnistik(ə)lē| *adv.*

an•a•co•lu•thon |ˌænəkəˈloŏˌTHän| • *n.* (pl. **anacolutha** |-THə|) a sentence or construction that lacks grammatical sequence, such as *while in the garden, the door banged shut.*
DERIVATIVES: **an•a•co•lu•thic** |-THik| *adj.*

an•a•gram |ˈænəˌgræm| • *n.* a word, phrase, or name formed by rearranging the letters of another, such as *cinema*, formed from *iceman*. • *v.* (**anagrammed**, **anagramming**) make an anagram of; anagrammatize.
DERIVATIVES: **an•a•gram•mat•ic** |ˌænəgrəˈmætik| *adj.* **an•a•gram•mat•i•cal** |ˌænəgrəˈmætikəl| *adj.*

a•nal |ˈānl| • *adj.* involving, relating to, or situated near the anus.
■ (in Freudian psychoanalysis) relating to or denoting a stage of infantile psychosexual development supposedly preoccupied with the

anus and defecation. ■ excessively orderly and fussy (anal-retentive): *he's anal about things like that.*

DERIVATIVES: **a•nal•ly** *adv.*

an•a•lects |'ænl‚ek(t)s| (also **analecta**) • *plural n.* a collection of short literary or philosophical extracts: *analects of Confucius.*

an•al•ge•sic |‚ænl'jēzik; -sik| • *adj.* (chiefly of a drug) acting to relieve pain. • *n.* an analgesic drug.

an•a•log |'ænl‚ôg; -‚äg| (also **analogue**) • *n.* a person or thing seen as comparable to another: *the idea that the fertilized egg contains a miniature analog of every adult structure.* ■ (in chemistry) a compound with a molecular structure closely similar to that of another. • *adj.* relating to or using signals or information represented by a continuously variable physical quantity such as spatial position or voltage. Often contrasted with DIGITAL. ■ (of a clock or watch) showing the time by means of hands rather than displayed digits.

a•nal•o•gous |ə'næləgəs| • *adj.* (often **analogous to**) comparable in certain respects, typically in a way that makes clearer the nature of the things compared: *they saw the relationship between a ruler and his subjects as analogous to that of father and children.* ■ (of organs, in biology) performing a similar function but having a different evolutionary origin, such as the wings of insects and birds. Often contrasted with HOMOLOGOUS.

DERIVATIVES: **a•nal•o•gous•ly** *adv.*

a•nal•o•gy |ə'næləjē| • *n.* (pl. **-ies**) a comparison between two things, typically on the basis of their structure and for the purpose of explanation or clarification: *an analogy between the workings of nature and those of human societies | interpreting logical functions by analogy with machines.* ■ a correspondence or partial similarity: *the syndrome is called deep dysgraphia because of its analogy to deep dyslexia.* ■ a thing that is comparable to something else in significant respects: *works of art were seen as an analogy for works of nature.* ■ (in logic) a process of arguing from similarity in known respects to similarity in other respects. ■ a process by which new words and inflections are created on the basis of regularities in the form of existing ones. ■ (in biology) the resemblance of function between organs that have a different evolutionary origin.

DERIVATIVES: **an•a•log•i•cal** |‚ænə'läjikəl| *adj.* **an•a•log•i•cal•ly** |‚ænə'läjik(ə)lē| *adv.* **analogize** *v.*

a•nal•y•sis |ə'næləsis| • *n.* (pl. **analyses** |-‚sēz|) detailed examination of the elements or structure of something, typically as a basis for discussion or interpretation: *statistical analysis | an analysis of popular culture.* ■ the process of separating something into its constituent elements. Often contrasted with SYNTHESIS. ■ the identification and measurement of the chemical constituents of a substance or specimen. ■ short for PSYCHOANALYSIS. ■ (in linguistics) the use of separate, short words and word order rather than in-

flection or agglutination to express grammatical structure. ■ the part of mathematics concerned with the theory of functions and the use of limits, continuity, and the operations of calculus.

DERIVATIVES: **an•a•lyt•i•cal** *adj.* **an•a•lyt•i•cal•ly** *adv.*

an•a•lyt•ic |‚ænl'itik| (also **analytical**) • *adj.* relating to or using analysis or logical reasoning. ■ (in logic) true by virtue of the meaning of the words or concepts used to express it, so that its denial would be a self-contradiction. ■ (of a language) tending not to alter the form of its words and to use word order rather than inflection or agglutination to express grammatical structure.

An•a•ni•as |‚ænə'nīəs| (in the New Testament) the husband of Sapphira, struck dead because he lied (Acts 5). ■ a liar.

an•a•pest |'ænə‚pest| (Brit. **anapaest**) • *n.* (in prosody) a metrical foot consisting of two short or unstressed syllables followed by one long or stressed syllable.

DERIVATIVES: **an•a•pes•tic** |‚ænə'pestik| *adj.*

a•naph•o•ra |ə'næfərə| • *n.* **1** the use of a word referring to or replacing a word used earlier in a sentence, to avoid repetition, such as *do* in *I like it and so do they.* **2** the repetition of a word or phrase at the beginning of successive clauses. **3** (in Christian ritual) the part of the Eucharist that contains the consecration, anamnesis, and communion.

DERIVATIVES: **an•a•phor•ic** |‚ænə'fôrik| *adj.*

an•aph•ro•dis•i•ac |‚æn‚æfrə'dizē‚æk| • *adj.* (chiefly of a drug) tending to reduce sexual desire. ■ *n.* an anaphrodisiac drug.

an•ar•chic |æ'närkik| • *adj.* with no controlling rules or principles to give order: *an anarchic and bitter civil war.* ■ (of comedy or a person's sense of humor) uncontrolled by convention: *anarchic wit.*

DERIVATIVES: **an•ar•chi•cal** |-ikəl| *adj.* **an•ar•chi•cal•ly** |-ik(ə)lē| *adv.*

an•ar•chist |'ænərkist| • *n.* a person who believes in or tries to bring about anarchy. • *adj.* relating to or supporting anarchy or anarchists: *an anarchist newspaper.*

DERIVATIVES: **an•ar•chis•tic** |‚ænər'kistik| *adj.* **an•ar•chism** *n.*

an•ar•chy |'ænərkē| • *n.* a state of disorder owing to absence or nonrecognition of authority: *we must ensure public order in a country threatened with anarchy.* ■ social or political confusion: *the futility and anarchy of modern city life.* ■ the absence of government as a political ideal, and absolute freedom of the individual: *liberty will arise, a liberty that in fact will be identical with anarchy.*

a•nath•e•ma |ə'næᴛHəmə| • *n.* **1** something or someone that one vehemently dislikes: *political correctness is anathema to her.* **2** a formal curse by a pope or a council of the Roman Catholic Church, excommunicating a person or denouncing a doctrine.

■ a strong curse: *the sergeant clutched the malfunctioning transmitter, muttering anathemas.*

an•cho•rite |ˈæNGkə,rīt| • *n.* a religious recluse.

DERIVATIVES: **an•cho•rit•ic** |,æNGkəˈriṯik| *adj.*

an•cil•lar•y |ˈænsə,lerē| • *adj.* providing necessary support to the primary activities or operation of an organization, institution, industry, or system: *the development of ancillary services to support its products.*

■ additional; subsidiary: *paragraph 19 was merely* **ancillary** *to paragraph 16.* • *n.* (pl. **-ies**) a person whose work provides necessary support to the primary activities of an organization, institution, or industry: *the employment of specialist teachers and ancillaries.*

■ something that functions in a supplementary or supporting role: *an undergraduate course of three main subjects with related ancillaries.*

an•dan•te |änˈdän,tā| • *adj.* & *adv.* (esp. as a musical direction) in a moderately slow tempo. • *n.* a movement or composition marked to be played andante.

an•drog•y•nous |ænˈdräjənəs| • *adj.* partly male and partly female in appearance; of indeterminate sex.

■ having the physical characteristics of both sexes; hermaphrodite.

DERIVATIVES: **an•dro•gyne** *n.* an androgynous individual. **an•drog•y•ny** |-nē| *n.*

an•droid |ˈæn,droid| • *n.* (in science fiction) a robot with a human appearance.

an•ec•do•tal |,ænikˈdōṯl| • *adj.* (of an account) not necessarily true or reliable, because based on personal accounts rather than facts or research: *while there was much anecdotal evidence there was little hard fact* | *these claims were purely anecdotal.*

■ characterized by or fond of telling anecdotes: *her book is anecdotal and chatty.* ■ [attrib.] (of a painting) depicting small narrative incidents: *nineteenth-century French anecdotal paintings.*

DERIVATIVES: **an•ec•do•tal•ist** |-ist| *n.* **an•ec•do•tal•ly** *adv.*

an•ec•dote |ˈænik,dōt| • *n.* a short and amusing or interesting story about a real incident or person: *he told anecdotes about his job* | *he had a rich store of anecdote.*

■ an account regarded as unreliable or hearsay: *his wife's death has long been the subject of rumor and anecdote.* ■ the depiction of a minor narrative incident in a painting.

DERIVATIVES: **an•ec•do•tal** *adj.*

a•ne•mi•a |əˈnēmēə| (Brit. **anaemia**) • *n.* a condition marked by a deficiency of red blood cells or of hemoglobin in the blood, resulting in pallor and weariness.

a•ne•mic |əˈnēmik| (Brit.**anaemic**) • *adj.* suffering from anemia.

■ lacking in color, spirit, or vitality: *an anemic rendering of mountain landscape.*

a•nent |əˈnent| • *prep.* concerning; about: *I'll say a few words anent the letter.*

an•er•o•bic |,æneˈrōbik| ,ænə-| • *adj.* relating to, involving, or requiring an absence of free oxygen: *anerobic bacteria.*

■ relating to or denoting exercise that does not improve or is not intended to improve the efficiency of the body's cardiovascular system in absorbing and transporting oxygen. *anerobic exercise like weightlifting requires short sudden bursts of energy.* Cf. AEROBIC.

DERIVATIVES: **an•er•o•bi•cal•ly** |-bik(ə)-lē| *adv.*

an•es•thet•ic |,ænəsˈTHeṯik| (Brit. **anaesthetic**) • *n.* **1** a substance that induces insensitivity to pain. **2** (**anesthetics**) [treated as sing.] the study or practice of anesthesia. • *adj.* inducing or relating to insensitivity to pain.

an•es•the•tist |əˈnesTHiṯist| (Brit. **anaesthetist**) • *n.* a medical specialist who administers anesthetics. (An **anesthesiologist** is a doctor trained in the science of anesthetics (anesthesiology).)

an•eu•rysm |ˈænyə,rizəm| (also **aneurism**) • *n.* an excessive localized and often dangerous enlargement of an artery caused by a weakening of the artery wall.

DERIVATIVES: **an•eu•rys•mal** |-,rizməl| *adj.*

an•gi•o•sperm |ˈænjēə,spərm| • *n.* a plant that has flowers and produces seeds enclosed within a seed vessel (carpel). Most herbaceous plants, shrubs, grasses, and trees are angiosperms.

an•gli•cize |ˈæNGgli,sīz| • *v.* [trans.] make English in form or character: *he anglicized his name to Goodman* | [as adj.] (**anglicized**) *an anglicized form of a Navajo word.*

DERIVATIVES: **an•gli•ci•za•tion** |,æNGglisi-ˈzāsHən| *n.*

an•glo•phone |ˈæNGglə,fōn| • *adj.* English-speaking: *anglophone students* | *the population of west Montreal is largely anglophone.* • *n.* an English-speaking person.

An•glo-Sax•on • *adj.* relating to or denoting the Germanic inhabitants of England from their arrival in the 5th century up to the Norman Conquest.

■ of English descent. ■ of, in, or relating to the Old English language. ■ (of an English word or expression) plain, in particular vulgar: *using a lot of good old Anglo-Saxon expletives.* • *n.* **1** a Germanic inhabitant of England between the 5th century and the Norman Conquest.

■ a person of English descent. ■ any white, English-speaking person. **2** another term for Old English, the language of the Anglo-Saxons to about 1150.

■ plain English, in particular vulgar slang.

angst |äNG(k)st; äNG(k)st| • *n.* a feeling of deep anxiety or dread, typically an unfocused one about the human condition or the state of the world in general: *adolescent angst.*

■ a feeling of persistent worry about something trivial: *my hair causes me angst.*

an•guine • *adj.* of or resembling a snake.

an•gu•lar |ˈæNGgyələr| • *adj.* **1** (of an object, outline, or shape) having angles or sharp corners: *angular chairs* | *Adam's angular black handwriting.*

■ (of a person or part of the body) lean and

having a prominent bone structure: *her angular face.* ■ (esp. of a person's way of moving) not flowing smoothly; awkward or jerky: *his movements were stiff and angular. the music is angular and sardonic.* ■ placed or directed at an angle: *he launched an angular shot across the face of the goal.* **2** denoting physical properties or quantities measured with reference to or by means of an angle, esp. those associated with rotation: *angular acceleration.*
DERIVATIVES: **an•gu•lar•i•ty** |ˌæNGgyə'læriṯē; -'ler-| *n.* **an•gu•lar•ly** *adv.*

an•i•mad•vert |ˌænəmæd'vərt| • *v.* [intrans.] (**animadvert on/upon/against**) pass criticism or censure on; speak out against: *we shall be obliged to animadvert most severely upon you in our report* | *many travelers animadvert against their own towns and cities.*
DERIVATIVES: **an•i•mad•ver•sion** *n.*

an•i•mat•ed |'ænəˌmāṯid| • *adj.* **1** full of life or excitement; lively: *an animated conversation.* **2** (of a movie) made using animation techniques: *an animated version of the classic fairytale.*
■ moving or appearing to move as if alive: *animated life-size figures.*
DERIVATIVES: **an•i•mat•ed•ly** *adv.*

an•i•ma•tion |ˌænə'māsHən| • *n.* **1** the state of being full of life or vigor; liveliness: *they started talking with animation.*
■ the state of being alive. **2** the technique of filming successive drawings or positions of puppets or models to create an illusion of movement when the movie is shown as a sequence: [as adj.] *animation techniques* | *animations as backdrops for live action.*
■ (also **computer animation**) the manipulation of electronic images by means of a computer in order to create moving images.

an•i•mism |'ænəˌmizəm| • *n.* **1** the attribution of a living soul to plants, inanimate objects, and natural phenomena. **2** the belief in a supernatural power that organizes and animates the material universe.
DERIVATIVES: **an•i•mist** *n.* **an•i•mis•tic** |ˌænə'mistik| *adj.*

an•i•mos•i•ty |ˌænə'mäsiṯē| • *n.* (pl. **-ies**) strong hostility: *he no longer felt any animosity toward her* | *the animosity between Norm and his brother* | *the five decided to put aside their animosities.*

an•i•mus |'ænəməs| • *n.* **1** hostility or ill feeling: *the author's animus toward her.* **2** motivation to do something: *the reformist animus came from within the Party.* **3** the psychologist C.G. Jung's term for the masculine part of a woman's personality. Often contrasted with *anima*, the feminine part of a man's personality.

an•nals |'ænlz| • *plural n.* a record of events year by year: *eighth-century annals for a small English town.*
■ historical records: *the annals of the famous European discoverers* | *the deed will live forever in the annals of infamy.* ■ (**Annals**) used in the titles of learned journals: *Annals of Internal Medicine.*

an•neal |ə'nēl| • *v.* [trans.] heat (metal or

glass) and allow it to cool slowly, in order to remove internal stresses and toughen it.
DERIVATIVES: **an•neal•er** *n.*

an•nex • *v.* |ə'neks; 'æneks| [trans.] (often **be annexed**) append or add as an extra or subordinate part, esp. to a document: *the first ten amendments were annexed to the Constitution in 1791* | [as adj.] (**annexed**) *the annexed diagram.*
■ add (territory) to one's own territory by appropriation: *Roxbury was annexed to Barton in 1868.* ■ take for oneself; appropriate: *it was bad enough that Richard should have annexed his girlfriend.* ■ add or attach as a condition or consequence. • *n.* |'æneks; -iks| (pl. **annexes**) **1** a building joined to or associated with a main building, providing additional space or accommodation. **2** an addition to a document: *an annex to the report.*
DERIVATIVES: **an•nex•a•tion** |ˌænek'sāsHən; ˌænik-| *n.* **an•nex•a•tion•ism** *n.* **an•nex•a•tion•ist** |ˌænek'sāsHənist; ˌænik-| *n. & adj.*

an•ni•hi•late |ə'nīəˌlāt| • *v.* [trans.] destroy utterly; obliterate: *a simple bomb of this type could annihilate them* | *a crusade to annihilate evil.*
■ defeat utterly: *the stronger force annihilated its opponent virtually without loss.*
DERIVATIVES: **an•ni•hi•la•tor** |-ˌlāṯər| *n.* **an•ni•hi•la•tion** |əˌnīə'lāsHən| *n.*

an•nu•al |'ænyəwəl| • *adj.* occurring once every year: *the union's annual conference* | *the sponsored walk became an annual event* | *an annual report.*
■ calculated over or covering a period of a year: *annual accounts* | *an annual rate of increase* | *his basic annual income.* ■ (of a plant) living only for a year or less, and perpetuating itself by seed: *annual flowers.* • *n.* a book or magazine that is published once a year under the same title but with different contents: *a Christmas annual* | *trade journals, annuals, and directories.*
■ an annual plant: *sow annuals in spring.* [as an adj.] *tending the annual beds.*
DERIVATIVES: **an•nu•al•ly** *adv.*

an•nu•i•ty |ə'n(y)ōōiṯē| • *n.* (pl. **-ies**) a fixed sum of money paid to someone each year, typically for the rest of his or her life: *he left her an annuity of $10,000 in his will.*
■ a form of insurance or investment entitling the investor to a series of annual sums: [as adj.] *an annuity scheme.*

an•nul |ə'nəl| • *v.* (**annulled, annulling**) [trans.] (usu. **be annulled**) declare (an official agreement, decision, or result) invalid: *the elections were annulled by the junta amid renewed protests.*
■ declare (a marriage) to have had no legal existence: *her first marriage was annulled by His Holiness.*
DERIVATIVES: **an•nul•ment** *n.*

an•nu•lar |'ænyələr| • *adj.* ring-shaped.
DERIVATIVES: **an•nu•lar•ly** *adv.*

an•nun•ci•ate |ə'nənsēˌāt| • *v.* [trans.] indicate as coming or ready; announce (something).

an•o•dyne |'ænə,dīn| • *adj.* not likely to provoke dissent or offense; uncontentious or inoffensive, often deliberately so: *anodyne piano music* | *I attempted to keep the conversation as anodyne as possible.* • *n.* a pain-killing drug or medicine.
■ something that alleviates a person's mental distress: *an anodyne to the misery she had put him through.*

a•noint |ə'noint| • *v.* [trans.] smear or rub with oil, typically as part of a religious ceremony: *bodies were anointed after death for burial.*
■ (**anoint something with**) smear or rub something with (any other substance): *they anoint the tips of their arrows with poison.* ■ ceremonially confer divine or holy office upon (a priest or monarch) by smearing or rubbing with oil:[with obj. and infinitive] *the Lord has anointed me to preach to the poor* | [with obj. and complement] *Samuel anointed him king.* ■ nominate or choose (someone) as successor to or leading candidate for a position: *he was anointed as the organizational candidate of the party* | [as adj.] (**anointed**) *his officially anointed heir.*

a•nom•a•lous |ə'nämələs| • *adj.* deviating from what is standard, normal, or expected: *an anomalous situation* | *sentences that are grammatically anomalous*
DERIVATIVES: **a•nom•a•lous•ly** *adv.* **a•nom•a•lous•ness** *n.*

a•nom•a•ly |ə'näməlē| • *n.* (pl. **-ies**) something that deviates from what is standard, normal, or expected: *there are a number of anomalies in the present system* | *a legal anomaly* | [with clause] *the apparent anomaly that those who produced the wealth were the poorest* | *the position abounds in anomaly.*
DERIVATIVES: **anomalous** *n.*

an•o•rex•i•a |,ænə'reksēə| • *n.* a lack or loss of appetite for food (as a medical condition).
■ (also **anorexia nervosa**) an emotional disorder characterized by an obsessive desire to lose weight by refusing to eat.

an•te•bel•lum |,æntē'beləm| • *adj.* [attrib.] occurring or existing before a particular war, esp. the US Civil War: *the conventions of the antebellum South.*

an•te•ced•ent |,ænti'sēdnt| • *n.* a thing or event that existed before or logically precedes another: *some antecedents to the African novel might exist in Africa's oral traditions.*
■ (**antecedents**) a person's ancestors or family and social background: *her early life and antecedents have been traced.* ■ a word, phrase, clause, or sentence to which another word (esp. a following relative pronoun) refers. ■ (in logic) the statement contained in the "if" clause of a conditional proposition. ■ the first term in a mathematical ratio. • *adj.* preceding in time or order; previous or preexisting: *the antecedent events that prompt you to break a diet.*
■ denoting a grammatical antecedent.
DERIVATIVES: **an•te•ced•ence** *n.*

an•te•date |'ænti,dāt| • *v.* [trans.] precede in time; come before (something) in date: *a civilization that antedated the Roman Empire.*

■ indicate that (a document or event) should be assigned to an earlier date: *there are no references to him that would antedate his birth.*

an•te•di•lu•vi•an |,æntēdə'lōōvēən| • *adj.* [attrib.] of or belonging to the time before the biblical Flood: *gigantic bones of antediluvian animals.*
■ ridiculously old-fashioned: *they maintain antediluvian sex-role stereotypes.*

an•te•ri•or |æn'tirēər| • *adj.* **1** nearer the front, esp. situated in the front of the body, or nearer to the head or forepart: *the veins anterior to the heart.* **2** coming before in time; earlier: *there are few examples of gold and silver work anterior to the dynasty of the Romanoffs.*
DERIVATIVES: **an•te•ri•or•i•ty** |æn,tirē'ôritē; -'är-| *n.* **an•te•ri•or•ly** *adv.*

an•thol•o•gy |æn'THäləjē| • *n.* (pl. **-ies**) a published collection of poems or other pieces of writing: *an anthology of Persian poetry.*
■ a similar collection of songs or musical compositions issued in one album.
DERIVATIVES: **an•thol•o•gist** |-jist| *n.* **an•thol•o•gize** *v.*

an•thro•poid |'ænTHrə,poid| • *adj.* resembling a human being in form: *cartoons of anthropoid frogs.*
■ of or relating to the group of higher primates, which includes monkeys, apes, and humans. ■ (of an ape) belonging to the family of great apes. ■ (of a person) apelike in appearance or behavior: *his crewcut sloped down to an anthropoid forehead.* • *n.* a higher primate, esp. an ape or one of the extinct relatives of early humans.
■ a person who resembles an ape in appearance or behavior: *anthropoids ruled the streets.*

an•thro•pol•o•gy |,ænTHrə'päləjē| • *n.* the study of humankind, in particular:
■ (also **cultural** or **social anthropology**) the comparative study of human societies and cultures and their development. ■ (also **physical anthropology**) the science of human zoology, evolution, and ecology.
DERIVATIVES: **an•thro•po•log•i•cal** |-pə'läjikəl| *adj.* **an•thro•pol•o•gist** |-jist| *n.*

an•thro•po•mor•phic |,ænTHrəpə'môrfik| • *adj.* relating to or characterized by anthropomorphism.
■ having human characteristics: *anthropomorphic bears and monkeys.*
DERIVATIVES: **an•thro•po•mor•phi•cal•ly** |-ik(ə)lē| *adv.*

an•thro•po•mor•phism |,ænTHrəpə'môr,fizəm| • *n.* the attribution of human characteristics or behavior to a god, animal, or object.
DERIVATIVES: **an•thro•po•mor•phize** |-,fīz| *v.*

an•thro•poph•a•gy |,ænTHrə'päfəjē| • *n.* the eating of human flesh by human beings; cannibalism.
DERIVATIVES: **an•thro•poph•a•gous** |-gəs| *adj.*

An•ti•christ |'æntē,krīst; 'æntī-| • *n.* (**the Antichrist**) a great personal opponent of Christ who will spread evil throughout the

world before being conquered at Christ's second coming.
■ a person or force seen as opposing Christ or the Christian Church.

an•ti•cler•i•cal |ˌæntēˈklərikəl; ˌæntī-| • *adj.* opposed to the power or influence of the clergy, esp. in politics. • *n.* a person holding such views.
DERIVATIVES: **an•ti•cler•i•cal•ism** |-ˌlizəm| *n.*

an•ti•cli•max |ˌæntēˈklī,mæks; ˌæntī-| • *n.* a disappointing end to an exciting or impressive series of events: *the rest of the journey was an anticlimax by comparison | a sense of anticlimax and incipient boredom.*
DERIVATIVES: **an•ti•cli•mac•tic** |-klī'mæktik| *adj.* **an•ti•cli•mac•ti•cal•ly** |-klī'mæktik(ə)lē| *adv.*

an•ti•gen |'æntijən| • *n.* a toxin or other foreign substance that induces an immune response in the body, esp. the production of antibodies (blood proteins that counteract alien organisms by combining with them).
DERIVATIVES: **an•ti•gen•ic** |ˌæntiˈjenik| *adj.*

an•ti•he•ro (also **anti-hero**) • *n.* a central character in a story, movie, or drama who lacks conventional heroic, and displays instead the opposite, attributes.

an•ti•ma•cas•sar |ˌæntēməˈkæsər| • *n.* a piece of cloth put over the back of a chair to protect it from grease and dirt or as an ornament.

an•ti•mo•ny |'æntə,mōnē| • *n.* the chemical element of atomic number 51, a brittle silvery-white metalloid. (Symbol: **Sb**)
DERIVATIVES: **an•ti•mo•ni•al** |ˌæntə'mōnēəl| *adj.* **an•ti•mo•nic** |ˌæntə'mänik| *adj.* **an•ti•mo•ni•ous** |ˌæntə'mōnēəs| *adj.*

an•tin•o•my |æn'tinəmē| • *n.* (pl. **-ies**) a contradiction between two beliefs or conclusions that are in themselves reasonable; a paradox.
DERIVATIVES: **an•tin•o•mic** *adj.*

an•ti•ox•i•dant |ˌæntē'äksidənt; ˌæntī-| • *n.* a substance that inhibits oxidation, esp. one used to counteract the deterioration of stored food products.
■ a substance such as vitamin C or E that removes potentially damaging oxidizing agents in a living organism.

an•ti•pa•thet•ic |æn,tipə'THetik| • *adj.* showing or feeling a strong aversion: *it is human nature to be **antipathetic to** change.*

an•tip•a•thy |æn'tipəTHē| • *n.* (pl. **-ies**) a deep-seated feeling of dislike; aversion: *his fundamental **antipathy to** capitalism | a thinly disguised mutual antipathy.*

an•tiph•o•nal |æn'tifənl| • *adj.* (esp. in traditional western Christian liturgy) (of a short sentence or its musical setting [an *antiphon*]) sung, recited, or played alternately by two groups. • *n.* another term for *antiphonary*, a book of antiphons.
DERIVATIVES: **an•tiph•o•nal•ly** *adv.*

an•tip•o•des |æn'tipədēz| • *plural n.* (**the Antipodes**) places on the surface of the earth directly or diametically opposite to each other, or those who live there.

■ the direct opposite of something: *we are the very **antipodes of** trades unions.*
DERIVATIVES: **an•tip•o•de•an** |-'dēən| *adj.*, *n.*

an•ti•quar•i•an |ˌænti'kwerēən| • *adj.* relating to or dealing in antiques or rare books.
■ valuable because rare or old: *out-of-print and antiquarian books.* • *n.* (also **antiquary**) a person who studies or collects antiques or antiquities.
DERIVATIVES: **an•ti•quar•i•an•ism** |-ˌnizəm| *n.*

an•tiq•ui•ty |æn'tikwitē| • *n.* (pl. **-ies**) **1** the ancient past, esp. the period before the Middle Ages: *the great civilizations of antiquity.*
■ [with adj.] a specified historical period during the ancient past: *cameos dating from classical antiquity.* ■ (usu. **antiquities**) an object, building, or work of art from the ancient past: *a collection of Islamic antiquities.* **2** great age: *a church of great antiquity.*

an•ti-Sem•i•tism • *n.* hostility to or prejudice against Jews.
DERIVATIVES: **an•ti-Sem•ite** *n.* **an•ti-Se•mit•ic** *adj.*

USAGE: Although the term **Semitic** applies to Arabs and other peoples as well as to Jews (see SEMITE), the term **anti-Semitism** is used only of prejudice against the latter.

an•ti•sep•tic |ˌænti'septik| • *adj.* of, relating to, or denoting substances that prevent the growth of disease-causing microorganisms.
■ (of medical techniques) based on the use of such substances. ■ scrupulously clean or pure, esp. so as to be bland or characterless: *the antiseptic modernity of a conference center.* • *n.* an antiseptic compound or preparation.
DERIVATIVES: **an•ti•sep•ti•cal•ly** |-ik(ə)-lē| *adv.*

an•ti•so•cial |ˌæntē'sōSHəl; ˌæntī-| • *adj.* **1** contrary to or rejecting the laws and customs of society; devoid of or antagonistic to sociable instincts or practices: *a dangerous, antisocial teenager | antisocial acts like vandalism.* **2** not wanting the company of others; unsociable.

an•tis•tro•phe |æn'tistrəfē| • *n.* the second section of an ancient Greek choral ode or of one division of it. Cf. STROPHE and EPODE.
■ the repetition of words in inverse order. ■ an inverse relation or correspondence.

an•tith•e•sis |æn'tiTHəsis| • *n.* (pl. **antitheses** |-ˌsēz|) a person or thing that is the direct opposite of someone or something else: *love is the antithesis of selfishness.*
■ a contrast or opposition between two things: *the **antithesis between** occult and rational mentalities* ■ a figure of speech in which an opposition or contrast of ideas is expressed by parallelism of words that are the opposites of, or strongly contrasted with, each other, such as "hatred stirs up strife, but love covers all sins": *his sermons were full of startling antitheses.* ■ (in Hegelian philosophy) the negation of the *thesis* as the second stage in the process of dialectical reasoning. Cf. SYNTHESIS.

an•ti•trust |ˌæntētrəst; ˌæntī-| • *adj.* [attrib.] (of legislation) preventing or controlling trusts or other monopolies, with the intention of promoting competition in business.

■ connected with, or engaged in the enforcement of, such legislation: *an antitrust suit* | *antitrust lawyers*.

an•to•nym |ˈæntəˌnim| • *n.* a word opposite in meaning to another (e.g., *bad* and *good*). Cf. SYNONYM.

DERIVATIVES: **an•ton•y•mous** |ænˈtänəməs| *adj.*

anx•ious |ˈæNG(k)SHəs| • *adj.* 1 experiencing worry, unease, or nervousness, typically about an imminent event or something with an uncertain outcome: *she was extremely anxious about her exams.*

■ [attrib.] (of a period of time or situation) causing or characterized by worry or nervousness: *there were some anxious moments.* 2 [usu with infinitive] wanting something very much, typically with a feeling of unease: *the company was anxious to avoid any trouble* | [with clause] *my parents were anxious that I get an education.*

DERIVATIVES: **anx•ious•ly** *adv.* **anx•ious•ness** *n.*

USAGE: **Anxious** and **eager** both mean 'looking forward to something,' but they have different connotations. **Eager** suggests enthusiasm about something, a positive outlook: *I'm eager to get started on my vacation.* **Anxious** implies worry about something: *I'm anxious to get started before it rains.*

a•o•rist |ˈāərist| • *n.* (esp. in Greek) an unqualified past tense of a verb without reference to duration or completion of the action. • *adj.* relating to or denoting this tense.

DERIVATIVES: **a•o•ris•tic** |ˌāəˈristik| *adj.*

ap•a•thy |ˈæpəTHē| • *n.* lack of interest, enthusiasm, or concern: *widespread apathy among students.*

DERIVATIVES: **ap•a•thet•ic** *adj.* **ap•a•thet•i•cal•ly** *adv.*

a•per•çu |äperˈso͞o| • *n.* (pl. **aperçus** pronunc. same) a comment or brief reference that makes an illuminating or entertaining point.

a•pe•ri•tif |äˌperiˈtēf| • *n.* an alcoholic drink taken before a meal to stimulate the appetite. Cf. LIQUEUR.

a•pex[1] |ˈāˌpeks| • *abbr.* (in the UK) Association of Professional, Executive, Clerical, and Computer Staff.

a•pex[2] |ˈāpeks| • *n.* (pl. **apexes** |ˈāˌpeksəz| or **apices** |ˈāpəˌsēz; ˈæpə-|) the top or highest part of something, esp. one forming a point: *the apex of the roof* | *the apex of his career.*

■ the highest point in a plane or solid figure, relative to a base line or plane. ■ the growing point of a shoot. ■ (in botany) the highest level of a hierarchy, organization, or other power structure regarded as a triangle or pyramid: *the central bank is at the apex of the financial system.* • *v.* [intrans.] reach a high point or climax: *melodic lines build up to the chorus and it apexes at the solo.*

a•pha•sia |əˈfāZHə| • *n.* loss of ability to understand or express speech or written language, caused by brain damage.

DERIVATIVES: **a•pha•sic** |-zik| *adj. & n.*

a•pher•e•sis |əˈfərisis| • *n.* **1** the loss of a sound or sounds at the beginning of a word, e.g., in the derivation of *adder* from *nadder.* **2** the removal of blood plasma from the body by the withdrawal of blood, its separation into plasma and cells, and the reintroduction of the cells, used esp. to remove antibodies in treating autoimmune diseases.

aph•o•rism |ˈæfəˌrizəm| • *n.* a pithy observation that contains a general truth, such as, "if it ain't broke, don't fix it."

■ a concise statement of a scientific principle, typically by an ancient classical author.

DERIVATIVES: **aph•o•rist** *n.* **aph•o•ris•tic** |ˌæfəˈristik| *adj.* **aph•o•ris•ti•cal•ly** |ˌæfəˈristik(ə)lē| *adv.* **aph•o•rize** |-ˌrīz| *v.*

aph•ro•dis•i•ac |ˌæfrəˈdizē,æk; -ˈdēzē-; -ˈdēzHē-| • *n.* a food, drink, or drug that stimulates sexual desire: *the Romans worshiped the apple as an aphrodisiac* | [as adj.] *aphrodisiac powers.*

■ a thing that causes excitement: *for a few seconds she'd fallen for the aphrodisiac of music* | *power is an aphrodisiac.*

DERIVATIVES: **aph•ro•dis•i•a•cal** *adj.*

a•pi•ar•y |ˈāpēˌerē| • *n.* (pl. **-ies**) a place where bees are kept; a collection of beehives.

DERIVATIVES: **a•pi•ar•i•an** |ˌāpēˈerēən| *adj.* **a•pi•a•rist** |-rist| *n.*

a•plomb |əˈpläm; əˈpləm| • *n.* self-confidence or assurance, esp. when in a demanding situation: *Diana handled the interview with aplomb.*

a•poc•a•lypse |əˈpäkəˌlips| • *n.* (often **the Apocalypse**) the complete final destruction of the world, esp. as described in the biblical book of Revelation.

■ an event involving destruction or damage on an awesome or catastrophic scale: *a stock market apocalypse* | *an era of ecological apocalypse.* ■ (**the Apocalypse**) (esp. in the Vulgate Bible) the book of Revelation.

DERIVATIVES: **a•poc•a•lyp•tic** *adj.* **a•poc•a•lyp•ti•cal•ly** *adv.*

A•poc•ry•pha |əˈpäkrəfə| • *plural n.* [treated as sing. or pl.] biblical or related writings not forming part of the accepted canon of Christian Scripture.

■ (**apocrypha**) writings or reports not considered genuine.

a•poc•ry•phal |əˈpäkrəfəl| • *adj.* (of a story or statement) of doubtful authenticity, although widely circulated as being true: *an apocryphal story about a former president.*

■ (also **Apocryphal**) of or belonging to the Apocrypha: *the apocryphal Gospel of Thomas.*

ap•o•dic•tic |ˌæpəˈdiktik| (also **apodeictic**) • *adj.* clearly established or beyond dispute.

ap•o•gee |ˈæpəjē| • *n.* the point in the orbit of the moon or a satellite at which it is farthest from the earth. The opposite of PERIGEE.

■ the highest point in the development of something; the climax or culmination of something: *the White House is considered the apogee of American achievement.*

Ap•ol•lo•ni•an |ˌæpə'lōnēən| • *adj.* **1** of or relating to the classical god Apollo. **2** of or relating to the rational, ordered, and self-disciplined aspects of human nature: *the struggle between cold Apollonian categorization and Dionysian lust and chaos.* Cf. DIONYSIAN.

a•pol•o•get•ics | əˌpälə'jetiks| • *plural n.* [treated as sing. or pl.] reasoned arguments or writings in justification of something, typically a theory or religious doctrine.

ap•o•lo•gi•a |ˌæpə'lōj(ē)ə| • *n.* a formal written defense of one's opinions or conduct: *an apologia for book-banning.*

ap•o•logue |'æpəˌlôg; -ˌläg| • *n.* a moral fable, esp. one with animals as characters.

a•pol•o•gy |ə'päləjē| • *n.* (pl. **-ies**) **1** a regretful acknowledgment of an offense or failure: *we owe you an apology | my apologies for the delay | I make no apologies for supporting that policy.*
■ a formal, public statement of regret, such as one issued by a newspaper, government, or other organization: *the government demanded an apology from the ambassador.* ■ (**apologies**) used to express formally one's regret at being unable to attend a meeting or social function: *apologies for absence were received from Miss Brown.* **2** (**an apology for**) a very poor or inadequate example of: *we were shown into an apology for a bedroom.* **3** a reasoned argument or writing in justification of something, typically a theory or religious doctrine: *a specious apology for capitalism.*
PHRASES: **with apologies to** used before the name of an author or artist to indicate that something is a parody or adaptation of their work: *here, with apologies to Rudyard Kipling, is a more apt version of "If."*

ap•o•plec•tic |ˌæpə'plektik| • *adj.* overcome with anger; extremely indignant: *Mark was apoplectic with rage at the decision.*
■ relating to or denoting apoplexy (stroke): *an apoplectic attack.*
DERIVATIVES: **ap•o•plec•ti•cal•ly** |-ik(ə)-lē| *adv.*

a•po•ri•a |ə'pôrēə| • *n.* an irresolvable internal contradiction or logical disjunction in a text, argument, or theory: *the celebrated aporia whereby a Cretan declares all Cretans to be liars.*
■ the expression of doubt.

a•pos•ta•sy |ə'pästəsē| • *n.* the abandonment or renunciation of a religious or political belief.
DERIVATIVES: **a•pos•tate** *adj. & n.* **a•po•stat•i•cal** *adj.* **a•pos•ta•tize** *v.*

a pos•te•ri•o•ri |'ä pä ˌstirē'ôˌrē; -ˌrī; 'ä| • *adj.* relating to or denoting reasoning or knowledge that proceeds from observations or experiences to the deduction of probable causes. Cf. A PRIORI.
■ [sentence adverb] (loosely) of the nature of an afterthought or subsequent rationalization. • *adv.* in a way based on reasoning from known facts or past events rather than by making assumptions or predictions.
■ (loosely) with hindsight; as an afterthought.

a•pos•tro•phe |ə'pästrəfē| • *n.* an exclamatory passage in a speech or poem addressed to a person (typically one who is dead or absent) or thing (typically one that is personified).

a•poth•e•car•y |ə'päTHiˌkerē| • *n.* (pl. **-ies**) formerly, a person who prepared and sold medicines and drugs.

ap•o•thegm |'æpəˌTHem| (Brit. **apophthegm**) • *n.* a concise saying or maxim; an aphorism.
DERIVATIVES: **ap•o•theg•mat•ic** |ˌæpə-THeg'mætik| *adj.*

a•poth•e•o•sis |əˌpäTHē'ōsis| • *n.* (pl. **apotheoses** |-sēz|) [usu. in sing.] the highest point in the development of something; culmination or climax: *his appearance as Hamlet was the apotheosis of his career.*
■ the elevation of someone to divine status; deification.

ap•pall |ə'pôl| • *v.* (**appalled, appalling**) [trans.] (usu. **be appalled**) greatly dismay or horrify: *bankers are appalled at the economic incompetence of some ministers* | [as adj.] (**appalled**) *Alison looked at me, appalled.*

ap•pa•rat•chik |ˌäpə'räCHik| • *n.* (pl. **apparatchiks** or **apparatchiki**) an official in a large organization, typically a political one: *Republican apparatchiks.*
■ a member of a Communist Party political machine.

ap•pa•rat•us |ˌæpə'rætəs; -'rātəs| • *n.* (pl. **apparatuses**) **1** the equipment needed for a particular activity or purpose: *laboratory apparatus.*
■ the organs used to perform a particular bodily function: *the specialized male and female sexual apparatus.* **2** a complex structure within an organization or system: *the apparatus of government.* **3** (also **critical apparatus** or **apparatus criticus**) a collection of notes, variant readings, and other matter accompanying a printed text.

ap•pa•ri•tion |ˌæpə'risHən| • *n.* a ghost or ghostlike image of a person.
■ the appearance of something remarkable or unexpected, typically an image of this type: *twentieth-century apparitions of the Virgin.*
DERIVATIVES: **ap•pa•ri•tion•al** |-sHənl| *adj.*

ap•pease |ə'pēz| • *v.* [trans.] **1** pacify or placate (someone) by acceding to demands: *amendments have been added to appease local pressure groups.* **2** relieve or satisfy (a demand or a feeling): *we give to charity because it appeases our guilt.*
DERIVATIVES: **ap•pease•ment** *n.* **ap•peas•er** *n.*

ap•pel•late |ə'pelit| • *adj.* [attrib.] (typically of a court) concerned with or dealing with applications for decisions to be reversed (appeals).

ap•pel•la•tion |ˌæpə'lāsHən| • *n.* a name or title: *the city fully justifies its appellation "the Pearl of the Orient."*
■ the action of giving a name to a person or thing.

ap•per•tain |ˌæpər'tān| • *v.* [intrans.] **1** (**appertain to**) relate to; concern: *the answers generally appertain to improvements in stan-*

dards of service. **2** be appropriate or applicable: *the institutional arrangements that appertain under this system.*

ap•pli•qué |ˌæpliˈkā| • *n.* a technique of ornamental needlework in which pieces of fabric are sewn or stuck onto a large piece of fabric to form pictures or patterns.
■ a piece of such work. • *v.* (**appliqués, appliquéd, appliquéing**) [trans.] (usu. **be appliquéd**) decorate (a piece of fabric) in such a way: *the coat is **appliquéd with** exotic-looking cloth* | [as adj.] (**appliquéd**) *19th-century appliquéd silks.*
■ sew or stick (pieces of fabric) onto a large piece of fabric to form pictures or patterns: *the floral motifs are **appliquéd to** christening robes.*

ap•por•tion |əˈpôrSHən| • *v.* [trans.] divide and allocate: *voting power will be apportioned according to population.*
■ assign: *they did not **apportion** blame or liability to any one individual.*

ap•por•tion•ment |əˈpôrSHənmənt| • *n.* the action or result of apportioning something: *an exercise in apportionment of blame.*
■ the determination of the proportional number of members each state sends to the U.S. House of Representatives, based on population figures.

ap•po•site |ˈæpəzit| • *adj.* apt in the circumstances or in relation to something: *searched for an apposite quotation* | *the observations are **apposite to** the discussion.*
DERIVATIVES: **ap•po•site•ly** *adv.* **ap•po•site•ness** *n.*

ap•praise |əˈprāz| • *v.* [trans.] assess the value or quality of: *she stealthily appraised him in a pocket mirror* | [intrans.] *the interviewer's job is to appraise and evaluate.*
■ (of an official or expert) set a price on; value: *they appraised the painting at $200,000.*
DERIVATIVES: **ap•prais•al** *n.* **ap•prais•er** *n.* **ap•prais•ing•ly** *adv.*

USAGE: **Appraise,** meaning 'evaluate,' should not be confused with *apprise,* which means 'inform': *The painting was appraised at $3,000,000. They gasped when apprised of this valuation.*

ap•pre•hen•sion |ˌæpriˈhenCHən| • *n.* **1** anxiety or fear that something bad or unpleasant will happen: *he felt sick with apprehension* | *she had some apprehensions about the filming.* **2** intellectual faculty or action; understanding; grasp: *a writer with a real apprehension of poverty* | *the pure apprehension of the work of art.* **3** the action of arresting someone: *they ran to avoid apprehension.*

ap•prise |əˈprīz| • *v.* [trans.] inform or tell (someone): *I thought it right to **apprise** Chris of what had happened.*

ap•pro•ba•tion |ˌæprəˈbāSHən| • *n.* approval or praise: *the opera met with high approbation.*
DERIVATIVES: **ap•pro•ba•tive** |ˈæprəˌbākhtiv| *adj.* **ap•pro•ba•to•ry** |əˈpröbəˌtôrē| *adj.*

ap•pro•pri•ate • *adj.* |əˈprōprē-it| suitable or proper in the circumstances: *a measure appro-*

priate to a wartime economy | *take appropriate precautions.* • *v.* |-ˌāt| [trans.] **1** take (something) for one's own use, typically without the owner's permission: *his images have been appropriated by advertisers.* **2** set aside (money or assets) for a special purpose: *there can be problems in **appropriating** funds for legal expenses.*
DERIVATIVES: **ap•pro•pri•ate•ly** |-itlē| *adv.* [sentence adverb] *appropriately, the first recital will be given at the festival.* **ap•pro•pri•ate•ness** |-itnis| *n.* **ap•pro•pri•a•tor** |-ˌātər| *n.*

ap•pur•te•nance |əˈpərt'n-əns| • *n.* (usu. **appurtenances**) an accessory or other item associated with a particular activity or style of living: *all the appurtenances of luxurious travel.*

a pri•o•ri |ˈä prēˈôrē; prīˈ ôrī; ˈä| • *adj.* relating to or denoting reasoning or knowledge that proceeds from theoretical deduction rather than from observation or experience: *data challenging a priori assumptions about human nature.* • *adv.* in a way based on theoretical deduction rather than empirical observation: *sexuality may be a factor but it cannot be assumed a priori.* | [sentence adverb] *a priori, it would seem that his government was an extension of Syrian power.*
DERIVATIVES: **a•pri•o•rism** |ˌäprīˈôrizəm; -prē-; ˌäprē-| *n.*

ap•ro•pos |ˌæprəˈpō| • *prep.* with reference to; concerning: *she remarked **apropos of** the initiative, "It's not going to stop the abuse."* • *adv.* [sentence adverb] (**apropos of nothing**) used to state a speaker's belief that someone's comments or acts are unrelated to any previous discussion or situation: *Isabel kept smiling apropos of nothing.* • *adj.* [predic.] very appropriate to a particular situation: *the composer's reference to child's play is apropos.*

apse |æps| • *n.* **1** a large semicircular or polygonal recess in a church, arched or with a domed roof and typically at the eastern (altar) end. **2** another term for APSIS.
DERIVATIVES: **ap•si•dal** |ˈæpsidl| *adj.*

ap•sis |ˈæpsis| • *n.* (pl. **apsides** |-ˌdēz|) either of two points on the orbit of a planet or satellite that are nearest to or farthest from the body around which it moves.
DERIVATIVES: **ap•si•dal** |ˈæpsidl| *adj.*

ap•ti•tude |ˈæptiˌt(y)ōod| • **1** *n.* (often **aptitude for**) a natural ability to do something: *the child's remarkable **aptitude for** learning words.*
■ a natural tendency: *the team's natural **aptitude for** failure.* **2** suitability or fitness; aptness: *aptitude of resources.*

aq•ua•cul•ture |ˈäkwəˌkəlCHər; ˈæk-| • *n.* the rearing of aquatic animals or the cultivation of aquatic plants for food. Cf. HYDROPONICS.

aq•ua•plane |ˈäkwəˌplān; ˈæk-| • *n.* a board for riding on water, pulled by a speedboat. • *v.* [intrans.] [often as *n.*] (**aquaplaning**) ride standing on an aquaplane.
■ (of a vehicle) slide uncontrollably on a wet surface; hydroplane: *the plane is believed to have aquaplaned on the runway.*

aq•ue•duct |ˈäkwəˌdəkt; ˈæk-| • *n.* an artifi-

cial channel for conveying water, typically in the form of a bridge supported by tall columns across a valley. Cf. VIADUCT.
■ a small body canal containing fluid.

aq•ui•line | ˈækwəˌlīn; -lin | • *adj.* like an eagle.
■ (of a person's nose) hooked or curved like an eagle's beak.

ar•a•besque |ˌærəˈbesk; ˌer- | • *n.* **1** an ornamental design consisting of intertwined flowing lines, originally found in Arabic or Moorish decoration: [as adj.] *arabesque scrolls.*
■ a musical passage or composition with fanciful ornamentation of the melody. **2** a ballet posture in which the body is bent forward and supported on one leg, with the other leg extended horizontally backward and the arms extended one forward and one backward.

ar•a•ble | ˈærəbəl; ˈer- | • *adj.* (of land) used or suitable for growing crops.
■ (of crops) able to be grown on such land.
■ concerned with growing such crops: *arable farming.* • *n.* land or crops of this type.

ar•bi•ter | ˈärbitər | • *n.* a person or force that settles a dispute or has ultimate authority in a matter: *the military acted as arbiter of conflicts between political groups.* Cf. ARBITRATOR.
■ (usu. **arbiter of**) someone whose views or actions have great influence over trends in social behavior: *an arbiter of taste.*

ar•bi•trage | ˈärbəˌträzH | • *n.* the simultaneous buying and selling of securities, currency, or commodities in different markets or in derivative forms in order to take advantage of differing prices for the same asset. • *v.* [intrans.] buy and sell assets in such a way.

ar•bi•trar•y | ˈärbiˌtrerē | • *adj.* based on random choice or personal whim, rather than any reason or system: *his mealtimes were entirely arbitrary.*
■ (of power or a ruling body) unrestrained and autocratic in the use of authority: *the commission has been criticized as arbitrary in its regulation of the sport.* ■ (of a mathematical constant or other quantity) of unspecified value.
DERIVATIVES: **ar•bi•trar•i•ly** |ˌärbəˈtrerəlē | *adv.* **ar•bi•trar•i•ness** *n.*

ar•bi•trate | ˈärbiˌtrāt | • *v.* [intrans.] (of an independent person or body) reach an authoritative judgment or settlement: *the board has the power to arbitrate in disputes* | [trans.] *it set up a commission to arbitrate border tensions.* Cf. MEDIATE.
DERIVATIVES: **ar•bi•tra•tion** *n.*

ar•bi•tra•tor | ˈärbiˌtrātər | • *n.* an independent person or body officially appointed to settle a dispute. Cf. ARBITER.

ar•bor•i•cul•ture | ˈärbəriˌkəlCHər; ärˈbôri- | • *n.* the cultivation of trees and shrubs. Cf. SILVICULTURE.
DERIVATIVES: **ar•bor•i•cul•tur•al** |ˌärbərəˈkəlCHərəl; ärˈbôriˌkəlCHərəl | *adj.* **ar•bor•i•cul•tur•ist** |ˌärbərəˈkəlCHərist; ärˈbôrəˌkəlCHərist | *n.*

ar•cade | ärˈkād | • *n.* **1** a covered passageway with arches along one or both sides.
■ a covered walk with stores along one or both

sides. ■ a series of arches supporting a wall, or set along it. Cf. COLONNADE. **2** (short for **video arcade**) a building or establishment containing electronic entertainment devices.
DERIVATIVES: **ar•cad•ed** *adj.* **ar•cad•ing** *n.*

Ar•ca•di•a | ärˈkādēə | a mountainous district in the Peloponnese of southern Greece. In poetic fantasy it represents a pastoral paradise and in Greek mythology it is the home of Pan.
■ an ideal region of rural contentment.

ar•ca•na | ärˈkänə | • *plural n.* [treated as sing. or pl.] (sing. **arcanum** |-nəm |) secrets or mysteries: *his knowledge of federal budget arcana is legendary.*
■ [treated as sing.] either of the two groups of cards in a tarot pack: the twenty-two trump cards (the **major arcana**) and the fifty-six suit cards (the **minor arcana**).

ar•cane | ärˈkān | • *adj.* understood by few; mysterious or secret: *modern math and its arcane notation.*
DERIVATIVES: **ar•cane•ly** *adv.*

ar•chae•ol•o•gy |ˌärkēˈäləjē | (also **archeology**) • *n.* the study of human history and prehistory through the excavation of sites and the analysis of artifacts and other physical remains.
DERIVATIVES: **ar•chae•o•log•ic** |-əˈläjik | *adj.* **ar•chae•o•log•i•cal** |-əˈläjikəl | *adj.* **ar•chae•o•log•i•cal•ly** |-əˈläjik(ə)lē | *adv.* **ar•chae•ol•o•gist** |-jist | *n.*

ar•cha•ic | ärˈkāik | • *adj.* very old or old-fashioned; primitive: *prisons are run on archaic methods.*
■ (of a word or a style of language) no longer in everyday use but sometimes used to impart an old-fashioned flavor. ■ of an early period of art or culture, esp. the 7th–6th centuries BC in Greece: *the archaic temple at Corinth.*
DERIVATIVES: **ar•cha•i•cal•ly** |-ik(ə)lē | *adv.*

ar•cha•ism | ˈärkēˌizəm; ˈärkā- | • *n.* a thing that is very old or old-fashioned.
■ an archaic word or style of language or art.
■ the use or conscious imitation of very old or old-fashioned styles or features in language or art.
DERIVATIVES: **ar•cha•is•tic** |ˌärkēˈistik; ˌärkā- | *adj.*

ar•che•type | ˈärk(ə)ˌtīp | • *n.* a very typical example of a certain person or thing: *the book is a perfect archetype of the genre.*
■ an original that has been imitated: *the archetype of faith is Abraham.* ■ a recurrent symbol or motif in literature, art, or mythology: *mythological archetypes of good and evil.* ■ (in Jungian psychology) a primitive mental image inherited from the earliest human ancestors, and supposed to be present in the COLLECTIVE UNCONSCIOUS.
DERIVATIVES: **ar•che•typ•al** *adj.* **ar•che•typ•i•cal** |ˌärk(ə)ˈtipikəl | *adj.*

ar•chi•pel•a•go |ˌärkəˈpeləˌgō | • *n.* (pl. **-os** or **-oes**) a group of islands.
■ a sea or stretch of water containing many islands.

ar•chi•tec•ton•ic |ˌärkiˌtek'tänik| • *adj.* of or relating to architecture or architects.
■ (of an artistic composition or physical appearance) having a clearly defined structure, esp. one that is artistically pleasing: *the painting's architectonic harmony.* ■ *n.* (**architectonics**) [usu. treated as sing.] the scientific study of architecture.
■ musical, literary, or artistic structure: *the architectonics of Latin prose.*
DERIVATIVES: **ar•chi•tec•ton•i•cal•ly** |-ik(ə)lē| *adv.*
ar•chive |'är,kīv| (usu. **archives**) • *n.* a collection of historical documents or records providing information about a place, institution, activity, or group of people: *source materials in local archives* | [as adj.] *a section of archive film.*
■ the place where such documents or records are kept: *to get into the archives I had to fill in a request form.* • *v.* [trans.] place or store (something) in such a collection or place.
■ (in computing) transfer (data) to a less frequently used storage medium such as magnetic tape, typically external to the computer system and having a greater storage capacity.
DERIVATIVES: **ar•chi•val** |är'kīvəl| *adj.* **ar•chi•vist** *n.*
ar•cu•ate |'ärkyəwit; -,wāt| • *adj.* shaped like a bow; curved: *the arcuate sweep of the chain of islands.*
ar•dent |'ärdnt| • *adj.* enthusiastic or passionate: *an ardent baseball fan* | *an ardent suitor.*
■ burning; glowing: *ardent flames.*
DERIVATIVES: **ar•dent•ly** *adv.*
ar•dor |'ärdər| (Brit. **ardour**) • *n.* enthusiasm or passion: *the stirrings of revolutionary ardor* | *with the ardor of a lover.*
ar•du•ous |'ärjəwəs| • *adj.* involving or requiring strenuous effort; difficult and tiring: *an arduous journey.*
DERIVATIVES: **ar•du•ous•ly** *adv.* **ar•du•ous•ness** *n.*
a•re•o•la |ə'rēələ| • *n.* (pl. **areolae** |-,lē|) Anatomy a small circular area, in particular the ring of pigmented skin surrounding a nipple.
■ any of the small spaces between lines or cracks on a leaf or an insect's wing. ■ (in medicine) a reddened patch around a spot or papule.
DERIVATIVES: **a•re•o•lar** *adj.*, **a•re•o•late** |-lit; -,lāt| *adj.*
a•rête |ə'rāt| • *n.* a sharp mountain ridge.
ar•gent |'ärjənt| • *adj.* silver; silvery white: *the argent moon.* • *n.* silver as a heraldic tincture.
Ar•go•nauts |'ärgə,nôts| (in Greek mythology) a group of heroes who accompanied Jason on board the ship *Argo* in the quest for the Golden Fleece.
■ (**argonaut**) an adventurer with a quest, esp. for gold; an explorer.
ar•go•sy |'ärgəsē| • *n.* (pl. **-ies**) a large merchant ship, originally one from Ragusa (now Dubrovnik) or Venice.
ar•got |'ärgō; -gət| • *n.* the jargon or slang of a particular group or class: *teenage argot.*
a•ri•a |'ärēə| • *n.* a long, accompanied song

for a solo voice, typically one in an opera or oratorio.
ar•id |'ærid; 'er-| • *adj.* (of land or a climate) having little or no precipitation; too dry or barren to support vegetation: *hot and arid conditions.*
■ lacking in interest, excitement, or meaning: *his arid years in suburbia.* | *the second piece was an arid rhythmic exercise*
DERIVATIVES: **a•rid•i•ty** |ə'riditē| *n.* **ar•id•ly** *adv.* **ar•id•ness** *n.*
ar•is•toc•ra•cy |ˌæri'stäkrəsē; ,er-| • *n.* (pl. **-ies**) [treated as sing. or pl.] (usu. **the aristocracy**) the highest class in certain societies, esp. those holding hereditary titles or offices, and usually landed estates: *the ancient Polish aristocracy had hereditary right to elect the king.*
■ a form of government in which power is held by the nobility. ■ a state governed in this way. ■ a group regarded as privileged or superior in a particular sphere: *high-level technocrats make up a large part of this "technical aristocracy."*
DERIVATIVES: **a•ris•to•crat** *n.* **a•ris•to•crat•ic** *adj.* **a•ris•to•crat•i•cal•ly** *adv.*

USAGE: **Aristocracy, oligarchy,** and **plutocracy** are sometimes confused. All mean some form of rule by a small elite. **Aristocracy** is rule by a traditional elite, held to be made up of 'the best' people, and is usually hereditary. **Oligarchy** is literally rule by a few. **Plutocracy** is rule by the (necessarily few) very rich.

ar•ma•da |är'mädə| • *n.* a fleet of warships: *an armada of destroyers, minesweepers, and gunboats.*
■ (**the Spanish Armada**) a Spanish naval invasion force sent against England and defeated in 1588. ■ any fleet of boats, or the like: *an armada of inflatable rafts* | *the snow-removal armada will grow to 135 plows.*
Ar•ma•ged•don |ˌärmə'gedn| • *n.* (in the New Testament) the last battle between good and evil before the Day of Judgment.
■ the place where this will be fought. ■ a dramatic and catastrophic conflict, typically seen as likely to destroy the world or the human race: *nuclear Armageddon.*
ar•ma•ture |'ärmə,cʜo͝or; -,cʜər| • *n.* **1** the rotating coil or coils of a dynamo or electric motor.
■ any moving part of an electrical machine in which a voltage is induced by a magnetic field. ■ a piece of iron or other object acting as a keeper for a magnet. **2** a metal framework on which a sculpture is molded with clay or similar material. **3** the protective covering of an animal or plant.
■ formerly, armor.
ar•o•mat•ic |ˌærə'mætik; ,er-| • *adj.* **1** having a pleasant and distinctive smell: *a massage with aromatic oils.* **2** (of an organic chemical compound) containing a planar unsaturated ring of atoms that is stabilized by an interaction of the bonds forming the ring. Such compounds are typified by benzene and its

derivatives. • *n.* **1** a substance or plant emitting a pleasant and distinctive smell. **2** (usu. **aromatics**) an aromatic chemical compound.
DERIVATIVES: **ar•o•mat•i•cal•ly** |-ik(ə)lē| *adv.* **ar•o•ma•tic•i•ty** |-məˈtisitē| *n.*

ar•peg•gi•o |ärˈpejē͞ō| • *n.* (pl. **-os**) the notes of a musical chord played in succession, either ascending or descending.
DERIVATIVES: **ar•peg•gi•ate** *v.* **ar•peg•gi•a•tion** *n.*

ar•raign |əˈrān| • *v.* (often **be arraigned**) call or bring (someone) before a court to answer a criminal charge; indict: *Nick was arraigned on Thursday* | *her sister was arraigned on attempted murder charges.*
■ find fault with (someone or something); censure: *the soldiers bitterly arraigned the government for failing to keep its word.*
DERIVATIVES: **ar•raign•ment** *n.*

ar•rant |ˈærənt; ˈer-| • *adj.* [attrib.] **1** complete, utter: *what arrant nonsense!* **2** public, notorious: *an arrant liar.*

ar•ras |ˈærəs; ˈer-| • *n.* a rich tapestry, typically hung on the walls of a room or used to conceal an alcove.

ar•ray |əˈrā| • *n.* **1** an impressive display or range of a particular type of thing: *there is a vast array of literature on the topic* | *a bewildering array of choices.* **2** an ordered arrangement, in particular:
■ an arrangement of troops. ■ (in mathematics) an arrangement of quantities or symbols in rows and columns; a matrix. ■ (in computing) an ordered set of related elements. ■ (in law) a list of jurors empaneled. **3** elaborate or beautiful clothing: *he was clothed in fine array.* • *v.* **1** [with obj. and adverbial of place] (usu. **be arrayed**) display or arrange (things) in a particular way: *arrayed across the table was a buffet* | *the forces arrayed against him.* **2** [trans.] (usu. **be arrayed in**) dress someone in (the clothes specified): *they were arrayed in Hungarian national dress.* **3** [trans.] empanel (a jury).

ar•rears |əˈrirz| • *plural n.* money that is owed and should have been paid earlier: *he was suing the lessee for the arrears of rent.*
PHRASES: **in arrears** behind in paying money that is owed: *two out of three tenants are in arrears.*
■ (of payments made or due for wages, rent, etc.) at the end of each period of work or occupancy: *you will be paid monthly in arrears.*
DERIVATIVES: **ar•rear•age** |əˈririj| *n.*

ar•rhyth•mi•a |āˈriᴛʜmēə; əˈriᴛʜ-| • *n.* Medicine a condition in which the heart beats with an irregular or abnormal rhythm.
DERIVATIVES: **ar•rhyth•mic** |-mik| *adj.* .

ar•rière-pen•sée |ärēˌer pänˈsā| • *n.* a concealed thought or intention; an ulterior motive.

ar•ri•viste |ˌärēˈvēst| • *n.* an ambitious or ruthlessly self-seeking person, esp. one who has recently acquired wealth or social status: *the transition from ingenue to arriviste.*

ar•ro•gant |ˈærəgənt; ˈer-| • *adj.* having or revealing an exaggerated sense of one's own importance; unduly assuming authority; overly proud: *he's arrogant and opinionated* | *a typically arrogant assumption.*
DERIVATIVES: **ar•ro•gance** *n.* **ar•ro•gant•ly** *adv.*

ar•ro•gate |ˈærəˌgāt; ˈer-| • *v.* [trans.] take or claim (something) for oneself without justification: *they arrogate to themselves the ability to divine the nation's true interests.*
DERIVATIVES: **ar•ro•ga•tion** |ˌærəˈgāSHən; ˈer-| *n.*

ar•son |ˈärsən| • *n.* the criminal act of deliberately setting fire to property: *police are treating the fire as arson* | [as adj.] *an arson attack.*
DERIVATIVES: **ar•son•ist** |-nist| *n.*

art dec•o • *n.* the predominant decorative art style of the 1920s and 1930s, characterized by precise and boldly delineated geometric shapes and strong colors, and used most notably in household objects and in architecture: *art deco furniture* | *the Art Deco district of Miami Beach*

ar•te•sian |ärˈtēzʜən| • *adj.* relating to or denoting a well bored perpendicularly into water-bearing strata lying at an angle, so that natural pressure produces a constant supply of water with little or no pumping.

ar•tic•u•late • *adj.* |ärˈtikyəlit| **1** having or showing the ability to speak fluently and coherently: *an articulate account of their experiences.* **2** having joints or jointed segments.
■ denoting a brachiopod that has projections and sockets that form a hinge joining the two halves of the shell. • *v.* |-ˌlāt| **1** [trans.] express (an idea or feeling) fluently and coherently: *they were unable to articulate their emotions.*
■ pronounce (something) clearly and distinctly: *he articulated each word with precision* | [intrans.] *people who do not articulate well are more difficult to lip-read.* **2** [intrans.] form a joint: *the mandible is a solid piece articulating with the head.*
■ (**be articulated**) be connected by joints: *the wing is articulated to the thorax.*
DERIVATIVES: **ar•tic•u•la•ble** *adj.* **ar•tic•u•la•cy** |-ləsē| *n.* **ar•tic•u•late•ly** |-litlē| *adv.* **ar•tic•u•late•ness** |-litnis| *n.* **ar•tic•u•la•tor** |-ˌlātər| *n.*

ar•ti•fact |ˈärtəˌfækt| (Brit. **artefact**) • *n.* **1** an object made by a human being, typically an item of cultural or historical interest: *gold and silver artifacts.*
■ such an object as distinguished from a similar object naturally produced. **2** something observed in a scientific investigation or experiment that is not naturally present but occurs as a result of the preparative or investigative procedure: *widespread tissue infection may be a technical artifact.*
DERIVATIVES: **ar•ti•fac•tu•al** |ˌärtəˈfækCHəwəl| *adj.*

ar•ti•fice |ˈärdifis| • *n.* clever or cunning devices or expedients, esp. as used to trick or deceive others: *filmmakers were often forced to rely on artifice and outright fakery* | *the artifices of a crafty charlatan.* | *the style is not free from the artifices of the period.*

ar•ti•san |'ärṭizən| • *n.* a worker in a skilled trade, esp. one that involves making things by hand.
DERIVATIVES: **ar•ti•san•al** |-zənl| *adj.*
ar•tiste |är'tēst| • *n.* a professional entertainer, esp. a singer or dancer: *cabaret artistes.*
art•less |'ärtləs| • *adj.* without guile or deception: *an artless, naive girl* | *artless sincerity.* ■ without effort or artificiality; natural and simple: *an artless literary masterpiece.* ■ without skill or finesse: *his awkward, artless prose.*
DERIVATIVES: **art•less•ly** *adv.* **artlessness** *n.*
art nou•veau • *n.* a style of decorative art, architecture, and design prominent from the 1890s through the early 1900s and characterized by intricate linear designs based on natural asymmetric forms and flowing curves.
Ar•y•an |'erēən; 'ær-| • *n.* a member of a people speaking an Indo-European language who invaded northern India in the 2nd millennium BC, displacing the Dravidian and other aboriginal peoples. ■ dated term for Proto-Indo-European (a lost language from which all Indo-European languages are thought to derive) or for Indo-Iranian (a subgroup of Indo-European languages). ■ (in Nazi ideology) a person of Caucasian race not of Jewish descent.

The idea that there was an "Aryan" race corresponding to the parent Indo-European language was proposed by certain 19th-century writers and was taken up by Hitler and other proponents of racist ideology, but it has been generally rejected by scholars.

• *adj.* of or relating to this people or their language.
as•cend•an•cy |ə'sendənsē| (also **ascendency**) • *n.* occupation of a position of dominant power or influence: *the ascendancy of good over evil* | *they have a moral ascendancy over the rich.*
as•cend•ant |ə'sendənt| (also **ascendent**) • *adj.* **1** rising in power or influence: *ascendant moderate factions in the party.* **2** (in astrology, of a planet, zodiacal degree, or sign) just above the eastern horizon. • *n.* (in astrology) the point on the ecliptic at which it intersects the eastern horizon at a particular time, typically that of a person's birth. ■ the point on an astrological chart representing this.
PHRASES: **in the ascendant** rising in power or influence: *the reformers are in the ascendant.*
as•cer•tain |ˌæsər'tān| • *v.* [trans.] find (something) out for certain; make sure of: *an attempt to ascertain the cause of the accident* | [with clause] *management should ascertain whether adequate funding can be provided.*
DERIVATIVES: **as•cer•tain•a•ble** *adj.* **as•cer•tain•ment** *n.*
as•ce•sis |ə'sēsis| • *n.* the practice of severe self-discipline, typically for religious reasons.
as•cet•ic |ə'seṭik| • *adj.* characterized by or suggesting the practice of severe self-

discipline (*ascesis*) and abstention from all forms of indulgence, typically for religious reasons: *an ascetic life of prayer, fasting, and manual labor* | *a narrow, humorless, ascetic face.* • *n.* a person who practices such self-discipline and abstention.
DERIVATIVES: **as•cet•i•cal•ly** |-ik(ə)lē| *adv.* **as•cet•i•cism** |-ˌsizəm| *n.*
as•cribe |ə'skrīb| • *v.* [trans.] (**ascribe something to**) attribute something to (a cause): *he ascribed Jane's short temper to her upset stomach.* ■ (usu. **be ascribed to**) attribute (a text, quotation, or work of art) to a particular person or period: *a quotation ascribed to Thoreau.* ■ (usu. **be ascribed to**) regard (a quality) as belonging to: *tough-mindedness is a quality commonly ascribed to top bosses.*
DERIVATIVES: **a•scrib•a•ble** *adj.*
Ash•ke•naz•i |ˌæsHkə'næzē; ˌäsHkə'näzē| • *n.* (pl. **Ashkenazim** |-zim|) a Jew of central or eastern European descent. More than 80 percent of Jews today are Ashkenazim; they preserve Palestinian rather than Babylonian Jewish traditions, and some still use Yiddish.
DERIVATIVES: **Ash•ke•naz•ic** |-zik| *adj.*
ash•ram |'äsHrəm| • *n.* (in the Indian subcontinent) a hermitage, monastic community, or other place of religious retreat for Hindus. ■ a place of religious retreat or community life modeled on the Indian ashram.
A•si•at•ic |ˌāzHē'æṭik; ˌāzē-| • *adj.* relating to or deriving from Asia: *Asiatic cholera* | *Asiatic coastal regions.* • *n.* offensive an Asian person.
USAGE: The standard and accepted term when referring to individual people is **Asian** rather than **Asiatic**, which can be offensive. However, **Asiatic** is standard in scientific and technical use, for example in biological and anthropological classifications. See **usage** at ORIENTAL.
as•i•nine |'æsəˌnīn| • *adj.* extremely stupid or foolish: *Lydia decided to ignore his asinine remark.*
DERIVATIVES: **as•i•nin•i•ty** |ˌæsə'niniṭē| *n.*
a•so•cial |ā'sōsHəl| • *adj.* avoiding social interaction; inconsiderate of or hostile to others: *the cat's independence has encouraged a view that it is asocial.*
as•per•i•ty |ə'speriṭē| • *n.* (pl. **-ies**) harshness of tone or manner: *he pointed this out with some asperity.* ■ (**asperities**) harsh qualities or conditions: *the asperities of society.* ■ (usu. **asperities**) a rough edge on a surface.
as•perse |ə'spərs| • *v.* [trans.] attack or criticize the reputation or integrity of: *he aspersed their organization.*
as•per•sion |ə'spərzHən| • *n.* (usu. **aspersions**) an attack on the reputation or integrity of someone or something: *I don't think anyone is **casting aspersions on** you.*
as•phalt |'æsfôlt| • *n.* a mixture of dark bituminous pitch with sand or gravel, used for

surfacing roads, flooring, roofing, etc. Cf. CONCRETE.

■ the pitch used in this mixture, sometimes found in natural deposits but usually made by the distillation of crude oil. • v. [trans.] cover with asphalt.
DERIVATIVES: **as•phal•tic** |æs'fôltik| adj.
as•pir•ant |'æspərənt; ə'spī-| • adj. [attrib.] (of a person) having ambitions to achieve something, typically to follow a particular career: an aspirant politician. • n. a person who has ambitions to achieve something: an aspirant to the throne.
as•pi•rate • v. |'æspə‚rāt| [trans.] **1** pronounce (a sound) with an exhalation of breath: [as adj.] (**aspirated**) the aspirated allophone of p occurs in "pie."
■ [intrans.] pronounce the sound of h at the beginning of a word. **2** (usu. **be aspirated**) (in medicine) draw (fluid) by suction from a vessel or cavity.
■ draw fluid in such a way from (a vessel or cavity). ■ breathe (something) in; inhale. **3** [usu. as adj.] (**aspirated**) provide (an internal combustion engine) with air: aspirated engines. • n. |'æsp(ə)rit| **1** an aspirated consonant.
■ a sound of h. **2** matter that has been drawn from the body by aspiration: gastric aspirate | esophageal aspirates. • adj. |'æsp(ə)rit| (of a sound) pronounced with an exhalation of breath; aspirated.
■ blended with the sound of h.
as•pi•ra•tion |‚æspə'rāsʜən| • n. **1** (usu. **aspirations**) a hope or ambition of achieving something: he had literary aspirations.
■ the object of such an ambition; a goal. **2** the action of pronouncing a sound with an exhalation of breath. **3** the action of drawing fluid by suction from a vessel or cavity.
DERIVATIVES: **as•pi•ra•tion•al** |-sʜənl| adj. (in sense 1).
as•pire |ə'spīr| • v. [intrans.] direct one's hopes or ambitions toward achieving something: we never thought that we might **aspire to** those heights | [with infinitive] other people will aspire to be like you | [as adj.] (**aspiring**) an aspiring artist.
■ rise high; tower: above the domes of loftiest mosques, these pinnacles of death aspire.
as•sail |ə'sāl| • v. [trans.] make a concerted or violent attack on: there were only two directions from which the hideout could be assailed | Christmas songs assailed us from the radio.
■ (usu. **be assailed**) come upon (one) suddenly and strongly: she was assailed by doubts and regrets. ■ criticize (someone) strongly.
DERIVATIVES: **as•sail•a•ble** adj. **assailant** n.
as•sas•sin |ə'sæsin| • n. a murderer of an important person in a planned attack.
as•sault |ə'sôlt| • v. [trans.] make a physical attack on: he pleaded guilty to assaulting a police officer.
■ attack or bombard (someone or the senses) with something undesirable or unpleasant: her right ear was assaulted with a tide of music.
■ carry out a military attack or raid on (an en-

emy position): they left their strong position to assault the hill. ■ molest sexually or rape. • n. **1** a physical attack: his imprisonment for an **assault on** the film director | sexual assaults.
■ (in legal use) an act that threatens physical harm to a person and puts that person in fear, whether or not actual harm is done: ■ a military attack or raid on an enemy position: an **assault on** the city | [as adj.] an assault boat.
■ a strong verbal attack: the **assault on** the party's tax policies. **2** a concerted attempt to do something demanding: a winter **assault on** Mt. Everest.
DERIVATIVES: **as•sault•er** n.
as•sault and bat•ter•y • n. the criminal act of threatening a person together with the act of making physical contact with him or her.
as•say |'æ‚sā; æ'sā| • n. the testing of a metal or ore to determine its ingredients and quality: submission of test rocks for assay.
■ a procedure for measuring the biochemical or immunological activity of a sample: each assay was performed in duplicate | sequential assay of serum. • v. [trans.] **1** determine the content or quality of (a metal or ore).
■ determine the biochemical or immunological activity of (a sample): cell contents were **assayed for** enzyme activity. ■ examine (something) in order to assess its nature: stepping inside, I quickly assayed the clientele. **2** attempt: I assayed a little humor in my remarks.
DERIVATIVES: **as•say•er** n.
as•sent |ə'sent| • n. the expression of approval or agreement: a loud murmur of assent | he **nodded assent**.
■ official agreement or sanction: the governor has power to withhold his assent from a bill. • v. [intrans.] express approval or agreement, typically officially: Roosevelt assented to the agreement | [with direct speech] "your house, then," Frank assented cheerfully.
DERIVATIVES: **as•sent•er** n.
as•sert |ə'sərt| • v. state a fact or belief confidently and forcefully: [with clause] the company asserts that the cuts will not affect development | [trans.] he asserted his innocence | [with direct speech] "I don't know why she came," he asserted.
■ [trans.] cause others to recognize (one's authority or a right) by confident and forceful behavior: the good librarian is able to assert authority when required. ■ (**assert oneself**) behave or speak in a confident and forceful manner: it was time to assert himself.
DERIVATIVES: **as•sert•er** n. **as•ser•tive** adj. **as•ser•tive•ly** adv. **as•ser•tive•ness** n.
as•ser•tion |ə'sərsʜən| • n. a confident and forceful statement of fact or belief: [with clause] his **assertion that** his father had deserted the family.
■ the action of stating something or exercising authority confidently and forcefully: the assertion of legal rights.
as•sess•ment |ə'sesmənt| • n. the evaluation or estimation of the nature, quality, or ability of someone or something.
as•sev•er•a•tion |ə‚sevə'rāsʜən| • n. the solemn or emphatic declaration or statement of

something: *I fear that you offer only unsupported asseveration | the dogmatic outlook marks many of his asseverations.*

DERIVATIVES: **as•sev•er•ate** |ə'sevə,rāt| *v.*

as•si•du•i•ty |,æsi'd(y)ōōitē| • *n.* (pl. **-ies**) constant or close attention to what one is doing.

■ (**assiduities**) constant attentions to someone.

as•sid•u•ous |ə'sijəwəs| • *adj.* showing great care and perseverance: *she was **assiduous in** pointing out every feature.*

DERIVATIVES: **as•sid•u•ous•ly** adv. **as•sid•u•ous•ness** *n.*

as•sign |ə'sīn| • *v.* [trans.] **1** allocate (a job or duty): *Congress **assigned** the task to the agency* | [with two objs.] *the agency assigned me this mission.*

■ (often **be assigned**) appoint (someone) to a particular job, task, or organization: [with obj. and infinitive] *he was assigned to prosecute the case.* **2** designate or set (something) aside for a specific purpose: *managers happily **assign** large sums of money to travel budgets.*

■ (**assign something to**) attribute something as belonging to: *it is difficult to decide whether to assign the victory to Goodwin.* **3** transfer (legal rights or liabilities): *they will ask you to assign your rights against the airline.* • *n.* (also **assignee**) the person to whom a legal right is assigned.

DERIVATIVES: **as•sign•a•ble** adj. (in sense 3 of the verb). **as•sign•er** *n.* **as•sign•or** |ə 'sīnər| *n.* (in sense 3 of the verb).

as•sig•na•tion |,æsig'nāsHən| • *n.* **1** an appointment to meet someone in secret, typically one made by lovers: *his **assignation** with an older woman.* **2** the allocation or attribution of someone or something as belonging to something.

as•sim•i•late |ə'simə,lāt| • *v.* [trans.] **1** take in (information, ideas, or culture) and understand fully: *Marie tried to assimilate the week's events.*

■ (usu. **be assimilated**) absorb and integrate (people, ideas, or culture) into a wider society or culture: *pop trends are **assimilated** into the mainstream with alarming speed* | [intrans.] *the converts were assimilated into the society of their conquerors.* ■ (usu. **be assimilated**) (of the body or any biological system) absorb and digest (food or nutrients): *the sugars in the fruit are readily assimilated by the body.* **2** cause (something) to resemble; liken: *philosophers had **assimilated** thought to perception.*

■ [intrans.] come to resemble: *the churches **assimilated to** a certain cultural norm.* ■ make (a speech sound) more like another in the same or next word.

DERIVATIVES: **as•sim•i•la•ble** |-ləbəl| adj. **as•sim•i•la•tion** |ə,simə'lāsHən| *n.* **as•sim•i•la•tive** |-,lātiv; -,lətiv| adj. **as•sim•i•la•tor** |-,lātər| *n.* **as•sim•i•la•to•ry** |-lə,tôrē| adj.

as•sim•i•la•tion•ist |ə,simə'lāsHə,nist| • *n.* a person who advocates or participates in racial or cultural integration (*assimilationism*): [as adj.] *the assimilationist policies of the right.*

as•so•nance |'æsənəns| • *n.* the resemblance of sound between syllables in nearby words, arising particularly from the rhyming of two or more stressed vowels, but not consonants (e.g., *sonnet, porridge*), but also from the use of identical consonants with different vowels (e.g., *killed, cold, culled*).

DERIVATIVES: **as•so•nant** adj. **as•so•nate** |-,nāt| *v.*

as•suage |ə'swāj| • *v.* [trans.] make (an unpleasant feeling) less intense: *the letter assuaged the fears of most members.*

■ satisfy (an appetite or desire): *an opportunity occurred to assuage her desire for knowledge.*

DERIVATIVES: **as•suage•ment** *n.*

as•sur•ance |ə'sHoŏrəns| • *n.* **1** a positive declaration intended to give confidence; a promise: [with clause] *he gave an assurance that work would not start until Wednesday.* **2** confidence or certainty in one's own abilities.

■ certainty about something. **3** chiefly Brit. insurance, specifically life insurance.

a•stig•ma•tism |ə'stigmə,tizəm| • *n.* a defect in the eye or in a lens caused by a deviation from spherical curvature, which results in distorted images, as light rays are prevented from meeting at a common focus.

DERIVATIVES: **as•tig•mat•ic** |,æstig'mæt-ik| adj.

as•tral |'æstrəl| • *adj.* [attrib.] of, connected with, or resembling the stars: *astral navigation.*

■ of or relating to a supposed nonphysical realm of existence to which various psychic and paranormal phenomena are ascribed, and in which the physical human body is said to have a counterpart.

as•trin•gent |ə'strinjənt| • *adj.* **1** causing the contraction of body tissues, typically of the cells of the skin: *an astringent skin lotion.* **2** sharp or severe in manner or style: *her astringent words had their effect.*

■ (of taste or smell) sharp or bitter: *an astringent smell of creosote.* • *n.* a substance that causes the contraction of body tissues, typically used to protect the skin and to reduce bleeding from minor abrasions.

DERIVATIVES: **as•trin•gen•cy** *n.* **as•trin•gent•ly** adv. (in sense 2 of the adjective).

as•trol•o•gy |ə'sträləjē| • *n.* the study of the movements and relative positions of celestial bodies interpreted as having an influence on human affairs and the natural world.

DERIVATIVES: **as•trol•o•ger** |-jər| *n.* **as•tro•log•i•cal** |,æstrə'läjikəl| adj. **as•trol•o•gist** |-jist| *n.*

a•sy•lum |ə'sīləm| • *n.* **1** (also **political asylum**) the protection granted by a nation to someone who has left their native country as a political refugee: *granting asylum to foreigners persecuted for political reasons*

■ shelter or protection from danger: *asylum for those too ill to care for themselves.* **2** dated an institution offering shelter and care to the mentally ill: *committed to an asylum.*

at•a•rax•y |'æţə,ræksē| • (also **ataraxia**) • *n.* a state of serene calmness.

DERIVATIVES: **at•a•rac•tic** |ˌætəˈræktik| *adj.* **at•a•rax•ic** |ˌætəˈræksik| *adj.*

at•a•vis•tic |ˌætəˈvistik| • *adj.* relating to or characterized by reversion to something ancient or ancestral: *atavistic fears and instincts.*
DERIVATIVES: **at•a•vism** |ˈætəˌvizəm| *n.* **at•a•vis•ti•cal•ly** |-tik(ə)lē| *adv.*

at•el•ier |ˌætlˈyā| • *n.* a workshop or studio, esp. one used by an artist or designer.

a•the•ism |ˈāTHēˌizəm| • *n.* the theory or belief that God does not exist. Cf.:AGNOSTIC.
DERIVATIVES: **a•the•ist** *n.* **a•the•is•tic** |ˌāTHēˈistik| *adj.* **a•the•is•ti•cal** |ˌāTHē ˈistikəl| *adj.*

ath•e•nae•um |ˌæTHəˈnēəm| (also **atheneum**) • *n.* used in the names of libraries or institutions for literary or scientific study: *the Boston Athenaeum.*
■ used in the titles of periodicals concerned with literature, science, and art.

a•thwart |əˈTHwôrt| • *prep.* **1** from side to side of (something); across: *a wooden bar athwart the entranceway.* **2** in opposition to; counter to: *these statistics* **run** *sharply* **athwart** *conventional presumptions.* • *adv.* **1** across from side to side; transversely: *one table running athwart was all the room would hold.* **2** so as to be perverse or contradictory: *our words* **ran athwart** *and we ended up at cross purposes.*

at•man |ˈätmən| (also **Atman**) • *n.* (in Hinduism) the spiritual life principle of the universe, esp. when regarded as inherent in the real self of the individual.
■ a person's soul.

at•om•ism |ˈætəˌmizəm| • *n.* a theoretical approach that regards something as interpretable through analysis into distinct, separable, and independent elementary components. The opposite of HOLISM.
DERIVATIVES: **at•om•ist** *n.* **at•om•is•tic** |ˌætəˈmistik| *adj.*

at•om•ize |ˈætəˌmīz| • *v.* [trans.] convert (a substance) into very fine particles or droplets: *the CO_2 depressurized, atomizing the paint into a mist.*
■ reduce (something) to atoms or other small distinct units: *crime atomizes society.*
DERIVATIVES: **at•om•i•za•tion** |ˌætəmi ˈzāSHən| *n.* **at•om•iz•er** *n.*

a•ton•al |āˈtōnl| • *adj.* (of music) not written or preformed in any key or mode.
DERIVATIVES: **a•ton•al•ism** |-ˌizəm| *n.* **a•ton•al•ist** |-ist| *n.* **a•to•nal•i•ty** |ˌātōˈnæl-itē| *n.*

a•tone |əˈtōn| • *v.* [intrans.] make amends or reparation: *he was being helpful, to atone for his past mistakes.*

a•tone•ment |əˈtōnmənt| • *n.* reparation for a wrong or injury: *she wanted to* **make atonement** *for her husband's behavior.*
■ reparation or expiation for sin: *the High Priest offered the sacrifice as atonement for all the sins of Israel.* ■ **(the Atonement)** (in Christian theology) the reconciliation of God and humankind through Jesus Christ.

a•tri•um |ˈātrēəm| • *n.* (pl. **atria** |ˈātrēə| or **atriums**) **1** an open-roofed entrance hall or central court in an ancient Roman house.
■ a central hall or court in a modern building, with rooms or galleries opening off it. **2** each of the two upper cavities of the heart from which blood is passed to the ventricles. The right atrium receives deoxygenated blood from the veins of the body; the left atrium receives oxygenated blood from the pulmonary vein. Also called *auricle.*
DERIVATIVES: **a•tri•al** |ˈātrēəl| *adj.*

a•tro•cious |əˈtrōSHəs| • *adj.* **1** horrifyingly wicked: *atrocious cruelties.*
■ of a very poor quality; extremely bad or unpleasant: *he attempted an atrocious imitation of my English accent* | *atrocious weather.*
DERIVATIVES: **a•tro•cious•ly** *adv.* **a•tro•cious•ness** *n.*

a•troc•i•ty |əˈträsitē| • *n.* (pl. **-ies**) an extremely wicked or cruel act, typically one involving physical violence or injury: *war atrocities* | *scenes of hardship and atrocity.*
■ a highly unpleasant or distasteful object.

at•ro•phy |ˈætrəfē| • *v.* (**-ies, -ied**) [intrans.] (of body tissue or an organ) waste away, typically due to the degeneration of cells, or become vestigial during evolution: *without exercise, the muscles will atrophy* | [as adj.] **(atrophied)** *in some beetles, the hind wings are atrophied.*
■ gradually decline in effectiveness or vigor due to underuse or neglect: *her artistic skills atrophied.* • *n.* the condition or process of atrophying: *gastric atrophy.*
■ the gradual decline of effectiveness or vigor due to underuse or neglect: *the atrophy of imagination.*
DERIVATIVES: **a•troph•ic** |āˈtrōfik; āˈträf-| *adj.*

At•ro•pos |ˈætrəˌpäs| one of the three Fates of Greek mythology, the one who cut the thread of life.

at•ta•ché |ˌætəˈSHā ˌætæ-| • *n.* **1** a person on the staff of an ambassador, typically with a specialized area of responsibility: *military attachés.* **2** short for *attaché case*, a small case for carrying documents.

at•tain•der |əˈtāndər| • *n.* the forfeiture of land and civil rights formerly suffered as a consequence of a sentence of death for treason or felony.
PHRASES: **bill of attainder** a piece of legislation inflicting attainder without judicial process.

at•ten•u•ate |əˈtenyəˌwāt| • *v.* [trans.] (often **be attenuated**) reduce the force, effect, or value of: *her intolerance was attenuated by a rather unexpected liberalism.*
■ reduce the amplitude of (a signal, electric current, or other oscillation). ■ [intrans.] (of a signal, electric current, or other oscillation) be reduced in amplitude. ■ [usu. as adj.] **(attenuated)** reduce the virulence of (a pathogenic organism or vaccine): *attenuated strains of rabies virus.* ■ reduce in thickness; make thin: *the trees are attenuated from growing too close together.* • *adj.* |-wit; -ˌwāt| reduced in force, effect, or physical thickness.

DERIVATIVES: **at•ten•u•a•tion** |ə,tenyə'wāsHən| n.
at•ten•u•at•ed |ə'tenyə,wātid| • adj. unnaturally thin.
■ weakened in force or effect.
at•test |ə'test| • v. [trans.] provide or serve as clear evidence of: his status is attested by his promotion | [intrans.] his drawings **attest to** his fascination with ships.
■ [intrans.] declare that something exists or is the case: I can **attest to** his tremendous energy | [with clause] the deceased's attorney attested that he had been about to institute divorce proceedings. ■ be a witness to; certify formally: the witnesses must attest and sign the will.
DERIVATIVES: **at•tes•ta•tion** |,æte'stāsHən| n. **at•tes•tor** n.
At•tic |'ætik| • adj. of or relating to Athens or Attica, or the dialect of Greek spoken there in ancient times. • n. the dialect of Greek used by the ancient Athenians, the chief literary form of classical Greek.
at•ti•cism |'ætə,sizəm| (often **Atticism**) • n. a word or form characteristic of Attic Greek.
at•ti•tu•di•nize |,æti't(y)oōdn,īz| • v. [intrans.] adopt or express a particular attitude or attitudes, typically just for effect.
DERIVATIVES: **at•ti•tu•di•niz•er** n.
at•trib•ute |ə'tri,byoōt| • v. [trans.] (**attribute something to**) regard something as being caused by (someone or something): he attributed the firm's success to the efforts of the vice president | the bombing was attributed to the IRA.
■ ascribe a work or remark to (a particular author, artist, or speaker): the building was attributed to Palladio. ■ regard a quality or feature as characteristic of or possessed by (someone or something): ancient peoples attributed magic properties to certain stones. • n. |'ætrə,byoōt| a quality or feature regarded as a characteristic or inherent part of someone or something: flexibility and mobility are the key attributes of our army.
■ a material object recognized as symbolic of a person, esp. a conventional object used in art to identify a saint or mythical figure. ■ an attributive adjective or noun. ■ a real property that a statistical analysis is attempting to describe.
DERIVATIVES: **at•trib•ut•a•ble** |ə'tribyətəbəl| adj. **at•tri•bu•tion** |,ætrə'byoōsHən| n.
at•trib•u•tive |ə'tribyətiv| • adj. (of an adjective or noun) preceding the word it qualifies or modifies and expressing an attribute, as old in the old dog (but not in the dog is old) and expiration in expiration date (but not in date of expiration). Often contrasted with predicative, in the PREDICATE.
DERIVATIVES: **at•trib•u•tive•ly** adv.
at•tri•tion |ə'trisHən| • n. 1 the action or process of gradually reducing the strength or effectiveness of someone or something through sustained attack or pressure: the council is trying to wear down the opposition by attrition | the squadron suffered severe attrition through mechanical failure.

■ the gradual reduction of a workforce by employees' leaving and not being replaced, rather than by their being laid off: with few retirements since March, the year's attrition was insignificant. ■ wearing away by friction; abrasion: the skull shows attrition of the edges of the teeth. 2 (in scholastic theology) sorrow, but not contrition, for sin.
DERIVATIVES: **at•tri•tion•al** |-sHənl| adj.
a•typ•i•cal |ā'tipikəl| • adj. not representative of a type, group, or class: a sample of people who are atypical of the target audience | there were atypical results in May and November.
DERIVATIVES: **a•typ•i•cal•ly** adv.
au cou•rant |,ō 'koōrän| • adj. aware of what is going on; well informed: they were **au courant with** the literary scene.
■ fashionable: light, low-fat, au courant recipes.
au•da•cious |ô'dāsHəs| • adj. 1 showing a willingness to take surprisingly bold risks: a series of audacious takeovers. 2 showing an impudent lack of respect: an audacious remark.
DERIVATIVES: **au•da•cious•ly** adv. **au•da•cious•ness** n.
au•dac•i•ty |ô'dæsitē| • n. 1 the willingness to take bold risks: her audacity came in handy during our most recent emergency. 2 rude or disrespectful behavior; impudence: she **had the audacity to** pick up the receiver and ask me to hang up.
au•dit |'ôdit| • n. an official inspection of an individual's or organization's accounts, typically by an independent body.
■ a systematic review or assessment of something: a complete audit of flora and fauna at the site. • v. (**audited, auditing**) [trans.] 1 conduct an official financial examination of (an individual's or organization's accounts): companies must have their accounts audited.
■ conduct a systematic review of: auditing obstetrical and neonatal care. 2 attend (a class) informally, without working for academic credit.
au•di•tion |ô'disHən| • n. an interview for a particular role or job as a singer, actor, dancer, or musician, consisting of a practical demonstration of the candidate's suitability and skill. • v. [intrans.] perform an audition: **auditioning for** the lead role in the play.
■ [trans.] assess the suitability of (someone) for a role by means of an audition: she was **auditioning** people **for** her new series.
au•di•to•ry |'ôdi,tôrē| • adj. of or relating to the sense of hearing: the auditory nerves | teaching methods use both visual and auditory stimulation.
au fait |,ō 'fe| • adj. (**au fait with**) having a good or detailed knowledge of something: you should be reasonably **au fait with** the company and its products.
aught |ôt| (also **ought**) • pron. anything at all: know you aught of this fellow, young sir? | For aught I know, he's there still.
aug•ment |ôg'ment| • v. make (something) greater by adding to it; increase: he augmented his summer income by painting houses. | the noise augments as the crowd grows.

DERIVATIVES: **aug·men·ta·tion** *n.* **aug·ment·er** *n.*

au·gur |ˈôgər| • *v.* [intrans.] (**augur well/badly/ill**) (of an event or circumstance) portend a good or bad outcome: *the end of the Cold War seemed to augur well* | *the return to the gold standard augured badly for industry.*
■ [trans.] portend or bode (a specified outcome): *they feared that these happenings augured a neo-Nazi revival.* ■ [trans.] foresee or predict. • *n.* (in ancient Rome) a religious official who observed natural signs, esp. the behavior of birds, interpreting these as an indication of divine approval or disapproval of a proposed action.
DERIVATIVES: **au·gu·ral** |ˈôgyərəl| *adj.*

au·gu·ry |ˈôgyərē| • *n.* (pl. **-ies**) a sign of what will happen in the future; an omen: *they heard the sound as an augury of death.*
■ the work of an augur; the interpretation of omens.

au·gust |ôˈgəst| • *adj.* respected and impressive: *she was in august company.*
■ venerable by birth, status, age, or reputation; eminent.
DERIVATIVES: **au·gust·ly** *adv.* **au·gust·ness** *n.*

au na·tu·rel |ˌō ˌnæCHəˈrel| • *adj. & adv.* with no elaborate treatment, dressing, or preparation: [as adv.] *I wear my hair au naturel these days* | [as adj.] *the cheese is delicious whether au naturel or seasoned.* ■ without clothing; naked: *appeared on the beach au naturel.*

au·ra |ˈôrə| • *n.* (pl. **auras** |ˈôrē| or **aurae**) [usu. in sing.] the distinctive atmosphere or quality that seems to surround and be generated by a person, thing, or place: *the ceremony retains **an aura of** mystery.*
■ a supposed emanation surrounding the body of a living creature, viewed by mystics, spiritualists, and some practitioners of nonscientific medicine as the essence of the individual, and allegedly discernible by people with special sensibilities. ■ any invisible emanation, esp. a scent or odor. ■ (pl. also **aurae**) a warning sensation experienced before an attack of epilepsy or migraine.

au·ral |ˈôrəl| • *adj.* of or relating to the ear or the sense of hearing: *aural anatomy.*
■ received by ear: *information held in written, aural, or database form.*
DERIVATIVES: **au·ral·ly** *adv.*

USAGE: The words **aural** and **oral** ('spoken rather than written') have the same pronunciation in standard English, which is sometimes a source of confusion.

au·re·ate |ˈôrēit; -ˌāt| • *adj.* denoting, made of, or having the color of gold.
■ (of language) highly ornamented or elaborate. *aureate diction frequently conceals the tritest sentiments.*

au·re·ole |ˈôrēˌōl| (also **aureola**) • *n.* a circle of light or brightness surrounding something, esp. as depicted in art around the head or body of a person represented as holy. *her hair framed her face in a golden aureole.*

au·ro·ra |əˈrôrə; ôˈrôrə| • *n.* (pl. **auroras** or aurorae |ôˈrôrē|) **1** a natural electrical phenomenon characterized by the appearance of streamers of reddish or greenish light in the sky, usually near the northern or southern magnetic pole.

The effect is caused by the interaction of charged particles from the sun with atoms in the upper atmosphere. In northern and southern regions it is respectively called **aurora borealis** or **northern lights** and **aurora australis** or **southern lights**. [ORIGIN: *borealis* from Latin, 'northern,' based on Greek *Boreas*, the god of the north wind; *australis* from Latin, 'southern,' from *Auster* 'the south, the south wind.']

2 [in sing.] the dawn.
DERIVATIVES: **au·ro·ral** *adj.*

aus·pice |ˈôspis| • *n.* archaic a divine or prophetic token. Cf.:AEGIS.
PHRASES: **under the auspices of** with the help, support, or protection of.

aus·pi·cious |ôˈspiSHəs| • *adj.* conducive to success; favorable: *it was not the most auspicious moment to open a new business.*
■ giving or being a sign of future success: *they said it was an auspicious moon—it was rising.* ■ characterized by success; prosperous: *he was respectful to his auspicious customers.*
DERIVATIVES: **aus·pi·cious·ly** *adv.* **aus·pi·cious·ness** *n.*

aus·tere |ôˈstir| • *adj.* (**austerer, austerest**) severe or strict in manner, attitude, or appearance: *an austere man, with a rigidly puritanical outlook* | *an austere expression.*
■ (of living conditions or a way of life) having no comforts or luxuries; harsh or ascetic: *conditions in the camp could hardly be more austere.*
■ having an extremely plain and simple style or appearance; unadorned: *the cathedral is impressive in its austere simplicity.* ■ (of an economic policy or measure) designed to reduce a budget deficit, esp. by cutting public expenditure.
DERIVATIVES: **aus·tere·ly** *adv.*

aus·ter·i·ty |ôˈsteriṭē| • *n.* (pl. **-ies**) sternness or severity of manner or attitude: *he was noted for his austerity and his authoritarianism.*
■ extreme plainness and simplicity of style or appearance: *the room was decorated with a restraint bordering on austerity.* ■ (**austerities**) conditions characterized by severity, sternness, or asceticism: *his austerities had undermined his health.* ■ difficult economic conditions, as during wartime or as created by government measures to reduce a budget deficit, esp. by reducing public spending: *a period of austerity* | [as adj.] *the austerity program was built around a massive increase in interest rates.*

aus·tral |ˈôstrəl| • *adj.* of or relating to the south, in particular:
■ of the southern hemisphere: *the austral spring.* ■ (**Austral**) of Australia or Australasia.

au·tar·chy |ˈôˌtärkē| • *n.* (pl. **-ies**) **1** another term for AUTOCRACY. **2** variant spelling of AUTARKY.
DERIVATIVES: **au·tar·chic** |ôˈtärkik| *adj.*

au•tar•ky |'ô,tärkē| • *n.* economic independence or self-sufficiency.
■ a country, state, or society that is economically independent.
DERIVATIVES: **au•tar•kic** |ô'tärkik| *adj.*

au•teur |ô'tər| • *n.* a filmmaker whose movies are characterized by his or her creative influence and control over all aspects of production.
DERIVATIVES: **au•teur•ism** |-,izəm| *n.* **au•teur•ist** |-ist| *adj.*

au•then•tic |ô'THentik| • *adj.* **1** of undisputed origin; genuine: *the letter is now accepted as an authentic document* | *authentic 14th-century furniture.*
■ made or done in the traditional or original way, or in a way that faithfully resembles an original: *the restaurant serves authentic Italian meals* | *every detail of the movie was totally authentic.* ■ based on facts; accurate or reliable: *an authentic depiction of the situation.* ■ (in existentialist philosophy) relating to or denoting an emotionally appropriate, significant, purposive, and responsible mode of human life. **2** (in music, of a church mode) comprising the notes lying between the principal note or final and the note an octave higher.
DERIVATIVES: **au•then•ti•cal•ly** |-ik(ə)lē| *adv.* [as submodifier] *the food is authentically Cajun.* **au•then•tic•i•ty** |,ôTHen'tisitē| *n.*

au•then•ti•cate |ô'THenti,kāt| • *v.* [trans.] prove or show (something, esp. a claim or an artistic work) to be true or genuine.
■ establish as valid.
DERIVATIVES: **au•then•ti•ca•tion** |ô,THenti'kāSHən| *n.*

au•thor•i•tar•i•an |ə,THôri'terēən; ə,THär-| • *adj.* favoring or enforcing strict obedience to authority, esp. that of the government, at the expense of personal freedom: *an authoritarian regime.*
■ showing a lack of concern for the wishes or opinions of others; domineering; dictatorial. • *n.* an authoritarian person.
DERIVATIVES: **au•thor•i•tar•i•an•ism** |-,nizəm| *n.*

au•thor•i•ta•tive |ə'THôri,tātiv; ə'THär-| • *adj.* **1** able to be trusted as being accurate or true; reliable: *clear, authoritative information and advice* | *an authoritative source.*
■ (of a text) considered to be the best of its kind and unlikely to be improved upon: *the authoritative study of mollusks.* **2** commanding and self-confident; likely to be respected and obeyed: *his voice was authoritative.*
■ proceeding from an official source and requiring compliance or obedience: *authoritative directives.*
DERIVATIVES: **au•thor•i•ta•tive•ly** *adv.* **au•thor•i•ta•tive•ness** *n.*

au•tism |'ô,tizəm| • *n.* a mental condition, present from early childhood, characterized by great difficulty in communicating and forming relationships with other people and in using language and abstract concepts.
■ a mental condition in which fantasy dominates over reality, as a symptom of schizophrenia and other disorders.

DERIVATIVES: **au•tis•tic** |ô'tistik| *adj. & n.*

au•toch•thon |ô'täkTHən| • *n.* (pl. **autochthons** or **autochthones** |-THə,nēz|) an original or indigenous inhabitant of a place; an aborigine.
DERIVATIVES: **au•toch•tho•nous** *adj.*

au•toch•tho•nous |ô'täkTHənəs| • *adj.*
■ (of an inhabitant of a place) indigenous rather than descended from migrants or colonists. ■ (of a geologic deposit or formation) formed in its present position. Often contrasted with *allochthonous* (originating at a distance from its present position).

au•toc•ra•cy |ô'täkrəsē| • *n.* (pl. **-ies**) a system of government by one person with absolute power.
■ a regime based on such a principle of government. ■ a country, state, or society governed in such a way. ■ domineering rule or control.

au•to•crat |'ôtə,kræt| • *n.* a ruler who has absolute power.
■ someone who insists on complete obedience from others; an imperious or domineering person.
DERIVATIVES: **au•to•crat•ic** *adj.* **au•to•crat•i•cal•ly** *adv.*

au•to•di•dact |,ôtō'dī,dækt| • *n.* a self-taught person.
DERIVATIVES: **au•to•di•dac•tic** |-,dī'dæktik| *adj.*

au•tom•a•tism |ô'tämə,tizəm| • *n.* the performance of actions without conscious thought or intention.
■ the avoidance of conscious intention in producing works of art, esp. by using mechanical techniques or subconscious associations. ■ an action performed unconsciously or involuntarily.

au•tom•a•ton |ô'tämətən| • *n.* (pl. **automata** |-ətə| or **automatons**) a moving mechanical device made in imitation of a human being.
■ a machine that performs a function according to a predetermined set of coded instructions, esp. one capable of a range of programmed responses to different circumstances.

au•to•nom•ic |,ôtə'nämik| • *adj.* [attrib.] involuntary or unconscious; relating to the autonomic nervous system (which controls bodily functions not consciously directed, e.g., breathing, the heartbeat, and digestion). Cf. SYMPATHETIC.

au•ton•o•my |ô'tänəmē| • *n.* (pl. **-ies**) the right or condition of self-government, esp. in a particular sphere: *Tatarstan demanded greater autonomy within the Russian Federation.*
■ a self-governing country or region. ■ freedom from external control or influence; independence: *economic autonomy is still a long way off for many women.* ■ (in Kantian moral philosophy) the capacity of an agent to act in accordance with objective morality rather than under the influence of desires.
DERIVATIVES: **au•ton•o•mist** |-mist| *n. & adj.* **au•ton•o•mous** *adj.* **au•ton•o•mous•ly** *adv.*

au•top•sy |ˈôˌtäpsē| • *n.* (pl. **-ies**) a postmortem examination to discover the cause of death or the extent of disease: [as adj.] *an autopsy report.* • *v.* (**-ies, -ied**) [trans.] perform a postmortem examination on (a body or organ): [as adj.] (**autopsied**) *an autopsied brain.*

aux•il•ia•ry |ôgˈzilyərē; -ˈzil(ə)rē| • *adj.* providing supplementary or additional help and support: *an auxiliary nurse* | *auxiliary airport staff.* ▪ (of equipment) held in reserve: *the ship has an auxiliary power source.* ▪ (of troops) engaged in the service of a nation at war but not part of the regular army, and often of foreign origin. ▪ (of a sailing vessel) equipped with a supplementary engine. • *n.* (pl. **-ies**) a person or thing providing supplementary or additional help and support: *a nursing auxiliary* | *there are two main fuel tanks and two auxiliaries.* ▪ a group of volunteers giving supplementary support to an organization or institution: *members of the Volunteer Fire Department's auxiliary.* ▪ (**auxiliaries**) troops engaged in the service of a nation at war but not part of the regular army, and often of foreign origin. ▪ Grammar an auxiliary verb. ▪ a naval vessel with a supporting role, not armed for combat.

a•vail |əˈvāl| • *v.* **1** (**avail oneself of**) use or take advantage of (an opportunity or available resource): *my daughter did not avail herself of my advice.* **2** help or benefit: [trans.] *no amount of struggle availed Charles* | [intrans.] *the dark and narrow hiding place did not avail to save the fugitives.*

a•vant-garde |ˈävänt ˈgärd| • *n.* (usu. **the avant-garde**) new and unusual or experimental ideas, esp. in the arts, or the people introducing them: *works by artists of the Russian avant-garde.* • *adj.* favoring or introducing such new ideas: *a controversial avant-garde composer.*
DERIVATIVES: **a•vant-gard•ism** |-ˌdizəm| *n.* **a•vant-gard•ist** |-dist| *n.*

av•a•rice |ˈævəris| • *n.* extreme greed for wealth or material gain.
DERIVATIVES: **av•a•ri•cious** *adj.* **av•a•ri•cious•ly** *adv.* **av•a•ri•cious•ness** *n.*

av•a•tar |ˈævəˌtär| • *n.* (originally in Hinduism) a manifestation of a deity or released soul in bodily form on earth; an incarnate divine teacher. ▪ an incarnation, embodiment, or manifestation of a person or idea: *he set himself up as a new avatar of Arab radicalism.*

a•venge |əˈvenj| • *v.* [trans.] inflict harm in return for (an injury or wrong done to oneself or another): *his determination to avenge the murder of his brother* | *they are eager to avenge last year's Super Bowl defeat.* ▪ inflict such harm on behalf of (oneself or someone else previously wronged or harmed): *we must avenge our dead* | *she avenged herself after he broke off their engagement* | *the warrior swore he would be avenged on their prince.*
DERIVATIVES: **a•veng•er** *n.*

a•ver |əˈvər| • *v.* (**averred, averring**) state

or assert to be the case: [with clause] *he averred that he was innocent of the allegations* | [with direct speech] *"You're the most beautiful girl in the world," he averred.* ▪ [trans.] (in legal use) allege as a fact in support of a plea.

a•verse |əˈvərs| • *adj.* [predic.] [usu. with negative] (**averse to**) having a strong dislike of or opposition to something: *he is not averse to secrecy* | [in combination] *the bank's approach has been risk-averse.*

USAGE: The widespread idiom for expressing dislike, opposition, or hostility (to things, usually not people) is *averse to.* Similarly, one may be said to have an *aversion to* (usually not *from*) certain things or activities (but usually not people): *Katherine was known for her aversion to flying. Averse from* is found more often in British than American English, following the prescription of Samuel Johnson and other traditionalists, who condemned *averse* as nonsensical (its Latin meaning is 'turn from'). See also **usage** at ADVERSE.

a•ver•sion |əˈvərzнən| • *n.* a strong dislike or disinclination: *he had a deep-seated aversion to most forms of exercise.* ▪ someone or something that arouses such feelings.
DERIVATIVES: **a•ver•sive** |-siv; -ziv| *adj.*

a•vert |əˈvərt| • *v.* [trans.] **1** turn away (one's eyes or thoughts): *she averted her eyes during the more violent scenes.* **2** prevent or ward off (an undesirable occurrence): *talks failed to avert a strike.*

a•vi•ar•y |ˈāvēˌerē| • *n.* (pl. **-ies**) a large cage, building, or enclosure for keeping birds in.

av•id |ˈævid| • *adj.* having or showing a keen interest in or enthusiasm for something: *an avid reader of science fiction* | *she took an avid interest in the project.* ▪ (**avid for**) having an eager desire for something: *she was avid for information about the murder inquiry.*
DERIVATIVES: **av•id•i•ty** *n.* **av•id•ly** *adv.*

av•o•ca•tion |ˌævəˈkāsнən| • *n.* a hobby or secondary occupation: *famed as an actor, Mostel was a painter by avocation.*
DERIVATIVES: **av•o•ca•tion•al** |-sнənl| *adj.*

av•oir•du•pois |ˌävərdəˈpoiz| • *n.* a system of weights based on a pound of 16 ounces or 7,000 grains, widely used in English-speaking countries: [as adj.] *avoirdupois weights* | [postpositive] *150 pounds avoirdupois.* ▪ weight; heaviness: *she was putting on the avoirdupois like nobody's business.*

a•vow |əˈvow| • *v.* assert or confess openly: [with clause] *he avowed that he had voted Republican in every election* | [trans.] *he avowed his change of faith* | [as adj.] (**avowed**) *an avowed Marxist.*
DERIVATIVES: **a•vow•al** |əˈvowəl| *n.* **a•vow•ed•ly** |əˈvowidlē| *adv.*

a•vun•cu•lar |əˈvəNGkyələr| • *adj.* **1** (of a man) kind and friendly toward a younger or less experienced person: *an avuncular man-*

ner. **2** of or relating to the relationship between men and their siblings' children.

awe | • *n.* a feeling of reverential respect mixed with fear or wonder: *they gazed in awe at the president.* | *the sight filled me with awe* | *his staff* **are in awe of** *him.*

■ capacity to inspire awe: *has Christmas Eve lost its awe?* • *v.* [trans.] (usu. **be awed**) inspire with awe: *they were both awed by the vastness of the forest* | [as adj.] (**awed**) *he spoke in a hushed, awed whisper.*

awe•some | 'ôsəm | • *adj.* extremely impressive or daunting; inspiring great admiration, apprehension, or fear: *the awesome power of the atomic bomb.*

■ extremely good; excellent: *the band is awesome, dude!*

DERIVATIVES: **awe•some•ly** *adv.* **awe•some•ness** *n.*

a•wry | ə'rī | • *adv.* & *adj.* away from the appropriate, planned, or expected course; amiss: [as adv.] *many youthful romances* **go awry** | [as predic. adj.] *I got the impression that something was awry.*

■ out of the normal or correct position; askew: [as predic. adj.] *he was hatless, his silver hair awry.*

ax•i•om | 'æksēəm | • *n.* a statement or proposition that is regarded as being established, accepted, or self-evidently true: *the axiom that supply equals demand.*

■ a statement or proposition (in mathematics, etc.) on which an abstractly defined structure is based.

ax•is | 'æksis | • *n.* (pl. **axes** | -,sēz |) **1** an imaginary line about which a body rotates: *the earth rotates on its axis once every 24 hours.*

■ an imaginary straight line passing through the center of a symmetrical solid, and about which a plane figure can be conceived as rotating to generate the solid. ■ an imaginary line that divides something into equal or roughly equal halves, esp. in the direction of its greatest length. **2** a fixed reference line for the location of mathematical coordinates. **3** a straight central part in a structure to which other parts are connected.

■ the central column of an inflorescence or other plant growth. ■ the skull and backbone of a vertebrate animal. **4** the second cervical vertebra, below the atlas at the top of the backbone. **5** an agreement or alliance between two or more countries that forms a center for an eventual larger grouping of nations: *the Anglo-American axis.*

■ (**the Axis**) the alliance of Germany and Italy formed before and during World War II, later extended to include Japan and other countries: [as adj.] *the Axis Powers.*

a•ya•tol•lah | ,īə'tōlə | • *n.* a Shi'ite religious leader in Iran. ■ a dogmatic, powerful leader.

az•i•muth | 'æzəməTH | • *n.* the direction of a celestial object from the observer, expressed as the angular distance from the north or south point of the horizon to the point at which a vertical circle passing through the object intersects the horizon.

■ the horizontal angle or direction of a compass bearing.

DERIVATIVES: **az•i•muth•al** | ,æzə'məTH-əl | *adj.*

Bb

ba•bel | 'bæbəl; 'bā- | • *n.* [in sing.] a confused noise, typically that made by a number of voices: *the babel of voices on the road.*

■ a scene of noisy confusion.

Bab•ism | 'bäbizəm | • *n.* a religion founded in 1844 by the Persian Mirza Ali Muhammad of Shiraz (1819–50) (popularly known as "the Bab"), who taught that a new prophet would follow Muhammad. See also BAHA'I.

bac•ca•lau•re•ate | ,bækə'lôrē-t | • *n.* **1** a university bachelor's degree. **2** a religious service held at some educational institutions before commencement, containing a farewell sermon to the graduating class.

bac•cha•nal | ,bäkə'näl; ,bæk-; 'bækənl | • *n.* **1** an occasion of wild and drunken revelry.

■ a drunken reveler. **2** a priest, worshiper, or follower of the Roman god Bacchus (Greek, Dionysus), the god of wine.

DERIVATIVES: **bac•cha•na•li•an** *adj.* **bac•cha•nal** *adj.*

bad•i•nage | ,bædn'äzH | • *n.* humorous or witty conversation: *cultured badinage about art and life.*

baf•fle | 'bæfəl | • *n.* (in engineering, architecture, acoustics, etc.) a device used to restrain the flow of a fluid, gas, or loose material or to prevent the spreading of sound or light in a particular direction.

DERIVATIVES: **baf•fle** *v.* [trans.]

bag•a•telle | ,bægə'tel | • *n.* **1** a thing of little importance; a very easy task: *he played so well that winning the tournament seemed* **a mere bagatelle** *for him.* **2** a short, light piece of music, esp. one for the piano.

bagn•io | 'bænyō; 'bän- | • *n.* (pl. **-os**) **1** a brothel. **2** an oriental prison. **3** a bathhouse in Turkey or Italy.

Ba•ha'i | bə'hī | • (also **Bahai**) • *n.* (pl. **Baha'is**) a monotheistic religion founded in the 19th century as a development of Babism, emphasizing the essential oneness of humankind and of all religions and seeking world peace. The Baha'i faith was founded by the Persian

Baha'ullah (1817–92) and his son Abdul Baha (1844–1921).
■ an adherent of the Baha'i faith.
DERIVATIVES: **Ba•ha•'ism** |-,izəm| *n.*
bail•iff |'bālif| • *n.* a person who performs certain actions under legal authority, in particular:
■ an official in a court of law who keeps order, looks after prisoners, etc.
bail•i•wick |'bālə,wik| • *n.* Law the district or jurisdiction of a bailiff or bailie (a municipal officer and magistrate in Scotland).
■ (**one's bailiwick**) informal one's sphere of operations or particular area of interest: *you don't give the presentations—that's my bailiwick.*
bak•sheesh |'bæksHēsH; bæk'sHēsH| (also **backsheesh**) • *n.* (in parts of Asia) a small sum of money given as alms, a tip, or a bribe.
bal•der•dash |'bôldər,dæsH| • *n.* senseless talk or writing; nonsense.
bale•ful |'bālfəl| • *adj.* threatening harm; menacing: *Bill shot a baleful glance in her direction.| the baleful light cast trembling shadows.*
■ having a harmful or destructive effect.
DERIVATIVES: **bale•ful•ly** *adv.* **bale•ful•ness** *n.*
balk |bôk| (Brit. also **baulk**) • *v.* [intrans.] **1** hesitate or be unwilling to accept an idea or undertaking: *any gardener will at first balk at enclosing the garden.*
■ [trans.] thwart or hinder (a plan or person): *all of his influence will be invoked to balk the law.*
■ [trans.] (**balk someone of**) prevent a person or animal from having (something): *the lions, fearing to be balked of their prey.* ■ (of a horse) refuse to go on. ■ [trans.] miss or refuse (a chance or invitation). **2** (of a baseball pitcher) make an illegal motion, penalized by an advance of the base runners: *the rookie balked and permitted Robinson to score.* • *n.* **1** an illegal motion made by a pitcher that may deceive a base runner. **2** a roughly squared timber beam. **3** any area on a pool or billiard table in which play is restricted in some way. **4** a ridge left unplowed between furrows.
bal•lad |'bæləd| • *n.* a poem or song narrating a story in short stanzas. Traditional ballads are typically of unknown authorship, having been passed on orally from one generation to the next as part of the folk culture.
■ a slow sentimental or romantic song.
bal•lade |bə'läd| • *n.* **1** a poem consisting of one or more triplets of stanzas with a repeated refrain and an envoi (a short stanza at the end). **2** a short, lyrical piece of music, esp. one for piano.
bal•last |'bæləst| • *n.* **1** heavy material, such as gravel, sand, iron, or lead, placed low in a vessel to improve its stability.
■ a substance of this type carried in an airship or on a hot-air balloon to stabilize it, and jettisoned when greater altitude is required.
■ something that gives stability or substance: *the film is an entertaining comedy with some serious ideas thrown in for ballast.* **2** gravel or coarse stone used to form the bed of a railroad track or road.

■ a mixture of coarse and fine aggregate for making concrete. **3** a passive component used in an electric circuit to moderate changes in current. • *v.* [trans.] (usu. **be ballasted**) **1** give stability to (a ship) by putting a heavy substance in its bilge: *the vessel has been ballasted with gravel.* **2** form (the bed of a railroad line or road) with gravel or coarse stone.
PHRASES: **in ballast** (of a ship) laden only with ballast.
bal•lis•tic |bə'listik| • *adj.* [attrib.] **1** of or relating to projectiles or their flight. **2** moving under the force of gravity only.
PHRASES: **go ballistic** fly into a rage.
DERIVATIVES: **bal•lis•ti•cal•ly** |-ik(ə)lē| *adv.*
balm |bä(l)m| • *n.* **1** a fragrant ointment or preparation used to heal or soothe the skin.
■ something that has a comforting, soothing, or restorative effect: *the murmur of the water can provide balm for troubled spirits.* **2** any of several trees that yield a fragrant resinous substance, typically one used in medicine.
■ such a substance. **3** (also **lemon balm** or **sweet balm**) a bushy herb (*Melissa officinalis*) of the mint family, with leaves smelling and tasting of lemon.
■ used in names of other aromatic herbs of the mint family, e.g., **bee balm.**
balm•y |'bä(l)mē| • *adj.* (**balmier, balmiest**) **1** (of the weather) pleasantly warm. **2** extremely foolish.
DERIVATIVES: **balm•i•ness** *n.*
bal•us•trade |'bælə,strād| • *n.* a railing supported by balusters (short pillars or columns), esp. an ornamental parapet on a balcony, bridge, or terrace.
DERIVATIVES: **bal•us•trad•ed** *adj.*
ba•nal |'bānl; bə'næl; -'näl| • *adj.* so lacking in originality as to be obvious and boring: *banal songs.*
DERIVATIVES: **ba•nal•i•ty** |bə'nælitē| *n.* (pl. **-ies**) **ba•nal•ly** *adv.*
ban•dy • *v.* (**-ies, -ied**) [trans.] (usu. **be bandied about/around**) pass on or discuss an idea or rumor in a casual way: *$40 million is the figure that has been bandied about.*
■ exchange; pass back and forth: *they bandied words and laughs from one to another.* • *n.* a game similar to field hockey.
■ the stick used to play this game.
bane•ful • *adj.* causing great distress or annoyance: *a baneful influence | baneful depression.*
■ archaic poisonous; causing death.
banns |bænz| • *plural n.* a notice read out on three successive Sundays in a parish church, announcing an intended marriage and giving the opportunity for objections.
PHRASES: **forbid the banns** raise an objection to an intended marriage, esp. in church following the reading of the banns.
ban•ter |'bæntər| • *n.* the playful and friendly exchange of teasing remarks: *good-natured banter.* • *v.* [intrans.] talk or exchange remarks in a good-humored teasing way: *the men bantered and joked with each other | [as adj.] (bantering) a bantering tone.*

ban•zai |'bæn'zī| • *exclam.* **1** a Japanese battle cry. [ORIGIN: early 20th cent.] **2** a form of greeting used to the Japanese emperor. [ORIGIN: late 19th cent.] • *adj.* (esp. of Japanese troops) attacking fiercely and recklessly: *a banzai charge.*

bap•tist |'bæptist| • *n.* **1** (**Baptist**) a member of a Protestant Christian denomination advocating baptism only of adult believers by total immersion. Baptists form one of the largest Protestant bodies and are found throughout the world and esp. in the US. **2** a person who baptizes someone.

bap•tis•ter•y |'bæptəstrē| (also **baptistry**) • *n.* (pl. **-ies**) the part of a church used for baptism. ■ a building next to a church, used for baptism. ■ (in a Baptist chapel) a sunken receptacle used for baptism by total immersion.

bar•ba•rism |'bärbə,rizəm| • *n.* **1** absence of culture and civilization: *the collapse of civilization and the return to barbarism.* ■ a word or expression that is badly formed according to traditional philological rules, for example a word formed from elements of different languages, such as *breathalyser* (English and Greek) or *television* (Greek and Latin). **2** extreme cruelty or brutality: *an act of barbarism* | *barbarisms from the country's past.*

bar•ba•rous |'bärbərəs| • *adj.* **1** savagely cruel; exceedingly brutal: *many early childrearing practices were barbarous by modern standards.* **2** primitive; uncivilized: *a remote and barbarous country.* ■ (esp. of language) coarse and unrefined. DERIVATIVES: **bar•ba•rous•ly** *adv.* **bar•ba•rous•ness** *n.*

bar•ca•role |'bärkə,rōl| (also **barcarolle**) • *n.* a song traditionally sung by Venetian gondoliers (canal boatmen). ■ a musical composition in the style of such a song.

bard[1] |bärd| • *n.* a poet, traditionally one reciting epics and associated with a particular oral tradition. ■ (**the Bard** or **the Bard of Avon**) Shakespeare. DERIVATIVES: **bard•ic** |-dik| *adj.*

bar mitz•vah |,bär 'mitsvə| • *n.* the religious initiation ceremony of a Jewish boy who has reached the age of 13 and is regarded as ready to observe religious precepts and eligible to take part in public worship. Cf. BAT MITZVAH. ■ the boy undergoing this ceremony. • *v.* [trans.] (usu. **be bar mitzvahed**) celebrate the bar mitzvah of (a boy).

ba•roque |bə'rōk| • *adj.* relating to or denoting a style of European architecture, music, and art of the 17th and 18th centuries that followed mannerism and is characterized by ornate detail. ■ highly ornate and extravagant in style. • *n.* the baroque style. ■ the baroque period.

bar•rage[1] |bə'räzH| • *n.* a concentrated artillery bombardment over a wide area. ■ a concentrated outpouring, as of questions or blows: *a **barrage of** questions* | *a barrage*

of *60-second television spots.* • *v.* [trans.] (usu. **be barraged**) bombard (someone) with something: *his doctor was **barraged with** unsolicited advice.*

bar•rage[2] |bə'räzH| • *n.* a concentrated artillery bombardment over a wide area. ■ figurative a concentrated outpouring, as of questions or blows: *she was not prepared for his **barrage of** questions* | *a barrage of 60-second television spots.* • *v.* [trans.] (usu. **be barraged**) bombard (someone) with something: *his doctor was **barraged with** unsolicited advice.*

bar•ri•o |'bärē,ō| • *n.* (pl. **-os**) a district of a town in Spain and Spanish-speaking countries. ■ the Spanish-speaking quarter of an American town or city. ■ a poor neighborhood populated by Spanish-speaking people.

bar•ris•ter |'bærəstər;'ber-| (also **barrister-at-law**) • *n.* chiefly Brit. a lawyer entitled to practice as an advocate, particularly in the higher courts. Cf. SOLICITOR.

ba•sil•i•ca |bə'silikə| • *n.* a large oblong hall or building with double colonnades and a semicircular apse, used in ancient Rome as a court of law or for public assemblies. ■ a similar building used as a Christian church. ■ the name given to certain Roman Catholic churches granted special privileges by the pope. DERIVATIVES: **ba•sil•i•can** *adj.*

bas•i•lisk |'bæsə,lisk;'bæz-| • *n.* a mythical reptile with a lethal gaze or breath, hatched by a serpent from a cock's egg. ■ (in heraldry) another term for COCKATRICE.

bas-re•lief |,bä rə'lēf| • *n.* another term for **low relief** (see RELIEF). ■ a sculpture, carving, or molding in low relief.

bas•tille |bæ'stēl| • *n.* a tower or bastion of a castle; a small fortress. ■ in siege operations, a wooden tower on wheels, or an entrenched protective hut used by the besiegers. ■ (**the Bastille**) a fortress in Paris built in the 14th century and used in the 17th–18th centuries as a state prison. Its storming by a mob on July 14, 1789 marked the start of the French Revolution.

bas•ti•na•do |,bæstə' nädō; -'nädō| • *n.* a form of torture that involves beating the soles of someone's feet with a stick. • *v.* (**-oes, -oed**) [trans.] (usu. **be bastinadoed**) punish or torture (someone) in such a way.

bas•tion |'bæscHən| • *n.* a projecting part of a fortification built at an angle to the line of a wall, so as to allow defensive fire in several directions. ■ a natural rock formation resembling such a fortification. ■ an institution, place, or person strongly defending or upholding particular principles, attitudes, or activities: *the **last** bastion of male privilege.*

bat•ed |'bātid| • *adj.* (in phrase **with bated breath**) in great suspense; very anxiously or excitedly: *he waited for a reply to his offer with bated breath.*

USAGE: The spelling *baited breath* instead of **bated breath** is a common mistake.

ba•thos |'bāTHäs| • n. (esp. in a work of literature) an effect of anticlimax created by an unintentional lapse in mood from the sublime to the trivial or ridiculous.
DERIVATIVES: **ba•thet•ic** |bə'THetik| adj.

bat mitz•vah |bät 'mitsvə| (also **bas mitzvah**) • n. a religious initiation ceremony for a Jewish girl aged twelve years and one day, regarded as the age of religious maturity.
■ the girl undergoing such a ceremony.

bat•ten[1] |'bætn| • v. [trans.] strengthen or fasten (something) with battens (strips of wood): *Stephen was battening down the shutters.*

bat•ten[2] • v. [intrans.] (**batten on**) thrive or prosper at the expense of (someone): *multinational monopolies batten on the working classes.*

bau•ble |'bôbəl| • n. 1 a small, showy trinket or decoration.
■ something of no importance or worth. 2 a baton formerly used as an emblem by jesters.

Bau•haus |'bow͵hows| a school of design established by Walter Gropius in Weimar in 1919, best known for its designs of objects based on functionalism and simplicity.

bawd•y |'bôdē| • adj. (**bawdier, bawdiest**) dealing with sexual matters in a comical way; humorously indecent. • n. humorously indecent talk or writing.
DERIVATIVES: **bawd•i•ly** |-dəlē| adv. **bawd•i•ness** n.

bear mar•ket • n. (regarding stocks) a market in which prices are falling, encouraging selling.

beat gen•er•a•tion a movement of young people in the 1950s (*beats*; later they and their followers were also called *beatniks*) who rejected conventional society and espoused Zen Buddhism, modern jazz, free sexuality, and recreational drugs. Among writers associated with the movement were Jack Kerouac (1922-69) and Allen Ginsberg (1926-97).

be•a•tif•ic |͵bēə'tifik| • adj. blissfully happy: *a beatific smile.*
DERIVATIVES: **be•a•tif•i•cal•ly** |-ik(ə)lē| adv.

be•at•i•fi•ca•tion |bē͵ætəfi'kāsHən| • n. (in the Roman Catholic Church) declaration by the pope that a dead person is in a state of bliss, constituting a step toward canonization and permitting public veneration.

be•at•i•fy |bē'ætə͵fī| • v. (**-ies, -ied**) [trans.] (in the Roman Catholic Church) announce the beatification of.
■ make (someone) blissfully happy.

be•at•i•tude |bē'ætə͵t(y)ōod| • n. supreme blessedness.
■ (**the Beatitudes**) the blessings listed by Jesus in the Sermon on the Mount (Matt. 5:3–11). ■ (**his/your Beatitude**) a title given to patriarchs in the Orthodox Church.

beau geste |͵bō 'zHest| • n. (pl. **beaux gestes** pronunc. same) a noble and generous act.

beau monde |͵bō 'mônd| • n. (**the beau monde**) fashionable society.

beaux arts |bōz 'är| • plural n. 1 fine arts.

2 (usu. **Beaux Arts**) [as adj.] relating to the classical decorative style maintained by the École des Beaux-Arts in Paris, esp. in the 19th century and important in America esp. in the early 20th century.

be•drag•gled |bi'drægəld| • adj. dirty and disheveled: *bedraggled refugees | we got there, tired and bedraggled.*
DERIVATIVES: **be•drag•gle** v.

be•get |bi'get| • v. (**begetting** ; past **begot** |-'gät| or archaic **begat** |-'gæt| ; past part. **begotten** |-'gätn|) [trans.] 1 (typically of a man, sometimes of a man and a woman) bring (a child) into existence by the process of reproduction: *they hoped that the king might beget an heir.* 2 give rise to; bring about: *success begets further success.*
DERIVATIVES: **be•get•ter** n.

be•grudge |bi'grəj| • v. 1 [with two objs.] envy (someone) the possession or enjoyment of (something): *she begrudged Martin his affluence.* 2 [trans.] give reluctantly or resentfully: *doesn't begrudge a single penny spent on her health.*
DERIVATIVES: **be•grudg•ing•ly** adv.

be•guile |bi'gīl| • v. [trans.] 1 charm or enchant (someone), sometimes in a deceptive way: *an artist beguiled by Maine* | [as adj.] (**beguiling**) *a beguiling smile.*
■ trick (someone) into doing something: *they were beguiled into signing a peace treaty.* 2 dated help (time) pass pleasantly: *to beguile some of the time they went to the cinema.*
DERIVATIVES: **be•guile•ment** n. **be•guiler** n. **be•guil•ing•ly** adv.

be•hav•ior•ism |bi'hāvyə͵rizəm| • n. the theory that human and animal behavior can be explained in terms of conditioning, without appeal to thoughts or feelings, and that psychological disorders are best treated by altering behavior patterns.
■ such study and treatment in practice.
DERIVATIVES: **be•hav•ior•ist** n. & adj. **be•hav•ior•is•tic** |bi͵hāvyə'ristik| adj.

be•he•moth |bi'hēməTH; 'bēəmɒTH| • n. a huge or monstrous creature.
■ something enormous, esp. a big and powerful organization: *shoppers loyal to their local stores rather than to faceless behemoths* | [as adj.] *behemoth telephone companies.*

be•hest |bi'hest| • n. a person's orders or command: *they had assembled at his behest | the slaughter of the male children at the behest of Herod.*

be•hold•en |bi'hōldən| • adj. [predic.] owing thanks or having a duty to someone in return for help or a service: *I don't like to be beholden to anybody.*

be•hoove |bi'hōōv| • v. [trans.] (**it behooves someone to do something**) it is a duty or responsibility for someone to do something; it is incumbent on: *it behooves any coach to study his predecessors.*
■ [with negative] it is appropriate or suitable; it befits: *it ill behooves them to decry the country's war effort.*

be•la•bor |bi'lābər| • v. [trans.] 1 argue or elaborate (a subject) in excessive detail:

critics thought they belabored the obvious. **2** attack or assault (someone) physically or verbally: *he seized every opportunity to belabor the Roman Church.*

be•lat•ed | bi'lātid | • *adj.* coming or happening later than should have been the case: *a belated apology.*
DERIVATIVES: **be•lat•ed•ly** *adv.* **be•lat•ed•ness** *n.*

bel•dam | 'beldəm; -,dæm | (also **beldame**) • *n.* an old woman.
■ a malicious and ugly woman, esp. an old one; a witch.

be•lea•guer | bi'lēgər | • *v.* [trans.] [usu. as adj.] (**beleaguered**) lay siege to: *a beleaguered city.*
■ beset with difficulties: *the board is supporting the beleaguered director amid calls for her resignation.*

bel es•prit | ,bel e'sprē | • *n.* (pl. **beaux esprits** | ,bōz e'sprē |) a witty person.

be•lie | bi'lī | • *v.* (**belying**) [trans.] **1** (of an appearance) fail to give a true notion or impression of (something); disguise or contradict: *his lively alert manner belied his years.* **2** fail to fulfill or justify (a claim or expectation); betray: *the notebooks belie Darwin's later recollection.*

be•lit•tle | bi'litl | • *v.* [trans.] make (someone or something) seem unimportant: *this is not to belittle his role.*
DERIVATIVES: **be•lit•tle•ment** *n.* **be•lit•tler** *n.*

bell curve • *n.* (in mathematics and statistics) a graph of a normal distribution, with a large rounded peak tapering away at each end, showing that the vast majority of variables fall within the 'bell', or within a relatively limited range.

belle é•poque | ,bel ā'pôk | • *n.* the period of settled and comfortable life preceding World War I: [as adj.] *a romantic, belle-époque replica of a Paris bistro.*

belles-let•tres | ,bel 'letrə | • *plural n.* [also treated as sing.] **1** essays, particularly of literary and artistic criticism, written and read primarily for their aesthetic effect. **2** literature considered as a fine art.
DERIVATIVES: **bel•let•rism** | bel'le,trizəm | *n.* **bel•let•rist** | bel'letrist | *n.* **bel•let•ris•tic** | ,belə'tristik | *adj.*

bel•li•cose | 'beli,kōs | • *adj.* demonstrating aggression and willingness to fight: *a group of bellicose patriots.*
DERIVATIVES: **bel•li•cos•i•ty** | ,belə'käsitē | *n.*

bel•lig•er•ent | bə'lijərənt | • *adj.* hostile and aggressive.
■ engaged in a war or conflict, as recognized by international law. • *n.* a nation or person engaged in war or conflict, as recognized by international law: *belligerents were denied access to the port.*
DERIVATIVES: **bel•lig•er•ent•ly** *adv.*

bell•weth•er | 'bel,weT͟Hər | • *n.* the leading sheep (*wether*, originally 'ram') of a flock, with a bell on its neck.
■ an indicator or predictor of something: *campuses are often the bellwether of change* | [as adj.] *the market's bellwether stock.*

belt•way | 'belt,wā | • *n.* a highway encircling an urban area.
■ (**Beltway**) [often as adj.] Washington, DC, esp. as representing the perceived insularity of the US government: *conventional beltway wisdom. that's how it looks from inside the Beltway.* [ORIGIN: transferred use by association with the beltway encircling Washington.]

bel•ve•dere | 'belvə,dir | • *n.* a summerhouse or open-sided gallery, usually at rooftop level, commanding a fine view.

be•muse | bi'myo͞oz | • *v.* [trans.] [usu. as adj.] (**bemused**) puzzle, confuse, or bewilder (someone): *her bemused expression.*
DERIVATIVES: **be•mus•ed•ly** | -zidlē | *adv.* **be•muse•ment** *n.*

bench•mark | 'bench,märk | • *n.* **1** a standard or point of reference against which things may be compared or assessed: | [as adj.] *a benchmark case.*
■ a problem designed to evaluate the performance of a computer system. **2** (also **bench mark**) a surveyor's mark cut in a wall, pillar, or building and used as a reference point in measuring altitudes. • *v.* [trans.] evaluate or check (something) by comparison with a standard: *we are benchmarking our performance against external criteria.*
■ [intrans.] evaluate or check something in this way: *we continue to benchmark against the competition.* ■ [intrans.] show particular results during a benchmark test: *the device should benchmark at between 100 and 150 MHz.*

ben•e•dic•tion | ,beni'dikSHən | • *n.* the utterance or bestowing of a blessing, esp. at the end of a religious service.
■ (**Benediction**) a service in which the congregation is blessed with the Blessed Sacrament, held mainly in the Roman Catholic Church. ■ devout or formal invocation of blessedness: *her arms outstretched in benediction.* ■ the state of being blessed: *he eventually wins benediction.*

ben•e•fac•tion | ,benə'fækSHən | • *n.* a donation or gift.
■ a good deal.

ben•e•fac•tor | 'benə,fæktər; ,benə'fæktər | • *n.* a person who gives money or other help to a person or cause.

ben•e•fice | 'benəfis | • *n.* a permanent church appointment, for which property and income are provided in respect of pastoral duties.
DERIVATIVES: **ben•e•ficed** *adj.*

be•nef•i•cent | bə'nefisənt | • *adj.* (of a person) generous or doing good.
■ resulting in good: *a beneficent democracy.*
DERIVATIVES: **be•nef•i•cence** *n.* **be•nef•i•cent•ly** *adv.*

ben•e•fi•ci•ar•y | ,benə'fiSHē,erē | • *n.* (pl. **-ies**) a person who derives advantage from something, esp. a trust, will, or life insurance policy.

be•nev•o•lent | bə'nevələnt | • *adj.* well meaning and kindly: *a benevolent smile.*
■ (of an organization) serving a charitable rather than a profit-making purpose: *a benevolent fund.*

DERIVATIVES: **be•nev•o•lence** n. **be•nev•o•lent•ly** adv.

be•night•ed |bi'nītid| • adj. 1 in a state of pitiful or contemptible intellectual or moral ignorance, typically owing to a lack of opportunity: *they saw themselves as bringers of culture to poor benighted peoples.* 2 overtaken by darkness: *a storm developed and we were forced to wait benighted near the summit.*
DERIVATIVES: **be•night•ed•ness** n.

be•nign |bi'nīn| • adj. 1 gentle; kindly: *her face was calm and benign | his benign but firm manner.* ■ (of a climate or environment) mild and favorable. ■ not harmful to the environment: [in combination] *an ozone-benign refrigerant.* 2 (of a disease) not harmful in effect: in particular, (of a tumor) not malignant.
DERIVATIVES: **be•nign•ly** adv.

be•nig•nant |bi'nignənt| • adj. 1 kindly and benevolent. 2 less common medical term for BENIGN. ■ having a good effect; beneficial: *the benignant touch of love and beauty.*
DERIVATIVES: **be•nig•nan•cy** n. **be•nig•nant•ly** adv.

be•nign ne•glect • n. a noninterference that is intended to benefit someone or something more than continual attention would: *they claimed that benign neglect would allow the city to rebuild itself.*

ben trovato |ˌben trə'vätō| • adj. (of an anecdote) invented but plausible.

be•queath |bi'kwēTH; -'kwēTH| • v. [trans.] leave (a personal estate or one's body) to a person or other beneficiary by a will: *an identical sum was bequeathed by Margaret | he bequeathed his art collection to the town.* ■ pass (something) on or leave (something) to someone else: *he is ditching the unpopular policies bequeathed to him.*
DERIVATIVES: **be•queath•er** n.

be•quest |bi'kwest| • n. a thing bequeathed; a legacy: *her $135,000 was the largest bequest the library ever has received.* ■ the action of bequeathing something: *a painting acquired by bequest.*

be•rate |bi'rāt| • v. [trans.] scold or criticize (someone) angrily: *my son berated me for not giving him a Jewish upbringing.*

be•reave |bi'rēv| • v. (**be bereaved**) be deprived of a loved one through a profound absence, esp. due to the loved one's death: *the year after they had been bereaved | [as adj.] (bereaved) bereaved families | [as plural n.] (the bereaved) those who counsel the bereaved.*
DERIVATIVES: **be•reave•ment** n.

be•reft |bi'reft| archaic past participle of BEREAVE. • adj. deprived of or lacking something, esp. a nonmaterial asset: *her room was stark and bereft of color.* ■ (of a person) lonely and abandoned, esp. through someone's death or departure.

ber•serk |bər'zərk;-'sərk| • adj. (of a person or animal) out of control with anger or excitement; wild or frenzied: *after she left, he went berserk, throwing things around the apartment.* ■ (of a mechanical device or system) operating in a wild or erratic way; out of control: *the climate control went berserk and either roasted or froze us.* ■ (of a procedure, program, or activity) act unpredictably; appear out of control: *the stock market went berserk.*

be•seech |bi'sēCH| • v. (past and past part. **besought** |-'sôt| or **beseeched**) ask (someone) urgently and fervently to do something; implore; entreat: [with obj. and infinitive] *they beseeched him to stay* | [with obj. and direct speech] *"You have got to believe me," Gloria beseeched him* | [trans.] *they earnestly beseeched his forgiveness* | [as adj.] (**beseeching**) *a beseeching gaze.*
DERIVATIVES: **be•seech•ing•ly** adv.

be•set |bi'set| • v. (**besetting**; past and past part. **beset**) [trans.] 1 (of a problem or difficulty) trouble or threaten persistently: *the social problems that beset the inner city | he was beset with self-doubt* ■ surround and harass; assail on all sides: *I was beset by clouds of flies.* ■ hem in; enclose: *a ship beset by ice.* 2 (**be besetwith**) be covered or studded with: *blades of grass beset with glistening drops of dew.*
PHRASES: **besetting sin** a fault to which a person or institution is especially prone; a characteristic weakness.

be•smirch |bi'smərCH| • v. [trans.] damage the reputation of (someone or something) in the opinion of others: *he had besmirched the good name of his family.* ■ make (something) dirty or discolored: *the ground was besmirched with blood.*

be•sot•ted |bi'sätid| • adj. 1 strongly infatuated: *he became besotted with his best friend's sister.* 2 intoxicated; drunk.

bes•tial |'besCHəl; 'bes-| • adj. of or like an animal or animals: *Darwin's revelations about out bestial beginnings.* ■ savagely cruel and depraved: *bestial and barbaric acts.*
DERIVATIVES: **bes•tial•ly** adv.

bes•ti•al•i•ty |ˌbesCHē'ælitē; ˌbes-| • n. 1 savagely cruel or depraved behavior: *there seems no end to the bestiality of human beings.* 2 sexual intercourse between a person and an animal.

bes•ti•ar•y |'besCHē,erē; 'bes-| • n. (pl. **-ies**) a descriptive or anecdotal treatise on various real or mythical kinds of animals, esp. a medieval work with a moralizing tone.

be•stir |bi'stər| • v. (**bestirred, bestirring**) (**bestir oneself**) make a physical or mental effort; exert or rouse oneself: *they rarely bestir themselves except in the most pressing circumstances.*

be•stow |bi'stō| • v. [trans.] confer or present (an honor, right, or gift): *thank you for this honor that you have bestowed upon me | she bestowed her nicest smile on Jim.*
DERIVATIVES: **be•stow•al** |-əl| n.

be•stride |bi'strīd| • v. (past **bestrode** |-'strōd|; past part. **bestridden** |-'stridn|) [trans.] stand astride over; span or straddle: *creatures that bestride the dividing line between amphibians and reptiles.*

■ sit astride on: *he bestrode his horse with easy grace.*

bête noire |ˌbāt ˈnwär; ˌbet | • *n.* (pl. **bêtes noires** |ˈnwärz| pronunc. same) the bane of one's life; a person or thing that one particularly dislikes: *great-uncle Edward was my father's bête noire.*

be•think |biˈTHiNGk| • *v.* (past and past part. **bethought** |-ˈTHôt|) (**bethink oneself**) think on reflection; come to think: *he bethought himself of the verse from the Book of Proverbs* | [with clause] *the council bethought itself that this plan would leave room for future expansion.*

be•tide |biˈtīd| • *v.* [intrans.] happen: *I waited with beating heart, as yet not knowing what would betide.*

■ [trans.] happen to (someone): *she was trembling with fear lest worse might betide her.*

be•to•ken |biˈtōkən| • *v.* [trans.] be a sign of; indicate: *she wondered if his cold, level gaze betokened indifference.*

■ be a warning or indication of (a future event): *the falling comet betokened the true end of Merlin's powers.*

bev•el |ˈbevəl| • *n.* a slope from the horizontal or vertical in carpentry and stonework; a sloping surface or edge.

■ (in full **bevel square**) a tool for marking angles in carpentry and stonework. • *v.* (**beveled, beveling** or **bevelled, bevelling**) [trans.] [often as adj.] (**beveled**) reduce (a square edge on an object) to a sloping edge: *a beveled mirror.*

bev•y |ˈbevē| • *n.* (pl. **-ies**) a large group of people or things of a particular kind: *he was surrounded by a bevy of beautiful girls.*

■ a group of birds, particularly when closely gathered on the ground: *a bevy of quail.*

bi•an•nu•al |bīˈænyəwəl| • *adj.* occurring twice a year: *the biannual meeting of the planning committee.* Cf. BIENNIAL.
DERIVATIVES: **bi•an•nu•al•ly** *adv.*

bi•be•lot |ˈbib(ə)ˌlō| • *n.* a small, decorative ornament or trinket.

bib•li•o•phile |ˈbiblēəˌfil| • *n.* a person who collects or has a great love of books.
DERIVATIVES: **bib•li•o•phil•ic** |ˌbiblēəˈfilik| *adj.* **bib•li•oph•i•ly** |ˌbiblēˈäfəlē| *n.*

bib•u•lous |ˈbibyələs| • *adj.* excessively fond of drinking alcohol.

bi•cam•er•al |bīˈkæmərəl| • *adj.* (of a legislative body) having two branches or chambers.
DERIVATIVES: **bi•cam•er•al•ism** |-ˌlizəm| *n.*

bi•det |biˈdā| • *n.* a low oval basin used for washing one's genital and anal area.

bi•en•ni•al |bīˈenēəl| • *adj.* **1** taking place every other year: *summit meetings are normally biennial.* Cf. BIANNUAL. **2** (esp. of a plant) living or lasting for two years. • *n.* **1** a plant that takes two years to grow from seed to fruition (which occurs in the second year) and die. Compare with ANNUAL, PERENNIAL. **2** an event celebrated or taking place every two years.
DERIVATIVES: **bi•en•ni•al•ly** *adv.*

USAGE: **Biennial** means 'lasting or occurring every two years': *Congressional elections are a biennial phenomenon.* A *biennial plant* is one that lives a two-year cycle, flowering and producing seed in the second year. **Biannual** means 'twice a year': *The solstice is a biannual event.*

bi•fur•cate • *v.* |ˈbīfərˌkāt| divide into two branches or forks: [intrans.] *just below Cairo the river bifurcates* | [trans.] *the trail was bifurcated by a mountain stream.* • *adj.* |bīˈfərkāt; ˈbīfərkit| forked; branched: *a bifurcate tree.*

big•a•my |ˈbigəmē| • *n.* the crime of going through a marriage ceremony while already married to another person.

■ (in some churches) the act of remarriage after the death of a spouse, divorce, or other change of condition.
DERIVATIVES: **big•a•mist** |-mist| *n.* **big•a•mous** |-məs| *adj.*

big bang (also **Big Bang**) • *n.* the explosion of dense matter that, according to current cosmological theories, marked the origin of the universe.

In the beginning a fireball of radiation at extremely high temperature and density, but occupying a tiny volume, is believed to have formed. This expanded and cooled, extremely fast at first, but more slowly as subatomic particles condensed into matter that later accumulated to form galaxies and stars. The galaxies are currently still retreating from one another. What was left of the original radiation continued to cool and has been detected as a uniform background of weak microwave radiation.

bight |bīt| • *n.* a curve or recess in a coastline, river, or other geographical feature.

■ a loop of rope, as distinct from the rope's ends.

big•ot |ˈbigət| • *n.* a person who is bigoted: *religious bigots.*

big•ot•ed |ˈbigətid| • *adj.* obstinately convinced of the superiority or correctness of one's own opinions and prejudiced against those who hold different opinions: *a bigoted group of reactionaries.*

■ expressing or characterized by prejudice and intolerance: *a thoughtless and bigoted article.*

big•ot•ry |ˈbigətrē| • *n.* bigoted attitudes; intolerance toward those who hold different opinions from oneself: *the report reveals racism and right-wing bigotry.*

bi•jou |ˈbēzHōō| • *adj.* (esp. of a residence or business establishment) small and elegant: *bijou restaurants.* • *n.* (pl. **bijoux** |-zHōō(z)|) a jewel or trinket.

bi•lat•er•al |bīˈlætərəl| • *adj.* having or relating to two sides; affecting both sides: *bilateral hearing is essential for sound location.*

■ involving two parties, usually countries: *the recently concluded bilateral agreements with Japan.*
DERIVATIVES: **bilaterality** *n.* **bi•lat•er•al•ly** *adv.*

bile |bīl| • *n.* a bitter greenish-brown alkaline

fluid that aids digestion and is secreted by the liver and stored in the gallbladder. ■ anger; irritability: *that topic is sure to stir up plenty of bile.*

bil•ious |'bilyəs| • *adj.* affected by or associated with nausea or vomiting: *feeling a little bilious | a bilious attack.* ■ (of a color) lurid or sickly: *a bilious olive hue.* ■ spiteful; bad-tempered. ■ of or relating to bile.
DERIVATIVES: **bil•ious•ly** *adv.* **bil•ious•ness** *n.*

bilk |bilk| • *v.* [trans.] **1** obtain or withhold money from (someone) by deceit or without justification; cheat or defraud: *government waste has bilked the taxpayer of billions.* ■ obtain (money) fraudulently: *some businesses bilk thousands of dollars from unsuspecting elderly consumers.* **2** evade; elude: *I ducked into the pantry, bilking Edward.*
DERIVATIVES: **bilk•er** *n.*

bil•let-doux |'bilā 'doo| • *n.* (pl. **billets-doux** |-'doo(z)|) a love letter.

bi•na•ry |'bī,nerē| • *adj.* **1** relating to, using, or expressed in a system of numerical notation that has 2 rather than 10 as abase. ■ in binary format: *it is stored as a binary file.* **2** relating to, composed of, or involving two things: *testing the so-called binary, or dual chemical, weapons.* • *n.* (pl. **-ies**) **1** the binary system: binary notation: *the device is counting in binary.* **2** something having two parts. ■ a binary star(a system of two stars, one revolving around the other or both revolving around a common center).

bi•no•mi•al |bī'nōmēəl| • *n.* **1** an algebraic expression of the sum or the difference of two mathematical terms. **2** a two-part name, esp. the Latin name of a species of living organism (consisting of the genus followed by the specific epithet, e.g., *Canis familiaris* the common dog). **3** a noun phrase with two heads joined by a conjunction, in which the order is relatively fixed (as in *knife and fork*). • *adj.* **1** (in mathematics) consisting of two terms. ■ of or relating to a binomial or to the binomial theorem. **2** having or using two names, (used esp. of the Latin name of a species of living organism).

bi•o•de•grad•a•ble |,bīōdi'grādəbəl| • *adj.* (of a substance or object) capable of being decomposed by bacteria or other living organisms.
DERIVATIVES: **bi•o•de•grad•a•bil•i•ty** |-,grādə'bilitē| *n.*

bi•o•di•ver•si•ty |,bīōdi'vərsitē| • *n.* the variety of plant and animal life in the world or in a particular habitat.

bi•o•en•gi•neer•ing |,bīō,enjə'niriNG| • *n.* **1** (also **genetic engineering**) the deliberate modification of the characteristics of an organism by manipulating its genetic material. **2** the use of artificial tissues, organs, or organ components to replace damaged or absent parts of the body, such as artificial limbs and heart pacemakers. **3** the use in engineering or industry of biological organisms or processes.
DERIVATIVES: **bi•o•en•gi•neer** *n. & v.*

bi•o•eth•ics |,bīō'eTHiks| • *plural n.* [treated as sing.] the ethics of medical and biological research.
DERIVATIVES: **bi•o•eth•i•cal** |'eTHikəl| *adj.* **bi•o•eth•i•cist** |-'eTHəsist| *n.*

bi•o•feed•back |,bīō'fēd,bæk| • *n.* the use of electronic monitoring of a normally automatic bodily function in order to train someone to acquire voluntary control of that function.

bi•o•gen•e•sis |,bīō'jenəsis| • *n.* the synthesis of substances by living organisms. ■ the hypothesis that living matter arises only from other living matter.
DERIVATIVES: **bi•o•ge•net•ic** |-jə'netik| *adj.*

bi•o•mass |'bīō,mæs| • *n.* the total quantity or weight of organisms in a given area or volume. ■ organic matter used as a fuel, esp. in a power station for the generation of electricity.

bi•ome |'bīōm| • *n.* a large naturally occurring community of flora and fauna occupying a major habitat, e.g., forest or tundra.

bi•on•ic |bī'änik| • *adj.* having artificial body parts, esp. electromechanical ones. ■ having ordinary human powers increased by or as if by the aid of such devices (real or fictional). ■ of or relating to bionics.
DERIVATIVES: **bi•on•i•cal•ly** |-ik(ə)lē| *adv.*

bi•on•ics |bī'äniks| • *plural n.* [treated as sing.] the study of mechanical systems that function like living organisms or parts of living organisms.

bi•op•sy |'bäpsē| • *n.* (pl. **-ies**) an examination of tissue removed from a living body to discover the presence, cause, or extent of a disease.

bi•o•rhythm |'bīō,riTHəm| • *n.* a recurring cycle in the physiology or functioning of an organism, such as the daily cycle of sleeping and waking. ■ a cyclic pattern of physical, emotional, or mental activity said to occur in the life of a person.
DERIVATIVES: **bi•o•rhyth•mic** |,bīō 'riTHmik| *adj.*

bi•o•sphere |'bīə,sfir| • *n.* the regions of the surface and atmosphere of the earth or other planet occupied by living organisms.
DERIVATIVES: **bi•o•spher•ic** |,bīə'sferik| *adj.*

bi•o•ta |bī'ōtə| • *n.* the animal and plant life of a particular region, habitat, or geological period: *the biota of the river.*

bi•o•tech•nol•o•gy |,bīōtek'näləjē| • *n.* the exploitation of biological processes for industrial and other purposes, esp. the genetic manipulation of microorganisms for the production of antibiotics, hormones, etc.

bi•po•lar |bī'pōlər| • *adj.* having or relating to two poles or extremities: *a sharply bipolar division of affluent and underclasses.* ■ (of a plant or animal species) of or occurring in both polar regions. ■ (of a nerve cell) having two axons (long, threadlike parts), one on either side of the cell body. ■ (of a transistor

or other electronic device) using both positive and negative charge carriers.
DERIVATIVES: **bi•po•lar•i•ty** |ˌbīpōˈleritē| n.

bi•po•lar dis•or•der • n. a mental disorder marked by alternating periods of elation and depression. Also called, esp. formerly, *manic depression*

bi•sex•u•al |bīˈsekshəwəl| • adj. sexually attracted to both men and women.
■ (in biology) having characteristics of both sexes. • n. a person who is sexually attracted to both men and women.
DERIVATIVES: **bi•sex•u•al•i•ty** |ˌbīseksha-ˈwælitē| n.

biv•ou•ac |ˈbivo͞oˌæk;ˈbivwæk| • n. a temporary camp without tents or cover, used esp. by soldiers or mountaineers. • v. [no obj., with adverbial of place] (**bivouacked, bivouacking**) stay in such a camp: *the battalion was now bivouacked in a cornfield.*

bi•zarre |biˈzär| • adj. very strange or unusual, esp. so as to cause interest or amusement: *her bizarre dresses and outrageous hairdos.*
DERIVATIVES: **bi•zarre•ly** adv. **bi•zarre•ness** n. **bizarrerie** n. a bizarre quality.

black |blæk| • adj. (also **Black**) of any human group having dark-colored skin, esp. of African or Australian Aboriginal ancestry: *black adolescents of Jamaican descent.*
■ of or relating to black people: *black culture.* • n. (also **Black**) a member of a dark-skinned people, esp. one of African or Australian Aboriginal ancestry: *a coalition of blacks and whites against violence.*

USAGE: **Black**, designating Americans of African heritage, became the most widely used and accepted term in the 1960s and 1970s, replacing **Negro**. It is not usually capitalized: *black Americans.* Through the 1980s, the more formal **African American** replaced **black** in much usage, but both are now generally acceptable. (The noun form is sometimes hyphenated, and the adjective form should be: *the African-American novelist Ralph Ellison*). **Afro-American**, an earlier alternative to **black**, is heard mostly in anthropological and cultural contexts. 'Colored people,' common earlier in the twentieth century, is now usually regarded as derogatory, although the phrase survives in the full name of the NAACP, the National Association for the Advancement of Colored People. An inversion, 'people of color,' has gained some favor, but is also used in reference to other nonwhite ethnic groups.

black Eng•lish • n. any of various nonstandard forms of English spoken by black people.
■ a dialect spoken by black Americans that displays consistent syntactical forms theorized as arising from African languages.

black•guard |ˈblægərd; ˈblækˌgärd| • n. a person, particularly a man, who behaves in a dishonorable or contemptible way. • v. [trans.] abuse or disparage (someone) scurrilously.

DERIVATIVES: **black•guard•ly** adj.

blackhole • n. **1** (inastronomy) a region of space having a gravitational field so intense thatno matter or radiation can escape. Black holes are probably formed when a massive star exhausts its nuclear fuel and collapses under its own gravity. If the star is massive enough, no known force can counteract the increasing gravity, and it will collapse to a point of infinite density. Before this stage is reached, within a certain radius (the event horizon) light itself becomes trapped and the object becomes invisible.
■ a figurative place of emptiness or aloneness: *they think he's sitting in a black hole with no interaction with his people.* ■ a place where money, lost items, etc., are supposed to go, never to be seen again: *the moribund economy has been a black hole for federal funds | I wouldn't dare go in that black hole he calls a "garage."* ■ (of a system, practice, or institution) a state of inadequacy or excessive bureaucracy in which hopes, progress, etc., become futile: *juveniles lost in the black hole of the criminal justice system.* **2** a dreadful place of confinement or imprisonment, esp. in the armed services.

black•mail |ˈblækˌmāl| • n. the action, treated as a criminal offense, of demanding money from a person in return for not revealing compromising or injurious information about that person: *they were acquitted of charges of blackmail.*
■ money demanded in this way: *we do not pay blackmail.* ■ the use of threats or the manipulation of someone's feelings to force them to do something: *out of fear, she submitted to Jim's emotional blackmail | they are trying to blackmail us with hunger.* • v. [trans.] demand money from (a person) in return for not revealing compromising or injurious information about that person: *trying to blackmail him for $400,000.*
■ force (someone) to do something by using threats or manipulating their feelings: *he had blackmailed her into sailing with him.*
DERIVATIVES: **black•mail•er** n.

black mar•ket • n. (**the black market**) an illegal traffic or trade in officially controlled or scarce commodities: *they planned to sell the meat on the black market.* The gray market invloves traffic or trade that is not illegal but is questionable, e.g., trade in securities not yet quoted on the Stock Exchange.
DERIVATIVES: **black mar•ke•teer** (also **black-mar•ke•teer**) n. **black-mar•ke•teer** v.

black tie • n. a black bow tie worn with a dinner jacket.
■ formal evening dress: *the audience wears black tie.* Cf. WHITE TIE. • adj. (**black-tie**) (of an event) requiring formal evening dress: *evening meals were black-tie affairs.*

bland•ish•ment |ˈblændishmənt| • n. a flattering or pleasing statement or action used to persuade someone gently to do something: *the blandishments of a travel brochure.*

bla•sé |bläˈzā| • adj. unimpressed or indifferent to something because one has experienced or seen it so often before: *she was becoming quite blasé about the dangers of city life.*

blas•phe•my | 'blæsfəmē | • *n.* (pl. **-ies**) the act or offense of speaking sacrilegiously about God or sacred things; profane talk: *he was detained on charges of blasphemy* | *screaming incomprehensible blasphemies.*
DERIVATIVES: **blas•phe•mous** *adj.* **blas•phe•mous•ly** *adv.*

bla•tant | 'blātnt | • *adj.* (of bad behavior) done openly and unashamedly: *blatant lies.*
■ completely lacking in subtlety; very obvious: *forcing herself to resist his blatant charm* | *blatant appeals to ethnicity.*
DERIVATIVES: **bla•tan•cy** | 'blātnsē | *n.*

blath•er | 'blæTHər | (also **blether** or **blither**) • *v.* [intrans.] talk long-windedly without making very much sense: *she began blathering on about her previous lives* | [as n.] (**blathering**) *stop your blathering.* • *n.* long-winded talk with no real substance.

blath•er•skite | 'blæTHər,skīt | • *n.* **1** a person who talks at great length without making much sense.
■ foolish talk; nonsense: *politicians get away all the time with their blatherskite.* **2** a scoundrel: *you lousy, thieving blatherskite!*

bla•zon | 'blāzən | • *v.* [trans.] **1** [with adverbial of place] display prominently or vividly: *they saw their company name blazoned all over the media.*
■ report (news), esp. in a sensational manner: *accounts of their ordeal blazoned to the entire nation.* **2** describe or depict (armorial bearings) in a correct heraldic manner.
■ inscribe or paint(an object) with arms or a name. • *n.* a correct heraldic description of armorial bearings.
■ a coat of arms.

blear | blir | • *v.* [trans.] make dim; blur: *you would blear your eyes with books.* • *adj.* dim, dull, or filmy: *a medicine to lay to sore and blear eyes.* • *n.* a film over the eyes; a blur: *he forced his eyes open and shut to rid them of blear.*
DERIVATIVES: **bleary** *adj.*

blench | blenCH | • *v.* [intrans.] make a sudden flinching movement out of fear or pain: *he blenched and struggled to regain his composure.*

blight | blīt | • *n.* a plant disease, esp. one caused by fungi such as mildews, rusts, and smuts: *a blight that attacks grapevines* | [with adj.] *potato blight.*
■ informal anything that causes a plant disease or interferes with the healthy growth of a plant.
■ [in sing.] a thing that spoils or damages something: *her remorse could be a blight on their happiness.* ■ an ugly or neglected urban area, or its condition: *the depressing urban blight in the south of the city.* • *v.* [trans.] (usu. **be blighted**) infect (plants or a planted area) with blight: *a peach tree blighted by leaf curl.*
■ spoil, harm, or destroy: *the scandal blighted the careers of several leading politicians* | [as adj.] (**blighted**) *his blighted ambitions.* ■ [usu. as adj.] (**blighted**) subject (an urban area) to neglect: *blighted neighborhoods.*

blithe | blīTH; blīTH | • *adj.* showing a casual and cheerful indifference considered to be

callous or improper: *a blithe disregard for the rules of the road.*
■ happy or joyous: *a blithe comedy.*
DERIVATIVES: **blithe•ly** *adv.* **blithe•ness** *n.* **blithesome** | -səm | *adj. a blithesome spirit.*

blitz•krieg | 'blits,krēg | • *n.* an intense military campaign intended to bring about a swift victory.

bloc | bläk | • *n.* a combination of countries, parties, or groups sharing a common purpose: *a larger, stronger European bloc* | *a center-left voting bloc* | *the upstate dairy bloc.*

blond | bländ | (also **blonde**) • *adj.* (of hair) fair or pale yellow: *short-cropped blond hair* | *her hair was dyed blond.*
■ (of a person) having hair of a fair or pale yellow color: *a slim blond woman.* ■ (of a person) having fair hair and a light complexion, typically regarded as a racial characteristic. ■ (of wood and other substances) light in color or tone: *a New York office full of blond wood.* • *n.* a person with fair hair and skin.
DERIVATIVES: **blond•ish** *adj.* **blond•ness** *n.*

blood•less | 'blədlis | • *adj.* (of a person) cold or unemotional: *a shrewd and bloodless Hollywood mogul.* ■ lacking in vitality; feeble: *their occasionally bloodless chamber jazz.*
DERIVATIVES: **blood•less•ly** *adv.* **blood•less•ness** *n.*

blue blood • *n.* noble birth: *blue blood is no guarantee of any particular merit, competence, or expertise.*
■ (also **blueblood**) a person of noble birth: *a comforting figure among that crowd of blue bloods.*
DERIVATIVES: **blue-blood•ed** *adj.*

blue law • *n.* a law prohibiting certain activities, such as shopping, on a Sunday.
■ (in colonial New England) a strict religious law, particularly one preventing entertainment or leisure activities on a Sunday.

blue•nose | 'bloō,nōz | • *n.* **1** a priggish or puritanical person: [as adj.] *the most restrictive, bluenose standards.* **2** (**Bluenose**) a person from Nova Scotia.
DERIVATIVES: **blue•nosed** *adj.* (in sense 1).

blues | bloōz | • *plural n.* **1** [treated as sing. or pl.] (often **the blues**) an often melancholic music of black American folk origin, typically in a twelve-bar sequence. It developed in the rural South toward the end of the 19th century, finding a wider audience from the 1920s as blacks migrated to the cities. This urban blues gave rise to rhythm and blues and rock and roll.
■ [treated as sing.] a piece of such music: *now we're going to play a blues in C.* **2** (**the blues**) feelings of melancholy, sadness, or depression: *she's got the blues.*
DERIVATIVES: **blues•y** *adj.* (in sense 1).

blue-sky (also **blue-skies**) • *adj.* [attrib.] not yet practical or profitable: *blue-sky research.*

blue•stock•ing | 'bloō,stäkiNG | • *n.* an intellectual or literary woman.

bluff • *adj.* direct in speech or behavior but in a good-natured way: *a big, bluff, hearty man.*
DERIVATIVES: **bluff•ly** *adv.* **bluff•ness** *n.*

blus•ter | ˈbləstər | • v. [intrans.] talk in a loud, aggressive, or indignant way with little effect: *you threaten and bluster, but you won't follow through* | [with direct speech] *"I don't care what he says," I blustered* | [as adj.] (**blustering**) *a blustering bully.*
■ (of a storm, wind, or rain) blow or beat fiercely and noisily: [as adj.] (**blustering**) *the blustering wind.* • n. loud, aggressive, or indignant talk with little effect: *their threats contained a measure of bluster.*
DERIVATIVES: **blus•ter•er** n.

boat•swain | ˈbōsən | (also **bo'sun** or **bo-sun**) • n. a ship's officer in charge of equipment and the crew.

bo•da•cious | bōˈdāsHəs | • adj. excellent, admirable, or attractive: *this restaurant serves bodacious grilled lobster!*
■ audacious in a way considered admirable: *a bunch of bodacious dudes playing games with death.*

bode | bōd | • v. [intrans.] (**bode well/ill**) be an omen of a particular outcome: *their argument did not bode well for the future* | [trans.] *high interest rates bode dark days ahead for retailers.*

bo•dhi•satt•va | ˌbōdiˈsätvə; -ˈsət- | (also **Bo-dhisattva**) • n. (in Mahayana Buddhism) a person who is able to reach nirvana but delays doing so out of compassion in order to save suffering beings.

bo•gus | ˈbōgəs | • adj. not genuine or true; fake: *a bogus insurance claim.*
DERIVATIVES: **bo•gus•ly** adv. **bo•gus•ness** n.

bo•he•mi•an | bōˈhēmēən | • n. a person who has informal and unconventional social habits, esp. an artist or writer: *the young bohemians with their art galleries and sushi bars.* [ORIGIN: mid 19th cent.: from French *bohémien* 'gypsy' (because gypsies were thought to come from Bohemia, or because they perhaps entered the West through Bohemia).] • adj. having informal and unconventional social habits.
DERIVATIVES: **bo•he•mi•an•ism** | -ˌnizəm | n.

bois•ter•ous | ˈboist(ə)rəs | • adj. (of a person, event, or behavior) noisy, energetic, and cheerful; rowdy: *the boisterous conviviality associated with taverns of that period.*
■ (of wind, weather, or water) wild or stormy.
DERIVATIVES: **bois•ter•ous•ly** adv. **bois•ter•ous•ness** n.

bo•lus | ˈbōləs | • n. (pl. **boluses**) a small rounded mass of a substance, esp. of chewed food at the moment of swallowing.
■ a type of large pill used in veterinary medicine. ■ a single dose of a drug or other medicinal preparation given all at once.

bom•bast | ˈbämbæst | • n. high-sounding language with little meaning, used to impress people.
DERIVATIVES: **bom•bas•tic** | bämˈbæstik | adj. **bom•bas•ti•cal•ly** | bämˈbæstik(ə)lē | adv.

bo•na fide | ˈbōnə ˌfīd; ˈbänə | • adj. genuine; real: *only bona fide members of the company may use the logo.* • adv. sincerely; without inten-

tion to deceive: *the court will assume that they have acted bona fide.*

bo•na fi•des | ˈbōnə ˌfīdz; ˈfīdēz; ˈbänə- | • n. a person's honesty and sincerity of intention: *he went to great lengths to establish his liberal bona fides.*
■ [treated as pl.] documentary evidence showing a person's legitimacy; credentials: *are you satisfied with my bona fides?* [ORIGIN: mid 20th cent.]

bond•age | ˈbändij | • n. 1 the state of being a slave: *the deliverance of the Israelites from bondage in Egypt.*
■ a state of being greatly constrained by circumstances or obligations: *young women lost to the bondage of early motherhood.* 2 sexual practice that involves the tying up or restraining of one partner.

bon•ho•mie | ˈbänəˌmē; ˌbänəˈmē | • n. cheerful friendliness; geniality: *he exuded good humor and bonhomie.*

bon•sai | bänˈsī; ˈbänsī | • n. (pl. same) (also **bonsai tree**) an ornamental tree or shrub grown in a pot and artificially prevented from reaching its normal size.
■ the art of growing trees or shrubs in such a way.

bon vi•vant | ˈbän vēˈvänt | • n. (pl. **bon vivants** | -ˈvänt(s) | or **bons vivants** | -ˈvänt(s) | pronunc. same) a person who enjoys a sociable and luxurious lifestyle.

boon•dog•gle | ˈbōōnˌdägəl; -ˌdôgəl | • n. work or activity that is wasteful or pointless but gives the appearance of having value: *writing off the cold fusion phenomenon as a boondoggle best buried in literature.* ■ a public project of questionable merit that typically involves political patronage and graft. • v. [intrans.] waste money or time on such projects.

boor | ˈbōōr | • n. a rude, unmannerly person: *a big, obnoxious boor.* ■ a clumsy person. ■ a peasant; a yokel.
DERIVATIVES: **boor•ish** adj. **boor•ish•ly** adv. **boor•ish•ness** n.

boot•less | ˈbōōtlis | • adj. (of a task or undertaking) ineffectual; useless: *words at this pass were vain and bootless* | *bootless efforts.*

bore[1] | bôr | • v. 1 [trans.] make (a hole) in something, esp. with a revolving tool: *they bored holes in the sides* | [intrans.] *the drill can bore through rock.*
■ [trans.] hollow out (a tube or tunnel): *try to bore the tunnel at the correct angle.* ■ [intrans.] (**bore into**) (of a person's eyes) stare harshly at: *your terrible blue eyes bore into me.* ■ [trans.] hollow out (a gun barrel or other tube). 2 [intrans.] make one's way through (a crowd). • n. 1 the hollow part inside a gun barrel or other Cf. GAUGE.tube.
■ [often in combination] the diameter of this; the caliber: *a small-bore rifle.* ■ [in combination] a gun of a specified bore: *he shot a guard in the leg with a twelve-bore.* 2 short for boreHole, a hole bored into the ground to find water, oil, etc.

bore[2] • n. a person whose talk or behavior is dull and uninteresting: *she found him a bore.*

■ [in sing.] a tedious situation or thing: *going out to dinner alone is such a bore.* • *v.* [trans.] make (someone) feel weary and uninterested by tedious talk or dullness: *rather than bore you with all the details, I'll hit some of the bright spots.*

bore³ • *n.* a steep-fronted wave caused by the meeting of two tides or by the constriction of a tide rushing up a narrow estuary.

bo•re•al |'bôrēəl| • *adj.* of the North or northern regions.

■ relating to or characteristic of the climatic zone south of the Arctic, esp. the cold temperate region dominated by taiga and forests of birch, poplar, and conifers: *northern boreal forest.* ■ (**Boreal**) (in botany) relating to or denoting a phytogeographical kingdom comprising the arctic and temperate regions of Eurasia and North America. ■ (**Boreal**) (in geology) relating to or denoting the second climatic stage of the postglacial period in northern Europe, between the Preboreal and Atlantic stages (about 9,000 to 7,500 years ago).

born-a•gain • *adj.* converted to a personal faith in Christ (with reference to John 3:3): *a born-again Christian.*

■ having the extreme enthusiasm of the newly converted or reconverted: *born-again environmentalists.* • *n.* a born-again Christian.

bor•ough |'bərō| • *n.* a town or district that is an administrative unit, in particular: ■ a municipal corporation in certain states. ■ each of five divisions of New York City. ■ in Alaska, a district corresponding to a county elsewhere in the US. ■ Brit. a town (as distinct from a city) with a corporation and privileges granted by a royal charter. ■ Brit. a town historically sending representatives to Parliament.

bos•cage |'bäskij| (also **boskage**) • *n.* massed trees or shrubs: *the lush subtropical boscage.*

bosk•y |'bäskē| • *adj.* wooded; covered by trees or bushes: *a river meandering between bosky banks.*

bo•tan•i•cal |bə'tænikəl| • *n.* (usu. **botanicals**) a substance obtained from a plant and used as an additive, esp. in gin or cosmetics.

bou•doir |'bōōdwär| • *n.* a woman's bedroom or private room.

bour•geois |bōōr'zHwä; 'bōōrzHwä| • *adj.* of or characteristic of the middle class, typically with reference to its perceived materialistic values or conventional attitudes: *a rich, bored, bourgeois family* | *these views will shock the bourgeois critics.*

■ (in Marxist contexts) upholding the interests of capitalism; not communist. • *n.* (pl. same) a bourgeois person: *a self-confessed and proud bourgeois.*

bour•geoi•sie |,bōōrzHwä'zē| • *n.* (usu. **the bourgeoisie**) the middle class, typically with reference to its perceived materialistic values or conventional attitudes. Cf. HAUFE BOURGEOISIE; PETIT BOURGEOIS.

■ (in Marxist contexts) the capitalist class who

own most of society's wealth and means of production.

bourse |bōōrs| • *n.* a stock market in a non-English-speaking country, esp. France.

■ (**Bourse**) the Paris stock exchange.

boutonnière |,bōōtn'ir| • *n.* a spray of flowers worn in a buttonhole.

bo•vine |'bōvīn; -vēn| • *adj.* of, relating to, or affecting cattle: *bovine tuberculosis.*

■ (of a person) slow-moving and dull-witted: *amiable bovine faces.* • *n.* an animal of the cattle group, which also includes buffaloes and bisons.

DERIVATIVES: **bo•vine•ly** *adv.*

bowd•ler•ize |'bōdlə,rīz; 'bowd-| • *v.* [trans.] remove material that is considered improper or offensive from (a text or account), esp. with the result that it becomes weaker or less effective: [as *adj.*] (**bowdlerized**) *a bowdlerized version of the story.*

DERIVATIVES: **bowd•ler•ism** |-,rizəm| *n.* **bowd•ler•i•za•tion** |,bōdləri'zāsHən; ,bowd-| *n.*

boy•cott |'boikät| • *v.* [trans.] withdraw from commercial or social relations with (a country, organization, or person) as a punishment or protest.

■ refuse to buy or handle (goods) as a punishment or protest. ■ refuse to cooperate with or participate in (a policy or event). • *n.* a punitive ban that forbids relations with other bodies, cooperation with a policy, or the handling of goods. In labor law, a **primary boycott** is a union's campaign to urge consumers not to buy an employer's products. A **secondary boycott** (usually illegal) is aimed at products of another producer who is seen as supporting the primary target.

bra•chi•al |'brākēəl; 'bræk-| • *adj.* of or relating to the arm, specifically the upper arm, or an armlike structure: *the brachial artery.*

■ like an arm.

bra•chi•ate • *v.* |'brākē,āt; 'bræk-| [no obj., usu. with adverbial of direction] (of certain apes) move by using the arms to swing from branch to branch: *the gibbons brachiate energetically across their enclosure.* • *adj.* |'brākē,āt; 'bræk; -it| branched, esp. having widely spread paired branches on alternate sides.

■ having arms.

DERIVATIVES: **bra•chi•a•tion** |,brākē 'āsHən; ,bræk-| *n.* **bra•chi•a•tor** |,āt̬ər| *n.*

brach•y•ce•phal•ic |,brækēsə'fælik| • *adj.* having a relatively broad, short skull (usually with the breadth at least 80 percent of the length). Often contrasted with DOLICHOCEPHALIC.

DERIVATIVES: **brach•y•ceph•a•ly** |-'sefəlē| *n.* .

brack•ish |'brækisH| • *adj.* (of water) slightly salty, as in river estuaries.

■ (of fish or other organisms) living in or requiring such water. ■ unpleasant or distasteful: *a brackish mixture unsuitable for consumption.*

DERIVATIVES: **brack•ish•ness** *n.*

bract |brækt| • *n.* a modified leaf or scale, typically small, with a flower or flower cluster in its axil. Bracts are sometimes larger and more brightly colored than the true flower, as in poinsettia and dogwood.

brag•ga•do•ci•o | ˌbrægə'dōsHē͵ō | • *n.* boastful or arrogant behavior.

Brah•ma | 'brämə | **1** the creator god in later Hinduism, who forms a triad with Vishnu the preserver and Shiva the destroyer. **2** another term for BRAHMAN (sense 2).

Brah•man | 'brämən | (also **Brahmin**) • *n.* (pl. **-mans** or **-mins**) **1** a member of the highest Hindu caste, that of the priesthood. [ORIGIN: from Sanskrit *brāhmaṇa*.] **2** (in Hinduism) the ultimate reality underlying all phenomena. [ORIGIN: from Sanskrit *brahman*.] **3** an ox of a humped breed (*Bos indicus* or *B. taurus*) originally domesticated in India that is tolerant of heat and drought and is now kept widely in tropical and warm-temperate countries. (Also called **zebu**) .
DERIVATIVES: **Brah•man•ic** | brä'mænik | *adj.* **Brah•man•i•cal** | brä'mænikəl | *adj.*

Brah•man•ism | 'brämə͵nizəm | (also **Brahminism**) • *n.* the complex sacrificial religion that emerged in post-Vedic India (*c.*900 BC) under the influence of the dominant priesthood (Brahmans), an early stage in the development of Hinduism.

Brah•min | 'brämin | • *n.* **1** variant spelling of BRAHMAN. **2** a socially or culturally superior person, esp. a member of the upper classes from New England.
DERIVATIVES: **Brah•min•i•cal** | brä 'minikəl | *adj.* (in sense 1).

brain death • *n.* irreversible brain damage causing the end of independent respiration, regarded as indicative of death.

brain•wash | 'brān͵wôsH; -͵wäsH | • *v.* [trans.] make (someone) adopt radically different beliefs by using systematic and often forcible pressure: *the organization could brainwash young people* | *they have been **brainwashed into** conformity and subservience.*
DERIVATIVES: **brainwashing** *n.*

bran•dish | 'brændisH | • *v.* [trans.] wave or flourish (something, esp. a weapon) as a threat or in anger or excitement.
DERIVATIVES: **bran•dish•er** *n.*

brash | bræsH | • *adj.* self-assertive in a rude, noisy, or overbearing way: *he could be brash, cocky, and arrogant.*
■ strong, energetic, or irreverent: *I like brash, vibrant flavors.* ■ (of a place or thing) having an ostentatious or tasteless appearance: *a brash new building.*
DERIVATIVES: **brash•ly** *adv.* **brash•ness** *n.*

brass•y | 'bræsē | • *adj.* (**brassier**, **brassiest**) resembling brass, in particular:
■ bright or harsh yellow. ■ sounding like a brass musical instrument; harsh and loud. ■ (of a person, typically a woman) tastelessly showy or loud in appearance or manner: *her brassy, audacious exterior.*
DERIVATIVES: **brass•i•ly** | 'bræsəlē | *adv.* **brass•i•ness** *n.*

bra•va•do | brə'vädō | • *n.* a bold manner or a show of boldness intended to impress or intimidate.

bra•vo | 'brävō | • *exclam.* used to express approval when a performer or other person has done something well: *people kept on clapping and shouting "bravo!"* • *n.* (pl. **-os**) a cry of bravo: *bravos rang out.*

A female performer may be saluted *brava!* For extra effect, the superlative *bravissimo!* (or *bravissima!*) is sometimes employed.

bra•vu•ra | brə'v(y)o͞orə | • *n.* great technical skill and brilliance shown in a performance or activity: *the recital ended with a blazing display of bravura* | [as adj.] *a bravura performance.*
■ the display of great daring: *his show of bravura hid a guilty timidity.*

bra•zen | 'brāzən | • *adj.* **1** bold and without shame: *he went about his illegal business with a brazen assurance* | *that brazen hussy!* **2** made of brass.
■ harsh in sound: *the music's brazen chords.*
▶**brazen it** (or **something**) **out** endure an embarrassing or difficult situation by behaving with apparent confidence and lack of shame.
DERIVATIVES: **bra•zen•ly** *adv.* **bra•zen•ness** *n.*

breach | brēcH | • *n.* **1** an act of breaking or failing to observe a law, agreement, or code of conduct: *a breach of confidence* | *I sued for breach of contract.*
■ a break in relations: *a sudden **breach between** father and son.* **2** a gap in a wall, barrier, or defense, esp. one made by an attacking army. • *v.* [trans.] **1** make a gap in and break through (a wall, barrier, or defense): *the river breached its bank.*
■ break or fail to observe (a law, agreement, or code of conduct). **2** [intrans.] (of a whale) rise and break through the surface of the water. Cf. BROACH.

break•ing and en•ter•ing • *n.* (inlegal use) the crime of entering a building by force so as to commit burglary.

bre•vet | brə'vet; 'brevit | • *n.* [often as adj.] a former type of military commission conferred esp. for outstanding service by which an officer was promoted to a higher rank without the corresponding pay: *a brevet lieutenant.* • *v.* (**breveted** or **brevetted**, **breveting** or **brevetting**) [trans.] confer a brevet rank on: *he was breveted for bravery in the campaign.*

brev•i•ty | 'brevitē | • *n.* concise and exact use of words in writing or speech.
■ shortness of time: *the brevity of human life.*

bric-a-brac | 'brik ə ͵bræk | • *n.* miscellaneous objects and ornaments of little value.

brick•bat | 'brik͵bæt | • *n.* a piece of brick, typically when used as a weapon.
■ a remark or comment that is highly critical and typically insulting: *the plaudits were beginning to outnumber the brickbats.*

bric•o•lage | ͵brikō'läzH; ͵brikə- | • *n.* (pl. same or **bricolages**) (in art or literature) construction or creation from a diverse range of available things: *the chaotic bricolage of the novel is brought together in a unifying gesture.*

■ something constructed or created in this way: *bricolages of painted junk.*

brig•and |'brigənd| • *n.* a member of a gang that ambushes and robs people in forests and mountains.
DERIVATIVES: **brig•and•age** |-dij| *n.* **brig•and•ry** |-drē| *n.*

brink•man•ship |'briNGkmən,SHip| (also **brinksmanship**) • *n.* the art or practice of pursuing a dangerous policy to the limits of safety (the *brink* before stopping, typically in politics.

bri•o |'brēō| • *n.* vigor or vivacity of style or performance: *she told her story with some brio.*

Brit•i•cism |'britə,sizəm| (also **Britishism**) • *n.* an idiom used in Britain but not in other English-speaking countries.

brit•tle |'britl| • *adj.* (of a sound, esp. a person's voice) unpleasantly hard and sharp and showing signs of instability or nervousness: *a brittle laugh.*
■ (of a person or behavior) appearing aggressive or hard but unstable or nervous within: *her manner was artificially bright and brittle.*
DERIVATIVES: **brit•tle•ly** *adv.* **brit•tle• ness** *n.*

broach |brōCH| • *v.* [trans.] **1** raise (a sensitive or difficult subject) for discussion: *he broached the subject he had been avoiding all evening.* **2** pierce (a cask) to draw liquor.
■ open and start using the contents of (a bottle or other container). **3** [intrans.] (of a fish or sea mammal) rise through the water and break the surface: *the salmon broach, then fall to slap the water.* Cf. BREACH.

broad•side |'brôd,sīd| • *n.* **1** a nearly simultaneous firing of all the guns from one side of a warship.
■ a strongly worded critical attack: *broadsides against the Christian faith.* ■ the set of guns that can fire on each side of a warship. ■ the side of a ship above the water between the bow and quarter. **2** (also **broadsheet**) a sheet of paper printed on one side only, forming one large page: *a broadside of Lee's farewell address.*
■ in 16th- and 17th-century England, a popular ballad. (Also called **broadside ballad**) . • *adv.* with the side turned to a particular thing: *the yacht was drifting broadside to the wind.*
■ on the side: *her car was hit broadside by another vehicle.* • *v.* [trans.] collide with the side of (a vehicle): *I had to skid sideways to avoid broadsiding her.*

bro•chure |brō'SHŏŏr| • *n.* a small book or magazine containing pictures and information about a product or service.

bro•gan |'brōgən| • *n.* a coarse, stout leather shoe reaching to the ankle.

brogue[1] |brōg| • *n.* a strong outdoor shoe with ornamental perforated patterns in the leather.
■ a rough shoe of untanned leather, formerly worn in parts of Ireland and the Scottish Highlands.

brogue[2] • *n.* [usu. in sing.] a marked accent,

esp. Irish or Scottish, when speaking English: *a fine Irish brogue | a sweet lilt of brogue in her voice.*

bro•mide |'brōmīd| • *n.* **1** a sedative preparation containing the compound potassium bromide. **2** a trite and unoriginal idea or remark, typically intended to soothe or placate: *feel-good bromides create the illusion of problem solving.*
DERIVATIVES: **bro•mid•ic** |brō'midik| *adj.* (sense 2).

brou•ha•ha |'brōohä,hä; brōo'hähä| • *n.* [usu. in sing.] a noisy and overexcited critical response, display of interest, or trail of publicity: *24 members resigned over the election brouhaha.*

brown•field |'brown,fēld| • *adj.* [attrib.] (of an urban site for potential building development) having had previous development on it.

bruit |brōot| • *v.* [with obj. and adverbial] spread (a report or rumor) widely: *I didn't want to have our relationship bruited about the office.* • *n.* **1** a report or rumor. **2** a sound, typically an abnormal one, heard through a stethoscope; a murmur.

brunt |brənt| • *n.* (**the brunt**) the worst part or chief impact of a specified thing: *education will bear the brunt of the cuts.*

brusque |brəsk| • *adj.* abrupt or offhand in speech or manner: *she could be brusque and impatient.*
DERIVATIVES: **brusque•ly** *adv.* **brusque• ness** *n.* **brus•que•rie** |'brəskərē| *n.* (archaic).

brut |'brōot| • *adj.* (of sparkling wine) unsweetened; very dry.

bru•tal•ism |'brōotl,izəm| • *n.* a style of architecture or art characterized by a deliberate plainness, crudity, or violence of imagery. The term was first applied to functionalist buildings of the 1950s and 1960s that made much use of steel and concrete in starkly massive blocks.
DERIVATIVES: **bru•tal•ist** *n.* & *adj.*

buc•cal |'bəkəl| • *adj.* of or relating to the mouth: *the buccal cavity.*
■ of or relating to the cheek: *the buccal side of the molars.*

buc•ca•neer |,bəkə'nir| • *n.* a pirate, originally off the Spanish-American coasts.
■ a daring, adventurous, and sometimes reckless person, esp. in business: [as adj.] *a shrewd and buccaneering businessman.*

bu•col•ic |byōo'kälik| • *adj.* of or relating to the pleasant aspects of the countryside and country life: *the church is known for its bucolic setting.* • *n.* (usu. **bucolics**) a pastoral poem.

buf•foon |bə'fōon| • *n.* a ridiculous but amusing person; a clown.
DERIVATIVES: **buf•foon•ish** *adj.* **buf•foon• er•y** *n.*

bug•a•boo |'bəgə,bōo| • *n.* an object of fear or alarm; a bugbear.

bug•bear |'bəg,ber| • *n.* a cause of obsessive fear, irritation, or loathing.
■ an imaginary being invoked to frighten children, typically a sort of hobgoblin supposed to devour them.

bug•ger |'bəgər; 'bo͝og-| chiefly Brit. • n. [with adj.] a contemptible or pitied person, typically a man.
■ a person with a particular negative quality or characteristic. ■ used as a term of affection or respect, typically grudgingly: *all right, let the little buggers come in.*

bug•ger•y |'bəgərē; 'bo͝og-| • n. anal intercourse.

bu•lim•i•a |bo͝o'lēmēə| • n. insatiable overeating as a medical condition, in particular: ■ (also **bulimia nervosa**) an emotional disorder involving distortion of body image and an obsessive desire to lose weight, in which bouts of extreme overeating are followed by depression and self-induced vomiting, purging, or fasting. Cf. ANOREXIA.
DERIVATIVES: **bu•lim•ic** |-'lēmik| adj. & n.

bull • n. a papal edict.

bul•lion |'bo͝olyən| • n. 1 gold or silver in bulk before coining, or valued by weight. 2 (also **bullion fringe**) ornamental braid or trimming made with twists of gold or silver thread.

bull mar•ket • n. a stock market in which share prices are rising, encouraging buying.

bul•ly•rag |'bo͝olē,ræg| (also **ballyrag**) • v. (**-ragged, -ragging**) [trans.] treat (someone) in a scolding or intimidating way: *he would bullyrag his staff around but then kiss up to his superiors.*

bul•wark |'bo͝ol,wərk| • n. a defensive wall. ■ a person, institution, or principle that acts as a defense: *the security forces are a bulwark against the breakdown of society.* ■ (usu. **bulwarks**) an extension of a ship's sides above the level of the deck.

bump•tious |'bəmpSHəs| • adj. self-assertive or proud to an irritating degree: *these bumptious young boys today.*
DERIVATIVES: **bump•tious•ly** adv. **bump•tious•ness** n.

bun•co |'bəNGkō| • n. (pl. **-os**) [often as adj.] a swindle or confidence trick: *a bunco artist* | *he was out to make a buck using fraud or bunco.* • v. (**-oes, -oed**) [trans.] swindle or cheat.

bun•kum |'bəNGkəm| (also **buncombe, bunk**) • n. nonsense: *they talk a lot of bunkum about their products.*

bur•den |'bərdn| • n. (**the burden**) the main theme or gist of a speech, book, or argument: *the burden of his views.* ■ the refrain or chorus of a song.

bu•reauc•ra•cy |byo͝o'räkrəsē| • n. (pl. **-ies**) a system of government in which most of the important decisions are made by appointed or career officials rather than by elected representatives. ■ a state or organization governed or managed according to such a system. ■ the officials in such a system, considered as a group or hierarchy. ■ excessively complicated administrative procedure, seen as characteristic of such a system: *the unnecessary bureaucracy in local government.*

burg |bərg| • n. an ancient or medieval fortress or walled town. [ORIGIN: from late Latin *burgus* 'castle, fort.']

■ a town or city: *what goes on after dark in this burg?*

bur•geon |'bərjən| • v. [intrans.] [often as adj.] (**burgeoning**) begin to grow or increase rapidly; flourish: *manufacturers are keen to cash in on the burgeoning demand.*

burgh |bərg; 'bərə| • n. a borough or chartered town.
DERIVATIVES: **burgh•al** |'bərgəl| adj.

bur•lesque |bər'lesk| • n. 1 a parody or comically exaggerated imitation of something, esp. in a literary or dramatic work: *the funniest burlesque of opera* | [as adj.] *burlesque Shakespearean stanzas.* ■ humor that depends on comic imitation and exaggeration; absurdity: *the argument descends into burlesque.* 2 a variety show, typically including striptease: [as adj.] *burlesque clubs.* • v. (**burlesques, burlesqued, burlesquing**) [trans.] cause to appear absurd by parodying or copying in an exaggerated form: *she struck a ridiculous pose that burlesqued her own vanity.*

bur•nish |'bərniSH| • v. [trans.] [usu. as adj.] (**burnished**) polish (something, esp. metal) by rubbing: *highly burnished armor.* ■ enhance or perfect (something such as a reputation or a skill). • n. [in sing.] the shine on a highly polished surface.
DERIVATIVES: **bur•nish•er** n.

bu•shi•do |'bo͝osHēdō| • n. the code of honor and morals developed by the Japanese samurai.

bush•whack |'bo͝osH,(h)wæk| • v. 1 [intrans.] [often as n.] (**bushwhacking**) live or travel in wild or uncultivated country: *I have not seen a bear yet after seven days of bushwhacking.* ■ [with adverbial of direction] cut or push one's way in a specified direction through dense vegetation: *he'd bushwhacked down the steep slopes.* 2 [intrans.] fight as a guerrilla in the bush. ■ [trans.] make a surprise attack on (someone) from a hidden place; ambush.

bus•kin |'bəskin| • n. a calf-high or knee-high boot of cloth or leather. ■ a thick-soled laced boot worn by an ancient Athenian tragic actor to gain height. ■ (**the buskin**) the style or spirit of tragic drama.
DERIVATIVES: **bus•kined** adj.

butte |byo͝ot| • n. an isolated hill with steep sides and a flat top (similar to but narrower than a MESA).

but•tress |'bətris| • n. a projecting support of stone or brick built against a wall. ■ a projecting portion of a hill or mountain. ■ a source of defense or support: *demand for a new economic order as a buttress against social collapse.* • v. [trans.] provide (a building or structure) with projecting supports built against its walls: [as adj.] (**buttressed**) *a buttressed wall.* ■ increase the strength of or justification for; reinforce: *authority buttressed by religious belief.*

bux•om |'bəksəm| • adj. (of a woman) plump, esp. with large breasts.
DERIVATIVES: **bux•om•ness** n.

buzz•word |'bəz,wərd| • n. a technical word

or phrase that has become fashionable, typically as a slogan.

bye |bī| • *n.* **1** the transfer of a competitor directly to the next round of a competition in the absence of an assigned opponent. **2** one or more holes remaining unplayed after a golf match has been decided.

by•gone |ˈbīˌgôn| • *adj.* belonging to an earlier time: *relics of a bygone society.* • *n.* (usu. **bygones**) a thing dating from an earlier time.

by•law |ˈbīˌlô| (also **by-law**) • *n.* **1** a rule made by a company or society to control the actions of its members. **2** a regulation made by a local government; an ordinance.

Byz•an•tine |ˈbizənˌtēn; -ˌtīn| • *adj.* of or relating to ancient Byzantium, the Byzantine Empire, or the Eastern Orthodox Church.
■ of an ornate artistic and architectural style that developed in the Byzantine Empire and spread esp. to Italy and Russia. The art is generally rich and stylized (as in religious icons) and the architecture typified by many-domed, highly decorated churches. ■ (of a system or situation) excessively complicated, typically involving a great deal of administrative detail: *Byzantine insurance regulations.* ■ characterized by deviousness or underhanded procedure: *Byzantine intrigues.* • *n.* a citizen of Byzantium or the Byzantine Empire.
DERIVATIVES: **By•zan•tin•ism** |-ˌnizəm| *n.*

Cc

ca•bal |kəˈbäl; kəˈbæl| • *n.* a secret intrigue or conspiracy; petty plotting.
■ a secret political clique or faction: *a cabal of dissidents.*

ca•bal•le•ro |ˌkæbə(l)ˈyerō; ˌkæbəˈlerō| • *n.* (pl. **-os**) **1** a Spanish or Mexican gentleman. **2** (in the southwestern US) a horseman.

cab•a•ret |ˌkæbəˈrā; ˈkæbəˌrā| • *n.* entertainment held in a nightclub or restaurant while the audience eats or drinks at tables: *she was seen recently in cabaret* | [as adj.] *a cabaret act.*
■ a nightclub or restaurant where such entertainment is performed.

cab•o•chon |ˈkæbəˌsHän| • *n.* a gem polished but not faceted:[as adj.] *a necklace of cabochon rubies.* Cf. CHATOYANT.
PHRASES: **en cabochon** |äN| (of a gem) treated in this way.

cab•o•tage |ˈkæbəˌtäzH; -bəˌtij| • *n.* the right to operate sea, air, or other transportation services within a particular territory.
■ restriction of the operation of sea, air, or other transportation services within or into a particular country to that country's own services.

cab•ri•o•let |ˌkæbrēəˈlā| • *n.* **1** a car with a roof that folds down. **2** a light, two-wheeled carriage with a hood, drawn by one horse.

ca•ca•o |kəˈkow; kəˈkāō| • *n.* (pl. **-os**) **1** beanlike seeds from which cocoa, cocoa butter, and chocolate are made. **2** the small tropical American evergreen tree (*Theobroma cacao*) that bears these seeds, which is now cultivated mainly in West Africa.

cache |kæsH| • *n.* a collection of items of the same type stored in a hidden or inaccessible place: *an arms cache* | *a cache of gold coins.*
■ a hidden or inaccessible storage place for valuables, provisions, or ammunition. ■ (also **cache memory**) an auxiliary computer memory from which high-speed retrieval of frequently used data is possible. • *v.* [trans.] store away in hiding or for future use.

■ store (data) in a cache memory. ■ provide (hardware) with a cache memory.

ca•chet |kæˈsHā| • *n.* **1** the state of being respected or admired; prestige: *no other shipping company had quite the cachet of Cunard.* **2** a distinguishing mark or seal.
■ Philately a printed design added to an envelope to commemorate a special event. **3** a flat capsule enclosing a dose of unpleasant-tasting medicine.

ca•chex•i•a |kəˈkeksēə| • *n.* weakness and wasting of the body due to severe chronic illness.

cach•in•nate |ˈkækəˌnāt| • *v.* [intrans.] laugh loudly.
DERIVATIVES: **cach•in•na•tion** |ˌkækəˈnā-sHən| *n.*

ca•cique |kəˈsēk| • *n.* **1** (in Latin America or the Spanish-speaking Caribbean) a native chief. **2** (in Spain or Latin America) a local political boss.

cac•o•de•mon |ˌkækəˈdēmən| • *n.* a malevolent spirit or person.

cac•o•e•thes |ˌkækəˈwēтнēz| • *n.* [in sing.] an irresistible urge to do something inadvisable.

ca•coph•o•ny |kəˈkäfənē; kæ-| • *n.* (pl. **-ies**) a harsh, discordant mixture, orig. of sounds: *a cacophony of deafening alarm bells* | *a cacophony of architectural styles.*
DERIVATIVES: **ca•coph•o•nous** |-nəs| *adj.*

ca•das•tral |kəˈdæstrəl| • *adj.* (of a map or survey) showing the extent, value, and ownership of land, esp. for taxation.

ca•dence |ˈkādns| • *n.* **1** a modulation or inflection of the voice: *the measured cadences he employed in the Senate.*
■ such a modulation in reading aloud as implied by the structure and ordering of words and phrases in written text: *the dry cadences of the essay.* ■ a fall in pitch of the voice at the end of a phrase or sentence. ■ measured movement; beat; rhythm: *the thumping cadence of the engines.* **2** a sequence of notes or

chords comprising the close of a musical phrase: *the final cadences of the Prelude.*
DERIVATIVES: **ca•denced** *adj.*

ca•den•za |kəˈdenzə| • *n.* a virtuoso solo passage inserted into a movement in a concerto or other work, typically near the end: *the famous violin cadenza.*

ca•det |kəˈdet| • *n.* **1** (in older use) a younger son or daughter.
▪ [usu. as adj.] a junior branch of a family: *a cadet branch of the family.*
DERIVATIVES: **ca•det•ship** |-ˌSHip| *n.*

ca•dre |ˈkædrē; ˈkäd-; -ˌrä| • *n.* a small group of people specially trained for a particular purpose or profession: *a small cadre of scientists.*
▪ a group of activists in a communist or other revolutionary organization. ▪ a member of such a group.

ca•du•ce•us |kəˈd(y)o͞osēəs; -sHəs| • *n.* (pl. **caducei** |-sē,ī; -sHē,ī|) an ancient Greek or Roman herald's wand, typically one with two serpents twined around it, carried by the messenger god Hermes or Mercury. Cf. FASCES.
▪ a representation of this, traditionally associated with healing.

ca•du•ci•ty |kəˈd(y)o͞osəṭē| • *n.* the infirmity of old age; senility.
▪ frailty or transitory nature: *read these books and reflect on their caducity.*

Cae•sar |ˈsēzər| • *n.* a title used by Roman emperors, esp. those from Augustus (63 BC–AD 14) to Hadrian (AD 117–138).
▪ an autocrat: *they complained that he was behaving like a Caesar.* Cf. CZAR, KAISER.
PHRASES: **Caesar's wife** a person (orig., Calpurnia) who is required to be above suspicion. [ORIGIN: with reference to Plutarch's *Caesar* (x. 6) 'I thought my wife ought not even to be under suspicion.']

cae•su•ra |siˈZHo͝orə; -ˈzo͝orə| • *n.* (in Greek and Latin verse) a break between words within a metrical foot.
▪ (in modern verse) a pause near the middle of a line. ▪ any interruption or break: *an unaccountable caesura: no deaths were reported in the newspapers.*
DERIVATIVES: **cae•su•ral** *adj.*

cairn |kern| • *n.* a mound of rough stones built as a memorial or landmark, typically on a trail, hilltop, or skyline.
▪ a prehistoric burial mound made of stones.

cais•son |ˈkä,sän; ˈkāsən| • *n.* **1** a large watertight chamber, open at the bottom, from which the water is kept out by air pressure and in which construction work may be carried out under water.
▪ a floating vessel or watertight structure used as a gate across the entrance of a dry dock or basin. **2** a chest or wagon for holding or conveying ammunition.

ca•jole |kəˈjōl| • *v.* [trans.] persuade someone to do something by sustained coaxing or flattery: *he hoped to cajole her into selling the house* | [intrans.] *she pleaded and cajoled as she tried to win his support.* Cf. INVEIGLE.
DERIVATIVES: **ca•jole•ment** *n.* **ca•jol•er•y** *n.*

Ca•jun |ˈkājən| • *n.* a member of any of the largely self-contained communities in the bayou areas of southern Louisiana formed by descendants of French Canadians (Acadians), speaking an archaic form of French.
• *adj.* of or relating to the Cajuns, esp. with reference to their folk music or spicy cuisine. Cf. ZYDECO.

cal•a•boose |ˈkælə,bo͞os| • *n.* a prison.

ca•lam•i•ty |kəˈlæməṭē| • *n.* (pl. **-ies**) an event causing great and often sudden damage or distress; a disaster.
▪ disaster and distress: *the journey had led to calamity and ruin.*
DERIVATIVES: **ca•lam•i•tous** |-əṭəs| *adj.* **ca•lam•i•tous•ly** |-əṭəslē| *adv.*

cal•car•e•ous |kælˈkerēəs| • *adj.* containing calcium carbonate; chalky.
▪ (of vegetation) occurring on chalk or limestone.

cal•ci•fy |ˈkælsə,fī| • *v.* (**-ies, -ied**) [trans.] [usu. as adj.] (**calcified**) harden by deposition of or conversion into calcium carbonate or some other insoluble calcium compounds: *calcified cartilage.*
▪ become or make rigid or inflexible: *views that are calcifying in face of demands for change.*
DERIVATIVES: **cal•cif•ic** |kælˈsifik| *adj.* **cal•ci•fi•ca•tion** |ˌkælsəfəˈkāSHən| *n.*

cal•cu•lus |ˈkælkyələs| • *n.* **1** (pl. **calculuses**) the branch of mathematics that deals with the finding and properties of derivatives and integrals of functions, by methods originally based on the summation of infinitesimal differences. The two main types are **differential calculus**, dealing with derivative and differentiation, and **integral calculus**, dealing with integrals and integration. **2** (pl. **calculuses**) a particular method or system of calculation or reasoning. **3** (pl. **calculi** |-ˌlī; -ˌlē|) a concretion of minerals formed within the body, esp. in the kidney or gallbladder.

cal•de•ra |kælˈderə; kôl-; -ˈdirə| • *n.* a large volcanic crater, typically one formed by a major eruption leading to the collapse of the mouth of the volcano.

Cal•e•do•ni•an |ˌkæləˈdōnēən| • *adj.* (chiefly in names or geographical or geological terms) of or relating to Scotland or the Scottish Highlands. • *n.* a person from Scotland.

cal•ends |ˈkælendz; ˈkā-| (also **kalends**) • *plural n.* the first day of the month in the ancient Roman calendar.

cal•i•ber |ˈkæləbər| (Brit. **calibre**) • *n.* **1** the quality of someone's character or the level of someone's ability: *they could ill afford to lose a man of his caliber.*
▪ the standard reached by something: *educational facilities of a very high caliber.* **2** the internal diameter of a gun barrel: [in combination] *a .22 caliber rifle.*
▪ the diameter of a bullet, shell, or rocket. ▪ the diameter of a body of circular section, such as a tube, blood vessel, or fiber.
DERIVATIVES: **cal•i•bered** *adj.* [also in combination].

cal•i•brate |'kælə,brāt| • v. [trans.] (often **be calibrated**) mark (a gauge or instrument) with a standard scale of readings.
■ correlate the readings of (an instrument) with those of a standard in order to check the instrument's accuracy. ■ adjust (experimental results) to take external factors into account or to allow comparison with other data.
DERIVATIVES: **cal•i•bra•tor** |-brātər| n.

cal•i•per |'kæləpər| (also **calliper**) • n. (**calipers**) an instrument for measuring external or internal dimensions, having two hinged legs resembling compasses and in-turned or out-turned points.
■ (also **caliper rule**) an instrument performing a similar function but having one linear component sliding along another, with two parallel jaws and a moveable, graduated scale. ■ (also **brake caliper**) a motor-vehicle or bicycle brake consisting of two or more hinged components.

ca•liph |'kāləf; 'kæləf| • n. the chief Muslim civil and religious ruler, regarded as the successor of Muhammad. Caliphs ruled in Baghdad until 1258 and then in Egypt until the Ottoman conquest of 1517; the title was then held by the Ottoman sultans until it was abolished in 1924 by Atatürk.
DERIVATIVES: **cal•iph•ate** |'kālə,fāt; 'kæl-; -fət| n.

cal•is•then•ics |,kæləs'THeniks| (Brit. **callisthenics**) • plural n. gymnastic exercises to achieve bodily fitness and grace of movement.
DERIVATIVES: **cal•is•then•ic** adj.

cal•lig•ra•phy |kə'ligrəfē| • n. decorative handwriting or handwritten lettering.
■ the art of producing decorative handwriting or lettering with a pen or brush.
DERIVATIVES: **cal•lig•ra•pher** |-fər| n. **cal•lig•ra•phist** |-fist| n.

cal•li•pyg•i•an |,kælə'pijēən| (also **callipygean**) • adj. having well-shaped buttocks.
DERIVATIVES: **cal•li•py•gous** |-'pīgəs| adj.

cal•los•i•ty |kə'läsəṭē| • n. (pl. **-ies**) a thickened and hardened part of the skin; a callus.

cal•lous |'kæləs| • adj. showing or having an insensitive and cruel disregard for others: *his callous comments about the murder made me shiver.* • n. variant spelling of CALLUS.
DERIVATIVES: **cal•lous•ly** adv. **cal•lous•ness** n.

cal•low |'kælō| • adj. (esp. of a young person) inexperienced and immature: *callow undergraduates.*
DERIVATIVES: **cal•low•ly** adv. **cal•low•ness** n.

cal•lus |'kæləs| (also **callous**) • n. a thickened and hardened part of the skin or soft tissue, esp. in an area that has been subjected to friction.
■ the bony healing tissue that forms around the ends of broken bone. ■ a hard formation of tissue, esp. new tissue formed over a wound on a plant.

ca•lor•ic |kə'lôrik; -'lär-; 'kælərik| • adj. (also **calorific**) of or relating to heat: *a caloric value of 7 calories per gram.* • n. (in the late 18th and early 19th centuries) a hypothetical fluid substance that was thought to be responsible for the phenomenon of heat.
DERIVATIVES: **ca•lor•i•cal•ly** |kə'lôrik(ə)-lē; -'lär-| adv.

cal•o•rie |'kæl(ə)rē| • n. (pl. **-ies**) either of two units of heat energy:
■ (also **small calorie**) (abbr.: **cal**) the energy needed to raise the temperature of 1 gram of water through 1 °C. ■ (also **large calorie**, **kilocalorie**) (abbr.: **Cal**) the energy needed to raise the temperature of 1 kilogram of water through 1 °C, equal to one thousand small calories and often used to measure the energy value of foods.

calque |kælk| • n. an expression adopted by one language from another in a more or less literally translated form. • v. (**be calqued on**) originate or function as a loan translation of.

cal•u•met |'kælyə,met; -mət| • n. a North American Indian peace pipe.

cal•um•ny |'kæləmnē| • n. (pl. **-ies**) the making of false and defamatory statements in order to damage someone's reputation; slander.
■ a false and slanderous statement.
DERIVATIVES: **cal•um•ni•ate** v. **ca•lum•ni•ous** |-nēəs| adj.

Cal•va•ry |'kælv(ə)rē| the hill outside Jerusalem on which Jesus was crucified.
■ [as n.] (**a calvary**) a sculpture or picture representing the scene of the Crucifixion. ■ a place of crucifixion.

Cal•vin•ism |'kælvə,nizəm| • n. the Protestant theological system of John Calvin (1509–64) and his successors, which develops Martin Luther's doctrine of justification by faith alone and emphasizes the grace of God and the doctrine of predestination.
DERIVATIVES: **Cal•vin•ist** n. **Cal•vin•is•tic** |,kælvə'nistik| adj. **Cal•vin•is•ti•cal** |,kælvə'nistikəl| adj.

ca•lyx |'kaliks; 'kæl| (also **calix**) • n. (pl. **ca•lyces** |'kālə,sēz; 'kæl-| or **calyxes**) 1 the sepals of a flower, typically forming a whorl that encloses the petals and forms a protective layer around a flower in bud. 2 a cuplike cavity or structure in various animals or organs.

ca•ma•ra•de•rie |,käm(ə)'rädərē; ,kæm-; -'ræd-| • n. mutual trust and friendship among people who spend a lot of time together: *the genuine camaraderie of the hockey team.*

cam•ber |'kæmbər| • n. a slightly convex or arched shape of a road or other horizontal surface: *a flat roof should have a slight camber to allow water to run off.*
■ Brit. a tilt built into a road at a bend or curve, enabling vehicles to maintain speed. ■ the slight sideways inclination of the front wheels of a motor vehicle. ■ the extent of curvature of a section of an airfoil.
DERIVATIVES: **cam•bered** adj.

Cam•bri•an |'kæmbrēən; 'käm-| • adj. 1 (chiefly in names or geographical terms) Welsh: *the Cambrian Railway.* 2 of, relating to, or denoting the first period in the Paleozoic era, between the end of the Precambrian eon and the beginning of the Ordovician period. ▪ [as n.] (**the Cambrian**) the Cambrian period or the system of rocks deposited during it.

The Cambrian lasted from about 570 million to 510 million years ago and was a time of widespread seas. It is the earliest period in which fossils, notably trilobites, can be used in geological dating.

cam•er•a ob•scu•ra |əb'skyo͞orə| • n. a darkened box with a convex lens or aperture for projecting the image of an external object on to a screen inside. It is important historically in the development of photography. ▪ a small round building with a rotating angled mirror at the apex of the roof, projecting an image of the landscape on to a horizontal surface inside.

camp • adj. deliberately exaggerated and theatrical in style, typically for humorous effect: *the movie seems more camp than shocking or gruesome.* ▪ (of a man or his manner) ostentatiously and extravagantly effeminate: *a heavily made-up and highly camp actor.* • n. deliberately exaggerated and theatrical behavior or style: *Hollywood camp.* • v. [intrans.] (of a man) behave in an ostentatiously effeminate way: *he camped it up a bit for the cameras.*
DERIVATIVES: **camp•i•ly** |'kæmpəlē| adv. **camp•i•ness** n. **camp•y** adj.

cam•pa•ni•le |ˌkæmpə'nēlē; -'nēl| • n. a bell tower, esp. a tall freestanding one.

cam•pe•si•no |ˌkæmpə'sēnō; ˌkäm-| • n. (pl. **-os**) (in Spanish-speaking regions) a peasant farmer.

ca•naille |kə'nī; -'näl| • n. (**the canaille**) the common people; the masses, regarded contemptuously: *the haughty contempt of a grandee sneering at the canaille.*

ca•nard |kə'närd; -'när| • n. an unfounded rumor or story: *the old canard that LA is a cultural wasteland.*

can•did |'kændid| • adj. **1** truthful and straightforward; frank: *a candid discussion.* **2** (of a photograph of a person) taken informally, esp. without the subject's knowledge.
DERIVATIVES: **can•did•ly** adv. **can•did•ness** n.

can•dor |'kændər; -ˌdôr| (Brit. **candour**) • n. the quality of being open and honest in expression; frankness: *a man of refreshing candor.*

ca•nine |'kā,nīn| • adj. of, relating to, or resembling a dog or dogs: *canine distemper virus.* ▪ of or relating to animals of the dog family (Canidae). • n. **1** a dog. ▪ another term for *canid*, a member of the dog family. **2** (also **canine tooth**) either of two pointed teeth of a mammal, often greatly enlarged in carnivores. (Also, **eye tooth**.)

can•is•ter |'kænəstər| • n. a round or cylindrical container, typically one made of metal, used for storing such things as food, chemicals, or rolls of film.

▪ a cylinder of pressurized gas, typically one that explodes when thrown or fired from a gun: *riot police fired tear-gas canisters into the crowd.* ▪ small bullets formerly packed in cases that fit the bore of an artillery piece or gun: *another deadly volley of canister.*

can•ny |'kænē| • adj. (**cannier**, **canniest**) **1** having or showing shrewdness and good judgment, esp. in money or business matters: *canny shoppers came early for a bargain.* **2** N. English & Scottish pleasant; nice: *she's a canny lass.*
DERIVATIVES: **can•ni•ly** |'kænl-ē| adv. **can•ni•ness** n.

can•on |'kænən| • n. **1** a general law, rule, principle, or criterion by which something is judged: *the appointment violated the canons of fair play and equal opportunity.* ▪ a church decree or law: *a set of ecclesiastical canons.* **2** a collection or list of sacred books accepted as genuine: *the formation of the biblical canon.* ▪ the works of a particular author or artist that are recognized as genuine: *the Shakespearean canon.* ▪ a list of literary or artistic works considered to be permanently established as being of the highest quality: *Hopkins was firmly established in the canon of English poetry.* **3** (also **canon of the Mass**) (in the Roman Catholic Church) the part of the Mass containing the words of consecration. **4** a piece of music in which the same melody is begun in different parts successively, so that the imitations overlap.

cant[1] |kænt| • n. **1** hypocritical and sanctimonious talk, typically of a moral, religious, or political nature: *the liberal case against all censorship is often cant.* **2** [as adj.] denoting a phrase or catchword temporarily current or in fashion: *they are misrepresented as, in the cant word of our day, uncaring.* ▪ language peculiar to a specified group or profession and regarded with disparagement: *thieves' cant.* • v. [intrans.] talk hypocritically and sanctimoniously about something: *if they'd stop canting about "honest work," they might get somewhere.*

cant[2] • v. [trans.] cause (something) to be in a slanting or oblique position; tilt: *he canted his head to look at the screen.* ▪ [intrans.] take or have a slanting position: *mismatched slate roofs canted at all angles.* • n. **1** [in sing.] a slope or tilt: *the outward cant of the curving walls.* **2** a wedge-shaped block of wood, esp. one remaining after the better-quality pieces have been cut off.

can•tan•ker•ous |kæn'tæŋkərəs| • adj. bad-tempered, argumentative, and uncooperative: *a crusty, cantankerous old man.*
DERIVATIVES: **can•tan•ker•ous•ly** adv. **can•tan•ker•ous•ness** n.

can•ta•ta |kən'tätə| • n. a medium-length narrative or descriptive piece of music, sacred or secular, with vocal solos and usually a chorus and orchestra.

can•ti•cle |'kæn(t)əkəl| • n. **1** a hymn or chant, typically with a biblical text, forming a regular part of a church service. **2** (**Canticles** or **Canticle of Canticles**) another name for

Song of Songs or Song of Solomon (esp. in the Vulgate Bible).

can•ti•le•ver | ˈkæntlˌēvər; -ˌevər | • n. a long projecting beam fixed at only one end, used chiefly in bridge construction. ■ a long bracket or beam projecting from a wall to support a balcony, cornice, or similar structure. • v. [trans.] [usu. as adj.] (**cantilevered**) support by a cantilever or cantilevers: *a cantilevered deck.* ■ [no obj., with adverbial of direction] project as or like a cantilever: *a conveyor cantilevered out over the river.*

can•tor | ˈkæntər | • n. **1** an official who sings liturgical music and leads prayer in a synagogue. Also called *hazzan* **2** (in formal Christian worship) a person who sings solo verses or passages to which the choir or congregation respond.

can•vass | ˈkænvəs | • v. **1** [trans.] solicit votes from (electors in a constituency): *in each ward, two workers canvassed some 2,000 voters* | [intrans.] *she **canvassed for** votes.* ■ question (someone) in order to ascertain the person's opinion on something: *they promised to canvass all member clubs for their views.* ■ ascertain (someone's opinion) through questioning: *opinions on the merger were canvassed.* ■ try to obtain; request: *they're canvassing support among shareholders.* **2** [trans.] (often **be canvassed**) discuss thoroughly: *the issues that were canvassed are still unresolved.* • n. [usu. in sing.] an act or process of attempting to secure votes or ascertain opinions: *a house-to-house canvass.*

DERIVATIVES: **can•vass•er** n.

caou•tchouc | ˈkow͵CHo͝ok; -ˌCHo͞o(k) | • n. unvulcanized natural rubber.

ca•pa•cious | kəˈpāSHəs | • adj. having a lot of space inside; roomy: *she rummaged in her capacious handbag.*

DERIVATIVES: **ca•pa•cious•ly** adv. **ca•pa•cious•ness** n.

ca•pac•i•tance | kəˈpæsətəns | • n. the ability to store an electric charge. ■ the ratio of the change in an electric charge in a system to the corresponding change in its electric potential. (Symbol: **C**)

ca•pac•i•ty | kəˈpæsətē | • n. (pl. **-ies**) **1** [in sing.] the maximum amount that something can contain: *the capacity of the freezer is 1.1 cubic feet* | *the stadium's seating capacity* | *the room was **filled to capacity**.* ■ [as adj.] fully occupying the available area or space: *they played to a capacity crowd.* ■ the amount that something can produce: *the company aimed to double its electricity-generating capacity* | *when running **at full capacity**, the factory will employ 450 people.* ■ the total cylinder volume that is swept by the pistons in an internal combustion engine. ■ former term for CAPACITANCE. **2** the ability or power to do, experience, or understand something: *I was impressed by her **capacity for** hard work* | [with infinitive] *his capacity to inspire trust in others* | *their intellectual capacities.* ■ [in sing.] a person's legal competence: *cases where a patient's testamentary capacity is in*

doubt. **3** [in sing.] a specified role or position: *I was engaged in a voluntary capacity* | *writing **in his capacity as** legal correspondent.*

DERIVATIVES: **ca•pac•i•tive** | -ətiv | (also **ca•pac•i•ta•tive**) adj. (chiefly Physics).

ca•par•i•son | kəˈpærəsən | • n. an ornamental covering spread over a horse or other animal's saddle or harness. • v. (**be caparisoned**) (of a horse or other animal) be decked out in rich decorative coverings. ■ ostentatiously ornate or decorated: [as adj.] *the use of caparisoned language to disguise a dearth of substance.*

cap•il•lar•y | ˈkæpəˌlerē | • n. **1** any of the smallest branching blood vessels that form a network between the ends of the arteries and veins. **2** (also **capillary tube**) a tube that has an internal diameter of hairlike thinness. • adj. [attrib.] of or relating to capillaries, esp. of their ability to take up liquid through the mechanism of surface tension (capillarity or capillary action).

cap•i•tal[1] | ˈkæpətl | • n. **1** (also **capital city** or **town**) the most important city or town of a country or region, usually its seat of government and administrative center. ■ [with adj.] a place associated more than any other with a specified activity or product: *Milan is the fashion capital of Europe.* **2** wealth in the form of money or other assets owned by a person or organization or available or contributed for a particular purpose such as starting a company or investing: *rates of return on invested capital were high.* ■ the excess of a company's assets over its liabilities. ■ people who possess wealth and use it to control a society's economic activity, considered collectively: *a conflict of interest between capital and labor.* ■ [with adj.] a valuable resource of a particular kind: *there is insufficient investment in **human capital**.* **3** (also **capital letter**) a letter of the size and form used to begin sentences and names: *he wrote the name in capitals.* • adj. **1** [attrib.] (of an offense or charge) liable to the death penalty: *murder was a capital crime.* **2** of or relating to wealth: *capital losses.* **3** of greatest political importance: *the capital city.* **4** [attrib.] (of a letter of the alphabet) large in size and of the form used to begin sentences and names.

DERIVATIVES: **cap•i•tal•ly** adv.

cap•i•tal[2] • n. (in architecture) the distinct, typically broader section at the head of a pillar or column.

cap•i•tal•ism | ˈkæpətlˌizəm | • n. an economic and political system in which a country's trade and industry are controlled by private owners for profit, rather than by the state.

DERIVATIVES: **cap•i•tal•ist** n. **cap•i•tal•is•tic** adj.

cap•i•ta•tion | ˌkæpəˈtāSHən | • n. the payment of a fee or grant to a doctor, school, or other person or body providing services to a number of people, such that the amount paid is determined by the number of patients, pupils, or customers: *the increased capitation* *enabled schools to offer pupils an enhanced curriculum* | [as adj.] *income capitation fees.*

Cap•i•tol | ˈkæpətl | (usu. **the Capitol**) **1** the seat of the US Congress in Washington, DC.
■ **(capitol)** a building housing a legislative assembly: *50,000 people marched on New Jersey's capitol.* **2** the temple of Jupiter on the Capitoline Hill in ancient Rome.

ca•pit•u•late | kəˈpicHəˌlāt | • v. [intrans.] cease to resist an opponent or an unwelcome demand; surrender: *the patriots had to capitulate to the enemy forces.*
DERIVATIVES: **ca•pit•u•la•tion** n. **ca•pit•u•la•tor** | -ˈlātər | n. **ca•pit•u•la•to•ry** adj.

ca•pric•ci•o | kəˈprēCHē,ō; -CHō | • n. (pl. **-os**) a lively piece of music, typically one that is short and free in form.
■ a painting or other work of art representing a fantasy or a mixture of real and imaginary features.

ca•price | kəˈprēs | • n. **1** a sudden and unaccountable change of mood or behavior: *her caprices had made his life impossible* | *ruled by law and not by caprice.* **2** another term for a musical CAPRICCIO.

ca•pri•cious | kəˈprisHəs;-ˈprē- | • adj. given to sudden and unaccountable changes of mood or behavior: *a capricious and often brutal administration* | *a capricious climate.*
DERIVATIVES: **ca•pri•cious•ly** adv. **ca•pri•cious•ness** n.

cap•tion | ˈkæpsHən | • n. a title or brief explanation appended to an article, illustration, cartoon, or poster.
■ a piece of text appearing on a movie or television screen as part of a movie or broadcast. ■ the heading of a legal document. • v. [trans.] (usu. **be captioned**) provide (an illustration) with a title or explanation: *the drawings were captioned with humorous texts* | [with two objs.] *the photograph was captioned "Three little maids."*

cap•tious | ˈkæpsHəs | • adj. (of a person) tending to find fault or raise petty objections.
DERIVATIVES: **cap•tious•ly** adv. **cap•tious•ness** n.

Cap•u•chin | ˈkæp(y)əsHən; kəˈp(y)ōō- | • n. **1** a friar belonging to a branch of the Franciscan order that observes a strict rule drawn up in 1529. **2** a cloak and hood formerly worn by women. **3** (**capuchin** or **capuchin monkey**) a South American monkey (genus *Cebus*) with a cap of hair on the head that has the appearance of a monk's hood.

car•a•pace | ˈkærəˌpās | • n. the hard upper shell of a turtle or crustacean.

car•a•van•sa•ry | ˌkærəˈvænsərē | (also **caravanserai** | -səˌrī |) • n. (pl. **caravansaries** or **caravanserais** | -ˌrīz |) **1** an inn with a central courtyard for travelers and their animals in the desert regions of Asia or North Africa. **2** a group of people traveling together; a caravan.

car•a•vel | ˈkærəˌvel; -vəl | (also **carvel**) • n. a small, fast Spanish or Portuguese ship of the 15th–17th centuries.

car•bo•hy•drate | ˌkärbəˈhīˌdrāt | • n. any of a large group of organic compounds occurring

in foods (notably in breads, pastas, and other plant-based foods) and living tissues and including sugars, starch, and cellulose.

car•bun•cle | ˈkär,bəNGkəl | • n. **1** a severe abscess or multiple boil in the skin, typically infected with bacteria. **2** a bright red gem, in particular a garnet cut en cabochon.
DERIVATIVES: **car•bun•cu•lar** | kär ˈbəNGkyələr | adj.

car•ci•no•ma | ˌkärsəˈnōmə | • n. (pl. **carcinomas** or **carcinomata** | -ˈnōmətə |) a cancer arising in the epithelial tissue of the skin or of the lining of the internal organs.
DERIVATIVES: **car•ci•no•ma•tous** | -ˈnōmətəs | adj.

car•di•ac | ˈkärdē,æk | • adj. [attrib.] **1** of or relating to the heart: *a cardiac arrest.* **2** of or relating to the part of the stomach nearest the esophagus. • n. a person with heart disease: *there's a cardiac in room 106.*

car•di•nal | ˈkärdnəl; ˈkärdn-əl | • n. a high priest of the Roman Catholic Church. Cardinals are nominated by the pope and form the Sacred College, which elects succeeding popes (now invariably from among their own number).
■ (also **cardinal red**) a deep scarlet color like that of a cardinal's cassock. • adj. [attrib.] **1** of the greatest importance; fundamental: *two cardinal points must be borne in mind.* **2** relating to or denoting numbers that express an amount, such as one, two, three, etc. Cf. ORDINAL.
DERIVATIVES: **car•di•nal•ate** | ˈkärdnələt; ˈkärdn-ələt; -ˌlāt | n. (in sense 1 of the noun). **car•di•nal•ly** adv. **car•di•nal•ship** | -ˌsHip | n. (in sense 1 of the noun).

ca•reen | kəˈrēn | • v. **1** [trans.] turn (a ship) on its side for cleaning, caulking, or repair.
■ [intrans.] (of a ship) tilt; lean over: *a heavy flood tide caused my vessel to careen dizzily.* **2** [no obj., with adverbial of direction] move swiftly and in an uncontrolled way in a specified direction: *an electric golf cart careened around the corner.* [ORIGIN: influenced by the verb CAREER.]

ca•reer | kəˈrir | • v. [no obj., with adverbial of direction] move swiftly and in an uncontrolled way in a specified direction: *the car careered across the road.*

ca•reer•ist | kəˈririst | • n. a person whose main concern is for professional advancement, esp. one willing to achieve this by any means: [as adj.] *a careerist politician.*
DERIVATIVES: **ca•reer•ism** | -ˌizəm | n.

car•et | ˈkærət | • n. a mark (∧, ⋀) placed below the line to indicate a proposed insertion in a printed or written text.

car•i•ca•ture | ˈkærikə,CHŏŏr; -CHər | • n. a picture, description, or imitation of a person or thing in which certain striking characteristics are exaggerated in order to create a comic or grotesque effect.
■ the art or style of such exaggerated representation: *there are elements of caricature in the portrayal of the hero.* ■ a ludicrous or grotesque version of someone or something: *he looked a caricature of his normal self.* • v. [trans.] (usu.

be **caricatured**) make or give a comically or grotesquely exaggerated representation of (someone or something): *he was caricatured on the cover of* TV Guide | *a play that caricatures the legal profession.*
DERIVATIVES: **car•i•ca•tur•al** |ˌkærikə ˈCHŏŏrəl| *adj.* **car•i•ca•tur•ist** |-CHŏŏrist| *n.*
car•ies |ˈkerēz| • *n.* decay and crumbling of a tooth or bone.
car•min•a•tive |kär'minəṯiv; 'kärmə,näṯiv| • *adj.* (chiefly of a drug) relieving flatulence. • *n.* a drug of this kind.
car•nage |ˈkärnij| • *n.* the killing of a large number of people or animals: *the carnage at Antietam.*
car•nal |ˈkärnl| • *adj.* relating to physical, esp. sexual, needs and activities: *carnal desire.*
DERIVATIVES: **car•nal•i•ty** |kär'nælətē| *n.* **car•nal•ly** *adv.*
carnal know•ledge • *n.* sexual intercourse.
car•niv•o•rous |kär'nivərəs| • *adj.* (of an animal) feeding on other animals.
■ (of a plant) able to trap and digest small animals, esp. insects.
DERIVATIVES: **car•niv•ore** *n.* **car•niv•o•rous•ly** *adv.* **car•niv•o•rous•ness** *n.*
ca•rouse |kə'rowz| • *v.* [intrans.] drink plentiful amounts of alcohol and enjoy oneself with others in a noisy, lively way: *they danced and caroused until the drink ran out* | [as n.] (**carousing**) *a night of carousing.* • *n.* a noisy, lively drinking party: *a three-day carouse.*
DERIVATIVES: **ca•rous•al** |-zəl| *n.* **ca•rous•er** *n.*
carp • *v.* [intrans.] complain or find fault continually, typically about trivial matters: *I won't carp about the way you did it* | *he was constantly carping at me.*
DERIVATIVES: **carp•er** *n.*
car•pal |ˈkärpəl| • *n.* any of the eight small bones forming the wrist.
■ any of the equivalent bones in an animal's forelimb. • *adj.* of or relating to these bones.
car•pe• di•em |ˌkärpe 'dē,em| • *exclam.* used to urge someone to make the most of the present time and give little thought to the future.
car•pet•bag•ger |ˈkärpət,bægər| • *n.* a political candidate who seeks election in an area where they have no local connections.
■ a person from the Northern states who went to the South after the Civil War to profit from the Reconstruction. They carried their possessions in bags made from carpet, hence the name. ■ a person perceived as an unscrupulous opportunist.
car•rel |ˈkærəl| • *n.* a small cubicle with a desk for the use of a reader or student in a library.
■ a small enclosure or study in a cloister.
car•ri•on |ˈkærēən| • *n.* the decaying flesh of dead animals.
carte blanche |ˈkärt 'bläNSH; 'blänCH| • *n.* complete freedom to act as one wishes or thinks best: *we were given carte blanche to redecorate.*
car•tel |kär'tel| • *n.* an association of manufacturers or suppliers with the purpose of maintaining prices at a high level and restricting competition: *the development of an energy cartel.*
■ a coalition or cooperative arrangement between political parties intended to promote a mutual interest.
DERIVATIVES: **car•tel•ism** *n.* **car•tel•i•za•tion** *n.*
Car•te•sian |kär'tēZHən| • *adj.* of or relating to the 17th-century French thinker René Descartes and his philosophical or mathematical ideas. • *n.* a follower of Descartes.
DERIVATIVES: **Car•te•sian•ism** |-,nizəm| *n.*
car•ti•lage |ˈkärtl-ij| • *n.* firm, whitish, flexible connective tissue found in various forms in the human larynx and respiratory tract, in structures such as the external ear, and in the articulating surfaces of joints. It is more widespread in the infant skeleton, being replaced by bone during growth. Some fish, including sharks, have skeletons of cartilage.
■ a particular structure made of this tissue.
DERIVATIVES: **car•ti•lag•i•noid** |ˌkärtl'æjə ,noid| *adj.* **car•ti•lag•i•nous** *adj.*
car•tog•ra•phy |kär'tägrəfē| • *n.* the science or practice of drawing maps.
DERIVATIVES: **car•tog•ra•pher** |-fər| *n.* **car•to•graph•ic** |ˌkärtə'græfik| *adj.* **car•to•graph•i•cal** |ˌkärtə'græfikəl| *adj.* **car•to•graph•i•cal•ly** |ˌkärtə'græfik(ə)lē| *adv.*
cartomancy |ˈkärtə,mænsē| • *n.* fortune-telling by interpreting a random selection of playing cards.
car•toon |kär'tōōn| • *n.* **1** a simple drawing showing the features of its subjects in a humorously exaggerated way, esp. a satirical one in a newspaper or magazine.
■ a comic strip. ■ a simplified or exaggerated version or interpretation of something: *this movie is a cartoon of rural life* | [as adj.] *Dolores becomes a cartoon housewife, reading glossy magazines in a bathrobe.* **2** a motion picture using computer graphics or a photographed sequence of drawings rather than real people or objects. Cf. ANIMATION. **3** a full-size drawing made by an artist as a preliminary design for a painting or other work of art. • *v.* [trans.] (usu. **be cartooned**) make a drawing of (someone) in a simplified or exaggerated way: *she has a face with enough character to be cartooned.*
DERIVATIVES: **car•toon•ish** *adj.* **car•toon•ist** |-ist| *n.* **car•toon•y** *adj.*
car•touche |kär'tōōSH| • *n.* a carved tablet or drawing representing a scroll with rolled-up ends, used ornamentally or bearing an inscription.
■ an oval or oblong figure enclosing a group of Egyptian hieroglyphs, typically representing the name and title of a monarch.
car•un•cle |kə'rəNGkəl| 'kær,əNG-| • *n.* a fleshy outgrowth, in particular:
■ a wattle of a bird such as a turkey. ■ the red prominence at the inner corner of the human eye.
DERIVATIVES: **ca•run•cu•lar** |kə'rəNGkyə-lər| *adj.*

car•y•at•id |ˌkærēˈætəd; ˈkærēəˌtid| • n. (pl. **caryatids** or **caryatides** |ˌkærēˈætəˌdēz|) a stone carving of a draped female figure, used as pillar to support the entablature of a Greek or Greek-style building. The male equivalent is an *atlas* (pl. *atlantes*).

cas•cade |kasˈkād| • n. **1** a small waterfall, typically one of several that fall in stages down a steep rocky slope.
■ a mass of something that falls or hangs in copious or luxuriant quantities: *a cascade of bougainvillea.* ■ a large number or amount of something occurring or arriving in rapid succession: *a cascade of antiwar literature.* **2** a process whereby something, typically information or knowledge, is successively passed on: [as adj.] *the greater the number of people who are well briefed, the wider the cascade effect.*
■ a succession of devices or stages in a process, each of which triggers or initiates the next.
• v. **1** [no obj., with adverbial of direction] (of water) pour downward rapidly and in large quantities: *water was cascading down the stairs.*
■ fall or hang in copious or luxuriant quantities: *blonde hair cascaded down her back.* **2** [trans.] arrange (a number of devices or objects) in a series or sequence.
■ arrange (windows on a computer monitor) to overlap partially, so that a part of each is visible.

case•mate |ˈkāsˌmāt| • n. a small room in the thickness of the wall of a fortress, with embrasures from which guns or missiles can be fired.
■ an armored enclosure for guns on a warship.

case•ment |ˈkāsmənt| • n. a window or part of a window set on a hinge so that it opens like a door: [as adj.] *casement windows.*
■ any window. ■ the sash of a sash window.

cash•ier • v. [trans.] (usu. **be cashiered**) dismiss someone from the armed forces in disgrace because of a serious misdemeanor: *he was found guilty and cashiered* | [as adj.] (**cashiered**) *a cashiered National Guard major.*
■ suspend or dismiss someone from an office, position, or membership: *the team owner had been cashiered for consorting with a gambler.*

casque |kæsk| • n. **1** a helmet. **2** a helmetlike anatomical structure, such as that on the bill of a hornbill or the head of a cassowary.

Cas•san•dra |kəˈsændrə| • a daughter of the legendary Trojan king Priam, who was given the gift of prophecy by Apollo. When she cheated him, however, he turned this into a curse by causing her prophecies, though true, to be disbelieved.
■ [as n.] (**a Cassandra**) a prophet of disaster, esp. one who is disregarded.

caste |kæst| • n. each of the hereditary classes of Hindu society, distinguished by relative degrees of ritual purity or pollution and of social status: *members of the lower castes* | *a man of high caste.*
■ the system of dividing society into such classes. ■ any class or group of people who in-

herit exclusive privileges or are perceived as socially distinct: *those educated in private schools belong to a privileged caste.* ■ (in some social insects) a physically distinct individual with a particular function in the society: *the caste of worker bees.*

There are four basic classes, or varnas, in Hindu society: Brahman (priest), Kshatriya (warrior), Vaishya (merchant or farmer), and Shudra (laborer).

cas•tel•lat•ed |ˈkæstəˌlātid| • adj. **1** having battlements: *a castellated tower.*
■ (of a nut or other mechanical part) having grooves or slots on its upper face. **2** having a castle or several castles: *the castellated hills along the east bank.* Cf. CRENELLATIONS.

cas•ti•gate |ˈkæstəˌgāt| • v. [trans.] reprimand (someone) severely: *he was castigated for not setting a good example.*
DERIVATIVES: **cas•ti•ga•tion** |ˌkæstəˈgāSHən| n. **cas•ti•ga•tor** |-ˌgātər| n. **cas•ti•ga•to•ry** |-gəˌtôrē| adj.

Cas•til•ian |kəˈstilyən| • n. **1** a native of the Spanish province (formerly, the kingdom) of Castile. **2** the dialect of Spanish spoken in Castile, which is standard Spanish. • adj. of or relating to Castile, Castilians, or the Castilian form of Spanish.

cas•u•al•ty |ˈkæzH(ə)wəltē; ˈkæzHəl-| • n. (pl. -ies) a person killed or injured in a war or accident.
■ a person or thing badly affected by an event or situation: *the building industry has been one of the casualties of the recession.* ■ (chiefly in insurance) an accident, mishap, or disaster.

cas•u•ist |ˈkæzHəwəst| • n. a person who uses clever but unsound reasoning, esp. in relation to moral questions; a sophist.
■ a person who resolves moral problems by the application of theoretical rules to particular instances.
DERIVATIVES: **cas•u•is•tic** |ˌkæzHəˈwistik| adj. **cas•u•is•ti•cal** |ˌkæzHəˈwistikəl| adj. **cas•u•is•ti•cal•ly** |ˌkæzHəˈwistik(ə)lē| adv. **cas•u•ist•ry** n.

ca•sus bel•li |ˈkäsəs ˈbelē; ˈkäsəs ˈbelˌī| • n. (pl. same) an act or situation provoking or justifying war.

cat•a•chre•sis |ˌkætəˈkrēsis| • n. (pl. **catachreses**) the use of a word in a way that is not correct, for example, the use of *mitigate* for *militate.*
DERIVATIVES: **cat•a•chres•tic** |-ˈkrestik| adj.

cat•a•clysm |ˈkætəˌklizəm| • n. a large-scale and violent event in the natural world.
■ a sudden violent upheaval, esp. in a political or social context: *the cataclysm of the First World War.*
DERIVATIVES: **cat•a•clys•mic** adj. **cat•a•clys•mi•cal•ly** adv.

cat•a•comb |ˈkætəˌkōm| • n. (usu. **catacombs**) an underground cemetery consisting of a subterranean gallery with recesses for tombs, as constructed by the ancient Romans.

■ a single crypt or gallery in such a cemetery.
■ an underground construction resembling or compared to such a cemetery.

cat•a•falque | ˈkætəˌfô(l)k; -ˌfælk | • n. a decorated framework supporting the coffin of a distinguished person during a funeral or while lying in state.

cat•a•lep•sy | ˈkætlˌepsē | • n. a medical condition characterized by a trance or seizure with a loss of sensation and consciousness accompanied by rigidity of the body.
DERIVATIVES: **cat•a•lep•tic** | ˌkætlˈeptik | adj. & n. **cat•a•lep•ti•cal•ly** adv.

ca•ta•logue rai•son•né | ˌkætlˌôg ˌrāzəˈnä -ˌäg | • n. (pl. **catalogues raisonnés** | ˈkætl ˌôg(z) ˌrāzəˈnä -ˌäg(z) |) a descriptive catalog of works of art with explanations and scholarly comments: *a catalogue raisonné of Miró's work.*

cat•a•lyst | ˈkætl-əst | • n. a substance that increases the rate of a chemical reaction (causes *catalysis*) without itself undergoing any permanent chemical change.
■ a person or thing that precipitates an event: *the governor's speech acted as a catalyst for debate.*

cat•a•lyt•ic | ˌˈkætlˈidik | • adj. relating to or involving the action of a catalyst.
DERIVATIVES: **cat•a•lyt•i•cal•ly** | -ik(ə)lē | adv.

cat•a•mite | ˈkætəˌmīt | • n. a boy kept for homosexual practices; the younger partner in a homosexual relationship, esp. the passive partner in anal intercourse.

cat•a•pult | ˈkædəˌpəlt; -ˌpo͞olt | • n. a device in which accumulated tension is suddenly released to hurl an object some distance, in particular:
■ an ancient military machine worked by a lever and ropes for hurling large stones or other missiles. ■ a mechanical device for launching a glider or other aircraft, esp. from the deck of a ship. ■ chiefly Brit. a slingshot. • v. [with obj. and adverbial of direction] hurl or launch (something) in a specified direction with or as if with a catapult: *the explosion catapulted the car 30 yards along the road* | *their music catapulted them to the top of the charts.*
■ [no obj., with adverbial of direction] move suddenly or at great speed as though hurled by a catapult: *the horse catapulted away from the fence.*

cat•a•ract | ˈkætəˌrækt | • n. **1** a large waterfall. Cf. CASCADE.
■ a sudden rush of water; a downpour: *the rain enveloped us in a deafening cataract.* **2** a medical condition in which the lens of the eye becomes progressively opaque, resulting in blurred vision: *she had cataracts in both eyes.*

ca•tarrh | kəˈtär | • n. excessive discharge or buildup of mucus in the nose or throat, associated with inflammation of the mucous membrane.
DERIVATIVES: **ca•tarrh•al** | kəˈtärəl | adj.

ca•tas•tro•phe | kəˈtæstrəfē | • n. an event causing great and often sudden damage or suffering; a disaster: *a national economic catastrophe* | *leading inexorably to catastrophe.*

■ the denouement of a drama, esp. a classical tragedy.
DERIVATIVES: **cat•a•stroph•ic** adj. **cat•a•stroph•i•cal•ly** adv.

ca•tas•tro•phism | kəˈtæstrəˌfizəm | • n. the theory that changes in the earth's crust during geological history have resulted chiefly from sudden violent and unusual events. Often contrasted with UNIFORMITARIANISM.
DERIVATIVES: **ca•tas•tro•phist** n. & adj.

cat•a•to•ni•a | ˌkætəˈtōnēə | • n. abnormality of movement and behavior arising from a disturbed mental state (typically schizophrenia). It may involve repetitive or purposeless overactivity, or catalepsy, resistance to passive movement, and negativism.
■ a state of immobility and stupor.
DERIVATIVES: **cat•a•ton•ic** adj.

catch-22 • n. a dilemma or difficult circumstance from which there is no escape because of mutually conflicting or dependent conditions.

cat•e•chet•ics | ˌkætəˈketiks | • plural n. [treated as sing.] the branch of theology that deals with the instruction given to Christians before baptism or confirmation.
■ religious teaching in general, typically that given to children in the Roman Catholic Church.
DERIVATIVES: **cat•e•chet•ic** adj. **cat•e•chet•i•cal** adj. **cat•e•chet•i•cal•ly** adv.

cat•e•chism | ˈkætəˌkizəm | • n. a summary of the principles of Christian religion in the form of questions and answers, used for instruction.
■ a series of fixed questions, answers, or precepts used for instruction in other situations.
DERIVATIVES: **cat•e•chis•mal** | ˌkætəˈkizəməl | adj.

cat•e•chize | ˈkætəˌkīz | • v. [trans.] instruct (someone) in the principles of Christian religion by means of question and answer, typically by using a catechism.
■ put questions to or interrogate (someone).
DERIVATIVES: **cat•e•chiz•er** n.

cat•e•chu•men | ˌkætəˈkyo͞omən | • n. a Christian convert under instruction before baptism.
■ a young Christian preparing for confirmation.

cat•e•nar•y | ˈkætəˌnerē; ˈkætnˌerē | • n. (pl. -ies) a curve formed by a wire, rope, or chain hanging freely from two points that are on the same horizontal level.
■ a wire, rope, or chain forming such a curve. • adj. [attrib.] having the form of, involving, or denoting a curve of this type.

cat•e•nat•ed | ˈkætəˌnātid; ˈkætnˌātid | • adj. connected in a chain or series: *catenated molecules.* Cf. CONCATENATE.
DERIVATIVES: **cat•e•na•tion** | ˌkætəˈnāsHən; ˌkætnˈāsHən | n.

cat•er-cor•nered | ˈkætē ˌkôrnərd; ˈkætər | (also **cater-corner** or **catty-cornered** or **kitty-corner**) • adj. & adv. situated diagonally opposite someone or something: [as adj.] *a restaurant cater-cornered from the movie* *theater* | [as adv.] *motorcyclists cut **cater-cornered across** his yard.*

cat•er•waul |ˈkætər,wôl| • *v.* [intrans.] [often as *n.*] (**caterwauling**) make a shrill howling or wailing noise: *the caterwauling of a pair of bobcats* | [as adj.] (**caterwauling**) *a caterwauling guitar.* • *n.* a shrill howling or wailing noise.

ca•thar•sis |kəˈTHärsis| • *n.* the process of releasing, and thereby providing or obtaining relief relief from, strong or repressed emotions.

ca•the•dral |kəˈTHēdrəl| • *n.* the principal church of a diocese, with which the bishop is officially associated: [in names] *St. John's Cathedral.* Cf. BASILICA

ca•thex•is |kəˈTHeksis| • *n.* the concentration of mental energy on one particular person, idea, or object (esp. to a pathological degree).
DERIVATIVES: **ca•thec•tic** *adj.*

cath•o•lic |ˈkæTH(ə)lik| • *adj.* (of tastes, interests, etc.) including a wide variety of things; all-embracing: *birds that are catholic in choice of habitat.*
DERIVATIVES: **cath•o•lic•i•ty** |ˌkæTH(ə)ˈlisəṯē| *n.* **ca•thol•ic•ly** *adv.*

cat's-paw • *n.* a person who is used by another, typically to carry out an unpleasant or dangerous task.

Cau•ca•sian |kôˈkāZHən| • *adj.* **1** of or relating to one of the traditional divisions of humankind, covering a broad group of peoples from Europe, western Asia, and parts of India and North Africa. [ORIGIN: so named because the German physiologist Johann Blumenbach (1752–1840) believed that it originated in the Caucasus region of southeastern Europe.]
■ white-skinned; of European origin. **2** of or relating to the Caucasus. **3** of or relating to a group of languages spoken in the region of the Caucasus, of which thirty-eight are known, many not committed to writing. The most widely spoken is Georgian. • *n.* a Caucasian person.
■ a white person; a person of European origin.

USAGE: In the racial classification as developed by anthropologists in the 19th century, **Caucasian** (or **Caucasoid**) included peoples whose skin color ranged from light (in northern Europe) to dark (in parts of North Africa and India). Although the classification is outdated and the categories are now not generally accepted as scientific, the term **Caucasian** has acquired a more restricted meaning. It is now used as a synonym for 'white or of European origin,' as in: *the police are looking for a **Caucasian** male in his forties.*

cau•cus |ˈkôkəs| • *n.* (pl. **caucuses**) **1** a meeting of the members of a legislative body who are members of a particular political party, to select candidates or decide policy.
■ the members of such a body. **2** a group of people with shared concerns within a political party or larger organization.

■ a meeting of such a group. • *v.* (**caucused, caucusing**) [intrans.] hold or form such a group or meeting.

cau•dal |ˈkôdl| • *adj.* of or like a tail.
■ at or near the tail or the posterior part of the body.
DERIVATIVES: **cau•dal•ly** *adv.*

caul |kôl| • *n.* **1** the amniotic membrane enclosing a fetus.
■ part of this membrane occasionally found on a child's head at birth, thought to bring good luck. **2** a woman's close-fitting indoor headdress or hairnet, as worn in former times.

caus•al |ˈkôzəl| • *adj.* of, relating to, or acting as a cause: *the causal factors associated with illness.*
■ expressing or indicating a cause: *a causal conjunction.*
DERIVATIVES: **caus•al•ly** *adv.*

cau•sal•i•ty |kôˈzæləṯē| • *n.* **1** the relationship between cause and effect.
■ the fact or state of acting as a cause. **2** the principle that everything has a cause.

cause cé•lè•bre |ˈkôz səˈleb(rə); ˈkōz| • *n.* (pl. **causes célèbres** pronunc. same) a controversial issue that attracts a great deal of public attention.

cau•se•rie |ˌkōz(ə)ˈrē| • *n.* (pl. **-ies** pronunc. same) an informal article or talk, typically one on a literary subject.

caus•tic |ˈkôstik| • *adj.* able to burn or corrode organic tissue by chemical action: *a caustic cleaner.*
■ sarcastic in a scathing and bitter way: *the players were making caustic comments about the referee.* ■ (of an expression or sound) expressive of such sarcasm: *a caustic smile.*
DERIVATIVES: **caus•ti•cal•ly** |-ik(ə)lē| *adv.* **caus•tic•i•ty** |kôˈstisəṯē| *n.*

cau•ter•ize |ˈkôṯə,rīz| • *v.* [trans.] burn the skin or flesh of (a wound) with a heated instrument or caustic substance, typically to stop bleeding or prevent the wound from becoming infected.
DERIVATIVES: **cau•ter•i•za•tion** |ˌkôṯərəˈzāSHən| *n.*

cav•al•cade |ˌkævəlˈkād| • *n.* a formal procession of people walking, on horseback, or riding in vehicles.
■ a large group of people with some shared characteristic: *I refuse to be one of your cavalcade of doting admirers.*

cav•a•lier |ˌkævəˈlir| • *n.* (**Cavalier**) a supporter of King Charles I in the English Civil War (1642–49).
■ a courtly gentleman, esp. one acting as a lady's escort. ■ a horseman, esp. a cavalryman. • *adj.* showing a lack of proper concern; offhand: *irritated by his cavalier attitude.*
DERIVATIVES: **cav•a•lier•ly** *adv.*

cav•al•ry |ˈkævəlrē| • *n.* (pl. **-ies**) [usu. treated as pl.] formerly, soldiers who fought on horseback.
■ a branch of an army made up of such soldiers. ■ modern soldiers who fight in armored vehicles.
DERIVATIVES: **cav•al•ry•man** |-mən| *n.* (pl. **-men**) .

ca•ve•at |ˈkævēˌät; ˈkäv-| • n. a warning or proviso of specific stipulations, conditions, or limitations.
■ a legal notice, esp. in a probate proceeding, that certain actions may not be taken without informing the person who gave the notice.

ca•ve•at emp•tor |ˈempˌtôr| • n. the principle that the buyer alone is responsible for checking the quality and suitability of goods before a purchase is made.

cav•il |ˈkævəl| • v. [intrans.] make petty or unnecessary objections: they caviled at the cost. • n. an objection of this kind.
DERIVATIVES: **cav•il•er** n.

cay |kē; kā| • n. a low bank or reef of coral, rock, or sand.

cede |sēd| • v. [trans.] give up (power or territory): they have had to cede control of the schools to the government | Poland ceded land to Russia and Prussia.

cei•lidh |ˈkālē| • n. a social event at which there is Scottish or Irish folk music and singing, traditional dancing, and storytelling.

cel•a•don |ˈseləˌdän| • n. a willow-green color: [as adj.] paneling painted in celadon green.
■ a gray-green glaze used on pottery, esp. that from China. ■ pottery made with this glaze.

cel•e•brant |ˈseləbrənt| • n. 1 a person who performs a rite, esp. a priest at the Christian Eucharist. 2 a person who celebrates something.

ce•ler•i•ty |səˈlerətē| • n. swiftness of movement.

ce•les•ta |səˈlestə| • n. (also celeste) a small keyboard musical instrument in which felted hammers strike a row of steel plates suspended over wooden resonators, giving an ethereal bell-like sound.

ce•les•tial |səˈlesCHəl| • adj. [attrib.] positioned in or relating to the sky, or outer space as observed in astronomy: a celestial body.
■ belonging or relating to heaven: the celestial city. ■ supremely good: the celestial beauty of music.
DERIVATIVES: **ce•les•tial•ly** adv.

cel•i•bate |ˈseləbət| • adj. abstaining from marriage and sexual relations, typically for religious reasons: a celibate priest.
■ having or involving no sexual relations: I'd rather stay single and celibate. • n. a person who abstains from marriage and sexual relations.
DERIVATIVES: **cel•i•ba•cy** |-bəsē| • n.

cel•lu•lar |ˈselyələr| • adj. 1 of, relating to, or consisting of living cells: cellular proliferation. 2 denoting or relating to a mobile telephone system that uses a number of short-range radio stations to cover the area that it serves, the signal being automatically switched from one station to another as the user travels about. 3 (of a fabric item, such as a blanket or vest) knitted so as to form extra holes or hollows that trap air and provide extra insulation. 4 consisting of small compartments or rooms: cellular accommodations.
DERIVATIVES: **cel•lu•lar•i•ty** |ˌselyəˈlerətē| n.

cel•lu•loid |ˈselyəˌloid| • n. a transparent flammable plastic made in sheets from camphor and nitrocellulose, formerly used for cinematographic film.
■ motion pictures as a genre: having made the leap from theater to celluloid, she can now make more money.

cel•lu•lose |ˈselyəˌlōs; -ˌlōz| • n. 1 an insoluble substance that is the main constituent of plant cell walls and of vegetable fibers such as cotton. It is a polysaccharide consisting of chains of glucose monomers. 2 paint or lacquer consisting principally of cellulose acetate or nitrate in solution.
DERIVATIVES: **cel•lu•lo•sic** |ˌselyəˈlōsik; -ˈlōzik| adj.

Cel•si•us |ˈselsēəs; ˈselsHəs| (abbr.: C) • adj. [postpositive when used with a numeral] of or denoting a scale of temperature on which water freezes at 0° and boils at 100° under standard conditions. • n. (also Celsius scale) this scale of temperature.
USAGE: **Celsius** rather than **centigrade** is the standard accepted term when giving temperatures: use 25° **Celsius** rather than 25° **centigrade**.

Celt |kelt; selt| • n. (also Kelt) a member of a group of peoples inhabiting much of Europe and Asia Minor in pre-Roman times. Their culture developed in the late Bronze Age around the upper Danube, and reached its height in the La Tène culture (5th to 1st centuries BC) before being overrun by the Romans and various Germanic peoples.
■ a native of any of the modern nations or regions in which Celtic languages are (or were until recently) spoken; a person of Irish, Highland Scottish, Manx, Welsh, Breton, or Cornish descent.

Celt•ic |ˈkeltik; ˈsel-| • adj. of or relating to the Celts or their languages, which constitute a branch of the Indo-European family and include Irish, Scottish Gaelic, Welsh, Breton, Manx, Cornish, and several extinct pre-Roman languages such as Gaulish. • n. the Celtic language group.
DERIVATIVES: **Celt•i•cism** |ˈkeltəˌsizəm; ˈsel-| n. **Celt•i•cist** |ˈkeltəˌsist; ˈsel-| n.
USAGE: **Celt** and **Celtic** can be pronounced either with an initial k- or s-, but in standard English the normal pronunciation is with a k-, except in the name of the Boston basketball team.

cen•a•cle |ˈsenikəl| • n. 1 a group of people, such as a discussion group or literary clique. 2 the room in which the biblical Last Supper was held.

ce•no•bite |ˈsenəˌbīt| (also coenobite) • n. a member of a monastic community.
DERIVATIVES: **ce•no•bit•ic** |ˌsenəˈbitik| adj. **ce•no•bit•i•cal** |ˌsenəˈbitikəl| adj.

cen•o•taph |ˈsenəˌtaf| • n. a tomblike monument to someone buried elsewhere, esp. one commemorating people who died in a war.

Ce•no•zo•ic |ˌsenəˈzōik| (also Cainozoic) • adj. relating to or denoting the most recent geologic era, following the Mesozoic era and comprising the Tertiary and Quaternary periods.

■ [as n.] (**the Cenozoic**) the Cenozoic era, or the system of rocks deposited during it.

> The Cenozoic has lasted from about 65 million years ago to the present day. It has seen the rapid evolution and rise to dominance of mammals, birds, and flowering plants.

cen•ser |'sensər| • *n.* a container in which incense is burned, typically during a religious ceremony: *priests swinging censers.*

cen•sor |'sensər| • *n.* **1** an official who examines material that is about to be released, such as books, movies, news, and art, and suppresses any parts that are considered obscene, politically unacceptable, or a threat to security. ■ a person who exercises supervision or judgment over the conduct of morals of others.

■ in Freudian psychology, an aspect of the superego that is said to prevent certain ideas and memories from emerging into consciousness. [ORIGIN: from a mistranslation of German *Zensur* 'censorship,' coined by Freud.] **2** (in ancient Rome) either of two magistrates who held censuses and supervised public morals. • *v.* [trans.] (often **be censored**) examine (a book, movie, etc.) officially and suppress unacceptable parts of it: *my mail was being censored.*
DERIVATIVES: **cen•so•ri•al** |sen'sôrēəl| *adj.*

> USAGE: Both **censor** and **censure** are both verbs and nouns, but **censor** means 'to scrutinize, revise, or cut unacceptable parts from a book, movie, etc.' or 'a person who does this,' while **censure** means 'to criticize harshly' or 'harsh criticism:' *a resolution of censure to express strong disapproval of the president's behavior.*

cen•so•ri•ous |sen'sôrēəs| • *adj.* severely critical of others: *charitable in his judgments and never censorious, Jim carried tolerance almost too far.*
DERIVATIVES: **cen•so•ri•ous•ly** *adv.* **cen•so•ri•ous•ness** *n.*

cen•sure |'senCHər| • *v.* [trans.] (often **be censured**) express severe disapproval of (someone or something), typically in a formal statement: *a judge was censured in 1983 for injudicious conduct.* • *n.* the expression of formal disapproval: *a resolution of censure against the offenders.*
DERIVATIVES: **cen•sur•a•ble** *adj.*

cen•sus |'sensəs| • *n.* (pl. **censuses**) an official count or survey of a population, typically recording various details of individuals: *population estimates extrapolated from the 1981 census* | [as adj.] *census data.*

cen•ten•ar•y |sen'tenərē; 'sentn,erē| chiefly Brit. • *n.* (pl. **-ies**) the hundredth anniversary of a significant event; a centennial.

■ a celebration of such an anniversary. • *adj.* of or relating to a hundredth anniversary; centennial.

cen•ten•ni•al |sen'tenēəl| • *adj.* of or relating to a hundredth anniversary: *centennial celebrations.* • *n.* a hundredth anniversary: *the museum's centennial.*

■ a celebration of such an anniversary.

cen•ti•grade |'sentə,grād| • *adj.* [postpositive when used with a numeral] another term for CELSIUS.

■ having a scale of a hundred degrees.

cen•trif•u•gal |sen'trif(y)əgəl| • *adj.* moving or tending to move away from a center. The opposite of CENTRIPETAL.
DERIVATIVES: **cen•trif•u•gal•ly** *adv.*

cen•trip•e•tal |sen'tripətl| • *adj.* moving or tending to move toward a center. The opposite of CENTRIFUGAL.
DERIVATIVES: **cen•trip•e•tal•ly** *adv.*

ce•phal•ic |sə'fælik| • *adj.* of, in, or relating to the head.

cer•e•bel•lum |,serə'beləm| • *n.* (pl. **cerebellums** or **cerebella** |-'belə|) the part of the brain at the back of the skull in vertebrates. Its function is to coordinate and regulate muscular activity.
DERIVATIVES: **cer•e•bel•lar** |-'belər| *adj.*

ce•re•bral |sə'rēbrəl; 'serəbrəl| • *adj.* of the cerebrum of the brain: *a cerebral hemorrhage* | *the cerebral cortex.*

■ intellectual rather than emotional or physical: *criticism is a cerebral process.*
DERIVATIVES: **ce•re•bral•ly** *adv.*

cer•e•bra•tion |,serə'brāsHən| • *n.* the working of the brain; thinking.
DERIVATIVES: **cer•e•brate** |'serə,brāt| *v.*

ce•re•brum |sə'rēbrəm; 'serə-| • *n.* (pl. **cerebra**) the principal and forward-most part of the brain in vertebrates, situated in the front area of the skull and consisting of two hemispheres, left and right, separated by a fissure.

cer•e•mo•ni•al |,serə'mōnēəl| • *adj.* **1** relating to or used for formal events of a religious or public nature: *ceremonial headgear* | *ceremonial occasions.* **2** (of a position or role) involving only nominal authority or power: *originally a ceremonial post, it is now a position with executive power.* • *n.* the system of rules and procedures to be observed at a formal or religious occasion: *the procedure was conducted with all due ceremonial.*

■ a rite or ceremony: *a ceremonial called the ghost dance.*
DERIVATIVES: **cer•e•mo•ni•al•ism** |-,lizəm| *n.* **cer•e•mo•ni•al•ist** |-list| *n.* **cer•e•mo•ni•al•ly** *adv.*

cer•e•mo•ni•ous |,serə'mōnēəs| • *adj.* relating or appropriate to grand and formal occasions: *a Great Hall where ceremonious and public appearances were made.*

■ excessively polite; punctilious: *he accepted the gifts with ceremonious dignity.*
DERIVATIVES: **cer•e•mo•ni•ous•ly** *adv.* **cer•e•mo•ni•ous•ness** *n.*

ce•rise |sə'rēs; sə'rēz| • *n.* a bright or deep red color: *a vivid cerise lampshade.* • *adj.* of a bright or deep red color.

cer•ti•fi•a•ble |,sərtə'fīəbəl| • *adj.* **1** able or needing to be certified: *encephalitis was a certifiable condition* | *financial reports showed cer-*

tifiable progress. **2** officially recognized as needing treatment for a mental disorder.

■ crazy: *the world of fashion is almost entirely insane, the people who work in it mainly certifiable.*

DERIVATIVES: **cer•ti•fi•a•bly** |-blē| *adj.*

cer•ti•fy |'sərtə,fī| • *v.* (**-ies, -ied**) [trans.] (often **be certified**) attest or confirm in a formal statement: *the profits for the year had been certified by the auditors*| [with clause] *the medical witness certified that death was due to cerebral hemorrhage.*

■ [often as adj.] (**certified**) officially recognize (someone or something) as possessing certain qualifications or meeting certain standards: *a certified scuba instructor* | **board certified** *in obstetrics and gynecology.* ■ officially declare insane.

ce•ru•le•an |sə'rōōlēən| • *adj.* deep blue in color like a clear sky: *cerulean waters and golden sands.* • *n.* a deep sky-blue color.

ce•ru•men |sə'rōōmən| • *n.* technical term for earwax.

cervine |'s@:vVIn| • *ADJ.* OF OR RELATING TO DEER; DEERLIKE.

ce•sar•e•an sec•tion • *n.* a surgical operation for delivering a child by cutting through the wall of the mother's abdomen.

ces•sa•tion |se'sāSHən| • *n.* a ceasing; an end: *the cessation of hostilities* | *a cessation of animal testing of cosmetics.*

■ a pause or interruption: *a cessation of respiration requiring resuscitation.*

ces•sion |'seSHən| • *n.* the formal giving up of rights, property, or territory by a state: *the cession of a coastal strip.*

ce•ta•cean |si'tāSH(ē)ə| • *adj.* belonging or relating to an order (Cetacea) of marine mammals that comprises the whales, dolphins, and porpoises. These have a streamlined hairless body, no hind limbs, a horizontal tail fin, and a blowhole on top of the head for breathing. • *n.* a member of this order.

chad•or |'CHədər; 'CHäd,ôr| (also **chadar** or **chuddar**) • *n.* a large piece of dark-colored cloth, typically worn by Muslim women, wrapped around the head and upper body to leave only the face exposed.

chafe |CHāf| • *v.* **1** [trans.] (of something restrictive or too tight) make (a part of the body) sore by rubbing against it: *the collar chafed his neck.*

■ [intrans.] (of a part of the body) be or become sore as a result of such rubbing: *shook hands until the skin chafed.* ■ [intrans.] (of an object) rub abrasively against another object: *the grommet stops the cable from chafing on the metal.* **2** [trans.] rub (a part of the body) to restore warmth or sensation.

■ restore (warmth or sensation) in this way: *he chafed some feeling into his frozen hands.* **3** become or make annoyed or impatient because of a restriction or inconvenience:[intrans.] *the bank chafed at the restrictions imposed upon it* | [trans.] *it chafed him to be confined like this.* • *n.* wear or damage caused by rubbing: *to prevent chafe the ropes should lie flat.*

chaff |CHæf| • *n.* the husks of grain or other seed separated by winnowing or threshing.

■ chopped hay and straw used as fodder. ■ worthless things; trash. ■ strips of metal foil released in the atmosphere from aircraft, or deployed as missiles, to obstruct radar detection.

DERIVATIVES: **chaff•y** *adj.*

cha•grin |SHə'grin| • *n.* distress or embarrassment at having failed or been humiliated: *Jeff, much to his chagrin, wasn't invited.* • *v.* (**be chagrined**) feel distressed or humiliated: *he was chagrined when his friend poured scorn on him.*

chain |CHān| • *n.* (in measuring) a jointed line consisting of linked metal rods.

■ the length of such a measuring line (66 ft.). ■ a measuring chain of ten yards, used in football in the determination of first downs.

chaise longue |'SHāz 'lôNG| • *n.* (pl.**chaises longues** |'SHāz 'lôNG(z)|) a reclining chair with a lengthened seat forming a leg rest.

chal•ced•o•ny |kæl'sedn,ē; CHæl-; 'kælsə,dōnē; 'CHælsə-| • *n.* (pl. **-ies**) a type of quartz in microscopic crystals occurring in several different forms, including onyx, agate, and jasper.

DERIVATIVES: **chal•ce•don•ic** |,kælsə'dänik| *adj.*

chal•ice |'CHæləs| • *n.* a large cup or goblet, typically used in former times for drinking wine.

■ the wine cup used in the Christian Eucharist.

chal•lah |'hälə; 'KHälə| • *n.* (pl. **challahs** |'häləz; 'KHäləz| or **chalot(h)** |hä'lōt; KHä-; -'lōs|) a loaf of white leavened bread, typically braided in form, traditionally baked to celebrate the Jewish sabbath.

chal•lenged |'CHælənjd| • *adj.* [with submodifier or in combination] (used euphemistically) impaired or disabled in a specified respect: *physically challenged.*

■ lacking or deficient in a specified respect: *today's attention-challenged teens.*

USAGE: The use with a preceding adverb, e.g., **physically challenged**, originally intended to give a more positive tone than such terms as **disabled** or **handicapped**, arose in the US in the 1980s. Despite the originally serious intention, the term rapidly became stalled by uses whose intention was to make fun of the attempts at euphemism and whose tone was usually clearly ironic: examples include **cerebrally challenged**, **follicularly challenged**, etc.

chal•lis |'SHælē| • *n.* a soft lightweight clothing fabric made from silk and wool.

cha•me•le•on |kə'mēlyən; -lēən| (chiefly Brit. also **chamaeleon**) • *n.* a small slow-moving Old World lizard with a prehensile tail, long extensible tongue, protruding eyes that rotate independently, and a highly developed ability to change color.

■ a changeable or inconstant person, esp. one who adapts to a changed situation for personal advantage.

DERIVATIVES: **cha•me•le•on•ic** |kə‚mēlē 'änik| adj.

cham•ois |'sнæmē| • n. 1 (pl. same) an agile goat-antelope (genus *Rupicapra*) with short hooked horns, found in mountainous areas of Europe from Spain to the Caucasus. 2 (pl. same) (also **chamois leather**) soft pliable leather made from the skin of sheep, goats, or deer. ■ a piece of such leather, or cloth treated to resemble it, used typically for washing windows or cars.

cham•paign |sнæm'pān| • n. open level countryside.

chan•cel |'cнænsəl| • n. the part of a church near the altar, reserved for the clergy and choir, and typically separated from the nave by steps or a screen.

chan•cel•ler•y |'cнæns(ə)lərē| • n. (pl. -ies) 1 the position, office, or department of a chancellor. ■ the official residence of a chancellor. 2 an office attached to an embassy or consulate.

chan•cel•lor |'cнæns(ə)lər| • n. a senior state or legal official. ■ the head of the government in some European countries, such as Germany. ■ the presiding judge of a chancery court. ■ the president or chief administrative officer of a university. ■ chiefly Brit. the nonresident honorary head of a university. ■ a bishop's law officer. DERIVATIVES: **chan•cel•lor•ship** |-‚sнip| n.

chan•cre |'kæNGkər; 'sнæNG-| • n. a painless ulcer, particularly one developing on the genitals as a result of syphilis.

chan•dler |'cнæn(d)lər| • n. 1 (also **ship chandler**) a dealer in supplies and equipment for ships and boats. 2 a dealer in household items such as oil, soap, paint, and groceries. ■ a person who makes and sells candles.

change•ling |'cнānjliNG| • n. a child believed to have been secretly substituted by fairies for the parents' real child in infancy. ■ any child secretly substituted for another in infancy.

chan•nel |'cнænl| • v. (**channeled, channeling** ; Brit. **channelled, channelling**) (in spiritualism) serve as a medium for (a spirit): *she channels Ramtha, a 30,000-year-old spirit* | [as adj.] *a channeling session.*

chan•teuse |‚sнän'tœz; 'tœz | • n. a female singer of popular songs, esp. in a nightclub. The male equivalent is a **chanteur**.

chant•ey |'sнæntē| • n. (also **chanty, shanty,** or **sea chantey**) • n. a song with alternating solo and chorus, of a kind originally sung by sailors while performing physical labor together.

cha•os |'kā‚äs| • n. complete disorder and confusion. ■ (in physics) behavior so unpredictable as to appear random, owing to great sensitivity to small changes in conditions. ■ the formless matter supposed to have existed before the creation of the universe.

DERIVATIVES: **chaotic** adj. **chaotically** adv.

chap•ar•ral |‚sнæpə'ræl| • n. vegetation consisting chiefly of tangled shrubs and thorny bushes, characteristic of parts of the American Southwest.

chap•let |'cнæplət| • n. 1 a garland or wreath for a person's head. 2 a string of 55 beads (one third of the rosary number) for counting prayers, or used as a necklace. DERIVATIVES: **chap•let•ed** adj.

chaps |cнæps; sнæps| • plural n. leather pants without a seat, worn by a cowboy over ordinary pants to protect the legs, as in chaparral conditions.

char•gé d'af•faires |‚sнär‚zнə dä'fer | (also **chargé**) • n. (pl. **chargés d'affaires** |sнär 'zā(z)|) a diplomatic official who temporarily takes the place of an ambassador. ■ a state's diplomatic representative in a minor country.

charg•er • n. a large, flat dish; a platter.

cha•ris•ma |kə'rizmə| • n. 1 compelling attractiveness or charm that can inspire devotion in others: *she enchanted guests with her charisma.* 2 (pl. **charismata** |-‚mətə|) (also **charism**) a divinely conferred power or talent.

char•is•mat•ic |‚kærəz'mæṭik| • adj. 1 exercising a compelling charm that inspires devotion in others: *a charismatic leader.* 2 of or relating to the charismatic movement in various Christian churches, which emphasizes talents held to be conferred by the Holy Spirit, such as speaking in tongues and healing of the sick (faith healing). ■ (of a power or talent) divinely conferred: *charismatic prophecy.* • n. an adherent of the charismatic movement. ■ a person who claims divine inspiration. DERIVATIVES: **char•is•mat•i•cal•ly** |-ik(ə)-lē| adv.

cha•ri•va•ri |‚sнivə'rē; 'sнivə‚rē| (also **shivaree**) • n. (pl. **charivaris**) a cacophonous mock serenade, typically performed by a group of people in derision of an unpopular person or in celebration of a marriage. ■ a series of discordant noises.

char•la•tan |'sнärlətən; 'sнärlətn| • n. a person falsely claiming to have a special knowledge or skill; a fraud: *who could buy into this charlatan and his charade?* Cf.: MOUNTEBANK. DERIVATIVES: **char•la•tan•ism** |-lətə‚nizəm; -lətn‚izəm| n. **char•la•tan•ry** |'sнärlə tənrē; -lətnrē| n.

char•nel |'cнärnl| • n. (also **charnel house**) a house or vault in which dead bodies or bones are piled. • adj. associated with death: *I gagged on the charnel stench of the place.*

char•y |'cнerē| • adj. (**charier, chariest**) cautious; wary: *most people are chary of allowing themselves to be photographed.* ■ cautious about the amount one gives or reveals: *he was chary with specifics about the script.* DERIVATIVES: **char•i•ly** |'cнerəlē| adv.

chase • v. [trans.] [usu. as adj.] (**chased**) engrave (metal, or a design on metal): *a minia-*

ture container with a delicately chased floral design.

chasm |ˈkæzəm| • *n.* a deep fissure in the earth, rock, or another surface.

■ a profound difference between people, viewpoints, feelings, etc.: *the chasm between rich and poor.* Cf. SCHISM.
DERIVATIVES: **chas•mic** |ˈkæzmik| *adj.* (rare).

chas•sé |SHæˈsā| • *n.* a gliding step in dancing in which one foot displaces the other. • *v.* (**chasséd, chasséing**) [intrans.] make such a step.

chas•sis |ˈCHæsē; ˈSHæsē| • *n.* (pl. same) the base frame of a motor vehicle or other wheeled conveyance.

■ the outer structural framework of a piece of audio, radio, or computer equipment.

chaste |CHāst| • *adj.* abstaining from extramarital, or from all, sexual intercourse. Cf. CELIBATE; VIRGIN.

■ not having any sexual nature or intention: *a chaste, consoling embrace.* ■ without unnecessary ornamentation; simple or restrained: *the dark, chaste interior was lightened by tile-work.*
DERIVATIVES: **chaste•ly** *adv.* **chaste•ness** *n.* **chas•ti•ty** *n.*

chas•ten |ˈCHāsən| • *v.* [trans.] (usu. be **chastened**) (of a reproof or misfortune) have a restraining or moderating effect on: *the director was somewhat chastened by his recent flop.* | [as adj.] (**chastening**) *a chastening experience.*

■ (esp. of God) discipline; punish.
DERIVATIVES: **chas•ten•er** |ˈCHās(ə)nər| *n.*

chas•tise |CHæsˈtīz| • *v.* [trans.] rebuke or reprimand severely: *he chastised his colleagues for their laziness.*

■ punish, esp. by beating.
DERIVATIVES: **chas•tise•ment** |CHæsˈtīzmənt; ˈCHæstəz-| *n.* **chas•tis•er** |ˈCHæs,tīzər| *n.*

chas•ti•ty |ˈCHæstətē| • *n.* the state or practice of refraining from extramarital, or esp. from all, sexual intercourse: *vows of chastity.*

chas•u•ble |ˈCHæzəbəl; ˈCHæzH-; ˈCHæs-| • *n.* a sleeveless outer vestment worn by a priest when celebrating Mass, typically ornate and having a simple hole for the head.

cha•toy•ant |SHəˈtoiənt| • *adj.* (of a gem, esp. when cut en cabochon) showing a band of bright reflected light caused by aligned impurities in the stone.
DERIVATIVES: **cha•toy•ance** *n.* **cha•toy•an•cy** |-ənsē| *n.*

chat•tel |ˈCHætl| • *n.* (in general use) a personal possession.

■ an item of property other than real estate or a freehold. ■ (also **chattel slave**) a human being treated as a chattel.

chau•tau•qua |SHəˈtôkwə| (also **Chautauqua**) • *n.* a cultural and educational program of lectures, performances, etc., originally held outdoors in the summer.

chau•vin•ism |ˈSHōvə,nizəm| • *n.* exaggerated or aggressive patriotism.

■ excessive or prejudiced loyalty or support for one's own cause, group, or sex: *a bastion of male chauvinism.*

chau•vin•ist |ˈSHōvənist| • *n.* a person displaying aggressive or exaggerated patriotism.

■ a person displaying excessive or prejudiced loyalty or support for a particular cause, group, or sex: *gained a reputation as a religious chauvinist.* ■ (also **male chauvinist**) a man displaying a complacent belief in the superiority of the male sex: *she wrote off all the local males as hopeless chauvinists.* • *adj.* showing or relating to such excessive or prejudiced support or loyalty: *a chauvinist slur.*
DERIVATIVES: **chau•vin•ism** *n.* **chau•vin•is•tic** |,SHōvə'nistik| *adj.* **chau•vin•is•ti•cal•ly** |,SHōvə'nistik(ə)lē| *adv.*

chef-d'œu•vre |SHā ˈdœv(rə); ˈdə(r)v | • *n.* (pl. **chefs-d'œuvre** |ˈdœv(rə); ˈdə(r)v(z) |) a masterpiece.

che•mo•ther•a•py |,kēmō'THerəpē; ,kemō-| • *n.* the treatment of disease by the use of chemical substances, esp. the treatment of cancer by drugs that kill cells.
DERIVATIVES: **che•mo•ther•a•peu•tic** *adj.* **che•mo•ther•a•pist** |-pist| *n.*

che•nille |SHə'nēl| • *n.* a tufted velvety cord or yarn, used for trimming furniture and making carpets and clothing.

■ fabric made from such yarn.

cher•no•zem |ˈCHernə,zHôm; -,zem| • *n.* a fertile black soil rich in humus, with a lighter lime-rich layer beneath. Such soils typically occur in temperate grasslands such as the Russian steppes and North American prairies.

cher•ub |ˈCHerəb| • *n.* (pl. **cherubim**) a winged angelic being described in biblical tradition as attending on God. It is represented in ancient Middle Eastern art as a lion or bull with eagles' wings and a human face, and regarded in traditional Christian angelology as an angel of the second highest order of the ninefold celestial hierarchy. Cf. SERAPH.

■ (pl. **cherubim** |ˈCHer(y)ə,bim| or **cherubs**) a representation of a cherub in art, depicted as a chubby, healthy-looking child with wings. ■ (pl. **cherubs**) a beautiful or innocent-looking child.
DERIVATIVES: **cherubic** *adj.*

chest•y |ˈCHestē| • *adj.* **1** (of a sound) produced deep in the chest: *a chesty growl.* **2** (of a woman) having large or prominent breasts. **3** conceited and arrogant.
DERIVATIVES: **chest•i•ly** |ˈCHestəlē| *adv.* **chest•i•ness** *n.*

chev•a•lier |,SHevə'lir| • *n.* a knight, esp. when mounted on a horse.

■ a chivalrous man. ■ a member of certain orders of knighthood or of modern French orders such as the Legion of Honor.
■ (**Chevalier**) Brit. the title of James (1688–1766) and Charles (1720–88) Stuart, pretenders to the British throne.

chev•ron |ˈSHevrən| • *n.* a line or stripe in the shape of a V or an inverted V, esp. one on the sleeve of a uniform indicating rank or length of service.

■ (in heraldry) a shape in the form of a broad inverted V.

chez |sнā| • *prep.* at the home of (used in imitation of French, often humorously): *I spent one summer chez Grandma.*

chi |kē| (also **qi** or **ki**) • *n.* the circulating life force whose existence and properties are the basis of much Chinese philosophy and medicine.

chi•a•ro•scu•ro |kē,ärə'sk(y)o͞orō; kē,ærə-| • *n.* the treatment of light and shade in drawing and painting.
■ an effect of contrasted light and shadow created by light falling unevenly or from a particular direction on something: *the chiaroscuro of cobbled streets.*

chi•as•mus |kī'æzməs| • *n.* a rhetorical or literary figure in which words, grammatical constructions, or concepts are repeated in reverse order, in the same or a modified form; e.g. 'Poetry is the record of the best and happiest moments of the happiest and best minds.'
DERIVATIVES: **chi•as•tic** |kī'æstik| *adj.*

chic |sнēk| • *adj.* (**chicer, chicest**) elegantly and stylishly fashionable: *your outfit is très chic!* • *n.* stylishness and elegance, typically of a specified kind: *biker chic.*
DERIVATIVES: **chic•ly** *adv.*

chi•cane |sнi'kān; cнi-| • *n.* **1** an artificial narrowing or turn on a road or automobile racecourse. **2** (in card games) a hand without cards of one particular suit; a void. **3** chicanery. • *v.* employ trickery or chicanery.

chi•can•er•y |sнi'kānərē; cнi-| • *n.* the use of trickery to achieve a political, financial, or legal purpose: *political chicanery behind closed doors.*

Chi•ca•no |cнi'känō; sнi-| (fem. **chicana**) • *n.* (pl. **-os**) a person of Mexican origin or descent.

USAGE: The term **Chicano** (derived from the Mexican Spanish *mexicano* 'Mexican'), denoting a Mexican-American male, and the feminine form **Chicana**, became current in the early 1960s. Sometimes spelled with a small *c-*. The plural forms are **Chicanos, Chicanas. Hispanic** is a more generic term denoting persons in the US of Latin-American or Spanish descent. See also **usage** at HISPANIC. See also LATINO.

chi•chi |'sнēsнē; 'cнēcнē| • *adj.* attempting stylish elegance but achieving only an overelaborate affectedness: *the chichi world of Manhattan cultural privilege.* • *n.* pretentious and overelaborate refinement: *the relentless chichi of late-eighties dining.*

chic•le |'cнikəl; 'cнiklē| • *n.* the milky latex of the tropical American sapodilla tree, used to make chewing gum.

chide |cнīd| • *v.* (past **chided** or archaic **chid** |cнid| ; past part. **chided** or archaic **chidden** |'cнidn|) [trans.] scold or rebuke: *she chided him for not replying to her letters* | [with direct speech] *"You mustn't speak like that," she chided gently.*
DERIVATIVES: **chid•er** *n.* **chid•ing•ly** *adv.*

chif•fo•nier |,sнifə'nir| • *n.* **1** a tall chest of drawers, often with a mirror on top. **2** Brit. a low cupboard, sometimes with a raised bookshelf on top.

chi•gnon |'sнēn,yän; sнēn'yän| • *n.* a knot or coil of hair arranged on the back of a woman's head.

chil•blain |'cнil,blān| • *n.* a painful, itching swelling on the skin, typically on a hand or foot, caused by poor circulation in the skin when exposed to cold.
DERIVATIVES: **chil•blained** *adj.*

child•ish |'cнildisн| • *adj.* of, like, or appropriate to a child: *childish enthusiasm.*
■ silly and immature: *a childish outburst.*
DERIVATIVES: **child•ish•ly** *adv.* **child•ish•ness** *n.*

child•like |'cнīld,līk| • *adj.* (of an adult) having good qualities associated with a child: *she speaks with a childlike directness.*

chil•i |'cнilē| (also **chili pepper** or **chile** or Brit.**chilli**) • *n.* (pl. **chilies** or **chiles** or Brit. **chillies**) a small hot-tasting pod of a variety of capsicum (C. annuum), used chopped (and often dried) in sauces, relishes, and spice powders. There are various forms with pods of differing size, color, and strength of flavor, such as cascabels and jalapeños.
■ short for *chili powder*, mixed from powdered chilies and other spices. ■ short for *chili con carne*, a stew made with chilies, beans, and ground beef.

chil•i•ad |'kilē,æd; -əd| • *n.* a thousand (of something).
■ a thousand years; a millennium.

chil•i•ast |'kilē,æst| • *n.* another term for MILLENARIAN.
DERIVATIVES: **chil•i•as•tic** *adj.* **chil•i•asm** |-,æzəm| *n.*

chi•me•ra |kī'mirə; kə-| (also **chimaera**) • *n.* **1** (**Chimera**) (in Greek mythology) a fire-breathing female monster with a lion's head, a goat's body, and a serpent's tail.
■ any mythical animal with parts taken from various animals. **2** a thing that is hoped or wished for but in fact is illusory or impossible to achieve: *the economic sovereignty you claim to defend is a chimera.* **3** an organism containing a mixture of genetically different tissues, formed by processes such as fusion of early embryos, grafting, or mutation: *the sheeplike goat chimera.*
■ a DNA molecule with sequences derived from two or more different organisms, formed by laboratory manipulation.
DERIVATIVES: **chi•mer•ic** |kī'mirik; kə-; -'merik| *adj.* **chi•mer•i•cal** |kī'merikəl; kə-; -'mir-| *adj.* **chi•mer•i•cal•ly** |kī'merik(ə)lē; kə-; -'mir-| *adv.*

chin•less |'cнinlis| • *adj.* (of a person) lacking a well-defined chin.
■ lacking strength of character; ineffectual.

chi•noi•se•rie |,sнēn,wäz(ə)'rē; ,sнēn'wäzə-rē| • *n.* (pl. **-ies**) the imitation or evocation of Chinese motifs and techniques in Western art, furniture, and architecture, esp. in the 18th century.
■ objects or decorations in this style: *a piece of*

chinoiserie | one room has red velvet and chinoiseries.

chi•nook | SHə'nŏŏk; CHə-| • *n.* **1** (also **chinook wind**) a warm dry wind that blows down the east side of the Rocky Mountains at the end of winter. **2** (also **chinook salmon**) a large North Pacific salmon (Oncorhynchus tshawytscha) that is an important commercial food fish.

chintz•y |'CHintsē| • *adj.* (**chintzier, chintziest**) **1** of, like, or decorated with chintz (a printed, multicolored cotton fabric with a glazed surface): *brighten the room with fresh paint and chintzy fabrics.*
■ brightly colorful but gaudy and tasteless. **2** miserly: *a chintzy salary increase.*
DERIVATIVES: **chintz•i•ly** |'CHintsəlē| *adv.* **chintz•i•ness** *n.*

Chip•e•wy•an |,CHipə'wīən| • *n.* (pl. same or **Chipewyans**) **1** a member of a Dene (native) people of northwestern Canada. Do not confuse with Chippewa (Ojibwa). **2** the Athabaskan language of this people. • *adj.* of or relating to this people or their language.

chi•rog•ra•phy |kī'rägrəfē| • *n.* handwriting, esp. as distinct from typography. Cf. CALLIGRAPHY.
DERIVATIVES: **chi•ro•graph•ic** |,kīrə'græfik| *adj.*

chi•ro•man•cy |'kīrə,mænsē| • *n.* the prediction of a person's future from the lines on the palms of his or her hands; palmistry.

chi•ro•prac•tic |,kīrə'præktik| • *n.* a system of nonscientific medicine based on the diagnosis and manipulative treatment of misalignments of the joints, esp. those of the spinal column, which are held to cause other disorders by affecting the nerves, muscles, and organs. Cf. OSTEOPATHY.
DERIVATIVES: **chi•ro•prac•tor** |'kīrə,præktər| *n.*

chit |CHit| • *n.* a short official note, memorandum, or voucher, typically recording a sum owed.

chit•ter•lings |'CHitlənz| (also **chitlins** or **chitlings**) • *plural n.* the smaller intestines of a pig, cooked for food.

chiv•al•rous |'SHivəlrəs| • *adj.* (of a man or his behavior) courteous and gallant, esp. toward women.
■ of or relating to the historical notion of chivalry.
DERIVATIVES: **chiv•al•rous•ly** *adv.*

chiv•al•ry |'SHivəlrē| • *n.* the medieval knightly system with its religious, moral, and social code.
■ knights, noblemen, and horsemen collectively: *I fought against the cream of French chivalry.* ■ the combination of qualities expected of an ideal knight, esp. courage, honor, courtesy, justice, and a readiness to help the weak. ■ courteous behavior, esp. that of a man toward women: *their relations with women were models of chivalry and restraint.*
DERIVATIVES: **chi•val•ric** |SHə'vælrik| *adj.*

chlo•ro•fluor•o•car•bon |,klôrō,flŏŏrō'kärbən| (abbr.: **CFC**) • *n.* any of a class of compounds of carbon, hydrogen, chlorine, and

fluorine, typically gases used chiefly in refrigerants and aerosol propellants. They are harmful to the ozone layer in the earth's atmosphere owing to the release of chlorine atoms upon exposure to ultraviolet radiation.

chlo•ro•phyll |'klôrə,fil| • *n.* a green pigment, present in all green plants and in cyanobacteria, responsible for the absorption of light to provide energy for photosynthesis.
DERIVATIVES: **chlo•ro•phyl•lous** |,klôrə'filəs| *adj.*

cho•co•la•tier |,SHôkələ'tyä; ,CHÔ-| • *n.* (pl. or pronunc. same) a maker or seller of chocolate.

USAGE: *Chocolatier* is used primarily by higher-priced sellers of chocolate.

chol•er |'kälər| • *n.* (in medieval science and medicine) one of the four bodily humors, identified with BILE, believed to be associated with a peevish or irascible temperament.
■ anger or irascibility.

chol•er•ic |'kälərik; kə'lerik| • *adj.* bad-tempered or irritable.
■ influenced by or predominating in the supposed humor choler: *a choleric disposition.*
DERIVATIVES: **chol•er•i•cal•ly** |-ik(ə)lē| *adv.*

cho•les•ter•ol |kə'lestə,rôl; -,rōl| • *n.* a compound found in most body tissues, including the blood and the nerves. Cholesterol and its derivatives are important constituents of cell membranes and precursors of other steroid compounds, but high concentrations in the blood (**serum cholesterol**) are thought to promote atherosclerosis (clogging of the arteries by fatty deposits).

cho•rale |kə'ræl; -'räl| • *n.* **1** a musical composition (or part of one) consisting of or resembling a harmonized version of a simple, stately hymn tune. **2** a choir or choral society.

chord |kôrd| • *n.* a group of (typically three or more) musical notes sounded together, as a basis of harmony: *the triumphal opening chords | a G major chord.* Cf. INTERVAL. • *v.* [intrans.] [usu. as n.] (**chording**) play, sing, or arrange notes in chords.
DERIVATIVES: **chord•al** |'kôrdl| *adj.*

cho•re•a |kə'rēə| • *n.* a neurological disorder characterized by jerky involuntary movements affecting esp. the shoulders, hips, and face. **Huntington's chorea** involves progressive degeneration of brain cells. **Sydenham's chorea** (also called *St. Vitus's dance*) is a neurological form of rheumatic fever.

cho•re•og•ra•phy |,kôrē'ägrəfē| • *n.* the sequence of steps and movements in dance or figure skating, esp. in a ballet or other staged dance: *the lively choreography reflects the themes of the original play.*
■ the art or practice of designing such sequences. ■ the written notation for such a sequence. ■ arrangement, as of an event or ritual: *the masterful choreography of the convention.*
DERIVATIVES: **cho•re•o•graph•ic** |-ə'græfik| *adj.* **cho•re•o•graph•i•cal•ly** |-ə'græfik(ə)lē| *adv.*

cho•rog•ra•phy |kə'rägrəfē| • *n.* the systematic description and mapping of regions or districts.
DERIVATIVES: **cho•rog•ra•pher** |-fər| *n.* **cho•ro•graph•ic** |ˌkôrə'græfik| *adj.*

chres•tom•a•thy |kre'stäməTHē| • *n.* (pl. **-ies**) a selection of passages from an author or authors, designed to help in learning a language.

chrism |'krizəm| • *n.* a mixture of oil and balsam, consecrated and used for anointing at baptism and in other rites of Catholic, Orthodox, and Anglican churches.

chris•om |'krizəm| • *n.* a white robe put on a child at baptism.

Chris•tian |'krisCHən| • *adj.* of, relating to, or professing Christianity or its teachings: *the Christian Church.*
■ having or showing qualities traditionally associated with Christians, esp. those of decency, kindness, and fairness. ■ of or relating to places, etc., dominated by Christianity: *Christian lands.* • *n.* a person who has received Christian baptism or is a believer in Jesus Christ and his teachings.
DERIVATIVES: **Chris•tian•i•za•tion** |ˌkris-CHənə'zāSHən| *n.* **Chris•tian•ize** |-ˌnīz| *v.* **Chris•tian•ly** *adv.*

chro•mat•ic |krō'mæṭik| • *adj.* **1** relating to or using notes not belonging to the diatonic scale of the key in which a musical passage is written.
■ (of a scale) ascending or descending by half tones. ■ (of an instrument) able to play all the notes of the chromatic scale. Cf. DIATONIC. **2** of, relating to, or produced by color.
DERIVATIVES: **chro•mat•i•cal•ly** |-ik(ə)-lē| *adv.* **chro•mat•i•cism** |-əˌsizəm| *n.*

chrome |krōm| • *n.* a decorative or protective finish on motor-vehicle fittings and other objects made from the lustrous metallic element chromium: [as adj.] *a chrome bumper.*
■ [as adj.] denoting compounds or alloys of chromium: *chrome dyes.*

chro•mo•some |'krōməˌsōm| • *n.* Biology a threadlike structure of DNA or RNA and protein found in the nucleus of most living cells, carrying genetic information in the form of genes.
DERIVATIVES: **chro•mo•so•mal** |ˌkrōmə'sōməl| *adj.*

chron•ic |'kränik| • *adj.* (of an illness) persisting for a long time or constantly recurring: *chronic bronchitis.* Cf. ACUTE.
■ (of a person) having such an illness: *a chronic asthmatic.* ■ (of a problem) long-lasting and difficult to eradicate: *the school suffers from chronic overcrowding.* ■ (of a person) having a particular bad habit: *a chronic liar.*
DERIVATIVES: **chron•i•cal•ly** |-ik(ə)lē| *adv.* **chro•nic•i•ty** |krä'nisəṭē| *n.*

USAGE: **Chronic** is often used to mean 'habitual, inveterate,' e.g., *a chronic liar.* Some consider this use incorrect. The precise meaning of **chronic** is 'persisting for a long time,' and it is used chiefly of illnesses or other problems.

chron•i•cle |'kränikəl| • *n.* a factual written account of important or historical events in the order of their occurrence.
■ a work of fiction or nonfiction that describes a particular series of events. • *v.* [trans.] record (a related series of events) in a factual and detailed way: *his work chronicles 20th-century displacement and migration.*
DERIVATIVES: **chron•i•cler** |-iklər| *n.*

chro•nol•o•gy |krə'näləjē| • *n.* (pl. **-ies**) the study of historical records to establish the dates of past events.
■ the arrangement of events or dates in the order of their occurrence: *the novel abandons the conventions of normal chronology.* ■ a table or document displaying such an arrangement.
DERIVATIVES: **chron•o•log•i•cal** *adj.* **chro•nol•o•gist** |-jist| *n.*

chro•nom•e•try |krə'nämətrē| • *n.* the science of accurate time measurement.
DERIVATIVES: **chron•o•met•ric** |ˌkränə-'metrik; ˌkrō-| *adj.* **chron•o•met•ri•cal** |ˌkränə'metrikəl; ˌkrō-| *adj.* **chron•o•met•ri•cal•ly** |ˌkränə'metrik(ə)lē| *adv.*

chrys•a•lis |'krisələs| • *n.* (pl. **chrysalises**) a quiescent insect PUPA, esp. of a butterfly or moth.
■ the hard outer case of this, esp. after being discarded. ■ a preparatory or transitional state: *she emerged from the chrysalis of self-conscious adolescence.*

chthon•ic |'THänik| (also **chthonian**) • *adj.* concerning, belonging to, or inhabiting the underworld: *a chthonic deity.*

churl•ish |'CHərliSH| • *adj.* rude in a mean-spirited and surly way: *it seems churlish to complain.*
DERIVATIVES: **churl•ish•ly** *adv.* **churl•ish•ness** *n.*

churn |CHərn| • *v.* [trans.] (of a broker) encourage frequent turnover of (investments) in order to generate commissions.

chutz•pah |'hŏŏtspə; 'KHŏŏtspə; -spä| (also **chutzpa** or **hutzpah** or **hutzpa**) • *n.* shameless audacity; impudence.

chyle |kīl| • *n.* a milky fluid consisting of fat droplets and lymph. It drains from minute vessels in the small intestine into the lymphatic system during digestion.
DERIVATIVES: **chy•lous** |'kīləs| *adj.*

chyme |kīm| • *n.* the pulpy acidic fluid that passes from the stomach to the small intestine, consisting of gastric juices and partly digested food.
DERIVATIVES: **chy•mous** |'kīməs| *adj.*

cia•o |CHow| • *exclam.* used as a greeting at meeting or parting.

ci•bo•ri•um |sə'bôrēəm| • *n.* (pl. **ciboria** |-rēə|) **1** a receptacle shaped like a shrine or a cup with an arched cover, used in the Christian Church for the reservation of (a portion of) the Eucharist. **2** a canopy over an altar in a church, standing on four pillars.

cic•a•trix |'sikəˌtriks| (also **cicatrice**) • *n.* (pl. **cicatrices** |ˌsikə'trīsēz; sə'kātrəˌsēz|) the scar of a healed wound.
■ a scar on the bark of a tree. ■ a mark on a

plant stem left after a leaf or other part has become detached.

DERIVATIVES: **cic•a•tri•cial** |ˌsikəˈtriSHəl| adj.

cic•e•ro•ne |ˌsisəˈrōnē; ˌCHēCHə-| • n. (pl. **ciceroni** |-nē| pronunc. same) a guide who gives information about antiquities and places of interest to sightseers.

Cic•e•ro•ni•an |ˌsisəˈrōnēən| • adj. characteristic of the work and thought of Cicero (1st cent. BC). The Roman politician and orator.

■ (of a piece of speech or writing) in an eloquent and rhythmic style similar to that of Cicero.

ci-de•vant |ˌsē dəˈväN | • adj. [attrib.] from or in an earlier time (used to indicate that someone or something once possessed a specified characteristic but no longer does so): her cidevant pupil, now her lover.

cinc•ture |ˈsiNG(k)CHər| • n. **1** a girdle or belt. **2** (in architecture) a ring at either end of a column shaft.

cin•e•ast |ˈsinēˌæst| (also **cinéaste** or **cineaste**) • n. a filmmaker.

■ an enthusiast for or devotee of movies or filmmaking.

cin•e•rar•i•um |ˌsinəˈrerēəm| • n. (pl. **cinerariums**) a place where the ashes of the cremated dead are kept.

DERIVATIVES: **cin•e•rar•y** |ˈsinəˌrerē| adj.

ci•ne•re•ous |səˈnirēəs| • adj. (esp. of hair or feathers) ash-gray.

cin•que•cen•to |ˌCHiNGkwiˈCHentō| • n. (**the cinquecento**) the 16th century as a period of Italian art, architecture, or literature, with a reversion to classical forms.

ci•pher |ˈsīfər| (also **cypher**) • n. **1** a secret or disguised way of writing; a code: cryptic notes in a cipher | the information may be given in cipher.

■ a thing written in such a code. ■ a key to such a code. **2** a zero; a figure 0.

■ a person or thing of no importance, esp. a person who does the bidding of others and seems to have no will of his or her own. **3** a monogram. • v. **1** [trans.] put (a message) into secret writing; encode. **2** [intrans.] do arithmetic.

cir•ca•di•an |sərˈkādēən| • adj. (of biological processes) recurring naturally on a twenty-four-hour cycle, even in the absence of fluctuations of light: a circadian rhythm.

cir•cu•i•tous |sərˈkyo͞oətəs| • adj. (of a route or journey) longer than the most direct way: the canal followed a circuitous route | a circuitous line of reasoning.

DERIVATIVES: **cir•cu•i•tous•ly** adv. **cir•cu•i•tous•ness** n.

cir•cuit rid•er • n. a clergyman who traveled on horseback from church to church, esp. within a rural Methodist circuit in the 19th cent.

■ a public official or service provider required to travel extensively within an area.

cir•cum•am•bi•ent |ˌsərkəmˈæmbēənt| • adj. surrounding: he could not see them clearly by reason of the circumambient water.

DERIVATIVES: **cir•cum•am•bi•ence** n. **cir•cum•am•bi•en•cy** n.

cir•cum•cise |ˈsərkəmˌsīz| • v. [trans.] cut off the foreskin of (a young boy or man, esp. a baby) as a religious rite, esp. in Judaism and Islam, or as a medical treatment.

■ cut off the clitoris, and sometimes the labia, of (a girl or young woman) as a traditional practice among some peoples.

DERIVATIVES: **cir•cum•ci•sion** n.

cir•cum•flex |ˈsərkəmˌfleks| • n. (also **circumflex accent**) a mark (ˆ) placed over a vowel in some languages to indicate contraction, length, or pitch or tone. • adj. (of a body part) bending around something else; curved: circumflex coronary arteries.

cir•cum•lo•cu•tion |ˌsərkəmlōˈkyo͞oSHən| • n. the use of many words where fewer would do, esp. in a deliberate attempt to be vague or evasive: his admission came after years of circumlocution | he used a number of poetic circumlocutions. Cf. PERIPHRASIS.

DERIVATIVES: **cir•cum•loc•u•to•ry** |-ˈläkyəˌtôrē| adj.

cir•cum•scribe |ˈsərkəmˌskrīb| • v. [trans.] (often **be circumscribed**) **1** restrict (something) within limits: their movements were strictly monitored and circumscribed. **2** draw (a figure) around another, touching it at points but not cutting it.

DERIVATIVES: **cir•cum•scrib•er** n. **cir•cum•scrip•tion** |ˌsərkəmˈskripSHən| n.

cir•cum•spect |ˈsərkəmˌspekt| • adj. wary and unwilling to take risks: the officials were very circumspect in their statements.

DERIVATIVES: **cir•cum•spec•tion** |ˌsərkəmzˈpekSHən| n. **cir•cum•spect•ly** adv.

cir•cum•stan•tial |ˌsərkəmˈstænCHəl; ˈsərkəmˈstæn(t)SHəl| • adj. **1** (of evidence or a legal case) pointing toward proof by inference from known facts rather than by introduction of direct evidence. **2** (of a description) containing full details: the picture was circumstantial and therefore convincing.

DERIVATIVES: **cir•cum•stan•ti•al•i•ty** |-ˌstænCHēˈælətē| n. **cir•cum•stan•tial•ly** adv.

cir•cum•vent |ˌsərkəmˈvent| • v. [trans.] find a way around (an obstacle).

■ overcome (a problem or difficulty), typically in a clever and surreptitious way: terrorists found the airport checks easy to circumvent. ■ deceive; outwit: he circumvented them with one of his stories.

DERIVATIVES: **cir•cum•ven•tion** |ˌsərkəmˈvenCHən| n.

cirque |sərk| • n. **1** a half-open steep-sided hollow at the head of a valley or on a mountainside, formed by glacial erosion. **2** a ring, circlet, or circle.

cir•rho•sis |səˈrōsəs| • n. a chronic disease of the liver marked by degeneration of cells, inflammation, and fibrous thickening of tissue. It is typically a result of alcoholism or hepatitis.

DERIVATIVES: **cir•rhot•ic** |səˈrätik| adj.

cit•a•del |ˈsitədl; ˈsidəˌdel| • n. a fortress, typically on high ground, protecting or dominating a city.

ci•ta•tion |sī'tāsHən| • *n.* **1** a quotation from or reference to a book, paper, or author, esp. in a scholarly work.
■ a mention of a praiseworthy act or achievement in an official report, esp. that of a member of the armed forces in wartime. ■ a note accompanying an award, describing the reasons for it: *the Nobel citation noted that the discovery would be useful for energy conversion technology.* ■ a reference to a former tried legal case, used as guidance in the trying of comparable cases or in support of an argument. **2** a legal summons: *a traffic citation.*

cite |sīt| • *v.* [trans.] (often **be cited**) **1** quote (a passage, book, or author) as evidence for or justification of an argument or statement, esp. in a scholarly work.
■ mention as an example: *medics have been cited as a key example of a modern breed of technical expert.* ■ praise (someone, typically a member of the armed forces) for a courageous act in an official dispatch. **2** summon (someone) to appear in a court of law: *the summons cited four defendants.* • *n.* a citation.
DERIVATIVES: **cit•a•ble** *adj.*

cit•i•zen |'sitizən; -sən| • *n.* a legally recognized national or subject of a state or nation, either native or naturalized.
■ an inhabitant of a particular town or city: *the **citizens of** Los Angeles.*
DERIVATIVES: **cit•i•zen•ry** |-rē| *n.:* a body of citizens; citizens collectively. **cit•i•zen•ship** |-,sHip| *n.*

cit•ron |'sitrən| • *n.* a shrubby Asian tree(*Citrus medica*) that bears large fruits similar to lemons, but with less acid flesh and thicker, more fragrant peels.
■ the fruit of this tree.

cit•ron•el•la |,sitrə'nelə| • *n.* **1** (also **citronella oil**) a fragrant natural oil used as an insect repellent and in perfume and soap manufacture. **2** the South Asian grass (*Cymbopogon nardus*) from which this oil is obtained.

civ•et |'sivət| • *n.* (also **civet cat**) a slender nocturnal carnivorous mammal (of the family Viverridae) with a barred and spotted coat and well-developed anal scent glands, native to Africa and Asia.
■ a strong musky perfume obtained from the secretions of the civet's scent glands.

civ•il |'sivəl| • *adj.* **1** [attrib.] of or relating to ordinary citizens and their concerns, as distinct from military or ecclesiastical matters: *civil aviation.*
■ (of disorder or conflict) occurring between citizens of the same country. ■ (in law) relating to private relations between members of a community; noncriminal: *a civil action.* **2** courteous and polite: *we tried to be **civil to** him.* **3** (of time measurement or a point in time) fixed by custom or law rather than being natural or astronomical: *civil twilight starts at sunset.*
DERIVATIVES: **civ•il•ly** *adv.*

ci•vil•i•ty |sə'vilətē| • *n.* (pl. **-ies**) conventional politeness and courtesy in behavior or speech: *I hope we can treat each other with civility and respect.*
■ (**civilities**) polite remarks used in formal conversation: *she was exchanging civilities with his mother.*

civ•il law • *n.* the system of law concerned with private relations between members of a community rather than criminal, military, or religious affairs.

cla•dis•tics |klə'distiks| • *plural n.* [treated as sing.] a method of classification of animals and plants according to the proportion of measurable characteristics that they have in common. It is assumed that the higher the proportion of characteristics two organisms share, the more recently they diverged from a common ancestor.
DERIVATIVES: **clad•ism** |'klăd,izəm| *n.* **cla•dis•tic** *adj.*

clair•au•di•ence |kler'ôdēəns| • *n.* the supposed faculty of perceiving, as if by hearing, what is inaudible.
DERIVATIVES: **clair•au•di•ent** *adj.* & *n.*

clair•voy•ance |kler'voiəns| • *n.* the supposed faculty of seeing things or events in the future or beyond normal sensory contact: *she stared at the card as if she could contact its writer by clairvoyance.*
■ keenness of mental perception; exceptional insight.
DERIVATIVES: **clair•voy•ant** *n.*, *adj.*

cla•mant |'klāmənt; 'klæm-| • *adj.* forcing itself urgently on the attention: *the proper use of biotechnology has become a clamant question.*
DERIVATIVES: **cla•mant•ly** *adv.*

clam•my |'klæmē| • *adj.* (**clammier, clammiest**) unpleasantly damp and sticky or slimy to touch: *his skin felt cold and clammy.*
■ (of air or atmosphere) damp, cool, and unpleasant: *the clammy atmosphere of the cave.*
DERIVATIVES: **clam•mi•ly** |'klæməlē| *adv.* **clam•mi•ness** *n.*

USAGE: *Clammy* is sometimes confused with *muggy*, which means "*warm* and humid."

clam•or |'klæmər| (Brit. **clamour**) • *n.* [in sing.] a loud and confused noise, esp. that of people shouting vehemently: *the questions rose to a clamor.*
■ a strongly expressed protest or demand, typically from a large number of people: *the growing **clamor for** more police on the beat.* • *v.* [intrans.] (of a group of people) shout loudly and insistently: *the surging crowds **clamored** for attention.*
■ make a vehement protest or demand: *scientists are **clamoring for** a ban on the pesticide.*
DERIVATIVES: **clam•or•ous** |-ərəs| *adj.* **clam•or•ous•ly** |-ərəslē| *adv.* **clam•or•ous•ness** |-ərəsnəs| *n.*

clan•des•tine |klæn'destən; -,tīn; -,tēn; 'klændəs-| • *adj.* kept secret or done secretively, esp. because illicit: *she deserved better than these clandestine meetings.*
DERIVATIVES: **clan•des•tine•ly** *adv.* **clan•des•tin•i•ty** |,klændes'tinitē| *n.*

clang•or |'klæNGər| (Brit **clangour**) • *n.* [in

sing.] a continuous loud banging or ringing sound: *the deafing clangor of steam hammers.*
DERIVATIVES: **clang•or•ous** | ˈklæNGərəs | *adj.* **clang•or•ous•ly** | ˈklæNGərəslē | *adv.*

claque | klæk | • *n.* a group of people hired to applaud (or heckle) a performer or public speaker.
■ a group of sycophantic followers: *the president was surrounded by a claque of scheming bureaucrats.*

clar•i•on | ˈklærēən | • *n.* a shrill, narrow-tubed war trumpet used in ancient times.
■ an organ stop with a quality resembling that of such a trumpet. • *adj.* loud and clear: *clarion trumpeters.*
PHRASES: **clarion call** a strongly expressed demand or request for action: *a clarion call to young people to join the party.*

clas•sic | ˈklæsik | • *adj.* judged over a period of time to be of the highest quality and outstanding of its kind: *a classic novel* | *a classic car.*
■ (of a garment or design) of a simple elegant style not greatly subject to changes in fashion: *this classic navy blazer.* ■ remarkably and instructively typical: *I had all the classic symptoms of flu.* • *n.* **1** a work of art of recognized and established value: *his books have become classics.*
■ a garment of a simple, elegant, and long-lasting style. ■ a thing that is memorable and a very good example of its kind: *yesterday's game will be remembered as a classic.* **2** (usu. **Classics**) a school subject that involves the study of ancient Greek and Latin literature, philosophy, and history.
■ (usu. **the classics**) the works of ancient Greek and Latin writers and philosophers. **3** a major sports tournament or competition, as in golf or tennis: *the Bob Hope Desert Classic.*

USAGE: Traditionally, **classic** means 'typical; excellent as an example; timeless,' and **classical** means 'of (esp. Greek or Roman) antiquity.' Thus: *John Ford directed many classic Westerns. The temple was built in the classical style.* Great art is considered **classic**, not **classical**, unless it is created in the forms of antiquity. *Classical music* is formal and sophisticated music adhering to certain stylistic principles, esp. European symphonic and chamber music of the late 18th and early 19th century, but *a classic folk song* is one that well expresses its culture. A *classical education* exposes a student to *classical* literature, history, and languages (esp. Latin and Greek), but the study of Greek and Latin languages and their literatures is also referred to as *classics*, as in *I majored in classics.*

clas•si•cal | ˈklæsikəl | • *adj.* **1** of or relating to ancient Greek or Latin literature, art, or culture: *classical mythology.*
■ (of art or architecture) influenced by ancient Greek or Roman forms or principles. ■ (of language) having the form used by the ancient standard authors: *classical Latin.*
■ based on the study of ancient Greek and

Latin: *a classical education.* **2** (typically of a form of art) regarded as representing an exemplary standard; traditional and long-established in form or style: *a classical ballet.* **3** of or relating to the first significant period of an area of study: *classical Marxism.*
■ relating to or based upon concepts and theories in physics that preceded the theories of relativity and quantum mechanics; Newtonian: *classical physics.*
DERIVATIVES: **clas•si•cal•ism** | -ˌlizəm | *n.* **clas•si•cal•i•ty** | ˌklæsəˈkælətē | *n.* **clas•si•cal•ly** | -ik(ə)lē | *adv.*

clas•si•cism | ˈklæsəˌsizəm | • *n.* the following of ancient Greek or Roman principles and style in art and literature, generally associated with harmony, restraint, and adherence to recognized standards of form and craftsmanship, esp. from the Renaissance to the 18th century. Often contrasted with RO-MANTICISM.
■ the following of traditional and long-established theories or styles.

class•ism | ˈklæsˌizəm | • *n.* prejudice against or in favor of people belonging to a particular social class.
DERIVATIVES: **class•ist** *adj. & n.*

clas•tic | ˈklæstik | • *adj.* denoting rocks composed of broken pieces of older rocks.

claus•tral | ˈklôstrəl | • *adj.* of or relating to a cloister or religious house: *claustral buildings.*
■ enveloping; confining: *this claustral heat.*

claus•tro•pho•bi•a | ˌklôstrəˈfōbēə | • *n.* extreme or irrational fear of confined places.
DERIVATIVES: **claus•tro•phobe** | ˈklôstrə ˌfōb | *n.* **claus•tro•pho•bic** *adj.*

cleave[1] | klēv | • *v.* (past **clove** | klōv | or **cleft** | kleftkleft | or **cleaved** | klēvd | ; past part. **cloven** | ˈklōvən | or **cleft** or **cleaved**) [trans.] split or sever (something), esp. along a natural line or grain: *a large ax used to cleave wood for the fire.*
■ split (a molecule) by breaking a particular chemical bond. ■ make a way through (something) forcefully, as if by splitting it apart: *they watched a swan cleave the smooth water* | [intrans.] *an unstoppable warrior clove through their ranks.* ■ [intrans.] (of a cell) divide: *the egg cleaves to form a cluster of cells.*
DERIVATIVES: **cleav•a•ble** *adj.*

cleave[2] • *v.* [intrans.] (**cleave to**) stick fast to: *Rose's mouth was dry, her tongue cleaving to the roof of her mouth.*
■ adhere strongly to (a particular pursuit or belief): *part of why we cleave to sports is that in them excellence is so measurable.* ■ become very strongly involved with or emotionally attached to (someone): *it was his choice to cleave to the Roosevelts.*

cleft | kleft | past participle of CLEAVE[1]. • *adj.* split, divided, or partially divided into two: *a cleft chin.* | *a cleft lip.*

clem•en•cy | ˈklemənsē | • *n.* mildness in the exercise of authority or power; mercy; lenience: *an appeal for clemency.*

clem•ent | ˈklemənt | • *adj.* **1** (of weather) mild. **2** (of a person or a person's actions) merciful.

clere•sto•ry |ˈklir,stôrē| (also **clearstory**) • n. (pl. **-ies**) the upper part of the nave, choir, and transepts of a large church, containing a series of windows. It is clear of the roofs of the aisles and admits light to the central parts of the building.
■ such a series of windows in a church or similar windows in another building. ■ a raised section of roof running down the center of a railroad car, with small windows or ventilators.

cler•ic |ˈklerik| • n. a priest or minister of a Christian church.
■ a priest or religious leader in any religion.

cler•i•cal |ˈklerikəl| • adj. 1 (of a job or person) concerned with or relating to work in an office, esp. routine documentation and administrative tasks: she felt stifled by clerical work. 2 of or relating to the clergy: attired in his clerical outfit.
DERIVATIVES: **cler•i•cal•ism** |-,lizəm| n. (in sense 2). **cler•i•cal•ist** |-ist| n. (in sense 2). **cler•i•cal•ly** |-ik(ə)lē| adv.

cli•ché |klēˈsHā kli-; ˈklēˌsHā| (also **cliche**) • n. a phrase or opinion that is overused and betrays a lack of original thought: the old cliché "one man's meat is another man's poison."
■ a very predictable or unoriginal thing or person.

cli•ent |ˈklīənt| • n. 1 a person or organization using the services of a lawyer or other professional person or company: insurance tailor-made to a client's requirements.
■ a person receiving social or medical services: a client referred for counseling. ■ (also **client state**) a nation that is dependent on another, more powerful nation. 2 (in a network) a desktop computer or workstation that is capable of obtaining information and applications from a server.
■ (also **client application** or **program**) a program that is capable of obtaining a service provided by another program. 3 (in ancient Rome) a plebeian under the protection of a patrician.
■ a dependent; a hanger-on.
DERIVATIVES: **cli•ent•ship** |-,sHip| n.

cli•en•tele |,klīən,tel; ,klē-| • n. [treated as sing. or pl.] clients collectively: the doctor has an upscale clientele.
■ the customers of a shop, bar, or place of entertainment: the dancers don't mix with the clientele.

cli•mac•ter•ic |klīˈmæktərik; ,klī,mækˈterik| • n. a critical period or event: the first real climacteric in twentieth-century poetry.
■ the period of life when fertility and sexual activity are in decline; (in women) menopause.
■ the ripening period of certain fruits such as apples, involving increased metabolism and only possible while still on the tree. • adj. having extreme and far-reaching implications or results; critical: so climacteric a weapon as nerve gas.
■ occurring at, characteristic of, or undergoing the climacteric; (in women) menopausal.
■ (of a fruit) undergoing a climacteric.

cli•mac•tic |klīˈmæktik; klə-| • adj. (of an action, event, or scene) exciting or thrilling and acting as a climax to a series of events: the film's climactic scenes.
DERIVATIVES: **cli•mac•ti•cal•ly** |-ik(ə)lē| adv.

cli•mate |ˈklīmit| • n. the weather conditions prevailing in an area in general or over a long period: our cold, wet climate.
■ a region with particular prevailing weather conditions: vacationing in a warm climate.
■ the prevailing trend of public opinion or of another aspect of public life: the current economic climate.
DERIVATIVES: **cli•mat•ic** |klīˈmætik| adj. **cli•mat•i•cal** |klīˈmætikəl| adj. **cli•mat•i•cal•ly** |klīˈmætik(ə)lē| adv.

clime |klīm| • n. (usu. **climes**) a region considered with reference to its climate: Florida and other sunny climes.

clin•ic |ˈklinik| • n. 1 a place or hospital department where outpatients are given medical treatment or advice, esp. of a specialist nature: a mental health clinic.
■ an occasion or time when such treatment or advice is given: we're now holding regular clinics. ■ a gathering at a hospital bedside for the teaching of medicine or surgery. 2 a conference or short course on a particular subject: a ski clinic.

cli•ni•cian |kləˈnisHən| • n. a doctor having direct contact with and responsibility for patients, rather than one involved with theoretical or laboratory studies.

clique |klēk; klik| • n. a small group of people with shared interests or other features in common who spend time together and do not readily allow others to join them.
DERIVATIVES: **cli•quish** adj. **cli•quish•ness** n.

clit•o•ri•dec•to•my |,klidərəˈdektəmē| • n. (pl. **-ies**) excision of the clitoris; female circumcision.

clit•o•ris |ˈklitərəs| • n. a small sensitive and erectile part of the female genitals at the front end of the vulva.
DERIVATIVES: **clit•o•ral** |ˈklitərəl| adj.

clo•a•ca |klōˈākə| • n. (pl. **cloacae** |-,kē; -,sē|) a common cavity at the end of the digestive tract for the release of both excretory and genital products in vertebrates (except most mammals) and certain invertebrates.
■ a sewer.
DERIVATIVES: **clo•a•cal** adj.

cloi•son•né |,kloizəˈnā ,klwäz-| (also **cloisonné enamel**) • n. enamelwork in which the different colors are separated by strips of flattened wire placed edgewise on a metal backing.

clois•ter |ˈkloistər| • n. a covered walk in a convent, monastery, college, or cathedral, typically with a wall on one side and a colonnade open to a quadrangle on the other.
■ (**the cloister**) monastic life: he was inclined more to the cloister than the sword. ■ a convent or monastery. ■ any place or position of seclusion: college is a cloister apart from the cares of the world. • v. [trans.] seclude or shut up in or as if in a convent or monastery: they clois-

tered their children in boarding schools | *she cloisters herself at home.*
DERIVATIVES: **clois•tered** adj. **clois•tral** |ˈkloistrəl| adj.

clone |klōn| • n. a group of organisms or cells produced asexually from one ancestor or stock, to which they are genetically identical. ■ an individual organism or cell so produced. ■ a person or thing regarded as identical to another: *successful women don't want to be male clones.* ■ a microcomputer designed to simulate exactly the operation of another, typically more expensive, model: *an IBM PC clone.* • v. [trans.] propagate (an organism or cell) as a clone. ■ make an identical copy of. ■ replicate (a fragment of DNA placed in an organism) so that there is enough to analyze or use in protein production. ■ illegally copy the security codes from (a cell phone) to one or more others as a way of obtaining free calls.
DERIVATIVES: **clon•al** |ˈklōnl| adj.

closed shop • n. a place of work where all employees must belong to a labor union.

closeted | | • adj. keeping something secret, esp. the fact of being homosexual: *among those who voted against it were some closeted gays.* | *he remained closeted through his twenties.*

clo•sure |ˈklōzHər| • n. an act or process of closing something, esp. an institution, thoroughfare, or frontier, or of being closed: *road closures* | *hospitals that face closure.* ■ a thing that closes or seals something, such as a cap or zipper. ■ a resolution or conclusion to a work or process: *he brings modernistic closure to his narrative.* ■ the state of arriving at a sense of completion, or of coming to terms with an emotional loss: *he felt that he couldn't obtain closure without seeing her again.*

Clo•tho |ˈklōTHō| one of the three Fates of Greek mythology, the one who spins the thread of life.

clo•ture |ˈklōCHər| • n. [mass noun] (in a legislative assembly) a procedure for ending a debate and taking a vote: [as adj.] *a cloture motion.* • v. [trans.] apply cloture to (a debate or speaker) in a legislative assembly.

cloy |kloi| • v. [trans.] [usu. as adj.] (**cloying**) disgust or sicken (someone) with an excess of sweetness, richness, or sentiment: *a romantic, rather cloying story* | *a curious bittersweetness that cloys the senses* | *the first long sip gives a malty taste that never cloys.*
DERIVATIVES: **cloy•ing•ly** adv.

co•ag•u•late |kōˈægyəˌlāt| • v. [intrans.] (of a fluid, esp. blood) change to a solid or semisolid state: *blood had coagulated around the edges of the wound.* ■ [trans.] cause (a fluid) to change to a solid or semisolid state: *epinephrine coagulates the blood.*
DERIVATIVES: **co•ag•u•la•ble** |-ləbəl| adj. **co•ag•u•lant** n. **co•ag•u•la•tion** |kōˌægyəˈlāsHən| n. **co•ag•u•la•tive** |-ˌlātiv| adj. **co•ag•u•la•tor** |-ˌlātər| n.

co•a•lesce |ˌkōəˈles| • v. [intrans.] come together and form one mass or whole: *the puddles had coalesced into shallow streams* | [with infinitive] *the separate details coalesce to form a single body of scientific thought.* ■ [trans.] combine (elements) in a mass or whole: *to help coalesce the community, they established an office.*
DERIVATIVES: **co•a•les•cence** |-ˈlesəns| n. **co•a•les•cent** |-ˈlesənt| adj.

co•a•li•tion |ˌkōəˈlisHən| • n. an alliance for combined action, esp. a temporary alliance of political parties or of states: *a coalition of moderate Republicans and disaffected Democrats* | [as adj.] *a coalition government.*
DERIVATIVES: **co•a•li•tion•al** adj. **co•a•li•tion•ist** |-nist| n.

co•ax•i•al |kōˈæksēəl| • adj. having a common axis. ■ (of a cable or line) transmitting by means of two concentric conductors separated by an insulator.
DERIVATIVES: **co•ax•i•al•ly** adv.

co-bel•lig•er•ent |ˌkōbəˈlijərənt| • n. any of two or more nations engaged in war as allies.
DERIVATIVES: **co-bel•lig•er•ence** n.

co•ca |ˈkōkə| • n. a tropical American shrub (*Erythroxylum coca*) that is widely grown for its leaves, which are the source of cocaine. Cf. CACAO. ■ the dried leaves of this shrub, which are mixed with lime and chewed as a stimulant by native peoples of western South America.

coc•cyx |ˈkäksiks| • n. (pl. **coccyges** |ˈkäkˌsəˌjēz| or **coccyxes** |ˈkäksiksiz|) a small, triangular bone at the base of the spinal column in humans and some apes, formed of fused vestigial vertebrae.
DERIVATIVES: **coc•cyg•e•al** |käkˈsijēəl| adj.

coch•i•neal |ˈkäCHəˌnēəl; ˈkō-| • n. **1** a scarlet dye used chiefly for coloring food. ■ the dried bodies of a female scale insect, which are crushed to yield this dye. ■ a similar dye or preparation made from the oak kermes insect (see KERMES). **2** (**cochineal insect**) the scale insect (*Dactylopius coccus*) that is used for cochineal, native to Mexico and formerly widely cultivated on cacti.

cock•a•ma•mie |ˈkäkəˌmāmē; ˌkäkəˈmāmē| (also **cockamamy**) • adj. ridiculous; implausible.

cock•a•trice |ˈkäkətris; -ˌtrīs| • n. a mythical reptile with a lethal gaze or breath; a basilisk. ■ a mythical animal depicted in heraldry as a two-legged dragon (wyvern) with a cock's head.

cock•le[1] |ˈkäkəl| • n. **1** an edible, burrowing bivalve mollusk (genus *Cardium*) with a strong ribbed shell. **2** (also **cockleshell**) a small shallow boat.
PHRASES: **warm the cockles of one's heart** give one a comforting feeling of pleasure or contentment.

cock•le[2] • v. [intrans.] (of paper) bulge out in certain places so as to present a wrinkled or creased surface; pucker.

cock•ney |ˈkäknē| • n. (pl. **-eys**) a native of East London. ■ the dialect or accent typical of such people.

- *adj.* of or characteristic of cockneys or their dialect or accent: *cockney humor.*

co•coa |'kōkō| • *n.* a powder made from roasted and ground cacao seeds.
■ a hot drink made from such a powder mixed with milk or water.

co•cotte |kō'kôt; kə'kät| • *n.* **1** (usu. **en cocotte**) a heatproof dish or small casserole in which individual portions of food can be both cooked and served. **2** a fashionable prostitute.

co•da |'kōdə| • *n.* the concluding passage of a piece of music or movement, typically forming an addition to the basic structure.
■ the concluding section of a dance, esp. of a pas de deux or the finale of a ballet in which the dancers parade before the audience. ■ a concluding event, remark, or section: *his new novel is a kind of coda to his career.*

cod•dle |'kädl| • *v.* [trans.] **1** treat in an indulgent or overprotective way: *I was coddled and cosseted.* **2** cook (an egg) in water below boiling point.
DERIVATIVES: **cod•dler** |'kädlər; 'kädl-ər| *n.*

co•de•pend•en•cy |ˌkōdə'pendənsē| (also **codependence** |-dəns|) • *n.* excessive emotional or psychological reliance on a partner, typically one with an illness or addiction who requires support.
DERIVATIVES: **co•de•pend•ent** |-dənt| *adj. & n.*

co•dex |'kō,deks| • *n.* (pl. **codices** |'kōdə ,sēz; 'käd-| or **codexes**) an ancient manuscript text in book form.
■ an official list of medicines, chemicals, etc.

cod•i•cil |'kädəsəl; -,sil| • *n.* an addition or supplement that explains, modifies, or revokes a will or part of one.
DERIVATIVES: **cod•i•cil•la•ry** |ˌkädə 'silərē| *adj.*

cod•i•fy |'kädə,fī; 'kōd-| • *v.* (**-ies, -ied**) [trans.] arrange (laws or rules) into a systematic code.
■ arrange according to a plan or system: *Verdi helped codify an international operatic culture.*
DERIVATIVES: **cod•i•fi•ca•tion** |ˌkädəfə 'kāsHən; ˌkōd-| *n.* **cod•i•fi•er** |'kädə,fīər; 'kōd-| *n.*

co•ef•fi•cient |ˌkōə'fisHənt| • *n.* **1** a numerical or constant quantity placed before and multiplying the variable in an algebraic expression (e.g., 4 in $4x$). **2** a multiplier or factor that measures some physical or dynamic property: *coefficients of elasticity.*

co•e•qual |kō'ēkwəl| • *adj.* equal with one another; having the same rank or importance: *coequal partners.* • *n.* a person or thing equal with another.
DERIVATIVES: **co•e•qual•i•ty** |ˌkō-i'kwäl-itē| *n.*

co•erce |kō'ərs| • *v.* [trans.] persuade (an unwilling person) to do something by using force or threats: *they were coerced into silence.*
■ obtain (something) by such means: *their confessions were allegedly coerced by torture.*
DERIVATIVES: **co•er•ci•ble** |kō'ərsəbəl| *adj.* **co•er•cion** |kō'ərzHən; -sHən| *n.*

co•e•ter•nal |ˌkō-i'tərnl| • *adj.* equally eternal; existing with something else eternally: *creation is not coeternal with God.*
DERIVATIVES: **co•e•ter•nal•ly** *adv.* **co•e•ter•ni•ty** *n.*

co•e•val |kō'ēvəl| • *adj.* having the same age or date of origin; contemporary: *these lavas were coeval with the volcanic activity.* • *n.* a person of roughly the same age as oneself; a contemporary: *like his coevals, he yearned for stability.*
DERIVATIVES: **co•e•val•i•ty** |ˌkō-ē'vælitē| *n.* **co•e•val•ly** *adv.*

co•gen•e•ra•tion |ˌkō,jenə'rāsHən| • *n.* the generation of electricity and useful heat jointly, esp. the utilization of the steam left over from electricity generation for heating.

co•gent |'kōjənt| • *adj.* (of an argument or case) clear, logical, and convincing.
DERIVATIVES: **co•gen•cy** *n.* **co•gent•ly** *adv.*

cog•i•tate |'käjə,tāt| • *v.* [intrans.] think deeply about something; meditate or reflect: *he stroked his beard and retired to cogitate.*
DERIVATIVES: **cog•i•ta•tion** |ˌkäjə'tāsHən| *n.* **cog•i•ta•tive** |-,tātiv| *adj.* **cog•i•ta•tor** |-,tātər| *n.*

cog•nate |'käg,nāt| • *adj.* **1** (of a word) having the same linguistic derivation as another; from the same original word or root (e.g., English *is*, German *ist*, Latin *est* from Indo-European *esti*.) **2** related; connected: *cognate subjects such as physics and chemistry.*
■ related to or descended from a common ancestor. • *n.* **1** a cognate word. **2** (in legal contexts) a blood relative.
DERIVATIVES: **cog•nate•ly** *adv.* **cog•nate•ness** *n.*

cog•ni•tion |ˌkäg'nisHən| • *n.* the mental action or process of acquiring knowledge and understanding through thought, experience, and the senses.
■ a result of this; a perception, sensation, notion, or intuition.
DERIVATIVES: **cog•ni•tion•al** |-sHənl| *adj.* **cog•ni•tive** *adj.*

cog•ni•tive dis•so•nance • *n.* the state of having inconsistent thoughts, beliefs, or attitudes, esp. as relating to behavioral decisions and attitude change.
■ psychological conflict resulting from irreconcilable disparity from sensory imputs.

cog•ni•za•ble |'kägnəzəbəl; käg'nīz-| • *adj.* **1** perceptible; clearly identifiable. **2** within the jurisdiction of a court of law.

cog•ni•zance |'kägnəzəns| • *n.* **1** knowledge, awareness, or notice: *he was deputed to bring the affair to the cognizance of the court.*
■ the action of taking judicial notice. **2** a distinctive heraldic device or mark, esp. an emblem or badge formerly worn by retainers of a noble house.
DERIVATIVES: **cog•ni•zant** *adj.*

cog•no•men |käg'nōmən; 'kägnəmən| • *n.* an extra personal name given to an ancient Roman citizen, functioning rather like a nickname and typically passed down from father to son:
■ a name; a nickname.

cog·no·scen·ti |ˌkänyōˈsHentē; ˌkägnə-| • *plural n.* people who are considered to be especially well informed about a particular subject: *it was hailed by the cognoscenti as one of the best golf courses in Europe.*

co·hab·it |kōˈhæbit| • *v.* (**cohabited, cohabiting**) [intrans.] **1** live together and have a sexual relationship without being married. **2** live together (with); coexist: *animals that can cohabit with humans thrive.*
DERIVATIVES: **co·hab·it·ant** *n.* **co·hab·i·ta·tion** |kō,hæbəˈtāsHən| *n.* **co·hab·it·er** *n.*

co·here |kōˈhir| • *v.* [intrans.] **1** be united; form a whole: *our mixed physical and spiritual natures cohere and mature.* **2** (of an argument or theory) be logically consistent: *this view does not cohere with their other beliefs.*

co·her·ent |kōˈhirənt| • *adj.* **1** (of an argument, theory, or policy) logical and consistent: *they failed to develop a coherent economic strategy.*
■ (of a person) able to speak clearly and logically: *she was lucid and coherent and did not appear to be injured.* **2** united as or forming a whole: *divided into a number of geographically coherent kingdoms.* **3** (in physics, of waves) having a constant phase relationship (relationship in time between successive states or cycles).
DERIVATIVES: **co·her·ence** *n.* **co·her·en·cy** *n.* (rare) **co·her·ent·ly** *adv.*

co·he·sion |kōˈhēzHən| • *n.* the action or fact of forming a united whole: *the work at present lacks cohesion.*
■ (in physics) the sticking together of particles of the same substance.
DERIVATIVES: **co·he·sive** *adj.*

co·hort |ˈkō,hôrt| • *n.* **1** [treated as sing. or pl.] an ancient Roman military unit, comprising six hundred men (six *centuries*), equal to one tenth of a legion. **2** [treated as sing. or pl.] a group of people banded together or treated as a group: *a cohort of civil servants patiently drafting legislation.*
■ a group of people with a common statistical characteristic: *the 1940–44 birth cohort of women.* **3** a supporter or companion: *with his cohorts he stormed the building.*
■ an accomplice or conspirator: *his three cohorts each had pled guilty.*

USAGE: The *co-* in **cohort** is not a prefix signifying a 'joint' or auxiliary relationship (as in *coauthor* or *codependency*). The word derives from the Latin *cohors*, an ancient Roman military unit, and also 'band of people with a common interest.' Careful writers will restrict the use of **cohort** to numerous groups of a kind, as in a demographic context (*the 1946–60 birth cohort*), and will not use it, as is commonly done, to denote an individual.

coign |koin| • *n.* a projecting corner or angle of a wall or building.
PHRASES: **coign of vantage** a favorable position for observation or action.

co·i·tus |ˈkōətəs; kōˈētəs| (also **coition**) • *n.* sexual intercourse.
DERIVATIVES: **co·i·tal** |ˈkōətl; kōˈētl| *adj.*

co·i·tus in·ter·rup·tus |intəˈrəptəs| • *n.* sexual intercourse in which the penis is withdrawn before ejaculation.

col·ic |ˈkälik| • *n.* severe, often fluctuating pain in the abdomen caused by wind or obstruction in the intestines and suffered esp. by babies.
DERIVATIVES: **col·ick·y** *adj.*

col·lab·o·rate |kəˈlæbə,rāt| • *v.* [intrans.] work jointly on an activity, esp. to produce or create something: *he collaborated with a distinguished painter on the designs.*
■ cooperate traitorously with an enemy: *during the war they collaborated with the Nazis.*
DERIVATIVES: **col·lab·o·ra·tion** *n.* **col·lab·o·ra·tive** *adj.* **col·lab·o·ra·tive·ly** *adv.* **col·lab·o·ra·tor** |-,rātər| *n.*

col·lage |kəˈläzH; kō-| • *n.* a form of art in which various materials such as photographs and pieces of paper or fabric are arranged and stuck to a backing.
■ a composition made in this way. ■ a combination or collection of various things.
DERIVATIVES: **col·lag·ist** |-läzHist| *n.*

col·late |kəˈlāt; ˈkō,lāt; ˈkäl,āt| • *v.* [trans.] **1** collect and combine (texts, information, or sets of figures) in proper order.
■ compare and analyze (texts or other data): *these accounts had collated with his own experience.* ■ (in printing) verify the order of (sheets of a book) by their signatures (groups of pages). **2** appoint (a clergyman) to a benefice.
DERIVATIVES: **col·la·tor** |-ər| *n.*

col·lat·er·al |kəˈlætərəl; kəˈlætrəl| • *n.* **1** something pledged as security for repayment of a loan, to be forfeited in the event of a default. **2** a person having the same descent as another but by a different line. • *adj.* **1** descended from the same stock but by a different line: *a collateral descendant of John Adams.* **2** additional but subordinate; secondary: *the collateral meanings of a word.*
■ situated side by side; parallel: *collateral veins.*
DERIVATIVES: **col·lat·er·al·i·ty** |kə,lætəˈrælitē| *n.* **col·lat·er·al·ly** *adv.*

col·la·tion |kəˈlāsHən; kō-; kä-| • *n.* **1** the action of collating something: *data management and collation.* **2** a light, informal meal.
■ (in the Roman Catholic Church) a light meal allowed during a fast.

col·league |ˈkäl,ēg| • *n.* a person with whom one works, esp. in a profession or business.

col·lec·ta·ne·a |ˌkäl,ek'tānēə| • *plural n.* [-also treated as sing.] passages, remarks, and other pieces of text collected from various sources.

col·lec·tive |kəˈlektiv| • *adj.* done by or relating to people or organizations acting as a group: *a collective protest | collective security.*
■ belonging or relating to all the members of a group: *ministers who share collective responsibility.* ■ (esp. of feelings or memories) common to the members of a group: *a collective sigh of relief from parents.* ■ taken as a whole; aggregate: *the collective power of the workforce.* • *n.* a cooperative enterprise.

■ a collective farm (the holdings of several farmers run as a joint enterprise) or similar organization: *an office collective.*
DERIVATIVES: **col•lec•tive•ly** *adv.* **col•lec•tive•ness** *n.* **col•lec•tiv•i•ty** |kə,lek'tivitē; ,käl,ek-| *n.*
col•lec•tive noun • *n.* a count noun that denotes a group of individuals (e.g., *assembly, family, crew*).

USAGE: Examples of collective nouns include *group, crowd, family, committee, class,* and *crew.* In American English collective nouns are usually followed by a singular verb (*the crowd was nervous*), while in Britain it is more common to follow a collective noun with a plural verb (*the band were late for their own concert*). Notice that if the verb is singular, any following pronouns must also be singular: *The council is prepared to act, but not until it has taken a poll.* When preceded by the definite article *the,* the collective noun *number* is usually treated as a singular (*the number of applicants was beyond belief*), whereas it is treated as a plural when preceded by the indefinite article *a* (*a number of proposals were considered*).

col•lec•tive un•con•scious • *n.* (in Jungian psychology) the part of the unconscious mind that is derived from ancestral memory and experience and is common to all humankind or to some race or people, as distinct from the individual's unconscious.
col•le•giate |kə'lējət| • *adj.* 1 belonging or relating to or characteristic of a college or its students: *collegiate life.* 2 (of a university) composed of different colleges.
■ (of a church) in the joint charge of two ministers.
col•lier |'kälyər| • *n.* 1 a coal miner. 2 a ship carrying coal.
DERIVATIVES: **colliery** *n.* a place where coal is mined.
col•lo•cate |'kälə,kāt| • *v.* 1 [intrans.] (of a word) be habitually juxtaposed with another with a frequency greater than chance: *"maiden" collocates with "voyage."* 2 [trans.] place side by side or in a particular relation: [as adj.] (**collocated**) *McAndrew was a collocated facility with Argentia Naval Station.* • *n.* a word that is habitually juxtaposed with another with a frequency greater than chance: *collocates for "mortgage" include "lend" and "property."*
col•loid |'kälˌoid| • *n.* a homogeneous, noncrystalline substance consisting of large molecules or ultramicroscopic particles of one substance dispersed uniformly through a second substance. Colloids include gels (semisolids in liquid), sols (solids in liquid), and emulsions (liquids in liquid); the particles do not settle and cannot be separated out by ordinary filtering or centrifuging like those in a suspension.
■ a substance of gelatinous consistency. • *adj.* [attrib.] of the nature of, relating to, or characterized by a colloid or colloids.
DERIVATIVES: **col•loi•dal** |kə'loidl| *adj.*

col•lo•qui•al |kə'lōkwēəl| • *adj.* (of language) used in ordinary or familiar conversation; not formal or literary.
DERIVATIVES: **col•lo•qui•al•ly** *adv.*
col•lo•qui•al•ism |kə'lōkwēə,lizəm| • *n.* 1 colloquial style. 2 a colloquial expression.
col•lo•qui•um |kə'lōkwēəm| • *n.* (pl. **colloquiums** or **colloquia** |-kwēə|) an academic conference or seminar.
col•lo•quy |'käləkwē| • *n.* (pl. **-ies**) 1 a discourse or conversation: *they broke off their colloquy at once* | *an evening of sophisticated colloquy.* 2 a gathering for discussion of theological questions.
col•lude |kə'lōōd| • *v.* [intrans.] come to a secret understanding for a harmful purpose; conspire: *industry leaders colluded in price-fixing* | *the president accused his opponents of colluding with foreigners.*
DERIVATIVES: **col•lud•er** *n.*
col•lu•sion |kə'lōōZHən| • *n.* secret or illegal cooperation or conspiracy, esp. in order to cheat or deceive others: *the armed forces were working in collusion with drug traffickers* | *collusion between media owners and political leaders.*
■ such cooperation or conspiracy between ostensible opponents in a lawsuit.
DERIVATIVES: **col•lu•sive** |-siv; -ziv| *adj.* **col•lu•sive•ly** |-ivlē; -zivlē| *adv.*
co•lon•ic |kō'länik; kə-| • *adj.* of, relating to, or affecting the colon. • *n.* an act or instance of fluid cleansing (via the anus) of the colon (colonic irrigation), performed for its supposed therapeutic benefits.
col•on•nade |,kälə'nād| • *n.* a row of columns supporting a roof, an entablature, or arches. Cf. ARCADE.
■ a row of trees or other tall objects.
DERIVATIVES: **col•on•nad•ed** *adj.*
col•o•ra•tu•ra |,kälərə'tŏŏrə; ,käl-| • *n.* elaborate ornamentation of a vocal melody, esp. in operatic singing by a soprano.
■ (also **coloratura soprano**) a soprano skilled in such singing.
col•ored |'kələrd| (Brit. **coloured**) • *adj.* 1 having or having been given a color or colors, esp. as opposed to being black, white, or neutral: *brightly colored birds are easier to see* | [in combination] *a peach-colored sofa.*
■ imbued with an emotive or exaggerated quality: *highly colored examples were used by both sides.* 2 (also **Colored**) wholly or partly of nonwhite descent (now usually offensive in the US). ■ relating to people who are wholly or partly of nonwhite descent: *a colored club.*
■ (also **Coloured**) S. African used as an ethnic label for people of mixed ethnic origin, including African slave, Malay, Chinese, and white. • *n.* 1 (also **Colored**) (dated and usually offensive) a person who is wholly or partly of nonwhite descent.
■ S. African a person of mixed ethnic origin speaking Afrikaans or English as his or her mother tongue. 2 (**coloreds**) clothes, sheets, etc., that are any color but white (used esp. in the context of washing and color fastness).

USAGE: **Colored** referring to skin color is first recorded in the early 17th century and was adopted in the US by emancipated slaves as a term of racial pride after the end of the Civil War. For the term's later history, see usage at **black**.

col•or-field paint•ing (also **colorfield**) • *n.* a style of abstract painting prominent from the late 1940s to the 1960s that features large expanses of unmodulated color covering the greater part of the canvas. Barnett Newman and Mark Rothko were considered its chief exponents.

col•or•ist |ˈkələrist| (Brit. **colourist**) • *n.* an artist or designer who uses color in a special or skillful way.
■ a person who tints black-and-white prints, photographs, or movies. ■ a hairdresser who specializes in dyeing people's hair.

co•los•sal |kəˈläsəl| • *adj.* extremely large: *a colossal amount of mail* | *a colossal mistake.*
■ (of an arrangement of columns) having more than one story. ■ (of a statue) at least twice life size.
DERIVATIVES: **co•los•sal•ly** *adv.*

colt•ish |ˈkōltisH| • *adj.* energetic but awkward in one's movements or behavior.
DERIVATIVES: **colt•ish•ly** *adv.* **colt•ish•ness** *n.*

col•u•brine |ˈkäl(y)əˌbrīn| • *adj.* of or belonging to a snake; snakelike: *colubrine coils.*

col•um•bar•i•um |ˌkäləmˈbereəm| • *n.* (pl. **columbaria** |-ˈbereə|) a room or building with niches for funeral urns to be stored.

co•ma |ˈkōmə| • *n.* a state of deep unconsciousness that lasts for a prolonged or indefinite period, caused esp. by severe injury or illness: *the crash left him in a coma*|
■ a similar apparent lack of consciousness: *a victim of a legislative coma.*

com•a•tose |ˈkōməˌtōs; ˈkämə-| • *adj.* of or in a state of deep unconsciousness (coma), for a prolonged or indefinite period, esp. as a result of severe injury or illness: *she had been comatose for seven months* | *lying in a comatose state.*
■ (of a person or thing) extremely exhausted, lethargic, or sleepy: *the economy remains almost comatose.*

com•bus•ti•ble |kəmˈbəstəbəl| • *adj.* able to catch fire and burn easily: *highly combustible paint thinner.*
■ excitable; easily annoyed: *combustible personalities.* • *n.* a combustible substance.
DERIVATIVES: **com•bus•ti•bil•i•ty** |kəmˌbəstəˈbilitē| *n.*

com•bus•tion |kəmˈbəscHən| • *n.* the process of burning something: *the combustion of fossil fuels.*
■ rapid chemical combination of a substance with oxygen, involving the production of heat and light. ■ violent excitement or commotion.
DERIVATIVES: **com•bus•tive** |-ˈbəstiv| *adj.*

com•e•dy of man•ners • *n.* a comedy that satirizes behavior in a particular social group, esp. upper-class society.

come•ly |ˈkəmlē| • *adj.* (**comelier, comeliest**) (typically of a woman) pleasant to look at; attractive.
■ agreeable; suitable.
DERIVATIVES: **come•li•ness** *n.*

co•mes•ti•ble |kəˈmestəbəl| • *n.* (usu. **comestibles**) an item of food: *a fridge groaning with comestibles.* • *adj.* edible: *comestible plants.*

com•ic re•lief • *n.* comic episodes in a dramatic or literary work that offset more serious portions.
■ a character or characters providing this. ■ comical episodes that serve to release tension in real life.

com•i•ty |ˈkämitē| • *n.* (pl. **-ies**) **1** courtesy and considerate behavior toward others. **2** an association of nations for their mutual benefit.
■ (also **comity of nations**) the mutual recognition by nations or other jurisdictions of the laws and customs of others.

com•man•deer |ˌkämənˈdir| • *v.* [trans.] officially take possession or control of (something), esp. for military purposes: *telegraph and telephone lines were commandeered by the generals.*
■ take possession of (something) without authority: *he hoisted himself onto a table, commandeering it as a speaker's platform.* ■ [with obj. and infinitive] enlist (someone) to help in a task, typically against the person's will: *he commandeered the men to find a table.* Cf. APPROPRIATE.

com•me•dia dell'ar•te |kəˈmādēə dəl ˈärtē| • *n.* an improvised kind of popular comedy in Italian theaters in the 16th–18th centuries, based on stock characters. Actors adapted their comic dialogue and action according to a few basic plots (commonly love intrigues) and to topical issues.

com•men•sal•ism |kəˈmensəˌlizəm| • *n.* (in biology) an association between two organisms in which one benefits and the other derives neither benefit nor harm. Cf. SYMBIOSIS.
DERIVATIVES: **commensal** *adj.* **commensality** *n.*

com•men•su•ra•ble |kəˈmensərəbəl; kəˈmencHərəbəl| • *adj.* **1** measurable by the same standard: *the finite is not commensurable with* the infinite. **2** [predic.] (**commensurable to**) proportionate to. **3** (of numbers) in a ratio equal to a ratio of integers.
DERIVATIVES: **com•men•su•ra•bil•i•ty** |kəˌmensərəˈbilitē; -ˌmenCHə-| *n.* **com•men•su•ra•bly** |kəˈmensərəblē; -ˈmenCHə-| *adv.*

com•men•su•rate |kəˈmensərət; -ˈmenCHə-| • *adj.* corresponding in size or degree; in proportion: *salary will be commensurate with experience* | *such heavy responsibility must receive commensurate reward.*
DERIVATIVES: **com•men•su•rate•ly** *adv.* **com•men•su•ra•tion** *n.*

com•mi•na•tion |ˌkäməˈnāsHən| • *n.* the action of threatening divine vengeance.
■ the recital of divine threats against sinners in the Anglican Liturgy for Ash Wednesday.

com•min•gle |kə'miNGgəl; kä-| • *v.* mingle together; mix; blend: [intrans.] *the dust had* **commingled with** *the rain* | [trans.] *publicly reproved for commingling funds.*

com•mis•er•ate |kə'mizə,rāt| • *v.* [intrans.] express or feel sympathy or pity; sympathize: *she went over to* **commiserate with** *Rose on her unfortunate circumstances.*

DERIVATIVES: **com•mis•er•a•tion** |kə,mizə 'rāSHən| *n.* **com•mis•er•a•tive** |-rətiv| *adj.*

com•mis•sar |'kämə,sär; ,kämə'sär| • *n.* an official of the Communist Party, esp. in the former Soviet Union or present-day China, responsible for political education and organization.
■ a head of a government department (commissariat) in the former Soviet Union before 1946. ■ a strict or prescriptive figure of authority: *our academic commissars.*

com•mis•sar•i•at |,kämə'serēət| • *n.* **1** a department for the supply of food and equipment, esp. in the military. **2** a government department of the USSR before 1946.

com•mis•sar•y |'kämə,serē| • *n.* (pl. **-ies**) **1** a restaurant in a movie studio, military base, prison, or other institution.
■ a store that sells food and drink to soldiers or other members of an organization. **2** a deputy or delegate.
DERIVATIVES: **com•mis•sar•i•al** |,kämə 'serēəl| *adj.*

com•mit•tal |kə'mitl| • *n.* **1** the action of sending a person to an institution, esp. prison or a psychiatric hospital: *his committal to prison* | [as adj.] *committal proceedings.* **2** the burial of a corpse. **3** commitment.

com•mod•i•fy |kə'mädə,fī| • *v.* (**-ies, -ied**) [trans.] turn into or treat as a commodity: [as adj.] (**commodified**) *art has become commodified.*
DERIVATIVES: **com•mod•i•fi•ca•tion** |kə ,mädəfə'kāSHən| *n.*

com•mo•di•ous |kə'mōdēəs| • *adj.* **1** formal (esp. of furniture or a building) roomy and comfortable. **2** convenient.
DERIVATIVES: **com•mo•di•ous•ly** *adv.* **com•mo•di•ous•ness** *n.*

com•mod•i•ty |kə'mädite| • *n.* (pl. **-ies**) a raw material or primary agricultural product that can be bought and sold, such as copper or coffee.
■ a useful or valuable thing, such as water or time.

com•mon•al•i•ty |'kämən,ælite| • *n.* (pl. **-ies**) **1** [in sing.] the state of sharing features or attributes: *a commonality of interest insures cooperation.*
■ a shared feature or attribute: *we discern the commonalities between these writers.* **2** (**the commonality**) another term for COMMON-ALTY.

com•mon•al•ty |'kämənl-tē| • *n.* [treated as pl.] (**the commonalty**) people without special rank or position; common people: *a petition by the earls, barons, and commonalty of the realm.*
■ the general body of a group.

com•mon law • *n.* the part of English law that is derived from custom and judicial precedent rather than statutes.
■ the body of English law adopted, beginning in the 1770s, by all US states except Louisana (which follows a form of CIVIL LAW), and subsequently adapted. Federal law has also developed in this way. Compare with CIVIL LAW. ■ [as adj.] (**common-law**) denoting a partner in a marriage recognized under common law, not by a civil or ecclesiastical ceremony. Such marriages are now recognized in only a few states of the US. ■ [as adj.] denoting a partner in a long-term relationship of cohabitation.

com•mon•place |'kämən,plās| • *adj.* not unusual; ordinary: *unemployment was commonplace in his profession.*
■ not interesting or original; trite: *the usual commonplace remarks.* • *n.* **1** a usual or ordinary thing: *bombing has become almost a commonplace of life there.*
■ a trite saying or topic; a platitude: *it is a commonplace to talk of the young being alienated.* **2** a quotation copied into a commonplace book, a collection of notable extracts from other works for personal use.
DERIVATIVES: **com•mon•place•ness** *n.*

com•mon•weal |'kämən,wēl| • *n.* (**the commonweal**) the welfare of the public.

com•mon•wealth |'kämən,welTH| • *n.* **1** an independent country or community, esp. a democratic republic.
■ an aggregate or grouping of countries or other bodies. ■ a community or organization of shared interests in a nonpolitical field: *the Christian commonwealth* | *the commonwealth of letters.* ■ a self-governing unit voluntarily grouped with the US, such as Puerto Rico. ■ the formal title of four states of the US: Kentucky, Massachusetts, Pennsylvania, and Virginia. ■ the title of the federated Australian states. ■ (**the Commonwealth**) the republican period of government in Britain between the execution of Charles I in 1649 and the Restoration of Charles II in 1660. **2** (**the Commonwealth**) (in full **the Commonwealth of Nations**) an international association consisting of the UK together with states that were previously part of the British Empire, and dependencies. The British monarch is the symbolic head of the Commonwealth. **3** (**the commonwealth**) archaic the general good.

com•mu•nal |kə'myo͞onl| • *adj.* **1** shared by all members of a community; for common use: *a communal bathroom.*
■ of, relating to, or done by a community: *communal pride.* ■ involving the sharing of work and property: *communal living.* **2** (of conflict) between different communities, esp. those having different religions or ethnic origins: *violent communal riots.*
DERIVATIVES: **com•mu•nal•i•ty** |,kämyə 'nælite| *n.* **com•mu•nal•ly** *adv.*

com•mune[1] |'käm,yo͞on| • *n.* **1** a group of people living together and sharing possessions and responsibilities.
■ a communal settlement in a communist

country. **2** the smallest French territorial division for administrative purposes. **3** (**the Commune**) the group that seized the municipal government of Paris in the French Revolution and played a leading part in the Reign of Terror until suppressed in 1794. ■ (also **the Paris Commune**) the municipal government organized on communalistic principles elected in Paris in 1871. It was soon brutally suppressed by government troops.

com•mune² |kə'myo͞on| • *v.* [intrans.] **1** (**commune with**) share one's intimate thoughts or feelings with (someone or something), esp. when the exchange is on a spiritual level: *to commune with God.* ■ feel in close spiritual contact with: *communing with nature on the bank of a stream.* **2** receive Holy Communion.

com•mu•nism |'kämyə,nizəm| • *n.* (often **Communism**) **1** a political theory derived from Karl Marx, advocating class war and leading to a society in which all property is publicly owned and each person works and is paid according to his or her abilities and needs. See also MARXISM, SOCIALISM. **2** a system of society with property vested in the community and each member working for the common benefit: *the primitive communism of the tribe* | *Shaker communism.* DERIVATIVES: **com•mu•nist** *n. & adj.* **com•mu•nis•tic** |,kämyə'nistik| *adj.*

communitarianism |kə,myo͞onə'terēə,nizəm| • *n.* a theory or system of social organization based on small self-governing communities. ■ an ideology that emphasizes the responsibility of the individual to the community and the social importance of the family unit. DERIVATIVES: **com•mu•ni•tar•i•an** *adj. & n.* .

com•mu•ta•tion |,kämyə'tāsHən| • *n.* (in law) the action or process, or an instance, of commuting a judicial sentence: *was sentenced to life in prison but got a commutation.* ■ the conversion of a legal obligation or entitlement into another form, e.g., the replacement of an annuity or series of payments by a single payment.

com•mute |kə'myo͞ot| • *v.* **1** [intrans.] travel some distance between one's home and place of work on a regular basis: *she commuted from Westport in to Grand Central.* **2** [trans.] reduce (a judicial sentence, esp. a sentence of death) to another less severe one: *the governor recently commuted the sentences of several women convicted of killing their husbands.* **3** [intrans.] (of two mathematical operations or quantities) have a commutative relationship (in which the order of the quantics involved does not affect the result of an operation, e.g., *a*×*b* gives the same result as *b*×*a*). • *n.* a regular journey

of some distance to and from one's place of work.
DERIVATIVES: **com•mut•er** *n.* (in sense 1).

com•pact¹ |kəm'pækt; käm-; 'käm,pækt| • *adj.* closely and neatly packed together; dense: *a compact cluster of houses.* ■ having all the necessary components or features neatly fitted into a small space: *a compact car.* ■ (of a person or animal) small, solid, and well-proportioned. ■ (of speech or writing) concise in expression: *a compact summary of the play.* • *v.* [trans.] (often **be compacted**) exert force on (something) to make it more dense; compress: *the waste is compacted before disposal* | [as adj.] (**compacted**) *compacted paper.* ■ [intrans.] (of a substance) become compressed in this way: *the snow hardened and compacted.*
DERIVATIVES: **com•pac•tion** |kəm'pæksHən| *n.* **com•pact•ly** *adv.* **com•pact•ness** *n.* **com•pac•tor** |kəm'pæktər; käm-; 'käm,pæktər| (also **com•pact•er**) *n.*

com•pact² |'käm,pækt| • *n.* a formal agreement or contract between two or more parties. • *v.* |kəm'pækt; käm-; 'käm,pækt| [trans.] make or enter into (a formal agreement) with another party or parties: *the Democratic Party compacted an alliance with dissident groups.*

com•pa•dre |kəm'pädrā| • *n.* (pl. **compadres**) a way of addressing or referring to a friend or companion.

com•pan•ion•a•ble |kəm'pænyənəbəl| • *adj.* (of a person) friendly and sociable: *a companionable young man.* ■ (of a shared situation) relaxed and pleasant: *they walked in companionable silence.*
DERIVATIVES: **com•pan•ion•a•ble•ness** *n.* **com•pan•ion•a•bly** |-blē| *adv.*

com•par•a•tive |kəm'pærətiv| • *adj.* **1** perceptible by comparison; relative: *he returned to the comparative comfort of his own home.* **2** of or involving comparison between two or more branches of science or subjects of study: *comparative religion.* **3** (of an adjective or adverb) expressing a higher degree of a quality, but not the highest possible (e.g., *braver, more fiercely*). Cf. POSITIVE, SUPERLATIVE. ■ (of a clause) involving comparison (e.g., *my memory is not as good as it used to be*). • *n.* a comparative adjective or adverb. ■ (**the comparative**) the middle degree of comparison.

com•part•men•tal•ize |kəm,pärt'mentl,īz| • *v.* [trans.] divide into sections or categories: *he had the ability to compartmentalize his life.*
DERIVATIVES: **com•part•men•tal•i•za•tion** |kəm,pärt,mentl-ə'zāsHən| *n.*

com•pass |'kəmpəs| • *n.* **1** (also **magnetic compass**) an instrument containing a magnetized pointer that shows the direction of magnetic north and bearings from it. **2** (also **pair of compasses**) an instrument for drawing circles and arcs and measuring distances between points, consisting of two arms linked by a movable joint, one arm ending in a point and the other usually carrying a pen-

cil or pen. **3** [in sing.] the range or scope of something: *the event had political repercussions* **beyond the compass of** *this book.*
■ the enclosing limits of an area: *this region had within its compass many types of agriculture.*
■ the range of notes that can be produced by a voice or a musical instrument: *the cellos were playing in a rather somber part of their compass.*
• *v.* [trans.] **1** go around (something) in a circular course: *the ship wherein Magellan compassed the world.*
■ surround or hem in on all sides: *they were compassed with numerous fierce and cruel tribes.*
2 contrive to accomplish (something): *he compassed his end only by the exercise of violence.*
com•pat•i•ble |kəm'pætəbəl| • *adj.* (of two things) able to exist or occur together without conflict: *the fruitiness of Beaujolais is* **compatible with** *a number of meat dishes.*
■ (of two people) able to have a harmonious relationship: well-suited: *it's a pity we're not compatible.* ■ (of one thing) consistent with another: *symptoms compatible with gastritis or a peptic ulcer.* ■ (of a computer, a piece of software, or other device) able to be used with a specified piece of equipment or software without special adaptation or modification: [in combination] *IBM-compatible laptops.*
DERIVATIVES: **com•pat•i•bil•i•ty** |kəm‚pætə'bilitē| *n.* **com•pat•i•bly** |-blē| *adv.*
com•pa•tri•ot |kəm'pātrēət| • *n.* a fellow citizen or national of a country: *Stich defeated his compatriot Boris Becker in the quarterfinals.*
com•peer |'käm‚pir; käm'pir| • *n.* a person of equal rank, status, or ability: *he was better versed in his profession than his compeers.*
com•pel |kəm'pel| • *v.* (**compelled, compelling**) [with obj. and infinitive] force or oblige (someone) to do something: *a sense of duty compelled Harry to answer her questions.* Cf. CO-ERCE, IMPEL.
■ [trans.] bring about (something) by the use of force or pressure: *they may compel a witness's attendance at court by issue of a summons.*
■ [with obj. and adverbial of direction] drive forcibly: *by heav'n's high will compell'd from shore to shore.*
com•pen•di•ous |kəm'pendēəs| • *adj.* containing or presenting the essential facts of something in a comprehensive but concise way: *a compendious study.*
DERIVATIVES: **com•pen•di•ous•ly** *adv.* **com•pen•di•ous•ness** *n.*
com•pen•di•um |kəm'pendēəm| • *n.* (pl. **compendiums** or **compendia** |-dēə|) a collection of concise but detailed information about a particular subject, esp. in a book or other publication.
■ a collection of things, esp. one systematically gathered: *a compendium of documents from our archives.*
com•pen•sa•to•ry |kəm'pensə‚tôrē| • *adj.* providing compensation, in particular:
■ (of a payment) intended to compensate someone who has experienced loss, suffering, or injury: *$50 million in compensatory damages.* ■ reducing or offsetting the unpleasant or unwelcome effects of something:

compensatory actions to keep the interest rate constant.
com•pi•la•tion |‚kämpə'lāsHən| • *n.* **1** the act of putting together (compiling) independent parts to form a whole: *great care has been taken in the compilation of this guidebook.* **2** a thing, esp. a book, record, or broadcast program, that is put together by assembling previously separate items: *there are thirty-three stories in this compilation* | [as adj.] *a compilation album.* Cf. ANTHOLOGY.
com•pla•cent |kəm'plāsənt| • *adj.* showing smug or uncritical satisfaction with oneself or one's achievements: *you can't afford to be complacent about security.*
DERIVATIVES: **com•pla•cen•cy** *n.* **com•pla•cent•ly** *adv.*

USAGE: **Complacent** means 'smugly self-satisfied:' *After four consecutive championships the team became complacent.* **Complaisant**, a much rarer word, means 'deferential, willing to please:' *Once released from the pen, the barking dogs become peaceful and complaisant.* The noun **complacence** is a variant of the much more common **complacency**.

com•plai•sant |kəm'plāsənt| • *adj.* willing to please others; obliging; agreeable.
DERIVATIVES: **com•plai•sance** *n.* **com•plai•sant•ly** *adv.*
com•pleat |kəm'plēt| • *adj. & v.* archaic spelling of **complete**.
com•ple•ment • *n.* |'kämpləmənt| **1** a thing that completes or brings to perfection: *the libretto proved a perfect* **complement to** *the music.* **2** [in sing.] a number or quantity of something required to make a group complete: *at the moment we have* **a full complement of** *staff.*
■ the number of people required to crew a ship: *almost half the ship's complement of 322 were wounded.* ■ (in geometry) the amount in degrees by which a given angle is less than 90°. ■ (in mathematics) the members of a set that are not members of a given subset. **3** one or more words, phrases, or clauses governed by a verb (or by a noun or a predicative adjective) that complete the meaning of the predicate. **4** a group of proteins present in blood plasma and tissue fluid that combine with an antigen–antibody complex to bring about the destruction of foreign cells. • *v.* |-‚ment; -mənt| [trans.] add to (something) in a way that enhances or improves it; make perfect: *a classic blazer complements a look that's smart or casual.*
■ add to or make complete: *the proposals complement the incentives already available.*
DERIVATIVES: **com•ple•men•tal** |‚kämplə'mentl| *adj.*

USAGE: **Complement** and **compliment** (and the related words **complementary** and **complimentary**) are frequently confused. Although pronounced alike, they have quite different meanings. As a verb **complement** means 'to add to (something) in a way that completes, enhances, or improves,' as in

The vice president's experience in military and foreign affairs complemented the president's expertise in domestic policy. **Compliment** means 'admire and praise (someone) for something,' as in *They complimented Janet on her new necklace.* **Complementary** means 'forming a complement or addition; completing': *I purchased a suit with a complementary tie and handkerchief.* It can be confused with **complimentary**, for which one sense is 'given freely, as a courtesy': *You must pay for the suit, but the tie and the handkerchief are complimentary.* A trick for remembering which is which: **complement** is similar in meaning to *supplement*, and there is always an 'I' in a **compliment**.

com•plex |käm'pleks; kəm'pleks; 'käm ‚pleks| • *adj.* **1** consisting of many different and connected parts: *a complex network of water channels.*
■ not easy to analyze or understand; complicated or intricate: *a complex personality | the situation is more complex than it appears.* **2** (in mathematics) denoting or involving numbers or quantities containing both a real and an imaginary part. **3** (in chemistry) denoting an ion or molecule in which one or more groups are linked to a metal atom by coordinate bonds. • *n.* |'käm‚pleks| **1** a group of similar buildings or facilities on the same site: *a new apartment complex | a complex of hotels.*
■ a group or system of different things that are linked in a close or complicated way; a network: *a complex of mountain roads.* **2** (in psychoanalysis) a related group of emotionally significant ideas that are completely or partly repressed and that cause psychic conflict leading to abnormal mental states or behavior.
■ a disproportionate concern or anxiety about something: *there's no point having a* **complex about** *losing your hair.* **3** an ion or molecule in which one or more groups are linked to a metal atom by coordinate bonds.
■ any loosely bonded species formed by the association of two molecules: *cross-linked protein–DNA complexes.* • *v.* |käm'pleks; kəm 'pleks; 'käm‚pleks| [trans.] (usu. **be complexed**) make (an atom or compound) form a complex with another: *the DNA was* **complexed with** *the nuclear extract | [as adj.]* (**complexed**) *the complexed metal ion.*
■ [intrans.] form a complex: *these proteins are capable of complexing with VP16.*
DERIVATIVES: **com•plex•a•tion** |käm‚plek 'sāSHən; kəm-| *n.* (Chemistry) **com•plex•ly** *adv.*

com•pli•ance |kəm'plīəns| • *n.* **1** the action or fact of according with a wish or command: *they must secure each other's cooperation or compliance.*
■ (**compliance with**) the state or fact of according with or meeting rules or standards: *all imports of timber are* **in compliance with** *regulations.* ■ unworthy or excessive yielding; giving in: *the appalling compliance with* **the governor's** *views shown by the commission.*

com•plic•it |kəm'plisit| • *n.* involved with others in an illegal activity or wrongdoing: *all*

of these people are **complicit in** some criminal conspiracy.
DERIVATIVES: **com•plic•i•ty** |-ty| *n.*

com•pli•ment • *n.* |'kämpləmənt| a polite expression of praise or admiration: *she paid me an enormous compliment..*
■ an act or circumstance that implies praise or respect: *it's a compliment to the bride to dress up on her special day.* ■ (**compliments**) congratulations or praise expressed to someone: *my* **compliments on** *your cooking.* ■ (**compliments**) greetings or expressions of friendliness, esp. when sent as a message. • *v.* |'kämplə‚ment| [trans.] politely congratulate or praise (someone) for something: *he* **complimented** *Erica* **on** *her appearance.*
■ praise (something) politely.

USAGE: See **usage** at COMPLEMENT.

com•po•nent |kəm'pōnənt| • *n.* **1** a part or element of a larger whole, esp. a part of a machine or vehicle. • *adj.* [attrib.] constituting part of a larger whole; constituent: *purchase component parts and assemble them.*

com•port |kəm'pôrt| • *v.* **1** (**comport oneself**) conduct oneself; behave: *articulate students who comported themselves well in television interviews.* **2** [intrans.] (**comport with**) accord with; agree with: *actions that comport with her liberal views.*

com•pose[1] |kəm'pōz| • *v.* [trans.] **1** write or create (a work of art, esp. music or poetry): *he had composed the First Violin Sonata four years earlier.*
■ write or phrase (a letter or piece of writing) with care and thought: *the first sentence is so hard to compose.* ■ form (a whole) by ordering or arranging the parts, esp. in an artistic way: *compose and draw a still life.* ■ order or arrange (parts) to form a whole, esp. in an artistic way: *make an attempt to compose your images.* **2** (usu. **be composed**) (of elements) constitute or make up (a whole): *the system is* **composed of** *a group of machines.* Cf. COMPRISE.
■ be (a specified number or amount) of a whole: *Christians compose 40 percent of the population.* **3** calm or settle (oneself or one's features or thoughts): *she tried to* **compose herself.**
■ settle (a dispute): *the king, with some difficulty, composed this difference.* **4** prepare (a text) for printing by manually, mechanically, or electronically setting up the letters and other characters in the order to be printed.
■ set up (letters and characters) in this way.

USAGE: **Compose** and **comprise** are often confused, but can be sorted out. The parts **compose** (make up) the whole; the whole **comprises** (contains) the parts. *Citizens who have been chosen at random and screened for prejudices compose a jury. Each crew comprises a commander, a gunner, and a driver.* In passive constructions, the whole *is composed of* the parts, and the parts *are comprised in* the whole. (**Compose** = put together; **comprise** = contain, consist of.) The usage "is comprised of" is avoided by careful speakers and writers.

com•pose[2] |kəm'pōz| • v. [trans.] **1** write or create (a work of art, esp. music or poetry): *he composed the First Violin Sonata four years earlier.* ■ write or phrase (a letter or piece of writing) with care and thought: *the first sentence is so hard to compose.* ■ form (a whole) by ordering or arranging the parts, esp. in an artistic way: *compose and draw a still life.* ■ order or arrange (parts) to form a whole, esp. in an artistic way: *make an attempt to compose your images.* **2** (usu. **be composed**) (of elements) constitute or make up (a whole): *the system is composed of a group of machines.* ■ be (a specified number or amount) of a whole: *Christians compose 40 percent of the state's population.* **3** calm or settle (oneself or one's features or thoughts): *she tried to compose herself.* ■ archaic settle (a dispute): *the king, with some difficulty, composed this difference.* **4** prepare (a text) for printing by manually, mechanically, or electronically setting up the letters and other characters in the order to be printed. ■ set up (letters and characters) in this way.

USAGE: **Compose** and **comprise** are often confused, but can be sorted out. The parts **compose** (make up) the whole; the whole **comprises** (contains) the parts. *Citizens who have been been chosen at random and screened for prejudices compose a jury. Each crew comprises a commander, a gunner, and a driver.* In passive constructions, the whole *is composed of* the parts, and the parts *are comprised in* the whole. (**Compose** = put together; **comprise** = contain, consist of.) The usage "is comprised of" is avoided by careful speakers and writers.

com•pos•ite |kəm'päzət; käm-| • adj. **1** made up of various parts or elements. ■ (esp. of a constructional material) made up of recognizable constituents: *a new composite material—a blend of plastic and ceramic resins.* ■ (of a mathematical integer) being the product of two or more factors greater than one; not prime. **2** (**Composite**) relating to or denoting a classical order of architecture consisting of elements of the Ionic and Corinthian orders. **3** relating to or denoting plants of the daisy family (Compositae or Asteraceae), whose so-called flowers are composed of many florets and surrounding bracts. • n. **1** a thing made up of several parts or elements: *the English legal system is a composite of legislation and judicial precedent.* ■ a composite constructional material. **2** a plant of the daisy family (Compositae). **3** (**Composite**) the Composite order of architecture. • v. [trans.] [usu. as n.] (**compositing**) combine (two or more images) to make a single picture, esp. electronically: *photographic compositing by computer.*
DERIVATIVES: **com•pos•ite•ly** adv. **com•pos•ite•ness** n.
com•pos•i•tor |kəm'päzitər| • n. a person who arranges type for printing or keys text into a composing machine.

com•po•sure |kəm'pōzʜər| • n. the state or feeling of being calm and in control of oneself.
com•pote |'käm,pōt| • n. **1** fruit preserved or cooked in syrup. **2** a bowl-shaped dessert dish with a stem.
com•pre•hen•si•ble |,kämpri'hensəbəl| (also **comprehendible**) • adj. able to be understood; (comprehended): *clear and comprehensible English.*
DERIVATIVES: **com•pre•hen•si•bil•i•ty** |-,hensə'bilitē| n. **com•pre•hen•si•bly** |-blē| adv.
com•pre•hen•sive |,kämpri'hensiv| • adj. complete; including all or nearly all elements or aspects of something: *a comprehensive list of sources.* ■ of large content or scope; wide-ranging: *a comprehensive collection of photographs.* ■ (of automobile insurance) providing coverage for most risks, including damage to the policyholder's own vehicle: *comprehensive and collision insurance.* ■ (also **comprehensive examination** or **comp**) an examination testing a student's command of a field of knowledge.
DERIVATIVES: **com•pre•hen•sive•ly** adv. **com•pre•hen•sive•ness** n.
com•press • v. |kəm'pres| [trans.] (often **be compressed**) flatten by pressure; squeeze; press: *the skirt can be folded and compressed into a small bag* | [as adj.] (**compressed**) *compressed gas.* ■ [intrans.] be squeezed or pressed together or into a smaller space: *the land is sinking as the soil compresses.* ■ squeeze or press (two things) together: *Violet compressed her lips grimly.* ■ express in a shorter form; abridge: *compress the main findings into summary form.* ■ alter the form of (computer data) to reduce the amount of storage necessary. ■ [as adj.] (**compressed**) having a narrow shape as if flattened, esp. sideways: *most sea snakes have a compressed tail.* • n. |'käm,pres| a pad of absorbent material pressed onto part of the body to relieve inflammation or stop bleeding: *a cold compress.*
DERIVATIVES: **com•press•i•bil•i•ty** |kəm,presə'bilitē| n. **com•press•i•ble** adj. **com•pres•sive** |-'presiv| adj.
com•prise |kəm'prīz| • v. [trans.] consist of; be made up of: *the country comprises fifty states and a federal district.* ■ make up; constitute: *this single breed comprises 50 percent of Swiss cattle* | (**be comprised of**) *documents are comprised of words.*

USAGE: **1** On the differences between **comprise** and **compose**, see usage at COMPOSE.

com•pro•mise |'kämprə,mīz| • n. an agreement or a settlement of a conflict that is reached by each side making concessions: *an ability to listen to two sides in a dispute, and devise a compromise acceptable to both.* ■ a middle state between conflicting opinions or actions reached by mutual concession or modification: *a compromise between com-*

munism and private enterprise. ∎ the acceptance of standards that are lower than is desirable: *we should allow no compromise on reading scores.* • *v.* **1** [intrans.] settle a conflict by mutual concession: *in the end we compromised and deferred the issue.*
∎ [trans.] settle (a dispute) by mutual concession: *I should compromise the matter with my father.* **2** [trans.] weaken (a reputation or principle) by accepting standards that are lower than is desirable: *commercial pressures could compromise safety.*
∎ [intrans.] accept standards that are lower than is desirable: *we were not prepared to compromise on safety.* ∎ bring into disrepute or danger by indiscreet, foolish, or reckless behavior: *situations in which our troops could be compromised.*
DERIVATIVES: **com•pro•mis•er** *n.*

comp•trol•ler |kənˈtrōlər; ˌkäm(p)ˈtrōlər; ˈkäm(p)ˌtrōlər| • *n.* a controller (used in the title of some financial officers).

com•pul•sion |kəmˈpəlSHən| • *n.* **1** the action or state of forcing or being forced to do something: constraint: *the payment was made under compulsion.* **2** an irresistible urge to behave in a certain way, esp. against one's conscious wishes: *he felt a compulsion to babble on about what had happened.*

com•pul•sive |kəmˈpəlsiv| • *adj.* **1** resulting from or relating to an irresistible urge, esp. one that is against one's conscious wishes: *compulsive eating.*
∎ (of a person) acting as a result of such an urge: *a compulsive liar.* Cf. IMPULSIVE. **2** irresistibly interesting or exciting; compelling: *this play is compulsive viewing.*
DERIVATIVES: **com•pul•sive•ly** *adv.* **com•pul•sive•ness** *n.*

com•pul•so•ry |kəmˈpəlsərē| • *adj.* required by law or a rule; obligatory.
∎ involving or exercising compulsion; coercive.
DERIVATIVES: **com•pul•so•ri•ly** |-sərəlē| *adv.* **com•pul•so•ri•ness** *n.*

com•punc•tion |kəmˈpəNG(k)SHən| • *n.* [usu. with negative] a feeling of guilt or moral scruple that accompanies or follows the doing of something bad: *they used insider information without compunction.*
DERIVATIVES: **com•punc•tion•less** *adj.* **com•punc•tious** |-SHəs| *adj.* **com•punc•tious•ly** |-SHəslē| *adv.*

co•na•tion |kōˈnāSHən| • *n.* (in philosophy and psychology) the mental faculty of purpose, desire, or will to perform an action; volition.
DERIVATIVES: **con•a•tive** *adj.*

con bri•o |kän ˈbrēō; kōn| • *adv.* (esp. as a musical direction) with vigor.

con•cat•e•nate |kənˈkatnˌāt| • *v.* [trans.] link (things) together in a chain or series: *a programming function that concatenates text strings.*
DERIVATIVES: **con•cat•e•na•tion** *n.*

con•cave |känˈkāv; ˈkänˌkāv| • *adj.* having an outline or surface that curves inward like the interior of a circle or sphere. Cf. CONVEX.

DERIVATIVES: **con•cave•ly** *adv.* **con•cav•i•ty** |känˈkavitē| *n.*

con•cede |kənˈsēd| • *v.* **1** admit that something is true or valid after first denying or resisting it: [with clause] *I had to concede that I'd overreacted* | [trans.] *that principle now seems to have been conceded.*
∎ [trans.] admit (defeat) in a contest: *he conceded defeat.* ∎ [trans.] admit defeat in (a contest): *ready to concede the semifinal.* **2** [trans.] surrender or yield (something that one possesses); cede: *to concede all the territory he'd won.*
∎ grant (a right, privilege, or demand): *their rights to redress of grievances were conceded once more.* ∎ (in sports) fail to prevent the scoring of (a goal or point) by an opponent: *conceded a field goal in the third quarter.* ∎ allow (a lead or advantage) to slip: *he took an early lead that he never conceded.*
DERIVATIVES: **con•ced•er** *n.*

con•ceit |kənˈsēt| • *n.* **1** excessive pride in oneself: *he was puffed up with conceit.* **2** a fanciful expression in writing or speech; an elaborate metaphor: *the idea of the wind's singing is a prime romantic conceit.*
∎ an artistic effect or device: *the director's brilliant conceit was to film this tale in black and white.* ∎ a fanciful notion: *the widespread conceit that he spent most of the 1980s drunk.*

con•cen•tric |kənˈsentrik; kän-| • *adj.* of or denoting circles, arcs, or other shapes that share the same center, the larger often completely surrounding the smaller. Cf. ECCENTRIC.
DERIVATIVES: **con•cen•tri•cal•ly** |-ik(ə)lē| *adv.* **con•cen•tric•i•ty** |ˌkänˌsenˈtrisitē| *n.*

con•cep•tu•al•ism |kənˈsepCHəwəˌlizəm| • *n.* (in philosophy) the theory that universal statements or categories can be said to exist, but only as concepts in the mind.
DERIVATIVES: **con•cep•tu•al•ist** *n.*

con•cert • *n.* |ˈkänˌsərt; ˈkänsərt| **1** a musical performance given in public, typically by several performers or of several separate works: *symphony concerts* | [as adj.] *a concert pianist.*
∎ [as adj.] of, relating to, or denoting the performance of music written for opera, ballet, or theater on its own without the accompanying dramatic action: *the concert version of Verdi's opera.* **2** agreement, accordance, or harmony: *critics' inability to describe with any precision and concert the characteristics of literature.* • *v.* |kənˈsərt| [trans.] arrange (something) by mutual agreement or coordination: *they started meeting regularly to concert their tactics.*

con•cert•ed |kənˈsərtəd| • *adj.* [attrib.] jointly arranged, planned, or carried out; coordinated: *determined to begin concerted action against them.*
∎ strenuously carried out; done with great effort: *it would take a concerted effort.*

con•cer•ti•na |ˌkänsərˈtēnə| • *n.* a small musical instrument, typically polygonal in form, played by stretching and squeezing between the hands, to work a central bellows that

blows air over reeds, each note being sounded by a button.
- [as adj.] opening or closing in multiple folds or coils: *concertina doors* | *concertina wire.* • *v.* (**concertinas, concertinaed** |-'tēnəd| or **concertina'd, concertinaing** |-'tēnə-iNG|) [trans.] extend, compress, or collapse in symmetrical creased folds: [as adj.] (**concertinaed**) *negotiations concertinaed into a week-long session.*

con•cer•to |kən'CHerṯō| • *n.* (pl. **concertos** or **concerti** |kən'CHerṯē|) a musical composition for a solo instrument or instruments accompanied by an orchestra, esp. one conceived on a relatively large scale.

con•cer•to gros•so |'grōsō; 'grôsō| • *n.* (pl. **concerti grossi** |'grōsē; 'grôsē|) a musical composition for a group of solo instruments accompanied by an orchestra. The term is used mainly of baroque works.

con•ces•sion |kən'seSHən| • *n.* **1** a thing that is granted, esp. in response to demands; a thing conceded.
- the action of conceding, granting, or yielding something. ■ (**a concession to**) a gesture, esp. a token one, made in recognition of a demand or prevailing standard: *the hat was her concession to fashion.* **2** a preferential allowance or rate given by an organization: *tax concessions.* **3** the right to use land or other property for a specified purpose, granted by a government, company, or other controlling body: *new logging concessions.*
- a commercial operation within the premises of a larger one, typically selling refreshments. DERIVATIVES: **con•ces•sion•aire** *n.* **con•ces•sion•er** *n.*

con•ces•sive |kən'sesiv| • *adj.* **1** characterized by, or tending to concession: *we must look for a more concessive approach.* **2** (of a preposition or conjunction) introducing a phrase or clause denoting a circumstance that might be expected to make the action of the main clause impossible, but does not (e.g., *in spite of, although*).
- (of a phrase or clause) introduced by a concessive preposition or conjunction.

con•cierge |kôN'syerZH| ˌkänsē'erZH| • *n.* **1** (esp. in France) a caretaker of an apartment complex or a small hotel, typically one living on the premises. **2** a hotel employee whose job is to assist guests by arranging tours, making theater and restaurant reservations, etc.

con•cil•i•a•to•ry |kən'silēə,tôrē| • *adj.* intended or likely to placate or pacify: *a conciliatory approach.* DERIVATIVES: **con•cil•i•a•tive** *adj.* **con•cil•i•a•to•ri•ness** *n.*

con•cise |kən'sīs| • *adj.* giving a lot of information clearly and in a few words; brief but comprehensive: *a concise account of the country's history.* DERIVATIVES: **con•cise•ly** *adv.* **con•cise•ness** *n.* **con•ci•sion** |-'siZHən| *n.*

con•clave |'kän,klāv| • *n.* a private meeting.
- (in the Roman Catholic Church) the assembly of cardinals for the election of a pope.
- the meeting place for such an assembly.

con•clu•sive |kən'klo͞osiv; -ziv| • *adj.* (of evidence or argument) serving to prove a case; decisive or convincing.
- (of a victory) achieved easily or by a large margin. DERIVATIVES: **con•clu•sive•ly** *adv.* **con•clu•sive•ness** *n.*

con•coct |kən'käkt| • *v.* [trans.] make (a dish or meal) by combining various ingredients.
- create or devise (said esp. of a story or plan). DERIVATIVES: **con•coct•er** *n.* **con•coc•tion** *n.*

con•com•i•tant |kən'kämətənt| • *adj.* naturally accompanying or associated: *she loved travel, with all its concomitant worries.* • *n.* a phenomenon that naturally accompanies or follows something: *pain is as concomitant of life.* DERIVATIVES: **con•com•i•tant•ly** *adv.*

con•cord |'käNG,kôrd; 'kän-| • *n.* **1** agreement or harmony between people or groups: *a pact of peace and concord.*
- a treaty. **2** agreement between words in gender, number, case, person, or any other grammatical category that affects the forms of the words. **3** (in music) a chord that is pleasing or satisfactory in itself.

con•cord•ance |kən'kôrdns| • *n.* **1** an alphabetical list of the words (esp. the important ones) in a text, usually with citations of the passages concerned: *a concordance to the Bible.* **2** agreement. • *v.* [trans.] [often as adj.] (**concordanced**) make a concordance of: *the value of concordanced information.*

con•cord•ant |kən'kôrdnt| • *adj.* in agreement or harmony; consistent: *the answers were roughly concordant.* DERIVATIVES: **con•cord•ant•ly** *adv.*

con•cor•dat |kän'kôr,dæt| • *n.* an agreement or treaty, esp. one between the Vatican and a secular government relating to matters of mutual interest.

con•course |'kän,kôrs; 'käNG-| • *n.* **1** a large open area inside or in front of a public building, as in an airport or train station: *the domestic arrivals concourse.* **2** a crowd or assembly of people: *a vast **concourse of** learned men.*

con•crete • *adj.* |kän'krēt; 'kän,krēt; kən 'krēt| **1** existing in a material or physical form; real or solid; not abstract: *concrete objects like stones* | *it exists as a physically concrete form.*
- specific; definite: *I haven't got any concrete proof.* ■ (of a noun) denoting a material object as opposed to an abstract quality, state, or action. **2** formed by cohesion of parts into a mass; solidified.
- (of music) constructed by mixing recorded sounds. ■ (of poetry) in which meaning is conveyed visually, by means of patterns of words and letters and other typographical devices. • *n.* |'kän,krēt; kän'krēt| a heavy, rough building material made from a mixture of broken stone or gravel, sand, cement, and water, that can be spread or poured into molds and that forms a stonelike mass on hardening: *slabs of concrete* | [as adj.] *the*

concrete sidewalk. • v. | 'kän,krēt; kän'krēt | [trans.] (often **be concreted**) **1** cover (an area) with concrete: *the precious English countryside may soon be concreted over.*
■ [with obj. and adverbial of place] fix in position with concrete: *the post is concreted into the ground.* **2** form (something) into a mass; solidify: *the juices of the plants are concreted upon the surface.*
■ make real or concrete instead of abstract: *concreting God into actual form of man.*
PHRASES: **be set in concrete** (of a policy or idea) be fixed and unalterable: *I do not regard the Constitution as set in concrete.*
DERIVATIVES: **con•crete•ly** *adv.* **con• crete•ness** *n.*
con•cre•tion | kən'krēsHən; kän- | • *n.* a hard solid mass formed by the local accumulation of matter, esp. within the body or within a mass of sediment.
■ the formation of such a mass.
DERIVATIVES: **con•cre•tion•ar•y** |-sHə ,nerē | *adj.*
con•cu•bine | 'käNGkyōō,bīn | • *n.* (in polygamous societies) a woman who lives with a man but has lower status than his wife or wives.
■ a mistress.
DERIVATIVES: **con•cu•bin•age** *n.* **con•cu• bi•nar•y** | kən'kyōōbə,nerē; kän- | *adj.*
con•cu•pis•cence | kän'kyōōpəsəns; kən- | • *n.* strong sexual desire; lust.
DERIVATIVES: **con•cu•pis•cent** *adj.*
con•cur | kən'kər | • *v.* (**concurred, concurring**) [intrans.] **1** be of the same opinion; agree: *the authors concurred with the majority* | *they concurred in the creation of the disciplinary procedures* | [with direct speech] *"That's right," the chairman concurred.*
■ (**concur with**) agree with (a decision, opinion, or finding): *we strongly concur with this recommendation.* **2** happen or occur at the same time; coincide.
DERIVATIVES: **con•cur•rence** |-'kərəns | *n.* **con•cur•ren•cy** |-'kərənsē | *n.* **con•cur• ring** *adj.* (of a judicial opinion) agreeing with the result of a case (but not with all of the majority's reasoning).
con•cur•rent | kən'kərənt | • *adj.* existing, happening, or done at the same time: *there are three concurrent art fairs around the city.*
■ (of two or more prison sentences) to be served at the same time. ■ (in mathematics, of three or more lines) meeting at or tending toward one point.
DERIVATIVES: **con•cur•rent•ly** *adv.*
con•cus•sion | kən'kəsHən | • *n.* **1** temporary unconsciousness caused by a blow to the head. The term is also used loosely of the aftereffects such as confusion or temporary incapacity. **2** a violent shock as from a heavy blow: *the ground shuddered with the concussion of the blast.* [as adj.] *a concussion grenade.*
con•den•sa•tion | ,kän,den'sāsHən; -dən- | • *n.* **1** water that collects as droplets on a cold surface when humid air is in contact with it. **2** the process of becoming more dense, in particular:

■ the conversion of a vapor or gas to a liquid.
■ (also **condensation reaction**) a chemical reaction in which two molecules combine to form a larger molecule, producing a small molecule such as H_2O as a by-product. ■ (in psychology) the fusion of two or more images, ideas, or symbolic meanings into a single composite or new image, as a primary process in unconscious thought exemplified in dreams. **3** a concise version of something, esp. a text: *a readable condensation of the recent literature.*
con•dense | kən'dens | • *v.* **1** [trans.] make (something) denser or more concentrated: *the limestones of the Jurassic age are condensed into a mere 11 feet* | [as adj.] (**condensed**) *check that your printer can cope with wide text or condensed characters.*
■ [usu. as adj.] (**condensed**) thicken (a liquid) by reducing the water content, typically by boiling: *condensed soup.* ■ express (a piece of writing or speech) in fewer words; make concise: *he condensed the three plays into a three-hour drama.* **2** [intrans.] be changed from a gas or vapor to a liquid: *the vapor in the air condenses into droplets of water.*
■ [trans.] cause (a gas or vapor) to be changed to a liquid: *the cold air was condensing my breath.*
DERIVATIVES: **con•den•sa•ble** *adj.*
con•de•scend | ,kändi'send | • *v.* [intrans.] show feelings of superiority; patronize: *take care not to condescend to your reader.*
■ [with infinitive] do something in a haughty way, as though it is below one's dignity or level of importance: *we'll be waiting for twenty minutes before she condescends to appear.*
DERIVATIVES: **con•de•scend•ing** *adj.* **con• de•scend•ing•ly** *adv.* **con•de•scen•dence** |-'sendəns | *n.* **con•de•scen•sion** |-'sen-cHən | *n.*
con•dign | kən'dīn | • *adj.* (of punishment or retribution) appropriate to the crime or wrongdoing; fitting and deserved.
DERIVATIVES: **con•dign•ly** *adv.*
con•di•tion•al | kən'disHənl | • *adj.* (of a clause, phrase, conjunction, or verb form) expressing a condition. • *n.* **1** a clause or logical conjunction that expresses a condition and in English typically begins with 'if.'
■ a statement or sentence containing a conditional clause. **2** Grammar the conditional mood of a verb, for example *should* in *if I should die.*
DERIVATIVES: **con•di•tion•al•i•ty** | kən ,disHə'nælitē | *n.* **con•di•tion•al•ly** *adv.*
con•do•min•i•um | ,kändə'minēəm | • *n.* (pl. **condominiums**) **1** a building or complex of buildings containing a number of individually owned apartments or houses.
■ (also **condo**) each of the individual apartments or houses in such a building or complex. ■ the system of ownership by which these operate, in which owners have full title to the individual apartment or house and an undivided interest in the shared parts of the property. **2** the joint control of a country's or territory's affairs by other countries.
■ a state so governed.

con•done |kən'dōn| • v. [trans.] [often with negative] accept and allow (behavior that is considered morally wrong or offensive) to continue: *the college cannot condone any behavior that involves illicit drugs.*
■ approve or sanction (something), esp. with reluctance: *the practice is not officially condoned by any airline.*
DERIVATIVES: **con•don•a•ble** adj. **con•do•na•tion** |-'nāsHən; -dō-| n. **con•don•er** n.

con•duce |kən'd(y)ōōs| • v. [intrans.] (**conduce to**) help to bring about (a particular situation or outcome): *every care was taken that could conduce to their comfort.*

con•du•cive |kən'd(y)ōōsiv| • adj. making a certain situation or outcome likely or possible: *the harsh lights and cameras were hardly* **conducive** *to a relaxed atmosphere.*

con•duc•tive |kən'dəktiv| • adj. having the ability to serve as a channel or medium for something (esp. heat or electricity): *to induce currents in conductive coils.*
■ of or relating to this process.
DERIVATIVES: **con•duc•tive•ly** adv. **con•duc•tiv•i•ty** n.

con•duit |'kän,d(y)ōōət; 'känd(w)ət| • n. a channel for conveying something, esp. water or another fluid: *a conduit takes water to the power plant* | *the office acts as a conduit for ideas to flow throughout the organization.*
■ a tube or trough for protecting electric wiring: *the gas pipe should not be close to any electrical conduit.*

con•fab•u•late |kən'fæbyə,lāt| • v. [intrans.] **1** engage in conversation; talk: *on the telephone confabulating with someone.* **2** (in psychiatry) fabricate imaginary experiences as compensation for loss of memory.
DERIVATIVES: **con•fab•u•la•tion** |-,fæbyə'lāsHən| n. **con•fab•u•la•to•ry** |-lə,tôrē| adj.

con•fec•tion |kən'feksHən| • n. **1** a dish or delicacy made with sweet ingredients: *a whipped chocolate and cream confection.*
■ an elaborately constructed thing, esp. a frivolous one: *the city is a confection of shimmering gold.* **2** the action of mixing or compounding something.
DERIVATIVES: **con•fec•tion•ar•y** |-,nerē| adj.

con•fed•er•ate • adj. |kən'fedərət| [attrib.] joined by an agreement or treaty: *confederate councils.*
■ (**Confederate**) of or relating to the Confederate States of America (1861–65): *the Confederate flag.* • n. **1** a person one works with, esp. in something secret or illegal; an accomplice. **2** (**Confederate**) a supporter, soldier, etc., of the Confederate States of America. • v. |-,rāt| [trans.] [usu. as adj.] (**confederated**) bring (states or groups of people) into an alliance: *Switzerland is a model for the new confederated Europe.*
DERIVATIVES: **con•fed•er•a•cy** n.

con•fi•dant |'känfə,dænt; -,dänt| (fem. **confidante** pronunc. same) • n. a person with whom one shares a secret or private matter, trusting them not to repeat it to others.

con•fi•den•tial |,känfə'denCHəl| • adj. intended to be kept secret: *knowledge that was privileged and confidential.*
■ (of a person's tone of voice) indicating that what one says is private or secret: *he dropped his voice to a confidential whisper.* ■ [attrib.] entrusted with private or restricted information: *a confidential secretary.*
DERIVATIVES: **con•fi•den•ti•al•i•ty** |-,denCHē'ælițē| n. **con•fi•den•tial•ly** adv.

con•fig•u•ra•tion |kən,fig(y)ə'rāsHən| • n. an arrangement of elements in a particular form, figure, or combination: *the broad configuration of the economy.*
■ the fixed three-dimensional relationship of the atoms in a molecule, defined by the bonds between them. ■ the arrangement in which items of computer hardware or software are interconnected. ■ (in psychology) another term for GESTALT.
DERIVATIVES: **con•fig•u•ra•tion•al** |-sHənl| adj. **con•fig•u•ra•tion•al•ly** |-sHənl-ē| adv. **con•fig•u•ra•tive** |-'fig(y)ərəṭiv| adj.

con•fig•ure |kən'figyər| • v. [trans.] (often be **configured**) shape or put together in a particular form or configuration: *two of the aircraft will be configured as VIP transports.*
■ (in computing) arrange or order (a computer system or an element of it) so as to fit it for a designated task: *expanded memory can be configured as a virtual drive.*
DERIVATIVES: **con•fig•ur•a•ble** adj.

con•fir•ma•tion |,känfər'māsHən| • n. (in the Christian Church) the rite at which a baptized person, esp. one baptized as an infant, affirms Christian belief and is admitted as a full member of the church.
■ the Jewish ceremony of bar mitzvah or bat mitzvah. ■ [as adj.] *a confirmation dress.*

con•firmed |kən'fərmd| • adj. (of a person) firmly established in a particular habit, belief, or way of life and unlikely to change: *a confirmed teetotaler.*

con•fis•cate |'känfə,skāt| • v. [trans.] take or seize (someone's property) with authority: *the guards confiscated his camera* | [as adj.] (**confiscated**) *confiscated equipment.*
■ seize private property with legal authority as a penalty against its owner: *the government confiscated their truck.*
DERIVATIVES: **con•fis•ca•tion** |,känfə'skāsHən| n. **con•fis•ca•tor** |-,skāṭər| n. **con•fis•ca•to•ry** |kən'fiskə,tôrē| adj.

con•fla•gra•tion |,känflə'grāsHən| • n. an extensive fire that burns over a great deal of land or destroys much property.

con•flate |kən'flāt| • v. [trans.] combine (two or more texts, ideas, etc.) into one: *the urban crisis conflates a number of different economic and social issues.*
DERIVATIVES: **con•fla•tion** |-'flāsHən| n.

con•flu•ence |'kän,flōōəns; kən'flōōəns| • n. the junction of two rivers, esp. rivers of approximately equal width: *here at the* **confluence** *of the Laramie and North Platte rivers.*
■ an act or process of merging: *a major confluence of the world's financial markets.*

con•form•ist |kən'fôrmist| • n. a person who

acts in accordance with accepted behavior or established practices.
■ Brit. a person who conforms to the practices of the Church of England. • *adj.* (of a person or activity) acting in accordance with accepted behavior or established practices; conventional.
DERIVATIVES: **con•form•ism** |-,mizəm| *n.*
con•form•i•ty |kən'fôrmiṯē| • *n.* compliance with standards, rules, or laws: *conformity to regulations* | *the goods were in conformity with the contract.*
■ behavior in accordance with accepted conventions or standards: *loyalty to one's party need not imply unquestioning conformity.* ■ Brit. compliance with the practices of the Church of England. ■ similarity in form or type; agreement in character: *these changes are intended to ensure conformity between all procedures.*
con•found |kən'fownd| • *v.* [trans.] **1** cause surprise or confusion in (someone), esp. by acting against their expectations: *the inflation figure confounded economic analysts.*
■ prove (a theory, expectation, or prediction) wrong: *the rise in prices confounded expectations.* ■ defeat (a plan, aim, or hope): *we will confound these tactics by the pressure groups.*
■ overthrow (an enemy). **2** (often **be confounded with**) mix up (something) with something else so that the individual elements become difficult to distinguish: *"nuke" is now a cooking term, as microwave radiation is confounded with nuclear radiation.*
DERIVATIVES: **con•found•er** *n.*
con•frère |'kän,frer; kän'frer; kôn'frer| (also **confrere**) • *n.* a fellow member of a profession; a colleague.
con•fute |kən'fyōōt| • *v.* [trans.] prove (a person or an assertion) to be wrong: *those who sought to confute this view were accused of ignorance.*
DERIVATIVES: **con•fu•ta•tion** |,känfyōō 'tāSHən| *n.* **con•fut•er** *n.*
con•geal |kən'jēl| • *v.* [intrans.] solidify or coagulate, esp. by cooling: *the blood had congealed into blobs* | [as adj.] **(congealed)** *congealed egg white.*
■ take shape or coalesce, esp. to form a satisfying whole: *the ballet failed to congeal as a single oeuvre.*
DERIVATIVES: **con•geal•a•ble** *adj.* **con•gel•a•tion** *n.*
con•gen•ial |kən'jēnyəl| • *adj.* pleasant or agreeable because well suited to one's own taste or inclination: *he went back to a climate more congenial to his cold stony soul.*
■ good-natured; amiable.
DERIVATIVES: **con•ge•ni•al•i•ty** |-,jēnē'æl-iṯē| *n.* **con•gen•ial•ly** *adv.*
con•gen•i•tal |kən'jenəṯl| • *adj.* (esp. of a disease or physical abnormality) present from birth.
■ (of a person) having a particular trait from birth or by firmly established habit: *a congenital liar.*
DERIVATIVES: **con•gen•i•tal•ly** *adv.*
con•glom•er•ate • *n.* |kən'glämərət| **1** a

number of different things or parts that are put or grouped together to form a whole but remain distinct entities: *the Earth is a specialized conglomerate of organisms.*
■ [often with adj.] a large corporation formed by the merging of separate and diverse firms: *a media conglomerate.* **2** (in geology) a coarse-grained sedimentary rock composed of rounded fragments embedded in a matrix of cementing material. • *adj.* of or relating to a conglomerate, esp. a large corporation: *conglomerate businesses.* • *v.* |-,rāt| [intrans.] gather together into a compact mass.
■ form a conglomerate by merging diverse businesses.
DERIVATIVES: **conglomeratic** |kən,glämə 'ræṯik| *adj.* **con•glom•er•a•tion** |kən,glämə 'rāSHən| *n.*
con•gre•ga•tion•al |,käNGgrə'gāSHənl| • *adj.* **1** of or relating to an assembly of worshippers (a congregation): *congregational singing.* **2** **(Congregational)** of or adhering to Congregationalism: *the Congregational Church.*
con•gru•ent |kən'grōōənt; 'käNGgrəwənt| • *adj.* **1** in agreement or harmony: *institutional and departmental objectives are largely congruent* | *the rules may not be congruent with the requirements of the law.* **2** (of geometrical figures) identical in form; coinciding exactly when superimposed.
DERIVATIVES: **con•gru•ence** *n.* **con•gru•en•cy** *n.* **con•gru•ent•ly** *adv.*
co•ni•fer |'känəfər; kō-| • *n.* a tree that bears cones and usu. evergreen needlelike or scalelike leaves. Conifers of major importance as the source of softwood, and also supply resins and turpentine.
DERIVATIVES: **co•nif•er•ous** |kə'nifərəs| *adj.*
con•jec•ture |kən'jekCHər| • *n.* an opinion or conclusion formed on the basis of incomplete information: *conjectures about the newcomer were many and varied* | *the purpose of the structure is open to conjecture.*
■ an unproven mathematical or scientific theorem. ■ the suggestion or reconstruction of a reading of a text not present in the original source. • *v.* [trans.] form an opinion or supposition about (something) on the basis of incomplete information: *he conjectured the existence of an otherwise unknown feature* | [with clause] *many conjectured that she had a second husband in mind.*
■ (in textual criticism) propose (a reading).
DERIVATIVES: **con•jec•tur•a•ble** *adj.* **con•jec•tur•er** *n.*
con•join |kən'join; kän-| • *v.* [trans.] join; combine: *an approach that conjoins theory and method.*
con•joint |kən'joint; kän-| • *adj.* [attrib.] combining all or both people or things involved: *conjoint family therapy.*
DERIVATIVES: **con•joint•ly** *adv.*
con•ju•gate • *v.* |'känjə,gāt| **1** [trans.] give the different forms of (a verb in an inflected language) as they vary according to voice, mood, tense, number, and person. **2** [intrans.] (of bacteria or unicellular organisms) become

temporarily united in order to exchange genetic material.
■ (of sex cells) become fused. **3** [trans.] (in chemistry) be combined with or joined to reversibly: *bilirubin is conjugated by liver enzymes.* • *adj.* | ˈkänjigət; -jə,gāt | coupled, connected, or related. • *n.* | ˈkänjigət; -jə,gāt | a thing that is conjugate or conjugated, in particular:
■ a chemical substance formed by the reversible combination of two or more others. ■ a mathematical value or entity having a reciprocal relation with another.
DERIVATIVES: **con•ju•ga•cy** | ˈkänjəgəsē | *n.* **con•ju•ga•tion** *n.* **con•ju•ga•tive** | ˈkänjə ,gātiv | *adj.*

con•junc•tive | kənˈjəNG(k)tiv | • *adj.* serving to join; connective: *the conjunctive tissue.*
■ involving the combination or co-occurrence of two or more conditions or properties: *conjunctive hypotheses are simpler to process than negative or disjunctive ones.* ■ of the nature of or relating to a grammatical conjunction. • *n.* a word or expression acting as a conjunction.
DERIVATIVES: **con•junc•tive•ly** *adv.*

con•jure • *v.* **1** | ˈkänjər; ˈkən- | [trans.] make (something) appear unexpectedly or seemingly from nowhere as if by magic: *Anne conjured up a most delicious stew.*
■ call (an image) to mind: *she was no longer able to conjure up the image of her mother's face.* ■ (of a word, sound, smell, etc.) cause someone to feel or think of (something): *one scent can conjure up a childhood summer beside a lake.* ■ call upon (a spirit or ghost) to appear, by means of a magic ritual: *they hoped to conjure up the spirit of their dead friend.* **2** | kən ˈjŏŏr | [with obj. and infinitive] archaic implore (someone) to do something.
DERIVATIVES: **con•jur•er con•ju•ror** *n.*

con•nate | ˈkän,āt; kä'nāt | • *adj.* (esp. of ideas or principles) existing in a person or thing from birth; innate.
■ of the same or similar nature; allied; congenial.

con•nat•u•ral | kəˈnæCH(ə)rəl; kä- | • *adj.* belonging naturally; innate: *religion is connatural with man.*
DERIVATIVES: **con•nat•u•ral•ly** *adv.*

con•niv•ance | kəˈnīvəns | • *n.* willingness to secretly allow or be involved in an immoral or illegal act: *this infringement of the law had taken place with the connivance of officials.*

con•nive | kəˈnīv | • *v.* [intrans.] (**connive at/in**) secretly allow (something considered immoral, illegal, or harmful) to occur: *you have it in your power to connive at my escape.*
■ conspire to do something considered immoral, illegal, or harmful: *the government had connived with security forces in permitting murder* | [as adj.] (**conniving**) *a conniving partner.*
DERIVATIVES: **con•niv•er** *n.*

con•nois•seur | ,känəˈsər; -ˈsŏŏr | • *n.* an expert judge in matters of taste: *a connoisseur of music.*
DERIVATIVES: **con•nois•seur•ship** | -,SHip | *n.*

con•no•ta•tion | ,känəˈtāSHən | • *n.* an idea or feeling that a word invokes for a person in addition to its literal or primary meaning (denotation): *the word "discipline" has unhappy connotations of punishment and repression.*
■ (in philosophy and logic) the abstract meaning or intension of a term, which forms a principle determining which objects or concepts it applies to.

con•note | kəˈnōt | • *v.* [trans.] (of a word) imply or suggest (an idea or feeling) in addition to the literal or primary meaning: *the term "modern science" usually connotes a complete openness to empirical testing.*
■ (of a fact) imply as a consequence or condition: *in that period a log cabin connoted hard luck.*
DERIVATIVES: **con•no•ta•tive** | ˈkänə,tākh tiv | *adj.*

USAGE: **Connote** does not mean the same as **denote**. **Denote** refers to the literal, primary meaning of something; **connote** refers to other characteristics suggested or implied by that thing. Thus, one might say that a word like **mother** *denotes* 'a woman who is a parent' but *connotes* qualities such as protection and affection. **Connotate** is a needless variant of **connote** that, if anything, only adds to the confusion: avoid it.

con•nu•bi•al | kəˈn(y)ŏŏbēəl | • *adj.* of or relating to marriage or the relationship of husband and wife; conjugal: *their connubial bed.*
DERIVATIVES: **con•nu•bi•al•i•ty** | kə ,n(y)ŏŏbēˈælitē | *n.* **con•nu•bi•al•ly** *adv.*

con•san•guin•e•ous | ,kän,sæNGˈgwinēəs | • *adj.* relating to or denoting people descended from the same ancestor: *consanguineous marriages.*
DERIVATIVES: **con•san•guin•i•ty** | -ˈgwin itē | *n.*

con•science | ˈkänCHəns | • *n.* an inner feeling or voice viewed as acting as a guide to the rightness or wrongness of one's behavior: *he had a guilty conscience about his desires* | *Ben was suffering a pang of conscience.*
DERIVATIVES: **con•science•less** *adj.*

con•sci•en•tious | ,känCHēˈenCHəs | • *adj.* (of a person) wishing to do what is right, esp. to do one's work or duty well and thoroughly.
■ (of work or a person's manner) showing such an attitude: *a conscientious look on her face.* ■ relating to a person's conscience. *conscientious beliefs.*
DERIVATIVES: **con•sci•en•tious•ly** *adv.* **con•sci•en•tious•ness** *n.*

con•scious | ˈkänCHəs | • *adj.* aware of and responding to one's surroundings; awake.
■ having knowledge of something; aware: *we are conscious of the extent of the problem.* ■ [predic.] (**conscious of**) painfully aware of; sensitive to: *he was very conscious of his appearance.* ■ [in combination] concerned with or worried about a particular matter: *they were growing increasingly security-conscious.* ■ (of an action or feeling) deliberate and intentional:

a conscious effort to walk properly. ■ (of the mind or a thought) directly perceptible to and under the control of the person concerned. *n.* (in psychology) the conscience mind. Cf. SUBCONSCIOUS, UNCONSCIOUS, PRECONSCIOUS.
DERIVATIVES: **con•scious•ly** *adv.*

con•script • *v.* |kənˈskript| [trans.] (often be **conscripted**) enlist (someone) compulsorily, typically into the armed services: *they were conscripted into the army.* • *n.* |ˈkänˌskript| a person enlisted compulsorily.
DERIVATIVES: **con•scrip•tion** *n.*

con•se•crate |ˈkänsiˌkrāt| • *v.* [trans.] (usu be **consecrated**) make or declare (something, typically a church) sacred; dedicate formally to a religious or divine purpose: *the present Holy Trinity church was consecrated in 1845* | [as adj.] (**consecrated**) *consecrated ground.* ■ (in Christian belief) make (bread or wine) into the body or blood of Christ: [as adj.] (**consecrated**) *they received the host but not the consecrated wine.* ■ ordain (someone) to a sacred office, typically that of bishop: [with obj. and complement] *in 1969 he was consecrated bishop of Northern Uganda.* ■ devote (something) exclusively to a particular purpose: *they'd decided to consecrate all their energies to this purposeful act.*
DERIVATIVES: **con•se•cra•tion** |ˌkänsiˈkrāsHən| *n.* **con•se•cra•tor** |-ˌkrātər| *n.* **con•se•cra•to•ry** |-krəˌtôrē| *adj.*

con•sec•u•tive |kənˈsekyətiv| • *adj.* following continuously: *five consecutive months of serious decline.* ■ in unbroken or logical sequence. ■ (in grammar) expressing consequence or result: *a consecutive clause.* ■ (in music) denoting intervals of the same kind (esp. fifths or octaves) occurring in succession between two parts or voices. ■ (of two or more prison sentences) to be served one after the other. Cf. CONCURRENT.
DERIVATIVES: **con•sec•u•tive•ly** *adv.* **con•sec•u•tive•ness** *n.*

con•sen•su•al |kənˈsenCHəwəl| • *adj.* relating to or involving consent, esp. mutual consent: *he admitted to having consensual sex with two women.* ■ relating to or involving consensus: *all decision-making was consensual.*
DERIVATIVES: **con•sen•su•al•ly** *adv.*

con•sen•sus |kənˈsensəs| • *n.* [usu. in sing.] general agreement: *a consensus of opinion among judges* | [as adj.] *a consensus view.*

con•se•quent |ˈkänsikwənt| -ˌkwent| • *adj.* following as a result or effect: *labor shortages would be created with a consequent increase in wages.* Cf. SUBSEQUENT. ■ (of a stream or valley) having a direction or character determined by the original slope of the land before erosion. ■ logically consistent. • *n.* 1 a thing that follows another. ■ (in logic) the second part of a conditional proposition, whose truth is stated to be implied by that of the antecedent. ■ the second term of a mathematical ratio.

con•se•quen•tial |ˌkänsəˈkwenCHəl| • *adj.* 1 following as a result or effect: *a loss of confidence and a consequential withdrawal of funds.* ■ (in law) resulting from an act, but not immediately and directly: *consequential damages.* 2 of great consequence; important; significant.
DERIVATIVES: **con•se•quen•ti•al•i•ty** |ˌkänsə,kwenCHēˈælitē| *n.* **con•se•quen•tial•ly** *adv.*

con•serv•an•cy |kənˈsərvənsē| • *n.* (pl. **-ies**) [in names] a body concerned with the preservation of natural resources: *the Nature Conservancy.*

con•serv•a•tive |kənˈsərvətiv; -vəˌtiv| • *adj.* holding to traditional attitudes and values and cautious about change or innovation, typically in relation to politics or religion. ■ (of Jews and Judaism) between Orthodox and Reform with regard to observation of traditional religious law and obligation. • *n.* a person who is averse to change and holds to traditional values and attitudes, typically in relation to politics. ■ (**Conservative**) a supporter or member of the Conservative Party of Great Britain or a similar party in another country.
DERIVATIVES: **con•serv•a•tism** |kənˈsərvəˌtizəm| *n.* **con•serv•a•tive•ly** *adv.* **con•serv•a•tive•ness** *n.*

con•ser•va•tor |kənˈsərvətər; kənˈsərvəˌtôr; ˈkänsərˌvātər| • *n.* a person responsible for the repair and preservation of works of art, buildings, or other things of cultural or environmental interest. ■ a guardian or protector: *the court appointed a conservator to handle the couple's affairs.*
DERIVATIVES: **con•serv•a•to•ri•al** *adj.* **con•ser•va•tor•ship** *n.*

con•serv•a•to•ry |kənˈsərvəˌtôrē| • *n.* (pl. **-ies**) 1 a college for the study of classical music or other arts. 2 a room with a glass roof and walls, attached to a house, typically at one side, and used as a greenhouse or a sun parlor.

con•serve |kənˈsərv| • *v.* [trans.] protect (something, esp. an environmentally or culturally important place or thing) from harm or destruction: *the funds raised will help conserve endangered meadowlands.* ■ prevent the wasteful or harmful overuse of (a resource): *industry should conserve more water.* ■ (in physics) maintain (a quantity such as energy or mass) at a constant overall total. ■ (usu. **be conserved**) retain (a particular amino acid, nucleotide, or sequence of these) unchanged in different protein or DNA molecules. ■ preserve (food, typically fruit) with sugar. • *n.* |ˈkänˌsərv| a sweet food made by preserving fruit with sugar; jam.

con•sid•er•a•tion |kənˌsidəˈrāsHən| • *n.* 1 careful thought, typically over a period of time: *a long process involving a great deal of careful consideration.* ■ a fact or a motive taken into account in deciding or judging something: *the idea was motivated by political considerations.* ■ thoughtfulness and sensitivity toward others: *companies should show more consideration for their* _employees._ **2** a payment or reward: _you can buy the books for a small consideration._

■ (in a contractual agreement) anything given or promised or forborne by one party in exchange for the promise or undertaking of another. **3** importance; consequence.

con•sign |kən'sīn| • _v._ [trans.] deliver (something) to a person's custody, typically in order for it to be sold: _he **consigned** three paintings **to** Sotheby's._

■ send (goods) by a public carrier. ■ (**consign someone/something to**) assign; commit decisively or permanently: _she consigned the letter to the wastebasket._

DERIVATIVES: **con•sign•ee** |ˌkänsəˈnē; ˌkänˌsīˈnē; kənˌsīˈnē| _n._ **con•sign•ment** _n._ **con•sign•or** |kənˈsīnər| _n._

con•sist • _v._ |kənˈsist| [intrans.] **1** (**consist of**) be composed or made up of: _the exhibition consists of 180 drawings._

■ (**consist in**) have as an essential feature: _his duties consist in taking the condition of the barometer._ **2** (**consist with**) be consistent with: _the information perfectly consists with our friend's account._ • _n._ (in railroading) the set of cars following the locomotive and making up a train.

con•so•nance |ˈkänsənəns| • _n._ agreement or compatibility between opinions or actions: _consonance between conservation measures and existing agricultural practice._

■ the recurrence of similar sounds, esp. consonants, in close proximity (chiefly as used in prosody). ■ combination of musical notes that are in harmony with each other owning to the relationship between their frequencies.

con•so•nant |ˈkänsənənt| • _n._ a basic speech sound in which the breath is at least partly obstructed and which can be combined with a vowel (made with relatively unobstructed breath) to form a syllable.

■ a letter representing such a sound. • _adj._ **1** [attrib.] denoting or relating to such a sound or letter: _a consonant phoneme._ **2** [predic.] (**consonant with**) in agreement or harmony with: _the findings are consonant with other research._

■ (in music) making a harmonious interval or chord: _the bass is consonant with all the upper notes._

DERIVATIVES: **con•so•nan•tal** |ˌkänsəˈnæntl| _adj._ **con•so•nant•ly** _adv._

con•sort[1] • _n._ |ˈkänˌsôrt| a wife, husband, or companion, in particular the spouse of a reigning monarch. • _v._ |kənˈsôrt; ˈkänˌsôrt| [intrans.] (**consort with**) habitually associate with (someone), typically with the disapproval of others: _you chose to consort with the enemy._

con•sort[2] |ˈkänˌsôrt| • _n._ a small group of musicians performing together, typically playing instrumental music of the Renaissance period: _a consort of viols._

con•sor•ti•um |kənˈsôrtēəm; -ˈsôrSH(ē)əm| • _n._ (pl. **consortia** |-ˈsôrtēə; -ˈsôrSH(ē)ə| or **consortiums**) **1** an association, typically of several companies. **2** (in law) the right of association and companionship with one's husband or wife.

con•spec•tus |kənˈspektəs| • _n._ a summary or overview of a subject: _five of his works give a rich conspectus of his art._

con•spic•u•ous |kənˈspikyəwəs| • _adj._ standing out so as to be clearly visible: _a conspicuous Adam's apple._

■ attracting notice or attention: _conspicuous bravery._

DERIVATIVES: **con•spi•cu•i•ty** |ˌkänspiˈkyo͞oitē| _n._ **con•spic•u•ous•ly** _adv._ **con•spic•u•ous•ness** _n._

con•spir•a•cy |kənˈspirəsē| • _n._ (pl. **-ies**) a secret plan by a group to do something unlawful or harmful: _a conspiracy to destroy evidence._

■ the action of plotting or conspiring.

con•sta•ble |ˈkänstəbəl| • _n._ **1** a peace officer with limited policing authority, typically in a small town.

■ Brit. a police officer. **2** the governor of a royal castle.

■ formerly, the highest-ranking official in a royal household.

con•stab•u•lar•y |kənˈstæbyəˌlerē| • _n._ (pl. **-ies**) the constables of a district, collectively.

■ an armed police force organized as a military unit. ■ a police force covering a particular area or city. • _adj._ [attrib.] of or relating to a constabulary.

con•ster•na•tion |ˌkänstərˈnāSHən| • _n._ feelings of anxiety or dismay, typically at something unexpected: _I let the lawn grow long, much **to the consternation of** the neighbors._

con•stit•u•en•cy |kənˈstiCHəwənsē| • _n._ (pl. **-ies**) a body of voters in a specified area who elect a representative to a legislative body: _the politician who wishes to remain in the good graces of his constituency._

■ the area represented in this way. ■ a body of customers or supporters: _a constituency of racing fans._

con•stit•u•ent |kənˈstiCHəwənt| • _adj._ [attrib.] **1** being a part of a whole: _the constituent minerals of the rock._ **2** being a voting member of an organization and having the power to appoint or elect: _the constituent body has a right of veto._

■ able to make or change a political constitution: _a constituent assembly._ • _n._ **1** a member of a constituency. **2** a component part of something: _the essential constituents of the human diet._

con•sti•tute |ˈkänstəˌt(y)o͞ot| • _v._ [trans.] **1** be (a part) of a whole: _single parents constitute a great proportion of the poor._

■ (of people or things) combine to form (a whole): _there were enough members present to constitute a quorum._ ■ be or be equivalent to (something): _his failure to act constituted a breach of duty._ **2** (usu. **be constituted**) give legal or constitutional form to (an institution); establish by law.

con•sti•tu•tion |ˌkänstəˈt(y)o͞oSHən| • _n._ **1** a body of fundamental principles or established precedents according to which a state or other organization is acknowledged to be governed.

■ a written record of this: _the preamble to the_

constitution of UNESCO. ■ (**the Constitution**) the basic written set of principles of federal government in the US, which came into operation in 1789 and has since been modified by twenty-seven amendments. **2** the composition of something: *the genetic constitution of a species.*

■ the forming or establishing of something: *the constitution of a police authority.* **3** a person's physical state with regard to vitality, health, and strength: *pregnancy had weakened her constitution.*

■ a person's mental or psychological makeup.

con•sti•tu•tion•al |ˌkänstəˈt(y)o͞osHənl| • *adj.* **1** of or relating to an established set of principles governing a state: *a constitutional amendment.*

■ in accordance with or allowed by such principles: *a constitutional monarchy* | *actions that were ruled not constitutional.* **2** of or relating to someone's physical or mental condition: *a constitutional weakness.* • *n.* a walk, typically one taken regularly to maintain or restore good health.
DERIVATIVES: **con•sti•tu•tion•al•i•ty** |-ˌt(y)o͞osHəˈnælitē| *n.* **con•sti•tu•tion•al•ly** *adv.*

con•sti•tu•tive |ˈkänstəˌt(y)o͞otiv; kən'stiCHətiv| • *adj.* **1** having the power to establish or give organized existence to something: *the state began to exercise a new and constitutive function.* **2** forming a part or constituent of something; component: *poverty is a constitutive element of a particular form of economic growth.*

■ forming an essential element of something: *language is constitutive of thought.* **3** (in biochemistry) relating to an enzyme or enzyme system that is continuously produced in an organism, regardless of the needs of cells.
DERIVATIVES: **con•sti•tu•tive•ly** *adv.*

con•strain |kənˈstrān| • *v.* [trans.] (often **be constrained**) severely restrict the scope, extent, or activity of: *agricultural development is constrained by climate.*

■ compel or force (someone) toward a particular course of action: [with obj. and infinitive] *children are constrained to work in the way the book dictates.* ■ [usu. as adj.] (**constrained**) cause to appear unnaturally forced, typically because of embarrassment: *he was acting in a constrained manner.* ■ confine forcibly; imprison. ■ bring about (something) by compulsion.
DERIVATIVES: **con•strain•a•ble** *adj.* **con•strain•ed•ly** |-nədlē| *adv.*

con•straint |kənˈstrānt| • *n.* a limitation or restriction: *the availability of water is the main constraint on food production* | *time constraints make it impossible to do everything.*

■ inhibition in relations between people: *they would be able to talk without constraint.*

con•struc•tiv•ism |kənˈstrəkti‚vizəm| • *n.* a style or movement in art in which assorted mechanical objects are combined into an abstract mobile structural forms. The movement originated in Russia in the 1920s and has influenced many aspects of modern ar-

chitecture and design. [ORIGIN: Russian *konstruktivizm.*]
DERIVATIVES: **con•struc•tiv•ist** *n.*, *adj.*

con•strue |kənˈstro͞o| • *v.* (**construes, construed, construing**) [trans.] (often **be construed**) interpret (a word or action) in a particular way: *his words could hardly be construed as an apology.*

■ analyze the syntax of (a text, sentence, or word): *both verbs can be construed with either infinitive.* ■ translate (a passage or author) word for word, typically aloud.
DERIVATIVES: **con•stru•a•ble** *adj.* **con•stru•al** |-ˈstro͞oəl| *n.*

con•sue•tude |ˈkänswəˌt(y)o͞od| • *n.* established custom, esp. when having legal force.
DERIVATIVES: **con•sue•tud•i•nal** *adj.* **con•sue•tu•di•nar•y** |ˌkänswəˈt(y)o͞odnˌerē| *adj.*

con•sul |ˈkänsəl| • *n.* **1** an official appointed by a government to live in a foreign city and protect the government's citizens and interests there (as distinguished from an ambassador, who represents one country's interests in another, and is usually stationed in the second country's capital). **2** (in ancient Rome) one of the two annually elected chief magistrates who jointly ruled the republic.

■ any of the three chief magistrates of the first French republic (1799–1804).
DERIVATIVES: **con•su•lar** |ˈkäns(y)ələr| *adj.* **con•sul•ship** |-ˌsHip| *n.*

con•sum•er•ism |kənˈso͞oməˌrizəm| • *n.* **1** the protection or promotion of the interests of consumers. **2** in economics, the idea that ever increasing growth in the consumption of goods is viable and beneficial. **3** the preoccupation of society with the acquisition of consumer goods.
DERIVATIVES: **con•sum•er•ist** *adj.* & *n.* **con•sum•er•is•tic** |kənˌso͞oməˈristik| *adj.*

con•sum•mate • *v.* |ˈkänsəˌmāt| [trans.] make (a marriage or relationship) complete by having sexual intercourse: *refused to consummate their marriage, which subsequently was annulled.*

■ complete (a transaction or attempt); make perfect: *their scheme of colonization was consummated through bloodshed.* • *adj.* |ˈkänsəmət; kənˈsəmət| showing a high degree of skill and flair; complete or perfect: *she dressed with consummate elegance.*
DERIVATIVES: **con•sum•mate•ly** |ˈkänsəmətlē; kənˈsəmətlē| *adv.* **con•sum•ma•tion** *n.* **con•sum•ma•tor** |ˈkänsəˌmātər| *n.*

con•sump•tive |kənˈsəm(p)tiv| • *adj.* **1** affected with a wasting disease, esp. pulmonary tuberculosis (formerly called **consumption**): *from birth he was sickly and consumptive.* **2** of or relating to the using up of resources: *tourism represents an insidious form of consumptive activity.* • *n.* a person with a wasting disease, esp. pulmonary tuberculosis.
DERIVATIVES: **con•sump•tive•ly** *adv.*

con•ta•gion |kənˈtājən| • *n.* the communication of disease from one person to another by close contact: *the rooms held no risk of contagion.*

■ a disease spread in such a way. ■ the spreading of a harmful idea or practice: *the contagion of disgrace.*

con·ta·gious |kənˈtājəs| • *adj.* (of a disease) spread from one person or organism to another by direct or indirect contact; communicable: *a contagious infection.* Cf. INFECTIOUS ■ (of a person or animal) likely to transmit a disease by contact with other people or animals. ■ (of an emotion, feeling, or attitude) likely to spread to and affect others: *her enthusiasm is contagious.*

DERIVATIVES: **con·ta·gious·ly** *adv.* **con·ta·gious·ness** *n.*

USAGE: **Contagious** and **infectious** (not-*infectuous*) are often misused. In the strict medical sense, a **contagious** disease is transmitted by direct physical contact, whereas an **infectious** disease is carried by germs in air or water, or by a specific kind of physical contact (as with venereal diseases). In figurative, nontechnical senses, **contagious** may describe the spread of things good or bad, such as laughter and merriment, or corruption, violence, panic, etc.: *The chief's paranoia had a contagious effect on the officers.* **Infectious,** in figurative senses, usually refers to the spread of only pleasant, positive things, such as good humor, optimism: *Sharon's infectious enthusiasm for the project attracted many volunteers.*.

con·tam·i·nate |kənˈtæməˌnāt| • *v.* [trans.] (often **be contaminated**) make (something) impure, often dangerous, by exposure to or addition of a poisonous or polluting substance: *the site was found to be contaminated by radioactivity | the juice has been contaminated with fine rust flakes | the entertainment industry is able to contaminate the mind of the public | [as adj.] (**contaminated**) contaminated blood products.*

DERIVATIVES: **con·tam·i·nant** |-ˈtæmənənt| *n.* **con·tam·i·na·tion** |-ˌtæməˈnāSHən| *n.* **con·tam·i·na·tor** |-nātər| *n.*

con·te |kôNt| • *n.* a short story as a form of literary composition.
■ a medieval narrative tale.

con·temn |kənˈtem| • *v.* [trans.] treat or regard with contempt.

DERIVATIVES: **con·tem·ni·ble** *adj.* **con·temn·er, contemnor** |-ˈtem(n)ər| *n.*

con·tem·po·ra·ne·ous |kənˌtempəˈrānēəs| • *adj.* existing or occurring in the same period of time: *Pythagoras was* **contemporaneous** *with the Buddha.*

DERIVATIVES: **con·tem·po·ra·ne·i·ty** |-rə ˈnēitē; -rəˈnāitē| *n.* **con·tem·po·ra·ne·ous·ly** *adv.* **con·tem·po·ra·ne·ous·ness** *n.*

con·tempt |kənˈtem(p)t| • *n.* the feeling that a person or a thing is not worthy of consideration, worthless, or deserving scorn: *he showed his contempt for his job by doing it very badly.*
■ disregard for something that should be taken into account: *an arrogant* **contempt** *for the wishes of the majority.* ■ (also **contempt of court**) the offense of being disobedient to or disrespectful of a court of law, its orders, or

its officers: *several unions were* **held** *to be* **in contempt** *and were fined.*

con·tempt·i·ble |kənˈtem(p)təbəl| • *adj.* **1** deserving contempt; despicable: *a display of contemptible cowardice.* **2** displaying contempt; contemptuous: *a contemptible sneer.*

DERIVATIVES: **con·tempt·i·bly** |-blē| *adv.*

con·temp·tu·ous |kənˈtem(p)CHəwəs| • *adj.* showing contempt; scornful: *she was intolerant and* **contemptuous** *of fellow students.*

DERIVATIVES: **con·temp·tu·ous·ly** *adv.* **con·temp·tu·ous·ness** *n.*

con·tend |kənˈtend| • *v.* **1** [intrans.] (**contend with/against**) struggle to overcome (a difficulty or danger): *she had to contend with his uncertain temper.*
■ (**contend for**) engage in a competition or campaign in order to win or achieve (something): *the local team should contend for a division championship* | [as adj.] (**contending**) *disputes continued between the contending parties.* **2** [with clause] assert something as a position in an argument: *he contends that the judge was wrong.*

DERIVATIVES: **con·tend·er** *n.*

con·ten·tious |kənˈtenCHəs| • *adj.* causing or likely to cause an argument; controversial: *a contentious issue.*
■ involving heated argument: *the subject of contentious debate.* ■ (of a person) given to arguing or provoking argument. ■ (in law) relating to or involving differences between contending parties.

DERIVATIVES: **con·ten·tious·ly** *adv.* **con·ten·tious·ness** *n.*

con·ter·mi·nous |känˈtərmənəs; kən-| • *adj.* sharing a common boundary: *the forty-eight conterminous states.*
■ having the same area, context, or meaning: *a genealogy conterminous with the history of the US.* Cf. COTERMINOUS.

DERIVATIVES: **con·ter·mi·nous·ly** *adv.* **con·ter·mi·nous·ness** *n.*

con·tes·ta·tion |ˌkän,təsˈtāSHən| • *n.* formal the action or process of disputing or arguing.

con·text |ˈkän,tekst| • *n.* the circumstances that form the setting for an event, statement, or idea, and in terms of which it can be fully understood and evaluated: *the decision was taken within the context of planned cuts in spending.*
■ the parts of something written or spoken that immediately precede and follow a word or passage and clarify its meaning: *word processing is affected by the context in which words appear.*

DERIVATIVES: **con·text·less** *adj.* **con·tex·tu·al** |kənˈteksCHəwəl| *adj.* **con·tex·tu·al·ly** |kənˈteksCHəwəlē| *adv.*

con·tex·tu·al·ism |kənˈteksCHəwə,lizəm| • *n.* **1** a philosophical doctrine that emphasizes the importance of the context of inquiry in a particular question. **2** the theory that works of art and literature should be viewed and judged with reference to the social, political, and cultural context in which they were made.

DERIVATIVES: **con·tex·tu·al·ist** *n.*

con•tex•tu•al•ize |kən'teksCHəwə,līz| • v. [trans.] place or study in context: *the book contextualizes Melville's short fiction and poetry.* DERIVATIVES: **con•tex•tu•al•i•za•tion** |kən,teksCHəwələ'zāsHən| n.

con•tig•u•ous |kən'tigyəwəs| • adj. sharing a common border; touching: *Maine and New Hampshire are contiguous states.* ■ next or together in sequence: *five hundred contiguous dictionary entries.* DERIVATIVES: **con•ti•gu•i•ty** n. **con•tig•u•ous•ly** adv. **con•tig•u•ous•ness** n.

con•ti•nent • adj. **1** able to control movements of the bowels and bladder. **2** exercising self-restraint, esp. sexually. DERIVATIVES: **con•ti•nence** n. **con•ti•nent•ly** adv.

con•ti•nen•tal |,käntn'entl| • adj. **1** [attrib.] coming from or characteristic of mainland Europe: *traditional continental cuisine.* **2** (also **Continental**) pertaining to the 13 original colonies of the US; colonial: *in 1783 the officers and men of the continental forces had little to celebrate.* • n. **1** an inhabitant of mainland Europe, as distinguished from Britain and Ireland. **2** (**Continental**) a member of the colonial army in the American Revolution.

con•tin•gen•cy |kən'tinjənsē| • n. (pl. **-ies**) a future event or circumstance that is possible but cannot be predicted with certainty: *a detailed contract that attempts to provide for all contingencies.* ■ a provision for such an events or circumstance: [as adj.] *a contingency reserve.* ■ an incidental expense: *allow an extra fifteen percent in the budget for contingencies.* ■ the absence of certainty in events: *the island's public affairs can be invaded by contingency.* ■ (in philosophy) the absence of necessity; the fact of being so without having to be so.

con•tin•gent |kən'tinjənt| • adj. **1** subject to chance: *the contingent nature of the job.* ■ (of losses, liabilities, etc.) that can be anticipated to arise if a particular event occurs: *businesses need to be aware of their liabilities, both actual and contingent.* ■ verifiable by observation, without reference to logical necessity: Cf. EMPIRICAL. **2** [predic.] (**contingent on/upon**) occurring or existing only if (certain other circumstances) are the case; dependent on: *resolution of the conflict was contingent on the signing of a cease-fire agreement.* DERIVATIVES: **con•tin•gent•ly** adv.

con•tin•u•al |kən'tinyəwəl| • adj. frequently recurring; always happening: *the city capitulated after continual attacks.* ■ having no interruptions: *some patients need continual safeguarding.* DERIVATIVES: **con•tin•u•al•ly** adv.

USAGE: For the difference between **continual** and **continuous**, see **usage** at CONTINUOUS.

con•ti•nu•i•ty |,käntn'(y)o͞oətē| • n. (pl. **-ies**) **1** the unbroken and consistent existence or operation of something over a period of time: *pension rights accruing through continuity of employment.*

■ a state of stability and the absence of disruption. ■ (often **continuity between/with**) a connection or line of development with no sharp breaks: *woven blanket designs that provide continuity with the past.* **2** the maintenance of continuous action and self-consistent detail in the various scenes of a movie or broadcast: [as adj.] *a continuity error.* ■ the linking of broadcast items, esp. by a spoken commentary.

con•tin•u•o |kən'tinyə,wō| (also **basso continuo**) • n. (pl. **-os**) (in baroque music) an accompanying part that includes a bass line and harmonies, typically played on a keyboard instrument and with other instruments such as cello or bass viol.

con•tin•u•ous |kən'tinyəwəs| • adj. **1** forming an unbroken whole; without interruption: *the whole performance is enacted in one continuous movement.* ■ forming a series with no exceptions or reversals: *there have been continuous advances in design and production.* **2** denoting an aspect or tense of a verb that expresses an action in progress. DERIVATIVES: **con•tin•u•ous•ly** adv. **con•tin•u•ous•ness** n.

USAGE: In precise usage, **continual** means 'frequent, repeating at intervals' and **continuous** means 'going on without pause or interruption': *We suffered from the continual attacks of mosquitoes. The waterfall's continuous flow creates an endless roar.* **Continuous** is the word to use in decribing spatial relationships, as in *a continuous* (not **continual**) *series of rooms; a continuous plain of arable land.* Avoid using **continuous** or **continuously** as a way of describing something that occurs at regular or seasonal intervals: *Our holiday ceremony has been held continuously* (should be *annually*) *since 1925.*

con•tin•u•um |kən'tinyəwəm| • n. (pl. **continua** |-yəwə|) [usu. in sing.] a continuous sequence in which adjacent elements are not perceptibly different from each other, although the extremes are quite distinct.

con•tort |kən'tôrt| • v. twist or bend out of its normal shape: [trans.] *a spasm of pain contorted his face* | [intrans.] *her face contorted with anger* | [as adj.] (**contorted**) *contorted limbs* | *a contorted version of the truth.* DERIVATIVES: **con•tor•tion** |kən'tôrsHən| n.

con•tor•tion•ist |kən'tôrsHənist| • n. an entertainer who twists and bends his or her body into strange and unnatural positions.

con•tra•band |'käntrə,band| • n. something that has been imported or exported illegally: *the police looked for drugs, guns, and other contraband.* ■ trade in smuggled goods: *the government has declared a nationwide war on contraband.* ■ (also **contraband of war**) goods forbidden to be supplied by neutrals to those engaged in war. • adj. imported or exported illegally, either in defiance of a total ban or without payment of duty: *contraband cigarettes.*

■ relating to traffic in illegal goods: *the contraband market.*
DERIVATIVES: **con•tra•band•ist** |-ist| *n.*
con•tra•bass |ˈkäntrəˌbäs| ▪ *n.* another term for double bass, the largest and lowest member of the violin family. ▪ *adj.* [attrib.] denoting a musical instrument with a range an octave lower than the normal bass range: *a contrabass clarinet.*
con•tract•a•ble |kənˈtraktəbəl| ▪ *adj.* (of a disease) able to be caught.
con•tract•i•ble |kənˈtraktəbəl| ▪ *adj.* able to be shrunk or capable of contracting.
con•trac•tile |kənˈtraktəl; -ˌtīl| ▪ *adj.* capable of or producing muscular contraction: *the contractile activity of the colon.*
DERIVATIVES: **con•trac•til•i•ty** |ˌkänˌtrak ˈtiliṯē| *n.*
con•trac•tion |kənˈtrakSHən| ▪ *n.* the process of becoming smaller: *the general contraction of the industry did further damage to morale.*
■ the process in which a muscle becomes or is made shorter and tighter: *neurons control the contraction of muscles* | *repeat the exercise, holding each contraction for one second.* ▪ (usu. **contractions**) a shortening of the uterine muscles occurring at intervals before and during childbirth. ■ a word or group of words resulting from shortening an original form: *"goodbye" is a contraction of "God be with you."* ■ the process of shortening a word by combination or elision.
con•tra•dance |ˈkäntrəˌdäns| ▪ *n.* a country dance in which the couples form lines facing each other.
con•tra•dis•tinc•tion |ˌkäntrədəˈstiNGk SHən| ▪ *n.* distinction made by contrasting the different qualities of two things: *the bacterium is termed "rough" in contradistinction to its ordinary smooth form.*
con•tra•in•di•cate |ˌkäntrəˈindəˌkāt| ▪ *v.* [trans.] (usu. **be contraindicated**) (of a condition or circumstance) suggest or indicate that (a particular technique or drug) should not be used in the case in question: *dosages over 500 mg are contraindicated in the presence of hypertension.*
DERIVATIVES: **con•tra•in•di•ca•tion** |-ˌin dəˈkāSHən| *n.*
con•tral•to |kənˈtraltō| ▪ *n.* (pl. **-os**) the lowest female singing voice: *the voice was a round, full contralto.*
■ a singer with such a voice. ■ a part written for such a voice.
con•tra•po•si•tion |ˌkäntrəpəˈzisHən| ▪ *n.* conversion of a logical proposition from *all A is B* to *all not-B is not-A.*
DERIVATIVES: **con•tra•pos•i•tive** |-ˈpäz ətiv| *adj.* & *n.*
con•tra•pun•tal |ˌkäntrəˈpəntl| ▪ *adj.* of or in musical COUNTERPOINT.
■ (of a piece of music) with two or more independent melodic lines.
DERIVATIVES: **con•tra•pun•tal•ly** *adv.* **con•tra•pun•tist** |-tist| *n.*
con•trar•i•an |kənˈtrerēən; kän-| ▪ *n.* a person who opposes or rejects popular opinion.

▪ *adj.* opposing or rejecting popular opinion; going against current practice.
DERIVATIVES: **con•trar•i•an•ism** |-ˌniz əm| *n.*
con•tra•ri•e•ty |ˌkäntrəˈrīəṯē| ▪ *n.* opposition or inconsistency between two or more things: *questions that involved much contrariety of opinion.*
con•tra•vene |ˌkäntrəˈvēn| ▪ *v.* [trans.] violate the prohibition or order of (a law, treaty, or code of conduct): *this would contravene the rule against hearsay.*
■ conflict with (a right, principle, etc.), and thereby compromise it.
DERIVATIVES: **con•tra•ven•er** *n.*
con•tre•danse |ˈkäntrəˌdäns; ˌkôNtrəˈdäNs| ▪ *n.* (pl. same) a French form of country dance, originating in the 18th century and related to the quadrille.
■ a piece of music for such a dance. ■ another term for CONTRADANCE.
con•tre•temps |ˈkäntrəˌtäN; ˌkôNtrəˈtäN| ▪ *n.* (pl. same |-ˌtäN(z); -ˈtäN(z)|) an unexpected and unfortunate occurrence.
■ a minor dispute or disagreement.
con•trib•u•to•ry |kənˈtribyəˌtôrē| ▪ *adj.*
1 playing a part in bringing something about: *smoking is a contributory cause of lung cancer.*
2 (of a pension or insurance plan) operated by means of a fund into which people pay: *contributory benefits.*
con•trite |kənˈtrīt| ▪ *adj.* feeling or expressing remorse or penitence; affected by guilt.
DERIVATIVES: **con•trite•ly** *adv.* **con•trite• ness** *n.*
con•tri•tion |kənˈtrisHən| ▪ *n.* the state of feeling remorseful and penitent.
■ (in the Roman Catholic Church) the repentance of past sins during or after confession.
con•triv•ance |kənˈtrīvəns| ▪ *n.* a thing that is created skillfully and inventively to serve a particular purpose: *an assortment of electronic equipment and mechanical contrivances.*
■ the use of skill to bring about something or create something: *the requirements of the system, by happy chance and some contrivance, can be summed up in an acronym.* ■ a device, esp. in literary or artistic composition, that gives a sense of artificiality.
con•trol |kənˈtrōl| ▪ *n.* (in science, medicine, etc.) a group or individual used as a standard of comparison for checking the results of a survey or experiment: *they saw no difference between the cancer patients and the controls.* ▪ *v.* [intrans.] (**control for**) take into account (an extraneous factor that might affect results) when performing an experiment: *no attempt was made to control for variations* | [as adj.] (**controlled**) *a controlled trial.*
DERIVATIVES: **con•trol•la•bil•i•ty** |kən ˌtrōlə ˈbiliṯē| *n.* **con•trol•la•ble** *adj.* **con• trol•la•bly** *adv.*
con•trol•ler |kənˈtrōlər| ▪ *n.* (in institutions, etc.) a person in charge of an organization's finances.
DERIVATIVES: **con•trol•ler•ship** |-ˌSHip| *n.*
con•tro•vert |ˈkäntrəˌvərt; ˌkäntrəˈvərt| ▪ *v.* [trans.] deny or contradict the truth of (some-

thing): *subsequent work from the same laboratory controverted these results.* ■ argue about (something): *the views in the article have been controverted.*

DERIVATIVES: **con•tro•vert•i•ble** *adj.*

con•tu•ma•cious |ˌkänt(y)əˈmāsHəs| • *adj.* stubbornly or willfully disobedient to authority, esp. legal authority.

DERIVATIVES: **con•tu•ma•cy** *n.* **con•tu•ma•cious•ly** *adv.*

con•tu•me•ly |kənˈt(y)o͞oməlē; ˈkänt(y)ə ˌmēlē; ˈkän,t(y)o͞omlē| • *n.* (pl. **-ies**) insolent or insulting language or treatment: *elderly neighbors should not be exposed to gossip and contumely.*

DERIVATIVES: **con•tu•me•li•ous** *adj.*

con•tu•sion |kənˈto͞ozHən| • *n.* a region of injured tissue or skin in which blood capillaries have been ruptured; a bruise.

co•nun•drum |kəˈnəndrəm| • *n.* (pl. **conundrums**) a confusing and difficult problem or question: *one of the most difficult conundrums for the experts.* ■ a question asked for amusement, typically one with a pun in its answer; a riddle.

con•ur•ba•tion |ˌkänərˈbāsHən| • *n.* an extended urban area, typically consisting of several towns merging with the suburbs of one or more cities.

con•va•lesce |ˌkänvəˈles| • *v.* [intrans.] recover one's health and strength over a period of time after an illness or operation: *he spent eight months convalescing after the stroke.*

DERIVATIVES: **con•va•les•cence** *n.* **con•va•les•cent** *adj., n.*

con•vec•tion |kənˈveksHən| • *n.* **1** the movement caused within a fluid by the tendency of hotter and therefore less dense material to rise, and of colder, denser material to sink under the influence of gravity, which consequently results in transfer of heat. **2** the upward movement of atmospheric properties. Cf. ADVECTION.

DERIVATIVES: **con•vect** *v.* **con•vec•tion•al** |-SHənl| *adj.* **con•vec•tive** |kənˈvektiv| *adj.*

con•ve•nance |ˈkänvənəns| • *n.* (also **convenances**) conventional social propriety: *adhered to the convenances of colonial society.*

con•vene |kənˈvēn| • *v.* [trans.] call people together for (a meeting): *convened a secret meeting.* ■ assemble or cause to assemble for a common purpose: [trans.] *convened a group of well-known scientists and philosophers* | [intrans.] *the committee had convened for its final plenary session.*

DERIVATIVES: **con•ven•a•ble** *adj.* **con•ven•er** *n.* **con•ve•nor** |-ˈvēnər| *n.*

con•ven•tion |kənˈvencHən| • *n.* **1** a way in which something is usually done, esp. within a particular area or activity: *the conventions of children's literature.* ■ behavior that is considered acceptable or polite to most members of a society: *an upholder of convention and correct form.* ■ (in bridge) an artificial bid by which a bidder tries to convey specific information about the hand to his or her partner. **2** an agreement between countries covering particular matters, esp.

one less formal than a treaty. **3** a large meeting or conference, esp. of members of a political party or a particular profession: *a convention of retail merchants.* ■ an assembly of the delegates of a political party to select candidates for office. ■ an organized meeting of enthusiasts for a television program, movie, or literary genre: *a Star Trek convention.* ■ a body set up by agreement to deal with a particular issue. *the convention is a UN body responsible for the regulation of sea dumping.*

con•ven•tion•al |kənˈvencHənl| • *adj.* based on or in accordance with what is generally done or believed. ■ (of a person) behaving in a way that is generally held to be acceptable, at the expense of individuality and sincerity. ■ (of a work of art or literature) following traditional forms and genres: *conventional love poetry.* ■ (of weapons or power) nonnuclear: *agreement on reducing conventional forces in Europe.* ■ (of a bid in bridge) intended to convey a particular meaning according to an agreed upon convention.

DERIVATIVES: **con•ven•tion•al•ism** |-ˌiz-əm| *n.* **con•ven•tion•al•ist** |-ist| *n.* **con•ven•tion•al•i•ty** |-ˌvencHəˈnælitē| *n.* **con•ven•tion•al•ize** |-ˌīz| *v.* **con•ven•tion•al•ly** *adv.*

con•verge |kənˈvərj| • *v.* [intrans.] (of several people or things) come together from different directions so as eventually to meet: *convoys from several eastern ports converged in the Atlantic* | *two people whose lives converge briefly from time to time.* ■ (**converge on/upon**) come from different directions and meet at (a place): *half a million sports fans will converge on the capital.* ■ (of a number of things) gradually change so as to become similar or develop something in common: *two cultures converged as the French settled Vermont.* ■ (of lines) tend to meet at a point: *lines of longitude are parallel at the equator but converge toward the poles.*

con•ver•sant |kənˈvərsənt| • *adj.* [predic.] familiar with or knowledgeable about something: *fully conversant with the principles of word processing.*

DERIVATIVES: **con•ver•sance** *n.* **con•ver•san•cy** |-sənsē| *n.*

con•ver•sion |kənˈvərzHən| • *n.* **1** (in religion) the fact of changing one's faith or beliefs or the action of persuading someone else to change theirs: *my conversion to the Catholic faith.* ■ (in Christian theology) repentance and change to a godly life. **2** (in law) the changing of real into personal property, or of joint into separate property, or vice versa. **3** (in psychiatry) the manifestation of a mental disturbance as a physical disorder or disease: [as adj.] *conversion disorders.* ■ the transposition of the subject and predicate of a logical proposition according to certain rules to form a new proposition by inference. **4** the illegal action of wrongfully dealing with goods in a manner inconsistent with the owner's rights: *the conversion of clients' monies.*

con•vert•i•ble |kən'vərt̮əbəl| • *adj.* able to be changed in form, function, or character: *a living room that is convertible into a bedroom.* ■ (of a car) having a folding or detachable roof: *a white convertible Mercedes.* ■ (of currency) able to be converted into other forms, esp. into gold or US dollars. ■ (of a bond or stock) able to be converted into ordinary or preference shares. ■ (of logical terms) synonymous. • *n.* **1** a car with a folding or detachable roof. **2** (usu. **convertibles**) a convertible security. DERIVATIVES: **con•vert•i•bil•i•ty** |-,vərt̮-əbiliṯē| *n.*

con•vex |kän'veks; 'kän,veks; kən'veks| • *adj.* **1** having an outline or surface curved like the exterior of a circle or sphere. Cf. CONCAVE. **2** (of a polygon) not having any interior angles greater than 180°. DERIVATIVES: **con•vex•i•ty** |kän'veksiṯē; kən-| *n.* **con•vex•ly** *adv.*

con•vic•tion |kən'viksHən| • *n.* **1** a formal declaration that someone is guilty of a criminal offense, made by judicial procedure, esp. by the verdict of a jury or the decision of a judge in a court of law: *a previous conviction for a similar offense.* **2** a firmly held belief or opinion: [with clause] *his conviction that the death was no accident* | *she takes pride in stating her political convictions.* ■ the quality of showing that one is firmly convinced of what one believes or says: *his voice lacked conviction.*

con•viv•i•al |kən'vivēəl; kən'vivyəl| • *adj.* (of an atmosphere or event) friendly, lively, and enjoyable. ■ (of a person) cheerful and friendly; jovial. DERIVATIVES: **con•viv•i•al•i•ty** |kən,vivē'æliṯē| *n.* **con•viv•i•al•ly** *adv.*

con•vo•ca•tion |,känvə'kāsHən| • *n.* **1** a large formal assembly of people. ■ a formal ceremony at a college or university, as for the conferring of awards and degrees. **2** the action of calling people together for a large formal assembly: *the convocation of the first congress.* DERIVATIVES: **con•vo•ca•tion•al** |-SHənl| *adj.*

con•vo•lut•ed |'känvə,loōt̮əd| • *adj.* (esp. of an argument, story, or sentence) extremely complex and difficult to follow: *its convoluted narrative encompasses all manner of digressions.* ■ intricately folded, twisted, or coiled: *walnuts come in hard and convoluted shells.* DERIVATIVES: **con•vo•lut•ed•ly** *adv.* **con•vo•lu•tion** *n.*

con•vul•sion |kən'vəlsHən| • *n.* (often **convulsions**) a sudden, violent, irregular movement of a limb or of the body, caused by involuntary contraction of muscles and associated esp. with brain disorders such as epilepsy, the presence of certain toxins or other agents in the blood, or fever in children. ■ (**convulsions**) uncontrollable laughter: *the audience collapsed in convulsions.* ■ an earthquake or other violent or major movement of the earth's crust: *the violent convulsions of tec-*

tonic plates. ■ a violent social or political upheaval: *the convulsions of 1939–45.* DERIVATIVES: **convulse** *v.*

con•vul•sive |kən'vəlsiv| • *adj.* producing or consisting of convulsions: *a convulsive disease* | *she gave a convulsive sob.* DERIVATIVES: **con•vul•sive•ly** *adv.*

co•op•er•a•tive |kō'äp(ə)rəṯiv| (also **co-operative**) • *adj.* involving mutual assistance in working toward a common goal. ■ willing to be of assistance: *they have been extremely considerate, polite, and cooperative.* ■ (of a farm, dwelling, business, etc.) owned and run jointly by its members, with profits or benefits shared among them. • *n.* a farm, business, dwelling, or other organization that is owned and run jointly by its members, who share the profits or benefits. DERIVATIVES: **co•op•er•a•tive•ly** *adv.*

co-opt |kō'äpt; 'kō,äpt| • *v.* [trans.] (often **be co-opted**) appoint to membership of a committee or other body by invitation of the existing members. ■ divert to or use in a role different from the usual or original one:[with obj. and infinitive] *social scientists were co-opted to work with the development agencies.* ■ adopt (an idea or policy) for one's own use: *they have had most of their ideas co-opted by bigger parties.* DERIVATIVES: **co-op•tion** |,kō'äpsHən| *n.* **co-op•tive** |-'äptiv| *adj.*

co•pa•cet•ic |,kōpə'seṯik| • *adj.* satisfactory and in good order: *don't worry — everything is copacetic.*

Co•per•ni•can sys•tem *n.* **1** a model of the solar system in which the planets orbit in circles around the sun (as proposed by Nicolaus Copernicus 1473–1543). Cf. PTOLEMAIC SYSTEM.

co•pi•ous |'kōpēəs| • *adj.* abundant in supply or quantity: *she took copious notes.* ■ profuse in speech or ideas: *I had been a little too copious in talking of my country.* DERIVATIVES: **co•pi•ous•ly** *adv.* **co•pi•ous•ness** *n.*

cop•pice |'käpəs| • *n.* an area of woodland in which the trees or shrubs are, or formerly were, periodically cut back to ground level to stimulate growth and provide firewood or timber. • *v.* [trans.] cut back (a tree or shrub) to ground level periodically to stimulate growth: [as adj.] (**coppiced**) *an oak wood with some coppiced hazel and ash.*

copse |käps| • *n.* a small group of trees.

cop•u•late |'käpyə,lāt| • *v.* [intrans.] have sexual intercourse. DERIVATIVES: **cop•u•la•tion** |,käpyə'lāsHən| *n.* **cop•u•la•to•ry** |-lə,tôrē| *adj.*

cop•y•writ•er |'käpi,rīṯər| • *n.* a person who writes the text of advertisements or publicity material. DERIVATIVES: **cop•y•writ•ing** |-,rīṯiNG| *n.*

co•quet•ry |'kōkətrē; kō'ke-trē| • *n.* flirtatious behavior or a flirtatious manner.

co•quette |kō'ket| • *n.* a woman who flirts. DERIVATIVES: **co•quet•tish** *adj.* **co•quet•tish•ly** *adv.* **co•quet•tish•ness** *n.*

cor•beil |'kôrbəl; kôr'bā| • *n.* (in architecture) a representation in stone of a basket of flowers.

cor•bel |'kôrbəl| • *n.* a projection jutting out from a wall to support a structure above it. • *v.* (**corbeled, corbeling; chiefly Brit. corbelled, corbelling**) [trans.] (often **be corbeled out**) support (a structure such as an arch or balcony) on corbels.

cord•age |'kôrdij| • *n.* **1** cords or ropes, esp. in a ship's rigging. **2** a quantity of wood divided into cords.

cor•dial |'kôrjəl| • *adj.* warm and friendly. ■ strongly felt: *I earned his cordial loathing.* • *n.* **1** another term for LIQUEUR. **2** a comforting or pleasant-tasting medicine.
DERIVATIVES: **cor•dial•i•ty** |,kôrjē'æli̯tē| *n.* **cor•dial•ly** *adv.*

cor•dil•le•ra |,kôrdl'(y)erə| • *n.* a system or group of parallel mountain ranges together with the intervening plateaus and other features, esp. in the Andes or the Rockies.

cor•don bleu |,kôrdōn 'blœ| • *adj.* (of cooking) of the highest class: *a cordon bleu chef.* ■ [postpositive] denoting a dish consisting of an escalope of veal or chicken rolled, filled with cheese and ham, and then fried in breadcrumbs. • *n.* a cook of the highest class.

cor•don sa•ni•taire |kôrdôN ,sänē'ter| • *n.* (pl. **cordons sanitaires** pronunc. same) a guarded line preventing anyone from leaving an area infected by a disease and thus spreading it. ■ a measure designed to prevent communication or the spread of undesirable influences: *these rules help to reinforce the cordon sanitaire around the Pentagon.*

co•re•spond•ent |,kō ri'spändənt| (also **corespondent**) • *n.* a person cited in a divorce case as having committed adultery with the RESPONDENT.

Co•rin•thi•an |kə'rinTHēən| • *adj.* **1** relating to or denoting the lightest and most ornate of the classical orders of architecture (used esp. by the Romans), characterized by flared capitals with rows of acanthus leaves. **2** given to luxurious indulgence. **3** involving or displaying the highest standards of sportsmanship: *a club embodying the Corinthian spirit.* • *n.* **1** a native of Corinth. ■ a wealthy amateur in sports. **2** the Corinthian order of architecture.

cork |kôrk| • *n.* the buoyant, light brown substance obtained from the outer layer of the bark of the cork oak: [as adj.] *cork tiles.* ■ a bottle stopper, esp. one made of cork. ■ a piece of cork used as a float for a fishing line or net. ■ a protective layer of dead cells immediately below the bark of woody plants. • *v.* [trans.] (often **be corked**) **1** close or seal (a bottle) with a cork. ■ [as adj.] (**corked**) (of wine) spoiled by tannin from the cork. **2** draw with burnt cork. **3** illicitly hollow out (a baseball bat) and fill it with cork to make it lighter.
DERIVATIVES: **cork•like** |-,līk| *adj.*

cork•age |'kôrkij| • *n.* a charge made by a restaurant or hotel for serving wine that has been brought in by a customer.

cor•mo•rant |'kôrmərənt| • *n.* a large diving bird (genus *Phalacrocorax*) with a long neck, long hooked bill, short legs, and mainly dark plumage. It typically breeds on coastal cliffs and is noted for its voracious appetite. ■ an insatiably greedy person or thing.

cor•nice |'kôrnis| • *n.* **1** an ornamental molding around the wall of a room just below the ceiling. ■ a horizontal molded projection crowning a building or structure, esp. the uppermost member of the entablature of an order, surmounting the frieze. **2** an overhanging mass of hardened snow at the edge of a mountain precipice.
DERIVATIVES: **cor•niced** *adj.* **cor•nic•ing** *n.*

cor•niche |'kôrnisH; kôr'nēsH| • *n.* a road running along a coast with scenic views, esp. one cut into the edge of a cliff.

cor•nu•co•pi•a |,kôrn(y)ə'kōpēə| • *n.* a symbol of plenty consisting of a goat's horn overflowing with flowers, fruit, and grains. ■ an ornamental container shaped like such a horn. ■ an abundant supply of good things of a specified kind: *the festival offers a cornucopia of pleasures.*
DERIVATIVES: **cor•nu•co•pi•an** *adj.*

cor•ol•lar•y |'kôrə,lerē; 'kärə-| • *n.* (pl. **-ies**) a proposition that follows from (and is often appended to) one already proved. ■ a direct or natural consequence or result: *the huge increases in unemployment were the corollary of spending cuts.* • *adj.* forming a proposition that follows from one already proved. ■ associated; supplementary.

co•ro•na |kə'rōnə| • *n.* (pl. **coronae** |kə'rōnē; -,nī|) **1** the rarefied gaseous envelope of the sun and other stars. The sun's corona is normally visible only during a total solar eclipse, when it is seen as an irregularly shaped pearly glow surrounding the darkened disk of the moon. ■ (also **corona discharge**) (in physics) the glow around a conductor at high potential. ■ a small circle of light seen around the sun or moon, due to diffraction by water droplets. **2** crownlike anatomical structure. ■ (in botany) the cup-shaped or trumpet-shaped outgrowth at the center of a daffodil or narcissus flower. **3** a part of an exterior CORNICE having a broad vertical face.
DERIVATIVES: **cor•o•nal** *adj.*

cor•o•nar•y |'kôrə,nerē; 'kär-| • *adj.* relating to or denoting the arteries that surround and supply blood to the heart. ■ relating to or denoting a structure that encircles a part of the body. • *n.* (pl. **-ies**) short for *coronary thrombosis*, a THROMBOSIS in a coronary artery.

cor•o•net |,kôrə,net; ,kär-| • *n.* a small or relatively simple crown, esp. as worn by minor royalty and nobles. ■ a circular decoration for the head, esp. one made of flowers.
DERIVATIVES: **cor•o•net•ed** *adj.*

cor•po•ral[1] |'kôrp(ə)rəl| • *n.* a rank of noncommissioned officer in the US Army or

Marine Corps, above lance corporal or private first class and below sergeant.

cor•po•ral² • *adj.* of or relating to the human body: *corporal punishment.* Cf. CORPOREAL.
DERIVATIVES: **cor•po•ral•ly** *adv.*

cor•po•rate |ˈkôrp(ə)rət| • *adj.* of or relating to a large company or group: *airlines seeking to enhance their corporate image.*
■ (of a large company or group) authorized to act as a single entity and recognized as such in law. ■ of or shared by all the members of a group: *the service emphasizes the corporate responsibility of the congregation.*
DERIVATIVES: **cor•po•rate•ly** *adv.*

cor•po•ra•tion |ˌkôrpəˈrāSHən| • *n.* a large group of people, company, or group of companies given an existence distinct from the individuals who compose it, authorized to act as a single entity and recognized as such in law.
■ a group of people elected to govern a city, town, or borough. ■ a large abdomen; paunch.

cor•po•rat•ism |ˈkôrp(ə)rəˌtizəm| • *n.* the control of a state or organization by large interest groups.
DERIVATIVES: **cor•po•rat•ist** *adj. & n.*

cor•po•ra•tive |ˈkôrp(ə)rətiv| • *adj.* relating to or denoting a state, typically a fascist one, organized into corporations representing both employers and employed in various spheres.
DERIVATIVES: **cor•po•ra•tiv•ism** |-p(ə)rətəˌvizəm| *n.* **cor•po•ra•tiv•ist** |-p(ə)rətəvist| *adj. & n.* .

cor•po•re•al |kôrˈpôrēəl| • *adj.* of or relating to the body, as opposed to the spirit: *he was frank about his corporeal appetites.*
■ having a body: *a corporeal God.* ■ (in law) consisting of material objects; tangible: *corporeal property.*
DERIVATIVES: **cor•po•re•al•i•ty** |kôrˌpôrēˈælitē| *n.* **cor•po•re•al•ly** *adv.*

corps de bal•let |ˌkôr də bæˈlā| • *n.* [treated as sing. or pl.] the members of a ballet company who dance together as a group.
■ the members of the lowest rank of dancers in a ballet company.

cor•pu•lent |ˈkôrpyələnt| • *adj.* (of a person) fat.
DERIVATIVES: **cor•pu•lence** *n.* **cor•pu•len•cy** *n.*

cor•pus |ˈkôrpəs| • *n.* (pl. **corpora** |-pərə| or **corpuses**) **1** a collection of written texts, esp. the entire works of a particular author or a body of writing on a particular subject: *the Darwinian corpus.*
■ a collection of written or spoken material, esp. in electronic form, assembled for the purpose of studying linguistic structures, frequencies, etc. **2** the main body or mass of an anatomical structure.

cor•pus•cle |ˈkôrˌpəsəl| • *n.* a minute body or cell in an organism, esp. a red or white cell in the blood of vertebrates.
■ a minute particle formerly regarded as the basic constituent of matter or light.
DERIVATIVES: **cor•pus•cu•lar** |kôrˈpəskyələr| *adj.*

cor•pus de•lic•ti |dəˈlikˌtī; -tē| • *n.* the facts and circumstances constituting a breach of a law.
■ concrete evidence of a crime, esp. a corpse.

cor•rec•tion |kəˈrekSHən| • *n.* (in law) punishment, esp. that of criminals in prison intended to rectify their behavior.
■ **corrections** the practice, profession, methods, etc. of punishing criminals: [as adj.] *a corrections officer.*

cor•rec•tion•al |kəˈrekSHənl| • *adj.* of or relating to the punishment of criminals in a way intended to rectify (correct) their behavior: *a correctional institution.*

cor•rec•ti•tude |kəˈrektəˌt(y)ood| • *n.* correctness, esp. conscious correctness in one's behavior.

cor•re•la•tion |ˌkôrəˈlāSHən| • *n.* a mutual relationship or connection between two or more things: *research showed a clear correlation between recession and levels of property crime.*
■ (in statistics) interdependence of variable quantities. ■ a quantity measuring the extent of such interdependence. ■ the process of establishing a relationship or connection between two or more things.
DERIVATIVES: **cor•rel•a•tive** *adj.* **cor•re•la•tion•al** |-SHənl| *adj.*

cor•ri•gi•ble |ˈkôrəjəbəl| • *adj.* capable of being corrected, rectified, or reformed. Cf. INCORRIGIBLE.
DERIVATIVES: **cor•ri•gi•bil•i•ty** |ˌkôrəjəˈbilitē| *n.*

cor•rob•o•rate |kəˈräbəˌrāt| • *v.* [trans.] confirm or give support to (a statement, theory, or finding): *the witness had corroborated the boy's account of the attack.*
DERIVATIVES: **cor•rob•o•ra•tion** |kəˌräbəˈrāSHən| *n.* **cor•rob•o•ra•tive** |-ˈräb(ə)rətiv| *adj.* **cor•rob•o•ra•tor** |-ˌrātər| *n.* **cor•rob•o•ra•to•ry** |-ˈräb(ə)rəˌtôrē| *adj.*

cor•rode |kəˈrōd| • *v.* [trans.] destroy or damage (metal, stone, or other materials) slowly by chemical action: *acid rain poisons fish and corrodes buildings.*
■ [intrans.] (of metal or other materials) be destroyed or damaged in this way: *over the years copper tubing corrodes.* ■ destroy or weaken (something) gradually: *the self-centered climate corrodes ideals and concerns about social justice.*
DERIVATIVES: **cor•rod•i•ble** *adj.* **corro•sion** *n.*

cor•ro•sive |kəˈrōsiv; -ziv| • *adj.* tending to corrode. ■ harmful and destructive of integrity: *a corrosive desire.* ■ extremely sarcastic or caustic: *corrosive criticism.* • *n.* a corrosive substance.
DERIVATIVES: **cor•ro•sive•ly** *adv.* **cor•ro•sive•ness** *n.*

cor•ru•gate |ˈkôrəˌgāt| • *v.* contract or cause to contract into wrinkles or folds: [intrans.] *Micky's brow corrugated in a simian frown* | as [adj.] *corrugated iron.*

cor•sage |kôrˈsäzH; -ˈsäj| • *n.* **1** a spray of flowers worn pinned to a woman's clothes. **2** the upper part of a woman's dress.

cor•sair |ˈkôrˌser| • *n.* **1** a pirate.
■ a privateer, esp. one operating along the southern coast of the Mediterranean in the 17th century. **2** a pirate ship.

cor•tège |kôrˈtezH ˈkôrˌtezH| • *n.* a solemn procession, esp. for a funeral.
■ a person's entourage or retinue.

cor•ti•sone |ˈkôrtəˌsōn| • *n.* a hormone produced by the adrenal cortex. It is also made synthetically for use as an anti-inflammatory and anti-allergy agent.

cor•us•cate |ˈkôrəˌskāt; ˈkär-| • *v.* [intrans.] (of light) flash or sparkle: *the light was coruscating through the walls.*
DERIVATIVES: **cor•us•ca•tion** |ˌkôrˈskā-sHən| *n.*

cor•vée |ˈkôrˌvā kôrˈvā| • *n.* (in the feudal system) a day's unpaid labor owed by a vassal to his lord.
■ forced labor exacted in lieu of taxes, in particular labor on public roads. ■ an unpleasant duty or onerous task.

cor•vette |kôrˈvet| • *n.* a small warship designed for convoy escort duty.
■ a sailing warship with one tier of guns.

cos•met•ic |kazˈmeṭik| • *adj.* involving or relating to treatment intended to restore or improve a person's appearance: *cosmetic surgery.*
■ designed or serving to improve the appearance of the body, esp. the face: *lens designs can improve the cosmetic effect of your glasses.* ■ affecting only the appearance of something rather than its substance: *the reform package was merely a cosmetic exercise.* • *n.* (usu. **cosmetics**) a product applied to the body, esp. the face, to improve its appearance.
DERIVATIVES: **cos•met•i•cal•ly** |-ik(ə)lē| *adv.*

cos•me•ti•cian |ˌkazmə'tisHən| • *n.* a person who sells or applies cosmetics as an occupation.

cos•me•tol•o•gy |ˌkazmə'täləjē| • *n.* the professional skill or practice of beautifying the face, hair, and skin.
DERIVATIVES: **cos•me•to•log•i•cal** |-ṭə'läjikəl| *adj.* **cos•me•tol•o•gist** |-jist| *n.*

cos•mic |ˈkazmik| • *adj.* of or relating to the universe or cosmos, esp. as distinct from the earth: *cosmic matter.*
■ inconceivably vast. ■ sweeping in grasp or intent; grandiose (often used ironically): *the lyrics to this song are cosmic!*
DERIVATIVES: **cos•mi•cal** *adj.* **cos•mi•cal•ly** |-ik(ə)lē| *adv.*

cos•mog•o•ny |kazˈmägənē| • *n.* (pl. **-ies**) a theory or story regarding the origin of the universe, esp. the solar system: *in their cosmogony, the world was thought to be a square, flat surface.*
DERIVATIVES: **cos•mo•gon•ic** |ˌkazmə'gänik| *adj.* **cos•mo•gon•i•cal** |ˌkazmə'gänikəl| *adj.* **cos•mog•o•nist** |-nist| *n.*

cos•mol•o•gy |kazˈmäləjē| • *n.* (pl. **-ies**) the science of the origin and development of the universe.
■ an account or theory of the origin of the universe.

DERIVATIVES: **cos•mo•log•i•cal** |ˌkazmə'läjikəl| *adj.* **cos•mol•o•gist** |-jist| *n.*

cos•mop•o•lis |käzˈmäpələs| • *n.* a city inhabited by people from many different countries.

cos•mo•pol•i•tan |ˌkazmə'pälətn| • *adj.* familiar with and at ease in many different countries and cultures: *his knowledge of French, Italian, and Spanish made him genuinely cosmopolitan.*
■ including people from many different countries: *immigration transformed the city into a cosmopolitan capital.* ■ having an exciting and glamorous character associated with travel and a mixture of cultures: *their designs became a byword for cosmopolitan chic.* ■ (of a plant or animal) found all over the world. • *n.* a cosmopolitan person.
■ a cosmopolitan plant or animal.
DERIVATIVES: **cos•mo•pol•i•tan•ism** |-ˌizəm| *n.* **cos•mo•pol•i•tan•ize** |-ˌīz| *v.*

cos•mop•o•lite |käzˈmäpəˌlīt| • *n.* a cosmopolitan person.

cos•mos |ˈkazməs; -ˌmōs; -ˌmäs| • *n.* (**the cosmos**) the universe seen as a well-ordered whole: *investigating the design of the cosmos.*
■ a system of thought: *the new gender-free intellectual cosmos.*

Cos•sack |ˈkäs,æk; -ək| • *n.* a member or soldier of a people of southern Russia, Ukraine, and Siberia, long noted for their horsemanship and military skill. Under the czars they were allowed considerable autonomy in return for protecting the frontiers. • *adj.* of, relating to, or characteristic of the Cossacks.

cos•set |ˈkäsət| • *v.* (**cosseted, cosseting**) [trans.] care for and protect in an overindulgent way.

cos•tal |ˈkästəl| • *adj.* of or relating to the ribs.

co•te•rie |ˈkōṭərē; ˌkōṭə'rē| • *n.* (pl. **-ies**) a small group of people with shared interests or tastes, esp. one that is exclusive of other people: *a coterie of friends.*

co•ter•mi•nous |kō'tərmənəs| • *adj.* **1** having the same boundaries or extent in space, time, or meaning: *the southern frontier was coterminous with the French Congo colony.* **2** meeting precisely at the ends. Cf. CONTERMINOUS.
DERIVATIVES: **co•ter•mi•nous•ly** *adv.*

co•til•lion |kə'tilyən| • *n.* **1** a dance with elaborate steps and figures, in particular:
■ an 18th-century French dance based on the contredanse. ■ a quadrille. **2** a formal ball, esp. one at which debutantes are presented.

Cou•é•ism |koo'ā,izəm| • *n.* a system of self-improvement using optimistic autosuggestion that enjoyed popularity in the 1920s.

cou•lee |ˈkoolē| • *n.* a deep ravine.

cou•loir |kool'wär| • *n.* a steep, narrow gully on a mountainside.

coun•ci•lor |ˈkowns(ə)lər| (also **councillor**) • *n.* a member of a council.
DERIVATIVES: **coun•ci•lor•ship** |-ˌsHip| *n.*

coun•se•lor |ˈkowns(ə)lər| (also **counsellor**) • *n.* **1** a person trained to give guidance on personal, social, or psychological problems: *a marriage counselor.* ■ [often with adj.] a person who gives advice on a specified subject: *a debt counselor.* **2** a person who supervises children at a camp. **3** a trial lawyer. **4** a senior officer in the diplomatic service. **5** a school or university official who advises students.

USAGE: A **counselor** is someone who gives advice or counsel, esp. an attorney. A **councilor** is a member of a council, such as a town or city council. Confusion arises because many *counselors* sit on councils, and *councilors* are often called on to give counsel.

coun•te•nance | 'kowntn-əns | • *n.* **1** a person's face or facial expression: *his impenetrable eyes and inscrutable countenance give little away.* **2** support: *she was giving her specific countenance to the occasion.* • *v.* [trans.] admit as acceptable or possible; allow: *he was reluctant to countenance the use of force.*

coun•ter•blast | 'kowntər,blæst | • *n.* a strongly worded reply to someone else's views: *a counterblast to the growing propaganda of the extreme Right.*

coun•ter•cul•ture | 'kowntər,kəlCHər | • *n.* a way of life and set of attitudes opposed to or at variance with values of the prevailing culture: *the idealists of the 60s counterculture.*

coun•ter•es•pi•o•nage | ,kowntər'espiə ,näzH; -,näj | • *n.* activities designed to prevent or thwart spying by an enemy.

coun•ter•feit | 'kowntər,fit | • *adj.* made in exact imitation of something valuable or important with the intention to deceive or defraud: *passing counterfeit $50 bills.* ■ pretended; sham: *the filmmakers created a counterfeit world using smoke and mirrors.* • *n.* a fraudulent imitation of something else; a forgery: *he knew the tapes to be counterfeits.* • *v.* [trans.] imitate fraudulently: *my signature is extremely hard to counterfeit.* ■ pretend to feel or possess (an emotion or quality): *no pretense could have counterfeited such terror.* ■ resemble closely: *sleep counterfeited Death so well.* Cf. FORGERY.

DERIVATIVES: **coun•ter•feit•er** *n.*

coun•ter•in•tel•li•gence | ,kowntərin'telə jəns | • *n.* another term for COUNTERESPIONAGE.

coun•ter•mand • *v.* | ,kowntər'mænd; 'kowntər,mænd | [trans.] revoke (an order): *an order to arrest the strike leaders had been countermanded.* ■ cancel an order for (goods): *she decided she had been extravagant and countermanded the outfit.* ■ revoke an order issued by (another person): *they were already countermanding her.*

coun•ter•part | 'kowntər,pärt | • *n.* **1** a person or thing holding a position or performing a function that corresponds to that of another person or thing in a different area: *the officials held talks with their French counterparts.* **2** one of two copies of a legal document.

coun•ter•point | 'kowntər,point | • *n.* **1** the art or technique of setting, writing, or playing a melody or melodies in conjunction with

another, according to fixed rules, esp. those that began to develop in western music in the 15th century. ■ a melody played in conjunction with another. **2** an argument, idea, or theme used to create a contrast with the main element: *I have used my interviews with parents as a counterpoint to a professional judgment.* • *v.* [trans.] **1** add counterpoint to (a melody): *the orchestra counterpoints the vocal part.* **2** (often **be counterpointed**) emphasize by contrast: *the cream walls and maple floors are counterpointed by black accents.* ■ compensate for: *fanciful excesses that are counterpointed with some unsentimental dialogue.*

coun•ter•poise | 'kowntər,poiz | • *n.* a factor, force, or influence that balances or neutralizes another: *money can be a counterpoise to beauty.* ■ a state of equilibrium. ■ a counterbalancing weight. • *v.* [trans.] have an opposing and balancing effect on: *our ideals are often counterpoised by the actual human condition we are in.* ■ bring into contrast: *the stories counterpoise a young recruit with an old-timer.*

Coun•ter-Ref•or•ma•tion the reform of the Church of Rome in the 16th and 17th centuries that was stimulated by, and opposed the spread of, the Protestant Reformation. It was spearheaded by the Jesuit order.

coun•ter•sign | 'kowntər,sin | • *v.* [trans.] add a signature to (a document already signed by another person): *each check had to be signed and countersigned.* • *n.* a signal or password given in reply to a soldier on guard.

DERIVATIVES: **coun•ter•sig•na•ture** | ,kowntər'signəCHər; -,CHŏŏr | *n.*

coun•ter•sink | 'kowntər,siNGk | • *v.* (past and past part. **-sunk** | -,səNGk |) [trans.] enlarge and bevel the rim of (a drilled hole) so that a screw, nail, or bolt can be inserted flush with the surface. ■ drive (a screw, nail, or bolt) into such a hole.

coun•ter•ten•or | 'kowntər,tenər | • *n.* the highest male adult singing voice (sometimes distinguished from the male alto voice by its strong, pure tone). ■ a singer with such a voice.

coun•ter•vail | ,kowntər'vāl | • *v.* [trans.] [usu. as adj.] (**countervailing**) offset the effect of (something) by countering it with something of equal force: *the dominance of the party was mediated by a number of countervailing factors.*

coup | kŏŏ | • *n.* (pl. **coups** | kŏŏz |) **1** (also **coup d'état**) a sudden, violent, and illegal seizure of power from a government: *a democracy overthrown by an army coup.* **2** a notable or successful stroke or move: *it was a coup to get such a prestigious contract.* ■ an unusual or unexpected but successful tactic in card play. **3** (among North American Indians) an act of touching an armed enemy in battle as a deed of bravery, or an act of first touching an item of the enemy's in order to claim it.

coup de grâce | ,kŏŏ də 'gräs | • *n.* (pl. **coups de grâce** pronunc. same) a final blow or shot given to kill a wounded person or animal: *he administered the* coup de grâce *with a knife* | *the party won another term and delivered the* coup de grâce *to socialism.*

coup de maî•tre |ˌko͞o də 'met(rə) | • *n.* (pl. **coups de maître** pronunc. same) a master stroke; an outstanding skillful and opportune act.

coup d'é•tat |ˌko͞o dā'tä | • *n.* (pl. **coups d'é•tat** |-'tä(z)| pronunc. same) another term for COUP (sense 1).

coupe[1] |ko͞op| (also **coupé** |ko͞o'pā|) • *n.* **1** a car with a fixed roof, two doors, and a sloping rear that is shorter than a sedan of the same model. **2** a four-wheeled enclosed horse-drawn carriage for two passengers and a driver.

coupe[2] |ko͞op| • *n.* a shallow glass or glass dish, typically with a stem, in which desserts or champagne are served.

■ a dessert served in such a dish.

cou•plet |'kəplət| • *n.* a pair of successive lines of verse, typically rhyming and of the same length.

cour•i•er |'ko͝orēər; 'kərēər| • *n.* a messenger who transports goods or documents, in particular:

■ a company or employee of a company that transports commercial packages and documents: *the check was dispatched by courier* | [as adj.] *a courier service.* ■ a messenger for an underground or espionage organization. • *v.* [trans.] (often **be couriered**) send or transport (goods or documents) by courier.

course |kôrs| • *n.* **1** (in architecture) a continuous horizontal layer of brick, stone, or other material in a building. **2** (in hunting) a pursuit of game (esp. hares) with greyhounds by sight rather than scent. • *v.* [trans.] pursue (game, esp. hares) with greyhounds using sight rather than scent: *many of the hares coursed escaped unharmed* | [intrans.] *she would course for hares with her greyhounds.*

DERIVATIVES: **courser** *n.* a person who hunts with hounds by sight.

cour•te•san |'kôrtəzən; 'kərtəzən| • *n.* a prostitute, esp. one with wealthy or aristocratic clients.

cour•ti•er |'kôrtēər; 'kôrCHər| • *n.* a person who attends a royal court as a companion or adviser to the king or queen.

■ a person who fawns and flatters in order to gain favor or advantage.

couth |ko͞oTH| • *adj.* [predic.] cultured, refined, and well mannered: *it is more couth to hold your shrimp by the tail.* • *n.* good manners; refinement: *their hockey team had more talent but less couth.*

cou•ture |ko͞o'to͞o(ə)r; -'tyr| • *n.* the design and manufacture of fashionable clothes to a client's specific requirements and measurements.

■ such clothes: *they were dressed in printed-silk couture.*

DERIVATIVES: **cou•tu•ri•er** *n.*

cou•vade |ko͞o'väd| • *n.* the custom in some cultures in which a man takes to his bed and goes through certain rituals when his child is being born, as though he were physically affected by the birth.

cov•en |'kəvən| • *n.* a group or gathering of witches who meet regularly.

■ a secret or close-knit group of associates: *covens of militants within the party.*

cov•e•nant |'kəvənənt| • *n.* an agreement.

■ a legal contract drawn up by deed. ■ a clause in such a contract: *restrictive covenants based on race.* ■ (in monotheistic religion) an agreement that brings about a relationship of commitment between God and his people. The Jewish faith is based on the biblical covenants made with Abraham, Moses, and David. • *v.* [intrans.] agree, esp. by lease, deed, or other legal contract: [with infinitive] *the landlord covenants to repair the property.*

PHRASES: **Old Covenant** (in Christianity) the covenant between God and Israel in the Old Testament. **New Covenant** (in Christianity) the covenant between God and the followers of Christ.

DERIVATIVES: **cov•e•nan•tal** |ˌkəvə'næntl| *adj.* **cov•e•nant•er** (also chiefly Law **cov•e•nan•tor**) *n.*

cov•er charge • *n.* (also **cover**) a flat fee paid for admission to a restaurant, bar, club, etc. It differs from a **minimum**, which is the required purchase of, typically, a minimum amount of food or drink.

cov•er crop • *n.* a crop grown for the protection and enrichment of the soil, esp. one grown outside the normal growing season.

co•vert • *adj.* |'kōvərt; kō'vərt; 'kəvərt| not openly acknowledged or displayed: *covert operations against the dictatorship* | *covert longing for change.* • *n.* |'kəvər(t); 'kōvərt| **1** a shelter or hiding place.

■ a thicket in which game can hide. **2 coverts** the feathers covering the bases of the main flight or tail feathers of a bird.

DERIVATIVES: **co•vert•ly** |'kōvərtlē; kō'vərtlē; 'kəvərtlē| *adv.* **co•vert•ness** *n.*

cov•er•ture |ˌkəvər,CHo͝or; -CHər| • *n.* **1** protective or concealing covering. **2** under common law, the legal status (now abolished by statute) of a married woman, considered to be under her husband's protection and authority.

cov•et |'kəvət| • *v.* (**coveted, coveting**) [trans.] yearn to possess or have (something): *the president-elect covets time for exercise and fishing* | [as adj.] (**coveted**) *she won the coveted Booker Prize for fiction.*

DERIVATIVES: **cov•et•a•ble** *adj.*

cov•et•ous |'kəvətəs| • *adj.* having or showing a great desire to possess something, typically something belonging to someone else: *fingered the linen with covetous hands* | *a grin that seemed entirely covetous.*

DERIVATIVES: **cov•et•ous•ly** *adv.* **cov•et•ous•ness** *n.*

cow • *v.* [trans.] (usu. **be cowed**) cause (someone) to submit to one's wishes by intimidation: *the intellectuals had been* **cowed into** *silence.*

cow•er |kowər| • *v.* [intrans.] crouch down in fear.

coy |koi| • *adj.* (**coyer, coyest**) (esp. of a woman) making a pretense of shyness or modesty that is intended to be alluring but is often regarded as irritating: *she treated him to a coy smile of invitation.*
■ reluctant to give details, esp. about something regarded as sensitive: *he is coy about his age.* ■ quiet and reserved; shy.
DERIVATIVES: **coy•ly** *adv.* **coy•ness** *n.*

coz•en |'kəzən| • *v.* [trans.] trick or deceive: *do not think to cozen your contemporaries.*
■ obtain by deception: *he was able to cozen a profit.*
DERIVATIVES: **coz•en•age** |-nij| *n.* **coz•en•er** *n.*

crabbed |kræbəd| • *adj.* **1** (of handwriting) ill-formed and hard to decipher.
■ (of style) contorted and difficult to understand: *crabbed legal language.* **2** ill-humored: *a crabbed, unhappy middle age.*
DERIVATIVES: **crab•bed•ly** *adv.* **crab•bed•ness** *n.*

crape |krāp| • *n.* archaic spelling of CREPE.
DERIVATIVES: **crap•y** *adj.*

crap•u•lent |'kræpyələnt| • *adj.* of or relating to the drinking of alcohol or drunkenness.
DERIVATIVES: **crap•u•lence** *n.* **crap•u•lous** |-yələs| *adj.*

cra•que•lure |kræ'kloŏr; 'kræk,loŏr| • *n.* a network of fine cracks in the paint or varnish of a painting.

crass |kræs| • *adj.* lacking sensitivity, refinement, or intelligence: *the crass assumptions that men make about women | the crass commercialization of historic sites.*
DERIVATIVES: **cras•si•tude** |'kræsə,t(y)oŏd| *n.* **crass•ly** *adv.* **crass•ness** *n.*

cra•ven |'krāvən| • *adj.* contemptibly lacking in courage; cowardly: *a craven abdication of his moral duty.* • *n.* archaic a cowardly person.
DERIVATIVES: **cra•ven•ly** *adv.* **cra•ven•ness** *n.*

craze |krāz| • *v.* (often **be crazed**) produce a network of fine cracks on (a surface): *the lake was frozen over but crazed with cracks.*
■ [intrans.] develop such cracks.

crease |krēs| • *v.* [trans.] (of a bullet) graze (someone or something), causing little damage: *a bullet creased his thigh.*

cre•a•tion•ism |krē'āsHə,nizəm| • *n.* the belief that the universe and living organisms originate from specific acts of divine creation, as in the biblical account, rather than by natural processes such as evolution.
DERIVATIVES: **cre•a•tion•ist** *n.* & *adj.*

crèche |kresH| • *n.* **1** a representation of the Christian nativity scene. **2** Brit. a nursery where babies and young children are cared for during the working day.

cre•dence |'krēdns| • *n.* **1** belief in or acceptance of something as true or valid: *psychoanalysis finds little credence among laymen.*
■ the likelihood of something being true; plausibility: *being called upon by the media as an expert lends credence to one's opinions.* **2** [usu. as adj.] a small side table, shelf, or niche in a church for holding the elements of the Eucharist before they are consecrated: *a credence table.*

cre•den•za |krə'denzə| • *n.* a sideboard or cupboard.

cred•i•ble |'kredəbəl| • *adj.* able to be believed; convincing: *few people found his story credible | a credible witness.*
■ capable of persuading people that something will happen or be successful: *a credible threat.*
DERIVATIVES: **cred•i•bil•i•ty** *n.* **cred•i•bly** |-blē| *adv.*

cred•it•a•ble |'kreditəbəl| • *adj.* (of a performance, effort, or action) deserving public acknowledgment and praise but not necessarily outstanding or successful: *a very creditable 4–2 loss.*
DERIVATIVES: **cred•it•a•bil•i•ty** |,kreditə'bilitē| *n.* **cred•it•a•bly** |'kreditəblē| *adv.*

cred•i•tor |'kreditər| • *n.* a person or company to whom money is owed.

cre•do |'krēdō; 'krādō| • *n.* (pl. **-os**) a statement of the beliefs or aims that guide someone's actions: *he announced his credo in his first editorial.*
■ (**Credo**) a creed of the Christian Church in Latin. ■ (**Credo**) a musical setting of the Nicene Creed, typically as part of a mass.

cre•du•li•ty |krə'd(y)oŏlitē| • *n.* a tendency to be too ready to believe that something is real or true.

cred•u•lous |'krejələs| • *adj.* having or showing too great a readiness to believe things.
DERIVATIVES: **cred•u•lous•ly** *adv.* **cred•u•lous•ness** *n.*

creed |krēd| • *n.* a system of religious belief; a faith: *people of many creeds and cultures.*
■ (often **the Creed**) a formal statement of Christian beliefs, esp. the Apostles' Creed or the Nicene Creed. ■ a set of beliefs or aims that guide someone's actions: *liberalism was more than a political creed.*

cren•el•la•tions |,krenl'āsHənz| • *plural n.* the battlements of a castle or other building.

cren•u•lated |'krenyələt; -yə,lāt| (also **crenulate**) • *adj.* having a finely scalloped or notched outline or edge.
DERIVATIVES: **cren•u•la•tion** |,krenyə'lāsHən| *n.*

Cre•ole |'krē,ōl| (also **creole**) • *n.* **1** a person of mixed European and black descent, esp. in the Caribbean.
■ a descendant of Spanish or other European settlers in the Caribbean or Central or South America. ■ a white descendant of French or Spanish settlers in Louisiana and other parts of the southern US. **2** a mother tongue formed from the contact of two languages through an earlier PIDGIN stage: *a Portuguese-based Creole.* • *adj.* of or relating to a Creole or Creoles.

crepe (also **crape, crêpe**) • *n.* **1** |krāp| a light, thin fabric with a wrinkled surface: [as adj.] *a crepe bandage.*
■ (also **crepe rubber**) hard-wearing wrinkled rubber, used esp. for the soles of shoes. **2** |krāp| black silk or imitation silk, formerly used for mourning clothes.
■ a band of such fabric formerly worn around

a person's hat as a sign of mourning. **3** |krāp; krep| a thin pancake.
DERIVATIVES: **crep•ey** adj.

crep•i•tate |'krepə,tāt| • v. [intrans.] make a crackling sound: *the night crepitates with an airy, whistling cacophony* | [as adj.] (**crepitating**) *spidery fingers of crepitating electricity.*
DERIVATIVES: **crep•i•tant** |'krepətənt| adj. **crep•i•ta•tion** n.

cre•pus•cu•lar |krə'pəskyələr| • adj. of, resembling, or relating to twilight.
■ (of an animal) appearing or active at twilight.

cre•scen•do |krə'sHendō| • n. **1** (pl. **crescendos** or **crescendi** |-dē|) a gradual increase in loudness in a piece of music.
■ a passage of music marked to be performed in this way. ■ the loudest point reached in a gradually increasing sound: *Deborah's voice was rising to a crescendo.* ■ a progressive increase in force or intensity: *a crescendo of misery.* ■ the most intense point reached in this; a climax: *the negative reviews reached a crescendo in mid-February.* • adv. & adj. (in music) with a gradual increase in loudness: [as adj.] *a short crescendo kettledrum roll.* • v. (**-oes, -oed**) [intrans.] increase in loudness or intensity: *the reluctant cheers began to crescendo.*

cres•cent |'kresənt| • adj. **1** [attrib.] having the shape of a curved sickle (a crescent): *a crescent moon.* **2** growing, increasing, or developing.

crest•fal•len |'krest,fôlən| • adj. sad and disappointed; dejected; abashed: *he came back empty-handed and crestfallen.* Cf. CHAPFALLEN.

cre•tin |'krētn| • n. a stupid person (used as a general term of abuse).
■ (in former medical use) a person who is deformed and mentally handicapped (suffers *cretinism*) because of congenital thyroid deficiency.
DERIVATIVES: **cre•tin•ous** |-əs| adj.

cre•vasse |kri'væs| • n. a deep open crack, esp. one in a glacier.
■ a breach in the embankment of a river or canal.

crev•ice |'krevəs| • n. a narrow opening or fissure, esp. in a rock or wall.

crim•i•nal•ize |'krimənl,īz| • v. [trans.] turn (an activity) into a criminal offense by making it illegal: *the law that criminalizes assisted suicide.*
■ turn (someone) into a criminal by making their activities illegal: *these measures would criminalize migrant workers for their way of life.*
DERIVATIVES: **crim•i•nal•i•za•tion** |,krimənl-ə'zāsHən| n.

cringe |krinj| • v. (**cringing**) [intrans.] bend one's head and body in fear or in a servile manner: *he cringed away from the blow* | [as adj.] (**cringing**) *we are surrounded by cringing yes-men and sycophants.*
■ experience an inward shiver of embarrassment or disgust: *I cringed at the speaker's stupidity.* • n. an act of cringing in fear.
■ a feeling of embarrassment or disgust.
DERIVATIVES: **cring•er** n.

cri•te•ri•on |krī'tirēən| • n. (pl. **criteria** |-'ti-rēə|) a principle or standard by which some-

thing may be judged or decided: *the launch came too close to violating safety criteria.*
DERIVATIVES: **cri•te•ri•al** |-'tirēəl| adj.

USAGE: Strictly speaking, the singular form (following the original Greek) is **criterion** and the plural form is **criteria**. It is a common mistake to use **criteria** as if it were a singular, as in *a further **criteria** needs to be considered.*

crit•ic |'kritik| • n. **1** a person who expresses an unfavorable opinion of something: *critics say many schools are not prepared to handle the influx of foreign students.* **2** a person who judges the merits of literary, artistic, or musical works, esp. one who does so professionally: *a film critic.*

crit•i•cal |'kritikəl| • adj. **1** (of a published literary or musical text) incorporating a detailed and scholarly analysis and commentary: *a critical edition of a Bach sonata.* **2** (of a situation or problem) having the potential to become disastrous; at a point of crisis: *the flood waters had not receded, and the situation was still critical.*
■ (of a person) extremely ill and at risk of death: *he had been in critical condition since undergoing surgery.* ■ having a decisive or crucial importance in the success or failure of something: *temperature is a critical factor in successful fruit storage.* **3** [attrib.] (in mathematics and physics) relating to or denoting a point of transition from one state to another.
■ (of a nuclear reactor or fuel) maintaining a self-sustaining chain reaction: *the reactor is due to go critical in October.*
DERIVATIVES: **crit•i•cal•i•ty** |,kritə'kæl-itē| n. (in senses 2 and 3). **crit•i•cal•ly** |'kri-tik(ə)lē| adv. [as submodifier] *he's critically ill.* **crit•i•cal•ness** n.

crit•i•cal mass • n. (in physics) the minimum amount of fissile material needed to maintain a nuclear chain reaction.
■ the minimum size or amount of something required to start or maintain a venture or activity.

cri•tique |kri'tēk| • n. a detailed analysis and assessment of something, esp. a literary, philosophical, or political theory. • v. (**critiques, critiqued, critiquing**) [trans.] evaluate in a detailed and analytical way: *the authors critique the methods and practices used in the research.*

cro•chet |krō'sHā| • n. a handicraft in which a patterned fabric is created by looping yarn with a single hooked needle: [as adj.] *a crochet hook.*
■ fabric or items made in such a way. • v. (**crocheted** |-'sHād|, **crocheting** |-'sHā-iNG|) [trans.] make (a garment or piece of fabric) in such a way: *she crocheted the shawl* | [intrans.] *her mother crochets.*
DERIVATIVES: **cro•chet•er** |-'sHāər| n.

crois•sant |k(r)wä'sänt; -'säN| • n. a French crescent-shaped roll made of sweet flaky pastry.

Cro-Mag•non man |krō'mægnən; 'mænyən| • n. the earliest form of modern human in

Europe. Their appearance *c.* 35,000 years ago marked the beginning of the Upper Paleolithic and the apparent decline and disappearance of Neanderthal man; the group persisted at least into the Neolithic period.

cro•ny•ism |'krōnē,izəm| • *n.* the appointment of friends and associates (cronies) to positions of authority, without proper regard to their qualifications.

crop•per |'kräpər| • *n.*
PHRASES: **come a cropper** fall heavily.
■ suffer a defeat or disaster: *the team's challenge for the championship has come a cropper.*

cross•hatch |'krôs,hæCH| • *v.* [trans.] [often as *n.*] (**crosshatching**) (in drawing or graphics) shade (an area) with intersecting sets of parallel lines.

cross•o•ver |'krôs,ōvər| • *n.* **1** the process of achieving success in a different field or style, esp. in popular music: [as adj.] *a jazz-classical crossover album.* **2** a person who votes for a candidate in a different political party than the one he or she usually supports: [adj.] *crossover voters.* **3** [as adj.] relating to or denoting trials of medical treatment in which experimental subjects and control groups are exchanged after a set period: *a crossover study.*

cross•patch |'krôs,pæCH| • *n.* a bad-tempered person.

crotch•et |'kräCHət| • *n.* **1** (in music) a quarter note. **2** a perverse or unfounded belief or notion: *the natural crotchets of inveterate bachelors.*

croup•i•er |'krōōpē,ā; -pēər| • *n.* the person in charge of a gambling table, gathering in and paying out money or tokens.

cro•zier |'krōzHər| (also **crosier**) • *n.* a hooked staff carried by a bishop as a symbol of pastoral office.

cru•cial |'krōōsHəl| • *adj.* decisive or critical, esp. in the success or failure of something: *negotiations were at a crucial stage.*
■ of great importance: *this game is crucial to our survival.*
DERIVATIVES: **cru•ci•al•i•ty** |,krōōsHē'æl-itē| *n.* **cru•cial•ly** *adv.*

USAGE: **Crucial** is used in formal contexts to mean 'decisive, critical,' e.g., *The testimony of the only eyewitness was crucial to the case.* Its broader use to mean 'very important,' as in *It is crucial to get good light for your photographs,* should be restricted to informal contexts.

cru•ci•ble |'krōōsəbəl| • *n.* a ceramic or metal container in which metals or other substances may be melted or subjected to very high temperatures.
■ a place or occasion of severe test or trial: *the crucible of combat.* ■ a place or situation in which different elements interact to produce something new: *the crucible of the new Romantic movement.*

cru•ci•form |'krōōsə,fôrm| • *adj.* having the shape of a cross: *a cruciform sword.*
■ of or denoting a church having a cross-shaped plan.

cru•di•tés |,krōōdə'tā| • *plural n.* assorted raw vegetables served as an hors d'oeuvre, typically with a dip.

cru•et |'krōōət| • *n.* **1** a small container for salt, pepper, oil, or vinegar for use at a dining table. **2** (in Christian church use) a small container for the wine or water to be used in the celebration of the Eucharist.

crustacean |krə'stāsHən| a member of a large group of mainly aquatic arthropods (the **Crustacea**) that include crabs, lobsters, shrimps, wood lice, barnacles, and many minute forms. They are very diverse, but most have four or more pairs of limbs and several other appendages.
DERIVATIVES: **crus•ta•ceous** |-sHəs| *adj.*

crux |krəks; krŏŏks| • *n.* (pl. **cruxes** or **cruces** |'krōō,sēz|) (**the crux**) the decisive or most important point at issue: *the crux of the matter is that attitudes have changed.*
■ a particular point of difficulty: *both cruces can be resolved by a consideration of the manuscripts.*

cry•o•gen•ics |,krī'jeniks| • *plural n.* [treated as sing.] the branch of physics dealing with the production and effects of very low temperatures.
■ another term for CRYONICS.
DERIVATIVES: **cry•o•gen•ic** *adj.* **cry•o•gen•i•cal•ly** |-ik(ə)lē| *adv.*

cry•on•ics |krī'äniks| • *plural n.* [treated as sing.] the practice or technique of deep-freezing the bodies of those who have just died of an incurable disease, in the hope of reviving them if and when a cure is developed.
DERIVATIVES: **cry•on•ic** *adj.*

crypt |kript| • *n.* an underground room or vault beneath a church, used as a chapel or burial place.

crypt•a•nal•y•sis |,kriptə'næləsəs| • *n.* the art or process of deciphering coded messages without the aid of the key.
DERIVATIVES: **crypt•an•a•lyst** |,krip'tænl-əst| *n.* **crypt•an•a•lyt•ic** |-,tænl'itik| *adj.* **crypt•an•a•lyt•i•cal** |-,tænl'itikəl| *adj.*

cryp•tic |'kriptik| • *adj.* **1** having a meaning that is mysterious or obscure: *he found her utterances too cryptic.*
■ (of a crossword puzzle) having difficult clues that indicate the solutions indirectly. **2** (of coloration or markings) serving to camouflage an animal in its natural environment.
DERIVATIVES: **cryp•ti•cal•ly** |-ik(ə)lē| *adv.*

cryp•tog•ra•phy |krip'tägrəfē| • *n.* the art of writing or solving codes.
DERIVATIVES: **cryp•tog•ra•pher** |-fər| *n.* **cryp•to•graph•ic** |,kriptə'græfik| *adj.* **cryp•to•graph•i•cal•ly** |,kriptə'græfik(ə)lē| *adv.*

cub•ism |'kyōō,bizəm| • *n.* an early 20th-century style and movement in art, esp. painting, in which perspective with a single viewpoint was abandoned and use was made of simple geometric shapes, interlocking planes, and, later, collage.
DERIVATIVES: **cub•ist** *n.* & *adj.* **cub•is•tic** |kyōō'bistik| *adj.*

cu•bit |'kyōōbit| • *n.* an ancient measure of

length, approximately equal to the length of a forearm. It was typically about 18 inches or 44 cm, though there was a **long cubit** of about 21 inches or 52 cm.

cuck•old |'kəkəld; -ōld| • *n.* the husband of an adulteress, often regarded as an object of derision. • *v.* [trans.] (of a man) make (another man) a cuckold by having a sexual relationship with his wife.
■ (of a man's wife) make (her husband) a cuckold.
DERIVATIVES: **cuck•old•ry** |-drē| *n.*

cues•ta |'kwestə| • *n.* (in geology) a ridge with a gentle slope (dip) on one side and a steep slope (scarp) on the other.

cui bo•no? |kwē 'bōnō| • *exclam.* who stands, or stood, to gain (typically, from a crime, and so might have been responsible for it)?

cui•rass |kwi'ræs; kyŏŏr'æs| • *n.* **1** a piece of medieval armor consisting of breastplate and backplate fastened together. **2** an artificial ventilator that encloses the body, leaving the limbs free, and forces air in and out of the lungs by changes in pressure.

cul-de-sac |'kəl di ,sæk| • *n.* (pl. **cul-de-sacs** or **culs-de-sac** |'kəl(z)| pronunc. same) a street or passage closed at one end; a dead end.
■ a route or course leading nowhere: *the prodemocracy forces found themselves in a political cul-de-sac.* ■ (in anatomy) a vessel, tube, or sac, e.g., the cecum, open at only one end.

cu•li•nar•y |'kələ,nerē; 'kyŏŏlə-| • *adj.* of or for cooking: *culinary skills.*
DERIVATIVES: **cu•li•nar•i•ly** |-,nerəlē| *adv.*

cul•mi•nate |'kəlmə,nāt| • *v.* [intrans.] reach a climax or point of highest development: *the tensions and disorders that culminated in World War II.*
■ [trans.] be the climax or point of highest development of: *her book culminated long researches on the symmetry studies of Escher.*
DERIVATIVES: **cul•mi•na•tion** *n.*

cul•pa•ble |'kəlpəbəl| • *adj.* deserving blame: *sometimes you're just as culpable when you watch something as when you actually participate.*
DERIVATIVES: **cul•pa•bil•i•ty** |,kəlpə'bilitē| *n.* **cul•pa•bly** |-blē| *adv.*

cul•ti•var |'kəltə,vär| • *n.* a plant variety that has been produced in cultivation by selective breeding.

cul•tured |'kəlCHərd| • *adj.* (of tissue cells, bacteria, etc.) grown or propagated in an artificial medium.
■ (of a pearl) formed around a foreign body inserted into an oyster.

cum•ber•some |'kəmbərsəm| (also **cumbrous**) • *adj.* large or heavy and therefore difficult to carry or use; unwieldy: *cumbersome diving suits.*
■ slow or complicated and therefore inefficient: *organizations with cumbersome hierarchical structures.*
DERIVATIVES: **cum•ber•some•ly** *adv.* **cum•ber•some•ness** *n.*

cu•mu•la•tive |'kyŏŏmyələtiv; -,lātiv| • *adj.* increasing or increased in quantity, degree, or force by successive additions: *the cumulative effect of two years of drought.* ■ (of interest or dividends) accruing in value until paid, even if not paid when due.
DERIVATIVES: **cu•mu•la•tive•ly** *adv.* **cu•mu•la•tive•ness** *n.*

cu•ne•i•form |kyŏŏ'nēə,fôrm; 'kyŏŏn(ē)ə-| • *adj.* denoting or relating to the wedge-shaped characters used in the ancient writing systems of Mesopotamia, Persia, and Ugarit, surviving mainly impressed on clay tablets: *a cuneiform inscription.*
■ denoting three bones of the tarsus (ankle) between the navicular bone and the metatarsals. ■ (in biology) wedge-shaped: *the eggs are cuneiform.* • *n.* cuneiform writing.

cu•pid•i•ty |kyŏŏ'piditē| • *n.* greed for money or possessions.

cu•pre•ous |'k(y)ŏŏprēəs| • *adj.* of or like copper.

cu•rate[1] |'kyŏŏrət; -,rāt| • *n.* (also **assistant curate**) chiefly Brit. a member of the clergy engaged as assistant to a vicar, rector, or parish priest.
■ a minister with pastoral responsibility.

cu•rate[2] |'kyŏŏ,rāt| • *v.* [trans.] (usu. **be curated**) select, organize, and look after the items in (a collection or exhibition): *both exhibitions are curated by the museum's director.*
DERIVATIVES: **cu•ra•tion** |kyə'rāSHən| *n.*

cur•a•tive |'kyŏŏrətiv| • *adj.* able to cure something, typically disease: *the curative properties of herbs.* • *n.* a medicine or agent of this type.
DERIVATIVES: **cur•a•tive•ly** *adv.* .

cu•ra•tor |'kyŏŏr,ātər; kyŏŏ'rātər; 'kyŏŏrətər| • *n.* a keeper or custodian of a museum or other collection.
DERIVATIVES: **cu•ra•to•ri•al** |,kyŏŏrə 'tôrēəl| *adj.* **cu•ra•tor•ship** |-,SHip| *n.*

curd |kərd| • *n.* (also **curds**) a soft, white substance formed when milk coagulates, used as the basis for cheese.
DERIVATIVES: **curd•y** *adj.*

cu•ret•tage |,kyŏŏrə'täZH| • *n.* the use of a **curette** (a scoop-shaped surgical knife), esp. on the lining of the uterus.

Cu•ri•a |'kyŏŏrēə| the papal court at the Vatican, by which the Roman Catholic Church is governed.
DERIVATIVES: **Cu•ri•al** *adj.*

cu•ri•o |'kyŏŏrē,ō| • *n.* (pl. **-os**) a rare, unusual, or intriguing object.

cu•ri•o•sa |,kyŏŏrē'ōsə; -'ōzə| • *plural n.* curiosities, esp. erotic or pornographic books or articles.

cur•mudg•eon |kər'məjən| • *n.* a bad-tempered or surly person.
DERIVATIVES: **cur•mudg•eon•li•ness** *n.* **cur•mudg•eon•ly** *adj.*

cur•ric•u•lum |kə'rikyələm| • *n.* (pl. **curricula** |-lə| or **curriculums**) the subjects comprising a course of study in a school or college.
DERIVATIVES: **cur•ric•u•lar** |-lər| *adj.*

cur·ric·u·lum vi·tae |kə'rik(y)ələm 'vē,tī; 'vītē| (abbr.: **CV**) • *n.* (pl. **curricula vitae** |-'rik(y)əlī|) a brief account of a person's education, qualifications, and previous occupations, typically sent with a job application.

cur·ry • *v.* (**-ies, -ied**) [trans.] **1** groom (a horse) with a rubber or plastic curry-comb. **2** treat (tanned leather) to improve its properties.
■ thrash; beat.
PHRASES: **curry favor** ingratiate oneself with someone through obsequious behavior: *a wimpish attempt to* **curry favor with** *the new bosses.* [ORIGIN: alteration of Middle English *curry favel*, from the name (*Favel* or *Fauvel*) of a chestnut horse in a 14th-cent. French romance who became a symbol of cunning and duplicity; hence 'to rub down Favel' meant to use the cunning that he personified.]

cur·sive |'kərsiv| • *adj.* written with the characters joined: *cursive script.* • *n.* writing with such a style.
DERIVATIVES: **cur·sive·ly** *adv.*

cur·so·ry |'kərsərē| • *adj.* hasty and therefore not thorough or detailed: *a cursory glance at the figures.*
DERIVATIVES: **cur·so·ri·ly** |'kərsərəlē| *adv.* **cur·so·ri·ness** *n.*

cur·tail |kər'tāl| • *v.* [trans.] (often **be curtailed**) reduce in extent or quantity; impose a restriction on: *civil liberties were further curtailed.*
DERIVATIVES: **cur·tail·ment** |kər'tālmənt| *n.*

cur·tal |'kərt̩l| • *adj.* shortened, abridged, or curtailed.

cur·vet |kər'vet| • *n.* a graceful or energetic leap. • *v.* (**curvetted, curvetting** or **curveted, curveting**) [intrans.] leap gracefully or energetically.

cur·vi·lin·e·ar |,kərvə'linēər| • *adj.* contained by or consisting of a curved line or lines: *these designs employ flowing, curvilinear forms.* Cf. RECTILINEAR.
DERIVATIVES: **cur·vi·lin·e·ar·i·ty** *n.* **cur·vi·lin·e·ar·ly** *adv.*

cush·y |'koŏshē| • *adj.* (**cushier, cushiest**) **1** (of a job, task, or situation) undemanding, easy, or secure: *cushy jobs that pay you to ski.* **2** (of furniture) comfortable.
DERIVATIVES: **cush·i·ness** *n.*

cusp |kəsp| • *n.* **1** a pointed end where two curves meet, in particular:
■ a projecting point between small arcs in Gothic tracery. ■ a cone-shaped prominence on the surface of a tooth, esp. of a molar or premolar. ■ a pocket or fold in the wall of the heart or a major blood vessel that fills and distends if the blood flows backward, so forming part of a valve. ■ a point at which the direction of a geometric curve is abruptly reversed. ■ each of the pointed ends of a crescent, esp. of the moon. **2** the initial point of an astrological sign or house: *he was Aries on the cusp with Taurus.*
■ a point between two different situations or

states, when a person or thing is poised between the two or just about to move from one to the other: *those on the cusp of adulthood.*
DERIVATIVES: **cus·pate** |'kəspət; -,pāt| *adj.* **cusped** *adj.* **cus·pi·date** |'kəspə,dāt| *adj.*

cus·pi·dor |'kəspə,dôr| • *n.* a pot for spitting into; spittoon.

cy·an |'sī,æn; 'sīən| • *n.* a greenish-blue color, which is one of the primary colors arrived at by selectively filtering parts of the spectrum, and is complementary to red.

cy·ber·naut |'sībər,nôt; -,nät| • *n.* a person who wears sensory devices in order to experience VIRTUAL REALITY.
■ a person who uses the Internet.

cy·ber·net·ics |,sībər'netiks| • *plural n.* [treated as sing.] the science of communications and automatic control systems in both machines and living things.
DERIVATIVES: **cy·ber·net·ic** *adj.* **cy·ber·net·i·cian** |-nə'tishən| *n.* **cy·ber·net·i·cist** |-'netəsəst| *n.*

cy·ber·space |'sībər,spās| • *n.* the notional environment in which communication over computer networks occurs: *my last message got lost in cyberspace.*

cy·borg |'sī,bôrg| • *n.* a fictional or hypothetical person whose physical abilities are extended beyond normal human limitations by mechanical elements built into the body.

cyg·net |'signət| • *n.* a young swan.

Cym·ric |'kəmrik| • *adj.* Welsh in language or culture. • *n.* the Welsh language.

cyn·ic |'sinik| • *n.* **1** a person who believes that people are motivated purely by self-interest rather than acting for honorable or unselfish reasons: *some cynics thought that the controversy was all a publicity stunt.*
■ a person who questions whether something will happen or whether it is worthwhile: *the cynics were silenced when the factory opened.* **2** (**Cynic**) a member of a school of ancient Greek philosophers (which flourished in the 3rd cent. BC and revived in the 1st cent. AD) founded by Antisthenes, marked by an ostentatious contempt for ease and pleasure. The movement stressed virtue as its own reward. Cf. STOIC.
DERIVATIVES: **cyn·i·cal** *adj.* **cyn·i·cal·ly** *adv.* **cyn·i·cism** |'sinə,sizəm| *n.*

cy·no·sure |'sīnə,sHŏŏr; 'sin-| • *n.* [in sing.] a person or thing that is the center of attention or admiration: *the queen was the cynosure of all eyes.*

Cyr·e·na·ic |,sirə'nāik| • *adj.* of or denoting the hedonistic school of philosophy, which was founded *c.*400 BC by Aristippus the Elder of Cyrene (in North Africa) and which holds that pleasure is the highest good and that virtue is to be equated with the ability to enjoy. • *n.* a follower of this school of philosophy. Cf. HEDONISM.
DERIVATIVES: **Cyr·e·na·i·cism** |-'nāə,sizəm| *n.*

Cy·ril·lic |sə'rilik| • *adj.* denoting the alphabet used by many Slavic peoples, chiefly those with a historical allegiance to the Orthodox Church. Ultimately derived from Greek uncials (script), it is now used for Russian, Bulgarian, Serbian, Ukrainian, and some other Slavic languages. • *n.* the Cyrillic alphabet.

cyst |sist| • *n.* in an animal or plant, a thin-walled, hollow organ or cavity containing a liquid secretion; a sac, vesicle, or bladder. ■ in the body, a membranous sac or cavity of abnormal character containing fluid. ■ a tough protective capsule enclosing the larva

of a parasitic worm or the resting stage of an organism.

czar |zär; (t)sär| (also **tsar** or **tzar**) • *n.* an emperor of Russia before 1917: [as title] *Czar Nicholas II.* ■ a South Slav ruler in former times, esp. one reigning over Serbia in the 14th century. ■ [usu. with adj.] a person with great authority or power in a particular area: *America's new drug czar.* DERIVATIVES: **czar•dom** |'-dəm| *n.* **czar•ism** |-,izəm| *n.* **czar•ist** |-ist| *n. & adj.*

Dd

da ca•po |dä 'käpō| • *adv.* (as a musical direction) repeat from the beginning. Cf. DAL SEGNO.

da•cha |'däCHə| (also **datcha**) • *n.* a country house or cottage in Russia, typically used as a second or vacation home.

dac•tyl |'dæktl| • *n.* a metrical prosodic foot consisting of one stressed syllable followed by two unstressed syllables or (in Greek and Latin) one long syllable followed by two short syllables.

Da•da |'dädä| (also **dada**) • *n.* an early 20th-century international movement in art, literature, music, and film, repudiating and mocking artistic and social conventions and emphasizing the illogical and absurd. ■ the products of this movement: *an exhibition of Dada.* ■ an example or the atmosphere of illogicality and absurdity: *the whole evening was dada.* DERIVATIVES: **Da•da•ism** |-,izəm| *n.* **Da•da•ist** |-ist| *n. & adj.* **Da•da•is•tic** |,dädä'istik| *adj.*

da•do |'dädō| • *n.* (pl. **-os**) the lower part of the wall of a room, below about waist height, if it is a different color or has a different covering than the upper part. ■ short for *dado rail*; a decorative molding at waist height, which protects the wall of a room from damage. ■ a groove cut in the face of a board, into which the edge of another board is fixed. ■ the part of a pedestal between the base and the cornice.

dae•mon[1] |'dēmən| (also **daimon**) • *n.* **1** (in ancient Greek belief) a divinity or supernatural being of a nature between gods and humans. ■ an inner or attendant spirit or inspiring force. **2** archaic spelling of *demon.* DERIVATIVES: **dae•mon•ic** |di'mänik| *adj.*

dae•mon[2] (also **demon**) • *n.* (in computing) a background process that handles requests for services such as print spooling and file transfers, and is dormant when not required.

daft |dæft| • *adj.* silly; foolish: *don't ask such daft questions.* ■ crazy: *have you gone daft?* ■ [predic.] (**daft**

about) infatuated with: *we were all daft about him.*

da•guerre•o•type |də'gerə,tīp| (also **daguerrotype**) • *n.* a photograph taken by an early photographic process employing an iodine-sensitized silvered plate and mercury vapor.

dai•myo |'dīmyō| (also **daimio**) • *n.* (pl. **-os**) (in feudal Japan) one of the great lords who were vassals of the shogun.

dal•li•ance |'dælēəns; 'dælyəns| • *n.* a casual romantic or sexual relationship. ■ brief or casual involvement with something: *college was my last dalliance with the education system.*

dal se•gno |däl 'sänyō| • *adv.* (esp. as a musical direction) repeat from the point marked by a sign. Cf. DA CAPO.

Dam•a•scene |'dæmə,sēn; ,dæmə'sēn| • *adj.* of or relating to the city of Damascus (Syria). ■ of, relating to, or resembling the conversion of St. Paul on the road to Damascus: *a transformation of Damascene proportions.* ■ of or relating to Damascus steel (which had a wavy hammer-welded pattern) or its manufacture. ■ (often **damascene**) relating to or denoting a process of inlaying a metal object with gold or silver decoration. • *n.* a native or inhabitant of Damascus. DERIVATIVES: **dam•a•scened** *adj.*

dam•ask |'dæməsk| • *n.* **1** a figured woven fabric with a pattern visible on both sides, typically used for table linen and upholstery. ■ a tablecloth made of this material. **2** short for *damask rose (Rosa damascena,* a sweet-scented old pink or light red variety (or hybrid) used for attar. **3** (also **damask steel**) another term for *Damascus steel,* a steel with welded iron parts and a wavy surface pattern, used in weapons and once marketed, if not made, in Damascus. • *adj.* made of or resembling damask. ■ having the velvety pink or light red color of a damask rose. • *v.* [trans.] weave with figured designs. ■ decorate with or as if with a variegated pattern.

dame |dām| • *n.* **1** (**Dame**) (in the UK) the title given to a woman equivalent to the rank of knight.

■ a woman holding this title. **2** a woman: *every guy on the block was watching this dame.*

■ an elderly or mature woman.

damn |dæm| • *v.* [trans.] (in Christian belief) (of God) condemn (a person) to suffer eternal punishment in hell: *be forever damned with Lucifer.*

■ (**be damned**) be doomed to misfortune or failure: *the enterprise was damned.* ■ condemn, esp. by the public expression of disapproval: *intellectuals whom he damns as doctrinaire idealists.* ■ curse (someone or something): *she cleared her throat, damning it for its huskiness | damn him for making this sound trivial.* • informal expressing anger, surprise, or frustration: *Damn! I completely forgot!* • *adj.* [attrib.] used for emphasis, esp. to express anger or frustration: *turn that damn thing off! | [as submodifier] don't be so damn silly!*

DERIVATIVES: **damnable** *adj.* **damnation** *n.*

dam•na•to•ry |ˈdæmnəˌtôrē| • *adj.* conveying or causing censure or damnation: *the case against him was most damnatory.*

Dam•o•cles |ˈdæməˌklēz| • a legendary courtier who extravagantly praised the happiness of Dionysius I, ruler of Syracuse. To show him how precarious this happiness was, Dionysius seated him at a banquet with a sword hung by a single hair over his head. PHRASES: **sword of Damocles** a precarious situation.

dan•der[1] |ˈdændər| • *n.* (in phrase **get/have one's dander up**) lose one's temper.

dan•der[2] • *n.* skin flakes in an animal's fur or hair.

dan•dle |ˈdændl| • *v.* [trans.] move (a baby or young child) up and down in a playful or affectionate way.

■ move (something) lightly up and down: *dandling the halter rope, he gently urged the pony's head up.*

dank |dæNGk| • *adj.* disagreeably damp, musty, and typically cold: *a dank cellar.*

DERIVATIVES: **dank•ly** *adv.* **dank•ness** *n.*

danse ma•ca•bre |ˈdäns məˈkäbrə| • *n.* another term for the **Dance of Death** an allegorical representation of Death leading people in the dance to the grave, popular in the Middle Ages.

dan•seur |dän'sər| • *n.* a male ballet dancer.

dan•seuse |dän'so͞oz| • *n.* a female ballet dancer.

dark•ling |ˈdärkliNG| • *adj.* of or relating to growing darkness: *the darkling sky.*

das•tard |ˈdæstərd| • *n.* a dishonorable or despicable person.

da•ta |ˈdætə; ˈdātə| • *n.* facts and statistics collected together for reference or analysis. See also DATUM.

■ the quantities, characters, or symbols on which operations are performed by a computer, being stored and transmitted in the form of electrical signals and recorded on magnetic, optical, or mechanical recording media. ■ (in philosophy) things known or assumed as facts, making the basis of reasoning or calculation.

USAGE: **Data** was originally the plural of the Latin word *datum*, 'something (e.g., a piece of information) given.' **Data** is now used as a singular where it means 'information': *This data was prepared for the conference.* It is used as a plural in technical contexts and when the collecion of bits of information is stressed: *All recent data on hurricanes are being compared.* Avoid *datas* and *datae*, which are false plurals, neither English nor Latin.

da•tive |ˈdātiv| • *adj.* (in Latin, Greek, German, and other languages) denoting a case of nouns and pronouns, and words in grammatical agreement with them, indicating an indirect object or recipient. • *n.* a noun or other word of this type.

■ (**the dative**) the dative case.

da•tum |ˈdætəm; ˈdā-| • *n.* (pl. **data** |-tə|) **1** a single piece of information.

■ an assumption or premise from which inferences may be drawn. **2** a fixed starting point of a scale or operation.

daub |dôb| • *v.* [trans.] coat or smear (a surface) with a thick or sticky substance in a carelessly rough or liberal way: *she daubed her face with cold cream.*

■ spread (a thick or sticky substance) on a surface in such a way: *a canvas with paint daubed on it.* ■ paint (words or drawings) on a surface in such a way: *they daubed graffiti on the walls.* • *n.* **1** plaster, clay, or another substance used for coating a surface, esp. when mixed with straw and applied to laths or wattles to form a wall: *square huts, mostly daub and wattle.*

■ a patch or smear of a thick or sticky substance: *a daub of paint.* **2** a painting executed without much skill.

DERIVATIVES: **daub•er** *n.* **1** an implement used for daubing. **2** a crude or inartistic painter.

daunt |dônt; dänt| • *v.* [trans.] (usu. **be daunted**) make (someone) feel intimidated or apprehensive: *some people are daunted by technology.*

PHRASES: **nothing daunted** without having been made fearful or apprehensive: *nothing daunted, the committee set to work.*

daunt•less |ˈdôntlis; ˈdänt-| • *adj.* showing fearlessness and determination: *a dauntless hero.*

DERIVATIVES: **daunt•less•ly** *adv.* **daunt•less•ness** *n.*

dau•phin |ˈdôfin| • *n.* the eldest son of the king of France, used as a title from 1349 to 1830.

dea•con |ˈdēkən| • *n.* (in Catholic, Anglican, and Orthodox churches) an ordained minister of an order ranking below that of priest.

■ (in some Protestant churches) a lay officer appointed to assist a minister, esp. in secular affairs. ■ (in the early church) an appointed minister of charity. • *v.* [trans.] appoint or ordain as a deacon.

DERIVATIVES: **deaconate** n. **deaconry** n. **dea•con•ship** |-ˌSHip| n.
dead•head |ˈdedˌhed| (also **dead-head**) • n.
1 (**Deadhead**) a fan and follower of the rock group The Grateful Dead: **2** a passenger or member of an audience with a free ticket.
■ a boring or unenterprising person. **3** a sunken or partially submerged log. • v.
1 [intrans.] (of a commercial driver, etc.) travel a route with no paying passengers or freight: *trucks deadheading into California to pick up outbound loads.*
■ ride in a plane or other vehicle without paying for a ticket: *the westbound crew boarded the red-eye to deadhead to Boston.* **2** [trans.] remove dead flowerheads from (a plant): *weeding and deadheading the roses.*
dead•lock |ˈdedˌläk| • n. [in sing.] a situation, typically one involving opposing parties, in which no progress can be made: *an attempt to* **break the deadlock.** • v. [trans.] (usu. **be deadlocked**) cause (a situation or opposing parties) to come to a point where no progress can be made because of fundamental disagreement: *the jurors were deadlocked on six charges.*
■ cause (a contest or game) to be in a tie: *Purdue deadlocked the game with a third-period field goal.*
dead•pan |ˈdedˌpæn| • adj. deliberately impassive or expressionless: *deadpan humor.* • adv. in a deadpan manner. • v. (**-panned**, **-panning**) [with direct speech] say something amusing while affecting a serious manner: *"I'm an undercover dentist," he deadpanned.*
dead reck•on•ing • n. the process of calculating one's position, esp. at sea, by estimating the direction and distance traveled rather than by using landmarks, astronomical observations, or electronic navigation methods.
dearth |dərTH| • n. [in sing.] a scarcity or lack of something: *a* **dearth of** *evidence* | *a* **dearth of** *good teachers.*
de•ba•cle |diˈbäkəl; ˈbäkəl| • n. a sudden and ignominious failure; a fiasco: *the economic debacle that became known as the Great Depression.*
de•bar |dēˈbär| • v. (**debarred**, **debarring**) [trans.] (usu. **be debarred**) exclude or prohibit (someone) officially from doing something: *people declaring that they were HIV-positive could be debarred from the country.* Cf. DISBAR.
DERIVATIVES: **de•bar•ment** n.
de•base |diˈbās| • v. [trans.] reduce (something) in quality or value; degrade: *commercialism has debased the meaning of the holiday* | [as adj.] (**debased**) *the debased traditions of sportsmanship.*
■ lower the moral character of (someone): *war debases people.* ■ lower the value of (coinage) by reducing the content of precious metal.
DERIVATIVES: **de•base•ment** n. **de•bas•er** n.
de•bauch |diˈbôCH| • v. [trans.] destroy or debase the moral purity of; corrupt.
■ seduce: *he debauched several schoolgirls.* • n. a

bout of excessive indulgence in sensual pleasures, esp. eating and drinking.
■ the habit or practice of such indulgence; debauchery: *his life had been spent in debauch.*
DERIVATIVES: **de•bauch•er** n.
de•bauch•er•y |diˈbôCHərē| • n. excessive indulgence in sensual pleasures.
de•bil•i•tate |diˈbiləˌtāt; dēˈbiləˌtāt| • v. [trans.] [often as adj.] (**debilitating**) make (someone) weak and infirm: *a debilitating disease* | [as adj.] (**debilitated**) *she had felt chronically debilitated and unwell for years.*
■ hinder, delay, or weaken: [adj.] *the debilitating effects of underinvestment.*
DERIVATIVES: **de•bil•i•tat•ing•ly** adv. **de•bil•i•ta•tion** |diˌbiləˈtāSHən| n. **de•bil•i•ta•tive** |diˌbiləˌtātiv| adj.
deb•o•nair |ˌdebəˈner| • adj. (of a man) confident, stylish, and charming.
DERIVATIVES: **deb•o•nair•ly** adv.
de•bouch |diˈbouCH; ˈbooSH| • v. [no obj., with adverbial of direction] emerge from a narrow or confined space into a wide, open area: *the soldiers debouched from their jeeps and dispersed among the trees* | *the stream finally debouches into a silent pool.*
DERIVATIVES: **de•bouch•ment** n.
de•bride•ment |diˈbrēdmənt| • n. the removal of damaged tissue or foreign objects from a wound.
de•brief |dēˈbrēf| • v. [trans.] question (someone, typically a soldier or spy) about a completed mission or undertaking: *together they debriefed their two colleagues* | [as n.] (**debriefing**) *during his debriefing he exposed two Russian spies.* • n. a series of questions about a completed mission or undertaking.
DERIVATIVES: **de•brief•er** n.
de•bris |dəˈbrē; ˌdā-| • n. scattered fragments, typically of something broken down or destroyed: *the streets were littered with debris from the explosion.*
■ loose natural material consisting esp. of broken pieces of rock: *planets, comets, and debris orbiting the sun.* ■ dirt or refuse: *clean away any collected dust or debris.*
debt•or |ˈdetər| • n. a person or institution that owes a sum of money.
■ (in the biblical sense) a person who has offended or sinned against another.
dec•a•dence |ˈdekədəns| • n. moral or cultural decline, esp. after a peak or culmination of achievement: *he denounced Western decadence.*
■ behavior reflecting such a decline: *the rituals of grief had become so ornate as to verge on decadence.* ■ luxurious self-indulgence.
DERIVATIVES: **dec•a•dent** adj. **dec•a•dent•ly** adv.
de•cal•co•ma•ni•a |dēˌkælkəˈmānēə| • n. the process of transferring designs (decals) from prepared paper to glass, china, metal, etc.
■ a technique used by some surrealist artists that involves pressing paint between sheets of paper.
Dec•a•logue |ˈdekəˌlôg; ˌläg| • n. (usu. **the Decalogue**) the biblical Ten Commandments.

de•cant |di'kænt| • v. [trans.] gradually pour (liquid, typically wine or a solution) from one container into another, esp. without disturbing the sediment: *the wine was decanted one hour before being served.*
■ empty out; move as if by pouring: *the bus broke down and we were decanted into another vehicle.*

de•cap•i•tate |di'kæpi,tāt| • v. [trans.] cut off the head of (a person or animal): *the guillotine decapitated its victims* | [as adj.] (**decapitated**) *a decapitated body.*
■ cut the end or top from (something). ■ attempt to undermine (a group or organization) by removing its leaders.
DERIVATIVES: **de•cap•i•ta•tion** |di,kæpi 'tāSHən| n. **de•cap•i•ta•tor** |-,tātər| n.

de•ce•dent |di'sēdnt| • n. (in legal use) a deceased person: *the decedent's property passed to his children.*

de•cel•er•ate |dē'selə,rāt| • v. [intrans.] (of a vehicle, machine, or process) reduce speed; slow down: *international growth rates decelerated in the early 1970s.*
■ [trans.] cause to move more slowly: *gravity decelerates the cosmic expansion.*
DERIVATIVES: **de•cel•er•a•tion** |-,selə'rā-SHən| n. **de•cel•er•a•tor** |-,rātər| n.

dec•i•bel |'desə,bəl| (abbr.: **dB**) • n. a unit used to measure the intensity of a sound or the power level of an electrical signal by comparing it with a given level on a logarithmic scale.
■ (in general use) a degree of loudness: *his voice went up several decibels.*

de•cid•u•ous |di'sijŏŏəs| • adj. (of a tree or shrub) shedding its leaves annually. Cf. EVERGREEN; CONIFER.
■ (of a tree or shrub) broad-leaved. ■ denoting the milk teeth of a mammal, which are shed after a time.
DERIVATIVES: **de•cid•u•ous•ly** adv. **de•cid•u•ous•ness** n.

dec•i•mate |'desə,māt| • v. [trans.] (often **be decimated**) 1 kill, destroy, or remove a large percentage of: *the project would decimate the fragile wetland wilderness* | *a population decimated by plague.*
■ drastically reduce the strength or effectiveness of (something): *plant viruses that can decimate yields.* 2 kill one in every ten of (a group of soldiers or others) as a punishment for the whole group.
DERIVATIVES: **dec•i•ma•tion** |,desə'mā-SHən| n. **dec•i•ma•tor** |-,mātər| n.

USAGE: Historically, the meaning of the word **decimate** is 'kill one in every ten of (a group of people).' This sense has been superseded by the later, more general sense 'kill or destroy (a large percentage of),' as in *the virus has **decimated** the population.* Some traditionalists argue that this and other later senses are incorrect. **Decimate** should not be used to mean 'defeat utterly.'

de•ci•pher |di'sīfər| • v. [trans.] convert (a text written in code, or a coded signal) into normal language: *enable the government to decipher coded computer transmissions.*

■ succeed in understanding, interpreting, or identifying (something): *an expression she could not decipher.*
DERIVATIVES: **de•ci•pher•a•ble** adj. **de•ci•pher•ment** n.

dec•la•ma•tion |,deklə'māsHən| • n. the action or art of speaking aloud or reciting with studied rhetorical expression (declaiming): *Shakespearean declamation* | *declamations of patriotism.*
■ a rhetorical exercise or set speech. ■ forthright or distinct projection of words set to music: *a soprano soloist with wonderfully clear declamation.*
DERIVATIVES: **declamatory** adj.

dé•clas•sé |,dāklä'sā| (also **déclassée**) • adj. having fallen in social rank or position: *his parents were now poor and déclassé.*
■ of inferior status: *a déclassé restaurant.*

de•clen•sion |di'klensHən| • n. 1 (in the grammar of Latin, Greek, and other languages) the variation of the form of a noun, pronoun, or adjective, by which its grammatical case, number, and gender are identified.
■ the class to which a noun or adjective is assigned according to the manner of this variation. 2 a condition of decline or moral deterioration: *the declension of the new generation.*
DERIVATIVES: **de•clen•sion•al** |-SHənl| adj.

dec•li•na•tion |,deklə'nāsHən| • n. 1 the angular distance of a point north or south of the celestial equator.
■ the angular deviation of a compass needle from true north (because the magnetic north pole and the geographic north pole do not coincide). 2 formal refusal: *in the face of this declination of the proposition.*
DERIVATIVES: **dec•li•na•tion•al** |-SHənl| adj.

de•cliv•i•ty |di'klivitē| • n. (pl. **-ies**) a downward slope: *a thickly wooded declivity.*
DERIVATIVES: **de•cliv•i•tous** |-təs| adj.

de•coct |di'käkt| • v. [trans.] extract the essence from (something) by heating or boiling it.
DERIVATIVES: **de•coc•tion** n.

dé•colle•tage |dā,kälə'täzH ,dekələ-| • n. a low neckline on a woman's dress or top.

dé•colle•té |dā,kälə'tā ,dekələ-| • adj. (also **décolletée**) (of a woman's dress or top) having a low neckline. • n. a low neckline on a woman's dress or top.

de•com•pose |,dēkəm'pōz| • v. [intrans.] (of a dead body or other organic matter) decay; become rotten: *leaves stuffed in plastic bags do not decompose* | [as adj.] (**decomposed**) *the body was badly decomposed.*
■ [trans.] cause (something) to decay or rot: *dead plant matter can be completely decomposed by microorganisms.* ■ [intrans.] (of a chemical compound) break down into component elements or simpler constituents: *many chemicals decompose rapidly under high temperature.*
■ [trans.] break down (a chemical compound) into its component elements or simpler constituents: *to decompose the compound by means of an acid.* ■ [trans.] (in mathematics) express

(a number or function) as a combination of simpler components.

DERIVATIVES: **de•com•pos•a•ble** *adj.* **de•com•po•si•tion** |dē͵kämpə'ziSHən| *n.*

de•con•struc•tion |͵dēkən'strəksHən| • *n.* a method of critical analysis of philosophical and literary language that emphasizes the internal workings of language and conceptual systems, the relational quality of meaning, and the assumptions implicit in forms of expression.

DERIVATIVES: **de•con•struc•tion•ism** |-͵nizəm| *n.* **de•con•struc•tion•ist** |-ist| *adj.* & *n.*

dec•o•rous |'dekərəs; di'kôrəs| • *adj.* in keeping with good taste and propriety; polite and restrained: *dancing with decorous space between partners.*

DERIVATIVES: **dec•o•rous•ly** *adv.* **dec•o•rous•ness** *n.*

de•co•rum |di'kôrəm| • *n.* behavior in keeping with good taste and propriety: *you exhibit remarkable modesty and decorum.*

■ etiquette: *he had no idea of funeral decorum.* ■ (usu. **decorums**) a particular requirement of good taste and propriety. ■ suitability to the requirements of a person, rank, or occasion.

de•cou•page |͵dākoo'päzH| • *n.* the decoration of the surface of an object with paper cutouts.

dec•re•ment |'dekrəmənt| • *n.* a reduction or diminution: *relaxation produces a decrement in sympathetic nervous activity.*

■ an amount by which something is reduced or diminished: *the dose was reduced by 10 mg weekly decrements.* ■ (in physics) the ratio of the amplitudes in successive cycles of a damped oscillation. • *v.* [trans.] cause a discrete reduction in (a numerical quantity): *the instruction decrements the accumulator by one.*

de•crep•it |di'krepit| • *adj.* elderly and infirm: *a decrepit old drunk.*

■ worn out or ruined because of long use or neglect; dilapidated: *centuries-old buildings, now decrepit and black with soot.*

DERIVATIVES: **de•crep•i•tude** |-͵t(y)ood| *n.*

de•cre•tal |di'krētl| • *n.* a papal decree concerning a point of canon law. • *adj.* of the nature of a decree.

de•crim•i•nal•ize |dē'kriminə͵līz| • *v.* [trans.] cease to treat (something) as illegal: *they argue that we should decriminalize drugs, not legalize them.*

DERIVATIVES: **de•crim•i•nal•i•za•tion** |-͵kriminəli'zāsHən| *n.*

de•cry |di'krī| • *v.* (**-ies, -ied**) [trans.] publicly denounce: *they decried human rights abuses.*

DERIVATIVES: **de•cri•er** *n.*

de•cus•sate |'dekə͵sāt; di'kəsät| • *v.* [reciprocal] (of two or more things) cross or intersect each other to form an X: *the fibers decussate in the collar.* • *adj.* shaped like an X.

■ (of leaves) arranged in opposite pairs, each pair being at right angles to the pair below.

DERIVATIVES: **de•cus•sa•tion** |͵dekə'sāsHən| *n.*

de•duce |di'd(y)oos| • *v.* [trans.] arrive at (a fact or a conclusion) by reasoning; draw as a logical conclusion: *little can be safely deduced from these figures* | [with clause] *they deduced that the fish died because of water pollution.*

■ trace the course or derivation of: *he cannot deduce his descent wholly by male heirs.*

DERIVATIVES: **de•duc•i•ble** |-səbəl| *adj.*

de•duct |di'dəkt| • *v.* [trans.] subtract or take away (an amount or part) from a total: *tax has been deducted from the payments.*

de•duc•tion |di'dəksHən| • *n.* **1** the action of deducting or subtracting something: *the dividend will be paid without deduction of tax.*

■ an amount that is or may be deducted from something, esp. from taxable income or tax to be paid: *tax deductions.* **2** the inference of particular instances by reference to a general law or principle: *if you are not a citizen, then by deduction I can list legal hurdles you may encounter.*

■ a conclusion that has been deduced.

de•fal•cate |di'fælkāt; 'fôl-| • *v.* [trans.] embezzle (funds with which one has been entrusted): *the officials were charged with defalcating government money.*

DERIVATIVES: **de•fal•ca•tion** |͵dēfæl'kāsHən; fôl-| *n.* **de•fal•ca•tor** |-kātər| *n.*

de•fame |di'fām| • *v.* [trans.] damage the good reputation of (someone); SLANDER or LIBEL: *he claimed that the article defamed his family.*

DERIVATIVES: **def•a•ma•tion** |͵defə'māsHən| *n.* **de•fam•a•to•ry** |-'fæmə͵tôrē| *adj.* **de•fam•er** *n.*

de•fault |di'fôlt| • *n.* **1** failure to fulfill an obligation, esp. to repay a loan or appear in a court of law: *the company will have to restructure its debts to avoid default.* **2** a preselected option adopted by a computer program or other mechanism when no alternative is specified by the user or programmer: *the default is 10-point type* | [as adj.] *default settings.* • *v.* [trans.] **1** fail to fulfill an obligation, esp. to repay a loan or to appear in a court of law: *some had defaulted on student loans.*

■ [trans.] declare (a party) in default and give judgment against that party: *the possibility that plaintiffs would be defaulted and the case dismissed.* **2** (**default to**) (of a computer program or other mechanism) revert automatically to (a preselected option): *when you start a fresh letter the system will default to its own style.*

PHRASES: **by default** because of a lack of opposition: *they won the third round by default.*

■ through lack of positive action rather than conscious choice: *legislation dies by default if the governor fails to act on it.*

de•fea•sance |di'fēzəns| • *n.* (in legal use) the action or process of rendering something null and void.

■ a clause or condition that, if fulfilled, renders a deed or contract null and void.

de•feat•ist |di'fētist| • *n.* a person who expects or is excessively ready to accept failure. • *adj.* demonstrating expectation or

acceptance of failure: *we have a duty not to be so defeatist.*
DERIVATIVES: **de•feat•ism** |-ˌtizəm| *n.*

def•e•cate |'defəˌkāt| • *v.* [intrans.] discharge feces from the body.
DERIVATIVES: **def•e•ca•tion** |ˌdefə'kāsHən| *n.* **def•e•ca•tor** |-ˌkātər| *n.* **def•e•ca•to•ry** |-kəˌtôrē| *adj.*

de•fect |di'fekt| • *v.* [intrans.] abandon one's country or cause in favor of an opposing one: *he defected to the Soviet Union after the war.*
DERIVATIVES: **de•fec•tion** |di'feksHən| *n.* **de•fec•tor** |di'fektər| *n.*

de•fen•es•tra•tion |dēˌfenə'strāsHən| • *n.* the action of throwing someone out of a window.
DERIVATIVES: **de•fen•es•trate** |-'fenəˌstrāt| *v.*

def•er•ence |'defərəns| • *n.* humble submission and respect: *he addressed her with the deference due to age.*

de•fib•ril•la•tor |dē'fibrəˌlātər| • *n.* a device used to restore normal rhythm to a heart in fibrillation by application of an electric current to the chest wall or heart.
DERIVATIVES: **de•fib•ril•late** |-ˌlāt| *v.* **de•fib•ril•la•tion** |dēˌfibrə'lāsHən| *n.*

de•file[1] |di'fīl| • *v.* [trans.] make dirty or foul; sully, mar, or spoil: *the land was defiled by a previous owner.*
■ desecrate or profane (something sacred): *the tomb had been defiled and looted.* ■ violate the chastity of (a woman).
DERIVATIVES: **de•file•ment** *n.* **de•fil•er** *n.*

de•file[2] |di'fīl; 'dēˌfīl| • *n.* a steep-sided, narrow gorge or passage (originally one requiring troops to march in single file). • *v.* [no obj., with adverbial of direction] (of troops) march in single file: *we emerged after defiling through the mountainsides.*

de•fine |di'fīn| • *v.* [trans.] **1** state or describe exactly the nature, scope, or meaning of: *the contract will seek to define the client's obligations.*
■ give the meaning of (a word or phrase), esp. in a dictionary. ■ make up or establish the character of: *for some, the football team defines their identity.* **2** mark out the boundary or limits of: [as adj.] (**defined**) *clearly defined boundaries.*
■ make clear the outline of; delineate: *she defined her eyes by applying eyeshadow.*
DERIVATIVES: **de•fin•a•ble** *adj.* **de•fin•er** *n.*

def•i•nite |'defənit| • *adj.* clearly stated or decided; not vague or doubtful: *we had no definite plans.*
■ clearly true or real; unambiguous: *no definite proof has emerged.* ■ [predic.] (of a person) certain or sure about something: *you're very definite about that!* ■ clear or undeniable (used for emphasis): *video is a definite asset in the classroom.* ■ having exact and discernible physical limits or form.
DERIVATIVES: **def•i•nite•ness** *n.*

de•fin•i•tive |di'finitiv| • *adj.* (of a conclusion or agreement) done or reached decisively and with authority: *a definitive diagnosis.*

■ (of a book or other text) the most authoritative of its kind: *the definitive biography of Harry Truman.* • *n.* a definitive postage stamp.
DERIVATIVES: **de•fin•i•tive•ly** *adv.*

USAGE: **Definitive** in the sense 'decisive, unconditional, final' is sometimes confused with **definite**. **Definite** means 'clearly defined, precise, having fixed limits,' but **definitive** goes further, meaning 'most complete, satisfying all criteria, most authoritative,' as in *Although some critics found a few definite weak spots in the author's interpretations, his book was nonetheless widely regarded as the definitive history of the war.* A **definite** decision is simply one that has been made clearly and is without doubt, whereas a **definitive** decision is one that is not only conclusive but also carries the stamp of authority or is a benchmark for the future, as in a Supreme Court ruling.

def•la•grate |'defləˌgrāt| • *v.* burn away or cause (a substance) to burn away with a sudden flame and rapid, sharp combustion: [trans.] *the current will deflagrate some of the particles.*
DERIVATIVES: **def•la•gra•tion** *n.* **def•la•gra•tor** |-ˌtər| *n.*

de•flate |di'flāt| • *v.* **1** [trans.] let air or gas out of (a tire, balloon, or similar object): *he deflated one of the tires.*
■ [intrans.] be emptied of air or gas: *the balloon deflated.* **2** cause (someone) to suddenly lose confidence or feel less important: [as adj.] (**deflated**) *the news left him feeling utterly deflated.*
■ reduce the level of (an emotion or feeling): *her anger was deflated.* **3** bring about a general reduction of price levels in (an economy).
DERIVATIVES: **de•fla•tor** |-ˌtər| *n.*

de•fla•tion |di'flāsHən| • *n.* **1** the action or process of deflating or being deflated: *deflation of the illusion that the 1960s were a perpetual party.* **2** a contraction of available money or credit resulting in a reduction of the general level of prices in an economy.
DERIVATIVES: **de•fla•tion•ar•y** |-ˌnerē| *adj.* **de•fla•tion•ist** |-ist| *n.* & *adj.*

de•flect |di'flekt| • *v.* [with obj., and usu. with adverbial of direction] cause (something) to change direction by interposing something; turn aside from a straight course: *the bullet was deflected harmlessly into the ceiling.*
■ [no obj., with adverbial of direction] (of an object) change direction after hitting something: *the pebble deflected off the windshield.* ■ cause (someone) to deviate from an intended purpose: *she refused to be deflected from anything she had set her mind on.* ■ cause (something) to change orientation: *the compass needle is deflected from magnetic north by metal in the aircraft.*

de•flow•er |dē'flowər| • *v.* [trans.] **1** deprive (a woman) of her virginity. **2** [usu. as adj.] (**deflowered**) strip (a plant or garden) of flowers: *deflowered rose bushes.*

de•fo•li•ate |dē'fōlēˌāt| • *v.* [trans.] remove leaves from (a tree, plant, or area of land) for

agricultural purposes or as a military tactic: *the area was defoliated and napalmed many times.*
DERIVATIVES: **de•fo•li•ant** *n.* **de•fo•li•a•tion** |dē͵fōli'ashən| *n.*
de•form |di'fôrm| • *v.* [trans.] distort the shape or form of; make misshapen: [as adj.] (**deformed**) *deformed hands.*
■ [intrans.] become distorted or misshapen; undergo deformation: *the suspension deforms slightly on corners.*
DERIVATIVES: **de•form•a•ble** *adj.* **deformation** *n.*
de•form•i•ty |di'fôrmitē| • *n.* (pl. **-ies**) a deformed part, esp. of the body; a malformation: *children born with deformities.*
■ the state of being deformed or misshapen: *respiratory problems caused by spinal deformity.*
de•fray |di'frā| • *v.* [trans.] provide money to pay (a cost or expense): *the proceeds from the raffle help to defray the expenses of the evening.*
DERIVATIVES: **de•fray•a•ble** *adj.* **de•fray•al** |-'frāəl| *n.* **de•fray•ment** *n.*
deft |deft| • *adj.* neatly skillful in one's movements: *a deft piece of footwork.*
■ demonstrating skill and cleverness: *the script was both deft and literate.*
DERIVATIVES: **deft•ly** *adv.* **deft•ness** *n.*
de•funct |di'fəngkt| • *adj.* no longer existing or functioning: *the now defunct Communist common market.*
dé•ga•gé |͵dāgä'zhā| • *adj.* unconcerned or unconstrained; relaxed. • *n.* (pl. pronunc. same) (in ballet) a movement in which weight is shifted from one foot to the other in preparation for the execution of a step.
de•gauss |dē'gows| • *v.* [trans.] [often as n.] (**degaussing**) remove unwanted magnetism from (a television or monitor) in order to correct color disturbance.
■ neutralize the magnetic field of (a ship) by encircling it with a conductor carrying electric currents.
DERIVATIVES: **de•gauss•er** *n.*
de•gen•er•ate • *adj.* |di'jenərit| **1** having lost the physical, mental, or moral qualities considered normal and desirable; showing evidence of decline: *a degenerate form of a higher civilization.* **2** lacking some property, order, or distinctness of structure previously or usually present, in particular:
■ (in mathematics) relating to or denoting an example of a particular type of equation, curve, or other entity that is equivalent to a simpler type, often occurring when a variable or parameter is set to zero. ■ (in physics) relating to or denoting an energy level that corresponds to more than one quantum state. ■ (in physics) relating to or denoting matter at densities so high that gravitational contraction is counteracted. ■ (in biology) having reverted to a simpler form as a result of losing a complex or adaptive structure present in the ancestral form. • *n.* an immoral or corrupt person. • *v.* |di'jenə͵rāt| [intrans.] decline or deteriorate physically, mentally, or morally: *the quality of life had degenerated| the debate* **degenerated into** *a brawl.*

DERIVATIVES: **de•gen•er•a•cy** |-rəsē| *n.* **de•gen•er•ate•ly** |-ritlē| *adv.*
deg•ra•da•tion |͵degrə'dāshən| • *n.* the condition or process of degrading or being degraded: *a trail of human misery and degradation.*
■ the wearing down of rock by disintegration.
de•grade |di'grād| • *v.* **1** [trans.] treat or regard (someone) with contempt or disrespect: *she thought that many supposedly erotic pictures degraded women.*
■ lower the character or quality of: *devices that clean up and amplify the degraded signal.* ■ reduce (someone) to a lower rank, esp. as a punishment: *he was degraded from his high estate.* **2** break down or deteriorate chemically: [intrans.] *when exposed to light, the materials will degrade* | [trans.] *the bacteria will degrade hydrocarbons.*
■ [trans.] reduce (energy) to a less readily convertible form. ■ [trans.] wear down (rock) and cause it to disintegrate.
DERIVATIVES: **de•grad•a•bil•i•ty** |di͵grādə'bilitē| *n.* **de•grad•a•ble** *adj.* **deg•ra•da•tive** |'degrə͵dātiv| *adj.* **de•grad•ed** *adj.* **de•grad•er** *n.* **de•grad•ing** *adj.*
de•gree |di'grē| • *n.* **1** [in sing.] the amount, level, or extent to which something happens or is present: *a degree of caution is probably wise| a question of degree.* **2** a unit of measurement of angles, (one three-hundred-and-sixtieth) of the circumference of a circle: *set at an angle of 45 degrees.* (Symbol: °) **3** a stage in a scale or series, in particular:
■ a unit in any of various scales of temperature, intensity, or hardness: *water boils at 100 degrees Celsius.* (Symbol: °) ■ [in combination] each of a set of grades (usually three) used to classify burns according to their severity, from *first-degree* (least serious) to *third-degree* (most serious) ■ [in combination] a legal grade of crime or offense, esp. murder: *second-degree murder.* ■ [often in combination] a step in direct genealogical descent: *second-degree relatives.* ■ a position in a musical scale, counting upward from the tonic or fundamental note: *the lowered third degree of the scale.* ■ the class into which a mathematical equation falls according to the highest power of unknowns or variables present: *an equation of the second degree.* ■ any of the three steps on the scale of comparison of gradable adjectives and adverbs, namely positive, comparative, and superlative. ■ a thing placed like a step in a series; a tier or row. **4** an academic rank conferred by a college or university after examination or after completion of a course of study, or conferred as an honor on a distinguished person: *a degree in zoology.*
■ social or official rank: *persons of unequal degree.* ■ a rank in an order of freemasonry.
PHRASES: **by degrees** a little at a time; gradually: *rivalries and prejudice were by degrees fading out.* **to a degree** to some extent: *to a degree, it is possible to educate oneself.* **to the nth degree** to the utmost: *tested our patience to the nth degree.*

de•hisce |diˈhis| • v. [intrans.] (of a pod or seed vessel, or of a cut or wound) gape or burst open: *after the anther lobes dehisce, the pollen is set free.*
DERIVATIVES: **de•his•cence** |-ˈhisəns| n. **de•his•cent** |-ˈhisənt| adj.

de•i•fy |ˈdēəˌfī| • v. (-ies, -ied) [trans.] (usu. **be deified**) worship, regard, or treat (someone or something) as a god: *she was deified by the early Romans as a fertility goddess.* | *they virtually deify efficiency.*
DERIVATIVES: **de•i•fi•ca•tion** |ˌdēəfiˈkāSHən| n.

deign |dān| • v. [no obj., with infinitive] do something that one considers to be beneath one's dignity: *she did not deign to answer the maid's question.*
■ [trans.] condescend to give (something): *he deigned no apology.*

de•ism |ˈdēizəm| • n. belief in the existence of a supreme being, specifically of a creator who does not intervene in the universe. The term is used chiefly of an intellectual movement of the 17th and 18th centuries that accepted the existence of a creator on the basis of reason but rejected belief in a supernatural deity who interacts with humankind. Cf. THEISM.
DERIVATIVES: **de•ist** n. **de•is•tic** |dēˈistik| adj. **de•is•ti•cal** |dēˈistikəl| adj.

dé•jà vu |ˌdāZHä ˈvoō| • n. the illusion of having already experienced the present situation.
■ something tediously familiar.

de ju•re |di ˈjoŏrē; dä ˈjoŏrä| • adv. according to rightful entitlement or claim; by right; according to law. • adj. denoting something or someone that is rightfully such: *he had been de jure king since his father's death.*

de•le |ˈdēlē| • v. (deled, deleing) [trans.] delete or mark (a part of a text) for deletion. • n. a proofreader's sign indicating matter to be deleted.

de•lec•ta•ble |diˈlektəbəl| • adj. (esp. of food or drink) delicious; delightful: *delectable handmade chocolates.*
■ extremely beautiful or attractive: *the delectable Ms. Davis.*
DERIVATIVES: **de•lec•ta•bil•i•ty** |-ˌlektəˈbilitē| n. **de•lec•ta•bly** |-blē| adv.

de•lec•ta•tion |ˌdēlekˈtāSHən| • n. pleasure and delight: *a box of chocolates for their delectation.*

del•e•gate • n. |ˈdeligit| a person sent or authorized to represent others, in particular an elected representative sent to a conference.
■ a member of a committee. • v. |ˈdeləˌgāt| [trans.] entrust (a task or responsibility) to another person, typically one who is less senior than oneself: *he delegates routine tasks* | *the power delegated to him must never be misused.* | [intrans.] *her chief strength as a boss is that she delegates well.*
■ [with obj. and infinitive] send or authorize (someone) to do something as a representative: *Edward was delegated to meet new arrivals.*
DERIVATIVES: **del•e•ga•ble** |-gəbəl| adj. **del•e•ga•tor** |-ˌgātər| n.

de•lete |diˈlēt| • v. [trans.] remove or obliterate (written or printed matter), esp. by drawing a line through it or marking it with a delete sign: *the passage was deleted.* • n. a command or key on a computer that erases text.
■ remove (data) from a computer's memory.
■ (**be deleted**) (of a section of genetic code, or its product) be lost or excised from a nucleic acid or protein sequence: *if one important gene is deleted from an animal's DNA, other genes can stand in.* ■ remove (a product, esp. a recording) from the catalog of those available for purchase: *their EMI release has already been deleted.*

del•e•te•ri•ous |ˌdeliˈtirēəs| • adj. causing harm or damage: *divorce is assumed to have deleterious effects on children.*
DERIVATIVES: **del•e•te•ri•ous•ly** adv.

de•lib•er•ate • adj. |diˈlibərit| done consciously and intentionally: *a deliberate attempt to provoke conflict.*
■ fully considered; not impulsive: *a deliberate decision.* ■ done or acting in a careful and unhurried way: *a careful and deliberate worker.* • v. |-ˌrāt| [intrans.] engage in long and careful consideration: *she deliberated over the menu.*
■ [trans.] consider (a question) carefully: *jurors deliberated the fate of those charged* | [with clause] *deliberating what she should do.*
DERIVATIVES: **de•lib•er•ate•ly** |-ritlē| adv. **de•lib•er•ate•ness** |-ritnis| n. **de•lib•er•a•tor** |-ˌrātər| n.

de•lict |diˈlikt| • n. (in civil law systems) a violation of the law; a tort: *an international delict.*

De•li•lah |diˈlīlə| a seductive and treacherous woman; a temptress (from the biblical woman who betrayed Samson to the Philistines [Judges 16] by revealing to them that the secret of his strength lay in his long hair).

de•lim•it |diˈlimit| • v. (**delimited, delimiting**) [trans.] determine the limits or boundaries of: *agreements delimiting fishing zones.*
DERIVATIVES: **de•lim•i•ta•tion** |-ˌlimiˈtāSHən| n. **de•lim•it•er** n.

de•lin•e•ate |diˈlinēˌāt| • v. [trans.] describe or portray (something) precisely: *the law should delineate and prohibit behavior that is socially abhorrent.*
■ indicate the exact position of (a border or boundary).
DERIVATIVES: **de•lin•e•a•tion** |-ˌlinēˈāSHən| n. **de•lin•e•a•tor** |-ˌātər| n.

de•lin•quent |diˈliNGkwənt| • adj. (typically of a young person or that person's behavior) showing or characterized by a tendency to commit crime, particularly minor crime: *delinquent children.*
■ in arrears; past due: *delinquent accounts.* ■ failing in one's duty: *delinquent in caring for his elderly parents.* • n. a delinquent person: *juvenile delinquents.*
DERIVATIVES: **de•lin•quen•cy** n. **de•lin•quent•ly** adv.

del•i•quesce |ˌdeliˈkwes| • v. [intrans.] (of organic matter) become liquid, typically during decomposition.

■ (of a solid) become liquid by absorbing moisture from the air. ■ waste away; dissolve: *the melody seemed to deliquesce rather than end.*

de•lude |di'lo͞od| • *v.* [trans.] impose a misleading belief upon (someone); deceive; fool: *too many theorists have deluded the public* | [as adj.] (**deluded**) *the poor deluded creature.*
DERIVATIVES: **de•lud•ed•ly** *adv.* **de•lud•er** *n.*

del•uge |'del(y)o͞oj| • *n.* a severe flood. ■ (**the Deluge**) the biblical Flood (recorded in Genesis 6–8). ■ a heavy fall of rain: *an April deluge hit the plains.* ■ a great quantity of something arriving at the same time: *a deluge of complaints.* • *v.* [trans.] (usu. **be deluged**) inundate with a great quantity of something: *he has been deluged with offers of work.* ■ flood: *vacation cottages were deluged by the heavy rains.*

de•lu•sion |di'lo͞ozнən| • *n.* an idiosyncratic belief or impression that is firmly maintained despite being contradicted by what is generally accepted as reality or rational argument, typically a symptom of mental disorder: *the delusion of being watched.* ■ the action of deluding someone or the state of being deluded: *what a capacity television has for delusion.*
PHRASES: **delusions of grandeur** an exaggerated impression of one's own importance.
DERIVATIVES: **de•lu•sion•al** |-zнənl| *adj.*

de•lu•sive |di'lo͞osiv| • *adj.* giving a false or misleading impression: *the delusive light of Venice.*
DERIVATIVES: **de•lu•sive•ly** *adv.* **de•lu•sive•ness** *n.*

dem•a•gogue |'demə,gäg| • *n.* a political leader who seeks support by appealing to popular desires and prejudices rather than through rational argument. ■ (in ancient Greece and Rome) a leader or orator who espoused the cause of the common people.
DERIVATIVES: **dem•a•gog•ic** |,demə'gäjik; 'gägik; 'gōjik| *adj.* **dem•a•gogu•er•y** |'demə,gägərē| *n.* **dem•a•go•gy** |'demə,gäjē; ,gōjē| *n.*

de•mar•ca•tion |,dēmär'käsнən| • *n.* the action of fixing the boundary or limits of something: *the demarcation of the maritime border.* ■ a dividing line: *a horizontal band that produces a distinct demarcation two inches from the top.*
DERIVATIVES: **demarcate** *v.* **demarcative** *adj.* **de•mar•ca•tor** |di'märkātər| *n.*

dé•marche |dā'märsн| • *n.* a political step or initiative: *foreign policy démarches.*

de•mean[1] |di'mēn| • *v.* [trans.] [often as adj.] (**demeaning**) cause a severe loss in the dignity of and respect for (someone or something): *he has demeaned the profession* | *the poster was not demeaning to women.* ■ (**demean oneself**) do something that is beneath one's dignity: *he demeaned himself by accepting a bribe.*

de•mean[2] • *v.* (**demean oneself**) conduct oneself in a particular way: *no man demeaned himself so honorably.*

de•mean•or |di'mēnər| (Brit. **demeanour**) • *n.* outward behavior or bearing: *his demeanor was quiet and somber.*

de•men•tia |di'mensнə| • *n.* a chronic or persistent disorder of the mental processes caused by brain disease or injury and marked by memory disorders, personality changes, and impaired reasoning.

de•mesne |di'mān| • *n.* **1** (in the feudal system) land attached to a manor and retained for the owner's own use. ■ the lands of an estate. ■ a region or domain: *she may one day queen it over that fair demesne.* **2** possession of real property in one's own right.
PHRASES: **held in demesne** (of an estate) occupied by the owner, not by tenants.

dem•i•god |'demē,gäd| • *n.* (fem. **demigoddess** |-,gädis|) a being with partial or lesser divine status, such as a minor deity, the offspring of a god and a mortal, or a mortal raised to divine rank. ■ a person who is greatly admired or feared.

dem•i•john |'demē,jän| • *n.* a bulbous, narrow-necked bottle holding from 3 to 10 gallons of liquid, typically enclosed in a wicker cover.

dem•i•monde |'demē,mänd | (also **demimonde**) • *n.* (in 19th-century France) the class of women considered to be of doubtful morality and social standing. ■ a group of people considered to be on the fringes of respectable society: *the demimonde of arms dealers.*
DERIVATIVES: **dem•i•mon•daine** *n.*

de•mise |di'mīz| • *n.* [in sing.] **1** a person's death: *Mr. Grisenthwaite's tragic demise.* ■ the end or failure of an enterprise or institution: *the demise of the record industry.* **2** (in legal use) conveyance or transfer of property or a title by demising. • *v.* [trans.] (in legal use) convey or grant (an estate) by will or lease. ■ transmit (a sovereign's title) by death or abdication.

de•mit |di'mit| • *v.* (**demitted, demitting**) [trans.] resign from (an office or position): *arguments within his congregation led to his demitting his post.*
DERIVATIVES: **de•mis•sion** |-'misнən| *n.*

dem•i•urge |'demē,ərj| • *n.* a being responsible for the creation of the universe, in particular: ■ (in Platonic philosophy) the Maker or Creator of the world. ■ (in Gnosticism and other theological systems) a heavenly being, subordinate to the Supreme Being, that is considered to be the controller of the material world and antagonistic to all that is purely spiritual.
DERIVATIVES: **dem•i•ur•gic** |,demē'ərjik| *adj.* **dem•i•ur•gi•cal** |,demē'ərjikəl| *adj.*

de•moc•ra•cy |di'mäkrəsē| • *n.* (pl. **-ies**) a system of government by the whole population or all the eligible members of a state, typically through elected representatives: *capitalism and democracy are ascendant as the 21st century begins.* ■ a state governed in such a way: *a multiparty democracy.* ■ control of an organization or group by the majority of its members: *the intended extension of union democracy.* ■ the practice or principles of social equality: *demands for greater economic democracy.*

dem•o•crat |'deməˌkræt| • *n.* **1** an advocate or supporter of democracy. **2** (**Democrat**) a member of the Democratic Party. ■ a member of any other political party styled 'democratic.'
DERIVATIVES: **democratic, Democratic** *adj.*

dem•o•graph•ics |ˌdemə'græfiks| • *plural n.* statistical data relating to the population and particular groups within it: *the demographics of book buyers.* ■ conditions reflected by these data: *the demographics just didn't keep the business afloat.*
DERIVATIVES: **demographic** *adj.* **demographically** *adv.*

de•mog•ra•phy |di'mägrəfē| • *n.* the study of statistics such as births, deaths, income, or the incidence of disease, which illustrate the changing structure of human populations. ■ the composition of a particular human population: *Europe's demography is changing.*
DERIVATIVES: **de•mog•ra•pher** |-fər| *n.*

de•mon |'dēmən| • *n.* **1** an evil spirit or devil, esp. one thought to take possession of a person or act as a tormentor in hell. ■ a cruel, evil, or destructive person or thing. ■ a mischievous child: *I was a little demon, I can tell you.* ■ [often as adj.] a forceful, fierce, or skillful performer of a specified activity: *a friend of mine is a demon cook* | *a demon for work.* **2** another spelling for DAEMON[1] (sense 1).

de•mon•e•tize |dē'mäniˌtīz| • *v.* [trans.] (usu. **be demonetized**) deprive (a coin or precious metal) of its status as money.
DERIVATIVES: **de•mon•e•ti•za•tion** |-ˌmäniti'zāSHən| *n.*

de•mo•ni•ac |di'mōnēˌæk| • *adj.* of, like, or characteristic of a demon or demons: *a goddess with both divine and demoniac qualities* | *demoniac rage.* • *n.* a person believed to be possessed by an evil spirit.
DERIVATIVES: **de•mo•ni•a•cal** |ˌdēmə'nīəkəl| *adj.* **de•mo•ni•a•cal•ly** |ˌdēmə'nīək(ə)lē| *adv.*

de•mon•ic |di'mänik| • *adj.* of, resembling, or characteristic of demons or evil spirits: *demonic possession* | *her laughter was demonic.* ■ fiercely energetic or frenzied: *in a demonic hurry.*
DERIVATIVES: **de•mon•i•cal•ly** |-ik(ə)lē| *adv.*

de•mot•ic |di'mätik| • *adj.* relating to or denoting the kind of language used by ordinary people; popular or colloquial: *a demotic idiom.* ■ relating to or denoting the form of modern Greek used in everyday speech and writing. ■ relating to or denoting a simplified, cursive form of ancient Egyptian script, dating from *c.*650 BC and replaced by Greek in the Ptolemaic period (323–30 BC). • *n.* ordinary colloquial speech. ■ demotic Greek. ■ demotic Egyptian script.

de•mul•cent |di'məlsənt| • *adj.* (of a substance) relieving inflammation or irritation. • *n.* a substance that relieves irritation of the mucous membranes in the mouth by forming a protective film.

de•mur |di'mər| • *v.* (**demurred, demurring**) [intrans.] raise doubts or objections or show reluctance: *normally she would have accepted the challenge, but here she demurred.* ■ (in legal use) put forward a demurrer. • *n.* [usu. with negative] the action or process of objecting to or hesitating over something: *they accepted this ruling without demur.*
DERIVATIVES: **de•mur•ral** *n.*

de•mure |di'myo͝or| • *adj.* (**demurer, demurest**) (of a woman or her behavior) reserved, modest, and shy. ■ (of clothing) lending such an appearance. ■ sober, grave, and composed: *awaiting the interview with demure calm.*
DERIVATIVES: **de•mure•ly** *adv.* **de•mure•ness** *n.*

de•mur•rer |di'mərər| • *n.* an objection. ■ (in law) an objection that an opponent's point is irrelevant or invalid, while granting the factual basis of the point: *on demurrer it was held that the plaintiff's claim succeeded.*

de•mys•ti•fy |dē'mistəˌfī| • *v.* (**-ies, -ied**) [trans.] make (a difficult or esoteric subject) clearer and easier to understand: *this book attempts to demystify astronomy.*
DERIVATIVES: **de•mys•ti•fi•ca•tion** |-ˌmistəfi'kāSHən| *n.*

de•my•thol•o•gize |ˌdēmi'THäləˌjīz| • *v.* [trans.] reinterpret (a subject or text) so that it is free of mythical or heroic elements: *he undertakes to demythologize the man who has been for many the modern counterpart of St. Augustine.* ■ reinterpret what are considered to be mythological elements of (the Bible).

de•na•ture |dē'nāCHər| • *v.* [trans.] [often as adj.] (**denatured**) take away or alter the natural qualities of: *empty verbalisms and denatured ceremonies.* ■ make (alcohol) unfit for drinking by the addition of toxic or foul-tasting substances. ■ destroy the characteristic properties of (a protein or other biological macromolecule) by heat, acidity, or other effects that disrupt its molecular conformation. ■ [intrans.] (of a substance) undergo this process.
DERIVATIVES: **de•na•tur•a•tion** |dē,nāCHə'rāSHən| *n.*

den•i•grate |'deniˌgrāt| • *v.* [trans.] criticize unfairly, defame, or disparage: *an attempt to denigrate his opponent's character* | *there is a tendency to denigrate the poor.*
DERIVATIVES: **den•i•gra•tion** |ˌdeni'grāSHən| *n.* **den•i•gra•tor** |-ˌgrātər| *n.* **den•i•gra•to•ry** |-grəˌtôrē| *adj.*

den•i•zen |'denəzən| • *n.* an inhabitant or occupant of a particular place: *denizens of field and forest.* ■ a foreigner allowed certain rights in the adopted country.
DERIVATIVES: **den•i•zen•ship** |-ˌSHip| *n.*

de•nom•i•nate |di'nämə‚nāt| • *v.* **1** (**be denominated**) (of sums of money) be expressed in a specified monetary unit: *the amounts borrowed were denominated in US dollars.* **2** [with obj. and complement] call; name: *the plane was denominated a supersonic transport.*

de•nom•i•na•tion |di‚nämə'nāsHən| • *n.* **1** a distinctive, generally recognized autonomous branch of the Christian Church. Cf. SECT.
■ a group or branch of any religion: *Jewish clergy of all denominations.* **2** the face value of a banknote, a coin, or a postage stamp: *a hundred dollars in small denominations.*
■ the rank of a playing card within a suit, or of a suit relative to others: *two cards of the same denomination.* **3** a characteristic name or designation, esp. one serving to classify a set of things.
■ the action of naming or classifying something: *denomination of oneself as a career woman.*

de•no•ta•tion |‚dēnō'tāsHən| • *n.* the literal or primary meaning of a word, in contrast to the feelings or ideas that the word suggests: *beyond their immediate denotation, the words have a connotative power.*
■ the action or process of indicating or referring to something by means of a word, symbol, etc. ■ (in philosophy) the object or concept to which a term refers, or the set of objects of which a predicate is true. Cf. CONNOTATION.
DERIVATIVES: **de•no•ta•tion•al** |-sHənl| *adj.* .

de•note |di'nōt| • *v.* [trans.] be a sign of; indicate: *this mark denotes purity and quality.*
■ (often **be denoted**) stand as a name or symbol for: *the level of output per firm, denoted by X.*
DERIVATIVES: **de•no•ta•tion** *n.* **de•no•ta•tive** |'dēnō‚tātiv; di'nōtətiv| *adj.*

USAGE: For the difference between **denote** and **connote**, see **usage** at CONNOTE.

de•noue•ment |‚dānoo'mäN| • *n.* the final part of a play, movie, or narrative in which the strands of the plot are drawn together and matters are explained or resolved.
■ the climax of a chain of events, usually when something is decided or made clear: *I waited by the eighteenth green to see the denouement.*

de•nounce |di'nowns| • *v.* [trans.] publicly declare to be wrong or evil: *the mayor denounced the use of violence* | *he was widely denounced as a traitor.*
■ inform against: *some of his own priests denounced him for heresy.*
DERIVATIVES: **de•nounce•ment** *n.* **de•nounc•er** *n.* **de•nun•ci•a•tion** *n.*

de nouveau |də noo'vō | • *adv.* starting again from the beginning; anew.

de no•vo |dā 'nōvō; de | • *adv. & adj.* starting from the beginning; anew: [as adv.] *in a pure meritocracy, everyone must begin de novo* | [as adj.] *a general strategy for de novo protein design.*

De•o vo•len•te |'dāō və'lentē| • *adv.* God willing; if nothing prevents it.

de•pend•ent |di'pendənt| • *adj.* **1** [predic.] (**dependent on/upon**) contingent on or determined by: *the various benefits will be dependent on length of service.* **2** requiring someone or something for financial, emotional, or other support: *an economy heavily dependent on oil exports* | *households with dependent children.*
■ unable to do without: *dependent on drugs* | [in combination] *welfare-dependent families.*
■ Grammar (of a clause, phrase, or word) subordinate to another clause, phrase, or word. • *n.* a person who relies on another, esp. a family member, for financial support: *a single man with no dependents.* **dependent variable** (in mathematics) having a value depending on that of another variable.
DERIVATIVES: **de•pend•ent•ly** *adv.*

de•pict |di'pikt| • *v.* [trans.] show or represent by a drawing, painting, or other art form.
■ portray in words; describe: *youth is depicted as a time of vitality and good health.*
DERIVATIVES: **de•pict•er** *n.* **de•pic•tion** |-'piksHən| *n.*

de•plete |di'plēt| • *v.* [often as adj.] (**depleted**) use up the supply of; exhaust the abundance of: *fish stocks are severely depleted.*
■ [intrans.] diminish in number or quantity: *supplies are depleting fast.* ■ exhaust: *avoid getting depleted and depressed.*
DERIVATIVES: **de•ple•tion** |-'plēsHən| *n.*

de•plor•a•ble |di'plôrəbəl| • *adj.* deserving strong condemnation: *the deplorable conditions in which most prisoners are held.*
■ shockingly bad in quality: *her spelling was deplorable.*
DERIVATIVES: **de•plor•a•bly** |-blē| *adv.*

de•plore |di'plôr| • *v.* [trans.] feel or express strong disapproval of (something): *we deplore this act of cowardice.*
DERIVATIVES: **de•plor•ing•ly** *adv.*

de•po•nent |di'pōnənt| • *adj.* (of a verb, esp. in Latin or Greek) passive or middle (reciprocal or reflexive) in form but active in meaning. • *n.* **1** a deponent verb. **2** (in legal use) a person who makes a deposition or affidavit under oath.

de•port |di'pôrt| • *v.* **1** [trans.] expel (a foreigner) from a country, typically on the grounds of illegal immigration status or for having committed a crime: *he was deported to his native Argentina.*
■ exile (a native) to another country. **2** (**deport oneself**) conduct oneself in a specified manner: *he has deported himself with great dignity.*
DERIVATIVES: **de•port•a•ble** *adj.* **de•por•ta•tion** |‚dēpôr'tāsHən| *n.*

de•pose |di'pōz| • *v.* [trans.] **1** remove from office suddenly and forcefully: *the president had been deposed by a military coup.* **2** (in legal use) testify to or give (evidence) on oath, typically in a written statement: *every affidavit shall state which of the facts deposed to are within the deponent's knowledge.*

dep•o•si•tion |‚depə'zisHən| • *n.* **1** the action of deposing someone, esp. a monarch: *Edward V's deposition.* **2** (in legal use) the

process of giving sworn evidence: *the deposition of four expert witnesses.*
■ a formal, usually written, statement to be used as evidence: *they took her deposition the next day.* **3** the action of depositing something: *pebbles formed by the deposition of calcium in solution.* **4** (**the Deposition**) the taking down of the body of Christ from the Cross.

de•prav•i•ty |di'prævitē| • *n.* (pl. **-ies**) moral corruption: *a tale of wickedness and depravity.*
■ a wicked or morally corrupt act. ■ (in Christian theology) the innate corruptness of human nature, due to original sin.
DERIVATIVES: **de•praved** *adj.*

dep•re•cate |'deprə,kāt| • *v.* [trans.] **1** express disapproval of: [as adj.] (**deprecating**) *he sniffed in a deprecating way.* **2** another term for DEPRECIATE (sense 2): *he deprecates the value of children's television.*
DERIVATIVES: **dep•re•cat•ing•ly** *adv.* **dep•re•ca•tion** |,deprə'kāSHən| *n.* **dep•re•ca•tive** |-,kātiv| *adj.* **dep•re•ca•tor** |-,kātər| *n.*

USAGE: The similarity of spelling and meaning of **deprecate** and **depreciate**, though they are etymologically unrelated, has led to confusion in their use. **Deprecate**, 'to express disapproval of,' has encroached on the meanings of **depreciate**, 'to lessen the value of; belittle.' **Deprecate** (originally from Latin *deprecari*, 'to try to avert by prayer,' was the opposite of 'pray for,' just as **depreciate** was the opposite of *appreciate*, 'to increase in value.' *Self-deprecating*, an old and common error (should be *self-depreciating*), has become the most prevalent way of saying 'modest, self-effacing.'

de•pre•ci•ate |di'prēSHē,āt| • *v.* **1** [intrans.] diminish in value over a period of time: *the pound is expected to depreciate against the dollar.*
■ reduce the recorded value in a company's books of (an asset) each year over a predetermined period: *the computers would be depreciated at 50 percent per annum.* **2** [trans.] disparage or belittle (something): *she was already depreciating her own aesthetic taste.*
DERIVATIVES: **de•pre•ci•a•to•ry** |-SHēə,tôrē| *adj.*

dep•re•da•tion |,deprə'dāSHən| • *n.* (usu. **depredations**) an act of attacking or plundering: *protecting grain from the depredations of rats and mice.*
DERIVATIVES: **dep•re•da•tor** *n.* **dep•re•da•to•ry** *adj.*

de•pres•sion |di'preSHən| • *n.* **1** severe despondency and dejection, typically felt over a period of time and accompanied by feelings of hopelessness and inadequacy.
■ a condition of mental disturbance characterized by such feelings to a greater degree than seems warranted by the external circumstances, typically with lack of energy and difficulty in maintaining concentration or interest in life: *clinical depression.* **2** a long and

severe recession in an economy or market: *the depression in the housing market.*
■ (**the Depression** or **the Great Depression**) the financial and industrial slump in the United States and other countries that began with the stock market crash in October 1929, and lasted through the 1930s. **3** the lowering or reducing of something: *the depression of prices.*
■ the action of pressing down on something: *depression of the plunger delivers two units of insulin.* ■ a sunken place or hollow on a surface: *the original shallow depressions were slowly converted to creeks.* ■ (in astronomy) the angular distance of an object below the horizon or a horizontal plane. ■ (in meteorology) a region of lower atmospheric pressure, esp. a cyclonic weather system.

de•pro•gram |dē'prōgræm| • *v.* (**deprogrammed, deprogramming** or **deprogramed, deprograming**) [trans.] release (someone) from apparent brainwashing (programming), typically that of a religious cult, by the systematic reindoctrination of conventional values.

de•rac•in•ate |di'ræsən,āt| • *v.* [trans.] tear (something) up by the roots.
■ uproot (someone) from his or her culture or environment.
DERIVATIVES: **de•rac•i•nat•ed** *adj.* **de•rac•i•na•tion** |-,ræsən'āSHən| *n.*

de•range |di'rānj| • *v.* [trans.] [usu. as adj.] (**deranged**) cause (someone) to become insane: *a deranged soldier.*
■ throw (something) into confusion; cause to act irregularly: *stress deranges the immune system.* ■ intrude on; interrupt: *I am sorry to have deranged you.*
DERIVATIVES: **de•range•ment** *n.*

de•reg•u•late |dē'regyə,lāt| • *v.* [trans.] remove regulations or restrictions from: *a law that would deregulate cable TV fees.*
DERIVATIVES: **de•reg•u•la•tion** |-,regyə'lāSHən| *n.* **de•reg•u•la•to•ry** |-lə,tôrē| *adj.*

der•e•lict |'derə,likt| • *adj.* in a very poor condition as a result of disuse and neglect: *the cities were derelict and dying.*
■ (of a person) shamefully negligent in not having done what one should have done: *he was derelict in his duty to his country.* • *n.* a person without a home, job, or property: *derelicts who could fit all their possessions in a paper bag.*
■ a piece of property, esp. a ship, abandoned by the owner and in poor condition.

der•e•lic•tion |,derə'likSHən| • *n.* the state of having been abandoned and become dilapidated: *the empty house had started the slow slide to dereliction.*
■ (usu. **dereliction of duty**) the shameful failure to fulfill one's obligations.

de ri•gueur |,də ri'gər| • *adj.* required by custom, etiquette, or current fashion: *it was de rigueur for band members to grow their hair long.*

de•ri•sion |di'riZHən| • *n.* contemptuous ridicule or mockery: *my stories were greeted with derision.*

DERIVATIVES: **de•ris•i•ble** |-'rizəbəl| adj.
de•ri•sive |di'rīsiv| • adj. expressing contempt or ridicule: painfully derisive comments.
DERIVATIVES: **de•ri•sive•ly** adv. **de•ri•sive•ness** n.
de•ri•so•ry |di'rīsərē; rīz-| • adj. 1 ridiculously small or inadequate: they were given a derisory pay rise. 2 another term for DERISIVE: his derisory gaze.

USAGE: Although the words **derisory** and **derisive** share similar roots, they have different core meanings. **Derisory** usually means 'ridiculously small or inadequate,' as in a **derisory** pay offer or the security arrangements were **derisory**. **Derisive**, on the other hand, is used to mean 'showing contempt,' as in he gave a **derisive** laugh.

der•i•va•tion |,derə'vāSHən| • n. 1 the obtaining or developing of something from a source or origin: the **derivation** of scientific laws **from** observation. ∎ the formation of a word from another word or from a root in the same or another language. ∎ (in generative grammar) the set of stages that link the abstract underlying structure of an expression to its surface form. ∎ (in mathematics) a sequence of statements showing that a formula, theorem, etc., is a consequence of previously accepted statements. ∎ (in mathematics) the process of deducing a new formula, theorem, etc., from previously accepted statements. 2 origin; extraction: music of primarily Turkish derivation. ∎ something derived; a derivative: the derivation "sheepish" has six definitions.
DERIVATIVES: **der•i•va•tion•al** |-SHənl| adj.
de•riv•a•tive |di'rivətiv| • adj. (typically of an artist or work of art) imitative of the work of another person, and usually disapproved of for that reason: an artist who is not in the slightest bit derivative. ∎ originating from, based on, or influenced by: Darwin's work is **derivative of** the moral philosophers. ∎ [attrib.] (of a financial product) having a value deriving from an underlying variable asset: equity-based derivative products. • n. something that is based on another source: a derivative of the system was chosen for the Marine Corps' V-22 tilt rotor aircraft. ∎ (often **derivatives**) an arrangement or instrument (such as a future, option, or warrant) whose value derives from and is dependent on the value of an underlying asset: [as adj.] the derivatives market. ∎ a word derived from another or from a root in the same or another language. ∎ a substance that is derived chemically from a specified compound: crack is a highly addictive cocaine derivative. ∎ (in mathematics) an expression representing the rate of change of a function with respect to an independent variable.
DERIVATIVES: **de•riv•a•tive•ly** adv.
de•rive |di'rīv| • v. [trans.] (**derive something from**) obtain something from (a specified source): they derived great comfort from this assurance.

∎ (**derive something from**) base a concept on a logical extension or modification of (another concept): Marx derived his philosophy of history from Hegel. ∎ [intrans.] (**derive from**) (of a word) have (a specified word, usually of another language) as a root or origin: the word "punch" derives from the Hindustani "pancha" | (**be derived from**) the word "man" is derived from the Sanskrit "manas." ∎ [intrans.] (**derive from**) arise from or originate in (a specified source): words whose spelling derives from Dr. Johnson's incorrect etymology. ∎ (**be derived from**) (in linguistics) an expression in a natural language) be linked by a set of stages to (its underlying abstract form). ∎ (**be derived from**) (of a substance) be formed or prepared by (a chemical or physical process affecting another substance): strong acids are derived from the combustion of fossil fuels. ∎ obtain (a mathematical function or equation) from another by a sequence of logical steps, for example by differentiation.
DERIVATIVES: **de•riv•a•ble** adj.
der•o•gate |'derə,gāt| • v. 1 [trans.] detract from or disparage (someone or something): it is typical of Pirandello to derogate the powers of reason. 2 [intrans.] (**derogate from**) detract from: this does not derogate from his duty to act honestly and faithfully. 3 [intrans.] (**derogate from**) deviate from (a set of rules or agreed form of behavior): one country has derogated from the Rome Convention.
DERIVATIVES: **de•rog•a•tive** |di'rägətiv| adj.
de•rog•a•to•ry |di'rägə,tôrē| • adj. showing a critical or disrespectful attitude: derogatory remarks.
DERIVATIVES: **de•rog•a•to•ri•ly** |-,tôrəlē| adv.
der•vish |'dərviSH| • n. a Muslim (specifically Sufi) religious man who has taken vows of poverty and austerity. Dervishes first appeared in the 12th century; they were noted for their wild or ecstatic rituals and were known as **dancing**, **whirling**, or **howling dervishes** according to the practice of their order.
des•cant • n. |'deskænt| an independent treble melody usually sung or played above a basic melody. ∎ a melodious song. ∎ a discourse on a theme or subject: his descant of deprivation. • v. |des 'kænt| [intrans.] talk tediously or at length: I have **descanted on** this subject before.
de•scry |di'skrī| • v. (**-ies, -ied**) [trans.] catch sight of: she descried two figures in the distance. ∎ discover by observation; perceive: I could not descry his intent.
des•e•crate |'desi,krāt| • v. [trans.] (often **be desecrated**) treat (a sacred place or thing) with violent disrespect; violate: many graves were desecrated.
DERIVATIVES: **des•e•cra•tion** |,desi'krāSHən| n. **des•e•cra•tor** |-,krātər| n.
de•sen•si•tize |dē'sensi,tīz| • v. [trans.] make less sensitive: a substance to desensitize the skin at the site of the injection. | the treatments should desensitize you to cat dander.

■ make (someone) less likely to feel shock or distress at scenes of cruelty, violence, or suffering by overexposure to such images: [as adj.] (**desensitized**) *people who view such movies become* **desensitized** *to violence.*
■ free (someone) from a phobia or neurosis by gradually exposing the person to the thing that is feared.
DERIVATIVES: **de•sen•si•ti•za•tion** |dē ˌsensiˌti'zāsHən| *n.* **de•sen•si•tiz•er** *n.*

desert |dizərt| • *n.* (usu. **deserts**) a person's worthiness or entitlement to reward or punishment; what one deserves: *the penal system fails to punish offenders in accordance with their deserts.*

de•sex |dē'seks| • *v.* [trans.] [usu. as adj.] (**desexed**) **1** deprive (someone) of sexual qualities or attraction: *he portrays feminists as shrill, humorless, and desexed.* **2** castrate or spay (an animal).

des•ic•cate |'desiˌkāt| • *v.* [trans.] [usu. as adj.] (**desiccated**) remove the moisture from (something, esp. food), typically in order to preserve it: *desiccated coconut.*
■ [as adj.] (**desiccated**) lacking interest, passion, or energy: *a desiccated history of ideas.*
DERIVATIVES: **des•ic•ca•tion** |-'kāsHən| *n.* **des•ic•ca•tive** |-ˌkātiv| *adj.*

de•sid•er•a•tive |di'sidərətiv, ˌrātiv| • *adj.* (in Latin and other inflected languages) denoting a verb formed from another and expressing a desire to do the act denoted by the root verb (such as Latin *esurire* 'want to eat,' from *edere* 'eat').
■ having, expressing, or relating to desire. • *n.* a desiderative verb.

de•sid•er•a•tum |diˌsidə'rätəm| • *n.* (pl. **desiderata** |-'rätə|) something that is needed or wanted: *integrity was a desideratum.*

des•o•late • *adj.* |'desəlit| (of a place) emptied of people and in a state of bleak and dismal emptiness: *a desolate moor.*
■ feeling or showing misery, unhappiness, or loneliness: *I suddenly felt desolate and bereft.* • *v.* |'desəˌlāt| [trans.] make (a place) bleakly and depressingly empty or bare: *the droughts that desolated the dry plains.*
■ (usu. **be desolated**) make (someone) feel utterly wretched and unhappy: *he was desolated by the deaths of his friends.*
DERIVATIVES: **des•o•late•ly** *adv.* **des•o•late•ness** |-litnis| *n.* **des•o•la•tor** |-ˌlātər| *n.*

des•pi•ca•ble |di'spikəbəl| • *adj.* deserving hatred and contempt; to be despised: *a despicable crime.*
DERIVATIVES: **des•pi•ca•bly** |-blē| *adv.*

de•spoil |di'spoil| • *v.* [trans.] (often **be despoiled**) steal or violently remove valuable or attractive possessions from; plunder: *the church was despoiled of its marble wall covering.*
DERIVATIVES: **de•spoil•er** *n.* **de•spoil•ment** *n.* **de•spo•li•a•tion** |-ˌspōlē'āsHən| *n.*

de•spond•en•cy |di'spändənsē| • *n.* a state of low spirits caused by loss of hope or courage; despond: *he hinted at his own deep despondency.*

DERIVATIVES: **de•spond•ence** |-dəns| *n.* **despondent** *adj.* **despondently** *adv.*

des•pot |'despət| • *n.* a ruler or other person who holds absolute power, typically one who exercises it in a cruel or oppressive way.
DERIVATIVES: **des•pot•ic** |di'spätik| *adj.* **des•pot•i•cal•ly** |di'spätik(ə)lē| *adv.*

des•pot•ism |'despəˌtizəm| • *n.* the exercise of absolute power, esp. in a cruel and oppressive way: *the King's arbitrary despotism.*
■ a political system in which the ruler holds absolute power.

des•ti•tute |'destiˌt(y)o͞ot| • *adj.* without the basic necessities of life: *the charity cares for destitute children.*
■ [predic.] (**destitute of**) not having: *towns destitute of commerce.*
DERIVATIVES: **des•ti•tu•tion** |ˌdesti't(y)o͞o sHən| *n.*

des•ue•tude |'deswiˌt(y)o͞od| • *n.* a state of disuse: *the docks fell into desuetude.*

des•ul•to•ry |'desəlˌtôrē| • *adj.* lacking a plan, purpose, or enthusiasm: *surfing the net in a desultory fashion.*
■ (of conversation or speech) going constantly from one subject to another in a halfhearted way; unfocused: *the desultory conversation faded.* ■ occurring randomly or occasionally: *desultory passengers.*
DERIVATIVES: **des•ul•to•ri•ly** |-ˌtôrəlē| *adv.* **des•ul•to•ri•ness** *n.*

dé•tente |dā'tänt| (also **detente**) • *n.* the easing of hostility or strained relations, esp. between countries: *a serious effort at détente with the eastern bloc.* Cf. ENTENTE.

de•ten•tion |di'tensHən| • *n.* the action of detaining someone or the state of being detained in official custody, esp. as a political prisoner: *he committed suicide while in police detention.*
■ the punishment of being kept in school after hours: *made students fear after-school detention* | *arbitrary after-school detentions.*

de•ter•mi•nate |də'tərmənit| • *adj.* having exact and discernible limits or form: *the phrase has lost any determinate meaning.*
■ (of a flowering shoot) having the main axis ending in a flower bud and therefore no longer extending in length, as in a cyme.
DERIVATIVES: **de•ter•mi•na•cy** |-minəsē| *n.* **de•ter•mi•nate•ly** *adv.* **de•ter•mi•nate•ness** *n.*

de•ter•min•er |di'tərminər| • *n.* **1** a person or thing that determines or decides something. **2** (in grammar) a modifying word that determines the kind of reference a noun or noun group has, for example *a, the, every.*

de•ter•min•ism |di'tərməˌnizəm| • *n.* the doctrine that all events, including human action, are ultimately determined by causes external to the will. Some philosophers have taken determinism to imply that individual human beings have no free will and cannot be held morally responsible for their actions.
DERIVATIVES: **de•ter•min•ist** *n.* & *adj.* **de•ter•min•is•tic** |-ˌtərmə'nistik| *adj.* **de•ter•min•is•ti•cal•ly** |-ˌtərmə'nistik(ə)lē| *adv.*

de•ter•rent |di'tərənt| • *n.* a thing that discourages or is intended to discourage someone from doing something.
▪ a weapon or weapons system regarded as deterring an enemy from attack. • *adj.* able or intended to deter: *the deterrent effect of heavy prison sentences.*
DERIVATIVES: **de•ter** *v.* **de•ter•rence** *n.*

de•tract |di'trækt| • *v.* **1** [intrans.] (**detract from**) reduce or take away the worth or value of: *these quibbles in no way detract from her achievement.*
▪ [trans.] deny or take away (a quality or achievement) so as to make its subject seem less impressive: *it detracts not one iota from the credit due to them.* **2** [trans.] (**detract someone/something from**) divert or distract (someone or something) away from: *the complaint was timed to detract attention from the ethics issue.*
DERIVATIVES: **de•trac•tion** |-'trækSHən| *n.* **de•trac•tive** |-'træktiv| *adj.*

det•ri•men•tal |,detrə'mentl| • *adj.* tending to cause harm (detriment): *releasing the documents would be detrimental to national security | moving her could have a detrimental effect on her health.*
DERIVATIVES: **det•ri•men•tal•ly** *adv.*

de•tri•tus |di'trītəs| • *n.* waste or debris of any kind.
▪ gravel, sand, silt, or other material produced by erosion. ▪ organic matter produced by the decomposition of organisms.
DERIVATIVES: **de•tri•tal** |-təl| *adj.*

de trop |də 'trō| • *adj.* not wanted; superfluous: *she had no grasp of the conversation and felt herself de trop.*

de•tu•mes•cence |,dēt(y)oo'mesəns| • *n.* the process of subsiding from a state of tension, swelling, or (esp.) sexual arousal.
DERIVATIVES: **de•tu•mesce** |-'mes| *v.* **de•tu•mes•cent** *adj.* .

de•us ex ma•chi•na |'dāəs eks 'mäkənə; 'mæk-| • *n.* an unexpected power or event saving a seemingly hopeless situation, esp. as a contrived plot device in a play or novel.

de•val•ue |dē'vælyoō| • *v.* (**devalues, devalued, devaluing**) [trans.] reduce or underestimate the worth or importance of: *people seem to devalue my achievement.*
▪ (often **be devalued**) reduce the official value of (a currency) in relation to other currencies: *the dinar was devalued by 20 percent.*
DERIVATIVES: **de•val•u•a•tion** |,dēvælyoō'āSHən| *n.*

de•vi•ant |'dēvēənt| • *adj.* departing from usual or accepted standards, esp. in social or sexual behavior: *deviant behavior | a deviant ideology.* • *n.* a deviant person or thing.
DERIVATIVES: **de•vi•ance** *n.* **de•vi•an•cy** *n.*

de•vi•ate • *v.* |'dēvē,āt| [intrans.] depart from an established course: *you must not deviate from the plan.*
▪ depart from usual or accepted standards: *those who deviate from society's values.* • *n.* & *adj.* old-fashioned term for DEVIANT.
DERIVATIVES: **de•vi•a•tor** |-,ātər| *n.*

de•vi•a•tion |,dēvē'āSHən| • *n.* **1** the action of departing from an established course or accepted standard: *deviation from a norm | sexual deviation* **2** (in statistics) the amount by which a single measurement differs from a fixed value such as the mean. **3** the deflection of a vessel's compass needle caused by iron in the vessel, which varies with the vessel's heading.
DERIVATIVES: **de•vi•a•tion•ism** |-,nizəm| *n.* **de•vi•a•tion•ist** |-ist| *n.*

dev•il's ad•vo•cate • *n.* a person who expresses a contentious opinion in order to provoke debate or test the strength of the opposing arguments: *we will play devil's advocate to put the other side's case forward.*
▪ an official appointed by the Roman Catholic Church to challenge a proposed beatification or canonization, or the verification of a miracle.

de•vi•ous |'dēvēəs| • *adj.* **1** showing a skillful use of underhanded tactics to achieve goals: *devious ways of making money.* **2** (of a route or journey) longer and less direct than the most straightforward way.
DERIVATIVES: **de•vi•ous•ly** *adv.* **de•vi•ous•ness** *n.*

de•vise |di'vīz| • *v.* [trans.] **1** plan or invent (a complex procedure, system, or mechanism) by careful thought: *a training program should be devised | a complicated game of his own devising.* **2** leave (real estate) to someone by the terms of a will. • *n.* a clause in a will leaving real estate to someone.
DERIVATIVES: **de•vis•a•ble** *adj.* **de•vi•see** |di,vī'zē| *n.* (in sense 2). **de•vis•er** *n.* **de•vi•sor** |-'vīzər| *n.* (in sense 2).

de•void |di'void| • *adj.* [predic.] (**devoid of**) entirely lacking or free from: *Lisa kept her voice devoid of emotion.*

de•voir |dəv'wär| • *n.* a person's duty: *you have done your devoir right well.*
▪ (**pay one's devoirs**) pay one's respects formally.

dev•o•lu•tion |,devə'loōSHən| • *n.* the transfer or delegation of power to a lower level, esp. by central government to local or regional administration.
▪ descent or degeneration to a lower or worse state: *the devolution of the gentlemanly ideal into a glorification of drunkenness.* ▪ the legal transfer of property from one owner to another. ▪ (in biology) evolutionary degeneration.
DERIVATIVES: **dev•o•lu•tion•ar•y** |-,nerē| *adj.* **dev•o•lu•tion•ist** |-ist| *n.*

de•volve |di'välv| • *v.* [trans.] transfer or delegate (power) to a lower level, esp. from central government to local or regional administration: *measures to devolve power to the provinces |* [as adj.] (**devolved**) *devolved and decentralized government.*
▪ [intrans.] (**devolve on/upon/to**) (of duties or responsibility) pass to (a body or person at a lower level): *his duties devolved on a comrade.* ▪ [intrans.] (**devolve on/upon/to**) (of property) be transferred from one owner to (another), esp. by inheritance. ▪ [intrans.]

(**devolve into**) degenerate or be split into: *the Empire devolved into separate warring states.*
DERIVATIVES: **de•volve•ment** *n.*

dev•o•tee |ˌdevəˈtē; -ˈtā| • *n.* a person who is very interested in and enthusiastic about someone or something: *a devotee of Chinese culture.*
■ a strong believer in a particular religion or god: *devotees of Krishna* | *devotees thronged the temple.*

de•vout |diˈvowt| • *adj.* having or showing deep religious feeling or commitment: *a devout Catholic.*
■ totally committed to a cause or belief: *the most devout environmentalist.*
DERIVATIVES: **de•vout•ly** *adv.* **de•vout• ness** *n.*

dew point • *n.* the atmospheric temperature (varying according to pressure and humidity) below which water droplets begin to condense and dew can form.

dex•ter |ˈdekstər| • *adj.* [attrib.] of, on, or toward the right-hand side (in a coat of arms, from the bearer's point of view, i.e., the left as it is depicted). The opposite of SINISTER.

dex•ter•ous |ˈdekstərəs| (also **dextrous**) • *adj.* demonstrating skill and adroitness with the hands: *dexterous accordion playing.*
■ mentally adroit; clever: *power users are dexterous at using software, rather than creating it.*
DERIVATIVES: **dex•ter•i•ty** |dekˈsteritē| *n.* **dex•ter•ous•ly** *adv.* **dex•ter•ous•ness** *n.*

dex•tral |ˈdekstrəl| • *adj.* of or on the right side or the right hand, in particular:
■ right-handed. ■ (in geology) relating to or denoting a strike-slip fault in which the motion of the block on the farther side of the fault from an observer is toward the right. ■ (of a spiral mollusk shell) with whorls rising to the right and coiling in a counterclockwise direction. • *n.* a right-handed person.
DERIVATIVES: **dex•tral•i•ty** |dekˈstrælitē| *n.* **dex•tral•ly** *adv.*

dhar•ma |ˈdärmə| • *n.* **1** (in Hinduism) the principle of cosmic order.
■ virtue, righteousness, and duty, esp. social and caste duty in accord with the cosmic order. **2** (in Buddhism) the teaching or religion of the Buddha.
■ one of the fundamental elements of which the world is composed.

diabolic |ˌdīəˈbälik| (also **diabolical**) • *adj.* relating to or characteristic of the devil: *the darkness of a diabolic world.*

di•a•crit•ic |ˌdīəˈkritik| • *n.* a sign, such as an accent or cedilla, which when written above or below a letter indicates a difference in pronunciation from the same letter when unmarked or differently marked. • *adj.* (of a mark or sign) indicating a difference in pronunciation.
DERIVATIVES: **di•a•crit•i•cal** *adj.* **di•a• crit•i•cal•ly** |-ik(ə)lē| *adv.*

di•a•dem |ˈdīəˌdem| • *n.* a jeweled crown or headband worn as a symbol of sovereignty.
■ (**the diadem**) the authority or dignity symbolized by a diadem: *the princely diadem.*
DERIVATIVES: **di•a•demed** *adj.*

di•ag•no•sis |ˌdīəgˈnōsis| • *n.* (pl. **diagnoses** |-ˌsēz|) **1** the identification of the nature of an illness or other problem by examination of the symptoms: *early diagnosis and treatment are essential* | *a diagnosis of Crohn's disease was made.* Cf. PROGNOSIS. **2** the distinctive characterization in precise terms of a genus, species, or phenomenon.

di•ag•nos•tic |ˌdīəgˈnästik| • *adj.* **1** concerned with the diagnosis of illness or other problems: *a diagnostic tool.*
■ (of a symptom) distinctive, and so indicating the nature of an illness: *there are a number of infections that are diagnostic of AIDS.* **2** characteristic of a particular species, genus, or phenomenon: *the diagnostic character of having not one but two pairs of antennae.* • *n.* **1** a distinctive symptom or characteristic.
■ a computer program or routine that helps a user to identify errors. **2** (**diagnostics**) the practice or techniques of diagnosis: *advanced medical diagnostics.*
DERIVATIVES: **di•ag•nos•ti•cal•ly** |-ik(ə)-lē| *adv.* **di•ag•nos•ti•cian** |-ˌnästiˈSHən| *n.*

di•a•lect |ˈdīəˌlekt| • *n.* a particular form of a language that is peculiar to a specific region or social group: *this novel is written in the dialect of Trinidad.*
■ a particular version of a computer programming language.
DERIVATIVES: **di•a•lec•tal** |ˌdīəˈlektəl| *adj.*

di•a•lec•tic |ˌdīəˈlektik| • *n.* (also **dialectics**) [usu. treated as sing.] **1** the art of investigating or discussing the truth of opinions. **2** inquiry into metaphysical contradictions and their solutions.
■ the existence or action of opposing social forces, concepts, etc. • *adj.* (also **dialectical**) of or relating to dialectic or dialectics.
DERIVATIVES: **di•a•lec•ti•cian** *n.*

di•a•logue |ˈdīəˌläg; -ˌlôg| (also **dialog**) • *n.* conversation between two or more people as a feature of a book, play, or movie: *the book consisted of a series of dialogues* | *passages of dialogue.*
■ a discussion between two or more people or groups, esp. one directed toward exploration of a particular subject or resolution of a problem: *the US would enter into a direct dialogue with Vietnam* | *interfaith dialogue.* • *v.* [intrans.] take part in a conversation or discussion to resolve a problem: *he stated that he wasn't going to dialogue with the guerrillas.*
■ [trans.] provide (a movie or play) with a dialogue.

di•al•y•sis |dīˈæləsis| • *n.* (pl. **dialyses** |-ˌsēz|) the separation of particles in a liquid on the basis of differences in their ability to pass through a membrane.
■ (also **hemodialysis**) the clinical purification of blood by this technique, as a substitute for the normal function of the kidneys.
DERIVATIVES: **di•a•lyt•ic** |ˌdīəˈlitik| *adj.* **di•a•lyze** *v.*

di•aph•a•nous |dīˈæfənəs| • *adj.* (esp. of fabric) light, delicate, and translucent: *a diaphanous dress of pale gold.*

di·a·pho·ret·ic |ˌdīəfə'retik| • *adj.* (chiefly of a drug) inducing perspiration.
■ (of a person) sweating heavily.
DERIVATIVES: **di·a·pho·re·sis** *n.*
di·a·phragm |'dīəˌfræm| • *n.* 1 a dome-shaped, muscular partition separating the thorax from the abdomen in mammals. It plays a major role in breathing, as its contraction increases the volume of the thorax and so inflates the lungs. 2 a thin sheet of material forming a partition.
■ a taut, flexible membrane in mechanical or acoustic systems. ■ a thin contraceptive cap fitting over the cervix. 3 a device for varying the effective aperture of the lens in a camera or other optical system.
DERIVATIVES: **di·a·phrag·mat·ic** |ˌdīə-fræg'mætik| *adj.*
di·ar·rhe·a |ˌdīə'rēə| (Brit.**diarrhoea**) • *n.* a condition in which feces are discharged from the bowels frequently and in a liquid form.
DERIVATIVES: **di·ar·rhe·al** *adj.* **di·ar·rhe·ic** |-'rēik| *adj.*
di·as·po·ra |dī'æspərə| • *n.* (often **the Diaspora**) Jews living outside Israel.
■ the dispersion of the Jews beyond Israel.
■ the dispersion of any people from their original homeland: *the diaspora of boat people from Asia.* ■ the people so dispersed: *the Ukrainian diaspora flocked back to Kiev.*

The main diaspora began in the 8th–6th centuries BC, and even before the sack of Jerusalem in AD 70 the number of Jews dispersed by the diaspora was greater than that living in Israel. Thereafter, Jews were dispersed even more widely throughout the Roman world and beyond.

di·a·ton·ic |ˌdīə'tänik| • *adj.* (of a musical scale, interval, etc.) involving only notes proper to the prevailing key without chromatic alteration. Cf. CHROMATIC.
■ (of a melody or harmony) constructed from such a scale.
DERIVATIVES: **di·a·ton·i·cal·ly** *adv.*
di·a·tribe |'dīəˌtrīb| • *n.* a forceful and bitter verbal attack against someone or something: *a diatribe against the Roman Catholic Church.*
di·chot·o·my |dī'kätəmē| • *n.* (pl. **-ies**) [usu. in sing.] a division or contrast between two things that are or are represented as being opposed or entirely different: *he argued that there was a rigid **dichotomy** between science and mysticism.*
■ (in botany) repeated branching into two equal parts.
DERIVATIVES: **di·chot·o·mize** *v.* **di·chot·o·mous** *adj.*
dic·tum |'diktəm| • *n.* (pl. **dicta** |-tə| or **dictums**) a formal pronouncement from an authoritative source: *the Politburo's dictum that the party will become a "left-wing parliamentary party."*
■ a short statement that expresses a general truth or principle: *the old dictum "might makes right."*
di·dac·tic |dī'dæktik| • *adj.* intended to teach, particularly in having moral instruc-

tion as an ulterior motive: *a didactic novel that set out to expose social injustice.*
■ in the manner of a teacher, particularly so as to treat someone in a patronizing way: *slow-paced, didactic lecturing.*
DERIVATIVES: **di·dac·ti·cal·ly** |-ik(ə)lē| *adv.* **di·dac·ti·cism** |-təˌsizəm| *n.*
di·er·e·sis |dī'erəsis| (also **diaeresis**) • *n.* (pl. **diereses** |-ˌsēz|) 1 a mark ([nfuml]) placed over a vowel to indicate that it is sounded separately, as in *nave, Brontë.*
■ the division of a sound into two syllables, esp. by sounding a diphthong as two vowels. 2 a natural rhythmic break in a line of verse where the end of a metrical foot coincides with the end of a word.
die·sel |'dēzəl; səl| • *n.* (also **diesel engine**) an internal combustion engine in which heat produced by the compression of air in the cylinder is used to ignite the fuel: [as adj.] *a diesel locomotive.* In a **diesel-electric** engine, electric motors are powered by current from a generator that is driven by a diesel engine.
■ a heavy petroleum fraction (component) used as fuel in diesel engines: *eleven liters of diesel.*
DERIVATIVES: **die·sel·ize** |-ˌlīz| *v.* **diesel·ing** *n.* the action of an internal combustion engine that continues to run after the ignition is turned off.
di·et • *n.* a legislative assembly in certain countries.
■ a regular meeting of the states of a confederation. ■ (in Scots law) a meeting or session of a court.
dif·fer·en·tial |ˌdifə'rensHəl| • *adj.* [attrib.] of, showing, or depending on a difference; differing or varying according to circumstances or relevant factors: *the differential achievements of boys and girls.*
■ constituting a specific difference; distinctive: *the differential features between benign and malignant tumors.* ■ (in mathematics) relating to infinitesimal differences or to the derivatives of functions. ■ of or relating to a difference in a physical quantity: *a differential amplifier.* • *n.* a difference between amounts of things: *the **differential between** gasoline and diesel prices.*
■ (in mathematics) an infinitesimal difference between successive values of a variable.
■ (also **differential gear**) a set of gears allowing a vehicle's driven wheels to revolve at different speeds when going around corners.
DERIVATIVES: **dif·fer·en·tial·ly** *adv.*
dif·fi·dent |'difidənt| • *adj.* modest or shy because of a lack of self-confidence: *a diffident youth.*
DERIVATIVES: **dif·fi·dence** *n.* **dif·fi·dent·ly** *adv.*
dif·frac·tion |di'fræksHən| • *n.* the process by which a beam of light or other system of waves is spread out as a result of passing through a narrow aperture or across an edge, typically accompanied by interference between the wave forms produced.
DERIVATIVES: **diffract** *v.* **diffractive** *adj.*

dif•fuse • *v.* |di'fyo͞oz| spread or cause to spread over a wide area or among a large number of people: [intrans.] *technologies diffuse rapidly* | [trans.] *the problem is how to diffuse power without creating anarchy.*
■ become or cause (a fluid, gas, individual atom, etc.) to become intermingled with a substance by movement, typically in a specified direction or at specified speed: [intrans.] *oxygen molecules* **diffuse** *across the membrane* | [trans.] *gas is* **diffused into** *the bladder.* ■ [trans.] cause (light) to glow faintly by dispersing it in many directions. • *adj.* |di'fyo͞os| spread out over a large area; not concentrated: *the diffuse community centered on the church* | *the light is more diffuse.*
■ (of disease) not localized in the body: *diffuse hyperplasia.* ■ lacking clarity or conciseness: *the second argument is more diffuse.*
DERIVATIVES: **dif•fuse•ly** |-'fyo͞oslē| *adv.* **dif•fuse•ness** |-'fyo͞osnis| *n.*

USAGE: The verbs **diffuse** and **defuse** sound similar but have different meanings. **Diffuse** means, broadly, 'disperse'; **defuse** means 'remove the fuse from a bomb, reduce the danger or tension in.' Thus *Cooper successfully* **diffused** *the situation* is wrong, and *Cooper successfully* **defused** *the situation* is right.

dif•fu•sion |di'fyo͞oZHən| • *n.* the spreading of something more widely: *the diffusion of knowledge.*
■ the action of spreading the light from a light source evenly so as to reduce glare and harsh shadows. ■ the intermingling of substances by the natural movement of their particles: *the rate of diffusion of a gas.* ■ the dissemination of elements of culture to another region or people.
DERIVATIVES: **dif•fu•sive** |-siv| *adj.*

dig•it•al |'dijitl| • *adj.* **1** relating to or using signals or information represented by discrete values of a physical quantity such as voltage or magnetic polarization: *digital TV.* Often contrasted with ANALOG.
■ (of a clock or watch) showing the time by means of displayed digits rather than hands or a pointer. **2** of or relating to a finger or fingers.
DERIVATIVES: **dig•it•al•ly** *adv.*

dig•i•ti•grade |'dijiti,grād| • *adj.* (of a mammal) walking on its toes and not touching the ground with its heels, as a dog, cat, or rodent.

dig•ni•tar•y |'digni,terē| • *n.* (pl. **-ies**) a person considered to be important because of high rank or office.

di•graph |'dī,græf| • *n.* a combination of two letters representing one sound, as in *ph* and *ng.*
■ a character consisting of two joined letters; a ligature as æ.
DERIVATIVES: **di•graph•ic** |dī'græfik| *adj.*

di•gress |dī'gres| • *v.* [intrans.] leave the main subject temporarily in speech or writing: *I have* **digressed** *a little from my outline.*
DERIVATIVES: **di•gress•er** *n.* **di•gres•sion** |-'greSHən| *n.* **di•gres•sive** |-'gresiv| *adj.*

di•gres•sive•ly |-'gresivlē| *adv.* **di•gres•sive•ness** |-'gresivnis| *n.*

dike |dīk| (also **dyke**) • *n.* **1** a long wall or embankment built to prevent flooding from the sea.
■ [often in place names] a low wall or earthwork serving as a boundary or defense: *Offa's Dike.* ■ a causeway. ■ an intrusion of igneous rock cutting across existing strata. Cf. SILL. **2** a ditch or watercourse. • *v.* [trans.] [often as adj.] (**diked**) provide (land) with a wall or embankment to prevent flooding.
PHRASES: **put one's finger in the dike** attempt to stem the advance of something undesirable.

di•lap•i•dat•ed |di'læpi,dātid| • *adj.* (of a building or object) in a state of disrepair or ruin as a result of age or neglect.

dil•a•ta•tion |,dilə'tāSHən; ,dī-| • *n.* (in medicine and physiology) the process of becoming dilated.
■ the action of dilating a vessel or opening. ■ a dilated part of a hollow organ or vessel.

di•late |'dī,lāt; dī'lāt| • *v.* **1** make or become wider, larger, or more open: [intrans.] *her eyes dilated with horror* | [trans.] *the woman dilated her nostrils.* **2** [intrans.] (**dilate on**) speak or write at length on (a subject).
DERIVATIVES: **di•lat•a•ble** *adj.* **di•la•tion** |dī'lāSHən| *n.*

dil•a•ta•tion |,dilə'tāSHən; ,dī-| • *n.* the process of becoming dilated.
■ the action of dilating a vessel or opening. ■ a dilated part of a hollow organ or vessel.

dil•a•to•ry |'dilə,tôrē| • *adj.* slow to act: *he had been dilatory in appointing a spokesman.*
■ intended to cause delay: *they resorted to dilatory procedural tactics, forcing a postponement.*
DERIVATIVES: **dil•a•to•ri•ly** |,dilə'tôrəlē| *adv.* **dil•a•to•ri•ness** *n.*

di•lem•ma |di'lemə| • *n.* a situation in which a difficult choice has to be made between two or more alternatives, esp. equally undesirable ones.
■ a difficult situation or problem: *the insoluble dilemma of adolescence.* ■ (in logic) an argument forcing an opponent to choose either of two unfavorable alternatives.

USAGE: **Dilemma** should be reserved for reference to a predicament in which a difficult choice must be made between undesirable alternatives, as in *You see his dilemma? If he chose one, his wife might never forgive him; if he chose the other, he'd break his mother's heart.* The weakened use of **dilemma** to mean simply 'a difficult situation or problem,' as in *the insoluble* **dilemma** *of adolescence* should be avoided.

dil•et•tante |,dili'tänt| • *n.* (pl. **dilettanti** |-tē| or **dilettantes**) a person who cultivates an area of interest, such as the arts, without real commitment or knowledge: [as adj.] *a dilettante approach to science.*
■ a person with an amateur interest in the arts.
DERIVATIVES: **dil•et•tan•tish** *adj.* **dil•et•tant•ism** |-,tizəm| *n.*

dil•i•gent |'dilǝjǝnt| • *adj.* having or showing care and conscientiousness in one's work or duties: *many caves are located only after a diligent search.*
DERIVATIVES: **dil•i•gence** *n.* **dil•i•gent•ly** *adv.*

di•lute |di'lo͞ot; dī-| • *v.* [trans.] (often **be diluted**) make (a liquid) thinner or weaker by adding water or another solvent to it: *bleach can be diluted with cold water.*
■ make (something) weaker in force, content, or value by modifying it or adding other elements to it: *the reforms have been diluted.* ■ reduce the value of (a shareholding) by issuing more shares in a company without increasing the values of its assets. • *adj.* (of a liquid) made thinner or weaker by having had water or another solvent added to it.
■ (of a chemical solution) having a relatively low concentration of solute: *a dilute solution of potassium permanganate.* ■ (of color or light) weak or low in concentration: *a short measure of dilute sun.*
DERIVATIVES: **di•lu•ent** *adj.*, *n.* **di•lut•er** *n.*

di•min•u•en•do |di,minyǝ'wendō| • *n.* (pl. **diminuendos** or **diminuendi**) (in music) a decrease in loudness: *the sudden diminuendos are brilliantly effective.*
■ a passage to be performed with such a decrease. • *adv. & adj.* (esp. as a direction) with a decrease in loudness: [as adj.] *the diminuendo chorus before the final tumult.* • *v.* (**-os, -oed**) [intrans.] decrease in loudness or intensity: *the singers left and the buzz diminuendoed.*

dim•i•nu•tion |,dimǝ'n(y)o͞osHǝn| • *n.* a reduction in the size, extent, or importance of something: *a permanent diminution in value* | *the disease shows no signs of diminution.*

di•min•u•tive |di'minyǝtiv| • *adj.* extremely or unusually small: *a diminutive figure dressed in black.*
■ (of a word, name, or suffix) implying smallness, either actual or imputed in token of affection, scorn, etc. (e.g., *teeny, -let, -kins*). • *n.* a smaller or shorter thing, in particular:
■ a diminutive word or suffix. ■ a shortened form of a name, typically used informally: *"Nick" is a diminutive of "Nicholas."*
DERIVATIVES: **di•min•u•tive•ly** *adv.* **di•min•u•tive•ness** *n.*

di•o•cese |'dīǝsis; ,sēs| • *n.* (pl. **dioceses**) a district under the pastoral care of a bishop in the Christian Church.
DERIVATIVES: **di•oc•e•san** *adj.*

Di•o•ny•sian |,dīǝ'nisēǝn; 'nisHǝn| (also **Dionysiac**) • *adj.* **1** (in Greek mythology) of or relating to Dionysus, the god of wine. **2** of or relating to the sensual, spontaneous, and emotional aspects of human nature: *Dionysian music.*

diph•thong |'dif,THäNG; 'dip-; ,THÔNG| • *n.* a sound formed by the combination of two vowels in a single syllable, in which the sound begins as one vowel and moves toward another (as in *coin, loud,* and *side*).
■ a digraph representing the sound of a diphthong or single vowel (as in *feat*). ■ a compound vowel character; a ligature (such as æ).

diph•thon•gal |dif'THäNGgǝl; dip-; 'THÔNG-| *adj.*

di•plo•ma•cy |di'plōmǝsē| • *n.* the profession, activity, or skill of managing international relations, typically by a country's representatives (*diplomats*) abroad: *an extensive round of diplomacy in the Middle East.*
■ the art of dealing with people in a sensitive and effective way: *he handled social difficulties with diplomacy.*
DERIVATIVES: **dip•lo•mat•ic** *adj.* **dip•lo•mat•i•cal•ly** *adv.*

dip•so•ma•ni•a |,dipsǝ'mānēǝ| • *n.* alcoholism, specifically in a form characterized by intermittent bouts of craving for alcohol.
DERIVATIVES: **dip•so•ma•ni•ac** |,-nē,æk| *n.* **dip•so•ma•ni•a•cal** |-mǝ'nīǝkǝl| *adj.* .

dire |'dīr| • *adj.* (of a situation or event) extremely serious or urgent: *dire consequences.*
■ (of a warning or threat) presaging disaster: *she cautioned us with dire warnings about breathing the fumes.*
DERIVATIVES: **dire•ly** *adv.* **dire•ness** *n.*

di•rect |di'rekt; dī-| • *adj.* **1** (of evidence or proof) bearing immediately and unambiguously upon the facts at issue: *there is no direct evidence that officials accepted bribes.* Cf. CIRCUMSTANTIAL. **2** (of government) conducted by the people or electorate without intermediaries: *the direct democracy of the town meeting.* Cf. REPRESENTATIVE.

di•rect ob•ject • *n.* a noun, pronoun, or phrase denoting a person or thing that is the recipient of the action of a transitive verb, for example *the dog* in *Jimmy fed the dog.*

dirge |dǝrj| • *n.* a lament for the dead, esp. one forming part of a funeral rite.
■ a mournful song, piece of music, or poem: *singers chanted dirges.*
DERIVATIVES: **dirge•ful** |-fǝl| *adj.*

dir•i•gi•ble |dǝ'rijǝbǝl; 'dirǝ-| • *n.* a power-driven aircraft that is kept buoyant by a body of gas (usu. helium) that is lighter than air; airship. • *adj.* capable of being steered, guided, or directed: *a dirigible spotlight.*

dis•a•buse |,disǝ'byo͞oz| • *v.* [trans.] persuade (someone) that an idea or belief is mistaken: *he quickly **disabused** me **of** my fanciful notions.*

dis•ad•van•taged |,disǝd'væntijd| • *adj.* (of a person or area) in unfavorable circumstances, esp. with regard to financial or social opportunities: *disadvantaged groups such as the elderly and unemployed* | [as plural n.] (**the disadvantaged**) *measures to help the disadvantaged.*

dis•af•fect•ed |,disǝ'fektid| • *adj.* dissatisfied with the people in authority and no longer willing to support them: *a military plot by disaffected elements in the army.*
DERIVATIVES: **dis•af•fect•ed•ly** *adv.* **dis•af•fec•tion** *n.*

dis•ap•pear |,disǝ'pir| • *v.* (in coded political language) intrans. be killed: *the family disappeared after being taken into custody.* [trans.] kill and conceal or destroy the body of (someone): *critics of the regime were disappeared by paramilitary units.*

dis•ar•ray |ˌdisəˈrā| • *n.* a state of disorganization or untidiness: *her gray hair was in disarray* | *his plans have been thrown into disarray.* • *v.* [trans.] **1** throw (someone or something) into a state of disorganization or untidiness: *the inspection disarrayed the usual schedule.* **2** strip (someone) of clothing: *attendant damsels to help to disarray her.*

dis•a•vow |ˌdisəˈvou| • *v.* [trans.] deny any responsibility or support for: *he disavowed the remarks attributed to him.*
DERIVATIVES: **dis•a•vow•al** |-ˈvouəl| *n.*

dis•band |disˈband| • *v.* [trans.] (usu. **be disbanded**) cause (an organized group) to break up.
■ [intrans.] (of an organized group) break up and stop functioning as an organization.
DERIVATIVES: **dis•band•ment** *n.*

dis•bar |disˈbär| • *v.* (**disbarred, disbarring**) [trans.] **1** (usu. **be disbarred**) expel (a lawyer) from the bar, so that he or she no longer has the right to practice law. **2** exclude (someone) from something: *competitors wearing rings will be disbarred from competition.*
DERIVATIVES: **dis•bar•ment** *n.*

dis•burse |disˈbərs| • *v.* [trans.] (often **be disbursed**) pay out (money from a fund): *$67 million of the pledged aid had already been disbursed.*
DERIVATIVES: **dis•bur•sal** |-səl| *n.* **dis•burse•ment** *n.* **dis•burs•er** *n.*

dis•cern |diˈsərn| • *v.* [trans.] perceive or recognize (something): *I can discern no difference between the two policies* | [with clause] *students quickly discern what is acceptable to the teacher.*
■ distinguish (someone or something) with difficulty by sight or with the other senses: *she could faintly discern the shape of a skull.*
DERIVATIVES: **dis•cern•er** *n.* **dis•cern•i•ble** *adj.* **dis•cern•i•bly** |-əblē| *adv.*

dis•cern•ing |diˈsərniNG| • *adj.* having or showing good judgment: *the restaurant attracts discerning customers.*
DERIVATIVES: **dis•cern•ing•ly** *adv.*

dis•claim |disˈklām| • *v.* [trans.] refuse to acknowledge; deny: *the school disclaimed any responsibility for his death.*
■ renounce a legal claim to (a property or title).

dis•claim•er |disˈklāmər| • *n.* a statement that denies something, esp. responsibility: *the novel carries the usual disclaimer about the characters bearing no relation to living persons.*
■ (in law) an act of repudiating another's claim or renouncing one's own.

dis•close |disˈklōz| • *v.* [trans.] make (secret or new information) known: *they disclosed her name to the press* | [with clause] *the magazine disclosed that he had served a prison sentence for fraud.*
■ allow (something) to be seen, esp. by uncovering it: *he cleared away the grass and disclosed a narrow opening descending into the darkness.*
DERIVATIVES: **dis•clos•er** *n.*

dis•com•bob•u•late |ˌdiskəmˈbäbyəˌlāt| • *v.* [trans.] disconcert or confuse (someone): *her question totally discombobulated him* | [as adj.]

(**discombobulated**) *he is looking a little pained and discombobulated.*

dis•com•fit |disˈkəmfit| • *v.* (**discomfited, discomfiting**) [trans.] (usu. **be discomfited**) make (someone) feel uneasy, uncertain, or embarrassed: *he was not noticeably discomfited by her tone.*
DERIVATIVES: **dis•com•fi•ture** |disˈkəmfiˌCHoͦr| *n.*

dis•com•fort |disˈkəmfərt| • *n.* lack of physical comfort: *the discomforts of too much sun in summer.*
■ slight pain: *the patient complained of discomfort in the left calf.* ■ a state of mental unease: *his remarks caused her discomfort.* • *v.* [trans.] make (someone) feel uneasy: *she liked to discomfort my mother by her remarks.*
■ [often as adj.] (**discomforting**) cause (someone) slight pain: *the patient's condition has discomforting symptoms.*

dis•con•cert |ˌdiskənˈsərt| • *v.* [trans.] disturb the composure of; unsettle: *the abrupt change of subject disconcerted her* | [as adj.] (**disconcerted**) *she was amused to see a disconcerted expression on his face.*
DERIVATIVES: **dis•con•cert•ed•ly** *adv.* **dis•con•cert•ing** *adj.* **dis•con•cer•tion** |-ˈsərsHən| *n.* **dis•con•cert•ment** *n.*

dis•con•so•late |disˈkänsəlit| • *adj.* without consolation or comfort; unhappy: *he'd met the man's disconsolate widow.*
■ (of a place or thing) causing or showing a complete lack of comfort; cheerless: *solitary, disconsolate clumps of cattails.*
DERIVATIVES: **dis•con•so•late•ly** *adv.* **dis•con•so•late•ness** *n.* **dis•con•so•la•tion** |-ˌkänsəˈlāsHən| *n.*

dis•cord |ˈdiskôrd| • *n.* **1** disagreement between people: *a prosperous family who showed no signs of discord.*
■ lack of agreement or harmony between things: *the discord between indigenous and Western cultures.* **2** lack of harmony between musical notes sounding together: *the theme faded in discord.*
■ a chord that (in conventional harmonic terms) is regarded as unpleasing or requiring resolution by another. ■ any interval except a unison, an octave, a perfect fifth or fourth, a major or minor third and sixth, or their octaves. ■ a single note dissonant with another. • *v.* [intrans.] (of people) disagree: *we discorded commonly on two points.*
■ (of things) be different or in disharmony: *the party's views were apt to discord with those of the leading members of the administration.*
DERIVATIVES: **discordance** *n.* **discordant** *adj.* **discordantly** *adv.*

dis•count • *n.* |ˈdiskount| a deduction from the usual cost of something, typically given for prompt or advance payment or to a special category of buyers: *many stores will offer a discount on bulk purchases.*
■ a percentage deducted from the face value of a bill of exchange or promissory note when it changes hands before the due date. • *v.* |ˈdiskount; disˈkount| [trans.] **1** deduct an amount from (the usual price of something):

[as adj.] (**discounted**) *existing users qualify for a discounted price.*
■ reduce (a product or service) in price: *merchandise that was deeply discounted—up to 50 percent* | [as adj.] (**discounted**) *discounted books.* ■ buy or sell (a bill of exchange) before its due date at less than its maturity value.
2 regard (a possibility, fact, or person) as being unworthy of consideration because it lacks credibility: *I'd heard rumors but discounted them.* • *adj.* |'diskownt| (of a store or business) offering goods for sale at discounted prices: *a discount drugstore chain.*
■ at a price lower than the usual one: *a discount flight.*
DERIVATIVES: **dis•count•a•ble** |dis'kowntəbəl| *adj.* **dis•count•er** |'diskowntər| *n.*
dis•coun•te•nance |dis'kowntn-əns| • *v.* [trans.] (usu. **be discountenanced**) **1** refuse to approve of (something): *alcohol consumption was discountenanced in their home.* **2** disturb the composure of: *Amanda was not discountenanced by the accusation.*
dis•course • *n.* |'dis,kôrs| written or spoken communication or debate: *the language of political discourse* | *an imagined discourse between two people traveling in France.*
■ a formal discussion of a topic in speech or writing: *a discourse on critical theory.* ■ (in linguistics) a connected series of utterances; a text or conversation. • *v.* |dis'kôrs| [intrans.] speak or write authoritatively about a topic: *she could* **discourse** *at great length* **on** *the history of Europe.*
■ engage in conversation: *he spent an hour* **discoursing with** *his supporters in the courtroom.*
dis•cred•it |dis'kredit| • *v.* (**discredited, discrediting**) [trans.] harm the good reputation of (someone or something): *his remarks were taken out of context in an effort to discredit him* | [as adj.] (**discredited**) *a discredited former governor.*
■ cause (an idea or piece of evidence) to seem false or unreliable: *recent attempts to discredit evolution.* • *n.* loss or lack of reputation or respect: *they committed crimes that brought discredit upon the administration.*
■ a person or thing that is a source of disgrace: *the house is a discredit to the neighborhood.*
dis•creet |dis'krēt| • *adj.* (**discreeter, discreetest**) careful and circumspect in one's speech or actions, esp. in order to avoid causing offense or to gain an advantage: *we made some discreet inquiries.*
■ intentionally unobtrusive: *a discreet cough.*
DERIVATIVES: **dis•creet•ly** *adv.* **dis•creet•ness** *n.*

USAGE: The words **discrete** and **discreet** are pronounced in the same way and share the same origin but they do not mean the same thing. **Discrete** means 'separate, distinct,' while **discreet** means 'careful, judicious, circumspect.'

dis•crep•an•cy |dis'krepənsē| • *n.* (pl. **-ies**) a lack of compatibility or similarity between two or more facts: *there's a* **discrepancy** *between your account and his.*

DERIVATIVES: **dis•crep•ant** |-pənt| *adj.*
dis•crete |dis'krēt| • *adj.* individually separate and distinct: *now let us treat the New England states as six discrete communities.*
DERIVATIVES: **dis•crete•ly** *adv.* **dis•crete•ness** *n.*
dis•cre•tion |dis'kreSHən| • *n.* **1** the quality of behaving or speaking in such a way as to avoid causing offense or revealing private information: *she knew she could rely on his discretion.* **2** the freedom to decide what should be done in a particular situation: *it is up to local authorities to* **use their discretion** *in setting the charges* | *a pass-fail grading system may be used* **at the discretion** *of the department.*
PHRASES: **discretion is the better part of valor** it is better to avoid a dangerous situation than to confront it.
dis•cre•tion•ar•y |dis'kreSHə,nerē| • *adj.* available for use at the discretion of the user: *rules are inevitably less flexible than a discretionary policy.*
■ denoting or relating to investment funds placed with a broker or manager who has discretion to invest them on the client's behalf: *discretionary portfolios.*
PHRASES: **discretionary income** income remaining after deduction of taxes, other mandatory charges, and expenditure on necessities.
dis•crim•i•nant |dis'krimənənt| • *n.* an agent or characteristic that enables things, people, or classes to be distinguished from one another: *anemia is commonly present in patients with both conditions, and is therefore not a helpful discriminant.*
dis•crim•i•nate |dis'krimə,nāt| • *v.* [intrans.] **1** recognize a distinction; differentiate: *babies can* **discriminate between** *different facial expressions of emotion.*
■ [trans.] perceive or constitute the difference in or between: *bats can discriminate a difference in echo delay of between 69 and 98 millionths of a second* | *features that* **discriminate** *this species* **from** *other gastropods.* **2** make an unjust or prejudicial distinction in the treatment of different categories of people or things, esp. on the grounds of race, sex, or age: *existing employment policies* **discriminate against** *women.*
DERIVATIVES: **dis•crim•i•nate•ly** |-nitlē| *adv.* **dis•crim•i•na•tive** |-,nātiv| *adj.*
dis•crim•i•nat•ing |dis'krimə,nātiNG| • *adj.* (of a person) having or showing refined taste or good judgment: *a discriminating collector and patron of the arts.*
DERIVATIVES: **dis•crim•i•nat•ing•ly** *adv.*
dis•crim•i•na•tion |dis,krimə'nāSHən| • *n.* **1** the unjust or prejudicial treatment of different categories of people or things, esp. on the grounds of race, age, or sex: *victims of racial discrimination* | *discrimination against homosexuals.* **2** recognition and understanding of the difference between one thing and another: *discrimination between right and wrong* | *young children have difficulties in making fine discriminations.*
■ the ability to discern what is of high quality;

good judgment or taste: *those who could afford to buy showed little taste or discrimination.* ■ (in psychology) the ability to distinguish between different stimuli: [as adj.] *discrimination learning.* **3** (in electronics) the selection of a signal having a required characteristic, such as frequency or amplitude, by means of a discriminator that rejects all unwanted signals.

dis•cur•sive |dis'kərsiv| • *adj.* **1** passing rapidly or indiscriminately from subject to subject: *students often write dull, secondhand, discursive prose.*
■ (of a style of speech or writing) fluent and expansive rather than formulaic or abbreviated: *the short story is concentrated, whereas the novel is discursive.* **2** of or relating to discourse or modes of discourse: *the attempt to transform utterances from one discursive context to another.* **3** proceeding by argument or reasoning rather than by intuition.
DERIVATIVES: **dis•cur•sive•ly** *adv.* **dis•cur•sive•ness** *n.*

dis•dain |dis'dān| • *n.* the feeling that someone or something is unworthy of one's consideration or respect; contempt: *her upper lip curled in disdain* | *an aristocratic disdain for manual labor.* • *v.* [trans.] consider to be unworthy of one's consideration: *gamblers disdain four-horse races.*
■ refuse or reject (something) out of feelings of pride or superiority: *she remained standing, pointedly disdaining his invitation to sit down* | [with infinitive] *he disdained to discuss the matter further.*

dis•em•bod•ied |ˌdisem'bädēd| • *adj.* separated from or existing without the body: *a disembodied ghost.*
■ (of a sound) lacking any obvious physical source: *a disembodied voice at the end of the phone.*

dis•em•bogue |ˌdisem'bōg| • *v.* (**disembogues, disembogued, disemboguing**) [intrans.] (of a river or stream) emerge or be discharged in quantity; pour out.

dis•en•chant |ˌdisen'CHænt| • *v.* [trans.] (usu. **be disenchanted**) free (someone) from illusion; disappoint: *he may have been disenchanted by the loss of his huge following* | [as adj.] (**disenchanted**) *he became disenchanted with his erstwhile ally.*
DERIVATIVES: **dis•en•chant•ing•ly** *adv.* **dis•en•chant•ment** *n.*

dis•en•fran•chise |ˌdisen'frænCHīz| (also **disfranchise**) • *v.* [trans.] deprive (someone) of the right to vote: *the law disenfranchised some 3,000 voters on the basis of a residence qualification.*
■ [as adj.] (**disenfranchised**) deprived of power; marginalized: *a hard core of kids who are disenfranchised and don't feel connected to the school.* ■ deprive (someone) of a right or privilege: *the move would disenfranchise the disabled from using the town center.* ■ deprive (someone) of the rights and privileges of a free inhabitant of a borough, city, or country.
DERIVATIVES: **dis•en•fran•chise•ment** *n.*

dis•es•tab•lish |ˌdisi'stæblisH| • *v.* [trans.] (usu. **be disestablished**) deprive (an organi-

zation, esp. a country's national church) of its official status.
DERIVATIVES: **dis•es•tab•lish•ment** *n.*

dis•fa•vor |dis'fāvər| (Brit. **disfavour**) • *n.* disapproval or dislike: *the headmaster regarded her with disfavor.*
■ the state of being disliked: *raises could be taken away if an employee fell into disfavor.* • *v.* [trans.] regard or treat (someone or something) with disfavor: *the hypothesis was favored and disfavored by approximately equal numbers of scientists.*

dis•fig•ure |dis'figyər| • *v.* [trans.] spoil the attractiveness of: *litter disfigures the countryside* | [as adj.] (**disfiguring**) *a disfiguring birthmark.*
DERIVATIVES: **dis•fig•u•ra•tion** |-ˌfigyə'rāsHən| *n.* **dis•fig•ure•ment** *n.*

dis•grun•tled |dis'grəntld| • *adj.* angry or dissatisfied: *judges receive letters from disgruntled members of the public.*
DERIVATIVES: **dis•grun•tle•ment** *n.*

dis•ha•bille |ˌdisə'bēl| (also **deshabille**) • *n.* the state of being only partly or scantily clothed: *the paintings of Venus all shared the same state of dishabille.*

dis•heart•en |dis'härtn| • *v.* [trans.] (often **be disheartened**) cause (someone) to lose determination or confidence: *the farmer was disheartened by the damage to his crops.*
DERIVATIVES: **dis•heart•en•ing•ly** *adv.* **dis•heart•en•ment** *n.*

dis•in•cli•na•tion |dis,iNGklə'nāsHən| • *n.* [in sing.] a reluctance or lack of enthusiasm: *Lucy felt a strong disinclination to talk about her engagement.*
DERIVATIVES: **dis•in•clined** *adj.*

dis•in•gen•u•ous |ˌdisin'jenyəwəs| • *adj.* not candid or sincere, typically by pretending that one knows less about something than one really does.
DERIVATIVES: **dis•in•gen•u•ous•ly** *adv.* **dis•in•gen•u•ous•ness** *n.* **dis•in•ge•nu•i•ty** *n.*

dis•in•her•it |ˌdisin'herit| • *v.* (**disinherited, disinheriting**) [trans.] change one's will or take other steps to prevent (someone) from inheriting one's property.
DERIVATIVES: **dis•in•her•i•tance** |-'heritəns| *n.*

dis•in•te•grate |dis'intə,grāt| • *v.* [intrans.] break up into small parts, typically as the result of impact or decay: *when the missile struck, the car disintegrated in a sheet of searing flame.*
■ (of a society, family, or other social group) weaken or break apart: *the marriage disintegrated amid allegations that she was having an affair.* ■ deteriorate mentally or physically: *I thought that when I finished working on the book I would disintegrate.* ■ (in physics) undergo or cause to undergo disintegration at a subatomic level: [intrans.] *a meson can spontaneously disintegrate* | [trans.] *it has become a relatively easy matter to disintegrate almost any atom.*
DERIVATIVES: **disintegration** *n.* **dis•in•te•gra•tive** |-ˌgrāṭiv| *adj.* **dis•in•te•gra•tor** |-ˌgrāṭər| *n.*

dis•in•ter•est•ed |dis'intə,restid; tristid|

• *adj.* **1** not influenced by considerations of personal advantage: *a broker is under an obligation to give disinterested advice.* **2** having or feeling no interest in something: *her father was so disinterested in her progress that he only visited the school once.*

DERIVATIVES: **dis•in•ter•est•ed•ly** *adv.* **dis•in•ter•est•ed•ness** *n.*

USAGE: Nowhere have the battle lines been more deeply drawn in usage questions than over the difference between **disinterested** and **uninterested**. **Disinterested**, to formalists, means 'not having a personal interest, impartial': *A juror must be **disinterested** in the case being tried.* **Uninterested** means 'not interested; indifferent': *On the other hand, a juror must not be **uninterested**.*

dis•joint•ed |disˈjointid| • *adj.* lacking a coherent sequence or connection: *piecing together disjointed fragments of information.*

DERIVATIVES: **dis•joint•ed•ly** *adv.* **dis•joint•ed•ness** *n.*

dis•junct |disˈjəNGkt| • *adj.* disjoined and distinct from one another: *these items of evidence are just phrases and clauses, often wildly disjunct.* ■ of or relating to the movement of a melody from one note to another by a leap. • *n.* |ˈdisjəNGkt| **1** (in logic) each of the terms of a disjunctive proposition. **2** another term for sentence adverb, an adverb that expresses the speaker's attitude toward the sentence.

dis•junc•tion |disˈjəNGksHən| • *n.* **1** the process or an act of putting apart (disjoining), or an act of disjoining; separation: *the Indians emphasized the disjunction between themselves and the invaders.* ■ a lack of correspondence or consistency: *there is a **disjunction between** the skills taught in schools and those demanded in the labor market.* **2** (in logic) the relationship between two distinct alternatives. ■ a statement expressing this relationship (esp. one using the word "or.").

dis•junc•tive |disˈjəNGktiv| • *adj.* **1** lacking connection: *the novel's disjunctive detail.* **2** (of a conjunction) expressing a choice between two mutually exclusive possibilities, for example *or in was he going or staying?* ■ (of a proposition in logic) expressing alternatives. • *n.* a disjunctive conjunction or other word. ■ a disjunctive proposition.

DERIVATIVES: **dis•junc•tive•ly** *adv.*

dis•lo•ca•tion |ˌdisləˈkāsHən| • *n.* disturbance from a proper, original, or usual place or state: *he fell prey to loneliness and a wrenching sense of dislocation* | *the social dislocations caused by government policies.* ■ injury or disability caused when the normal position of a joint or other part of the body is disturbed: *dislocation of the hip* | *a specialist dealing with fractures and dislocations.*

dis•man•tle |disˈmæntl| • *v.* [trans.] (often **be dismantled**) take to pieces; pull down: *the sheds were dismantled and the beams piled in a heap* | *the old regime was dismantled.*

DERIVATIVES: **dis•man•tle•ment** *n.* **dis•man•tler** |-t(ə)lər| *n.*

dis•miss |disˈmis| • *v.* [trans.] order or allow to leave; send away: *she dismissed the taxi at the corner.* ■ discharge from employment or office, typically on the grounds of unsatisfactory performance or dishonorable behavior: *he dismissed five members of his Cabinet.* ■ treat as unworthy of serious consideration: *it would be easy to **dismiss** him **as** all brawn and no brain.* ■ deliberately cease to think about: *he suspected a double meaning in her words, but dismissed the thought.* ■ [intrans.] (of a group assembled under someone's authority) disperse: *he told his company to dismiss.* ■ refuse further hearing to (a legal case): *the judge dismissed the case for lack of evidence.* ■ (in sports) defeat or end the turn of (an opponent).

DERIVATIVES: **dis•miss•al** |-əl| *n.* **dis•miss•i•ble** *adj.* **dis•mis•sive** *adj.*

dis•par•age |disˈpærij| • *v.* [trans.] represent or regard as being of little worth: *he never missed an opportunity to disparage his competitors* | [as adj.] (**disparaging**) *disparaging remarks.*

DERIVATIVES: **dis•par•age•ment** *n.* **dis•par•ag•ing•ly** *adv.*

dis•pa•rate |ˈdispərit; disˈpærit| • *adj.* essentially different in kind; not allowing comparison: *they inhabit disparate worlds of thought.* ■ containing elements very different from one another: *a culturally disparate country.* • *n.* (**disparates**) things so unlike that there is no basis for comparison.

DERIVATIVES: **dis•pa•rate•ly** *adv.* **dis•pa•rate•ness** *n.*

dis•par•i•ty |disˈpæritē| • *n.* (pl. **-ies**) a great difference: *economic **disparities between** different regions of the country* | *the great disparity of weight between the sun and the planets.*

dis•pas•sion•ate |disˈpæsHənit| • *adj.* not influenced by strong emotion, and so able to be rational and impartial: *she dealt with life's disasters in a calm, dispassionate way.*

DERIVATIVES: **dis•pas•sion** |-sHən| *n.* **dis•pas•sion•ate•ly** *adv.* **dis•pas•sion•ate•ness** *n.*

dis•pel |disˈpel| • *v.* (**dispelled**, **dispelling**) [trans.] make (a doubt, feeling, or belief) disappear: *the brightness of the day did nothing to dispel Elaine's dejection.* ■ drive (something) away; scatter: *sprinkle catnip tea to dispel beetles from garden plants.*

DERIVATIVES: **dis•pel•ler** *n.*

dis•pen•sa•ry |disˈpensərē| • *n.* (pl. **-ies**) **1** a room where medicines are prepared and provided. **2** a clinic provided by public or charitable funds.

dis•pen•sa•tion |ˌdispənˈsāsHən; pen-| • *n.* **1** exemption from a rule or usual requirement: *although she was too young, she was given special dispensation to play in the games* | *they were given a dispensation to take most of the first week off.* ■ permission to be exempted from the laws or observances of a church: *he received papal dispensation to hold a number of benefices.* **2** a

system of order, government, or organization of a nation, community, etc., esp. as existing at a particular time: *scholarship is conveyed to a wider audience than under the old dispensation.* ■ (in Christian theology) a divinely ordained order prevailing at a particular period of history: *the Mosaic dispensation.* ■ an act of divine providence: *the laws to which the creator in all his dispensations conforms.* **3** the action of distributing or supplying something: *regulations controlling dispensation of medications.*
DERIVATIVES: **dis·pen·sa·tion·al** |-sHənl| *adj.*

dis·perse |dis'pərs| • *v.* [trans.] distribute or spread over a wide area: *storms can disperse seeds at high altitudes | camping sites could be dispersed among trees so as to be out of sight.* ■ go or cause to go in different directions or to different destinations: [intrans.] *the crowd dispersed |* [trans.] *the police used tear gas to disperse the protesters.* ■ cause (gas, smoke, mist, or cloud) to thin out and eventually disappear: *winds dispersed the radioactive cloud high in the atmosphere.* ■ [intrans.] thin out and disappear: *the earlier mist had dispersed.* ■ [trans.] (in physics) divide (light) into constituents of different wavelengths. • *adj.* [attrib.] (in chemistry) denoting a phase dispersed in another phase, as in a colloid: *emulsions should be examined after storage for droplet size of the disperse phase.*
DERIVATIVES: **dis·pers·er** *n.* **dis·pers·i·ble** *adj.* **dis·per·sive** |-siv| *adj.* **dis·per·sion** *n.*

dis·pir·it |dis'pirit| • *v.* [trans.] (often be **dispirited**) cause (someone) to lose enthusiasm or hope: *the army was dispirited by the severe winter conditions |* [as adj.] (**dispiriting**) *it was a dispiriting occasion.*
DERIVATIVES: **dis·pir·it·ed·ly** *adv.* **dis·pir·it·ed·ness** *n.* **dis·pir·it·ing·ly** *adv.*

dis·place·ment |dis'plāsmənt| • *n.* **1** the moving of something from its place or position: *vertical displacement of the shoreline.* ■ the removal of someone or something by someone or something else that takes their place: *males may be able to resist displacement by other males.* ■ the enforced departure of people from their homes, typically because of war, persecution, or natural disaster: *the displacement of farmers.* ■ the amount by which a thing is moved from its normal position: *a displacement of 6.8 meters along the San Andreas Fault.* **2** the occupation by a submerged body or part of a body of a volume that would otherwise be occupied by a fluid. ■ the amount or weight of fluid that would fill such a volume in the case of a floating ship, used as a measure of the ship's size: *the submarine has a surface displacement of 2,185 tons.* ■ the volume of the space moved through by the piston of a reciprocating system, as in a pump or engine. **3** the unconscious transfer of an intense emotion from its original object to another one: *this phobia was linked with the displacement of fear of his father.* **4** (in physics) the component of an electric field due to free separated charges, regardless of any polarizing effects.

■ the vector representing such a component. ■ the flux density of such an electric field.

dis·port |dis'pôrt| • *v.* enjoy oneself unrestrainedly; frolic: *a painting of lords and ladies disporting themselves by a lake.* • *n.* diversion from work or serious matters; recreation or amusement. ■ a pastime, game, or sport.

dis·pos·a·ble |dis'pōzəbəl| • *adj.* **1** (of an article) intended to be used, typically once, and then thrown away: *disposable diapers | a disposable razor.* ■ (of a person or idea) able to be dispensed with; easily dismissed: *disposable personnel.* **2** (chiefly of financial assets) readily available for the owner's use as required. • *n.* an article designed to be thrown away after use: *don't buy disposables, such as razors, cups, and plates.* ■ (**disposable income**) income remaining after deduction of taxes and other mandatory charges.
DERIVATIVES: **dis·pos·a·bil·i·ty** |-,pōzə 'bilitē| *n.*

dis·pos·sess |',dispə'zes| • *v.* [trans.] (often be **dispossessed**) deprive (someone) of something that they own, typically land or property: *they were dispossessed of lands and properties at the time of the Reformation |* [as plural n.] (**the dispossessed**) *a champion of the poor and the dispossessed.* ■ oust (a person) from a dwelling or position: *he used to dispossess his tenants as the spirit moved him.*
DERIVATIVES: **dis·pos·ses·sion** |-'zesHən| *n.*

dis·pro·por·tion·ate |,disprə'pôrsHənit| • *adj.* too large or too small in comparison with something else: *sentences disproportionate to the offenses committed.*
DERIVATIVES: **dis·pro·por·tion·ate·ly** *adv.* **dis·pro·por·tion·ate·ness** *n.*

dis·pu·ta·tious |,dispyōō',tāsHəs| • *adj.* (of a person) fond of having heated arguments: *a congenial hangout for disputatious academics.* ■ (of an argument or situation) motivated by or causing strong opinions: *disputatious council meetings.*
DERIVATIVES: **dis·pu·ta·tious·ly** *adv.* **dis·pu·ta·tious·ness** *n.*

dis·qui·et |dis'kwī-it| • *n.* a feeling of anxiety or worry: *public disquiet about animal testing.* • *v.* [trans.] [usu. as adj.] (**disquieted**) make (someone) worried or anxious.
DERIVATIVES: **dis·qui·e·tude** *n.*

dis·qui·si·tion |,diskwi'zisHən| • *n.* a long or elaborate essay or discussion on a particular subject.
DERIVATIVES: **dis·qui·si·tion·al** |-sHənl| *adj.*

dis·sect |di'sekt; dī-| • *v.* [trans.] (often be **dissected**) methodically cut up (a body, part, or plant) in order to study its internal parts. ■ analyze (something) in minute detail: *novels that dissect our obsession with urban angst.*
DERIVATIVES: **dis·sec·tion** |-'seksHən| *n.* **dis·sec·tor** |-ər| *n.*

dis•sem•ble |di'sembəl| • v. [intrans.] conceal one's true motives, feelings, or beliefs: *an honest, sincere person with no need to dissemble.*
■ [trans.] disguise or conceal (a feeling or intention): *she smiled, dissembling her true emotion.*
DERIVATIVES: **dis•sem•blance** |-bləns| n. **dis•sem•bler** |-b(ə)lər| n.

dis•sem•i•nate |di'semə,nāt| • v. [trans.] spread or disperse (something, esp. information) widely: *health authorities should concentrate more on disseminating information.*
■ [usu. as adj.] **(disseminated)** spread throughout an organ or the body: *disseminated colon cancer.*
DERIVATIVES: **dis•sem•i•na•tion** |-,semə'nāSHən| n. **dis•sem•i•na•tor** |-,nātər| n.

dis•sen•sion |di'sensHən| • n. disagreement that leads to discord: *this maneuver caused dissension within feminist ranks.*

dis•sent |di'sent| • v. [intrans.] hold or express opinions that are at variance with those previously, commonly, or officially expressed: *two members **dissented from** the majority* | [as adj.] **(dissenting)** *there were only a couple of dissenting voices.*
■ separate from an established or orthodox church because of doctrinal disagreement. • n. the expression or holding of opinions at variance with those previously, commonly, or officially held: *there was no **dissent from** this view.*
■ (also **Dissent**) refusal to accept the doctrines of an established or orthodox church; nonconformity.

dis•sen•tient |di'sensHənt| • adj. in opposition to a majority or official opinion: *dissentient voices were castigated as hopeless bureaucrats.* • n. a person who opposes a majority or official opinion.

dis•ser•ta•tion |,disər'tāSHən| • n. a long essay on a particular subject, esp. one written as a requirement for the Doctor of Philosophy degree: *he had considered writing his doctoral dissertation on Kant.*
■ a long discourse: *she went on into a dissertation on her family's love of Ireland.*
DERIVATIVES: **dis•ser•ta•tion•al** |-SHənl| adj.

dis•sim•u•late |di'simyə,lāt| • v. [trans.] conceal or disguise (one's thoughts, feelings, or character): *a country gentleman who dissimulates his wealth beneath ragged pullovers* | [intrans.] *now that they have power, they no longer need to dissimulate.*
DERIVATIVES: **dis•sim•u•la•tion** |-,simyə'lāSHən| n. **dis•sim•u•la•tor** |-,lātər| n.

dis•si•pate |'disə,pāt| • v. 1 [intrans.] disperse or scatter: *the cloud of smoke dissipated.*
■ (of a feeling or other intangible thing) disappear or be dispelled: *the concern she'd felt for him had wholly dissipated.* ■ [trans.] cause (a feeling or other intangible thing) to disappear or disperse: *he wanted to dissipate his anger.* 2 [trans.] squander or fritter away (money, energy, or resources): *he had dissipated his entire fortune.*
■ (usu. **be dissipated**) (in physics) cause (energy) to be lost, typically by converting it to heat.
DERIVATIVES: **dis•si•pa•tive** |-,pātiv| adj. **dis•si•pa•tor** |-,pātər| (also **dis•si•pat•er**) n.

dis•si•pat•ed |'disə,pātid| • adj. (of a person or way of life) overindulging in sensual pleasures: *dissipated behavior.*

dis•si•pa•tion |,disə'pāSHən| • n. 1 a dissolute manner of living; immoderation and laxity: *a descent into drunkenness and sexual dissipation.* 2 squandering of money, energy, or resources: *the dissipation of the country's mineral wealth.*
■ (in physics) loss of energy, esp. by its conversion into heat. ■ scattering or dispersion: *the complete dissipation of paint fumes.*

dis•so•ci•ate |di'sōSHē,āt; 'sōsē-| • v. [trans.] 1 disconnect or separate (used esp. in abstract contexts): *opinions should not be **dissociated from** their social context.*
■ **(dissociate oneself from)** declare that one is not connected with or a supporter of (someone or something): *he took pains to dissociate himself from religious radicals.* ■ [intrans.] become separated or disconnected: *the region would **dissociate from** the country.* ■ (usu. **be dissociated**) (in psychiatry) split off (a component of mental activity) to act as an independent part of mental life. 2 (usu. **be dissociated**) (in chemistry) cause (a molecule) to split into separate smaller atoms, ions, or molecules, esp. reversibly: *these compounds are dissociated by solar radiation to yield atoms of chlorine.*
■ [intrans.] (of a molecule) undergo this process.
DERIVATIVES: **dis•so•ci•a•tive** |-,ātiv; sHə-tiv| adj.

dis•so•lute |'disə,lōot| • adj. lax in morals; licentious: *a dissolute, drunken, disreputable rogue.*
DERIVATIVES: **dis•so•lute•ly** adv. **dis•so•lute•ness** n.

dis•so•lu•tion |,disə'lōoSHən| • n. 1 the closing down or dismissal of an assembly, partnership, or official body: *the dissolution of their marriage* | *Henry VIII declared the abbey's dissolution in 1540.*
■ the action or process of dissolving or being dissolved: *minerals susceptible to dissolution.*
■ breaking down; disintegration; decomposition: *the dissolution of the flesh* ■ death. 2 debauched living; dissipation: *an advanced state of dissolution.*

dis•solve |di'zälv| • v. 1 [intrans.] (of a solid) become incorporated into a liquid so as to form a solution: *glucose dissolves easily in water.*
■ [trans.] cause (a solid) to become incorporated into a liquid in this way: *dissolve a bouillon cube in a pint of hot water.* ■ (of something abstract, esp. a feeling) disappear: *my courage dissolved.* ■ deteriorate or degenerate: *the community policy could **dissolve into** chaos.*
■ subside uncontrollably into (an expression of strong feelings): *she suddenly dissolved into floods of tears.* ■ (in a movie) change

gradually to (a different scene or picture): *dissolve to side view, looking down the street.* **2** [trans.] close down or dismiss (an assembly or official body): *the country's president can dissolve parliament under certain circumstances.*

■ annul or put an end to (a partnership or marriage): *it only takes 28 days to dissolve a domestic partnership.* • *n.* (in a film) an act or instance of moving gradually from one picture to another.

DERIVATIVES: **dis•solv•a•ble** *adj.* **dis•solv•er** *n.*

dis•so•nant |ˈdisənənt| • *adj.* (in music) lacking harmony: *irregular, dissonant chords.*

■ unsuitable or unusual in combination; clashing: *Jackson employs both harmonious and dissonant color choices.*

DERIVATIVES: **dis•so•nance** *n.* **dis•so•nant•ly** *adv.*

dis•suade |dəˈswād| • *v.* [trans.] persuade (someone) not to take a particular course of action: *his friends tried to **dissuade** him from flying.*

DERIVATIVES: **dis•suad•er** *n.* **dis•sua•sion** |diˈswāZHən| *n.* **dis•sua•sive** |-ˈswāsiv| *adj.*

dis•taff side • *n.* the female side of a family: *the family title could be passed down through the distaff side.* The opposite of *spear side.*

■ the female members of a group: *this fascination was not limited to the distaff side of society.*

dis•tem•per[1] |disˈtempər| • *n.* **1** a viral disease of some animals, esp. dogs, causing fever, coughing, and catarrh. **2** political disorder: *an attempt to illuminate the moral roots of the modern world's distemper.*

dis•tem•per[2] • *n.* a kind of paint using glue or size instead of an oil base, for use on walls or for scene-painting.

■ a method of mural and poster painting using this. • *v.* [trans.] [often as adj.] (**distempered**) paint (something) with distemper: *the distempered roof timbers.*

dis•tend |disˈtend| • *v.* [trans.] cause (something) to swell by stretching it from inside: *air is introduced into the stomach to distend it* | [as adj.] (**distended**) *a distended belly.*

■ [intrans.] swell out because of pressure from inside: *the abdomen distended rapidly.*

DERIVATIVES: **dis•ten•si•bil•i•ty** |-ˌtensəˈbilitē| *n.* **dis•ten•si•ble** |-ˈtensəbəl| *adj.* **dis•ten•sion** |-ˈtensHən| *n.*

dis•tich |ˈdistik| • *n.* a pair of verse lines; a couplet.

dis•tin•gué |ˌdistæNGˈgā| • *adj.* (fem. **distinguée** pronunc. same) having a distinguished manner or appearance: *he was lean and distingué, with a small goatee.*

dis•tort |disˈtôrt| • *v.* [trans.] pull or twist out of shape: *a grimace distorted her fine mouth* | [as adj.] (**distorted**) *his face was **distorted** with rage.*

■ [intrans.] become twisted out of shape: *the pipe will distort as you bend it.* ■ give a misleading or false account or impression of: *many factors can distort the results* | [as adj.] (**distorted**) *his report gives a distorted view of the meeting.*

■ change the form of (an electrical signal or sound wave) during transmission, amplifica-

tion, or other processing: *you're distorting the sound by overloading the amp.*

DERIVATIVES: **dis•tort•ed•ly** *adv.* **dis•tort•ed•ness** *n.* **dis•tor•tion** |-ˈtôrsHən| *n.* **dis•tor•tion•al** |-ˈtôrsHənl| *adj.* **dis•tor•tion•less** |-ˈtôrsHənləs| *adj.*

dis•train |disˈtrān| • *v.* [trans.] seize (someone's property) in order to obtain payment of rent or other money owed: *legislation has restricted the right to distrain goods found on the premises.* Cf. CONFISCATE.

■ seize the property of (someone) for this purpose: *the government applied political pressure by distraining debtors.*

DERIVATIVES: **dis•train•er** *n.* **dis•train•ment** *n.*

dis•trait |disˈtrā| • *adj.* (fem. **distraite** |-ˈtrāt|) [predic.] distracted or absentminded: *he seemed oddly distrait.*

dis•traught |disˈtrôt| • *adj.* deeply upset and agitated: *a distraught woman sobbed and screamed for help* | *he appeared on television, grief-ravaged and distraught.*

dis•tressed |disˈtrest| • *adj.* suffering from anxiety, sorrow, or pain: *I was distressed at the news of his death.*

■ impoverished: *women in distressed circumstances.* ■ (of furniture, leather, or clothing) having simulated marks of age and wear: *a distressed leather jacket.*

dis•trib•u•tar•y |disˈtribyōˌterē| • *n.* (pl. **-ies**) a branch of a river that does not return to the main stream after leaving it (as in a delta), rather distributes part of its water.

dis•tri•bu•tive |disˈtribyətiv| • *adj.* **1** concerned with the supply of goods to stores and other businesses that sell to consumers: *transportation and distributive industries.*

■ concerned with the way in which things are shared among people: *the distributive effects of public expenditure* | *distributive justice.* **2** (of a grammatical determiner or pronoun) referring to each individual of a class, not to the class collectively, e.g., *each, either.* **3** (of a mathematical operation) fulfilling the condition that, when it is performed on two or more quantities already combined by another operation, the result is the same as when it is performed on each quantity individually and the products then combined. • *n.* a distributive word.

DERIVATIVES: **dis•trib•u•tive•ly** *adv.*

dith•er |ˈdiTHər| • *v.* [intrans.] **1** act hesitantly; be indecisive: *he was dithering about how to vote.* **2** [trans.] display or print (a computer image) without sharp edges so that there appear to be more colors in it than are really available: [as adj.] (**dithered**) *dithered bit maps.* • *n.* **1** indecisive behavior: *after months of dither they had still not agreed.* **2** [in sing.] a state of agitation: *buses are jammed and dirty and everyone is **in a dither** over taxis.*

DERIVATIVES: **dith•er•er** *n.* **dith•er•y** *adj.*

dith•y•ramb |ˈdiTHəˌræm| • *n.* a wild choral hymn of ancient Greece, esp. one dedicated to Dionysus.

■ a passionate or inflated speech, poem, or other writing.

DERIVATIVES: **dith•y•ram•bic** |ˌdiTHə'ræmbik| *adj.*

di•u•ret•ic |ˌdīyə'reṯik| • *adj.* (chiefly of drugs) causing increased passing of urine. • *n.* a diuretic drug.

di•ur•nal |dī'ərnl| • *adj.* **1** of or during the day.
■ (of animals) active in the daytime. ■ (of flowers) open only during the day. **2** daily; of each day: *diurnal rhythms.* ■ of or resulting from the daily rotation of the earth.
DERIVATIVES: **di•ur•nal•ly** *adv.*

di•va |'dēvə| • *n.* a famous female opera singer: *your average opera isn't over till the diva trills her high notes.*
■ a female singer who has enjoyed great popular success: *a chance to create a full-blown pop diva.* ■ an admired, glamorous, or distinguished woman: *the former director of the association is still a downtown diva.* ■ a haughty, spoiled woman.

di•va•gate |'dīvəˌgāt| • *v.* [intrans.] wander about; stray; digress: *Yeats divagated into Virgil's territory only once.*
DERIVATIVES: **di•va•ga•tion** |ˌdīvə'gāSHən| *n.*

di•var•i•cate |dī'værəˌkāt; di-| • *v.* [intrans.] stretch or spread apart; diverge widely: *her crow's feet are divaricating like deltas.* • *adj.* |-kit; ˌkāt| (of a tree branch) coming off the stem almost at a right angle.
DERIVATIVES: **di•var•i•ca•tion** |-ˌværə'kāSHən| *n.*

di•ver•gent |dī'vərjənt; di-| • *adj.* **1** tending to be different or develop in different directions: *divergent interpretations* | *varieties of English can remain astonishingly divergent from one another.*
■ (of thought) using a variety of premises, esp. unfamiliar premises, as bases for inference, and avoiding common limiting assumptions in making deductions. **2** (of a mathematical series) increasing indefinitely as more of its terms are added; not convergent.
DERIVATIVES: **di•ver•gen•cy** *n.* **di•ver•gent•ly** *adv.*

di•vers |'dīvərz| • *adj.* [attrib.] of varying types; several: *in divers places.*

di•verse |dī'vərs; dī-| • *adj.* showing a great deal of variety: *a culturally diverse population.*
■ (of two or more things) markedly different from one another: *subjects as diverse as architecture, language teaching, and paleobotany.*
DERIVATIVES: **di•verse•ly** *adv.* **diverseness** *n.*

di•ver•sion |dī'vərZHən; dī-| • *n.* **1** an instance of turning something aside from its course: *a diversion of resources from defense to basic research.*
■ Brit. an alternative route for use by traffic when the usual road is temporarily closed; detour: *the road was closed and diversions put into operation.* **2** an activity that diverts the mind from tedious or serious concerns; a recreation or pastime: *our chief diversion was reading.*
■ something intended to distract someone's

attention from something more important: *a raid was carried out on a nearby airfield to create a diversion.*

di•vert |di'vərt; dī-| • *v.* [trans.] **1** cause (someone or something) to change course or turn from one direction to another: *a scheme to divert water from the river to irrigate agricultural land.*
■ [intrans.] (of a vehicle or person) change course: *an aircraft has diverted and will be with you shortly.* ■ reallocate (something, esp. money or resources) to a different purpose: *more of their advertising budget was diverted into promotions.* **2** distract (someone or their attention) from something: *public relations policies are sometimes intended to divert attention away from criticism.*
■ [usu. as adj.] (**diverting**) draw the attention of (someone) away from tedious or serious concerns; entertain or amuse: *a diverting book* | *nursery rhymes can calm and divert all but the most fractious child.*
DERIVATIVES: **di•vert•er** *n.* **di•vert•ing•ly** *adv.*

di•ver•ti•men•to |di,vərtə'mentō| • *n.* (pl. **divertimenti** |-,tē| or **divertimentos**) a light and entertaining musical composition, typically one in the form of a suite for chamber orchestra.

di•ver•tisse•ment |di'vərṯismənt| • *n.* a minor entertainment or diversion: *as a Sunday divertissement Wittgenstein would play Schubert quartets.*
■ a short dance within a ballet that displays a dancer's technical skill without advancing the plot or character development.

di•vest |di'vest; dī-| • *v.* [trans.] deprive (someone) of power, rights, or possessions: *men are unlikely to be divested of power without a struggle.*
■ deprive (something) of a particular quality: *he has divested the original play of its charm.* ■ rid oneself of something that one no longer wants or requires, such as a business interest or investment: *it appears easier to carry on in the business than to divest* | *the government's policy of divesting itself of state holdings.* ■ relieve (someone) of something being worn or carried: *she divested him of his coat.*

div•i•dend |'diviˌdend| • *n.* **1** a sum of money paid regularly (typically annually) by a company to its shareholders out of its profits (or reserves).
■ a payment divided among a number of people, e.g., members of a cooperative or creditors of an insolvent estate. ■ an individual's share of a dividend. ■ (**dividends**) a benefit from an action or policy: *persistence pays dividends.* **2** a number to be divided by another number.

div•i•na•tion |ˌdivə'nāSHən| • *n.* the practice of seeking knowledge of the future or the unknown by supernatural means (divining).
DERIVATIVES: **di•vin•a•to•ry** |di'vinəˌtôrē| *adj.*

di•vine[1] |di'vīn| • *adj.* (**diviner, divinest**) **1** of, from, or like God or a god: *heroes with*

divine powers | *paintings of shipwrecks being prevented by divine intervention.* ■ devoted to God; sacred: *divine liturgy.* **2** excellent; delightful: *that succulent pastry tasted divine* | *he had the most divine smile.* ▪ *n.* **1** a cleric or theologian. **2** (**the Divine**) providence or God.
DERIVATIVES: **di•vine•ly** *adv.* **di•vine•ness** *n.*

di•vine[2] ▪ *v.* [trans.] discover (something) by guesswork or intuition: *his brother usually divined his ulterior motives* | [with clause] *they had divined that he was a fake.* ■ have supernatural or magical insight into (future events): *claimed to divine the future in chicken's entrails.* ■ discover (water) by dowsing, as with a *divining rod.*
DERIVATIVES: **di•vin•er** *n.*

di•vulge |di'vəlj; dī-| ▪ *v.* [trans.] make known (esp. private or sensitive information): *I am too much of a gentleman to divulge her age.*
DERIVATIVES: **div•ul•ga•tion** |ˌdivəl'gāsHən| *n.* **di•vul•gence** |-jəns| *n.*

DNA ▪ *n.* deoxyribonucleic acid, a self-replicating material present in nearly all living organisms as the main constituent of chromosomes. It is the carrier of genetic information. Cf. RNA.

Each molecule of DNA consists of two strands coiled around each other to form a double helix, a structure like a spiral ladder. Each rung of the ladder consists of a pair of chemical groups called bases (of which there are four types), which combine in specific pairs so that the sequence on one strand of the double helix is complementary to that on the other. It is the specific sequence of bases that constitutes the genetic information.

do•cent |'dōsənt| ▪ *n.* **1** a person who acts as a guide, typically on a voluntary basis, in a museum, art gallery, or zoo. **2** (in certain universities and colleges) a member of the teaching staff immediately below professorial rank.

Do•ce•tism |dō'sēˌtizəm; 'dōsi-| ▪ *n.* the doctrine, important in Gnosticism, that Christ's body was not human but either a phantasm or of real but celestial substance, and that his sufferings were therefore, only apparent.
DERIVATIVES: **Do•ce•tist** *n.*

doc•ile |'däsəl| ▪ *adj.* ready to accept control or instruction; submissive: *a cheap and docile work force.*
DERIVATIVES: **doc•ile•ly** *adv.* **do•cil•i•ty** |dä'silitē| *n.*

doc•tri•naire |ˌdäktrə'ner| ▪ *adj.* seeking to impose a doctrine in all circumstances without regard to practical considerations: *a doctrinaire socialist.* ▪ *n.* a person who seeks to impose a theory in such a way.
DERIVATIVES: **doc•tri•nair•ism** |-ˌizəm| *n.*

doc•tri•nal |'däktrənl| ▪ *adj.* concerned with a doctrine or doctrines: *doctrinal disputes.*
DERIVATIVES: **doc•tri•nal•ly** *adv.*

doc•trine |'däktrin| ▪ *n.* a belief or set of beliefs held and taught by a church, political party, or other group: *the doctrine of predestination.* ■ a stated principle of government policy, mainly in foreign or military affairs: *the Monroe Doctrine.*

doc•u•ment ▪ *n.* |'däkyəmənt| a piece of written, printed, or electronic matter that provides information or evidence or that serves as an official record. ▪ *v.* |'däkyəˌment| [trans.] record (something) in written, photographic, or other form: *the photographer spent years documenting the lives of miners.* ■ support or accompany with documentation.
DERIVATIVES: **doc•u•ment•a•ble** |ˌdäkyə'mentəbəl| *adj.* **doc•u•ment•al** |ˌdäkyə'mentl| *adj.* **doc•u•ment•er** |-ˌmentər| *n.*

doc•u•men•ta•ry |ˌdäkyə'mentərē| ▪ *adj.* consisting of pieces of written, printed, or other matter, esp. official materials: *his book is based on documentary sources.* ■ (of a movie, a television or radio program, or photography) using pictures or interviews with people involved in real events to provide a factual record or report: *he has directed documentary shorts and feature films.* ▪ *n.* (pl. **-ies**) a movie or a television or radio program that provides a factual record or report.
DERIVATIVES: **documentarist, documentarian** *n.* a person who produces documentaries.

doc•u•men•ta•tion |ˌdäkyəmen'tāsHən| ▪ *n.* **1** material that provides official information or evidence or that serves as a record: *you will have to complete the relevant documentation.* ■ the written specification and instructions accompanying a computer program or hardware. **2** the process of classifying and annotating texts, photographs, etc.: *she arranged the collection and documentation of photographs.*

doge |dōj| ▪ *n.* the chief magistrate in the former republics of Venice or Genoa.

dog•ger•el |'dôgərəl; 'däg-| ▪ *n.* comic verse composed in irregular rhythm. ■ verse or words that are badly written or expressed: *the last stanza deteriorates into doggerel.*

dog•ma |'dôgmə| ▪ *n.* a principle or set of principles laid down by an authority as incontrovertibly true: *the Christian dogma of the Trinity* | *the rejection of political dogma.*

dog•mat•ic |dôg'maɾik| ▪ *adj.* inclined to lay down principles as incontrovertibly true: *he gives his opinion without trying to be dogmatic.*
DERIVATIVES: **dog•mat•i•cal•ly** |-ik(ə)lē| *adv.*

dol•ce vi•ta |ˌdōlCHä 'vēɾə| ▪ *n.* [in sing.] (usu. **la dolce vita**) a life of heedless pleasure and luxury.

dol•drums |'dōldrəmz; 'däl-; 'dôl-| ▪ *plural n.* (**the doldrums**) low spirits; a feeling of boredom or depression: *color catalogs will rid you of February doldrums.* ■ a period of inactivity or a state of stagnation: *the mortgage market has been* **in the doldrums** *for three months.* ■ an equatorial region of the Atlantic and Pacific oceans with pronounced calms, sudden storms, and light unpredictable winds.

dole•ful |ˈdōlfəl| • *adj.* expressing sorrow; mournful: *a doleful look.*
■ causing grief or misfortune: *doleful consequences.*
DERIVATIVES: **dole•ful•ly** *adv.* **dole•ful•ness** *n.*

dol•i•cho•ce•phal•ic |ˌdälikōsəfælik| • *adj.* having a relatively long skull (typically with the breadth less than 80 (or 75) percent of the length). Often contrasted with BRACHY-CEPHALIC.
DERIVATIVES: **dol•i•cho•ceph•a•ly** |-ˈsefəlē| *n.*

dol•men |ˈdōlmən; ˈdäl-| • *n.* a megalithic tomb with a large flat stone laid on upright ones, found chiefly in Britain and France. Cf. MENHIR.

do•lor |ˈdōlər| (Brit. **dolour**) • *n.* a state of great sorrow or distress: *they squatted, hunched in visible dolor.*

do•main |dōˈmān| • *n.* an area of territory owned or controlled by a ruler or government: *the southwestern French domains of the Plantagenets.* Cf. EMINENT DOMAIN.
■ an estate or territory held in legal possession by a person or persons. ■ a specified sphere of activity or knowledge: *the expanding domain of psychology | visual communication is the domain of the graphic designer.* ■ (in physics) a discrete region of magnetism in ferromagnetic material. ■ a distinct subset of the Internet with addresses sharing a common suffix, such as the part in a particular country or used by a particular group of users. ■ (in mathematics) the set of possible values of the independent variable or variables of a function. ■ (**domaine**) a vineyard.
DERIVATIVES: **do•ma•ni•al** |-nēəl| *adj.*

do•mes•tic |dəˈmestik| • *adj.* **1** of or relating to the running of a home or to family relations: *domestic chores | domestic violence.*
■ of or for use in the home rather than in an industrial or office environment: *domestic appliances.* ■ (of a person) fond of family life and running a home: *she was not at all domestic.* ■ (of an animal) tame and kept by humans: *domestic cattle.* **2** existing or occurring inside a particular country; not foreign or international: *Korea's domestic affairs.* • *n.* **1** (also **domestic worker** or **domestic help**) a person who is paid to do menial tasks such as cleaning. **2** a product not made abroad.
DERIVATIVES: **do•mes•ti•cal•ly** |-ik(ə)lē| *adv.* **domesticity** *n.* the quality or state of being domestic, esp. (attachment to) home life.

do•mes•ti•cate |dəˈmestiˌkāt| • *v.* [trans.] (usu. **be domesticated**) tame (an animal) and keep it as a pet or for farm produce: *mammals were first domesticated for their milk.*
■ cultivate (a plant) for food. ■ make (someone) fond of and good at home life and the tasks that it involves: *you've finally domesticated him* | [as adj.] (**domesticated**) *he is thoroughly domesticated.*
DERIVATIVES: **do•mes•ti•ca•ble** |-kəbəl| *adj.* **do•mes•ti•ca•tion** |-ˌmestiˈkāSHən| *n.*

dom•i•cile |ˈdäməˌsīl; ˈdō-; ˈdäməsəl| (also **domicil**) • *n.* (in legal use) the country or place that a person treats as his or her permanent home, or lives in and has a substantial connection with.
■ a person's residence or home: *the builder I've hired to renovate my new domicile.* ■ the place at which a company or other body is registered, esp. for tax purposes. • *v.* [with adverbial of place] (**be domiciled**) treat a specified country or place as a permanent home: *the tenant is domiciled in the United States.*
■ reside; be based: *he was domiciled in a frame house on the outskirts of town.*

dom•i•nant |ˈdämənənt| • *adj.* most important, powerful, or influential: *they are now in an even more dominant position in the market.*
■ (of a high place or object) overlooking others. ■ relating to or denoting heritable characteristics controlled by genes that are expressed in offspring even when inherited from only one parent. ■ denoting the predominant species in a plant (or animal) community. ■ in decision theory, (of a choice) at least as good as the alternatives in all circumstances, and better in some: *a dominant strategy.* • *n.* a dominant thing, in particular:
■ a dominant trait or gene. ■ a dominant species in a plant (or animal) community. ■ the fifth note of the diatonic scale of any musical key, or the key based on this, considered in relation to the key of the tonic.
DERIVATIVES: **dom•i•nant•ly** *adv.*

dom•i•na•trix |ˌdäməˈnātriks| • *n.* (pl. **dominatrices** |-trəˌsēz| or **dominatrixes**) a dominating woman, esp. one who takes the sadistic role in sadomasochistic sexual activities.

dom•i•neer |ˌdäməˈnir| • *v.* [intrans.] [usu. as adj.] (**domineering**) assert one's will over another in an arrogant way: *they had survived years with a gruff, domineering father.*
DERIVATIVES: **dom•i•neer•ing•ly** *adv.*

do•min•ion |dəˈminyən| • *n.* **1** sovereignty; control: *man's attempt to establish dominion over nature.* **2** (usu. **dominions**) the territory of a sovereign or government: *the Angevin dominions.*
■ (**Dominion**) each of the self-governing territories of the historical British Commonwealth: *the Dominion of Canada.* **3** (**dominions**) (in Christianity) another term for *domination*, the fourth highest order of angel.

dom•i•no ef•fect • *n.* the effect of the domino theory, which, in politics, holds that events in one country will cause similar events in neighboring countries, like a falling domino causing a row of upended dominos to fall in turn.

don•a•tive |ˈdōnətiv; ˈdän-| • *n.* a donation, esp. one given formally or officially as largesse. • *adj.* given as a donation.

don•jon |ˈdänjən; ˈdən-| • *n.* the great tower or innermost keep of a castle.

don•née |däˈnā| (also **donné**) • *n.* **1** a subject or theme of a narrative. **2** a basic fact or assumption.

don•ny•brook |ˈdänēˌbro͝ok| • *n.* a scene of uproar and disorder; an uproarious meeting.

■ a heated argument: *raucous ideological donny-brooks.*

dop•pel•gäng•er |ˈdäpəl,gæNGər| • *n.* an apparition or double of a living person.

Dor•ic |ˈdôrik; ˈdär-| • *adj.* **1** relating to or denoting a classical order of architecture characterized by a plain, sturdy column and a thick square slab (abacus) resting on a rounded molding. **2** relating to or denoting the ancient Greek dialect of the Dorians.
■ (of a dialect) broad; rustic. • *n.* **1** the Doric order of architecture. **2** the ancient Greek dialect of the Dorians.
■ a broad or rustic dialect, esp. the dialect spoken in northeastern Scotland.

dork |dôrk| • *n.* a dull, slow-witted, or socially inept person.
■ the penis.
DERIVATIVES: **dork•y** *adj.*

dor•mant |ˈdôrmənt| • *adj.* (of an animal) having normal physical functions suspended or slowed down for a period of time; in or as if in a deep sleep: *dormant butterflies.*
■ in a state of rest or inactivity: *the event evoked memories that she would rather had lain dormant.* ■ (of a plant or bud) alive but not actively growing. ■ (of a volcano) temporarily inactive. ■ (of a disease) causing no symptoms but not cured and liable to recur.
■ [usu. postpositive] (in heraldry, of an animal) depicted lying with its head on its paws.
DERIVATIVES: **dor•man•cy** *n.*

dor•mer |ˈdôrmər| (also **dormer window**) • *n.* a window that projects vertically from a sloping roof.
■ the projecting structure that houses such a window: *the windowed dormer above the sink.* Cf. GABLE.

dor•sal |ˈdôrsəl| • *adj.* of, on, or relating to the upper side or back of an animal, plant, or organ: *a dorsal view of the body | the dorsal aorta. a dorsal fin broke the surface.* Cf. VENTRAL.
DERIVATIVES: **dor•sal•ly** *adv.*

dos•si•er |ˈdôsē,ā; ˈdäs-| • *n.* a collection of documents about a particular person, event, or subject: *we have a dossier on him | a dossier of complaints.*

dot•age |ˈdōtij| • *n.* [in sing.] the period of life in which a person is old and weak: *you could live here and look after me in my dotage.*
■ the state of having the intellect impaired, esp. through old age; senility.

do•tard |ˈdōtərd| • *n.* an old person, esp. one who has become weak or senile.

dote |dōt| • *v.* [intrans.] **1** (**dote on/upon**) be extremely and uncritically fond of: *she doted on her two young children* | [as adj.] (**doting**) *she was spoiled outrageously by her doting father.* **2** be silly or feebleminded, esp. as a result of old age: *the parson is now old and dotes.*
DERIVATIVES: **dot•er** *n.* **dot•ing•ly** *adv.*

dou•ble-blind • *adj.* [attrib.] denoting a test or trial, esp. of a drug, in which any information that may influence the behavior of the tester or the subject is withheld until after the test.

dou•ble en•ten•dre |än'tändrə| • *n.* (pl. **double entendres** pronunc. same) a word or phrase open to two interpretations, one of which is usually risqué or indecent.
■ humor using such words or phrases.

dou•ble jeop•ard•y • *n.* (in law) the prosecution of a person twice for the same offense.
■ risk or disadvantage incurred from two sources simultaneously: *he is in double jeopardy, unable to speak either language adequately.*

dou•blet |ˈdəblət| • *n.* **1** either of a pair of similar things, in particular:
■ either of two words of the same historical source but with two different stages of entry into the language, for example *regal* and *royal*, *yard* and *garden*. ■ (**doublets**) the same number on two dice thrown at once. **2** a man's short close-fitting padded jacket, commonly worn from the 14th to the 17th century.

dou•ble•think |ˈdəbəl,THiNGk| • *n.* the acceptance of or mental capacity to accept contrary opinions or beliefs at the same time, esp. as a result of political indoctrination.

dour |dowr| • *adj.* relentlessly severe, stern, or gloomy in manner or appearance: *a hard, dour, humorless fanatic | harsh weather in a dour landscape.*
DERIVATIVES: **dour•ly** *adv.* **dour•ness** *n.*

douse |dows| (also **dowse**) • *v.* [trans.] pour a liquid over; drench: *he doused the car with gasoline and set it on fire.*
■ extinguish (as a fire or light): *stewards appeared and the fire was doused | nothing could douse her sudden euphoria.* ■ lower (a sail) quickly.

dow•a•ger |ˈdowəjər| • *n.* a widow with a title or property derived from her late husband: [as adj.] *the dowager duchess* | [postpositive] *the queen dowager.*
■ a dignified elderly woman.

dow•dy |ˈdowdē| • *adj.* (**dowdier, dowdiest**) (of a person, typically a woman, or their clothes) unfashionable and without style in appearance: *her casual chic made other women around her look dowdy.* • *n.* (pl. **-ies**) (also **dowd**) a woman who is unfashionably and unattractively dressed.
DERIVATIVES: **dow•di•ly** |ˈdowdəlē| *adv.* **dow•di•ness** *n.*

dow•er |ˈdowər| • *n.* a widow's share for life of her husband's estate.
■ a dowry. • *v.* [trans.] give a dowry to.

down•beat |ˈdown,bēt| • *adj.* pessimistic; gloomy: *the assessment of current economic prospects is downbeat.* • *n.* (in music) an accented beat, usually the first of the bar.

Down syn•drome (also **Down's syndrome**) • *n.* a congenital disorder arising from a chromosome defect, causing intellectual impairment and physical abnormalities including short stature and a broad facial profile. It arises from a defect involving chromosome 21, usually an extra copy (trisomy-21).

USAGE: Of relatively recent coinage, **Down syndrome** is the accepted term in modern use, and former terms such as **mongol**, **Mongoloid**, and **mongolism**, which are likely to cause offense, should be avoided. See also **usage** at MONGOLOID.

dows•ing |dowziNG| • *n.* a technique for searching for underground water, minerals, or anything invisible, by observing the motion of a pointer (traditionally a forked stick, now often paired bent wires) or the changes in direction of a pendulum, supposedly in response to unseen influences: [as adj.] *a dowsing rod.*
DERIVATIVES: **dowse** *v.* **dows•er** *n.*

dox•ol•o•gy |däk'sälәjē| • *n.* (pl. **-ies**) a Christian liturgical formula of praise to God.
DERIVATIVES: **dox•o•log•i•cal** |,däksә'läjikәl| *adj.*

dox•y |'däksē| • *n.* (pl. **-ies**) a lover or mistress.
■ a prostitute.

doy•en |doi'en; 'doi-en| • *n.* (fem. **doyenne**) the most respected or prominent person in a particular field: *the doyen of academic critics.*

dra•co•ni•an |drә'kōnēәn; drā-| • *adj.* (of laws or their application) excessively harsh and severe.
DERIVATIVES: **dra•con•ic** |-'känik| *adj.*

drag |dræg| • *n.* (of dress) clothing more conventionally worn by the opposite sex, esp. women's clothes worn by a man: *a fashion show, complete with men in drag* | [as adj.] *a live drag show. a drag queen.*

drag•o•man |'drægәmәn| • *n.* (pl. **dragomans** or **dragomen**) an interpreter or guide, esp. in countries speaking Arabic, Turkish, or Persian.

dra•goon |drә'gōōn| • *n.* a member of any of several cavalry regiments in the household troops of the British army.
■ a mounted infantryman armed with a short rifle or musket. • *v.* [trans.] coerce (someone) into doing something: *she had been dragooned into helping with the housework.*

dram•a•tis per•so•nae |'drämәtis pәr'sōnē| • *plural n.* the characters of a play, novel, or narrative.
■ the participants in a series of events.

dram•a•tur•gy |'drämә,tәrjē| • *n.* the theory and practice of dramatic composition: *studies of Shakespeare's dramaturgy.*
DERIVATIVES: **dram•a•tur•gic** |-jik| *adj.* **dram•a•tur•gi•cal** |,drämә'tәrjikәl| *adj.* **dram•a•tur•gi•cal•ly** |,drämә'tәrjik(ә)lē| *adv.*

dregs |dregz| • *n.* the remnants of a liquid left in a container, together with any sediment or grounds: *coffee dregs.* Cf. DROSS.
■ the most worthless part or parts of something: *the dregs of society.*
DERIVATIVES: **dreg•gy** |'dregē| *adj.*

dres•sage |drә'säzH| • *n.* the art of riding and training a horse in a manner that develops obedience, flexibility, and balance.

dri•ly • *adv.* variant spelling of DRYLY.

droll |drōl| • *adj.* curious or unusual in a way that provokes dry amusement: *his unique brand of droll self-mockery.* • *n.* a jester or humorous entertainer; a buffoon.
DERIVATIVES: **droll•er•y** |'drōlәrē| *n.* **droll•ness** *n.* **drol•ly** *adv.*

drone |drōn| • *v.* [intrans.] make a continuous low humming sound: *in the far distance a machine droned.*

■ speak tediously in a dull monotonous tone: *he reached for another beer while Jim droned on.* ■ [with adverbial of direction] move with a continuous humming sound: *traffic droned up and down the street.* • *n.* 1 a low continuous humming sound: *he nodded off to the drone of the engine.*
■ a monotonous speech: *only twenty minutes of the hour-long drone had passed.* ■ a continuous musical note, typically of low pitch. ■ a musical instrument, or part of one, sounding such a continuous note, in particular (also **drone pipe**) a pipe in a bagpipe or (also **drone string**) a string in an instrument such as a hurdy-gurdy or a sitar. 2 a male bee in a colony of social bees, which does no work but can fertilize a queen.
■ a person who does no useful work and lives off others. 3 a remote-controlled pilotless aircraft or missile.

drop•sy |'dräpsē| • *n.* (pl. **-ies**) old-fashioned or less technical term for EDEMA.
DERIVATIVES: **drop•si•cal** *adj.*

dross |drôs; dräs| • *n.* something regarded as worthless; rubbish: *there are bargains if you have the patience to sift through the dross.*
■ foreign matter, dregs, or mineral waste, in particular scum formed on the surface of molten metal.
DERIVATIVES: **dross•y** *adj.*

Dru•id |'drōoid| • *n.* a priest, magician, or soothsayer in the ancient Celtic religion.
■ a member of a present-day group claiming to represent or be derived from this religion.
DERIVATIVES: **Dru•id•ic** |drōo'idik| *adj.* **Dru•id•i•cal** |drōo'idikәl| *adj.* **Dru•id•ism** |-,izәm| *n.*

Druze |drōoz| (also **Druse**) • *n.* (pl. same, **Druzes**, or **Druses** |-ziz|) a member of a political and religious sect of Islamic origin, living chiefly in Lebanon and Syria. The Druze broke away from the (Shiite) Ismaili Muslims in the 11th century; they are regarded as heretical by the Muslim community at large.

dry |drī| • *adj.* (**drier**, **driest**) (of a joke or sense of humor) subtle, expressed in a matter-of-fact way, and having the appearance of being unconscious or unintentional: *he delighted his friends with a dry, covert sense of humor.*

Dry•ad |'drī,æd; әd| (also **dryad**) • *n.* (in folklore and Greek mythology) a nymph inhabiting a forest or a tree, esp. an oak tree.

dry•ly |'drīlē| (also **drily**) • *adv.* 1 in a matter-of-fact or ironically humorous way: *"How very observant," he said dryly.* 2 in a dry way or condition: *Evans swallowed dryly.*

du•al•ism |'d(y)ōoә,lizәm| • *n.* 1 the division of something conceptually into two opposed or contrasted aspects, or the state of being so divided: *a dualism between man and nature.*
■ (in philosophy) a theory or system of thought that regards a domain of reality in terms of two independent principles, esp. mind and matter (**Cartesian dualism**). Cf. IDEALISM, MATERIALISM, and MONISM. ■ the religious doctrine (as in Manichaeism) that the

universe contains opposed powers of good and evil, esp. seen as balanced equals. ■ in Christian theology, the heresy that in the incarnate Christ there were two coexisting persons, human and divine. **2** the quality or condition of being dual; duality.
DERIVATIVES: **du·al·ist** n. & adj. **du·al·is·tic** |ˌd(y)ōōə'listik| adj. **du·al·is·ti·cal·ly** |ˌd(y)ōōə'listik(ə)lē| adv.

du·bi·e·ty |d(y)ōō'bīitē| • n. the state or quality of being doubtful; uncertainty: *his enemies made much of the dubiety of his paternity.*

du·bi·ous |'d(y)ōōbēəs| • adj. **1** hesitating or doubting: *Alex looked dubious, but complied.* **2** not to be relied upon; suspect: *extremely dubious assumptions.*
■ morally suspect: *timesharing has been brought into disrepute by dubious sales methods.* ■ of questionable value: *she earned the dubious distinction of being the lowest-paid teacher in the county.*
DERIVATIVES: **du·bi·ous·ly** adv. **du·bi·os·i·ty** n. **du·bi·ous·ness** n.

duc·tile |'dəktl; ˌtīl| • adj. (of a metal) able to be drawn out into a thin wire.
■ able to be deformed without losing toughness; pliable, not brittle. ■ (of a person) able to be led or drawn; docile or gullible.
DERIVATIVES: **duc·til·i·ty** |dək'tilitē| n.

dude |dōōd| informal • n. a man; a guy: *if some dude smacked me, I'd smack him back.*
■ a stylish, fastidious man: *cool dudes.* ■ a city-dweller, esp. one vacationing on a ranch in the western US. • v. [intrans.] (**dude up**) dress up elaborately: [as adj.] (**duded**) *my brother was all duded up in silver and burgundy.*
DERIVATIVES: **dud·ish** adj.

dudg·eon |'dəjən| • n. a feeling of offense or deep resentment: *the manager walked out in high dudgeon.*

duen·de |dōō'endä| • n. a quality of passion and inspiration; charisma.
■ a spirit or demon.

due proc·ess (also **due process of law**) • n. fair treatment through the normal judicial system, esp. as a citizen's entitlement. In American law, **procedural due process** is proper adherence to rules and principles by courts. **Substantive due process** is proper relation of laws to legitimate government objectives; it protects against arbitrary treatment of individuals. Due process is guaranteed under the 5th and 14th Amendments to the U.S. Constitution.

du jour |də 'ZHŌŌr; ˌdōō| • adj. [postpositive] (of food in a restaurant) available and being served on this day: *what is the soup du jour?*
■ used to describe something that is enjoying great but probably short-lived popularity or publicity: *attention deficit is the disorder du jour.*

dul·cet |'dəlsit| • adj. (esp. of sound) sweet and soothing (often used ironically): *record the dulcet tones of your family and friends.*

dul·ci·fy |'dəlsəˌfī| • v. (-ies, -ied) [trans.] sweeten: *cider pap dulcified with molasses.*
■ calm or soothe: *his voice dulcified the panic.*

DERIVATIVES: **dul·ci·fi·ca·tion** |ˌdəlsəfi'kāsHən| n.

dumb·found |'dəmˌfownd| (also **dumfound**) • v. [trans.] (usu. **be dumbfounded**) greatly astonish or amaze: *they were dumbfounded at his popularity.*

du·plic·i·ty |d(y)ōō'plisitē| • n. **1** the quality of instance of being deceitful; double-dealing. **2** doubleness.

du·ress |d(y)ōō'res| • n. threats, violence, constraints, or other action brought to bear to force someone to do something against his or her will or better judgment: *confessions extracted under duress.*
■ (in legal use) constraint illegally exercised to force someone to perform an act. ■ forcible restraint or imprisonment.

du·ti·ful |'d(y)ōōtəfəl| • adj. conscientiously or obediently fulfilling one's duty: *a dutiful daughter.*
■ motivated by duty rather than desire or enthusiasm: *dutiful applause | a dutiful visit.*
DERIVATIVES: **du·ti·ful·ly** adv. **du·ti·ful·ness** n.

dwarf |dwôrf| • n. (pl. **dwarfs** or **dwarves** |dwôrvz|) **1** (in folklore or fantasy literature) a member of a mythical race of short, stocky humanlike creatures who are generally skilled in mining and metalworking.
■ an abnormally small person. Cf. MIDGET. ■ [as adj.] denoting something, esp. an animal or plant, that is much smaller than the usual size for its type or species: *a dwarf conifer.* **2** (also **dwarf star**) a star of relatively small size and low luminosity, including the majority of main sequence stars. • v. [trans.] cause to seem small or insignificant in comparison: *the buildings surround and dwarf All Saints Church.*
■ stunt the growth or development of: [as adj.] (**dwarfed**) *the dwarfed but solid branch of a tree.*
DERIVATIVES: **dwarf·ish** adj.

USAGE: As applied to a person, both **dwarf** and **midget** are normally considered offensive. A **dwarf** has generally been defined as a very small person who is not well-proportioned, while a **midget** is merely very small.

dy·ad |'dīæd| • n. something that consists of two elements or parts: *the mother–child dyad.*
DERIVATIVES: **dy·ad·ic** |dī'ædik| adj.

dyb·buk |'dibōōk| • n. (pl. **dybbuks** or **dybbukim** |di'bōōkim|) (in Jewish folklore) a malevolent wandering spirit that enters and possesses the body of a living person until exorcized.

dy·nam·ic |dī'næmik| • adj. **1** (of a process or system) characterized by constant change, activity, or progress: *a dynamic economy.*
■ (of a person) positive in attitude and full of energy and new ideas: *a dynamic new leader.* ■ (of a thing) stimulating development or progress: *the dynamic forces of nature.* ■ (in physics) of or relating to forces producing motion. Cf. STATIC. ■ (of a verb) expressing an action, activity, event, or process. Cf.

STATIVE. ■ (of an electronic memory device) needing to be refreshed by the periodic application of a voltage. **2** relating to the volume of sound produced by an instrument, voice, or recording: *an astounding dynamic range.* • *n.* **1** a force that stimulates change or progress within a system or process: *evaluation is part of the basic dynamic of the project.* **2** (in music) another term for DYNAMICS.
DERIVATIVES: **dy•nam•i•cal** *adj.* **dy•nam•i•cal•ly** |-ik(ə)lē| *adv.*

dy•nam•ics |dī'næmiks| • *plural n.* **1** [treated as sing.] the branch of mechanics concerned with the motion of bodies under the action of forces. Cf. STATICS.
■ [usu. with adj.] the branch of any science in which forces or changes are considered: *chemical dynamics.* **2** the forces or properties that stimulate growth, development, or change within a system or process: *the dynamics of changing social relations.* **3** the varying levels of volume of sound in different parts of a musical performance.
DERIVATIVES: **dy•nam•i•cist** |-'næməsist| *n.* (in sense 1).

dy•na•mism |'dīnə,mizəm| • *n.* **1** the quality of being characterized by vigorous activity and progress: *the dynamism and strength of the economy.*
■ the quality of being dynamic and positive in attitude: *he was known for his dynamism and strong views.* **2** (in philosophy) the theory that phenomena of matter or mind are due to the action of forces rather than to motion or matter.
DERIVATIVES: **dy•na•mist** *n.*

dy•nast |'dī,næst; nəst| • *n.* a member of a powerful family or dynasty, esp. a hereditary ruler.

dy•nas•ty |'dīnəstē| • *n.* (pl. **-ies**) a line of hereditary rulers of a country: *China's Tang dynasty.*
■ a succession of people from the same family who play a prominent role in business, politics, or another field: *the Guinness dynasty.* ■ a succession of leaders or winners in any sphere: *the Yankee dynasty led by Ruth and Gehrig.*
DERIVATIVES: **dy•nas•tic** |dī'næstik| *adj.* **dy•nas•ti•cal•ly** |dī'næstik(ə)lē| *adv.*

dys•func•tion•al |dis'fəNGkSHənl| • *adj.* not operating normally or properly: *a dysfunctional economy.*
■ deviating from the norms of social behavior in a way regarded as bad: *dysfunctional families.*
DERIVATIVES: **dys•func•tion•al•ly** *adv.*

dys•gen•ic |dis'jenik| • *adj.* exerting a detrimental effect on later generations through the inheritance of undesirable characteristics: *dysgenic breeding.* Cf. EUGENICS.

dys•lex•i•a |dis'leksēə| • *n.* a general term for disorders that involve difficulty in learning to read or interpret words, letters, and other symbols, but that do not affect general intelligence.
DERIVATIVES: **dys•lec•tic** |-'lektik| *adj.* & *n.* **dys•lex•ic** |-'leksik| *adj.* & *n.*

dys•pep•tic |dis'peptik| • *adj.* of or having indigestion (dyspepsia) or consequent irritability or depression. • *n.* a person who suffers from indigestion or irritability.

dys•pha•sia |dis'fāZHə| • *n.* language disorder marked by deficiency in the generation of speech, and sometimes also in its comprehension, owing to brain disease or damage.
DERIVATIVES: **dys•pha•sic** |-'fāzik| *adj.*

dys•phe•mism |'disfə,mizəm| • *n.* a derogatory or unpleasant term used instead of a pleasant or neutral one, such as "loony bin" for "mental hospital." Cf. EUPHEMISM.

dys•pho•ri•a |dis'fôrēə| • *n.* a state of unease or generalized dissatisfaction with life. Cf. EUPHORIA.
DERIVATIVES: **dys•phor•ic** |-'fôrik| *adj.* & *n.*

dys•to•pi•a |dis'tōpēə| • *n.* an imagined place or state in which everything is unpleasant or bad, typically a totalitarian or environmentally degraded one. Cf. UTOPIA.
DERIVATIVES: **dys•to•pi•an** *adj.* & *n.*

Ee

earth•bound |'ərTH,bownd| • *adj.* **1** attached or restricted to the earth: *a flightless earthbound bird.*
■ attached or limited to material existence as distinct from a spiritual or heavenly one: *her earthbound view of the sacrament.* ■ lacking in imaginative reach or drive: *an earthbound performance.* **2** moving toward the earth: *an earthbound spaceship.*

earth•ly |'ərTHlē| • *adj.* of or relating to the earth or human life on the earth: *water is liquid at normal earthly temperatures.*
■ of or relating to humankind's material existence as distinct from a spiritual or heavenly one: *all earthly happiness is but vanity.*
DERIVATIVES: **earth•li•ness** *n.*

earth•y |'ərTHē| • *adj.* (**earthier**, **earthiest**) resembling or suggestive of earth or soil: *an earthy smell.*
■ (of a person) direct and uninhibited; hearty: *the storefront is given over to a young, earthy crowd.* ■ (of humor) somewhat coarse or crude: *an earthy story that shocked some listeners.*
DERIVATIVES: **earth•i•ly** *adv.* **earth•i•ness** *n.*

east |ēst| • *n.* (usu. **the east**) (in geography and politics) the eastern part of the world or of a specified country, region, or town: *a factory in the east of the city.*
■ (usu. **the East**) the regions or countries lying to the east of Europe, esp. China, Japan, and India: *the mysterious East.* The **Near East**, originally Balkan states of SE Europe, is now generally regarded as including the countries of SW Asia between the Mediterranean and India. The **Middle East**, in SW Asia and N Africa, includes the Arabian Peninsula and stretches to Pakistan. The **Far East** includes China, Japan, and other E Asian countries. ■ (usu. **the East**) the former communist states of eastern Europe.
DERIVATIVES: **east•ern, East•ern** *adj.*

ebb |eb| • *n.* (usu. **the ebb**) the movement of the tide out to sea: *I knew the tide would be on the ebb* | [as adj.] *the ebb tide.* • *v.* [intrans.] (of tidewater) move away from the land; recede: *the tide began to ebb.*
■ (of an emotion or quality) gradually lessen or reduce: *my enthusiasm was ebbing away.*
PHRASES: **at a low ebb** in a poor state: *the country was at a low ebb due to the recent war.*
ebb and flow a recurrent or rhythmical pattern of coming and going or decline and regrowth.

eb•on |'ebən| • *n.* dark brown or black; ebony: [as adj.] *the dark shadows of the mountains gave the river an ebon hue.*

e•bul•lient |i'boolyənt; i'bəlyənt| • *adj.*
1 bubbling over with enthusiasm or excitement; exuberant: *she sounded ebullient and happy.* **2** (of liquid or other matter) boiling or agitated as if boiling: *misted and ebullient seas.*
DERIVATIVES: **e•bul•lience** *n.* **e•bul•lient•ly** *adv.*

ec•cen•tric |ik'sentrik| • *adj.* **1** (of a person or personal behavior) unconventional or odd: *a whimsical, sometimes eccentric style of dressing.* **2** (of a thing) not placed centrally or not having its axis or other part placed centrally.
■ (of a circle) not centered on the same point as another. ■ (of an orbit) not circular. • *n.*
1 a person of unconventional and slightly strange views or behavior: *he enjoys a colorful reputation as an engaging eccentric.* **2** a disc or wheel mounted eccentrically on a revolving shaft in order to transform rotation into backward-and-forward motion, e.g., a cam in an internal combustion engine.
DERIVATIVES: **ec•cen•tri•cal•ly** *adv.* **ec•cen•tric•i•ty** *n.*

ec•cle•si•as•ti•cal |i,klēzē'æstikəl| (also **ecclesial, ecclesiastic**) • *adj.* of or relating to the Christian Church or its clergy: *the ecclesiastical hierarchy.*
DERIVATIVES: **ec•cle•si•as•ti•cal•ly** *adv.*

ec•dys•i•ast |ek'dēzēəst| • *n.* a striptease performer.
DERIVATIVES: **ec•dys•i•asm** *n.*

ech•e•lon |'esHə,län| • *n.* **1** a level or rank in an organization, a profession, or society: *the upper echelons of the business world.*
■ [often with adj.] a part of a military force dif-

ferentiated by position in battle or by function: *the rear echelon.* **2** a formation of troops, ships, aircraft, or vehicles in parallel rows with the end of each row projecting farther than the one in front. • *v.* [trans.] arrange in an echelon formation: [as n.] (**echeloning**) *the echeloning of equipment.*

ech•o•la•li•a |,ekō'lālēə| • *n.* meaningless repetition of another person's spoken words as a symptom of psychiatric disorder.
■ repetition of speech by a child learning to talk.

echt |ekt| • *adj.* authentic and typical: *the film's opening was an echt pop snob event.* • *adv.* [as submodifier] authentically and typically: *such echt-American writers as Hawthorne and Cooper and Mark Twain.*

é•clair•cisse•ment |ā,klersēs'mänt| • *n.* an enlightening explanation of something, typically someone's conduct, that has been hitherto inexplicable.

é•clat |ā'klä| • *n.* brilliant display or effect: *she came into prominence briefly but with éclat.*
■ social distinction or conspicuous success: *such action bestows more éclat upon a warrior than success by other means.*

ec•lec•tic |i'klektik| • *adj.* **1** deriving ideas, style, or taste from a broad and diverse range of sources: *her musical tastes are eclectic.* **2** (**Eclectic**) of, denoting, or belonging to a class of ancient philosophers who did not belong to or found any recognized school of thought but selected such doctrines as they wished from various schools. • *n.* a person who derives ideas, style, or taste from a broad and diverse range of sources.
DERIVATIVES: **ec•lec•ti•cal•ly** *adv.* **ec•lec•ti•cism** |i'klekti,sizəm| *n.* : *an architect known for his eclecticism.*

e•clipse |i'klips| • *n.* an obscuring of the light from one celestial body by the passage of another between it and the observer or between it and its source of illumination: *an eclipse of the sun.*
■ a loss of significance, power, or prominence in relation to another person or thing: *the election result marked the eclipse of the party's right wing.* • *v.* [trans.] (often **be eclipsed**) (of a celestial body) obscure the light from or to (another celestial body): *as the last piece of the sun was eclipsed by the moon.*
■ obscure or block out (light): *a sea of blue sky violently eclipsed by showers.* ■ deprive (someone or something) of significance, power, or prominence: *health care has eclipsed the environment as the main issue.*

ec•logue |'ek,lôg; 'ek,läg| • *n.* a short poem, esp. a pastoral dialogue.

e•col•o•gy |i'käləjē| • *n.* the branch of biology that deals with the relations of organisms to one another and to their physical surroundings.
DERIVATIVES: **ec•o•log•i•cal** |,ekə'läjəkəl; ,ēkə'läjəkəl| *adj.* **ec•o•log•i•cal•ly** *adv.* **e•col•o•gist** |i'käləjist| *n.*

e•con•o•met•rics |i,känə'metriks| • *plural n.* [treated as sing.] the branch of economics concerned with the use of mathematical methods (esp. statistics) in describing economic systems.

DERIVATIVES: **e•con•o•met•ric** adj. **e•con•o•met•ri•cal** adj. **e•con•o•me•tri•cian** |i‚känəmə'trisHən| n. **e•con•o•met•rist** |i‚känə'metrəst| n.

ec•o•nom•ic |‚ekə'nämik; ‚ēkə-| • adj. of or relating to economics or the economy: *the government's economic policy* | *species of great economic importance.*
■ (of a subject) considered in relation to trade, industry, and the creation of wealth: *economic history.*

USAGE: **Economic** means 'concerning economics': *He's rebuilding a solid economic base for the country's future.* **Economical** is commonly used to mean 'thrifty; avoiding waste': *Small cars should be inexpensive to buy and economical to run.*

ec•o•nom•i•cal |‚ekə'nämikəl; ‚ēkə'nämikəl| • adj. giving good value or service in relation to the amount of money, time, or effort spent: *a small, economical car.*
■ (of a person or lifestyle) careful not to waste money or resources. ■ using no more of something than is necessary: *this chassis is economical in metal and therefore light in weight.*
■ justified in terms of profitability: *many organizations must become larger if they are to remain economic.*

e•con•o•mism |i'känə‚mizəm| • n. belief in the primacy of economic causes or factors.

e•con•o•my |i'känəmē| • n. (pl. **-ies**) **1** the wealth and resources of a country or region, esp. in terms of the production and consumption of goods and services.
■ a particular system or stage of an economy: *a free-market economy* | *the less-developed economies.* **2** careful management of available resources: *effects on heat distribution and fuel economy.*
■ sparing or careful use of something: *economy of words.* ■ (usu. **economies**) a financial saving: *there were many economies to be made by giving up our offices in Manhattan.* ■ (also **economy class**) the cheapest class of air or rail travel: *we flew economy.* • adj. [attrib.] (of a product) offering the best value for the money: [in comb.] *an economy pack.*
■ designed to be economical to use: *an economy car.*

ec•o•sys•tem |'ekō‚sistəm; 'ēkō-| • n. a biological community of interacting organisms and their physical environment.

ec•ru |'ekrōō| • n. the light fawn color of unbleached linen.

ec•sta•sy |'ekstəsē| • n. (pl. **-ies**) **1** an overwhelming feeling of great happiness or joyful excitement. **2** an emotional or religious frenzy or trancelike state, originally one involving an experience of mystic self-transcendence.

ec•to•morph |'ektə‚môrf| • n. a person with a lean and delicate body build. Cf. ENDOMORPH; MESOMORPH.
DERIVATIVES: **ec•to•mor•phic** |‚ektə'môrfik| adj. **ec•to•morph•y** n.

ec•top•ic |ek'täpik| • adj. (in medicine) in an abnormal place or position. • n. an ectopic pregnancy, in which a fetus develops outside the womb, typically in a Fallopian tube.

ec•to•plasm |'ektə‚plæzəm| • n. **1** the viscous, clear outer layer of the material in some cells (e.g., in the amoeba). **2** a supernatural viscous substance that is supposed to exude from the body of a medium during a spiritualistic trance and form the material for the manifestation of spirits.
DERIVATIVES: **ec•to•plas•mic** |‚ektə'plæzmik| adj.

ec•u•men•i•cal |‚ekyə'menikəl| • adj. representing a number of different Christian churches.
■ promoting or relating to unity among the world's Christian churches: *ecumenical dialogue.*
DERIVATIVES: **ec•u•men•i•cal•ly** adv.

ec•u•me•nism |'ekyəmə‚nizəm; e'kyōōmə‚nizəm| • n. the principle or aim of promoting unity among the world's Christian churches.

e•da•cious |i'dāsHəs| • adj. of, relating to, or given to eating.
■ voracious; greedy.
DERIVATIVES: **e•dac•i•ty** |ə'dæsədē; ē'dæsədē| n.

e•de•ma |i'dēmə| (Brit. also **oedema**) • n. a condition characterized by an excess of watery fluid collecting in the cavities or tissues of the body. Also called *dropsy.*
DERIVATIVES: **e•dem•a•tous** |ə'demədəs| adj.

ed•i•fice |'edəfis| • n. a building, esp. a large, imposing one.
■ a complex system of beliefs: *the concepts on which the edifice of capitalism was built.*

ed•i•fy |'edə‚fī| • v. (**-ies, -ied**) [trans.] instruct or improve (someone) morally or intellectually.

e•duce |i'd(y)ōōs| • v. [trans.] bring out or develop (something latent or potential): *out of love obedience is to be educed.*
■ infer (something) from data: *more information can be educed from these statistics.*
DERIVATIVES: **e•duc•i•ble** |ē'd(y)ōōsəbəl; i'd(y)ōōs-| adj. **e•duc•tion** |i'dəksHən| n.

Ed•ward•i•an |ed'wôrdēən; -'wär-| • adj. of, relating to, or characteristic of the reign (1901-10) of Edward VII of England: *the Edwardian era* | *a fine Edwardian house.* • n. a person who lived during this period.

ee•rie |'irē| • adj. (**eerier, eeriest**) strange and frightening: *an eerie green glow in the sky.*
DERIVATIVES: **ee•ri•ly** adv. [as submodifier] *it was eerily quiet.* **ee•ri•ness** n.

ef•face |i'fās| • v. [trans.] erase (a mark) from a surface; cause (something) to disappear: *with time, the words are effaced by the frost and the rain* | *his anger was effaced when he stepped into the open air.*
■ (**efface oneself**) make oneself appear insignificant or inconspicuous.
DERIVATIVES: **ef•face•ment** n.

ef•fect |i'fekt| • n. **1** a change that is a result or consequence of an action or other cause: *the lethal effects of hard drugs.*

■ used to refer to the state of being or becoming operative: *they succeeded in putting their strategies into effect.* ■ the extent to which something succeeds or is operative: *wind power can be used to great effect.* ■ [with adj.] a physical phenomenon, typically named after its discoverer: *the Doppler effect.* ■ an impression produced in the mind of a person: *gentle music can have a soothing effect.* 2 [often in pl.] (**effects**) the lighting, sound, or scenery used in a play, movie, or broadcast: *the production relied too much on spectacular effects.* ■ (**special effects**) illusions created for movies and television by props, camerawork, computer graphics, etc. 3 (**effects**) personal belongings: *the insurance covers personal effects.* • v. [trans.] (often **be effected**) cause (something) to happen; bring about: *budget cuts that were quietly effected over four years.*

USAGE: For the differences in use between **effect** and **affect**, see **usage** at AFFECT.

ef•fec•tive |i'fektiv| • *adj.* 1 successful in producing a desired or intended result: *effective solutions to environmental problems.* ■ (esp. of a law or policy) operative; in force: *the agreements will be effective from November.* 2 [attrib.] fulfilling a specified function in fact, though not formally acknowledged as such: *the companies were under effective government control.* ■ assessed according to actual rather than face value: *an effective price of $176 million.* ■ making a strong impression; striking: *an effective finale.* • *n.* a soldier fit and available for service.
DERIVATIVES: **ef•fec•tive•ness** *n.* **ef•fec•tiv•i•ty** |ˌefek'tivitē; ˌēfek'tivitē| *n.*

ef•fec•tu•al |i'fekCHəwəl| • *adj.* (typically of something inanimate or abstract) successful in producing a desired or intended result; effective: *tobacco smoke is an effectual protection against the mosquito.* ■ (of a legal document) valid or binding.
DERIVATIVES: **ef•fec•tu•al•i•ty** |i,fekCHə'wælitē| *n.* **ef•fec•tu•al•ly** *adv.* **ef•fec•tu•al•ness** *n.*

ef•fec•tu•ate |i'fekCHə,wāt| • *v.* [trans.] put into force or operation: *school choice would effectuate a transfer of power from government to individuals.*
DERIVATIVES: **ef•fec•tu•a•tion** |i,fekCHə'wāSHən| *n.*

ef•fem•i•nate |i'femənət| • *adj.* (of a man) having or showing characteristics regarded as typical of a woman; unmanly.
DERIVATIVES: **ef•fem•i•na•cy** |i'femənə-sē| *n.* **ef•fem•i•nate•ly** *adv.*

ef•fer•ent |'efərənt| • *adj.* (in physiology) conducted or conducting outward or away from something (for nerves, the central nervous system; for blood vessels, the organ supplied).

ef•fer•ves•cent |ˌefər'vesənt| • *adj.* (of a liquid) giving off bubbles; fizzy. ■ (of a person or personal behavior) vivacious and enthusiastic.

DERIVATIVES: **ef•fer•vesce** *v.* **ef•fer•ves•cence** *n.*

ef•fete |i'fēt| • *adj.* 1 affected, overrefined, and ineffectual: *effete trendies from art college.* ■ no longer capable of effective action: *the authority of an effete aristocracy began to dwindle.* 2 no longer fertile; past producing offspring.
DERIVATIVES: **ef•fete•ness** *n.*

ef•fi•ca•cious |ˌefi'kāSHəs| • *adj.* (typically of something inanimate or abstract) successful in producing a desired or intended result; effective: *the vaccine has proved both efficacious and safe.*
DERIVATIVES: **ef•fi•ca•cious•ly** *adv.* **ef•fi•ca•cious•ness** *n.*

ef•fi•ca•cy |'efikəsē| • *n.* the ability to produce a desired or intended result: *there is little information on the efficacy of this treatment.*

ef•fi•cient |i'fiSHənt| • *adj.* (esp. of a system or machine) achieving maximum productivity with minimum effort or expense: *fluorescent lamps are efficient at converting electricity into light.* ■ (of a person) working in a well-organized and competent way: *an efficient administrator.* ■ [in combination] preventing the wasteful use of a particular resource: *an energy-efficient heating system.*
DERIVATIVES: **ef•fi•cien•cy** *n.* **ef•fi•cient•ly** *adv.*

ef•fleu•rage |ˌeflə'räzH| • *n.* a form of massage involving a circular stroking movement made with the palm of the hand. • *v.* [trans.] massage with such a circular stroking movement: *effleurage the shoulders and press gently.*

ef•flo•resce |ˌeflə'res| • *v.* 1 [intrans.] (of a substance) lose moisture and turn to a fine powder upon exposure to air. ■ (of salts) come to the surface of brickwork, rock, or other material and crystallize there. ■ (of a surface) become covered with salt particles. 2 reach a peak of development; blossom: *simple concepts that effloresce into testable conclusions.*
DERIVATIVES: **ef•flo•res•cence** |-'resəns| *n.* **ef•flo•res•cent** *adj.*

ef•flu•ent |'efləwənt| • *n.* liquid waste or sewage discharged into a river or the sea: *the bay was contaminated with the effluent from an industrial site.* • *adj.* that flows forth or out.

ef•flu•vi•um |i'flōōvēəm| • *n.* (pl. **effluvia** |i'flōōvēə|) an unpleasant or harmful odor, secretion, or discharge: *the unwholesome effluvia of decaying vegetable matter.*

ef•fron•ter•y |i'frəntərē| • *n.* insolent or impertinent behavior: *had the effrontery to challenge the coroner's decision.*

ef•ful•gent |i'foŏljənt; i'fəljənt| • *adj.* shining brightly; radiant. ■ (of a person or personal expression) emanating joy or goodness.
DERIVATIVES: **ef•ful•gence** *n.* **ef•ful•gent•ly** *adv.*

ef•fuse • *v.* |i'fyōōz; i'fyōōs| [trans.] give off (a liquid, light, smell, or quality). ■ [intrans.] talk in an unrestrained, excited manner: *this was the type of material that they effused about.*

DERIVATIVES: **ef•fu•sive** *adj.*

ef•fu•sion |iˈfyo͞oZHən| • *n.* an instance of giving off something such as a liquid, light, or smell: *a massive effusion of poisonous gas.* ■ an escape of fluid into a body cavity. Cf. IN-FUSION. ■ an act of talking or writing in an unrestrained or heartfelt way: *literary effusions.*

e•gal•i•tar•i•an |iˌɡæləˈterēən| • *adj.* of, relating to, or believing in the principle that all people are equal and deserve equal rights and opportunities: *a fairer, more egalitarian society.* • *n.* a person who advocates or supports such a principle.

DERIVATIVES: **e•gal•i•tar•i•an•ism** *n.*

e•go |ˈēɡō| • *n.* (pl. **-os**) a person's sense of self-esteem or self-importance: *a boost to my ego.* ■ (in psychoanalysis) the part of the mind that mediates between the conscious and the unconscious and is responsible for reality testing and a sense of personal identity. Cf. ID and SUPEREGO. ■ an overly high opinion of oneself: *some major players with really big egos.* ■ (in metaphysics) a conscious thinking subject.

DERIVATIVES: **e•go•less** *adj.*

e•go•cen•tric |ˌēɡōˈsentrik| • *adj.* thinking only of oneself, without regard for the feelings or desires of others; self-centered: *an egocentric tendency to think of oneself as invulnerable.* ■ centered in or arising from a person's own existence or perspective: *egocentric spatial perception.* • *n.* an egocentric person.

DERIVATIVES: **e•go•cen•tric•al•ly** |-(ə)lē| *adv.* **e•go•cen•tric•i•ty** |ˌēɡōsenˈtrisitē| *n.* **e•go•cen•trism** |ˌēɡōˈsentrizəm| *n.*

e•go•ism |ˈēɡəˌwizəm| • *n.* an ethical theory that treats self-interest as the foundation of morality. ■ another term for EGOTISM.

DERIVATIVES: **e•go•ist** *n.* **e•go•is•tic** |-ˈwistik| *adj.* **e•go•is•ti•cal** |-ˈwistikəl| *adj.* **e•go•is•ti•cal•ly** *adv.*

USAGE: The words **egoism** and **egotism** are frequently confused, as though interchangeable, but there are distinctions worth noting. **Egotism** denotes an excessive sense of self-importance, too-frequent use of the word 'I,' and general arrogance and boastfulness. **Egoism**, a more subtle term, is perhaps best left to ethicists, for whom it denotes a view or theory of moral behavior in which self-interest is the root of moral conduct. An **egoist**, then, might devote considerable attention to introspection, but could be modest about it, whereas an **egotist** would have an exaggerated sense of the importance of his or her self-analysis, and would have to tell everyone.

e•go•ma•ni•a |ˌēɡōˈmānēə| • *n.* obsessive egotism or self-centeredness.

DERIVATIVES: **e•go•ma•ni•ac** |-nē,æk| *n.* **e•go•ma•ni•a•cal** |-məˈnīəkəl| *adj.*

e•go•tism |ˈēɡəˌtizəm| • *n.* the practice of

talking and thinking about oneself excessively because of an undue sense of self-importance: *in his arrogance and egotism, he underestimated others.*

DERIVATIVES: **e•go•tist** *n.* **e•go•tis•tic** |-ˌtistik| *adj.* **e•go•tis•ti•cal** |ˈtistikəl| *adj.* **e•go•tis•ti•cal•ly** |ˈtistik(ə)lē| *adv.* **e•go•tize** |ˈēɡə,tīz| *v.*

e•gre•gious |iˈɡrējəs| • *adj.* **1** outstandingly bad; shocking: *egregious abuses of copyright.* **2** remarkably good.

DERIVATIVES: **e•gre•gious•ly** *adv.* **e•gre•gious•ness** *n.*

e•gress |ˈē,ɡres| • *n.* the action of going out of or leaving a place: *direct means of access and egress for passengers.* ■ a way out: *a narrow egress.* ■ another term for *emersion* (the reappearance of a celestial object after its eclipse). • *v.* [trans.] go out of or leave (a place): *they'd egress the area by heading southwest.*

ei•det•ic |īˈdetik| • *adj.* relating to or denoting mental images having unusual vividness and detail, as if actually visible: *eidetic memory.* • *n.* a person able to form or recall eidetic images.

DERIVATIVES: **ei•det•i•cal•ly** *adv.*

ei•do•lon |īˈdōlən| • *n.* (pl. **eidolons** or **eidola** |īˈdōlə|) **1** an idealized person or thing. **2** a specter or phantom.

ei•dos |ˈīdäs; ˈādäs| • *n.* (pl. **eide** |ˈīdē; ˈādā|) the distinctive expression of the cognitive or intellectual character of a culture or social group.

e•jac•u•late • *v.* |iˈjækyə,lāt| **1** [intrans.] (of a male) eject semen from the body at the moment of sexual climax. **2** [with direct speech] say something quickly and suddenly: *"Indeed?" ejaculated the stranger.* • *n.* |-,lit| semen that has been ejected from the body.

DERIVATIVES: **e•jac•u•la•tion** |iˌjækyə ˈlāSHən| *n.* **e•jac•u•la•tor** |-,lādər| *n.* **e•jac•u•la•to•ry** |-lə,tôrē| *adj.*

e•ject |iˈjekt| • *v.* [trans.] (often **be ejected**) force or throw (something) out, typically in a violent or sudden way: *many types of rock are ejected from volcanoes as solid, fragmentary material.* ■ compel (someone) to leave a place: *angry demonstrators were forcibly ejected from the court.* ■ dismiss (someone), esp. from political office: *he was ejected from office in July.* ■ emit; give off: *plants utilize carbon dioxide in the atmosphere that animals eject* | [as adj.] (**ejected**) *ejected electrons.* ■ [intrans.] (of a pilot) escape from an aircraft by being explosively propelled out of it.

DERIVATIVES: **e•jec•tion** |iˈjekSHən| *n.*

eke |ēk| • *v.* [trans.] (**eke something out**) manage to support oneself or make a living with difficulty: *they eked out their livelihoods from the soil.* ■ make an amount or supply of something last longer by using or consuming it frugally: *the remains of yesterday's stew could be eked out to make another meal.* ■ obtain or create, but just barely: *Tennessee eked out a 74–73 overtime victory.*

e•lab•o•rate • *adj.* |i'læb(ə)rit| involving many carefully arranged parts or details; detailed and complicated in design and planning: *elaborate security precautions | elaborate wrought-iron gates.*
■ (of an action) lengthy and exaggerated: *he made an elaborate pretense of yawning.* • *v.* |i'læbə,rāt| [trans.] develop or present (a theory, policy, or system) in detail: *the key idea of the book is expressed in the title and elaborated in the text.*
■ [intrans.] add more detail concerning what has already been said: *he would not elaborate on his news.*
DERIVATIVES: **e•lab•o•rate•ly** *adv.* **e•lab•o•rate•ness** *n.* **e•lab•o•ra•tion** |i,læbə'rā-SHən| *n.* **e•lab•o•ra•tive** |i'læbə,rātiv| *adj.* **e•lab•o•ra•tor** *n.*

é•lan |ā'län; ā'læn| • *n.* energy, style, and enthusiasm: *a rousing march, played with great élan.*

e•las•tic |i'læstik| • *adj.* (of an object or material) able to resume its normal shape spontaneously after contraction, expansion, or distortion.
■ able to encompass variety and change; flexible and adaptable: *the definition of nationality is elastic in this cosmopolitan country.* ■ springy and buoyant: *Annie returned with beaming eyes and elastic step.* ■ (of demand or supply) sensitive to changes in price or income: *the labor supply is elastic | the somewhat more elastic demand for lawn services.* ■ (in physics, of a collision) involving no decrease of kinetic energy. • *n.* cord, tape, or fabric, typically woven with strips of rubber, that returns to its original length or shape after being stretched.
DERIVATIVES: **e•las•ti•cal•ly** |-(ə)lē| *adv.* **e•las•tic•i•ty** |i,læ'stisitē; ē,læ-| *n.* **e•las•ti•cize** |i'læstə,sīz| *v.*

e•late |i'lāt| • *v.* [trans.] [usu. as adj.] (**elated**) make (someone) ecstatically happy: *I felt elated at beating Dennis.* • *adj.* in high spirits; exultant or proud: *the ladies returned with elate and animated faces.*
DERIVATIVES: **e•lat•ed•ly** |i'lātidlē| *adv.* **e•lat•ed•ness** *n.*

el•dritch |'eldriCH| • *adj.* weird and sinister or ghostly: *an eldritch screech.*

e•lect |i'lekt| • *v.* [trans.] (in Christian theology, of God) choose (someone) in preference to others for salvation. • *adj.* chosen by God for salvation.

e•lec•tor•al |i'lektərəl| • *adj.* of or relating to elections or electors: *electoral reform.*
DERIVATIVES: **e•lec•tor•al•ly** *adv.*

e•lec•tron |i'lekträn| • *n.* (in physics) a stable subatomic particle with a charge of negative electricity, found in all atoms and acting as the primary carrier of electricity in solids.

e•lec•tron•ic |ilek'tränik; ,ēlek-| • *adj.* **1** (of a device) having, or operating with the aid of, many small components, esp. microchips and transistors, that control and direct an electric current: *an electronic calculator.*
■ (of music) produced by electronic instruments. ■ of or relating to electronics: *a degree in electronic engineering.* **2** of or relating to electrons. **3** relating to or carried out using a computer or other electronic device, esp. over a network: *electronic banking.*
DERIVATIVES: **e•lec•tron•i•cal•ly** |-(ə)lē| *adv.*

e•lec•tron•ics |ilek'träniks; ,ēlek-| • *plural n.* [usu. treated as sing.] the branch of physics and technology concerned with the design of circuits using transistors and microchips, and with the behavior and movement of electrons in a semiconductor, conductor, vacuum, or gas: *electronics is seen as a growth industry |* [as adj.] *electronics engineers.*
■ [treated as pl.] circuits or devices using transistors, microchips, and other components.

el•ee•mos•y•nar•y |,elə'mäsə,nerē; ,elēə-| • *adj.* of, relating to, or dependent on charity; charitable.

el•e•gi•ac |,elə'jīək; e'lējē,æk| • *adj.* (esp. of a work of art) having a mournful quality: *the movie score is a somber effort, elegiac in its approach.*
■ (of a poetic meter) used for elegies. • *plural n.* (**elegiacs**) verses in an elegiac meter.
DERIVATIVES: **el•e•gi•a•cal•ly** *adv.*

el•e•gy |'eləjē| • *n.* (pl. **-ies**) **1** a poem of serious reflection, typically a lament for the dead. Cf. EULOGY.
■ a piece of music in a mournful style. **2** (in Greek and Roman poetry) a poem written in elegiac couplets, as notably by Catullus and Propertius.

el•e•phan•tine |,elə'fæntēn; -,tīn; 'eləfən,tēn; -,tīn| • *adj.* of, resembling, or characteristic of an elephant or elephants, as in being large, clumsy, or awkward; in strength; or in supposed power of memory: *there was an elephantine thud from the bathroom. | elephantine recall of detail.*

e•lic•it |i'lisit| • *v.* (**elicited, eliciting**) [trans.] evoke or draw out (a response, answer, or fact) from someone in reaction to one's own actions or questions: *they invariably elicit exclamations of approval from guests.*
■ draw forth (something that is latent or potential) into existence: *a corrupt heart elicits in an hour all that is bad in us.*
DERIVATIVES: **e•lic•i•ta•tion** |i,lisi'tāSHən| *n.* **e•lic•i•tor** |-itər| *n.*

e•lide |i'līd| • *v.* [trans.] omit (a sound or syllable) when speaking: [as adj.] (**elided**) *these marks indicate elided consonants or vowels.*
■ join; merge: *whole periods of time are elided into a few seconds of screen time |* [intrans.] *the two things elided in his mind.*

USAGE: The standard meaning of the verb **elide** is 'omit,' most frequently used as a term to describe the way that some sounds or syllables are dropped in speech, as for example in contractions such as **I'll** or **he's.** The result of such omission (or **elision**) is that the two surrounding syllables are merged; this fact has given rise to a new sense, with the meaning 'join; merge,' as in *the two things **elided** in his mind.* This new sense is now common in general use.

e•lite |ə'lēt; ā'lēt| • *n.* **1** a group of people considered to be the best in a particular society or category, esp. because of their power, talent, or wealth: *China's educated elite* | [as adj.] *an elite combat force.* **2** a size of letter in typewriting, with 12 characters to the inch (about 4.7 to the centimeter).
DERIVATIVES: **e•lit•ist** *adj., n.*

e•lit•ism |ə'lētizəm| • *n.* **1** advocacy or existence of an elite as a dominant element in a system or society. **2** the attitude or behavior or a person or group who regard themselves as belonging to an elite.

e•lix•ir |i'liksər| • *n.* a magical or medicinal potion: *an elixir guaranteed to induce love.*
■ a preparation that was supposedly able to change metals into gold, sought by alchemists. ■ (also **elixir of life**) a preparation supposedly able to prolong life indefinitely. ■ a medicinal solution of a specified type: *the cough elixir is a natural herbal expectorant.*

el•lipse |i'lips| • *n.* a regular oval shape, traced by a point moving in a plane so that the sum of its distances from two other points (the foci) is constant, or resulting when a cone is cut by an oblique plane that does not intersect the base.

el•lip•sis |i'lipsis| • *n.* (pl. **ellipses** |i'lipsēz|) the omission from speech or writing of a word or words that are superfluous or able to be understood from contextual clues.
■ a set of dots indicating such an omission.

el•lip•ti•cal (also **elliptic**) |i'liptik| • *adj.* **1** of, relating to, or having the form of an ellipse. **2** (usu. **elliptical**) (of speech or writing) lacking a word or words, esp. when the sense can be understood from contextual clues.
■ difficult to understand because not clearly or fully expressed; cryptic.
DERIVATIVES: **el•lip•ti•cal•ly** |-(ə)lē| *adv.*

el•o•cu•tion |,elə'kyōōSHən| • *n.* the skill of clear and expressive speech, esp. of distinct pronunciation and articulation. Cf. LOCUTION.
■ a particular style of speaking.
DERIVATIVES: **el•o•cu•tion•ar•y** |-,nerē| *adj.* **el•o•cu•tion•ist** |-ist| *n.*

el•o•quence |'eləkwəns| • *n.* fluent or persuasive speaking or writing: *a preacher of great power and eloquence.*
■ the art or manner of such speech or writing.
DERIVATIVES: **el•o•quent** *adj.* **el•o•quent•ly** *adv.*

e•lu•ci•date |i'lōōsi,dāt| • *v.* [trans.] make (something) clear; explain: *a work that helps to elucidate this issue* | [with clause] *in what follows I shall try to elucidate what I believe the problems to be* | [intrans.] *they would not elucidate further.*
DERIVATIVES: **e•lu•ci•da•tion** |i,lōōsi 'dāSHən| *n.* **e•lu•ci•da•tive** |-,dātiv| *adj.* **e•lu•ci•da•tor** |-,dātər| *n.* **e•lu•ci•da•to•ry** |-də,tôrē| *adj.*

e•lu•sive |i'lōōsiv| (also **elusory**) • *adj.* difficult to find, catch, or achieve: *success will become ever more elusive.*
■ difficult to remember or recall: *the elusive thought he had had moments before.*
DERIVATIVES: **e•lu•sive•ly** *adv.* **e•lu•sive• ness** *n.*

E•ly•sian |i'lizHən; i'lēzHən| • *adj.* of, relating to, or characteristic of heaven or paradise: *Elysian visions.*
PHRASES: **the Elysian Fields** another name for *Elysium* (in Greek mythology, the home of the blessed after death).

e•ma•ci•ate |i'māsHē,āt| • *v.* [trans.] [usu. as adj.] (**emaciated**) make abnormally thin or weak, esp. because of illness or a lack of food: *she was so emaciated she could hardly stand.*
DERIVATIVES: **e•ma•ci•a•tion** |i,māsHē'ā-sHən| *n.*

em•a•nate |'emə,nāt| • *v.* [intrans.] (**emanate from**) (of something intangible but perceptible, or abstract) issue or spread out from (a source): *warmth emanated from the fireplace* | *she felt an undeniable charm emanating from him.*
■ originate from; be produced by: *the proposals emanated from a committee.* ■ [trans.] give out or emit (something intangible or abstract but perceptible): *he emanated a powerful brooding air.*
DERIVATIVES: **em•a•na•tive** |-,nativ| *adj.* **em•a•na•tor** |-,nātər| *n.*

em•a•na•tion |,emə'nāSHən| • *n.* an intangible or abstract but perceptible thing that issues or originates from a source: *she saw the insults as emanations of his own tortured personality.* | *the fetid emanation from a pile of old clothes.*
■ the action or process of issuing from a source: *the risk of radon gas emanation.* ■ a tenuous substance or form of radiation given off by something: *vaporous emanations surround the mill's foundations.* ■ a radioactive gas formed by radioactive decay of a solid. ■ a body or organization that has its source or takes its authority from another: *the commission is an emanation of the state.* ■ (in various mystical traditions) a being or force that is a manifestation of God.

e•man•ci•pate |i'mansə,pāt| • *v.* [trans.] set free, esp. from legal, social, or political restrictions: *the citizen must be emancipated from the obsessive secrecy of government* | [as adj.] (**emancipated**) *emancipated young women.*
■ (in law) set (a child) free from the authority of its father or parents. ■ free from slavery: *it is estimated that he emancipated 8,000 slaves.*
DERIVATIVES: **e•man•ci•pa•tion** |i,mansə 'pāSHən| *n.* **e•man•ci•pa•tor** |-,pātər| *n.* **e•man•ci•pa•to•ry** |-pə,tôrē| *adj.*

e•mas•cu•late |i'mæskyə,lāt| • *v.* [trans.] make (a person, idea, or piece of legislation) weaker or less effective: *our winner-take-all elections emasculate third parties.*
■ [usu. as adj.] (**emasculated**) deprive (a man) of his male role or identity: *he feels emasculated, because he cannot control his sons' behavior.* ■ castrate (a man or male animal). ■ remove the anthers from a flower.
DERIVATIVES: **e•mas•cu•la•tion** |i,mæs-kyə'lāSHən| *n.* **e•mas•cu•la•tor** |-,lātər| *n.* **e•mas•cu•la•to•ry** |-lə,tôrē| *adj.*

em•balm |em'bä(l)m| • *v.* [trans.] **1** [often as n.] (**embalming**) preserve (a corpse) from decay, originally with spices and now usually by arterial injection of a preservative: *the Egyptian method of embalming.* ■ preserve (someone or something) in an unaltered state: *the band was all about embalming the legacy of certain pop greats.* **2** give a pleasant fragrance to: *the sweetness of the linden trees embalmed all the air.* DERIVATIVES: **em•balm•er** *n.* **em•balm•ment** *n.*

em•bar•go |em'bärgō| • *n.* (pl. **-oes**) an official ban on trade or other commercial activity with a particular country: *an embargo on grain sales* | *the oil embargo of 1973.* ■ an official prohibition on any (specified) activity. ■ an order of a state forbidding foreign ships to enter, or any ships to leave, its ports. ■ a stoppage, prohibition, or impediment. • *v.* (**-oes, -oed**) [trans.] **1** (usu. **be embargoed**) impose an official ban on (trade or a country or commodity): *the country has been virtually embargoed since the 1960s.* ■ officially ban the publication of: *documents of national security importance are routinely embargoed.* **2** seize (a ship or goods) for state service.

em•bed |em'bed| (also **imbed**) • *v.* (**embedded, embedding**) [trans.] (often **be embedded**) fix (an object) firmly and deeply in a surrounding mass: *there was shrapnel embedded in his chest.* ■ implant (an idea or feeling) within something else so it becomes an ingrained or essential characteristic of it: *the Victorian values embedded in Tennyson's poetry.* ■ place (a phrase or clause) within another clause or sentence. ■ incorporate (a text or code) within the body of a computer file or document. ■ [often as adj.] (**embedded**) design and build (a microprocessor) as an integral part of a computer system or device. DERIVATIVES: **em•bed•ment** *n.*

em•bel•lish |em'belisH| • *v.* [trans.] make (something) more attractive by the addition of decorative details or features: *blue silk embellished with golden embroidery.* ■ make (a statement or story) more interesting or entertaining by adding extra details, esp. ones that are not true: *she had difficulty telling the truth because she liked to embellish things.* DERIVATIVES: **em•bel•lish•er** *n.* **em•bel•lish•ment** *n.*

em•bez•zle |em'bezəl| • *v.* [trans.] steal or misappropriate (money placed in one's trust or belonging to the organization for which one works): *she had embezzled $5,600,000 in company funds.* DERIVATIVES: **em•bez•zle•ment** *n.* **em•bez•zler** |em'bezlər|.

em•bla•zon |em'blāzn| • *v.* [with obj. and adverbial of place] (often **be emblazoned**) conspicuously inscribe or display (a design) on something: *T-shirts emblazoned with the names of baseball teams.* ■ depict (a heraldic device): *the Queen's coat of arms is emblazoned on the door panel.* ■ celebrate or extol publicly. DERIVATIVES: **em•bla•zon•ment** *n.*

em•blem |'embləm| • *n.* a heraldic device or symbolic object as a distinctive badge of a nation, organization, or family: *America's national emblem, the bald eagle.* ■ (**emblem of**) a thing serving as a symbolic representation of a particular quality or concept: *our child would be a dazzling emblem of our love.* DERIVATIVES: **em•blem•at•ic** |,emblə'mætik| *adj.* **em•blem•at•i•cal** *adj.* **em•blem•at•i•cal•ly** *adv.*

em•bod•i•ment |em'bädēmənt; im-| • *n.* a tangible or visible form of an idea, quality, or feeling: *she seemed a living embodiment of vitality.* ■ the representation or expression of something in such a form: *it was in Germany alone that his hope seemed capable of embodiment.*

em•bo•lism |'embə,lizəm| • *n.* obstruction of an artery, typically by a clot of blood or an air bubble.

em•bon•point |,änbôN'pwæN| • *n.* the plump or fleshy part of a person's body, in particular a woman's bosom. ■ plumpness.

em•boss |em'bôs; -'bäs| • *v.* [trans.] [usu. as adj.] (**embossed**) carve or mold a design on (a surface) so that it stands out in relief: *an embossed brass dish.* ■ decorate (a surface) with a raised design. DERIVATIVES: **em•boss•er** *n.* **em•boss•ment** *n.*

em•bou•chure |,änboō'sHoōr| • *n.* **1** the way in which a player applies the mouth to the mouthpiece of a brass or wind musical instrument. ■ the mouthpiece of a flute or a similar instrument. ■ the quality of a brass or wind player's lip or mouth control: *trying to get his embouchure back.* **2** the mouth of a river or valley.

em•bra•sure |em'brāzHər| • *n.* the beveling or splaying of a wall at the sides of a door or window. ■ a small opening in a parapet of a fortified building, splayed on the inside. DERIVATIVES: **em•bra•sured** *adj.*

em•bro•ca•tion |,embrə'kāsHən| • *n.* a liquid used for rubbing on the body to relieve pain from sprains and strains. DERIVATIVES: **em•bro•cate** *v.*

em•broil |em'broil| • *v.* [trans.] [often as adj.] (**embroiled**) involve (someone) deeply in an argument, conflict, or difficult situation: *she became embroiled in a dispute with her landlord.* ■ bring into a state of confusion or disorder. DERIVATIVES: **em•broil•ment** *n.*

em•bry•o |'embrē,ō| • *n.* (pl. **-os**) an unborn or unhatched offspring in the process of development. ■ an unborn human baby, esp. in the first eight weeks from conception, after implantation but before all the organs are developed. Cf. FETUS. ■ the part of a seed that develops into a plant, consisting (in the mature embryo of a higher plant) of a plumule, a radicle, and one or two cotyledons. ■ a thing at a rudimentary stage that shows potential for development: *a simple commodity economy is merely the embryo of a capitalist economy.*

em•bry•on•ic |ˌembrēˈänik| • *adj.* (also **embryonal**) of or relating to an embryo.
■ (of a system, idea, or organization) in a rudimentary stage with potential for further development: *the plan is still in its embryonic stages.*
DERIVATIVES: **em•bry•on•i•cal•ly** |-(ə)lē| *adv.*

e•mend |iˈmend| • *v.* [trans.] make corrections and improvements to (a text).
■ alter (something) in such a way as to correct it: *the year of his death might need to be emended to 652* | [with clause] *he hesitated and quickly emended what he had said.*
DERIVATIVES: **e•mend•a•ble** *adj.* **e•men•da•tion** |ˌēmənˈdāsʜən; ˌemən-| *n.* **e•mend•er** *n.*

e•mer•i•tus |iˈmerətəs| • (fem. **emerita**) *adj.* (of the former holder of an office, esp. a university professor) having retired but allowed to retain his or her title as an honor: *emeritus professor of microbiology* | [postpositive] *the gallery's director emeritus.*

e•met•ic |iˈmetik| • *adj.* (of a substance) causing vomiting.
■ nauseating or revolting: *the emetic music played in department stores.* • *n.* a medicine or other substance that causes vomiting.

em•i•grate |ˈemiˌgrāt| • *v.* [intrans.] leave one's own country in order to settle permanently in another: *Rose's parents emigrated to Australia.*
DERIVATIVES: **em•i•gra•tion** |ˌemiˈgrāsʜən| *n.*

USAGE: To **emigrate** is to leave a country, esp. one's own, intending to remain away. To **immigrate** is to enter a country, intending to remain there. From the point of view of the receiving country, one might say: *My aunt emigrated from Poland and immigrated into Canada.*

é•mi•gré |ˈemiˌgrā| • *n.* a person who has left their own country in order to settle in another, usually for political reasons.

em•i•nence |ˈemənəns| • *n.* **1** fame or recognized superiority, esp. within a particular sphere or profession: *her eminence in cinematography.*
■ an important, influential, or distinguished person: *they canvassed the views of various legal eminences.* ■ **(His/Your Eminence)** a title given to a Roman Catholic cardinal, or used in addressing him: *His Eminence, John Cardinal O'Connor.* **2** a piece of rising ground: *an eminence commanding a view of the river.*
■ a slight projection from the surface of a part of the body.

éminence grise |ˌemənəns ˈgrēz| • *n.* (pl. **éminences grises** pronunc. same) a person who exercises power or influence in a certain sphere without holding an official position.

em•i•nent |ˈemənənt| • *adj.* (of a person) famous and respected within a particular

sphere or profession: *one of the world's most eminent statisticians.*
■ used to emphasize the presence of a positive quality: *the guitar's eminent suitability for recording-studio work.*
DERIVATIVES: **em•i•nent•ly** *adv.* [as submodifier] *an eminently readable textbook.*

USAGE: **Eminent** means 'outstanding; famous': *The book was written by an **eminent** authority on folk art.* **Imminent** means 'about to happen': *People brushed aside the possibility that war was **imminent**.* **Immanent**, often used in religious or philosophical contexts, means 'inherent': *He believed in the **immanent** unity of nature taught by the Hindus.*

em•i•nent do•main • *n.* (in law) the power of a government or its agent to expropriate private property for public use, with payment of compensation. In the US it is used of federal and state governments.

em•is•sar•y |ˈeməˌserē| • *n.* (pl. **-ies**) a person sent on a special mission, usually as a diplomatic representative.

e•mol•lient |iˈmälyənt| • *adj.* having the quality of softening or soothing the skin: *an emollient cream.*
■ attempting to avoid confrontation or anger; soothing or calming: *the president's emollient approach to disputes.* • *n.* a preparation that softens the skin: *formulated with rich emollients.*
DERIVATIVES: **e•mol•lience** *n.*

e•mol•u•ment |iˈmälyəmənt| • *n.* (usu. **emoluments**) a salary, fee, or profit from employment or office: *the directors' emoluments.*

e•mo•tive |iˈmōtiv| • *adj.* arousing or able to arouse intense feeling: *an emotive subject* | *the issue has proved highly emotive.*
■ expressing one's feelings rather than being neutrally or objectively descriptive: *the comparisons are emotive rather than analytic.*
DERIVATIVES: **e•mo•tive•ly** *adv.* **e•mo•tive•ness** *n.* **e•mo•tiv•i•ty** |ˌēmōˈtivitē| *n.*

USAGE: The words **emotive** and **emotional** share similarities but are not interchangeable. **Emotive** is used to mean 'arousing intense feeling,' while **emotional** tends to mean 'characterized by intense feeling.' Thus an **emotive** issue is one likely to arouse people's passions, while an **emotional** response is one that is itself full of passion.

em•pa•thy |ˈempəᴛʜē| • *n.* the ability to understand and share the feelings of another. Cf. SYMPATHY.
DERIVATIVES: **em•pa•thet•ic** |ˌempəˈᴛʜetik| *adj.* **em•pa•thet•i•cal•ly** |ˌempəˈᴛʜetik(ə)lē| *adv.* **em•path•ic** |emˈpæᴛʜik| *adj.* **em•path•i•cal•ly** |emˈpæᴛʜik(ə)lē| *adv.* **em•pa•thize** *v.*

em•phat•ic |emˈfætik| • *adj.* showing or giving emphasis; expressing something forcibly and clearly: *the children were emphatic that they wanted to go with us* | *an emphatic movement of his hand.*

■ (of an action or event or its result) definite and clear: *he walked stiffly, with an emphatic limp.* ■ (of word or syllable) bearing the stress.

em•pir•i•cal |em'pirikəl| • *adj.* based on, concerned with, or verifiable by observation or experience rather than theory or pure logic: *they provided considerable empirical evidence to support their argument.*
DERIVATIVES: **em•pir•i•cal•ly** *adv.*

em•pir•i•cism |em'pirə,sizəm| • *n.* the theory that all knowledge is derived from sense-experience. Stimulated by the rise of experimental science, it developed in the 17th and 18th centuries, expounded in particular by John Locke, George Berkeley, and David Hume.
■ practice based on experiment and observation. ■ formerly, ignorant or unscientific practice; quackery.
DERIVATIVES: **em•pir•i•cist** *n.* & *adj.*

em•po•ri•um |em'pôrēəm| • *n.* (pl. **emporiums** or **emporia** |em'pôrēə|) a large retail store selling a wide variety of goods.
■ a business establishment that specializes in products or services on a large scale (often used for humorously formal effect): *a Chinese food emporium.* ■ a principal center of commerce; a market.

em•py•re•an |em'pirēən|; ,empə'rēən| (also **empyreal**) • *adj.* belonging to or deriving from heaven. • *n.* (**the empyrean**) heaven, in particular the highest part of heaven.
■ the visible heavens; the sky.

em•u•late |'emyə,lāt| • *v.* [trans.] match or surpass (a person or achievement), typically by imitation: *lesser men trying to emulate his greatness.*
■ imitate: *hers is not a hairstyle I wish to emulate.*
DERIVATIVES: **em•u•la•tion** |,emyə'lā-shən| *n.* **em•u•la•tive** |-,lātiv| *adj.* **em•u•la•tor** |-,lātər| *n.*

e•mul•sion |i'məlshən| • *n.* a fine dispersion of minute droplets of one liquid in another in which it is not soluble or miscible.
■ a light-sensitive coating for photographic films and plates, containing crystals of a silver compound dispersed in a medium such as gelatin.
DERIVATIVES: **e•mul•si•fy** *v.* **e•mul•si•fi•er** *n.* **e•mul•si•fi•ca•tion** *n.* **e•mul•sive** |-siv| *adj.*

en•am•or |i'næmər| (chiefly Brit. **enamour**) • *v.* (**be enamored of/with/by**) be filled with a feeling of love for: *it is not difficult to see why Edward is enamored of her.*
■ be charmed or delighted by: *she was truly enamored of New York.*

en•ceinte • *adj.* pregnant.

en•clave |'en,klāv; 'äNG-| • *n.* a portion of territory within or surrounded by a larger territory whose inhabitants are culturally or ethnically distinct.
■ a place or group that is different in character from those surrounding it: *the engineering department is traditionally a male enclave.* • *v.* [trans.] surround and isolate; make an enclave of.

en•clit•ic |en'klitik| • *n.* (in linguistics) a word pronounced with so little emphasis that it is shortened and forms part of the preceding word, e.g., *n't* in *can't*. • *adj.* denoting or relating to such a word.
DERIVATIVES: **en•clit•i•cal•ly** |-(ə)lē| *adv.*

en•co•mi•ast |en'kōmē,æst| • *n.* a person who publicly praises or flatters someone else.
DERIVATIVES: **en•co•mi•as•tic** |en,kōmē 'æstik| *adj.* **en•co•mi•as•ti•cal•ly** |en,kōmē 'astik(ə)lē| *adv.*

en•co•mi•um |en'kōmēəm| • *n.* (pl. **encomiums** or **encomia** |-mēə|) a speech or piece of writing that praises someone or something highly.

en•com•pass |en'kəmpəs| • *v.* **1** [trans.] surround and have or hold within: *a vast halo encompassing the Milky Way galaxy.*
■ include comprehensively: *no studies encompass all aspects of medical care.* **2** cause (something) to take place: *an act designed to encompass the death of the king.*
DERIVATIVES: **en•com•pass•ment** *n.*

en•croach |en'krōCH| • *v.* [intrans.] (**encroach on/upon**) intrude on (a person's territory or a thing considered to be a right): *he didn't want his privacy encroached upon.*
■ advance gradually and in a way that causes damage: *the sea has encroached all around the coast.*
DERIVATIVES: **en•croach•er** *n.* **en•croach•ment** *n.*

en•crypt |en'kript| • *v.* [trans.] convert (information or data) into a cipher or code, esp. to prevent unauthorized access.
■ (**encrypt something in**) conceal information or data in something by this means.
DERIVATIVES: **en•cryp•tion** |-'kripshən| *n.*

en•cum•ber |en'kəmbər| • *v.* [trans.] (often **be encumbered**) restrict or burden (someone or something) in such a way that free action or movement is difficult: *she was encumbered by her heavy skirts | they had arrived encumbered with families.*
■ saddle (a person or estate) with a debt or mortgage: *an estate heavily encumbered with debt.* ■ fill or block up (a place): *we tripped over sticks and stones, which encumber most of the trail.*
DERIVATIVES: **en•cum•brance** *n.*

en•cy•clo•pe•dic |en,sīklə'pēdik| (also chiefly Brit. **encyclopaedic**) • *adj.* comprehensive in terms of information: *he has an almost encyclopedic knowledge of food.*
■ relating to or containing names of famous people and places and information about words that is not simply linguistic: *a dictionary with encyclopedic material.*
DERIVATIVES: **en•cy•clo•pe•di•cal•ly** *adv.*

en•dem•ic |en'demik| • *adj.* **1** (of a disease or condition) regularly found among particular people or in a certain area: *areas where malaria is endemic | complacency is endemic in industry today.* **2** (of a plant or animal) native or restricted to a certain country or area: *a marsupial endemic to northeastern Australia.* • *n.* an endemic plant or animal.

■ an endemic disease.
DERIVATIVES: **en•dem•i•cal•ly** |-(ə)lē|
adv. **en•de•mic•i•ty** |ˌendəˈmisiṯē| *n.* **en•de•mism** |ˈendəˌmizəm| *n.* (in sense 2 of the adjective).

USAGE: On the difference between **endemic, epidemic,** and **pandemic,** see usage at EPIDEMIC.

en•do•crine |ˈendəkrin| • *adj.* of, relating to, or denoting glands that secrete hormones or other products directly into the blood: *the endocrine system.* • *n.* an endocrine gland: *the pituitary is sometimes called the "master gland" of the endocrines.*

en•dog•a•my |enˈdägəmē| • *n.* the custom of marrying only within the limits of a local community, clan, or tribe. Cf. EXOGAMY.
■ (in biology) the fusion of reproductive cells from related individuals; inbreeding; self-pollination.
DERIVATIVES: **en•do•gam•ic** |ˌendōˈgæmik| *adj.* **en•dog•a•mous** |-gəməs| *adj.*

en•dog•e•nous |enˈdäjənəs| • *adj.* having an internal cause or origin: *the expected rate of infection is endogenous to the system.* Cf. EXOGENOUS.
■ growing or originating from within an organism: *endogenous gene sequences.* ■ (of a disease or symptom) not attributable to any external or environmental factor: *endogenous depression.* ■ confined within a group or society.
DERIVATIVES: **en•dog•e•nous•ly** *adv.*

en•do•morph |ˈendəˌmôrf| • *n.* **1** a person with a soft round body build and a high proportion of fat tissue. Cf. ECTOMORPH, MESOMORPH. **2** a mineral or crystal enclosed within another.
DERIVATIVES: **en•do•mor•phic** |ˌendəˈmôrfik| *adj.* **en•do•mor•phy** |ˈendəˌmôrfē| *n.*

en•do•plasm |ˈendōˌplæzəm| • *n.* Biology, dated the more fluid, granular inner layer of the cytoplasm in amoeboid cells. Cf. ECTOPLASM (sense 1).

en•dor•phin |enˈdôrfin| • *n.* any of a group of hormones secreted within the brain and nervous system and having a number of physiological functions. They are peptides (amino acid compounds) that activate the body's opiate receptors and inhibit pain.

en•dorse |enˈdôrs| (also **indorse**) • *v.* [trans.] **1** declare one's public approval or support of: *the report was endorsed by the college.*
■ recommend (a product) in an advertisement. **2** sign (a check or bill of exchange) on the back to make it payable to someone other than the stated payee or to accept responsibility for paying it.
■ (usu. **be endorsed on**) write (a comment) on the front or back of a document.
DERIVATIVES: **en•dors•a•ble** *adj.* **en•dors•er** *n.*

en•due |enˈd(y)o͞o| • *v.* (**endues, endued, enduing**) [trans.] endow or provide with a quality or ability: *our sight would be endued with a far greater sharpness.*

en•er•gize |ˈenərˌjīz| • *v.* [trans.] give vitality and enthusiasm to: *people were energized by his ideas.*
■ supply energy, typically kinetic or electrical energy, to (something).
DERIVATIVES: **en•er•giz•er** *n.*

en•er•vate |ˈenərˌvāt| • *v.* [trans.] cause (someone) to feel drained of energy or vitality; weaken. • *adj.* lacking in energy or vitality: *the enervate slightness of his frail form.*
DERIVATIVES: **en•er•va•tion** |ˌenərˈvāSHən| *n.* **en•er•va•tor** |-ˌvāṯər| *n.*

en•fant ter•ri•ble |änˌfän teˈrēbl(ə)| • *n.* (pl. **enfants terribles** pronunc. same) a person whose unconventional or controversial behavior or ideas shock, embarrass, or annoy others.

en•fi•lade |ˈenfəˌlād; -ˌläd| • *n.* **1** a volley of gunfire directed along a line from end to end. **2** a suite of rooms with doorways in line with each other. • *v.* [trans.] direct a volley of gunfire along the length of (a target).

en•fran•chise |enˈfrænˌCHīz| • *v.* [trans.] give the right to vote to: *a proposal that foreigners should be enfranchised for local elections.*
■ (in British history) give (a town) the right to be represented in Parliament. ■ free (a slave).
DERIVATIVES: **en•fran•chise•ment** *n.*

en•gage |enˈgāj| • *v.* **1** [trans.] occupy, attract, or involve (someone's interest or attention): *he plowed on, trying to outline his plans and engage Sutton's attention.*
■ (**engage someone in**) cause someone to become involved in (a conversation or discussion). ■ arrange to employ or hire (someone): *she was engaged as a copywriter.* ■ [with infinitive] pledge or enter into a contract to do something: *he engaged to pay them $10,000 against a bond.* ■ reserve (accommodations, a place, etc.) in advance: *he had engaged a small boat.* **2** [intrans.] (**engage in**) participate or become involved in: *organizations engage in a variety of activities* | (**be engaged in**) *some are actively engaged in crime.*
■ (**engage with**) establish a meaningful contact or connection with: *all our branches need to engage with local communities.* ■ (of a part of a machine or engine) move into position so as to come into operation: *the clutch will not engage.* ■ [trans.] cause (a part of a machine or engine) to do this. ■ [trans.] (of fencers or swordsmen) bring (weapons) together preparatory to fighting. ■ [trans.] enter into conflict or combat with (an adversary).

en•ga•gé |ˌänGgäˈzHā| • *adj.* (of a writer, artist, or works) morally committed to a particular aim or cause.

en•gen•der |ənˈjendər| • *v.* [trans.] cause or give rise to (a feeling, situation, or condition): *the issue engendered continuing controversy.*
■ (of a father) beget (offspring). ■ [intrans.] come into being; arise.

en•gorge |enˈgôrj| • *v.* **1** [trans.] cause to swell with blood, water, or another fluid: *the river was engorged by a day-long deluge.*
■ [intrans.] become swollen in this way. **2** (**engorge oneself**) eat to excess.
DERIVATIVES: **en•gorge•ment** *n.*

en•gram |'engræm| • *n.* a hypothetical permanent change in the brain accounting for the existence of memory; a memory trace.
DERIVATIVES: **en•gram•mat•ic** |,engrə'mætik| *adj.*

en•gross |en'grōs| • *v.* [trans.] **1** absorb all the attention or interest of: *the notes totally engrossed him.*
■ gain or keep exclusive possession of (something): *the country had made the best of its position to engross trade.* [ORIGIN: from Old French *en gros*, from medieval Latin *in grosso* 'wholesale.'] **2** produce (a legal document) in its final or definitive form.
■ reproduce (a document, etc.) in larger letters or larger format. [ORIGIN: from Anglo-Norman French *engrosser*, medieval Latin *ingrossare* (from Old French *grosse*, medieval Latin *grossa* 'large writing').]
DERIVATIVES: **en•gross•ment** *n.*

en•hance |en'hæns| • *v.* [trans.] intensify, increase, or further improve the quality, value, or extent of: *his refusal does nothing to enhance his reputation* | *computer techniques that enhance images.*
DERIVATIVES: **en•hance•ment** *n.* **en•hanc•er** *n.*

e•nig•ma |i'nigmə| • *n.* (pl. **enigmas** or **enigmata** |-mətə|) a person or thing that is mysterious, puzzling, or difficult to understand.
■ a riddle or paradox.
DERIVATIVES: **e•nig•mat•ic** *adj.*

en•join |en'join| • *v.* [with obj. and infinitive] instruct or urge (someone) to do something: *the code enjoined members to trade fairly.*
■ [trans.] prescribe (an action or attitude) to be performed or adopted: *the charitable deeds enjoined on him by religion.* ■ [trans.] (**enjoin someone from**) (in law) prohibit someone from performing (a particular action) by issuing an INJUNCTION.
DERIVATIVES: **en•join•er** *n.* **en•join•ment** *n.*

en•light•en |en'lītn| • *v.* [trans.] give (someone) greater knowledge and understanding about a subject or situation.
■ give (someone) spiritual knowledge or insight. ■ illuminate or make clearer (a problem or area of study): *this will enlighten the studies of origins of myths and symbols.* ■ shed light on (an object).
DERIVATIVES: **en•light•en•er** *n.*

en•light•en•ment |en'lītnmənt| • *n.* **1** the action of enlightening or the state of being enlightened: *Robbie looked to me for enlightenment.*
■ the action or state of attaining or having attained spiritual knowledge or insight, in particular (in Buddhism) awareness that frees a person from the cycle of rebirth. **2** (**the Enlightenment**) a European intellectual movement of the late 17th and 18th centuries emphasizing reason and individualism rather than tradition.

en masse |än 'mæs| • *adv.* in a group; all together: *the board of directors resigned en masse.*

en•mi•ty |'enmitē| • *n.* (pl. **-ies**) the state or feeling of being actively opposed or hostile to someone or something: *enmity between Protestants and Catholics* | *family feuds and enmities.*

en•ne•ad |'enē,æd| • *n.* a group or set of nine.

en•no•ble |en'nōbəl| • *v.* [trans.] give (someone) a noble rank or title.
■ lend greater dignity or nobility of character to: *the theater is an instrument to ennoble the mind* | [as adj.] (**ennobling**) *ennobling acts of charity.*
DERIVATIVES: **en•no•ble•ment** *n.*

en•nui |än'wē| • *n.* a feeling of listlessness and dissatisfaction arising from a lack of occupation or excitement.

e•nor•mi•ty |i'nôrmitē| • *n.* (pl. **-ies**) **1** (**the enormity of**) the great or extreme scale, seriousness, or extent of something perceived as bad or morally wrong: *a thorough search disclosed the full enormity of the crime.*
■ (in neutral use) the large size or scale of something: *the enormity of his intellect.* See **usage** below. **2** a grave crime or sin: *the enormities of the Hitler regime.*

USAGE: This word is imprecisely used to mean 'great size,' as in *it is difficult to comprehend the **enormity** of the continent,* but the original and preferred meaning is 'extreme wickedness,' as in *the **enormity** of the mass murders.*

e•nor•mous |i'nôrməs| • *adj.* very large in size, quantity, or extent: *her enormous blue eyes* | *the possibilities are enormous.*
DERIVATIVES: **e•nor•mous•ly** *adv.* [as submodifier] *she has been enormously successful.* **e•nor•mous•ness** *n.*

en plein air |än plen 'er| • *adv.* (chiefly with reference to painting) in the open air: *the young girls were posed en plein air.*

en•quire |en'kwīr| • *v.* alternate spelling for inquire.
DERIVATIVES: **en•quir•er** *n.*

en•rap•ture |en'ræpCHər| • *v.* [trans.] (usu. **be enraptured**) give intense pleasure or joy to: *Ruth was enraptured by the child who was sleeping in her arms so peacefully.*

en•sconce |en'skäns| • *v.* [with obj. and adverbial of place] establish or settle (someone) in a comfortable, safe, or secret place: *Agnes ensconced herself in their bedroom.*

en•shrine |en'sHrīn| • *v.* [with obj. and adverbial of place] (usu. **be enshrined**) place (a revered or precious object) in an appropriate receptacle: *relics are enshrined under the altar.*
■ preserve (a right, tradition, or idea) in a form that ensures it will be protected and respected: *the right of all workers to strike was enshrined in the new constitution.*
DERIVATIVES: **en•shrine•ment** *n.*

en•sign • *n.* **1** |'ensən; 'en,sīn| a flag or standard, esp. military or naval, indicating nationality.
■ a sign or emblem of a particular thing: *all the ensigns of our greatness.* **2** |'ensən| the lowest rank of commissioned officer in the US Navy and Coast Guard, ranking above chief warrant officer and below lieutenant.

■ formerly, the lowest rank of commissioned infantry officer in the British army. ■ a standard-bearer.

en•sure |en'sHŏŏr| • v. [trans.] make certain that (something) will occur or be the case: [with clause] *the client must ensure that accurate records are kept.*
■ make certain of obtaining or providing (something): [with two objs.] *would ensure him a place in society.* ■ [intrans.] (**ensure against**) make sure that (a problem) does not occur.

USAGE: On the difference between **ensure** and **insure**, see usage at INSURE.

en•tab•la•ture |en'tæblə,cHŏŏr| • n. the upper part of a classical building supported by columns or a colonnade, comprising the architrave, frieze, and cornice.

en•tail |en'tāl| • v. [trans.] **1** involve (something) as a necessary or inevitable part or consequence: *a situation that entails considerable risks.*
■ have as a logically necessary consequence. **2** (in law) settle the inheritance of (property) over a number of generations so that ownership remains within a particular group, usually one family: *her father's estate was entailed on a cousin.*
■ cause to experience or possess in a way perceived as permanent or inescapable: *I cannot get rid of the disgrace that you have entailed upon us.* • n. |'en,tāl| (in law) a settlement of the inheritance of property over a number of generations so that it remains within a family or other group.
■ a property that is bequeathed under such conditions.
DERIVATIVES: **en•tail•ment** n.

en•tente |än'tänt| • n. (also **entente cordiale**) a friendly understanding or informal alliance between states or factions: *the growing entente between former opponents.* Cf. DÉTENTE.

en•thrall |en'THrôl| (Brit. also **enthral**) • v. (**enthralled, enthralling**) [trans.] (often be **enthralled**) capture the fascinated attention of: *she had been so enthralled by the adventure that she had hardly noticed the cold* | [as adj.] (**enthralling**) *an enthralling best seller.*
■ (also **inthrall**) enslave.
DERIVATIVES: **en•thrall•ment** (Brit also **en•thral•ment**) n.

en•tice |en'tīs| • v. [trans.] attract or tempt by offering pleasure or advantage: *a show that should entice a new audience into the theater* | [with obj. and infinitive] *the whole purpose of bribes is to entice governments to act against the public interest* | [as adj.] (**enticing**) *the idea of giving up sounds enticing but would be a mistake.*
DERIVATIVES: **en•tice•ment** n. **en•tic•er** n. **en•tic•ing•ly** |-siNGlē| adv.

en•ti•tle•ment |en'tītlmənt| • n. the fact of having a right to something: *full entitlement to fees and maintenance should be offered* | *you should be fully aware of your legal entitlements.*
■ the amount to which a person has a right: *annual leave entitlement.*

en•ti•ty |'entitē| • n. (pl. **-ies**) a thing with distinct and independent existence: *church and empire were fused in a single entity.*
■ existence; being: *entity and nonentity.*
DERIVATIVES: **en•ti•ta•tive** |-,tātiv| adj.

en•to•mol•o•gy |,entə'mäləjē| • n. the branch of zoology concerned with the study of insects.
DERIVATIVES: **en•to•mo•log•i•cal** |-mə'läjikəl| adj. **en•to•mol•o•gist** |-jist| n.

en•tr'acte |'än,trækt; än'trækt| • n. an interval between two acts of a play or opera.
■ a piece of music or a dance performed during such an interval.

en•trap |en'træp| • v. (**entrapped, entrapping**) [trans.] catch (someone or something) in or as in a trap: *she was entrapped by family expectations.*
■ trick or deceive (someone), esp. by inducing them to commit a crime in order to secure their prosecution.
DERIVATIVES: **en•trap•ment** n. **en•trap•per** n.

en•treat |en'trēt| • v. **1** ask someone earnestly or anxiously to do something: [with obj. and infinitive] *his friends entreated him not to go.*
■ [trans.] ask earnestly or anxiously for (something): *a message had been sent, entreating aid for the Navajos.* **2** [with obj. and adverbial] treat (someone) in a specified manner: *the King, I fear, hath ill entreated her.*
DERIVATIVES: **en•treat•ing•ly** adv. **en•treat•ment** n.

en•tre•chat |,äntrə'sHä| • n. (in ballet) a vertical jump during which the dancer repeatedly crosses the feet and beats them together.

en•trée |'än,trā ,än'trā| (also **entree**) • n. **1** the main course of a meal.
■ a dish served between the fish and meat courses at a formal dinner. **2** the right to enter a domain or join a particular social group: *an actress with an entrée into the intellectual society of Berlin.*
■ an entrance, esp. of performers onto a stage.

en•tre•pôt |'äntrə,pō| • n. a port, city, or other center to which goods are brought for import and export, and for collection and distribution.

en•tre•pre•neur |,äntrəprə'nŏŏr; ,äntrəprə'nər| • n. a person who organizes and operates a business or businesses, taking on greater than normal financial risks in order to do so.
DERIVATIVES: **en•tre•pre•neur•i•al** |-'nər-ēəl; -'nŏŏrēəl| adj. **en•tre•pre•neur•i•al•ism** |-'nərēə,lizəm; -'nŏŏrēə,lizəm| n. **en•tre•pre•neur•i•al•ly** |-'nərēəlē; 'nŏŏrēəlē| adv. **en•tre•pre•neur•ism** |-,izəm| n. **en•tre•pre•neur•ship** |-,sHip| n.

en•tro•py |'entrəpē| • n. (in physics) a thermodynamic quantity representing the unavailability of a system's thermal energy for conversion into mechanical work, often interpreted as the degree of disorder or randomness in the system. (Symbol: **S**)
■ lack of order or predictability; gradual decline into disorder: *a marketplace where entropy reigns supreme.* ■ a logarithmic measure

of the rate of transfer of information in a particular message or language.

DERIVATIVES: **en•tro•pic** |en'träpik| *adj.* **en•tro•pi•cal•ly** |en'träpik(ə)lē| *adv.*

e•nu•mer•ate |i'n(y)o͞omə,rāt| • *v.* [trans.] mention (a number of things) one by one: *there is not space to enumerate all the possibilities.* ■ establish the number of: *the 1981 census enumerated 19,493,000 households.*

DERIVATIVES: **e•nu•mer•a•ble** *adj.* **e•nu•mer•a•tion** |i,n(y)o͞omə'rāsHən| *n.* **e•nu•mer•a•tive** |-rətiv; i'n(y)o͞omə,rātiv| *adj.* **e•nu•mer•a•tor** *n.*

e•nun•ci•ate |i'nənsē,āt| • *v.* [trans.] say or pronounce clearly: *she enunciated each word slowly.* ■ express (a proposition or theory) in clear or definite terms: *a written document enunciating this policy.* ■ state publicly; proclaim: *a prophet enunciating the Lord's wisdom.*

DERIVATIVES: **e•nun•ci•a•tion** |i,nənsē'ā-sHən| *n.* **e•nun•ci•a•tive** |i'nənsēətiv; -,ātiv| *adj.* **e•nun•ci•a•tor** |-,ātər| *n.*

en•ure |i'n(y)o͞or| • *v.* **1** [intrans.] (**enure for/to**) (in law, of a right or other advantage) belong or be available to. **2** variant spelling of INURE.

en•u•re•sis |,enyə'rēsis| • *n.* involuntary urination, esp. by children at night.

DERIVATIVES: **en•u•ret•ic** |-'retik| *adj. & n.*

en•vi•a•ble |'envēəbəl| • *adj.* arousing or likely to arouse envy: *an enviable reputation for academic achievement.*

DERIVATIVES: **en•vi•a•bly** |-əblē| *adv.*

en•vi•ous |'envēəs| • *adj.* feeling or showing envy: *I'm* **envious** *of their happiness* | *an envious glance.*

DERIVATIVES: **en•vi•ous•ly** *adv.*

en•vi•ron•ment |en'vīrənmənt; -'vīrn-| • *n.* **1** the surroundings or conditions in which a person, animal, or plant lives or operates. ■ [usu. with adj.] the setting or conditions in which a particular activity is carried on: *a good learning environment.* **2** (**the environment**) the natural world, as a whole or in a particular geographical area, esp. as affected by human activity.

en•vi•rons |en'vīrənz; -'vīrnz| • *plural n.* the surrounding area or district: *the picturesque environs of the lake.*

en•vis•age |en'vizij| • *v.* [trans.] contemplate or conceive of as a possibility or a desirable future event: *the North American Free Trade Agreement envisaged free movement across borders.* ■ form a mental picture of (something not yet existing or known): *he knew what he liked but had difficulty envisaging it.*

en•zyme |'enzīm| • *n.* a substance produced by a living organism that acts as a catalyst to bring about a specific biochemical reaction.

Most enzymes are large complex molecules whose action depends on their particular molecular shape. Some enzymes control reactions within cells and some, such as the enzymes involved in digestion, reactions outside them.

DERIVATIVES: **en•zy•mat•ic** |,enzə'mætik| *adj.* **en•zy•mat•i•cal•ly** |,enzə'mætik(ə)lē| *adv.* **en•zy•mic** |en'zīmik; -'zimik| *adj.* **en•zy•mi•cal•ly** |en'zīmik(ə)lē; -zim-| *adv.*

E•o•cene |'ēə,sēn| • *adj.* of, relating to, or denoting the second epoch of the Tertiary period, between the Paleocene and Oligocene epochs. ■ [as n.] (**the Eocene**) the Eocene epoch or the system of rocks deposited during it.

The Eocene epoch lasted from 56.5 million to 35.4 million years ago. It was a time of rising temperatures, and there was an abundance of mammals, including the first horses, bats, and whales.

e•on |'ēən; 'ē,än| (chiefly Brit. also **aeon**) • *n.* (often **eons**) an indefinite and very long period of time, often a period exaggerated for humorous or rhetorical effect: *they haven't won the pennant in eons* | *his eyes searched her face for what seemed like eons.* ■ (in astronomy and geology) a unit of time equal to a billion years. ■ a major division of geological time, subdivided into eras: *the Precambrian eon.* ■ (in Neoplatonism, Platonism, and Gnosticism) a power existing from eternity; an emanation or phase of the supreme deity.

DERIVATIVES: **e•o•ni•an** (also **aeonian**) *adj.*

é•pa•ter • *v.* (in phrase **épater les bourgeois**) shock people who are conventional or complacent.

e•phebe |'efēb; i'fēb| • *n.* (in ancient Greece) a young man 18–20 years old undergoing military training.

DERIVATIVES: **e•phe•bic** |i'fēbik; e'fēbik| *adj.*

e•phem•er•a |ə'fem(ə)rə| • *plural n.* (sing. **ephemeron** |-ə,rän|) things that exist or are used or enjoyed for only a short time. ■ items of collectible memorabilia, typically written or printed ones, that were originally expected to have only short-term usefulness or popularity: *Mickey Mouse ephemera.*

e•phem•er•al |ə'fem(ə)rə| • *adj.* lasting for a very short time: *fashions are ephemeral.* ■ (chiefly of plants) having a very short life cycle. ■ *n.* an ephemeral plant.

DERIVATIVES: **e•phem•er•al•i•ty** |ə,femə'rælitē| *n.* **e•phem•er•al•ly** *adv.* **e•phem•er•al•ness** *n.*

ep•ic |'epik| • *n.* a long poem, typically one derived from ancient oral tradition, narrating the deeds and adventures of heroic or legendary figures or the history of a nation. ■ the genre of such poems: *the romances display gentler emotions not found in Greek epic.* ■ a long film, book, or other work portraying heroic deeds and adventures or covering an extended period of time: *a Hollywood biblical epic.* • *adj.* of, relating to, or characteristic of an epic or epics: *England's national epic poem* Beowulf. ■ heroic or grand in scale or character: *his epic journey around the world* | *a tragedy of epic proportions.*

DERIVATIVES: **ep•i•cal** |'epikəl| *adj.* **ep•i•cal•ly** |-(ə)lē| *adv.*

ep•i•cene |'epi,sēn| • *adj.* having characteristics of both sexes or no characteristics of either sex; of indeterminate sex: *the epicene beauty of certain children.*
■ lacking masculine character; effeminate; effete: *the actor infused the role with an epicene languor.* ■ (of a noun or pronoun) denoting either sex without change of gender. • *n.* an epicene person.

ep•i•cen•ter |'epi,sentər| • *n.* the point on the earth's surface directly above the focus of an earthquake.
■ the central point of something, typically a difficult or unpleasant situation: *this region is at the epicenter of the growing conflict.* DERIVATIVES: **ep•i•cen•tral** |,epi'sentrəl| *adj.*

ep•i•cure |'epi,kyŏor| • *n.* a person who takes particular pleasure in fine food and drink. DERIVATIVES: **ep•i•cur•ism** |-,rizəm; ,epi 'kyŏo-| *n.*

Ep•i•cu•re•an |,epikyə'rēən; ,epi'kyŏorēən| • *n.* a disciple or student of the Greek philosopher Epicurus (341-270 BC), who held that the highest good is pleasure.
■ (**epicurean**) a person devoted to sensual enjoyment, esp. that derived from fine food and drink. • *adj.* of or concerning Epicurus or his ideas: *Epicurean philosophers.*
■ (**epicurean**) relating to or suitable for an epicure: *epicurean feasts.*

ep•i•dem•ic |,epi'demik| • *n.* a widespread occurrence of an infectious disease in a community at a particular time: *a flu epidemic.*
■ a disease occurring in such a way. ■ a sudden, widespread occurrence of a particular undesirable phenomenon: *an epidemic of violent crime.* • *adj.* of, relating to, or of the nature of an epidemic: *shoplifting has reached epidemic proportions.* Cf. ENDEMIC and PANDEMIC.

USAGE: A disease that quickly and severely affects a large number of people and then subsides is an **epidemic**: *Throughout the Middle Ages, successive epidemics of the plague killed millions.* **Epidemic** is also used as an adjective: *She studied the causes of epidemic cholera.* A disease that is continually present in an area and affects a relatively small number of people is **endemic**: *Malaria is endemic in* (or *to*) *hot, moist climates.* A **pandemic** is a widespread epidemic that may affect entire continents or even the world, as in *The influenza pandemic of 1918 ushered in a period of frequent epidemics of gradually diminishing severity.*

ep•i•de•mi•ol•o•gy |,epi,dēmē'äləjē| • *n.* the branch of medicine that deals with the incidence, distribution, and possible control of diseases and other factors relating to health. DERIVATIVES: **ep•i•de•mi•o•log•i•cal** |-ə 'läjikəl| *adj.* **ep•i•de•mi•ol•o•gist** |-jist| *n.*

ep•i•der•mis |,epi'dərmis| • *n.* the outer layer of cells covering an organism, in particular:
■ the surface epithelium of the skin of an animal, overlying the dermis. ■ the outer layer of tissue in a plant, except where it is replaced by periderm (a corky secondary layer). DERIVATIVES: **ep•i•der•mal** |-'dərməl| *adj.* **ep•i•der•mic** |-'dərmik| *adj.* **ep•i•der•moid** |-'dər,moid| *adj.*

ep•i•du•ral |,epi'd(y)ŏorəl| • *adj.* on or around the dura mater, in particular (of an anesthetic), introduced into the space around the dura mater of the spinal cord. • *n.* an epidural anesthetic, used esp. in childbirth to produce loss of sensation below the waist.

ep•i•gram |'epi,græm| • *n.* a pithy saying or remark expressing an idea in a clever and amusing way.
■ a short poem, esp. a satirical one, having a witty or ingenious ending. DERIVATIVES: **e•pi•gram•mat•ic** *adj.* **e•pi•gram•mat•i•cal** *adj.* **ep•i•gram•ma•tist** |,epi'græmətist| *n.* **ep•i•gram•ma•tize** |,epi'græmə,tiz| *v.*

ep•i•graph |'epi,græf| • *n.* an inscription on a building, statue, or coin.
■ a short quotation or saying at the beginning of a book or chapter, intended to suggest its theme.

ep•i•logue |'epə,lôg; -,läg| (also **epilog**) • *n.* a section or speech at the end of a book or play that serves as a comment on or a conclusion to what has happened.

ep•i•neph•rine |,epi'nefrin| • *n.* a hormone secreted by the adrenal glands, esp. in conditions of stress, increasing rates of blood circulation, breathing, and carbohydrate metabolism and preparing muscles for exertion. Also called ADRENALINE.

e•piph•a•ny |i'pifənē| • *n.* (pl. **-ies**) (**Epiphany**) the manifestation of Christ to the Gentiles as represented by the Magi (Matthew 2:1-12).
■ the festival commemorating this on January 6. ■ a manifestation of a divine or supernatural being. ■ a moment of sudden revelation or insight. DERIVATIVES: **ep•i•phan•ic** |,epə'fænik| *adj.*

ep•i•phyte |'epə,fīt| • *n.* a plant that grows on another plant but is not parasitic, such as the numerous ferns, bromeliads, air plants, and orchids growing on tree trunks in tropical rain forests. DERIVATIVES: **ep•i•phyt•al** |,epə'fītl| *adj.* **ep•i•phyt•ic** |,epə'fitik| *adj.*

e•pis•co•pa•lian |i,piskə'pālēən| • *adj.* of or advocating government of a church by bishops.
■ of or belonging to an episcopal church. ■ (**Episcopalian**) of or belonging to the Episcopal Church. • *n.* an adherent of episcopacy (the government of a church by bishops). ■ (**Episcopalian**) a member of the Episcopal Church. DERIVATIVES: **e•pis•co•pa•lian•ism** |-,nizəm| *n.*

ep•i•ste•mic |,epə'stemik; -'stē-| • *adj.* of or relating to knowledge or to the degree of its validation.

DERIVATIVES: **ep•i•ste•mi•cal•ly** |-(ə)lē| adv.

e•pis•te•mol•o•gy |i,pistə'mäləjē| • n. the branch of philosophy that deals with knowledge, esp. with regard to its methods, validity, and scope.
DERIVATIVES: **e•pis•te•mo•log•i•cal** |-mə 'läjikəl| adj. **e•pis•te•mo•log•i•cal•ly** |-mə 'läjik(ə)lē| adv. **e•pis•te•mol•o•gist** |-jist| n.

e•pis•tle |i'pisəl| • n. a letter. ■ a poem or other literary work in the form of a letter or series of letters. ■ (also **Epistle**) a book of the New Testament in the form of a letter from an Apostle: *St. Paul's epistle to the Romans.* ■ an extract from an Epistle (or another New Testament book not a Gospel) that is read in a church service.

e•pis•to•lar•y |i'pistə,lerē| • adj. relating to or denoting the writing of letters or literary works in the form of letters: *an epistolary novel.*

ep•i•taph |'epi,tæf| • n. a phrase or statement written in memory of a person who has died, esp. as an inscription on a tombstone.

ep•i•the•li•um |,epə'THēlēəm| • n. (pl. **epithelia** |-lēə|) the thin tissue forming the outer layer of a body's surface and lining the alimentary canal and other hollow structures.
DERIVATIVES: **ep•i•the•li•al** |-lēəl| adj.

ep•i•thet |'epə,THet| • n. an adjective or descriptive phrase expressing a quality characteristic of the person or thing mentioned: *old men are often unfairly awarded the epithet "crotchety."*
■ such a word or phrase as a term of abuse: *he felt an urge to hurl epithets in her face.* ■ a descriptive title: *the epithet "Father of Waters," used for the Mississippi River.*
DERIVATIVES: **ep•i•thet•ic** |-'THetik| adj. **ep•i•thet•i•cal** |-'THetikəl| adj. **ep•i•thet•i•cal•ly** |-'THetik(ə)lē| adv.

e•pit•o•me |i'pitəmē| • n. 1 (**the epitome of**) a person or thing that is a perfect example of a particular quality or type: *she looked the epitome of elegance and good taste.* 2 a summary of a written work; an abstract.
■ a thing representing something else in miniature.
DERIVATIVES: **e•pit•o•mist** |-mist| n. **e•pit•o•mize** v.

ep•och |'epək| • n. a period of time in history or a person's life, typically one marked by notable events or particular characteristics: *the Victorian epoch.*
■ the beginning of a distinctive period in the history of someone or something: *reimmigration to Palestine marked an epoch in the history of Jewry.* ■ (in geology) a division of time that is a subdivision of a period and is itself subdivided into ages: *the Pliocene epoch.* ■ (in astronomy) an arbitrarily fixed date relative to which planetary or stellar measurements are expressed.

ep•och•al |'epəkəl| • adj. forming or characterizing an epoch; epoch-making.

ep•ode |'epōd| • n. 1 a form of lyric poem written in couplets, in which a long line is fol-

lowed by a shorter one. 2 the third section of an ancient Greek choral ode, or of one division of such an ode. Cf. STROPHE and ANTI-STROPHE.

ep•o•nym |'epə,nim| • n. a person after whom a discovery, invention, place, etc., is named or thought to be named.
■ a name or noun formed in such a way.
DERIVATIVES: **ep•on•y•mous** adj.

eq•ua•ble |'ekwəbəl| • adj. (of a person) not easily disturbed or angered; calm and eventempered.
■ not varying or fluctuating greatly: *an equable climate.*
DERIVATIVES: **eq•ua•bil•i•ty** |,ekwə'bilitē| n. **eq•ua•bly** |-blē| adv.

e•qua•nim•i•ty |,ēkwə'nimitē; ,ekwə-| • n. mental calmness, composure, and evenness of temper, esp. in a difficult situation: *she accepted both the good and the bad with equanimity.*
DERIVATIVES: **e•quan•i•mous** |i'kwänəməs| adj.

e•ques•tri•an |i'kwestrēən| • adj. of or relating to horse riding: *his amazing equestrian skills.*
■ depicting or representing a person on horseback: *an equestrian statue.* • n. (fem. **equestrienne** |-'en|) a rider or performer on horseback.

e•quil•i•brate |i'kwilə,brāt| • v. [trans.] bring into or keep in equilibrium.
■ [intrans.] approach or attain a state of equilibrium.
DERIVATIVES: **e•quil•i•bra•tion** |i,kwilə 'brāSHən| n.

e•qui•lib•ri•um |,ēkwə'librēəm; ,ekwə-| • n. (pl. **equilibria** |-'librēə|) a state in which opposing forces or influences are balanced: *the maintenance of social equilibrium.*
■ a state of physical balance: *I stumbled over a rock and recovered my equilibrium.* ■ a calm state of mind: *his intensity could unsettle his equilibrium.* ■ (in chemistry) a state in which a process and its reverse are occurring at equal rates so that no overall change is taking place: *ice is in equilibrium with water.* ■ (in economics) a situation in which supply and demand are matched and prices stable.
DERIVATIVES: **e•qui•lib•ri•al** |-'librēəl| adj.

e•quine |'ekwīn; 'ē,kwīn| • adj. of, relating to, or affecting horses or other members of the horse family: *equine infectious anemia.*
■ resembling a horse, esp. facially: *her somewhat equine features.* • n. a horse or other member of the horse family.

e•qui•noc•tial |,ēkwə'näksHəl; ,ekwə-| • adj. happening at or near the time of an equinox.
■ of or relating to equal day and night. ■ at or near the equator. • n. (also **equinoctial line** or **equinoctial circle**) another term for *celestial equator,* the projection into space of the earth's equator.

e•qui•nox |'ekwə,näks; 'ēkwə-| • n. the time or date (twice each year) at which the sun crosses the celestial equator, when day and night are of equal length (about September 22 and March 20).

eq•ui•page |'ekwəpij| • *n.* **1** the equipment for a particular purpose. **2** a carriage and horses with attendants.

e•qui•poise |'ekwə,poiz| • *n.* balance of forces or interests: *this temporary equipoise of power.*
■ a counterbalance or balancing force: *capital flows act as an* **equipoise** *to international imbalances in savings.* • *v.* [trans.] balance or counterbalance (something).

eq•ui•ta•ble |'ekwitəbəl| • *adj.* **1** fair and impartial: *an equitable balance of power.* **2** (in law) valid in equity as distinct from law: *the beneficiaries have an equitable interest in the property.*
DERIVATIVES: **eq•ui•ta•bil•i•ty** |,ekwitə'bilitē| *n.* **eq•ui•ta•ble•ness** *n.* **eq•ui•ta•bly** |-əblē| *adv.*

eq•ui•ty |'ekwitē| • *n.* (pl. **-ies**) **1** the quality of being fair and impartial: *equity of treatment.*
■ a branch of law that developed alongside common law in order to remedy some of its defects in fairness and justice by allowing recourse to general principles of justice, formerly administered in special courts. ■ (**Equity**) (in the US, Britain, and several other countries) a trade union to which professional actors belong. **2** the value of the shares issued by a company: *he owns 62% of the group's equity.*
■ (**equities**) shares that carry no fixed interest. **3** the value of a mortgaged property after deduction of charges against it: *they're building equity in their house month by month.*

e•quiv•o•cal |i'kwivəkəl| • *adj.* open to more than one interpretation; ambiguous: *the equivocal nature of her remarks* | *an equivocal expression.*
■ uncertain or questionable in nature: *the results of the investigation were equivocal.*
DERIVATIVES: **e•quiv•o•cal•i•ty** |i,kwivə'kælitē| *n.* **e•quiv•o•cal•ly** *adv.* **e•quiv•o•cal•ness** *n.*

e•quiv•o•cate |i'kwivə,kāt| • *v.* [intrans.] use ambiguous language so as to conceal the truth or avoid committing oneself: [with direct speech] *"Not that we are aware of," she equivocated.*
DERIVATIVES: **e•quiv•o•ca•tion** |i,kwivə'kāSHən| *n.* **e•quiv•o•ca•tor** |-,kātər| *n.* **e•quiv•o•ca•to•ry** |i'kwivəkə,tôrē| *adj.*

e•rad•i•cate |i'rædi,kāt| • *v.* [trans.] destroy completely; put an end to: *this disease has been eradicated from the world.*
DERIVATIVES: **e•rad•i•ca•ble** |-kəbəl| *adj.* **e•rad•i•cant** |-kant| *n.* **e•rad•i•ca•tion** |i,rædi'kāSHən| *n.* **e•rad•i•ca•tor** |-,kātər| *n.*

er•e•mite |'erə,mīt| • *n.* a Christian hermit or recluse.
DERIVATIVES: **er•e•mit•ic** |,erə'mitik| *adj.* **er•e•mit•i•cal** |,erə'mitikəl| *adj.*

er•ga•tive |'ərgətiv| • *adj.* relating to or denoting a case of nouns, in some languages, e.g., Basque and Eskimo, that identifies the subject of a transitive verb and is different from the case that identifies the subject of an intransitive verb.

■ (of a language) possessing this case. ■ (in English) denoting verbs that can be used both transitively and intransitively to describe the same action, with the object in the former case being the subject in the latter, as in *I boiled the water* and *the water boiled.* • *n.* an ergative word.
■ (**the ergative**) the ergative case.
DERIVATIVES: **er•ga•tiv•i•ty** |,ərgə'tivitē| *n.*

er•go•nom•ics |,ərgə'nämiks| • *plural n.* [treated as sing.] the study of people's efficiency, comfort, and well-being in their working environment.
DERIVATIVES: **er•go•nom•ic** |-'nämik| *adj.* **er•gon•o•mist** |ər'gänəmist| *n.*

e•rode |i'rōd| • *v.* [trans.] (often **be eroded**) (of wind, water, or other natural agents) gradually wear away (soil, rock, or land): *the cliffs have been eroded by the sea.*
■ [intrans.] (of soil, rock, or land) be gradually worn away by such natural agents. ■ gradually destroy or be gradually destroyed: [trans.] *this humiliation has eroded what confidence Jean had* | [intrans.] *profit margins are eroding.* ■ (of a disease) gradually destroy (bodily tissue).
DERIVATIVES: **e•rod•i•ble** |i'rōdəbəl| *adj.* **e•ro•sion** *n.* **e•ro•sive** *adj.*

e•rog•e•nous |i'räjənəs| • *adj.* (of a part of the body) sensitive to sexual stimulation: *erogenous zones.*

E•ros |'eräs; 'iräs| **1** (in Greek mythology) the god of love, son of Aphrodite. Roman equivalent *Cupid*
■ sexual love or desire. Cf. AGAPE ■ (in Freudian theory) the life instinct. Often contrasted with *Thanatos*, the death instinct. ■ (in Jungian psychology) the principle of personal relatedness in human activities, associated with the anima.

e•rot•ic |i'rätik| • *adj.* of, relating to, or tending to arouse sexual desire or excitement. Cf. PLATONIC.
DERIVATIVES: **e•rot•i•cal•ly** |-ik(ə)lē| *adv.* **eroticism** *n.* **eroticist** *n.*

e•rot•i•ca |i'rätikə| • *n.* literature or art intended to arouse sexual desire.

er•rant |'erənt| • *adj.* **1** [attrib.] erring or straying from the proper course or standards: *a novel about errant husbands and unfaithful wives.* **2** [often postpositive] traveling in search of adventure: *a knight errant.*
DERIVATIVES: **er•ran•cy** |'erənsē| *n.* (in sense 1) **er•rant•ry** |-trē| *n.* (in sense 2).

er•rat•ic |i'rætik| • *adj.* not even or regular in pattern or movement; unpredictable: *her breathing was erratic.*
■ deviating from the normal or conventional in behavior or opinions: *neighbors were alarmed by this increasingly erratic behavior.* • *n.* (also **erratic block** or **boulder**) a rock or boulder that differs from the surrounding rock and is believed to have been brought from a distance by glacial action.
DERIVATIVES: **er•rat•i•cal•ly** *adv.* **er•rat•i•cism** |i'ræti,sizəm| *n.*

er•ra•tum |i'rätəm; -'rä-; 'ræt-| • *n.* (pl. **er•rata** |-tə|) an error in printing or writing.

■ (**errata**) a list of corrected errors appended to a book or published in a subsequent issue of a journal.

er•ro•ne•ous |i'rōnēəs| • adj. containing errors or based on errors; wrong; incorrect: *employers sometimes make erroneous assumptions.*

DERIVATIVES: **er•ro•ne•ous•ly** adv. **er•ro•ne•ous•ness** n.

er•satz |'er,säts; -,zäts; er'zäts| • adj. (of a product) made or used as a substitute, typically an inferior one: *ersatz coffee.*

■ not real or genuine: *ersatz emotion.*

erst |ərst| • adv. long ago; formerly: *the friends whom erst you knew.*

erst•while |'ərst,(h)wīl| • adj. [attrib.] former: *his erstwhile rivals.* • adv. formerly: *Mary Anderson, erstwhile the queen of America's stage.*

e•ruc•ta•tion |irək'tāsHən| • n. a belch.

er•u•dite |'er(y)ə,dīt| • adj. having or showing great knowledge or learning.

DERIVATIVES: **er•u•dite•ly** adv. **er•u•di•tion** |,er(y)oŏ'disHən| n.

es•ca•pade |'eskə,pād| • n. an act or incident involving excitement, daring, or adventure.

es•cap•ism |i'skāp,izəm| • n. the tendency to seek distraction and relief from unpleasant realities, esp. by seeking entertainment or engaging in fantasy.

DERIVATIVES: **es•cap•ist** n. & adj.

es•carp•ment |i'skärpmənt| • n. a long, steep slope, esp. one at the edge of a plateau or separating areas of land at different heights.

es•cha•tol•o•gy |,eskə'täləjē| • n. the part of theology concerned with death, judgment, and the final destiny of the soul and of humankind.

DERIVATIVES: **es•cha•to•log•i•cal** |e,skætl 'äjikəl; ,eskətl-| adj. **es•cha•to•log•i•cal•ly** adv. **es•cha•tol•o•gist** |-jist| n.

es•cheat |es'CHēt| • n. the reversion of property to the state, or (in feudal law) to a lord, on the owner's dying without legal heirs.

■ an item of property affected by this. • v. [intrans.] (of land) revert to a lord or the state by escheat.

■ [trans.] [usu. as adj.] (**escheated**) hand over (land) as an escheat.

es•chew |es'CHoō| • v. [trans.] deliberately avoid using; abstain from: *he appealed to the crowd to eschew violence.*

DERIVATIVES: **es•chew•al** n.

es•cri•toire |,eskri'twär| • n. a small writing desk with drawers and compartments.

es•crow |'eskrō| • n. (in law) a bond, deed, or other document kept in the custody of a third party, taking effect only when a specified condition has been fulfilled.

■ [usu. as adj.] a deposit or fund held in trust or as a security: *an escrow account.* ■ the state of being kept in custody or trust in this way: *the board holds funds in escrow.* • v. [trans.] place in custody or trust in this way.

es•cu•lent |'eskyələnt| formal • adj. fit to be eaten; edible. • n. a thing, esp. a vegetable, that is fit to be eaten.

es•cutch•eon |i'skəCHən| • n. **1** a shield or emblem bearing a coat of arms. **2** (also **escutcheon plate**) a flat piece of metal for protection and often ornamentation, around a keyhole, door handle, or light switch.

PHRASES: **a blot on one's escutcheon** a stain on one's reputation or character.

DERIVATIVES: **es•cutch•eoned** adj.

Es•ki•mo |'eskə,mō| • n. (pl. same or **-os**) **1** a member of an indigenous people inhabiting northern Canada, Alaska, Greenland, and eastern Siberia, traditionally living by hunting (esp. of seals) and by fishing. **2** either of the two main languages of this people (Inuit and Yupik), forming a major division of the Eskimo-Aleut family. • adj. of or relating to the Eskimos or their languages.

USAGE: **1** In recent years **Eskimo** has come to be regarded as offensive because of one of its possible etymologies (Abnaki *askimo* 'eater of raw meat'), but this descriptive name is accurate since Eskimos traditionally derived their vitamins from eating raw meat. This dictionary gives another possible etymology above, but the etymological problem is still unresolved.
2 The peoples inhabiting the regions from northwestern Canada to western Greenland call themselves **Inuit** (see **usage** at INUIT), and that term is also used by many in Alaska, but **Eskimo** is the only term that can be properly applied to all of the peoples as a whole, and it is still widely used in anthropological and archaeological contexts. The broader term **Native American** is sometimes used to refer to Eskimo and Aleut peoples in the US. See **usage** at NATIVE AMERICAN.

es•o•ter•ic |,esə'terik| • adj. intended for or likely to be understood by only a small number of people with a specialized knowledge or interest: *esoteric philosophical debates.* Cf. ARCANE; RECONDITE.

DERIVATIVES: **es•o•ter•i•cal•ly** |-(ə)lē| adv. **es•o•ter•i•cism** |-'terə,sizəm| n. **es•o•ter•i•cist** |-'terəsist| n.

es•o•ter•i•ca |,esə'terikə| • n. esoteric or highly specialized subjects or publications.

es•pal•ier |i'spælyər; -yā| • n. a fruit tree or ornamental shrub whose branches are trained to grow flat against a wall, supported on a lattice or a framework of stakes.

■ a lattice or framework of this type. • v. [trans.] train (a tree or shrub) in such a way.

Es•pe•ran•to |,espə'räntō| • n. an artificial language devised in 1887 as an international medium of communication, based on roots from the chief European languages.

DERIVATIVES: **Es•pe•ran•tist** |-tist| n.

es•pi•o•nage |'espēə,näzH| • n. the practice of spying or of using spies, typically by governments to obtain political and military information.

es•pla•nade |'esplə,näd; -,nād| • n. a long, open, level area, typically beside the sea, along which people may walk for pleasure.

■ an open, level space separating a fortress from a town.

es•pouse |i'spowz| • v. [trans.] **1** adopt or support (a cause, belief, or way of life): *her writings espoused world communism.* **2** marry: *Edward had espoused the lady Grey.*

■ (**be espoused to**) (of a woman) be engaged to (a particular man).

DERIVATIVES: **espousal** n. **es•pous•er** n.

es•prit de corps |e‚sprē də 'kôr| • n. a feeling of pride, fellowship, and common loyalty shared by the members of a particular group.

es•quire |'eskwīr; i'skwīr| • n. **1** (**Esquire**) (abbr.: **Esq.**) a title appended to a lawyer's surname.

■ in Britain, a polite title appended to a man's name when no other title is used, typically in the address of a letter or other documents: *J. C. Pearson Esquire.* **2** a young nobleman who, in training for knighthood, acted as an attendant to a knight.

■ an officer in the service of a king or nobleman. ■ [as title] a landed proprietor or country squire.

es•say • n. |'esā| **1** a short piece of writing on a particular subject. **2** an attempt or effort: *a misjudged essay in job preservation.* • v. |e'sā| [trans.] attempt or try: *Donald essayed a smile.*

Es•sene |i'sēn; 'esēn| • n. a member of an ancient Jewish ascetic sect of the 2nd century BC–2nd century AD in Palestine, who lived in highly organized groups and held property in common. The Essenes are widely regarded as the authors of the Dead Sea Scrolls.

es•sen•tial•ism |i'senSHə‚lizəm| • n. a belief that things have a set of characteristics that make them what they are, and that the task of science and philosophy is their discovery and expression; the doctrine that essence is prior to existence. Cf. EXISTENTIALISM.

■ the view that all children should be taught on traditional lines the ideas and methods regarded as essential to the prevalent culture. ■ the view that categories of people, such as women and men, or heterosexuals and homosexuals, or members of ethnic groups, have intrinsically different and characteristic natures or dispositions.

DERIVATIVES: **es•sen•tial•ist** n. & adj.

es•teem |i'stēm| • n. respect and admiration, typically for a person: *he was held in high esteem by colleagues.* • v. [trans.] (usu. **be esteemed**) respect and admire: *many of these qualities are esteemed by managers* | [as adj., with submodifier] (**esteemed**) *a highly esteemed scholar.*

■ consider; deem: [with two objs.] *I should esteem it a favor if you could speak to them.*

es•ter |'estər| • n. an organic chemical compound made by replacing the hydrogen of an acid by an alkyl or other organic group. Many naturally occurring fats and essential oils (distilled oils with the characteristic odor of the plant or other source from which they are extracted) are esters of fatty acids.

es•ti•val |'estəvəl; e'stī-; | (also **aestival**) • adj. technical belonging to or appearing in summer.

es•ti•vate |'estə‚vāt| (also **aestivate**) • v. [intrans.] (of an animal, particularly an insect, fish, or amphibian) spend a hot or dry period in a prolonged state of torpor or dormancy. Cf. HIBERNATE.

es•top•pel |e'stäpəl| • n. (in law) the principle that precludes a person from asserting something contrary to what is implied by a previous action or statement of that person or by a previous pertinent judicial determination.

DERIVATIVES: **es•top** v.

es•trange |i'strānj| • v. [trans.] cause (someone) to be no longer close or affectionate to someone; alienate: *are you deliberately seeking to estrange your readers?* | [as adj.] (**estranged**) *his estranged wife.*

DERIVATIVES: **es•trange•ment** n.

es•trus |'estrəs| (also **estrum** or **oestrus**) • n. a recurring period of sexual receptivity and fertility in many female mammals; heat: *a mare in estrus.*

DERIVATIVES: **es•trous** (also **oestrous**) |'estrəs| adj.

es•tu•ar•y |'esCHə‚werē| • n. (pl. **-ies**) the tidal mouth of a large river, where the tide meets the stream.

DERIVATIVES: **es•tu•ar•i•al** |‚esCHə'werēəl| adj. **es•tu•a•rine** |-wə‚rīn; -wə‚rēn| adj.

é•ta•gère (also **etagere**) • n. (pl. same or **étagères**) a piece of furniture with a number of open shelves for displaying ornaments.

e•the•re•al |i'THirēəl| • adj. **1** extremely delicate and light in a way that seems too perfect for this world: *ethereal beauty* | *an ethereal voice.*

■ heavenly or spiritual: *ethereal, otherworldly visions.* **2** (of a solution) having diethyl ether as a solvent.

DERIVATIVES: **e•the•re•al•i•ty** |i‚THirēə'ælitē| n. **e•the•re•al•ize** |-‚īz| v. **e•the•re•al•ly** adv.

eth•ic |'eTHik| • n. [in sing.] a set of moral principles, esp. ones relating to or affirming a specified group, field, or form of conduct: *the puritan ethic was being replaced by the hedonist ethic.* • adj. of or relating to moral principles or the branch of knowledge dealing with these.

DERIVATIVES: **eth•i•cal** adj.

eth•ics |'eTHiks| • plural n. **1** [usu. treated as pl.] moral principles that govern a person's or group's behavior: *Judeo-Christian ethics.*

■ the moral correctness of specified conduct: *the ethics of euthanasia.* **2** [usu. treated as sing.] the branch of knowledge that deals with moral principles.

Schools of ethics in Western philosophy can be divided, very roughly, into three sorts. The first, drawing on the work of Aristotle, holds that the virtues (such as justice, charity, and generosity) are dispositions to act in ways that benefit both the person possessing them and that person's society. The second, defended particularly by Kant, makes the concept of duty central to morality: humans are bound, from a knowledge of their duty as rational beings, to obey the categorical imperative to respect other rational beings. Thirdly, utilitarianism asserts that the guiding principle of conduct should be the greatest happiness or benefit of the greatest number.

DERIVATIVES: **eth•i•cist** |'ɛTHisist| *n.*

eth•nic |'ɛTHnik| • *adj.* of or relating to a population subgroup (within a larger or dominant national or cultural group) with a common national or cultural tradition: *leaders of ethnic communities.*
■ of or relating to national and cultural origins: *we recruit our employees regardless of ethnic origin.* ■ denoting origin by birth or descent rather than by present nationality: *ethnic Albanians in Kosovo.* ■ characteristic of or belonging to a non-Western cultural tradition: *folk and ethnic music.* ■ neither Christian nor Jewish; pagan or heathen. • *n.* a member of an ethnic group, esp. a minority.
DERIVATIVES: **eth•ni•cal•ly** |-(ə)lē| *adv.* [sentence adverb] *Denmark is ethnically Scandinavian.*

eth•no•cen•tric |ˌɛTHnō'sentrik| • *adj.* evaluating other peoples and cultures according to the standards of one's own culture.
DERIVATIVES: **eth•no•cen•tri•cal•ly** |-(ə)lē| *adv.* **eth•no•cen•tric•i•ty** |-ˌsen'trisiṭē| *n.* **eth•no•cen•trism** |-ˌtrizəm| *n.*

eth•nog•ra•phy |ɛTH'nägrəfē| • *n.* the scientific description of the customs of individual peoples and cultures.
DERIVATIVES: **eth•nog•ra•pher** |-fər| *n.* **eth•no•graph•ic** |ˌɛTHnə'græfik| *adj.* **eth•no•graph•i•cal** |ˈˌɛTHnə'græfikəl| *adj.* **eth•no•graph•i•cal•ly** |ˈˌɛTHnə'græfik(ə)lē| *adv.*

eth•nol•o•gy |ɛTH'näləjē| • *n.* the study of the characteristics of various peoples and the differences and relationships between them.
DERIVATIVES: **eth•no•log•ic** |ˌɛTHnə'läjik| *adj.* **eth•no•log•i•cal** |ˌɛTHnə'läjikəl| *adj.* **eth•no•log•i•cal•ly** |ˌɛTHnə'läjik(ə)lē| *adv.* **eth•nol•o•gist** |-jist| *n.*

e•thol•o•gy |ē'THäləjē| • *n.* the science of animal behavior.
■ the study of human behavior and social organization from a biological perspective.
DERIVATIVES: **e•tho•log•i•cal** |ˌēTHə'läjikəl| *adj.* **e•thol•o•gist** |-jist| *n.*

e•thos |'ɛTHäs| • *n.* the characteristic spirit of a culture, era, or community as manifested in its beliefs and aspirations: *a challenge to the ethos of the 1960s.*

e•ti•ol•o•gy |ˌēṭē'äləjē| (Brit. **aetiology**) • *n.* **1** the cause, set of causes, or manner of causation of a disease or condition: *a disease of unknown etiology* | *a group of distinct diseases with different etiologies.*
■ the causation of diseases and disorders as a subject of investigation. **2** the investigation or attribution of the cause or reason for something, often expressed in terms of historical or mythical explanation.

DERIVATIVES: **e•ti•o•log•ic** |ˌēṭēə'läjik| *adj.* **e•ti•o•log•i•cal** |ˌēṭēə'läjikəl| *adj.* **e•ti•o•log•i•cal•ly** |ˌēṭēə'läjik(ə)lē| *adv.*

et•y•mol•o•gy |ˌeṭə'mäləjē| • *n.* (pl. **-ies**) the study of the origin of words and the way in which their meanings have changed through time.
■ the origin of a word and the historical development of its meaning.
DERIVATIVES: **et•y•mo•log•i•cal** |-mə'läjikəl| *adj.* **et•y•mo•log•i•cal•ly** *adv.* **et•y•mol•o•gist** |-jist| *n.*

Eu•cha•rist |'yōōkərəst| • *n.* the Christian ceremony commemorating the Last Supper, in which bread and wine are consecrated and consumed.
■ the consecrated elements, esp. the bread.
DERIVATIVES: **Eu•cha•ris•tic** |ˌyōōkə'ristik| *adj.* **Eu•cha•ris•ti•cal** |ˌyōōkə'ristikəl| *adj.*

eu•gen•ics |yōō'jeniks| • *plural n.* [treated as sing.] the science of improving a population by controlled breeding to increase the occurrence of desirable heritable characteristics. Developed largely by Francis Galton (1822–1911) as a method of improving the human race, it fell into disfavor after the perversion of its doctrines by the Nazis.
DERIVATIVES: **eu•gen•ic** |-'jenik| *adj.* **eu•gen•i•cal•ly** |-ik(ə)lē| *adv.* **eu•gen•i•cist** |-'jenisist| *n.* & *adj.* **eu•gen•ist** |-'jenist| *n.* & *adj.*

eu•kar•y•ote |yōō'kærē,ōt; -'kerē-; -ēət| (also **eucaryote**) • *n.* an organism consisting of a cell or cells in which the genetic material is DNA in the form of chromosomes contained within a distinct nucleus. Eukaryotes include all living organisms other than the eubacteria and archaea. Cf. PROKARYOTE.
DERIVATIVES: **eu•kar•y•ot•ic** |yōō,kærē'äṭik; -,kerē-| *adj.*

eu•lo•gy |'yōōləjē| • *n.* (pl. **-ies**) a speech or piece of writing that praises someone or something highly, typically someone who has just died: *his good friend delivered a brief eulogy.* Cf. ELEGY.
DERIVATIVES: **eu•lo•gist** *n.* **eu•lo•gize** *v.*

eu•phe•mism |'yōōfə,mizəm| • *n.* a mild or indirect word or expression substituted for one considered to be too harsh or blunt when referring to something unpleasant or embarrassing: *"downsizing" as a euphemism for job cuts.* Cf. DYSPHEMISM.

eu•pho•ni•ous |yōō'fōnēəs| • *adj.* (of sound, esp. speech) pleasing to the ear: *the candidate delivered a stream of fine, euphonious phrases.*
DERIVATIVES: **eu•pho•ni•ous•ly** *adv.*

eu•pho•ny |'yōōfənē| • *n.* (pl. **-ies**) the quality of being pleasing to the ear, esp. through a harmonious combination of words.
■ the tendency to make phonetic change for ease of pronunciation.
DERIVATIVES: **eu•phon•ic** |yōō'fänik| *adj.* **eu•pho•nize** |-,nīz| *v.*

eu•pho•ri•a |yōō'fōrēə| • *n.* a feeling or state of intense excitement and happiness: *the euphoria of success.*

eu•phu•ism |'yōōfyə,wizəm| • *n.* an artificial, highly elaborate way of writing or speaking.

DERIVATIVES: **eu·phu·ist** n. **eu·phu·is·tic** |ˌyōōfyəˈwistik| adj. **eu·phu·is·ti·cal·ly** |ˌyōōfyəˈwistik(ə)lē| adv.

Eu·ro·cen·tric |ˌyərōˈsentrik; ˌyōōrō-| • adj. focusing on European culture or history to the exclusion of a wider view of the world; implicitly regarding European culture as preeminent.

DERIVATIVES: **Eu·ro·cen·tric·i·ty** |-ˌsen ˈtrisiṭē| n. **Eu·ro·cen·trism** |-ˈsen,trizəm| n.

eu·sta·sy |ˈyōōstəsē| (also **Eustacy**) • n. a change of sea level throughout the world, caused by fluctuations in the total volume of water in the oceans (esp. those caused by changes in the size of the ice caps), or by the changes in volume of the ocean basins.

DERIVATIVES: **eu·sta·tic** |yōōˈstæṭik| adj.

eu·tha·na·sia |ˌyōōThəˈnāzhə| • n. the painless killing of a patient suffering from an incurable and painful disease or in an irreversible coma.

DERIVATIVES: **eu·tha·nize** v.

eu·troph·i·ca·tion |yōō,träfiˈkāSHən| • n. excessive richness of nutrients in a lake or other body of water, frequently due to runoff from the land, which causes a dense growth of plant life, killing animal life by depriving it of oxygen.

DERIVATIVES: **eutrophic** adj. rich in organic material, etc. **eu·troph·i·cate** |yōō ˈträfi,kāt| v.

ev·a·nes·cent |ˌevəˈnesənt| • adj. soon passing out of sight, memory, or existence; quickly fading or disappearing: a shimmering evanescent bubble.

■ (in physics) denoting a field or wave that extends into a region where it cannot propagate and whose amplitude therefore decreases with distance.

DERIVATIVES: **ev·a·nesce** v. **ev·a·nes·cence** n. **ev·a·nes·cent·ly** adv.

e·van·gel·i·cal |ˌivænˈjelikəl| • adj. of or according to the teaching of the gospel or the Christian religion.

■ of or denoting a tradition within Protestant Christianity emphasizing the authority of the Bible, personal conversion, and the doctrine of salvation by faith alone. ■ zealous in advocating something. • n. a member of the evangelical tradition in the Christian Church.

DERIVATIVES: **e·van·gel·ic** |-ˈjelik| adj. **e·van·gel·i·cal·ism** |-izəm| n. **e·van·gel·i·cal·ly** adv.

e·van·ge·list |iˈvænjəlist| • n. 1 a person who seeks to convert others to the Christian faith, esp. by public preaching.

■ a layperson engaged in Christian missionary work. ■ a zealous advocate of something: he is an evangelist of junk bonds. 2 the writer of one of the four Gospels (Matthew, Mark, Luke, or John): St. John the Evangelist.

DERIVATIVES: **e·van·ge·lis·tic** |i,vænjəˈlistik| adj.

e·van·ge·lize |iˈvænjə,līz| • v. [trans.] convert or seek to convert (someone) to Christianity.

■ [intrans.] preach the Christian gospel: the

Church's mission to evangelize and declare the faith.

DERIVATIVES: **e·van·ge·li·za·tion** |i,vænjəli'zāSHən| n. **e·van·ge·liz·er** n.

e·va·sive |iˈvāsiv| • adj. tending to avoid commitment or self-revelation, esp. by responding only indirectly: she was evasive about her positions when interviewed.

■ directed toward avoidance or escape: they decided to take evasive action.

DERIVATIVES: **e·va·sive·ly** adv. **e·va·sive·ness** n.

e·ven·tu·ate |iˈvenCHə,wāt| • v. [intrans.] occur as a result: you never know what might eventuate.

■ (**eventuate in**) lead to as a result: circumstances that eventuate in crime.

DERIVATIVES: **e·ven·tu·a·tion** |i,venCHə ˈwāSHən| n.

e·vince |iˈvins| • v. [trans.] reveal the presence of (a quality or feeling): his letters evince the excitement he felt at undertaking this journey.

■ be evidence of; indicate: man's inhumanity to man as evinced in the use of torture.

e·vis·cer·ate |iˈvisə,rāt| • v. [trans.] disembowel (a person or animal): the goat had been skinned and neatly eviscerated.

■ deprive (something) of its essential content: myriad concessions that would eviscerate the project. ■ (in surgery) remove the contents of (a body organ).

DERIVATIVES: **e·vis·cer·a·tion** |i,visə'rā-SHən| n.

e·voke |iˈvōk| • v. [trans.] 1 bring or recall to the conscious mind: the sight of autumn asters evokes pleasant memories of childhood.

■ elicit (a response): the awkward kid who evoked giggles from his sisters. 2 call on; invoke (a spirit or deity).

DERIVATIVES: **ev·o·ca·tion** |ˌēvō'kāSHən; ˌevə-| n. **e·vok·er** n.

e·volve |iˈvälv| • v. 1 develop gradually, esp. from a simple to a more complex form: [intrans.] the company has evolved into a major chemical manufacturer | the Gothic style evolved steadily and naturally from the Romanesque | [trans.] each school must evolve its own way of working.

■ (with reference to an organism or biological feature) develop over successive generations, esp. as a result of natural selection: [intrans.] the populations are cut off from each other and evolve independently. 2 [trans.] Chemistry give off (gas or heat).

DERIVATIVES: **e·volv·a·ble** |-əbəl| adj. **e·volve·ment** n.

ex·ac·er·bate |igˈzæsər,bāt| • v. [trans.] make (a problem, bad situation, or negative feeling) worse: the forest fire was exacerbated by the lack of rain.

DERIVATIVES: **ex·ac·er·ba·tion** |ig,zæsər ˈbāSHən| n.

USAGE: On the difference between **exacerbate** and **exasperate**, see usage at EXASPERATE.

ex·act |igˈzækt| • v. [trans.] demand and obtain (something, esp. a payment) from someone: *tributes exacted from the Slav peoples* | *William's advisers exacted an oath of obedience from the clergy.*

■ inflict (revenge) on someone: *a frustrated woman bent on exacting a cruel revenge for his rejection.*

DERIVATIVES: **ex•act•a•ble** *adj.* **ex•ac•tor** |-tər| *n.*

ex•alt |ig'zôlt| • *v.* [trans.] hold (someone or something) in very high regard; think or speak very highly of: *the party will continue to exalt its hero.*

■ raise to a higher rank or a position of greater power: *this naturally exalts the peasant above his brethren in the same rank of society.*

■ make noble in character; dignify: *romanticism liberated the imagination and exalted the emotions.*

ex•a•men |ig,zāmən| • *n.* a formal examination of the soul or conscience, made usually daily by Jesuits and some other Roman Catholics.

ex•as•per•ate |ig'zæspə,rāt| • *v.* [trans.] irritate intensely; infuriate: *this futile process exasperates prison officials* | [as adj.] (**exasperated**) *she grew exasperated with his inability to notice anything* | [as adj.] (**exasperating**) *they suffered a number of exasperating setbacks.*

DERIVATIVES: **ex•as•per•at•ed•ly** *adv.* **ex•as•per•at•ing•ly** |-,rāṭiNGlē| *adv.* **ex•as•per•a•tion** |ig,zæspə'rāsHən| *n.*

USAGE: The verbs **exasperate** and **exacerbate** are sometimes confused. **Exasperate**, the more common of the two, means 'to irritate or annoy to an extreme degree,' (*He calls me three times a day asking for money. It's exasperating!*); **exacerbate** means 'to increase the bitterness or severity' of something (*The star shortstop's loud self-congratulation only exacerbated his teammates' resentment*).

ex ca•the•dra |,eks kə'THēdrə| • *adv. & adj.* with the full authority of office (esp. of the pope's infallibility as defined in Roman Catholic doctrine): [as adv.] *for an encyclical to be infallible the pope must speak ex cathedra.*

ex•cept |ik'sept| • *v.* [trans.] specify as not included in a category or group; exclude: *he excepted from his criticism a handful of distinguished writers.*

■ [intrans.] make objection (against); object (to).

ex•cep•tion |ik'sepsHən| • *n.* a person or thing that is excluded from a general statement or does not follow a rule: *the drives between towns are a delight, and the journey to Graz is **no exception*** | *while he normally shies away from introducing resolutions, he **made an exception** in this case.*

■ (in law) an objection made to a ruling of the court during the course of a trial, e.g., to the admission of evidence.

ex•cise[1] |'ek,sīz| • *n.* [usu. as adj.] a tax levied on certain goods and commodities produced or sold within a country or state and on licenses granted for certain activities: *excise taxes on cigarettes.* • *v.* |ik'sīz; ek-| [trans.]

[usu. as adj.] (**excised**) charge excise on (goods): *excised goods.*

ex•com•mu•ni•cate • *v.* |,ekskə'myōōni,kāt| [trans.] officially exclude (someone) from participation in the sacraments and services of the Christian Church. • *adj.* excommunicated: *all violators were to be pronounced excommunicate.* • *n.* an excommunicated person.

DERIVATIVES: **ex•com•mu•ni•ca•tion** |,ekskə,myōōni'kāsHən| *n.* **ex•com•mu•ni•ca•tive** |-,kādiv| *adj.* **ex•com•mu•ni•ca•tor** |-,kāṭər| *n.* **ex•com•mu•ni•ca•to•ry** |-kə,tôrē| *adj.*

ex•co•ri•ate |ik'skôrē,āt| • *v.* [trans.] **1** censure or criticize severely: *the papers that had been excoriating him were now lauding him.* **2** (in medicine) damage or remove part of the surface of (the skin).

DERIVATIVES: **ex•co•ri•a•tion** |ik,skôrē'āsHən| *n.*

ex•cres•cence |ik'skresəns| • *n.* a distinct outgrowth on a human or animal body or on a plant, esp. one that is the result of disease or abnormality.

■ an unattractive or superfluous addition or feature: *removing an architectural excrescence.*

ex•cre•tion |ik'skrēsHən| • *n.* (in living organisms and cells) the process of eliminating or expelling waste matter.

■ a product of this process: *bodily excretions.*
DERIVATIVES: **ex•crete** *v.* **ex•cre•tive** *adj.* **ex•cre•to•ry** *adj.*

ex•cru•ci•at•ing |ik'skrōōsHē,āṭiNG| • *adj.* intensely painful: *excruciating back pain.*

■ mentally agonizing; very embarrassing, awkward, or tedious: *excruciating boredom.*

DERIVATIVES: **ex•cru•ci•at•ing•ly** *adv.* [as submodifier] *the sting can prove excruciatingly painful.*

ex•cul•pate |'ekskəl,pāt| • *v.* [trans.] show or declare that (someone) is not guilty of wrongdoing: *the article exculpated the mayor.*

DERIVATIVES: **ex•cul•pa•tion** |,ekskəl'pā-sHən| *n.* **ex•cul•pa•to•ry** |,eks'kəlpə,tôrē| *adj.*

ex•cur•sive |ik'skərsiv| • *adj.* of the nature of an excursion; ranging widely; digressive: *an excursive piece of writing.*

DERIVATIVES: **ex•cur•sive•ly** *adv.* **ex•cur•sive•ness** *n.*

ex•e•cra•ble |'eksikrəbəl| • *adj.* extremely bad or unpleasant: *execrable cheap wine.*

DERIVATIVES: **ex•e•cra•bly** |-blē| *adv.*

ex•e•crate |'eksi,krāt| • *v.* [trans.] feel or express great loathing for: *they were execrated as dangerous and corrupt.*

■ [intrans.] curse; swear.

DERIVATIVES: **ex•e•cra•tion** |,eksi'krā-sHən| *n.* **ex•e•cra•tive** |-,krātiv| *adj.* **ex•e•cra•to•ry** |-krə,tôrē| *adj.*

ex•e•cute |'eksi,kyōōt| • *v.* [trans.] **1** carry out or put into effect (a plan, order, or course of action): *the corporation executed a series of financial deals.*

■ produce (a work of art): *she designs and executes detailed embroideries.* ■ perform (an activity or maneuver requiring care or skill): *they had to execute their dance steps with the*

greatest precision. ■ make (a legal instrument) valid by signing or sealing it. ■ carry out (a judicial sentence, the terms of a will, or other order): *police executed a search warrant* | *sentence was executed on November 5th.* **2** (often **be executed**) carry out a sentence of death on (a legally condemned person): *he was convicted of treason and executed.*
■ kill (someone) as a political act.
ex•ec•u•tor • *n.* **1** |igˈzekyətər| (in law) a person or institution appointed by a testator to carry out the terms of a will: *my father named me as his executor.*
■ a person who executes a particular plan or command: *a literary executor.* **2** |ˈeksəˌkyōōtər| a person who produces something or puts something into effect: *the makers and executors of policy.*
DERIVATIVES: **ex•ec•u•to•ri•al** |igˌzekyəˈtôrēəl| *adj.* **ex•ec•u•tor•ship** |igˈzekyətərˌSHip| *n.* **ex•ec•u•to•ry** |igˈzekyə͟torē| *adj.*
ex•e•ge•sis |ˌeksiˈjēsis| • *n.* (pl. **exegeses** |-sēz|) critical explanation or interpretation of a text, esp. of scripture: *the task of biblical exegesis* | *an exegesis of Marx.*
DERIVATIVES: **ex•e•get•ic** |-ˈjetik| *adj.* **ex•e•get•i•cal** *adj.*
ex•em•plar |igˈzemplər; -plär| • *n.* a person or thing serving as a typical example or excellent model: *he became the leading exemplar of conservative philosophy.*
ex•em•pla•ry |igˈzemplərē| • *adj.* **1** serving as a desirable model; representing the best of its kind: *an award for exemplary community service.*
■ characteristic of its kind or illustrating a general rule: *her works are exemplary of certain feminist arguments.* **2** (of a punishment) serving as a warning or deterrent: *exemplary sentencing may discourage the ultraviolent minority.*
■ (in law, of damages) exceeding the amount needed for simple compensation, and awarded to mark disapproval of the defendant's conduct. (Also called **punitive damages**).
DERIVATIVES: **ex•em•pla•ri•ly** |-rəlē| *adv.* **ex•em•pla•ri•ness** |-rēnis| *n.* **ex•em•plar•i•ty** |ˌegzemˈplæri͟tē; -ˈpler-| *n.*
ex•em•pli•fy |igˈzempləˌfī| • *v.* (**-ies, -ied**) [trans.] be a typical example of: *rock bands that exemplify the spirit of the age.*
■ give an example of; illustrate by giving an example.
DERIVATIVES: **ex•em•pli•fi•er** *n.* **ex•em•pli•fi•ca•tion** |igˌzempləfiˈkāSHən| *n.*
ex•em•plum |igˈzempləm| • *n.* (pl. **exempla** |-plə|) an example or model, esp. a moralizing or illustrative story.
ex•empt |igˈzem(p)t| • *adj.* free from an obligation or liability imposed on others: *these patients are exempt from all charges* | *they are not exempt from criticism.* Cf. IMMUNE. • *v.* [trans.] free (a person or organization) from an obligation or liability imposed on others: *they were exempted from paying the tax.* • *n.* a person who is exempt from something, esp. the payment of tax.
ex•e•quy |ˈeksikwē| • *n.* (**exequies**) funeral

rites; obsequies: *he attended the exequies for the dead pope.*
ex•er•tion |igˈzərSHən| • *n.* **1** physical or mental effort: *she was panting with the exertion* | *a well-earned rest after their mental exertions.* **2** the application of a force, influence, or quality: *the exertion of authority.*
ex•fo•li•ate |eksˈfōlēˌāt| • *v.* [intrans.] (of a material) come apart or be shed from a surface in scales or layers: *the bark exfoliates in papery flakes.*
■ [trans.] cause to do this: *salt solutions exfoliate rocks on evaporating.* ■ [intrans.] (of a tree) throw off layers of bark: *the plane tree exfoliates most noticeably.* ■ [trans.] wash or rub (a part of the body) with a granular substance to remove dead cells from the surface of the skin: *exfoliate your legs to get rid of dead skin.* ■ [trans.] (often **be exfoliated**) shed (material) in scales or layers.
DERIVATIVES: **ex•fo•li•ant** *n.* *this cream is an effective exfoliant.* **ex•fo•li•a•tion** |eksˌfōlēˈāSHən| *n.* **ex•fo•li•a•tive** |-ˌātiv| *adj.* **ex•fo•li•a•tor** *n.* .
ex•haus•tive |igˈzôstiv| • *adj.* examining, including, or considering all elements or aspects; fully comprehensive: *she has undergone exhaustive tests since becoming ill.*
DERIVATIVES: **ex•haus•tive•ly** *adv.* **ex•haus•tive•ness** *n.*
ex•hi•bi•tion•ism |ˌeksəˈbiSHəˌnizəm| • *n.* extravagant behavior that is intended to attract attention to oneself.
■ a mental condition characterized by the compulsion to display one's genitals in public.
DERIVATIVES: **ex•hi•bi•tion•ist** *n.* **ex•hi•bi•tion•is•tic** |-ˌbiSHəˈnistik| *adj.* **ex•hi•bi•tion•is•ti•cal•ly** |-ˌbiSHəˈnistik(ə)lē| *adv.*
ex•hil•a•rate |igˈziləˌrāt| • *v.* (usu. **be exhilarated**) make (someone) feel very happy, animated, or elated: *the children were exhilarated by a sense of purpose* | [as adj.] (**exhilarated**) *this fresh mountain air makes me feel exhilarated* | [as adj.] (**exhilarating**) *riding was one of the most exhilarating experiences he knew.*
DERIVATIVES: **ex•hil•a•rat•ing•ly** |-ˌrātiNGlē| *adv.* **ex•hil•a•ra•tion** |igˌziləˈrāSHən| *n.*
ex•hort |igˈzôrt| • *v.* [with obj. and infinitive] strongly encourage or urge (someone) to do something: *they've been exhorting people to turn out for the demonstration* | [with direct speech] *"Come on, you guys," exhorted Linda.*
DERIVATIVES: **ex•hor•ta•tion** *n.* **ex•hort•a•tive** |-ˌtətiv| *adj.* **ex•hort•a•to•ry** |-ˌtəˌtôrē| *adj.* **ex•hort•er** *n.*
ex•i•gen•cy |ˈeksijənsē; igˈzijənsē| • *n.* (pl. **-ies**) urgent need or demand: *women worked long hours when the exigencies of the family economy demanded it* | *he put financial exigency before personal sentiment.*
ex•i•gent |ˈeksijənt| • *adj.* pressing; demanding: *the exigent demands of the music took a toll on her voice.*
ex•ig•u•ous |igˈzigyəwəs; ikˈsig-| • *adj.* very small in size or amount: *my exiguous musical resources.*

DERIVATIVES: **ex•i•gu•i•ty** |ˌeksi'gyōōiṭē| *n.* **ex•ig•u•ous•ly** *adv.* **ex•ig•u•ous•ness** *n.*
ex•is•ten•tial |ˌegzi'stenCHəl| • *adj.* of or relating to existence.
■ (in philosophy) concerned with existence, esp. human existence as viewed in the theories of existentialism. ■ (of a logical proposition) affirming or implying the existence of a thing.
DERIVATIVES: **ex•is•ten•tial•ly** *adv.*
ex•is•ten•tial•ism |ˌegzi'stenCHəˌlizəm| • *n.* a philosophical theory or approach that emphasizes the existence of the individual person as a free and responsible agent determining his or her own development through acts of the will.

Generally taken to originate with Kierkegaard and Nietzsche, existentialism tends to be atheistic, to disparage scientific knowledge, and to deny the existence of objective values, stressing instead the reality and significance of human freedom and experience. The approach was developed chiefly in 20th-century Europe, notably by Martin Heidegger, Jean-Paul Sartre, Albert Camus, and Simone de Beauvoir.

DERIVATIVES: **ex•is•ten•tial•ist** *n. & adj.*
ex of•fi•ci•o |'eks ə'fishēō| • *adv. & adj.* by virtue of one's position or status: [as adj.] *an ex officio member of the committee.*
ex•og•a•my |ek'sägəmē| • *n.* (in anthropology) the custom of marrying outside a community, clan, or tribe. Cf. ENDOGAMY.
■ (in biology) the fusion of reproductive cells from distantly related or unrelated individuals; outbreeding; cross-pollination.
DERIVATIVES: **ex•og•a•mous** |-məs| *adj.*
ex•og•e•nous |ek'säjənəs| • *adj.* of, relating to, or developing from external factors. Cf. ENDOGENOUS.
■ growing or originating from outside an organism: *an exogenous hormone.* ■ (of a disease, symptom, etc.) caused by an agent or organism outside the body: *exogenous depression.* ■ relating to an external group or society: *exogenous marriage.*
DERIVATIVES: **ex•og•e•nous•ly** *adv.*
ex•on•er•ate |ig'zänəˌrāt| • *v.* [trans.] **1** (esp. of an official body) absolve (someone) from blame for a fault or wrongdoing, esp. after due consideration of the case: *the court-martial exonerated her* | *they should exonerate these men from this crime.* **2** (**exonerate someone from**) release someone from (a duty or obligation).
DERIVATIVES: **ex•on•er•a•tion** | igˌzänə'rāSHən| *n.* **ex•on•er•a•tive** |-ˌrātiv| *adj.*
ex•or•bi•tant |ig'zôrbitənt| • *adj.* (of a price or amount charged) unreasonably high: *the exorbitant price of tickets.*
DERIVATIVES: **ex•or•bi•tance** |eg'zôrbə-tns| *n.* **ex•or•bi•tant•ly** *adv.*
ex•or•cise |'eksôr,sīz; 'eksər-| (also **-ize**) • *v.* [trans.] drive out or attempt to drive out (as an evil spirit) from a person or place: *an attempt to exorcise an unquiet spirit* | *inflation has been exorcised.*

■ (often **be exorcised**) rid (a person or place) of anevil spirit: *infants were exorcised prior to baptism.*
ex•o•sphere |ˌeksō'sfir| • *n.* the outermost region of a planet's atmosphere.
DERIVATIVES: **ex•o•spher•ic** |ˌeksō'sfirik; -'sferik| *adj.* .
ex•o•ter•ic |ˌeksə'terik| • *adj.* (esp. of a doctrine or mode of speech) intended for or likely to be understood by the general public: *an exoteric, literal meaning and an esoteric, inner teaching.* Cf. ESOTERIC.
■ relating to the outside world; external: *the exoteric and esoteric aspects of life.* ■ current or popular among the general public.
ex•ot•ic |ig,zätik| • *adj.* originating in or characteristic of a distant foreign country: *exotic birds* | *the exotic scenery of Patagonia.*
■ attractive or striking because colorful or out of the ordinary: *an exotic outfit* | [as n.] (**the exotic**) *there was a touch of the exotic in her appearance.* ■ of a kind not used for ordinary purposes or not ordinarily encountered: *exotic elementary particles as yet unknown to science.* • *n.* an exotic plant or animal: *we planted exotics in a sheltered garden.* ■ a thing that is imported or unusual: *the market in exotics has gone crazy with speculators.*
DERIVATIVES: **ex•ot•i•cal•ly** |-(ə)lē| *adv.* **ex•ot•i•cism** |ig'zätəˌsizəm| *n.*
ex par•te |eks 'pärtē| • *adj. & adv.* (in law) with respect to or in the interests of one side only or of an interested outside party: *an exparte hearing.*
ex•pa•ti•ate |ik'spāSHē,āt| • *v.* [intrans.] speak or write at length or in detail: *she expatiated on working-class novelists.*
DERIVATIVES: **ex•pa•ti•a•tion** |ikˌspāSHē 'āSHən| *n.*
ex•pa•tri•ate • *n.* |eks'pātreit| a person who lives outside his or her native country: *American expatriates in London.*
■ (in earlier use) a person exiled from his or her native country. • *adj.* [attrib.] (of a person) living outside one's native country: *expatriate workers.*
■ expelled from one's native country. • *v.* |eks 'pātrē,āt| [intrans.] settle oneself abroad: *candidates for the position should be willing to expatriate.*
DERIVATIVES: **ex•pa•tri•a•tion** |eksˌpātrē 'āSHən| *n.*
ex•pec•to•rant |ik'spektərənt| • *n.* a medicine that promotes the secretion of sputum (saliva and mucus) by the air passages, used esp. to treat coughs.
ex•pec•to•rate |ik'spektə,rāt| • *v.* [intrans.] cough or spit out phlegm from the throat or lungs.
■ [trans.] spit out (phlegm) in this way.
DERIVATIVES: **ex•pec•to•ra•tion** |ikˌspek-tə'rāSHən| *n.* **ex•pec•to•rant** *n.*
ex•pe•di•ent |ik'spēdēənt| • *adj.* (of an action) convenient and practical, although possibly improper or immoral: *either side would break the agreement if it were expedient to do so.*
■ (of an action) suitable or appropriate in the circumstances, or for the matter at hand:

holding a public inquiry into the scheme was not expedient. ▪ *n.* a means of attaining an end, esp. one that is convenient but considered improper or immoral: *the current policy is a political expedient.*
DERIVATIVES: **ex•pe•di•ence** *n.* **ex•pe•di•en•cy** *n.* **ex•pe•di•ent•ly** *adv.*
ex•pe•dite |'ekspə‚dīt| ▪ *v.* [trans.] make (an action or process) happen sooner or be accomplished more quickly: *he promised to expedite economic reforms.*
DERIVATIVES: **ex•pe•dit•er** (also **ex•pe•di•tor**) *n.* **ex•pe•di•tion** *n.*
ex•pe•di•tious |‚ekspə'disHəs| ▪ *adj.* done with speed and efficiency (expedition): *an expeditious investigation.*
DERIVATIVES: **ex•pe•di•tious•ly** *adv.* **ex•pe•di•tious•ness** *n.*
ex•pe•ri•en•tial |ek‚spirē'encHəl| ▪ *adj.* involving or based on experience and observation: *the experiential learning associated with employment.*
DERIVATIVES: **ex•pe•ri•en•tial•ly** *adv.*
ex•per•tise |‚ekspər'tēz; -'tēs| ▪ *n.* expert skill or knowledge in a particular field: *technical expertise.*
ex•pi•ate |'ekspē‚āt| ▪ *v.* [trans.] atone or make amends for (guilt or sin): *their sins must be expiated by sacrifice.*
DERIVATIVES: **ex•pi•a•ble** |'ekspēəbəl| *adj.* **ex•pi•a•tion** |‚ekspē'āsHən| *n.* **ex•pi•a•tor** |-‚ātər| *n.* **ex•pi•a•to•ry** |'ekspēə‚tôrē| *adj.*
ex•ple•tive |'eksplitiv| ▪ *n.* **1** an oath or swear word. **2** a word or phrase used to fill out a sentence or a line of verse without adding to the sense. ▪ *adj.* (of a word or phrase) serving to fill out a sentence or line of verse.
ex•pli•cate |'ekspli‚kāt| ▪ *v.* [trans.] analyze and develop (an idea or principle) in detail: *attempting to explicate the relationship between crime and economic forces.* ▪ analyze (a literary work) in order to reveal its meaning.
DERIVATIVES: **ex•pli•ca•tion** |‚ekspli'kā-sHən| *n.* **ex•pli•ca•tive** |-‚kātiv| *adj.* **ex•pli•ca•tor** |-‚kātər| *n.* **ex•pli•ca•to•ry** |ik'splikə‚tôrē| *adj.*
ex•plic•it |ik'splisit| ▪ *adj.* stated clearly and in detail, leaving no room for confusion or doubt: *the speaker's intentions were not made explicit.* ▪ (of a person) stating something in such a way: *let me be explicit.* ▪ describing or representing sexual activity in a graphic fashion: *explicit photos.*
DERIVATIVES: **ex•plic•it•ly** *adv.* **ex•plic•it•ness** *n.*
ex•ploit ▪ *v.* |ik'sploit| [trans.] make full use of and derive benefit from (a resource): *500 companies sprang up to exploit this new technology.* ▪ use (a situation or person) in an unfair or selfish way: *the company was exploiting a legal loophole.* ▪ benefit unfairly from the work of (someone), typically by overworking or underpaying them: *making money does not always mean exploiting others.* ▪ *n.* |'ek‚sploit| a

bold or daring feat: *the most heroic exploits of the war.*
DERIVATIVES: **ex•ploit•a•ble** *adj.* **ex•ploi•ta•tion** |‚eksploi'tāsHən| *n.* **ex•ploit•a•tive** |ik'sploitətiv| *adj.* **ex•ploit•er** |ik'sploitər| *n.* **ex•ploit•ive** |ik'sploitiv| *adj.*
ex•po•nent |ik'spōnənt; 'ekspōnənt| ▪ *n.* **1** a person who believes in and promotes the truth or benefits of an idea or theory: *an early exponent of the teachings of Thomas Aquinas.* ▪ a person who has and demonstrates a particular skill, esp. to a high standard: *the world's leading exponent of country rock guitar.* **2** (in mathematics) a quantity representing the power to which a given number or expression is to be raised, usually expressed as a raised symbol beside the number or expression (e.g., 3 in $2^3 = 2 \times 2 \times 2$).
ex•po•nen•tial |‚ekspə'nencHəl| ▪ *adj.* of or expressed by a mathematical exponent: *an exponential curve.* ▪ (of an increase) becoming more and more rapid: *the military budget was rising at an exponential rate.*
DERIVATIVES: **ex•po•nen•tial•ly** *adv.*
ex•po•si•tion |‚ekspə'zisHən| ▪ *n.* **1** a comprehensive description and explanation of an idea or theory: *an exposition and defense of Marx's writings.* ▪ (in music) the part of a movement, esp. in sonata form, in which the principal themes are first presented. ▪ the part of a play or work of fiction in which the background to the main conflict is introduced. **2** a large public exhibition of art or trade goods. ▪ the action of making public; exposure: *the country squires dreaded the exposition of their rustic conversation.*
DERIVATIVES: **ex•po•si•tion•al** |-zisHənl| *adj.*
ex•pos•i•tor |ik'späzitər| ▪ *n.* a person or thing that explains complicated ideas or theories: *a lucid expositor of difficult ideas.*
ex post fac•to |‚ek‚spōst 'fæktō| ▪ *adj.* & *adv.* with retroactive effect or force: [as adj.] *ex post facto laws, which punish actions of long ago.*
ex•pos•tu•late |ik'späscHə‚lāt| ▪ *v.* [intrans.] express strong disapproval or disagreement: *I expostulated with him in vain.*
DERIVATIVES: **ex•pos•tu•la•tion** |ik‚späs-cHə'lāsHən| *n.* **ex•pos•tu•la•tor** |-‚lātər| *n.* **ex•pos•tu•la•to•ry** |ik‚späscHələ‚tôrē| *adj.*
ex•pres•sion•ism |ik'spresHə‚nizəm| ▪ *n.* a style of painting, music, or drama in which the artist or writer seeks to express emotional experience rather than impressions of the external world.
DERIVATIVES: **ex•pres•sion•ist** *n.* & *adj.* **ex•pres•sion•is•tic** |ik‚spresHə'nistik| *adj.* **ex•pres•sion•is•ti•cal•ly** |ik‚spresHə'nistək-(ə)lē| *adv.*
ex•pro•pri•ate |‚eks'prōprē‚āt| ▪ *v.* [trans.] (esp. of the state) take away (property) from its owner: *government plans to expropriate farmland.* ▪ dispossess (someone) of property: *the land reform expropriated the Irish landlords.*

DERIVATIVES: **ex•pro•pri•a•tion** |,eks ,prōprē'āsHən| *n.* **ex•pro•pri•a•tor** |-,āṭər| *n.*

ex•punge |ik'spənj| • *v.* [trans.] erase or remove completely (something unwanted or unpleasant): *he asked that his statement be expunged from the record.*
DERIVATIVES: **ex•punc•tion** |ik'spəNG(k)-sHən| *n.* **ex•punge•ment** *n.* **ex•pung•er** *n.*

ex•pur•gate |'ekspər,gāt| • *v.* [trans.] [often as adj.] (**expurgated**) remove matter thought to be objectionable or unsuitable from (a book or account): *efforts to expurgate several works by Mark Twain.*
DERIVATIVES: **ex•pur•ga•tion** |,ekspər 'gāsHən| *n.* **ex•pur•ga•tor** |-,gāṭər| *n.* **ex•pur•ga•to•ry** |ik'spərgə,tôrē| *adj.*

ex•tant |'ekstənt; ek'stænt| • *adj.* (esp. of a document) still in existence; surviving: *the original manuscript is no longer extant* | *are your grandparents extant?*

ex•tem•po•ra•ne•ous |ik,stempə'rānēəs| • *adj.* spoken or done without preparation: *an extemporaneous speech.*
DERIVATIVES: **ex•tem•po•ra•ne•ous•ly** *adv.* **ex•tem•po•ra•ne•ous•ness** *n.*

ex•tem•po•rar•y |ik'stempə,rerē| • *adj.* another term for EXTEMPORANEOUS.
DERIVATIVES: **ex•tem•po•rar•i•ly** |ik ,stempə'rerəlē| *adv.* **ex•tem•po•rar•i•ness** |-,rerēnis| *n.*

ex•tem•po•re |ik'stempərē| • *adj. & adv.* spoken or done without preparation: [as adj.] *extempore public speaking* | [as adv.] *he recited the poem extempore.*

ex•ten•u•ate |ik'stenyə,wāt| • *v.* [trans.] **1** [usu. as adj.] (**extenuating**) make (guilt or an offense) seem less serious or more forgivable: *there were **extenuating circumstances** that tended to help the defendants.* **2** [usu. as adj.] (**extenuated**) make (someone) thin: *drawings of extenuated figures.*
DERIVATIVES: **ex•ten•u•a•tion** |ik,stenyə 'wāsHən| *n.* **ex•ten•u•a•to•ry** |-wə,tôrē| *adj.*

ex•ter•nal•ize |ik'stərnə,līz| • *v.* [trans.] (usu. **be externalized**) give external existence or form to: *elements of the internal construction were externalized onto the façade.* ■ express (a thought or feeling) in words or actions: *an urgent need to externalize the experience.* ■ project (a mental image or process) onto a figure outside oneself: *such neuroses are externalized as interpersonal conflicts.*
DERIVATIVES: **ex•ter•nal•i•za•tion** |ik ,stərnəli'zāsHən| *n.*

ex•tir•pate |'ekstər,pāt| • *v.* [trans.] root out and destroy completely: *the dream of extirpating racism.*
DERIVATIVES: **ex•tir•pa•tion** |,ekstər 'pāsHən| *n.* **ex•tir•pa•tor** |-,pāṭər| *n.*

ex•tol |ik'stōl| • *v.* (**extolled, extolling**) [trans.] praise enthusiastically: *he extolled the virtues of the Russian peoples.*
DERIVATIVES: **ex•tol•ler** *n.* **ex•tol•ment** *n.*

ex•tort |ik'stôrt| • *v.* obtain (something) by force, threats, or other unfair means: *he was convicted of trying to extort $3 million from a developer.*
DERIVATIVES: **ex•tort•er** *n.* **ex•tor•tive** |-ṭiv| *adj.*

ex•tor•tion |ik'stôrsHən| • *n.* the practice or crime of obtaining something, esp. money, through force or threats.
DERIVATIVES: **ex•tor•tion•er** *n.* **ex•tor•tion•ist** |-əst| *n.*

ex•tra•di•tion |,ekstrə'disHən| • *n.* the action of delivering (*extraditing*) a person to another state or country where he or she has been accused or convicted of a crime: *they fought to prevent his extradition to the US* | *extraditions of drug suspects.*
DERIVATIVES: **ex•tra•dite** *v.* **ex•tra•dit•a•ble** *adj.*

ex•tra•dos |'ekstrə,däs| • *n.* (in architecture) the upper or outer curve of an arch.

ex•tra•ne•ous |ik'strānēəs| • *adj.* irrelevant or unrelated to the subject being dealt with: *one is obliged to wade through many pages of extraneous material.* ■ of external origin: *when the transmitter pack is turned off, no extraneous noise is heard.* ■ separate from the object to which it is attached: *other insects attach extraneous objects or material to themselves.*
DERIVATIVES: **ex•tra•ne•ous•ly** *adv.* **ex•tra•ne•ous•ness** *n.*

ex•trap•o•late |ik'stræpə,lāt| • *v.* [trans.] extend the application of (a method or conclusion, esp. one based on statistics) to an unknown situation by assuming that existing trends will continue or similar methods will be applicable: *the results cannot be extrapolated to other patient groups* | [intrans.] *it is always dangerous to **extrapolate from** a sample.* ■ estimate or conclude (something) in this way: *attempts to extrapolate likely human cancers from laboratory studies.* ■ (in mathematics) extend (a graph, curve, or range of values) by inferring unknown values from trends in the known data: [as adj.] (**extrapolated**) *a set of extrapolated values.*
DERIVATIVES: **ex•trap•o•la•tion** |ik,stræp-ə'lāsHən| *n.* **ex•trap•o•la•tive** |-,lāṭiv| *adj.* **ex•trap•o•la•tor** |-,lāṭər| *n.*

ex•tra•sen•so•ry per•cep•tion |,ekstrə'sen-sərē| (abbr.: **ESP**) • *n.* the supposed faculty of perceiving things by means other than the known senses, e.g., by telepathy or clairvoyance: *twins often seem connected by extrasensory perception.*

ex•treme unc•tion • *n.* (in the Roman Catholic Church) a former name for the sacrament of anointing of the sick, esp. when administered to the dying.

ex•tri•cate |'ekstri,kāt| • *v.* [trans.] free (someone or something) from a constraint or difficulty: *they raced to extricate him from the car* | *he was trying to **extricate** himself **from** official duties.*
DERIVATIVES: **ex•tri•ca•ble** |ek'strikəbəl; ik-| *adj.* **ex•tri•ca•tion** |,ekstri'kāsHən| *n.*

ex•trin•sic |ik'strinzik; -sik| • *adj.* not part of the essential nature of someone or something; coming or operating from outside: *extrinsic factors that might affect budgets* | *the idea that power is **extrinsic to** production and profits.*

DERIVATIVES: **ex•trin•si•cal•ly** |-(ə)lē| adv.

ex•tro•vert |'ekstrə,vərt| (also **extravert**) • n. an outgoing, overtly expressive person. ■ (in psychology) a person predominantly concerned with external things or objective considerations. Cf. INTROVERT. • adj. of, denoting, or typical of an extrovert: his extrovert personality made him the ideal host. DERIVATIVES: **ex•tro•ver•sion** |,ekstrə 'vərzHən| n. **ex•tro•vert•ed** adj.

USAGE: The original spelling **extravert** is now rare in general use but is found in technical use in psychology.

ex•trude |ik'strо̄о̄d| • v. [trans.] (usu. be **extruded**) thrust or force out: lava was being extruded from the volcano. ■ shape (a material such as metal or plastic) by forcing it through a die: [as adj.] extruded plastic forms. DERIVATIVES: **ex•trud•a•ble** |-əbəl| adj. **ex•tru•sile** |ik'strо̄о̄səl; -,sīl| adj. **ex•tru•sion** |ik'strо̄о̄zHən| n.

ex•u•ber•ant |ig'zо̄о̄bərənt| • adj. filled with or characterized by a lively energy and excitement: giddily exuberant crowds | flamboyant and exuberant architectural invention. ■ growing luxuriantly or profusely: exuberant foliage.

DERIVATIVES: **ex•u•ber•ance** n. **ex•u•ber•ant•ly** adv.

ex•ude |ig'zо̄о̄d| • v. [trans.] discharge (moisture or a smell) slowly and steadily: the beetle exudes a caustic liquid. ■ [intrans.] (of moisture or a smell) be discharged by something in such a way: slime **exudes from** the fungus. ■ (of a person) display (an emotion or quality) strongly and openly: they exuded friendship and goodwill. ■ [intrans.] (of an emotion or quality) be displayed by someone in such a way: sexuality **exuded from** him. ■ (of a place) have a strong atmosphere of: the building exudes an air of tranquility. DERIVATIVES: **ex•u•da•tion** |,eksyо̄о̄'dā-sHən; ,eksə-| n. **ex•u•da•tive** |ig'zо̄о̄dətiv; 'eksə,dātiv; 'eksyо̄о̄-| adj.

ex•ult |ig'zəlt| • v. [intrans.] show or feel elation or jubilation, esp. as the result of a success: **exulting in** her escape, Leonora closed the door behind her. DERIVATIVES: **ex•ul•ta•tion** |,eksəl'tā-sHən; ,egzəl-| n. **ex•ult•ing•ly** adv.

ex•urb |'eksərb| • n. a district outside a city, esp. a prosperous area beyond the suburbs. DERIVATIVES: **ex•ur•ban** |ek'sərbən| adj. **ex•ur•ban•ite** |ek'sərbə,nīt| n. & adj.

ey•rie |'erē; 'irē| • n. variant spelling of AERIE.

Ff

fab•li•au |'fæblē,ō| • n. (pl. **fabliaux** |-ōz|) a story in verse form, typically a bawdily humorous one, of a type found chiefly in early French poetry.

fab•ri•cate |'fæbrə,kāt| • v. [trans.] invent or concoct (something), typically with deceitful intent: officers fabricated evidence. ■ construct or manufacture (something, esp. an industrial product), esp. from prepared components: you will have to fabricate an exhaust system. DERIVATIVES: **fab•ri•ca•tion** |,fæbrə'kā-sHən| n. **fab•ri•ca•tor** |-,kātər| n.

fab•u•list |'fæbyələst| • n. a person who composes or relates fables. ■ a liar, esp. a person who invents elaborate dishonest stories.

fa•cade |fə'säd| (also **façade**) • n. the face of a building, esp. the principal front that looks onto a street or open space. ■ an outward appearance that is maintained to conceal a less pleasant or creditable reality: her flawless public facade masked private despair.

fac•et |'fæsət| • n. one side of a many-sided thing, esp. of a cut gem. ■ a particular aspect or feature of something: participation by the laity in all facets of church life.

DERIVATIVES: **fac•et•ed** |'fæsətid| adj. [in combination] multifaceted.

fa•ce•ti•ae |fə'sēsHē,ē; -sHē,ī| • plural n. **1** pornographic literature. **2** humorous or witty sayings.

fa•ce•tious |fə'sēsHəs| • adj. treating serious issues with deliberately inappropriate humor; flippant. DERIVATIVES: **fa•ce•tious•ly** adv. **fa•ce•tious•ness** n.

fac•ile |'fæsəl| • adj. **1** (esp. of a theory or argument) appearing neat and comprehensive only by ignoring the true complexities of an issue; superficial. ■ having or revealing a superficial or simplistic knowledge or approach: a facile and shallow intellect. **2** (of success, esp. in sports) easily achieved; effortless: a facile victory. ■ acting or done in a quick, fluent, and easy manner: he was revealed to be a facile liar. DERIVATIVES: **fac•ile•ly** |'fæsəl(l)ē| adv. **fac•ile•ness** n.

fa•cil•i•tate |fə'silə,tāt| • v. make (an action or process) easy or easier: schools were located on the same campus to facilitate the sharing of resources. ■ act as a catalyst to (a conversation, discussion, conference, etc.) without leading it. DERIVATIVES: **fa•cil•i•ta•tive** |-,tātiv| adj.

fa·cil·i·ta·tor |-ˌtātər| *n.* **fa·cil·i·ta·to·ry** |fə'silətəˌtôrē| *adj.*

fac·sim·i·le |fæk'siməlē| • *n.* an exact copy, esp. of written or printed material. • *v.* (**fac-similed, facsimileing**) [trans.] make a copy of: *the ride was facsimiled for Disney World.*

fac·tion |'fækSHən| • *n.* a small, organized, dissenting group within a larger one, esp. in politics: *the left-wing faction of the party.*
■ a state of conflict within an organization; dissension.
DERIVATIVES: **fac·tion·al** *adj.* **fac·tion·al·ism** *n.*

fac·tious |'fækSHəs| • *adj.* relating or inclined to a state of faction: *a factious country.*
DERIVATIVES: **fac·tious·ly** *adv.* **fac·tious·ness** *n.*

fac·ti·tious |fæk'tiSHəs| • *adj.* artificially created or developed: *a largely factitious national identity.*
DERIVATIVES: **fac·ti·tious·ly** *adv.* **fac·ti·tious·ness** *n.*

fac·toid |'fækˌtoid| • *n.* a brief or trivial item of news or information.
■ an assumption or speculation that is reported and repeated so often that it becomes accepted as fact.

fac·to·tum |fæk'tōtəm| • *n.* (pl. **factotums**) an employee who does all kinds of work: *he was employed as the general factotum.*

fac·ul·ty |'fækəltē| • *n.* (pl. **-ies**) **1** an inherent mental or physical power: *her critical faculties.*
■ an aptitude or talent for doing something: *the author's faculty for philosophical analysis.*
2 the teaching staff of a university, college, or school or of one of its departments or divisions, viewed as a body.
■ a group of university departments concerned with a major division of knowledge: *the Faculty of Arts and Sciences.* **3** a license or authorization, esp. from a Church authority.

fa·er·ie |'ferē| (also **faery**) • *n.* the imaginary world of fairies.
■ a fairy. ■ [as adj.] imaginary; mythical: *faerie dragons.*

fa·ience |fī'äns; fä-| • *n.* glazed ceramic ware, in particular decorated tin-glazed earthenware of the type that includes delftware and maiolica.

fai·né·ant |'fānēənt| • *adj.* idle or ineffective.

fait ac·com·pli |'fet əkäm'plē; 'fāt | • *n.* [in sing.] a thing that has already happened or been decided before those affected hear about it, leaving them with no option but to accept: *the results were presented to shareholders as a fait accompli.*

fa·kir |fə'kir; 'fākər| (also **faquir**) • *n.* a Muslim (or, loosely, a Hindu) religious ascetic who lives solely on alms. Cf. DERVISH.

fal·la·cy |'fæləsē| • *n.* (pl. **-ies**) a mistaken belief, esp. one based on unsound argument or information.
■ a failure in reasoning that renders an argument illogical and invalid. ■ faulty reasoning; misleading or unsound argument: *the potential for fallacy that lies behind the notion of self-esteem.*
DERIVATIVES: **fal·la·cious** |fə'läSHəs| *adj.*

fal·la·cious·ly |fə'läSHəslē| *adv.* **fal·la·cious·ness** |fə'läSHəsnəs| *n.*

fal·li·ble |'fæləbəl| • *adj.* capable of making mistakes or being erroneous: *experts can be fallible.*
DERIVATIVES: **fal·li·bil·i·ty** |ˌfælə'bilətē| *n.* **fal·li·bly** |-blē| *adv.*

fal·low |'fælō| • *adj.* (of farmland) plowed and harrowed but left unsown for a period in order to restore its fertility as part of a crop rotation or to avoid surplus production: *incentives for farmers to let land lie fallow in order to reduce grain surpluses.*
■ inactive or uncreative: *long fallow periods when nothing seems to happen.* • *n.* a piece of fallow or uncultivated land. • *v.* [trans.] leave (land) fallow for a period after it has been plowed and harrowed.
DERIVATIVES: **fal·low·ness** *n.*

fal·set·to |fôl'setō| • *n.* (pl. **-os**) a method of voice production used by male singers, esp. tenors, to sing notes higher than their normal range: *he sang in a piercing falsetto | he was singing falsetto in this role.*
■ a singer using this method. ■ a voice or sound that is unusually or unnaturally high.

fal·ter |'fôltər| • *v.* [intrans.] start to lose strength or momentum: *her smile faltered and then faded* | [as adj.] (**faltering**) *his faltering career.*
■ speak in a hesitant or unsteady voice: [with direct speech] *"A-Adam?" he faltered.* ■ move unsteadily or in a way that shows lack of confidence: *he faltered and finally stopped in midstride.*
DERIVATIVES: **fal·ter·er** *n.* **fal·ter·ing·ly** *adv.*

fan·fa·ron·ade |ˌfænˌferə'näd| • *n.* arrogant or boastful talk.

fan·ta·sia |fæn'tāZHə; fæntə'zēə| • *n.* a musical composition with a free form and often an improvisational style.
■ a musical composition that is based on several familiar tunes. ■ a thing that is composed of a mixture of different forms or styles: *the theater is a kind of Moorish and Egyptian fantasia.*

fan·tas·tic |fæn'tæstik| • *adj.* (in literature, etc.) imaginative or fanciful; remote from reality: *novels are capable of mixing fantastic and realistic elements.*
■ (of a shape or design) bizarre or exotic; seeming more appropriate to a fairy tale than to reality or practical use: *visions of a fantastic, mazelike building.*
DERIVATIVES: **fan·tas·ti·cal** |-kəl| *adj.* . **fan·tas·ti·cal·i·ty** |ˌfæn,tæstə'kælətē| *n.* . **fan·tas·ti·cal·ly** |-k(ə)lē| *adv.*

farce |färs| • *n.* a comic dramatic work using buffoonery and boisterous play and typically including crude characterization and ludicrously improbable situations.
■ the genre of such works. ■ an absurd event: *the debate turned into a drunken farce.*
DERIVATIVES: **far·ci·cal** *adj.* **far·ci·cal·i·ty** *n.* **far·ci·cal·ly** *adv.*

far·ceur |fär'sər| • *n.* a writer of or performer in farces.

■ a joker or comedian.

fa•rouche |fə'rōōsн| • *adj.* sullen or shy in company. Cf. DIFFIDENT

far•ra•go |fə'rägō; -'rä-| • *n.* (pl. **-oes**) a confused mixture: *a farrago of fact and myth about Abraham Lincoln.*
DERIVATIVES: **far•rag•i•nous** |fə'ræjənəs| *adj.*

far•ri•er |'færēər; 'fer-| • *n.* a blacksmith who shoes horses.
DERIVATIVES: **far•ri•er•y** *n.*

far•ther |'färᴛʜər| • *adv.* (also **further** |'fər-ᴛʜər|) **1** at, to, or by a greater distance (used to indicate the extent to which one thing or person is or becomes distant from another): *the farther away you are from your home, the better you should behave* | *his action pushes Haiti even farther away from democratic rule.* **2** over a greater expanse of space or time; for a longer way: *the stream fills the passage, and only a cave diver can explore farther* | *people were trying to get their food dollars to go farther.* • *adj.* more distant in space than another item of the same kind: *the farther side of the mountain.*
■ more remote from a central point: *the farther stretches of the diocese.*

USAGE: Traditionally, **farther** and **farthest** were used in referring to physical distance: *the falls were still two or three miles farther up the path.* **Further** and **furthest** were restricted to figurative or abstract senses: *we decided to consider the matter further.* Although **farther** and **farthest** are still restricted to measurable distances, **further** and **furthest** are now common in both senses: *put those plants the furthest from the window.*

fas•ces |'fæs͵ēz| • *plural n.* (in ancient Rome) a bundle of rods with a projecting ax blade, carried by attendants (lictors) of chief magistrates as a symbol of a magistrate's power.
■ (in Fascist Italy) such items used as emblems of authority.

fas•ci•cle |'fæsikəl| • *n.* **1** (also **fascicule** |-͵kyōōl|) a separately published installment of a book or other printed work. **2** (also **fasciculus** |fə'sikyələs|) a bundle of structures, such as nerve or muscle fibers or conducting vessels in plants.
DERIVATIVES: **fas•ci•cled** *adj.* **fas•cic•u•lar** |fə'sikyələr| *adj.* **fas•cic•u•late** |fə'sikyə͵lat; -yəlit| *adj.*

fas•cism |'fæsн͵izəm| (also **Fascism**) • *n.* an authoritarian and nationalistic right-wing system of government and social organization.
■ (in general use) extreme right-wing, authoritarian, or intolerant views or practice.
DERIVATIVES: **fas•cist** *n.* & *adj.* **fa•scis•tic** |fæ'sнistik| *adj.*

fas•tid•i•ous |fæs'tidēəs| • *adj.* very attentive to and concerned about accuracy and detail: *he chooses his words with fastidious care.*
■ very concerned about matters of cleanliness: *fastidious about getting her fingers sticky or dirty.*
DERIVATIVES: **fas•tid•i•ous•ly** *adv.* **fas•tid•i•ous•ness** *n.*

fas•tig•i•ate |fə'stijēət| • *adj.* (of a tree or shrub) having the branches more or less parallel to the main stem: *fastigiate poplars.*

fa•tal•ism |'fātl͵izəm| • *n.* the belief that all events are predetermined and therefore inevitable.
■ a submissive attitude to events, resulting from such a belief.
DERIVATIVES: **fa•tal•ist** *n.* **fa•tal•is•tic** |͵fātl'istik| *adj.* **fa•tal•is•ti•cal•ly** |͵fātl'is-tik(ə)lē| *adv.*

Fata Morgana |'fätə môr'gänə| • *n.* a mirage.

fath•om |'fæᴛʜəm| • *n.* a unit of length equal to six feet (1.8 meters), chiefly used in reference to the depth of water: *according to our latest sonar readings, we're in eighteen fathoms.* • *v.* [trans.] **1** [usu. with negative] understand (a difficult problem or an enigmatic person) after much thought: *he could scarcely fathom the idea that people actually lived in Las Vegas.* **2** measure the depth of (water): *an attempt to fathom the ocean.*
DERIVATIVES: **fath•om•a•ble** *adj.* **fath•om•less** *adj.*

fat•u•ous |'fæcнəwəs| • *adj.* silly and pointless: *a fatuous comment* | *a fatuous young man.*
DERIVATIVES: **fa•tu•i•ty** |fə't(y)ōōəṭē| *n.* (pl. **-ies**) **fat•u•ous•ly** *adv.* **fat•u•ous•ness** *n.*

faun |fôn| • *n.* (in classical mythology) one of a class of lustful rural gods, represented as a man with a goat's horns, ears, legs, and tail.
DERIVATIVES: **fau•nal** *adj.*

fau•na |'fônə; 'fänə| • *n.* (pl. **faunas** |'fônəz; 'fänəz| or **faunae** |'fô͵nē|) the animals of a particular region, habitat, or geological period: *the flora and fauna of Siberia.* Cf. FLORA.
■ a book or other work describing or listing the animal life of a region.
DERIVATIVES: **fau•nal** |'fônl; 'fänl| *adj.* **fau•nis•tic** |-'nistik| *adj.*

Faus•ti•an • *adj.* **1** involving the sacrifice of morals for power or material gain. **2** involving spiritual torment.

fauv•ism |'fō͵vizəm| • *n.* a style of painting with vivid expressionistic and exaggerated use of color that flourished in Paris from 1905 and, although short-lived, had an important influence on subsequent artists, esp. the German expressionists. Matisse was regarded as the movement's leading figure.
DERIVATIVES: **fauve** *n.* **fauv•ist** *n.* & *adj.*

faux pas |fō 'pä| • *n.* (pl. same) an embarrassing or tactless act or remark in a social situation. Cf. GAFFE.

fawn • *v.* [intrans.] (of a person) give a servile display of exaggerated flattery or affection, typically in order to gain favor or advantage: *congressmen fawn over the President.*
■ (of an animal, esp. a dog) show slavish devotion, esp. by crawling and rubbing against someone.
DERIVATIVES: **fawn•ing•ly** *adv.*

fay |fā| • *n.* literary term for a fairy.

fe•al•ty |'fēltē| • *n.* a feudal tenant's or vassal's sworn loyalty to a lord: *they owed fealty to the Earl rather than the King.*

■ allegiance or fidelity to any authority: *The unions have lost their ability to command fealty from the Democratic party.*

fea•si•ble |ˈfēzəbəl| • *adj.* possible to do easily or conveniently: *it is not feasible to put most finds from excavations on public display.*

■ likely; probable: *the most feasible explanation.*
DERIVATIVES: **fea•si•bly** |-zəblē| *adv.*

USAGE: The primary meaning of **feasible** is 'capable of being done, effected.' There is rarely a need to use **feasible** to mean 'likely' or 'probable' when those words can do the job. There are cases, however, in which a careful writer finds that the sense of likelihood or probability (as with an explanation or theory) is more naturally or idiomatically expressed with **feasible** than with *possible* or *probable. They've settled on the Libertarians as their only feasible ally.*

feb•ri•fuge |ˈfebrəˌfyo͞oj| • *n.* a medicine used to reduce fever.
DERIVATIVES: **fe•brif•u•gal** |ˌfəbrəˈf(y)o͞ogəl| *adj.*

fe•brile |ˈfebˌrīl; ˈfēˌbril| • *adj.* having or showing the symptoms of a fever: *a febrile illness.*

■ having or showing a great deal of nervous excitement or energy: *a febrile imagination.*
DERIVATIVES: **fe•bril•i•ty** |fēˈbrilətē| *n.*

fe•cal |ˈfēkəl| (Brit. **faecal**) • *adj.* consisting of or pertaining to waste matter (**feces**, Brit. **faeces**) discharged from the bowels after food has been digested.

feck•less |ˈfekləs| • *adj.* (of a person) lacking in efficiency or vitality: *a feckless mama's boy.*

■ unthinking and irresponsible: *the feckless exploitation of the world's natural resources.*
DERIVATIVES: **feck•less•ly** *adv.* **feck•less•ness** *n.*

fec•u•lent |ˈfekyələnt| • *adj.* of or containing dirt, sediment, or waste matter: *their feet were forever slipping on feculent bog.*
DERIVATIVES: **fec•u•lence** |-ləns| *n.*

fe•cund |ˈfekənd; ˈfē-| • *adj.* producing or capable of producing an abundance of offspring or new growth; fertile: *a lush and fecund garden* | *a fecund imagination.*

■ (of a woman or women) capable of becoming pregnant and giving birth.
DERIVATIVES: **fe•cun•di•ty** |feˈkəndətē; fiˈkən-| *n.*

fed•er•ate • *v.* |ˈfedəˌrāt| [intrans.] (of a number of states or organizations) form a single centralized unit, within which each keeps some internal autonomy.

■ [trans.] [usu. as adj.] (**federated**) form (states or organizations) into such a centralized unit: *the establishment of 20 federated states in Mindanao.* • *adj.* of or relating to such an arrangement: *federate armies.* Cf. CONFEDERATE.
DERIVATIVES: **fed•er•a•tive** |ˈfedəˌrātiv; -rə,tiv| *adj.*

feign |fān| • *v.* [trans.] pretend to be affected by (a feeling, state, or injury): *she feigned nervousness.*

■ archaic invent (a story or excuse). ■ [intrans.] archaic indulge in pretense.

feint |fānt| • *n.* a deceptive or pretended blow, thrust, or other movement, esp. in boxing or fencing: *a brief feint at the opponent's face.*

■ a mock attack or movement in warfare, made in order to distract or deceive an enemy. • *v.* make a deceptive or distracting movement, typically during a fight: *he feinted left, drawing a punch and slipping it.*

feist•y |ˈfīstē| • *adj.* (**feistier, feistiest**) having or showing exuberance and strong determination: *a feisty, outspoken, streetwise teenager.*

■ touchy and aggressive: *got a bit feisty as reporters continued their questions.*
DERIVATIVES: **feist•i•ly** |ˈfīstəlē| *adv.* **feist•i•ness** |ˈfīstēnis| *n.*

fe•lic•i•tate |fəˈlisəˌtāt| • *v.* [trans.] congratulate: *the award winner was felicitated by the cultural association.*

fe•lic•i•tous |fəˈlisətəs| • *adj.* well chosen or suited to the circumstances: *a felicitous phrase.*

■ pleasing and fortunate: *the view was the room's only felicitous feature.*
DERIVATIVES: **fe•lic•i•tous•ly** *adv.* **fe•lic•i•tous•ness** *n.*

fe•lic•i•ty |fəˈlisətē| • *n.* (pl. **-ies**) **1** intense happiness: *domestic felicity.* **2** the ability to find appropriate expression for one's thoughts: *speech which pleased by its felicity.*

■ a particularly effective feature of a work of literature or art: *the King James version, with its felicities of language.*

fe•line |ˈfēˌlīn| • *adj.* of, relating to, or affecting cats or other members of the cat family: *feline leukemia.*

■ catlike, esp. in beauty or slyness: *feline elegance feline in her grace* • *n.* a cat or other member of the cat family.
DERIVATIVES: **fe•lin•i•ty** |fēˈlinətē| *n.*

fell /fel/ • *adj.* of terrible evil or ferocity; deadly: *sorcerers use spells to achieve their fell ends.*
PHRASES: **in** (or **at**) **one fell swoop** all at one time: *seeking to topple the government in one fell swoop.*

fel•la•ti•o |fəˈlāsh(ē)ˌō| • *n.* oral stimulation of a man's penis.
DERIVATIVES: **fel•la•tor** |ˈfelˌātər| *n.*

fel•o•ny |ˈfelənē| • *n.* (pl. **-ies**) a crime, typically one involving violence, regarded as more serious than a misdemeanor and typically punished by imprisonment for at least one year. A **felon** is one who has committed a felony: *he pleaded guilty to six felonies* | *an accusation of felony* | [as adj.] *felony assault.* Cf. MISDEMEANOR.
DERIVATIVES: **fe•lo•ni•ous** *adj.*

fem•i•nism |ˈfeməˌnizəm| • *n.* the advocacy of women's rights on the grounds of political, social, and economic equality to men.

fem•i•nist |ˈfemənist| • *n.* a person who advocates or supports feminism. • *adj.* of, relating to, or supporting feminism: *feminist literature.*

fem•i•nize |ˈfeməˌnīz| • *v.* [trans.] make (something) more characteristic of or associated with women: *as office roles changed, clerical work was increasingly feminized.*

DERIVATIVES: **fem•i•ni•za•tion** |ˌfemənə 'zāsHən| *n.*

fen•es•tra•tion |ˌfenə'strāsHən| • *n.* (in architecture) the design and arrangement of windows in a building.

feng shui |ˈfəNG 'sHwē; -sHwä| • *n.* (in Chinese thought) a system of laws considered to govern spatial arrangement and orientation in relation to the flow of energy (chi), and whose favorable or unfavorable effects are taken into account when siting and designing buildings and their surroundings and furnishings. Cf. GEOMANCY.

fe•ral |ˈfirəl; ˈferəl| • *adj.* (esp. of an animal) in a wild state after escape from captivity or domestication: *a feral cat.*
■ resembling or pertaining to a wild animal: *a feral snarl.*

fer•ment • *v.* |fər'ment| **1** [intrans.] (of a substance) undergo fermentation, the conversion of carbohydrates, esp. sugars, to alcohol and carbon dioxide by the action of enzymes.
■ [trans.] cause the fermentation of (a substance). **2** [trans.] incite or stir up (trouble or disorder): *the politicians and warlords who are fermenting this chaos.* Cf. FOMENT.
■ [intrans.] (of a negative feeling or memory) fester and develop into something worse: *it had been fermenting in my subconscious for a while.* • *n.* **1** agitation and excitement among a group of people, typically concerning major change and leading to trouble or violence: *Germany at this time was in a state of religious ferment.*
DERIVATIVES: **fer•ment•a•ble** |fər'mentəbəl| *adj.* **fer•men•ta•tion** *n.*

fer•rous |ˈferəs| • *adj.* (chiefly of metals) containing or consisting of iron.

fer•rule |ˈferəl| • *n.* a ring or cap, typically a metal one, that strengthens the end of a handle, stick, or tube and prevents it from splitting or wearing.
■ a metal band strengthening or forming a joint.

fer•tile |ˈfərtl| • *adj.* (of soil or land) producing or capable of producing abundant vegetation or crops: *fields along the fertile flood plains of the river*
■ similarly productive in social, intellectual, etc. fields: *Germany in the 1920s and 30s was **fertile ground** for such ideas.*
■ (of a seed or egg) capable of becoming a new individual. ■ (of a person, animal, or plant) able to conceive young or produce seed: *Karen carefully calculated the period when she was most fertile.* ■ (of a person's mind or imagination) producing many new and inventive ideas with ease. ■ (of a situation or subject) being fruitful and productive in generating new ideas: *a series of fertile debates within the social sciences.* ■ (in physics, of nuclear material) able to become fissile by the capture of neutrons.
DERIVATIVES: **fer•til•i•ty** |fər'tilətē| *n.*

fer•vent |ˈfərvənt| • *adj.* having or displaying a passionate intensity: *a fervent disciple of tax reform.*
■ burning, hot, or glowing.

DERIVATIVES: **fer•ven•cy** |-vənsē| *n.* **fer•vent•ly** *adv.*

fer•vid |ˈfərvid| • *adj.* intensely enthusiastic or passionate, esp. to an excessive degree: *an expression of fervid devotion.* Cf. PERFERVID.
■ burning, hot, or glowing.
DERIVATIVES: **fer•vid•ly** *adv.*

fer•vor |ˈfərvər| (Brit.**fervour**) • *n.* intense and passionate feeling: *he talked with all the fervor of a new convert.*
■ intense heat.

fes•tal |ˈfestəl| • *adj.* of, like, or relating to a celebration or festival: *he appeared in festal array.*
DERIVATIVES: **fes•tal•ly** |ˈfestəlē| *adv.*

fes•ter |ˈfestər| • *v.* [intrans.] (of a wound or sore) become septic; suppurate: *I developed a tropical sore that festered badly* | [as adj.] (**festering**) *a festering abscess.*
■ (of food or garbage) become rotten and offensive to the senses: *a gully full of trash that festered in the sun.* ■ (of a negative feeling or a problem) become worse or more intense, esp. through long-term neglect or indifference: *anger that festers and grows in the heart.* ■ (of a person) undergo physical and mental deterioration in isolated inactivity: *I might be **festering in** jail now.*

fes•tive |ˈfestiv| • *adj.* of or relating to a festival: *parties are held and festive food is served.*
■ cheerful and jovially celebratory: *the somber atmosphere has given way to a festive mood.*
DERIVATIVES: **fes•tive•ly** *adv.* **fes•tive•ness** *n.*

fes•toon |fes'tōōn| • *n.* a chain or garland of flowers, leaves, or ribbons, hung in a curve as a decoration.
■ a carved or molded ornament representing such a garland. • *v.* [trans.] (often **be festooned with**) adorn (a place) with chains, garlands, or other decorations: *the classroom was festooned with balloons and streamers.*

fête |fāt; fet| (also **fete**) • *n.* a celebration or festival. A **fête champêtre** is a rural, outdoor festival. A **fête galante** is a representation of this in art. • *v.* [trans.] (usu. **be fêted**) honor or entertain (someone) lavishly: *she was an instant celebrity, fêted by the media.*

fe•ti•cide |ˈfetəˌsīd| • *n.* destruction or abortion of a fetus.

fet•id |ˈfetid| (Brit. also **foetid**) • *adj.* smelling extremely unpleasant: *the fetid water of the marsh.*
DERIVATIVES: **fet•id•ly** *adv.* **fet•id•ness** *n.*

fet•ish |ˈfetisH| • *n.* an inanimate object worshiped for its supposed magical powers or because it is considered to be inhabited by a spirit.
■ a course of action to which one has an excessive and irrational commitment: *he **had a fetish** for writing more opinions each year than any other justice.* ■ a form of sexual desire in which gratification is linked to an abnormal degree to a particular object, item of clothing, part of the body, etc.: *Victorian men developed fetishes focusing on feet, shoes, and boots.*
DERIVATIVES: **fet•ish•ism** |-ˌizəm| *n.* **fet•ish•ist** *n.* **fet•ish•is•tic** |ˌfetiˈsHistik| *adj.*

fet•ter |'fetər| • *n.* (usu. **fetters**) a chain or manacle used to restrain a prisoner, typically placed around the ankles: *he lay bound with fetters of iron.*
■ a restraint or check on someone's freedom to do something, typically one considered unfair or overly restrictive: *the fetters of discipline and caution.* • *v.* [trans.] restrain with chains or manacles, typically around the ankles: [as adj.] (**fettered**) *a ragged and fettered prisoner.*
■ (often **be fettered**) restrict or restrain (someone) in an unfair or undesirable fashion: *he was not fettered by tradition.*

fet•tle |'fetl| • *n.* condition: *the team is in fine fettle.*

fe•tus |'fētəs| (Brit. (in nontechnical use) also **foetus**) • *n.* (pl. **fetuses**) an unborn or unhatched offspring of a mammal, in particular an unborn human baby more than eight weeks after conception. Cf. EMBRYO.

feud |fyōōd| • *n.* a state of prolonged mutual hostility, typically between two families or communities, characterized by murderous assaults in revenge for a previous injuries: *the incident rekindled a long-term feud between two ethnic groups.*
■ a prolonged and bitter quarrel or dispute: *one of the most volatile feuds that currently rock the scientific community.* • *v.* [intrans.] take part in such a quarrel or violent conflict: *Hoover feuded with the CIA for decades.*
DERIVATIVES: **feudist** *n.* a person who takes part in a feud.

feu•dal |'fyōōdl| • *adj.* according to, resembling, or denoting the system of feudalism: *feudal barons.*
■ absurdly outdated or old-fashioned: *his views are more than old-fashioned—they're positively feudal.*
DERIVATIVES: **feu•dal•i•za•tion** |,fyōōdli 'zāsHən| *n.* **feu•dal•ize** |'fyōōdl,īz| *v.* **feu•dal•ly** |'fyōōdl-ē| *adv.*

feu•dal•ism |'fyōōdl,izəm| • *n.* the dominant social system in medieval Europe, in which the nobility held lands from the Crown in exchange for military service, and vassals were in turn tenants of the nobles, while the peasants (villeins or serfs) were obliged to live on their lord's land and give him homage, labor, and a share of the produce, notionally in exchange for military protection.
DERIVATIVES: **feu•dal•ist** *n.* **feu•dal•is•tic** |,fyōōdl'istik| *adj.*

fey |fā| • *adj.* giving an impression of vague unworldliness: *his mother was a strange, fey woman.*
■ having supernatural powers of clairvoyance.
■ fated to die or at the point of death: *now he is fey, he sees his own death, and I see it too.*
DERIVATIVES: **fey•ly** *adv.* **fey•ness** *n.*

fi•as•co |fē'æskō| • *n.* (pl. **-os**) a thing that is a complete failure, esp. in a ludicrous or humiliating way: *the event, not carefully organized, turned into a fiasco.*

fi•at |'fēat; 'fē,ät| • *n.* a formal authorization or proposition; a decree: *adopting a legislative review program, rather than trying to regulate by fiat.*

■ an arbitrary order: *the appraisal dropped the value from $75,000 to $15,000, rendering it worthless by bureaucratic fiat.*

fi•bril•late |'fibrə,lāt| • *v.* [intrans.] **1** (of a muscle, esp. in the heart) make a quivering movement due to uncoordinated contraction of individual small fibers (fibrils): *the atria ceased to fibrillate when the temperature was reduced.* **2** (of a fiber) split up into smaller subdivisions (fibrils).
■ [trans.] break (a fiber) into fibrils.
DERIVATIVES: **fi•bril•la•tion** |,fibrə'lā-sHən| *n.* Cf. DEFIBRILLATOR

fick•le |'fikəl| • *adj.* changing frequently, esp. as regards one's loyalties, interests, or affection: *Web users are a notoriously fickle lot, bouncing from one site to another on a whim | the weather at this time of year is fickle.*
DERIVATIVES: **fick•le•ness** *n.* **fick•ly** |'fik-(ə)lē| *adv.*

fic•ti•tious |fik'tisHəs| • *adj.* not real or true, having been fabricated with the intent to deceive: *she pleaded guilty to stealing thousands of taxpayer dollars by having a fictitious employee on her payroll.*
■ of, relating to, or denoting the imaginary characters and events found in fiction: *the people in this novel are fictitious; the background of public events is not.*
DERIVATIVES: **fic•ti•tious•ly** *adv.* **fic•ti•tious•ness** *n.*

fic•tive |'fiktiv| • *adj.* creating or created by imagination: *the novel's fictive universe.*
DERIVATIVES: **fic•tive•ness** *n.*

fi•del•i•ty |fə'delətē| • *n.* **1** faithfulness to a person, cause, or belief, demonstrated by continuing loyalty and support: *he sought only the strictest fidelity to justice.*
■ sexual faithfulness to a spouse or partner.
■ the degree of exactness with which something is copied or reproduced: *the 1949 recording provides reasonable fidelity.*

fi•du•ci•ar•y |fə'dōōsHē,erē; -sHərē| • *adj.* (in legal matters) involving trust, esp. with regard to the relationship between a trustee and a beneficiary: *the company has a fiduciary duty to shareholders.*
■ (of a paper currency) depending for its value on securities (as opposed to gold) or the reputation of the issuer. Cf. CONVERTIBLE. • *n.* (pl. **-ies**) a trustee.

fief |fēf| • *n.* (also, **fiefdom**) **1** an estate of land, esp. one held on condition of feudal service. **2** a person's sphere of operation or control.

fifth col•umn • *n.* a group within a country at war who are sympathetic to or working for its enemies.
DERIVATIVES: **fifth col•umn•ist** *n.*

fig•ur•a•tive |'fig(y)ərətiv| • *adj.* **1** departing from a literal use of words; metaphorical: *gold, in the figurative language of the people, was "the tears wept by the sun."* **2** (of an artist or work of art) representing forms that are recognizably derived from life.
DERIVATIVES: **fig•ur•a•tive•ly** *adv.* **fig•ur•a•tive•ness** *n.*

fil•a•ment |'filəmənt| • *n.* a slender thread-

like object or fiber, esp. one found in animal or plant structures: *a filament of cellulose.*
■ a conducting wire or thread with a high melting point, forming part of an electric bulb and heated or made incandescent by an electric current.
DERIVATIVES: **fil•a•men•ta•ry** |ˌfiləˈmentərē| *adj.* **fil•a•ment•ed** *adj.* **fil•a•men•tous** |-ˌmentəs| *adj.*

fi•let |fiˈlā; ˈfilā| • *n.* **1** French spelling of FIL-LET, used esp. in the names of French or French-sounding dishes: *filet de boeuf.* **2** a kind of net or lace with a square mesh.

fil•i•al |ˈfilēəl; ˈfilyəl| • *adj.* of or due from a son or daughter: *a display of filial affection.*
DERIVATIVES: **fil•i•al•ly** *adv.*

fil•i•bus•ter |ˈfiləˌbəstər| • *n.* **1** an action such as a prolonged speech that obstructs progress in a legislative assembly while not technically contravening the required procedures: *the bill was defeated by a Senate filibuster in June.* **2** a person engaging in unauthorized warfare against a foreign country. • *v.* [intrans.] [often as n.] (**filibustering**) act in an obstructive manner in a legislature, esp. by speaking at inordinate length: *several measures were killed by Republican filibustering.*
■ [trans.] obstruct (a measure) in such a way.

fil•i•gree |ˈfiləˌgrē| • *n.* ornamental work of fine (typically gold or silver) wire formed into delicate tracery: [as adj.] *silver filigree earrings.*
■ a thing resembling such fine ornamental work: *a wedding cake of gold and white filigree.*
DERIVATIVES: **filigreed** *adj.*

fil•let • *n.* **1** (also **filet**) |fiˈlā; ˈfilā| a fleshy boneless piece of meat from near the loins or the ribs of an animal: *a chicken breast fillet | roast **fillet** of lamb.*
■ (also **fillet steak**) a beef steak cut from the lower part of a sirloin. ■ a boned side of a fish. **2** |ˈfilit| a band or ribbon worn around the head, esp. for binding the hair.
■ a narrow flat band separating two architectural moldings. ■ a small band between the flutes of a column. ■ a plain or decorated line impressed on the cover of a book. ■ a roller used to impress such a line. **3** |ˈfilit| a roughly triangular strip of material that rounds off an interior angle between two surfaces: *a splayed mortar fillet at the junction of the roof with the chimney stack* | [as adj.] *a fillet weld.* • *v.* |fiˈlā; ˈfilā| (**filleted, filleting**, also **filet, fileted, fileting**) [trans.] remove the bones from (a fish).
■ cut (fish or meat) into boneless strips.
DERIVATIVES: **fil•let•er** *n.*

fil•lip |ˈfiləp| • *n.* **1** something that acts as a stimulus or boost to an activity: *the halving of the title fees would provide a fillip to sales.* **2** archaic a movement made by bending the last joint of a finger against the thumb and suddenly releasing it; a flick of the finger: *the Prince, by a fillip, made some of the wine fly in Oglethorpe's face.*
■ a slight smart stroke or tap given in such a way: *she began to give him dainty fillips on the nose with a soft forepaw.* • *v.* (**filliped, fillipping**) [trans.] propel (a small object) with a flick

of the finger: *our aforesaid merchant filliped a nut sharply against his bullying giant.*
■ strike (someone or something) slightly and smartly: *he filliped him over the nose.* ■ stimulate or urge (someone or something): *pour, that the draft may fillip my remembrance.*

fils |fēs| • *n.* used after a surname to distinguish a son from a father of the same name: *Alexandre Dumas fils.* Cf. PÈRE.

fin•an•cier • *n.* |ˌfinənˈsir; fəˈnænˌsir| a person concerned with the management of large amounts of money on behalf of governments, corporations, banks, or other large organizations. • *v.* [intrans.] manage large amounts of money.

fin de siè•cle |ˌfæn də sēˈəkl(ə)| • *adj.* relating to or characteristic of the end of a century, esp. the 19th century: *fin-de-siècle art.*
■ decadent: *there was a fin-de-siècle air in the club last night.* • *n.* the end of a century, esp. the 19th century.

fi•nesse |fəˈnes| • *n.* **1** intricate and refined delicacy: *orchestral playing of great finesse.*
■ artful subtlety, typically that needed for tactful handling of a difficulty: *action that calls for considerable finesse.* ■ subtle or delicate manipulation: *a certain amount of finesse is required to fine-tune the sound system.* **2** (in bridge and whist) an attempt to win a trick with a card that is not a certain winner. • *v.* [trans.] **1** do (something) in a subtle and delicate manner: *his third shot, which he attempted to finesse, failed.*
■ slyly attempt to avoid blame or censure when dealing with (a situation or action): *the administration's attempts to finesse its mishaps.* **2** (in bridge and whist) play (a card that is not a certain winner) in the hope of winning a trick with it: *the declarer finesses ♦♥.*

fin•i•al |ˈfinēəl| • *n.* a distinctive section or ornament at the apex of a roof, pinnacle, canopy, or similar structure in a building.
■ an ornament at the top, end, or corner of an object: *ornate curtain poles with decorative finials.*

fi•nite |ˈfīnīt| • *adj.* **1** having limits or bounds: *every computer has a finite amount of memory.*
■ not infinitely small: *one's chance of winning may be small, but it is finite.* **2** (of a verb form) having a specific tense, number, and person.
DERIVATIVES: **fi•nite•ly** *adv.* **fi•nite•ness** *n.* **finitude** *n.*

fir•ma•ment |ˈfərməmənt| • *n.* the heavens or the sky, esp. when regarded as a tangible thing.
■ a sphere or world viewed as a collection of people: *one of the great **stars in the** American golfing firmament.*
DERIVATIVES: **fir•ma•men•tal** |ˌfərməˈmentl| *adj.*

fis•cal |ˈfiskəl| • *adj.* of or relating to government revenue, esp. taxes: *monetary and fiscal policy.*
■ of or relating to financial matters: *the domestic fiscal crisis.* ■ used to denote a 12-month accounting period that is not synchronous with the calendar year: *the company's fiscal 1996 begins on Oct. 1, 1995.*
DERIVATIVES: **fis•cal•ly** |ˈfiskəlē| *adv.*

fis•sile |'fisəl; 'fis,īl| • *adj.* (of an atom or element) able to undergo nuclear fission: *a fissile isotope.*
■ (chiefly of rock) easily split: *flat-bedded and very highly fissile shale.*
DERIVATIVES: **fis•sil•i•ty** |fi'silətē| *n.*

fis•sion |'fisHən; 'fizHən| • *n.* the action of dividing or splitting into two or more parts: *the party dissolved into fission and acrimony.*
■ (also **nuclear fission**) the splitting of an atomic nucleus into lighter atoms as a source of energy. Cf. FUSION ■ reproduction by means of a cell or organism dividing into two or more new cells or organisms. • *v.* [intrans.] (chiefly of atoms) undergo fission: *these heavy nuclei can also fission.*

fit•ful |'fitfəl| • *adj.* active or occurring spasmodically or intermittently; not regular or steady: *a few hours' fitful sleep* | *business was fitful.*
DERIVATIVES: **fit•ful•ly** *adv.* **fit•ful•ness** *n.*

fix•a•tion |fik'sāsHən| • *n.* **1** an obsessive interest in or feeling about someone or something: *his fixation on the details of other people's erotic lives* | *our fixation with diet and fitness.*
■ (in psychoanalysis) the arresting of part of the libido at an immature stage, causing an obsessive attachment: *fixation at the oral phase might result in dependence on others* | *a maternal fixation.* **2** the action of making something firm or stable: *sand dune fixation.*
■ the process by which some plants and microorganisms combine chemically with atmospheric nitrogen to form stable compounds that are available in soil as plant nutrients: *his work on nitrogen fixation in plants.* ■ the process of preserving or stabilizing (a specimen) with a chemical substance prior to microscopic or other examination: *biopsy specimens were placed in cassettes before fixation in formalin.*

fix•a•tive |'fiksətiv| • *n.* **1** a chemical substance used to preserve or stabilize biological material prior to microscopic or other examination: *an alcoholic fixative* | *ten double drops of fixative.*
■ a substance used to stabilize the volatile components of perfume. ■ a liquid sprayed on to a pastel or charcoal drawing to fix colors or prevent smudging. **2** a substance used to keep things in position or stick them together: *the bird glues these thin twigs to a wall using its own saliva as a fixative.* • *adj.* (of a substance) used to fix or stabilize something.

fjord |fē'ôrd; fyôrd| (also **fiord**) • *n.* a long, narrow, deep inlet of the sea between high cliffs, as in Norway, typically formed by submergence of a glaciated valley.

flac•cid |'flæ(k)səd| • *adj.* (of part of the body) soft and hanging loosely or limply, esp. so as to look or feel unpleasant: *she took his flaccid hand in hers.*
■ (of plant tissue) drooping or inelastic through lack of water. ■ lacking force or effectiveness: *the flaccid leadership of the campaign was causing concern.*

DERIVATIVES: **flac•cid•i•ty** |flæ(k)'sidətē| *n.* **flac•cid•ly** *adv.*

flack[1] |flæk| • *n.* a publicity agent: *a public relations flack.* • *v.* [trans.] publicize or promote (something or someone): *a crass ambulance-chaser who flacks himself in TV commercials* | [intrans.] *the local news media shamelessly flack for the organizing committee.*
DERIVATIVES: **flack•er•y** |-ərē| *n.* .

flack[2] • *n.* variant spelling of FLAK.

flac•on |'flækən; flæ'kôN| • *n.* (pl. **flacons** pronunc. same) a small stoppered bottle, esp. one for perfume. Cf. FLAGON

flag•el•late |'flæjə,lāt| • *v.* [trans.] flog (someone), either as a religious discipline or for sexual gratification. The medieval sects who practiced this as a religious discipline were called the Flagellants: *he flagellated himself with branches.*
DERIVATIVES: **flag•el•la•tion** |,flæjə'lā-sHən| *n.* **flag•el•la•tor** |-,lātər| *n.* **flag•el•la•to•ry** |flə'jelə,tôrē| *adj.*

fla•gi•tious |flə'jisHəs| • *adj.* (of a person or their actions) extremely wicked; criminal; villainous.
DERIVATIVES: **fla•gi•tious•ly** *adv.* **fla•gi•tious•ness** *n.*

flag•on |'flægən| • *n.* a large container in which drink is served, typically with a handle and spout: *there was a flagon of beer in his vast fist.*
■ the amount of liquid held in such a container. ■ a similar container used to hold the wine for the Eucharist. ■ a large bottle in which wine or cider is sold, typically holding 1.13 liters (about 2 pints). Cf. FLACON

fla•grant |'flāgrənt| • *adj.* (of something considered wrong or immoral) conspicuously or obviously offensive: *his flagrant bad taste* | *a flagrant violation of the law.*
DERIVATIVES: **fla•gran•cy** |-grənsē| *n.* **fla•grant•ly** *adv.*

flair |fler| • *n.* **1** [in sing.] a special or instinctive aptitude or ability for doing something well: *she had a flair for languages* | *none of us had much artistic flair.* **2** stylishness and originality: *she dressed with flair.*

flak |flæk| (also **flack**) • *n.* antiaircraft fire.
■ strong criticism: *you must be strong enough to take the flak if things go wrong.*

flam•bé |fläm'bā| • *adj.* **1** [postpositive] (of food) covered with liquor and set alight briefly: *crêpes flambé.* **2** denoting or characterized by a red copper-based porcelain glaze with purple streaks. • *v.* (**flambés, flambéed** |fläm'bād|, **flambéing**) [trans.] cover (food) with liquor and set it alight briefly.

flam•beau |'flæm,bō| • *n.* (pl. **flambeaus** or **flambeaux** |-,bōz|) a flaming torch, esp. one made of several thick wicks dipped in wax.
■ a large candlestick with several branches.

flam•boy•ant |flæm'boiənt| • *adj.* **1** (of a person or personal behavior) tending to attract attention because of exuberance, confidence, and stylishness: *a flamboyant display of aerobatics* | *she is outgoing and flamboyant, continuously talking and joking.*

■ (esp. of clothing) noticeable because brightly colored, highly patterned, or unusual in style. **2** of or denoting a style of French Gothic architecture marked by wavy flamelike tracery and ornate decoration.
DERIVATIVES: **flam•boy•ance** n. **flam• boy•an•cy** |-'boiənsē| n. **flam•boy•ant•ly** adv.

flam•ma•ble |'flæməbəl| • adj. easily set on fire: *the use of highly flammable materials.* Cf. INFLAMMABLE.
DERIVATIVES: **flam•ma•bil•i•ty** |ˌflæmə'bilətē| n.

flap•per |'flæpər| • n. (in the 1920s) a fashionable young woman intent on enjoying herself and flouting conventional standards of behavior.

flat•u•lent |'flæCHələnt| • adj. suffering from or marked by an accumulation of gas in the alimentary canal: *treat flatulent cows with caustic soda.*
■ related to or causing this condition: *the flatulent effect of beans.* ■ inflated or pretentious in speech or writing: *the days of flatulent oratory are gone.*
DERIVATIVES: **flat•u•lence** n. **flat•u•len• cy** n. **flat•u•lent•ly** adv.

fla•tus |'flāṭəs| • n. gas in or from the stomach or intestines, produced by swallowing air or by bacterial fermentation.

flaunt |flônt; flänt| • v. [trans.] display (something) ostentatiously, esp. in order to provoke envy or admiration or to show defiance: *newly rich consumers eager to flaunt their prosperity.*
■ **(flaunt oneself)** dress or behave in a sexually provocative way.
DERIVATIVES: **flaunt•er** n. **flaunt•y** adj.

USAGE: **Flaunt** and **flout** may sound similar but they have different meanings. **Flaunt** means 'display ostentatiously,' as in *visitors who liked to **flaunt** their wealth,* while **flout** means 'openly disregard (a rule or convention),' as in *new recruits growing their hair and **flouting** convention.*

fledge |flej| • v. **1** [intrans.] (of a young bird) develop wing feathers that are large enough for flight.
■ [trans.] bring up (a young bird) until its wing feathers are developed enough for flight. ■ [as adj.] **(fledged)** having developed feathers sufficient for flight. ■ **(fully fledged)** fully trained and properly qualified. **2** [trans.] provide (an arrow) with feathers.

fledg•ling |'flejliNG| (also **fledgeling**) • n. a young bird that has just fledged.
■ [usu. as adj.] a person or organization that is immature, inexperienced, or underdeveloped: *the fledgling democracies of eastern Europe.*

fleece |flēs| • n. **1** the woolly covering of a sheep or goat: *as the sheep came on board, we grabbed their long shaggy fleeces.*
■ the amount of wool cut (shorn) from a sheep in a single piece at one time. **2** a thing resembling a sheep's woolly covering, in particular:

■ a soft warm fabric with a texture similar to sheep's wool, used as a lining material. ■ a jacket or other garment made from such a fabric. ■ Heraldry a representation of a fleece suspended from a ring. • v. [trans.] **1** obtain a great deal of money from (someone), typically by overcharging or swindling them: *authorities say he fleeced well-to-do acquaintances.* **2** cover as if with a fleece: *the sky was half blue, half fleeced with white clouds.*
DERIVATIVES: **fleeced** adj.

flesh•ly |'fleSHlē| • adj. **(fleshlier, fleshliest)** **1** of or relating to human desire or bodily appetites; sensual: *fleshly pleasures.* **2** having an actual physical presence.

flesh•y |'fleSHē| • adj. **(fleshier, fleshiest)** **1** (of a person or part of the body) having a substantial amount of flesh; plump: *her torso was full, fleshy, and heavy.*
■ (of plant or fruit tissue) soft and thick: *fleshy, greeny-gray leaves.* ■ (of a wine) full-bodied. **2** resembling flesh in appearance or texture.
DERIVATIVES: **flesh•i•ness** |-ēnis| n.

flim•flam |'flim,flæm| • n. nonsensical or insincere talk: *I suppose that you suspect me of pseudointellectual flimflam.*
■ a confidence game: *flimflams perpetrated against us by our elected officials.* • v. **(flimflammed, flimflamming)** [trans.] swindle (someone) with or as with a confidence game: *the tribe was flimflammed out of its land.*
DERIVATIVES: **flim•flam•mer** n. **flim• flam•mer•y** |-,flæmərē| n.

flint•y |'flintē| • adj. **(flintier, flintiest)** of, containing, or reminiscent of flint: *flinty soil.*
■ (of a person or their expression) very hard and unyielding: *a flinty stare.*
DERIVATIVES: **flint•i•ly** |'flintl-ē| adv. **flint•i•ness** |-tēnis| n.

flip•pant |'flipənt| (also **flip**) • adj. not showing a serious or respectful attitude: *a flippant remark.*
DERIVATIVES: **flip•pan•cy** |'flipənsē| n. **flip•pant•ly** adv.

floc•cu•lent |'fläkyələnt| • adj. having or resembling tufts of wool: *the first snows of winter lay thick and flocculent.*
■ having a loosely clumped texture: *a brown flocculent precipitate.*
DERIVATIVES: **floc•cu•lence** n.

floe |flō| (also **ice floe**) • n. a sheet of floating ice: *seated on a floe* | [as adj.] *floe ice.*

flo•ra |'flôrə| • n. (pl. **floras** or **florae** |'flôr,ē; 'flôr,ī|) the plants of a particular region, habitat, or geological period: *the desert flora give way to oak woodlands* | *the river's **flora and fauna** have been inventoried and protected.* Cf. FAUNA.
■ a treatise on or list of such plant life.

flor•id |'flôrid; 'flärid| • adj. **1** having a red or flushed complexion: *a stout man with a florid face.* **2** elaborately or excessively intricate or complicated: *florid operatic-style music was out.*
■ (of language) using unusual words or complicated rhetorical constructions: *the florid prose of the nineteenth century.* **3** (of a disease or its manifestations) occurring in a fully

developed form: *florid symptoms of psychiatric disorder.*
DERIVATIVES: **flo•rid•i•ty** |flə'ridətē| *n.* **flor•id•ly** *adv.* **flor•id•ness** *n.*
flo•ri•le•gi•um |ˌflôrē'lējēəm| • *n.* (pl. **florilegia** |-'lējēə| or **florilegiums**) a collection of literary extracts; an anthology.
flo•ru•it |'flôrəwət| (abbr.: **fl.** or **flor.**) • *v.* used in conjunction with a specified period or set of dates to indicate when a particular historical figure lived, worked, or was most active. • *n.* such a period: *they place Nicander's floruit in the middle of the 2nd century BC.*
flot•sam |'flätsəm| • *n.* the wreckage of a ship or its cargo found floating on or washed up by the sea. Cf. JETSAM.
■ people or things that have been rejected and are regarded as worthless: *the room was cleared of boxes and other flotsam.*
PHRASES: **flotsam and jetsam** useless or discarded objects.
flounce[1] |flowns| • *v.* go or move in an exaggeratedly impatient or angry manner: *he stood up in a fury and flounced out.*
■ move with exaggerated motions: *she flounced around, playing the tart and flirting.* • *n.* [in sing.] an exaggerated action, typically intended to express one's annoyance or impatience: *she left the room with a flounce.*
flounce[2] • *n.* a wide ornamental strip of material gathered and sewn to a piece of fabric, typically on a skirt or dress; a frill. • *v.* [as adj.] (**flounced**) trimmed with a flounce or flounces: *a flounced skirt.*
DERIVATIVES: **flounc•y** |'flownsē| *adj.*
floun•der |'flowndər| • *v.* [intrans.] struggle or stagger helplessly or clumsily in water or mud: *he was floundering about in the shallow offshore waters.*
■ struggle mentally; show or feel great confusion: *she floundered, not knowing quite what to say.* ■ be in serious difficulty: *many firms are floundering.*
DERIVATIVES: **floun•der•er** *n.*

USAGE: See usage at FOUNDER.

flour•ish |'flərisH| • *v.* **1** [intrans.] (of a person, animal, or other living organism) grow or develop in a healthy or vigorous way, esp. as the result of a supportive environment: *wild plants flourish by the lake.*
■ develop rapidly and successfully: *the organization has continued to flourish.* ■ [with adverbial] (of a person) be working or at the height of one's career during a specified period: *the caricaturist and wit who flourished in the early years of the 20th century.* **2** [trans.] (of a person) wave (something) around to attract the attention of others: *"Happy New Year!" he yelled, flourishing a bottle.* • *n.* **1** a bold or extravagant gesture or action, made esp. to attract the attention of others: *with a flourish, she ushered them inside.*
■ an instance of suddenly performing or developing in an impressively successful way: *the Bulldogs produced a late second-half flourish.* ■ an elaborate rhetorical or literary expression. ■ an ornamental flowing curve in hand-

writing or scrollwork: *spiky gothic letters with an emphatic flourish beneath them.* **2** a fanfare played by brass instruments: *a flourish of trumpets.*
■ an ornate musical passage. ■ an improvised addition played esp. at the beginning or end of a composition.
DERIVATIVES: **flour•ish•er** *n.*
flout |flowt| • *v.* [trans.] openly disregard (a rule, law or convention): *these same companies still flout basic ethical practices.*
■ [intrans.] mock; scoff: *the women pointed and flouted at her.*

USAGE: **Flout** and **flaunt** do not have the same meaning: see **usage** at FLAUNT.

fluc•tu•ate |'fləkCHə,wāt| • *v.* [intrans.] rise and fall irregularly in number or amount: *trade with other countries tends to fluctuate from year to year* | [as adj.] (**fluctuating**) *a fluctuating level of demand.*
DERIVATIVES: **fluc•tu•a•tion** |ˌfləkCHə'wāsHən| *n.*
flu•ent |'floōənt| • *adj.* (of a person) able to express oneself easily and articulately: *a fluent speaker and writer on technical subjects.*
■ (of a person) able to speak or write a particular foreign language easily and accurately: *she became fluent in French and German.* ■ (of a foreign language) spoken accurately and with facility: *he spoke fluent Spanish.* ■ (of speech, language, movement, or style) smoothly graceful and easy: *his style of play was fast and fluent.* ■ able to flow freely; fluid: *a fluent discharge from the nose.*
DERIVATIVES: **flu•en•cy** *n.* **flu•ent•ly** *adv.*
flume |floōm| • *n.* a deep narrow channel or ravine with a stream running through it.
■ an artificial channel conveying water, typically used for transporting logs or timber. ■ a water chute ride at an amusement park.
flum•mer•y |'fləmərē| • *n.* (pl. **-ies**) **1** empty compliments; nonsense: *she hated the flummery of public relations.* **2** a sweet dish, typically made with beaten eggs, sugar, and flavorings.
flum•mox |'fləməks| • *v.* [trans.] (usu. be **flummoxed**) perplex (someone) greatly; bewilder: *he was completely flummoxed by the question.*
flun•ky |'fləNGkē| (also **flunkey**) • *n.* (pl. **-ies** or **-eys**) a person who performs relatively menial tasks for someone else, esp. obsequiously.
DERIVATIVES: **flun•ky•ism** |-ˌizəm| *n.*
fluo•res•cence |floŏ(ə)'resəns; flôr'esəns| • *n.* the visible or invisible radiation produced from certain substances as a result of incident radiation of a shorter wavelength such as X-rays or ultraviolet light.
■ the property of absorbing light of short wavelength and emitting light of longer wavelength.
DERIVATIVES: **fluo•resce** *v.*
fluo•res•cent |ˌfloō(ə)'resənt; flôr'esənt| • *adj.* (of a substance) having or showing fluorescence: *a fluorescent dye.*
■ containing a fluorescent tube, which radiates

light when phosphor on its inside surface is made to flouresce by ultraviolet radiation from mercury vapor: *fluorescent lighting.* Cf. INCANDESCENT. ■ vividly colorful: *a fluorescent T-shirt.* • *n.* a fluorescent tube or lamp.

flut•ing |ˈflo͞otiNG| • *n.* (in architcture and design) a groove or set of grooves forming a surface decoration: *a hollow stem with vertical flutings* | *pieces decorated with fluting.*

flu•vi•al |ˈflo͞ovēəl| • *adj.* of or found in a river. Cf. RIPARIAN

flux |fləks| • *n.* **1** the action or process of flowing or flowing out: *the flux of people entering and leaving the theater.*
■ an abnormal discharge of blood or other matter from or within the body. ■ (usu. **the flux**) diarrhea or dysentery. **2** continuous change: *the whole political system is in a state of flux.* **3** (in physics) the rate of flow of a fluid, radiant energy, or particles striking an area.
■ the amount of radiation or particles striking on an area in a given time. ■ the total electric or magnetic field passing through a surface. **4** a substance mixed with a solid to lower its melting point, used esp. in soldering and brazing metals or to promote vitrification in glass or ceramics.
■ a substance added to a furnace during metal smelting or glassmaking that combines with impurities to form slag. • *v.* [trans.] treat (a metal object) with a flux to promote melting.

fo•gey |ˈfōgē| (also **fogy**) • *n.* (pl. **-eys** or **-ies**) a person, typically an old one, who is considered to be old-fashioned or conservative in attitude or tastes: *a bunch of old fogeys.*
DERIVATIVES: **fo•gey•dom** |-dəm| *n.* **fo•gey•ish** *adj.* **fo•gey•ism** |-ˌizəm| *n.*

foi•ble |ˈfoibəl| • *n.* **1** a minor weakness or eccentricity in someone's character: *they have to tolerate each other's little foibles.* **2** the weaker part of a fencing sword blade, from the middle to the point. Compare with FORTE[1], sense 2.

foi•deur |frwäˈdər | • *n.* coolness or reserve between people.

foil[1] |foil| • *v.* [trans.] prevent (something considered wrong or undesirable) from succeeding: *a brave policewoman foiled the robbery.*
■ frustrate the efforts or plans of: *Errol Flynn is a dashing Mountie foiling Nazi agents.*

foil[2] • *n.* **1** metal hammered or rolled into a thin flexible sheet, used chiefly for covering or wrapping food: *aluminum foil.* **2** a person or thing that contrasts with and so emphasizes and enhances the qualities of another: *the earthy taste of grilled vegetables is a perfect foil for the tart bite of creamy goat cheese.*
■ a thin leaf of metal placed under a precious stone to increase its brilliance.

foil[3] • *n.* a light fencing sword without cutting edges and with a blunt point.
■ the sport of fencing with a foil: *in épée and foil, hits must be made with the point.*
DERIVATIVES: **foil•ist** |-ist| *n.*

foist |foist| • *v.* [trans.] (**foist someone/ something on**) impose an unwelcome or un-

necessary person or thing on: *don't let anyone foist inferior goods on you.*
■ (**foist someone/something into**) introduce someone or something surreptitiously or unwarrantably into: *he attempted to foist a new delegate into the conference.*

fo•li•ate • *adj.* |ˈfōlēət; -ˌāt| decorated with leaves or leaflike motifs: *foliate scrolls.* • *v.* |ˈfōlēˌāt| [trans.] **1** decorate with leaves or leaflike motifs: *the dome is to be foliated.* **2** number the leaves of (a book) rather than the pages.

fo•li•o |ˈfōlēˌō| • *n.* (pl. **-os**) an individual leaf of paper or parchment, numbered on the recto or front side only, occurring either loose as one of a series or forming part of a bound volume.
■ the leaf number or page number in a printed book. ■ a sheet of paper folded once to form two leaves (four pages) of a book. ■ a size of book made up of such sheets: *copies in folio.*
■ a book or manuscript made up of sheets of paper folded in such a way; a volume of the largest possible size: *old vellum-bound folios* | [as adj.] *a folio volume.*

fo•ment |ˈfōˌment; fōˈment| • *v.* [trans.] instigate or stir up (an undesirable or violent sentiment or course of action): *they accused him of fomenting political unrest.*
DERIVATIVES: **fo•ment•er** *n.*

foot•print |ˈfo͝otˌprint| • *n.* (in figurative use) the area covered by something, in particular:
■ the area in which a broadcast signal from a particular source can be received. ■ the space taken up on a surface by a piece of computer hardware. ■ the area beneath an aircraft or a land vehicle that is affected by its noise or weight. ■ the area taken up by the ground level of a building.

for•ay |ˈfôrˌā; ˈfärˌā| • *n.* a sudden attack or incursion, esp. into enemy territory, to obtain something; a raid: *the garrison made a foray against Richard's camp* | *he made another foray to the bar.*
■ an attempt to become involved in a new activity or sphere: *my first foray into journalism.* • *v.* [no obj., with adverbial of direction] make or go on a foray: *the place into which they were forbidden to foray.*
DERIVATIVES: **for•ay•er** *n.*

for•bear•ance |fôrˈberəns; fər-| • *n.* patient self-control; restraint and tolerance: *forbearance from taking action.*
■ the action of refraining (forbearing) from exercising a legal right, esp. enforcing the payment of a debt.

for•ci•ble |ˈfôrsəbəl| • *adj.* done by force: *signs of forcible entry.*
■ vigorous and strong; forceful: *they could only be deterred by forcible appeals.*
DERIVATIVES: **for•ci•bly** |-blē| *adv.*

fore•bod•ing |fôrˈbōdiNG| • *n.* fearful apprehension; a feeling that something bad will happen: *with a sense of foreboding she read the note.* • *adj.* implying or seeming to imply that something bad is going to happen: *when the doctor spoke, his voice was dark and foreboding.*
DERIVATIVES: **fore•bod•ing•ly** *adv.*

fore•cas•tle |ˈfōksəl; ˈfôrˌkæsəl| (also **fo'c's'le**) • *n.* the forward part of a ship below the deck, traditionally used as the crew's living quarters.
■ a raised deck at the front of a ship.

fo•ren•sic |fəˈrenzik; -sik| • *adj.* of, relating to, or denoting the application of scientific methods and techniques to the investigation of crime: *a forensic psychologist* | *forensic evidence.*
■ of or relating to courts of law. • *n.* (**forensics**) scientific tests or techniques used in connection with the detection of crime.
DERIVATIVES: **fo•ren•si•cal•ly** |-(ə)lē| *adv.*

fore•short•en |fôrˈSHôrtn| • *v.* [trans.] portray or show (an object or view) as closer than it is or as having less depth or distance, as an effect of perspective or the angle of vision: *seen from the road, the mountain is greatly foreshortened.*
■ prematurely or dramatically shorten or reduce (something) in time or scale:[as adj.] (**foreshortened**) *foreshortened careers.*

fore•skin |ˈfôrˌskin| • *n.* the retractable roll of skin covering the end of the (uncircumcised) penis. Also called PREPUCE.

fore•word |ˈfôrˌwərd| • *n.* a short introduction to a book, typically by a person other than the author. Cf. PREFACE.

for•feit |ˈfôrfit| • *v.* (**forfeited, forfeiting** |ˈfôrfiṭiNG|) [trans.] lose or be deprived of (property or a right or privilege) as a penalty for wrongdoing: *those unable to meet their taxes were liable to forfeit their property.* Cf. WAIVE, CONFISCATE.
■ lose or give up (something) as a necessary consequence of something else: *she didn't mind forfeiting an extra hour in bed to get up and clean the stables.* • *n.* a fine or penalty for wrongdoing or for a breach of the rules in a club or game. ■ The loss of a game owing to breach of the rules, failure to field a team, or the like. ■ an item of property or a right or privilege lost as a legal penalty. ■ the action of forfeiting something. • *adj.* [predic.] lost or surrendered as a penalty for wrongdoing or neglect: *the lands he had acquired were automatically forfeit.*
DERIVATIVES: **for•feit•a•ble** |ˈfôrfədəbəl| *adj.* **for•feit•er** |ˈfôrfiṭər| *n.* **for•fei•ture** |ˈfôrfəCHər| *n.*

for•ger•y |ˈfôrjərē| • *n.* (pl. **-ies**) the action of producing a copy of a document, signature, banknote, or work of art with the intention of profiting by presenting it as genuine. Cf. COUNTERFEIT
■ a document, signature, banknote, or work of art produced in this way.
DERIVATIVES: **forge** *v.* **forg•er** *n.*

for•mal•ism |ˈfôrməˌlizəm| • *n.* **1** excessive adherence to prescribed forms: *academic dryness and formalism.*
■ the use of forms of worship without regard to inner significance. ■ the basing of ethics on the form of the moral law without regard to intention or consequences. ■ concern or excessive concern with form and technique rather than with content in artistic creation. ■ (in

the theater) a symbolic and stylized manner of production. ■ the treatment of mathematics as a manipulation of meaningless symbols. **2** a description of something in formal mathematical or logical terms.
DERIVATIVES: **for•mal•ist** *n.* **for•mal•is•tic** |-ˈlistik| *adj.*

for•mal•i•ty |fôrˈmæləṭē| • *n.* (pl. **-ies**) the rigid observance of rules of convention or etiquette: *the formality of his social background inhibited him.*
■ stiffness of behavior or style: *with disconcerting formality the brothers shook hands.* ■ (usu. **formalities**) a thing that is done simply to comply with requirements of etiquette, regulations, or custom: *legal formalities.* Cf. PROTOCOL ■ (**a formality**) something that is done as a matter of course and without question; an inevitability: *her saying no was just a formality, and both of them knew it.*

for•mi•ca•tion |ˌfôrmiˈkāSHən| • *n.* a sensation like insects crawling over the skin.

for•mi•da•ble |ˈfôrmədəbəl; fôrˈmidəbəl; fər ˈmid-| • *adj.* inspiring fear or respect through being impressively large, powerful, intense, or capable: *a formidable opponent.*
DERIVATIVES: **for•mi•da•ble•ness** *n.* **for•mi•da•bly** |-əblē| *adv.*

for•mu•la•ic |ˌfôrmyəˈlāik| • *adj.* constituting or containing a verbal formula or set form of words: *a formulaic greeting.*
■ produced in accordance with a slavishly followed rule or style; predictable: *much romantic fiction is stylized, formulaic, and unrealistic.*
DERIVATIVES: **for•mu•la•i•cal•ly** |ˈ(ə)lē| *adv.*

for•ni•cate |ˈfôrniˌkāt| • *v.* [intrans.] have sexual intercourse with someone one is not married to.
DERIVATIVES: **for•ni•ca•tion** |ˌfôrniˈkā-SHən| *n.* **for•ni•ca•tor** |-ˌkāṭər| *n.*

for•swear |fôrˈswer| • *v.* (past **forswore** |-ˈswôr|; past part. **forsworn** |ˈswôrn|) [trans.] agree to give up or do without (something): *he would never forswear the religion of his people.*
■ (**forswear oneself/be forsworn**) swear falsely: *I swore that I would lead us safely home and I do not mean to be forsworn.*

forte¹ |ˈfôrˌtā; fôrt| • *n.* **1** [in sing.] a thing at which someone excels: *small talk was not his forte.* **2** the stronger part of a fencing sword blade, from the hilt to the middle. Compare with FOIBLE.

forte² |ˈfôrˌtā| • *adv. & adj.* (in music, esp. as a direction) loud or loudly. • *n.* a passage performed or marked to be performed loudly.

forth•com•ing |fôrTHˈkəmiNG; ˈfôrTHˌkəm- iNG| • *adj.* **1** planned for or about to happen in the near future: *the forthcoming Broadway season.* **2** [predic.] [often with negative] (of something required) ready or made available when wanted or needed: *financial support was not forthcoming.*
■ (of a person) willing to divulge information: *their daughter had never been forthcoming about her time in Europe.*
DERIVATIVES: **forth•com•ing•ness** *n.*

forth•with |fôrTHˈwiTH| • *adv.* (esp. in official

use) immediately; without delay: *we undertake to pay forthwith the money required.*

for•ti•tude |ˈfôrtəˌto͞od| • *n.* courage in pain or adversity: *she endured her illness with great fortitude.*

for•tu•i•tous |fôrˈto͞oətəs| • *adj.* happening by accident or chance rather than design: *the similarity between the paintings may not be simply fortuitous.*
■ happening by a lucky chance; fortunate: *from a cash standpoint, the company's timing is fortuitous.* See **usage** below.
DERIVATIVES: **for•tu•i•tous•ly** *adv.* **for•tu•i•tous•ness** *n.*

USAGE: The traditional, etymological meaning of **fortuitous** is 'happening by chance': a *fortuitous meeting* is a chance meeting, which might turn out to be either a good thing or a bad thing. In modern uses, however, **fortuitous** tends to be often used to refer only to fortunate outcomes, and the word is regarded by many as a synonym for 'lucky' or 'fortunate.'

found•er • *v.* [no obj., with adverbial] (of a ship) fill with water and sink: *six drowned when the yacht foundered off the Florida coast.*
■ (of a plan or undertaking) fail or break down, typically as a result of a particular problem or setback: *the talks foundered on the issue of reform.* ■ (of a horse or its rider) stumble or fall from exhaustion, lameness, or because of uneven or boggy ground. ■

USAGE: It is easy to confuse the words **founder** and **flounder**, not only because they sound similar but also because the contexts in which they are used tend to overlap. **Founder** means, in its general and extended use, 'fail or come to nothing; sink out of sight' as in *the plan foundered because of lack of organizational backing.* **Flounder**, on the other hand, means 'struggle; move clumsily; be in a state of confusion,' as in *new recruits floundering in their first week.*

found•ling |ˈfoundliNG| • *n.* an infant that has been abandoned by its parents and is discovered and cared for by others. Cf. CHANGE-LING

foy•er |ˈfoiər; ˈfoiˌā| • *n.* an entrance hall or other open area in a building used by the public, esp. a hotel or theater.
■ an entrance hall in a house or apartment.

fra•cas |ˈfrākəs; ˈfræk-| • *n.* (pl. **fracases**) a noisy disturbance or quarrel.

frac•tious |ˈfrækSHəs| • *adj.* easily irritated; bad-tempered: *they fight and squabble like fractious children.*
■ (of an organization) difficult to control; unruly: *the fractious coalition of populists.*
DERIVATIVES: **frac•tious•ly** *adv.* **frac•tious•ness** *n.*

frail•ty |ˈfrāltē| • *n.* (pl. **-ies**) the condition of being weak and delicate: *the increasing frailty of old age.*
■ weakness in character or morals: *all drama begins with human frailty.*

fran•chise |ˈfrænˌCHīz| • *n.* **1** an authoriza-

tion granted by a government or company to an individual or group enabling them to carry out specified commercial activities, for example, providing a broadcasting service or acting as a dealer in a company's products.
■ a business or service given such authorization to operate. ■ an authorization, given by a league, to own a sports team. ■ a professional sports team. ■ (also **franchise player**) a star player on a team, usually regarded as the most important. **2** (usu. **the franchise**) the right to vote.
■ the rights of citizenship. • *v.* [trans.] grant a franchise to (an individual or group).
■ grant a franchise for the sale of (goods) or the operation of (a service): *all the catering was franchised out.* Cf. ENFRANCHISE
DERIVATIVES: **fran•chis•a•ble** *adj.* **fran•chis•a•bil•i•ty** *n.* **fran•chi•see** |ˌfrænˌCHīˈzē| *n.* **fran•chis•er** (also **fran•chi•sor**) *n.*

Fran•cis•can |frænˈsiskən| • *n.* a friar, sister, or lay member of a Christian religious order, originally mendicant, founded in 1209 by St. Francis of Assisi or based on its rule, and noted for its preachers, teachers, and missionaries. • *adj.* of, relating to, or denoting St. Francis or the Franciscans.

fran•co•phone |ˈfræNGkəˌfōn| (also **Francophone**) • *adj.* French-speaking: *a summit of francophone countries| Ontario's francophone minority.* • *n.* a person who speaks French.

fran•gi•ble |ˈfrænjəbəl| • *adj.* able to be broken; fragile; brittle.

frap•pé |fræˈpā| • *adj.* [postpositive] (of a drink) iced or chilled: *a crème de menthe frappé.* • *n.* a drink served with ice or frozen to a slushy consistency.
■ (usu. **frappe**) |fræp| (chiefly in New England) a milkshake, esp. one made with ice cream.

frat•er•nize |ˈfrætərˌnīz| • *v.* [intrans.] associate or form a friendship with someone, esp. when one is not supposed to: *fraternizing with the enemy.*
DERIVATIVES: **frat•er•niz•er** *n.* **frat•er•ni•za•tion** |ˌfrætərniˈzāSHən| *n.*

frat•ri•cide |ˈfrætrəˌsīd| • *n.* the killing of one's brother or sister. The killing of one's sister is, less commonly, also called **sororicide**.
■ a person who kills his or her brother or sister. ■ the accidental killing of one's own forces in war.
DERIVATIVES: **frat•ri•cid•al** *adj.*

fraud |frôd| • *n.* wrongful or criminal deception intended to result in financial or personal gain: *he was convicted of fraud| prosecutions for social security frauds.*
■ a person or thing intended to deceive others, typically by unjustifiably claiming or being credited with accomplishments or qualities: *mediums exposed as tricksters and frauds.*

fraud•u•lent |ˈfrôjələnt| • *adj.* obtained, done by, or involving deception, esp. criminal deception: *fraudulent copying of the company's software.*
■ unjustifiably claiming or being credited with particular accomplishments or qualities: *he unmasked fraudulent psychics.*

DERIVATIVES: **fraud•u•lence** *n.* **fraud•u•lent•ly** *adv.*

fraught |frôt| • *adj.* **1** [predic.] (**fraught with**) (of a situation or course of action) filled with or destined to result in (something undesirable): *marketing any new product is fraught with danger.* **2** causing or affected by great anxiety or stress: *a fraught silence* | *she sounded a bit fraught.*

freak |frēk| • *n.* **1** a very unusual and unexpected event or situation: *the accident was a total freak* | [as adj.] *a freak storm.*
■ (also **freak of nature**) a person, animal, or plant with an unusual physical abnormality. ■ a person regarded as strange because of unusual appearance or behavior. ■ [with adj.] a person who is obsessed with or unusually enthusiastic about a specified interest: *a fitness freak.* ■ [usu. with adj.] a person addicted to a drug of a particular kind: *the twins were cocaine freaks.* ■ an unconventional person, esp. a hippie: *a community of late-sixties freaks.* **2** a sudden arbitrary change of mind; a whim: *follow this way or that, as the freak takes you.* • *v.* **1** [intrans.] react or behave in a wild and irrational way, typically because of the effects of extreme emotion, mental illness, or drugs: *I could have freaked out and started smashing the place up.*
■ [trans.] cause to act in such a way: *he freaks guest stars out on show day.* **2** [trans.] fleck or streak randomly: *the white pink and the pansy freaked with jet.*

free•base |ˈfrēˌbās| (also **freebase cocaine**) • *n.* cocaine that has been converted from its salt to its base form by heating with ether or boiling with sodium bicarbonate, taken by inhaling the fumes or smoking the residue. • *v.* [trans.] prepare or take (cocaine) in such a way.

free•boot•er |ˈfrēˌbo͞otər| • *n.* a pirate or lawless adventurer.
DERIVATIVES: **free•boot** |ˈfrēˌbo͞ot| *v.*

free•hold |ˈfrēˌhōld| • *n.* permanent and absolute tenure of land or property with freedom to dispose of it at will. Often contrasted with *leasehold*, tenure under the terms of a lease.
■ (**the freehold**) the ownership of a piece of land or property by such tenure. ■ a piece of land or property held by such tenure. • *adj.* held by or having the status of freehold.
DERIVATIVES: **free•hold•er** *n.*

free mar•ket • *n.* an economic system in which prices are determined by unrestricted competition between privately owned businesses.
DERIVATIVES: **free mar•ket•eer** (also **free-mar•ket•eer**) *n.*

USAGE: The **free market** is often spoken of as 'free' from the effects of government action, but speakers refer chiefly to regulations and other controls on private action. Few freemarket advocates would, for instance, do away with laws protecting copyrights or trademarks.

Free•ma•son•ry |ˈfrēˈmāsənrē| • *n.* **1** the system and institutions of the Freemasons, a worldwide secret society of men dedicated to mutual support and the promotion of brotherly love. **2** instinctive sympathy or fellow feeling between people with something in common: *the unshakable freemasonry of actors in a crisis.*

fre•net•ic |frəˈnetik| • *adj.* fast and energetic in a wild and uncontrolled way: *a frenetic pace of activity.*
DERIVATIVES: **fre•net•i•cal•ly** |-ik(ə)lē| *adv.*

fre•quen•ta•tive |frēˈkwentətiv| • *adj.* (of a verb or verbal form) expressing frequent repetition or intensity of action. • *n.* a verb or verbal form of this type, e.g., *chatter* in English.

fres•co |ˈfreskō| • *n.* (pl. **-oes** or **-os**) a painting done rapidly in watercolor on wet plaster on a wall or ceiling, so that the colors penetrate the plaster and become fixed as it dries.
■ this method of painting, used esp. in Roman times and by the masters of the Italian Renaissance. • *v.* [trans.] paint in fresco: *four scenes had been frescoed on the wall* | [as adj.] *frescoed ceilings.*

fresh•et |ˈfreSHət| • *n.* the flood of a river from heavy rain or melted snow.
■ a rush of fresh water flowing into the sea.

Freud•i•an |ˈfroidēən| • *adj.* relating to or influenced by Sigmund Freud and his methods of psychoanalysis, esp. with reference to the importance of sexuality in human behavior.
■ susceptible to analysis in terms of unconscious desires: *he wasn't sure whether his passion for water power had some deep Freudian significance.* • *n.* a follower of Freud or his methods.
DERIVATIVES: **Freud•i•an•ism** |-ˌnizəm| *n.*

fri•a•ble |ˈfrīəbəl| • *adj.* easily crumbled: *the soil was friable between her fingers.*
DERIVATIVES: **fri•a•bil•i•ty** |ˌfrīəˈbilətē| *n.* **fri•a•ble•ness** *n.*

fri•ar |ˈfrīər| • *n.* a member of any of certain religious orders of men, esp. the four originally mendicant Roman Catholic orders (Augustinians, Carmelites, Dominicans, and Franciscans).

fric•a•tive |ˈfrikətiv| • *adj.* denoting a type of consonant made by the friction of breath in a narrow opening, producing a turbulent air flow. • *n.* a consonant made in this way, e.g., *f* and *th.* Cf. PLOSIVE.

fric•tion |ˈfrikSHən| • *n.* the resistance that one surface or object encounters when moving over another: *a lubrication system that reduces friction.*
■ the action of one surface or object rubbing against another: *the friction of braking.* ■ conflict or animosity caused by a clash of wills, temperaments, or opinions: *friction between father and son.*
DERIVATIVES: **fric•tion•less** *adj.*

frieze |frēz| • *n.* a broad horizontal band of sculpted or painted decoration, esp. on a wall near the ceiling.

■ a horizontal paper strip mounted on a wall to give a similar effect. ■ the part of an entablature between the architrave and the cornice.

frig•id | 'frijid | • *adj.* very cold in temperature: *frigid water.*

■ (esp. of a woman) unable or unwilling to be sexually aroused and responsive. ■ showing no friendliness or enthusiasm; stiff or formal in behavior or style: *Henrietta looked back with a frigid calm.*

DERIVATIVES: **fri•gid•i•ty** | frə'jidətē | *n.* **frig•id•ly** *adv.* **frig•id•ness** *n.*

frip•per•y | 'fripərē | • *n.* (pl. **-ies**) showy or unnecessary ornament in architecture, dress, or language.

■ a tawdry or frivolous thing.

fris•son | 'frē'sôN | • *n.* a sudden strong feeling of excitement or fear; a thrill: *a frisson of excitement.*

friv•o•lous | 'frivələs | • *adj.* not having any serious basis, purpose, or value: *rules to stop frivolous lawsuits.*

■ (of a person) carefree and not serious.

DERIVATIVES: **fri•vol•i•ty** | fri'välətē | *n.* **friv•o•lous•ly** *adv.* **friv•o•lous•ness** *n.*

frot•tage | frô'täzH | • *n.* **1** the technique or process of taking a rubbing from an uneven surface to form the basis of a work of art.

■ a work of art produced in this way. **2** the practice of touching or rubbing against the clothed body of another person in a crowd as a means of obtaining sexual gratification.

DERIVATIVES: **frot•teur** | -'tər | *n.* (pl. same) (in sense 2). **frot•teur•ism** | -'tər,izəm | *n.* (in sense 2).

frou-frou | 'frōō,frōō | (also **frou-frou**) • *n.* a rustling noise made by someone walking in a dress.

■ frills or other ornamentation, particularly of women's clothes: [as adj.] *a little froufrou skirt.*

fro•ward | 'frō(w)ərd | • *adj.* (of a person) difficult to deal with; contrary.

DERIVATIVES: **fro•ward•ly** *adv.* **fro•ward•ness** *n.*

frowz•y | 'frowzē | (also **frowsy**) • *adj.* (**frowzier, frowziest**) scruffy and neglected in appearance.

■ dingy and stuffy: *a frowzy nightclub.*

DERIVATIVES: **frowz•i•ness** | -zēnis | *n.*

fruc•ti•fy | 'frəktə,fī | • *v.* (**-ies, -ied**) [trans.] make (something) fruitful or productive.

■ [intrans.] bear fruit or become productive.

DERIVATIVES: **fruc•tif•er•ous** *adj.*

fruc•tu•ous | 'frəkcHəwəs; 'frōōK- | • *adj.* full of or producing a great deal of fruit.

fru•gal | 'frōōgəl | • *adj.* sparing or economical with regard to money or food: *he led a remarkably frugal existence.*

■ simple and plain and costing little: *a frugal meal.*

DERIVATIVES: **fru•gal•i•ty** | frōō'gælətē | *n.* **fru•gal•ly** *adv.* **fru•gal•ness** *n.*

fruit•ar•i•an | frōō'terēən | • *n.* a person who eats only fruit.: (as adj.) *a fruitarian diet.*

DERIVATIVES: **fruit•ar•i•an•ism** | -,nizəm | *n.*

fru•i•tion | frōō'isHən | • *n.* **1** the point at

which a plan or project is realized: *the plans have come to fruition sooner than expected.*

■ [in sing.] the realization of a plan or project: *the fruition of years of research.* **2** the state or action of producing fruit.

frus•trate • *v.* | 'frəs,trāt | [trans.] prevent (a plan or attempted action) from progressing, succeeding, or being fulfilled: *his attempt to frustrate the merger.*

■ prevent (someone) from doing or achieving something: *an increasingly popular way to frustrate car thieves.* ■ cause (someone) to feel upset or annoyed, typically as a result of being unable to change or achieve something: [as adj.] (**frustrating**) *it can be very frustrating to find that the size you want isn't there.* • *adj.* archaic frustrated.

DERIVATIVES: **frus•trat•er** *n.* **frus•trat•ing•ly** *adv.* [as submodifier] *progress turned out to be frustratingly slow.* **frus•tra•tion** *n.*

fu•ga•cious | fyōō'gāsHəs | • *adj.* tending to disappear; fleeting: *the fugacious years of youth.*

DERIVATIVES: **fu•ga•cious•ly** *adv.* **fu•ga•cious•ness** *n.*

fugue | fyōōg | • *n.* **1** a musical contrapuntal composition in counterpoint in which a short melody or phrase (the subject) is introduced by one part and successively taken up by others and developed by interweaving the parts. **2** (in psychiatry) a state or period of loss of awareness of one's identity, often coupled with flight from one's usual environment, associated with certain forms of hysteria and epilepsy.

DERIVATIVES: **fu•gal** *adj.* **fugu•ist** | 'fyōō-gist | *n.*

füh•rer | 'fyōōrər | (also **fuehrer**) • *n.* a (ruthless or tyrannical) leader.

ful•crum | 'fŏŏlkrəm; 'fəl- | • *n.* (pl. **fulcra** or **fulcrums**) the point on which a lever rests or is supported.

■ a thing that plays a central or essential role in an activity, event, or situation: *research is the fulcrum of the university community.*

ful•gu•ra•tion | ,fŏŏlg(y)ə'räsHən | • *n.* **1** (in medicine) the therapeutic destruction of small growths or areas of tissue using direct application of heat. **2** a flash like that of lightning.

DERIVATIVES: **ful•gu•rant** | 'fŏŏlg(y)ərənt | *adj.* (in sense 2). **ful•gu•rate** | 'fŏŏlg(y)ə,rāt | *v.* (in sense 2). **ful•gu•rous** | 'fŏŏlg(y)ərəs | *adj.* (in sense 2).

fu•lig•i•nous | fyōō'lijənəs | • *adj.* sooty; dusky: *the hut's fuliginous interior.*

full /fŏŏl/ • *v.* [trans.] [often as n.] (**fulling**) clean, shrink, and felt (cloth) by heat, pressure, and moisture.

DERIVATIVES: **full•er** *n.*

ful•mi•nant | 'fŏŏlmənənt; 'fəl- | • *adj.* (of a disease or symptom) severe and sudden in onset.

ful•mi•nate | 'fŏŏlmə,nāt; 'fəl- | • *v.* [intrans.] express vehement protest: *they **fulminated** **against** the new curriculum.*

■ explode violently or flash like lightning: *thunder fulminated around the house.* ■ [usu. as

adj.] (**fulminating**) (of a disease or symptom) develop suddenly and severely: *fulminating appendicitis.*
DERIVATIVES: **ful•mi•na•tion** *n.* **ful•mi•na•tor** *n.* **ful•mi•na•to•ry** *adj.*

ful•some | 'fŏolsəm | • *adj.* **1** complimentary or flattering to an excessive degree: *they are almost embarrassingly fulsome in their appreciation.* **2** of large size or quantity; generous or abundant: *a fulsome harvest.*
DERIVATIVES: **ful•some•ly** *adv.* **ful•some•ness** *n.*

USAGE: The earliest recorded use of **fulsome**, in the 13th century, had the meaning 'abundant,' but in modern use this is held by many to be incorrect. The correct current meaning is 'disgusting because overdone; excessive.' The word is still often used to mean 'abundant; copious,' but this use can give rise to ambiguity: the possibility that while for one speaker **fulsome praise** will be a genuine compliment, for others it will be interpreted as an insult.

ful•vous | 'fŏolvəs; 'fəl- | • *adj.* reddish yellow; tawny.
fu•mi•gate | 'fyŏomə,gāt | • *v.* [trans.] apply the fumes of certain chemicals to (an area) to disinfect it or to rid it of vermin.
DERIVATIVES: **fu•mi•gant** |-gənt| *n.* **fu•mi•ga•tion** |,fyŏomə'gāsHən| *n.* **fu•mi•ga•tor** |-,gātər| *n.*
fu•nam•bu•list | fyŏo'næmbyələst | • *n.* a tightrope walker.
func•tion•al•ism | 'fəNGksHənl,izəm | • *n.* belief in or stress on the practical application of a thing, in particular: ■ (in the arts) the doctrine that the design of an object should be determined solely by its function, rather than by aesthetic considerations, and that anything practically designed will be inherently beautiful. ■ (in the social sciences) the theory that all aspects of a society serve a function and are necessary for the survival of that society. ■ (in the philosophy of mind) the theory that mental states can be sufficiently defined by their cause, their effect on other mental states, and their effect on behavior.
DERIVATIVES: **func•tion•al•ist** *n.* & *adj.*
fun•da•ment | 'fəndəmənt | • *n.* **1** the foundation or basis of something. **2** a person's buttocks or anus.
fun•da•men•tal•ism | ,fəndə'mentl,izəm | • *n.* a form of Protestant Christianity that upholds belief in the strict and literal interpretation of the Bible, including its narratives, doctrines, prophecies, and moral laws. ■ strict maintenance of ancient or fundamental doctrines of any religion or ideology, notably Islam.
DERIVATIVES: **fun•da•men•tal•ist** *n.* & *adj.*
fu•ner•ar•y | 'fyŏonə,rerē | • *adj.* relating to a funeral or the commemoration of the dead: *funerary ceremonies.*
fu•ne•re•al | fyə'nēriəl | • *adj.* having the mournful, somber character appropriate to a

funeral: *Lincoln's funereal gloominess was legendary.*
DERIVATIVES: **fu•ne•re•al•ly** *adv.*
fun•gi•ble | 'fənjəbəl | • *adj.* (esp. of goods contracted for without an individual specimen being specified) able to replace or be replaced by another identical item; mutually interchangeable.
DERIVATIVES: **fun•gi•bil•i•ty** | ,fənjə'bilətē | *n.*
fu•nic•u•lar | fyŏo'nikyələr | • *adj.* **1** (of a railway, esp. one on a mountainside) operating by cable with ascending and descending cars counterbalanced. **2** of or relating to a rope or its tension. • *n.* a railway operating in such a way.
funk[1] | fəNGk | informal • *n.* **1** (also **blue funk**) [in sing.] a state of depression: *I sat absorbed in my own blue funk.* ■ a state of great fear or panic: *are you in a funk about running out of things to say?* **2** chiefly Brit. a coward. • *v.* [trans.] chiefly Brit. avoid (a task or thing) out of fear: *I could have seen him this morning but I funked it.*
funk[2] • *n.* **1** a style of popular dance music of black origin, based on elements of blues and soul and having a strong rhythm that typically accentuates the first beat in the bar. ■ a style of jazz music that is uncomplicated, soulful, and blues-infused. **2** [in sing.] a strong musty smell of sweat or tobacco.
funk•y | 'fəNGkē | • *adj.* (**funkier, funkiest**) informal **1** (of music) having or using a strong dance rhythm, in particular that of funk: *some excellent funky beats.* ■ (of jazz music) incorporating earthy, bluesy elements. ■ modern and stylish in an unconventional or earthy way: *she likes wearing funky clothes.* **2** strongly musty: *cooked greens make the kitchen smell really funky.*
DERIVATIVES: **funk•i•ly** |-kəlē| *adv.* **funk•i•ness** |-kēnis| *n.*
fur•be•low | 'fərbə,lō | • *n.* a gathered strip or pleated border of a skirt or petticoat. ■ (**furbelows**) showy ornaments or trimmings: *frills and furbelows just made her look stupid.* • *v.* [trans.] [usu. as adj.] (**furbelowed**) adorn with trimmings.
fur•lough | 'fərlō | • *n.* leave of absence, esp. that granted to a member of the armed services: *a six-week furlough in Guam.* ■ a temporary release of a convict from prison: *after three years they were allowed weekend furloughs.* ■ a layoff, esp. a temporary one, from a place of employment. • *v.* [trans.] grant such leave of absence to. ■ lay off (workers), esp. temporarily: *President Reagan furloughed "nonessential" employees* | [as adj.] (**furloughed**) *factories are apt to recall some furloughed workers.*
fu•ror | 'fyŏor,ôr; 'fyŏorər | (also chiefly Brit. **furore**) • *n.* [in sing.] an outbreak of public anger or excitement: *the article raised a furor among mathematicians.* ■ archaic a wave of enthusiastic admiration; a craze.
fur•tive | 'fərtiv | • *adj.* attempting to avoid notice or attention, typically because of guilt or

a belief that discovery would lead to trouble; secretive: *they spent a furtive day together* | *he stole a furtive glance.*
■ suggestive of guilty nervousness: *the look in his eyes became furtive.*
DERIVATIVES: **fur•tive•ly** *adv.* **fur•tive•ness** *n.*

fus•cous |ˈfəskəs| • *adj.* dark and somber in color.

fu•se•lage |ˈfyo͞osəˌläzH; -zə-| • *n.* the main body of an aircraft.

fu•sil•lade |ˈfyo͞osəˌläd; -ˌlād| • *n.* a series, as of shots fired or missiles thrown all at the same time or in quick succession: *marchers had to dodge a fusillade of missiles* | *a fusillade of accusations.*

fu•sion |ˈfyo͞ozHən| • *n.* the process or result of joining two or more things together to form a single entity: *a fusion of an idea from anthropology and an idea from psychology* | *malformation or fusion of the three bones in the middle ear.*
■ Physics (also **nuclear fusion**) a nuclear reaction in which atomic nuclei of low atomic number fuse to form a heavier nucleus with the release of energy. ■ The union of atomic nuclei to form a heavier nucleus as a source of energy. Cf. FISSION ■ the process of causing a material or object to melt with intense heat, esp. so as to join with another: *the fusion of resin and glass fiber in the molding process.*
■ music that is a mixture of different styles, esp. jazz and rock.
DERIVATIVES: **fu•sion•al** |-zHnl| *adj.*

fus•tian |ˈfəsCHən| • *n.* **1** thick, durable twilled cloth with a short nap, usually dyed in dark colors. **2** pompous or pretentious speech or writing: *a smoke screen of fustian and fantasy.*

fus•ty |ˈfəstē| • *adj.* (**fustier, fustiest**) smelling stale, damp, or stuffy: *the fusty odor of decay.*
■ old-fashioned in attitude or style: *grammar in the classroom became a fusty notion.*
DERIVATIVES: **fus•ti•ly** |ˈfəstəlē| *adv.* **fus•ti•ness** |ˈfəstēnis| *n.*

fu•tile |ˈfyo͞otl; ˈfyo͞oˌtil| • *adj.* incapable of producing any useful result; pointless: *a futile attempt to keep fans from mounting the stage.*
DERIVATIVES: **fu•tile•ly** *adv.* **fu•til•i•ty** |ˈfyo͞oˈtiləṭē| *n.*

fu•tur•ism |ˈfyo͞oCHəˌrizəm| • *n.* concern with events and trends of the future or which anticipate the future.
■ (**Futurism**) a short-lived artistic movement begun in Italy in 1909, and also influential in Russia, which violently rejected traditional forms so as to celebrate and incorporate into art the energy and dynamism of modern technology. ■ more broadly, futuristic tendencies in any sphere; belief or interest in human progress.

fu•tur•is•tic |ˌfyo͞oCHəˈristik| • *adj.* having or involving modern technology or design: *a swimming pool and futuristic dome.*
■ (of a film or book) set in the future, typically in a world of advanced or menacing technology.
DERIVATIVES: **fu•tur•is•ti•cal•ly** |-ik(ə)lē| *adv.*

fu•tu•ri•ty |fyo͞oˈto͞oˌrəṭē; -CHo͞oˌrəṭē| • *n.* (pl. **-ies**) the future time: *the tremendous shadows futurity casts upon the present.*
■ a future event. ■ renewed or continuing existence: *the snowdrops were a promise of futurity.*
■ (also **futurity race, futurity stake**) a horse race held long after its entrants are nominated.

Gg

gab•ar•dine |ˈgæbərˌdēn| (chiefly Brit. also **gaberdine**) • *n.* a smooth, durable twillwoven cloth, typically of worsted or cotton.
■ Brit. a raincoat made of such cloth. ■ (usu. **gaberdine**) a loose long upper garment, worn particularly by Jewish men.

ga•ble |ˈgābəl| • *n.* the part of a wall that encloses the end of a pitched roof.
■ (also **gable end**) a wall topped with a gable. ■ a gable-shaped canopy over a window or door. Cf. DORMER.
DERIVATIVES: **ga•bled** *adj.*

gad•fly |ˈgædˌflī| • *n.* (pl. **-flies**) an annoying person, esp. one who provokes others into action by criticism.

gaffe |gæf| • *n.* an unintentional act or remark causing embarrassment to its origina-

tor; a blunder: *an unforgivable social gaffe.* Cf. FAUX PAS.

gage[1] |gāj| archaic • *n.* a valued object deposited as a guarantee of good faith.
■ a pledge, esp. a glove, thrown down as a symbol of a challenge to fight. Cf. GAUNTLET[1].
• *v.* [trans.] offer (a thing or one's life) as a guarantee of good faith.

gage[2] • *n.* & *v.* variant spelling of GAUGE.

gain•say |ˌgānˈsā; ˈgānˌsā| • *v.* (past and past part. **-said** |-ˈsed; -ˌsed|) [trans.] [with negative] deny or contradict (a fact or statement): *the impact of the railroads cannot be gainsaid.*
■ speak against or oppose (someone).
DERIVATIVES: **gain•say•er** *n.*

gait |gāt| • *n.* a person's manner of walking: *the easy gait of an athlete.*

■ the paces of an animal, esp. a horse or dog. • *v.* [intrans.] (of a dog or horse) walk in a trained gait, as at a show: *the dogs are gaiting in a circle.*
DERIVATIVES: **gait•ed** *adj.* (in combination): *double-gaited.*

Gal•a•had |ˈɡæləˌhæd| • *n.* (also **Sir Galahad**) the noblest of King Arthur's legendary knights; renowned for immaculate purity and destined to find the Holy Grail.
■ a man characterized by nobility, courtesy, integrity, etc.

gal•ax•y |ˈɡæləksē| • *n.* (pl. **-ies**) a system of millions or billions of stars, together with gas and dust, held together by gravitational attraction.
■ (**the Galaxy**) the galaxy of which our solar system is a part; the Milky Way. ■ a large or impressive group of people or things: *a galaxy of young talent.*
DERIVATIVES: **ga•lac•tic** *adj.*

ga•lère |ɡæˈler| • *n.* a (usu. undesirable) group or coterie: *the repulsive galère of Lolita's admirers.*

gall¹ |ɡôl| • *n.* **1** bold, impudent behavior: *the bank had the gall to demand a fee.* **2** the contents of the gallbladder; bile (proverbial for its bitterness).
■ an animal's gallbladder. ■ used to refer to something bitter or cruel: *accept life's gall without blaming somebody else.*

gall² • *n.* **1** annoyance; irritation: *he imagined Linda's gall as she found herself still married and not rich.* **2** (esp. of a horse) a sore on the skin made by chafing. • *v.* [trans.] **1** make (someone) feel annoyed: *he knew he was losing, and it galled him.* **2** make sore by rubbing: *the straps galled their shoulders.*

gall³ • *n.* an abnormal growth formed in response to the presence of insect larvae, mites, or fungi on plants and trees, esp. oaks.
■ [as adj.] denoting insects or mites that produce such growths: *gall flies.*

gal•lant•ry |ˈɡæləntrē| • *n.* (pl. **-ies**) **1** courageous behavior, esp. in battle: *a medal awarded for outstanding gallantry during the raid.* **2** polite attention or respect given by men (sometimes called *gallants*) to women.
■ (**gallantries**) actions or words used when paying such attention.

gal•le•on |ˈɡælēən; ˈɡælyən| • *n.* a sailing ship in use (esp. by Spain) from the 15th through 17th centuries, originally as a warship, later for trade. Galleons were mainly square-rigged and usually had three or more decks and masts.

gal•liard |ˈɡælyərd| • *n.* a lively dance of former times in triple time for two people, involving complicated turns and steps.

Gal•li•cism |ˈɡæliˌsizəm| • *n.* a French expression, esp. one adopted by speakers of another language.
■ a (typically) French characteristic, custom, or outlook.

gal•li•mau•fry |ˌɡæləˈmôfrē| • *n.* (pl. **-ies**) a confused jumble or medley of things.
■ a dish made from diced or minced meat, esp. a hash or ragout.

gal•li•vant |ˈɡæləˌvænt| • *v.* [no obj., with adverbial] go around from one place to another in the pursuit of pleasure or entertainment: *she quit her job to go gallivanting around the globe.*

gal•van•ic |ɡælˈvænik| • *adj.* **1** relating to or involving electric currents produced by chemical action. **2** sudden and dramatic: *hurry with awkward galvanic strides.*
DERIVATIVES: **gal•van•i•cal•ly** |-ik(ə)lē| *adv.*

gal•va•nize |ˈɡælvəˌnīz| • *v.* [trans.] **1** shock or excite (someone), typically into taking action: *the urgency of his voice galvanized them into action.* **2** [often as adj.] (**galvanized**) coat (iron or steel) with a protective layer of zinc: *an old galvanized bucket.*
DERIVATIVES: **gal•va•ni•za•tion** |ˌɡælvəni ˈzāSHən| *n.* **gal•va•niz•er** *n.*

gam•ba•do |ɡæmˈbädō; -ˈbä-| (also **gambade** |-ˈbäd; -ˈbäd|) • *n.* (pl. **-os** or **-oes**) a leap or bound on a horse, esp. an exaggerated one. ■ any sudden or fantastic action.

gam•bit |ˈɡæmbit| • *n.* (in chess) an opening in which a player makes a sacrifice, typically of a pawn, for the sake of some compensating advantage.
■ a device, action, or opening remark, typically one entailing a degree of risk, that is calculated to gain an advantage: *his resignation was a tactical gambit.*

gam•bol |ˈɡæmbəl| • *v.* (**gamboled, gamboling**; Brit. **gambolled, gambolling**) [no obj., usu. with adverbial] run or jump about playfully: *the mare gamboled toward Connie.* • *n.* [usu. in sing.] an act of running or jumping about playfully.

gam•brel |ˈɡæmbrəl| (also **gambrel roof**) • *n.* a roof with two sides, each of which has a shallower slope above a steeper one.
■ a hip roof with a small gable forming the upper part of each end. Cf. MANSARD

gam•ete |ˈɡæmēt; ɡəˈmēt| • *n.* a mature haploid (having a single set of unpaired chromosomes) male or female germ cell that is able to unite with another of the opposite sex in sexual reproduction to form a zygote (a fertilized ovum).
DERIVATIVES: **ga•met•ic** |ɡəˈmetik| *adj.*

gam•ine |ˈɡæmēn| • *n.* a girl with mischievous or boyish charm.
■ a female street urchin. • *adj.* characteristic of or relating to such a girl.

gam•mon |ˈɡæmən| • *n.* ham that has been cured or smoked like bacon.
■ the bottom piece of a side of bacon, including a hind leg.

gam•ut |ˈɡæmət| • *n.* (**the gamut**) **1** the complete range or scope of something: *the whole gamut of human emotion.* **2** a complete scale of musical notes; the compass or range of a voice or instrument.
■ a scale consisting of seven overlapping six-note scales (hexachords), containing all the recognized notes used in western medieval music, covering almost three octaves from bass G to treble E. ■ the lowest note in this scale.
PHRASES: **run the gamut** experience, dis-

play, or perform the complete range of something: *wines that run the gamut from dry to sweet.*

USAGE: Do not confuse **run the gamut** with **run the gauntlet** (see GAUNTLET[2]).

gan•gli•on |ˈgæNGglēən| • *n.* (pl. **ganglia** |-glēə| or **ganglions**) **1** a structure containing a number of nerve cell bodies, typically linked by synapses, and often forming a swelling on a nerve fiber. ■ a network of cells forming a nerve center in the nervous system of an invertebrate. ■ a well-defined mass of gray matter within the central nervous system. **2** (in medicine) an abnormal benign swelling on a tendon sheath.
DERIVATIVES: **gan•gli•on•ic** |ˌgæNGglēˈänik| *adj.*

Gan•y•mede |ˈgænəˌmēd| • *n.* a legendary Trojan youth who was so beautiful that he was carried off by Zeus to be the cupbearer for the Olympic gods. ■ a cupbearer. ■ a boy retained for sexual purposes.

gar•bol•o•gy |gärˈbäləjē| • *n.* the study of a community or culture by analyzing its waste.
DERIVATIVES: **gar•bol•o•gist** |-jist| *n.*

garde•robe |ˈgärdˌrōb| • *n.* a toilet in a medieval building. ■ a wardrobe or small storeroom, esp. in a medieval building.

gar•gan•tu•an |gärˈgænCHəwən| • *adj.* enormous: *a gargantuan appetite.*

gar•goyle |ˈgärgoil| • *n.* a grotesque carved human or animal face or figure projecting from the gutter of a building, typically acting as a spout to carry water clear of a wall.
DERIVATIVES: **gar•goyled** *adj.*

gar•ish |ˈgeriSH| • *adj.* obtrusively and unpleasantly bright and showy; lurid: *garish shirts in all sorts of colors.*
DERIVATIVES: **gar•ish•ly** *adv.* **gar•ish•ness** *n.*

gar•ner |ˈgärnər| • *v.* [trans.] gather or collect (something, esp. information or approval): *the police struggled to garner sufficient evidence.* ■ store; deposit: *the crop was ready to be reaped and garnered.* • *n.* a storehouse; a granary.

gar•nish |ˈgärniSH| • *v.* [trans.] **1** decorate or embellish (something, esp. food): *salad garnished with an orange slice.* **2** serve notice of seizure of (a person's) money to settle debt or claim. ■ seize (money, esp. part of a person's salary) to settle a debt or claim: *the IRS garnished his earnings.* • *n.* a decoration or embellishment for something, esp. food: *the custard is served with a garnish of fresh mint.*
DERIVATIVES: **gar•nish•ment** *n.*

gar•rote |gəˈrät; -ˈrōt| (also **garrotte** or **garotte**) • *v.* [trans.] kill (someone) by strangulation, typically with an iron collar or a length of wire or cord: *he had been garroted with piano wire.* • *n.* a wire, cord, or apparatus used for such a killing.

gar•ru•lous |ˈgærələs| • *adj.* excessively talk-

ative, esp. on trivial matters: *Polonius is portrayed as a foolish, garrulous old man.*
DERIVATIVES: **gar•ru•li•ty** |gəˈro͞olitē| *n.* **gar•ru•lous•ly** *adv.* **gar•ru•lous•ness** *n.*

gas•con•ade |ˌgæskəˈnād| • *n.* extravagant boasting.

gas•ket |ˈgæskit| • *n.* **1** a shaped piece or ring of rubber or other material sealing the junction between two surfaces in an engine or other device. **2** a cord securing a furled sail of a sailing vessel.
PHRASES: **blow a gasket 1** lose one's temper. **2** suffer a leak in a gasket of an engine.

gas•tro•nome |ˈgæstrəˌnōm| • *n.* a gourmet.

gauche |gōSH| • *adj.* lacking ease or grace; unsophisticated and socially awkward.
DERIVATIVES: **gauche•ly** *adv.* **gauche•ness** *n.*

gau•che•rie |ˌgōSHəˈrē| • *n.* awkward, embarrassing, or unsophisticated ways: *she had long since gotten over gaucheries such as blushing.*

gau•cho |ˈgowCHō| • *n.* (pl. **-os**) a cowboy of the South American plains (*pampas*).

gaud•y |ˈgôdē| • *adj.* (**gaudier, gaudiest**) extravagantly bright or showy, typically so as to be tasteless: *silver bows and gaudy ribbons.*
DERIVATIVES: **gaud•i•ly** |-dəlē| *adv.* **gaud•i•ness** *n.*

gauge |gāj| (also **gage**) • *n.* **1** an instrument or device for measuring the magnitude, amount, or contents of something, typically with a visual display of such information. ■ a tool for checking whether something conforms to a desired dimension. ■ a means of estimating something; a criterion or test: *emigration is perhaps the best gauge of public unease.* **2** the thickness, size, or capacity of something, esp. as a standard measure, in particular: ■ the diameter of a string, fiber, tube, etc.: [as adj.] *a fine 0.018-inch gauge wire.* ■ [in combination] a measure of the diameter of a gun barrel, or of its ammunition, expressed as the number of spherical pieces of shot of the same diameter as the barrel that can be made from 1 lb (454 g) of lead: [as adj.] *a 12-gauge shotgun.* ■ [in combination] the thickness of sheet metal or plastic: [as adj.] *500-gauge polyethylene.* ■ the distance between the rails of a line of railroad track: *the line was laid to a gauge of 2 ft. 9 in.* **3** (usu. **the gage**) the position of a sailing vessel to windward (**weather gage**) or leeward (**lee gage**) of another. • *v.* [trans.] **1** estimate or determine the magnitude, amount, or volume of: *astronomers can gauge the star's intrinsic brightness.* ■ form a judgment or estimate of (a situation, mood, etc.): *she was unable to gauge his mood.* **2** measure the dimensions of (an object) with a gauge: *when dry, the assemblies can be gauged exactly and planed to width.* ■ [as adj.] (**gauged**) made in standard dimensions: *gauged sets of strings.*
DERIVATIVES: **gauge•a•ble** *adj.* **gaug•er** *n.*

Gaull•ism |ˈgô,lizəm| • *n.* the principles and policies of French statesman Charles de Gaulle (1890-1970), characterized by their conservatism, nationalism, and advocacy of centralized government.

DERIVATIVES: **Gaull•ist** *n.* & *adj.*

gaunt |gônt| • *adj.* (of a person) lean and haggard, esp. because of suffering, hunger, or age.
■ (of a building or place) grim or desolate in appearance.

DERIVATIVES: **gaunt•ly** *adv.* **gaunt•ness** *n.*

gaunt•let[1] |'gôntlit; 'gänt-| • *n.* a stout glove with a long loose wrist.
■ an armored glove, as worn by a medieval knight. ■ the part of a glove covering the wrist.

PHRASES: **take up** (or **throw down**) **the gauntlet** accept (or issue) a challenge.

gaunt•let[2] (also **gantlet**) • *n.* (in phrase **run the gauntlet**) **1** go through an intimidating or dangerous crowd, place, or experience in order to reach a goal: *they had to run the gauntlet of television cameras.* **2** undergo the former military punishment of receiving blows while running between two rows of men with sticks. Do not confuse with *run the gamut* (see GAMUT).

gauze |gôz| • *n.* a thin translucent fabric of silk, linen, or cotton.
■ (also **wire gauze**) a very fine wire mesh. ■ (in medicine) thin, loosely woven cloth used for dressing and swabs. ■ [in sing.] a transparent haze or film: *they saw the grasslands through a gauze of golden dust.*

DERIVATIVES: **gauz•i•ly** |-zəlē| *adv.* **gauz•i•ness** *n.* **gauz•y** |-zē| *adj.*

ga•vage |gə'väzн| • *n.* the administration of food or drugs by force, esp. to an animal, typically through a tube leading down the throat to the stomach.

ga•votte |gə'vät| • *n.* a medium-paced French dance, popular in the 18th century.
■ a piece of music accompanying or in the rhythm of such a dance, composed in $^4/_4$ time beginning on the third beat of the bar.

gay |gā| • *adj.* (**gayer, gayest**) **1** (of a person, esp. a man) homosexual: *that friend of yours, is he gay?*
■ relating to or used by homosexuals: *feminist, black, and gay perspectives.* **2** lighthearted and carefree: *Nan had a gay disposition and a very pretty face.*
■ characterized by cheerfulness or pleasure: *we had a gay old time.* ■ brightly colored; showy; brilliant: *a gay profusion of purple and pink sweet peas.* **3** foolish; stupid: *making students wait for the light is kind of a gay rule.* • *n.* a homosexual, esp. a man: *straights and gays alike spoke out against intolerance.*

DERIVATIVES: **gaily** *adv.* with cheerfulness, pleasure, etc.; brightly, showily. **gay•ness** *n.*

USAGE: **Gay** meaning 'homosexual,' dating back to the 1930s (if not earlier), became established in the 1960s as the term preferred by homosexual men to describe themselves. It is now the standard accepted term throughout the English-speaking world. As a result, the centuries-old other senses of **gay** meaning either 'carefree' or 'bright and showy,' once common in speech and literature, are much less frequent. The word **gay** cannot be readily used unselfconsciously today in these older senses without sounding old-fashioned or arousing a sense of double entendre, despite concerted attempts by some to keep them alive.
Gay in its modern sense typically refers to men (**lesbian** being the standard term for homosexual women) but in some contexts it can be used of both men and women.

ga•ze•bo |gə'zēbō| • *n.* (pl. **-os** or **-oes**) a roofed structure that offers an open view of the surrounding area, typically used for relaxation or entertainment.

gaz•et•teer |,gæzə'tir| • *n.* a geographical index or dictionary.

geek |gēk| • *n.* **1** an unfashionable or socially inept person.
■ [with adj.] a person with an obssesive devotion to a particular interest esp. one connected with technology: *a computer geek.* **2** a carnival performer who does wild or disgusting acts.

DERIVATIVES: **geek•y** *adj.*

ge•gen•schein |'gāgən,sнīn| • *n.* a patch of very faint nebulous light sometimes seen in the night sky opposite the position of the sun. It is thought to be the image of the sun reflected from gas and dust outside the atmosphere.

gei•sha |'gāsнə; 'gē-| (also **geisha girl**) • *n.* (pl. same or **geishas**) a Japanese hostess trained to entertain men with conversation, dance, and song. ■ (loosely) a Japanese prostitute.

gel |jel| • *n.* a jellylike substance containing a cosmetic, medicinal, or other preparation: *try rubbing some teething gel onto sore gums.*
■ a substance of this consistency used for setting the hair. ■ (in chemistry) a semisolid colloidal suspension of a solid dispersed in a liquid. ■ a semirigid slab or cylinder of an organic polymer used as a medium for the separation of macromolecules. • *v.* (**gelled, gelling**) [intrans.] (in chemistry) form into a gel: *the mixture gelled at 7 degrees Celsius.*
■ [trans.] treat (the hair) with gel.

geld |geld| • *v.* [trans.] castrate (a male animal).
■ deprive of vitality or vigor: *the English version of the book has been gelded.*

DERIVATIVES: **gelding** *n.* a castrated male animal, esp. a horse.

gel•id |'jelid| • *adj.* icy; extremely cold: *the gelid pond* | *she gave a gelid reply.*

gen•darme |'zнändärm| • *n.* an armed police officer in France and other French-speaking countries.

DERIVATIVES: **gen•dar•me•rie** *n.* a force of gendarmes.

gen•der |'jendər| • *n.* **1** (in languages such as Latin, Greek Russian, and German) each of the classes (typically masculine, feminine, common, neuter) of nouns and pronouns distinguished by the different inflections that they have and require in words syntactically associated with them. Grammatical gender is

only very loosely associated with natural distinctions of sex.
■ the property (in nouns and related words) of belonging to such a class: *adjectives usually agree with the noun in gender and number.* **2** the state of being male or female (typically used with reference to social and cultural differences rather than biological ones): *traditional concepts of gender* | [as adj.] *gender roles.*
■ the members of one or other sex: *differences between the genders.*

USAGE: The word **gender** has been used since the 14th century primarily as a grammatical term, referring to the classes of noun in Latin, Greek, German, and other languages designated as *masculine, feminine,* or *neuter.* It has also been used since the 14th century in the sense 'the state of being male or female,' but this did not become a standard use until the mid 20th century. Although the words **gender** and **sex** both have the sense 'state of being male or female,' they are typically used in slightly different ways: **sex** tends to refer to biological differences, while **gender** tends to refer to cultural or social ones.

ge•ne•al•o•gy |ˌjēnēˈäləjē; -ˈæl-| • *n.* (pl. **-ies**) a line of descent traced continuously from an ancestor: *combing through the birth records and genealogies.*
■ the study and tracing of lines of descent or development. ■ a plant's or animal's line of evolutionary development from earlier forms.
DERIVATIVES: **ge•ne•al•o•gist** |-jist| *n.* **ge•ne•al•o•gize** |-ˌjīz| *v.*
gen•er•al•is•si•mo |ˌjenərəˈlisəˌmō| • *n.* (pl. **-os**) the commander of a combined military force consisting of army, navy, and air force units.
gen•er•al•ist |ˈjenərəlist| • *n.* a person competent in several different fields or activities: *with a generalist's education and some specific skills.* • *adj.* able to carry out a range of activities, or adapt to different situations: *a generalist doctor.*
gen•er•al•i•ty |ˌjenəˈrælitē| • *n.* (pl. **-ies**) **1** a statement or principle having general rather than specific validity or force: *he confined his remarks to generalities.*
■ the quality or state of being general: *policy should be formulated at an appropriate level of generality.* **2** (**the generality**) the majority: *appropriate to the generality of laymen.*
Gen•er•a•tion X (also **Gen X**) • *n.* the generation born after that of the baby boomers (roughly from the early 1960s to mid 1970s), often perceived to be disaffected and directionless.
DERIVATIVES: **Gen•er•a•tion X•er** |ˈeksər| *n.* **Gen X•er** *n.*
gen•er•a•tive |ˈjenərətiv; -ˌrātiv;| • *adj.* of or relating to reproduction.
■ able to produce: *the generative power of the life force.* ■ applying principles of generative grammar, which aims to formulate rules that are able to generate all and only the permissible sequences of a language.

ge•ner•ic |jəˈnerik| • *adj.* **1** characteristic of or relating to a class or group of things; not specific: *chèvre is a generic term for all goats' milk cheese.*
■ (of commercial products, esp. medicinal drugs) having no brand name; not protected by a registered trademark: *generic aspirin.* **2** of or relating to a biological genus. • *n.* a consumer product having no brand name or trademark: *substituting generics for brand-name drugs.*
DERIVATIVES: **ge•ner•i•cal•ly** |-ik(ə)lē| *adv.*
gen•e•sis |ˈjenəsis| • *n.* [in sing.] the origin or mode of formation of something: *this tale had its genesis in fireside stories.*
ge•ni•al |ˈjēnyəl; -nēəl| • *adj.* friendly and cheerful: *waved to them in genial greeting.*
■ (esp. of air or climate) pleasantly mild and warm.
DERIVATIVES: **ge•ni•al•i•ty** |ˌjēnēˈælitē| *n.* **gen•ial•ly** *adv.*
gen•i•tive |ˈjenitiv| • *adj.* relating to or denoting a case of nouns and pronouns (and words in grammatical agreement with them) indicating possession or close association. • *n.* a word in the genitive case.
■ (**the genitive**) the genitive case.
DERIVATIVES: **gen•i•ti•val** |ˌjeniˈtīvəl| *adj.* **gen•i•ti•val•ly** |ˌjeniˈtīvəlē| *adv.*
ge•ni•us lo•ci |ˈjēnēəs ˈlōsī; -kī| • *n.* [in sing.] the prevailing character or atmosphere of a place.
■ the presiding god or spirit of a place.
gen•o•cide |ˈjenəˌsīd| • *n.* the deliberate killing of a large group of people, esp. those of a particular ethnic group or nation.
DERIVATIVES: **gen•o•cid•al** |ˌjenəˈsīdl| *adj.*
ge•nome |ˈjēnōm| • *n.* a single set of chromosomes in a gamete or microorganism, or in each cell of a multicellular organism.
■ the complete set of genes or genetic material present in a cell or organism: *the human genome.*
DERIVATIVES: **ge•no•mic** |jēˈnämik; -ˈnō-; ji-| *adj.*
gen•o•type |ˈjēnəˌtīp; ˈjen-| • *n.* (in biology) the genetic constitution of an individual organism. Often contrasted with PHENOTYPE.
DERIVATIVES: **gen•o•typ•ic** |ˌjenəˈtipik| *adj.*
gen•re |ˈZHänrə| • *n.* a category of artistic composition, as in music or literature, characterized by similarities in form, style, or subject matter: *a master in the genre of film noir.* ■ (also **genre painting**) a style of painting depicting scenes of ordinary life.
gen•teel |jenˈtēl| • *adj.* polite, refined, or respectable, often in an affected or ostentatious way. Cf. GENTILITY
DERIVATIVES: **gen•teel•ly** *adv.* **gen•teel•ness** *n.*
gen•tile |ˈjentīl| • *adj.* (**Gentile**) not Jewish: *Christianity spread from Jewish into Gentile cultures.*

■ (of a person) not belonging to one's own religious community. ■ (in the Mormon church) non-Mormon. • n. (**Gentile**) a person who is not Jewish.

gen•til•i•ty |jen'tilitē| • n. social superiority as demonstrated by genteel manners, behavior, or appearances: *her grandmother's pretensions to gentility.*
■ genteel manners, behavior, or appearances.

gen•tri•fy |'jentrə,fī| • v. (**-ies, -ied**) [trans.] renovate and improve (esp. a house or district) so that it conforms to middle-class taste.
■ [usu. as adj.] (**gentrified**) make (someone or their way of life) more refined or dignified. DERIVATIVES: **gen•tri•fi•ca•tion** |,jentrəfi 'kāSHən| n. **gen•tri•fi•er** n.

gen•try |'jentrē| • n. (often **the gentry**) people of good social position, specifically (in Britain) the class of people next below the nobility in position and birth: *a member of the landed gentry.*
■ [with adj.] people of a specified class or group: *a New Orleans family of Creole gentry.*

gen•u•flect |'jenyə,flekt| • v. [intrans.] lower one's body briefly by bending one knee to the ground, typically in worship or as a sign of respect: *she genuflected and crossed herself.*
■ [with adverbial] show deference or servility: *politicians had to genuflect to the far left to advance their careers.* DERIVATIVES: **gen•u•flec•tion** |,jenyə 'flekSHən| n. (also **gen•u•flex•ion** archaic) **gen•u•flec•tor** |-tər| n.

ge•nus |'jēnəs| • n. (pl. **genera** |'jenərə| or **genuses**) (in biology) a grouping of organisms having common characteristics distinct from those of other such groupings. The genus is a principal taxonomic category that ranks above species and below family, and is denoted by a capitalized Latin name, e.g., *Leo.*
■ (in philosophical and general use) a class of things that have common characteristics and that can be divided into subordinate kinds.

ge•o•cen•tric |,jēō'sentrik| • adj. having or representing the earth as the center, as in former astronomical systems. Cf. HELIOCENTRIC.
■ measured from or considered in relation to the center of the earth. DERIVATIVES: **ge•o•cen•tri•cal•ly** |-trik(ə)lē| adv. **ge•o•cen•trism** |-trizəm| n.

ge•o•des•ic |,jēə'desik; -'dē-| • adj. **1** of, relating to, or denoting the shortest possible line between two points on a sphere or other curved surface. **2** another term for GEODETIC.
• n. a geodesic line or structure. PHRASES: **geodesic dome** a dome constructed of short struts following geodesic lines and forming an open framework of triangles or polygons. The principles of its construction were described by Buckminster Fuller (1895–1983).

ge•od•e•sy |jē'ädəsē| • n. the branch of mathematics dealing with the shape and area of the earth or large portions of it. DERIVATIVES: **ge•od•e•sist** |-sist| n.

ge•o•det•ic |,jēə'detik| • adj. of or relating to geodesy, esp. as applied to land surveying.

ge•o•man•cy |'jēə,mansē| • n. divination from configurations seen in a handful of earth thrown on the ground, or by interpreting lines or textures on the ground. Cf. FENG SHUI.
DERIVATIVES: **ge•o•man•cer** |-sər| n. **ge•o•man•tic** |,jēə'mæntik| adj.

ge•o•met•ric |,jēə'metrik| • adj. **1** of or relating to geometry, or according to its methods. **2** (of a design) characterized by or decorated with regular lines and shapes: *traditional Hopi geometric forms.*
■ (**Geometric**) of or denoting a period of Greek culture (around 900–700 BC) characterized by geometrically decorated pottery. DERIVATIVES: **ge•o•met•ri•cal** adj. **ge•o•met•ri•cal•ly** |-ik(ə)lē| adv.

ge•o•met•ric pro•gres•sion • n. a progression of numbers with a constant ratio between each number and the one before (e.g., each subsequent number is increased by a factor of 3 in the progression *1, 3, 9, 27, 81*).

geor•gic |'jôrjik| • n. a poem or book dealing with agriculture or rural topics.
■ (**Georgics**) the title of a didactic poem on farming by the Roman poet Virgil (70-19 BC). • adj. rustic; pastoral.

ge•o•ther•mal |,jēō'THərməl| (also **geothermic**) • adj. of, relating to, or produced by the internal heat of the earth: *some 70% of Iceland's energy needs are met from geothermal sources.*

ger•i•at•ric |,jerē'ætrik| • adj. [attrib.] of or relating to old people, esp. with regard to their health care: *a geriatric hospital.* • n. an old person, esp. one receiving special care: *a rest home for geriatrics.*

USAGE: **Geriatric** is the normal, semiofficial term used in the US and Britain when referring to the health care of old people (*a geriatric ward*; *geriatric patients*). When used outside such contexts, it typically carries overtones of being worn out and decrepit and can therefore be offensive if used with reference to people.

ger•mane |jər'mān| • adj. relevant to a subject under consideration: *that is not germane to our theme.* Cf. PERTINENT, APROPOS. DERIVATIVES: **ger•mane•ly** adv. **ger•mane•ness** n.

ger•mi•nal |'jərmənl| • adj. [attrib.] relating to or of the nature of a germ cell or embryo.
■ in the earliest stage of development. ■ providing material for future development: *the subject was revived in a germinal article by Charles Ferguson.* Cf. SEMINAL DERIVATIVES: **ger•mi•nal•ly** adv.

ger•mi•nate |'jərmə,nāt| • v. [intrans.] (of a seed or spore) begin to grow and put out shoots after a period of dormancy.
■ [trans.] cause (a seed or spore) to sprout in such a way. ■ come or bring into existence and develop: *the idea germinated and slowly grew into an obsession.* | *the group is constantly germinating new proposals.*

DERIVATIVES: **ger•mi•na•ble** |-nəbəl| *adj.* **ger•mi•na•tion** |ˌjərmə'nāsHən| *n.* **ger•mi•na•tive** |-ˌnātiv| *adj.* **ger•mi•na•tor** |-ˌnā-tər| *n.*

ger•on•tol•o•gy |ˌjerən'täləjē| • *n.* the scientific study of old age, the process of aging, and the particular problems of old people. DERIVATIVES: **ge•ron•to•log•i•cal** |jə ˌräntl'äjikəl| *adj.* **ger•on•tol•o•gist** |-jist| *n.*

ger•ry•man•der |'jerē,mændər| • *v.* [trans.] [often as n.] (**gerrymandering**) manipulate the boundaries of (an electoral district) so as to favor one party or class. ■ achieve (a result) by such manipulation: *a freedom to gerrymander the results they want.* • *n.* an instance of such a practice. DERIVATIVES: **ger•ry•man•der•er** *n.*

ger•und |'jerənd| • *n.* a word form that is derived from a verb but that functions as a noun, in English ending in -*ing*, e.g., *asking* in *do you mind my asking you?.* DERIVATIVES: **ge•run•dive** *adj.*

ge•stalt |gə'sHält; -'stôlt| (also **Gestalt**) • *n.* (pl. **-stalten** |-tn| or **-stalts**) (in psychology) an organized whole that is perceived as more than the sum of its parts. PHRASES: **Gestalt therapy** a psychotherapeutic approach developed by Fritz Perls (1893–1970). It focuses on insight into gestalts in patients and their relations to the world, and often uses role-playing to aid the resolution of past conflicts. DERIVATIVES: **ge•stalt•ism** |-ˌtizəm| *n.* **ge•stalt•ist** |-tist| *n.*

ges•ta•tion |je'stāsHən| • *n.* the process of carrying or being carried in the womb between conception and birth. ■ the duration of such a process. ■ the development of something over a period of time: *various ideas are in the process of gestation.* DERIVATIVES: **ges•tate** *v.* **ges•ta•tion•al** |-sHənl| *adj.*

ges•tic•u•late |je'stikyəˌlāt| • *v.* [intrans.] use gestures, esp. dramatic ones, instead of speaking or to emphasize one's words: *they were shouting and gesticulating frantically at drivers who did not slow down.* DERIVATIVES: **ges•tic•u•la•tion** |jeˌstikyə 'lāsHən| *n.* **ges•tic•u•la•tive** |-ˌlātiv| *adj.* **ges•tic•u•la•tor** |-ˌlātər| *n.* **ges•tic•u•la•to•ry** |-lə,tôrē| *adj.*

gey•ser |'gīzər| • *n.* a hot spring in which water intermittently boils, sending a tall column of water and steam into the air. ■ a jet or stream of liquid: *the pipe sent up a geyser of sewer water into the street.* • *v.* [no obj., with adverbial of direction] (esp. of water or steam) gush or burst out with great force: *yellow smoke geysered upward.*

ghet•to |'getō| • *n.* (pl. **-os** or **-oes**) a part of a city, esp. a slum area, occupied by a minority group or groups. ■ a former designation for the Jewish quarter in a city: *the Warsaw Ghetto.* ■ an isolated or segregated group or area: *the relative security of the gay ghetto.* DERIVATIVES: **ghet•to•ize** *v.* *rental practices had the effect of ghettoizing Hispanics.*

ghoul |gōōl| • *n.* an evil spirit or phantom, esp. one supposed to rob graves and feed on dead bodies. ■ a person morbidly interested in death or disaster. ■ a grave robber: *19th-century medical students were sometimes accused of being ghouls.* DERIVATIVES: **ghoul•ish** *adj.* **ghoul•ish•ly** *adv.* **ghoul•ish•ness** *n.*

gib•ber |'jibər| • *v.* [intrans.] speak rapidly and unintelligibly, typically through fear or shock: *they shrieked and gibbered as flames surrounded them* |[as adj.] (**gibbering**) *a gibbering idiot.*

gib•bet |'jibit| • *n.* a gallows. ■ an upright post with an arm on which the bodies of executed criminals were left hanging as a warning or deterrent to others. ■ (**the gibbet**) execution by hanging: *sentenced to the gibbet.* • *v.* (**gibbeted**, **gibbeting**) [trans.] hang up (a body) on a gibbet. ■ execute (someone) by hanging. ■ hold up to contempt: *poor Melbourne is gibbeted in the Times.*

gib•bous |'gibəs| • *adj.* (of the moon) having the illuminated part greater than a semicircle and less than a circle. ■ convex or protuberant: *gibbous eyes.* DERIVATIVES: **gib•bos•i•ty** |gi'bäsitē| *n.* **gib•bous•ly** *adv.* **gib•bous•ness** *n.*

gibe |jīb| (also **jibe**) • *n.* an insulting or mocking remark; a taunt: *a gibe at his old rivals.* • *v.* [intrans.] make insulting or mocking remarks; jeer: *some cynics in the media might gibe.*

gi•gan•tism |jī'gæntizəm| • *n.* unusual or abnormal largeness in living things. ■ excessive growth due to hormonal imbalance. ■ excessive size in plants due to expression of excess chromosomes.

gig•o•lo |'jigəˌlō| • *n.* (pl. **-os**) a young man paid or financially supported by an older woman to be her escort or lover. ■ a professional male dancing partner or escort.

gild |gild| • *v.* [trans.] cover thinly with gold. ■ give a specious or false brilliance to: *the useless martyrs' deaths of the pilots gilded the operation.* PHRASES: **gild the lily** try to improve what is already beautiful or excellent. DERIVATIVES: **gild•er** *n.*

gim•let |'gimlit| • *n.* **1** a small T-shaped tool with a screw-tip for boring holes. A **gimlet** (or **gimlety**) **eye** is a sharp, piercing, often skeptical eye or glance: *she greeted the suggestion with the gimlet eye.* **2** a cocktail of gin (or sometimes vodka) and lime juice.

gird |gərd| • *v.* (past and past part. **girded** or **girt** |gərt|) [trans.] encircle (a person or part of the body) with a belt or band: *a young man was to be girded with the belt of knighthood.* ■ secure (a garment or sword) on the body with a belt or band: *a white robe girded with a magenta sash.* ■ surround; encircle: *the mountains girding Kabul.* PHRASES: **gird (up) one's loins** prepare and strengthen oneself for what is to come. ▶**gird oneself for** prepare oneself for (dangerous or difficult future actions).

gist |jist| • *n.* [in sing.] **1** the substance or essence of a speech or text: *she noted the gist of each message.* **2** the real point of a legal action: *damage is the gist of the action and without it the plaintiff must fail.*

giz•zard |ˈgizərd| • *n.* a muscular, thick-walled part of a bird's stomach for grinding food, typically with grit.
■ a muscular stomach of some fish, insects, mollusks, and other invertebrates. ■ a person's stomach or throat.

gla•brous |ˈglābrəs| • *adj.* (chiefly of the skin or a leaf) free from hair or down; smooth.

gla•cé |glæˈsā| • *adj.* [attrib.] **1** (of fruit) having a glossy surface due to preservation in sugar: *a glacé cherry.* **2** (of cloth or leather) smooth and highly polished. • *v.* [trans.] glaze with a thin sugar-based coating: [as adj.] *glacéed orange slices.*

gla•cial |ˈglāsHəl| • *adj.* relating to, resulting from, or denoting the presence or agency of ice, esp. in the form of glaciers: *thick glacial deposits | a glacial lake.*
■ extremely cold: *glacial temperatures. | gave him a glacial look.* ■ extremely slow (like the movement of a glacier): *described progress in the talks as glacial.*
DERIVATIVES: **gla•cial•ly** *adv.*

gla•cis |ˈglāsis; ˈglæs-| • *n.* (pl. same |-sēz| or **glacises**) a gently sloping bank, in particular one that slopes down from a fort, exposing attackers to the defenders' missiles.

glas•nost |ˈglæz,nōst; ˈglæs-; ˈgläz-; ˈgläs-| • *n.* (in the former Soviet Union) the policy or practice of more open consultative government and wider dissemination of information, initiated by leader Mikhail Gorbachev from 1985.

glass ceil•ing • *n.* [usu. in sing.] a barrier to advancement in a profession that affects only a particular group, such as women.

glau•cous |ˈglôkəs| • *adj.* **1** of a dull grayish-green or blue color. **2** covered with a powdery bloom like that on grapes.

glean |glēn| • *v.* [trans.] extract (information) from various sources: *the information is gleaned from press clippings.*
■ collect gradually and piece by piece: *objects gleaned from local markets.* ■ gather (leftover grain or other produce) after a harvest: [as n.] (**gleaning**) *the conditions of farm workers in the 1890s made gleaning essential.*
DERIVATIVES: **glean•er** *n.* **glean•ing** *n.*

glen•gar•ry |glenˈgærē| • *n.* (pl. **-ies**) a brimless boat-shaped hat with a cleft down the center, typically having two ribbons hanging at the back, worn as part of Scottish Highland dress.

glib |glib| • *adj.* (**glibber, glibbest**) (of words or the person speaking them) fluent and voluble but insincere and shallow: *she was careful not to sound too glib.*
DERIVATIVES: **glib•ly** *adv.* **glib•ness** *n.*

glint |glint| • *v.* [intrans.] give out or reflect small flashes of light: *her glasses were glinting in the firelight.*
■ (of a person's eyes) shine with a particular emotion: *his eyes glinted angrily.* • *n.* a small flash of light, esp. as reflected from a shiny surface: *the glint of gold in his teeth.*
■ [in sing.] a brightness in someone's eyes seen as a sign of enthusiasm or a particular emotion: *the glint of excitement in his eyes.*

glis•sade |gliˈsäd; säd| • *n.* **1** a way of sliding down a steep slope of snow or ice, typically on the feet with the support of an ice ax. **2** a ballet movement, typically used as a joining step, in which one leg is brushed outward from the body, which then takes the weight while the second leg is brushed in to meet it. • *v.* [intrans.] slide down a steep slope of snow or ice with the support of an ice ax.

glis•san•do |gliˈsändō| • *n.* (pl. **glissandi** |-dē| or **glissandos**) a continuous slide upward or downward between two musical notes.

glitch |glicH| *informal* • *n.* a sudden, usually temporary malfunction or irregularity of equipment: *a draft version was lost in a computer glitch.*
■ an unexpected setback in a plan: *the first real glitch they've encountered.* ■ (in astronomy) a brief irregularity in the rotation of a pulsar. • *v.* [intrans.] suffer a sudden malfunction or irregularity: *her job involves troubleshooting when systems glitch.*
DERIVATIVES: **glitch•y** *adj.*

glit•te•ra•ti |ˌglitəˈrätē| • *plural n.* the fashionable set of people engaged in show business or some other glamorous activity.

glitz•y |ˈglitsē| • *adj.* (**glitzier, glitziest**) ostentatiously attractive (often used to suggest superficial glamour): *I wanted something glitzy to wear to the launch party. | a glitzy group of movie bigwigs.*
DERIVATIVES: **glitz•i•ly** |-səlē| *adv.* **glitz•i•ness** *n.*

gloam•ing |ˈglōmiNG| • *n.* (**the gloaming**) twilight; dusk.

gloat |glōt| • *v.* [intrans.] contemplate or dwell on one's own success or another's misfortune with smugness or malignant pleasure: *his enemies gloated over his death.* • *n.* [in sing.] an act of gloating. Cf. SCHADENFREUDE
DERIVATIVES: **gloat•er** *n.* **gloat•ing•ly** *adv.*

glob•al•ist |ˈglōbəlist| • *n.* a person who advocates the interpretation or planning of economic and foreign policy in relation to events and developments throughout the world.
■ a person or organization advocating or practicing operations across national divisions.
DERIVATIVES: **glob•al•ism** |-ˌlizəm| *n.*

glob•u•lar |ˈgläbyələr| • *adj.* **1** globe-shaped; spherical. **2** composed of globules.

glob•ule |ˈgläbyo͞ol| • *n.* a small round particle of a substance; a drop: *globules of fat.*
DERIVATIVES: **glob•u•lous** |-yələs| *adj.*

glom |gläm| • *v.* (**glommed, glomming**) **1** [intrans.] (**glom onto**) take possession of something in a peremptory way, denying others' access: *she glommed onto me as soon as I walked into the room.* ■ become stuck or attached to: *The molecules glom onto the virus and destroy it.* **2** steal: *I thought he was about to glom my wallet.*

gloss[1] |gläs; glôs| • *n.* shine or luster on a smooth surface: *hair with a healthy gloss.*
■ (also **gloss paint**) a type of paint that dries to a bright shiny surface. ■ [in sing.] a superficially attractive appearance or impression: *beneath the gloss of success lay a tragic private life.* • *v.* [trans.] apply a cosmetic gloss to.
■ apply gloss paint to. ■ (**gloss over**) try to conceal or disguise (something embarrassing or unfavorable) by treating it briefly or representing it misleadingly: *the social costs of this growth are glossed over.*
DERIVATIVES: **gloss•er** *n.*
gloss[2] • *n.* a translation or explanation of a word or phrase.
■ an explanation, interpretation, or paraphrase: *the chapter acts as a helpful gloss on Pynchon's general method.* • *v.* [trans.] (usu. be **glossed**) provide an explanation, interpretation, or paraphrase for (a text, word, etc.).
glos•so•la•li•a |ˌgläsəˈlālēə; ˌglô-| • *n.* the phenomenon of (apparently) speaking in an unknown language during religious worship. (Also called **speaking in tongues**) .
■ a similar phenomenon as a symptom of mental illness.
DERIVATIVES: **glos•so•la•lic** |-ˌlälik| *adj.*
glow•er |ˈglowər| • *v.* [intrans.] have an angry or sullen look on one's face; scowl: *she glowered at him suspiciously.* • *n.* [in sing.] an angry or sullen look.
DERIVATIVES: **glow•er•ing** *adj.* **glow•er•ing•ly** *adv.*
glut |glət| • *n.* an excessively abundant supply of something: *there is a glut of cars on the market.* • *v.* (**glutted, glutting**) [trans.] (usu. be **glutted**) supply or fill to excess: *the paper recycling plants are glutted* | *he was glutting himself on junk food.*
■ archaic satisfy fully: *he planned a treacherous murder to glut his desire for revenge.*
glu•ten |ˈgloŏtn| • *n.* a substance present in cereal grains, esp. wheat, that is responsible for the elastic texture of dough. Intolerance to it is the chief factor in celiac (small intestine) disease.
glu•te•us |ˈgloŏtēəs| (also **gluteus muscle**) • *n.* (pl. **glutei** |-tē,ī|) any of three muscles (informally called the **glutes**) in each buttock that move the thigh, the largest of which is the **gluteus maximus.**
DERIVATIVES: **glu•te•al** |ˈgloŏtēəl| *adj.*
glu•ti•nous |ˈgloŏtn-əs| • *adj.* like glue in texture; sticky: *glutinous mud.*
DERIVATIVES: **glu•ti•nous•ly** *adv.* **glu•ti•nous•ness** *n.*
glut•ton |ˈglətn| • *n.* an excessively greedy eater.
■ a person who is excessively fond of or always eager for something: *a glutton for adventure.*
DERIVATIVES: **glut•ton•ize** |-,īz| *v.* **glut•ton•ous** |-əs| *adj.* **glut•ton•ous•ly** |-əslē| *adv.*
glyph |glif| • *n.* **1** a hieroglyphic character or symbol; a pictograph: *walls painted with esoteric glyphs.*
■ strictly, a sculptured symbol (e.g., as forming the ancient Mayan writing system). ■ a

graphic symbol that appears as part of a computer screen display. Cf. ICON ■ an alphabetic or other character that is printed or displayed as a single unit. **2** an ornamental carved groove or channel, as on a Greek frieze.
DERIVATIVES: **glyph•ic** |ˈglifik| *adj.*
glyp•tic |ˈgliptik| • *adj.* of or concerning carving or engraving, esp. on stones.
gnarled |närld| • *adj.* knobbly, rough, and twisted, esp. with age: *the gnarled old oak tree.*
gnarl•y |ˈnärlē| • *adj.* (**-ier, -iest**) **1** gnarled. **2** difficult, dangerous, or challenging: *she battled through the gnarly first sequence.*
■ unpleasant; unattractive: *bus stations can be pretty gnarly places.*
gnath•ic |ˈnæThik| • *adj.* of or relating to the jaws.
gnome[1] |nōm| • *n.* a legendary dwarfish creature supposed to guard the earth's treasures underground.
■ a small ugly person. ■ a person regarded as having secret or sinister influence, esp. in financial matters: *the gnomes of Zurich.*
DERIVATIVES: **gnom•ish** *adj.*
gnome[2] • *n.* a short statement encapsulating a general truth; a maxim.
gno•mic |ˈnōmik| • *adj.* expressed in or of the nature of short, pithy maxims or aphorisms: *that most gnomic form, the aphorism.*
■ enigmatic; ambiguous: *I had to have their gnomic response interpreted for me.*
DERIVATIVES: **gno•mi•cal•ly** |-ik(ə)lē| *adv.*
gno•mon |ˈnōmän| • *n.* **1** the projecting piece on a sundial that shows the time by the position of its shadow.
■ a structure, esp. a column, used in observing the sun's meridian altitude. **2** the part of a parallelogram left when a similar parallelogram has been taken from its corner.
DERIVATIVES: **gno•mon•ic** |nōˈmänik| *adj.*
gno•sis |ˈnōsis| • *n.* knowledge of spiritual mysteries.
Gnos•tic • *n.* relating to a prominent heretical movement (Gnosticism) of the 2nd-century Christian Church, partly of pre-Christian origin. Gnostic doctrine taught that the world was created and ruled by a lesser divinity, the demiurge, and that Christ was an emissary of the remote supreme divine being, esoteric knowledge (gnosis) of whom enabled the redemption of the human spirit.
goad |gōd| • *n.* a spiked stick used for driving cattle.
■ a thing that stimulates someone into action: *for him the visit was a goad to renewed effort.* • *v.* [trans.] provoke or annoy (someone) so as to stimulate some action or reaction: *he goaded her on to more daring revelations.*
■ [with obj. and adverbial of direction] drive or urge (an animal) on with a goad.
gob•bet |ˈgäbit| • *n.* a piece or lump of flesh, food, or other matter: *they lobbed gobbets of fresh bonito off the side of the boat.*
god•head |ˈgäd,hed| • *n.* (usu. **the Godhead**) God.
■ divine nature. ■ an adored, admired, or influential person; an idol.

go•fer |ˈgōfər| (also **gopher**) • *n.* a person who runs errands, esp. on a movie set or in an office.

Gol•con•da |gälˈkändə| • *n.* a source of wealth, advantages, or happiness: *posters calling emigrants from Europe to the Golconda of the American West.*

gold brick • *n.* a thing that looks valuable, but is in fact worthless.
■ (also **goldbrick** or **goldbricker**) a con man.
■ a lazy person: [as adj.] *two goldbrick watchmen sat drinking in the shed.*. • *v.* (usu. **goldbrick**) [intrans.] invent excuses to avoid a task; shirk: *he wasn't goldbricking; he was really sick.*
■ [trans.] swindle (someone).

go•lem |ˈgōləm| • *n.* (in European Jewish legend) a clay figure brought to life by magic.
■ an automaton or robot.

gon•fa•lon |ˈgänfələn| • *n.* a banner or pennant, esp. one with streamers, hung from a crossbar.
■ a pennant awarded to baseball league champions.
DERIVATIVES: **gon•fa•lon•ier** |ˌgänfələˈnir| *n.*

gon•if |ˈgänəf| (also **goniff**) • *n.* a disreputable or dishonest person (often used as a general term of abuse).

gon•zo |ˈgänzō| • *adj.* informal of or associated with journalistic writing of an exaggerated, subjective, and fictionalized style.
■ bizarre or crazy: *the woman was either gonzo or stoned.*

Gor•di•an knot |ˈgôrdēən| • *n.* an extremely difficult or involved problem.
PHRASES: **cut the Gordian knot** solve or remove a problem in a direct or forceful way, rejecting gentler or more indirect methods.

Gor•gon |ˈgôrgən| (also **gorgon**) • *n.* each of three sisters of Greek mythology, Stheno, Euryale, and Medusa, with snakes for hair, who had the power to turn anyone who looked at them to stone. Medusa was killed by Perseus.
■ a fierce, frightening, or repulsive woman.

gorm•less |ˈgôrmlis| • *adj.* chiefly Brit. lacking sense or initiative; foolish.
DERIVATIVES: **gorm•less•ly** *adv.* **gorm•less•ness** *n.*

gos•pel |ˈgäspəl| • *n.* **1** the teaching or revelation of Christ: *it is the Church's mission to preach the gospel.*
■ (also **gospel truth**) a thing that is absolutely true: *they say it's sold out, but don't take that as gospel.* ■ a set of principles or beliefs: *the new economics unit has produced what it intends to be the approved gospel.* **2** (**Gospel**) the record of Jesus' life and teaching in the first four books of the New Testament.
■ each of these books. ■ a portion from one of these read at a church service.

The four Gospels ascribed to St. Matthew, St. Mark, St. Luke, and St. John all give an account of the ministry, crucifixion, and resurrection of Christ, although the Gospel of John differs greatly from the other three. There are also several later, apocryphal accounts that are recorded as Gospels.

3 (also **gospel music**) a fervent style of black evangelical religious singing, developed from spirituals sung in Southern Baptist and Pentecostal churches: [as adj.] *gospel singers.*

gos•sa•mer |ˈgäsəmər| • *n.* a fine, filmy substance consisting of cobwebs spun by small spiders, which is seen esp. in autumn when dew is clinging to it.
■ used to refer to something very light, thin, and insubstantial or delicate: *in the light from the table lamp, his hair was gossamer.* • *adj.* [attrib.] made of or resembling gossamer: *gossamer wings.*
DERIVATIVES: **gos•sa•mer•y** *adj.*

Goth |gäth| • *n.* **1** a member of a Germanic people that invaded the Roman Empire from the east between the 3rd and 5th centuries. The eastern division, the Ostrogoths, founded a kingdom in Italy, while the Visigoths went on to found one in Spain. **2** (**goth**) a style of rock music derived from punk, typically with apocalyptic or mystical lyrics.
■ a member of a subculture favoring black clothing, white and black makeup, and goth music.

Goth•ic |ˈgäthik| • *adj.* **1** of or relating to the Goths or their extinct East Germanic language, which provides the earliest manuscript evidence of any Germanic language (4th–6th centuries AD). **2** of or in the style of architecture prevalent in western Europe in the 12th–16th centuries, characterized by pointed arches, rib vaults, and flying buttresses, together with large windows and elaborate tracery. The **Gothic revival** of the mid 18th through the early 20th centuries focused again on this style. **3** belonging to or redolent of the Dark Ages; portentously gloomy or horrifying: *19th-century Gothic horror.* **4** (of lettering) of or derived from the angular style of handwriting with broad vertical downstrokes used in western Europe from the 13th century, including black-letter typefaces. **5** (**gothic**) of or relating to goths or their rock music. • *n.* **1** the language of the Goths. **2** the Gothic style of architecture. **3** Gothic type.
DERIVATIVES: **Goth•i•cal•ly** |-ik(ə)lē| *adv.* **Goth•i•cism** |ˈgäthəˌsizəm| *n.*

gouache |gwäsh; go͞oˈäsh| • *n.* a method of painting using opaque pigments ground in water and thickened with a gluelike substance.
■ paint of this kind; opaque watercolor. ■ a picture painted in this way. Cf. TEMPERA

gour•mand |go͝orˈmänd| • *n.* a person who enjoys eating and often eats too much.
■ a connoisseur of good food. See **usage** below. Cf. EPICURE
DERIVATIVES: **gour•man•dise** *n.: they spent their days in gourmandise and drinking.* **gour•man•dism** |ˈgo͝ormənˌdizəm| *n.*

USAGE: The words **gourmand** and **gourmet** overlap in meaning but are not identical. Both mean 'a connoisseur of good food' but **gourmand** more usually means 'a person who enjoys eating and often overeats.'

gour•met |ˌgôr'mā; ˌgŏor-| • *n.* a connoisseur of good food; a person with a discerning palate.
■ [as adj.] of a kind or standard suitable for a gourmet: *a gourmet meal.*

gout |gowt| • *n.* **1** a disease in which defective metabolism of uric acid causes arthritis, esp. in the smaller bones of the feet and episodes of acute pain. **2** poetic/literary a drop or spot, esp. of blood, smoke, or flame: *gouts of flame and phlegm.*
DERIVATIVES: **gout•i•ness** |-t̠ēnis| *n.* **gout•y** *adj.*

goy |goi| • *n.* (pl. **goyim** |'goi-im| or **goys**) a Jewish name (generally derogatory) for a non-Jew.
DERIVATIVES: **goy•ish** *adj.*

grace |grās| • *n.* **1** simple elegance or refinement of movement: *she moved through the water with effortless grace.*
■ courteous goodwill: *at least he has the grace to admit his debt to her.* ■ (**graces**) an attractively polite manner of behaving: *she has all the social graces.* **2** (in Christian belief) the free and unmerited favor of God, as manifested in the salvation of sinners and the bestowal of blessings.
■ a divinely given talent or blessing: *the graces of the Holy Spirit.* ■ the condition or fact of being favored by someone: *he fell from grace because of drug use at the Olympics.* **3** (also **grace period**) a period officially allowed for payment of a sum due or for compliance with a law or condition, esp. an extended period granted as a special favor: *another three days' grace.* **4** a short prayer of thanks said before or after a meal: *before dinner the Reverend Newman said grace.* **5** (**His, Her,** or **Your Grace**) used as forms of description or address for a duke, duchess, or archbishop: *His Grace, the Duke of Atholl.* • *v.* [with obj. and adverbial] do honor or credit to (someone or something) by one's presence: *she bowed out from the sport she has graced for two decades.*
■ [trans.] (of a person or thing) be an attractive presence in or on; adorn: *Ms. Pasco has graced the front pages of magazines like Elle and Vogue.*
PHRASES: **the (Three) Graces** Greek Mythology three beautiful goddesses (Aglaia, Thalia, and Euphrosyne), daughters of Zeus. They were believed to personify and bestow charm, grace, and beauty.

gra•cious |'grāsHəs| • *adj.* **1** courteous, kind, and pleasant, esp. toward someone of lower social status: *smiling and gracious in defeat.*
■ elegant and tasteful, esp. as exhibiting wealth or high social status: *the painter specialized in gracious Victorian interiors | gracious living.* **2** (in Christian belief) showing divine grace: *I am saved by God's gracious intervention on my behalf.* **3** Brit. a polite epithet used of royalty or their acts: *the accession of Her present gracious Majesty.* • *exclam.* expressing polite surprise.
DERIVATIVES: **gra•cious•ly** *adv.* **gra•cious•ness** *n.*

gra•da•tion |grā'dāsHən| • *n.* a scale or a series of successive changes, stages, or degrees: *within the woodpecker family, there is a gradation of drilling ability.*
■ a stage or change in a such a scale or series: *minute gradations of distance.* ■ a minute change from one shade, tone, or color to another: *amorphous shapes in subtle gradations of green and blue.* ■ (in historical linguistics) another term for ABLAUT.
DERIVATIVES: **gra•date** *v.* **gra•da•tion•al** |-sHənl| *adj.* **gra•da•tion•al•ly** |-sHnl-ē| *adv.*

gra•di•ent |'grādēənt| • *n.* **1** an inclined part of a road or railway; a slope: *fail-safe brakes for use on steep gradients.*
■ the degree of such a slope: *the path becomes very rough as the gradient increases.* ■ the degree of steepness of a plotted graph at any point. **2** an increase or decrease in the magnitude of a property (e.g., temperature, pressure, or concentration) observed in passing from one point or moment to another.
■ the rate of such a change.

grad•u•ate • *n.* |'græjəwit| a person who has successfully completed a course of study or training, esp. a person who has been awarded an undergraduate academic degree.
■ a person who has received a high school diploma: *she is 19, a graduate of Lincoln High.* • *v.* |'græjə,wāt| **1** [intrans.] successfully complete an academic degree, course of training, orhigh school: *I graduated from West Point in 1939.*
■ [trans.] confer a degree or other academic qualification on: *the school graduated more than one hundred arts majors in its first year.* ■ (**graduate to**) move up to (a more advanced level or position): *he started with rummy and graduated to high-stakes poker.* **2** [trans.] arrange in a series or according to a scale: [as adj.] (**graduated**) *a graduated tax.*
■ mark out (an instrument or container) in degrees or other proportionate divisions: *the stem was graduated with marks for each hour* | [as adj.] *graduated cylinders.* **3** [trans.] change (something, typically color or shade) gradually or step by step: *the color is graduated from the middle of the frame to the top.* • *adj.* [attrib.] relating to graduate school (postgraduate) education: *the graduate faculty.*
■ having graduated from a school or academic program: *a graduate electrical engineer.*

USAGE: The traditional use is "to be graduated from": *She will be graduated from medical school in June.* It is now more common to say "graduate from": *He will graduate from high school next year.* Avoid using **graduate** as a transitive verb, as in "He graduated high school last week."

graf•fi•ti |grə'fētē| • plural *n.* (sing. **graffito** |-tō|) [treated as sing. or pl.] writing or drawings scribbled, scratched, or sprayed illicitly on a wall or other surface in a public place: *the walls were covered with graffiti* | [as adj.] *a graffiti artist.* • *v.* [trans.] **1** write or draw graffiti on (something): *he and another teenager graffitied an entire train.*

■ write (words or drawings) as graffiti.
DERIVATIVES: **graf•fi•tist** |-ţist| *n.*

USAGE: In Italian the word **graffiti** is a plural noun, and its singular form is **graffito**. Traditionally, the same distinction has been maintained in English, so that **graffiti**, being plural, would require a plural verb: *the graffiti were all over the wall.* By the same token, the singular would require a singular verb: *there was a graffito on the wall.* The most common modern use is to treat **graffiti** as if it were a mass noun, similar to a word like **writing**. In this case **graffiti** takes a singular verb, as in *the graffiti was all over the wall.* Such uses are now widely accepted as standard and may be regarded as part of the natural development of the language, rather than as mistakes.

graft[1] |græft| • *n.* **1** a shoot or scion inserted into a slit of rooted stock, from which it receives sap.
■ an instance of inserting a shoot or scion in this way. **2** a piece of living tissue that is transplanted surgically.
■ a surgical operation in which tissue is transplanted. • *v.* [with obj. and adverbial] **1** insert (a scion) as a graft: *graft different varieties onto a single tree trunk.*
■ insert a graft on (a stock). **2** transplant (living tissue) as a graft: *they can graft a new hand onto the arm.*
■ insert or fix (something) permanently to something else, typically in a way considered inappropriate: *western-style government could not easily be grafted onto a profoundly different country.*

graft[2] • *n.* practices, esp. bribery, used to secure illicit gains in politics or business; corruption: *measures to curb official graft.*
■ such gains: *grow fat off bribes and graft.* • *v.* [intrans.] make money by shady or dishonest means.
DERIVATIVES: **graft•er** *n.*

gran•deur |ˈgrænjər; ˈgrændyoor| • *n.* splendor and impressiveness, esp. of appearance or style: *the austere grandeur of mountain scenery.*
■ high rank or social importance: *for all their grandeur, the chancellors were still officials of the household.*

gran•dil•o•quent |grænˈdiləkwənt| • *adj.* pompous or extravagant in language, style, or manner, esp. in a way that is intended to impress: *a grandiloquent celebration of Spanish glory.*
DERIVATIVES: **gran•dil•o•quence** *n.* **gran•dil•o•quent•ly** *adv.*

gran•di•ose |ˈgrændēˌōs; ˌgrændēˈōs| • *adj.* impressive or magnificent in appearance or style, esp. pretentiously so: *the court's grandiose facade.*
■ excessively grand or ambitious: *grandiose plans to reform the world.*
DERIVATIVES: **gran•di•ose•ly** *adv.* **gran•di•os•i•ty** |ˌgrændēˈäsiţē| *n.*

grand ju•ry • *n.* a jury, normally of twenty-three jurors, selected to examine the validity of a criminal accusation prior to trial; if the accusation is found to be supported by facts meriting a trial, the grand jury issues an indictment. The case may then be heard by a **petit** (or **petty**) jury, or by a judge, at trial.

grand mal |ˌgræn(d) ˈmäl; ˈmæl| • *n.* a serious form of epilepsy with muscle spasms and prolonged loss of consciousness. Cf. PETIT MAL.
■ an epileptic seizure of this kind.

gran•ite |ˈgrænit| • *n.* a very hard, granular, crystalline, igneous rock consisting mainly of quartz, mica, and feldspar and often used as a building stone.
■ used in similes and metaphors to refer to something very hard and impenetrable: [as adj.] *a man with granite determination.*
DERIVATIVES: **gra•nit•ic** |grəˈnitik| *adj.* **gran•it•oid** |ˈgræniˌtoid| *adj. & n.*

graph•ic |ˈgræfik| • *adj.* **1** of or relating to visual art, esp. involving drawing, engraving, or lettering: *his mature graphic work.*
■ giving a vivid picture with explicit detail: *a graphic description of the torture.* ■ (in computing) of, relating to, or denoting a visual image. **2** of or in the form of a graph. **3** [attrib.] of or denoting rocks having a surface texture resembling cuneiform writing. • *n.* a graphical item prepared for reproduction in printing ■ a graphical item displayed on a screen or stored as data.
DERIVATIVES: **graph•i•cal•ly** |-ik(ə)lē| *adv.* **graph•ic•ness** *n.*

graph•ol•o•gy |græˈfäləjē| • *n.* **1** the study of handwriting, for example as used to infer a person's character. **2** the study of written and printed symbols and of writing systems as a discipline of linguistics.
DERIVATIVES: **graph•o•log•i•cal** |ˌgræfəˈläjikəl| *adj.* **graph•ol•o•gist** |-jist| *n.*

grat•i•fy |ˈgrætiˌfī| • *v.* (**-ies, -ied**) [trans.] (often **be gratified**) give (someone) pleasure or satisfaction: *I was gratified to see the coverage in May's issue* | [as adj.] (**gratifying**) *the results were gratifying.*
■ indulge or satisfy (a desire): *not all the sexual impulses can be gratified.*
DERIVATIVES: **grat•i•fi•ca•tion** |ˌgrætəfiˈkāSHən| *n.* **grat•i•fi•er** *n.* **gra•ti•fy•ing•ly** *adv.*

grat•is |ˈgrætis| • *adv.* without charge; free: *a monthly program was issued gratis.* • *adj.* given or done for nothing; free: *gratis copies.*

gra•tu•i•tous |grəˈt(y)o͞oiţəs| • *adj.* **1** uncalled for; lacking good reason; unwarranted: *gratuitous violence.* **2** given or done free of charge: *gratuitous legal advice.*
DERIVATIVES: **gra•tu•i•tous•ly** *adv.* **gra•tu•i•tous•ness** *n.*

gra•tu•i•ty |grəˈt(y)o͞oiţē| • *n.* (pl. **-ies**) money given in return for some service or favor, in particular:
■ a tip given to a waiter, taxicab driver, etc.

grav•id |ˈgrævid| • *adj.* pregnant; carrying eggs or young.
■ full of meaning or a specified quality: *the scene is gravid with unease.*

grav•i•tas |ˈgræviˌtäs| • *n.* dignity, seriousness, or solemnity of manner: *a post for which he has the expertise and the gravitas.*

grav•i•tate |ˈɡrævɪˌtāt| • v. [no obj., with adverbial] move toward or be attracted to a place, person, or thing: *they gravitated to the Catholic faith in their hour of need.*
■ move, or tend to move, toward a center of gravity or other attractive force. ■ archaic descend or sink by the force of gravity.
DERIVATIVES: **grav•i•ta•tion** n. **grav•i•ta•tion•al** adj.

grav•i•ty |ˈɡrævɪtē| • n. 1 the force that attracts a body toward the center of the earth, or toward any other physical body having mass.
■ the degree of intensity of this, measured by acceleration. 2 extreme or alarming importance; seriousness: *crimes of the utmost gravity.*
■ seriousness or solemnity of manner: *has the poet ever spoken with greater eloquence or gravity?*

green•mail |ˈɡrēnˌmāl| • n. the practice of buying enough shares in a company to threaten a takeover, forcing the company's owners to buy them back at a higher price in order to retain control.
DERIVATIVES: **green•mail•er** n.

gre•gar•i•ous |ɡriˈɡerēəs| • adj. (of a person) fond of company; sociable: *a popular and gregarious man.*
■ (of animals) living in flocks or loosely organized communities: *gregarious species forage in flocks from colonies or roosts.* ■ (of plants) growing in open clusters or without intervention of other species.
DERIVATIVES: **gre•gar•i•ous•ly** adv. **gre•gar•i•ous•ness** n.

grid•lock |ˈɡridˌläk| • n. 1 a traffic jam affecting a whole network of intersecting streets, esp. because vehicles entering one or more intersections are unable to leave them (as, by turning through oncoming traffic). 2 another term for DEADLOCK.
DERIVATIVES: **grid•locked** adj.

griev•ance |ˈɡrēvəns| • n. a real or imagined wrong or other cause for complaint or protest, esp. unfair treatment: *failure to redress genuine grievances.*
■ an official statement of a complaint over something believed to be wrong or unfair: *three pilots have filed grievances against the company.* | [as adj.] *are they following grievance procedures?* ■ a feeling of resentment over something believed to be wrong or unfair: *he was nursing a grievance.*

grift |ɡrift| • v. [intrans.] engage in petty swindling. • n. a petty swindle.
DERIVATIVES: **grift•er** n.

grille |ɡril| (also **grill**) • n. a grating or screen of metal bars or wires, placed in front of something as protection or to allow ventilation or discreet observation.
■ a grating at the front of a motor vehicle allowing air to circulate to the radiator to cool it.

grim•ace |ˈɡriməs| • n. an ugly, twisted expression on a person's face, typically expressing disgust, pain, or wry amusement: *she gave a grimace of pain.* • v. [intrans.] make a grimace: *I sipped the coffee and grimaced.*
DERIVATIVES: **grim•ac•ing•ly** adv.

grin•go |ˈɡriNɡō| • n. (pl. **-os**) a sometimes offensive term for a white person from an English-speaking country (used in Spanish-speaking communities).

grip |ɡrip| • n. an assistant in a theater; a stagehand.
■ a member of a camera crew responsible for moving and setting up equipment.

grippe |ɡrip| • n. old-fashioned term for *influenza.*

gri•saille |ɡriˈzī; -ˈzäl| • n. a method of painting in gray monochrome, typically to imitate sculpture.
■ a painting or stained-glass window in this style.

gris•ly |ˈɡrizlē| • adj. (**grislier, grisliest**) causing horror or disgust: *the town was shaken by a series of grisly crimes.*
DERIVATIVES: **gris•li•ness** n.

grist |ɡrist| • n. grain that is ground to make flour.
■ malt crushed to make mash for brewing. ■ useful material, esp. to back up an argument: *the research provided the most sensational grist for opponents of tobacco.*
PHRASES: **grist for the mill** useful experience, material, or knowledge.

gro•tesque |ɡrōˈtesk| • adj. comically or repulsively ugly or distorted: *grotesque facial distortions.*
■ incongruous or inappropriate to a shocking degree: *a lifestyle of grotesque luxury.* • n. a very ugly or comically distorted figure, creature, or image: *the cups are carved in the form of a series of grotesques.*
■ (**the grotesque**) that which is grotesque: *images of the macabre and the grotesque.* ■ a style of decorative painting or sculpture consisting of the interweaving of human and animal forms with flowers and foliage.
DERIVATIVES: **gro•tesque•ly** adv. **gro•tesque•ness** n.

ground ze•ro • n. [in sing.] the point on the earth's surface directly above or below an exploding nuclear bomb.
■ a starting point or base for some activity: *if you're starting at ground zero in terms of knowledge, go to the library.*

group•think |ˈɡro͞opˌTHiNGk| • n. the practice of thinking or making decisions as a group in a way that discourages creativity or individual resonsibility: *there's always a danger of groupthink when two leaders are so alike.*

grov•el |ˈɡrävəl; ˈɡrə-| • v. (**groveled, groveling**; Brit. **grovelled, grovelling**) [intrans.] lie or move abjectly on the ground with one's face downward: *she was groveling on the floor in fear.*
■ act in an obsequious manner in order to obtain someone's forgiveness or favor: *everyone expected me to grovel with gratitude* | [as adj.] (**groveling**) *his groveling references to "great" historians and their "brilliant" works.*
DERIVATIVES: **grov•el•er** n. **grov•el•ing•ly** adv.

grudg•ing |'grəjiNG| • adj. given, granted, or allowed only reluctantly or resentfully: a grudging apology.
■ (of a person) reluctant or resentfully unwilling to give, grant, or allow something: Oliver was grudging about accepting Wickham's innocence.
DERIVATIVES: **grudg•ing•ly** adv. **grudg•ing•ness** n.

gruel•ing |'grōōəliNG| (Brit. **gruelling**) • adj. extremely tiring and demanding: a grueling schedule.
DERIVATIVES: **gruel•ing•ly** adv.

grunge |grənj| • n. **1** grime; dirt. **2** (also **grunge rock**) a style of rock music characterized by a raucous guitar sound and lazy vocal delivery.
■ the fashion associated with this music, including loose, layered clothing and ripped jeans.
DERIVATIVES: **grun•gi•ness** n. **grun•gy** adj.

gua•no |'gwänō| • n. (pl. **-os**) the excrement of bats or seabirds, occurring in thick deposits notably in caves or on the islands off Peru and Chile, and used as fertilizer.
■ an artificial fertilizer resembling natural guano, esp. one made from fish.

guar•an•tee |ˌgerən'tē| • n. a formal promise or assurance (typically in writing) that certain conditions will be fulfilled, esp. that a product will be repaired or replaced if not of a specified quality and durability: we offer a 10-year **guarantee** against rusting.
■ something that gives a certainty of outcome: past performance is no **guarantee of** future results. ■ variant spelling of GUARANTY. ■ less common term for guarantor, a person who makes or gives a guarantee. • v. (**guarantees, guaranteed, guaranteeing**) [intrans.] provide a formal assurance or promise, esp. that certain conditions will be fulfilled relating to a product, service, or transaction: [with infinitive] the con artist guarantees that the dirt pile will yield at least 20 ounces of gold.
■ [trans.] provide such an assurance regarding (something, esp. a product): the repairs will be guaranteed for three years | [as adj.] (**guaranteed**) the guaranteed bonus is not very high.
■ [trans.] provide financial security for; underwrite: a demand that $100,000 be deposited to guarantee their costs. ■ [trans.] promise with certainty: no one can guarantee a profit on stocks.

USAGE: **Guarantee** and **guaranty** are interchangeable for both noun and verb, although the latter is now rare as a verb. **Warranty** is widely used in their place. Warrantee means 'person to whom a warranty is made'; it is not a spelling variant of warranty.

guar•an•ty |'gerənˌtē| (also **guarantee**) • n. (pl. **-ies**) a formal pledge to pay another person's debt or to perform another person's obligation in the case of default. ■ a person who acts in this capacity (also called a guarantor).
■ a thing serving as security for a such a pledge. Cf. WARRANTY.

guard•i•an |'gärdēən| • n. a defender, protector, or keeper: self-appointed guardians of public morality.
■ a person who looks after and is legally responsible for someone (ward) who is unable to manage his or her own affairs, esp. a child whose parents have died. ■ the superior of a Franciscan convent.
DERIVATIVES: **guard•i•an•ship** |-ˌSHip| n.

guer•don |'gərdn| • n. a reward or recompense. • v. [trans.] give a reward to (someone): there might come a time in which he should guerdon them.

gui•don |'gīdn| • n. a pennant that narrows to a point or fork at the free end, esp. one used as the standard of a light cavalry regiment.

guild |gild| (also **gild**) • n. a medieval association of craftsmen or merchants, often having considerable power.
■ an association of people for mutual aid or the pursuit of a common goal. ■ a group of species that have similar requirements and play a similar role within an ecosystem.

guile |gīl| • n. sly or cunning intelligence: he used all his guile to free himself from the muddle he was in.
DERIVATIVES: **guile•ful** |-fəl| adj. **guile•ful•ly** |-fəlē| adv.

guile•less |'gīllis| • adj. devoid of guile; innocent and without deception: a youthful face, so open and guileless.
DERIVATIVES: **guile•less•ly** adv. **guile•less•ness** n.

guise |gīz| • n. an external form, appearance, or manner of presentation, typically concealing the true nature of something: he visited **in the guise of** an inspector | telemarketing **under the guise of** market research.

Gu•lag |'gōōläg| • n. [in sing.] a system of labor camps maintained in the Soviet Union from 1930 to 1955 in which many people died.
■ (**gulag**) a camp in this system, or any political labor camp: the imprisonment of dissidents in a massive gulag.

gull • v. [trans.] fool or deceive (someone): workers had been **gulled into** inflicting poverty upon themselves. • n. a person who is fooled or deceived.

gul•li•ble |'gələbəl| • adj. easily persuaded to believe something; credulous: persuade a gullible public to spend their money.
DERIVATIVES: **gul•li•bil•i•ty** |ˌgələ'bilitē| n. **gul•li•bly** |-blē| adv.

gum•bo |'gəmbō| • n. (pl. **-os**) **1** okra, esp. the gelatinous pods used in cooking.
■ (in Cajun cooking) a spicy chicken or seafood soup thickened typically with okra or rice. **2** (**Gumbo**) a French-based patois spoken by some blacks and Creoles in Louisiana. **3** a fine, clayey soil that becomes sticky and impervious when wet. **4** a type of Cajun music consisting of a lively blend of styles and sounds.

gump•tion |'gəmpSHən| • n. shrewd or spirited initiative and resourcefulness: she **had the gumption to** put her foot down and stop those crazy schemes.

gung-ho |ˈɡəNG ˈhō| • *adj.* unthinkingly enthusiastic and eager, esp. about taking part in fighting or warfare: *the gung-ho soldier who wants all the big military toys.*

gun•sel |ˈɡənsəl| • *n.* A criminal carrying a gun.

gu•ru |ˈɡo͝oro͞o; ɡo͞oˈro͞o| • *n.* (in Hinduism and Buddhism) a spiritual teacher, esp. one who imparts initiation.
■ each of the ten first leaders of the Sikh religion. ■ an influential teacher or popular expert: *a management guru.*

gus•sy |ˈɡəsē| • *v.* (-ies, -ied) [trans.] (**gussy someone/something up**) make more attractive, esp. in a showy or gimmicky way: *shopkeepers gussied up their window displays.*

gus•ta•to•ry |ˈɡəstəˌtôrē| • *adj.* concerned with tasting or the sense of taste: *gustatory delights.* Cf. CULINARY

gus•to |ˈɡəstō| • *n.* (pl. **-os** or **-oes**) enjoyment or vigor in doing something; zest: *she sang it with gusto.*
■ [in sing.] a relish or liking: *he had a particular gusto for those sort of performances.*

gust•y |ˈɡəstē| • *adj.* (**gustier, gustiest**) 1 characterized by or blowing in gusts: *a gusty morning.* 2 having or showing gusto: *gusty female vocals.*
DERIVATIVES: **gust•i•ly** |ˈɡəstəlē| *adv.* **gust•i•ness** *n.*

gut•ta-per•cha |ˌɡətə ˈpərCHə| • *n.* a hard, tough thermoplastic substance that is the coagulated latex of certain Malaysian trees (genus *Palaquium*). It consists chiefly of a hydrocarbon isomeric with rubber and is now used chiefly in dentistry and for electrical insulation, having been replaced in many other uses by synthetics.

gut•ter |ˈɡətər| • *v.* 1 [intrans.] (of a candle or flame) flicker and burn unsteadily: *the candles had almost guttered out.* 2 [trans.] channel or furrow with something such as streams or tears: *my cheeks are guttered with tears.*
■ [intrans.] (**gutter down**) stream down: *the raindrops gutter down her visage.*

gut•tur•al |ˈɡətərəl| • *adj.* (of a speech sound) produced in the throat; harsh-sounding.
■ (of a manner of speech) characterized by the use of such sounds: *his parents' guttural central European accent.* • *n.* a guttural consonant (e.g., *k, g*) or other speech sound.
DERIVATIVES: **gut•tur•al•ly** *adv.*

gym•kha•na |jimˈkänə| • *n.* 1 an equestrian day event comprising races and other competitions on horseback, typically for children. 2 (in India) a public place with facilities for track and field.

gym•na•si•um |jimˈnāzēəm| • *n.* (pl. **gymnasiums** or **gymnasia** |-zēə|) 1 a room or building equipped for gymnastics, games, and other physical exercise. 2 |ɡimˈnäzē ˌo͝om| a school in Germany, Scandinavia, or central Europe that prepares pupils for university entrance.

DERIVATIVES: **gym•na•si•al** |-zēəl| *adj.* (in sense 2).

gym•nas•tics |jimˈnæstiks| • *plural n.* [also treated as sing.] exercises developing or displaying physical agility and coordination. The modern sport of gymnastics typically involves exercises on uneven bars, balance beam, floor, and vaulting horse (for women), and horizontal and parallel bars, rings, floor, and pommel horse (for men).
■ [with adj.] other physical or mental agility of a specified kind: *these vocal gymnastics make the music unforgettable.*

gym•no•sperm |ˈjimnəˌspərm| • *n.* a plant that has seeds unprotected by an ovary or fruit. Gymnosperms include the conifers, cycads, and ginkgo.
DERIVATIVES: **gym•no•sper•mous** |ˌjimnəˈspərməs| *adj.*

gy•ne•col•o•gy |ˌɡīnəˈkäləjē; ˌjinə-| (Brit. **gynaecology**) • *n.* the branch of physiology and medicine that deals with the functions and diseases specific to women and girls, esp. those affecting the reproductive system. Cf. OBSTETRICS.
DERIVATIVES: **gyn•e•co•log•ic** |-kəˈläjik| *adj.* **gyn•e•co•log•i•cal** |-kəˈläjikəl| *adj.* **gyn•e•co•log•i•cal•ly** |-kəˈläjik(ə)lē| *adv.* **gy•ne•col•o•gist** |-jist| *n.*

gyp |jip| *informal* • *v.* (**gypped, gypping**) [trans.] cheat or swindle (someone): *that's salesmanship, you have to gyp people into buying stuff they don't like.* • *n.* (also **gip**) an act of cheating; a swindle.

gyp•sy |ˈjipsē| (also **gipsy**) • *n.* (pl. **-ies**) a member of a traveling people with dark skin and hair who speak the Indo-European language Romany and traditionally live by seasonal work, itinerant trade, and fortune-telling. Gypsies are now found mostly in Europe, parts of North Africa, and North America, but are believed to have originated in the Indian subcontinent.
■ the language of the gypsies; Romany. ■ a person who leads an unconventional life. ■ a person who moves from place to place as required by employment. ■ (also **gypsy cab**) an unlicensed taxi, or one licensed to do business only by telephone or in certain areas of a large city. • *adj.* (of a business or business person) nonunion or unlicensed: *gypsy trucking firms.*
DERIVATIVES: **gyp•sy•ish** *adj.*

gy•rate • *v.* |ˈjīrāt| move or cause to move in a circle or spiral, esp. quickly: [intrans.] *their wings gyrate through the water like paddle wheels.*
■ [intrans.] dance in a wild or suggestive manner: *strippers gyrated on a low stage.*
DERIVATIVES: **gy•ra•tion** |jīˈrāSHən| *n.* **gy•ra•tor** |-ˌrātər| *n.*

gyre |ˈjīr| • *v.* [intrans.] whirl; gyrate: *a swarm of ghosts gyred around him.* • *n.* a circular movement; spiral; or a vortex.
■ a circular pattern of currents in an ocean basin: *the central North Pacific gyre.*

Hh

ha•be•as cor•pus |ˈhābēəˈskôrpəs| • *n.* (in law) a writ requiring a person under arrest to be brought before a judge or into court, esp. to secure the person's release unless lawful grounds are shown for his or her detention. ■ the legal right to apply for such a writ.

ha•bil•i•ment |həˈbiləmənt| • *n.* (usu. **habil-iments**) clothing, an outfit appropriate for an office or occasion, armor, or equipment: *the habiliments of war.*

ha•bil•i•tate |həˈbiləˌtāt| • *v.* [trans.] fit out; equip.
■ clothe; dress. ■ [intrans.] qualify for office.
DERIVATIVES: **ha•bil•i•ta•tion** |həˌbiləˈtā-sнən| *n.*

hab•it•a•ble |ˈhæbitəbəl| • *adj.* suitable for good enough to live in.
DERIVATIVES: **hab•it•a•bil•i•ty** |ˌhæbədə-ˈbilətē| *n.*

hab•i•tant |ˈhæbitənt; ˈhæbətnt| • *n.* 1 (often as adj.) an early French settler in Canada (esp. Quebec) or Louisiana: *the habitant farmhouses of old Quebec.* 2 an inhabitant.

ha•bit•u•al |həˈbiCHəwəl| • *adj.* done or doing constantly or as a habit: *a habitual late sleeper* | *this pattern of behavior can become habitual.*
■ regular; usual: *his habitual dress.*
DERIVATIVES: **ha•bit•u•al•ly** *adv.*

ha•bit•u•ate |həˈbiCHəˌwāt| • *v.* make or become accustomed or used to something: [trans.] *she had habituated the chimps to humans.*
DERIVATIVES: **ha•bit•u•a•tion** *n.*

ha•bit•u•é |həˈbiCHəˌwā| • *n.* a resident of or frequent visitor to a particular place: *his uncle was a habitué of the French theater.*

ha•ci•en•da |ˌhäsēˈendə| • *n.* (in Spanish-speaking regions) a large estate or plantation with a dwelling house.
■ the main house on such an estate. ■ a factory or other works on such an estate.

hack |hæk| • *n.* 1 a writer or journalist producing dull, unoriginal work: [as adj.] *a hack scriptwriter.*
■ a person who does dull routine work. 2 a horse for ordinary riding.
■ a good-quality lightweight riding horse, esp. one used in the show ring. ■ a ride on a horse. ■ an inferior or worn-out horse. ■ a horse rented out for riding. 3 a taxicab. • *v.* [intrans.] [usu. as n.] (**hacking**) ride a horse for pleasure or exercise.
DERIVATIVES: **hack•er•y** |ˈhækərē| *n.* (in sense 1)

hack•le |ˈhækəl| • *n.* 1 (**hackles**) erectile hairs along the back of a dog or other animal that rise when it is angry or alarmed.
■ the hairs on the back of a person's neck, thought of as being raised when the person is angry or hostile: *off-road vehicles have long raised the hackles of environmentalists.* 2 (often **hackles**) a long, narrow feather on the neck or saddle of a domestic cock or other bird.
■ a feather wound around a fishing fly so that its filaments are splayed out. ■ such feathers collectively. ■ a bunch of feathers in a military headdress. 3 a steel comb for separating flax fibers. • *v.* [trans.] dress or comb with a hackle.

hack•ney |ˈhæknē| • *n.* (pl. **-eys**) a horse or pony of a light breed with a high-stepping trot, used in harness.
■ [usu. as adj.] a horse-drawn vehicle kept for hire: *a hackney coach.*
DERIVATIVES: **hack•neyed** *adj.*

Ha•des |ˈhādēz| • *n.* (in Greek mythology) the underworld; the abode of the spirits of the dead.
■ the god of the underworld, one of the sons of the Titan Cronus. Also called Pluto.
DERIVATIVES: **Ha•de•an** |ˈhādēən| *adj.*

haec•ce•i•ty |hækˈsēətē| • *n.* (in philosophy) that property or quality of a thing by virtue of which it is unique or describable as "this (one)."
■ the property of being a unique and individual thing.

hag•gard |ˈhæɡərd| • *adj.* 1 looking exhausted and unwell, esp. from fatigue, worry, or suffering: *He trailed on behind, haggard and disheveled.* 2 (of a hawk) caught for training as a wild adult of more than twelve months. • *n.* a haggard hawk.
DERIVATIVES: **hag•gard•ly** *adv.* **hag•gard•ness** *n.*

hag•i•og•ra•phy |ˌhæɡēˈägrəfē; ˌhāɡē-| • *n.* the writing of the lives of saints.
■ adulatory writing about another person. ■ a biography idealizing its subject.
DERIVATIVES: **hag•i•o•graph•ic** |ˌhæɡēə-ˈɡræfik; ˌhāɡē-| *adj.* **hag•i•o•graph•i•cal** |ˌhæɡēəˈɡræfəkəl; ˌhāɡē-| *adj.*

hai•ku |ˈhīˌko͞o; ˈhīˈko͞o| (also **hokku**) • *n.* (pl. same or **haikus**) a Japanese poem of seventeen syllables, in three lines of five, seven, and five, traditionally evoking images of the natural world.
■ an English imitation of this.

hail-fel•low-well-met • *adj.* showing excessive familiarity: *We grew accustomed to hail-fellow-well-met salesmen.*

hajj |hæj| (also **haj**) • *n.* the Muslim pilgrimage to Mecca that takes place in the last month of the year, and that all Muslims are expected to make at least once during their lifetime. A **haji** (also **hajji**) is a Muslim who has made this pilgrimage.

hal•cy•on |ˈhælsēən| • *adj.* denoting a period of time in the past that is idyllically happy and peaceful: *the halcyon days of the mid-1980s, when profits were soaring.* • *n.* 1 a tropical Asian and African kingfisher (genus *Halcyon*) with brightly colored plumage. 2 a mythical bird said by ancient writers to breed in a nest floating at sea at the winter solstice, charming the wind and waves into calm.

hale[1] |hāl| • *adj.* (of a person, esp. an elderly one) strong and healthy: *only just sixty, very hale and hearty.*

hale[2] • *v.* [with obj. and adverbial of direction] drag or draw forcibly: *he haled an old man out of the audience. | the suspect was haled into court.*

hall•mark |ˈhôlˌmärk| • *n.* a mark stamped on articles of gold, silver, or platinum in Britain, certifying their standard of purity.
■ a distinctive feature, esp. one of excellence: *the tiny bubbles are the hallmark of fine champagnes.* • *v.* [trans.] stamp with a hallmark.
■ designate as distinctive, esp. for excellence.

hal•low |ˈhælō| • *v.* [trans.] honor as holy: *the Ganges is hallowed as a sacred, cleansing river* | [as adj.] (**hallowed**) *hallowed ground.*
■ make holy; consecrate. ■ [as adj.] (**hallowed**) greatly revered or respected: *in keeping with a hallowed American tradition.* • *n.* a saint or holy person.

hal•lu•ci•nate |həˈlo͞osənˌāt| • *v.* [intrans.] experience a seemingly real perception of something not actually present, typically as a result of a mental disorder or of taking drugs: *people sense themselves going mad and hallucinate about spiders.*
■ [trans.] experience a hallucination of (something): *I don't care if they're hallucinating purple snakes.*
DERIVATIVES: **hal•lu•ci•nant** |-sənənt| *adj. & n.* **hal•lu•ci•na•tion** *n.* **hal•lu•ci•na•tor** |-ˌātər| *n.* **hal•lu•ci•na•to•ry** *adj.*

hal•lu•ci•no•gen |həˈlo͞osənəˌjən| • *n.* a drug that causes hallucinations, such as LSD.
DERIVATIVES: **hal•lu•ci•no•gen•ic** |hə ˌlo͞osənəˈjenik| *adj.*

ha•lo |ˈhālō| • *n.* (pl. **-oes** or **-os**) a disk or circle of light shown surrounding or above the head of a saint or holy person to represent his or her holiness.
■ the glory associated with an idealized person or thing: *he has long since lost his halo for many ordinary Russians.* ■ a circle or ring of something resembling a halo: *their frizzy haloes of hair.* ■ a circle of white or colored light around the sun, moon, or other luminous body caused by refraction through ice crystals in the atmosphere. ■ a tenuous sphere of hot gas and old stars surrounding a spiral galaxy. • *v.* (**-oes, -oed**) [trans.] (usu. **be haloed**) surround with or as if with a halo.

hal•yard |ˈhælyərd| • *n.* a rope used for raising and lowering a sail, spar, flag, or yard on a sailing ship.

ham•a•dry•ad |ˌhæməˈdrīəd| • *n.* **1** (also **Hamadryad**) (in Greek & Roman mythology) a nymph who lives in a tree and dies when the tree dies. **2** another term for king cobra.

ha•mar•ti•a |həˈmärtēə| • *n.* a fatal flaw leading to the downfall of a tragic hero or heroine.

hap•haz•ard |ˌhæpˈhæzərd| • *adj.* lacking any obvious principle of organization: *the kitchen drawers contained a haphazard collection of silver souvenir spoons.*

DERIVATIVES: **hap•haz•ard•ly** *adv.* **hap• haz•ard•ness** *n.*

hap•less |ˈhæplis| • *adj.* (esp. of a person) unfortunate: *if you're one of the many hapless car buyers who've been shafted.*
DERIVATIVES: **hap•less•ly** *adv.* **hap•less• ness** *n.*

ha•ra-ki•ri |ˌhärə ˈkirē; ˌhærə-; ˌherē ˈkerē| • *n.* ritual suicide by disembowelment with a sword, formerly practiced in Japan by samurai as an honorable alternative to disgrace or execution. Also called SEPPUKU.
■ ostentatious or ritualized self-destruction: *you may wonder why you find this software hard to navigate, painfully slow, and prone to hara-kiri.*

ha•rangue |həˈræŋ| • *n.* a lengthy and aggressive speech. • *v.* [trans.] lecture (someone) at length in an aggressive and critical manner: *the kind of guy who harangued total strangers about PCB levels in fish.*
DERIVATIVES: **ha•rangu•er** *n.*

ha•rass |həˈræs; ˈhærəs; ˈher-| • *v.* [trans.] subject to aggressive pressure or intimidation: *a warning to men harassing women at work.*
■ make repeated small-scale attacks on (an enemy): *the squadron's task was to harass retreating enemy forces.* ■ [as adj.] (**harassed**) feeling or looking strained by having too many demands made on one.
DERIVATIVES: **ha•rass•er** *n.* **ha•rass•ing• ly** *adv.* **ha•rass•ment** *n.*

har•bin•ger |ˈhärbənjər| • *n.* a person or thing that announces or signals the approach of another: *witch hazels are the harbingers of spring.*
■ a forerunner of something: *these works were not yet opera but they were the most important harbinger of opera.*

har•bor |ˈhärbər| (Brit. **harbour**) • *v.* [trans.] **1** keep (a thought or feeling, typically a negative one) in one's mind, esp. secretly: *she started to harbor doubts about the wisdom of their journey.* **2** give a home or shelter to: *woodlands that once harbored a colony of red deer.*
■ shelter or hide (a criminal or wanted person). ■ carry the germs of (a disease). **3** [intrans.] (of a ship or its crew) moor in a harbor.
DERIVATIVES: **har•bor•er** *n.*

hard core • *n.* the most active, committed, or doctrinaire members of a group or movement: *there is always a hard-core of trusty stalwarts* | [as adj.] *a hard core following.*
■ popular music that is experimental in nature and typically characterized by high volume and aggressive presentation. ■ pornography of an explicit kind: [as adj.] *hard-core porn.*

har•em |ˈherəm| • *n.* **1** the separate part of a Muslim household reserved for wives, concubines, and female servants. **2** the wives (or concubines) of a polygamous man.
■ a group of female animals sharing a single mate.

har•le•quin |ˈhärlək(w)ən| • *n.* (**Harlequin**) a mute character in traditional pantomime,

typically masked and dressed in a diamond-patterned costume.
■ a stock comic character in Italian *commedia dell'arte*. ■ a mischievous buffoon. • *adj.* in varied colors; variegated.

har•mon•ic |här'mänik| • *adj.* **1** of, relating to, or characterized by musical harmony: *a basic four-chord harmonic sequence.*
■ (in music) relating to or denoting a harmonic or harmonics. **2** (in mathematics) of or relating to a harmonic progression.
■ (in physics) of or relating to component frequencies of a complex oscillation or wave.
■ (in astrology) using or produced by the application of a harmonic: *harmonic charts.* • *n.* **1** (in music) an overtone accompanying a fundamental tone at a fixed interval, produced by vibration of a string, column of air, etc., in an exact fraction of its length.
■ a note produced on a musical instrument as an overtone, e.g., by lightly touching a string while sounding it. **2** (in physics) a component frequency of an oscillation or wave.
■ (in astrology) a division of the zodiacal circle by a specified number, used in the interpretation of a birth chart.
DERIVATIVES: **har•mon•i•cal•ly** |-ik(ə)lē| *adv.*

har•mo•ni•um |här'mōnēəm| • *n.* a keyboard instrument in which the notes are produced by air driven through metal reeds by foot-operated bellows.

harp |härp| • *v.* [intrans.] talk or write persistently and tediously on a particular topic: *guys who are constantly harping on the war.*

har•py |'härpē| • *n.* (pl. **-ies**) (in Greek & Roman mythology) a rapacious monster described as having a woman's head and body and a bird's wings and claws or depicted as a bird of prey with a woman's face.
■ a grasping, unscrupulous woman.

har•ri•dan |'hæridn; 'heridn| • *n.* a strict, bossy, or belligerent old woman: *a bullying old harridan.*

har•ri•er[1] • *n.* a hound of a breed used for hunting hares.
■ a cross-country runner.

har•ri•er[2] • *n.* a long-winged, slender-bodied bird of prey (genus *circus*) with low quartering flight.

har•ry |'hærē; 'herē| • *v.* (**-ies, -ied**) [trans.] persistently carry out attacks on (an enemy or an enemy's territory).
■ persistently harass: *he bought the house for Jenny, whom he harries into marriage* | [as adj.] (**harried**) *harried reporters are frequently forced to invent what they cannot find out.*
DERIVATIVES: **har•ri•er** *n.*

har•um-scar•um |'herəm 'skerəm| • *adj.* reckless; impetuous: *she shall be frightened out of her wits by your harum-scarum ways.* • *n.* such a person. • *adv.* in a harum-scarum manner: *the tables were scattered harum-scarum around a small room.*

Ha•sid |KHä'sēd; 'KHäsid; 'häsid| (also **Chasid, Chassid,** or **Hassid**) • *n.* (pl. **Hasidim** |,KHäsē'dēm; KHäsēdim; hä 'sēdim|) **1** a member of a strictly orthodox Jewish sect in Palestine in the 3rd and 2nd centuries BC that opposed Hellenizing influences on their faith and supported the Maccabean revolt. **2** an adherent of Hasidism.
DERIVATIVES: **Ha•sid•ic** |KHä'sedik; häs-ēdik| *adj.*

has•sock |'hæsək| • *n.* **1** a thick, firmly padded cushion, in particular:
■ a footstool. ■ a cushion for kneeling on in church. **2** a firm clump of grass or matted vegetation in marshy or boggy ground.

haugh•ty |'hôt̯ē| • *adj.* (**haughtier** |'hô-dēər|, **haughtiest**) arrogantly superior and disdainful: *a look of haughty disdain* | *a haughty aristocrat.*
DERIVATIVES: **haugh•ti•ly** |-t̯əlē| *adv.* **haugh•ti•ness** *n.*

haute bour•geoi•sie |,ōt boōzHwä'zē| • *n.* (**the haute bourgeoisie**) [treated as sing. or pl.] the upper middle class.

haute cou•ture |,ōt ,koō'toŏr| • *n.* the designing and making of high-quality fashionable clothes by leading fashion houses, esp. to order.
■ fashion houses that engage in such work.
■ clothes of this kind.

haute cui•sine |,ōt ,kwə'zēn| • *n.* the preparation and cooking of high-quality food following the style of traditional French cuisine.
■ food produced in such a way.

hau•teur |hō'tər| • *n.* haughtiness of manner; disdainful pride.

haut monde |ō 'mōNd; ō 'mänd| • *n.* (**the haut monde**) fashionable society. Cf. BEAU MONDE, DEMIMONDE.

haut-re•lief |,ō ri'lēf| • *n.* another term for sculptural high relief (see RELIEF).
■ a sculpture or carving in high relief.

hav•er•sack |'hævər,sæk| • *n.* a small, sturdy bag carried on the back or over the shoulder, used esp. by soldiers and hikers.

head•y |'hedē| • *adj.* (**headier, headiest**) **1** (of liquor) potent; intoxicating: *several bottles of heady local wine.*
■ having a strong or exhilarating effect: *the heady days of the birth of the women's movement* | *a heady, exotic perfume.* **2** impetuous; violent; passionate; headstrong.
DERIVATIVES: **head•i•ly** |'hedl-ē| *adv.* **head•i•ness** *n.*

hear•say |'hir,sā| • *n.* information received from other people that one cannot adequately substantiate; rumor: *according to hearsay, Bob was about to be promoted.*
■ (in law) the report of another person's words by a witness, usually disallowed as evidence in court, primarily because it is not susceptible to cross-examination: *everything they had told him would have been ruled out as hearsay* | [as adj.] *hearsay evidence.*

heath |hēTH| • *n.* **1** an area of open uncultivated land, esp. in Britain, with characteristic vegetation of heather, gorse, and coarse grasses.
■ vegetation dominated by dwarf shrubs of the heath family: [as adj.] *heath vegetation.* **2** a dwarf shrub (*Erica* and related genera) with small leathery leaves and small pink or pur-

ple bell-shaped flowers, characteristic of heathland and moorland.
DERIVATIVES: **heath•y** adj.
heath•en |'hēᴛʜən| • n. a person who does not belong to a widely held religion (esp. one who is not a Christian, Jew, or Muslim) as regarded by those who do: *bringing Christianity to the heathens.*
■ a follower of a polytheistic religion. ■ (**the heathen**) heathen people collectively, esp. (in biblical use) those who did not worship the God of Israel. ■ an unenlightened person; a person regarded as lacking culture or moral principles. • adj. of or relating to heathens: *heathen gods.*
■ unenlightened or uncivilized.
DERIVATIVES: **heath•en•dom** |-dəm| n. **heath•en•ish** adj. **heath•en•ism** |-ˌnizəm| n.

heav•y wa•ter • n. water in which the hydrogen in the molecules is partly or wholly replaced by the isotope deuterium, used esp. as a moderator in nuclear reactors.

heb•dom•a•dal |heb'däməd l| • adj. weekly (used esp. of organizations that meet weekly): *hebdomadal clubs | hebdomadal journals.*

heb•e•tude |'hebəˌt(y)o͞od| • n. the state of being dull or lethargic.

hec•tare |'hekˌter| (abbr.: **ha**) • n. a metric unit of square measure, equal to 100 ares (2.471 acres or 10,000 square meters).
DERIVATIVES: **hec•tar•age** |'hektərij| n.

hec•tic |'hektik| • adj. **1** full of incessant or frantic activity: *a hectic business schedule.* **2** relating to, affected by, or denoting a regularly recurrent fever typically accompanying tuberculosis, with flushed cheeks and hot, dry skin. • n. a hectic fever or flush.
■ a patient suffering from such a fever.
DERIVATIVES: **hec•ti•cal•ly** |-tik(ə)lē| adv.

hec•tor |'hektər| • v. [trans.] talk to (someone) in a bullying way: *she hectored him into taking violin lessons.* | [as adj.] (**hectoring**) *a brusque, hectoring manner.*
DERIVATIVES: **hec•tor•ing•ly** |'hekt(ə)r-iNGlē| adv.

hedge |hej| • n. a contract entered into or asset held as a protection against possible financial loss: *inflation hedges such as real estate and gold* | [as adj.] *a hedge fund.*
■ a word or phrase used to allow for additional possibilities or to avoid overprecise commitment, for example, *etc., often, usually,* or *sometimes.* • v. [trans.] **1** limit or qualify (something) by conditions or exceptions: *experts usually hedge their predictions, just in case.*
■ [intrans.] avoid making a definite decision, statement, or commitment: *she hedged around the one question she wanted to ask.* **2** protect (one's investment or an investor) against loss by making balancing or compensating contracts or transactions: *the company hedged its investment position on the futures market.*
PHRASES: **hedge one's bets** avoid committing oneself when faced with a difficult choice.
DERIVATIVES: **hedg•er** n.

he•don•ism |'hēdnˌizəm| • n. the pursuit of pleasure; sensual self-indulgence.
■ the ethical theory that pleasure (in the sense of the satisfaction of desires) is the highest good and proper aim of human life.
DERIVATIVES: **he•don•ist** n. **he•don•is•tic** |ˌhēdn'istik| adj. **he•don•is•ti•cal•ly** |ˌhēdn'istik(ə)lē| adv.

heed•less |'hēdlis| • adj. showing a reckless lack of care or attention: *"Elaine!" she shouted, heedless of attracting unwanted attention* | *his heedless impetuosity.*
DERIVATIVES: **heed•less•ly** adv. **heed•less•ness** n.

he•gem•o•ny |hə'jemənē; 'hejəˌmōnē| • n. leadership or dominance, esp. by one country or social group over others: *Germany was united under Prussian hegemony after 1871.*
DERIVATIVES: **he•gem•o•nist** n.

He•gi•ra |hə'jīrə; 'hejərə| (also **Hejira** or **Hijra**) • n. Muhammad's departure from Mecca to Medina in AD 622, prompted by the opposition of the merchants of Mecca and marking the consolidation of the first Muslim community.
■ the Muslim era reckoned from this date: *the second century of the Hegira.* Muslim dates are computed in the year of the Hegira: a Koran dated 586 AH. ■ (**hegira**) an exodus or migration.

hei•nous |'hānəs| • adj. (of a person or wrongful act, esp. a crime) utterly odious or wicked: *a battery of heinous crimes.*
DERIVATIVES: **hei•nous•ly** adv. **hei•nous•ness** n.

heir ap•par•ent • n. (pl. **heirs apparent** |ˌe(ə)rz ə'perənt|) an heir whose claim cannot be set aside by the birth of another heir. An **heir presumptive** may have his or her claim thus set aside.
■ a person who is most likely to succeed to the place of another: *he was once considered heir apparent to the chairman.*

hel•i•cal |'helikəl; 'hē-| • adj. having the shape or form of a helix; spiral: *helical molecules.*
DERIVATIVES: **hel•i•cal•ly** |-ik(ə)lē| adv.

he•li•o•cen•tric |ˌhēlēə'sentrik| • adj. having or representing the sun as the center, as in the accepted astronomical model of the solar system.
■ (in astronomy) measured from or considered in relation to the center of the sun: *heliocentric distance.*
DERIVATIVES: **he•li•o•cen•tri•cal•ly** |-trik(ə)lē| adv.

he•lix |'hēliks| • n. (pl. **helices** |'hēləˌsēz|) an object having a three-dimensional shape like that of a wire wound uniformly in a single layer around a cylinder or cone, as in a corkscrew or spiral staircase.
■ (in geometry) a curve on a conical or cylindrical surface that would become a straight line if the surface were unrolled into a plane. ■ an extended spiral chain of atoms in a protein, nucleic acid, or other polymeric molecule. ■ (in architecture) a spiral ornament. ■ the rim of the external human ear.

Hel•len•is•tic |ˌhelə'nistik| • adj. of or relating to Greek history, language, and culture from the death of Alexander the Great in 323 BC to the defeat of Cleopatra and Mark Antony by Octavian in 31 BC. During this period Greek culture flourished, spreading through the Mediterranean and into the Near East and Asia and centering on Alexandria in Egypt and Pergamum in Turkey.

hel•ot |'helət| • n. a member of a class of serfs in ancient Sparta, intermediate in status between slaves and citizens.
■ a serf or slave.
DERIVATIVES: **hel•ot•age** |'helə,tij| n. **hel•ot•ism** |-,tizəm| n. **hel•ot•ry** |'helətrē| n.

helve |helv| • n. the handle of a weapon or tool.

hem•i•dem•i•sem•i•qua•ver |ˌhemē,demē 'semē,kwāvər| • n. a musical note with the time value of half a demisemiquaver; a sixty-fourth note.

Hem•ing•way•esque |'hemiNGg,wāesk| • adj. in the syle or tradition of Ernest (Miller) Hemingway (1899–1961), US novelist, short-story writer, and journalist, noted for the terseness of his writing and for his concern with manliness and vigor.

hem•or•rhage |'hem(ə)rij| (Brit. **haemorrhage**) • n. an escape of blood from a ruptured blood vessel, esp. when profuse.
■ a damaging loss of valuable people or resources suffered by an organization, group, or country: *a hemorrhage of highly qualified teachers.* • v. [intrans.] (of a person) suffer a hemorrhage: *he had begun hemorrhaging in the night.*
■ [trans.] expend (money) in large amounts in a seemingly uncontrollable manner: *the business was hemorrhaging cash.*

hem•or•rhoid |'hem(ə),roid| (Brit. **haemorrhoid**) • n. (usu. **hemorrhoids**) a swollen vein or group of veins in the region of the anus. Also (collectively) called *piles.*
DERIVATIVES: **hem•or•rhoi•dal** |ˌhem(ə) 'roidl| adj.

hen•di•a•dys |hen'dīədəs| • n. (in rhetoric) the expression of a single idea by two words connected with "and," e.g., *nice and warm,* when one could be used to modify the other, as in *nicely warm.*

hen•o•the•ism |'henōTHē,izəm; ,henō'THē-| • n. adherence to one particular god out of several, esp. by a family, tribe, or other group.

her•ald |'herəld| • n. **1** an official formerly employed to oversee state ceremony, precedence, and the use of armorial bearings, and to make proclamations, carry ceremonial messages, and oversee tournaments. **2** a person or thing viewed as a sign that something is about to happen: *they considered the first primroses as the herald of spring.* • v. [trans.] be a sign that (something) is about to happen: *the speech heralded a change in policy.*
■ (usu. **be heralded**) acclaim: *the band has been heralded as the industrial supergroup of the '90s.*

her•ald•ry |'herəldrē| • n. the system by which coats of arms and other armorial bearings are devised, described, and regulated.

■ armorial bearings or other heraldic symbols.
■ colorful ceremony: *all the pomp and heraldry provided a splendid pageant.*
DERIVATIVES: **her•ald•ist** |'herəldist| n.

her•ba•ceous |(h)ər'bāSHəs| • adj. of, denoting, or relating to herbs (in the botanical sense), especially plants not forming a woody stem but dying down to the root each year.

herb•al |'(h)ərbəl| • adj. relating to or made from herbs, esp. those used in cooking and medicine: *herbal remedies.* • n. a book that describes herbs and their culinary and medicinal properties.

her•bar•i•um |(h)ər'berēəm| • n. (pl. **herbaria** |-'berēə|) a systematically arranged collection of dried plants.
■ a room or building housing such a collection. ■ a box, cabinet, or other receptacle in which dried plants are kept.

herb•i•cide |'(h)ərbə,sīd| • n. a substance that is toxic to plants and is used to destroy unwanted vegetation.
DERIVATIVES: **herb•i•ci•dal** adj.

Her•cu•le•an |ˌhərkyə'lēən; hər'kyōōlēən| • adj. requiring great strength or effort: *a Herculean task.*
■ (of a person) muscular and strong.

he•red•i•tar•i•an |hə,redi'terēən| • adj. of or relating to the theory that heredity is the primary influence on human behavior, intelligence, or other characteristics. • n. an advocate of such a view.
DERIVATIVES: **he•red•i•tar•i•an•ism** |-,izəm| n.

he•red•i•tar•y |hə'redi,terē| • adj. (of a title, office, or right) conferred by or based on inheritance: *members of the Polish aristocracy had hereditary right to elect the king.*
■ [attrib.] (of a person) holding a position by inheritance: *I am the hereditary chief of the Piscataway people.* ■ (of a characteristic or disease) determined by genetic factors and therefore able to be passed on from parents to their offspring or descendants: *cystic fibrosis is our most common fatal hereditary disease.* Cf. CONGENITAL. ■ of or relating to inheritance: *a form of hereditary succession and dynastic rule became standard practice.* ■ (of a mathematical set) defined such that every element that has a given relation to a member of the set is also a member of the set.
DERIVATIVES: **he•red•i•tar•i•ly** |hə,redi 'terəlē| adv. **he•red•i•tar•i•ness** |hə,redi 'terēnis| n.

her•e•sy |'herəsē| • n. (pl. **-ies**) belief or opinion contrary to orthodox religious (esp. Christian) doctrine: *Huss was burned for heresy | the doctrine was denounced as a heresy by the pope.*
■ opinion profoundly at odds with what is generally accepted: *the politician's heresies became the conventional wisdom of the day.*

her•e•tic |'herə,tik| • n. a person believing in or practicing religious heresy.
■ a person holding an opinion at odds with what is generally accepted.
DERIVATIVES: **he•ret•i•cal** |hə'reṭikəl| adj. **he•ret•i•cal•ly** |hə'reṭiklē| adv.

her•it•a•ble |'heritəbəl| • adj. able to be inherited, in particular: ■ (of a characteristic) transmissible from parent to offspring. ■ (of real property) capable of being inherited by heirs-at-law (heirs by right of blood). DERIVATIVES: **her•it•a•bil•i•ty** |ˌheritə'biltē| n. **her•it•a•bly** |-blē| adv.

herm |hərm| • n. a squared stone pillar with a carved head on top (typically of the god Hermes), used in ancient Greece as a boundary marker or a signpost.

her•maph•ro•dite |hər'mæfrədīt| • n. a person or animal having both male and female sex organs or other sexual characteristics, either abnormally or (in the case of some organisms) as the natural condition. ■ a plant having stamens and pistils in the same flower. ■ a person or thing combining opposite qualities or characteristics. • adj. of or denoting a person, animal, or plant of this kind: *hermaphrodite creatures in classical sculpture.* DERIVATIVES: **her•maph•ro•dit•ic** |hər ˌmæfrə'ditik| adj. **her•maph•ro•dit•i•cal** |hər'ˌmæfrə'ditikəl| adj. **her•maph•ro•dit•ism** |hər'mæfrədiˌtizəm| n.

her•me•neu•tic |ˌhərmə'n(y) o͞otik| • adj. concerning interpretation, esp. of the Bible or literary texts. • n. a method or theory of interpretation. DERIVATIVES: **her•me•neu•ti•cal** |-tiəkəl| adj. **her•me•neu•ti•cal•ly** |-tik(ə)lē| adv.

her•met•ic |hər'metik| • adj. 1 (of a seal or closure) complete and airtight: *a hermetic seal that ensures perfect waterproofing.* ■ insulated or protected from outside influences: *a hermetic society.* 2 (also **Hermetic**) of or relating to an ancient occult tradition encompassing alchemy, astrology, and theosophy. ■ esoteric; cryptic: *obscure and hermetic poems.* DERIVATIVES: **her•met•i•cal•ly** |hər'metiklē; -ik(ə)lē| adv. **her•met•i•cism** |hər'metiˌsizəm| n.

her•mit |'hərmit| • n. a person living in solitude as a religious discipline. ■ any person living in solitude or seeking to do so. DERIVATIVES: **her•mit•ic** |hər'mitik| adj.

her•mit•age |'hərmətij| • n. 1 the dwelling of a hermit, esp. when small and remote. 2 (**the Hermitage**) a major art museum in St. Petersburg, Russia, containing among its collections those begun by Catherine the Great. 3 (**the Hermitage**) estate near Nashville, Tennessee, the former home of U.S. President Andrew Jackson (1767–1845).

her•ni•a |'hərnēə| • n. (pl. **hernias** or **herniae** |-nēˌē|) a condition in which part of an organ is displaced and protrudes through the wall of the cavity containing it (often involving the intestine at a weak point in the abdominal wall). A **hiatus** (or **hiatal**) **hernia** involves part of the stomach protruding through the esophagus and against the diaphragm. In an **inguinal hernia**, part of the intestine protrudes through the abdominal

wall in the groin area. An **umbilical hernia** involves protrusion in the area of the umbilicus (navel). DERIVATIVES: **her•ni•al** adj.

her•pe•tol•o•gy |ˌhərpə'täləjē| • n. the branch of zoology concerned with reptiles and amphibians. DERIVATIVES: **her•pe•to•log•i•cal** |-tə'läjəkəl| adj. **her•pe•tol•o•gist** |-jist| n.

Hes•sian boot • n. a mercenary soldier from the German state of Hesse, esp. one who fought for the British during the American Revolution. ■ a military hireling; mercenary.

het•er•o•clite |'hetərəˌklīt| • adj. abnormal or irregular. • n. an abnormal thing or person. ■ an irregularly declined word, esp. a Greek or Latin noun. DERIVATIVES: **het•er•o•clit•ic** |ˌhetərə'klitik| adj.

het•er•o•dox |'hetərəˌdäks| • adj. not conforming with accepted or orthodox standards or beliefs: *heterodox views.* DERIVATIVES: **het•er•o•dox•y** n.

het•er•o•ge•ne•ous |ˌhetərə'jēnēəs| • adj. diverse in character or content: *a large and heterogeneous collection.* ■ (in chemistry) of or denoting a process involving substances in different phases (solid, liquid, or gaseous). ■ (in mathematics) incommensurable through being of different kinds, degrees, or dimensions. DERIVATIVES: **het•er•o•ge•ne•i•ty** |-jə'nēətē| n. **het•er•o•ge•ne•ous•ly** adv. **het•er•o•ge•ne•ous•ness** n.

USAGE: The correct spelling is **heterogeneous** but a fairly common misspelling is **heterogenous.** The reason for the error probably relates to the pronunciation, which, in rapid speech, often leaves out the extra **e.** (The word **heterogenous**, used in specialized medical and biological senses, means 'originating outside the organism,' but that is a different word, altered from **heterogeneous.**)

het•er•o•nym |'hetərəˌnim| • n. 1 each of two or more words that are spelled identically but have different sounds and meanings, such as *tear* meaning "rip" and *tear* meaning "liquid from the eye." Cf. HOMONYM, HOMOPHONE. 2 each of two or more words that are used to refer to the identical thing in different geographical areas of a speech community, such as *submarine sandwich, hoagie,* and *grinder.* 3 each of two words having the same meaning but derived from unrelated sources, for example *preface* and *foreword.* Cf. PARONYM. DERIVATIVES: **het•er•o•nym•ic** |ˌhetərə'nimik| adj. **het•er•on•y•mous** |ˌhetə'ränəməs| adj.

heu•ris•tic |hyo͞o'ristik| • adj. enabling a person to discover or learn something for himself or herself: *a "hands-on" or interactive heuristic approach to learning.* ■ (in computing) proceeding to a solution by

trial and error or by rules that are only loosely defined. • *n.* a heuristic process or method.
■ (**heuristics**) [usu. treated as sing.] the study and use of heuristic techniques.
DERIVATIVES: **heu•ris•ti•cal•ly** |-ik(ə)lē| *adv.*

hew |hyōō| • *v.* (past part. **hewn** |hyōōn| or **hewed**) 1 [trans.] chop or cut (something, esp. wood) with an ax, pick, or other tool: *hauling and hewing timber.*
■ (usu. **be hewn**) make or shape (something) by cutting or chopping a material such as wood or stone: *a seat* **hewn out of** *a fallen tree trunk.* 2 [intrans.] (**hew to**) conform or adhere to: *some artists took photographs that hewed to more traditional ideas of art.*

hex•a•gram |ˈheksəˌgram| • *n.* a figure formed of straight lines, in particular:
■ a star-shaped figure formed by two intersecting equilateral triangles. ■ any of a set of sixty-four figures made up of parallel whole or broken lines, occurring in the ancient Chinese *I Ching.*

hi•a•tus |hīˈātəs| • *n.* (pl. **hiatuses**) [usu. in sing.] a pause or gap in a sequence, series, or process: *there was a brief hiatus in the war with France.*
■ (in prosody and grammar) a break between two vowels coming together but not in the same syllable, as in *the ear* and *cooperate.*
DERIVATIVES: **hi•a•tal** |-ˈātəl| *adj.*

hi•ber•nate |ˈhībərˌnāt| • *v.* [intrans.] (of an animal or plant) spend the winter in a dormant state.
■ (of a person) remain inactive or indoors for an extended period: *pilots who have been hibernating during the winter months get their gliders out again.*
DERIVATIVES: **hi•ber•na•tion** |ˌhībərˈnā-SHən| *n.* **hi•ber•na•tor** |-ˌnātər| *n.*

Hi•ber•ni•an |hīˈbərnēən| • *adj.* of or concerning Ireland (now chiefly used in names): *the Royal Hibernian Academy.* • *n.* a native of Ireland (now chiefly used in names): *the Ancient Order of Hibernians.*

hi•dal•go |hiˈdälgō| • *n.* (pl. **-os**) (in Spanish-speaking regions) a gentleman.

hi•dro•sis |hiˈdrōsəs; hī-| • *n.* (in medicine) sweating.
DERIVATIVES: **hi•drot•ic** |hiˈdrätik; hī-| *adj.*

hi•er•ar•chi•cal |ˌhī(ə)ˈrärkikəl| • *adj.* of the nature of a hierarchy; arranged in order of rank: *the hierarchical bureaucracy of local govenment.*
DERIVATIVES: **hi•er•ar•chi•cal•ly** *adv.*

hi•er•ar•chy |ˈhī(ə)ˌrärkē| • *n.* (pl. **-ies**) a system or organization in which people or groups are ranked one above the other according to status or authority.
■ (**the hierarchy**) the upper echelons of a hierarchical system; those in authority: *the magazine was read quite widely even by some of the hierarchy.* ■ an arrangement or classification of things according to relative importance or inclusiveness: *a taxonomic hierarchy of phyla, classes, orders, families, genera, and species.*
■ (**the hierarchy**) the clergy of the Catholic

or Episcopal church; the religious authorities. ■ (in Christian theology) the traditional system of orders of angels and other heavenly beings.
DERIVATIVES: **hi•er•ar•chic** |ˌhī(ə)ˈrärkik| *adj.* **hi•er•ar•chi•za•tion** |ˌhī(ə)ˌrärki ˈzāSHən| *n.* **hi•er•ar•chize** |-ˌkīz| *v.*

hi•er•oc•ra•cy |ˌhī(ə)ˈräkrəsē| • *n.* (pl. **-ies**) rule by priests.
■ a ruling body composed of priests.
DERIVATIVES: **hi•er•o•crat•ic** |ˌhī(ə)rə ˈkrætik| *adj.*

hi•er•o•glyph |ˈhī(ə)rəˌglif| • *n.* a stylized picture of an object representing a word, syllable, or sound, as found in ancient Egyptian and other writing systems.

hi•er•o•glyph•ic |ˌhī(ə)rəˈglifik| • *n.* (**hiero-glyphics**) writing consisting of hieroglyphs.
■ enigmatic or incomprehensible symbols or writing: *tattered notebooks filled with illegible hieroglyphics.* • *adj.* of or written in hieroglyphs.
■ (esp. in art) stylized, symbolic, or enigmatic in effect.
DERIVATIVES: **hi•er•o•glyph•i•cal** *adj.* **hi•er•o•glyph•i•cal•ly** |-ik(ə)lē| *adv.*

high•brow |ˈhīˌbrow| • *adj.* scholarly or rarefied in taste: *their art had a mostly highbrow following.* • *n.* a person of this type.

high•fa•lu•tin |ˌhīfəˈlōōtn| (also **highfalu-ting** |-ˈlōōtiNG|) • *adj.* (esp. of speech, writing, or ideas) pompous or pretentious: *you don't want any highfalutin jargon.*

High Mass • *n.* (in the Roman Catholic Church) formerly, a mass with full ceremonial, including music and incense and typically having the assistance of a deacon and subdeacon.

hi•lar•i•ty |həˈleritē| • *n.* extreme amusement, esp. when expressed by laughter: *his incredulous expression was the cause of much hilarity.*
■ boisterous merriment: *the noisy hilarity of the streets.*

hin•ter•land |ˈhintərˌlænd| (also **hinter-lands**) • *n.* the often uncharted areas beyond a coastal district or a river's banks: *early settlers were driven from the coastal areas into the hinterland.*
■ an area surrounding a town or port and served by it: *a city had grown prosperous by exploiting its western hinterland.* ■ the remote areas of a region: *the mountain hinterland.* ■ an area lying beyond what is visible or known: *in the hinterland of his mind these things rose, dark and ominous.*

hip-hop • *n.* a style of popular music of African-American and Hispanic origin, featuring rap with an electronic backing.
■ a subculture defined by its adherence to this music, graffiti art, and characteristic styles in clothing and dance, esp. break dancing. • *adj.* of or relating to hip-hop music or subculture.

hip•po•cam•pus |ˌhipəˈkæmpəs| • *n.* (pl. **hippocampi** |-ˈkæmˌpī; -ˈkæmˌpē|) the elongated ridges on the floor of each lateral ventricle of the brain, thought to be the center of emotion, memory, and the autonomic nervous system.

hip•po•drome |'hipə,drōm| • *n.* **1** an arena used for equestrian or other sporting events. **2** (in ancient Greece or Rome) a course for chariot or horse races.

hir•cine |'hər,sīn; -sən| • *adj.* of or resembling a goat.

hire•ling |'hīrliNG| • *n.* a person employed to undertake menial work, esp. on a casual basis.

hir•sute |'hər,sōōt; hər'sōōt; 'hir,sōōt| • *adj.* having rough or shaggy hair; hairy: *their hirsute chests.*

DERIVATIVES: **hir•sute•ness** *n.*

His•pan•ic |hi'spænik| • *adj.* of or relating to Spain or to Spanish-speaking countries, esp. those of Latin America.

■ of or relating to Spanish-speaking people or their culture, esp. in the US. • *n.* a Spanish-speaking person living in the US, esp. one of Latin American descent.

DERIVATIVES: **His•pan•i•cize** |hi'spæni ,sīz| *v.*

USAGE: In the US, **Hispanic** is the standard accepted term when referring to Spanish-speaking people living in the US. Other, more specific, terms such as **Latino** and **Chicano** are also used where occasion demands. See also **usage** at CHICANO.

his•tor•ic |hi'stôrik; -'stär-| • *adj.* **1** famous or important in history, or potentially so: *we are standing on a historic site | a time of historic change.*

■ of or concerning history; of the past: *eruptions in historic times.* **2** (of a tense) used in the narration of past events, esp. Latin and Greek imperfect and pluperfect.

USAGE: In general, **historic** means 'notable in history, significant in history,' as in a Supreme Court decision, a battlefield, or a great discovery. **Historical** means 'relating to history or past events,' as in an *historical society* or *document.* To write **historic** instead of **historical** may imply a greater significance than is warranted: an **historical** lecture may simply tell about something that happened, whereas an **historic** lecture would in some way change the course of human events. It would be correct to say, *Professor Suarez's historical lecture on the Old Southwest was given at the historic mission church.* Note also that both of these words, traditionally preceded by *a,* are now often used with *an: a historic moment, an historic moment.*

his•tor•i•cal |hi'stôrikəl; -'stär-| • *adj.* of or concerning history; concerning past events: *the historical background to such studies.*

■ belonging to the past, not the present: *famous historical figures.* ■ (esp. of a novel or movie) set in the past. ■ (of the study of a subject) based on an analysis of its development over a period: *for the Darwinians, biogeography became a historical science.*

his•tor•i•cism |hi'stôri,sizəm; -stär-| • *n.*

1 the theory that social and cultural phenomena are determined by history.

■ the belief that historical events are governed by laws. **2** the tendency to regard historical development as the most basic aspect of human existence. **3** (in artistic and architectural contexts) excessive regard for past styles.

DERIVATIVES: **his•tor•i•cist** *n.*

his•to•ri•og•ra•phy |hi,stôrē'ägrəfē; -stär-| • *n.* the study of historical writing.

■ the writing of history.

DERIVATIVES: **his•to•ri•og•ra•pher** |-'ägrəfər| *n.* **his•to•ri•o•graph•ic** |-ə'græfik| *adj.* **his•to•ri•o•graph•i•cal** |-ə'græfikəl| *adj.*

his•tri•on•ic |,histrē'änik| • *adj.* overly theatrical or melodramatic in character or style: *a histrionic outburst.*

■ of or concerning actors or acting: *histrionic talents.* ■ (in psychiatry) denoting a personality disorder marked by shallow, volatile emotions and attention-seeking behavior. • *n.* **1** (**histrionics**) exaggerated dramatic behavior designed to attract attention: *discussions around the issue have been based as much in histrionics as in history.*

■ dramatic performance; theater. **2** an actor.

DERIVATIVES: **his•tri•on•i•cal•ly** |-ik(ə)lē| *adv.*

hoar |hôr| • *adj.* grayish white; gray or gray-haired with age. • *n.* hoarfrost (a crystalline water-vapor deposit formed in clear, still freezing weaather on vegetation, etc.).

hoard |hôrd| • *n.* a stock or store of money or valued objects, typically one that is secret or carefully guarded: *he came back to rescue his little hoard of gold.*

■ an ancient store of coins or other valuable artifacts: *a hoard of Romano-British bronzes.*

■ an amassed store of useful information or facts, retained for future use: *a hoard of secret information about the work.* • *v.* [trans.] amass (money or valued objects) and hide or store away: *thousands of antiques hoarded by a compulsive collector.*

■ accumulate a supply of (something) in a time of scarcity: *many of the boat people had hoarded rations.* ■ reserve in the mind for future use: [as adj.] (**hoarded**) *a year's worth of hoarded resentments and grudges.*

DERIVATIVES: **hoard•er** *n.*

USAGE: The words **hoard** and **horde** have some similarities in meaning and are pronounced the same; so they are therefore sometimes confused. A **hoard** is 'a secret stock or store of something,' as in *a hoard of treasure,* while a **horde** is a disparaging word for 'a large group of people,' as in *hordes of fans descended on the stage,* or, in an old cliché, *the Mongol hordes of Genghis Khan.*

hoar•frost |'hôr,frôst; -,fräst| • *n.* a grayish-white crystalline deposit of frozen water vapor formed in clear still weather on vegetation, fences, etc.

hoar•y |'hôrē| • *adj.* (**hoarier, hoariest**) **1** grayish-white: *hoary cobwebs.*

■ (of a person) having gray or white hair; aged:

a hoary old fellow with a face of white stubble.
■ [attrib.] used in names of animals and plants covered with whitish fur or short hairs, e.g., **hoary bat, hoary cress**. **2** old and trite: *that hoary notion that bigger is better.*
DERIVATIVES: **hoar·i·ly** |'hôrəlē| *adv.* **hoar·i·ness** *n.*

hoax |hōks| • *n.* a humorous or malicious deception: *they recognized the plan as a hoax* | [as adj.] *he was accused of making hoax calls.* • *v.* [trans.] deceive with a hoax.
DERIVATIVES: **hoax·er** *n.*

hob·ble·de·hoy |'häbəldē,hoi| • *n.* a clumsy or awkward youth. • *adj.* awkward or clumsy: *his hobbledehoy hands.*

hodge·podge |'häj,päj| (Brit. **hotchpotch**) • *n.* [in sing.] a confused mixture: *a hodge-podge of modern furniture and antiques.*

hoi pol·loi |'hoi pə,loi| • *plural n.* (usu. **the hoi polloi**) the masses; the common people: *avoid mixing with the hoi polloi.*

USAGE: **1 Hoi** is the Greek word for **the**, and the phrase **hoi polloi** means 'the many.' This has led some traditionalists to insist that **hoi polloi** should not be used in English with **the**, since that would be to state the word twice. Such arguments miss the point: once established in English, expressions such as **hoi polloi** are treated as a fixed unit and are subject to the rules and conventions of English. Evidence shows that use with **the** has now become an accepted part of standard English usage.
2 Hoi polloi is sometimes used incorrectly to mean 'upper class,' i.e., the exact opposite of its normal meaning. It seems likely that the confusion arose by association with the similar-sounding but otherwise unrelated word **hoity-toity**.

hoi·ty-toi·ty |'hoitē 'toitē| • *adj.* **1** haughty; snobbish: *hoity-toity models.* **2** frolicsome.

Hol·arc·tic |häl'ärktik; hō'lärk-; -'artik| • *adj.* of, relating to, or denoting a zoogeographical region comprising the Nearctic and Palearctic regions combined (i.e. all the cold and temperate zones of the Northern Hemisphere). The two continents have been linked intermittently by the Bering land bridge, and the faunas are closely related.
■ [as n.] (**the Holarctic**) the Holarctic region.

ho·li·ness |'hōlēnis| • *n.* the state of being holy: *a life of holiness and total devotion to God.*
■ (**His/Your Holiness**) a title given to the pope, Orthodox patriarchs, and the Dalai Lama, or used in addressing them.

ho·lism |'hōl,izəm| • *n.* the theory that parts of a whole are in intimate interconnection, such that they cannot exist independently of the whole, or cannot be understood without reference to the whole, which is thus regarded as greater than the sum of its parts. Holism is often applied to mental states, language, and ecology. Cf. ATOMISM.
■ (in medicine) the treating of the whole person, taking into account mental and social factors, rather than just the physical symptoms of a disease.

DERIVATIVES: **ho·list** *adj. & n.*
ho·lis·tic |hō'listik| • *adj.* (in philosophy) characterized by comprehension of the parts of something as intimately interconnected and explicable only by reference to the whole.
■ (in medicine) characterized by the treatment of the whole person, taking into account mental and social factors, rather than just the physical symptoms of a disease.
DERIVATIVES: **ho·lis·ti·cal·ly** |-ik(ə)lē| *adv.*

hol·o·caust |'hälə,kôst; 'hōlə-| • *n.* **1** destruction or slaughter on a mass scale, esp. caused by fire or nuclear war: *a nuclear holocaust* | *the threat of imminent holocaust.*
■ (**the Holocaust**) the mass murder of Jews under the German Nazi regime during the period 1941–45. More than 6 million European Jews, as well as members of other persecuted groups, such as gypsies and homosexuals, were murdered, most at concentration camps. **2** a Jewish sacrificial offering that is burned completely on an altar.

Hol·o·cene |'hälə,sēn; 'hōlə-| • *adj.* (in geology) of, relating to, or denoting the present epoch, which is the second epoch in the Quaternary period and followed the Pleistocene. Also called *recent.*
■ [as n.] (**the Holocene**) the Holocene epoch or the system of deposits laid down during this time.

The Holocene epoch has lasted from about 10,000 years ago to the present day. It covers the period since the ice retreated after the last glaciation and is sometimes regarded as just another interglacial period.

hol·o·gram |'hälə,græm; 'hōlə-| • *n.* a three-dimensional image formed by the interference of light beams from a laser or other coherent light source.
■ a photograph of an interference pattern that, when suitably illuminated, produces a three-dimensional image.

hol·o·graph |'hälə,græf; 'hōlə-| • *n.* a manuscript handwritten by the person named as its author: [as adj.] *a holograph letter by Abraham Lincoln.*

hol·og·ra·phy |hō'lägrəfē| • *n.* the study or production of holograms.
DERIVATIVES: **hol·o·graph** *v.* **hol·o·graph·ic** |,hälə'græfik; ,hōlə-| *adj.* **hol·o·graph·i·cal·ly** |,hälə'græfiklē; ,hōlə-| *adv.*

hol·oph·ra·sis |hə'läfrəsis| • *n.* the expression of a whole phrase in a single word, for example *howdy* for *how do you do.*
■ the learning of linguistic elements as whole chunks by very young children acquiring their first language, for example *it's all gone* learned as *allgone.* Cf. POLYSYNTHETIC.
DERIVATIVES: **hol·o·phrase** |'hälə,frāz; 'hōlə-| *n.* **hol·o·phras·tic** |,hälə'fræstik; hōlə-| *adj.*

hom·age |'(h)ämij| • *n.* special honor or respect shown publicly: *they **paid homage** to the local boy who became president* | *a masterly work written **in homage to** Beethoven.*
■ formal public acknowledgment of feudal allegiance: *doing **homage to** his personal lord.*

home•ly |ˈhōmlē| • *adj.* (**homelier, homeliest**) **1** (of a person) unattractive in appearance. **2** Brit. (of a place or surroundings) simple but cozy and comfortable, as in one's own home; homey: *a modern hotel with a homely atmosphere.* ■ unsophisticated and unpretentious: *homely pleasures.*
DERIVATIVES: **home•li•ness** *n.*

ho•me•op•a•thy |ˌhōmēˈäpəтнē| (Brit. also **homoeopathy**) • *n.* a system of nonscientific medicine in which disease is treated by minute doses of natural substances that in a healthy person would produce symptoms of disease. Cf. ALLOPATHY.
DERIVATIVES: **ho•me•o•path•ic** |ˌhōmēə ˈpæтнik| *adj.* **ho•me•o•path•i•cal•ly** |ˌhōmēəˈpæтнik(ə)lē| *adv.*

ho•me•o•sta•sis |ˌhōmēəˈstāsis| • *n.* (pl. **homeostases**) the tendency toward a relatively stable equilibrium between interdependent elements, esp. as maintained by physiological processes.
DERIVATIVES: **ho•me•o•stat•ic** |-ˈstæṭik| *adj.*

Ho•mer•ic |hōˈmerik| • *adj.* of or in the style of Homer or the epic poems (the *Iliad* and the *Odyssey*) ascribed to him. ■ of Bronze Age Greece as described in these poems: *the mists of the Homeric age.* ■ epic and large-scale: *we will have to exert a Homeric effort.*

home•stead |ˈhōmˌsted| • *n.* **1** a house, esp. a farmhouse, and outbuildings. **2** an area of land (in 19th-century U.S. history usually 160 acres) granted to a settler as a home. **Urban homesteading** is the practice, under a federal program, of taking over and rehabilitating housing in poverty-stricken city areas, agreeing to live there for a certain period of time.
DERIVATIVES: **home•stead•er** *n.* **home•stead•ing** *n.*

hom•i•cide |ˈhäməˌsīd; ˈhōmə-| • *n.* the killing of one person by another: *he was charged with homicide* | *two thirds of homicides in the county were drug-related.* **Justifiable homicide** incurs neither blame nor criminal liability because it is commited in the execution of one's duties. Other kinds include **excusable homicide**, brought about in self-defense or by accident, and various grades of criminal homicide including murder and manslaughter. ■ (often **Homicide**) the police department that deals with such killings: *a man from Homicide.* ■ a killer; a murderer.

hom•i•let•ic |ˌhäməˈleṭik| • *adj.* of the nature of or characteristic of a homily: *homiletic literature.* • *n.* (**homiletics**) the art of preaching or writing sermons: *the teaching of homiletics.*

hom•i•ly |ˈhäməlē| • *n.* (pl. **-ies**) a religious discourse that is intended primarily for spiritual edification rather than doctrinal instruction; a sermon. ■ a tedious moralizing discourse: *she delivered her homily about the need for patience.*
DERIVATIVES: **hom•i•list** |-ist| *n.*

hom•i•nid |ˈhäməˌnid| • *n.* a primate of a family (Hominidae) that includes humans and their fossil ancestors.

hom•i•noid |ˈhäməˌnoid| • *n.* a primate of a group that includes humans, their fossil ancestors, and the great apes. •Superfamily Hominoidea: families Hominidae (hominids) and Pongidae. • *adj.* of or relating to primates of this group; hominid or pongid.

ho•mo•e•rot•ic |ˌhōmō-iˈräṭik| • *adj.* concerning or arousing sexual desire centered on a person of the same sex: *homoerotic images.*
DERIVATIVES: **ho•mo•e•rot•i•cism** |-ˌsizəm| *n.*

ho•mo•ge•ne•ous |ˌhōməˈjēnēəs| • *adj.* of the same kind; alike: *timbermen prefer to deal with homogeneous woods.* ■ consisting of parts all of the same kind: *culturally speaking the farmers constitute an extremely homogeneous group.* ■ (in mathematics) containing terms all of the same degree.
DERIVATIVES: **ho•mo•ge•ne•i•ty** |ˌhōməjə ˈnēitē; ˌhämə-| *n.* **ho•mo•ge•ne•ous•ly** *adv.* **ho•mo•ge•ne•ous•ness** *n.*

USAGE: **Homogeneous**, 'of the same kind,' should not be confused with the more specialized biological term **homogenous**, 'having a common descent.' **Homogenous** should be left to the biologists and geneticists. See also **usage** at HETEROGENEOUS.

ho•mog•e•nize |həˈmäjəˌnīz| • *v.* [trans.] **1** subject (milk) to a process in which the fat droplets are emulsified and the cream does not separate: [as adj.] (**homogenized**) *homogenized milk.* ■ (in biology) prepare a suspension of cell constituents from (tissue) by physical treatment in a liquid. **2** make uniform or similar.
DERIVATIVES: **ho•mog•e•ni•za•tion** |həˌmäjənizˈāsнən| *n.* **ho•mog•e•niz•er** *n.*

hom•o•graph |ˈhäməˌgræf; ˈhōmə-| • *n.* each of two or more words spelled the same but not necessarily pronounced the same and having different meanings and origins (e.g., *bow* 'arrow-firing weapon' and *bow* 'front of a ship').
DERIVATIVES: **hom•o•graph•ic** |ˌhämə ˈgræfik| *adj.*

ho•mol•o•gous |hōˈmäləgəs; hə-| • *adj.* having the same relation, relative position, or structure, in particular: ■ (of organs) similar in position, structure, and evolutionary origin but not necessarily in function: *a seal's flipper is **homologous with** the human arm.* Cf. ANALOGOUS. ■ (of chromosomes) pairing at meiosis and having the same structural features and pattern of genes. ■ (of a series of chemical compounds) having the same functional group but differing in composition by a fixed group of atoms.

hom•o•nym |ˈhäməˌnim| • *n.* each of two or more words having the same pronunciation but different meanings, origins, or spelling (e.g., *to, too,* and *two*); a homophone. ■ each of two or more words having the same spelling but different meanings and origins (e.g., *pole* 'a piece of wood' and *pole* 'place on the earth's surface'); a homograph. ■ (in biology) a Latin name that is identical to that of a different organism, the newer of the two names being invalid.

DERIVATIVES: **hom•o•nym•ic** |ˌhōmə'nimik| *adj.* **ho•mon•y•mous** |hō'mänəməs| *adj.* **ho•mon•y•my** |hō'mänəmē| *n.*

ho•mo•pho•bi•a |ˌhōmə'fōbēə| • *n.* an extreme and irrational aversion to homosexuality and homosexual people.

DERIVATIVES: **ho•mo•phobe** |'hōmə,fōb| *n.* **ho•mo•pho•bic** |-'fōbik| *adj.*

ho•mo•phone |'hämə,fōn; 'hōmə-| • *n.* each of two or more words having the same pronunciation but different meanings, origins, or spelling, e.g., *new* and *knew*.

■ each of a set of symbols denoting the same sound or group of sounds.

ho•mo•phon•ic |ˌhämə'fänik; ˌhōmə-| • *adj.* **1** (in music) characterized by the movement of accompanying parts in the same rhythm as the melody. Cf. POLYPHONIC. **2** another term for HOMOPHONOUS.

DERIVATIVES: **ho•mo•phon•i•cal•ly** |-ik-(ə)lē; ˌhōmə',fänək(ə)lē| *adv.*

ho•moph•o•nous |hō'mäfənəs; hə-| • *adj.* (of a word or words) having the same pronunciation as another or others but different meaning, origin, or spelling.

DERIVATIVES: **ho•moph•o•ny** |-'mäfənē| *n.*

hon•cho |'hänCHŌ| *informal* • *n.* (pl. **-os**) a leader or manager; the person in charge: *the company's **head honcho**.* • *v.* (**-oes, -oed**) [trans.] be in charge of (a project or situation): *the task at hand was to honcho an eighteen-wheeler to St. Louis.*

hone |hōn| • *v.* [trans.] sharpen with a whetstone.

■ (usu. **be honed**) make sharper or more focused or efficient: *their appetites were honed by fresh air and exercise.* • *n.* a whetstone, esp. one used to sharpen razors.

■ the fine-grained stone of which whetstones are made.

hon•ky |'häNGkē; 'hawNGkē| • *n.* (pl. **-ies**) a derogatory term used by black people for a white person or for white people collectively.

hon•o•rar•i•um |ˌänə'rerēəm| • *n.* (pl. **honorariums** or **honoraria** |-'rerēə|) a payment given for professional services that are rendered traditionally, or officially, without charge.

hon•or•ar•y |'änə,rerē| • *adj.* **1** conferred as an honor, without the usual requirements or functions: *an honorary doctorate.*

■ (of a person) holding such a title or position: *an honorary member of the club.* **2** *Brit.* (of an office or its holder) unpaid: *Honorary Secretary of the Association.*

hon•or•if•ic |ˌänə'rifik| • *adj.* given as a mark of respect: *an honorific award for military valor.*

■ (of an office or position) given as a mark of respect, but having few or no duties: *the post is merely honorific.* ■ denoting a form of address showing high status, politeness, or respect: *an honorific title for addressing women.* • *n.* a title or word implying or expressing

high status, politeness, or respect: *he will be able to put the honorific after his name:* licenciado, *"college graduate."*

DERIVATIVES: **hon•or•if•i•cal•ly** |ik(ə)lē| *adv.*

ho•no•ris cau•sa |ä'nōros 'kōzə; 'kowsə| • *adv.* (esp. of a degree awarded without examination) as a mark of esteem: *the artist has been awarded the degree honoris causa.*

hoose•gow |'hōōs,gow| • *n.* informal a jail: *the sheriff got ol' Loney in the hoosegow.*

hope•ful•ly |'hōpfəlē| • *adv.* **1** in a hopeful manner: *he rode on hopefully.* **2** [sentence adverb] it is to be hoped that: *hopefully it should be finished by next year.*

USAGE: The traditional sense of **hopefully**, 'in a hopeful manner,' has been used since 1593. The first recorded use of **hopefully** as a sentence adverb, meaning 'it is to be hoped that' (as in *hopefully, we'll see you tomorrow*), appears in 1702 the *Magnalia Christi Americana*, written by the Massachusetts theologian and writer Cotton Mather (1663–1728). This second use is now much commoner than the first use. The use as a sentence adverb, however, is widely held to be incorrect. It is not only **hopefully** that has the power to annoy, but the use of sentence adverbs in general (*frankly, honestly, regrettably, seriously*), a construction found in English since at least the 1600s, but more common in recent decades. Attentive ears are particularly bothered when the sentence that follows does not match the promise of the introductory adverb, as when "Frankly" is followed not by honesty but by a self-serving "spin" or twist. Follett's *Modern American Usage* points out that in sentence adverbs the point of view is obscured: "they fail to tell us who does the hoping, the sorrowing, or the being thankful."

horde |hôrd| • *n.* **1** a large group of people: *he was surrounded by **a horde of** tormenting relatives.*

■ an army or tribe of nomadic warriors: *Tartar hordes.* **2** (in anthropology) a loosely knit small social group typically consisting of about five families.

USAGE: The words **hoard** and **horde** are quite distinct; see **usage** at HOARD.

ho•rol•o•gy |hə'räləjē| • *n.* the study and measurement of time.

■ the art of making clocks and watches.

DERIVATIVES: **ho•rol•o•ger** |-jər| *n.* **hor•o•log•ic** |ˌhôrə'läjik| *adj.* **hor•o•log•i•cal** |ˌhôrə'läjikəl| *adj.* **ho•rol•o•gist** |-jist| *n.*

hors d'oeuvre |ôr 'dərv| • *n.* (pl. same or **hors d'oeuvres** |'dərv; 'dərvz|) a small savory dish, typically one served as an appetizer at the beginning of a meal.

horse lat•i•tudes • *plural n.* a belt of calm air and sea occurring in both the northern and southern hemispheres between the trade winds and the westerlies.

hor•ta•to•ry |'hôrtə,tôrē| • *adj.* tending or

aiming to exhort: *the central bank relied on hortatory messages and voluntary compliance.*
DERIVATIVES: **hor•ta•tion** |ˌhôrˈtāSHən| *n.* **hor•ta•tive** |ˈhôrtətiv| *adj.*

hor•ti•cul•ture |ˈhôrtəˌkəlCHər| • *n.* the art or practice of garden cultivation and management.
DERIVATIVES: **hor•ti•cul•tur•al** |ˌhôrtəˈkəlCHərəl| *adj.* **hor•ti•cul•tur•al•ist** |ˌhôrtəˈkəlCHərəlist| *n.* **hor•ti•cul•tur•ist** |ˌhôrtəˈkəlCHərist| *n.*

hos•pice |ˈhäspis| • *n.* a home providing care for the sick, esp. the terminally ill.
■ a lodging for travelers, esp. one run by a religious order.

host • *n.* (usu. **the Host**) (in Christianity) the bread consecrated in the Eucharist: *the elevation of the Host.*

hos•tel |ˈhästl| • *n.* an establishment that provides cheap food and lodging for a specific group of people, such as students, workers, or travelers, esp. those on foot or bicycle.
■ an inn providing accommodation.

hos•tel•ry |ˈhästlrē| • *n.* (pl. **-ies**) older term for an inn (providing lodging and entertainment).

hos•tile wit•ness • *n.* (in law) a witness who is antagonistic to the party calling him or her and, if the court permits, may be cross-examined by that party.

hos•tler |ˈ(h)äslər| (also **ostler**) • *n.* a person employed to look after the horses of people staying at an inn.
■ a person employed to service vehicles or other machinery when it is not in use.

ho•te•lier |ˌōtelˈyā; hōˈtelyər| • *n.* a person who owns or manages a hotel.

hoy•den |ˈhoidn| • *n.* a boisterous girl.
DERIVATIVES: **hoy•den•ish** *adj.*

hu•bris |ˈ(h)yo͞obris| • *n.* excessive pride or self-confidence.
■ (in Greek tragedy) excessive pride toward or defiance of the gods, leading to nemesis.
DERIVATIVES: **hu•bris•tic** |(h)yo͞oˈbristik| *adj.*

huck•ster |ˈhəkstər| • *n.* a person who sells small items, either door-to-door or from a stall or small store.
■ a mercenary person eager to make a profit out of anything. ■ a publicity agent or advertising copywriter, esp. for radio or television. Cf. FLACK[1]. • *v.* [trans.] promote or sell (something, typically a product of questionable value).
■ [intrans.] bargain; haggle.
DERIVATIVES: **huck•ster•ism** |-izəm| *n.*

hue and cry • *n.* a loud clamor or public outcry.
■ a loud cry calling for the pursuit and capture of a criminal. In former English law, the cry had to be raised by the inhabitants of a hundred (a subdivision of a county or shire) in which a robbery had been committed, if they were not to become liable for the damages suffered by the victim.

Hu•gue•not |ˈhyo͞ogəˌnät| • *n.* a French Protestant of the 16th–17th centuries. Largely Calvinist, the Huguenots suffered severe persecution at the hands of the Catholic majority, and many thousands emigrated from France.

hu•mane |(h)yo͞oˈmān| • *adj.* **1** having or showing compassion or benevolence: *regulations ensuring the humane treatment of animals.*
■ inflicting the minimum of pain: *humane methods of killing.* **2** (of a branch of learning) intended to have a civilizing or refining effect on people: *the center emphasizes economics as a humane discipline.*
DERIVATIVES: **hu•mane•ly** *adv.* **hu•mane•ness** *n.*

hu•man•ism |ˈ(h)yo͞oməˌnizəm| • *n.* an outlook or system of thought attaching prime importance to human rather than divine or supernatural matters. Humanist beliefs stress the potential value and goodness of human beings, emphasize common human needs, and seek solely rational ways of solving human problems.
■ (often **Humanism**) a Renaissance cultural movement that turned away from medieval scholasticism and revived interest in ancient Greek and Roman thought. ■ (among some contemporary writers) a system of thought criticized as being centered on the notion of the rational, autonomous self and ignoring the unintegrated and conditioned nature of the individual.
DERIVATIVES: **hu•man•ist** *n.* & *adj.* **hu•man•is•tic** |ˌ(h)yo͞oməˈnistik| *adj.* **hu•man•is•ti•cal•ly** |ˌ(h)yo͞oməˈnistik(ə)lē| *adv.*

hu•man•i•tar•i•an |(h)yo͞oˌmænəˈterēən| • *adj.* concerned with or seeking to promote human welfare: *groups sending humanitarian aid* | *a humanitarian organization.* • *n.* a person who seeks to promote human welfare; a philanthropist.
DERIVATIVES: **hu•man•i•tar•i•an•ism** |-ˌnizəm| *n.*

USAGE: Sentences such as *this is the worst humanitarian disaster this country has seen* are a loose use of the adjective **humanitarian** to mean 'human.' This use is quite common, esp. in "live reports" on television, but is not generally considered good style.

hu•man•i•ty |(h)yo͞oˈmænitē| • *n.* (pl. **-ies**) **1** the human race; human beings collectively: *appalling crimes against humanity.*
■ the fact or condition of being human; human nature: *a few moments when Soviets and Canadians shared their common humanity.* **2** humaneness; benevolence: *he praised them for their standards of humanity, care, and dignity.* **3** (**humanities**) learning or literature concerned with human culture, esp. literature, history, art, music, and philosophy: *a curriculum based on the humanities.*

hu•man•oid |ˈ(h)yo͞oməˌnoid| • *adj.* having an appearance or character resembling that of a human. • *n.* (esp. in science fiction) a being resembling a human in its shape.

hum•bug |ˈhəmˌbəg| • *n.* deceptive or false talk or behavior: *the manufacturer's claims are sheer humbug.*

■ a hypocrite: *you see what a humbug I am.* • *v.* (**humbugged, humbugging**) [trans.] deceive; trick: *to humbug his humble neighbors was not difficult.*

■ [intrans.] act like a fraud or sham.
DERIVATIVES: **hum•bug•ger•y** |-,bəg(ə)rē| *n.*

hu•mec•tant |(h)yoo͞'mektənt| • *adj.* retaining or preserving moisture. • *n.* a substance, esp. a skin lotion or a food additive, used to reduce the loss of moisture.

hu•mid |'(h)yoo͞mid| • *adj.* marked by a relatively high level of water vapor in the atmosphere: *a hot and humid day.*
DERIVATIVES: **hu•mid•i•ty** *n.* **hu•mid•ly** *adv.*

hu•mid•i•ty |(h)yoo͞'miditē| • *n.* (pl. **-ies**) the state or quality of being humid.

■ a quantity representing the amount of water vapor in the atmosphere or a gas: *the temperature is seventy-seven, the humidity in the low thirties.* ■ atmospheric moisture. ■ (**relative humidity**) the amount of water vapor present in the air expressed as a percentage of the amount needed for saturation at the same temperature.

hu•mil•i•ty |(h)yoo͞'militē| • *n.* a modest or low view of one's own importance; humbleness.

hum•mock |'həmək| • *n.* a hillock, knoll, or mound.

■ a hump or ridge in an ice field. ■ (also **hammock**) a piece of forested ground rising above a marsh or plain.
DERIVATIVES: **hum•mock•y** *adj.*

hu•mor |'(h)yoo͞mər| (Brit.**humour**) • *n.* **1** the quality of being amusing or comic, esp. as expressed in literature or speech: *his tales are full of humor.*

■ the ability to perceive or express humor or to appreciate a joke: *their inimitable brand of humor* | *she has a great **sense of humor**.* **2** a mood or state of mind: *her **good humor** vanished* | *the clash hadn't improved his humor.*

■ an inclination or whim. **3** (also **cardinal humor**) (in medieval theory) each of the four chief fluids of the body (blood, phlegm, yellow bile (choler), and black bile (melancholy)) that were thought to determine a person's physical and mental qualities by the relative proportions in which they were present. • *v.* [trans.] comply with the wishes of (someone) in order to keep them content, however unreasonable such wishes might be: *she was always humoring him to prevent trouble.*

■ adapt or accommodate oneself to (something).
DERIVATIVES: **hu•mor•less** *adj.* **hu•mor•less•ly** *adv.* **hu•mor•less•ness** *n.*

hu•mor•esque |,(h)yoo͞mə'resk| • *n.* a short, lively piece of music. Cf. CAPRICE.

hu•mus |'(h)yoo͞məs| • *n.* the organic component of soil, formed by the decomposition of leaves and other plant material by soil microorganisms.

hus•band |'həzbənd| • *v.* [trans.] use (re-

sources) economically; conserve: *the need to husband his remaining strength.*
DERIVATIVES: **hus•band•er** *n.*

hus•band•man |'həzbəndmən| • *n.* (pl. **-men**) a person who cultivates the land; a farmer.

hus•band•ry |'həzbəndrē| • *n.* **1** the care, cultivation, and breeding of crops and animals: *crop husbandry.* **2** management and conservation of resources.

hus•sar |hə'zär| • *n.* (in the 15th century) a Hungarian light horseman.

■ a soldier in a light cavalry regiment in various European armies that had adopted a dress uniform modeled on that of the Hungarian hussars.

hy•brid |'hī,brid| • *n.* a thing made by combining two different elements; a mixture: *the final text is a **hybrid of** the stage play and the film.*

■ (in biology) the offspring of two plants or animals of different species or varieties, such as a mule (a hybrid of a donkey and a horse): *a **hybrid of** wheat and rye.* ■ a person of mixed racial or cultural origin. ■ a word formed from elements taken from different languages, for example *television* (tele- from Greek, *vision* from Latin). • *adj.* of mixed character; composed of mixed parts: *Mexico's hybrid culture.*

■ bred as a hybrid from different species or varieties: *a hybrid variety* | *hybrid offspring.*
DERIVATIVES: **hy•brid•ism** |'hībrə,dizəm| *n.* **hy•brid•i•ty** |hī'briditē| *n.*

Hy•dra |'hīdrə| **1** (in Greek mythology) a many-headed snake whose heads grew again as they were cut off, killed by Hercules.

■ [as *n.*] (**hydra**) a thing that is hard to overcome or resist because of its pervasive and enduring quality or its many aspects.

hy•drate • *n.* |'hī,drāt| a compound, typically a crystalline one, in which water molecules are chemically bound to another compound or an element. • *v.* [trans.] cause to absorb water.

■ combine chemically with water molecules: [as *adj.*] (**hydrated**) *hydrated silicate crystals.*
DERIVATIVES: **hy•drat•a•ble** *adj.* **hy•dra•tion** |hī'drāsHən| *n.* **hy•dra•tor** |-tər| *n.*

hy•drau•lic |hī'drôlik| • *adj.* **1** denoting, relating to, or operated by a liquid moving in a confined space under pressure: *hydraulic fluid* | *hydraulic lifting gear.* **2** of or relating to the science of hydraulics. **3** (of cement) hardening under water.
DERIVATIVES: **hy•drau•li•cal•ly** |-ik(ə)lē| *adv.*

hy•drau•lics |hī'drôliks| • *plural n.* **1** [usu. treated as sing.] the branch of science and technology concerned with the conveyance of liquids through pipes and channels, esp. as a source of mechanical force or control. **2** hydraulic systems, mechanisms, or forces.

hy•dro•e•lec•tric |,hīdrōə'lektrik| • *adj.* relating to or denoting the generation of electricity using flowing water (typically from a reservoir held behind a dam or other barrier) to drive a turbine that powers a generator.

DERIVATIVES: **hy·dro·e·lec·tric·i·ty** |-əlek 'trisiṯē| *n.*

hy·dro·foil |'hīdrə,foil| • *n.* a boat whose hull is fitted underneath with shaped vanes (foils) that lift the hull clear of the water to increase the boat's speed.
▪ another term for *foil*, the shaped vane used by such a boat.

hy·drog·ra·phy |hī'drägrəfē| • *n.* the science of surveying and charting bodies of water, such as seas, lakes, and rivers.
DERIVATIVES: **hy·drog·ra·pher** |-fər| *n.* **hy·dro·graph·ic** |,hīdrə'græfik| *adj.* **hy·dro·graph·i·cal** |,hīdrə'græfikəl| *adj.* **hy·dro·graph·i·cal·ly** |,hīdrə'græfik(ə)lē| *adv.*

hy·drol·o·gy |hī'dräləjē| • *n.* the branch of science concerned with the properties of the earth's water, esp. its movement in relation to land.
DERIVATIVES: **hy·dro·log·ic** |,hīdrə'läjik| *adj.* **hy·dro·log·i·cal** *adj.* **hy·dro·log·i·cal·ly** |,hīdrə'läjik(ə)lē| *adv.* **hy·drol·o·gist** |-jist|

hy·drop·a·thy |hī'dräpəTHē| • *n.* the treatment of illness through the use of water, either internally or through external means such as steam baths (not now a part of orthodox medicine).
DERIVATIVES: **hy·dro·path·ic** |,hīdrə 'pæTHik| *adj.* **hy·drop·a·thist** |-THist| *n.*

hy·dro·pho·bi·a |,hīdrə'fōbēə| • *n.* extreme or irrational fear of water, esp. as a symptom of rabies in humans.
▪ rabies, esp. in humans.

hy·dro·plane |'hīdrə,plān| • *n.* **1** a light fast motorboat designed to skim over the surface of water. **2** a finlike attachment that enables a moving submarine to rise or fall in the water. **3** a seaplane. • *v.* **1** (also, **aquaplane**) (of a vehicle or its tires) slide uncontrollably on the wet surface of a road: *a motorist whose car hydroplaned and crashed into a tree.* **2** (of a boat) skim over the surface of water with its hull lifted.

hy·dro·pon·ics |,hīdrə'päniks| • *plural n.* [treated as sing.] the process of growing plants in sand, gravel, or liquid, with added nutrients but without soil.
DERIVATIVES: **hy·dro·pon·ic** *adj.* **hy·dro·pon·i·cal·ly** |-,pänik(ə)lē| *adv.*

hy·men |'hīmən| • *n.* a membrane that partially closes the opening of the vagina and whose presence is traditionally taken to be a mark of virginity.
DERIVATIVES: **hy·men·al** |'hīmənl| *adj.* **hy·me·ne·al** |,hīmə'nēəl| • *adj.* of or concerning marriage.

hype |hīp| *informal* • *n.* extravagant or intensive publicity or promotion: *she relied on hype and headlines to build up interest in her music.*
▪ a deception carried out for the sake of publicity. • *v.* [trans.] promote or publicize (a product or idea) intensively, often exaggerating its importance or benefits: *an industry quick to hype its products.*

hy·per·bo·la |hī'pərbələ| • *n.* (pl. **hyperbolas** or **hyperbolae** |-bəlē|) a symmetrical open curve formed by the intersection of a cone with a plane at a smaller angle with its axis than the side of the cone.
▪ (in mathematics) the pair of such curves formed by the intersection of a plane with two equal cones on opposites of the same vertex.

hy·per·bo·le |hī'pərbəlē| • *n.* exaggerated statements or claims, typically not meant to be taken literally.
DERIVATIVES: **hy·per·bol·i·cal** |,hīpər'bä-likəl| *adj.* **hy·per·bol·i·cal·ly** |,hīpər'bäl-ik(ə)lē| *adv.* **hy·per·bo·lism** |-,lizəm| *n.*

hy·per·son·ic |,hīpər'sänik| • *adj.* **1** relating to or attaining speeds of more than five times the speed of sound (Mach 5). **2** relating to sound frequencies above about a thousand million hertz.
DERIVATIVES: **hy·per·son·i·cal·ly** |-ik(ə)-lē| *adv.*

hy·per·space |'hīpər,spās| • *n.* space of more than three dimensions.
▪ (in science fiction) a notional space-time continuum in which it is possible to travel faster than light.
DERIVATIVES: **hy·per·spa·tial** |,hīpər'spā-SHəl| *adj.*

hy·per·ten·sion |,hīpər'tensHən| • *n.* abnormally high blood pressure.
▪ a state of great psychological stress.

hy·per·ven·ti·late |,hīpər'ventl,āt| • *v.* [intrans.] breathe at an abnormally rapid rate, so increasing the rate of loss of carbon dioxide: *she started to hyperventilate under stress.*
▪ [trans.] (usu. **be hyperventilated**) cause to breathe in such a way: *the patients were hyperventilated for two minutes.* ▪ [intrans.] become unnecessarily or exaggeratedly excited or agitated: *now don't start hyperventilating until I explain the rest of the conditions.* ▪ [as adj.] (**hyperventilated**) inflated or pretentious in style; overblown: *hyperventilated prose.*
DERIVATIVES: **hy·per·ven·ti·la·tion** |-,ventl'āsHən| *n.*

hyp·na·gog·ic |,hipnə'gäjik; -'gō-| (also **hypnogogic**) • *adj.* of or relating to the state immediately before falling asleep.

hy·po·chon·dri·a |,hīpə'kändrēə| • *n.* abnormal anxiety about one's health, esp. with an unwarranted fear that one has a serious disease.
DERIVATIVES: **hy·po·chon·dri·ac** *n.* **hy·po·chon·dri·a·cal** *adj.*

hy·po·gly·ce·mi·a |,hīpōglī'sēmēə| (Brit. **hypoglycaemia**) • *n.* deficiency of glucose in the bloodstream. The opposite of **hyperglycemia**.
DERIVATIVES: **hy·po·gly·ce·mic** |-'sēmik| *adj.*

hy·pos·ta·sis |hī'pästəsis| • *n.* (pl. **hypostases** |-,sēz|) **1** (in medicine) the accumulation of fluid or blood in the lower parts of the body or organs under the influence of gravity, as occurs in cases of poor circulation or after death. **2** (in philosophy) an underlying reality or substance, as opposed to attributes or that which lacks substance.
▪ (in Christian theology) each of the three persons of the Trinity, as contrasted with the

unity of the Godhead. ■ [in sing.] the single person of Christ, as contrasted with his dual human and divine nature.

hy•po•ther•mi•a |ˌhīpəˈTHermēə| • *n.* the condition of having an abnormally low body temperature, typically one that is dangerously low. The opposite of **hyperthermia.**

hy•poth•e•sis |hīˈpäTHəsis| • *n.* (pl. **hypotheses** |-ˌsēz|) a supposition or proposed explanation made on the basis of limited evidence as a starting point for further investigation: *professional astronomers attacked him for popularizing an unconfirmed hypothesis.* ■ (in philosophy) a proposition made as a basis for reasoning, without any assumption of its truth.

hy•po•thet•i•cal |ˌhīpəˈTHetikəl| • *adj.* of, based on, or serving as a hypothesis: *that option is merely hypothetical at this juncture.* ■ supposed but not necessarily real or true: *a hypothetical cure.* ■ denoting or containing a

proposition of the logical form *if p then q.* • *n.* (usu. **hypotheticals**) a hypothetical proposition or statement: *Finn talked in hypotheticals, tossing what-if scenarios to Rosen.*

DERIVATIVES: **hy•po•thet•i•cal•ly** |-ik(ə)-lē| *adv.* [sentence adverb] *hypothetically, varying interpretations of the term are possible.*

hys•te•ri•a |hiˈsterēə; -ˈstirēə| • *n.* exaggerated or uncontrollable emotion or excitement, esp. among a group of people: *the mass hysteria that characterizes the week before Christmas.* ■ a psychological disorder (not now regarded as a single definite condition) whose symptoms include conversion of psychological stress into physical symptoms (somatization), selective amnesia, shallow volatile emotions, and overdramatic or attention-seeking behavior. The term has a controversial history as it was formerly regarded as a disease specific to women.

Ii

i•am•bi (also **iambus**) • *n.* a metrical foot consisting of one short or unstressed followed by one long or stressed syllable.

DERIVATIVES: **i•am•bic** *adj.*

i•chor |ˈīˌkôr| • *n.* (in Greek mythology) the fluid that flows like blood in the veins of the gods. ■ any bloodlike fluid: *tomatoes drooled ichor from their broken skins.* ■ a watery, fetid discharge from a wound.

DERIVATIVES: **i•chor•ous** |ˈīkərəs| *adj.*

ich•thy•ol•o•gy |ˌikTHēˈäləjē| • *n.* the branch of zoology that deals with fishes.

DERIVATIVES: **ich•thy•o•log•i•cal** |-əˈläjikəl| *adj.* **ich•thy•ol•o•gist** |-jist| *n.*

i•con |ˈīˌkän| • *n.* (also, in religious use, **ikon**) a painting of Christ or another holy figure, typically in a traditional style on wood, venerated and used as an aid to devotion in the Byzantine and other Eastern Churches. ■ a person or thing regarded as a representative symbol of something: *this iron-jawed icon of American manhood.* ■ a symbol or graphic representation on a video display terminal of a computer program, option, or window, esp. one of several for selection. Cf. GLYPH. ■ (in linguistics) a sign whose form directly reflects the thing it signifies, for example, the word *snarl* pronounced in a snarling way.

i•con•ic |īˈkänik| • *adj.* of, relating to, or of the nature of an icon: *language is not in general an iconic sign system.* ■ (of a classical Greek statue) depicting a victorious athlete in a conventional style.

DERIVATIVES: **i•con•i•cal•ly** |-ik(ə)lē| *adv.* **i•co•nic•i•ty** |ˌīkəˈnisitē| *n.* (esp. in linguistics).

i•con•o•clast |īˈkänəˌklæst| • *n.* **1** a person who attacks cherished beliefs or institutions. **2** a destroyer of images used in religious worship, in particular: ■ a supporter of the 8th- and 9th-century movement in the Byzantine Church that sought to abolish the veneration of icons and other religious images. ■ a Puritan of the 16th or 17th century.

DERIVATIVES: **i•con•o•clas•tic** |ˌīˌkänəˈklæstik| *adj.* **i•con•o•clas•ti•cal•ly** |ˌīˌkänəˈklæstik(ə)lē| *adv.*

ic•tus |ˈiktəs| • *n.* (pl. same or **ictuses**) **1** (in prose or poetry) a rhythmical or metrical stress. **2** (in medicine) a stroke or seizure.

id |id| • *n.* (in Freudian psychology) the part of the mind in which innate instinctive impulses and primary processes are manifest. Cf. EGO and SUPEREGO.

i•de•al•ism |īˈdē(ə)ˌlizəm| • *n.* **1** the practice of forming or pursuing ideals, esp. unrealistically: *the idealism of youth.* Cf. REALISM. ■ (in art or literature) the representation of things in ideal or idealized form. Cf. REALISM. **2** any of various philosophical systems in which the objects of knowledge are held to be in some way dependent on the activity of mind. Cf. REALISM; CONCEPTUALISM; NOMINALISM.

DERIVATIVES: **i•de•al•ist** *n.* **i•de•al•is•tic** |ˌīˌdē(ə)ˈlistik| *adj.* **i•de•al•is•ti•cal•ly** |ˌīˌdē(ə)ˈlistik(ə)lē| *adv.*

i•de•ate |ˈīdēˌāt| • *v.* [trans.] [often as adj.] (**ideated**) form an idea of; imagine or conceive: *the arc whose ideated center is a nodal point in the composition.* ■ [intrans.] form ideas; think.

DERIVATIVES: **i·de·a·tion** n.

id·e·o·gram |'idēə,græm; 'īdēə-| (also **ideograph**) • n. a written character symbolizing the idea of a thing without indicating the sounds used to say it, e.g., numerals and Chinese characters.

i·de·o·logue |'īdēə,lôg; -,läg; 'idēə-| • n. an adherent of an ideology, esp. one who is uncompromising and dogmatic: *a Nazi ideologue.*

i·de·ol·o·gy |,īdē'äləjē; ,idē-| • n. **1** (pl. **-ies**) a system of ideas and ideals, esp. one that forms the basis of economic or political theory and policy: *the ideology of republicanism.* ■ the ideas and manner of thinking characteristic of a group, social class, or individual: *a critique of bourgeois ideology.* ■ archaic visionary speculation, esp. of an unrealistic or idealistic nature. **2** archaic the science of ideas; the study of their origin and nature.

DERIVATIVES: **i·de·o·log·i·cal** |-ə'läjikəl| adj. **i·de·o·log·i·cal·ly** |-ə'läjik(ə)lē| adv. **i·de·ol·o·gist** |-jist| n.

ides |īdz| • plural n. (in the ancient Roman calendar) a day falling roughly in the middle of each month (the 15th day of March, May, July, and October, and the 13th of other months) from which other dates were calculated. Cf. NONES, CALENDS.

id·i·o·graph·ic |,idēə'græfik| • adj. of or relating to the study or discovery of particular scientific facts and processes, as distinct from general laws.

id·i·om |'idēəm| • n. **1** a group of words established by usage as having a meaning not deducible from the meaning of the individual words (e.g., *rain cats and dogs, see the light*). ■ a form of expression natural to a language, person, or group of people: *a feeling for phrase and idiom.* ■ the dialect of a people or part of a country: *the idiom of New York City.* **2** a characteristic mode of expression in music or art: *a neo-Impressionist idiom.*

id·i·o·mat·ic |,idēə'mætik| • adj. **1** using, containing, or denoting expressions that are natural to a native speaker: *idiomatic dialogue.* **2** appropriate to the style of art or music associated with a particular period, individual, or group: *a short Bach piece containing idiomatic motifs.*

DERIVATIVES: **id·i·o·mat·i·cal·ly** |-ik(ə)lē| adv.

id·i·o·path·ic |,idēə'pæTHik| • adj. relating to or denoting any disease or condition that arises spontaneously or for which the cause is unknown.

id·i·o·syn·cra·sy |,idēə'siNGkrəsē| • n. (pl. **-ies**) (usu. **idiosyncrasies**) a mode of behavior or way of thought peculiar to an individual: *one of his little idiosyncrasies was always having to be in the car first.* ■ a distinctive or peculiar feature or characteristic of a place or thing: *the idiosyncrasies of the prison system.* ■ an abnormal physical reaction by an individual to a food or drug.

DERIVATIVES: **id·i·o·syn·cra·tic** adj.

id·i·ot·rop·ic • adj. relating to or characterized by introspection.

id·i·ot sa·vant • n. (pl. **idiot savants** or **idiots savants** pronunc. same) a person who is considered to be mentally handicapped but displays brilliance in a specific area, esp. one involving memory.

i·dol·a·try |ī'dälətrē| • n. worship of idols. ■ extreme admiration, love, or reverence for something or someone: *we must not allow our idolatry of art to obscure issues of political significance.*

DERIVATIVES: **i·dol·a·ter** n. **idol·a·trous** adj.

i·dyll |'īdl| (also **idyl**) • n. an extremely happy, peaceful, or picturesque episode or scene, typically an idealized or unsustainable one: *the rural idyll remains strongly evocative in most industrialized societies.* ■ a short description in verse or prose of a picturesque scene or incident, esp. in rustic life.

DERIVATIVES: **i·dyl·lic** adj. **i·dyl·list** n. **i·dyl·lize** v.

ig·ne·ous |'ignēəs| • adj. (of rock) having solidified from lava or magma. Cf. METAMORPHIC; SEDIMENTARY. ■ relating to or involving volcanic processes: *igneous activity.*

ig·nis fat·u·us |'ignəs 'fæCHəwəs| • n. (pl. **ignes fatui** |'ignēz 'fæCHə,wī|) a phosphorescent light seen hovering or floating at night on marshy ground, thought to result from the combustion of natural gases. (Also called **will-o'-the-wisp**). ■ something deceptive or deluding.

ig·no·ble |ig'nōbəl| • adj. (**ignobler, ignoblest**) **1** not honorable in character or purpose: *ignoble feelings of intense jealousy.* **2** of humble origin or social status: *ignoble tillers of the soil.*

DERIVATIVES: **ig·no·bil·i·ty** |,ignō'bilitē| n. **ig·no·bly** |-blē| adv.

ig·no·min·i·ous |,ignə'minēəs| • adj. deserving or causing public disgrace or shame: *ignominious defeat.*

DERIVATIVES: **ig·no·min·i·ous·ly** adv. **ig·no·min·i·ous·ness** n.

ig·no·min·y |'ignə,minē; ig'näminē| • n. public shame or disgrace: *the ignominy of being imprisoned.*

il·e·um |'ilēəm`| • n. (pl. **ilea** |'ilēə|) the third portion of the small intestine, between the jejunum and the cecum. **Ileitis** is inflammation of the ileum.

DERIVATIVES: **il·e·ac** |-,æk| adj. **il·e·al** |-əl| adj.

il·i·um |'ilēəm| • n. (pl. **ilia** |'ilēə|) the large broad bone forming the upper part of each half of the pelvis.

ilk |ilk| • n. [in sing.] a type of people or things similar to those already referred to: *the veiled suggestions that reporters of his ilk seem to be so good at* | *fascists, racists, and others of that ilk.*

USAGE: In modern use, **ilk** is used in phrases such as *of his ilk, of that ilk,* to mean 'type' or 'sort.' The use arose out of a misunderstanding of the earlier, Scottish use in the phrase **of that ilk**, where it means 'of the same name or place.' For this reason, some traditionalists regard the modern use as incorrect. It is, however, the only common current use and is now part of standard English.

il•le•gal |i(l)'lēgəl| • *adj.* contrary to or forbidden by law, esp. criminal law: *illegal drugs.* • *n.* an illegal immigrant.
DERIVATIVES: **il•le•gal•i•ty** |ˌi(l)li'gælitē| *n.* (pl. **-ies**) **il•le•gal•ly** *adv.*

il•lic•it |i(l)'lisit| • *adj.* forbidden by law, rules, or custom: *illicit sex.*
DERIVATIVES: **il•lic•it•ly** *adv.* **il•lic•it•ness** *n.*

il•lit•er•ate |i(l)'litərit| • *adj.* unable to read or write: *his parents were illiterate.* Cf. INNUMERATE.
■ [with submodifier] ignorant in a particular subject or activity: *the extent to which voters are politically illiterate.* ■ uncultured or poorly educated: *an ignorant, illiterate Town Council.* ■ (esp. of a piece of writing) showing a lack of education, esp. an inability to read or write well. • *n.* a person who is unable to read or write.
PHRASES: **functionally illiterate** lacking the literacy necessary for coping with most jobs and many everyday situations.
DERIVATIVES: **il•lit•er•a•cy** |-əsē| *n.* **il•lit•er•ate•ly** *adv.* **il•lit•er•ate•ness** *n.*

il•lo•cu•tion |ˌilə'kyo͞oSHən| • *n.* an action performed by saying or writing something, e.g., ordering, warning, or promising.
DERIVATIVES: **il•lo•cu•tion•ar•y** |-ˌnerē| *adj.*

il•lu•mi•na•ti |iˌlo͞omə'nätē| • *plural n.* people claiming to possess special enlightenment or knowledge of something: *some mysterious standard known only to the illuminati of the organization.*
■ (**Illuminati**) a sect of 16th-century Spanish heretics who claimed special religious enlightenment. ■ (**Illuminati**) a Bavarian secret society founded in 1776, organized like the Freemasons. Cf. GNOSTIC.
DERIVATIVES: **il•lu•mi•nism** |i'lo͞omə,nizəm| *n.* **il•lu•mi•nist** |i'lo͞omənist| *n.*

il•lu•sion |i'lo͞oZHən| • *n.* a false idea or belief: *he had no illusions about the trouble she was in.*
■ a deceptive appearance or impression: *the illusion of family togetherness.* ■ a thing that is or is likely to be wrongly perceived or interpreted by the senses: *Zollner's illusion makes parallel lines seem to diverge by placing them on a zigzag-striped background.* Cf. ALLUSION; DELUSION.
PHRASES: **be under the illusion that** believe mistakenly that: *the world is under the illusion that the original painting still hangs in the Winter Palace.* **be under no illusion** (or **illusions**) be fully aware of the true state of affairs.
DERIVATIVES: **il•lu•sion•al** |-ZHənl| *adj.* **illusionary** *adj.*

il•lu•so•ry |i'lo͞osərē; -zərē| • *adj.* based on illusion; not real: *she knew the safety of her room was illusory.*

DERIVATIVES: **il•lu•so•ri•ly** |-rəlē| *adv.* **il•lu•so•ri•ness** *n.*

im•ag•ism |'imə,jizəm| • *n.* a movement in early 20th-century English and American poetry that sought clarity of expression through the use of precise images. The movement derived in part from the aesthetic philosophy of T. E. Hulme and involved Ezra Pound, James Joyce, Amy Lowell, and others.
DERIVATIVES: **im•ag•ist** *n.* **im•ag•is•tic** |ˌimə'jistik| *adj.*

i•ma•go |i'māgō; i'mä-| • *n.* (pl. **imagos**, **imagoes**, or **imagines** |-gə,nēz|) **1** the final and fully developed adult stage of an insect, typically winged. Cf. LARVA; METAMORPHOSIS; PUPA. **2** an unconscious, idealized mental image of someone, esp. a parent, that influences a person's behavior.

i•mam |i'mäm| • *n.* the person who leads prayers in a mosque.
■ (**Imam**) a title of various Muslim leaders, esp. of one succeeding Muhammad as leader of Shiite Islam.
DERIVATIVES: **i•mam•ate** |-ˌmāt| *n.*

im•be•cile |'imbəsəl; -ˌsil| • **1** *n.* a stupid person. **2** formerly, a classification for an adult with the mental age of a young child. • *adj.* [attrib.] stupid; idiotic: *try not to make imbecile remarks.*
DERIVATIVES: **im•be•cil•ic** |ˌimbə'silik| *adj.* **im•be•cil•i•ty** |ˌimbə'silitē| *n.* (pl. **-ies**).

im•bibe |im'bīb| • *v.* [trans.] drink (alcohol): *they were imbibing far too many pitchers of beer* | [intrans.] *having imbibed too freely, he fell over.*
■ absorb or assimilate (ideas or knowledge): *the Bolshevist propaganda which you imbibed in your youth.* ■ (esp. of seeds) absorb (water) into ultramicroscopic spaces or pores. ■ place (seeds) in water in order to absorb it.
DERIVATIVES: **im•bib•er** *n.* **im•bi•bi•tion** |ˌimbə'biSHən| *n.*

im•bri•cate |'imbri,kāt| • *v.* [usu. as adj.] (**imbricated**) arrange (scales, sepals, plates, etc.) so that they overlap like shingles: *these molds have spherical bodies composed of imbricated triangular plates.*
■ [intrans.] [usu. as adj.] (**imbricating**) overlap: *a coating of imbricating scales.* • *adj.* (of scales, sepals, plates, etc.) having adjacent edges overlapping.
DERIVATIVES: **im•bri•ca•tion** |ˌimbri'kāSHən| *n.*

im•bro•glio |im'brōlyō| • *n.* (pl. **-os**) an extremely confused, complicated, or embarrassing situation: *the Watergate imbroglio.*

im•brue |im'bro͞o| (also **embrue** |em-|) • *v.* (**imbrues**, **imbrued**, **imbruing**) [trans.] stain (something, esp. one's hands or sword): *they were unwilling to imbrue their hands in his blood.*

im•bue |im'byo͞o| • *v.* (**imbues**, **imbued**, **imbuing**) [trans.] (often **be imbued with**) inspire or permeate with a feeling or quality: *he was imbued with a deep Christian piety.*

im•mac•u•late |i'makyəlit| • *adj.* (esp. of a person or clothes) perfectly clean, neat, or tidy: *an immaculate white suit.*
■ free from flaws or mistakes; perfect: *an*

immaculate safety record. ■ (in the Roman Catholic Church) free from sin. ■ (in botony and zoology) uniformly colored without spots or other marks.
DERIVATIVES: **im·mac·u·la·cy** |-ləsē| *n.* **im·mac·u·late·ly** *adv.* **im·mac·u·late·ness** *n.*

im·ma·nent |'imənənt| • *adj.* existing or operating within; inherent: *the protection of liberties is **immanent in** constitutional arrangements.*
■ (of God) permanently pervading and sustaining the universe. Often contrasted with TRANSCENDENT.
DERIVATIVES: **im·ma·nence** *n.* **im·ma·nen·cy** *n.* **im·ma·nent·ism** |-,tizəm| *n.* **im·ma·nent·ist** |-tist| *n.*

USAGE: See **usage** at EMINENT.

im·ma·te·ri·al |,i(m)mə'tirēəl| • *adj.* **1** unimportant under the circumstances: *so long as the band kept the beat, what they played was immaterial.*
■ (in law) not consequential: *the evidence, while relevant, adds nothing to the case, and may be excluded as immaterial.* **2** spiritual, rather than physical: *we have immaterial souls.*
DERIVATIVES: **im·ma·te·ri·al·i·ty** |-,tirē 'ælitē| *n.* **im·ma·te·ri·al·ly** *adv.*

USAGE: **Immaterial** and **irrelevant** are familiar in legal, esp. courtroom, use. **Immaterial** means 'unimportant because not adding anything to the point.' **Irrelevant**, a much more common word, means 'beside the point; not speaking to the point.' Courts have long since ceased to demand precise distinctions, and evidence is often objected to with the blanket formula "immaterial, irrelevant, and incompetent ('offered by a witness who is not qualified to offer it')."

im·me·mo·ri·al |,i(m)mə'môrēəl| • *adj.* originating in the distant past; very old: *an immemorial custom.*
DERIVATIVES: **im·me·mo·ri·al·ly** *adv.*
im·mi·grate |'imi,grāt| • *v.* [intrans.] come to live permanently in a foreign country: *the Mennonites immigrated to western Canada in the 1870s.*

USAGE: See **usage** at EMIGRATE.

im·mi·nent |'imənənt| • *adj.* about to happen: *they were in imminent danger of being swept away.*
DERIVATIVES: **im·mi·nence** *n.* **im·mi·nent·ly** *adv.*

USAGE: See **usage** at EMINENT.

im·mo·late |'imə,lāt| • *v.* [trans.] kill or offer as a sacrifice, esp. by burning.
DERIVATIVES: **im·mo·la·tion** |,imə'lāSHən| *n.* **im·mo·la·tor** |-,lātər| *n.*
im·mor·al |i(m)'môrəl; -'märəl| • *adj.* not conforming to accepted standards of morality: *an immoral and unwinnable war.*
DERIVATIVES: **im·mo·ral·i·ty** |,imə'rælitē; ,imô-| *n.* (pl. **-ies**) **im·mor·al·ly** *adv.*

USAGE: See **usage** at AMORAL.

im·mune |i'myoon| • *adj.* resistant to a particular infection or toxin owing to the presence of specific antibodies or sensitized white blood cells: *they were naturally **immune to** hepatitis B.*
■ protected or exempt, esp. from an obligation or the effects of something: *they are **immune from** legal action.* Cf. EXEMPT. ■ [predic.] not affected or influenced by something: *no one is **immune to** his immense charm.* ■ [attrib.] of or relating to immunity: *the body's immune system.*
DERIVATIVES: **im·mu·nize** *v.* **im·mu·ni·za·tion** *n.*
im·mu·ni·ty |i'myoonitē| • *n.* (pl. **-ies**) the ability of an organism to resist a particular infection or toxin by the action of specific antibodies or sensitized white blood cells: *immunity to typhoid seems to have increased spontaneously.*
■ protection or exemption from something, esp. an obligation or penalty: *the rebels were given **immunity from** prosecution.* ■ officially granted exemption from legal proceedings. ■ (**immunity to**) lack of susceptibility, esp. to something unwelcome or harmful: *products must have an adequate level of immunity to interference.*
im·mure |i'myoor| • *v.* [trans.] (usu. **be immured**) enclose or confine (someone) forcibly: *her brother was immured in a lunatic asylum.*
DERIVATIVES: **immuration** *n.* **im·mure·ment** *n.*
im·mu·ta·ble |i'myootəbəl| • *adj.* unchanging over time or unable to be changed: *an immutable fact.*
DERIVATIVES: **im·mu·ta·bil·i·ty** |i,myootə'bilitē| *n.* **im·mu·ta·bly** |-blē| *adv.*
im·pact • *n.* |'im,pækt| the action of one object coming forcibly into contact with another: *bullets that expand on impact.*
■ the effect or influence of one person, thing, or action, on another: *the measures have had a significant **impact on** unemployment.* • *v.* |im 'pækt| **1** [intrans.] come into forcible contact with another object: *the shell impacted twenty yards away.*
■ [trans.] come into forcible contact with: *an asteroid impacted the earth some 60 million years ago.* ■ have a strong effect: *high interest rates have **impacted on** retail spending.* [trans.] *the move is not expected to impact the company's employees.* **2** [trans.] press firmly: *the animals' feet do not impact and damage the soil as cows' hooves do.*

USAGE: The phrasal verb **impact on**, as in *when produce is lost, it always **impacts on** the bottom line,* has been in the language since the 1960s. Many people disapprove of it despite its relative frequency, saying that **make an impact on** or other equivalent wordings should be used instead.

im·pair |im'per| • *v.* [trans.] weaken or damage (esp. a human faculty or function): *drug use that impairs job performance.*
im·pale |im'pāl| • *v.* [trans.] **1** pierce or transfix with a sharp instrument: *his head was*

impaled on a pike and exhibited for all to see. **2** display (a coat of arms) side by side with another on the same shield, separated by a vertical line: [as adj.] (**impaled**) *the impaled arms of her husband and her father.*
■ (of a coat of arms) adjoin (another coat of arms) in this way.
DERIVATIVES: **im•pale•ment** *n.* **im•pal•er** *n.*

im•pal•pa•ble |imˈpælpəbəl| • *adj.* unable to be felt by touch: *an impalpable ghost.* Cf. IM-MATERIAL.
■ not easily comprehended: *something so impalpable as personhood.*
DERIVATIVES: **im•pal•pa•bil•i•ty** |-ˌpælpə ˈbilitē| *n.* **im•pal•pa•bly** |-blē| *adv.*

im•par•tial |imˈpärSHəl| • *adj.* treating all parties equally; not partial; fair and just: *independent and impartial advice.*
DERIVATIVES: **im•par•ti•al•i•ty** |-ˌpärSHē ˈælitē| *n.* **im•par•tial•ly** *adv.*

im•passe |ˈimˌpæs; imˈpæs| • *n.* a situation in which no progress is possible, esp. because of disagreement; a deadlock: *the current political impasse.*

im•pas•sioned |imˈpæSHənd| • *adj.* filled with or showing great emotion: *she made an impassioned plea for help.*

im•pas•sive |imˈpæsiv| • *adj.* not feeling or showing emotion: *impassive passersby ignore the performers.*
DERIVATIVES: **im•pas•sive•ly** *adv.* **im•pas•sive•ness** *n.* **im•pas•siv•i•ty** |ˌimpə ˈsivitē| *n.*

im•peach |imˈpēCH| • *v.* [trans.] call into question the integrity or validity of (a practice or action): *there is no basis to Searle's motion to impeach the verdict.*
■ charge (the holder of a public office) with misconduct: *Presidents Andrew Johnson and Bill Clinton were both impeached, but neither was convicted on any charge.* ■ Brit. charge with treason or another crime against the state.
DERIVATIVES: **im•peach•a•ble** *adj.* **im•peach•ment** *n.*

im•pec•ca•ble |imˈpekəbəl| • *adj.* (of behavior, performance, or appearance) in accordance with the highest standards of propriety; faultless: *a man of impeccable character.*
■ Theology not liable to sin.
DERIVATIVES: **im•pec•ca•bil•i•ty** |-ˌpekə ˈbilitē| *n.* **im•pec•ca•bly** |-blē| *adv.*

im•pe•cu•ni•ous |ˌimpəˈkyoōnēəs| • *adj.* having little or no money: *a humble and impecunious family.*
DERIVATIVES: **im•pe•cu•ni•os•i•ty** |-ˌkyoō-nēˈäsitē| *n.* **im•pe•cu•ni•ous•ness** *n.*

im•ped•ance |imˈpēdns| • *n.* the effective resistance of an electric circuit or component to alternating current, arising from the combined effects of ohmic resistance and reactance.

USAGE: **Impedance** is a specialized electrical term, while **impediment** is an everyday term meaning 'a hindrance or obstruction,' e.g., *interpreting his handwriting was an impediment to getting business done.*

im•pede |imˈpēd| • *v.* [trans.] delay or prevent (someone or something) by obstructing them; hinder: *the sap causes swelling that can impede breathing.*

im•ped•i•ment |imˈpedəmənt| • *n.* a hindrance or obstruction in doing something: *a serious impediment to scientific progress.*
■ (also **speech impediment**) a defect in a person's speech, such as a lisp or stammer.
DERIVATIVES: **im•ped•i•men•tal** |-ˌpedə ˈmentl| *adj.*

USAGE: See usage at IMPEDANCE.

im•ped•i•men•ta |imˌpedəˈmentə| • *plural n.* equipment for an activity or expedition, esp. when considered as bulky or an encumbrance.

im•pel |imˈpel| • *v.* (**impelled, impelling**) [trans.] drive, force, or urge (someone) to do something: *financial difficulties impelled him to desperate measures* | [with obj. and infinitive] *a lack of equality impelled the oppressed to fight.*
■ drive forward; propel: *vital energies impel him in unforeseen directions.*

im•pend |imˈpend| • *v.* [intrans.] [usu. as adj.] (**impending**) be about to happen: *my impending departure.*
■ (of something bad) loom: *danger of collision impends.*

im•per•a•tive |imˈperətiv| • *adj.* **1** of vital importance; crucial: *immediate action was imperative* | [with clause] *it is imperative that standards be maintained.* **2** giving an authoritative command; peremptory: *the bell pealed again, a final imperative call.*
■ grammar denoting the mood of a verb that expresses a command or exhortation, as *come* in *come here!* • *n.* **1** an essential or urgent thing: *free movement of labor was an economic imperative.*
■ a factor or influence making something necessary: *the change came about through a financial imperative.* ■ a thing felt as an obligation: *the moral imperative of aiding Third World development.* **2** a verb or phrase in the imperative mood.
■ (**the imperative**) the imperative mood.
DERIVATIVES: **im•per•a•ti•val** |-ˌperə ˈtīvəl| *adj.* **im•per•a•tive•ly** *adv.* **im•per•a•tive•ness** *n.*

im•per•cep•ti•ble |ˌimpərˈseptəbəl| • *adj.* impossible to perceive: *his head moved in an almost imperceptible nod.*
DERIVATIVES: **im•per•cep•ti•bil•i•ty** |-ˌsep-təˈbilitē| *n.* **im•per•cep•ti•bly** |-blē| *adv.*

im•pe•ri•al•ism |imˈpirēəˌlizəm| • *n.* a policy of extending a country's power and influence through diplomacy or military force (or, by extension, through other forms of power).
■ rule by an emperor.
DERIVATIVES: **im•pe•ri•al•ist** *n.* **im•pe•ri•al•is•tic** |-ˌpirēəˈlistik| *adj.* **im•pe•ri•al•is•ti•cal•ly** |-ˌpirēəˈlistik(ə)lē| *adv.*

im•pe•ri•ous |imˈpirēəs| • *adj.* assuming power or authority without justification; arrogant and domineering: *his imperious demands.*

DERIVATIVES: **im•pe•ri•ous•ly** *adv.* **im•pe•ri•ous•ness** *n.*

im•per•me•a•ble |im'pərmēəbəl| • *adj.* not allowing fluid to pass through: *an impermeable membrane.* Cf. IMPERVIOUS.
■ not liable to be affected by pain or distress; not susceptible or not perturbable: *women who appear **impermeable** to pain.*
DERIVATIVES: **im•per•me•a•bil•i•ty** |-,pərmēə'bilitē| *n.*

im•per•ti•nent |im'pərtn-ənt| • *adj.* **1** not showing proper respect; rude: *an impertinent question.* Cf. INSOLENT, IRREVERENT. **2** not pertinent to a particular matter; irrelevant: *talk of "rhetoric" and "strategy" is **impertinent to** this process.*
DERIVATIVES: **im•per•ti•nence** *n.* **im•per•ti•nent•ly** *adv.*

im•per•vi•ous |im'pərvēəs| • *adj.* not allowing anything to pass through: *an impervious layer of basaltic clay.* Cf. IMPERMEABLE.
■ [predic.] (**impervious to**) unable to be affected by: *he worked on, apparently impervious to the heat.*
DERIVATIVES: **im•per•vi•ous•ly** *adv.* **im•per•vi•ous•ness** *n.*

im•pet•u•ous |im'pecHəwəs| • *adj.* acting or done quickly and without thought or care: *her friend was headstrong and impetuous.*
■ moving forcefully or rapidly: *an impetuous but controlled flow of water.*
DERIVATIVES: **im•pet•u•os•i•ty** |-,pecHə'wäsitē| *n.* **im•pet•u•ous•ly** *adv.* **im•pet•u•ous•ness** *n.*

im•pe•tus |'impitəs| • *n.* the force or energy with which a body moves: *hit the booster coil before the flywheel loses all its impetus.* Cf. MOMENTUM.
■ the force that makes something happen or happen more quickly: *the crisis of the 1860s provided the original **impetus for** the settlements.*

im•pinge |im'pinj| • *v.* (**impinging**) [intrans.] have an effect or impact, esp. a negative one: *Nora was determined that the tragedy would **impinge** as little as possible **on** Constance's life.*
■ advance over an area belonging to someone or something else; encroach: *the site **impinges on** a conservation area.* ■ (**impinge on/upon**) come into forcible contact with; strike: *the gases impinge on the surface of the liquid.*
DERIVATIVES: **im•pinge•ment** *n.* **im•ping•er** *n.*

im•plac•a•ble |im'plækəbəl| • *adj.* unable to be placated: *he was an implacable enemy of Ted's.*
■ relentless; unstoppable: *the implacable advance of the enemy.*
DERIVATIVES: **im•plac•a•bil•i•ty** |-,plækə'bilitē| *n.* **im•plac•a•bly** |-blē| *adv.*

im•plau•si•ble |im'plôzəbəl| • *adj.* (of an argument or statement) not seeming reasonable or probable; failing to convince: *a blatantly implausible claim | your suggested solution is implausible.*
DERIVATIVES: **im•plau•si•bil•i•ty** |-,plôzə'bilitē| *n.* **im•plau•si•bly** |-blē| *adv.*

im•pli•cate |'impli,kāt| • *v.* [trans.] **1** show (someone) to be involved in a crime: *police claims **implicated** him **in** many more killings.*
■ (**be implicated in**) bear some of the responsibility for (an action or process, esp. a criminal or harmful one): *a chemical implicated in ozone depletion.* ■ involve (something) in a necessary way: *cable franchise activities plainly implicate First Amendment interests.* **2** convey (a meaning or intention) indirectly through what one says, rather than stating it explicitly; imply: *by saying that coffee would keep her awake, Mary implicated that she didn't want any.* • *n.* a thing implied.
DERIVATIVES: **im•pli•ca•tive** |'impli,kākhtiv; im'plikətiv| *adj.* **im•pli•ca•tive•ly** *adv.*

im•pli•ca•tion |,impli'kāsHən| • *n.* **1** the conclusion that can be drawn from something, although it is not explicitly stated: *the implication is that no one person at the bank is responsible.*
■ a likely consequence of something: *a victory that had important political implications.* **2** the action or state of being involved in something: *our implication in the problems.*
DERIVATIVES: **im•pli•ca•tion•al** |-SHənl| *adj.*

im•plic•it |im'plisit| • *adj.* **1** implied though not plainly expressed: *comments seen as implicit criticism of the policies.*
■ [predic.] (**implicit in**) essentially or very closely connected with; always to be found in: *the values implicit in the school ethos.* **2** with no qualification or question; absolute: *an implicit faith in God.* **3** (of a mathematical function) not expressed directly in terms of independent variables.
DERIVATIVES: **im•plic•it•ly** *adv.* **im•plic•it•ness** *n.*

im•plode |im'plōd| • *v.* collapse or cause to collapse violently inward: [intrans.] *the windows on both sides of the room imploded* | [trans.] *these forces would implode the pellet to a density 100 times higher than that of lead.*
■ [intrans.] suffer sudden economic or political collapse: *can any amount of aid save the republic from imploding?*
DERIVATIVES: **im•plo•sion** |-zHən| *n.* **im•plo•sive** |-siv| *adj.*

im•plore |im'plôr| • *v.* beg someone earnestly or desperately to do something: *he implored her to change her mind | "Please don't talk that way," Ellen implored.*
■ [trans.] beg earnestly for: *I implore mercy.*
DERIVATIVES: **im•plor•ing•ly** *adv.*

im•ply |im'plī| • *v.* (**-ies, -ied**) [trans.] strongly suggest the truth or existence of (something not expressly stated): *salesmen who use jargon to imply superior knowledge* | [with clause] *the report implies that two million jobs may be lost.*
■ (of a fact or occurrence) suggest (something) as a logical consequence: *the predicted traffic increase implied more roads and more air pollution.*

USAGE: **Imply** and **infer** do not mean the same thing and should not be used interchangeably: see **usage** at INFER.

im•pol•i•tic |im'päli,tik| • adj. failing to possess or display prudence; unwise: *it was impolitic to pay the slightest tribute to the enemy.*
DERIVATIVES: **im•pol•i•tic•ly** adv.

im•por•tu•nate |im'pôrCHənit| • adj. persistent, esp. to the point of annoyance or intrusion: *importunate creditors.*
DERIVATIVES: **im•por•tu•nate•ly** adv. **im•por•tu•ni•ty** |,impôr't(y)o͞oni̯tē| n. (pl. -ies).

im•por•tune |,impôr't(y)o͞on; im'pôrCHən| • v. [trans.] ask (someone) pressingly and persistently for or to do something: *if he were alive now, I should importune him with my questions.*
■ approach (someone) to offer one's services as a prostitute.

im•post |'im,pōst| • n. a tax or similar compulsory payment.

im•pos•ture |im'päsCHər| • n. an instance of pretending to be someone else in order to deceive others.

im•po•tent |'impətnt| • adj. 1 unable to take effective action; helpless or powerless: *he was seized with an impotent anger.* 2 (of a man) abnormally unable to achieve a sexual erection.
■ (of a male animal) unable to copulate.
DERIVATIVES: **im•po•tence** n. **im•po•ten•cy** n. **im•po•tent•ly** adv.

im•pound |im'pownd| • v. [trans.] 1 seize and take legal custody of (something, esp. a vehicle, goods, or documents) because of an infringement of a law or regulation: *vehicles parked in the zone will be impounded.* 2 shut up (domestic animals) in a pound or enclosure.
■ (of a dam) hold back or confine (water): *the dam impounds the Feather River.*
DERIVATIVES: **im•pound•a•ble** adj. **im•pound•er** n. **im•pound•ment** n.

im•pov•er•ish |im'päv(ə)riSH| • v. [trans.] make (a person or area) poor: *they discourage investment and impoverish their people* | [as adj.] (**impoverished**) *impoverished peasant farmers.*
■ exhaust the strength, vitality, or natural fertility of: *the soil was impoverished by overplanting* | [as adj.] (**impoverished**) *an impoverished and debased language.*
DERIVATIVES: **im•pov•er•ish•ment** n.

im•prac•ti•ca•ble |im'præktikəbəl| • adj. (of a course of action) impossible in practice to do or carry out: *it was impracticable to widen the road here* | *an impracticable suggestion.*
DERIVATIVES: **im•prac•ti•ca•bil•i•ty** |-,præktikə'bilitē| n. **im•prac•ti•ca•bly** |-blē| adv.

USAGE: **Impracticable** and **impractical** are sometimes confused. **Impracticable** means 'impossible to carry out' and is normally used of a specific procedure or course of action, as in *poor visibility made the task difficult, even* **impracticable**. **Impractical**, on the other hand, tends to be used in more general senses, often to mean simply 'unrealistic' or 'not sensible,' as in *in windy weather an umbrella is* **impractical**. **Impractical** may be used in describing a person, but not **impracticable**.

im•prac•ti•cal |im'præktikəl| • adj. 1 (of an object or course of action) not adapted for use or action; not sensible or realistic: *impractical high heels* | *his impractical romanticism.*
■ (of a person) not skilled or interested in practical matters: *Paul was impractical and dreamy.* 2 impossible to do; impracticable.
DERIVATIVES: **im•prac•ti•cal•i•ty** |-,prækti'kælitē| n. **im•prac•ti•cal•ly** |-ik(ə)lē| adv.

im•pre•cate |'impri,kāt| • v. [trans.] utter (a curse) or invoke (evil) against someone or something.
DERIVATIVES: **im•pre•ca•tion** |,impri'kāsHən| n. **im•pre•ca•tor** n. **im•pre•ca•to•ry** |'imprikə,tôrē| adj.

im•preg•na•ble |im'pregnəbəl| • adj. (of a fortified position) unable to be captured or broken into: *an impregnable wall of solid sandstone* | *the companies are impregnable to takeovers.*
■ unable to be defeated or destroyed; unassailable: *the case against Simpson would have been almost impregnable.*
DERIVATIVES: **im•preg•na•bil•i•ty** |-,pregnə'bilitē| n. **im•preg•na•bly** |-blē| adv.

im•preg•nate |im'preg,nāt| • v. [trans.] 1 make (a woman or female animal) pregnant.
■ fertilize (a female reproductive cell or ovum). 2 (usu. **be impregnated with**) soak or saturate (something) with a substance: *wood that had been impregnated with preservative.*
■ imbue with feelings or qualities: *an atmosphere impregnated with tension.*
DERIVATIVES: **im•preg•na•tion** |,impreg'nāsHən| n.

im•pre•sa•ri•o |,imprə'särē,ō; -'ser-| • n. (pl. -os) a person who organizes and often finances concerts, plays, or operas.
■ formerly, the manager of a musical, theatrical, or operatic company.

im•press • v. [trans.] force (someone) to serve in an army or navy: *a number of Poles, impressed into the German army.*
■ commandeer (goods or equipment) for public service.
DERIVATIVES: **im•press•ment** n.

Im•pres•sion•ism |im'presHə,nizəm| • n. a style or movement in painting originating in France in the 1860s, characterized by a concern with depicting the visual impression of the moment, esp. in terms of the shifting effect of light and color.
■ a literary or artistic style that seeks to capture a feeling or experience rather than to achieve accurate depiction. ■ Music a style of composition (associated esp. with Debussy) in which clarity of structure and theme is subordinate to harmonic effects, characteristically using the whole-tone scale. Cf. EXPRESSIONISM.

im•pri•ma•tur |,imprə'mätər; -'mātər| • n. an official license granted by the Roman Catholic Church to print an ecclesiastical or religious book.
■ [in sing.] a person's acceptance or guarantee

that something is of a good standard: *the original LP enjoyed the imprimatur of the composer.*

im•print • *v.* |im'print| **1** [trans.] (usu. **be imprinted**) impress or stamp (a mark or outline) on a surface or body: *tire marks were imprinted in the snow.*

■ make an impression or mark on (something): *clothes imprinted with the logos of sports teams.* ■ fix (an idea) firmly in someone's mind: *he would always have this ghastly image imprinted on his mind.* **2** [intrans.] (**imprint on**) Zoology (of a young animal) come to recognize (another animal, person, or thing) as a parent or other object of habitual trust.

• *n.* |'imprint| **1** a mark made by pressing something on to a softer substance so that its outline is reproduced: *the signet ring left its imprint in the sealing wax.*

■ a lasting impression or effect: *years in the colonies had left their imprint.* **2** a printer's or publisher's name, address, and other details in a book or other printed item.

■ a brand name under which books are published, typically the name of a former publishing house that is now part of a larger group.

im•promp•tu |im'präm(p),t(y)o͞o| • *adj. & adv.* done without being planned, organized, or rehearsed: [as adj.] *an impromptu press conference* | [as adv.] *he spoke impromptu.* • *n.* (pl. **impromptus**) a short piece of instrumental music, esp. a solo, that is reminiscent of an improvisation.

im•pro•pri•e•ty |,imprə'prīitē| • *n.* (pl. **-ies**) a failure to observe standards or show due honesty or modesty; improper behavior or character: *she was scandalized at the impropriety of the question* | *there are no demonstrable diplomatic improprieties.*

im•prov•i•dent |im'prävidənt| • *adj.* not having or showing foresight; spendthrift or thoughtless: *improvident and undisciplined behavior.* Cf. PROVIDENT.
DERIVATIVES: **im•prov•i•dence** *n.* **im•prov•i•dent•ly** *adv.*

im•pro•vise |'imprə,vīz| • *v.* [trans.] create and perform (music, drama, or verse) spontaneously or without preparation: *the ability to improvise operatic arias in any given style* | [intrans.] *he was improvising over guitar chords.* Cf. AD LIB.

■ produce or make (something) from whatever is available: *I improvised a costume for myself out of an old blue dress* | [as adj.] (**improvised**) *we camped out, sleeping on improvised beds.*
DERIVATIVES: **im•prov•i•sa•tion** |im,prävi'zāsHən| *n.* **im•prov•i•sa•tion•al** |,prävi'zāsHənl| *adj.* **im•prov•i•sa•to•ri•al** |im,prävizə'tôrēəl| *adj.* **im•prov•i•sa•to•ry** |im,prävizə,tôrē| *adj.* **im•pro•vis•er** *n.*

im•pru•dent |im'pro͞odnt| • *adj.* not showing care for the consequences of an action; rash: *it would be imprudent to leave your coat behind.*
DERIVATIVES: **im•pru•dence** *n.* **im•pru•dent•ly** *adv.*

im•pu•dent |'impyəd(ə)nt| • *adj.* not showing due respect for another person; imperti-

nent: *he could have strangled this impudent upstart* | *impudent remarks from the children.* Cf. INSOLENT.
DERIVATIVES: **im•pu•dence** *n.* **im•pu•dent•ly** *adv.*

im•pugn |im'pyo͞on| • *v.* [trans.] dispute the truth, validity, or honesty of (a statement or motive); call into question: *the father does not impugn her capacity as a good mother* | *defendant's lawyer impugned this testimony.*
DERIVATIVES: **im•pugn•a•ble** *adj.* **im•pugn•ment** *n.*

im•pul•sive |im'pəlsiv| • *adj.* **1** acting or done without advance planning or thought: *they had married as impulsive teenagers* | *perhaps he's regretting his impulsive offer.* **2** (in physics) acting as an impulse: *impulsive forces.*
DERIVATIVES: **im•pul•sive•ly** *adv.* **im•pul•sive•ness** *n.* **im•pul•siv•i•ty** |,impəl'sivitē| *n.*

im•pu•ni•ty |im'pyo͞onitē| • *n.* exemption from punishment or freedom from the injurious consequences of an action: *the impunity enjoyed by military officers* | *protesters burned flags on the streets with seeming impunity.*

im•pute |im'pyo͞ot| • *v.* [trans.] represent (something, esp. something undesirable) as being done, caused, or possessed by someone; attribute: *the crimes imputed to Richard.*

■ assign (a value) to something by inference from the economic value of the products or processes to which it contributes: [as adj.] (**imputed**) *recovering the initial outlay plus imputed interest.* ■ ascribe a moral quality or attribute to someone by virtue of a similar quality in another: *Christ's righteousness has been imputed to us.*
DERIVATIVES: **im•put•a•ble** *adj.* **im•pu•ta•tion** |,impyə'tāsHən| *n.*

in•ad•vert•ent |,inəd'vərtnt| • *adj.* not resulting from or achieved through deliberate planning: *inadvertent spread of species through trade.*

■ (of a mistake) made through lack of care: *an inadvertent omission.*
DERIVATIVES: **in•ad•vert•ence** *n.* **in•ad•vert•en•cy** *n.* **in•ad•vert•ent•ly** *adv.*

in•al•ien•a•ble |in'ālēənəbəl| • *adj.* unable to be taken away from or given away by the possessor; not alienable: *freedom of thought, the most inalienable of all human rights.*
DERIVATIVES: **in•al•ien•a•bil•i•ty** |-,ālēənə'bilitē| *n.* **in•al•ien•a•bly** |-blē| *adv.*

in•am•o•ra•ta |in,æmə'rätə| • *n.* a person's female lover. The male is **inamorato.**

in•ane |i'nān| • *adj.* without sense or meaning; silly; stupid: *don't constantly badger people with inane questions.*
DERIVATIVES: **in•ane•ly** *adv.* **in•ane•ness** *n.* **in•an•i•ty** |i'nænitē| *n.* (pl. **-ies**) .

in•an•i•mate |in'ænimit| • *adj.* not alive, esp. not in the manner of animals and humans: *inanimate objects like stones.*

■ showing no sign of life; lifeless: *he was completely inanimate and it was difficult to tell if he was breathing.*
DERIVATIVES: **in•an•i•mate•ly** *adv.*

in•ar•tic•u•late | ˌinär'tikyəlit | • adj. **1** unable to speak distinctly or express oneself clearly: *he was inarticulate with abashment and regret.* ■ not clearly expressed or pronounced: *inarticulate complaints of inadequate remuneration.* ■ having no distinct meaning; unintelligible: *lurching up and down uttering inarticulate cries.* ■ not expressed; unspoken: *inarticulate resentment.* **2** without joints or articulations.
DERIVATIVES: **in•ar•tic•u•la•cy** |-ləsē| n. **in•ar•tic•u•late•ly** adv. **in•ar•tic•u•late•ness** n.

in•aus•pi•cious | ˌinô'spiSHəs | • adj. not conducive to success; unpromising: *an inauspicious beginning* Cf. AUSPICIOUS.
DERIVATIVES: **in•aus•pi•cious•ly** adv. **in•aus•pi•cious•ness** n.

in•born | 'in'bôrn | • adj. existing from birth: *an inborn defect in breathing capacity.* ■ natural to a person or animal: *people think doctors have inborn compassion.*

in•bred | 'in,bred | • adj. **1** produced by the interbreeding of closely related individuals (inbreeding): *a classic inbred English aristocrat.* **2** existing in a person, animal, or plant from birth; congenital: *inbred disease resistance in crops.*

in cam•er•a • adv. in private, esp. in the chambers of a judge: *the court retired to consider the motion in camera.*

in•can•des•cent | ˌinkən'desənt | • adj. emitting light as a result of being heated: *plumes of incandescent liquid rock.* ■ (of an electric light) containing a filament that glows white-hot when heated by a current passed through it. ■ of outstanding and exciting quality; brilliant: *an incandescent performance.*
DERIVATIVES: **in•can•des•cence** n. **in•can•des•cent•ly** adv.

in•can•ta•tion | ˌinkæn'tāSHən | • n. a series of words said as a magic spell or charm: *an incantation to raise the dead.* ■ the use of such words: *there was no magic in such incantation* | *incantations of old slogans.*
DERIVATIVES: **in•can•ta•to•ry** |-'kæntə,tôrē| adj.

in•ca•pac•i•tate | ˌinkə'pæsi,tāt | • v. [trans.] prevent from functioning in a normal way: *he was incapacitated by a heart attack.* ■ deprive (someone) of their legal capacity.
DERIVATIVES: **in•ca•pac•i•tant** |-'pæsətnt| n. **in•ca•pac•i•ta•tion** |-ˌpæsi'tāSHən| n.

in•car•cer•ate | in'kärsə,rāt | • v. [trans.] (usu. **be incarcerated**) put in jail or prison: *many are incarcerated for property offenses.* ■ confine (someone) in a particular place: *he spent a long evening incarcerated in his study.*
DERIVATIVES: **in•car•cer•a•tion** |-ˌkärsə'rāSHən| n. **in•car•cer•a•tor** |-ˌrātər| n.

in•car•nate | in'kärnit; -ˌnāt | • adj. [often postpositive] (esp. of a deity or spirit) embodied in flesh; in human form: *Krishna incarnate* | *he chose to be incarnate as a man.* ■ [postpositive] represented in the ultimate or most extreme form: *here is capitalism incarnate.* • v. |-ˌnāt| [trans.] **1** embody or represent (a deity or spirit) in human form: *the idea that God incarnates himself in man.* ■ put (an idea or other abstract concept) into concrete form: *a desire to make things that will incarnate their personality.* ■ (of a person) be the living embodiment of (a quality): *the woman who incarnates the suffering of all her people.*

in•cen•di•ar•y | in'sendē,erē | • adj. (of a device or attack) designed to cause fires: *incendiary bombs* | *an incendiary raid.* ■ tending to stir up conflict: *incendiary rhetoric.* ■ very exciting: *an incendiary live performer.* • n. (pl. **-ies**) an incendiary bomb or device. ■ a person who starts fires, esp. in a military context. ■ a person who stirs up conflict.
DERIVATIVES: **in•cen•di•a•rism** |-dēə,ri-zəm| n.

in•cense | in'sens | • v. [trans.] (usu. **be incensed**) make very angry: *she was incensed by the accusations.*

in•cen•tive | in'sentiv | • n. a thing that motivates or encourages one to do something: *give farmers an incentive to improve their land.* ■ a payment or concession to stimulate greater output or investment: *tax incentives for investing in depressed areas* | [as adj.] *incentive payments.*
DERIVATIVES: **incentivize** v. **incentivization** n.

in•cep•tion | in'sepSHən | • n. [in sing.] the establishment or starting point of an institution or activity: *she has been on the board since its inception two years ago.*

in•cer•ti•tude | in'sərti,t(y)ood | • n. a state of uncertainty or hesitation: *some schools broke down under the stresses of policy incertitude.*

in•ces•sant | in'sesənt | • adj. (of something regarded as unpleasant) continuing without pause or interruption: *the incessant beat of the music.*
DERIVATIVES: **in•ces•san•cy** n. **in•ces•sant•ly** adv. **in•ces•sant•ness** n.

in•cest | 'in,sest | • n. sexual relations between people classed as being too closely related to marry each other. ■ the crime of having sexual intercourse with a parent, child, sibling, or grandchild.

in•ces•tu•ous | in'sesCHəwəs | • adj. **1** involving or guilty of incest: *the child of an incestuous relationship.* **2** (of human relations generally) excessively close and resistant to outside influence: *the incestuous nature of literary journalism.*
DERIVATIVES: **in•ces•tu•ous•ly** adv. **in•ces•tu•ous•ness** n.

in•cho•ate • adj. | in'kō-it; -āt | just begun and so not fully formed or developed; rudimentary: *a still inchoate democracy.* ■ confused or incoherent: *inchoate political protest.* ■ (of an offense, such as incitement or conspiracy) anticipating a further criminal act.
DERIVATIVES: **in•cho•ate•ly** adv. **in•cho•ate•ness** n.

in•ci•dent | 'insidənt | • n. **1** an event or occurrence: *several amusing incidents.*

■ a violent event, such as a fracas or assault: *one person was stabbed in the incident.* ■ a hostile clash between forces of rival countries. ■ **(incident of)** a case or instance of something happening: *a single incident of rudeness does not support a finding of contemptuous conduct.* ■ the occurrence of dangerous or exciting things: *the winter passed without incident.* ■ a distinct piece of action in a play or a poem. **2** (in law) a privilege, burden, or right attaching to an office, estate, or other holding. • *adj.* **1** [predic.] **(incident to)** liable to happen because of; resulting from: *the changes incident to economic development.*
■ (in law) attaching to: *the costs properly incident to a suit for foreclosure or redemption.* **2** (esp. of light or other radiation) falling on or striking something: *when an ion beam is **incident on** a surface.*
■ of or relating to incidence: *the incident angle.*

in•ci•den•tal |ˌinsiˈdentl| • *adj.* **1** accompanying but not a major part of something: *incidental expenses.*
■ occurring by chance in connection with something else: *the incidental catch of dolphins in the pursuit of tuna.* **2** [predic.] **(incidental to)** liable to happen as a consequence of (an activity): *the ordinary risks incidental to a fireman's job.* • *n.* (usu. **incidentals**) an incidental detail, expense, event, etc.: *meals, taxis, and other incidentals.*
DERIVATIVES: **incidentally** *adv.*

in•cip•i•ent |inˈsipēənt| • *adj.* in an initial stage; beginning to happen or develop: *could feel incipient anger building up* | *an incipient black eye.*
■ (of a person) developing into a specified type or role: *we seemed more like friends than incipient lovers.*
DERIVATIVES: **in•cip•i•ence** *n.* **in•cip•i•en•cy** *n.* **in•cip•i•ent•ly** *adv.*

in•cise |inˈsīz| • *v.* [trans.] (usu. **be incised**) mark or decorate (an object or surface) with a cut or a series of cuts: *a button incised with the letter G.*
■ cut (a mark or decoration) into a surface: *figures incised on upright stones.* ■ cut (skin or flesh) with a surgical instrument: *the wound was incised and drained.*

in•ci•sive |inˈsīsiv| • *adj.* (of a person or mental process) intelligently analytical and clear-thinking: *she was an incisive critic.*
■ (of an account) accurate and sharply focused: *the songs offer incisive pictures of American ways.*
DERIVATIVES: **in•ci•sive•ly** *adv.* **in•ci•sive•ness** *n.*

in•cite |inˈsīt| • *v.* [trans.] encourage or stir up (violent or unlawful behavior): *the offense of inciting racial hatred.*
■ urge or persuade (someone) to act in a violent or unlawful way: *he incited loyal subjects to rebellion.*
DERIVATIVES: **in•ci•ta•tion** |ˌinsīˈtāSHən| *n.* **in•cite•ment** *n.* **in•cit•er** *n.*

in•ci•vil•i•ty |ˌinsiˈvilitē| • *n.* (pl. **-ies**) rude or unsociable speech or behavior; lack of civility or politeness.

■ (often **incivilities**) an impolite or offensive comment.

in•clem•ent |inˈklemənt| • *adj.* (of the weather) unpleasantly stormy, cold, or wet; not clement.
DERIVATIVES: **in•clem•en•cy** *n.* (pl. **-ies**) .

in•cog•ni•to |ˌinkägˈnētō; inˈkägniˌtō| • *adj.* & *adv.* (of a person) having one's true identity concealed: [as adj.] *in order to observe you have to be incognito* | [as adv.] *operating incognito.* • *n.* (pl. **-os**) an assumed or false identity.

in•co•her•ent |ˌinkōˈhirənt; -ˈher-; ˌiNG-| • *adj.* **1** (of spoken or written language) expressed in an incomprehensible or confusing way; not coherent; unclear: *he screamed some incoherent threat.*
■ (of a person) unable to speak intelligibly.
■ (of an ideology, policy, or system) internally inconsistent; illogical: *the film is ideologically incoherent.* **2** (of light or electromagnetic waves) having no definite or stable phase relationship.
DERIVATIVES: **in•co•her•ence** *n.* **in•co•her•en•cy** *n.* (pl. **-ies**) **in•co•her•ent•ly** *adv.*

in•com•mu•ni•ca•do |ˌinkəˌmyōōniˈkädō| • *adj.* & *adv.* not able, wanting, or allowed to communicate with other people: *they were separated and detained incommunicado* | *trying to arrange a few days incommunicado.*

in•com•pat•i•ble |ˌinkəmˈpætəbəl; ˌiNG-| • *adj.* (of two things) so opposed in character as to be incapable of existing together; not compatible: *cleverness and femininity were seen as incompatible.*
■ (of two people) unable to live together harmoniously. ■ [predic.] **(incompatible with)** (of one thing or person) not consistent or able to coexist with (another): *long hours are simply incompatible with family life.* ■ (of equipment, machinery, computer programs, etc.) not capable of being used in combination.
DERIVATIVES: **in•com•pat•i•bil•i•ty** |-ˌpætəˈbilitē| *n.* **in•com•pat•i•bly** |-blē| *adv.*

in•con•gru•ous |inˈkäNGgrōōəs| • *adj.* not in harmony or keeping with the surroundings or other aspects of something.
DERIVATIVES: **in•con•gru•i•ty** |ˌinkənˈgrōōitē; ˌiNGkäNG-| *n.* (pl. **-ies**) **in•con•gru•ous•ly** *adv.*

in•con•ti•nent |inˈkäntənənt; -ˈkäntn-ənt| • *adj.* **1** having no or insufficient voluntary control over urination or defecation. **2** lacking self-restraint; uncontrolled: *the incontinent hysteria of the fans.*
DERIVATIVES: **in•con•ti•nence** *n.* **in•con•ti•nent•ly** *adv.*

in•con•tro•vert•i•ble |ˌinˌkäntrəˈvərtəbəl| • *adj.* not able to be denied or disputed; not possible to controvert: *incontrovertible fact.*
DERIVATIVES: **in•con•tro•vert•i•bil•i•ty** |-ˌvərtəˈbilitē| *n.* **in•con•tro•vert•i•bly** |-blē| *adv.*

in•cor•po•rate • *v.* |inˈkôrpəˌrāt| [trans.] **1** put or take in (something) as part of a whole; include: *he has **incorporated in** his proposals a large number of measures* | *territo-*

ries that had been **incorporated into** *the Japanese Empire.* ■ contain or include (something) as part of a whole: *the guide incorporates all the recent changes in legislation.* ■ combine (ingredients) into one substance: *add the cheeses and butter and process briefly to incorporate them.* **2** (often **be incorporated**) constitute (a company, city, or other organization) as a legal corporation. • *adj.* |-'kôrp(ə)rit| **1** (also **incorporated**) (of a company or other organization) formed into a legal corporation. **2** having a bodily form; embodied.
DERIVATIVES: **in·cor·po·ra·tion** |-,kôrpə'rāSHən| *n.* **in·cor·po·ra·tor** |-,rātər| *n.*

in·cor·po·re·al |,inkôr'pôrēəl| • *adj.* not composed of matter; having no material existence: *millions believe in a supreme but incorporeal being they call God.* Cf. IMMATERIAL.
■ (in law) having no physical existence: *incorporeal hereditaments such as rights of way.*
DERIVATIVES: **in·cor·po·re·al·i·ty** |-,pôrē 'ælitē| *n.* **in·cor·po·re·al·ly** *adv.* **in·cor·po· re·i·ty** |-pə'rēitē| *n.*

in·cor·ri·gi·ble |in'kôrijəbəl| • *adj.* (of a person or their tendencies) not able to be corrected, improved, or reformed: *she's an incorrigible flirt.* • *n.* a person of this type. Cf. RECALCITRANT, REFRACTORY.
DERIVATIVES: **in·cor·ri·gi·bil·i·ty** |-,kôri jə'bilitē| *n.* **in·cor·ri·gi·bly** *adv.* [as submodifier] *the incorrigibly macho character of newsgathering operations.*

in·cred·i·ble |in'kredəbəl| • *adj.* **1** impossible to believe: *an almost incredible tale of triumph and tragedy.* **2** difficult to believe; extraordinary: *the noise from the crowd was incredible.*
■ amazingly good or beautiful: *she looked so incredible.*
DERIVATIVES: **in·cred·i·bil·i·ty** |-,kredə 'bilitē| *n.*

USAGE: The adjective **incredible** means 'unbelievable' or 'not convincing' and can be applied to a situation, statement, policy, or threat to a person, e.g., *I find this testimony incredible.* **Incredulous** means 'disinclined to believe; skeptical'—the opposite of *credulous, gullible*—and is usually applied to a person's attitude, e.g., *You shouldn't be surprised that I'm incredulous after all your lies.*

in·cre·du·li·ty |,inkrə'd(y)o͞olitē| • *n.* the state of being unwilling or unable to believe something: *he stared down the street in incredulity.*

in·cred·u·lous |in'krejələs| • *adj.* (of a person or their manner) unwilling or unable to believe something: *an incredulous gasp.*
DERIVATIVES: **in·cred·u·lous·ly** *adv.* **in· cred·u·lous·ness** *n.*

in·cre·ment |'iNGkrəmənt| • *n.* an increase or addition, esp. one of a series on a fixed scale: *the inmates' pay can escalate in five-cent increments to a maximum of 90 cents an hour.*
■ a regular increase in salary on such a scale.
■ (in mathematics) a small positive or nega-

tive change in a variable quantity or function. Cf. DECREMENT.
DERIVATIVES: **in·cre·men·tal** |,iNGkrə 'mentl; ,in-| *adj.* **in·cre·men·tal·ly** |,iNGkrə 'mentl-ē; ,in-| *adv.*

in·crim·i·nate |in'krimə,nāt| • *v.* [trans.] make (someone) appear guilty of a crime or wrongdoing; strongly imply the guilt of (someone): *he refused to answer questions in order not to incriminate himself* | [as adj.] (**incriminating**) *incriminating evidence.*
DERIVATIVES: **in·crim·i·na·tion** |-,krimə 'nāSHən| *n.* **in·crim·i·na·to·ry** |-nə,tôrē| *adj.*

in·cu·bate |'inkyə,bāt; 'iNG-| • *v.* [trans.] (of a bird) sit on (eggs) in order to keep them warm and bring them to hatching.
■ (esp. in a laboratory) keep (eggs, cells, bacteria, embryos, etc.) at a suitable temperature so that they develop: *the samples were incubated at 80°C for 3 minutes.* ■ (**be incubating something**) have an infectious disease developing inside one before symptoms appear: *the possibility that she was incubating syphilis.*
■ [intrans.] develop slowly without outward or perceptible signs: *unfortunately the bug incubates for around three years.*
DERIVATIVES: **in·cu·ba·tion** *n.* **in·cu·ba· tive** *adj.*

in·cu·bus |'iNGkyəbəs; 'in-| • *n.* (pl. **incubi** |-,bī|) a male demon believed to have sexual intercourse with sleeping women.
■ a cause of distress or anxiety: *debt is a big incubus in developing countries.* Cf. SUCCUBUS.

in·cul·cate |in'kəl,kāt; 'inkəl-| • *v.* [trans.] instill (an attitude, idea, or habit) by persistent instruction: *the failures of the churches to inculcate a sense of moral responsibility.*
■ teach (someone) an attitude, idea, or habit by such instruction: *they will try to* **inculcate** *you* **with** *a respect for culture.*
DERIVATIVES: **in·cul·ca·tion** |,inkəl'kā-SHən| *n.* **in·cul·ca·tive** *adj.* **in·cul·ca·tor** |-,kātər| *n.*

in·cul·pate |in'kəl,pāt; 'inkəl-| • *v.* [trans.] accuse or blame.
■ incriminate: *someone placed the pistol in your room in order to inculpate you.* Cf. EXCULPATE.
DERIVATIVES: **in·cul·pa·tion** |,inkəl'pā-SHən| *n.* **in·cul·pa·to·ry** |in'kəlpə,tôrē| *adj.*

in·cum·bent |in'kəmbənt| • *adj.* **1** [predic.] (**incumbent on/upon**) necessary for (someone) as a duty or responsibility: *it is incumbent on all decent people to concentrate on destroying this evil.* **2** [attrib.] (of an official or regime) currently holding office: *the incumbent president had been defeated.*
■ denoting a company having a relatively greater franchise or share of a market: *powerful incumbent airlines.* • *n.* the holder of an office or post.

in·de·fat·i·ga·ble |,ində'fætigəbəl| • *adj.* (of a person or personal efforts) persisting tirelessly: *an indefatigable defender of human rights.*
DERIVATIVES: **in·de·fat·i·ga·bil·i·ty** |-,fæt igə'bilitē| *n.* **in·de·fat·i·ga·bly** |-blē| *adv.*

in·del·i·ble |in'deləbəl| • *adj.* (of ink or a pen) making marks that cannot be removed.

■ not able to be forgotten or removed: *the story made an indelible impression on me.*
DERIVATIVES: **in•del•i•bil•i•ty** |-,delə'bil-itē| *n.* **in•del•i•bly** |-blē| *adv.*
in•del•i•cate |in'delikit| • *adj.* having or showing a lack of sensitive understanding or tact: *forgive me asking an indelicate question, but how old are you?*
■ slightly indecent: *an earthy, often indelicate sense of humor.*
DERIVATIVES: **in•del•i•ca•cy** |-kəsē| *n.* (pl. -ies) **in•del•i•cate•ly** *adv.*
in•dem•ni•fy |in'demnə,fī| • *v.* (-ies, -ied) [trans.] compensate (someone) for harm or loss: *the amount of insurance that may be carried to indemnify the owner in the event of a loss.*
■ secure (someone) against anticipated loss or liability: *a clause to indemnify the landlord against third-party claims.*
DERIVATIVES: **in•dem•ni•fi•ca•tion** |-,demnəfi'kāsHən| *n.* **in•dem•ni•fi•er** *n.*
in•dem•ni•ty |in'demnitē| • *n.* (pl. -ies) security or protection against a loss or other financial burden: *no indemnity will be given for loss of cash.*
■ security against or exemption from legal liability or anticipated loss: *a deed of indemnity | even warranties and indemnities do not provide complete protection.* ■ a sum of money paid as compensation, esp. a sum exacted by a victor in war as one condition of peace.
in•den•ture |in'denCHər| • *n.* a formal legal agreement, contract, or document, in particular:
■ formerly, a deed of contract of which copies were made for the contracting parties with the edges indented for identification. ■ a formal list, certificate, or inventory. ■ an agreement binding an apprentice to a master: *the 30 apprentices have received their indentures on completion of their training.* ■ the fact of being bound to service by such an agreement: *men in their first year after indenture to the Company.* • *v.* [trans.] (usu. **be indentured to**) bind (someone) by an indenture as an apprentice or laborer.
DERIVATIVES: **in•den•ture•ship** |-,SHip| *n.*
in•de•ter•mi•nate |,indi'tərmənit| • *adj.* not certain, known, or established: *the date of manufacture is indeterminate.*
■ left doubtful; vague: *the ending rendered the story incomplete, or at least indeterminate.* ■ (of a judicial sentence) such that the convicted person's conduct determines the date of release. ■ (of a quantity in mathematics) having no definite or definable value. ■ (of a medical condition) from which a diagnosis of the underlying cause cannot be made: *indeterminate colitis.* ■ (of a plant shoot) not having all the axes terminating in a flower bud and so producing a shoot of indefinite length.
DERIVATIVES: **in•de•ter•mi•na•cy** |-nəsē| *n.* **in•de•ter•mi•nate•ly** *adv.* **in•de•ter•mi•nate•ness** *n.*
In•di•an |'indēən| • *adj.* **1** of or relating to the indigenous peoples of America. **2** of or relat-

ing to India or to the subcontinent comprising India, Pakistan, and Bangladesh. • *n.* **1** an American Indian. **2** a native or national of India, or a person of Indian descent.
DERIVATIVES: **In•di•an•i•za•tion** |,indēəni'zāsHən| *n.* **In•di•an•ize** |-,nīz| *v.* **In•di•an•ness** *n.*

USAGE: **Indian**, meaning 'native of America before the arrival of Europeans,' is objected to by many who now favor **Native American**. There are others (including many members of these ethnic groups), however, who see nothing wrong with **Indian** or **American Indian**, which are long-established terms, although the preference where possible is to refer to specific peoples, as **Apache, Mohawk,**, and so on. The terms **Amerind** and **Amerindian**, once proposed as alternatives to **Indian**, are used in linguistics and anthropology, but have never gained widespread use. Newer alternatives, not widely used or established, include **First Nation** (esp. in Canada) and the more generic **aboriginal peoples**. It should be noted that **Indian** is held by many not to include some American groups, for example, prehistoric groups like the Anasazi, and the modern Aleut and Inuit. A further consideration is that **Indian** also (and in some contexts primarily) refers to inhabitants of India or their descendants, who may be referred to as "Asian Indians" to prevent misunderstanding. See also **usage** at NATIVE AMERICAN.

in•dic•a•tive |in'dikətiv| • *adj.* **1** serving as a sign or indication of something: *having recurrent dreams is not necessarily indicative of any psychological problem.* **2** denoting a mood of verbs expressing simple statement of a fact. Cf. SUBJUNCTIVE. • *n.* a verb in the indicative mood.
■ (**the indicative**) the indicative mood.
DERIVATIVES: **in•dic•a•tive•ly** *adv.*
in•di•ci•a |in'disH(ē)ə| • *plural n.* signs, indications, or distinguishing marks: *learned footnotes and other indicia of scholarship.*
in•dict |in'dīt| • *v.* [trans.] (usu. **be indicted**) formally accuse or charge (someone) with a serious crime: *his former manager was indicted for fraud. | In American law, indictments are issued by a grand jury.* Cf. ARRAIGN.
DERIVATIVES: **indictability** *n.* **indictable** *adj.* **indictor, in•dict•ee** |,indī'tē| *n.* **in•dict•er** *n.* **indictment** *n.*
in•dif•fer•ent |in'dif(ə)rənt| • *adj.* **1** having no particular interest or sympathy; unconcerned: *she seemed indifferent rather than angry | indifferent to foreign affairs.* **2** neither good nor bad; mediocre: *attempts to distinguish between good, bad, and indifferent work.*
■ not especially good; fairly bad: *several indifferent watercolors.*
DERIVATIVES: **in•dif•fer•ent•ly** *adv.*
in•dig•e•nous |in'dijənəs| • *adj.* originating or occurring naturally in a particular place;

native: *the indigenous peoples of Siberia* | *coriander is* **indigenous to** *southern Europe.* Cf. ABORIGINAL.
DERIVATIVES: **in•dig•e•nous•ly** *adv.* **in•dig•e•nous•ness** *n.*

in•di•gent |'indijənt| • *adj.* lacking the necessities of life; poor; needy. • *n.* a needy person.
DERIVATIVES: **in•di•gence** *n.* **in•di•gent•ly** *adv.*

in•dig•na•tion |,indig'nāsHən| • *n.* anger or annoyance provoked by what is perceived as injustice or unfair treatment: *the letter filled Lucy with indignation.*

in•dig•ni•ty |in'dignitē| • *n.* (pl. **-ies**) treatment or circumstances that cause one to feel shame or to lose one's dignity: *the indignity of needing financial help* | *he was subjected to all manner of indignities.*

in•dis•cre•tion |,indi'skresHən| • *n.* behavior or speech that displays a lack of prudence or good judgment; indiscreet talk or actions: *he knew himself all too prone to indiscretion* | *sexual indiscretions.*

in•dis•crim•i•nate |,indi'skrimənit| • *adj.* done at random or without careful judgment: *terrorist gunmen engaged in indiscriminate killing.*
■ (of a person) not using or exercising discrimination: *she was indiscriminate with her affections.*
DERIVATIVES: **in•dis•crim•i•nate•ly** *adv.* **in•dis•crim•i•nate•ness** *n.* **in•dis•crim•i•na•tion** |-,skrimə'nāsHən| *n.*

in•dis•pen•sa•ble |,indi'spensəbəl| • *adj.* unable to be dispensed with or done without; absolutely necessary: *he made himself indispensable to the parish priest.*
DERIVATIVES: **in•dis•pen•sa•bil•i•ty** |-,spensə'bilitē| *n.* **in•dis•pen•sa•ble•ness** *n.* **in•dis•pen•sa•bly** |-blē| *adv.*

in•dite |in'dīt| • *v.* [trans.] write; compose: *he indites the wondrous tale of Our Lord.*

in•di•vid•u•ate |,ində'vijə,wāt| • *v.* [trans.] distinguish from others of the same kind; single out: *it is easy to individuate and enumerate the significant elements.*
DERIVATIVES: **in•di•vid•u•a•tion** |-,vijə'wāsHən| *n.*

in•di•vis•i•ble |,ində'vizəbəl| • *adj.* unable to be divided or separated: *privilege was indivisible from responsibility.*
■ (of a number) unable to be divided by another number exactly without leaving a remainder.
DERIVATIVES: **in•di•vis•i•bil•i•ty** |-,vizə'bilitē| *n.* **in•di•vis•i•bly** |-blē| *adv.*

in•doc•tri•nate |in'däktrə,nāt| • *v.* [trans.] teach (a person or group) to accept a set of beliefs uncritically: *broadcasting was a vehicle for indoctrinating the masses.*
■ teach or instruct (someone): *he indoctrinated them in systematic theology.*
DERIVATIVES: **in•doc•tri•na•tion** |-,däktrə'nāsHən| *n.* **in•doc•tri•na•tor** |-,nātər| *n.* **in•doc•tri•na•to•ry** |-nə,tôrē| *adj.*

in•do•lent |'indələnt| • *adj.* **1** wanting to avoid activity or exertion; lazy. **2** (of a disease condition) causing little or no pain.
■ (esp. of an ulcer) slow to develop, progress, or heal; persistent.
DERIVATIVES: **in•do•lence** *n.* **in•do•lent•ly** *adv.*

in•dom•i•ta•ble |in'dämitəbəl| • *adj.* impossible to subdue or defeat: *a woman of indomitable spirit.*
DERIVATIVES: **in•dom•i•ta•bil•i•ty** |-,dämitə'bilitē| *n.* **in•dom•i•ta•ble•ness** *n.* **in•dom•i•ta•bly** |-blē| *adv.*

in•du•bi•ta•ble |in'd(y)ōōbitəbəl| • *adj.* impossible to doubt; unquestionable: *an indubitable truth.*
DERIVATIVES: **in•du•bi•ta•bly** |-blē| *adv.* [sentence adverb] *indubitably, liberalism parades under many guises.*

in•duce |in'd(y)ōōs| • *v.* [trans.] **1** [with obj. and infinitive] succeed in persuading or influencing (someone) to do something: *the pickets induced many workers to stay away.* **2** bring about or give rise to: *none of these measures induced a change of policy.*
■ produce (an electric charge or current or a magnetic state) by proximity to an already charged object (induction). ■ [usu. as adj.] (**induced**) cause (radioactivity) by bombardment with radiation. **3** bring on (childbirth or abortion) artificially, typically by the use of drugs.
■ bring on childbirth in (a pregnant woman) in this way. ■ bring on the birth of (a baby) in this way. **4** derive by inductive reasoning.
DERIVATIVES: **in•duc•er** *n.* **in•duc•i•ble** *adj.*

in•duct |in'dəkt| • *v.* [trans.] admit (someone) formally to a position or organization: *each worker, if formally inducted into the Mafia, was known as a "soldier."*
■ formally introduce (a member of the clergy) into possession of a benefice. ■ enlist (someone) for military service. ■ (**induct someone in/into**) introduce someone to (a difficult or obscure subject): *my master inducted me into the skills of magic.*
DERIVATIVES: **in•duc•tee** |,indək'tē| *n.*

in•duc•tion |in'dəksHən| • *n.* **1** the action or process of inducting someone to a position or organization: *the league's induction into the Baseball Hall of Fame.*
■ [usu. as adj.] a formal introduction to a new job or position: *an induction course.* ■ formal entry into military service. **2** the process or action of bringing about or giving rise to something: *isolation, starvation, and other forms of stress induction.*
■ the process of bringing on childbirth or abortion by artificial means, typically by the use of drugs. **3** (in logic) the inference of a general law from particular instances. Cf. DEDUCTION.
■ (**induction of**) the production of (facts) to prove a general statement. ■ (also **mathematical induction**) a means of proving a theorem by showing that if it is true of any particular case, it is true of the next case in a series, and then showing that it is indeed true in one particular case. **4** (in physics) the production of an electric or magnetic state by the

proximity (without contact) of an electrified or magnetized body.
■ the production of an electric current in a conductor by varying the magnetic field applied to the conductor. **5** the stage of the working cycle of an internal combustion engine in which the fuel mixture is drawn into the cylinders.

in•dulge |in'dəlj| • v. [intrans.] (**indulge in**) allow oneself to enjoy the pleasure of: *we indulged in a hot fudge sundae.*
■ become involved in (an activity, typically one that is undesirable or disapproved of): *I don't indulge in idle gossip.* ■ allow oneself to enjoy a particular pleasure, esp. that of alcohol: *I only indulge on special occasions.* ■ [trans.] satisfy or yield freely to (a desire or interest): *she was able to indulge a growing passion for literature.* ■ [trans.] allow (someone) to enjoy a desired pleasure: *I spent time indulging myself with secret feasts.*
DERIVATIVES: **indulgent** adj. **in•dulg•er** n.

in•du•rate |'ind(y)ə,rāt| • v. [trans.] [usu. as adj.] (**indurated**) harden; solidify: *a bed of indurated clay | a heart indurated from years of struggle.*
DERIVATIVES: **in•du•ra•tion** |,ind(y)ə'rāsHən| n. **in•du•ra•tive** |-,rātiv| adj.

in•e•bri•ate • v. |i'nēbrē,āt| [trans.] [often as adj.] (**inebriated**) make drunk; intoxicate. • n. |-brē-it| a drunkard. • adj. drunk; intoxicated.
DERIVATIVES: **in•e•bri•a•tion** |i,nēbrē'āsHən| n. **in•e•bri•e•ty** |,ini'brī-itē| n.

in•ef•fa•ble |in'efəbəl| • adj. too great or extreme to be expressed or described in words: *the ineffable beauty of the Everglades.*
■ not to be uttered: *the ineffable Hebrew name that gentiles write as Jehovah.*
DERIVATIVES: **in•ef•fa•bil•i•ty** |-efə'bilitē| n. **in•ef•fa•bly** |-blē| adv.

in•ef•fec•tive |,ini'fektiv| • adj. not producing any or the desired effect: *a weak and ineffective president.*
DERIVATIVES: **in•ef•fec•tive•ly** adv. **in•ef•fec•tive•ness** n.

in•ef•fec•tu•al |,ini'fekcHəwəl| • adj. not producing any or the desired effect: *an ineffectual campaign.*
■ (of a person) lacking the ability or qualities to cope with a role or situation: *she was neglectful and ineffectual as a parent.*
DERIVATIVES: **in•ef•fec•tu•al•i•ty** |-,fekcHə'wælitē| n. **in•ef•fec•tu•al•ly** adv. **in•ef•fec•tu•al•ness** n.

in•ept |i'nept| • adj. having or showing no skill; clumsy: *the inept handling of the threat.*
DERIVATIVES: **in•ept•i•tude** |-ti,t(y)o͞od| n. **in•ept•ly** adv. **in•ept•ness** n.

in•e•qual•i•ty |,ini'kwälitē| • n. (pl. **-ies**) difference in size, degree, circumstances, etc.; lack of equality: *social inequality | the widening inequalities in income.*
■ lack of smoothness or regularity in a surface: *the inequality of the ground hindered their footing.* ■ (in mathematics) the relation between two expressions that are not equal, employing a sign such as ≠ "not equal to," > "greater

than," or < "less than." ■ a symbolic expression of the fact that two quantities are not equal.

in•eq•ui•ty |in'ekwitē| • n. (pl. **-ies**) lack of fairness or justice: *inequities in school financing.*

in•ert |i'nərt| • adj. lacking the ability or strength to move: *she lay inert in her bed.*
■ lacking vigor: *an inert political system.*
■ chemically inactive: *inert ingredients.*
DERIVATIVES: **in•ert•ly** adv. **in•ert•ness** n.

in•er•tia |i'nərsHə| • n. **1** a tendency to do nothing or to remain unchanged: *the bureaucratic inertia of government.* **2** a property of matter by which it continues in its existing state of rest or uniform motion in a straight line, unless that state is changed by an external force.
■ [with adj.] resistance to change in some other physical property: *the thermal inertia of the oceans will delay the full rise in temperature for a few decades.*
DERIVATIVES: **inertial** adj. **in•er•tia•less** adj.

in•es•ti•ma•ble |in'estəməbəl| • adj. too great to calculate: *a treasure of inestimable value.*
DERIVATIVES: **in•es•ti•ma•bly** |-blē| adv.

in•ev•i•ta•ble |in'evitəbəl| • adj. certain to happen; unavoidable: *war was inevitable.*
■ so frequently experienced or seen that it is completely predictable: *the inevitable letter from the bank.* • n. (**the inevitable**) a situation that is unavoidable: *trying to hold off the inevitable.*
DERIVATIVES: **in•ev•i•ta•bil•i•ty** |-,evitə'bilitē| n. **in•ev•i•ta•bly** |-blē| adv. [sentence adverb] *inevitably, she turned her experiences into a book.*

in•ex•o•ra•ble |in'eksərəbəl| • adj. impossible to stop or prevent: *the seemingly inexorable march of new technology.*
■ (of a person) impossible to persuade by request or entreaty: *the doctors were inexorable, and there was nothing to be done.*
DERIVATIVES: **in•ex•o•ra•bil•i•ty** |-,eksərə'bilitē| n. **in•ex•o•ra•bly** |-blē| adv.

in•ex•pli•ca•ble |,inek'splikəbəl; in'eksplikəbəl| • adj. unable to be explained or accounted for: *for some inexplicable reason her mind went completely blank.*
DERIVATIVES: **in•ex•pli•ca•bil•i•ty** |'inek,splikə'bilitē| n. **in•ex•pli•ca•bly** |-blē| adv. [sentence adverb] *inexplicably, the pumps started to malfunction.*

in•fal•li•ble |in'fæləbəl| • adj. incapable of making mistakes or being wrong: *doctors are not infallible.*
■ never failing; always effective: *infallible cures.* ■ (in the Roman Catholic Church) credited with **papal infallibility**, the doctrine (promulgated in 1870) that in specified circumstances the Pope is incapable of error in pronouncing dogma: *for an encyclical to be infallible the pope must speak ex cathedra.*
DERIVATIVES: **in•fal•li•bil•i•ty** n. **in•fal•li•ble•ness** n. **in•fal•li•bly** |-blē| adv.

in•fa•mous |'infəməs| • adj. well known for

some bad quality or deed: *an infamous war criminal.* Cf. NOTORIOUS.
■ shamefully wicked; abominable: *the medical council disqualified him for infamous misconduct.* ■ (in former times, of a person) deprived of all or some citizens' rights as a consequence of conviction for a serious crime.
DERIVATIVES: **in•fa•mous•ly** *adv.* **in•fa•my** |-mē| *n.* (pl. **-ies**).

in•fan•til•ism |'infəntl,izəm; in'fæn-| • *n.* childish behavior.
■ (in psychology) the persistence of infantile characteristics or behavior in adult life.

in•farc•tion |in'färksHən| • *n.* the obstruction of the blood supply to an organ or region of tissue, typically by a thrombus or embolus, causing local death of the tissue.

in•fec•tious |in'feksHəs| • *adj.* (of a disease or disease-causing organism) liable to be transmitted to people, organisms, etc., through the environment.
■ liable to spread infection: *the dogs may still be infectious.* ■ likely to spread or influence others in a rapid manner: *her enthusiasm is infectious.*
DERIVATIVES: **in•fec•tious•ly** *adv.* **in•fec•tious•ness** *n.*

USAGE: On the differences in meaning between **infectious** and **contagious**, see **usage** at CONTAGIOUS.

in•fe•lic•i•tous |,infə'lisitəs| • *adj.* **1** unhappy or unfortunate. **2** not appropriate: *his illustration is singularly infelicitous.*
DERIVATIVES: **in•fe•lic•i•tous•ly** *adv.*

in•fer |in'fər| • *v.* (**inferred, inferring**) [trans.] deduce or conclude (information) from evidence and reasoning rather than from explicit statements:[with clause] *from these facts we can infer that crime has been increasing.*
DERIVATIVES: **in•fer•a•ble** (also **inferrable**) *adj.*

USAGE: There is a distinction in meaning between **infer** and **imply**. In the sentence *the speaker implied that the general had been a traitor,* **implied** means that something in the speaker's words **suggested** that this man was a traitor (though nothing so explicit was actually stated). However, in *we inferred from his words that the general had been a traitor,* **inferred** means that something in the speaker's words enabled the listeners to **deduce** that the man was a traitor. The two words **infer** and **imply** can describe the same event, but from different angles. Mistakes occur when **infer** is used to mean **imply,** as in *are you inferring that I'm a liar?* (instead of *are you implying that I'm a liar?*).

in•fer•ence |'inf(ə)rəns| • *n.* a conclusion reached on the basis of evidence and reasoning.
■ the process of reaching such a conclusion: *his emphasis on order and health, and by inference cleanliness.*
DERIVATIVES: **in•fer•en•tial** |,infə'ren-

CHəl| *adj.* **in•fer•en•tial•ly** |,infə'renCHəlē| *adv.*

in•fer•nal |in'fərnl| • *adj.* **1** of, relating to, or characteristic of hell or the underworld: *the infernal regions* | *the infernal heat of the forge.* **2** [attrib.] irritating and tiresome (used for emphasis): *you're an infernal nuisance.*
DERIVATIVES: **in•fer•nal•ly** *adv.*

in•fi•del |'infədl; -,del| • *n.* a person who does not believe in religion or who adheres to a religion other than one's own: [as plural n.] (**the infidel**) *they wanted to secure the Holy Places from the infidel.* • *adj.* adhering to a religion other than one's own: *the infidel foe.*

in•fi•del•i•ty |,infi'delitē| • *n.* (pl. **-ies**) **1** the action or state of being unfaithful to a spouse or other sexual partner: *her infidelity continued after her marriage* | *I ought not to have tolerated his many infidelities.* **2** unbelief in a particular religion, esp. Christianity.

in•fil•trate |'infil,trāt; in'fil-| • *v.* [trans.] **1** enter or gain access to (an organization, place, etc.) surreptitiously and gradually, esp. in order to acquire secret information.
■ permeate or become a part of (something) in this way: *computing has infiltrated most professions now.* ■ (of a tumor, cells, etc.) spread into or invade (a tissue or organ). **2** (of a liquid) permeate (something) by filtration: *virtually no water infiltrates deserts such as the Sahara.*
■ introduce (a liquid) into something in this way: *lignocaine was infiltrated into the wound.* • *n.* an infiltrating biochemical substance or a number of infiltrating cells.
DERIVATIVES: **in•fil•tra•tion** |,infil'trāsHən| *n.* **in•fil•tra•tor** |-,trātər| *n.*

in•fi•nite |'infənit| • *adj.* **1** limitless or endless in space, extent, or size; impossible to measure or calculate: *the infinite mercy of God* | *the infinite number of stars in the universe.*
■ very great in amount or degree: *he bathed the wound with infinite care.* ■ (in mathematics) greater than any assignable quantity or countable number. ■ (of a mathematical series) able to be continued indefinitely. **2** (in grammar) another term for *nonfinite,* 'not limited by tense, person, or number.' Cf. FINITE. • *n.* (**the infinite**) a space or quantity that is infinite.
■ (**the Infinite**) God.
DERIVATIVES: **in•fi•nite•ly** *adv.* [as submodifier] *the pay is infinitely better.* **in•fi•nite•ness** *n.*

in•fin•i•tes•i•mal |,infini'tes(ə)məl| • *adj.* extremely small: *an infinitesimal pause.* • *n.* an indefinitely small quantity; a value approaching zero.
DERIVATIVES: **in•fin•i•tes•i•mal•ly** *adv.*

USAGE: Although this long word is commonly assumed to refer to large numbers, **infinitesimal** describes only very small size. While there may be an *infinite* number of grains of sand on the beach, a single grain may be said to be *infinitesimal.*

in•fir•mi•ty |in'fərmitē| • *n.* (pl. **-ies**) the state or an aspect of physical or mental weakness: *the infirmities of old age.*

in·fla·gran·te de·lic·to |ˌin fləˈgräntā də ˈliktō; fləˈgræntē| (also **in flagrante**) • *adv.* in the very act of wrongdoing, esp. in an act of sexual misconduct: *he had been **caught in** flagrante with Joe's wife.*

in·flam·ma·ble |inˈflæməbəl| • *adj.* easily set on fire: *inflammable and poisonous gases.*
■ likely to provoke strong feelings.
DERIVATIVES: **in·flam·ma·bil·i·ty** |-ˌflæmə'bilitē| *n.* **in·flam·ma·ble·ness** *n.* **in·flam·ma·bly** |-blē| *adv.*

USAGE: Both **inflammable** and **flammable** mean 'easily set on fire.' The opposite is **nonflammable.** Where there is a danger that **inflammable** could be understood to mean its opposite, that is, 'not easily set on fire,' **flammable** should be used to avoid confusion. **Inflammable** is usually used figuratively or in nontechnical contexts (*inflammable temper*).

in·fla·tion |inˈflāsHən| • *n.* **1** the action of inflating something or the condition of being inflated: *the inflation of a balloon | the gross inflation of salaries.*
■ (in some theories of cosmology) a very brief exponential expansion of the universe postulated to have interrupted the standard linear expansion shortly after the big bang. **2** (in economics) a general increase in prices and fall in the purchasing value of money: *policies aimed at controlling inflation |* [as adj.] *high inflation rates.* Cf. DEFLATION; STAGFLATION.
DERIVATIVES: **inflationary** *adj.* **in·fla·tion·ism** |-ˌnizəm| *n.* **in·fla·tion·ist** |-nist| *n. & adj.*

in·flec·tion |inˈfleksHən| (chiefly Brit. also **inflexion**) • *n.* **1** a change in the form of a word (typically the ending) to express a grammatical function or attribute such as tense, mood, person, number, case, and gender.
■ the process or practice of inflecting words. **2** the modulation of intonation or pitch in the voice: *she spoke slowly and without inflection | the variety of his vocal inflections.*
■ the variation of the pitch of a musical note. **3** a change of curvature from convex to concave at a particular point on a curve.
DERIVATIVES: **in·flec·tion·al** |-sHənl| *adj.* **in·flec·tion·al·ly** |-sHənl-ē| *adv.* **in·flec·tion·less** *adj.*

in·flo·res·cence |ˌinflôˈresəns; -flə-| • *n.* the complete flowerhead of a plant including stems, stalks, bracts, and flowers.
■ the arrangement of the flowers on a plant.
■ the process of flowering.

in·form·er |inˈfôrmər| • *n.* a person who informs on another person to the police or other authority.

in·frac·tion |inˈfræksHən| • *n.* a violation or infringement of a law, agreement, or set of rules.
DERIVATIVES: **in·frac·tor** |-tər| *n.*

in·fra dig • *adj.* [predic.] beneath one; demeaning.

in·fran·gi·ble |inˈfrænjəbəl| • *adj.* unbreakable.
■ unable to be infringed; inviolable.
DERIVATIVES: **in·fran·gi·bil·i·ty** |-ˌfrænjəˈbilitē| *n.* **in·fran·gi·bly** |-blē| *adv.*

in·fra·struc·ture |ˈinfrəˌstrəkCHər| • *n.* the basic physical structures and facilities (e.g., buildings, roads, and power supplies) needed for the operation of a society or enterprise.
■ The underlying structure of a system or organization.
DERIVATIVES: **in·fra·struc·tur·al** |ˌinfrəˈstrəkCHərəl| *adj.*

in·fringe |inˈfrinj| • *v.* [trans.] actively break the terms of (a law, agreement, etc.): *making an unauthorized copy would infringe copyright.*
■ act so as to limit or undermine (something); encroach on: *his legal rights were being infringed |* [intrans.] *I wouldn't **infringe on** his privacy.*
DERIVATIVES: **in·fringe·ment** *n.* **in·fring·er** *n.*

in·fuse |inˈfyo͞oz| • *v.* [trans.] **1** fill; pervade: *her work is **infused with** an anger born of pain and oppression.*
■ instill (a quality) in someone or something: *he did his best to **infuse** good humor **into** his voice.* ■ allow (a liquid) to flow into a patient, vein, etc.: *saline was **infused into** the aorta.* **2** soak (tea, herbs, etc.) in liquid to extract the flavor or healing properties: *infuse the dried flowers in boiling water.*
■ [intrans.] (of tea, herbs, etc.) be soaked in this way: *allow the mixture to infuse for 15 minutes.* Cf. SUFFUSE.
DERIVATIVES: **in·fus·er** *n.*

in·fu·sion |inˈfyo͞oZHən| • *n.* **1** a drink, remedy, or extract prepared by soaking the leaves of a plant or herb in liquid.
■ the process of preparing such a drink, remedy, or extract. **2** the introduction of a new element or quality into something: *an infusion of youthful talent.*
■ the slow injection of a substance into a vein or tissue.

in·gen·ious |inˈjēnyəs| • *adj.* (of a person) clever, original, and inventive: *he was ingenious enough to overcome the limited budget.*
■ (of a machine or idea) cleverly and originally devised and well suited to its purpose.
DERIVATIVES: **in·gen·ious·ly** *adv.* **in·gen·ious·ness** *n.*

USAGE: **Ingenious** and **ingenuous** are often confused. **Ingenious** means 'clever, skillful, or resourceful,' (*an ingenious device*), while **ingenuous** means 'artless' or 'frank,' (*charmed by the ingenuous honesty of the child.*)

in·gé·nue |ˈænjəˌno͞o; ˈänzH-| • *n.* an innocent or unsophisticated young woman.
■ a part of this type in a play. ■ an actress who plays such a part.

in·ge·nu·i·ty |ˌinjəˈn(y)o͞oitē| • *n.* the quality of being clever, original, and inventive.

in·gen·u·ous |inˈjenyəwəs| • *adj.* (of a person or action) innocent and unsuspecting.
DERIVATIVES: **in·gen·u·ous·ly** *adv.* **in·gen·u·ous·ness** *n.*

in•glo•ri•ous |in'glôrēəs| • *adj.* (of an action or situation) causing shame or a loss of honor: *the events are inglorious and culminate in ostracism.*
■ not famous or renowned.
DERIVATIVES: **in•glo•ri•ous•ly** *adv.* **in•glo•ri•ous•ness** *n.*

in•grate |'in,grāt| • *n.* an ungrateful person. • *adj.* ungrateful.

in•gra•ti•ate |in'grāSHē,āt| • *v.* (**ingratiate oneself**) bring oneself into favor with someone by flattering or trying to please: *a social climber who had tried to ingratiate herself with the city gentry.*
DERIVATIVES: **in•gra•ti•a•tion** |-,grāSHē 'āSHən| *n.* **ingratiatory** *adj.*

in•her•ent |in'hirənt; -'her-| • *adj.* existing in something as a permanent, essential, or characteristic attribute: *any form of mountaineering has its inherent dangers* | *the symbolism inherent in all folk tales.* Cf. IMMANENT.
■ vested in (someone) as a legal right or privilege: *the president's inherent foreign affairs power.*
DERIVATIVES: **in•her•ence** *n.* **in•her•ent•ly** *adv.*

in•hib•it |in'hibit| • *v.* (**inhibited, inhibiting**) [trans.] hinder, restrain, or prevent (an action or process): *cold inhibits plant growth.*
■ prevent or prohibit someone from doing something: *the rule inhibited some retirees from working.* ■ make (someone) self-conscious and unable to act in a relaxed and natural way: *his mother's strictures would always inhibit him.* ■ (chiefly of a drug or other substance) slow down or prevent (a process, reaction, or function) or reduce the activity of (an enzyme or other agent). ■ (in ecclesiastical law) forbid (a member of the clergy) to exercise clerical functions.
DERIVATIVES: **in•hib•i•tive** |-div| *adj.* **in•hib•i•to•ry** |-,tôrē| *adj.*

in•hi•bi•tion |,in(h)i'biSHən| • *n.* a feeling that makes one self-conscious and unable to act in a relaxed and natural way.
■ a psychological restraint on the direct expression of an instinct. ■ the action of inhibiting, restricting, or hindering a process. ■ the slowing or prevention of a process, reaction, or function by a particular substance.

in•hu•man |in'(h)yŌŌmən| • *adj.* 1 lacking human qualities of compassion and mercy; cruel and barbaric. 2 not human in nature or character.
DERIVATIVES: **in•hu•man•ly** *adv.*

in•hu•mane |,in(h)yŌŌ'mān| • *adj.* without compassion for misery or suffering; cruel.
DERIVATIVES: **in•hu•mane•ly** *adv.*

in•im•i•cal |i'nimikəl| • *adj.* tending to obstruct or harm: *actions inimical to our interests.*
■ unfriendly; hostile: *an inimical alien power.*
DERIVATIVES: **in•im•i•cal•ly** |-ik(ə)lē| *adv.*

in•im•i•ta•ble |i'nimitəbəl| • *adj.* so good or unusual as to be impossible to copy; unique: *the inimitable ambience of the Vanguard.*
DERIVATIVES: **in•im•i•ta•bil•i•ty** |i,nimitə 'bilitē| *n.* **in•im•i•ta•bly** |-blē| *adv.*

in•iq•ui•ty |i'nikwitē| • *n.* (pl. **-ies**) immoral or grossly unfair behavior: *a den of iniquity* | *iniquities committed on our own doorstep.*
DERIVATIVES: **in•iq•ui•tous** |-witəs| *adj.* **in•iq•ui•tous•ly** |-witəslē| *adv.* **in•iq•ui•tous•ness** |-witəsnəs| *n.*

in•i•ti•ate • *v.* |i'niSHē,āt| [trans.] 1 cause (a process or action) to begin: *he proposes to initiate discussions on planning procedures.* 2 admit (someone) into a secret or obscure society or group, typically with a ritual: *she had been formally initiated into the movement.*
■ [as plural n.] (**the initiated**) a small group of people who share obscure knowledge: *she flies over an airway marker beacon, known as a "fix" to the initiated.* ■ (**initiate someone in/into**) introduce someone to a particular activity or skill, esp. a difficult or obscure one: *they were initiated into the mysteries of mathematics.* • *n.* a person who has been initiated into an organization or activity, typically recently: *initiates of the Shiva cult.*
DERIVATIVES: **in•i•ti•a•tion** |i,niSHē'āSHən| *n.* **in•i•ti•a•to•ry** |-ə,tôrē| *adj.*

in•i•ti•a•tive |i'niSH(ē)ətiv| • *n.* 1 the ability to take the first step independently, or to lead: *use your initiative, imagination, and common sense.* 2 [in sing.] the power or opportunity to act or take charge before others do: *we have lost the initiative and allowed our opponents to dictate the subject.* 3 an act or strategy intended to resolve a difficulty or improve a situation; a fresh approach to something: *a new initiative against crime.*
■ a proposal made by one nation to another in an attempt to improve relations: *diplomatic initiatives to end the war.* 4 the right of citizens outside the legislature to originate legislation.
■ a piece of legislation proposed in this way. Cf. REFERENDUM.

in•junc•tion |in'jəNG(k)SHən| • *n.* an authoritative warning or order.
■ a judicial order that restrains (enjoins) a person from beginning or continuing an action that threatens or invades the legal right of another, or an order that compels a person to carry out a certain act, e.g., to make restitution to an injured party.
DERIVATIVES: **in•junc•tive** |-'jəNG(k)tiv| *adj.*

in•ju•ri•ous |in'jŌŌrēəs| • *adj.* causing or likely to cause damage or harm.
■ (of language) maliciously insulting; libelous.
DERIVATIVES: **in•ju•ri•ous•ly** *adv.* **in•ju•ri•ous•ness** *n.*

ink•ling |'iNGkliNG| • *n.* a slight knowledge or suspicion; a hint: *the records give us an inkling of how people saw the world.*

in lo•co pa•ren•tis |in ,lōkō pə'rentis| • *adv. & adj.* (of a teacher or other adult responsible for children) in the place of a parent: [as adv.] *he was used to acting in loco parentis.*

in•ly |'inlē| • *adv.* inwardly: *inly stung with anger and disdain.*

in me•di•as res |in 'mēdēəs 'res; 'mādē,äs| • *adv.* into or in the middle of a narrative; without preamble: *having begun his story in medias res, he then interrupts it.*

■ into or in the midst of things.

in•nate |i'nāt| • adj. inborn; present at birth; natural: *her innate capacity for organization.*
■ originating in the mind naturally rather than as a result of experience.
DERIVATIVES: **in•nate•ly** adv. **in•nate•ness** n.

in•noc•u•ous |i'näkyəwəs| • adj. not harmful or offensive: *it was an innocuous question.*
DERIVATIVES: **in•noc•u•ous•ly** adv. **in•noc•u•ous•ness** n.

in•no•va•tive |'inə,vātiv| • adj. (of a product, idea, etc.) featuring new methods; advanced and original: *innovative designs| innovative ways to help unemployed people.*
■ (of a person) introducing new ideas; original and creative in thinking: *an innovative thinker.*

in•nu•en•do |,inyə'wendō| • n. (pl. **-oes** or **-os**) an allusive or oblique remark or hint, typically a suggestive or disparaging one: *she's always making sly innuendoes | a torrent of innuendo, gossip, lies, and half-truths.* Cf. INSINUATE.

in•nu•mer•ate |i'n(y)ōōmərit| • adj. without a basic knowledge of mathematics and arithmetic. • n. a person lacking such knowledge. Cf. ILLITERATE.
DERIVATIVES: **in•nu•mer•a•cy** |-rəsē| n.

in•oc•u•late |i'näkyə,lāt| • v. [trans.] treat (a person or animal) with a vaccine to produce immunity against a disease. A substance effecting this is an **inoculum** or **inoculant**: *he inoculated his tenants against smallpox.* Cf. VACCINATE.
■ introduce (an infective agent) into an organism: *it can be inoculated into laboratory animals.* ■ introduce (cells or organisms) into a culture medium.
DERIVATIVES: **in•oc•u•la•ble** |-ləbəl| adj. **in•oc•u•la•tion** |i,näkyə'lāsHən| n. **in•oc•u•la•tor** |-,lātər| n.

in•op•por•tune |,inäpər't(y)ōōn| • adj. occurring at an inconvenient time; not appropriate: *he spoke up at an inopportune moment.*
DERIVATIVES: **in•op•por•tune•ly** adv. **in•op•por•tune•ness** n.

in•or•di•nate |'nôrdn-it| • adj. unusually or disproportionately large; excessive: *inordinate amount of time.*
DERIVATIVES: **in•or•di•nate•ly** adv. [as submodifier] *an inordinately expensive business.*

in•quest |'in,kwest; 'iNG-| • n. a judicial inquiry to ascertain the facts relating to an incident, such as a death: *the coroner's inquest.*

in•qui•e•tude |in'kwīə,t(y)ōōd| • n. physical or mental restlessness or disturbance. Cf. DISQUIET.

in•qui•si•tion |,inkwi'zisHən; ,iNG-| • n. **1** a period of prolonged and intensive questioning or investigation: *she relented in her determined inquisition and offered help.*
■ in former times, a judicial or official inquiry. ■ the verdict or finding of an official inquiry. **2** (**the Inquisition**) an ecclesiastical tribunal established by Pope Gregory IX *c.*1232 for the suppression of heresy. It was active chiefly in northern Italy and southern France, becoming notorious for the use of torture. In

1542 the papal Inquisition was reinstituted to combat Protestantism, eventually becoming an organ of papal government. The **Spanish Inquisition**, established in 1478 and directed originally against converts from Judaism and Islam, later also against Protestants, and noted for its severity, was not suppressed until the early 19th century.
DERIVATIVES: **in•qui•si•tion•al** |-sHənl| adj.

in•road |'in,rōd| • n. **1** [usu. in pl.] progress; an advance: *make inroads in reducing spending.*
■ an instance of something being affected, encroached on, or destroyed by something else: *serious inroads had now been made into my pitiful cash reserves.* **2** a hostile attack; a raid.

in•sa•tia•ble |in'sāsHəbəl| • adj. (of an appetite or desire) impossible to satisfy: *an insatiable hunger for success.*
■ (of a person) having an insatiable appetite or desire for something, esp. sex.
DERIVATIVES: **in•sa•tia•bil•i•ty** |-,sāsHə'bilitē| n. **in•sa•tia•bly** |-blē| adv.

in•sa•ti•ate |in'sāsHē-it| • adj. never satisfied: *your strong desire is insatiate.*
DERIVATIVES: **insatiety** n. **insatiately** adv.

in•scru•ta•ble |in'skrōōtəbəl| • adj. impossible to understand or interpret: *her inscrutable handwriting.*
DERIVATIVES: **in•scru•ta•bil•i•ty** |-,skrōōtə'bilitē| n. **in•scru•ta•bly** |-blē| adv.

in•sen•sate |in'sen,sāt; -sit| • adj. lacking physical sensation: *a patient who was permanently unconscious and insensate.*
■ lacking sympathy or compassion; unfeeling. ■ completely lacking sense or reason: *insensate jabbering.*
DERIVATIVES: **in•sen•sate•ly** adv. **in•sen•sate•ness** n.

in•sen•si•ble |in'sensəbəl| • adj. **1** [usu. as complement] without one's mental faculties, typically a result of violence or intoxication; unconscious: *insensible with drink.*
■ (esp. of a body or bodily extremity) numb; without feeling: *the horny and insensible tip of the beak.* **2** [predic.] (**insensible of/to**) unaware of; indifferent to: *they slept on, insensible to the headlight beams.*
■ without emotion; callous. **3** too small or gradual to be perceived; inappreciable: *varying by insensible degrees.*
DERIVATIVES: **in•sen•si•bil•i•ty** n. **in•sen•si•bly** |-blē| adv.

in•sen•ti•ent |in'sensH(ē)ənt| • adj. incapable of feeling or understanding things; inanimate: *it's arrogant to presume animals be insentient.*
DERIVATIVES: **in•sen•ti•ence** n.

in•sid•i•ous |in'sidēəs| • adj. proceeding in a gradual, subtle way, but with harmful effects.
■ full of wiles or plots; treacherous; crafty: *tangible proof of an insidious alliance.*
DERIVATIVES: **in•sid•i•ous•ly** adv. **in•sid•i•ous•ness** n.

in•sin•u•ate |in'sinyə,wāt| • v. [trans.] **1** suggest or hint (something bad or reprehensible) in an indirect and unpleasant way:[with clause] *he was insinuating that she slept her way to the top.* **2** (**insinuate oneself into**) maneuver oneself into (a position of favor or office) by subtle manipulation: *she seemed to be taking over, insinuating herself into the family.*

■ [with obj. and adverbial of direction] slide (oneself or a thing) slowly and smoothly into a position: *the bugs insinuate themselves between one's skin and clothes.*
DERIVATIVES: **in•sin•u•at•ing•ly** *adv.* **in•sin•u•a•tive** *adj.* **in•sin•u•a•tion** *n.* **in•sin•u•a•tor** |-,wāṭər| *n.*
in•sip•id |in'sipid| • *adj.* lacking flavor: *mugs of insipid coffee.*

■ lacking vigor or interest: *many artists continued to churn out insipid, shallow works.*
DERIVATIVES: **in•si•pid•i•ty** |,insə'pidiṭē| *n.* **in•sip•id•ly** *adv.* **in•sip•id•ness** *n.*
in si•tu |,in 'sītoō; 'sē-| • *adv. & adj.* in its original place: [as adv.] *mosaics and frescoes have been left in situ* | [as adj.] *a collection of in situ pumping engines.*

■ in position: [as adv.] *her guests were all in situ.*
in•so•lent |'insələnt| • *adj.* showing a rude and arrogant lack of respect: *the insolent tone of his voice.*
DERIVATIVES: **in•so•lence** *n.* **in•so•lent•ly** *adv.*
in•sol•u•ble |in'sälyəbəl| • *adj.* **1** impossible to solve. **2** (of a substance) incapable of being dissolved: *insoluble in water.*
DERIVATIVES: **in•sol•u•bil•i•ty** |-,sälyə 'bilïṭē| *n.* **in•sol•u•bil•ize** |-,līz| *v.* **in•sol•u•bly** |-blē| *adv.*
in•sol•vent |in'sälvənt| • *adj.* unable to pay debts owed: *the company became insolvent.*

■ relating to insolvency: *insolvent liquidation.* • *n.* an insolvent person.
DERIVATIVES: **in•sol•ven•cy** *n.*
in•som•ni•a |in'sämnēə| • *n.* habitual sleeplessness; inability to sleep.
DERIVATIVES: **in•som•ni•ac** |-nē,æk| *n. & adj.*
In•sou•ci•ance |in'ɛoōsēəns; ,æNsoō'syäNs| • *n.* casual lack of concern; indifference.
DERIVATIVES: **in•sou•ci•ant** *adj.* **in•sou•ci•ant•ly** *adv.*
in•sti•gate |'insti,gāt| • *v.* [trans.] bring about or initiate (an action or event): *they instigated a reign of terror* | *instigating legal proceedings.*

■ (**instigate someone to do something**) incite someone to do something, esp. something bad: *instigating men to refuse allegiance to the civil powers.*
DERIVATIVES: **in•sti•ga•tion** *n.* **in•sti•ga•tor** |-,gāṭər| *n.*
in•sti•tute |'insti,t(y)oōt| • *n.* [usu. in names] **1** a society or organization having a particular object or common factor, esp. a scientific, educational, or social one: *a research institute.* **2** (usu. **institutes**) a commentary, treatise, or summary of principles, esp. concerning law. • *v.* [trans.] **1** set in motion or establish (something, esp. a program, system, or inquiry): *the award was instituted in 1900.*

■ begin (legal proceedings) in a court. **2** (often **be instituted**) appoint (someone) to a posi-

tion, esp. as a cleric: *his sons were instituted to the priesthood* | [with complement] *a testator who has instituted his daughter heir.*
in•sti•tu•tion |,insti't(y)oōsHən| • *n.* **1** a society or organization founded for a religious, educational, social, or similar purpose: *a certificate from a professional institution.*

■ an organization providing residential care for people with special needs: *an institution for the severely handicapped.* ■ an established official organization or company having an important role in the life or economy of a country, such as a bank, church, or legislature: *the institutions of democratic government* | *capitalist institutions.* **2** an established law, practice, or custom: *the institution of marriage.*

■ a well-established and familiar person, custom, or object: *the event soon became something of a national institution.* **3** the action of instituting something: *a delay in the institution of proceedings.*
in•sub•or•di•nate |,insə'bôrdn-it| • *adj.* defiant of authority; disobedient to superiors or their orders: *an insubordinate attitude.*
DERIVATIVES: **in•sub•or•di•nate•ly** *adv.* **in•sub•or•di•na•tion** |-,bôrdn'āsHən| *n.*
in•suf•flate |'insə,flāt| • *v.* [trans.] **1** blow (air, gas, or powder) into a cavity of the body.

■ blow something into (a part of the body) in this way. **2** blow or breathe on (someone, as at baptism) to symbolize spiritual influence.
DERIVATIVES: **in•suf•fla•tion** |,insə'flāsHən| *n.*
in•su•lar |'ins(y)ələr| • *adj.* **1** ignorant of or uninterested in cultures, ideas, or peoples outside one's own experience: *a stubbornly insular farming people.*

■ lacking contact with other people: *people living restricted and sometimes insular existences.* **2** of, relating to, or from an island: *the movement of goods of insular origin.*

■ (of climate) equable because of the influence of the sea. **3** Anatomy of or relating to a region of the brain at the base of the cerebrum (the *insula*).
DERIVATIVES: **in•su•lar•i•ty** |,ins(y)ə'læriṭē; -'ler-| *n.* **in•su•lar•ly** *adv.*
in•su•per•a•ble |in'soōp(ə)rəbəl| • *adj.* (of a difficulty or obstacle) impossible to overcome: *insuperable financial problems.*
DERIVATIVES: **in•su•per•a•bil•i•ty** |-,soōp(ə)rə'bilïṭē| *n.* **in•su•per•a•bly** |-blē| *adv.*
in•sure |in'sHoōr| • *v.* [trans.] arrange for compensation in the event of damage to or loss of (property), or injury to or the death of (someone), in exchange for regular advance payments to a company or government agency: *the table should be insured for $2,500* | *the company had insured itself against a fall of the dollar* | [intrans.] *businesses can insure against exchange rate fluctuations.*

■ provide insurance coverage with respect to: *subsidiaries set up to insure the risks of a group of companies.* ■ (**insure someone against**) secure or protect someone against (a possible contingency): *by appeasing Celia they might insure themselves against further misfortune* |

[intrans.] *such changes could insure against further violence and unrest.*

DERIVATIVES: **in•sur•a•bil•i•ty** |-ˌsʜᴏᴏrə 'bilitē| *n.* **in•sur•a•ble** *adj.* **in•sur•er** *n.*

USAGE: There is considerable overlap between the meaning and use of **insure** and **ensure**. In both American and British English, the primary meaning of **insure** is the commercial sense of providing financial compensation in the event of damage to property; **ensure** is not used at all in this sense. For the more general senses, **ensure** is more likely to be used, but **insure** and **ensure** are often interchangeable, particularly in American English, e.g., *bail is posted to* **insure** *that the defendant appears for trial; the system is run to* **ensure** *that a good quality of service is maintained.*

in•sur•gent |in'sərjənt| • *adj.* [attrib.] rising in active revolt: *alleged links with insurgent groups.* ■ of or relating to rebels: *a series of insurgent attacks.* • *n.* (usu. **insurgents**) a rebel or revolutionary.
DERIVATIVES: **in•sur•gence** *n.* **in•sur•gen•cy** *n.* (pl. **-ies**) .

in•sur•rec•tion |ˌinsə'rekʃən| • *n.* a violent uprising against an authority or government.
DERIVATIVES: **in•sur•rec•tion•ar•y** |-ˌner-ē| *adj.* **in•sur•rec•tion•ist** |-nist| *n.* & *adj.*

in•ta•glio |in'talyō; -'täl-| • *n.* (pl. **-os**) a design incised or engraved into a material: *the dies bore a design in intaglio.* ■ a gem with an incised design. ■ any printing process in which the type or design is etched or engraved, such as photogravure or drypoint. • *v.* (**-oes, -oed**) [trans.] [usu. as adj.] (**intaglioed**) engrave or represent by an engraving: *a carved box with little intaglioed pineapples on it.*

in•tan•gi•ble |in'tænjəbəl| • *adj.* unable to be touched or grasped; not having physical presence. ■ difficult or impossible to define or understand; vague and abstract. ■ (of an asset or benefit) not constituting or represented by a physical object and of a value not precisely measurable: *intangible business property like trademarks and patents.* • *n.* (usu. **intangibles**) an intangible thing.
DERIVATIVES: **in•tan•gi•bil•i•ty** |-ˌtænjə 'bilitē| *n.* **in•tan•gi•bly** |-blē| *adv.*

in•tar•si•a |in'tärsēə| • *n.* [often as adj.] **1** a method of knitting with a number of colors, in which a separate length or ball of yarn is used for each area of color. **2** an elaborate form of marquetry using inlays in wood, esp. as practiced in 15th-century Italy. ■ similar inlaid work in stone, metal, or glass.

in•te•gral • *adj.* |'intigrəl; in'teg-| **1** necessary to make a whole complete; essential or fundamental: *sports are an integral part of the school's curriculum | systematic training should be* **integral to** *library management.* ■ [attrib.] included as part of the whole rather than supplied separately: *the unit comes complete with integral pump and heater.* ■ [attrib.] having or containing all parts that are necessary to be complete: *the first integral recording of the ten Mahler symphonies.* **2** of or denoted by a positive or negative number, or zero (an integer). ■ involving only integers, esp. as coefficients of a function.
DERIVATIVES: **in•te•gral•i•ty** |ˌinti'grælitē| *n.* **in•te•gral•ly** *adv.*

in•te•grate • *v.* |'inti,grāt| [trans.] **1** combine (one thing) with another so that they become a whole: *transportation planning should be* **integrated with** *energy policy.* ■ combine (two things) so that they become a whole: *the problem of integrating the two approaches.* ■ [intrans.] (of a thing) combine with another to form a whole: *the stone will blend with the environment and* **integrate into** *the landscape.* **2** bring into equal participation in or membership of society or an institution or body: *integrating children with special needs into neighborhood schools.* ■ [intrans.] come into equal participation in or membership of society or an institution or body: *she was anxious to* **integrate** *well into her husband's family.* **3** end segregation (a school, neighborhood, etc.) esp. racially: *there was a national campaign under way to integrate the lunch counters.*
DERIVATIVES: **in•te•gra•bil•i•ty** |ˌintigrə 'bilitē| *n.* **in•te•gra•ble** |-grəbəl| *adj.* **in•te•gra•tive** |-ˌgrātiv| *adj.*

in•te•gra•tion |ˌinti'grāʃən| • *n.* **1** the action or process of integrating: *economic and political integration | integration of individual countries into trading blocs.* ■ the intermixing of people or groups previously segregated. **2** Mathematics the finding of an integral or integrals: *integration of an ordinary differential equation | mathematical integrations.* **3** the coordination of processes in the nervous system, including diverse sensory information and motor impulses: *visuomotor integration.* ■ (in Freudian psychology) the process by which a well-balanced psyche becomes whole as the developing ego organizes the id. ■ the state that results from this or that treatment seeks to create or restore by countering the fragmenting effect of defense mechanisms.
DERIVATIVES: **in•te•gra•tion•ist** |-nist| *n.*

in•teg•ri•ty |in'tegritē| • *n.* **1** the quality of being honest and having strong moral principles; moral uprightness: *he is known to be a man of integrity.* **2** the state of being whole and undivided: *upholding territorial integrity and national sovereignty.* ■ the condition of being unified, unimpaired, or sound in construction: *questions about the building's structural integrity.* ■ internal consistency or lack of corruption in electronic data: [as adj.] *integrity checking.*

in•teg•u•ment |in'tegyəmənt| • *n.* a tough outer protective layer, esp. that of an animal or plant.
DERIVATIVES: **in•teg•u•men•tal** |-ˌtegyə 'mentl| *adj.* **in•teg•u•men•ta•ry** |-ˌtegyə 'mentərē| *adj.*

in•tel•lect |'intl‚ekt| • *n*. the faculty of reasoning and understanding objectively, esp. with regard to abstract or academic matters. ▪ the understanding or mental powers of a particular person: *her keen intellect.* ▪ an intelligent or intellectual person.

in•tel•lec•tion |‚intl'ekSHən| • *n*. the action or process of understanding, as opposed to imagination.
DERIVATIVES: **in•tel•lec•tive** |-tiv| *adj.*

in•tel•lec•tu•al |‚intl'ekCHəwəl| • *adj.* of or relating to the intellect: *children need intellectual stimulation.* ▪ appealing to or requiring use of the intellect: *the movie wasn't very intellectual.* ▪ possessing a highly developed intellect. • *n*. a person possessing a highly developed intellect. ▪ a person whose interests and pursuits tend toward the analytical, rational, philosophical, aesthetic, etc., as contrasted with what are generally perceived to be the interests of 'average' people.
DERIVATIVES: **in•tel•lec•tu•al•i•ty** |-ə‚lek-CHə'wælițē| *n*. **in•tel•lec•tu•al•ly** *adv.*

in•tel•lec•tu•al•ize |‚intl'ekCHəwə‚līz| • *v*. [trans.] **1** give an intellectual character to. **2** [intrans.] talk, write, or think intellectually: *people who intellectualize about fashion.*
DERIVATIVES: **in•tel•lec•tu•al•i•za•tion** |-‚ekCHəwəli'zāSHən| *n*.

in•tel•li•gence |in'telijəns| • *n*. (in government) the collection of information of military or political value: *the chief of military intelligence* | [as adj.] *the intelligence department.* ▪ people employed in this, regarded collectively: *British intelligence has been able to secure numerous local informers.* ▪ information collected in this way. ▪ information in general; news.

in•tel•li•gent•si•a |in‚teli'jentsēə| • *n*. (usu. **the intelligentsia**) [treated as sing. or pl.] intellectuals or highly educated people as a group, esp. when regarded as possessing culture and political influence.

in•tem•per•ate |in'temp(ə)rit| • *adj.* having or showing a lack of self-control; immoderate: *intemperate outbursts concerning global conspiracies.* ▪ given to or characterized by excessive indulgence, esp. in alcohol: *an intemperate social occasion.*
DERIVATIVES: **in•tem•per•ance** |-rəns| *n*. **in•tem•per•ate•ly** *adv.* **in•tem•per•ate•ness** *n*.

in•ten•si•fi•er |in'tensə‚fīər| • *n*. (in grammar) an adverb used to give force or emphasis, for example *really* in *my feet are really cold.*

in•ten•sion |in'tensHən| • *n*. **1** (in logic) the internal content of a concept. Often contrasted with *extension* 'the range of a term or concept as measured by the objects it denotes or contains.' **2** resolution or determination.
DERIVATIVES: **in•ten•sion•al** |-sHənl| *adj.* **in•ten•sion•al•ly** |-sHənl-ē| *adv.*

in•ten•sive |in'tensiv| • *adj.* **1** (of agriculture) aiming to achieve the highest possible level of production within a limited area, esp. by using chemical and technological aids: *in-*tensive farming. **2** [usu. in combination] (typically in business and economics) concentrating on or making much use of a specified thing: *computer-intensive methods.* **3** Grammar (of an adjective, adverb, or particle) expressing intensity; giving force or emphasis. • *n*. an intensive adjective, adverb, or particle; an intensifier.
DERIVATIVES: **in•ten•sive•ly** *adv.* **in•ten•sive•ness** *n*.

in•ter |in'tər| • *v*. (**interred, interring**) [trans.] (usu. **be interred**) place (a corpse) in a grave or tomb, typically with funeral rites: *he was interred with the military honors due to him.*
DERIVATIVES: **in•ter•ment** *n*.

USAGE: **Interment**, which means 'burial,' should not be confused with **internment**, which means 'imprisonment.'

in•ter a•li•a |'intər ālēə; älēə| • *adv.* among other things: *the study includes, inter alia, computers, aircraft, and pharmaceuticals.* Cf. INTER SE.

in•ter•ca•lar•y |in'tərkə‚lerē; ‚intər'kælərē| • *adj.* (of a day or a month) inserted in the calendar to harmonize it with the solar year, e.g., February 29 in leap years. ▪ of the nature of an insertion: *elaborate intercalary notes and footnotes.*

in•ter•ca•late |in'tərkə‚lāt| • *v*. [trans.] **1** interpolate (an intercalary period) in a calendar. **2** (usu. **be intercalated**) insert (something) between layers in a crystal lattice, geological formation, or other structure.
DERIVATIVES: **in•ter•ca•la•tion** |-‚tərkə'lāsHən| *n*.

in•ter•cede |‚intər'sēd| [intrans.] • *v*. intervene on behalf of another: *I begged him to intercede for Theresa but he never did a thing.*
DERIVATIVES: **in•ter•ced•er** *n*. **in•ter•ces•sion** *n*.

in•ter•ces•sion |‚intər'sesHən| • *n*. the action of intervening on behalf of another: *through the intercession of friends, I was able to obtain her a sinecure.* ▪ the action of saying a prayer on behalf of another person: *prayers of intercession.*
DERIVATIVES: **in•ter•ces•sor** |'intər‚sesər| *n*. **in•ter•ces•so•ry** |-'sesərē| *adj.*

in•ter•dict • *n*. |'intər‚dikt| an authoritative prohibition: *an interdict against marriage of those of close kin.* ▪ (in the Roman Catholic Church) a sentence barring a person, or esp. a place, from ecclesiastical functions and privileges: *a papal interdict.* • *v*. |‚intər'dikt| [trans.] **1** prohibit or forbid (something): *society will never interdict sex.* ▪ (**interdict someone from**) prohibit someone from (doing something): *I have not been interdicted from consuming alcoholic beverages.* **2** intercept and prevent the movement of (a prohibited commodity or person): *the police established roadblocks for interdicting drugs.* ▪ impede (an enemy force), esp. by aerial bombing of lines of communication or supply.

DERIVATIVES: **in•ter•dic•tion** |ˌintərˈdik-SHən| *n.*

in•ter•face |ˈintərˌfās| • *n.* **1** a point where two systems, subjects, organizations, etc., meet and interact: *the interface between accountancy and the law.*

■ a surface forming a common boundary between two portions of matter or space, for example between two immiscible liquids: *the surface tension of a liquid at its air/liquid interface.* **2** a device or program enabling a user to communicate with a computer.

■ a device or program for connecting two items of hardware or software so that they can be operated jointly or communicate with each other. • *v.* [intrans.] (**interface with**) **1** interact with (another system, person, organization, etc.): *his goal is to get people interfacing with each other.* **2** connect with (another computer or piece of equipment) by an interface.

USAGE: The word **interface** is relatively new, having been in the language (as a noun) since the 1880s. However, in the 1960s it became widespread in computer use and, by analogy, began to enjoy a vogue as both a noun and a verb in all sorts of other spheres. Traditionalists object to it on the grounds that there are plenty of other words that are more exact and sound less like "vogue jargon." The verb **interface** is best restricted to technical references to computer systems, etc.

in•ter•fer•on |ˌintərˈfir,än| • *n.* a protein released by animal cells, usually in response to the entry of a virus, that has the property of inhibiting virus replication.

in•ter•im |ˈintərəm| • *n.* the intervening time; the meantime: *in the interim I'll just keep my fingers crossed.* • *adj.* in or for the intervening period; provisional or temporary: *an interim arrangement.*

■ relating to less than a full year's business activity: *an interim dividend | interim profit.*

in•ter•jec•tion |ˌintərˈjeksHən| • *n.* an abrupt remark, made esp. as an aside or interruption.

■ an exclamation, esp. as a part of speech, e.g., *ah!* or *dear me!* or *oh, man!*

DERIVATIVES: **in•ter•jec•tion•al** |-SHənl| *adj.*

in•ter•lard |ˌintərˈlärd| • *v.* [trans.] (**interlard something with**) intersperse or embellish speech or writing with different material: *a compendium of advertisements and reviews, interlarded with gossip.*

in•ter•loc•u•tor |ˌintərˈläkyətər| • *n.* a person who takes part in a dialogue or conversation.

DERIVATIVES: **in•ter•lo•cu•tion** |-ləˈkyoo-SHən| *n.*

in•ter•lop•er |ˈintərˌlōpər; ˌintərˈlōpər| • *n.* a person who becomes involved in a place or situation where he or she is not wanted or considered to belong.

DERIVATIVES: **in•ter•lope** |ˈintərˌlōp; ˌin-tərˈlōp| *v.*

in•ter•mez•zo |ˌintərˈmetsō| • *n.* (pl. **inter-mezzi** |-ˈmetsē| or **intermezzos**) a short connecting instrumental movement in an opera or other musical work.

■ a similar piece performed independently. ■ a short piece for a solo instrument. ■ a light dramatic, musical, or other performance inserted between the acts of a play.

in•ter•mi•na•ble |inˈtərmənəbəl| • *adj.* endless (often used hyperbolically): *interminable discussions.*

DERIVATIVES: **in•ter•mi•na•bil•i•ty** |-ˌtər-mənəˈbilitē| *n.* **in•ter•mi•na•ble•ness** *n.* **in•ter•mi•na•bly** |-blē| *adv.*

in•ter•mit•tent |ˌintərˈmitnt| • *adj.* occurring at irregular intervals; not continuous or steady: *intermittent rain.*

DERIVATIVES: **in•ter•mit•tence** *n.* **in•ter•mit•ten•cy** *n.* **in•ter•mit•tent•ly** *adv.*

in•tern • *n.* |ˈin,tərn| a recent medical graduate receiving supervised training in a hospital and acting as an assistant physician or surgeon.

■ a student or trainee who works, sometimes without pay, at a trade or occupation in order to gain work experience: *the garden's summer interns.* • *v.* |inˈtərn| **1** [trans.] confine (someone) as a prisoner, esp. for political or military reasons. **2** [intrans.] serve as an intern.

DERIVATIVES: **in•tern•ment** *n.* (in sense 1 of the verb).

in•ter•nal•ize |inˈtərnl,īz| • *v.* [trans.] **1** make (attitudes or behavior) part of one's nature by learning or unconscious assimilation.

■ acquire knowledge of (the rules of a language). **2** incorporate (costs) as part of a pricing structure, esp. social costs resulting from the manufacture and use of a product. Cf. EX-TERNALIZE.

DERIVATIVES: **in•ter•nal•i•za•tion** |in,tə-rnl-iˈzāsHən| *n.*

in•ter•ne•cine |ˌintərˈnesēn; -ˈnēsēn; -sin| • *adj.* destructive to both sides in a conflict: *the region's history of internecine warfare.*

■ of or relating to conflict within a group or organization: *the party shrank from further internecine strife.*

in•tern•ist |inˈtərnist; ˈintərn-| • *n.* a specialist in internal medicine.

in•ter•po•late |inˈtərpə,lāt| • *v.* [trans.] insert (something) between fixed points: *illustrations were interpolated in the text.*

■ insert (words) in a book or other text, esp. in order to give a false impression as to its date. ■ make such insertions in (a book or text). ■ interject (a remark) in a conversation. ■ insert (an intermediate value or term) into a series of numbers by estimating or calculating it from surrounding known values.

DERIVATIVES: **in•ter•po•la•tion** |-ˌtərpə-ˈlāsHən| *n.* **in•ter•po•la•tive** |-ˌlātiv| *adj.*

in•ter•pose |ˌintərˈpōz| • *v.* **1** [trans.] place or insert between one thing and another: *he interposed himself between the child and the top of the stairs.* **2** [intrans.] intervene between parties: [with infinitive] *the legislature interposed to suppress these amusements.*

■ [trans.] say (words) as an interruption: *if I may*

interpose a personal remark here. ■ [trans.] exercise or advance (a veto or objection) so as to interfere: *the memo interposes no objection to issuing a discharge.*
DERIVATIVES: **in•ter•pos•a•ble** *adj.* **in•ter•pos•er** *n.*

in•ter•reg•num |ˌintərˈregnəm| • *n.* (pl. **interregnums** or **interregna** |-nə|) a period when normal government is suspended, esp. between successive reigns or regimes.
■ (**the Interregnum**) the period in English history from the execution of Charles I in 1649 to the Restoration of Charles II in 1660. ■ an interval or pause: *the interregnum between the discovery of radioactivity and its detailed understanding.*

in•ter•ro•gate |inˈterəˌgāt| • *v.* [trans.] ask questions of (someone, esp. a suspect or a prisoner) closely, aggressively, or formally. ■ obtain data from (a computer file, database, storage device, or terminal). ■ (of an electronic device) transmit a signal to (another device, esp. one on a vehicle) to obtain a response giving information about identity, condition, etc.
DERIVATIVES: **interrogation** *n.* **in•ter•ro•ga•tor** |-ˌgāt̮ər| *n.*

in•ter•rog•a•to•ry |ˌintəˈrägəˌtôrē| • *adj.* conveying the force of a question; questioning: *the guard moved away with an interrogatory stare.* • *n.* (pl. **-ies**) a written question that is formally put to one party in a legal case by another party and that must be answered: *interrogatories must be filed by 5 p.m. Tuesday.*

in•ter se |ˈintər ˈsē; ˈsä| • *adv.* between or among themselves: *agreements entered into by all the shareholders inter se.* Cf. INTER ALIA.

in•ter•sperse |ˌintərˈspərs| • *v.* [trans.] (often **be interspersed**) scatter among or between other things; place here and there: *interspersed between tragic stories are a few songs supplying comic relief.* ■ diversify (a thing or things) with other things at intervals: *a patchwork of open fields interspersed with pine woods.*
DERIVATIVES: **in•ter•sper•sion** |-ˈspərZHən| *n.*

in•ter•stice |inˈtərstis| • *n.* (usu. **interstices**) an intervening space, esp. a very small one: *sunshine filtered through the interstices of the arching trees.*

in•ter•sti•tial |ˌintərˈstiSHəl| • *adj.* of, forming, or occupying interstices: *the interstitial space.* ■ (of minute animals) living in the spaces between individual sand grains in the soil or aquatic sediments: *the interstitial fauna of marine sands.*
DERIVATIVES: **in•ter•sti•tial•ly** *adv.*

in•ter•val |ˈintərvəl| • *n.* **1** an intervening time or space: *after his departure, there was an interval of many years without any meetings | the intervals between meals were very short.* **2** a pause; a break in activity: *an interval of mourning.* ■ Brit. an intermission separating parts of a theatrical or musical performance. ■ Brit. a break between the parts of an athletic contest: *lead-*

ing 3-0 at the interval. **3** a space between two things; a gap. ■ the difference in pitch between two musical sounds. ■ two sounds of different pitch played simultaneously (a **harmonic interval**) or in succession (a **melodic interval**) . Cf. CHORD.
DERIVATIVES: **in•ter•val•lic** |ˌintərˈvælik| *adj.*

in•ter•vene |ˌintərˈvēn| • *v.* [intrans.] **1** come between so as to prevent or alter a result or course of events: *he intervened in the dispute | [with infinitive] their forces intervened to halt the attack.* ■ (of an event or circumstance) occur as a delay or obstacle to something being done: *Christmas intervened and the investigation was suspended.* ■ interrupt verbally. ■ interpose in a lawsuit as a third party. **2** [usu. as adj.] (**intervening**) occur in time between events: *to occupy the intervening months she took a job in a hospital.* ■ be situated between things: *they heard the sound of distant gunfire, muffled by the intervening trees.*
DERIVATIVES: **in•ter•ven•er** *n.* **in•ter•ven•ient** |-ˈvēnyənt| *adj.* **in•ter•ve•nor** |-ˈvēnər| *n.*

in•tes•tate |inˈtestāt; -tit| • *adj.* [predic.] not having made a will before one dies: *he died intestate.* ■ [attrib.] of or relating to a person who dies without having made a will: *intestate heirs.* • *n.* a person who has died without having made a will.
DERIVATIVES: **in•tes•ta•cy** |-təsē| *n.*

in•ti•mate |ˈintəˌmāt| • *v.* [trans.] imply or hint: [with clause] *he intimated that he might not be able to continue.* ■ state or make known.
DERIVATIVES: **in•ti•ma•tion** |ˌintəˈmāsHən| *n.*

in•tim•i•date |inˈtimiˌdāt| • *v.* frighten or overawe (someone), esp. in order to make him or her do what one wants: *he tries to intimidate his rivals* | [as adj.] (**intimidating**) *the intimidating defense lawyer.*
DERIVATIVES: **in•tim•i•dat•ing•ly** *adv.* **in•tim•i•da•tion** |-ˈdāsHən| *n.* **in•tim•i•da•tor** |-ˌdāt̮ər| *n.* **in•tim•i•da•to•ry** |-dəˌtôrē| *adj.*

in•to•na•tion |ˌintəˈnāsHən; -tō-| • *n.* **1** the manner of utterance of the tones of the voice in speaking; accent: *she spoke English with a German intonation.* ■ the action of intoning or reciting in a singing voice. **2** accuracy of pitch in playing or singing: *poor woodwind intonation at the opening.* **3** the opening phrase of a plainsong melody.
DERIVATIVES: **in•to•na•tion•al** |-SHənl| *adj.*

in•tone |inˈtōn| • *v.* [trans.] say or recite with little rise and fall of the pitch of the voice: *he intoned a prayer.*
DERIVATIVES: **in•ton•er** *n.*

in•trac•ta•ble |inˈtræktəbəl| • *adj.* hard to control or deal with: *intractable economic problems.*

■ (of a person) difficult; stubborn. Cf. RECAL-CITRANT.
DERIVATIVES: **in•trac•ta•bil•i•ty** |-,træktə'bilitē| n. **in•trac•ta•ble•ness** n. **in•trac•ta•bly** |-blē| adv.
in•tran•si•gent |in'trænsijənt; -zi-| • adj. unwilling or refusing to change one's views or to agree about something. • n. an intransigent person.
DERIVATIVES: **in•tran•si•gence** n. **in•tran•si•gen•cy** n. **in•tran•si•gent•ly** adv.
in•tran•si•tive |in'trænsitiv; -zi-| • adj. (of a verb or a sense or use of a verb) not taking a direct object, e.g., look in look at the sky. The opposite of TRANSITIVE. • n. an intransitive verb.
DERIVATIVES: **in•tran•si•tive•ly** adv. **in•tran•si•tiv•i•ty** |-,trænsi'tivitē; -zi-| n.
in•tra•pre•neur |,intrəprə'nər; -'nŏor| • n. a manager within a company who promotes innovative product development and marketing.
DERIVATIVES: **in•tra•pre•neu•ri•al** |-ēəl| adj.
in•tra•ve•nous |,intrə'vēnəs| (abbr.: **IV**) • adj. existing or taking place within, or administered into, a vein or veins: an intravenous drip.
DERIVATIVES: **in•tra•ve•nous•ly** adv.
in•trep•id |in'trepid| • adj. fearless; adventurous (often used for rhetorical or humorous effect): our intrepid reporter.
DERIVATIVES: **in•tre•pid•i•ty** |,intrə'piditē| n. **in•trep•id•ly** adv. **in•trep•id•ness** n.
in•tri•cate |'intrikit| • adj. very complicated or detailed: an intricate network of canals.
DERIVATIVES: **in•tri•cate•ly** adv.
in•trigue • v. |in'trēg| (**intrigues, intrigued, intriguing**) **1** [trans.] arouse the curiosity or interest of; fascinate: I was intrigued by your question| [as adj.] (**intriguing**) the food is an intriguing combination of German and French. **2** [intrans.] make secret plans to do something illicit or detrimental to someone: intriguing for their own gains. • n. |'in,trēg| **1** the secret planning of something illicit or detrimental to someone: a nest of intrigue.
■ a secret love affair. **2** a mysterious or fascinating quality: within the region's borders is a wealth of interest and intrigue.
DERIVATIVES: **in•tri•guer** n. **in•tri•guing•ly** adv.
in•trin•sic |in'trinzik; -sik| • adj. belonging naturally; essential: access to the arts is **intrinsic to** a high quality of life.
■ (of a muscle) contained wholly within the organ on which it acts. Cf. EXTRINSIC.
DERIVATIVES: **in•trin•si•cal•ly** |-ik(ə)lē| adv.
in•tro•jec•tion |,intrə'jeksHən| • n. the unconscious adoption of the ideas or attitudes of others.
DERIVATIVES: **in•tro•ject** |-'jekt| v.
in•tro•mis•sion |,intrə'misHən| • n. the action or process of inserting the penis into the vagina in sexual intercourse.
in•tro•spec•tion |,intrə'speksHən| • n. the examination or observation of one's own

mental and emotional processes: quiet introspection can be extremely valuable.
DERIVATIVES: **in•tro•spec•tive** |-'spektiv| adj. **in•tro•spec•tive•ly** |-'spektəvlē| adv. **in•tro•spec•tive•ness** |-'spektivnis| n.
in•tro•vert • n. |'intrə,vərt| a shy, reticent, and typically self-centered person.
■ a person predominantly concerned with his or her own thoughts and feelings rather than with external things. [as adj.] introvert tendencies. Cf. EXTROVERT.
DERIVATIVES: **in•tro•ver•sion** |-,vərzHən| n. **in•tro•ver•sive** |-,vərsiv| adj. **introverted** adj.
in•tu•it |in't(y)ōō-it| • v. [trans.] understand or work out by instinct: I intuited his real identity.
DERIVATIVES: **in•tu•it•a•ble** adj.
in•tu•i•tion |,int(y)ōō'isHən| • n. the ability to understand something immediately, without the need for conscious reasoning: we shall allow intuition to guide us.
■ a thing that one knows or considers likely from instinctive feeling rather than conscious reasoning: your insights and intuitions as a native speaker are sought.
DERIVATIVES: **in•tu•i•tion•al** |-'isHənl| adj. **in•tu•i•tion•al•ly** |-'isHənl-ē| adv.
in•tu•i•tive |in't(y)ōōitiv| • adj. using or based on what one feels to be true even without conscious reasoning; instinctive: I had an intuitive conviction that there was something unsound in him.
■ (chiefly of computer software) easy to use and understand. ■ (of a person) possessing intuition, esp. to a notable or unusual degree: she is truly intuitive.
DERIVATIVES: **in•tu•i•tive•ly** adv. **in•tu•i•tive•ness** n.
in•tu•mesce |,int(y)ōō'mes| • v. [intrans.] swell or bubble up.
DERIVATIVES: **in•tu•mes•cence** |-'mesəns| n. **in•tu•mes•cent** adj.
In•u•it |'in(y)ōō-it| • n. **1** (pl. same or **-its**) a member of an indigenous people of northern Canada and parts of Greenland and Alaska. **2** the family of languages of this people, one of the three branches of the Eskimo-Aleut language family. It is also known as **Inupiaq** (from inuk 'person' + piaq 'genuine') or, esp. to its speakers, as **Inuktitut.** • adj. of or relating to the Inuit or their language.

USAGE: The peoples inhabiting the regions from northwestern Canada to western Greenland speak **Inuit** languages (**Inuit** in Canada, **Greenlandic** in Greenland) and call themselves **Inuit**, not **Eskimo**, and **Inuit** now has official status in Canada. By analogy **Inuit** is also used in the US, usually in an attempt to be politically correct, as a general synonym for **Eskimo**. This, however, is inaccurate because there are no **Inuit** in Alaska and **Inuit** therefore cannot include people from Alaska (who speak **Inupiaq** (from inuk 'person' + piaq 'genuine'), which is closely related to **Inuit**, or **Yupik**, which is also spoken in Siberia).

Since neither **Inupiaq** nor **Yupik** is in common US usage, only **Eskimo** includes all of these peoples and their languages.

in•un•date |'inən,dāt| • v. [trans.] (usu. **be inundated**) cover with water; flood: *the islands may be the first to be inundated as sea levels rise.*
■ overwhelm (someone) with things or people to be dealt with: *we've been inundated with complaints.*
DERIVATIVES: **in•un•da•tion** |,inən'dā-sHən| n.

in•ure |i'n(y)o͝or| (also **enure**) • v. [trans.] (usu. **be inured to**) accustom (someone) to something, esp. something unpleasant: *these children have been inured to violence.*
DERIVATIVES: **in•ure•ment** n.

in u•ter•o |in 'yo͞otərō| • adv. & adj. in a woman's uterus; before birth.

in•val•i•date |in'væli,dāt| • v. [trans.] **1** make (an argument, statement, or theory) unsound or erroneous: *these errors invalidate the entire thesis.* **2** deprive (an official document or procedure) of legal efficacy because of contravention of a regulation or law.
DERIVATIVES: **in•val•i•da•tion** |-,væli 'dāsHən| n. **in•val•i•da•tor** |-,dātər| n.

in•val•u•a•ble |in'vælyəwəbəl| • adj. beyond valuation; extremely useful; indispensable.
DERIVATIVES: **in•val•u•a•ble•ness** n. **in•val•u•a•bly** |-blē| adv.

in•vec•tive |in'vektiv| • n. insulting, abusive, or highly critical language: *a stream of invective.*

in•veigh |in'vā| • v. [intrans.] (**inveigh against**) speak or write about (something) with great hostility: *Marx inveighed against the evils of the property-owning classes.*

in•vei•gle |in'vāgəl| • v. [with obj. and adverbial] persuade (someone) to do something by means of deception or flattery: *we cannot inveigle him into putting pen to paper.*
■ (**inveigle oneself** or **one's way into**) gain entrance to (a place) by using such methods. Cf. CAJOLE.
DERIVATIVES: **in•vei•gle•ment** n.

in•ver•te•brate |in'vərtəbrit; -,brāt| • n. an animal lacking a backbone, such as an arthropod, mollusk, annelid, coelenterate, etc. The invertebrates constitute an artificial division of the animal kingdom, comprising 95 percent of animal species and about 30 different phyla. • adj. of, relating to, or belonging to this division of animals.
■ irresolute; spineless: *so invertebrate is today's Congress regarding foreign policy responsibilities.*

in•ves•ti•ture |in'vesti,CHo͝or; -CHər| • n. **1** the action of formally investing a person with honors or rank: *the investiture of bishops.*
■ a ceremony at which honors or rank are formally conferred on a particular person. **2** the action of clothing or robing.
■ a thing that clothes or covers.

in•vet•er•ate |in'vetərit| • adj. [attrib.] having a particular habit, activity, or interest that is long-established and unlikely to change: *an inveterate gambler.*

■ (of a feeling or habit) long-established and unlikely to change: *her inveterate optimism.*
DERIVATIVES: **in•vet•er•a•cy** |-rəsē| n. **in•vet•er•ate•ly** adv.

in•vid•i•ous |in'vidēəs| • adj. (of an action or situation) likely to arouse or incur resentment or anger in others: *she'd put herself in an invidious position.*
■ (of a comparison or distinction) unfairly discriminating; unjust: *it seems invidious to make special mention of one aspect of his work.*
DERIVATIVES: **in•vid•i•ous•ly** adv. **in•vid•i•ous•ness** n.

in•vin•ci•ble |in'vinsəbəl| • adj. too powerful to be defeated or overcome: *an invincible warrior.*
DERIVATIVES: **in•vin•ci•bil•i•ty** |-,vinsə 'bilitē| n. **in•vin•ci•bly** |-blē| adv.

in•vi•o•la•ble |in'vīələbəl| • adj. never to be broken, infringed, or dishonored: *an inviolable rule of chastity.*
DERIVATIVES: **in•vi•o•la•bil•i•ty** |-,vīələ 'bilitē| n. **in•vi•o•la•bly** |-blē| adv.

in•vi•o•late |in'vīəlit| • adj. free or safe from injury or violation: *an international memorial that must remain inviolate.*
DERIVATIVES: **in•vi•o•la•cy** |-ləsē| n. **in•vi•o•late•ly** adv.

in vi•tro |in 'vē,trō| • adj. & adv. (of processes or reactions) taking place in a test tube, culture dish, or elsewhere outside a living organism: [as adj.] *in vitro fertilization.*

in vi•vo |in 'vēvō| • adv. & adj. (of biological processes) taking place in a living organism. The opposite of IN VITRO.

in•vo•ca•tion |,invə'kāsHən| • n. the action of invoking something or someone for assistance or as an authority: *the invocation of new disciplines and methodologies.*
■ the summoning of a deity or the supernatural: *invocation of the ancient mystical powers.*
■ an incantation used for this. ■ (in the Christian Church) a form of words such as "In the name of the Father" introducing a prayer, sermon, etc.
DERIVATIVES: **in•voc•a•tive** adj. **in•voc•a•to•ry** |in'väkə,tôrē| adj.

in•voke |in'vōk| • v. [trans.] cite or appeal to (someone or something) as an authority for an action or in support of an argument: *the antiquated defense of insanity is rarely invoked today.*
■ call on (a deity or spirit) in prayer, as a witness, or for inspiration. ■ call earnestly for: *she invoked his help against this attack.*
■ summon (a spirit) by charms or incantation. ■ give rise to; evoke: *explain the accident without invoking his wrath.* ■ cause (a computational procedure) to be carried out.
DERIVATIVES: **in•vok•er** n.

in•vol•un•tar•y |in'välən,terē| • adj. **1** done without conscious control: *she gave an involuntary shudder.*
■ (esp. of muscles or nerves) concerned in bodily processes that are not under the control of the will. ■ caused unintentionally, esp. through negligence: *involuntary homicide.*

2 done against someone's will; compulsory: *a policy of involuntary repatriation.*
DERIVATIVES: **in•vol•un•tar•i•ly** |in,välən'terəlē; -'välən,ter-| *adv.* **in•vol•un•tar•i•ness** *n.*

in•vo•lute |ˈinvə,lo͞ot| • *adj.* **1** involved; entangled; intricate: *the art novel has grown increasingly involute.* **2** curled spirally.
■ (of a shell) having the whorls wound closely around the axis. ■ (of a leaf or the cap of a fungus) rolled inward at the edges.

in•vo•lu•tion |,invəˈlo͞osHən| • *n.* **1** the shrinkage of an organ in old age or when inactive, e.g., of the uterus after childbirth. **2** a mathematical function, transformation, or operator that is equal to its inverse. **3** the process of involving or complicating, or the state of being involved or complicated: *periods of artistic involution.*
DERIVATIVES: **in•vo•lu•tion•al** |-SHənl| *adj.* **in•vo•lu•tion•ar•y** |-,nerē| *adj.*

in•vul•ner•a•ble |inˈvəlnərəbəl| • *adj.* impossible to harm or damage.
DERIVATIVES: **in•vul•ner•a•bil•i•ty** |-,vəlnərə'bilitē| *n.* **in•vul•ner•a•bly** |-blē| *adv.*

i•o•ta |īˈōtə| • *n.* [in sing.] [usu. with negative] an extremely small amount: *nothing she said seemed to make an iota of difference.*

ip•se dix•it |ˈipsē ˈdiksit| • *n.* a dogmatic and unproven statement.

ip•so fac•to |ˈipsō ˈfæktō| • *adv.* by that very fact or act: *the enemy of one's enemy may be ipso facto a friend.*

i•ras•ci•ble |iˈræsəbəl| • *adj.* (of a person) easily made angry.
■ characterized by or arising from anger: *their rebukes got progressively more irascible.*
DERIVATIVES: **i•ras•ci•bil•i•ty** |i,ræsə'bilitē| *n.* **i•ras•ci•bly** |-blē| *adv.*

i•rate |īˈrāt| • *adj.* feeling or characterized by great anger: *a barrage of irate letters.*
DERIVATIVES: **i•rate•ly** *adv.* **i•rate•ness** *n.*

i•ren•ic |īˈrenik; īˈrē-| (also **eirenic**) • *adj.* aiming or aimed at peace. Cf. PACIFIC. • *n.* (**irenics**) a part of Christian theology concerned with reconciling different denominations and sects.
DERIVATIVES: **i•ren•i•cal** *adj.* **i•ren•i•cal•ly** |-ik(ə)lē| *adv.* **i•ren•i•cism** |-ni,sizəm| *n.*

ir•i•des•cent |,iri'desənt| • *adj.* showing luminous colors that seem to change when seen from different angles.
DERIVATIVES: **ir•i•des•cence** *n.* **ir•i•des•cent•ly** *adv.*

irk•some |ˈərksəm| • *adj.* tending to irritate (irk), esp. because repeated; tiresome.
DERIVATIVES: **irk•some•ly** *adv.* **irk•some•ness** *n.*

i•ron•ic |īˈränik| • *adj.* using or characterized by irony: *his mouth curved into an ironic smile | an ironic commentator.*
■ happening in a way opposite to what is expected, and typically causing wry amusement because of this: [with clause] *it was ironic that now that everybody had high-powered cars, they spent all their time sitting in traffic.*
DERIVATIVES: **i•ron•i•cal** *adj.*

i•ro•ny |ˈīrənē; ˈīərnē| • *n.* (pl. **-ies**) the expression of one's meaning by using language that normally signifies the opposite, typically for humorous or emphatic effect: *"Don't go overboard with the gratitude," he rejoined with irony.*
■ a state of affairs or an event that seems deliberately contrary to what one expects and is often amusing as a result. ■ (also **dramatic** or **tragic irony**) a literary technique, originally used in Greek tragedy, by which the full significance of a character's words or actions are clear to the audience or reader although unknown to the character. Cf. SOCRATIC IRONY.
DERIVATIVES: **i•ron•ist** *n.*

Ir•o•quoi•an |ˈirə,kwoiən| • *n.* a language family of eastern North America, including the languages of the Five Nations (Iroquos Confederacy), Tuscarora, Huron, Wyandot, and Cherokee. With the exception of Cherokee, all its members are extinct or nearly so. • *adj.* of or relating to the Iroquois people or the Iroquoian language family.

Ir•o•quois |ˈirə,kwoi| • *n.* (pl. same) **1** a member of a former confederacy of North American Indian peoples originally comprising the Cayuga, Mohawk, Oneida, Onondaga, and Seneca peoples (known as the Five Nations), and later including also the Tuscarora (thus forming the Six Nations). **2** any of the Iroquoian languages. • *adj.* of or relating to the Iroquois or their languages.

ir•ra•di•ate |iˈrādē,āt| • *v.* [trans.] **1** (often **be irradiated**) expose to radiation.
■ expose (food) to gamma rays (electromagnetic radiation of shorter wavelength than x-rays) to kill microorganisms. **2** illuminate (something) or as if by shining light on it: *sunlight streamed down through stained glass, irradiating the faces of family and friends.*
DERIVATIVES: **ir•ra•di•a•tion** *n.* **ir•ra•di•a•tive** *adj.* **ir•ra•di•a•tor** |-,ātər| *n.*

ir•ra•tion•al |iˈræSHənl| • *adj.* **1** not logical or reasonable.
■ not endowed with the power of reason. **2** (of a number, quantity, or expression) not expressible as a ratio of two integers, and having an infinite and nonrecurring expansion when expressed as a decimal. Examples of irrational numbers are the number π and the square root of 2. • *n.* Mathematics an irrational number.
DERIVATIVES: **ir•ra•tion•al•i•ty** |i,ræsHə'nælitē| *n.* **ir•ra•tion•al•ize** |-,īz| *v.* **ir•ra•tion•al•ly** *adv.*

ir•re•duc•i•ble |,iri'd(y)o͞osəbəl| • *adj.* not able to be reduced or simplified.
■ not able to be brought to a certain form or condition: *the imagery remains irreducible to textual structures.*
DERIVATIVES: **ir•re•duc•i•bil•i•ty** |-,d(y)o͞osə'bilitē| *n.* **ir•re•duc•i•bly** |-blē| *adv.*

ir•ref•ra•ga•ble |iˈrefrəgəbəl| • *adj.* not able to be refuted or disproved; indisputable.
DERIVATIVES: **ir•ref•ra•ga•bly** |-blē| *adv.*

ir•re•fran•gi•ble |,irə'frænjəbəl| • *adj.* (of a rule) inviolable: *an irrefrangible law of country etiquette.*

ir•re•gard•less |ˌiriˈgärdləs| • adj. & adv. regardless.

USAGE: **Irregardless**, with its illogical negative prefix, is widely heard, perhaps arising under the influence of such perfectly correct forms as *irrespective*. **Irregardless** is avoided by careful users of English. Use **regardless** to mean 'without regard or consideration for' or 'nevertheless': *I go walking every day regardless of season or weather.*

ir•reg•u•lar |iˈregyələr| • adj. 1 [attrib.] (of troops) not belonging to regular or established army units. 2 (of a verb or other word) having inflections that do not conform to the usual rules. • n. (usu. **irregulars**) a member of a military force not under the control of a legitimate or ruling government.
DERIVATIVES: **ir•reg•u•lar•ly** adv.

ir•rel•e•vant |iˈreləvənt| • adj. not connected with or relevant to something.
DERIVATIVES: **ir•rel•e•vance** n. **ir•rel•e•van•cy** n. (pl. **-ies**) **ir•rel•e•vant•ly** adv.

USAGE: See **usage** at IMMATERIAL.

ir•re•li•gious |ˌirəˈlijəs| • adj. indifferent or hostile to religion: *an irreligious world.*
DERIVATIVES: **ir•re•li•gion** |-ˈlijən| n. **ir•re•li•gious•ly** adv. **ir•re•li•gious•ness** n.

ir•rep•a•ra•ble |irˈrep(ə)rəbəl| • adj. (of an injury or loss) impossible to rectify or repair: *irreparable damage to the heart and lungs.*
DERIVATIVES: **ir•rep•a•ra•bil•i•ty** |iˌrep(ə)rəˈbilitē| n. **ir•rep•a•ra•bly** |-blē| adv.

ir•re•press•i•ble |ˌirəˈpresəbəl| • adj. not able to be repressed, controlled, or restrained: *a great shout of irrepressible laughter.*
DERIVATIVES: **ir•re•press•i•bil•i•ty** |-ˌpresəˈbilitē| n. **ir•re•press•i•bly** |-blē| adv.

ir•res•o•lute |i(r)ˈrezəˌlо͞ot| • adj. showing or feeling hesitancy; uncertain: *she stood irresolute outside his door.*
DERIVATIVES: **ir•res•o•lute•ly** adv. **ir•res•o•lute•ness** n. **ir•res•o•lu•tion** |-ˌrezəˈlо͞оSHən| n.

ir•re•spec•tive |ˌiriˈspektiv| • adj. [predic.] (**irrespective of**) not taking (something) into account; regardless of: *child benefit is paid irrespective of income levels.*
DERIVATIVES: **ir•re•spec•tive•ly** adv.

ir•rev•er•ent |iˈrev(ə)rənt| • adj. showing a lack of respect for people or things that are generally taken seriously.
DERIVATIVES: **ir•rev•er•ence** n. **ir•rev•er•en•tial** |iˌrevəˈrenSHəl| adj. **ir•rev•er•ent•ly** adv.

ir•re•vers•i•ble |ˌirəˈvərsəbəl| • adj. not able to be undone or altered; not reversible.
DERIVATIVES: **ir•re•vers•i•bil•i•ty** |-ˌvərsəˈbilitē| n. **ir•re•vers•i•bly** |-blē| adv.

ir•rev•o•ca•ble |iˈrevəkəbəl| • adj. not able to be changed, reversed, or recovered; final.
DERIVATIVES: **ir•rev•o•ca•bil•i•ty** |iˌrevəkəˈbilitē| n. **ir•rev•o•ca•bly** |-blē| adv.

ir•ri•gate |ˈiriˌgāt| • v. [trans.] supply water to (land or crops) to help growth, typically by means of channels.

■ (of a river or stream) supply (land) with water. ■ apply a continuous flow of water or liquid medication to (an organ or wound).
DERIVATIVES: **ir•ri•ga•ble** |-gəbəl| adj. **ir•ri•ga•tion** |ˌiriˈgāSHən| n. **ir•ri•ga•tor** |-ˌgātər| n.

i•so•bar |ˈīsəˌbär| • n. 1 Meteorology a line on a map connecting points having the same atmospheric pressure at a given time or on average over a given period.

■ (in physics) a curve or formula representing a physical system at constant pressure. 2 each of two or more isotopes of different elements, with the same atomic weight.
DERIVATIVES: **i•so•bar•ic** |ˌīsəˈbærik; -ˈbär-; -ˈber-| adj.

i•so•met•ric |ˌīsəˈmetrik| • adj. 1 of or having equal dimensions. 2 of, relating to, or denoting muscular action in which tension is developed without contraction of the muscle.

■ denoting a form of exercise (**isometrics**) in which muscles are strenthened by acting in equal opposition to each other. 3 (in technical or architectural drawing) incorporating a method of showing projection or perspective in which the three principal dimensions are represented by three axes 120° apart.
DERIVATIVES: **i•so•met•ri•cal•ly** |-ik(ə)lē| adv.

i•so•mor•phic |ˌīsəˈmôrfik| (also **isomorphous** |-fəs|) • adj. corresponding or similar in form and relations.

■ having the same crystalline form.
DERIVATIVES: **i•so•mor•phism** |-ˌfizəm| n.

i•sos•ta•sy |īˈsästəsē| • n. the equilibrium that exists between parts of the earth's crust, which behaves as if it consists of blocks floating on the underlying mantle, rising if material (such as an ice cap) is removed and sinking if material is deposited.
DERIVATIVES: **i•so•stat•ic** |ˌīsəˈstætik| adj.

i•so•tope |ˈīsəˌtōp| • n. each of two or more forms of the same element that contain equal numbers of protons but different numbers of neutrons in their nuclei, and hence differ in relative atomic mass but not in chemical properties; in particular, a radioactive form of an element.
DERIVATIVES: **i•so•top•ic** |ˌīsəˈtäpik| adj. **i•so•top•i•cal•ly** |ˌīsəˈtäpik(ə)lē| adv. **i•sot•o•py** |ˈīsəˌtōpē; īˈsätəpē| n.

is•sei |ˈē(s)ˌsā| • n. (pl. same) a Japanese immigrant to North America. Cf. NISEI and SANSEI.

isth•mus |ˈisməs| • n. (pl. **isthmuses**) a narrow strip of land with water on either side, forming a link between two larger areas of land.

■ (pl. **isthmi** |-mī|) (in anatomy) a narrow organ, passage, or piece of tissue connecting two larger parts.

it•er•ate |ˈitəˌrāt| • v. [trans.] perform or utter repeatedly.

■ [intrans.] make repeated use of a mathematical or computational procedure, applying it each time to the result of the previous application; perform iteration. • *n.* Mathematics a quantity arrived at by iteration.

it•er•a•tion |ˌitəˈrāSHən| • *n.* the repetition of a process or utterance.

■ repetition of a mathematical or computational procedure applied to the result of a previous application, typically as a means of obtaining successively closer approximations to the solution of a problem. ■ a new version of a piece of computer hardware or software.

it•er•a•tive |ˈitəˌrātiv; -rətiv| • *adj.* relating to or involving iteration, esp. of a mathematical or computational process.

■ denoting a grammatical rule that can be applied repeatedly. ■ another term for FREQUENTATIVE, in grammar.
DERIVATIVES: **it•er•a•tive•ly** *adv.*

i•tin•er•ant |īˈtinərənt; iˈtin-| • *adj.* traveling from place to place: *itinerant traders.* • *n.* a person who travels from place to place.
DERIVATIVES: **i•tin•er•a•cy** |-rəsē| *n.* **i•tin•er•an•cy** *n.* **i•tin•er•ant•ly** *adv.*

i•tin•er•ar•y |īˈtinəˌrerē; iˈtin-| • *n.* (pl. **-ies**) a planned route or journey.
■ a travel document recording these.

its |its| • *possessive adj.* belonging to or associated with a thing previously mentioned or easily identified: *turn the camera on its side.*
■ belonging to or associated with a child or animal of unspecified sex: *a baby in its mother's womb.*

USAGE: **Its** is the possessive form of *it* (*the dog licked its paw*), while **it's** is the contraction of *it is* (*Look, it's a dog licking its paw*) or *it has* (*It's been licking its paw*). The apostrophe in **it's** never denotes a possessive. The confusion is at least partly understandable since other possessive forms (singular nouns) do take an apostrophe + s, as in *the **girl's** bike*; *the **president's** smile.*

i•vo•ry tow•er • *n.* a state of privileged seclusion or separation from the facts and practicalities of the real world: *the ivory tower of academia.*

Jj

jab•ber•wock•y |ˈjæbərˌwäkē| • *n.* (pl. **-ies**) invented or meaningless language; nonsense. • *adj.* meaningless; nonsensical.

jack•al |ˈjækəl| • *n.* a slender, long-legged wild dog that feeds on carrion, game, and fruit and often hunts cooperatively, found in Africa and southern Asia.
■ a person who acts like a jackal, esp. one who serves or does subordinate preparatory work or drudgery for another.

jack•a•napes |ˈjækəˌnāps| • *n.* **1** an impertinent person. **2** a tame monkey.

jack•leg |ˈjækˌleg| • *n.* an incompetent, unskillful, or dishonest person: [as adj.] *a jackleg carpenter.* A person employed to break a strike: *jackleg laborers.* Cf. SCAB.

Jac•o•be•an |ˌjækəˈbēən| • *adj.* of or relating to the reign (1406-37) of James I of England: *a Jacobean mansion.*
■ (of furniture) in the style prevalent during the reign of James I, esp. being the color of dark oak. • *n.* a person who lived during this period.

Jac•o•bin |ˈjækəbən| • *n.* **1** a member of a democratic club established in Paris in 1789. The Jacobins were the most radical and ruthless of the political groups formed in the wake of the French Revolution, and in association with Maximilien Robespierre they instituted the Terror of 1793–4.
■ an extreme political radical. **2** a Dominican friar.
DERIVATIVES: **Jac•o•bin•ic** |ˌjækəˈbinik| *adj.* **Jac•o•bin•i•cal** |ˌjækəˈbinikəl| *adj.* **Jac•o•bin•ism** |-ˌnizəm| *n.*

Jac•o•bite |ˈjækəˌbīt| • *n.* a supporter of the deposed James II and his descendants in their claim to the British throne after the Revolution of 1688. Drawing most of their support from Catholic clans of the Scottish Highlands, Jacobites made attempts to regain the throne in 1689–90, 1715, 1719, and 1745–6, finally being defeated at the Battle of Culloden in 1746.
DERIVATIVES: **Jac•o•bit•i•cal** |ˌjækəˈbitikəl| *adj.* **Jac•o•bit•ism** |-bīˌtizəm| *n.*

jac•quard |ˈjæˌkärd; jəˈkärd| • *n.* an apparatus with perforated cards, fitted to a loom to facilitate the weaving of figured and brocaded fabrics.
■ a fabric made on a loom with such a device, with an intricate variegated pattern.

jad•ed |jādid| • *adj.* tired, bored, or lacking enthusiasm, typically after having had too much of something: *meals to tempt the most jaded appetites.*
DERIVATIVES: **jad•ed•ly** *adv.* **jad•ed•ness** *n.*

jal•ou•sie |ˈjæləˌsē| • *n.* a blind or shutter made of a row of angled slats.

Ja•nus |ˈjānəs| • *n.* an ancient Italian deity, guardian of doorways and gates and protector of the state in time of war. He is usually represented with two faces, so that he looks both forward and backward. • *adj.* (also **janus-faced**) having a dual function, purpose, attitude, etc.: *a Janus aspect.*
■ hypocritical; two-faced.

ja•pan |jəˈpæn| • *n.* a hard, dark, enamellike varnish containing asphalt, used to give a black gloss to metal objects.

■ a kind of varnish in which pigments are ground, typically used to imitate lacquer on wood. ■ articles made in a Japanese style, esp. when decorated with lacquer or enamellike varnish. • *v.* (**japanned, japanning**) [trans.] cover (something) with a hard black varnish: [as adj.] (**japanned**) *a japanned tin tray.*

jape |jāp| • *n.* a practical joke: *the childish jape of depositing a stink bomb in her locker.* • *v.* [intrans.] say or do something in jest or mockery: *children japing at policemen.*
DERIVATIVES: **jap•er•y** |ˈjāp(ə)rē| *n.*

jar•gon |ˈjärgən| • *n.* special words or expressions that are used by a particular profession or group and are difficult for others to understand: *legal jargon.*
■ a form of language regarded as barbarous, debased, or hybrid.
DERIVATIVES: **jar•gon•is•tic** |ˌjärgəˈnistik| *adj.* **jar•gon•ize** |-ˌnīz| *v.*

jaun•dice |ˈjôndis| • *n.* a medical condition with yellowing of the skin or whites of the eyes, arising from excess of the pigment bilirubin and typically caused by obstruction of the bile duct, by liver disease, or by excessive breakdown of red blood cells.
■ bitterness, resentment, or envy.

jaun•diced |ˈjôndist| • *adj.* having or affected by jaundice, in particular unnaturally yellow in complexion.
■ affected by bitterness, resentment, or envy: *they looked on politicians with a jaundiced eye.*

jaun•ty |ˈjôntē| • *adj.* (**-ier, -iest**) having or expressing a lively, cheerful, and self-confident manner: *there was no mistaking that jaunty walk.*
DERIVATIVES: **jaun•ti•ly** |-təlē| *adv.* **jaun•ti•ness** *n.*

jeal•ous |ˈjeləs| • *adj.* feeling or showing envy of someone or their achievements and advantages: *he grew jealous of her success.*
■ feeling or showing suspicion of someone's unfaithfulness in a relationship: *a jealous boyfriend.* ■ fiercely protective or vigilant of one's rights or possessions: *Howard is still a little jealous of his authority* | *they kept a jealous eye over their interests.* ■ (of God) demanding faithfulness and exclusive worship.
DERIVATIVES: **jeal•ous•ly** *adv.*

je•june |jiˈjōōn| • *adj.* **1** naive, simplistic, and superficial: *their entirely predictable and usually jejune opinions.* **2** (of ideas or writings) dry and uninteresting: *the poem seems rather jejune.*
DERIVATIVES: **je•june•ly** *adv.* **je•june•ness** *n.*

jell |jel| • *v.* [intrans.] (of jelly or a similar substance) set or become firmer: *the stew is jelling.*
■ (of a project or idea) take a definite shape; begin to work well: *everything seemed to jell for the magazine.*

je ne sais quoi |ˌZHə nə sā ˈkwä| • *n.* a quality that cannot be described or named easily: *that je ne sais quoi that makes a professional.*

jeop•ard•y |ˈjepərdē| • *n.* danger of loss, harm, or failure: *Michael's job was not in jeopardy.*
■ (in law) danger (of imprisonment, etc.) arising from being on trial for a criminal offense. Cf. DOUBLE JEOPARDY.
DERIVATIVES: **jeopardize** *v.*

jer•e•mi•ad |ˌjerəˈmīəd| • *n.* a long, mournful complaint or lamentation; a list of woes.

Jes•u•it |ˈjezHəwit; ˈjez(y)ə-| • *n.* a member of the Society of Jesus, a Roman Catholic order of priests founded by St. Ignatius Loyola, St. Francis Xavier, and others in 1534, to do missionary work. The order was zealous in opposing the Reformation.

jet•sam |ˈjetsəm| • *n.* unwanted material or goods that have been thrown overboard from a ship and washed ashore, esp. material that has been discarded to lighten a vessel in distress. Cf. FLOTSAM; LAGAN.

jet•ti•son |ˈjetisən; -zən| • *v.* [trans.] throw or drop (something) from an aircraft or ship: *six bombers jettisoned their loads in the sea.*
■ abandon or discard (someone or something that is no longer wanted): *he's ready to jettison his politics.* • *n.* the action of jettisoning something.

jeu d'es•prit |ˌZHə dəˈsprē; ˌZHœ| • *n.* (pl. **jeux d'esprit** pronunc. same) a lighthearted display of wit and cleverness, esp. in a work of literature.

Jew |jōō| • *n.* a member of the people and cultural community whose traditional religion is Judaism and who trace their origins through the ancient Hebrew people of Israel to Abraham.

Jew•ry |ˈjōōrē| • *n.* (pl. **-ies**) **1** Jews collectively. **2** a historical Jewish quarter in a town or city.

Je•ze•bel |ˈjezəˌbel; -bəl| • *n.* (*fl.* 9th century BC), a Phoenician princess, traditionally the great-aunt of Dido and in the Bible the wife of Ahab, king of Israel. She was denounced by Elijah for introducing the worship of Baal into Israel (1 Kings 16:31, 21:5–15, 2 Kings 9:30–7).
■ [as n.] (**a Jezebel**) a shameless or immoral woman.

jib¹ |jib| • *n.* **1** (in sailing) a triangular sail set forward of the forwardmost mast. **2** the projecting arm of a crane.

jib² • *v.* (**jibbed, jibbing**) [intrans.] (of an animal, esp. a horse) stop and refuse to go on: *he jibbed at the final fence.*
■ (of a person) be unwilling to do or accept something: *he jibs at paying large bills.*
DERIVATIVES: **jib•ber** *n.*

jibe¹ |jib| • *n.* & *v.* variant spelling of GIBE.

jibe² (Brit. **gybe**) • *v.* [intrans.] (in sailing) change course by swinging a fore-and-aft sail across a following wind: *they jibed, and headed closer to shore.*
■ [trans.] swing (a sail or boom) across the wind in such a way. ■ (of a sail or boom) swing or be swung across the wind: [as adj.] (**jibing**) *the skipper was hit by a jibing boom.* • *n.* an act or instance of jibing.

jibe³ • *v.* [intrans.] be in accord; agree: *the verdict does not jibe with the medical evidence.*

ji•had |jiˈhäd| • *n.* a holy war undertaken by Muslims against unbelievers.

■ a single-minded or obsessive campaign: *the quest for greater sales became a jihad.*

jin•go•ism |ˈjiNGgōˌizəm| • *n.* extreme patriotism, esp. in the form of aggressive or warlike foreign policy.
DERIVATIVES: **jin•go•ist** *n.* **jin•go•is•tic** |ˌjiNGgōˈistik| *adj.*

jinn |jin| (also **djinn** or **jinni** |jiˈnē; ˈjinē|) • *n.* (pl. same or **jinns**) (in Arabian and Muslim mythology) an intelligent spirit of lower rank than angels, able to appear in human and animal forms and to possess humans.

jive |jīv| • *n.* **1** a lively style of dance popular esp. in the 1940s and 1950s, performed to swing music or rock and roll.
■ swing music. **2** (also **jive talk**) a form of slang associated with black American jazz musicians.
■ a thing, esp. talk, that is deceptive or worthless: *a single image says more than any amount of blather and jive.* • *v.* **1** [intrans.] perform the jive or a similar dance to popular music. **2** [trans.] taunt or sneer at: *Willy kept jiving him until Jimmy left.*
■ [intrans.] talk nonsense: *he wasn't jiving about that.* • *adj.* deceitful or worthless: *jive talk.*
DERIVATIVES: **jiv•er** *n.* **jiv•ey** *adj.*

jo•cose |jōˈkōs| • *adj.* playful or humorous: *a jocose allusion.*
DERIVATIVES: **jo•cose•ly** *adv.* **jo•cose•ness** *n.* **jo•cos•i•ty** |-ˈkäsitē| *n.* (pl. **-ies**).

joc•u•lar |ˈjäkyələr| • *adj.* fond of or characterized by joking; humorous or playful: *she sounded in a jocular mood* | *his voice was jocular.*
DERIVATIVES: **joc•u•lar•i•ty** |ˌjäkyəˈlæritē; -ˈler-| *n.* **joc•u•lar•ly** *adv.*

joc•und |ˈjäkənd; ˈjō-| • *adj.* cheerful and lighthearted: *a jocund wedding party.*
DERIVATIVES: **jo•cun•di•ty** |jōˈkənditē| *n.* (pl. **-ies**) **joc•und•ly** *adv.*

joie de vi•vre |ˌZHwä də ˈvēvrə| • *n.* exuberant enjoyment of life.

join•der |ˈjoindər| • *n.* (esp. in law) the action of bringing parties together; union.

jol•li•ty |ˈjälitē| • *n.* (pl. **-ies**) lively and cheerful activity or celebration: *a night of riotous jollity.*
■ the quality of being cheerful: *he was full of false jollity.*

jos•tle |ˈjäsəl| • *v.* [trans.] push, elbow, or bump against (someone) roughly, typically in a crowd: *he was jostled in the subway and had his pocket picked.* | [intrans.] *people jostled against us.*
■ [intrans.] (**jostle for**) struggle or compete forcefully for: *a jumble of images jostled for attention.* • *n.* the action of jostling.

jour•ney•man |ˈjərnēmən| • *n.* (pl. **-men**) a trained worker who is employed by someone else.
■ a worker or professional athlete who is reliable but not outstanding: [as adj.] *a journeyman infielder.*

joust |joust| • *v.* [intrans.] [often as n.] (**jousting**) (of a medieval knight) engage in a sporting contest in which two opponents on horseback fight with lances.

■ compete closely for superiority: *the guerrillas jousted for supremacy.* • *n.* a medieval sporting contest in which two opponents on horseback fought with lances.
DERIVATIVES: **joust•er** *n.*

jo•vi•al |ˈjōvēəl| • *adj.* cheerful and friendly: *she was in a jovial mood.*
DERIVATIVES: **jo•vi•al•i•ty** |ˌjōvēˈælitē| *n.* **jo•vi•al•ly** *adv.*

ju•bi•lee |ˈjōōbəˌlē; ˌjōōbəˈlē| • *n.* a special anniversary of an event, esp. one celebrating twenty-five or fifty years of a reign or activity: [as adj.] *jubilee celebrations.*
■ (in Jewish history) a year of emancipation and restoration, observed every fifty years.
■ (in full **Jubilee Year**) a period of remission from the penal consequences of sin, granted by the Roman Catholic Church under certain conditions for a year, usually at intervals of twenty-five years. • *adj.* [postpositive] (of desserts) flambé: *cherries jubilee.*

ju•di•ca•ture |ˈjōōdikəˌCHŏŏr; -ˌkāCHər| • *n.* the administration of justice.
■ (**the judicature**) judges collectively; the judiciary.
DERIVATIVES: **ju•di•ca•to•ry** |-kəˌtôrē| *adj.*

ju•di•cial |jōōˈdisHəl| • *adj.* of, by, or appropriate to a law court or judge: *a judicial inquiry into the allegations* | *a judicial system.*
DERIVATIVES: **ju•di•cial•ly** *adv.*

USAGE: **Judicial** means 'relating to judgment and the administration of justice': *the judicial system; judicial robes.* Do not confuse it with **judicious**, which means 'prudent, reasonable': *getting off the highway the minute you felt tired was a judicious choice.* **Judiciary,** usually a noun and sometimes an adjective, refers to the judicial branch of government, the court system, or judges collectively.

ju•di•ci•ar•y |jōōˈdisHēˌerē; -ˈdisHərē| • *n.* (pl. **-ies**) (usu. **the judiciary**) the judicial authorities of a country; judges collectively.
USAGE: See usage at JUDICIAL.

ju•di•cious |jōōˈdisHəs| • *adj.* having, showing, or done with good judgment or sense: *the efficient and judicious use of pesticides.*
DERIVATIVES: **ju•di•cious•ly** *adv.* **ju•di•cious•ness** *n.*

ju•do |ˈjōōdō| • *n.* a sport of unarmed combat derived from jujitsu and intended to train the body and mind. It involves using holds and leverage to unbalance the opponent.
DERIVATIVES: **ju•do•ist** |-ist| *n.*

jug•ger•naut |ˈjəgərˌnôt| • *n.* a huge, powerful, and overwhelming force or institution: *a juggernaut of secular and commercial culture.*

jug•u•lar |ˈjəgyələr| • *adj.* **1** of the neck or throat. **2** (of fish's pelvic fins) located in front of the pectoral fins. • *n.* short for *jugular vein,* which conveys blood from the face and scalp (*external jugular vein*) or from the face, neck, and brain (*internal jugular vein*).
PHRASES: **go for the jugular** be aggressive or unrestrained in making an attack: *once stock prices started to drop, the corporate raiders decided to go for the jugular.*

ju•jit•su |ˌjo͞o'jitso͞o| (also **jiujitsu** or **jujut-su**) • *n.* a Japanese system of unarmed combat and physical training.

junc•ture |'jəNG(k)CHər| • *n.* a particular point in events or time: *it is difficult to say at this juncture whether this recovery can be sustained.*
■ a place where things join: *the plane crashed at the juncture of two mountains.* ■ the set of features in speech that enable a hearer to detect a word or phrase boundary, e.g., distinguishing *I scream* from *ice cream.*

jun•ket |'jəNGkit| • *n.* **1** a dish of sweetened and flavored curds of milk, often served with fruit. **2** an extravagant trip or celebration, in particular one enjoyed by a government official at public expense. • *v.* (**junketed, junketing**) [intrans.] [often as n.] (**junketing**) attend or go on such a trip or celebration.
DERIVATIVES: **jun•ke•teer** |ˌjəNGki'tir| *n.*

jun•ta |'ho͞ontə; 'jəntə| • *n.* **1** a military or political group that rules a country after taking power by force: *the right-wing military junta.* **2** a deliberative or administrative council in Spain or Portugal.

jun•to |'jəntō| • *n.* (pl. **-os**) a political or economic grouping or faction, esp. in 17th- and 18th-century Britain and America: *the Essex Junto.*

ju•ris•dic•tion |ˌjo͞oris'dikSHən| • *n.* the official power to make legal decisions and judgments: *federal courts had no **jurisdiction over** the case | the District of Columbia was placed under the **jurisdiction of** Congress.*
■ the extent of this power: *the claim will be **within the jurisdiction** of the military police.* ■ a system of law courts; a judicature. ■ the territory or sphere of activity over which the legal authority of a court or other institution extends.
DERIVATIVES: **ju•ris•dic•tion•al** |-SHənl| *adj.*

ju•ris•pru•dence |ˌjo͞oris'pro͞odns| • *n.* the theory or philosophy of law.
■ a legal system: *American jurisprudence.*
DERIVATIVES: **ju•ris•pru•dent** *adj. & n.* **ju•ris•pru•den•tial** |-pro͞o'denCHəl| *adj.*

ju•rist |'jo͞orist| • *n.* an expert in or writer on law.
■ a lawyer or a judge.
DERIVATIVES: **ju•ris•tic** |jo͞o'ristik| *adj.*

ju•ror |'jo͞orər; -ôr| • *n.* a member of a jury. Cf. JURIST.
■ a person taking an oath, esp. one of allegiance.

jus•sive |'jəsiv| • *adj.* (of a form of a verb) expressing a command.

jus•ti•fy |'jəstə,fī| • *v.* (**-ies, -ied**) [trans.] (in printing) adjust (a line of type or piece of text) so that the print fills a space evenly or forms a straight edge at the margin.
DERIVATIVES: **jus•ti•fi•ca•tion** |ˌjəstəfi'kāSHən| *n.*

ju•ve•nes•cence |ˌjo͞ovə'nesəns| • *n.* the state or period of being young.
DERIVATIVES: **ju•ve•nes•cent** *adj.*

ju•ve•nile¹ |'jo͞ovə,nīl; -vənl| • *adj.* of, for, or relating to young people: *juvenile entertainment.*
■ childish; immature: *she's bored with my juvenile conversation.* ■ of or denoting a theatrical or film role representing a young person: *the romantic juvenile lead.* ■ of or relating to young birds or other animals. • *n.* a young person.
■ a person below the age at which ordinary criminal prosecution is possible (18 in most countries): [as adj.] *juvenile justice, juvenile courts.* ■ a young bird or other animal. ■ an actor who plays juvenile roles.

ju•ve•nile² |ˌjo͞ovə'nilitē| • *n.* **1** youthfulness; juvenile manner, quality, or character. **2** (pl. **-ies**) a juvenile characteristic, act, or idea. **3** young people collectively.
DERIVATIVES: **ju•ve•nil•i•ty** *n.*

ju•ve•nil•i•a |ˌjo͞ovə'nilēə| • *plural n.* works produced by an author or artist while still young.

ju•ve•nil•ize |'jo͞ovənl,īz| • *v.* [trans.] make or keep young or youthful; arrest the development of.
■ [as adj.] (**juvenilized**) (of an insect or part of one) having a juvenile appearance or physiology; showing arrested or reversed development.

jux•ta•pose |'jəkstə,pōz; ˌjəkstə'pōz| • *v.* [trans.] place or deal with close together, as for contrasting effect: *black-and-white photos of slums were starkly **juxtaposed with** color images.*
DERIVATIVES: **jux•ta•po•si•tion** |ˌjəkstəpə'ziSHən| *n.* **jux•ta•po•si•tion•al** |ˌjəkstəpə'ziSHənl| *adj.*

Kk

Kab•ba•lah | ˈkæbələ; kəˈbä- | (also **Kabbala, Cabala, Cabbala,** or **Qabalah**) • *n.* the ancient Jewish tradition of mystical interpretation of the Bible, first transmitted orally and using esoteric methods (including ciphers). It reached the height of its influence in the later Middle Ages and remains significant in Hasidism.
DERIVATIVES: **Kab•ba•lism** | ˈkæbəˌlizəm | *n.* **Kab•ba•list** |-list| *n.* **Kab•ba•lis•tic** |ˌkæbəˈlistik| *adj.*
ka•bu•ki | kəˈbo͞okē | • *n.* a form of traditional Japanese drama with highly stylized song, mime, and dance, now performed only by male actors, using exaggerated gestures and body movements to express emotions, and including historical plays, domestic dramas, and dance pieces.
kaf•fee•klatsch | ˈkäfēˌkläCH; -ˌkläCH; ˈkôfē | • *n.* an informal social gathering at which coffee is served.
■ talking or gossip at such gatherings.
Kaf•fir | ˈkæfər | • *n.* chiefly S. African an insulting and contemptuous term for a black African.
kaf•fi•yeh | kəˈfē(y)ə | (also **keffiyeh**) • *n.* a Bedouin Arab's kerchief worn as a headdress.
kaf•ir | ˈkæfər | • *n.* a person who is not a Muslim (formerly used by Muslims).
Kaf•ka•esque |ˌkäfkəˈesk| • *adj.* characteristic or reminiscent of the oppressive or nightmarish qualities of the fictional world of Franz Kafka (1883–1924).
ka•hu•na | kəˈho͞onə | • *n.* (in Hawaii) a wise man or shaman.
■ an important person; the person in charge.
■ (in surfing) a very large wave.
kai•ser | ˈkīzər | • *n.* the German emperor, the emperor of Austria, or the head of the Holy Roman Empire: [as title] *Kaiser Wilhelm.*
DERIVATIVES: **kai•ser•ship** |-SHip| *n.*
Ka•ma Su•tra | ˈkämə ˈso͞otrə | an ancient Sanskrit treatise on the art of love and sexual technique.
ka•mi•ka•ze |ˌkämiˈkäzē | • *n.* (in World War II) a Japanese aircraft loaded with explosives and making a deliberate suicidal crash on an enemy target.
■ the pilot of such an aircraft. • *adj.* [attrib.] of or relating to such an attack or pilot.
■ reckless or potentially self-destructive: *he made a kamikaze run across three lanes of traffic.*
ka•nak•a | kəˈnäkə | • *n.* a native of Hawaii.
■ formerly, a Pacific Islander employed as an indentured laborer in Australia, esp. in the sugar and cotton plantations of Queensland.
kan•ga•roo court • *n.* an unofficial court held by a group of people in order to try someone regarded, esp. without good evidence, as guilty of a crime or misdemeanor.
■ any unfair or irregular court.
ka•put | kəˈpo͝ot; kä- | • *adj.* [predic.] broken and useless; no longer working or effective.

kar•a•o•ke |ˌkærēˈōkē; ˌker- | • *n.* a form of entertainment, offered typically by bars and clubs, in which people take turns singing popular songs into a microphone over prerecorded backing tracks.
kar•at | ˈkærət; ˈker- | (chiefly Brit. also **carat**) • *n.* a measure of the purity of gold, pure gold being 24 karats: *an ounce of 21-carat gold.*
kar•ma | ˈkärmə | • *n.* (in Hinduism and Buddhism) the sum of a person's actions in this and previous states of existence, viewed as deciding his or her fate in future existences.
■ destiny or fate, following as effect from cause.
DERIVATIVES: **kar•mic** |-mik| *adj.* **kar•mi•cal•ly** |-mik(ə)lē| *adv.*
karst |kärst| • *n.* landscape underlain by limestone that has been eroded by dissolution, producing ridges, towers, fissures, sinkholes, and other characteristic landforms: [as adj.] *karst topography* | *it was strange country, broken into hummocks and karsts and mesas.*
DERIVATIVES: **kars•tic** | ˈkärstik | *adj.* **kars•ti•fi•ca•tion** |ˌkärstəfiˈkāSHən | *n.* **kars•ti•fy** | ˈkärstəˌfī | *v.* (**-ies, -ied**) .
kat•a•bat•ic |ˌkætəˈbætik | • *adj.* (of a wind) caused by local downward motion of cool air. The opposite (upward, warm) movement is called *anabatic.*
keel•haul | ˈkēlˌhôl | • *v.* [trans.] punish (someone) by dragging him or her through the water under the keel of a ship, either across the width or from bow to stern.
■ punish or reprimand severely.
ker•a•tin | ˈkerətin | • *n.* a fibrous protein forming the main structural constituent of hair, feathers, hoofs, claws, horns, etc.
DERIVATIVES: **ke•rat•i•nous** | kəˈrætn-əs | *adj.*
ker•mes | ˈkermēz | • *n.* **1** a red dye used, esp. formerly, for coloring fabrics and manuscripts.
■ the dried bodies of a female scale insect, which are crushed to yield this dye. **2** (**oak kermes**) the scale insect (*kermes illicis*) that is used for this dye, forming berrylike galls on the kermes oak.
ker•mis | ˈkərmis | • *n.* a summer fair held in towns and villages in the Netherlands.
■ a fair or carnival, esp. one held to raise money for a charity.
kern¹ |kərn| • *v.* [trans.] **1** [usu. as n.] (**kerning**) adjust the spacing between (letters or characters) in a piece of text to be printed.
■ make (letters) overlap. **2** design (metal type) with a projecting part beyond the body or shank. • *n.* the part of a metal type projecting beyond its body or shank.
kern² (also **kerne**) • *n.* **1** a light-armed Irish foot soldier. **2** a peasant; a rustic.
ketch |kecH| • *n.* a two-masted, fore-and-aft rigged sailboat with a mizzenmast stepped

forward of the rudder and smaller than the foremast.

key • *n.* a low-lying island or reef, esp. in the Caribbean. Cf. CAY.

Keynesian |ˈkānzēən| • *adj. & n.* of or pertaining to the English economist John Maynard Keyes (1883–1946) or his economic theories, esp. regarding state control of the economy through money and taxes.
DERIVATIVES: **Keynes•i•an•ism** |ˈkānzēə ˌnizəm| *n.*

key•note |ˈkēˌnōt| • *n.* **1** a prevailing tone or central theme, typically one set or introduced at the start of a conference: *individuality was the keynote of the nineties* | [as adj.] *he delivered the keynote address at the launch.* **2** (in music) the note on which a key is based.
DERIVATIVES: **key•not•er** *n.*

key•stone |ˈkēˌstōn| • *n.* a central stone at the summit of an arch, locking the whole together.
■ [usu. in sing.] the central principle or part of a policy, system, etc., on which all else depends: *cooperation remains the keystone of the government's security policy.*

khan |kän| • *n.* a title given to rulers and officials in central Asia, Afghanistan, and certain other Muslim countries.
■ any of the successors of Genghis Khan (1162–1227), supreme rulers of the Turkish, Tartar, and Mongol peoples and emperors of China in the Middle Ages.
DERIVATIVES: **khan•ate** |ˈkänāt| *n.*

kib•butz |kiˈbo͞ots| • *n.* (pl. **kibbutzim** |ki ˌbo͞otˈsēm|) a communal settlement in Israel, typically a farm.

kib•itz |ˈkibits| • *v.* [intrans.] look on and offer unwelcome advice, esp. at a card game.
■ speak informally; chat: *she kibitzed with friends.*
DERIVATIVES: **kib•itz•er** *n.*

ki•bosh |kəˈbäsH; ˈkīˌbäsH| • *n.* (in phrase **put the kibosh on**) put an end to; dispose of decisively: *he put the kibosh on the deal.*

kin•dred |ˈkindrid| • *n.* [treated as pl.] one's family and relations.
■ relationship by blood: *ties of kindred.* • *adj.* [attrib.] similar in kind; related: *books on kindred subjects.*

ki•ne•sics |kəˈnēsiks; -ziks| • *plural n.* [usu. treated as sing.] the study of the way in which certain body movements and gestures serve as a form of nonverbal communication.
■ [usu. treated as pl.] certain body movements and gestures regarded in such a way.

ki•ne•si•ol•o•gy |kəˌnēsēˈäləjē; -zē-| • *n.* the study of the mechanics of body movements.
DERIVATIVES: **ki•ne•si•o•log•i•cal** |-sēə ˈläjikəl| *adj.* **ki•ne•si•ol•o•gist** |-jist| *n.*

kin•es•the•sia |ˌkinəsˈTHēZHə| (Brit. **kinaesthesia**) • *n.* awareness of the position and movement of the parts of the body by means of sensory organs (proprioceptors) in the muscles and joints.
DERIVATIVES: **kin•es•thet•ic** |-ˈTHetik| *adj.*

ki•net•ic |kəˈnetik| • *adj.* of, relating to, or resulting from motion.

■ (of a work of art) depending on movement for its effect.
DERIVATIVES: **ki•net•i•cal•ly** |-ik(ə)lē| *adv.*

ki•osk |ˈkēˌäsk| • *n.* a small open-fronted hut or cubicle from which newspapers, refreshments, tickets, etc., are sold.
■ (usu. **telephone kiosk**) Brit. a telephone booth. ■ (in Turkey and Iran) a light open pavilion or summerhouse.

kis•met |ˈkizmit; -ˌmet| • *n.* destiny; fate: *what chance did I stand against kismet?*

kitch•en cab•i•net • *n.* a group of unofficial advisers to the holder of an elected office (esp. the president) who are considered to be unduly influential.

kite |kīt| • *v.* [trans.] write or use (a check, bill, or receipt) fraudulently.

kith |kiTH| • *n.* (in phrase **kith and kin** or **kith or kin**) one's friends, acquaintances, and relations: *a widow without kith or kin.*

kitsch |kiCH| • *n.* art, objects, or design considered to be in poor taste because of excessive garishness or sentimentality, but sometimes appreciated in an ironic or knowing way: *the lava lamp is an example of sixties kitsch* | [as adj.] *kitsch decor.*
DERIVATIVES: **kitsch•i•ness** *n.* **kitsch•y** *adj.*

klatch |kläCH; klæCH| (also **klatsch**) • *n.* a social gathering, esp. for food and conversation. Cf. KAFFEEKLATSCH.

klep•to•ma•ni•a |ˌkleptəˈmānēə; -ˈmānyə| • *n.* a recurrent urge to steal, typically without regard for need or profit.
DERIVATIVES: **klep•to•ma•ni•ac** |-ˈmānē ˌæk| *n. & adj.*

klutz |kləts| • *n.* a clumsy, awkward, or foolish person.
DERIVATIVES: **klutz•i•ness** *n.* **klutz•y** *adj.*

knave |nāv| • *n.* a dishonest or unscrupulous man.
■ another term for *jack* in cards.
DERIVATIVES: **knav•er•y** |-vərē| *n.* (pl. **-ies**) . **knav•ish** *adj.* **knav•ish•ly** *adv.* **knav•ish•ness** *n.*

knee-jerk • *n.* a sudden involuntary reflex kick caused by a blow on the tendon just below the knee. • *adj.* [attrib.] (of a response) automatic and unthinking: *a knee-jerk reaction.*
■ (of a person) responding in this way: *knee-jerk conservatives.*

knell |nel| • *n.* the sound of a bell, esp. when rung solemnly for a death or funeral.
■ used with reference to an announcement, event, or sound that is regarded as a solemn warning of the end of something: *the decision will probably toll the knell for the facility.* • *v.* [intrans.] (of a bell) ring solemnly, esp. for a death or funeral.
■ [trans.] proclaim (something) by or as if by a knell.

knick•er•bock•er |ˈnikərˌbäkər| • *n.* **1** (**knickerbockers**) loose-fitting trousers gathered at the knee or calf. **2** (**Knickerbocker**) a New Yorker.
■ a descendant of the original Dutch settlers in New York.

DERIVATIVES: **knick•er•bock•ered** *adj.*
knock•off |ˈnäkˌôf| (also **knock-off**) • *n.* a copy or imitation, esp. of an expensive or designer product: [as adj.] *knockoff merchandise.*
knurl |nərl| • *n.* a small projecting knob or ridge, esp. in a series around the edge of something.
DERIVATIVES: **knurled** *adj.*
ko•sher |ˈkōsHər| • *adj.* (of food, or premises in which food is sold, cooked, or eaten) satisfying the requirements of Jewish law: *a kosher kitchen.*
■ (of a person) observing Jewish food laws. ■ genuine and legitimate: *do you really think this deal is kosher?* • *v.* [trans.] prepare (food) according to the requirements of Jewish law. ■ give (something) the appearance of being legitimate: *see them scramble to kosher illegal evidence.*
PHRASES: **keep** (or **eat**) **kosher** observe the Jewish food regulations (kashruth).
kow•tow |ˈkowˈtow| • *v.* [intrans.] kneel and touch the ground with the forehead in worship or submission as part of Chinese custom.
■ act in an excessively subservient manner: *she didn't have to kowtow to a boss.* • *n.* an act of kneeling and touching the ground with the forehead in such a way.
DERIVATIVES: **kow•tow•er** *n.*
krem•lin |ˈkremlin| • *n.* a citadel within a Russian town.
■ (**the Kremlin**) the citadel in Moscow. ■ the Russian or (formerly) Soviet government housed within this citadel.
ku•dos |ˈk(y)ooˌdōs; -ˌdōz; -ˌdäs| • *n.* praise and honor received for an achievement.

USAGE: **Kudos** comes from Greek and means 'glory.' Despite appearances, it is not a plural form. This means that there is no singular form **kudo** and that use as a plural, as in the following sentence, is, strictly, incorrect: *he received many kudos for his work* (correct use is *he received much kudos . . .*).

ku•lak |kooˈlæk; -ˈläk| • *n.* a peasant in Russia wealthy enough to own a farm and hire labor. Emerging after the emancipation of serfs in the 19th century, the kulaks resisted (1920s–30s) Stalin's forced collectivization, and millions were arrested, exiled, or killed.
kvetch |k(ə)vecH; kfecH| • *n.* a person who complains a great deal.
■ a complaint. • *v.* [intrans.] complain: *stop kvetching, already!*
Kwan•zaa |ˈkwänzə| (also **Kwanza**) • *n.* a secular festival observed by many African Americans from December 26 to January 1 as a celebration of their cultural heritage and traditional values.
kwash•i•or•kor |ˌkwäsHēˈôrkôr; -kər| • *n.* a form of malnutrition caused by protein deficiency in the diet, typically affecting young children in the tropics.

Ll

la•bi•a |ˈlābēə| • *plural n.* (in anatomy) the inner and outer folds of the vulva, at either side of the vagina.
la•bi•al |ˈlābēəl| • *adj.* **1** of or relating to the lips.
■ (of the surface of a tooth) adjacent to the lips. ■ (in zoology) of, resembling, or serving as a lip, liplike part, or labium (fused mouthpart of an insect). **2** (of a consonant) requiring complete or partial closure of the lips (e.g., *p, b, f, v, m, w*), or (of a vowel) requiring rounded lips (e.g., *oo* in moon). • *n.* a labial sound.
DERIVATIVES: **la•bi•al•ize** |-ˌlīz| *v.* (in sense 2). **la•bi•al•ly** *adv.*
la•bile |ˈlāˌbīl; -bəl| • *adj.* **1** liable to err or sin. **2** liable to change; easily altered.
■ of or characterized by emotions that are easily aroused or freely expressed, and that tend to alter quickly and spontaneously; emotionally unstable. ■ (in chemistry) easily broken down or displaced.
DERIVATIVES: **la•bil•i•ty** |ləˈbiləṭē; lə-| *n.*
lab•y•rinth |ˈlæb(ə)ˌrinTH| • *n.* **1** a complicated irregular network of passages or paths in which it is difficult to find one's way; a maze: *a labyrinth of passages and secret chambers.*
■ an intricate and confusing arrangement: *a labyrinth of conflicting laws and regulations.* **2** a complex structure in the inner ear that contains the organs of hearing and balance. It consists of bony cavities (the **bony labyrinth**) filled with fluid and lined with sensitive membranes (the **membranous labyrinth**).
DERIVATIVES: **lab•y•rin•thi•an** |ˌlæbəˈrinTHēən| *adj.* **lab•y•rin•thine** |ˌlæbəˈrin ˌTHēn; -ˈrinTHin; -ˈrinˌTHīn| *adj.*
lac•er•ate |ˈlæsəˌrāt| • *v.* [trans.] tear or deeply cut (something, esp. flesh or skin): *the point had lacerated his neck* | [as adj.] (**lacerated**) *his lacerated hands.*
■ (of feelings or emotions) wound or injure.
DERIVATIVES: **lac•er•a•tion** |ˌlæsəˈrāsHən| *n.*
Lach•e•sis |ˈlækəsis| in Greek mythology, one of the three Fates, who measures the length of the thread of life.
lach•ry•mal |ˈlækrəməl| (also **lacrimal** or **lacrymal**) • *adj.* **1** connected with weeping or tears. **2** (usu. **lacrimal**) concerned with the

secretion of tears: *lacrimal cells.* • *n.* (usu. **lacrimal** or **lacrimal bone**) a small bone forming part of the eye socket.

lach•ry•mose |ˈlækrəˌmōs; -ˌmōz| • *adj.* tearful or given to weeping: *she was pink-eyed and lachrymose.*

■ inducing tears; sad: *a lachrymose children's classic.*

DERIVATIVES: **lach•ry•mose•ly** *adv.* **lach•ry•mos•i•ty** |ˌlækrəˈmäsətē| *n.*

lack•a•dai•si•cal |ˌlækəˈdāzikəl| • *adj.* lacking enthusiasm and determination; carelessly lazy.

DERIVATIVES: **lack•a•dai•si•cal•ly** *adv.*

lack•ey |ˈlækē| • *n.* (pl. **-eys**) a servant, esp. a liveried footman or manservant.

■ a person who is obsequiously willing to obey or serve another person or group of people. Cf. SYCOPHANT. • *v.* (also **lacquey**) (**-eys, -eyed**) [trans.] behave servilely to; wait upon as a lackey.

lack•lus•ter |ˈlækˌləstər|) Brit. **lacklustre**) • *adj.* lacking in vitality, force, or conviction; uninspired or uninspiring: *no excuses were made for the lackluster performance.*

■ (of the hair or the eyes) not shining; dull.

la•con•ic |ləˈkänik| • *adj.* (of a person, speech, or style of writing) using very few words: *the laconic reply suggested a lack of interest in the topic.*

DERIVATIVES: **la•con•i•cal•ly** |-(ə)lē| *adv.* **la•con•i•cism** |ləˈkänəˌsizəm| *n.* **lac•o•nism** |ˈlækəˌnizəm| *n.*

lac•ta•tion |lækˈtāSHən| • *n.* the secretion of milk by the mammary glands.

■ the suckling of young; the period of milk secretion normally following childbirth.

DERIVATIVES: **lac•ta•tion•al** |-ˈtāSHənl| *adj.*

lac•to•veg•e•tar•i•an |ˌlæktōˌvejəˈterēən| • *n.* a person who abstains from eating meat and eggs, but who eats dairy products. An **ovolactovegetarian** also eats eggs.

la•cu•na |ləˈk(y)o͞onə| • *n.* (pl. **lacunae** |-nī; -nē| or **lacunas**) an unfilled space or interval; a gap: *the journal has filled a lacuna in Middle Eastern studies.*

■ a missing portion in a book or manuscript. ■ (in anatomy) a cavity or depression, esp. in bone.

DERIVATIVES: **la•cu•nal** |ləˈk(y)o͞onl| *adj.* **lac•u•nar•y** |ˈlækyəˌnerē; ləˈk(y)o͞onərē| *adj.* **la•cu•nate** |-ˌnāt; -nit; ˈlækyəˌnāt| *adj.* **la•cu•nose** |ˈlækyəˌnōs; -ˌnōz| *adj.*

la•cus•trine |ləˈkəstrin| • *adj.* of, relating to, or associated with lakes: *lacustrial vegetation.*

lade |lād| • *v.* (past part. **laden** |ˈlādn|) [trans.] load (a ship or other vessel).

■ ship (goods) as cargo. ■ [intrans.] (of a ship) take on cargo.

lag•gard |ˈlægərd| • *n.* a person who makes slow progress and falls behind others: *there was no time for laggards.* • *adj.* slower than desired or expected: *a bell to summon laggard children to school.*

DERIVATIVES: **lag•gard•ly** *adj. & adv.* **lag•gard•ness** *n.*

la•gniappe |lænˈyæp; ˈlænˌyæp| • *n.* something given as a bonus or extra gift.

la•goon |ləˈgo͞on| • *n.* a stretch of salt water separated from the sea by a low sandbank or coral reef.

■ the enclosed water of an atoll. ■ a small freshwater lake near a larger lake or river. ■ an artificial pool for the treatment of effluent or to accommodate an overspill from surface drains during heavy rain.

DERIVATIVES: **la•goon•al** |-ˈgo͞onl| *adj.*

la•ic |ˈlāik| • *adj.* of or pertaining to a layperson or the laity; nonclerical; lay. • *n.* a layperson; a noncleric.

DERIVATIVES: **la•i•cal** |-ikəl| *adj.* **la•i•cal•ly** |-(ə)lē| *adv.*

laird |lerd| • *n.* (in Scotland) a person who owns a large estate.

DERIVATIVES: **laird•ship** |-ˌSHip| *n.*

lais•sez-al•ler |ˌlesā äˈlā; ˌlezā| • *n.* absence of restraint; unconstrained freedom.

lais•sez-faire |ˌlesā ˈfer; ˌlezā| • *n.* a policy or attitude of leaving things to take their own course, without interfering.

■ abstention by governments from interfering in the workings of the **free market**: [as adj.] *laissez-faire capitalism.*

DERIVATIVES: **lais•ser-faire•ism** |ˈfer ˌizəm| *n.*

la•i•ty |ˈlāətē| • *n.* [usu. treated as pl.] (**the laity**) lay people, as distinct from the clergy.

■ ordinary people, as distinct from professionals or experts.

la•ma |ˈlämə| • *n.* **1** an honorific title applied to a spiritual leader in Tibetan Buddhism, whether a reincarnate lama (such as the Dalai Lama) or one who has earned the title in life. **2** a Tibetan or Mongolian Buddhist monk.

la•ma•ser•y |ˈläməˌserē| • *n.* (pl. **-ies**) a monastery of lamas.

lam•baste |læmˈbāst; -ˈbæst| (also **lambast** |-ˈbæst|) • *v.* [trans.] beat or thrash soundly; criticize (someone or something) harshly.

lam•bent |ˈlæmbənt| • *adj.* (of light or fire) glowing, gleaming, or flickering with a soft radiance: *the magical, lambent light of the north.*

■ (of wit, humor, etc.) lightly brilliant: *a touch of the lambent bitterness that sometimes surfaced in him.*

DERIVATIVES: **lam•ben•cy** |-bənsē| *n.* **lam•bent•ly** *adv.*

la•mé |læˈmā; lä-| • *n.* fabric with interwoven gold or silver threads. • *adj.* (of fabric or a garment) having such threads.

la•ment |ləˈment| • *n.* a passionate expression of grief or sorrow: *a song full of lament and sorrow.*

■ a song, piece of music, or poem expressing such emotions. ■ an expression of regret or disappointment; a complaint: *there were constant laments about work conditions.* • *v.* [trans.] mourn (a person's loss or death).

■ [intrans.] (**lament for/over**) express one's grief passionately about. ■ express regret or disappointment over something considered unsatisfactory, unreasonable, or unfair: [trans.] *she lamented the lack of bookstores in the town* | [with direct speech] *Jefferson later lamented, "Heaven remained silent."*

DERIVATIVES: **lam•en•ta•tion** |ˌlæmən
'tāSHən| *n.* **la•ment•er** *n.*

lam•i•na |'læmənə| • *n.* (pl. **laminae** |-ˌnē;
-ˌnī|) a thin layer, plate, or scale of sedimen-
tary rock, organic tissue, or other material.
DERIVATIVES: **lam•i•nal** *adj.* **lam•i•nar**
adj. **lam•i•nose** |-ˌnōs; -ˌnōz| *adj.*

lam•i•nate • *v.* |'læməˌnāt| [trans.] (often as
adj.] (**laminated**) overlay (a flat surface, esp.
paper) with a layer of plastic or some other
protective material. ■ manufacture by placing layer on layer. ■ split
into layers or leaves. ■ beat or roll (metal)
into thin plates. • *n.* |-nit; -ˌnāt| a laminated
structure or material, esp. one made of layers
fixed together to form a hard, flat, or flexible
material. • *adj.* |-nit; -ˌnāt| in the form of a
lamina or laminae.
DERIVATIVES: **lam•i•na•ble** |-nəbəl| *adj.*
lam•i•na•tion |ˌlæmə'nāSHən| *n.* **lam•i•na•
tor** |-ˌnātər| *n.*

lam•poon |læm'po͞on| • *v.* [trans.] publicly
criticize (someone or something) by using
ridicule, irony, or sarcasm. • *n.* a speech or
text criticizing someone or something in this
way: *a lampoon of student life.*
DERIVATIVES: **lam•poon•er** *n.* **lam•poon•
ist** |-ist| *n.*

lan•cet |'lænsit| • *n.* **1** a small, broad, two-
edged surgical knife or blade with a sharp
point. **2** a lancet arch or window (high and
narrow, with an acutely pointed head).
■ [as *adj.*] shaped like a lancet arch: *a lancet
clock.*
DERIVATIVES: **lan•cet•ed** |-tid| *adj.*

lan•guid |'læNGgwid| • *adj.* **1** (of a person,
manner, or gesture) displaying or having a
disinclination for physical exertion or effort;
slow and relaxed: *they turned with languid
movements from back to front so as to tan evenly.*
■ (of an occasion or period of time) pleasantly
lazy and peaceful: *languid days in the Italian
sun.* **2** weak or faint from illness or fatigue.
DERIVATIVES: **lan•guid•ly** *adv.* **lan•guid•
ness** *n.*

lan•guish |'læNGgwiSH| • *v.* [intrans.] **1** (of a
person or other living thing) lose or lack vitality; grow weak or feeble: *dormant plants
may appear to be languishing.*
■ fail to make progress or be successful: *many
Japanese works still languish unrecognized in
Europe.* ■ pine with love or grief: *she still lan-
guished after Richard.* ■ assume or display
a sentimentally tender or melancholy expression or tone: *when a visitor comes in, she smiles
and languishes.* **2** be forced to remain in an unpleasant place or situation: *has been languishing in a Mexican jail since 1974.*
DERIVATIVES: **lan•guish•er** *n.* **lan•guish•
ing•ly** *adv.*

lan•guor |'læNG(g)ər| • *n.* **1** the state or feel-
ing, often pleasant, of tiredness or inertia.
2 an oppressive stillness of the air:
DERIVATIVES: **lan•guor•ous** |-g(ə)rəs;
'læNGgrəs| *adj.* **lan•guor•ous•ly** |-g(ə)rəslē;
'læNGərəslē| *adv.*

lank |læNGk| • *adj.* (of hair) long, limp, and
straight.

■ (of a person) tall and lean; lanky.
DERIVATIVES: **lank•ly** *adv.* **lank•ness** *n.*

lan•yard |'lænyərd| • *n.* a rope threaded
through a pair of wooden blocks, used to adjust the tension in the rigging of a sailing vessel. Cf. HALYARD.
■ a cord passed around the neck, shoulder, or
wrist for holding a knife, whistle, or similar
object. ■ a cord attached to a breech mechanism for firing a gun.

La•od•i•ce•an |lāˌädə'sēən| • *adj.* lukewarm
or halfhearted, esp. with respect to religion
or politics. • *n.* a person with such an attitude.

lap•a•ros•co•py |ˌlæpə'räskəpē| • *n.* (pl.
-ies) a surgical procedure in which a fiber-
optic instrument is inserted through the ab-
dominal wall to view the organs in the abdomen or to perform minor surgery.
DERIVATIVES: **lap•a•ro•scope** |'læp(ə)rə
ˌskōp| *n.* **lap•a•ro•scop•ic** |ˌlæp(ə)rə'skäp-
ik| *adj.* **lap•a•ro•scop•i•cal•ly** |ˌlæp(ə)rə
'skäpik(ə)lē| *adv.*

lap•i•dar•y |'læpəˌderē| • *adj.* (of language)
engraved on or suitable for engraving on
stone and therefore elegant and concise: *a
lapidary statement intended to grace his own
gravestone.*
■ of or relating to stone and gems and the work
involved in engraving, cutting, or polishing.
• *n.* (pl. **-ies**) a person who cuts, polishes, or
engraves gems. ■ the art of cutting, polishing,
or engraving gems.

lar•ce•ny |'lärs(ə)nē| • *n.* (pl. **-ies**) theft of
personal property. Under various statutes, it
may be defined as **grand larceny** (of items
above a specified dollar value) or **petty larceny** (of items of lesser value).
DERIVATIVES: **lar•ce•nist** |-nist| *n.* **lar•
ce•nous** |-nəs| *adj.*

la•res |'läˌrēz; 'lerēz| • *plural n.* gods of the
household worshiped in ancient Rome. Cf.
PENATES.
PHRASES: **lares and penates** the home.

lar•gesse |lär'ZHes; -'jes| (also **largess**) • *n.*
generosity in bestowing money or gifts upon
others.
■ money or gifts given generously.

lar•go |'lärgō| • *adv. & adj.* (as a musical di-
rection) in a slow tempo and dignified in
style. • *n.* (often **Largo**) (pl. **-os**) a passage,
movement, or composition marked to be performed in this way.

lar•va |'lärvə| • *n.* (pl. **larvae** |-vē; -ˌvī|) the
active immature form of an insect, esp. one
that differs greatly from the adult and forms
the stage between egg and pupa, e.g., a cater-
pillar or grub. Cf. NYMPH.
■ an immature form of other animals that undergo some metamorphosis, e.g., a tadpole.
DERIVATIVES: **lar•val** |-vəl| *adj.* **lar•vi•
cide** |-ˌsīd| *n.*

las•civ•i•ous |lə'sivēəs| • *adj.* (of a person,
manner, or gesture) feeling or revealing an
overt and often offensive sexual desire: *he
gave her a lascivious wink.*
DERIVATIVES: **las•civ•i•ous•ly** *adv.* **las•
civ•i•ous•ness** *n.*

las•si•tude |ˈlæsəˌt(y)o͞od| • *n.* a state of physical or mental weariness; lack of energy.
la•ten•cy |ˌlātn ˈsē| see LATENT PERIOD.
la•tent |ˈlātnt| • *adj.* (of a quality or state) existing but not yet developed or manifest; hidden; concealed: *discovering her latent talent for diplomacy.*
■ (of a plant bud, resting stage, etc.) lying dormant or hidden until circumstances are suitable for development or manifestation. ■ (of a disease) in which the usual symptoms are not yet manifest. ■ (of a microorganism, esp. a virus) present in the body without causing disease, but capable of doing so at a later stage or when transmitted to another body.
DERIVATIVES: **la•tent•ly** *adv.*
la•tent pe•ri•od • *n.* **1** Medicine (also **latency period**) the period between infection with a virus or other microorganism and the onset of symptoms, or between exposure to radiation and the appearance of a cancer. **2** Physiology (also **latency**) the delay between the receipt of a stimulus by a sensory nerve and the response to it.
lat•er•al |ˈlætərəl; ˈlætrəl| • *adj.* of, at, toward, or from the side or sides: *the plant takes up water through its lateral roots.*
■ situated on one side or other of the body or of an organ, esp. in the region farthest from the median plane. The opposite of MEDIAL.
■ (of a disease or condition) affecting the side or sides of the body, or confined to one side of the body. ■ (in physics) acting or placed at right angles to the line of motion or of strain. ■ (of a consonant, esp. *l*, or its articulation) formed by or involving partial closure of the air passage by the tongue, which is so placed as to allow the breath to flow on one or both sides of the point of contact. • *n.* **1** a side part of something, esp. a shoot or branch growing out from the side of a stem. **2** (in phonetics) a lateral consonant. **3** (in football) a pass thrown either sideways or backward from the position of the passer. • *v.* [trans.] throw (a football) in a sideways or backward direction: *he tried to lateral the return but fumbled.*
■ [intrans.] throw a lateral pass: *he faked a handoff and then lateraled to the tailback.*
DERIVATIVES: **lat•er•al•ly** *adv.*
La•ti•no |ləˈtēnō; læ-| • *n.* (pl. **-os**) a Latin American inhabitant of the United States. Cf. HISPANIC; CHICANO. • *adj.* of or relating to these inhabitants.
lat•i•tude |ˈlætəˌt(y)o͞od| • *n.* **1** the angular distance of a place north or south of the earth's equator, or of the equator of a celestial object, usually expressed in degrees and minutes: *at a latitude of 51° N | lines of latitude.*
■ (**latitudes**) regions, esp. with reference to their temperature and distance from the equator: *temperate latitudes | northern latitudes.* **2** scope for freedom of action or thought: *journalists have considerable latitude in criticizing public figures.*
■ (in photography) the range of exposures for which an emulsion or printing paper will give

acceptable contrast: *a film with a latitude that is outstanding.*
DERIVATIVES: **lat•i•tu•di•nal** |ˌlætəˈt(y)o͞odn-əl; -ˈt(y)o͞odnəl| *adj.* **lat•i•tu•di•nal•ly** |ˌlætəˈt(y)o͞odn-əlē; -ˈt(y)o͞odnəlē| *adv.*
lat•i•tu•di•nar•i•an |ˌlætəˌt(y)o͞odnˈerēən| • *adj.* allowing latitude in religion; showing no preference among varying creeds and forms of worship. • *n.* a person with a latitudinarian attitude.
DERIVATIVES: **lat•i•tu•di•nar•i•an•ism** |-ˌnizəm| *n.*
lat•ter |ˈlætər| • *adj.* [attrib.] **1** situated or occurring nearer to the end of something than to the beginning: *the latter half of 1989.*
■ belonging to the final stages of something, esp. of a person's life: *heart disease dogged his latter years.* ■ recent: *the project has had low cash flows in latter years.* **2** (**the latter**) denoting the second or second mentioned of two people or things: *the Russians could advance into either Germany or Austria—they chose the latter option.*

USAGE: **Latter** means 'the second-mentioned of two.' Its use to mean 'the last-mentioned of three or more' is common, but is considered incorrect by some because **latter** means 'later' rather than 'latest.' *Last* or *last-mentioned* is preferred where three or more things are involved.

laud |lôd| • *v.* [trans.] praise (a person or his or her achievements) highly, esp. in a public context: *the obituary lauded him as a great statesman and soldier* | [as adj., with submodifier] (**lauded**) *her much lauded rendering of Lady Macbeth.* • *n.* praise: *all glory, laud, and honor to Thee.*
lau•da•num |ˈlôdn-əm; ˈlôdnəm| • *n.* an alcoholic solution containing morphine, prepared from opium and formerly used as a narcotic painkiller.
laud•a•to•ry |ˈlôdəˌtôrē| • *adj.* (of speech or writing) expressing praise and commendation.
laun•der |ˈlôndər; ˈlän-| • *v.* [trans.] (in finance) conceal the origins of (money obtained illegally) by transfers involving foreign banks or legitimate businesses.
■ alter (information) to make it appear more acceptable: *we began to notice attempts to launder the data.*
DERIVATIVES: **laun•der•er** *n.*
lau•re•ate |ˈlôrē-it; ˈlär-| • *n.* a person who is honored with an award for outstanding creative or intellectual achievement: *a Nobel laureate.*
■ (short for **poet laureate**) an eminent poet appointed to, or regarded unofficially as holding, an honorary representative position in a country, region, or group. The first official American poet laureate was Robert Penn Warren. • *adj.* wreathed with laurel as a mark of honor.
■ (of a crown or wreath) consisting of laurel.
DERIVATIVES: **lau•re•ate•ship** |-ˌSHip| *n.*
lau•rel |ˈlôrəl; ˈlär-| • *n.* (usu. **laurels**) the foliage of the bay tree woven into a wreath or

crown and worn on the head as an emblem of victory or mark of honor in classical times.
■ honor: *she has rightly won laurels for her first novel.* • *v.* (**laureled, laureling**; Brit. **laurelled, laurelling**) [trans.] adorn with or as if with a laurel: *they banish our anger forever when they laurel the graves of our dead.*

PHRASES: **look to one's laurels** be careful not to lose one's superior position to a rival. **rest on one's laurels** be so satisfied with what one has already achieved that one makes no further effort.

la•vage |ləˈväzh; ˈlævij| • *n.* washing out of a body cavity, such as the colon or stomach, with water or a medicated solution.

lav•ish |ˈlæviSH| • *adj.* sumptuously rich, elaborate, or luxurious: *a lavish banquet.*
■ (of a person) very generous or extravagant: *he was lavish with his hospitality.* ■ spent or given in profusion: *lavish praise.* • *v.* [trans.] (**lavish something on**) bestow something in generous or extravagant quantities upon: *the media couldn't lavish enough praise on the film.*
■ (**lavish something with**) cover something thickly or liberally with: *she lavished her son with kisses.*

DERIVATIVES: **lav•ish•ly** *adv.* **lav•ish•ness** *n.*

lax |læks| • *adj.* **1** not sufficiently strict or severe: *lax security arrangements at the airport* | *they've been lax about discipline in school lately.*
■ careless: *why do software developers do little more than parrot their equally lax competitors?* **2** (of the limbs or muscles) relaxed:
■ (of the bowels) loose. ■ (of a speech sound, esp. a vowel) pronounced with the vocal muscles relaxed. The opposite of *tense.*

DERIVATIVES: **lax•i•ty** |ˈlæksətē| *n.* **lax•ly** *adv.* **lax•ness** *n.*

lay¹ |lā| • *v.* (past and past part. **laid** |lād|)

USAGE: The verb **lay** means, broadly, 'put something down,' as in *they are going to lay the carpet.* The past tense and the past participle of this verb is **laid**, as in *they laid the groundwork* or *she had laid careful plans.* The verb **lie**, on the other hand, means 'be in a horizontal position to rest,' as in *why don't you lie on the floor?* The past tense of this verb is **lay**)*he lay on the floor*) and the past participle is **lain**)*she had lain on the bed for hours*). Thus, in correct use, **lay** can be either the past tense of **lie** or the base form of **lay**. In practice many speakers make the mistake of using **lay, laying,** and **laid** as if they meant **lie, lying, lay,** and **lain.** Examples of incorrect use: *why don't you lay on the bed* (correct form is **lie**); *she was laying on the bed* (correct form is **lying**); *he had laid on the floor for hours* (correct form is **lain**).

lay² • *adj.* [attrib.] **1** not ordained into or belonging to the clergy: *a lay preacher.* **2** not having professional qualifications or expert knowledge, esp. in law or medicine: *lay and professional views of medicine.*

leach |lēCH| • *v.* [with obj. and adverbial of direction] make (a soluble chemical or mineral) drain away from soil, ash, or similar material

by the action of percolating liquid, esp. rainwater: *the nutrient is quickly leached away.*
■ [no obj., with adverbial of direction] (of a soluble chemical or mineral) drain away from soil, ash, etc., in this way: *coats of varnish prevent the dye leaching out.* ■ [trans.] subject (soil, ash, etc.) to this process.

lead•ed |ˈledid| • *adj.* **1** (of windowpanes or a roof) framed, covered, or weighted with lead: *Georgian-style leaded windows.* **2** (of gasoline) containing tetraethyl lead: *leaded fuel.* **3** (of type) having the lines separated by leads.

league • *n.* a former measure of distance by land, usually about three miles.

lech•er |ˈleCHər| • *n.* a man of lewd and promiscuous sexual desires or behavior.

DERIVATIVES: **lech•er•ous** *adj.* **lech•er•ous•ly** *adv.* **lech•er•y** *n.*

lec•tern |ˈlektərn| • *n.* a tall stand with a sloping top to hold a book or notes, and from which someone, typically a preacher or lecturer, can read while standing up.

lec•tion |ˈlekSHən| • *n.* **1** a reading of a text found in a particular copy or edition. **2** an extract from a sacred book, appointed to be read at religious services; a lesson.

lec•tion•ar•y |ˈlekSHəˌnerē| • *n.* (pl. **-ies**) a list or book of portions of the Bible appointed to be read at a church service.

lee |lē| • *n.* shelter from wind or weather given by a neighboring object, esp. nearby land: *we pitch our tents in the lee of a rock.*
■ (also **lee side**) the sheltered side; the side away from the wind: *ducks were taking shelter on the lee of the island.* The opposite of *windward* or *weather* side.

leech |lēCH| • *n.* **1** an aquatic or terrestrial annelid worm with suckers at both ends. Many species are bloodsucking parasites, esp. of vertebrates, and others are predators. **2** a person who extorts profit from or sponges on others: *they are leeches feeding off the hardworking majority.* • *v.* [intrans.] habitually exploit or rely on: *he's leeching off the abilities of others.*

lees |lēz| • *plural n.* the sediment of wine in the barrel.
■ dregs; refuse: *the lees of the city's underworld.*

lee•ward |ˈlēwərd; ˈlo͞oərd| • *adj. & adv.* on or toward the side sheltered from the wind or toward which the wind is blowing; downwind: [as adj.] *the leeward side of the house* | [as adv.] *we pitched our tents leeward of a hill.* • *n.* the side sheltered or away from the wind: *the ship was drifting to leeward.*

lee•way |ˈlēˌwā| • *n.* **1** the amount of freedom to move or act that is available: *Congress had several months' leeway to introduce reforms.*
■ margin of safety: *there is little leeway if anything goes wrong.* **2** the sideways drift of a ship or an aircraft to leeward of the desired course: *the leeway is only about 2°.*

left wing • *n.* (**the left wing**) (in politics) the liberal, socialist, or radical section of a party or system. • *adj.* liberal, socialist, or radical: *left-wing activists.*

DERIVATIVES: **left-wing•er** *n.*

leg•a•cy |ˈlegəsē| • *n.* (pl. **-ies**) an amount of money or property left to someone in a will.
■ a thing handed down by a predecessor: *the legacy of centuries of neglect.* ■ a student or potential student who may be favored by a college or school as the child or relative of a graduate, esp. one likely to make financial gifts. • *adj.* denoting computer software or hardware that has been superseded but is difficult to replace because of its wide use.
DERIVATIVES: **leg•a•tee** *n.* one who receives a legacy.

le•gal•ism |ˈlēgəˌlizəm| • *n.* excessive adherence to law or formula.
■ (in theology) dependence on moral law rather than on personal religious faith.
DERIVATIVES: **le•gal•ist** *n.* & *adj.* **le•gal•is•tic** |ˌlēgəˈlistik| *adj.* **le•gal•is•ti•cal•ly** |ˌlēgəˈlistik(ə)lē| *adv.*

le•gal•ize |ˈlēgəˌlīz| • *v.* [trans.] make (something that was previously illegal) permissible by law: *a measure legalizing gambling in Deadwood.* Cf. DECRIMINALIZE.
DERIVATIVES: **le•gal•i•za•tion** |-ˌlēgələˈzāSHən; -ˌliˈzā-| *n.*

leg•ate |ˈlegit| • *n.* **1** a member of the Roman Catholic clergy, esp. a cardinal, representing the pope.
■ an ambassador or messenger. **2** a general or governor of an ancient Roman province, or his deputy: *the Roman legate of Syria.*
DERIVATIVES: **leg•ate•ship** |-ˌSHip| *n.* **leg•a•tine** |ˈlegəˌtēn; -ˌtin| *adj.*

le•ga•tion |liˈgāSHən| • *n.* **1** a diplomatic minister, esp. one below the rank of ambassador, and his or her staff.
■ the official residence of a diplomatic minister. **2** the position or office of legate; a legateship.
■ the sending of a legate, esp. a papal legate, on a mission.

le•ga•to |liˈgäto| • *adv.* & *adj.* (in music) in a smooth, flowing manner, without breaks between notes. Cf. STACCATO. • *n.* performance in this manner.

leg•end |ˈlejənd| • *n.* **1** a traditional story sometimes popularly regarded as historical but unauthenticated. **2** an extremely famous or notorious person, esp. in a particular field: *a living legend* | *a Wall Street legend.* **3** an inscription, esp. on a coin or medal.
■ a caption: *a picture of a tiger with the legend "Go ahead, make my day."* ■ the wording on a map or diagram explaining the symbols used: *see legend to Fig. 1.* **4** the story of a saint's life. • *adj.* [predic.] very well known: *his speed was legend.*

leg•er•de•main |ˌlejərdəˈmān; ˈlejərdəˌmān| • *n.* skillful use of one's hands when performing conjuring tricks.
■ deception; trickery.

le•gion |ˈlējən| • *n.* **1** a unit of 3,000–6,000 men (*legionaries*) in the ancient Roman army.
■ (**the Legion**) the French Foreign Legion. ■ (**the Legion**) any of the national associations of former servicemen and servicewomen (*Legionnaires*) instituted after World War I, such as the American Legion. **2** (**a legion/legions of**) a vast host, multitude, or number of people or things: *legions of photographers.* • *adj.* [predic.] great in number: *her fans are legion.*

le•git•i•mate • *adj.* |liˈjitəmit| conforming to the law or to rules: *claims to legitimate authority.*
■ able to be defended with logic or justification: *a legitimate excuse for being late.* ■ (of a child) born of parents lawfully married to each other. ■ (of a sovereign) having a title based on strict hereditary right: *the last legitimate Anglo-Saxon king.* ■ constituting or relating to serious drama as distinct from musical comedy, revue, etc.: *the legitimate theater.* • *v.* |-ˌmāt| [trans.] make legitimate; justify or make lawful: *the regime was not legitimated by popular support.*
DERIVATIVES: **le•git•i•ma•cy** |-məsē| *n.* **le•git•i•mate•ly** |-mitlē| *adv.* **le•git•i•ma•tion** |liˌjitəˈmāSHən| *n.* **le•git•i•ma•tize** |-məˌtīz| *v.*

le•git•i•mism |liˈjitəˌmizəm| • *n.* support for a ruler whose claim to a throne is based on direct descent.
DERIVATIVES: **le•git•i•mist** *n.* & *adj.*

leit•mo•tif |ˈlītmōˌtēf| (also **leitmotiv**) • *n.* a recurrent theme throughout a musical or literary composition, associated with a particular person, idea, or situation.

lem•ma |ˈlemə| • *n.* (pl. **lemmas** or **lemmata** |ˈlemətə|) **1** a subsidiary or intermediate theorem in an argument or proof. **2** a heading indicating the subject or argument of a literary composition, an annotation, or a dictionary entry.

le•ni•ent |ˈlēnēənt; ˈlēnyənt| • *adj.* **1** (of punishment or a person in authority) permissive, merciful, or tolerant. **2** having the quality of softening; emollient.
DERIVATIVES: **le•ni•ence** *n.* **le•ni•en•cy** *n.* **le•ni•ent•ly** *adv.*

len•i•tive |ˈlenətiv| • *adj.* (of a medicine) loosening the bowels; gently laxative. • *n.* a medicine of this type.

len•i•ty |ˈlenətē| • *n.* kindness; gentleness.

le•o•nine |ˈlēəˌnīn| • *adj.* of or resembling a lion or lions: *a handsome, leonine profile.*

lep•i•dop•ter•ist |ˌlepəˈdäptərist| • *n.* a person who studies or collects butterflies and moths. (members of the order Lepidoptera).
DERIVATIVES: **lep•i•dop•ter•ol•ogy** *n.* **lep•i•dop•ter•y** *n.*

lep•re•chaun |ˈleprəˌkän; -ˌkôn| • *n.* (in Irish folklore) a small, mischievous sprite.

les•bi•an |ˈlezbēən| • *n.* a homosexual woman. • *adj.* of or relating to homosexual women or to homosexuality in women: *a lesbian relationship.*
DERIVATIVES: **les•bi•an•ism** |-ˌnizəm| *n.*

lèse maj•es•ty |ˌlez ˈmäjəˈstā; ˌlēz; ˈmæjəstē| • *n.* the insulting of a monarch or other ruler; treason.

le•sion |ˈlēzHən| • *n.* a region in an organ or tissue that has suffered damage through injury or disease, such as a wound, ulcer, abscess, tumor, etc.

less |les| • *adj. & pron.* a smaller amount; not as much.

USAGE: In standard English **less** should only be used with uncountable things)*less money*, *less time*). With countable things it is incorrect to use **less**)*less people* and *less words*); strictly speaking, correct use is *fewer people* and *fewer words*.

les•see |le'sē| • *n.* a person who holds the lease of a property; a tenant or leaseholder.
DERIVATIVES: **les•see•ship** |-,SHip| *n.*

les•sor |'les,ôr; le'sôr| • *n.* a person who leases or lets a property to another; a landlord.

le•thal |'lēTHəl| • *adj.* sufficient to cause death: *a lethal cocktail of alcohol and drugs.* ■ harmful or destructive.
DERIVATIVES: **le•thal•i•ty** |lē'THælətē| *n.* **le•thal•ly** *adv.*

leth•ar•gy |'leTHərjē| • *n.* a lack of energy and enthusiasm: *periods of weakness and lethargy.* [in sing.] ■ a pathological state of sleepiness or deep unresponsiveness and inactivity.
DERIVATIVES: **le•thar•gic** *adj.*

let•tered |'letərd| • *adj.* formally educated: *though not lettered, he read widely.* ■ of or pertaining to learning, learned people, or literary culture: *a man of lettered tastes.*

let•ter of marque |märk| • *n.* (usu. **letters of marque**) a license to fit out an armed vessel and use it in the capture of enemy merchant shipping and to commit acts that would otherwise have constituted piracy. ■ a ship carrying such a license; a privateer.

lev•ee[1] |'levē| • *n.* a reception or assembly of people, in particular: ■ a formal reception of visitors or guests. ■ in Britain an afternoon assembly for men held at court and often attended by the monarch. ■ a reception of visitors just after rising from bed.

lev•ee[2] • *n.* an embankment built to prevent the overflow of a river. ■ a ridge of sediment deposited naturally alongside a river by overflowing water. ■ a landing place; a quay. ■ a ridge of earth surrounding a field to be irrigated.

lev•er•age |'lev(ə)rij; 'lēv(ə)rij| • *n.* **1** the exertion of force by means of a lever or an object used in the manner of a lever: *my spade hit something solid that wouldn't respond to leverage.* ■ mechanical advantage gained in this way: *use a metal bar to increase the leverage.* ■ the power to influence a person or situation to achieve a particular outcome: *the right wing had lost much of its political leverage in the Assembly.* **2** (in finance) the ratio of a company's loan capital (debt) to the value of its ordinary shares (equity). • *v.* [trans.] [usu. as adj.] (**leveraged**) use borrowed capital for (an investment), expecting the profits made to be greater than the interest payable: *a leveraged takeover bid.*

le•vi•a•than |lə'vīəTHən| • *n.* (in biblical use) a sea monster, identified in different passages with the whale and the crocodile (e.g., Job 41, Ps. 74:14), and with the Devil (after Isa. 27:1). ■ a very large aquatic creature, esp. a whale: *the great leviathans of the deep.* ■ a thing that is very large or powerful, esp. a ship. ■ an autocratic monarch or state.

lev•i•tate |'levə,tāt| • *v.* [intrans.] rise and hover in the air, esp. by means of supernatural or magical power: *he seems to levitate about three inches off the ground.* ■ [trans.] cause (something) to rise and hover in such a way.
DERIVATIVES: **lev•i•ta•tion** |,levə'tāSHən| *n.* **lev•i•ta•tor** |'-,tātər| *n.*

lev•i•ty |'levətē| • *n.* humor or frivolity, esp. the treatment of a serious matter with humor or in a manner lacking due respect: *as an attempt to introduce a note of levity, the words were a disastrous flop.*

lev•y |'levē| • *v.* (**-ies, -ied**) [trans.] **1** (often **be levied**) impose (a tax, fee, or fine): *a new tax could be levied on industry to pay for cleaning up contaminated land.* ■ impose a tax, fee, or fine on: *there will be powers to levy the owner.* ■ [intrans.] (**levy on/upon**) seize (property) to satisfy a legal judgment: *there were no goods to levy upon.* **2** enlist (someone) for military service: *he sought to levy one man from each parish for service.* ■ begin to wage (war). • *n.* (pl. **-ies**) **1** an act of levying a tax, fee, or fine: *union members were wit with a 2 percent levy on all pay.* ■ a tax so raised. ■ a sum collected for a specific purpose, esp. as a supplement to an existing amount pledged to an organization. ■ an item or set of items of property seized to satisfy a legal judgment. **2** an act of enlisting troops. ■ (usu. **levies**) a body of troops that have been enlisted: *lightly armed local levies.*
DERIVATIVES: **lev•i•a•ble** *adj.*

lewd |lood| • *adj.* crude in a sexual way: *she began to gyrate to the music and sing a lewd song.*
DERIVATIVES: **lewd•ly** *adv.* **lewd•ness** *n.*

lex•i•cal |'leksikəl| • *adj.* of or relating to the words or vocabulary of a language: *lexical analysis.* ■ relating to or of the nature of a lexicon or dictionary: *a lexical entry.*
DERIVATIVES: **lex•i•cal•ly** |ik(ə)lē| *adv.*

lex•i•cog•ra•phy |,leksə'kägrəfē| • *n.* the practice of compiling dictionaries.
DERIVATIVES: **lex•i•cog•ra•pher** *n.* **lex•i•co•graph•ic** |-kə'græfik| *adj.* **lex•i•co•graph•i•cal** |-kə'græfikəl| *adj.* **lex•i•co•graph•i•cal•ly** |-kə'græfik(ə)lē| *adv.*

lex•i•con |'leksi,kän; -kən| • *n.* (pl. **lexicons** or **lexica** |-kə|) **1** the vocabulary of a person, language, or branch of knowledge: *the size of the English lexicon.* ■ a dictionary, esp. of Greek, Hebrew, Syriac, or Arabic: *a Greek–Latin lexicon.* **2** the complete set of meaningful units (words, etc.) in a language (without definitions).

lex•is |'leksis| • *n.* the total stock of words in a language: *a notable loss of English lexis.* ■ the level of language consisting of vocabulary, as opposed to grammar or syntax.

lex lo•ci | ˈleks ˈlōsī; -ˌsē; -ˌkē; -ˌkī | • *n.* the law of the country in which a transaction is performed, an act is committed, or a property is situated.

li•a•bil•i•ty | ˌlīəˈbilətē | • *n.* (pl. **-ies**) **1** the state of being responsible for something, esp. by law: *the partners accept unlimited* **liability** *for any risks they undertake.*
■ (usu. **liabilities**) a thing for which someone is responsible, esp. a debt or financial obligation: *valuing the company's liabilities and assets.* **2** [usu. in sing.] a person or thing whose presence or behavior is likely to cause embarrassment or put one at a disadvantage: *he has become a political liability.*

li•a•ble | ˈlī(ə)bəl | • *adj.* [predic.] **1** responsible by law; legally answerable: *the supplier of goods or services can become* **liable** *for breach of contract in a variety of ways.* **2** [with infinitive] likely to do or to be something: *patients were liable to faint if they stood up too suddenly.*
■ (**liable to**) likely to experience (something undesirable): *areas liable to flooding.*

USAGE: **Liable** is commonly used to mean 'likely (to do something undesirable),' e.g., *without his glasses he's liable to run the car into a tree.* Precisely, however, **liable** means 'legally obligated,' as in *if he runs into another car, he may be liable for damages.*

li•aise | lēˈāz | • *v.* [intrans.] establish a working relationship, typically in order to cooperate on a matter of mutual concern: *she will* **liaise** *with teachers across the country.*

li•ai•son | ˈlēəˌzän; lēˈā- | • *n.* **1** communication or cooperation that facilitates a close working relationship between people or organizations: *the department works in close* **liaison** *with public relations.*
■ a person who acts as a link to assist communication or cooperation between groups of people. ■ a sexual relationship, esp. one that is secret and involves unfaithfulness to a partner. **2** the binding or thickening agent of a sauce, often based on egg yolks. **3** (in French and other languages) the sounding of a consonant that is normally silent at the end of a word because the next word begins with a vowel.

li•ba•tion | līˈbāsHən | • *n.* a drink poured out as an offering to a deity.
■ the pouring out of such a drink-offering: *wine was poured in libation.* ■ a drink: *free food and libations.*

li•bel | ˈlībəl | • *n.* **1** (in law) a published false statement that is damaging to a person's reputation; a written defamation. Cf. SLANDER.
■ the action or crime of publishing such a statement. ■ a false and malicious statement about a person. ■ a thing or circumstance that brings undeserved discredit on a person by misrepresentation. **2** (in admiralty and ecclesiastical law) a plaintiff's written declaration. • *v.* (**libeled**, **libeling**; Brit. **libelled**, **libelling**) [trans.] **1** defame (someone) by publishing a libel. Cf. DEFAME.
■ make a false and malicious statement about.

2 (in admiralty and ecclesiastical law) bring a suit against (someone).
DERIVATIVES: **li•bel•er** *n.* **li•bel•ous** *adj.*

lib•er•al | ˈlib(ə)rəl | • *adj.* **1** open to new behavior or opinions and willing to discard traditional values: *liberal views on marriage and divorce.*
■ favorable to or respectful of individual rights and freedoms: *liberal citizenship laws.* ■ (in a political context) favoring maximum individual liberty in political and social reform: *a liberal democratic state.* ■ (**Liberal**) of or characteristic of Liberals or a Liberal Party. ■ (in theology) regarding many traditional beliefs as dispensable, invalidated by modern thought, or liable to change. **2** [attrib.] (of education) concerned mainly with broadening a person's general knowledge and experience, rather than with technical or professional training. **3** (esp. of an interpretation of a law) broadly construed or understood; not strictly literal or exact. **4** given, used, or occurring in generous amounts: *liberal amounts of wine had been consumed.*
■ (of a person) giving generously: *Sam was too* **liberal** *with the wine.* • *n.* a person of liberal views.
■ (**Liberal**) a supporter or member of a Liberal Party.
DERIVATIVES: **lib•er•al•ism** | -ˌlizəm | *n.* **lib•er•al•ist** | -rəlist | *n.* **lib•er•al•is•tic** | ˌlib(ə)rəˈlistik | *adj.* **lib•er•al•ly** *adv.* **lib•er•al•ness** *n.*

lib•er•al arts • *plural n.* academic subjects such as literature, philosophy, mathematics, and social and physical sciences as distinct from professional and technical subjects.

lib•er•al•i•ty | ˌlibəˈralətē | • *n.* **1** the quality of giving or spending freely. **2** the quality of being open to new ideas and free from prejudice: *liberality toward bisexuality.*

lib•er•tar•i•an | ˌlibərˈterēən | • . (in philosophy) a person who holds to the doctrine of the freedom of the will, as opposed to that of necessity: [as *adj.*] *libertarian philosophy.* Cf. NECESSITARIAN, DETERMINISM.
■ a person who advocates civil liberty, esp. in opposition to the state action.

lib•er•tine | ˈlibərˌtēn | • *n.* **1** a person, esp. a man, who behaves without moral principles or a sense of responsibility, esp. in sexual matters. **2** a person who rejects accepted opinions in matters of religion; a freethinker. • *adj.* **1** characterized by a disregard of morality, esp. in sexual matters: *his more libertine impulses.* **2** freethinking in matters of religion.
DERIVATIVES: **lib•er•tin•age** | -ˌtēnij | *n.* **lib•er•tin•ism** | -ˌnizəm | *n.*

li•bid•i•nous | ləˈbidn-əs | • *adj.* showing excessive sexual drive; lustful.
DERIVATIVES: **li•bid•i•nous•ly** *adv.* **li•bid•i•nous•ness** *n.*

li•bi•do | ləˈbēdō | • *n.* (pl. **-os**) sexual desire.
■ (in psychoanalysis) the energy of the sexual drive as a component of the life instinct.
DERIVATIVES: **li•bid•i•nal** | -ˈbidn-əl | *adj.* **li•bid•i•nal•ly** | -ˈbidn-əlē | *adv.*

li•bret•to | ləˈbretō | • *n.* (pl. **libretti** | -ˈbretē |

or **librettos**) the text of an opera or other long vocal work.
DERIVATIVES: **li•bret•tist** |-'bretist| *n.*
li•cense | 'līsəns | • *n.* (Brit. **licence**) a permit from an authority to own or use something, do a particular thing, or carry on a trade (esp. in alcoholic beverages): *a gun license* | [as adj.] *vehicle license fees.*
■ formal or official permission to do something: *logging is permitted under license from the Forest Service.* ■ a writer's or artist's freedom to deviate from fact or from conventions such as grammar, meter, or perspective, for effect: *artistic license.* ■ freedom to behave as one wishes, esp. in a way that results in excessive or unacceptable behavior: *the government was criticized for giving the army too much license.* • *v.* (Brit. also **licence**) [trans.] (often **be licensed**) grant a license to (someone or something) to permit the use of something or to allow an activity to take place: *brokers must be licensed to sell health-related insurance* | [with obj. and infinitive] *he ought not to have been licensed to fly a plane* | [as adj.] (**licensing**) *a licensing authority.*
■ authorize the use, performance, or release of (something). ■ give permission to (someone) to do something.
DERIVATIVES: **li•cens•a•ble** *adj.* **li•cens•er** *n.* **li•cen•sor** |-sər; ,līsən'sôr| *n.*
li•cen•tious |lī'sensHəs| • *adj.* **1** promiscuous and unprincipled in sexual matters. **2** disregarding accepted rules or conventions, esp. in grammar or literary style.
DERIVATIVES: **li•cen•tious•ly** *adv.* **li•cen•tious•ness** *n.*
li•chen | 'līkən | • *n.* **1** a simple slow-growing plant that typically forms a low crustlike, leaflike, or branching growth on rocks, walls, and trees.

Lichens are complex plants consisting of a fungus that contains photosynthetic algal cells. They obtain their water and nutrients from the atmosphere and can be sensitive indicators of atmospheric pollution.

2 [usu. with adj.] a skin disease in which small round hard lesions occur close together.
DERIVATIVES: **li•chened** *adj.* (in sense 1) **li•chen•ol•o•gy** |,līkə'näləjē| *n.* (in sense 1) **li•chen•ous** |-nəs| *adj.* (in sense 2).
lic•it | 'lisit | • *adj.* not forbidden; lawful: *licit and illicit drugs.*
DERIVATIVES: **lic•it•ly** *adv.*
lie | līe | • *v.* See usage note at LAY[1].
liege | lēj; lēzH | historical • *adj.* [attrib.] concerned with or relating to the relationship between a feudal superior and a vassal: *an oath of fealty and liege homage.* • *n.* (also **liege lord**) a feudal superior or sovereign.
■ a vassal or subject: *the king's lieges.*
lien | 'lē(ə)n | • *n.* (in law) a right to keep possession of property belonging to another person until a debt owed by that person is discharged: *put a lien on something.*
lieu | lōō | • *n.* (in phrase **in lieu**) instead: *the company issued additional shares in lieu of a cash dividend.*

li•ga•tion |lī'gāsHən| • *n.* **1** the surgical procedure of closing off a blood vessel or other duct or tube in the body by means of a ligature or clip. **2** the joining of two DNA strands or other molecules by a phosphate ester linkage.
li•ga•ture | 'ligəCHər; -,CHŏŏr | • *n.* **1** a thing used for tying or binding something tightly.
■ a cord or thread used in surgery, esp. to tie up a bleeding artery. **2** (in music) a slur or tie, joining notes to be played without an interval. **3** (in printing) a character consisting of two or more joined letters, e.g., æ, fl.
■ a stroke that joins adjacent letters in writing or printing. • *v.* [trans.] bind or connect with a ligature.
Lil•li•pu•tian |,lilə'pyōōsHən| • *adj.* trivial or very small: *America's banks look Lilliputian in comparison with Japan's.* • *n.* a trivial or very small person or thing.
lim•bo[1] | 'limbō | • *n.* **1** (also **Limbo**) (in some Christian beliefs) the supposed abode of the souls of unbaptized infants, and of the just who died before Christ's coming. **2** an uncertain period of awaiting a decision or resolution; an intermediate state or condition: *the fate of the hostages is now in limbo.*
■ a state of neglect or oblivion: *children left in an emotional limbo.*
lim•bo[2] • *n.* (pl. **-os**) a West Indian dance in which the dancer bends backward to pass under a horizontal bar that is progressively lowered to a position just above the ground. • *v.* [intrans.] dance in such a way.
limn | lim | • *v.* [trans.] depict or describe in painting or words.
■ suffuse or highlight (something) with a bright color or light: *a crescent moon limned each shred with white gold.*
DERIVATIVES: **lim•ner** *n.* a painter, esp. of portraits or miniatures, and usu. regarded as not of the highest aesthetic standards.
linch•pin | 'linCH,pin | (also **lynchpin**) • *n.* **1** a pin passed through the end of an axle to keep a wheel in position. **2** a person or thing vital to an enterprise or organization: *regular brushing is the linchpin of all good dental hygiene.*
lin•e•age | 'linē-ij | • *n.* **1** lineal descent from an ancestor; ancestry or pedigree.
■ a social group tracing its descent from a single ancestor. **2** (in biology) a sequence of species each of which is considered to have evolved from its predecessor: *the chimpanzee and gorilla lineages.*
■ a sequence of cells in the body that developed from a common ancestral cell: *the myeloid lineage.*
lin•e•al | 'linēəl | • *adj.* **1** in a direct line of descent or ancestry: *a lineal descendant.* **2** of, relating to, or consisting of lines; linear.
DERIVATIVES: **lin•e•al•ly** *adv.*
lin•e•ar | 'linēər | • *adj.* **1** arranged in or extending along a straight or nearly straight line: *linear arrangements* | *linear in shape* | *linear movement.*
■ consisting of or predominantly formed using lines or outlines: *simple linear designs.* ■ (in

physics) involving one dimension only: *linear elasticity*. ■ (in mathematics) able to be represented by a straight line on a graph; involving or exhibiting directly proportional change in two related quantities: *linear functions* | *linear relationship*. **2** progressing from one stage to another in a single series of steps; sequential: *a linear narrative*.

■ doing this without adequately considering ideas or data that do not fit into the sequence: *linear thinking*.

DERIVATIVES: **lin•e•ar•i•ty** |ˌlinēˈærətē; -ˈer-| *n.* **lin•e•ar•ly** *adv.*

lin•e•a•tion |ˌlinēˈasHən| • *n.* the action or process of drawing lines or marking with lines.

■ a line or linear marking; an arrangement or group of lines: *magnetic lineations*. ■ a contour or outline. ■ the division of text into lines: *the punctuation and lineation are reproduced accurately*.

lin•ge•rie |ˌlänzHəˈrā; -jə-| • *n.* women's underwear and nightclothes.

lin•gua fran•ca |ˈliNGgwə ˈfræNGkə| • *n.* (pl. **lingua francas**) a language that is adopted as a common language among speakers whose native languages are different.

■ a mixture of Italian with French, Greek, Arabic, and Spanish, formerly used in the Eastern Mediterranean.

lin•gual |ˈliNGgwəl| • *adj.* **1** of or relating to the tongue.

■ (of a sound) formed by the tongue. ■ (in anatomy) near or on the side toward the tongue. **2** of or relating to speech or language: *his demonstrations of lingual dexterity*. • *n.* a lingual sound.

DERIVATIVES: **lin•gual•ly** *adv.*

lin•guist |ˈliNGgwist| • *n.* **1** a person skilled in foreign languages. **2** a person who studies linguistics; linguistician.

lin•guis•tic |liNGˈgwistik| • *adj.* of or relating to language or linguistics.

DERIVATIVES: **lin•guis•ti•cal•ly** |tik(ə)lē| *adv.*

lin•guis•tics |liNGˈgwistiks| • *plural n.* [treated as sing.] the scientific study of language and its structure, including the study of morphology, syntax, phonetics, semantics. Specific branches of linguistics include sociolinguistics, dialectology, psycholinguistics, computational linguistics, historical-comparative linguistics, and applied linguistics.

DERIVATIVES: **lin•guis•ti•cian** |ˌliNGgwəˈstisHən| *n.*

lin•i•ment |ˈlinəmənt| • *n.* a liquid or lotion, esp. one made with oil, for rubbing on the body to relieve pain.

Lin•nae•an |liˈnēən; -ˈnā-| (also **Linnean**) • *adj.* of or relating to the Swedish naturalist Carolus Linnaeus (Carl von Linné, 1707–78) or his classification system for plants and animals, which employs binomial nomenclature: *its Linnaean name is Magnolia tomentosa*. • *n.* a follower of Linnaeus.

lin•tel |ˈlintl| • *n.* a horizontal support of timber, stone, concrete, or steel across the top of a door or window. Cf. TRANSOM, MULLION.

DERIVATIVES: **lin•teled** (Brit. **lin•telled**) *adj.*

li•on•ize |ˈlīəˌnīz| • *v.* [trans.] give a lot of public attention and approval to (someone); treat as a celebrity: *the media lionize modern athletes*.

DERIVATIVES: **li•on•i•za•tion** |ˌlīənəˈzāsHən| *n.* **li•on•iz•er** *n.*

lip•id |ˈlipid| • *n.* any of a class of organic compounds that are fatty acids or their derivatives and are insoluble in water but soluble in organic solvents. They include many natural oils, waxes, and steroids.

lip•o•suc•tion |ˈlipōˌsəkSHən; ˈlī-| • *n.* a technique in cosmetic surgery for removing excess fat from under the skin by suction.

liq•ue•fy |ˈlikwəˌfī| (also **liquify**) • *v.* (**-ies, -ied**) make or become liquid: [trans.] *the minimum pressure required to liquefy a gas* | [intrans.] *as the fungus ripens, the cap turns black and liquefies*.

■ convert (solid food) into a liquid or purée, typically by using a blender.

DERIVATIVES: **liq•ue•fac•tion** |ˌlikwəˈfækSHən| *n.* **liq•ue•fac•tive** |ˌlikwəˈfæktiv| *adj.* **liq•ue•fi•a•ble** *adj.* **liq•ue•fi•er** *n.*

li•queur |liˈkər; -ˈk(y)o͝or| • *n.* a strong, sweet flavored alcoholic liquor, usually drunk after a meal. Cf. APERITIF.

liq•ui•date |ˈlikwiˌdāt| • *v.* [trans.] **1** wind up the affairs of (a company or firm) by ascertaining liabilities and apportioning assets.

■ [intrans.] (of a company) undergo such a process. ■ convert (assets) into cash: *a plan to liquidate $10,000,000 worth of property over seven years*. ■ pay off (a debt). **2** eliminate, typically by violent means; kill: *enemies of the state have been liquidated*.

DERIVATIVES: **liq•ui•da•tion** |ˌlikwəˈdāsHən| *n.*

liq•uid•i•ty |liˈkwidətē| • *n.* (in finance) the availability of liquid assets to a market or company.

■ liquid assets; cash. ■ a high volume of activity in a market.

lis•some |ˈlisəm| (also chiefly Brit. **lissom**) • *adj.* (of a person or the body) thin, supple, and graceful.

DERIVATIVES: **lis•some•ness** *n.*

list•less |ˈlis(t)lis| • *adj.* (of a person or personal manner) lacking energy or enthusiasm.

DERIVATIVES: **list•less•ly** *adv.* **list•less•ness** *n.*

lit•a•ny |ˈlitn-ē| • *n.* (pl. **-ies**) a series of supplications for use in church services or processions, usually recited by the clergy and responded to in a recurring formula by the people.

■ a tedious recital or repetitive series: *a litany of complaints*.

lit•er•a•cy |ˈlitərəsē; ˈlitrə-| • *n.* the ability to read and write. Cf. ILLITERATE.

■ competence or knowledge in a specified area: *wine literacy can't be taught in three hours*.

lit•er•al |ˈlitərəl; ˈlitrəl| • *adj.* **1** taking words in their usual or most basic sense without metaphor or allegory: *'dreadful' in its literal sense, full of dread*.

■ free from exaggeration or distortion: *you shouldn't take this as a literal record of events*.

■ absolute (used to emphasize that a strong expression is deliberately chosen to convey one's feelings): *years of literal hell.* **2** (of a translation) representing the exact words of the original text.

■ (of a visual representation) exactly copied; realistic as opposed to impressionistic. **3** (also **literal-minded**) (of a person or performance) lacking imagination; prosaic. **4** of, in, or expressed by a letter or the letters of the alphabet: *literal mnemonics.*
DERIVATIVES: **lit•er•al•ism** *n.* **lit•er•al•i•ty** | ˌlitəˈralətē | **lit•er•al•ize** | ˈlitərəˌlīz; ˈlitrə- | *v.* **lit•er•al•ness** *n.*
lit•er•ar•y | ˈlitəˌrerē | • *adj.* **1** [attrib.] concerning the writing, study, or content of literature, esp. of the kind valued for quality of form: *great literary works.*

■ concerned with literature as a profession: *it was signed by such literary figures as Maya Angelou.* **2** (of language) associated with literary works or other formal writing; having a marked style intended to create a particular emotional effect.
DERIVATIVES: **lit•er•ar•i•ly** | ˈlitəˈrerəlē | *adv.* **lit•er•ar•i•ness** *n.*
lit•e•ra•ti | ˌlitəˈrätē | • *plural n.* well-educated people who are interested in literature: *a favorite of the literati.*
lithe | līTH | (also **lithesome**) • *adj.* (esp. of a person's body) thin, supple, and graceful.
DERIVATIVES: **lithe•ly** *adv.* **lithe•ness** *n.*
lith•i•um | ˈliTHēəm | • *n.* (in psychiatry) lithium carbonate or another lithium salt, used as a mood-stabilizing drug.
li•thog•ra•phy | liˈTHägrəfē | • *n.* the process of printing from a flat surface treated so as to repel the ink except where it is required for printing.

■ (in electronics) an analogous method for making printed circuits.
DERIVATIVES: **li•thog•ra•pher** | -fər | *n.*
lit•i•gant | ˈlitəgənt | • *n.* a person involved in a lawsuit. • *adj.* [postpositive] involved in a lawsuit: *the parties litigant.*
lit•i•gate | ˈlitəˌgāt | • *v.* [intrans.] be a party to a lawsuit.

■ [trans.] take (a claim or a dispute) to a court of law.
DERIVATIVES: **lit•i•ga•tion** | ˌlitəˈgāsHən | *n.* **lit•i•ga•tive** | ˈlitəˌgātiv | *adj.* **lit•i•ga•tor** | -ˌgātər | *n.*
li•ti•gious | ləˈtijəs | • *adj.* concerned with lawsuits or litigation.

■ unreasonably prone to go to court to settle disputes. ■ suitable to become the subject of a lawsuit.
DERIVATIVES: **li•ti•gious•ly** *adv.* **li•ti•gious•ness** *n.*
lit•o•tes | ˈlitəˌtēz; ˈlit-; līˈtōtēz | • *n.* ironical understatement in which an affirmative is expressed by the negative of its contrary (e.g., *you won't be sorry,* meaning *you'll be glad*).
lit•to•ral | ˈlitərəl | • *adj.* of, relating to, or situated on the shore of the sea or a lake: *the littoral states of the Indian Ocean.*

■ of, relating to, or denoting the zone of the seashore between high- and low-water marks,

or the zone near a lake shore with rooted vegetation: *limpets and other littoral mollusks.* • *n.* a region lying along a shore: *irrigated regions of the Mediterranean littoral.*

■ the littoral zone.
lit•ur•gy | ˈlitərjē | • *n.* (pl. **-ies**) **1** a form or formulary according to which public religious worship, esp. Christian worship, is conducted.

■ a religious service conducted according to such a form or formulary. ■ (**the Liturgy**) the Eucharistic service of the Eastern Orthodox Church. **2** (in ancient Athens) a public office or duty performed voluntarily by a rich Athenian.
DERIVATIVES: **lit•ur•gist** | ˈlidərjəst | *n.*
liv•er•y[1] | ˈliv(ə)rē | • *n.* (pl. **-ies**) **1** special uniform worn by a servant or official.

■ a special design and color scheme used on the vehicles, aircraft, racehorses, or products of a particular company or owner. **2** short for *livery stable,* a stable where horses are kept at livery or let out for hire. **3** a provision of food or clothing for servants.
PHRASES: **at livery** (of a horse) kept for the owner and fed and cared for at a fixed charge.
DERIVATIVES: **liv•er•ied** | ˈliv(ə)rēd | *adj.* (in sense 1).
liv•er•y[2] • *adj.* resembling liver in color or consistency: *he was short with livery lips.*

■ liverish: *port wine always makes you livery.*
liv•id | ˈlivid | • *adj.* **1** furiously angry: *he was livid at being left out.* **2** (of a color or the skin) having a dark inflamed tinge: *his face went livid, then purple.*

■ of a bluish leaden color: *livid bruises.*
DERIVATIVES: **li•vid•i•ty** | ləˈvidətē | *n.* **liv•id•ly** *adv.* **liv•id•ness** *n.*
liv•ing will • *n.* a written statement detailing a person's desires regarding medical treatment in circumstances in which he or she is no longer able to express informed consent, esp. an advance directive.
lla•no | ˈlänō; ˈyä- | • *n.* (pl. **-os**) (in South America) a treeless grassy plain.
loath | lōTH; lōTH | (also **loth**) • *adj.* [predic., with infinitive] reluctant; unwilling: *I was loath to leave.*
loathe | lōTH | • *v.* [trans.] feel intense dislike or disgust for: *she loathed him on sight* | [as n.] (**loathing**) *the thought filled him with loathing.* Cf. abhor.
DERIVATIVES: **loath•er** *n.* **loath•some** *adj.*
lo•bot•o•mize | ləˈbätəˌmīz | • *v.* [trans.] (often **be lobotomized**) perform a lobotomy on.

■ reduce the mental or emotional capacity or ability to function of: *couples we knew who had been lobotomized by the birth of their children.*
DERIVATIVES: **lo•bot•o•mi•za•tion** | -ˌbätəməˈzāsHən | *n.*
lo•bot•o•my | ləˈbätəmē | • *n.* (pl. **-ies**) a surgical operation involving incision into the prefrontal lobe of the brain, formerly used to treat mental illness.
lo•cate | ˈlōˌkāt; lōˈkāt | • *v.* [trans.] discover the exact place or position of: *engineers were working to locate the fault.*

■ [with obj. and adverbial of place] (usu. **be**

located) situate in a particular place: *these apartments are centrally located.* ■ [with obj. and adverbial] place within a particular context: *they locate their policies in terms of wealth creation.* ■ [no obj., with adverbial of place] establish oneself or one's business in a specified place: *his marketing strategy has been to locate in small towns.*

USAGE: In formal English one should avoid using **locate** to mean 'find')*it drives him out of his mind when he can't locate something*). In precise usage **locate** means 'fix the position of, put in place')*the studio should be located on a north-facing slope*).

loc•a•tive |'läkətiv| • *adj.* relating to or denoting a case in some languages of nouns, pronouns, and adjectives, expressing location. • *n.* (**the locative**) the locative case. ■ a word in the locative case.

loch |läk; läкн| • *n.* Scottish a lake. Cf. LOUGH. ■ (also **sea loch**) an arm of the sea, esp. when narrow or partially landlocked.

lock•step |'läk,step| • *n.* a way of marching with each person as close as possible to the one in front: *the trio marched in lockstep* | [as adv.] *hundreds marched lockstep into the stadium.* ■ close adherence to and emulation of another's actions: *they raised prices in lockstep with those of competitors* | [as adj.] *lockstep unity.*

lo•cu•tion |lō'kyo͞osHən| • *n.* **1** a word or phrase, esp. with regard to style or idiom. ■ a person's style of speech: *his impeccable locution.* **2** an utterance regarded in terms of its intrinsic meaning or reference, as distinct from its function or purpose in context. Cf. ILLOCUTION, PERLOCUTION. ■ language regarded in terms of locutionary rather than illocutionary or perlocutionary acts.

DERIVATIVES: **lo•cu•tion•ar•y** |-,nerē| *adj.*

lode |lōd| • *n.* a vein of metal ore in the earth. ■ [in sing.] a rich source of something: *a lode of crime.*

lode•star |'lōd,stär| • *n.* a star that is used to guide the course of a ship, esp. Polaris. ■ a person or thing that serves as a guide: *she was his intellectual lodestar.*

lode•stone |'lōd,stōn| • *n.* a piece of magnetite or other naturally magnetized mineral, able to be used as a magnet. ■ a mineral of this kind; magnetite. ■ a thing that is the focus of attention or attraction.

loft•y |'lôftē; 'läf-| • *adj.* (**loftier, loftiest**) **1** of imposing height: *shaded by lofty palms.* ■ of a noble or exalted nature: *an extraordinary mixture of harsh reality and lofty ideals.* ■ proud, aloof, or self-important: *lofty intellectual disdain.* **2** (of wool and other textiles) thick and resilient.

DERIVATIVES: **loft•i•ly** |-təlē| *adv.* **loft•i•ness** *n.*

log•a•rithm |'lôgə,riTHəm; 'lägə-| (abbr.: **log**) • *n.* a quantity representing the power to which a fixed number (the base) must be raised to produce a given number.

Logarithms can be used to simplify calculations because the addition and subtraction of logarithms is equivalent to multiplication and division, though the use of printed tables of logarithms for this has declined with the spread of electronic calculators. They also allow a geometric relationship to be represented conveniently by a straight line. The base of a **common logarithm** is 10, and that of a **natural logarithm** is the number *e* (2.71828 . . .).

DERIVATIVES: **log•a•rith•mic** *adj.*

loge |lōzн| • *n.* a private box or enclosure in a theater. ■ the front section of the first balcony in a theater. ■ a similar section in an arena or stadium.

log•ic |'läjik| • *n.* **1** reasoning conducted or assessed according to strict principles of validity: *experience is a better guide to this than deductive logic* | *he explains his move with simple logic* | *the logic of the argument is faulty.* ■ a particular system or codification of the principles of proof and inference: *Aristotelian logic.* ■ the systematic use of symbolic and mathematical techniques to determine the forms of valid deductive argument. ■ the quality of being justifiable by reason: *there's no logic in telling her not to hit people when that's what you're doing.* ■ (**logic of**) the course of action or line of reasoning suggested or made necessary by: *if the logic of capital is allowed to determine events.* **2** a system or set of principles underlying the arrangements of elements in a computer or electronic device so as to perform a specified task. ■ logical operations collectively.

DERIVATIVES: **log•i•cal** *adj.* **log•i•cal•i•ty** *adv.* **log•i•cal•ly** *n.* **lo•gi•cian** |lə'jisHən; lō-| *n.*

lo•gis•tics |lə'jistiks; lō-| • *plural n.* [treated as sing. or pl.] the detailed coordination of a complex operation involving many people, facilities, or supplies: *the logistics and costs of a vaccination campaign.* ■ the organization of moving, housing, and supplying military troops and equipment.

lo•go |'lōgō| • *n.* (pl. **-os**) a symbol or other small design adopted by an organization to identify its products, uniform, vehicles, etc.: *the Olympic logo was emblazoned across the tracksuits.*

lo•gy |'lōgē| • *adj.* (**logier, logiest**) dull and heavy in motion or thought; sluggish.

loi•ter |'loitər| • *v.* [no obj., with adverbial of place] stand or wait around idly or without apparent purpose: *she saw Mary loitering near the entrance to the building.* ■ [with adverbial of direction] travel indolently and with frequent pauses: *they loitered along in the sunshine.*

DERIVATIVES: **loi•ter•er** *n.*

lol•la•pa•loo•za |,läləpə'lo͞ozə| (also **lala-palooza** or **lollapaloosa**) • *n.* a person or thing that is particularly impressive or attractive: *it's a lollapalooza, just like your other books.*

lol•ly•gag |ˈläle͞ˌgæg| (also **lallygag**) • v. (**lollygagged, lollygagging**) [intrans.] spend time aimlessly; idle: *he sends her to Arizona every January to lollygag in the sun.*
■ [with adverbial of direction] dawdle: *we're lollygagging along.*

lon•gev•i•ty |lônˈjevəˌtē; län-| • n. long life: *the greater longevity of women compared with men.*
■ long duration of service: *her longevity in office now appeared as a handicap to the party.*

lon•gi•tu•di•nal |ˌlänjəˈt(y)o͞odn-əl; ˌlôn-; -ˈt(y)o͞odnəl| • adj. 1 running lengthwise rather than across: *longitudinal stripes | longitudinal extent.*
■ (of research or data) involving information about an individual or group gathered over a long period of time: *a longitudinal study.* 2 of or relating to longitude; measured from east to west: *longitudinal positions.*
DERIVATIVES: **lon•gi•tu•di•nal•ly** adv.

long•shore |ˈlôNGˌSHôr; ˈläNG-| • adj. [attrib.] existing on, frequenting, or moving along the seashore: *longshore currents.*

lon•gueur |lôNGˈgər; läNG-| • n. a tedious passage in a book or other work: *its brilliant comedy passages do not cancel out the occasional longueurs.*
■ tedious periods of time: *the last act is sometimes marred by longueur.*

lo•qua•cious |lōˈkwāSHəs| • adj. given to much talking; talkative.
DERIVATIVES: **lo•qua•cious•ly** adv. **lo•qua•cious•ness** n. **lo•quac•i•ty** |ˈkwæsətē| n.

Lorelei |ˈlôrəˌlī| a rock on the bank of the Rhine, held by legend to be the home of a siren whose song lures boatmen to destruction.
■ the siren said to live on this rock. ■ a dangerously fascinating woman; a temptress or siren.

lor•gnette |lôrnˈyet| (also **lorgnettes**) • n. a pair of glasses or opera glasses held in front of a person's eyes by a long handle at one side.

Lo•thar•i•o |lōˈTHerēˌō; -ˈTHär-| • n. (pl. **-os**) a man who behaves selfishly and irresponsibly in his sexual relationships with women.

lo•tus-eat•er • n. a person who spends time indulging in pleasure and luxury rather than dealing with practical concerns.
DERIVATIVES: **lo•tus-eat•ing** adj.

louche |lo͞oSH| • adj. disreputable or sordid in a rakish or appealing way: *the louche world of the theater.*

lough |läk; läkH| • n. Anglo-Irish spelling of LOCH.

lour • v. see LOWER.

lou•ver |ˈlo͞ovər| (also **louvre**) • n. 1 each of a set of angled slats or flat strips fixed or hung at regular intervals in a door, shutter, or screen to allow air or light to pass through. 2 a domed structure on a roof, with side openings for ventilation.
DERIVATIVES: **lou•vered** adj.

low•brow |ˈlōˌbrow| • adj. not highly intellectual or cultured: *lowbrow tabloids.* • n. a person of such a type.

low•er |ˈlowər; ˈo͝or| (also **lour**) • v. [intrans.] look angry or sullen; frown.
■ (of the sky, weather, or landscape) look dark and threatening: [as adj.] (**lowering**) *lowering clouds.* • n. a scowl.
■ a dark and gloomy appearance of the sky, weather or landscape.
DERIVATIVES: **low•er•ing•ly** adv.

loy•al•ist |ˈloiəlist| • n. a person who remains loyal to the established ruler or government, esp. in the face of a revolt.
■ (**Loyalist**) a colonist of the American revolutionary period who supported the British cause. ■ (**Loyalist**) a supporter (typically Protestant) of union between Great Britain and Northern Ireland. ■ (**Loyalist**) a supporter of the republic and opposer of the fascist general Francisco Franco's revolt in the Spanish Civil War.
DERIVATIVES: **loy•al•ism** |-ˌlizəm| n.

lu•au |ˈlo͞oˌow| • n. (pl. same or **luaus**) a Hawaiian party or feast, esp. one accompanied by entertainment.

lu•bri•cious |lo͞oˈbriSHəs| (also **lubricous** |ˈlo͞obrikəs|) • adj. 1 offensively displaying or intended to arouse sexual desire. 2 smooth and slippery with oil or a similar substance.
DERIVATIVES: **lu•bri•cious•ly** adv. **lu•bric•i•ty** |-ˈbrisitē| n.

lu•cent |ˈlo͞osənt| • adj. glowing with or giving off light: *the moon was lucent in the background.*
DERIVATIVES: **lu•cen•cy** n.

lu•cid |ˈlo͞osid| • adj. 1 expressed clearly; easy to understand: *a lucid account | write in a clear and lucid style.*
■ showing ability to think clearly, esp. in the intervals between periods of confusion or insanity: *he has a few lucid moments every now and then.* ■ (of a dream) experienced with the dreamer feeling awake, aware of dreaming, and able to control events consciously. 2 bright or luminous:
DERIVATIVES: **lu•cid•i•ty** |lo͞oˈsidətē| n. **lu•cid•ly** adv. **lu•cid•ness** n.

Lu•ci•fer |ˈlo͞osəfər| • n. 1 another name for SATAN. 2 the planet Venus when it rises in the morning. 3 (**lucifer**) a match struck by rubbing it on a rough surface.

lu•cra•tive |ˈlo͞okrətiv| • adj. producing a great deal of profit: *a lucrative career as a stand-up comic.*
DERIVATIVES: **lu•cra•tive•ly** adv. **lu•cra•tive•ness** n.

lu•cre |ˈlo͞okər| • n. money, esp. when regarded as sordid or distasteful or gained in a dishonorable way: *officials getting their hands grubby with filthy lucre.*

lu•cu•brate |ˈlo͞ok(y)əˌbrāt| • v. [intrans.] discourse learnedly in writing.
DERIVATIVES: **lu•cu•bra•tor** |-ˌbrātər| n. **lu•cu•bra•tion** |ˌlo͞ok(y)əˈbrāSHən| • n. study; meditation.
■ (usu. **lucubrations**) a piece of writing, typically a pedantic or over-elaborate one.

lu•di•crous |ˈlo͞odəkrəs| • adj. so foolish, unreasonable, or out of place as to be amusing:

it's ludicrous that I have been fined | every night he wore a ludicrous outfit.
DERIVATIVES: **lu•di•crous•ly** adv. [as submodifier] *a ludicrously inadequate army.* **lu•di•crous•ness** n.

lu•gu•bri•ous |ləˈg(y)o͞obrēəs| • adj. looking or sounding sad and dismal.
DERIVATIVES: **lu•gu•bri•ous•ly** adv. **lu•gu•bri•ous•ness** n.

lum•bar |ˈləmbər; -ˌbär| • adj. [attrib.] relating to the lower part of the back: *pains in the lumbar region.*

lu•mi•nar•y |ˈlo͞oməˌnerē| • n. (pl. **-ies**) **1** a person who inspires or influences others, esp. one prominent in a particular sphere: *one of the luminaries of child psychiatry.* **2** an artificial light.
■ a natural light-giving body, esp. the sun or moon.

lu•mi•nes•cence |ˌlo͞oməˈnesəns| • n. the emission of light by a substance that has not been heated, as in fluorescence and phosphorescence.
DERIVATIVES: **lu•mi•nes•cent** adj.

lu•mi•nos•i•ty |ˌlo͞oməˈnäsətē| • n. (pl. **-ies**) luminous quality: *acrylic colors retain freshness and luminosity.*
■ the intrinsic brightness of a celestial object (as distinct from its apparent brightness diminished by distance). ■ (in physics) the rate of emission of radiation, visible or otherwise.

lu•mi•nous |ˈlo͞omənəs| • adj. full of or shedding light; bright or shining, esp. in the dark: *the luminous dial on his watch | a luminous glow.*
■ (of a person's complexion or eyes) glowing with health, vigor, or a particular emotion: *eyes **luminous with joy.*** ■ (of a color) very bright; harsh to the eye: *he wore luminous green socks.* ■ (in physics) relating to light as it is perceived by the eye, rather than in terms of its actual energy.
DERIVATIVES: **lu•mi•nous•ly** adv. **lu•mi•nous•ness** n.

lum•pen |ˈləmpən; ˈlo͞om-| • adj. (in Marxist contexts) uninterested in revolutionary advancement: *the lumpen public is enveloped in a culture of dependency.*
■ boorish and stupid: *growing ranks of lumpen, uninhibited, denim-clad youth.* • plural n. (**the lumpen**) the lumpenproletariat.

lum•pen•pro•le•tar•i•at |ˈləmpənˌprōlə ˈterēət; ˈlo͞om-| • n. [treated as sing. or pl.] (esp. in Marxist terminology) the unorganized and unpolitical lower orders of society who are not interested in revolutionary advancement.

lu•nar |ˈlo͞onər| • adj. of, determined by, or resembling the moon: *a lunar landscape. | a total lunar eclipse.*
■ having the character of the moon as opposed to that of the sun; not warmly bright; pale; pallid.

lu•nate |ˈlo͞oˌnāt| • adj. crescent-shaped. • n. (also **lunate bone**) a crescent-shaped carpal bone situated in the center of the wrist and articulating with the radius.

lu•nu•la |ˈlo͞onyələ| • n. (pl. **lunulae** |-ˌlē; -ˌlī|) a crescent-shaped object or mark, in particular:
■ the white area at the base of a fingernail. ■ (in printing) one of a pair of parentheses.
DERIVATIVES: **lu•nu•lar** |-lər| adj. **lu•nu•late** |-ˌlāt; lit| adj.

lu•pine |ˈlo͞oˌpīn| • adj. of, like, or relating to a wolf or wolves. ■ fierce or ravenous as a wolf.

lur•dan |ˈlərdn| (also **lurdane**) • n. an idle or incompetent person. • adj. lazy; good-for-nothing.

lu•rid |ˈlo͝orid| • adj. very vivid in color, esp. so as to create an unpleasantly harsh or unnatural effect.
■ (of a description) presented in vividly shocking or sensational terms, esp. giving explicit details of crimes or sexual matters: *lurid details of the murder.*
DERIVATIVES: **lu•rid•ly** adv. **lu•rid•ness** n.

lus•cious |ˈləSHəs| • adj. (of food or wine) having a pleasingly rich, sweet taste.
■ richly verdant or opulent. ■ (of a woman) very sexually attractive.
DERIVATIVES: **lus•cious•ly** adv. **lus•cious•ness** n.

lus•ter |ˈləstər| (Brit. **lustre**) • n. **1** a gentle sheen or soft glow, esp. that of a partly reflective surface: *the luster of the Milky Way | her hair had lost its luster.*
■ glory or distinction: *an all-star to **add luster** to the lineup.* ■ the manner in which the surface of a mineral reflects light. **2** a substance imparting or having a shine or glow, in particular:
■ a thin coating containing unoxidized metal that gives an iridescent glaze to ceramics. ■ ceramics with such a glaze; lusterware. ■ a type of finish on a photographic print, less reflective than a glossy finish. ■ a fabric or yarn with a sheen or gloss. **3** a prismatic glass pendant on a chandelier or other ornament.
■ a cut-glass chandelier or candelabra.
DERIVATIVES: **lus•ter•less** adj.

lus•tral |ˈləstrəl| • adj. relating to or used in ceremonial purification.

lus•trate |ˈləsˌtrāt| • v. [trans.] purify by expiatory sacrifice, ceremonial washing, or some other ritual action: *a soul lustrated in the baptismal waters.*
DERIVATIVES: **lus•tra•tion** |ˌləsˈtrāSHən| n.

lus•trous |ˈləstrəs| • adj. having luster; shining: *large, lustrous eyes.*
DERIVATIVES: **lus•trous•ly** adv. **lus•trous•ness** n.

lus•trum |ˈləstrəm| • n. (pl. **lustra** |-trə| or **lustrums**) a period of five years.

lux•ate |ˈləkˌsāt| • v. [trans.] (in medicine) dislocate; put out of joint.
DERIVATIVES: **lux•a•tion** |ˌləkˈsāSHən| n.

luxe |ləks; lo͝oks| • n. luxury: [as adj.] *the luxe life.*

lux•u•ri•ant |ləgˈZHo͝orēənt; ləkˈSHo͝or-| • adj. (of vegetation, etc.) rich and profuse in growth; lush: *forests of dark, luxuriant foliage | luxuriant prose.*

■ (of hair) thick and healthy.
DERIVATIVES: **lux•u•ri•ance** *n.* **lux•u•ri•ant•ly** *adv.*
USAGE: See usage at LUXURIOUS.

lux•u•ri•ate |ləɡˈzHŏŏrēˌāt; ləkˈsHŏŏr-| • *v.* [intrans.] (often **luxuriate in**) enjoy oneself in a luxurious way; take self-indulgent delight: *luxuriating in a long bath.*

lux•u•ri•ous |ləɡˈzHŏŏrēəs; ləkˈsHŏŏr-| • *adj.* extremely comfortable, elegant, or enjoyable, esp. in a way that involves great expense: *a luxurious marble bathroom* | *many of the leadership led luxurious lives.*
■ giving self-indulgent or sensuous pleasure: *a luxurious wallow in a scented bath.*
DERIVATIVES: **lux•u•ri•ous•ly** *adv.* **lux•u•ri•ous•ness** *n.*

USAGE: **Luxuriant** and **luxurious** are sometimes confused. **Luxuriant** means 'lush, profuse, prolific, ' (*forests of dark luxuriant foliage; luxuriant black eyelashes*). **Luxurious,** a more common word, means 'supplied with luxuries, extremely comfortable,' (*a luxurious mansion*).

ly•can•thro•py |līˈkænTHrəpē| • *n.* the supernatural transformation of a person into a wolf (werewolf), as recounted in folk tales.
■ a form of madness involving the delusion of being an animal, usually a wolf, with correspondingly altered behavior.
DERIVATIVES: **ly•can•throp•ic** |ˌlīkən ˈTHräpik| *adj.*

Ly•ce•um |līˈsēəm| the garden at Athens in which Aristotle taught philosophy.
■ [as n.] (**the Lyceum**) Aristotelian philosophy and its followers. ■ [as n.] (**a lyceum**) a literary institution, lecture hall, or teaching place.

lymph |limf| • *n.* **1** a colorless fluid containing white blood cells, that bathes the tissues and drains through the lymphatic system into the bloodstream.
■ fluid exuding from a sore or inflamed tissue. **2** poetic/literary pure water.
DERIVATIVES: **lymph•ous** |-fəs| *adj.*

lyr•ic |ˈlirik| • *adj.* **1** (of poetry) expressing the writer's emotions, usually briefly and in stanzas or recognized forms.
■ (of a poet) writing in this manner. **2** (of a singing voice) using a light register: *a lyric soprano with a light, clear timbre.* • *n.* (usu. **lyrics**) **1** a lyric poem or verse.
■ lyric poetry as a literary genre. **2** the words of a song: *she has published both music and lyrics for a number of songs.*

lyr•i•cal |ˈlirikəl| • *adj.* **1** (of literature, art, or music) expressing the writer's emotions in an imaginative and beautiful way: *the poet's combination of lyrical and descriptive power.*
■ (of poetry or a poet) lyric: *Wordsworth's Lyrical Ballads.* **2** of or relating to the words of a popular song: *the lyrical content of his songs.*
DERIVATIVES: **lyr•i•cal•ly** |-ik(ə)lē| *adv.*

lyr•i•cist |ˈlirəsist| • *n.* a person who writes the words to a popular song or musical.

Mm

ma•ca•bre |məˈkäbrə; -ˈkäb| • *adj.* disturbing and horrifying because of involvement with or depiction of death and injury: *a macabre series of murders.*

mac•a•ron•ic |ˌmækəˈränik| • *adj.* denoting language, esp. burlesque verse, containing words or inflections from one language introduced into the context of another. • *n.* (usu. **macaronics**) macaronic verse, esp. that which mixes the vernacular with Latin.

mac•er•ate |ˈmæsəˌrāt| • *v.* [trans.] **1** soften or break up (something, esp. food) by soaking in a liquid.
■ [intrans.] become softened or broken up by soaking. **2** cause to grow thinner or waste away, esp. by fasting.
DERIVATIVES: **mac•er•a•tion** |ˌmæsə ˈrāSHən| *n.* **mac•er•a•tor** |-ˌrātər| *n.*

Mach (also **Mach number**) • *n.* the ratio of the speed of a body to the speed of sound in the surrounding medium. It is often used with a numeral (as **Mach 1**, **Mach 2**, etc.) to indicate the speed of sound, twice the speed of sound, etc.

Mach•i•a•vel•li•an |ˌmækēəˈvelēən; ˌmäk-|

• *adj.* **1** cunning, scheming, and unscrupulous, esp. in politics or in advancing one's career. **2** of or relating to Niccolò Machiavelli (1469–1527), Italian political theorist who wrote *The Prince.* • *n.* (also **Machiavelli**) a person who schemes in such a way.
DERIVATIVES: **Mach•i•a•vel•li•an•ism** |-ˌnizəm| *n.*

mach•i•nate |ˈmækəˌnāt; ˈmæsHə-| • *v.* [intrans.] engage in plots and intrigues; scheme.
DERIVATIVES: **mach•i•na•tion** |ˌmækə ˈnāSHən; ˌmæsHə-| *n.* **mach•i•na•tor** |-ˌnātər| *n.*

ma•chis•mo |məˈCHēzmō; məˈkēzmō| • *n.* strong or aggressive masculine pride.
■ daring or bravado.

ma•cho |ˈmäCHō| • *adj.* showing aggressive pride in one's masculinity: *one big macho tough guy.* • *n.* (pl. **-os**) a man who is aggressively proud of his masculinity.
■ machismo.

mac•ro |ˈmækrō| • *n.* (pl. **-os**) **1** (also **macro instruction**) (in computing) a single instruction that expands automatically into a set of instructions to perform a particular task. **2** short for **macro lens,** a lens suitable for taking photographs unusually close to the subject. • *adj.* **1** large-scale; overall: *the analysis of social events at the macro level.* Often contrasted with *micro.* **2** relating to or used in macrophotography.

mac•ro•bi•ot•ic |ˌmækrōbī'ätik| • *adj.* constituting, relating to, or following a diet of whole pure prepared foods that is based on Taoist principles of the balance of yin and yang. • *plural n.* (**macrobiotics**) [treated as sing.] the use or theory of such a diet.

mac•ro•cosm |'mækrəˌkäzəm| (also **macrocosmos**) • *n.* the universe; the cosmos.
■ the whole of a complex structure, esp. as represented or epitomized in a small part of itself (a **microcosm**).
DERIVATIVES: **mac•ro•cos•mic** |ˌmækrə 'käzmik| *adj.* **mac•ro•cos•mi•cal•ly** |ˌmækrə'käzmik(ə)lē| *adv.*

mac•ro•ec•o•nom•ics |'mækrō,ekə'nämiks; -ˌēkə-| • *plural n.* [treated as sing.] the part of economics concerned with large-scale or general economic factors, such as interest rates and national productivity. Cf. MICROECONOMICS.
DERIVATIVES: **mac•ro•ec•o•nom•ic** |-'näm-ik| *adj.* **mac•ro•e•con•o•mist** |-i'känəmist| *n.*

mad•ri•gal |'mædrigəl| • *n.* a part-song for several voices, esp. one of the Renaissance period, typically arranged in elaborate counterpoint and without instrumental accompaniment. Originally used of a genre of 14th-century Italian songs, the term now usually refers to English or Italian songs of the late 16th and early 17th c., in a free style strongly influenced by the text.
DERIVATIVES: **mad•ri•gal•i•an** |ˌmædri 'gālēən| *adj.* **mad•ri•gal•ist** |-ist| *n.*

mael•strom |'māl,sträm; -strəm| • *n.* a powerful whirlpool in the sea or a river.
■ a scene or state of confused and violent movement or upheaval: *the train station was a maelstrom of crowds* | *a maelstrom of violence and recrimination.*

mae•nad |'mē,næd| • *n.* (in ancient Greece) a female follower of Bacchus, the god of wine, traditionally associated with divine possession and frenzied rites.
DERIVATIVES: **mae•nad•ic** |mē'nædik| *adj.*

ma•es•to•so |mī'stōsō; -'stōzō| • *adv. & adj.* (esp. as a musical direction) in a majestic manner. • *n.* (pl. **-os**) a movement or passage marked to be performed in this way.

maes•tro |'mīstrō| • *n.* (pl. **maestri** |-strē| or **maestros**) a distinguished musician, esp. a conductor of classical music.
■ a great or distinguished figure in any sphere: *a movie maestro.*

Ma•fi•a |'mäfēə| • *n.* (**the Mafia**) [treated as sing. or pl.] an organized international body of criminals, operating originally in Sicily and now esp. in Italy and the US and having a complex and ruthless behavioral code.
■ (usu. **mafia**) any similar group using extor-

tion and other criminal methods. ■ (usu. **mafia**) a closed group of people in a particular field, having a controlling influence: *the international tennis mafia.*

Ma•gi |'māgī; -jī; -gē| (**the Magi**) the "wise men" from the East who brought gifts to the infant Jesus (Matt. 2:1), said in later tradition to be kings named Caspar, Melchior, and Balthasar who brought gifts of gold, frankincense, and myrrh.

mag•is•te•ri•al |ˌmæjə'stirēəl| • *adj.* **1** having or showing great authority: *a magisterial pronouncement.*
■ domineering; dictatorial: *he dropped his somewhat magisterial style of questioning.* **2** relating to or conducted by a magistrate.
■ (of a person) holding the office of a magistrate.
DERIVATIVES: **mag•is•te•ri•al•ly** *adv.*

Mag•na Car•ta |ˌmægnə 'kärtə| a charter of liberty and political rights obtained from King John of England by his rebellious barons at Runnymede in 1215, which came to be seen as the seminal document of English constitutional practice.
■ any similar document of rights: *a Magna Carta for alternative broadcasters.*

mag•nan•i•mous |mæg'nænəməs| • *adj.* very generous or forgiving, esp. toward a rival or someone less powerful than oneself.
DERIVATIVES: **mag•na•nim•i•ty** |ˌmægnə 'nimətē| *n.* **mag•nan•i•mous•ly** *adv.*

mag•nate |'mæg,nāt; 'mægnət| • *n.* a wealthy and influential person, esp. in business: *a media magnate.*

mag•ne•to |mæg'nētō| • *n.* (pl. **-os**) a small electric generator containing a permanent magnet and used to provided high-voltage pulses, esp. (formerly) in the ignition systems of internal combustion engines.

mag•nil•o•quent |mæg'niləkwənt| • *adj.* using high-flown or bombastic language.
DERIVATIVES: **mag•nil•o•quence** *n.* **mag•nil•o•quent•ly** *adv.*

mag•ni•tude |'mægnəˌtood| • *n.* **1** the great size or extent of something: *they may feel discouraged at the magnitude of the task before them.*
■ great importance: *events of tragic magnitude.* **2** size: *electorates of less than average magnitude.*
■ a numerical quantity or value: *the magnitudes of all the economic variables could be determined. An order of magnitude is a difference between two quantities expressed as a power of ten.* **3** the degree of brightness of a star. The magnitude of an astronomical object is now reckoned as the negative logarithm of the brightness; a decrease of one magnitude (e.g., from magnitude 3 to magnitude 2) represents an increase in brightness of 2.512 times.
■ the class into which a star falls by virtue of its brightness. ■ a difference of one on a scale of brightness, treated as a unit of measurement.

mag•num o•pus |'mægnəm 'ōpəs| • *n.* (pl. **magnum opuses** or **magna opera** |'mæg-nə 'ōpərə; 'äpərə|) a large and important work of art, music, or literature, esp. one regarded as the most important work of an artist or writer. Cf. CHEF-D'ŒUVRE.

ma•ha•ra•ja |ˌmähəˈräjə; -ˈräzНə| (also **maharajah**) • *n.* an Indian prince ranking higher than a *rajah*, esp. one who ruled a Native State before independence (1947).

ma•ha•ri•shi |ˌmähəˈrēsHē; məˈhärəsHē| • *n.* a great Hindu sage or spiritual leader.

ma•hat•ma |məˈhätmə; -ˈhætmə| • *n.* (in the Indian subcontinent) a person regarded with reverence or loving respect; a holy person or sage.

■ **(the Mahatma)** Mahatma (Mohandas K.) Gandhi (1869–1948), Indian nationalist and spiritual leader. ■ (in some forms of theosophy) a person in India or Tibet said to have supernatural powers.

Ma•ha•ya•na |ˌmähəˈyänə| (also **Mahayana Buddhism**) • *n.* one of the two major traditions of Buddhism, now practiced in a variety of forms esp. in China, Tibet, Japan, and Korea. The tradition emerged around the 1st century AD and is typically concerned with altruistically oriented spiritual practice as embodied in the ideal of the BODHISATTVA. Cf. THERAVADA.

ma•ieu•tic |mäˈyo͞otik| • *adj.* of or denoting the Socratic mode of inquiry, which aims to bring a person's latent ideas into clear consciousness. • *plural n.* (**maieutics**) [treated as sing.] the maieutic method.

mail•lot |mīˈō| • *n.* (pl. pronunc. same) **1** a pair of tights worn for dancing or gymnastics.

■ a woman's tight-fitting one-piece swimsuit. **2** a jersey or top, esp. one worn in sports such as cycling.

maim |mām| • *v.* [trans.] wound or injure (someone) so that part of the body is permanently damaged: *100,000 soldiers were killed or maimed.*

ma•iol•i•ca |mīˈäləkə| • *n.* fine earthenware with colored decoration on an opaque white tin glaze, originating in Italy during the Renaissance. Cf. MAJOLICA.

maî•tre d'hô•tel |ˌmätrə dōˈtel; ˌmetrə| (also **maître d'** |ˌmätrə ˈdē; ˌmätər|) • *n.* (pl. **maîtres d'hôtel** pronunc. same or **maître d's**) the person in a restaurant who oversees the serving staff, and who typically handles reservations.

■ the manager of a hotel.

ma•jol•i•ca |məˈjälikə| • *n.* a kind of earthenware made in imitation of Italian maiolica, esp. in England during the 19th century.

ma•jor-do•mo |ˌmäjər ˈdōmō| • *n.* (pl. **-os**) the chief steward of a large household.

ma•jor•i•ty |məˈjôrətē; -ˈjär-| • *n.* (pl. **-ies**) **1** the greater number: *in the majority of cases all will go smoothly* | [as adj.] *it was a majority decision.*

■ the number by which votes for one candidate in an election are more than those for all other candidates combined. ■ Brit. the number by which the votes for one party or candidate exceed those of the next in rank. ■ a party or group receiving the greater number of votes. **2** the age when a person is legally considered a full adult, in most contexts either 18 or 21. **3** the rank or office of a major.

USAGE: **1** Strictly speaking, **majority** should be used with countable nouns to mean 'the greater number,' as in *the majority of cases.* Use with uncountable nouns to mean 'the greatest part,' as in *I spent the majority of the day reading* or *she ate the majority of the meal,* although common in informal contexts, is not considered good standard English.

2 Majority means more than half: *Fifty-one out of 100 is a majority.* A **plurality** is the largest number among three or more: *If Anne received 50 votes, Barry received 30, and Carlos received 20, then Anne received a plurality, and no candidate won a majority; if Anne got 35 votes, Barry 14, and Carlos 51, then Carlos won both the plurality and the majority.*

ma•jus•cule |ˈmæjəsˌkyo͞ol| • *n.* large lettering, either capital or uncial, in which all the letters are usually the same height.

■ a large letter. Cf. MINUSCULE.

DERIVATIVES: **ma•jus•cu•lar** |məˈjəskyələr| *adj.*

mal•a•droit |ˌmæləˈdroit| • *adj.* ineffective or bungling; clumsy.

DERIVATIVES: **mal•a•droit•ly** *adv.* **mal•a•droit•ness** *n.*

mal•a•dy |ˈmælədē| • *n.* (pl. **-ies**) a disease or ailment: *an incurable malady* | *the nation's maladies.*

ma•laise |məˈläz; -ˈlez| • *n.* a general feeling of discomfort, illness, or uneasiness whose exact cause is difficult to identify: *a society afflicted by a deep cultural malaise* | *a general air of malaise.*

mal•a•pert |ˌmæləˈpərt| • *adj.* boldly disrespectful to a person of higher standing. • *n.* an impudent person.

mal•a•prop |ˈmæləˌpræp| (also **malapropism**) • *n.* the mistaken use of a word in place of a similar-sounding one, often with unintentionally amusing effect, as in, for example, "dance a *flamingo*" (instead of *flamenco*).

mal•ap•ro•pos |ˌmælˌæprəˈpō| • *adv.* in an inopportune or awkward manner; inappropriately. • *adj.* inopportune; inappropriate: *these terms applied to him seem to me malapropos.* • *n.* (pl. same) something inappropriately said or done.

mal•con•tent |ˌmælkənˈtent; ˈmælkənˌtent| • *n.* a person who is dissatisfied and rebellious. • *adj.* dissatisfied and complaining or making trouble.

DERIVATIVES: **mal•con•tent•ed** *adj.*

mal•e•dic•tion |ˌmæləˈdiksHən| • *n.* a magical word or phrase uttered with the intention of bringing about evil; a curse. Cf. BENEDICTION.

DERIVATIVES: **mal•e•dic•tive** |-ˈdiktiv| *adj.* **mal•e•dic•to•ry** |-ˈdiktərē| *adj.*

mal•e•fac•tor |ˈmæləˌfæktər| • *n.* a person who commits a crime or some other wrong.

DERIVATIVES: **mal•e•fac•tion** |ˌmæləˈfæksHən| *n.*

ma•lef•ic |məˈlefik| • *adj.* causing or capable of causing harm or destruction, esp. by supernatural means.
■ relating to the planets Saturn and Mars, traditionally considered by astrologists to have an unfavorable influence.
DERIVATIVES: **ma•lef•i•cence** |-ˈlefəsəns| *n.* **ma•lef•i•cent** |-ˈlefəsənt| *adj.*

ma•lev•o•lent |məˈlevələnt| • *adj.* having or showing a wish to do evil to others: *malevolent eyes | some malevolent force of nature.* Cf. BENEVOLENT.
DERIVATIVES: **ma•lev•o•lence** *n.* **ma•lev•o•lent•ly** *adv.*

mal•fea•sance |mælˈfēzns| • *n.* wrongdoing, esp. by a public official when it affects his or her public duties.
DERIVATIVES: **mal•fea•sant** |-ˈfēznt| *n. & adj.*

mal•ice |ˈmæləs| • *n.* the intention or desire to do evil; ill will: *I bear no malice toward anybody.*
■ (in law) wrongful intention, esp. as increasing the guilt of certain offenses. **Malice aforethought** is the intention to kill or harm that is held to distinguish murder from other unlawful killing.

ma•lign |məˈlīn| • *adj.* evil in nature or effect: malevolent: *she had a strong and malign influence.* • *v.*
■ (of a disease) malignant. Cf. BENIGN. • *v.* [trans.] speak about (someone) in a spitefully critical manner: *don't you dare malign her in my presence.*
DERIVATIVES: **ma•lign•er** *n.* **ma•lig•ni•ty** |-ˈlignətē| *n.* **ma•lign•ly** *adv.*

ma•lig•nan•cy |məˈlignənsē| • *n.* (pl. **-ies**)
1 the state or presence of a malignant tumor; cancer: *in the biopsy, evidence of malignancy was found.*
■ a cancerous growth. ■ a form of cancer: *diffuse malignancies such as leukemia.* **2** the quality of being malign or malevolent: *her eyes sparkled with renewed malignancy.*

ma•lig•nant |məˈlignənt| • *adj.* **1** (of a disease) very virulent or infectious.
■ (of a tumor) tending to invade normal tissue or to recur after removal; cancerous. Cf. BENIGN. **2** characterized by intense ill will; malevolent: *in the hands of malignant fate.*
DERIVATIVES: **ma•lig•nant•ly** *adv.*

ma•lin•ger |məˈliNGgər| • *v.* [intrans.] exaggerate or feign illness in order to escape duty or work. Cf. GOLD BRICK.
DERIVATIVES: **ma•lin•ger•er** *n.*

mal•le•a•ble |ˈmæl(y)əbəl; ˈmælēə-| • *adj.* (of a metal or other material) able to be hammered or pressed permanently out of shape without breaking or cracking.
■ easily influenced; pliable: *Anna was shaken enough to be malleable.* Cf. DUCTILE; TENSILE.
DERIVATIVES: **mal•le•a•bil•i•ty** |ˌmæl(y)-əˈbilətē; ˌmælēə-| *n.* **mal•le•a•bly** |-blē| *adv.*

mal•o•dor•ous |mælˈōdərəs| • *adj.* smelling very unpleasant.

mal•prac•tice |mælˈpræktəs| • *n.* improper, illegal, or negligent professional activity or treatment, esp. by a medical practitioner, lawyer, or public official: *victims of medical malpractice.*

mal•ver•sa•tion |ˌmælvərˈsāsHən| • *n.* corrupt behavior in a position of trust, esp. in public office: *ineptitude and malversation were major factors in the trouncing of the party's candidates.*

mam•mon |ˈmæmən| (also **Mammon**) • *n.* wealth regarded as an evil influence or false object of worship and devotion. It was taken by medieval writers as the name of the devil of covetousness, and revived in this sense by John Milton.
DERIVATIVES: **mam•mon•ism** |-ˌizəm| *n.* **mam•mon•ist** |-ˌist| *n.*

man•a•cle |ˈmænikəl| • *n.* (usu. **manacles**) a metal band, chain, or shackle for fastening someone's hands or ankles: *the practice of keeping prisoners in manacles.* • *v.* [trans.] (usu. **be manacled**) fetter (a person or a part of the body) with manacles: *his hands were manacled behind his back.*

ma•ña•na |mənˈyänə| • *adv.* in the indefinite future (used to indicate procrastination): *the exhibition will be ready mañana.*

man•da•la |ˈmændələ; ˈmən-| • *n.* a geometric figure representing the universe in Hindu and Buddhist symbolism.
■ (in Jungian psychology) such a symbol in a dream, representing the dreamer's search for completeness and self-unity.
DERIVATIVES: **man•da•lic** |mænˈdælik; ˌmən-| *adj.*

man•da•mus |mænˈdāməs| • *n.* a judicial writ issued as a command to an inferior court or ordering a person to perform a public or statutory duty: *a writ of mandamus.*

man•da•rin |ˈmændərən| • *n.* **1** (**Mandarin**) the standard literary and official form of Chinese based on the Beijing dialect, spoken by over 730 million people: [as adj.] *Mandarin Chinese.* **2** an official in any of the nine top grades of the former imperial Chinese civil service.
■ [as adj.] (esp. of clothing) characteristic or supposedly characteristic of such officials: *a red-buttoned mandarin cap.* ■ porcelain decorated with Chinese figures dressed as mandarins. ■ a powerful official or senior bureaucrat, esp. one perceived as reactionary and secretive: *State Department mandarins.*
DERIVATIVES: **man•da•rin•ate** *n.* **man•da•rin•ism** *n.*

man•da•to•ry |ˈmændəˌtôrē| • *adj.* required by law or rules; compulsory: *wearing helmets was made mandatory for cyclists.*
■ of or conveying a command: *he did not want the guidelines to be mandatory.*
DERIVATIVES: **man•da•to•ri•ly** |-ˌtôrəlē| *adv.*

man•di•ble |ˈmændəbəl| • *n.* the jaw or a jawbone, esp. the lower jawbone in mammals and fishes.
■ either of the upper and lower parts of a bird's beak. ■ either half of the crushing organ in an arthropod's mouthparts. Cf. MAXILLA
DERIVATIVES: **man•dib•u•lar** |mænˈdib-

yəl|ər| *adj.* **man•dib•u•late** |ˌmænˈdibyəˌlāt| *adj.*

ma•nège |mæˈnezH; mə-| • *n.* an arena, school, or enclosed area in which horses and riders are trained.
■ the movements of a trained horse. ■ horsemanship.

ma•neu•ver |məˈn(ōō)vər| (Brit. **manoeuvre**) • *n.* **1** a movement or series of moves requiring skill and care: *spectacular jumps and other daring maneuvers.*
■ a carefully planned scheme or action, esp. one involving deception: *shady financial maneuvers.* ■ the fact or process of taking such action: *the economic policy provided no room for maneuver.* **2** (**maneuvers**) a large-scale military exercise of troops, warships, and other forces: *the Russian vessel was on maneuvers.* • *v.* (**maneuvered, maneuvering**) **1** perform or cause to perform a movement or series of moves requiring skill and care: [intrans.] *the truck was unable to maneuver comfortably in the narrow street* | [with obj. and adverbial of direction] *I'm maneuvering a loaded tray around the floor.* **2** [with obj. and adverbial] carefully guide or manipulate (someone or something) in order to achieve an end: *they were maneuvering him into a betrayal of his countryman.*
■ [intrans.] carefully manipulate a situation to achieve an end: [as n.] (**maneuvering**) *two decades of political maneuvering.*
DERIVATIVES: **ma•neu•ver•er** *n.*

ma•ni•ac |ˈmānēˌæk| • *n.* a person exhibiting extreme symptoms of wild behavior, esp. when violent and dangerous: *a homicidal maniac.*
■ [with adj.] an obsessive enthusiast: *a gambling maniac.* ■ a former technical designation for a person suffering from mental disturbance characterized by great excitement, delusions, or overactivity (mania).
DERIVATIVES: **ma•ni•a•cal** |məˈnīəkəl| *adj.* **ma•ni•a•cal•ly** |məˈnīək(ə)lē| *adv.*

Man•i•chae•ism |ˈmænəˌkēizəm| (also **Manicheism**) • *n.* a dualistic religious system with Christian, Gnostic, and pagan elements, founded in Persia in the 3rd century by Manes (*c.*216–*c.*276). The system was based on a supposed primeval conflict between light and darkness. It spread widely in the Roman Empire and in Asia, and survived in Chinese Turkestan until the 13th century.
■ religious or philosophical dualism.

man•i•fest¹ |ˈmænəˌfest| • *adj.* clear or obvious to the eye or mind: *the system's manifest failings.* • *v.* display or show (a quality or feeling) by one's acts or appearance; demonstrate: *Ray manifested signs of severe depression.*
■ (often **be manifested in**) be evidence of; prove: *bad industrial relations are often manifested in disputes and strikes.* ■ [intrans.] (of an ailment) become apparent through the appearance of symptoms: *a disorder that usually manifests in middle age.* ■ [intrans.] (of a ghost or spirit) appear: *one deity manifested in the form of a bird.*

DERIVATIVES: **man•i•fest•ly** *adv.*

man•i•fest² • *n.* a document giving comprehensive details of a ship and its cargo and other contents, passengers, and crew for the use of customs officers.
■ a list of passengers or cargo in an aircraft. ■ a list of the cars forming a freight train. • *v.* [trans.] record in such a manifest: *every passenger is manifested at the point of departure.*

man•i•fes•ta•tion |ˌmænəfəˈstāsHən; -ˌfesˈtāsHən| • *n.* an event, action, or object that clearly shows or embodies something, esp. a theory or an abstract idea: *the first obvious manifestations of global warming.*
■ the action or fact of showing something in such a way: *the manifestation of anxiety over the upcoming exams.* ■ a symptom or sign of an ailment: *a characteristic manifestation of Lyme disease.* ■ a version or incarnation of something or someone: *Purity and Innocence and Young Love in all their gentle manifestations.* ■ an appearance of a ghost or spirit.

man•i•fes•to |ˌmænəˈfestō| • *n.* (pl. **-os**) a public declaration of policy and aims, esp. one issued before an election by a political party or candidate.

man•i•fold |ˈmænəˌfōld| • *adj.* many and various: *the implications of this decision were manifold.*
■ having many different forms or elements: *the appeal of the crusade was manifold.* • *n.* **1** [often with adj.] a pipe or chamber branching into several openings: *the pipeline manifold.*
■ (in an internal combustion engine) the part conveying air and fuel from the carburetor to each cylinder, or that leading from the cylinders to the exhaust pipe: *the exhaust manifold.* **2** something with many different parts or forms, in particular:
■ (in mathematics) a collection of points forming a certain kind of set, such as those of a topologically closed surface or an analog of this in three or more dimensions. ■ (in Kantian philosophy) the sum of the particulars furnished by sense before they have been unified by the synthesis of the understanding.
DERIVATIVES: **man•i•fold•ly** *adv.* **man•i•fold•ness** *n.*

man•i•kin |ˈmænikən| (also **mannikin**) • *n.* **1** a person who is very small, esp. one not otherwise abnormal or deformed. **2** a jointed model of the human body, used in anatomy or as an artist's lay figure.

USAGE: See **usage** at MANNEQUIN.

ma•nip•u•late |məˈnipyəˌlāt| • *v.* [trans.] **1** handle or control (a tool, mechanism, etc.), typically in a skillful manner: *he manipulated the dials of the set.*
■ alter, edit, or move (text or data) on a computer. ■ examine or treat (a part of the body) by feeling or moving it with the hand: *a system of healing based on manipulating the ligaments of the spine.* **2** control or influence (a person or situation) cleverly, unfairly, or unscrupulously: *the masses were deceived and manipulated by a tiny group.*

- alter (data) or present (statistics) so as to mislead.

DERIVATIVES: **ma•nip•u•la•bil•i•ty** |-,nipyələ'bilətē| n. **ma•nip•u•la•ble** |-ləbəl| adj. **ma•nip•u•lat•a•ble** |-,lātəbəl| adj. **ma•nip•u•la•tion** |mə,nipyə'lāsHən| n. **ma•nip•u•la•tor** |-,lātər| n. **ma•nip•u•la•to•ry** |-lə,tôrē| adj.

ma•nip•u•la•tive |mə'nipyələtiv; -,lātiv| • adj. **1** characterized by unscrupulous control of a situation or person: *she was sly, selfish, and manipulative.* **2** of or relating to manipulation of an object or part of the body: *a manipulative skill.*

DERIVATIVES: **ma•nip•u•la•tive•ly** adv. **ma•nip•u•la•tive•ness** n.

man•na |'mænə| • n. (in the Bible) the substance miraculously supplied as food to the Israelites in the wilderness (Exod. 16).

- an unexpected or gratuitous benefit: *the cakes were manna from heaven.* ■ (in Christian contexts) spiritual nourishment, esp. the Eucharist.

man•ne•quin |'mænikən| • n. a dummy used to display clothes in a store window.

- a young woman or man employed to show clothes to customers.

USAGE: **Mannequin** occurs about five times more frequently than either of its relatives **manakin**, **manikin**, and **mannikin**. The source for all three words is the Middle Dutch *mannekijn* (modern Dutch *manneken*) 'little man,' 'little doll.'
Mannequin is the French spelling from the same Dutch source. One of its French meanings, dating from about 1830, is 'a young woman hired to model clothes' (even though the word means 'little *man*'). This sense—still current, but rare in English—first appears in 1902. The far more common sense of 'a life-size jointed figure or dummy used for displaying clothes' is first recorded in 1939.
Manikin has had the sense 'little man' (often contemptuous) since the mid 16th century. It occurs as a term of abuse in Shakespeare's *Twelfth Night* (spelled *manakin*). **Manikin's** sense of 'an artist's lay figure' also dates from the mid 16th century (first recorded with the Dutch spelling *Manneken*).
It is unfortunate that **manakin** and **mannikin** refer to birds of two different families. For the bird names **manakin** is the earlier spelling, dating from the mid 18th century. It has a variant spelling, *manikin*, identical with **manikin**. **Mannikin** dates from about 1875 and is merely a variant spelling of **manikin**. The more remote history of these bird names is obscure: **manakin** may come from the Portuguese *manaquim* 'mannikin,' a variant of *manequim* 'mannequin'; or **mannikin** may come directly from the source of the Portuguese words, the Middle Dutch *mannekijn*.

ma•no a ma•no |,mänō ä 'mänō| (also **mano-a-mano**) • adj. (of combat or compe-

tition) hand-to-hand: *the exhilaration of the mano-a-mano battle.* • adv. in the manner of hand-to-hand combat or a duel: *they want to settle this mano a mano.* • n. (pl. **-os**) an intense fight or contest between two adversaries; a duel: *a real courtroom mano-a-mano.*

man•or |'mænər| • n. (also **manor house**) a large country house with lands; the principal house of a landed estate.

- (esp. formerly in England and Wales) a unit of land, originally a feudal lordship, consisting of a lord's demesne and lands rented to tenants. ■ (formerly in North America) an estate or district leased to tenants, esp. one granted by royal charter in a British colony or by the Dutch governors of what is now New York.

DERIVATIVES: **ma•no•ri•al** |mə'nôrēəl| adj.

man•qué |mäNG'kā| • adj. [postpositive] having failed to become what one might have been; unfulfilled: *a poet manqué.*

man•sard |'mæn,särd; -sərd| • n. (also **mansard roof**) a roof that has four sloping sides, each of which becomes steeper halfway down.

- a story or apartment under a mansard roof. ■ Brit. another term for GAMBREL.

man•slaugh•ter |'mæn,slôtər| • n. the crime of killing a human being without malice aforethought, or otherwise in circumstances not amounting to murder: *the defendant was convicted of manslaughter.*

man•sue•tude |'mænswi,tōōd; mæn'sōōə-| • n. meekness; gentleness.

man•tic |'mæntik| • adj. of or relating to divination or prophecy.

man•tra |'mæntrə; 'män-| • n. (originally in Hinduism and Buddhism) a word or sound repeated to aid concentration in meditation.

- a Vedic (early Hindu) hymn. ■ a statement or slogan repeated frequently: *the environmentalist mantra that energy is too cheap.*

DERIVATIVES: **man•tric** |-trik| adj.

man•u•mit |,mænyə'mit| • v. (**manumitted, manumitting**) [trans.] release from slavery; set free.

DERIVATIVES: **man•u•mis•sion** |-'misHən| n. **man•u•mit•ter** n.

Mao•ism |'mow,izəm| • n. the communist doctrines of Mao Zedong (1893-1976) as formerly practiced in China, having as a central idea permanent revolution and stressing the importance of the peasantry, of small-scale industry, and of agricultural collectivization.

DERIVATIVES: **Mao•ist** |'mowist| n. & adj.

ma•qui•la•do•ra |,mækilə'dôrə| • n. a factory in Mexico run by a foreign company (typically, American) and exporting its products (typically, assembled from parts imported into Mexico) to the country of that company.

ma•raud |mə'rôd| • v. [intrans.] [often as adj.] (**marauding**) roam in search of things to steal or people to attack: *marauding gangs of looters.*

- [trans.] raid and plunder (a place).

DERIVATIVES: **ma•raud•er** n.

mar·chion·ess |ˈmärsH(ə)nəs| • n. the wife or widow of a marquess.
■ a woman holding the rank of marquess in her own right.

mare's nest • n. 1 a complex and difficult situation; a muddle: this dispute has become a mare's nest. 2 an illusory discovery: the mare's nest of perfect safety.

mar·gi·na·li·a |ˌmärjəˈnālēə| • plural n. marginal notes: among the marginalia are clues to the author's identity.

mar·gin·al·ize |ˈmärjənəˌlīz| • v. [trans.] treat (a person, group, or concept) as insignificant or peripheral: attempting to marginalize those who disagree | [as adj.] (**marginalized**) members of marginalized cultural groups.
DERIVATIVES: **mar·gin·al·i·za·tion** |ˌmärjənələˈzāsHən|.

mar·i·cul·ture |ˈmæriˌkəlCHər| • n. the cultivation of fish or other marine life for food.
DERIVATIVES: **mar·i·cul·tur·al** adj. **mar·i·cul·tur·ist** n.

Mar·i·ol·a·try |ˌmerēˈälətrē| • n. idolatrous worship of the Virgin Mary.

marque[1] |märk| • n. a make of car, as distinct from a specific model.

marque[2] • n. see LETTER OF MARQUE.

mar·quee |märˈkē| • n. 1 a rooflike projection over the entrance to a theater, hotel, or other building.
■ [as adj.] leading; preeminent: a marquee player. 2 a large tent used for social or commercial functions.

mar·quess |ˈmärkwəs| • n. a British nobleman ranking above an earl and below a duke. Cf. MARQUIS.

mar·que·try |ˈmärkətrē| (also **marqueterie** or **marquetery**) • n. inlaid work made from small pieces of variously colored wood or other materials, used chiefly for the decoration of furniture.

mar·quis |märˈkē; ˈmärkwəs| • n. (in some European countries) a nobleman ranking above a count and below a duke. Cf. MARQUESS.

mar·quise |märˈkēz| • n. 1 the wife or widow of a marquis. Cf. MARCHIONESS.
■ a woman holding the rank of marquis in her own right. 2 a finger ring set with a pointed oval gem or cluster of gems. 3 archaic term for MARQUEE (sense 2). 4 a chilled dessert similar to a chocolate mousse.

mar·shal |ˈmärsHəl| • n. 1 an officer of the highest rank in the armed forces of some countries, including France.
■ a high-ranking officer of state. 2 a federal or municipal law officer.
■ the head of a police department. ■ the head of a fire department. 3 an official responsible for supervising public events, esp. sports events or parades. • v. (**marshaled, marshaling**; chiefly Brit. **marshalled, marshalling**) [trans.] 1 arrange or assemble (esp. a group of people, such as soldiers) in order: the general marshaled his troops | he paused for a moment, as if marshaling his thoughts.
■ [with obj. and adverbial of direction] guide or usher (someone) ceremoniously: guests were

marshaled into position. ■ [trans.] correctly position or arrange (rolling stock). ■ [trans.] guide or direct the movement of (an aircraft) on the ground at an airport. 2 (in heraldry) combine (coats of arms), typically to indicate marriage, descent, or the bearing of office.
DERIVATIVES: **mar·shal·er** n. **mar·shal·ship** |-ˌsHip| n.

mar·su·pi·al |märˈsoōpēəl| • n. a mammal of an order (Marsupialia) whose members are born incompletely developed and are typically carried and suckled in a pouch on the mother's belly. • adj. of or relating to this order.

mar·tial |ˈmärsHəl| • adj. of or appropriate to war; warlike: martial bravery.
DERIVATIVES: **mar·tial·ly** adv.

mar·ti·net |ˌmärtnˈet| • n. a strict disciplinarian, esp. in the armed forces.

mar·tyr |ˈmärtər| • n. a person who is killed because of his or her religious or other beliefs.
■ a person who displays or exaggerates discomfort or distress to obtain sympathy or admiration: she played the martyr. ■ (**martyr to**) a constant sufferer from (an ailment): I'm a martyr to migraines! • v. [trans.] (usu. **be martyred**) kill (someone) because of his or her beliefs: she was martyred for her faith.
■ cause great pain or distress to: there was no need to martyr themselves again.
DERIVATIVES: **mar·tyr·i·za·tion** |ˌmärtərəˈzāsHən| n. **mar·tyr·ize** |ˈmärtəˌrīz| v. **mar·tyr·dom** n.

Marx·ism |ˈmärkˌsizəm| • n. the political and economic theories of Karl Marx and Friedrich Engels, later developed by their followers to form the basis for the theory and practice of communism.

Central to Marxist theory is an explanation of social change in terms of economic factors, according to which the means of production provide the economic base, which influences or determines the political and ideological superstructure. Marx and Engels predicted the revolutionary overthrow of capitalism by the proletariat and the eventual attainment of a classless communist society.

DERIVATIVES: **Marx·ist** |ˈmärksəst| n. & adj.

masque |mæsk| • n. a form of amateur dramatic entertainment, popular among the nobility in 16th- and 17th-century England, which consisted of dancing and acting performed by masked players.
■ a masked ball.
DERIVATIVES: **mas·quer** |ˈmæskər| n.

mas·sif |mæˈsēf| • n. a compact group of mountains, esp. one that is separate from other groups.

mast • n. the fruit of beech, oak, chestnut, and other forest trees, esp. as food for pigs and wild animals.

mas·ti·cate |ˈmæstiˌkāt| • v. [trans.] chew (food).
DERIVATIVES: **mas·ti·ca·tion** |ˌmæstiˈkāsHən| n. **mas·ti·ca·tor** |-ˌkātər| n. **mas·ti·ca·to·ry** |ˈmæstikəˌtôrē| adj.

mas·tur·bate |ˈmæstərˌbāt| • v. [intrans.] stimulate one's own genitals for sexual pleasure.

■ [trans.] stimulate the genitals of (someone) to give them sexual pleasure.
DERIVATIVES: **mas•tur•ba•tion** |ˌmæstər'bāsHən| *n.* **mas•tur•ba•tor** |-ˌbātər| *n.* **mas•tur•ba•to•ry** |-bəˌtôrē| *adj.*

ma•té |'mä,tā| (also **yerba maté**) • *n.* **1** (also **maté tea** or **Paraguay tea**) an infusion of the leaves of a South American shrub (*Ilex paraguariensis*), which is high in caffeine and bitter.
■ the leaves of this shrub. **2** the South American shrub of the holly family that produces these leaves.

ma•ter•fa•mil•i•as |ˌmātərfə'mileəs; ˌmätər-| • *n.* (pl. **matresfamilias** |ˌmä,träs-; ˌmātərz-|) the female head of a family or household.

ma•te•ri•al•ism |mə'tirēəˌlizəm| • *n.* **1** a tendency to consider material possessions and physical comfort as more important than spiritual, aesthetic, or cultural values.
■ a way of life based on material interests. **2** the philosophical doctrine that nothing exists except matter and its movements and modifications.
■ the doctrine that consciousness and will are due wholly to material agency. See also IDEALISM; MENTALISM.
DERIVATIVES: **ma•te•ri•al•ist** *n.* & *adj.* **ma•te•ri•al•is•tic** |mə,tirēə'listik| *adj.* **ma•te•ri•al•is•ti•cal•ly** |-tik(ə)lē| *adv.*

ma•te•ri•el |mə,tirē'el| (also **matériel**) • *n.* military materials and equipment: *moving material along muddy roads was a challenge.*

ma•ter•nal |mə'tərnl| • *adj.* of or relating to a mother, esp. during pregnancy or shortly after childbirth: *maternal age* | *maternal care.*
■ [attrib.] related through the mother's side of the family: *my maternal grandfather.* ■ denoting feelings associated with or typical of a mother; motherly: *maternal instincts.*
DERIVATIVES: **ma•ter•nal•ism** |-ˌizəm| *n.* **ma•ter•nal•ist** |-ist| *adj.* **ma•ter•nal•is•tic** |mə,tərnl'istik| *adj.* **ma•ter•nal•ly** *adv.*

mat•ins |'mætnz| • *n.* a service of morning prayer in various churches, esp. the Anglican (Episcopal) Church.
■ a service of the Western Christian Church, originally said (or chanted) at or after midnight, but historically often held with lauds on the previous evening.

ma•tri•arch |'mātrē,ärk| • *n.* a woman who is the head of a family or tribe.
■ an older woman who is powerful within a family or organization: *a domineering matriarch.*
DERIVATIVES: **ma•tri•ar•chal** |ˌmātrē'ärkəl| *adj.*

ma•tri•ar•chy |'mātrē,ärkē| • *n.* (pl. **-ies**) a system of society or government ruled by a woman or women.
■ a form of social organization in which descent and relationship are reckoned through the female line. ■ the state of being an older, powerful woman in a family or group.

mat•ri•cide |'mætrə,sīd; 'mā-| • *n.* the killing of one's mother: *a man suspected of matricide.*
■ a person who kills his or her mother.

DERIVATIVES: **mat•ri•cid•al** |ˌmætrə'sīdl; ˌmā-| *adj.*

ma•tric•u•late |mə'trikyə,lāt| • *v.* **1** [intrans.] be enrolled at a college or university: *he matriculated at Yale.*
■ [trans.] admit (a student) to membership of a college or university. **2** [trans.] record (a coat of arms) in an official register. • *n.* a person who has been matriculated.
DERIVATIVES: **ma•tric•u•lant** *n.* **ma•tric•u•la•tion** |mə,trikyə'lāsHən| *n.*

mat•ri•lin•e•al |ˌmætrə'lineəl; ˌmā-| • *adj.* of or based on kinship with the mother or the female line.
DERIVATIVES: **mat•ri•lin•e•al•ly** *adv.* **mat•ri•lin•e•al•i•ty** *n.*

ma•trix |'mātriks| • *n.* (pl. **matrices** |'mātrə,sēz| or **matrixes** |'mātriksiz|) **1** an environment or material in which something develops; a surrounding medium or structure: *free choices become the matrix of human life.*
■ a mass of fine-grained rock in which gems, crystals, or fossils are embedded. ■ the substance between living cells or in which biological structures are embedded. ■ the tissue from which a tooth, hair, feather, nail, etc. arises. ■ fine material: *the matrix of gravel paths is hoed regularly.* **2** a mold in which something, such as printing type or a phonograph record, is cast or shaped. **3** a rectangular array of numerical quantities or expressions in rows and columns that is treated as a single entity and manipulated according to particular mathematical rules.
■ an organizational structure in which two or more lines of command, responsibility, or communication may run through the same individual.

ma•tron |'mātrən| • *n.* **1** a married woman, esp. a dignified and sober middle-aged one.
■ a female prison officer. **2** a woman in charge of domestic and medical arrangements at a boarding school or other establishment.
DERIVATIVES: **ma•tron•hood** |-ˌho͝od| *n.* **ma•tron•ly** *adj.* (in sense 1 only).

matte¹ |mæt| (also **matt** or **mat**) • *adj.* (of a color, paint, or surface) dull and flat, without a shine: *matte black.* • *n.* **1** a matte color, paint, or finish: *the varnishes are available in gloss, satin, and matte.* **2** a sheet of cardboard placed on the back of a picture, either as a mount or to form a border around the picture. • *v.* (**matted, matting**) [trans.] (often **be matted**) give a matte appearance to (something).

matte² • *n.* a mask used to obscure part of an image in a film and allow another image to be substituted, combining the two.

maud•lin |'môdlin| • *adj.* self-pityingly or tearfully sentimental, often through drunkenness: *the drink made her maudlin* | *a maudlin ballad.* Cf. MAWKISH.

mau•so•le•um |ˌmôzə'lēəm; ˌmôsə-| • *n.* (pl. **mausolea** |-'lēə| or **mausoleums**) a building, esp. a large and stately one, housing a tomb or tombs.

ma•ven |'māvən| • *n.* [often with adj.] an expert or connoisseur: *fashion mavens.*

mav•er•ick |ˈmav(ə)rik| • n. 1 an unorthodox or independent-minded person: a free-thinking maverick.
■ a person who refuses to conform to a particular party or group: the maverick Connecticut Republican. 2 an unbranded calf or yearling. • adj. unorthodox: a maverick detective | a maverick approach to school financing.

mawk•ish |ˈmôkiSH| • adj. sentimental in a feeble or sickly way: a mawkish poem.
■ having a faint sickly flavor: the mawkish smell of beer.
DERIVATIVES: **mawk•ish•ly** adv. **mawk•ish•ness** n.

max•il•la |makˈsilə| • n. (pl. **maxillae** |-ˈsilē; -ˈsil,ī|) the jaw or jawbone, specifically the upper jaw in most vertebrates. In humans it also forms part of the nose and eye socket.
■ (in many arthropods) each of a pair of mouthparts used in chewing. Cf. MANDIBLE.

max•im |ˈmaksim| • n. a short, pithy statement expressing a general truth or rule of conduct: the maxim that actions speak louder than words.

ma•ya |ˈmīə; ˈmäyə| • n. the supernatural power wielded by Hindu gods and demons to produce illusions.
■ the power by which the universe becomes manifest. ■ the illusion or appearance of the phenomenal world.

may•hem |ˈmā,hem| • n. violent or damaging disorder; chaos: complete mayhem broke out.
■ a former designation for the crime of maliciously injuring or maiming someone, originally so as to render the victim defenseless.

ma•zel tov |ˈmäzəl ,tôv; ,tôf| • exclam. a Jewish phrase expressing congratulations or wishing someone good luck.

me•a cul•pa |,māə ˈko͞ol,pə; -,pä| • n. an acknowledgment of one's fault or error: [as exclam.] "Well, whose fault was that?" "Mea culpa!" Frank said.

mean • n. 1 the quotient of the sum of several quantities and their number; an average: acid output was calculated by taking the mean of all three samples. An **arithmetic mean** is calculated by adding a set of numerical values together and dividing them by the number of terms in the set. A **geometric mean** is the central number in a geometric progression (e.g. 9 in 3, 9, 27), also calculable as the nth root of a product of n numbers.
■ the term or one of the terms midway between the first and last terms of a progression. 2 a condition, quality, or course of action equally removed from two opposite (usually unsatisfactory) extremes: the mean between two extremes. • adj. [attrib.] 1 (of a quantity) calculated as a mean; average: by 1989, the mean age at marriage stood at 24.8 for women and 26.9 for men. 2 equally far from two extremes: hope is the mean virtue between despair and presumption.

me•an•der |mēˈandər| • v. (of a river or road) follow a winding course: a river that meandered gently through a meadow | [as adj.] (**meandering**) a meandering lane.
■ (of a person) wander at random: kids meandered in and out. ■ [intrans.] (of a speaker or text) proceed aimlessly or with little purpose: a stylish offbeat thriller that occasionally meanders. • n. (usu. **meanders**) a winding curve or bend of a river or road: the river flows in sweeping meanders.
■ [in sing.] a circuitous journey, esp. an aimless one: a leisurely meander around the twisting coastline road. ■ an ornamental pattern of winding or interlocking lines, e.g., in a mosaic.

me•di•a |ˈmēdēə| • n. 1 plural form of MEDIUM. 2 (usu. **the media**) [treated as sing. or pl.] the main means of mass communication (esp. television, radio, newspapers, and sometimes the Internet) regarded collectively: [as adj.] the campaign won media attention.

USAGE: The word **media** comes from the Latin plural of **medium**. The traditional view is that it should therefore be treated as a plural noun in all its senses in English and be used with a plural rather than a singular verb: the media **have** not followed the reports (rather than 'has'). In practice, in the sense 'television, radio, the press, and the Internet collectively,' it behaves as a collective noun (like **staff** or **clergy**, for example), which means that it is now acceptable in standard English for it to take either a singular or a plural verb.

me•di•a•cy |ˈmēdēəsē| • n. the quality of being mediate.

me•di•al |ˈmēdēəl| • adj. situated in the middle, in particular:
■ situated near the median plane of the body or the midline of an organ. The opposite of LATERAL. ■ (of a speech sound) in the middle of a word. ■ (esp. of a vowel) pronounced in the middle of the mouth; central.
DERIVATIVES: **me•di•al•ly** adv.

me•di•an |ˈmēdēən| • adj. [attrib.] 1 denoting or relating to a value or quantity lying at the midpoint of a range of observed values or quantities, such that there is an equal probability of a value falling above or below it: the median duration of this treatment was four months.
■ denoting the middle term of a series arranged in order of magnitude, or (if there is no middle term) the average of the middle two terms. For example, the median number of the series 55, 62, 76, 85, 93 is 76; of the series 23, 27, 29, 32 it is 28. 2 situated in the middle, esp. of the body: the median part of the sternum. • n. 1 the median value of a range of values: acreages ranged from one to fifty-two with a median of twenty-four. 2 (also **median strip**) the strip of land between the lanes of opposing traffic on a divided highway. 3 a straight line drawn from any vertex of a triangle to the midpoint of the opposite side.
DERIVATIVES: **me•di•an•ly** adv.

me•di•ate • v. |ˈmēdē,āt| 1 [intrans.] intervene between people in a dispute in order to bring about an agreement or reconciliation: Wilson

attempted to **mediate between** the powers to end the war.
■ [trans.] intervene in (a dispute) to bring about an agreement. ■ [trans.] bring about (an agreement or solution) by intervening in a dispute: *efforts to mediate a peaceful resolution of the conflict.* Cf. ARBITRATE. **2** [trans.] bring about (a result such as a physiological effect): *the right hemisphere plays an important role in mediating tactile perception of direction.*
■ be a means of conveying: *this important ministry of mediating the power of the word.* ■ form a connecting link between: *structures that mediate gender divisions.* ● adj. |'mēdēət| connected indirectly through another person or thing; involving an intermediate agency: *public law institutions are a type of mediate state administration.*
DERIVATIVES: **me·di·ate·ly** |'mēdēətlē| adv. **me·di·a·tion** |ˌmēdē'āsHən| n. **me·di·a·tor** |'mēdēˌātər| n. **me·di·a·to·ry** |'mēdēəˌtôrē| adj.
me·di·o·cre |ˌmēdē'ōkər| ● adj. of only moderate quality; not very good: *a mediocre actor.*
DERIVATIVES: **me·di·oc·ri·ty** n. : *the numbering mediocrity of radio music* | *neither candidate is more than a mediocrity.* **me·di·o·cre·ly** adv.
med·i·tate |'medəˌtāt| ● v. [intrans.] focus one's mind for a period of time, in silence or with the aid of chanting, for religious or spiritual purposes or as a method of relaxation.
■ (**meditate on/upon**) think deeply or carefully about (something): *he went off to meditate on the new idea.* ■ [trans.] plan mentally; consider: *they had suffered severely, and they began to meditate retreat.*
DERIVATIVES: **med·i·ta·tor** |-ˌtātər| n.
med·i·ta·tion |ˌmedə'tāsHən| ● n. the action or practice of meditating: *a life of meditation.*
■ a written or spoken discourse expressing considered thoughts on a subject: *his later letters are intense meditations on man's exploitation of his fellows.*
me·di·um |'mēdēəm| ● n. (pl. **media** |'mēdēə| or **mediums** |'mēdēəmz|) **1** an agency or means of doing something: *using the latest technology as a medium for job creation* | *their primitive valuables acted as a medium of exchange.*
■ a means by which something is communicated or expressed: *here the Welsh language is the medium of instruction.* **2** the intervening substance through which impressions are conveyed to the senses or a force acts on objects at a distance: *radio communication needs no physical medium between the two stations* | *the medium between the cylinders is a vacuum.*
■ the substance in which an organism lives or is cultured: *grow bacteria in a nutrient-rich medium.* **3** a liquid (e.g., oil or water) with which pigments are mixed to make paint.
■ the material or form used by an artist, composer, or writer: *oil paint is the most popular medium for glazing.* **4** (pl. **mediums**) a person claiming to be in contact with the spirits of the dead and to communicate between the dead and the living. **5** the middle quality or

state between two extremes; a reasonable balance: *you have to strike a happy medium between looking like royalty and looking like a housewife.* ● adj. about halfway between two extremes of size or another quality; average: *John is six feet tall, of medium build* | *medium-length hair.*
■ (of cooked meat) halfway between rare and well-done: *I wanted my burger to be medium.*
DERIVATIVES: **me·di·um·ism** |-ˌmizəm| n. (in sense 4). **me·di·um·is·tic** |ˌmēdēə'mistik| adj. (in sense 4). **me·di·um·ship** |-ˌsHip| n. (in sense 4).
med·ley |'medlē| ● n. (pl. **-eys**) a varied mixture of people or things; a miscellany: *a medley of flavors.*
■ a collection of songs or other musical items performed as a continuous piece: *a medley of Fats Waller songs.* ■ a swimming race in which contestants swim sections in different strokes, either individually or in relay teams: *the 400-meter individual medley.* ● adj. mixed; motley: *a medley range of vague and varied impressions.* ● v. (past and past part. **-eyed** or **-ied**) [trans.] make a medley of; intermix.
me·dul·la ob·lon·ga·ta |ˌäˌblôNG'gätə| ● n. the continuation of the spinal cord within the skull, forming the lowest and most primitive part of the brain and containing control centers for the heart and lungs.
Me·du·sa |mə'd(y)ōōsə; -zə| the only mortal gorgon of Greek mythology, whom Perseus killed by cutting off her head.
■ (**also medusa**) a terrifying or ugly woman.
meed |mēd| ● n. a deserved share or reward: *he must extract from her some meed of approbation.*
meet ● adj. suitable; fit; proper: *it is a theater meet for great events.*
DERIVATIVES: **meet·ly** adv. **meet·ness** n.
meg·a·lith |'megəˌliTH| ● n. a large stone that forms a prehistoric monument (e.g., a menhir) or part of one (e.g., a stone circle or dolmen).
meg·a·lith·ic |ˌmegə'liTHik| ● adj. of, relating to, or denoting prehistoric monuments made of or containing megaliths.
■ (often **Megalithic**) of, relating to, or denoting prehistoric cultures characterized by the erection of megalithic monuments. ■ massive or monolithic: *since June, the committee has become megalithic.*
meg·a·lo·ma·ni·a |ˌmegəlō'mānēə| ● n. obsession with the exercise of power, esp. in the domination of others.
■ delusion about one's own power or importance (typically as a symptom of psychiatric disorder); delusions of grandeur.
DERIVATIVES: **meg·a·lo·man·ic** |-'mænik| adj.
meg·a·lop·o·lis |ˌmegə'läpələs| ● n. a very large, heavily populated city or urban complex. Cf. CONURBATION; METROPLEX; METROPOLITAN AREA.
Me·gil·lah |mə'gilə| one of five books of the Hebrew scriptures (the Song of Solomon, Ruth, Lamentations, Ecclesiastes, and Esther) that are appointed to be read on cer-

tain Jewish notable days, esp. the Book of Esther, read at the festival of Purim.
■ [as n.] (also **the whole megillah**) something in its entirety, esp. a complicated set of arrangements or a long-winded story.

me•grim |'mēgrim| • n. 1 (**megrims**) depression; low spirits: *fresh air and exercise, she generally found, could banish most megrims.* 2 a whim or fancy. 3 old-fashioned term for MIGRAINE.

mei•o•sis |mī'ōsəs| • n. (pl. **meioses** |-'ō ,sēz|) 1 a type of cell division that results in two daughter cells each with half the chromosome number of the parent cell, as in the production of sex cells. Cf. MITOSIS. 2 another term for LITOTES.
DERIVATIVES: **mei•ot•ic** |mī'ätik| adj. **mei•ot•i•cal•ly** |-ik(ə)lē| adv.

mel•an•cho•li•a |,melən'kōlēə| • n. deep sadness or gloom; melancholy: *rain slithered down the windows, encouraging a creeping melancholia.*
■ formerly, a mental condition marked by persistent depression and ill-founded fears.
DERIVATIVES: **mel•an•cho•li•ac** |-'kōlē-æk| n. & adj.

mel•an•chol•y |'melən,kälē| • n. a deep, pensive, and long-lasting sadness.
■ another term for MELANCHOLIA (as a mental condition). ■ another term for black bile, one of the four bodily humors (fluids) formerly taken to be the foundation of character. • adj. sad, gloomy, or depressed: *the dog has a melancholy expression.*
■ causing or expressing sadness; depressing: *the study makes melancholy reading.*
DERIVATIVES: **mel•an•chol•ic** |,melən'kälik| adj. **mel•an•chol•i•cal•ly** |,melən'käl-ək(ə)lē| adv.

mé•lange |mā'länj| (also **melange**) • n. a mixture; a medley: *a mélange of tender vegetables and herbs.*

mel•a•nin |'melənin| • n. a dark brown to black pigment occurring in the hair, skin, and iris of the eye in people and animals. It is responsible for tanning of skin exposed to sunlight.

mel•a•nism |'melə,nizəm| • n. unusual darkening of body tissues caused by excessive production of melanin, esp. as a form of color variation in animals.
DERIVATIVES: **me•lan•ic** |mə'lænik| adj. **mel•a•nis•tic** |,melə'nistik| adj.

meld[1] |meld| • v. blend; combine: [trans.] *Australia's winemakers have melded modern science with traditional art* | [intrans.] *the nylon bristles shrivel and meld together.* • n. a thing formed by merging or blending: *a meld of many contributions.*

meld[2] • v. [trans.] (in rummy, canasta, and other card games) lay down or declare (a combination of cards) in order to score points: *my opponent melded four kings.* • n. a completed set or run of cards in any of these games.

me•lee |'mā,lā; mā'lā| (also **mêlée**) • n. a confused fight, skirmish, or scuffle: *several people were hurt in the melee.*

■ a confused mass of people: *the melee always thronging the streets.*

mel•io•rate |'mēlēə,rāt| • v. another term for AMELIORATE.
DERIVATIVES: **mel•io•ra•tion** |,mēlēə'rā-sHən| n. **mel•io•ra•tive** |'mēlēə,rātiv| adj.

mel•io•rism |'mēlēə,rizəm| • n. the belief that the world can be made better by human effort. Cf. OPTIMISM.
DERIVATIVES: **mel•io•rist** n. & adj. **mel•io•ris•tic** |,mēlēə'ristik| adj.

mel•lif•lu•ous |mə'lifləwəs| • adj. (of a voice or words) sweet or musical; pleasant to hear: *the voice was mellifluous and smooth.*
DERIVATIVES: **mel•lif•lu•ous•ly** adv. **mel•lif•lu•ous•ness** n.

me•lod•ic |mə'lädik| • adj. of, having, or producing melody: *melodic and rhythmic patterns.*
■ pleasant-sounding; melodious: *his voice was deep and melodic.*
DERIVATIVES: **me•lod•i•cal•ly** |-(ə)lē| adv.

me•lo•di•ous |mə'lōdēəs| • adj. of, producing, or having a pleasant tune; tuneful: *the melodious chant of the monks.*
■ pleasant-sounding: *a melodious voice.*
DERIVATIVES: **me•lo•di•ous•ly** adv. **me•lo•di•ous•ness** n.

mel•o•dra•ma |'melə,drämə| • n. 1 a sensational dramatic piece with exaggerated characters and exciting events intended to appeal to the emotions.
■ the genre of drama of this type. ■ language, behavior, or events that resemble drama of this kind: *what little is known of his early life is cloaked in melodrama.* 2 a play interspersed with songs and orchestral music accompanying the action, popular from the 17th to 19th cent.
DERIVATIVES: **mel•o•dram•a•tist** |,melə 'drämətist| n. **mel•o•dram•a•tize** |,melə 'drämə,tīz| v.

mem•brane |'mem,brān| • n. a pliable sheetlike structure acting as a boundary, lining, or partition in an organism.
■ a thin pliable sheet or skin of various kinds: *the concrete should include a membrane to prevent water seepage.* ■ (in biology) a microscopic double layer of lipids and proteins that bounds cells and organelles and forms structures within cells.
DERIVATIVES: **mem•bra•na•ceous** |,membrə'nāsHəs| adj. **mem•bra•ne•ous** |mem 'brānēəs| adj. **mem•bra•nous** |'membrən-əs; mem'brānəs| adj.

meme |mēm| • n. an element of a culture or system of behavior that may be considered to replicate by passing from one individual to another by nongenetic means, esp. imitation.
DERIVATIVES: **me•me•tic** |mē'metik; mə-| adj.

me•men•to |mə'men,tō| • n. (pl. **-os** or **-oes**) an object kept as a reminder or souvenir of a person or event: *you can purchase a memento of your visit.*

me•men•to mo•ri |mə'men,tō 'môrē| • n. (pl. same) an object serving as a warning or reminder of death, such as a skull.

mé•nage à trois |mā'näzH ä 't(r)wä; mə-|
• n. (pl. **ménages à trois**pronunc. same) an arrangement in which three people share a sexual relationship, typically a domestic situation involving a married couple and the lover of one of them.

men•da•cious |men'dāsHəs| • adj. not telling the truth; lying: *mendacious propaganda.*
DERIVATIVES: **men•da•cious•ly** adv. **men•da•cious•ness** n.

men•dac•i•ty |men'dæsiṯē| (pl. **-ies**) • n. untruthfulness: *a politician notorious for his mendacity* | *the mendacities of advertising.*

men•di•cant |'mendikənt| • adj. given to begging.
■ of, belonging to, or denoting one of the religious orders that originally relied solely on alms: *a mendicant friar.* • n. a beggar.
■ a member of a mendicant order.
DERIVATIVES: **men•di•can•cy** |-kənsē| n.

men•hir |'men,hir| • n. a tall upright stone of a kind erected in prehistoric times in western Europe.

me•ni•al |'mēnēəl| • adj. (of work) not requiring much skill and lacking prestige: *menial factory jobs.*
■ [attrib.] (of a servant) domestic. • n. a person with a menial job.
■ a domestic servant.
DERIVATIVES: **me•ni•al•ly** adv.

me•nor•ah |mə'nôrə| • n. (**the Menorah**) a sacred candleholder with seven branches used in the Temple in Jerusalem, originally that made by the craftsman Bezalel and placed in the sanctuary of the Tabernacle (Exod. 37:17–24).
■ a candleholder used in Jewish worship, esp. one with eight branches and a central socket used at Hanukkah.

mensch |'mencH| • n. (pl. **menschen** |'mencHən| or **mensches**) a person, esp. a man, of integrity and honor.

men•stru•ate |'menstrə,wāt; 'men,strāt| • v. [intrans.] (of a woman) discharge blood and other material from the lining of the uterus as part of the menstrual cycle (ovulation, or the usually monthly release of a reproductive egg or eggs [ovum or ova], followed by menstruation, which accompanies the elimination of an unfertilized egg from the system).

men•su•ral |'mensərəl; 'mencHərəl| • adj. of or involving measuring: *mensural investigations.*
■ (in music) involving notes of definite duration and usually a regular meter.
DERIVATIVES: **men•sur•a•ble** adj. **men•su•ra•tion** n.

men•tal•i•ty |men'tæliṯē| • n. (pl. **-ies**) 1 the characteristic attitude of mind or way of thinking of a person or group: *the yuppie mentality of the eighties.* 2 the capacity for intelligent thought.

men•tor |'men,tôr; -tər| • n. an experienced and trusted, usu. older, adviser: *he was her friend and mentor until his death in 1915.*
■ an experienced person in a company, college, or school who trains and counsels new

employees or students. • v. [trans.] to advise or train (someone, esp. a younger colleague).
DERIVATIVES: **men•tor•ship** |-,sHip| n.

me•phit•ic |mə'fiṯik| (also **mephitical**) • adj. (esp. of a gas or vapor) foul-smelling; noxious.

mer•can•tile |'mərkən,tēl; -,tīl| • adj. of or relating to trade or commerce; commercial: *the shift of wealth to the mercantile classes.*
■ of or relating to mercantilism. • n. old term for a general store: *we walked to the local mercantile.*

mer•can•til•ism |'mərkənti,lizəm; -,tē-; -,tī-| • n. belief in the benefits of profitable trading; commercialism.
■ the economic theory, developed in the late 18th cent., that trade generates wealth and is stimulated by the accumulation of profitable balances, which a government should encourage by means of protectionism.
DERIVATIVES: **mer•can•til•ist** n. & adj. **mer•can•til•is•tic** |,mərkənti'listik; -,tē-; -,tī-| adj.

mer•ce•nar•y |'mərsə,nerē| • adj. (of a person or personal behavior) primarily concerned with making money at the expense of ethics: *nothing but a mercenary dealmaker.* • n. (pl. **-ies**) a professional soldier hired to serve in a foreign army.
■ a person primarily concerned with material reward at the expense of ethics: *the sport's most infamous mercenary.*
DERIVATIVES: **mer•ce•nar•i•ly** adv. **mer•ce•nar•i•ness** n.

mer•cu•ri•al |mər,kyŏŏrēəl| • adj. 1 (of a person) subject to sudden or unpredictable changes of mood or mind: *his mercurial temperament.*
■ (of a person) sprightly; lively. 2 of or containing the element mercury. • n. (usu. **mercurials**) a drug or other compound containing mercury.
DERIVATIVES: **mer•cu•ri•al•i•ty** |mər,kyŏŏrē'ælədē| n. **mer•cu•ri•al•ly** adv.

mere • n. a lake, pond, or arm of the sea; often appearing in place names.

mer•e•tri•cious |merə'trisHəs| • adj. 1 apparently attractive but having in reality no value or integrity: *meretricious souvenirs for the tourist trade.* 2 of, relating to, or characteristic of a prostitute.
DERIVATIVES: **mer•e•tri•cious•ly** adv. **mer•e•tri•cious•ness** n.

me•rid•i•an |mə'ridēən| • n. 1 a circle of constant longitude passing through a given place on the earth's surface and the terrestrial poles.
■ (also **celestial meridian**) (in astronomy) a circle passing through the celestial poles and the zenith of a given place on the earth's surface. 2 (in acupuncture and Chinese medicine) each of a set of pathways in the body along which vital energy is said to flow. There are twelve such pathways associated with specific organs. • adj. [attrib.] relating to or situated at a meridian: *the meridian moon.*
■ of noon. ■ of the period of greatest splendor, vigor, etc.

mer•i•toc•ra•cy |ˌmerəˈtäkrəsē| • *n.* (pl. **-ies**) government or the holding of power by people selected on the basis of their ability. ▪ a society governed by such people or in which such people hold power. ▪ a ruling or influential class of educated or skilled people. DERIVATIVES: **mer•i•to•crat** *n.* **mer•i•to• crat•ic** |ˌmerətəˈkrætik| *adj.*

mer•o•nym |ˈmerəˌnim| • *n.* a term that denotes part of something but that is used to refer to the whole of it, e.g., *heads* when used to mean *people* in *some of the best heads in government have considered the issue.* Cf. METONYMY.
DERIVATIVES: **mer•on•y•mous** *adj.* **mer• on•y•my** |məˈränəmē| *n.*

me•sa |ˈmāsə| • *n.* a flat-topped hill or plateau with steep sides, found in landscapes with horizontal strata; a tableland. Cf. BUTTE.

mé•sal•li•ance |ˌmāzəˈlēəns; ˌmāˌzælˈyäNs| • *n.* a marriage with a person thought to be unsuitable or of a lower social position.

mes•ca•line |ˈmeskəlin; -ˌlēn| • *n.* a hallucinogenic and intoxicating compound present in mescal buttons from the peyote cactus.

me•shu•ga |məˈSHŌŌgə| (also **meshugga** or **meshugah**) • *adj.* (of a person) mad; idiotic: *either a miracle is taking place, or we're all meshuga.*
DERIVATIVES: **me•shug•ge•ner** *adj.*

me•shu•gaas |məSHŌŌgˈäs| • *n.* mad or idiotic ideas or behavior: *there's method in this man's meshugaas.*

mes•mer•ism |ˈmezməˌrizəm| • *n.* the therapeutic system of Austrian physician F. A. Mesmer (1734–1815), which was influential in the development of hypnotism. ▪ (in general use) hypnotism.
DERIVATIVES: **mes•mer•ist** |-ist| *n.*

mes•mer•ize |ˈmezməˌrīz| • *v.* [trans.] (often **be mesmerized**) hold the attention of (someone) to the exclusion of all else or so as to transfix: *she was mesmerized by the blue eyes that stared so intently into her own* | [as adj.] (**mesmerizing**) *a mesmerizing stare.* ▪ hypnotize (someone).
DERIVATIVES: **mes•mer•i•za•tion** |ˌmez- mərəˈzāSHən| *n.* **mes•mer•iz•er** *n.* **mes• mer•iz•ing•ly** *adv.*

mesne |mēn| • *adj.* (in law) intermediate; intervening: *mesne process.*

mes•o•morph |ˈmezəˌmôrf; ˈmē-| • *n.* a person with a compact and muscular body build. Cf. ECTOMORPH; ENDOMORPH.
DERIVATIVES: **mes•o•mor•phic** |ˌmezə ˈmôrfik; ˌmē-| *adj.*

Mes•si•ah |məˈsīə| • *n.* **1** (**the Messiah**) the promised deliverer of the Jewish nation prophesied in the Hebrew Bible. ▪ Jesus regarded by Christians as the Messiah of the Hebrew prophecies and the savior of humankind. **2** a leader or savior of a particular group or cause: *to Germany, Hitler was more a messiah than a political leader.*
DERIVATIVES: **mes•si•ah•ship** |-ˌSHip| *n.*

mes•si•an•ic |ˌmesēˈænik| • *adj.* (also **Messianic**) of or relating to the Messiah: *the messianic role of Jesus.*

▪ inspired by hope or belief in a messiah: *the messianic expectations of that time.* ▪ fervent or passionate: *a messianic zeal to reform the practice of politics.*
DERIVATIVES: **mes•si•a•nism** |ˈmesēə ˌnizəm; məˈsīə-| *n.*

mes•ti•zo |meˈstēzō| • *n.* (pl. **-os**) (feminine **mestiza**) (in Latin America) a man of mixed race, esp. the offspring of European (primarily Spanish) and native parents. Cf. MÉTIS.

me•tab•o•lism |məˈtæbəˌlizəm| • *n.* the chemical processes that occur within a living organism in order to maintain life.

Two kinds of metabolism are often distinguished, often called *anabolism*), the synthesis of the proteins, carbohydrates, and fats that form tissue and store energy, and **destructive metabolism** (formerly called *catabolism*), the breakdown of complex substances and the consequent production of energy and waste matter.

DERIVATIVES: **met•a•bol•ic** |ˈmetəˈbälik| *adj.* **met•a•bol•i•cal•ly** |ˌmetəˈbälik(ə)lē| *adv.*

met•a•fic•tion |ˈmetəˌfiksHən| • *n.* fiction in which the author self-consciously alludes to the artificiality or literariness of a work by parodying or departing from novelistic conventions (esp. naturalism) and traditional narrative techniques.
DERIVATIVES: **met•a•fic•tion•al** |ˌmetə ˈfiksHənl| *adj.*

met•a•lan•guage |ˈmetəˌlæNG(g)wij| • *n.* a form of language or set of terms used for the description or analysis of another language. ▪ (in logic) a system of propositions about propositions.

met•a•mor•phic |ˈmetəˈmôrfik| • *adj.* **1** denoting rocks or minerals that have undergone transformation by heat, pressure, or other natural agencies, e.g., in the folding of strata or the nearby intrusion of igneous rocks. ▪ of or relating to such rocks or changes affecting them: *metamorphic hardening.* **2** of or marked by metamorphosis: *the shift from dead calm to hurricane-force winds was as metamorphic as Jekyll to Hyde.*
DERIVATIVES: **met•a•mor•phism** *n.*

met•a•mor•pho•sis |ˌmetəˈmôrfəsəs| • *n.* (pl. **metamorphoses** |-fəˌsēz|) (in an insect or amphibian) the process of transformation from an immature form to an adult form in two or more distinct stages. Cf. IMAGO, LARVA, PUPA. ▪ a change of the form or nature of a thing or person into a completely different one, by natural or supernatural means: *his metamorphosis from presidential candidate to talk-show host.*

met•a•noi•a |ˌmetəˈnoiə| • *n.* change in one's way of life resulting from penitence or spiritual conversion.

met•a•phor |ˈmetəˌfôr; -fər| • *n.* a figure or style of speech or writing in which a word or phrase is applied to an object or action to which it is not literally applicable: *"I had*

fallen through the trapdoor of depression," said Mark, *who was fond of theatrical metaphors|* the poetry depends on suggestion and metaphor.
■ a thing regarded as representative or symbolic of something else, esp. something abstract: *the amounts of money being lost by the company were enough to make it a metaphor for an industry that was teetering.* Cf. SIMILE. DERIVATIVES: **met•a•phor•ic** |ˈmetəˈfôrik| *adj.* **met•a•phor•i•cal** |ˌmetəˈfôrikəl| *adj.* **met•a•phor•i•cal•ly** |ˌmetəˈfôrik(ə)lē| *adv.*

met•a•phys•i•cal |ˈmetəˈfizikəl| • *adj.* **1** of or relating to metaphysics: *the essentially metaphysical question of the nature of the mind.*
■ based on abstract (typically, excessively abstract) reasoning: *an empiricist rather than a metaphysical view of law.* ■ transcending physical matter or the laws of nature: *Good and Evil are inextricably linked in a metaphysical battle across space and time.* **2** of or characteristic of the English poets of the 17th century whose work exhibited subtlety of thought and complex imagery (the metaphysical poets). • *n.* (**the Metaphysicals**) the metaphysical poets. DERIVATIVES: **met•a•phys•i•cal•ly** |-ik(ə)-lē| *adv.*

met•a•phys•ics |ˈmetəˌfiziks| • *plural n.* [usu. treated as sing.] the branch of philosophy that deals with the first principles of things, including abstract concepts such as being, knowing, substance, cause, identity, time, and space.
■ abstract theory or talk with no basis in reality: *his concept of society as an organic entity is, for market liberals, simply metaphysics.* DERIVATIVES: **met•a•phy•si•cian** |-fəˈziSHən| *n.*

me•tas•ta•sis |məˈtæstəsəs| • *n.* (pl. **metastases** |-ˌsēz|) the development of secondary malignant growths at a distance from a primary site of a cancer.
■ a growth of this type. DERIVATIVES: **met•a•stat•ic** |ˌmetəˈstætik| *adj.* **me•tas•ta•size** *v.*

me•tath•e•sis |məˈtæTHəsəs| • *n.* (pl. **metatheses** |-ˌsēz|) **1** the transposition of sounds or letters in a word, esp. one occurring in the development of a language over time. **2** (also **metathesis reaction**) a chemical reaction in which two compounds exchange ions, typically with precipitation of an insoluble product. DERIVATIVES: **me•tath•e•size** *v.* **met•a•thet•ic** |ˌmetəˈTHetik| *adj.* **met•a•thet•i•cal** |ˌmetəˈTHetikəl| *adj.*

mete[1] |mēt| • *v.* [trans.] (**mete something out**) dispense or allot (justice, a punishment, or harsh treatment): *he denounced the maltreatment meted out to minorities.*
■ (in biblical use) measure out: *with what measure ye mete, it shall be measured to you again.*

mete[2] • *n.* (usu. **metes and bounds**) a boundary or boundary stone.

me•tem•psy•cho•sis |ˌmetəm,sīˈkōsəs; mə ˌtemsīˈkōsəs| • *n.* (pl. **metempsychoses** |-ˌsēz|) the supposed transmigration at death of the soul of a human being or animal into a new body of the same or a different species. DERIVATIVES: **me•tem•psy•chot•ic** |-ˈkätik| *adj.* **me•tem•psy•chot•i•cal•ly** |-ˈkätik(ə)lē| *adv.* **me•tem•psy•cho•sist** |-ˈkō-sist| *n.*

me•ter |ˈmētər| (Brit. **metre**) • *n.* the fundamental unit of length in the metric system, equal to 100 centimeters or approximately 39.37 inches.
■ (—— **meters**) a race over a specified number of meters: *he placed third in the 1,000 meters.* DERIVATIVES: **me•ter•age** |-ij| *n.*

me•thod•i•cal |məˈTHädikəl| • *adj.* done according to a systematic or established form of procedure: *a methodical approach to the evaluation of computer systems.*
■ (of a person) orderly or systematic in thought or behavior. DERIVATIVES: **me•thod•ic** *adj.* **me•thod•i•cal•ly** |-ik(ə)lē| *adv.*

Meth•od•ist |ˈmeTHədəst| • *n.* a member of a Christian Protestant denomination originating in the 18th-century evangelistic movement of Charles and John Wesley and George Whitefield.

The Methodist Church grew out of a religious society established within the Church of England, from which it formally separated in 1791. It is particularly strong in the US and now constitutes one of the largest Protestant denominations worldwide, with more than 30 million members. Methodism has a strong tradition of missionary work and concern with social welfare, and emphasizes the believer's personal relationship with God.

• *adj.* of or relating to Methodists or Methodism: *a Methodist chapel.* DERIVATIVES: **Meth•od•ism** |-ˌdizəm| *n.* **Meth•od•is•tic** |ˌmeTHəˈdistik| *adj.* **Meth•od•is•ti•cal** |ˌmeTHəˈdistikəl| *adj.*

meth•od•ol•o•gy |ˌmeTHəˈdäləjē| • *n.* (pl. **-ies**) a system of methods used in a particular area of study or activity: *a methodology for investigating the concept of focal points|* *courses in research methodology and practice.* DERIVATIVES: **meth•od•o•log•i•cal** |-də ˈläjikəl| *adj.* **meth•od•o•log•i•cal•ly** |dəˈläjik(ə)lē| *adv.* **meth•od•ol•o•gist** |-ˈdäləjist| *n.*

me•tic•u•lous |məˈtikyələs| • *adj.* showing great attention to detail; very careful and precise: *he had always been so meticulous about his appearance.* DERIVATIVES: **me•tic•u•lous•ly** *adv.* **me•tic•u•lous•ness** *n.*

mé•tier |meˈtyā; ˈme,tyā| • *n.* a trade, profession, or occupation: *those who work honestly at their métier.*
■ an occupation or activity that one is good at: *she decided that her real métier was grand opera.*
■ an outstanding or advantageous characteristic: *subtlety is not his métier.* Cf. FORTE[1].

mé•tis |māˈtēs| (also **Metis**) • *n.* (pl. same) (esp. in western Canada) a person of mixed

American Indian and Euro-American ancestry, in particular one of a group of such people who in the 19th century constituted the so-called **Métis nation** in the areas around the Red and Saskatchewan rivers. • adj. denoting or relating to such people.

me•ton•y•my |məˈtänəmē| • n. (pl. -ies) the substitution of the name of an attribute or adjunct for that of the thing meant, for example *suit* for *business executive*, or *the track* for *horse racing.* Cf. MERONYM.
DERIVATIVES: **met•o•nym** n. **met•o•nym•ic** |ˌmetəˈnimik| adj. **met•o•nym•i•cal** |ˌmetəˈnimikəl| adj. **met•o•nym•i•cal•ly** |ˌmetəˈnimik(ə)lē| adv.

met•ric[1] |ˈmetrik| • adj. **1** of or based on the meter as a unit of length; relating to the metric system: *all measurements are given in metric form.*
■ using the metric system: *we should have gone metric years ago.* **2** (in mathematics and physics) relating to or denoting a metric. • n. **1** a system or standard of measurement.
■ (in mathematics and physics) a binary function of a topological space that gives, for any two points of the space, a value equal to the distance between them, or to a value treated as analogous to distance for the purpose of analysis. **2** metric units, or the metric system: *it's easier to work in metric.*

met•ric[2] • adj. relating to or composed in a poetic meter. • n. (**metrics**) [treated as sing.] the meter of a poem.

met•ro•nome |ˈmetrəˌnōm| • n. a device used by musicians (esp. pianists) that marks time at a selected rate by giving a regular tick.
DERIVATIVES: **met•ro•nom•ic** |ˌmetrəˈnämik| adj. : *he appeared at my door with metronomic regularly.* **met•ro•nom•i•cal•ly** |ˌmetrəˈnämik(ə)lē| adv.

met•ro•plex |ˈmetrəˌpleks| • n. a very large metropolitan area, esp. one that is an aggregation of two or more cities.
■ (**the Metroplex**) popular name for the Dallas-Forth Worth area. Cf. CONURBATION; MEGALOPOLIS; METROPOLITAN AREA.

me•trop•o•lis |məˈträp(ə)ləs| • n. the capital or chief city of a country or region.
■ a very large and densely populated industrial and commercial city.

met•ro•pol•i•tan |ˌmetrəˈpälətn| • adj. **1** of, relating to, or denoting a metropolis. **2** of, relating to, or denoting the parent state of a colony or dependency: *metropolitan Spain.* **3** of, relating to, or denoting a metropolitan or his see: *a metropolitan bishop.* • n. **1** a bishop having authority over the bishops of a province, in particular (in many Orthodox Churches) one ranking above archbishop and below patriarch. **2** an inhabitant of a metropolis: *the sophisticated metropolitan.* Cf. COSMOPOLITAN.
DERIVATIVES: **me•tro•pol•i•tan•ate** |-ˈpälətnˌāt | n. (only of the noun). **met•ro•pol•i•tan•ism** |-ˌpälətnˌizəm| n. **met•ro•po•lit•i•cal** |-pəˈlitikəl| adj. (only of the noun).

met•tle |ˈmetl| • n. a person's ability to cope well with difficulties or to face a demanding

situation in a spirited and resilient way: *the team showed their true mettle in the second half.*
PHRASES: **be on one's mettle** be ready or forced to prove one's ability to cope well with a demanding situation.
DERIVATIVES: **met•tle•some** |-səm| adj.

mews |myōoz| • n. (pl. same) a row or street of houses or apartments that have been converted from stables or built to look like former stables.
■ a group of stables, typically with rooms above, built around a yard or along an alley.

me•zu•zah |məˈzoozə| (also **mezuza**) • n. (pl. **mezuzahs** or **mezuzas** or **mezuzot** |məˈzoozˌōt| or **mezuzoth** |məˈzoozˌōt|) a parchment inscribed with religious texts and attached in a case to the doorpost of a Jewish house as a sign of faith.
■ a small case containing such a parchment, sometimes used as a personal item: *she wore a mezuzah around her neck.*

mez•za•nine |ˈmezəˌnēn; ˌmezəˈnēn| • n. a low story between two others in a building, typically between the ground and second floors.
■ the lowest balcony of a theater, cinema, stadium, etc., or the front rows of the balcony. • adj. [attrib.] relating to or denoting unsecured, higher-yielding loans that are subordinate to bank loans and secured loans but rank above equity.

mez•zo |ˈmetsō; ˈmedzō| • n. (pl. **-os**) (also **mezzo-soprano**) a female singer with a voice pitched between soprano and contralto.
■ a singing voice of this type, or a part written for one. • adv. half, moderately.

mez•zo•tint |ˈmetsōˌtint; ˈmedzō-| • n. a print made from an engraved copper or steel plate on which the surface has been partially roughened, for shading, and partially scraped smooth, giving light areas. The technique was much used in the 17th, 18th, and early 19th centuries for the reproduction of paintings.
■ the technique or process of making pictures in this way. • v. [trans.] engrave (a picture) in mezzotint.
DERIVATIVES: **mez•zo•tint•er** n.

mi•as•ma |mīˈazmə; mē-| • n. (pl. **miasmas** or **miasmata** |-mətə|) a highly unpleasant or unhealthy smell or vapor: *a miasma of stale alcohol hung around him like marsh gas.*
■ an oppressive or unpleasant atmosphere that surrounds or emanates from something: *a miasma of despair rose from the black workshops.*
DERIVATIVES: **mi•as•mal** adj. **mi•as•mat•ic** |ˌmīəzˈmatik| adj. **mi•as•mic** |-mik| adj. **mi•as•mic•al•ly** |mik(ə)lē| adv.

mi•crobe |ˈmīˌkrōb| • n. a microorganism, esp. a bacterium causing disease or fermentation. Cf. PATHOGEN, VECTOR.
DERIVATIVES: **mi•cro•bi•al** |mīˈkrōbēəl| adj. **mi•cro•bic** |mīˈkrōbik| adj.

microcosm |ˈmīkrəˌkäzəm| (also **microcosmos**) • n. a community, place, or situation regarded as encapsulating in miniature the characteristic qualities or features of something much larger: *Berlin is a microcosm of Germany.*

■ humankind regarded as the epitome of the universe. Cf. MACROCOSM.
DERIVATIVES: **mi•cro•cos•mic** |ˌmīkrə'käzmik| *adj.* **mi•cro•cos•mi•cal•ly** |-'käzmik(ə)lē| *adv.*

mi•cro•ec•o•nom•ics |ˌmīkrō,ekə'nämiks; -,ēkə-| • *plural n.* [treated as sing.] the part of economics concerned with single factors and the effects of individual decisions. Cf. MACROECONOMICS.
DERIVATIVES: **mi•cro•ec•o•nom•ic** *adj.*

mi•cro•man•age |ˌmīkrō'mænij| • *v.* [trans.] control every part, however small, of (an enterprise or activity): *unable to delegate, he went on micromanaging.*
DERIVATIVES: **mi•cro•man•age•ment** |'mænijmənt| *n.* **mi•cro•man•ag•er** *n.*

mic•tu•rate |'mikCHəˌrāt| • *v.* [intrans.] urinate.
DERIVATIVES: **mic•tu•ri•tion** |ˌmikCHə'riSHən| *n.*

mid•den |'midn| • *n.* a dunghill or refuse heap.
■ (also **kitchen midden**) a prehistoric refuse heap associated with a site of human habitation, often a focus of scientific study.

mid•dle•brow |'midl'brow| • *adj.* (of art or literature or a system of thought) demanding or involving only a moderate degree of intellectual application, typically as a result of not deviating from convention: *middlebrow fiction, only a step above mass appeal.* • *n.* a person who is capable of or enjoys only a moderate degree of intellectual effort.

Mid•dle Eng•lish • *n.* the English language from *c.*1150 to *c.*1470, reflecting the post-conquest (post-1066) influence of Norman French on OLD ENGLISH.

midg•et |'mijit| • *n.* an extremely or unusually small person, usu. one with normal proportions. Cf. DWARF, MANIKIN. • *adj.* [attrib.] very small: *a midget submarine.*

mid•ship•man |'mid,SHipmən; mid'SHip-| • *n.* (pl. **-men**) a cadet in the US Navy or student at the US Naval Academy.
■ a rank of officer in the (British) Royal Navy, above naval cadet and below sublieutenant.

mid•wife |'mid,wīf| • *n.* (pl. **-wives**) a person (typically a woman) trained to assist women in childbirth.
■ a person or thing that helps to bring something into being or assists its development: *he survived to be one of the midwives of the Reformation.* • *v.* [trans.] assist (a woman) during childbirth.
■ bring into being: *revolutions midwifed by new technologies of communication.*
DERIVATIVES: **mid•wife•ry** |mid'wīf(ə)rē; -'wīf(ə)rē| *n.*

mien |mēn| • *n.* a person's look or manner, esp. one of a particular kind indicating character or mood: *he has a cautious, academic mien | her mien was somber.* Cf. COUNTENANCE.

miff |mif| • *v.* [trans.] (usu. **be miffed**) put out of humor; offend; annoy: *she was slightly miffed at not being invited.* • *n.* a petty quarrel or fit of pique.

DERIVATIVES: **mif•fy** *adj.*

mi•graine |'mī,grān| • *n.* a recurrent throbbing headache that typically affects one side of the head and is often accompanied by nausea and disturbed vision: *such severe migraines that she could not work.*
DERIVATIVES: **mi•grain•ous** |-,grānəs| *adj.*

mi•grate |'mī,grāt| • *v.* [intrans.] (of an animal, typically a bird or fish) move from one region or habitat to another, esp. regularly according to the seasons: *as autumn arrives, the birds migrate south.*
■ (of a person) move from one area or country to settle in another, esp. in search of work: *rural populations have **migrated to** urban areas.*
■ move from one specific part of something to another: *cells that can form pigment migrate beneath the skin.* ■ (in computing) change or cause to change from using one system to another: *we're planning to migrate from a standalone to a networked environment.* ■ [trans.] transfer (programs or hardware) from one system to another.
DERIVATIVES: **mi•gra•tion** |mī'grāSHən| *n.* **mi•gra•tion•al** |mī'grāSHənl| *adj.* **mi•gra•tor** |-,grātər| *n.* **mi•gra•to•ry** |'mīgrəˌtôrē| *adj.*

mik•veh |'mikvə| (also **mikva** or **mikvah**) • *n.* (pl. **mikvehs** or **mikvahs** or **mikvoth** |mēk'vōt| or **mikvot** |mēk'vōt| or **mikvos** |-vəz; -vōs|) a bath in which certain Jewish ritual purifications are performed.
■ the action of taking such a bath.

mi•la•dy |mə'lādē; mī-| • *n.* (pl. **-ies**) used, formerly or humorously, to address or refer to a noblewoman or great lady: *I went off to milady's boudoir.*

mi•lieu |mil'yōō; -'yə(r)| • *n.* (pl. **milieux** |mil'yōō(z); -'yə(r)(z)| or **milieus** |mil'yōō(z); -'yə(r)(z)|) an environment, esp. a person's social environment: *he grew up in a military milieu.*

mil•i•tant |'milətənt| • *adj.* combative and aggressive in support of a political or social cause, and typically favoring extreme, violent, or confrontational methods: *an uprising by militant Islamic fundamentalists.* • *n.* a person who is active in this way.
DERIVATIVES: **mil•i•tan•cy** |-tənsē| *n.* **mil•i•tant•ly** *adv.*

mil•i•ta•rism |'milətəˌrizəm| • *n.* the belief or desire of a government or people that a country should maintain a strong military capability and be prepared to use it aggressively to defend or promote national interests.
DERIVATIVES: **mil•i•ta•rist** *n. & adj.* **mil•i•ta•ris•tic** |ˌmilətə'ristik| *adj.*

mil•i•tate |'milə,tāt| • *v.* [intrans.] (**militate against**) (of a fact or circumstance) be a powerful or conclusive factor in preventing: *these fundamental differences will militate against the two communities coming together.*

USAGE: The verbs **militate** and **mitigate** are often confused. See **usage** at MITIGATE.

mi•li•tia |mə'liSHə| • *n.* a military force that is raised from the civil population to supplement a regular army in an emergency.

■ a military force that engages in rebel or terrorist activities, typically in opposition to a regular army. ■ all able-bodied civilians eligible by law for military service.

milk•sop |'milk,säp| • *n.* a person who is indecisive and lacks courage. Cf. MILQUETOAST.

mil•le•nar•i•an |ˌmiləˈnerēən| • *adj.* relating to or believing in the idea that Christ will return to earth and reign for one thousand years, as suggested in Rev. 20:1–5.
■ believing in the imminence or inevitability of a golden age of peace, justice, and prosperity: *millenarian Marxists.* ■ denoting a religious or political group seeking solutions to present crises through rapid and radical transformation of politics and society. • *n.* a person who believes in the Christian doctrine of the millennium.
DERIVATIVES: **mil•le•nar•i•an•ism** *n.* **mil•le•nar•y** *n.* and *adj.*

mil•len•ni•um |məˈlenēəm| • *n.* (pl. **millennia** |-ēə| or **millenniums**) a period of a thousand years, esp. when calculated from the traditional date of the birth of Christ.
■ an anniversary of a thousand years: *the millennium of the city of Warsaw.* ■ (**the millennium**) the point at which one period of a thousand years ends and another begins. ■ (**the millennium**) the prophesied thousand-year reign of Christ at the end of the age (Rev. 20:1–5). ■ (**the millennium**) a utopian period of good government, great happiness, and prosperity.
DERIVATIVES: **mil•len•ni•al** |-ēəl| *adj.* **mil•len•ni•al•ism** *n.*

USAGE: The spelling of **millennium** is less difficult if one remembers that it comes ultimately from two Latin words containing double letters: *mille,* 'thousand,' and *annum,*'year.'

mil•li•ner |'milənər| • *n.* a person who makes or sells women's hats.
DERIVATIVES: **mil•li•ner•y** *n.*

milque•toast |'milk,tōst| (also **Milquetoast**) • *n.* a person who is timid or submissive: [as adj.] *a soppy, milquetoast composer.* Cf. MILKSOP.

mime |mīm| • *n.* **1** the theatrical technique of suggesting action, character, or emotion without words, using only gesture, expression, and movement.
■ a theatrical performance or part of a performance using such a technique. ■ an action or set of actions intended to convey the idea of another action or an idea or feeling: *she performed a brief mime of someone fencing.* ■ a practitioner of mime or a performer in a mime. **2** (in ancient Greece and Rome) a simple farcical drama including mimicry. • *v.* [trans.] use gesture and movement without words in the acting of (a play or role).
■ convey an impression of (an idea or feeling) by gesture and movement, without using words; mimic (an action or set of actions) in this way: *he stands up and mimes throwing a spear.*
DERIVATIVES: **mim•er** *n.*

mi•me•sis |məˈmēsis; mī-| • *n.* imitation, in particular:
■ representation or imitation of the real world in art and literature. ■ the deliberate imitation of the behavior of one group of people by another as a factor in social change. ■ another term for MIMICRY.

mi•met•ic |məˈmetik| • *adj.* relating to, constituting, or habitually practicing mimesis: *mimetic patterns in butterflies.*
DERIVATIVES: **mi•met•i•cal•ly** |-ik(ə)lē| *adv.*

mim•ic•ry |'miməkrē| • *n.* (pl. **-ies**) the action or art of imitating someone or something, typically in order to entertain or ridicule: *the word was spoken with gently teasing mimicry | mimicry of the techniques of realist writers.*
■ the close external resemblance of an animal or plant (or part of one) to another animal, plant, or inanimate object, typically as an evolved characteristic that haas survival value.

mi•na•cious |məˈnāsHəs| • *adj.* menacing; threatening.

min•a•ret |ˌminəˈret| • *n.* a slender tower, typically part of a mosque, with a balcony from which a muezzin calls Muslims to prayer.
DERIVATIVES: **min•a•ret•ed** *adj.*

min•a•to•ry |'minəˌtôrē; 'mī-| • *adj.* expressing or conveying a threat: *he is unlikely to be deterred by minatory finger-wagging.*

mince |mins| • *v.* [intrans.] walk with an affected delicacy or fastidiousness, typically with short quick steps: *there were plenty of secretaries mincing about.*
DERIVATIVES: **minc•er** *n.* **minc•ing•ly** *adv.*

min•gy |'minjē| • *adj.* (**mingier, mingiest**) mean and stingy: *you've been mingy with the sunscreen.*
■ unexpectedly or undesirably small: *a mingy kitchenette tucked in the corner.*
DERIVATIVES: **ming•i•ly** |'minjəlē| *adv.*

min•i•mal•ism |'minəmə,lizəm| • *n.* **1** a trend in sculpture and painting that arose in the 1950s and used simple, typically massive, forms. **2** an avant-garde movement in music characterized by the repetition of very short phrases that change gradually, producing a hypnotic effect.
DERIVATIVES: **min•i•mal•ist** *adj.* and *n.*

min•ion |'minyən| • *n.* a follower or underling of a powerful person, esp. a servile or unimportant one. Cf. LACKEY, SYCOPHANT.

min•is•te•ri•al |ˌminəˈstirēəl| • *adj.* **1** of or relating to a minister of religion. **2** of or relating to a government minister or ministers: | *ministerial officials.* **3** acting as an agent, instrument, or means in achieving a purpose: *those words of conversation which are ministerial to intellectual culture.*
■ of or relating to delegate authority: *ministerial acts.*
DERIVATIVES: **min•is•te•ri•al•ly** *adv.*

min•is•tra•tion |ˌminəˈstrāsHən| • *n.* (usu. **ministrations**) the provision of assistance or care: *a kitchen made spotless by the ministrations of* a cleaning lady.

■ the services of a minister of religion or of a religious institution. ■ the action of administering a Christian sacrament.

DERIVATIVES: **min•is•trant** |'minəstrənt| n. **min•is•tra•tive** adj.

Min•o•taur |'minə,tôr; 'mī–| (in Greek mythology) a creature who was half man and half bull, the offspring of Pasiphaë and a bull with which she fell in love. Confined in Crete in a labyrinth made by Daedalus and fed on human flesh, it was eventually slain by Theseus.

min•strel |'minstrəl| • n. a medieval singer or musician, esp. one who (in the tradition of **minstrelsy**) sang or recited lyric or heroic poetry to a musical accompaniment for the nobility.
■ a member of a band of entertainers with blackened faces who (typically, in a **minstrel show**) perform songs and music ostensibly of black American origin.

mi•nus•cule |'minə,skyŏŏl; min'əs,kyŏŏl| • adj. **1** extremely small; tiny: a minuscule fragment of cloth.
■ so small as to be negligible or insufficient: the risk of infection was believed to be minuscule. **2** of or in lowercase letters, as distinct from capitals or uncials.
■ of or in a small cursive script of the Roman alphabet, developed in the 7th century AD. • n. minuscule script.
■ a small or lowercase letter. Cf. MAJUSCULE.

DERIVATIVES: **mi•nus•cu•lar** |mə'nəskyə-lər| adj.

USAGE: The correct spelling is **minuscule** rather than **miniscule**. The latter is a common error, which has arisen by analogy with other words beginning with **mini-**, where the meaning is similarly 'very small.'

mi•nute |mī'n(y)ŏŏt; mə–| • adj. (**minutest**) extremely small: a minute fraction of an inch.
■ so small as to verge on insignificance: he will have no more than a minute chance of exercising significant influence. ■ (of an inquiry or investigation, or an account of one) taking the smallest points into consideration; precise and meticulous: a minute examination of the islands.

DERIVATIVES: **mi•nute•ly** adv. **mi•nute•ness** n.

mi•nu•ti•ae |mə'n(y)ŏŏsHē,ē; –sHē,ī| (also **minutia** |–sHē,ə; –sHə|) • plural n. the small, precise, or trivial details of something: the minutiae of everyday life.

minx |miNGks| • n. an impudent, cunning, or boldly flirtatious girl or young woman.

DERIVATIVES: **minx•ish** adj.

min•yan |'minyən| • n. (pl. **minyanim** |,minyə'nēm|) a quorum of ten men over the age of 13 required for traditional Jewish public worship.
■ a meeting of Jews for public worship.

mire |'mīr| • n. a stretch of swampy or boggy ground.
■ soft and slushy mud or dirt. ■ a situation or state of difficulty, distress, or embarrassment from which it is hard to extricate oneself: left

to squirm in a mire of new allegations. ■ a wetland area or ecosystem based on peat. • v. [trans.] (usu. **be mired**) cause to become stuck in mud: sometimes a heavy truck gets mired down.
■ (**mire someone/something in**) involve someone or something in (difficulties): the economy is mired in its longest recession since World War II.

mirth |mərTH| • n. amusement, esp. as expressed in laughter: his six-foot frame shook with mirth.

DERIVATIVES: **mirth•ful** |–fəl| adj. **mirth•ful•ly** |–fəlē| adv.

mis•an•thrope |'misən,THrōp; 'miz| (also **misanthropist** |mis'ænTHrəpist|) • n. a person who dislikes people and avoids human society.

DERIVATIVES: **mis•an•throp•ic** |,misən 'THräpik| adj. **mis•an•throp•i•cal** |,misən 'THräpikəl| adj. **mis•an•throp•i•cal•ly** |,misən'THräpik(ə)lē| adv. **mis•an•thro•py** n.

mis•ap•pre•hen•sion |,mis,æpri'hensHən| • n. a mistaken belief about or interpretation of something: she must have been laboring under the misapprehension that I was in charge.

DERIVATIVES: **mis•ap•pre•hen•sive** |–'hensiv| adj.

mis•be•got•ten |,misbə'gätn| • adj. badly conceived, designed, or planned: a misbegotten journey to Indianapolis.
■ contemptible (used as a term of abuse): you misbegotten hound! ■ (of a child) illegitimate.

mis•car•riage |'mis,kerij; –,kærij| • n. **1** the expulsion of a fetus from the womb before it is able to survive independently, esp. spontaneously or as the result of accident: his wife had a miscarriage | some pregnancies result in miscarriage. Cf. STILLBIRTH. **2** an unsuccessful outcome of something planned: the miscarriage of the project.

mis•car•ry |mis'kerē| • v. (**-ies, -ied**) [intrans.] **1** (of a pregnant woman) have a miscarriage: Wendy conceived, but she miscarried at four months. | [trans.] an ultrasound scan showed that she had miscarried her baby. **2** (of something planned) fail to attain an intended or expected outcome: such a rash crime, and one so very likely to miscarry!
■ (of a letter) fail to reach its intended destination.

mis•ceg•e•na•tion |mi,sejə'nāsHən; ,misə-jə–| • n. the interbreeding of people considered to be of different races.

mis•ci•ble |'misəbəl| • adj. (of liquids) forming a homogeneous mixture when combined: sorbitol is miscible with glycerol.

DERIVATIVES: **mis•ci•bil•i•ty** |,misə'bil-ətē| n.

mis•con•ceive |,miskən'sēv| • v. [trans.] fail to understand correctly: she was frustrated by professors who consistently misconceived her essays.
■ (usu. **be misconceived**) judge or plan badly, typically on the basis of faulty under-

standing: *criticism of the trade surplus in Washington is misconceived* | [as adj.] (**misconceived**) *misconceived notions about gypsies.*
DERIVATIVES: **mis•con•ceiv•er** *n.* **mis•con•cep•tion** *n.*

mis•con•strue |ˌmiskən'strōō| • *v.* (**misconstrues, misconstrued, misconstruing**) [trans.] interpret (something, esp. a person's words or actions) wrongly: *my advice was deliberately misconstrued.*
DERIVATIVES: **mis•con•struc•tion** |-'strək-SHən| *n.*

mis•cre•ant |'miskrēənt| • *n.* a person who behaves badly or in a way that breaks the law.
■ a heretic. • *adj.* (of a person) behaving badly or in a way that breaks a law or rule: *her miscreant husband.*
■ heretical.

mis•de•mean•or |'misdiˌmēnər| (Brit. **misdemeanour**) • *n.* a minor wrongdoing: *the defenseman can expect a lengthy suspension for his latest misdemeanor.*
■ a crime regarded in the US (and formerly in the UK) as less serious than a felony, and typically punishable by fine or by imprisonment (usu. in a jail) for less than one year.

mis en scène |ˌmēz ˌäN 'sen| • *n.* [usu. in sing.] the arrangement of scenery and stage properties in a play.
■ the setting or surroundings of an event or action.

mis•giv•ing |mis'giviNG| • *n.* (usu. **misgivings**) a feeling of doubt or apprehension about the outcome or consequences of something: *misgivings about the way the campaign is being run* | *a sense of misgiving at the prospect of retirement.*

mis•no•mer |mis'nōmər| • *n.* a wrong or inaccurate name or designation: *"horseshoe crab" is a misnomer—these creatures are not crustaceans at all.*
■ a wrong or inaccurate use of a name or term: *to call this "neighborhood policing" would be a misnomer.*

mi•sog•a•my |məˈsägəmē| • *n.* the hatred of marriage.
DERIVATIVES: **mi•sog•a•mist** |-mist| *n.*

mi•sog•y•ny |məˈsäjənē| • *n.* the hatred of women by men: *she felt she was struggling against thinly disguised misogyny.*
DERIVATIVES: **mi•sog•y•nist** *n., adj.* **mi•sog•y•nis•tic** *adj.* **mi•sog•y•nous** |-nəs| *adj.*

mis•sal |'misəl| • *n.* a book containing the texts used in the Catholic Mass throughout the year.
■ any book of prayers.

mis•sile |'misəl| • *n.* an object that is forcibly propelled at a target, either by hand or from a mechanical weapon.
■ a weapon that is self-propelled or directed by remote control, carrying a conventional or nuclear explosive.

mis•sion•ar•y |'misHəˌnerē| • *n.* (pl. **-ies**) a person sent on a religious mission, esp. one sent to promote Christianity in a foreign country. • *adj.* of, relating to, or characteris-

tic of a missionary or a religious mission: *missionary work* | *they have lost the missionary zeal they once had.*

mis•sive |'misiv| • *n.* a letter, esp. a long or official one: *he hastily banged out electronic missives.*

mis•tri•al |'mis,trī(ə)l| • *n.* a trial rendered invalid through an error in the proceedings.
■ an inconclusive trial, such as one in which the jury cannot agree on a verdict.

mi•ter |'mītər| (Brit. **mitre**) • *n.* **1** a tall hat worn by bishops and senior abbots as a symbol of office, tapering to a point at front and back with a deep cleft between.
■ a hat formerly worn by a Jewish high priest.
■ a headband worn by women in ancient Greece. **2** (also **miter joint**) a joint made between two pieces of wood or other material cut at 45° angles to form an angle of 90°.
■ a diagonal seam of two pieces of fabric that meet at a corner joining. • *v.* [trans.] join by means of a miter.

mit•i•gate |'mitəˌgāt| • *v.* [trans.] make less severe, serious, or painful: *he wanted to mitigate misery in the world.*
■ lessen the gravity of (an offense or mistake): [as adj.] (**mitigating**) *he would have faced a prison sentence but for mitigating circumstances.*
DERIVATIVES: **mit•i•ga•ble** |-gibəl| *adj.* **mit•i•ga•tion** *n.* **mit•i•ga•tive** *adj.* **mit•i•ga•tor** |-ˌgātər| *n.* **mit•i•ga•to•ry** |-gəˌtôrē| *adj.*

USAGE: The verbs **mitigate** and **militate** do not have the same meaning although the similarity of the forms has led to them being often confused. **Mitigate** means 'make (something bad) less severe,' as in *he wanted to mitigate misery in the world,* while **militate** is nearly always used in constructions with **against** to mean 'be a powerful factor in preventing,' as in *these disagreements will militate against the two communities coming together.*

mi•to•sis |mī'tōsəs| • *n.* (pl. **mitoses** |-sēz|) a type of cell division that results in two daughter cells each having the same number and kind of chromosomes as the parent nucleus, typical of ordinary tissue growth. Cf. MEIOSIS.
DERIVATIVES: **mi•tot•ic** |mī'tätik| *adj.*

mix•ol•o•gist |mik'sälə jist| • *n.* a person who is skilled at mixing cocktails and other drinks.
■ a bartender.
DERIVATIVES: **mix•ol•o•gy** |-əjē| *n.*

miz•zen |'mizən| (also **mizen**) • *n.* **1** (also **mizzenmast**) the mast immediately behind a ship's mainmast. **2** (also **mizzensail**) the lowest sail on a mizzenmast.

mne•mon•ic |nə'mänik| • *n.* a device such as a pattern of letters, ideas, or associations that assists in remembering something. • *adj.* aiding or designed to aid the memory: *a mnemonic device.*
■ of or relating to the power of memory.
DERIVATIVES: **mne•mon•i•cal•ly** |-ik(ə)-lē| *adv.*

mo•bile |ˈmōbəl; -ˌbēl; -ˌbīl| • *adj.* able to move or be moved freely or easily: *he has a major weight problem and is not very mobile | highly mobile international capital.* ■ (of the face or its features) indicating feelings with fluid and expressive movements: *her mobile features working overtime to register shock and disapproval.* ■ (of a store, library, or other service) accommodated in a vehicle so as to travel around and serve various places. ■ (of a military or police unit) equipped and prepared to move quickly to any place it is needed: *mobile army combat units.* ■ able or willing to move easily or freely between occupations, places of residence, or social classes: *an increasingly mobile and polarized society.* • *n.* |ˈmō,bēl| **1** a decorative structure that is suspended so as to turn freely in the air.

mod•al |ˈmōdl| • *adj.* **1** of or relating to mode or form as opposed to substance. **2** (in grammar) of or denoting the mood of a verb. ■ relating to a verb that expresses the mood of an accompanying infinitive (a modal verb). **3** (in statistics) of or relating to a mode; occurring most frequently in a sample or population. **4** of or denoting music using melodies or harmonies based on modes other than the ordinary major and minor scales. **5** (of a logical proposition) in which the predicate is affirmed of the subject with some qualification, or which involves the affirmation of possibility, impossibility, necessity, or contingency. • *n.* a modal word or construction.
DERIVATIVES: **mod•al•ly** |ˈmōdl-ē| *adv.*

mo•dal•i•ty |mōˈdælətē| • *n.* (pl. **-ies**) **1** modal quality: *the harmony had a touch of modality.* **2** a particular mode in which something exists or is experienced or expressed. ■ a particular method or procedure: *questions concerning the modalities of troop withdrawals.* ■ a particular form of sensory perception: *the visual and auditory modalities.*

mode |mōd| • *n.* **1** a way or manner in which something occurs or is experienced, expressed, or done: *his preferred mode of travel was a kayak | differences between language modes, namely speech and writing.* ■ an option allowing a change in the method of operation of a computer or other electronic device: *a camcorder in automatic mode.* ■ any of the distinct kinds or patterns of vibration of an oscillating system. ■ the character of a modal proposition in logic (whether necessary, contingent, possible, or impossible). ■ another term for grammatical or logical MOOD. **2** a fashion or style in clothes, art, literature, etc.: *in the Seventies, the mode for activewear took hold.* **3** the value that occurs most frequently in a given set of statistical data. Cf. MEDIAN. **4** a set of musical notes forming a scale and from which melodies and harmonies are constructed.

mo•derne |məˈdern; mä-| • *adj.* of or relating to a popularization of the art deco style marked by bright colors and geometric shapes.

■ facetiously or disparagingly denoting an ultramodern style.

mod•ern•ism |ˈmädərˌnizəm| • *n.* modern character or quality of thought, expression, or technique: *when he waxes philosophical, he comes across as a strange mix of nostalgia and modernism.* ■ a style or movement in the arts that aims to break with classical and traditional forms. ■ a movement toward modifying traditional beliefs in accordance with modern ideas, esp. in the Roman Catholic Church in the late 19th and early 20th centuries.
DERIVATIVES: **mod•ern•ist** *n.*

mod•i•cum |ˈmädikəm; ˈmōd-| • *n.* [in sing.] a small quantity of a particular thing, esp. something considered desirable or valuable: *his statement had more than a modicum of truth.*

mo•diste |mōˈdēst| • *n.* a fashionable milliner or dressmaker.

mod•u•late |ˈmäjəˌlāt| • *v.* [trans.] exert a modifying or controlling influence on: *the state attempts to modulate private business's cash flow.* ■ vary the strength, tone, or pitch of (one's voice): *we all modulate our voice by hearing it.* ■ alter the amplitude or frequency of (an electromagnetic wave or other oscillation) in accordance with the variations of a second signal, typically one of a lower frequency: *radio waves are modulated to carry the analog information of the voice.* ■ [intrans.] (in music) change from one key to another: *the first half of the melody, modulating from E minor to G.* ■ [intrans.] (**modulate into**) change from one form or condition into (another): *ideals and opinions are not modulated into authoritative journalese.*
DERIVATIVES: **mod•u•la•tion** |ˌmäjəˈlāSHən| *n.* **mod•u•la•tor** |-ˌlātər| *n.*

mod•ule |ˈmäjo͞ol| • *n.* each of a set of standardized parts or independent units that can be used to construct a more complex structure, such as an item of furniture or a building. ■ [usu. with adj.] an independent self-contained unit of a spacecraft. ■ (in computing) any of a number of distinct but interrelated units from which a program may be built up or into which a complex activity may be analyzed.

mo•dus op•e•ran•di |ˈmōdəs ˌäpəˈrændē; -ˌdī| • *n.* (pl. **modi operandi** |ˈmō,dē; ˈmō ˌdī|) [usu. in sing.] a particular way or method of doing something, esp. one that is characteristic or well-established: *the volunteers were instructed to buy specific systems using our usual modus operandi—anonymously and with cash.* ■ the way something operates or works. Abbreviation: **MO** or **m.o.**

mo•gul |ˈmōgəl| • *n.* an important or powerful person, esp. in the motion picture or media industry.

moi•e•ty |ˈmoiətē| • *n.* (pl. **-ies**) each of two parts into which a thing is or can be divided. ■ each of two social or ritual groups into which a people is divided, esp. among Australian

Aboriginals and some American Indians. ■ a part or portion, esp. a lesser share. ■ a distinct part of a large molecule: *the enzyme removes the sulfate moiety.*

moire |mô'rā; mwä-; mwär| (also **moiré** |mwä'rā; mô-|) • *n.* silk fabric that has been subjected to heat and pressure rollers after weaving to give it a rippled appearance. • *adj.* (of silk) having a rippled, lustrous finish.
■ denoting or showing a pattern of irregular wavy lines like that of such silk, produced by the superposition at a slight angle of two sets of closely spaced lines.

mold•er |'mōldər| (Brit. **moulder**) • *v.* [intrans.] [often as adj.] (**moldering**) slowly decay or disintegrate, esp. because of neglect: *there was a mushroomy smell of disuse and moldering books.* | *I couldn't permit someone of your abilities to* **molder away** *in a backwater.*

mol•e•cule |'mälə,kyōōl| • *n.* a group of atoms bonded together, representing the smallest fundamental unit of a chemical compound that can take part in a chemical reaction.
DERIVATIVES: **mo•lec•u•lar** *adj.*

mol•li•fy |'mälə,fī| • *v.* (**-ies, -ied**) [trans.] appease the anger or anxiety of (someone): *nature reserves were set up around the power stations to mollify local conservationists.* | [as adj.] *removal of riders to the bill had a mollifying effect on critics.*
■ reduce the severity of (something); soften.
DERIVATIVES: **mol•li•fi•ca•tion** |,mäləfə'kāSHən| *n.* **mol•li•fi•er** *n.*

mol•ly•cod•dle |'mälē,kädl| • *v.* [trans.] treat (someone) very indulgently or protectively. • *n.* an effeminate or ineffectual man or boy; a milksop.

molt |mōlt| (Brit. **moult**) • *v.* [intrans.] (of an animal) shed old feathers, hair, or skin, or an old shell, to make way for a new growth: *the adult birds were already molting into their winter shades of gray* | [trans.] *the snake molts its skin.*
■ (of hair or feathers) fall out to make way for new growth: *the last of his juvenile plumage had molted.* • *n.* a loss of plumage, skin, or hair, esp. as a regular feature of an animal's life cycle.

mol•ten |'mōltn| • *adj.* (esp. of materials with a high melting point, such as metal and glass) liquefied by heat.

mo•men•tous |mō'men(t)əs; mə'-| • *adj.* (of a decision, event, or change) of great importance or significance, esp. in its bearing on the future: *a period of momentous changes in East-West relations.*
DERIVATIVES: **mo•men•tous•ly** *adv.* **mo•men•tous•ness** *n.*

mo•men•tum |mō'mentəm; mə-| • *n.* (pl. **momenta** or **momentums**) **1** the quantity of motion of a moving body, measured as a product of its mass and velocity. **2** the impetus gained by a moving object: *the vehicle* **gained momentum** *as the road dipped.*
■ the impetus and driving force gained by the development of a process or course of events: *the investigation* **gathered momentum** *in the spring.*

mon•ad |'mō,næd| • *n.* a single unit; the number one. Cf. DYAD; TRIAD.
■ (in the philosophy of Gottfried Leibniz, 1646–1716) an indivisible and hence ultimately simple entity, such as an atom or a person. ■ a name formerly used for a single-celled organism, esp. a flagellate protozoan, or a single cell.
DERIVATIVES: **mo•nad•ic** |mō'nædik; mə-| *adj.* **mon•ad•ism** |-,izəm| *n.* (in philosophy).

mo•nad•nock |mə'næd,näk| • *n.* an isolated hill or ridge of erosion-resistant rock rising above a peneplain.

mo•nas•tic |mə'næstik| • *adj.* of or relating to monks, nuns, or others living under religious vows, or the buildings in which they live: *a monastic order.*
■ resembling or suggestive of monks or their way of life, esp. in being austere, solitary, or celibate: *a monastic student bedroom.* • *n.* a monk or other follower of a monastic rule.
DERIVATIVES: **mo•nas•ti•cal•ly** |-ik(ə)lē| *adv.* **mo•nas•ti•cism** |-tə,sizəm| *n.*

mon•e•ta•rism |'mänətə,rizəm; 'mən-| • *n.* the theory or practice of controlling the supply of money as the chief method of stabilizing the economy.
DERIVATIVES: **mon•e•ta•rist** *n.* & *adj.* **mon•e•tar•is•tic** *adj.*

mon•e•tize |'mänə,tīz| • *v.* [trans.] convert into or express in the form of currency: *must we monetize everything, even relaxation?*
■ [usu. as adj.] (**monetized**) adapt (a society) to the use of money: *a fully monetized society.* Cf. DEMONETIZE.
DERIVATIVES: **mon•e•ti•za•tion** |,mänədə'zāSHən; ,mänə,tī'zāSHən| *n.*

Mon•gol•oid |'mäNGgə,loid| • *adj.* **1** of or relating to the broad and now somewhat dated division of humankind including the indigenous peoples of eastern Asia, Southeast Asia, and the Arctic region of North America. **2** (**mongoloid**) (older and now considered offensive) affected with Down syndrome. • *n.* **1** a person of a Mongoloid physical type. **2** offensive a person with Down syndrome.

USAGE: 1 The terms **Mongoloid**, **Negroid**, **Caucasoid**, and **Australoid** were introduced by 19th-century anthropologists attempting to classify human racial types, but today they are recognized as having limited validity as scientific categories. Although occasionally used when making broad generalizations about the world's populations, in most modern contexts they are potentially offensive, esp. when used of individuals. Instead, the names of specific peoples or nationalities should be used wherever possible.
2 The term **mongol**, or **Mongoloid**, was adopted in the late 19th century to refer to a person with **Down syndrome**, owing to the similarity of some of the physical symptoms of the disorder with the normal facial characteristics of eastern Asian people. In mod-

ern English this use is now considered offensive. It has been replaced in scientific as well as in most general contexts by the term **Down syndrome** (first recorded in the early 1960s).

mon•i•ker |'mänikər| (also **monicker**) • *n.* a name or nickname.
DERIVATIVES: **mon•i•kered** *adj.*

mon•ism |'män,izəm; 'mō,nizəm| • *n.* a theory or doctrine that denies the existence of a distinction or duality in some sphere, such as that between matter and mind, or God and the world.
■ the doctrine that only one supreme being exists. Cf. PLURALISM.
DERIVATIVES: **mon•ist** *n.* & *adj.* **mo•nis•tic** |män'istik; mō'nistik| *adj.*

mo•ni•tion |mə'nisHən| • *n.* a warning of impending danger.
■ a formal notice from a bishop or ecclesiastical court admonishing a person not to do something specified.

mon•i•to•ry |'mänə,tôrē| • *adj.* giving or serving as a warning: *the monitory wail of an air-raid siren.* • *n.* (pl. **-ies**) (in church use) a letter of admonition from the pope or a bishop.

mon•o•chro•mat•ic |,mänəkrō'mætik| • *adj.* containing or using only one color: *monochromatic light.*
■ lacking in variety; monotonous: *her typically monochromatic acting style.*
DERIVATIVES: **mon•o•chro•mat•i•cal•ly** |-ik(ə)lē| *adv.*

mon•o•coque |'mänə,kōk; -,käk| • *n.* an aircraft or vehicle structure in which the chassis is integral with the body.

mon•o•cul•ture |'mänə,kəlCHər| • *n.* the cultivation of a single crop in a given area.
DERIVATIVES: **mon•o•cul•tur•al** |,mänə 'kəlCHərəl| *adj.*

mon•o•dy |'mänədē| • *n.* (pl. **-ies**) **1** an ode sung by a single actor in a Greek tragedy. **2** a poem lamenting a person's death. **3** music with only one melodic line, esp. an early Baroque style with one singer and continuo accompaniment.
DERIVATIVES: **mo•nod•ic** |mə'nädik| *adj.* **mon•o•dist** |-dist| *n.*

mo•nog•a•my |mə'nägəmē| • *n.* the practice or state of being married to one person at a time.
■ the practice or state of having a sexual relationship with only one partner. ■ (in zoology) the habit of having only one mate at a time. Cf. BIGAMY; POLYGAMY.
DERIVATIVES: **mo•nog•a•mist** |-mist| *n.* **mo•nog•a•mous** |-məs| *adj.* **mo•nog•a•mous•ly** |-məslē| *adv.*

mon•o•graph |'mänə,græf| • *n.* a detailed written study of a single specialized subject or an aspect of it: *a series of monographs on music in late medieval and Renaissance cities.* • *v.* [trans.] write a monograph on; treat in a monograph.
DERIVATIVES: **mo•nog•ra•pher** |mə'nägrəfər| *n.* **mo•nog•ra•phist** |mə'nägrəfist| *n.*

mon•o•lith |'mänl-iTH| • *n.* **1** a large single upright block of stone, esp. one shaped into or serving as a pillar or monument. Cf. DOLMEN; MENHIR.
■ a very large and characterless building: *the 72-story monolith overlooking the waterfront.* ■ a large block of concrete sunk in water, e.g., in the building of a dock. **2** a large and impersonal political, corporate, or social structure regarded as intractably indivisible and uniform: *states struggling to break away from the Communist monolith.*

mon•o•ma•ni•a |,mänə'mānēə| • *n.* exaggerated or obsessive enthusiasm for or preoccupation with one thing.
DERIVATIVES: **mon•o•ma•ni•ac** |-'mānē ,æk| *n.* & *adj.* **mon•o•ma•ni•a•cal** |-mə'nī əkəl| *adj.*

mo•nop•o•ly |mə'näpəlē| • *n.* (pl. **-ies**) the exclusive possession or control of the supply or trade in a commodity or service: *his likely motive was to protect his regional monopoly on furs.* **Horizontal monopoly** is the control of all business at a certain level of production in a particular market or industry. **Vertical monopoly** is control of at least one business at each level of production in a market or industry.
■ [usu. with negative] the exclusive possession, control, or exercise of something: *men don't have a monopoly on unrequited love.* ■ a company or group having exclusive control over a commodity or service: *areas where cable companies operate as monopolies.* ■ a commodity or service controlled in this way: *electricity, gas, and water were considered to be natural monopolies.*

mo•not•o•ny |mə'nätn-ē| • *n.* lack of variety and interest; tedious repetition and routine: *you can become resigned to the monotony of captivity.*
■ sameness of pitch or tone in a sound or utterance: *depression flattens the voice almost to monotony.*

mons pu•bis |'mänz 'pyōōbəs| • *n.* (pl. **montes pubis**) the rounded mass of fatty tissue lying over the joint of the pubic bones, in women typically more prominent and also called the **mons veneris** ('Venus's mount').

mon•tage |män'täzH; mōn-; mōN-| • *n.* the process or technique of selecting, editing, and piecing together separate sections of film to form a continuous whole.
■ a sequence of film resulting from this: *a dazzling montage of the movie's central banquet scene.* ■ the technique of producing a new composite whole from fragments of pictures, text, or music: *the play often verged on montage.*

mon•u•men•tal |,mänyə'mentl| • *adj.* great in importance, extent, or size: *it's been a monumental effort.*
■ (of a work of art) great in ambition and scope: *the ballet came across as one of MacMillan's most monumental works.* ■ of or serving as a monument: *additional details are found in monumental inscriptions.*

DERIVATIVES: **mon•u•men•tal•ism** *n.*
mon•u•men•tal•i•ty |ˌmänyəˌmen'tælət̯ē|
n. **mon•u•men•tal•ly** |-'mentl-ē| *adv.*
mooch |mo͞oCH| • *v.* **1** [trans.] ask for or ob-
tain (something) without paying for it: *a
bunch of your friends will show up, mooching food*
| [intrans.] *I'm mooching off you all the time.*
2 [intrans.] (**mooch around/about**) loiter in a
bored or listless manner: *he didn't want them
mooching around all day.* • *n.* (also **moocher**)
a beggar or scrounger: *Frank was a mooch who
got everything from his dad.*
mood |mo͞od| • *n.* **1** Grammar a category of
verb use, typically expressing fact (indicative
mood), command (imperative mood), question (interrogative mood), wish (optative
mood), or conditionality (subjunctive
mood).
■ a form or set of forms of a verb in an inflected language such as French, Latin, or
Greek, serving to indicate whether it expresses fact, command, wish, or conditionality. **2** Logic any of the valid forms into which
each of the figures of a categorical syllogism
may occur.
moon |mo͞on| • *v.* **1** [no obj., with adverbial] be-
have or move in a listless and aimless man-
ner: *lying in bed eating candy, mooning around.*
■ act in a dreamily infatuated manner: *Tim's
mooning over her like a schoolboy.* **2** [trans.]
expose one's buttocks to (someone) in order
to insult or amuse them: *Dan whipped around,
bent over, and mooned the crowd.*
moon•y |'mo͞onē| • *adj.* (**moonier, mooni-
est**) (of a person) dreamy and unaware of
one's surroundings, for example because one
is in love: *she's not drunk, but still smiling in the
same moony way* | *little girls go moony over
horses.*
moot |mo͞ot| • *adj.* subject to debate, dispute,
or uncertainty, and typically not admitting of
a final decision: *whether the temperature rise
was mainly due to the greenhouse effect was **a
moot point**.*
■ having no practical significance, typically because the subject is too uncertain to allow a
decision: *it is moot whether this phrase should be
treated as metaphor or not.* ■ no longer relevant, typically because of a change of circumstances: *what it's worth is moot because it's no
longer for sale.* • *v.* [trans.] (usu. **be mooted**)
raise (a question or topic) for discussion; suggest (an idea or possibility): *Sylvia needed a
vacation, and a trip to Ireland had been mooted.*
• *n.* **1** Brit. an assembly held for debate, esp. in
Anglo-Saxon and medieval times.
■ a regular gathering of people having a common interest. **2** (also **moot court**) a mock
trial set up to examine a hypothetical case as
an academic exercise.
mor•al |'môrəl; 'mär-| • *adj.* concerned with
the principles of right and wrong behavior
and the goodness or badness of human character: *the moral dimensions of medical interven-
tion* | *a moral judgment.*
■ concerned with or adhering to the code of
interpersonal behavior that is considered
right or acceptable in a particular society: *an*

*individual's ambitions may get out of step with
the general moral code.* ■ holding or manifest-
ing high principles for proper conduct: *he is a
caring, efficient, moral man.* ■ derived from or
based on ethical principles or a sense of these:
*the moral obligation of society to do something
about the inner city's problems.* ■ [attrib.] examining the nature of ethics and the foundations
of good and bad character and conduct:
moral philosophers. • *n.* **1** a lesson, esp. one
concerning what is right or prudent, that can
be derived from a story, a piece of information, or an experience: *the moral of this
story was that one must see the beauty in what
one has.* **2** (**morals**) a person's standards of
behavior or beliefs concerning what is and is
not acceptable to do: *the corruption of public
morals.*
■ standards of behavior that are considered
good or acceptable: *they believe addicts have no
morals and cannot be trusted.*
mor•al•ist |'môrəlist| • *n.* a person who
teaches or promotes morality.
■ a person given to moralizing. ■ a person who
behaves in a morally commendable way.
DERIVATIVES: **mor•al•is•tic** |ˌmôrə'listik|
adj. **mor•al•is•ti•cal•ly** |ˌmôrə'listik(ə)lē|
adv.
mor•al•ize |'môrəˌlīz; 'mär-| • *v.* [intrans.]
[often as n.] (**moralizing**) comment on issues of right and wrong, typically with an
unfounded air of superiority: *the self-
righteous moralizing of his aunt was ringing in
his ears.*
■ [trans.] interpret or explain as giving lessons
on good and bad character and conduct:
*mythographers normally moralize Narcissus as
the man who wastes himself in pursuing worldly
goods.* ■ [trans.] reform the character and conduct of: *he endeavored to moralize an immoral
society.*
DERIVATIVES: **mor•al•i•za•tion** |ˌmôrələ
'zāSHən; ˌmär-| *n.* **mor•al•iz•er** *n.* **mor•al•
iz•ing•ly** *adv.*
mo•rass |mə'ræs; mô-| • *n.* an area of muddy
or boggy ground.
■ a complicated or confused situation: *lost in **a
morass** of lies and explanations.*
mor•a•to•ri•um |ˌmôrə'tôrēəm; ˌmär-| • *n.*
(pl. **moratoriums** |ˌmôrə'tôrēəmz| or **mor-
atoria** |-ēə|) a postponement or temporary
prohibition of an activity: *an indefinite mor-
atorium on the use of drift nets.*
■ a legal authorization to debtors to postpone payment. ■ the period of this postponement.
mor•bid |'môrbəd| • *adj.* **1** characterized by
or appealing to an abnormal and unhealthy
interest in disturbing and unpleasant subjects, esp. death and disease: *a morbid fascination with the horrors of warfare.* **2** of the nature
of or indicative of disease: *the treatment of morbid obesity.*
DERIVATIVES: **mor•bid•i•ty** |môr'bidət̯ē|
n. **1** the quality or conditioning of being dis-
eased or ill. **2** prevalence of disease, esp. in a
given area. **mor•bid•ly** *adv.* **mor•bid•ness**
n.

mor•da•cious |môr'dāsʜəs| • *adj.* **1** denoting or using biting sarcasm or invective. **2** (of a person or animal) given to biting.
DERIVATIVES: **mor•da•ci•ty** *n.*

mor•dant |'môrdnt| • *adj.* (esp. of humor) having or showing a sharp or critical quality; biting: *a mordant sense of humor.* • *n.* a substance, typically an inorganic oxide, that combines with a dye or stain and thereby fixes it in a material.
■ an adhesive compound for fixing gold leaf.
■ a corrosive liquid used to etch the lines on a printing plate. • *v.* [trans.] impregnate or treat (a fabric) with a mordant.
DERIVATIVES: **mor•dan•cy** |-dnsē| *n.* **mor•dant•ly** *adv.*

mor•dent |'môrdnt| • *n.* a musical ornament consisting of a rapid alternation of a written note with the note immediately below or above it in the scale (sometimes further distinguished as **lower mordent** and **upper mordent**). The term **inverted mordent** usually refers to the **upper mordent**.

mo•res |'môr,āz| • *plural n.* the essential or characteristic customs and conventions of a community: *an offense against social mores.*

mor•i•bund |'môrə,bənd; 'mär-| • *adj.* (of a person) at the point of death.
■ (of a thing) in terminal decline; lacking vitality or vigor: *the moribund farm property market.*
DERIVATIVES: **mor•i•bun•di•ty** |,môrə'bəndətē; ,mär-| *n.*

mo•ron |'môr,än| • *n.* a stupid person.
■ a formerly used classification fo an adult with a mental age of between 8 and 12.
DERIVATIVES: **mo•ron•ic** |mə'ränik; mô-| *adj.* **mo•ron•i•cal•ly** |mə'ränik(ə)lē; mô-| *adv.*

morph • *v.* change or cause to change smoothly from one image to another by small gradual steps using computer animation techniques: *3-D objects can be morphed into other objects* | *you see her face morphing into the creature's face.* • *n.* an image that has been processed in this way.
■ an instance of changing an image in this way.

mor•pheme |'môr,fēm| • *n.* a meaningful morphological unit of a language that cannot be further divided (e.g., the three units *in*, *come*, *-ing*, forming *incoming*).
■ a morphological element considered with respect to its functional relations in a linguistic system.
DERIVATIVES: **mor•phe•mic** |môwr'fēkʜ mik| *adj.* **mor•phe•mi•cal•ly** |môr 'fēmik(ə)lē| *adv.*

mor•phol•o•gy |môr'fäləjē| • *n.* (pl. **-ies**) the study of the forms of things, in particular:
■ the branch of biology that deals with the form of living organisms, and with relationships between their structures. ■ the study of the forms of words.
DERIVATIVES: **mor•pho•log•ic** |,môrfə 'läjik| *adj.* **mor•pho•log•i•cal** |,môrfə'läji-kəl| *adj.* **mor•pho•log•i•cal•ly** |,môrfə'läji-k(ə)lē| *adv.* **mor•phol•o•gist** |-jist| *n.*

mort•gage |'môrgij| • *n.* the charging of real (or personal) property by a debtor to a creditor as security for a debt (esp. one incurred by the purchase of the property), on the condition that it shall be returned on payment of the debt within a certain period.
■ a deed effecting such a transaction. ■ a loan obtained through the conveyance of property as security: *I put down a hundred thousand in cash and took out a mortgage for the rest.* • *v.* [trans.] (often **be mortgaged**) convey (a property) to a creditor as security on a loan: *the estate was mortgaged up to the hilt.*
■ expose to future risk or constraint for the sake of immediate advantage: *some people worry that selling off federal assets mortgages the country's future.*
DERIVATIVES: **mort•gage•a•ble** *adj.*

mort•ga•gee |,môrgə'jē| • *n.* the lender in a mortgage, typically a bank.

mort•ga•gor |,môrgə'jôr; 'môrgijər| • *n.* the borrower in a mortgage, typically a homeowner.

mor•ti•fy |'môrtə,fī| • *v.* (**-ies, -ied**) [trans.] **1** (often **be mortified**) cause (someone) to feel embarrassed, ashamed, or humiliated: [with obj. and infinitive] *she was mortified to see wrinkles in the mirror* | [as adj.] (**mortifying**) *he refused to accept this mortifying disgrace.* **2** subdue (the body or its needs and desires) by self-denial or discipline: *return to heaven by mortifying the flesh.* **3** [intrans.] (of flesh) be affected by gangrene or necrosis: *the cut in Henry's arm had mortified.*
DERIVATIVES: **mor•ti•fi•ca•tion** |,môrtəfə 'kāsʜən| *n.* **mor•ti•fy•ing•ly** *adv.*

mor•tise |'môrtəs| (also **mortice**) • *n.* a hole or recess cut into a part, designed to receive a corresponding projection (a tenon) on another part so as to join or lock the parts together. • *v.* [with obj. and adverbial] join securely by using a mortise and tenon.
■ [trans.] [often as adj.] (**mortised**) cut a mortise in or through: *the mortised ports.*
DERIVATIVES: **mor•tis•er** *n.*

mo•sa•ic |mō'zā-ik| • *n.* **1** a picture or pattern produced by arranging together small colored pieces of hard material, such as stone, tile, or glass: *the mosaic shows the baptism of Christ* | [as adj.] *a mosaic floor.*
■ decorative work of this kind: *the walls and vaults are decorated by marble and mosaic.* ■ a colorful and variegated pattern: *the bird's plumage was a mosaic of slate-gray, blue, and brown.* ■ a combination of diverse elements forming a more or less coherent whole: *a mosaic of competing interests.* ■ an arrangement of photosensitive elements in a television camera. **2** an individual (esp. an animal) composed of cells of two genetically different types. **3** (also **mosaic disease**) a viral disease that results in leaf variegation in tobacco, corn, sugar cane, and other plants. • *v.* (**mosaicked, mosaicking**) [trans.] decorate with a mosaic: [as adj.] (**mosaicked**) *the mosaicked swimming pool.*
■ combine (distinct or disparate elements) to

form a picture or pattern: *the digital data were combined, or mosaicked, to delineate counties.*
DERIVATIVES: **mo•sa•i•cist** |mō'zāəsist| *n.*
moss•back |'môs,bæk| • *n.* an old-fashioned or extremely conservative person.
DERIVATIVES: **moss•backed** *adj.*
mote |mōt| • *n.* a tiny piece of something: *the tiniest mote of dust.* Cf. IOTA.
PHRASES: **a mote in someone's eye** a fault in a person that is less serious than one in someone else who is being critical.
mo•tet |mō'tet| • *n.* a short piece of sacred choral music, typically polyphonic and unaccompanied. Cf. MADRIGAL.
mo•tif |mō'tēf| • *n.* a decorative design or pattern: *T-shirts featuring spiral motifs.*
■ a distinctive or dominant idea in an artistic or literary composition: *the nautical motif of his latest novel.* ■ a short succession of notes producing a single impression; a brief melodic or rhythmic formula out of which longer passages are developed: *the motif in the second violin is submerged by the first violin's countermelody.* ■ an ornament of lace, braid, etc., sewn separately on a garment. ■ a distinctive sequence in a protein or DNA, having a three-dimensional structure that allows binding interactions to occur.
mo•tile |'mōtl; 'mō,tīl| • *adj.* **1** (of cells) capable of motion: *highly motile sperm cells.* **2** of, relating to, or characterized by bodily responses that involve muscular rather than audiovisual sensations.
DERIVATIVES: **mo•til•i•ty** |mō'tilətē| *n.*
mot juste |,mō 'ZHyst| • *n.* (pl. **mots justes** pronunc. same) the exact, appropriate word.
mot•ley |'mätlē| • *adj.* (**motlier, motliest**) incongruously varied in appearance or character; disparate: *a motley crew of discontents and zealots.* • *n.* **1** [usu. in sing.] an incongruous mixture: *a motley of interacting interest groups.* **2** the multicolored costume of a jester: *life-size mannequins in full motley.*
mot•tle |'mätl| • *v.* [trans.] (usu. **be mottled**) mark with spots or smears of color: *the cow's coat was light red mottled with white* | [as adj.] (**mottled**) *a bird with mottled brown plumage.* • *n.* an irregular arrangement of spots or patches of color: *the ship was a mottle of khaki and black.*
■ (also **mottling**) a spot or patch forming part of such an arrangement: *the mottles on a trout* | *white marble with mottlings of black and gray.*
mot•to |'mätō| • *n.* (pl. **-oes** or **-os**) a short sentence or phrase chosen as encapsulating the beliefs or ideals guiding an individual, family, or institution: *the school motto, "Serve and obey"* | *he soon adopted the motto "work hard and play hard."*
■ a phrase that recurs throughout a musical work and has some symbolic significance.
moue |mōō| • *n.* a pouting expression used to convey annoyance or distaste: *she made a moue at the suggestion that she clean the house.*
moun•te•bank |'mownti,bæNGk| • *n.* a person who deceives others, esp. in order to trick them out of their money; a charlatan.

■ in former times, a person who sold patent medicines in public places.
DERIVATIVES: **moun•te•bank•er•y** |-,bæNGkərē| *n.*
mox•ie |'mäksē| • *n.* force of character, determination, or nerve: *when you've got moxie, you need the clothes to match.*
mu•ci•lage |'myōōs(ə)lij| • *n.* a viscous secretion or bodily fluid.
■ a polysaccharide substance extracted as a viscous or gelatinous solution from plant roots, seeds, etc., and used in medicines and adhesives. ■ an adhesive solution; gum, glue.
DERIVATIVES: **mu•ci•lag•i•nous** |,myōōsə'læjənəs| *adj.*
muck•rak•ing |'mək,rākiNG| • *n.* the action of searching out and publicizing scandalous information about famous people, sometimes in an underhanded way: *her candidacy was threatened by her opponent's muckraking* | [as adj.] *a muckraking journalist.*
DERIVATIVES: **muck•rake** |-,rāk| *v.* **muck•rak•er** |-,rākər| *n.*
mu•cous |'myōōkəs| • *adj.* relating to, producing, covered with, or of the nature of mucus.
DERIVATIVES: **mu•cos•i•ty** |,myōō'käsətē| *n.*
mu•cus |'myōōkəs| • *n.* a slimy substance, secreted by mucous membranes and glands for lubrication, protection, etc.
■ a gummy substance found in plants; mucilage.
mu•ez•zin |m(y)ōō'ezən; 'mōōəzən| • *n.* a man who calls Muslims to prayer from the minaret of a mosque.
muf•ti[1] |'məftē| • *n.* (pl. **muftis**) a Muslim legal expert who is empowered to give rulings on religious matters.
muf•ti[2] • *n.* plain clothes worn by a person who wears a uniform for his or her job, such as a soldier or police officer: *I was an officer in mufti.*
mug•wump |'məg,wəmp| • *n.* a person who remains aloof or independent, esp. from party politics.
■ a Republican who in 1884 refused to support James G. Blaine, the Republican nominee for president.
DERIVATIVES: **mug•wump•er•y** *n.*
mu•lat•to |m(y)ōō'lätō; -'lætō| • *n.* (pl. **-oes** or **-os**) a person of mixed white and black ancestry, esp. a person with one white and one black parent. • *adj.* relating to or denoting a mulatto or mulattoes. Cf. QUADROON.

USAGE: This term is now usually considered offensive and is rarely seen except in historical contexts.

mulct |məlkt| • *v.* [trans.] extract money from (someone) by fine or taxation: *no government dared propose to mulct the taxpayer for such a purpose.*
■ (**mulct someone of**) defraud (someone) of (money or possessions): *he mulcted Shelly of $75,000.* • *n.* a fine or compulsory payment.
mu•li•eb•ri•ty |,myōōlē'ebrətē| • *n.* womanly qualities; womanhood.

mull[1] • *v.* [trans.] think about (a fact, proposal, or request) deeply and at length: *she began to* **mull over** *the various possibilities.*

mull[2] • *v.* [trans.] [usu. as adj.] (**mulled**) warm (a beverage, esp. wine, beer, or cider) and add spices and sweetening to it: *a tankard of mulled ale.*

mul•lion | ˈməlyən | • *n.* a vertical bar between the panes of glass in a window. Cf. TRANSOM.
DERIVATIVES: **mul•lioned** *adj.*

mul•ti•dis•ci•pli•nar•y | ˌməlti'disəpli'nerē; ˌməl,tī– | • *adj.* combining or involving several academic disciplines or professional specializations in an approach to a topic or problem.

mul•ti•far•i•ous | ˌməlti'ferēəs | • *adj.* many and of various types: *multifarious activities.*
■ having many varied parts or aspects: *a vast and multifarious organization.*
DERIVATIVES: **mul•ti•far•i•ous•ly** *adv.* **mul•ti•far•i•ous•ness** *n.*

mul•ti•lat•er•al | ˌməlti'lætərəl | • *adj.* agreed upon or participated in by three or more parties, esp. the governments of different countries: *multilateral negotiations* | *multilateral nuclear disarmament.*
■ having members or contributors from several groups, esp. several different countries: *multilateral aid agencies.* Cf. BILATERAL, UNILATERAL.
DERIVATIVES: **mul•ti•lat•er•al•ism** |-,lizəm | *n.* **mul•ti•lat•er•al•ist** |-list| *adj.* & *n.* **mul•ti•lat•er•al•ly** *adv.*

mul•ti•plex | ˈməlti,pleks | • *adj.* consisting of many elements in a complex relationship: *multiplex ties of work and friendship.*
■ involving simultaneous transmission of several messages along a single channel of communication. ■ (of a movie theater) having several separate screens within one building. • *n.* **1** a system or signal involving simultaneous transmission of several messages along a single channel of communication. **2** a movie theater with several separate screens. • *v.* [trans.] incorporate into a multiplex signal or system.
DERIVATIVES: **mul•ti•plex•er** (also **mul•ti•plex•or**) *n.* **mul•ti•plex•i•ty** *n.*

mul•ti•task•ing | ˌməlti'tæskiNG; ˌməl,tī– | • *n.* the simultaneous execution of more than one program or task by a single computer processor.
■ Simultaneously undertaking two or more activities, such as eating while watching television and talking on the telephone.
DERIVATIVES: **mul•ti•task** | ˈməlti,tæsk; ˈməl,tī| *v.*

mul•ti•va•lent | ˌməlti'vālənt; ˌməl,tī– | • *adj.* **1** having or susceptible to many applications, interpretations, meanings, or values: *visually complex and multivalent work.* **2** (of an antigen or antibody) having several sites at which attachment to an antibody or antigen can occur: *a multivalent antiserum.* Cf. POLYVALENT. **3** (in chemistry) another term for POLYVALENT.
DERIVATIVES: **mul•ti•va•lence** *n.* **mul•ti•va•len•cy** *n.* Brit.

mum•mer•y | ˈməmərē | • *n.* (pl. **-ies**) a performance by mummers (masked actors in a mime show).
■ ridiculous ceremonial, esp. of a religious nature: *that's all it is, mere mummery.*

mun•dane | ˌmən'dān | • *adj.* **1** lacking interest or excitement; dull: *seeking a way out of a mundane existence.* **2** of this earthly world rather than a heavenly or spiritual one: *according to Shinto doctrine, spirits of the dead can act upon the mundane world.*
DERIVATIVES: **mun•dane•ly** *adv.* **mun•dane•ness** *n.* **mun•dan•i•ty** |-'dānəṯē | *n.* (pl. **-ies**).

mu•nif•i•cent | myoo'nifəsənt; myə– | • *adj.* (of a gift or sum of money) larger or more generous than is usual or necessary: *a munificent gesture.*
■ (of a person) very generous.
DERIVATIVES: **mu•nif•i•cence** *n.* **mu•nif•i•cent•ly** *adv.*

mu•ni•ment | ˈmyoonəmənt | • *n.* (usu. **muniments**) a document or record, esp. one kept in an archive.

mu•ni•tion | myoo'nisHən; myə– | • *plural n.* (**munitions**) military weapons, ammunition, equipment, and stores: *reserves of nuclear, chemical, and conventional munitions* | [as adj.] *a munitions expert* | [as adj.] *munitions factories.* • *v.* [trans.] supply with munitions.
DERIVATIVES: **mu•ni•tion•er** *n.*

mur•rain | ˈmərən | • *n.* **1** any of various infectious diseases affecting cattle or other animals. **2** a plague, epidemic, or crop blight.

Muse | myooz | • *n.* (in Greek and Roman mythology) each of nine goddesses, the daughters of Zeus and Mnemosyne, who preside over the arts and sciences.
■ (**muse**) a woman, or a force personified as a woman, who is the source of inspiration for a creative artist.

The Muses are generally listed as Calliope (epic poetry), Clio (history), Euterpe (flute playing and lyric poetry), Terpsichore (choral dancing and song), Erato (lyre playing and lyric poetry), Melpomene (tragedy), Thalia (comedy and light verse), Polyhymnia (hymns, and later mime), and Urania (astronomy).

muse | myooz | • *v.* [intrans.] be absorbed in thought: *he was* **musing on** *the problems he faced.*
■ (**muse on**) gaze thoughtfully at. • *n.* an instance or period of reflection.
DERIVATIVES: **mus•ing•ly** *adv.*

must[1] • *n.* grape juice before or during fermentation.

must[2] • *n.* a musty state; dampness or mold: *a pervasive smell of must.*

must[3] (also **musth**) • *n.* the frenzied state of certain male animals, esp. elephants or camels, that is associated with the season: *a big old bull elephant* **in must.** Cf. RUT.
• *adj.* (of a male elephant or camel) in such a state.

mus•ter | ˈməstər | • *v.* [trans.] **1** assemble

(troops), esp. for inspection or in preparation for battle.

■ [no obj., with adverbial] (of troops) come together in this way: *the cavalrymen mustered beside the other regiments.* ■ [no obj., with adverbial of place] (of a group of people) gather together: *reporters mustered outside her house.* **2** collect or assemble (a number or amount): *they could not muster a majority.*

■ summon up (a particular feeling, attitude, or response): *he replied with as much dignity as he could muster.* ▪ *n.* a formal gathering of troops, esp. for inspection, display, or exercise.

PHRASES: **pass muster** be accepted as adequate or satisfactory: *a treaty that might pass muster with the voters.*

mus•ty |ˈməstē| ▪ *adj.* (**mustier, mustiest**) having a stale, moldy, or damp smell: *a dark musty library filled with old books.*

■ having a stale taste: *the beer tasted sour, thin, and musty.* ■ lacking originality or interest: *when I read it again, the play seemed musty.* DERIVATIVES: **mus•ti•ly** |ˈməstəlē| *adv.* **mus•ti•ness** *n.*

mu•ta•ble |ˈmyo͞otəbəl| ▪ *adj.* liable to change: *the mutable nature of fashion.*

■ inconstant in one's affections: *youth is said to be fickle and mutable.* DERIVATIVES: **mu•ta•bil•i•ty** |ˌmyo͞otəˈbil-ətē| *n.* **mu•ta•bly** *adv.*

mu•ta•gen |ˈmyo͞otəjən| ▪ *n.* an agent, such as radiation or a chemical substance, that causes genetic mutation. DERIVATIVES: **mu•ta•gen•e•sis** |ˌmyo͞otə ˈjenəsəs| *n.* **mu•ta•gen•ic** |ˌmyo͞otəˈjenik| *adj.*

mu•ta•tion |myo͞oˈtāsHən| ▪ *n.* **1** the action or process of undergoing change (mutating): *the mutation of ethnic politics into nationalist politics* | *his first novel went through several mutations.* **2** the changing of the structure of a gene, resulting in a variant form that may be transmitted to subsequent generations, caused by the alteration of single base units in DNA, or the deletion, insertion, or rearrangement of larger sections of genes or chromosomes.

■ a distinct form resulting from such a change. **3** uniform change of a sound when it occurs adjacent to another, in particular:

■ (in Germanic languages) the process by which the quality of a vowel was altered in certain phonetic contexts. ■ (in Celtic languages) change of an initial consonant in a word caused (historically) by the preceding word. DERIVATIVES: **mu•ta•tion•al** |-sHənl| *adj.* **mu•ta•tion•al•ly** |-sHənl-ē| *adv.* **mu•ta•tive** |ˈmyo͞otətiv| *adj.*

mu•ta•tis mu•tan•dis |m(y)o͞oˈtätəs m(y)o͞o ˈtändəs; -ˈtātəs; -ˈtændəs| ▪ *adv.* (used when comparing two or more cases or situations) making necessary alterations of detail while not affecting the main point at issue: *what is true of undergraduate teaching in England is equally true, mutatis mutandis, of American graduate schools.*

mu•ti•late |ˈmyo͞otl,āt| ▪ *v.* [trans.] (usu. **be mutilated**) inflict a violent and disfiguring injury on: *the leg was badly mutilated* | [as adj.] (**mutilated**) *mutilated bodies.*

■ inflict serious damage on: *the 14th-century church had been partly mutilated in the 18th century.* ■ render imperfect by removing or severely damaging a part: *They couldn't suppress the book but they mutilated it almost beyond recognition.* DERIVATIVES: **mu•ti•la•tion** |ˌmyo͞otl'ā-sHən| *n.* **mu•ti•la•tor** |-ˌātər| *n.*

mu•ti•nous |ˈmyo͞otn-əs| ▪ *adj.* (of a soldier or sailor) refusing to obey the orders of a superior.

■ willful or disobedient: *the junior members seemed mutinous, but adhered to party policy in the end.* DERIVATIVES: **mu•ti•nous•ly** *adv.*

mu•ti•ny |ˈmyo͞otn-ē| ▪ *n.* (pl. **-ies**) an open rebellion against the proper authorities, esp. by soldiers or sailors against their officers: *a mutiny by those manning the weapons could trigger a global war* | *mutiny at sea.* ▪ *v.* (**-ies, -ied**) [intrans.] refuse to obey the orders of a person in authority.

mut•ism |ˈmyo͞ot,izəm| ▪ *n.* inability to speak, typically as a result of congenital deafness or brain damage.

■ (in full **elective mutism**) unwillingness or refusal to speak, arising from psychological causes such as depression or trauma.

mu•tu•al•ism |ˈmyo͞ocHəwə,lizəm| ▪ *n.* the doctrine that mutual dependence is necessary to social well-being.

■ symbiosis that is beneficial to both organisms involved. DERIVATIVES: **mu•tu•al•ist** *n.* & *adj.* **mu•tu•al•is•tic** |ˌmyo͞ocHəwə'listik| *adj.* **mu•tu•al•is•ti•cal•ly** |ˌmyo͞ocHəwə'listik(ə)lē| *adv.*

muz•zy |ˈməzē| ▪ *adj.* (**muzzier, muzziest**) **1** unable to think clearly; confused: *she was shivering and her head felt muzzy from sleep.*

■ not thought out clearly; vague: *society's muzzy notion of tolerance.* **2** (of a person's eyes or a visual image) blurred: *a slightly muzzy picture.*

■ (of a sound) indistinct: *the bass and drums are, even on CD, appallingly muzzy.* DERIVATIVES: **muz•zi•ly** |ˈməzəlē| *adv.* **muz•zi•ness** *n.*

my•col•o•gy |mīˈkäləjē| ▪ *n.* the scientific study of fungi. DERIVATIVES: **my•co•log•i•cal** |ˌmīkəˈläji-kəl| *adj.* **my•co•log•i•cal•ly** |ˌmīkəˈläji-k(ə)lē| *adv.* **my•col•o•gist** |-jist| *n.*

my•ol•o•gy |mīˈäləjē| ▪ *n.* the study of the structure, arrangement, and action of muscles. DERIVATIVES: **my•o•log•i•cal** |ˌmīəˈläji-kəl| *adj.* **my•ol•o•gist** |-jist| *n.*

my•op•ic |mīˈäpik| ▪ *adj.* (of a person or their eyes) affected by nearsightedness (myopia).

■ lacking imagination, foresight, or intellectual insight: *a myopic attitude toward public spending.* DERIVATIVES: **my•op•i•cal•ly** |-ik(ə)lē| *adv.*

myr•i•ad |ˈmirēəd| • *n.* **1** a countless or extremely great number: *networks connecting a* **myriad of** *computers.* **2** (chiefly in classical history) a unit of ten thousand. • *adj.* countless or extremely great in number: *the myriad lights of the city.*
■ having countless or very many elements or aspects: *the myriad music scene.*

USAGE: **Myriad**, derived from a Greek word meaning 'ten thousand,' is best used as an adjective (not as a noun) in the sense of 'countless' or 'innumerable,' in reference to a great but indefinite number. It should not be used in the plural or take the preposition *of* (*myriad opportunities*, not *myriads of opportunities*).

mys•ta•gogue |ˈmistə‚gäg| • *n.* a teacher or propounder of mystical doctrines.
DERIVATIVES: **mys•ta•gog•i•cal** *adj.* **mys•ta•go•gy** |-‚gōjē| *n.*

mys•ter•y |ˈmist(ə)rē| • *n.* (pl. **-ies**) **1** something that is difficult or impossible to understand or explain: *the mysteries of outer space* | *hoping that the inquest would solve the mystery.*
■ the condition or quality of being secret, strange, or difficult to explain: *much of her past is shrouded in mystery.* ■ a person or thing whose identity or nature is puzzling or unknown: *"He's a bit of a mystery,"* said Nina | [as adj.] *a mystery guest.* **2** a novel, play, or movie dealing with a puzzling crime, esp. a murder. **3** (**mysteries**) the secret rites of Greek and Roman pagan religion, or of any ancient or tribal religion, to which only initiates are admitted.
■ the practices, skills, or lore peculiar to a particular trade or activity and regarded as baffling to those without specialized knowledge: *the mysteries of analytical psychology.* ■ the Christian Eucharist. **4** a religious belief based on divine revelation, esp. one regarded as beyond human understanding: *the mystery of Christ.*
■ an incident in the life of Jesus or of a saint as a focus of devotion in the Roman Catholic Church, esp. each of those commemorated during recitation of successive decades of the rosary.

mys•tic |ˈmistik| • *n.* a person who seeks by contemplation and self-surrender to obtain unity with or absorption into God or the absolute, or who believes in the spiritual apprehension of truths that are beyond the intellect. • *adj.* another term for MYSTICAL.

mys•ti•cal |ˈmistikəl| • *adj.* **1** of or relating to mystics or religious mysticism: *the mystical experience.*
■ spiritually allegorical or symbolic; transcending human understanding: *the mystical body of Christ.* ■ of or relating to ancient religious mysteries or other occult or esoteric rites: *the mystical practices of the Pythagoreans.*
■ of hidden or esoteric meaning: *a geometric figure of mystical significance.* **2** inspiring a sense of spiritual mystery, awe, and fascination: *the mystical forces of nature.*

■ concerned with the soul or the spirit, rather than with material things: *the beliefs of a more mystical age.*
DERIVATIVES: **mys•ti•cal•ly** |-ik(ə)lē| *adv.*

mys•ti•cism |ˈmistə‚sizəm| • *n.* **1** belief that union with or absorption into God or the absolute, or the spiritual apprehension of knowledge inaccessible to the intellect, may be attained through contemplation and self-surrender. **2** belief characterized by self-delusion or dreamy confusion of thought, esp. when based on the assumption of occult qualities or mysterious agencies.

mys•tique |misˈtēk| • *n.* a fascinating aura of mystery, awe, and power surrounding someone or something: *the West is lately rethinking its cowboy mystique* | *the tiger has a mystique that man has always respected and revered.*
■ an air of secrecy surrounding a particular activity or subject that makes it impressive or baffling to those without specialized knowledge: *eliminating the mystique normally associated with computers.* Cf. DEMYSTIFY.

myth |miTH| • *n.* **1** a traditional story, esp. one concerning the early history of a people or explaining some natural or social phenomenon, and typically involving supernatural beings or events. Cf. LEGEND.
■ such stories collectively: *the heroes of Greek myth.* **2** a widely held but false belief or idea: *he wants to dispel the myth that sea kayaking is too risky or too strenuous* | *there is a popular myth that corporations are big people with lots of money.*
■ a misrepresentation of the truth: *attacking the party's irresponsible myths about privatization.* ■ a fictitious or imaginary person or thing. ■ an exaggerated or idealized conception of a person or thing: *the book is a scholarly study of the Kennedy myth.*

myth•ic |ˈmiTHik| • *adj.* of, relating to, or resembling myth: *we explain spiritual forces in mythic language.*
■ exaggerated or idealized: *a national hero of mythic proportions.* ■ fictitious: *a mythic land of plenty.*

myth•i•cal |ˈmiTHikəl| • *adj.* occurring in or characteristic of myths or folk tales: *one of Denmark's greatest mythical heroes.*
■ idealized, esp. with reference to the past: *a mythical age of contentment and social order.* ■ fictitious: *a mythical customer whose name appears in brochures.*
DERIVATIVES: **myth•i•cal•ly** |-ik(ə)lē| *adv.*

myth•i•cize |ˈmiTHə‚siz| • *v.* [trans.] turn into myth; interpret mythically.
DERIVATIVES: **myth•i•cism** |-‚sizəm| *n.* **myth•i•cist** |-sist| *n.*

my•thol•o•gy |məˈTHäləjē| • *n.* (pl. **-ies**) **1** a collection of myths, esp. one belonging to a particular religious or cultural tradition: *Ganesa was the god of wisdom and success in Hindu mythology.*
■ a set of stories or beliefs about a particular person, institution, or situation, esp. when exaggerated or fictitious: *in popular mythology, truckers are kings of the road.* **2** the study of myths.

DERIVATIVES: **my•thol•o•ger** |-jər| *n.* **myth•o•log•ic** |ˌmiTHə'läjik| *adj.* **myth•o•log•i•cal** |ˌmiTHə'läjikəl| *adj.* **myth•o•log•i•cal•ly** |ˌmiTHə'läjik(ə)lē| *adv.* **my•thol•o•gist** |-jist| *n.*

myth•o•ma•ni•a |ˌmiTHə'mānēə| • *n.* an abnormal or pathological tendency to exaggerate or tell lies.
DERIVATIVES: **myth•o•ma•ni•ac** |-'mānē ˌæk| *n.* & *adj.* **myth•o•mane** *n.*

Nn

na•bob |'nābäb| • *n.* a Muslim official or governor under the Mogul empire (16th–19th cents.) in India.
■ a person of conspicuous wealth or high status. ■ a person who returned from India to Europe with a fortune during the period (late 18th–early 20th cent.) of European, esp. British, colonization.

na•cre |'nākər| • *n.* mother-of-pearl.
DERIVATIVES: **na•cre•ous** |-krēəs| *adj.*

na•dir |'nādər; 'nādir| • *n.* [in sing.] the lowest point in the fortunes of a person or organization: *they had reached the nadir of their despair.*
■ the point on the celestial sphere directly below an observer. The opposite of ZENITH.

nai•ad |'nāæd; -əd; nī-| • *n.* (pl. **naiads** or **naiades** |ə,dēz|) **1** (also **Naiad**) (in classical mythology) a water nymph said to inhabit a river, spring, or waterfall. **2** the aquatic larva or nymph of a dragonfly, mayfly, or stonefly. **3** a submerged aquatic plant, genus *Najas*, with narrow leaves and minute flowers.
•Genus *Najas*, family Najadaceae.

na•if |nī'ēf| (also **naf**) • *adj.* naive or ingenuous. • *n.* a naive or ingenuous person.

na•ive |nī'ēv| (also **nave**) • *adj.* (of a person or action) showing a lack of experience, wisdom, or judgment: *the rather naive young man had been totally misled.*
■ (of a person) natural and unaffected; innocent: *Andy had a sweet, naive look when he smiled.* ■ of or denoting art produced in a straightforward style that deliberately rejects sophisticated artistic techniques and has a bold directness resembling a child's work, typically in bright colors with little or no perspective.
DERIVATIVES: **na•ive•ly** *adv.* **na•ive•ness** *n.*

na•ive•té |ˌnī,ēv(ə)'tā; nī'ēv(ə),tā| (also **na•ïveté**, Brit. **naivety**) • *n.* lack of experience, wisdom, or judgment: *the administration's naiveté in foreign policy.*
■ innocence or unsophistication: *they took advantage of his naiveté and deep pockets.*

name•sake |'nām,sāk| • *n.* a person or thing that has the same name as another: *Hugh Capet paved the way for his son and namesake to be crowned king of France.| I've been researching my 18th-century ancestor and namesake.*

nar•cis•sism |'närsə,sizəm| • *n.* excessive or erotic interest in oneself and one's physical appearance.

■ extreme selfishness, with a grandiose view of one's own talents and a craving for admiration, as characterizing a personality type. ■ (in psychoanalysis) self-centeredness arising from failure to distinguish the self from external objects, either in very young babies or as a feature of mental disorder. Cf. AUTISM
DERIVATIVES: **nar•cis•sist** |'närsəsəst| *n.* **nar•cis•sis•tic** |ˌ'närsə'sistik| *adj.* **nar•cis•sis•ti•cal•ly** |ˌ'närsə'sistək(ə)lē| *adv.*

nar•co•lep•sy |'närkə,lepsē| • *n.* a pathological condition characterized by an extreme tendency to fall asleep whenever in relaxing surroundings.
DERIVATIVES: **nar•co•lep•tic** |ˌnärkə'leptik| *adj.* & *n.*

nar•co•sis |när'kōsis| • *n.* a state of stupor, drowsiness, or unconsciousness produced by drugs. ■ (**nitrogen narcosis**) a drowsy state induced by breathing air under pressure, e.g., in deep-sea diving.

nar•cot•ic |när'kätik| • *n.* a drug or other substance affecting mood or behavior and sold for nonmedical purposes, esp. an illegal one.
■ (in medicine) a drug that relieves pain and induces drowsiness, stupor, or insensibility. • *adj.* relating to or denoting narcotics or their effects or use: *the substance has a mild narcotic effect.*
DERIVATIVES: **nar•cot•i•cal•ly** |-tik(ə)lē| *adv.* **nar•co•tism** |'närkə,tizəm| *n.*

nas•cent |'nāsənt; 'næsənt| • *adj.* (esp. of a process or organization) just coming into existence and beginning to display signs of future potential: *the nascent space industry.*
■ (in chemistry, chiefly of hydrogen) freshly generated in a reactive form.
DERIVATIVES: **nas•cence** *n.* **nas•cen•cy** *n.*

na•tion•al•ism |'næsHənə,lizəm| • *n.* feeling, principles, or efforts devoted to one's nation.
■ an extreme form of this, esp. marked by a feeling of superiority over other countries.
■ advocacy of political independence for a particular country: *Palestinian nationalism.*
DERIVATIVES: **na•tion•al•ist** *n.* **na•tion•al•is•tic** *adj.* **na•tion•al•is•ti•cal•ly** *adv.*

na•tion•al•ize |'næsHənə,līz| • *v.* [trans.] **1** transfer (a major branch of industry or commerce) from private to state ownership or control. **2** make distinctively national; give a national character to: *in the 13th and 14th centuries church designs were further nationalized.* **3** [usu. as adj.] (**nationalized**) natural-

ize (a foreigner): *he is now a nationalized Frenchman.*
DERIVATIVES: **na•tion•al•i•za•tion** |,næ-sHənəli'zāsHən| *n.* **na•tion•al•iz•er** *n.*
Na•tive A•mer•i•can • *n.* a member of any of the indigenous peoples of the Americas. • *adj.* of or relating to these peoples.

USAGE: **Native American** is now an accepted term in many contexts. The term **American Indian** is also used, by many American Indians themselves, among others. See **usage** at AMERICAN INDIAN.

na•tiv•ism |'nāṭi,vizəm| • *n.* **1** the policy of protecting the interests of native-born or established inhabitants against those of immigrants: *a deep vein of xenophobia and nativism.* **2** a return to or emphasis on traditional or local customs, in opposition to outside influences. **3** the theory or doctrine that concepts, mental capacities, and mental structures are innate rather than acquired or learned.
DERIVATIVES: **na•tiv•ist** *n.* & *adj.* **na•tiv•is•tic** |,nāṭi'vistik| *adj.*
nat•ter |'næṭər| • *v.* [intrans.] talk casually, esp. about unimportant matters; chatter: *they nattered away for hours.* • *n.* [in sing.] a casual and leisurely conversation.
DERIVATIVES: **nat•ter•er** *n.*
nat•u•ral•ism |'næCHərə,lizəm| • *n.* **1** (in art and literature) a style and theory of representation based on the accurate depiction of detail.

The name "Naturalism" was given to a 19th-century artistic and literary movement, influenced by contemporary ideas of science and society, that rejected the idealization of experience and adopted an objective and often uncompromisingly realistic approach to art. Notable figures include the novelist Émile Zola (1840–1902) and the painter Théodore Rousseau (1812–1867).

2 a philosophical viewpoint according to which everything arises from natural properties and causes, and supernatural or spiritual explanations are excluded or discounted.
■ (in moral philosophy) the theory that ethical statements can be derived from nonethical ones. ■ religion, esp. deism, based on reason rather than on divine revelation. (Also called **natural religion**).
nat•u•ral•ize |'næCHərə,līz| • *v.* [trans.] **1** (often **be/become naturalized**) admit (a foreigner) to the citizenship of a country: *he was born in Germany and had never been naturalized* | [as adj.] (**naturalized**) *a naturalized US citizen born in Germany.*
■ [intrans.] (of a foreigner) be admitted to the citizenship of a country: *the opportunity to naturalize as American.* ■ alter (an adopted foreign word) so that it conforms more closely to the phonology or orthography of the adopting language: *Al Kelly was naturalized in Nice as stocoficada.* **2** [trans.] [usu. as adj.] (**naturalized**) establish (a plant or animal) so that it lives wild in a re-

gion where it is not indigenous: *native and naturalized species* | *dandelions quickly became naturalized in America.*
■ establish (a cultivated plant) in a natural situation: *this species of crocus **naturalizes itself** very easily.* ■ [intrans.] (of a cultivated plant) become established in a natural situation: *these perennials should be planted where they can naturalize.* **3** regard as or cause to appear natural: *although women do more child care than men, feminists should beware of naturalizing that fact.*
■ explain (a phenomenon) as natural rather than supernatural.
DERIVATIVES: **na•t•ura•l•iz•ation** |,næ-CHərəli'zāsHən| *n.*
nat•u•ral se•lec•tion • *n.* the biological process whereby organisms better adapted to their environment tend to survive and produce more offspring. The theory of its action was first fully expounded by Charles Darwin and is now believed to be the main process that brings about EVOLUTION.
na•tur•ism |'nāCHə,rizəm| • *n.* **1** the practice of wearing no clothes in a vacation camp or for other leisure activities; nudism. **2** the worship of nature or natural objects.
DERIVATIVES: **na•tur•ist** *n.* & *adj.*
nau•se•a |'nôzēə; -zHə| • *n.* a feeling of sickness with an inclination to vomit.
■ feelings of loathing; revulsion: *his graphic account induced a feeling of nausea.*
nau•se•ate |'nôzē,āt; - zHē,āt| • *v.* [trans.] make (someone) feel sick; affect with nausea: *the thought of food nauseated her* | [as adj.] (**nauseating**) *the stench became nauseating.*
■ fill (someone) with revulsion; disgust: *I was nauseated by the vicious comment.*
DERIVATIVES: **nau•se•at•ing•ly** *adv.*

USAGE: A distinction has traditionally been drawn between **nauseated**, meaning 'affected with nausea,' and **nauseous**, meaning 'causing nausea.' Today, however, the use of **nauseous** to mean 'affected with nausea' is so common that it is generally considered to be standard.

nau•seous |'nôsHəs; -zHəs; -ēəs| • *adj.* **1** affected with nausea; inclined to vomit: *a rancid odor that made him nauseous.* **2** causing nausea; offensive to the taste or smell: *a nauseous smell of decay.*
■ disgusting, repellent, or offensive: *this nauseous account of a bloody case.*
DERIVATIVES: **nau•seous•ly** *adv.* **nau•seous•ness** *n.*
nave |nāv| • *n.* the central part of a church building, intended to accommodate most of the congregation. In traditional Western churches it is rectangular, separated from the chancel by a step or rail, and from adjacent aisles by pillars.
né |nā| • *adj.* originally called; born (used before the name by which a man was originally known): *Al Kelly, né Kabish.*
Ne•an•der•thal |nē'ændərТНôl| • *n.* (also **Neanderthal man**) an extinct species of human (*Homo neanderthalensis*) that was widely

distributed in ice-age Europe between *c.*120,000–35,000 years ago, with a receding forehead and prominent brow ridges. Neanderthals are now usually regarded as a separate species from *H. sapiens* and probably at the end of a different evolutionary line.

■ an uncivilized, unintelligent, or uncouth person, esp. a man. • *adj.* of or relating to this extinct human species.

■ (esp. of a man) uncivilized, unintelligent, or uncouth: *your attitude to women is Neanderthal.*

neap |nēp| • *n.* (usu. **neap tide**) a tide just after the first or third quarters of the moon when there is the least difference between high and low water. • *v.* (**be neaped**) (of a boat) be kept aground or in harbor by a neap tide.

■ [intrans.] (of a tide) tend toward or reach the highest point of a neap tide.

neb•bish | 'nebisH| (also **nebbich**) • *n.* a person, esp. a man, who is regarded as pitifully ineffectual, timid, or submissive; a nobody; a nonentity: [as adj.] *so where's your nebbish brother?*

DERIVATIVES: **neb•bish•y** *adj.*

neb•u•la | 'nebyələ| • *n.* (pl. **nebulae** |-lē| or **nebulas**) **1** a cloud of gas and dust in outer space, visible in the night sky either as an indistinct bright patch or as a dark silhouette against other luminous matter.

■ (in general use) any indistinct bright area in the night sky, e.g., a distant galaxy. **2** (in medicine) a clouded spot on the cornea causing defective vision. Cf. CATARACT.

neb•u•lar | 'nebyələr| • *adj.* of, relating to, or denoting a nebula or nebulae: *a vast nebular cloud.*

neb•u•lous | 'nebyələs| • *adj.* in the form of a cloud or haze; hazy: *a giant nebulous glow.*

■ (of a concept or idea) unclear, vague, or ill-defined: *nebulous concepts like quality of life.*

■ another term for NEBULAR.

DERIVATIVES: **neb•u•los•i•ty** |,nebyə'läsitē| *n.* **neb•u•lous•ly** *adv.* **neb•u•lous•ness** *n.*

ne•ces•si•tar•i•an |nə,sesə'terēən| • *n.* & *adj.* (in philosophy) another term for **determinist** (see DETERMINISM). Cf. LIBERTARIAN.

DERIVATIVES: **ne•ces•si•tar•i•an•ism** |-,nizəm| *n.*

ne•ces•si•tous |nə'sesitəs| • *adj.* (of a person) lacking the necessities of life; needy.

ne•ces•si•ty |nə'sesitē| • *n.* (pl. **-ies**) **1** the fact of being required or indispensable: *the **necessity of** providing parent guidance* | *the **necessity for** law and order.*

■ unavoidability: *the **necessity of** growing old.*

■ a state of things or circumstances enforcing a certain course: *created more by necessity than design.* **2** an indispensable thing: *a good book is a necessity when traveling.* **3** (in philosophy) the principle according to which something must be so, by virtue either of logic or of natural law.

■ a condition that cannot be otherwise, or a statement asserting this.

ne•crol•o•gy |ne'kräləjē| • *n.* (pl. **-ies**) **1** an obituary notice. **2** a list of deaths.

DERIVATIVES: **ne•cro•log•i•cal** |,nekrə'läjikəl| *adj.*

nec•ro•man•cy | 'nekrə,mænsē| • *n.* the supposed practice of communicating with the dead, esp. in order to predict the future.

■ witchcraft, sorcery, or black magic in general.

DERIVATIVES: **nec•ro•man•cer** |-sər| *n.* **nec•ro•man•tic** |,nekrə'mæntik| *adj.*

nec•ro•phil•i•a |,nekrə'filēə| • *n.* a morbid and esp. erotic attraction toward corpses.

■ sexual intercourse with a corpse.

DERIVATIVES: **nec•ro•phile** | 'nekrə,fīl| *n.* **nec•ro•phil•i•ac** |-'filē,æk| *n.* **nec•ro•phil•ic** |-filik| *adj.* **nec•ro•phil•ism** |ne'kräfə,lizəm| *n.* **nec•ro•phil•ist** |ne'kräfəlist| *n.*

ne•crop•o•lis |ne'kräpəlis| • *n.* a cemetery, esp. a large one belonging to an ancient city.

ne•cro•sis |ne'krōsis| • *n.* the death of most or all of the cells in an organ or tissue due to disease, injury, or failure of the blood supply.

DERIVATIVES: **ne•crot•ic** |-'krätik| *adj.*

née |nā| • *adj.* originally called; born (used esp. in adding a woman's maiden name after her married name): *Mary Toogood, née Johnson.*

ne•far•i•ous |ni'ferēəs| • *adj.* (typically of an action or activity) wicked or criminal: *the nefarious activities of the organized-crime syndicates.*

DERIVATIVES: **ne•far•i•ous•ly** *adv.* **ne•far•i•ous•ness** *n.*

ne•gate |nə'gāt| • *v.* [trans.] **1** nullify; make ineffective: *alcohol negates the effects of the drug.* **2** make (a clause, sentence, or proposition) negative in meaning. **3** deny the existence of (something): *negating the political nature of education.*

ne•ga•tion |nə'gāsHən| • *n.* **1** the contradiction or denial of something: *there should be confirmation—or negation—of the findings.*

■ (in grammar) denial of the truth of a clause or sentence, typically involving the use of a negative word (e.g., *not*, *no*, *never*) or a word or affix with negative force (e.g., *nothing*, *non-*). ■ (in logic) a proposition whose assertion specifically denies the truth of another proposition: *the negation of A is, briefly, "not A."* ■ (in mathematics) inversion: *these formulas and their negations.* **2** the absence or opposite of something actual or positive: *evil is not merely the negation of goodness.*

DERIVATIVES: **neg•a•to•ry** | 'negə,tôrē| *adj.*

neg•a•tive | 'negətiv| • *adj.* **1** consisting in or characterized by the absence rather than the presence of distinguishing features.

■ (of a statement or decision) expressing or implying denial, disagreement, or refusal: *that, I take it, was a negative answer.* ■ (of the results of a test or experiment) indicating that a certain substance is not present or a certain condition does not exist: *so far all the patients have tested negative for TB.* ■ [in combination] (of a person or their blood) not having a specified substance or condition: *HIV-negative.*

■ (of a person, attitude, or situation) not

optimistic; harmful or unwelcome: *the new tax was having a negative effect on car sales* | *not all the news is negative.* ∎ denoting a complete lack of something: *they were described as having negative vulnerability to water entry.* ∎ (of a word, clause, or proposition) expressing denial, negation, or refutation; stating or asserting that something is not the case. Contrasted with *affirmative* and *interrogative* **2** (of a quantity) less than zero; to be subtracted from others or from zero. ∎ denoting a direction of decrease or reversal: *the industry suffered negative growth in 1992.* **3** of, containing, producing, or denoting the kind of electric charge carried by electrons. **4** (of a photographic image) showing light and shade or colors reversed from those of the original. **5** (in astrology) relating to or denoting any of the earth or water signs, considered passive in nature. • *n.* **1** a word or statement that expresses denial, disagreement, or refusal: *she replied in the negative.* ∎ (often **the negative**) a bad, unwelcome, or unpleasant quality, characteristic, or aspect of a situation or person: *confidence will not be instilled by harping solely on the negative* | *the bus trip and the positive media have not had time to turn his significant negatives around.* ∎ (in grammar) a word, affix, or phrase expressing negation. ∎ (in logic) another term for NEGATION. **2** a photographic image made on film or specially prepared glass that shows the light and shade or color values reversed from the original, and from which positive prints can be made. **3** a result of a test or experiment indicating that a certain substance is not present or a certain condition does not exist: *the percentage of false negatives generated by the cancer test was of great concern.* **4** the part of an electric circuit that is at a lower electrical potential than another part designated as having zero electrical potential. **5** a number less than zero. • *exclam.* no (usually used in a military context): *"Any snags, Captain?" "Negative, she's running like clockwork."* • *v.* [trans.] **1** reject; refuse to accept; veto: *the bill was negatived by 130 votes to 129.* ∎ disprove; contradict: *the insurer's main arguments were negatived by Lawrence.* **2** render ineffective; neutralize: *should criminal law allow consent to negative what would otherwise be a crime?*
DERIVATIVES: **neg•a•tive•ly** *adv.* **neg•a•tive•ness** *n.* **neg•a•tiv•i•ty** |ˌnegəˈtivitē| *n.*
neg•a•tiv•ism |ˈnegətivˌizəm| • *n.* the practice of being or tendency to be negative or skeptical in attitude while failing to offer positive suggestions or views.
DERIVATIVES: **neg•a•tiv•ist** *n. & adj.* **neg•a•tiv•is•tic** *adj.*
neg•li•gence |ˈneglijəns| • *n.* failure to take proper care in doing something: *some of these accidents are due to negligence.* ∎ (in law) failure to use reasonable care, resulting in damage or injury to another. Cf. CONTRIBUTORY; MALPRACTICE.
neg•li•gi•ble |ˈneglijəbəl| • *adj.* so small or unimportant as to be not worth considering;

insignificant: *the additional costs were negligible.*
DERIVATIVES: **neg•li•gi•bil•i•ty** |ˌneglǝjǝˈbilitē| *n.* **neg•li•gi•bly** |-blē| *adv.*
ne•go•ti•a•ble |nəˈgōsHəbəl| • *adj.* open to discussion or modification: *the price was not negotiable.* ∎ (of a document) able to be transferred or assigned to the legal ownership of another person. ∎ (of an obstacle or pathway) able to be traversed; passable: *such walkways must be accessible and negotiable for all users.*
DERIVATIVES: **ne•go•ti•a•bil•i•ty** |nəˌgōsHəˈbilitē| *n.*
ne•gri•tude (also **Negritude**) • *n.* the quality or fact of being of black African origin. ∎ the affirmation or consciousness of the value of black or African culture, heritage, and identity: *Negritude helped to guide Senegal into independence with pride.*
Ne•gro |ˈnegrō| • *n.* (pl. **-oes**) a member of a dark-skinned group of peoples originally native to Africa south of the Sahara. • *adj.* of or relating to such people.

USAGE: The word **Negro** was adopted from Spanish and Portuguese and first recorded from the mid 16th century. It remained the standard term throughout the 17th–19th centuries and was used by such prominent black American campaigners as W.E.B. DuBois and Booker T. Washington in the early 20th century. Since the Black Power movement of the 1960s, however, when the term **black** was favored as the term to express racial pride, **Negro** (together with related words such as the feminine **Negress**) has dropped out of favor and now seems out of date or even offensive in both American and British English. Cf. AFRICAN AMERICAN, BLACK.

Ne•groid |ˈnegroid| • *adj.* of or relating to the division of humankind represented by the indigenous peoples of central and southern Africa.

USAGE: The term **Negroid** belongs to a set of terms introduced by 19th-century anthropologists attempting to categorize human races. Such terms are associated with outdated notions of racial types, and so are now potentially offensive and best avoided. See also MONGOLOID.

nem•e•sis |ˈneməsis| • *n.* (pl. **nemeses** |-ˌsēz|) (usu. **one's nemesis**) the inescapable or implacable agent of someone's or something's downfall: *the balance beam proved to be the team's nemesis.* ∎ a downfall caused by such an agent: *one risks nemesis by uttering such words.* ∎ (often **Nemesis**) retributive justice: *Nemesis is notoriously slow.*
ne•o•clas•si•cism |ˌnēōˈklæsiˌsizəm| • *n.* the revival of a classical style or treatment in art, literature, architecture, or music.

As an aesthetic and artistic style this originated in Rome in the mid-18th century, combining a reaction against the late baroque and rococo with a new interest in antiquity. In music, the term refers to a return by composers of the early 20th century to the forms and styles of the 17th and 18th centuries, as a reaction against 19th-century romanticism.

DERIVATIVES: **ne•o•clas•si•cal** adj, **ne•o•clas•si•cist** n. & adj.

ne•o•co•lo•ni•al•ism |ˌnēōkəˈlōnēəˌlizəm| • n. the use of economic, political, cultural, or other pressures to control or influence other countries, esp. former dependencies.

DERIVATIVES: **ne•o•co•lo•ni•al** adj. **ne•o•co•lo•ni•al•ist** n. & adj.

ne•o•con•serv•a•tive |ˌnēōkənˈsərvətiv| • adj. of or relating to an approach to politics, literary criticism, theology, history, or any other branch of thought, that represents a return to a modified form of a traditional viewpoint, in contrast with more radical or liberal schools of thought. • n. a person with neoconservative views.

DERIVATIVES: **ne•o•con•serv•a•tism** |-tizəm| n.

ne•o-Im•pres•sion•ism (also **Neo-Impressionism**) • n. a late 19th-century movement in French painting that sought to improve on Impressionism through a systematic approach to form and color, particularly using pointillist technique. The movement's leading figures included Georges Seurat, Paul Signac, and Camille Pissarro.

DERIVATIVES: **ne•o-Im•pres•sion•ist** adj. & n.

ne•o•lib•er•al |ˌnēōˈlibərəl| • adj. relating to or denoting a modified form of liberalism tending to favor free-market capitalism. • n. a person holding such views.

DERIVATIVES: **ne•o•lib•er•al•ism** n.

Ne•o•lith•ic |ˌnēəˈliTHik| • adj. of, relating to, or denoting the later part of the Stone Age, when ground or polished stone weapons and implements prevailed.

■ [as n.] (**the Neolithic**) the Neolithic period. (Also called **New Stone Age**.)

In the Neolithic period farm animals were first domesticated, and agriculture was introduced. It began in the Near East by the 8th millennium BC and spread to northern Europe by the 4th millennium BC.

ne•ol•o•gism |nēˈäləˌjizəm| • n. a newly coined word or expression.

■ the coining or use of new words.

DERIVATIVES: **ne•o•log•i•cal** adj. **ne•ol•o•gist** |-jist| n. **ne•ol•o•gize** |-ˌjīz| v.

ne•o•na•tal |ˌnēōˈnātl| • adj. of or relating to newborn children.

DERIVATIVES: **ne•o•na•tol•o•gist** |-nātäləjist| n. **ne•o•na•tol•o•gy** |-nāˈtäləjē| n.

ne•o•nate |ˈnēəˌnāt| • n. a newborn child.

■ an infant less than four weeks old.

ne•o•phyte |ˈnēəˌfīt| • n. a person who is new to a subject, skill, or belief: *four-day cooking classes are offered to neophytes and experts.*

■ a new convert to a religion. ■ a novice in

a religious order, or a newly ordained priest.

ne•o•ter•ic |ˌnēəˈterik| • adj. recent; new; modern: *another effort by the White House to display its neoteric wizardry went awry.* • n. a modern person; a person who advocates new ideas.

ne plus ul•tra |ˈnē ˌpləs ˈəltrə; ˈnä ˌplо̄о̄s ˈо̄о̄ltrə| • n. the perfect or most extreme example of its kind; the ultimate: *he was the ne plus ultra of trombonists.*

nep•o•tism |ˈnepəˌtizəm| • n. the practice among those with power or influence of favoring relatives or friends, esp. by giving them jobs.

DERIVATIVES: **nep•o•tist** n. **nep•o•tis•tic** |ˌnepəˈtistik| adj.

Ne•re•id |ˈnirēid| • (also **nereid**) (in Greek mythology) any of the sea nymphs, daughters of Nereus. They include Thetis, mother of Achilles.

nerve•less |ˈnərvlis| • adj. **1** lacking vigor or feeling; inert or lifeless: *the knife dropped from Grant's nerveless fingers.*

■ (of literary or artistic style) diffuse or insipid: *Wilde and his art have been described as "nerveless and effeminate."* **2** not nervous; confident: *with nerveless panache.*

DERIVATIVES: **nerve•less•ly** adv. **nerve•less•ness** n.

nerv•y |ˈnərvē| • adj. (**nervier, nerviest**) **1** bold or impudent: *it was nervy of Billy to tell him how to play.* **2** chiefly Brit. easily agitated or alarmed; nervous: *he was nervy and on edge.* **3** sinewy or strong.

DERIVATIVES: **nerv•i•ly** |-əlē| adv. **nerv•i•ness** n.

nes•cient |ˈnesH(ē)ənt| • adj. lacking knowledge; ignorant: *a product of nescient minds.*

DERIVATIVES: **nesc•ience** n.

neth•er |ˈneTHər| • adj. lower in position: *the ballast is suspended from its nether end.*

DERIVATIVES: **neth•er•most** |-ˌmōst| adj.

net•tle |ˈnetl| • v. [trans.] irritate or annoy (someone): *I was nettled by her tone of superiority.*

net•tle•some |ˈnetlsəm| • adj. causing annoyance or difficulty: *complicated and nettlesome regional disputes.*

neu•ral•gia |n(y)о̄о̄ˈraljə| • n. intense, typically intermittent pain along the course of a nerve, esp. in the head or face.

DERIVATIVES: **neu•ral•gic** |-jik| adj.

neur•as•the•ni•a |ˌn(y)о̄о̄rəsˈTHēnēə| • n. an ill-defined medical condition characterized by lassitude, fatigue, headache, and irritability, associated chiefly with emotional disturbance.

DERIVATIVES: **neur•as•then•ic** |-ˈTHenik| adj. & n.

neu•ri•tis |n(y)о̄о̄ˈrītis| • n. (in medicine) inflammation of a peripheral nerve or nerves, usually causing pain and loss of function.

■ (in general use) neuropathy (disease or dysfunction of one or more such nerves, typically causing numbness and weakness).

DERIVATIVES: **neu•rit•ic** |-ˈritik| adj.

neu•rol•o•gy |n(y)o͝oˈräləjē| • *n.* the branch of medicine or biology that deals with the anatomy, functions, and organic disorders of nerves and the nervous system.
DERIVATIVES: **neu•ro•log•i•cal** |-rəˈläjikəl| *adj.* **neu•ro•log•i•cal•ly** |-rəˈläjik(ə)lē| *adv.* **neu•rol•o•gist** |-jist| *n.*

neu•ro•sis |n(y)o͝oˈrōsis| • *n.* (pl. **neuroses** |-ˌsēz|) a relatively mild mental illness that is not caused by organic disease, involving symptoms of stress (depression, anxiety, obsessive behavior, hypochondria) but not a radical loss of touch with reality. Cf. PSYCHOSIS.
■ (in nontechnical use) excessive and irrational anxiety or obsession: *apprehension over mounting debt has become a collective neurosis in the business world.*

neu•ter |ˈn(y)o͞otər| • *adj.* **1** of or denoting a gender of nouns in some languages, typically contrasting with masculine and feminine or common: *it is a neuter word in Greek.* **2** (of an animal) lacking developed sexual organs, or having had them removed.
■ (of a plant or flower) having neither functional pistils nor functional stamens. ■ (of a person) apparently having no sexual characteristics; asexual. • *n.* **1** a neuter word.
■ (**the neuter**) the neuter gender. **2** a nonfertile caste of social insect, esp. a worker bee or ant.
■ a castrated or spayed domestic animal. ■ a person who appears to lack sexual characteristics. • *v.* [trans.] castrate or spay (a domestic animal): | [as adj.] (**neutered**) *a neutered tomcat.*
■ render ineffective; deprive of vigor or force: *disarmament negotiations that will neuter their military power.*

neu•tral |ˈn(y)o͞otrəl| • *adj.* **1** not helping or supporting either of two opposing sides, esp. countries at war; impartial: *during World War II, Portugal was neutral.*
■ belonging to an impartial party, country, or group: *on neutral ground.* ■ unbiased; disinterested: *neutral, expert scientific advice.* **2** having no strongly marked or positive characteristics or features: *the tone was neutral, devoid of sentiment | a fairly neutral background will make any small splash of color stand out.*
■ Chemistry neither acid nor alkaline; having a pH of about 7. ■ electrically neither positive nor negative. • *n.* **1** an impartial and uninvolved country or person: *he acted as a neutral between the parties | Sweden and its fellow neutrals.*
■ an unbiased person. **2** a neutral color or shade, esp. light gray or beige. **3** a disengaged position of gears in which the engine is disconnected from the driven parts: *she slipped the gear into neutral.* **4** an electrically neutral point, terminal, conductor, or wire.
DERIVATIVES: **neu•tral•i•ty** |n(y)o͞oˈtralitē| *n.* **neu•tral•ly** *adv.*

neu•tral•ize |ˈn(y)o͞otrəˌlīz| • *v.* [trans.] render (something) ineffective or harmless by applying an opposite force or effect: *impatience at his frailty began to neutralize her fear.*
■ make (an acidic or alkaline substance) chemically neutral. ■ disarm (a bomb or similar weapon). ■ (euphemistically) kill or destroy, esp. in a covert or military operation: *agents sent out to neutralize the opposition leader.*
DERIVATIVES: **neu•tral•i•za•tion** |ˌn(y)o͞otrəli'zāsHən| *n.* **neu•tral•iz•er** *n.*

ne•vus |ˈnēvəs| (Brit. **naevus**) • *n.* (pl. **nevi** |-ˌvī|) a birthmark or a mole on the skin, esp. a birthmark in the form of a raised red patch.

New Age • *n.* a broad movement characterized by alternative approaches to traditional Western culture, with an interest in spirituality, mysticism, holism, and environmentalism: [as adj.] *a New Age center.*
DERIVATIVES: **New Ag•er** *n.* **New Ag•ey** *adj.*

new•speak |ˈn(y)o͞oˌspēk| • *n.* ambiguous euphemistic language used chiefly in political propaganda.

New•to•ni•an |n(y)o͞oˈtōnēən| • *adj.* relating to or arising from the work of Sir Isaac Newton (1642-1727), esp. in physics and optics.
■ formulated or behaving according to the principles of CLASSICAL physics.

nex•us |ˈneksəs| • *n.* (pl. same or **nexuses**) a connection or series of connections linking two or more things: *the nexus between industry and political power.*
■ a connected group or series: *a nexus of ideas.* ■ the central and most important point or place: *the nexus of all this activity was the college campus.*

ni•ce•ty |ˈnīsitē| • *n.* (pl. **-ies**) (usu. **niceties**) a fine detail or distinction, esp. one regarded as intricate and fussy: *absorbed in the niceties of Greek and Latin.*
■ accuracy or precision: *she prided herself on her nicety of pronunciation.* ■ a minor aspect of polite social behavior; a detail of etiquette: *we were brought up to observe the niceties.*
PHRASES: **to a nicety** precisely.

nic•ti•tate |ˈnikˌtitāt| (also **nictate**) • *v.* [intrans.] blink; wink.

nig•gard•ly |ˈnigərdlē| • *adj.* not generous; stingy: *serving out fodder with a niggardly hand.*
■ meager; scanty: *their share is a niggardly 2.7 percent.* • *adv.* in a stingy or meager manner.
DERIVATIVES: **nig•gard•li•ness** *n.*
USAGE: This word, along with its noun form **niggard**, should be used only with caution. Although the noun has been used since the fourteenth century, in recent years, because of the similarity in sound of these words and the highly inflammatory racial epithet **nigger**, confusion or offense can result.

nig•gling |ˈnig(ə)liNG| • *adj.* troublesome or irritating in a slight but persistent way: *gripped by a niggling feeling of premonition | niggling aches and pains.*
■ trifling or petty: *he picked up on the most niggling, tedious details.*

ni•hil•ism |ˈnīəˌlizəm; ˈnē-| • *n.* the rejection of all religious and moral principles, often in the belief that life is meaningless.
■ (in philosophy) extreme skepticism main-

taining that nothing in the world has a real existence. ■ the doctrine of an extreme Russian revolutionary party *c.*1900, which found nothing to approve of in the established social order.
DERIVATIVES: **ni•hil•ist** *n.* **ni•hil•is•tic** |ˌnīə'listik; ˌnēə-| *adj.*

nil |nil| • *n.* zero, esp. as a score in certain games: *they beat us three-nil.* • *adj.* nonexistent: *his chances for survival were slim, almost nil.*

nim•bus |'nimbəs| • *n.* (pl. **nimbi** |-ˌbī| or **nimbuses**) **1** a luminous cloud or a halo surrounding a supernatural being or a saint.
■ a light, aura, color, etc., that surrounds someone or something. **2** a large gray rain cloud: [as adj.] *nimbus clouds.*

nim•rod |'nimräd| • *n.* a skillful hunter.

nir•va•na |nər'vänə; nir-| • *n.* (in Buddhism) a transcendent state in which there is neither suffering, desire, nor sense of self, and the subject is released from the effects of karma and samsara. It represents the final goal of Buddhism. ■ (in Hinduism) liberation of the soul from the effects of karma and from bodily existence.
■ a state of perfect happiness; an ideal or idyllic place. *Hollywood's dearest dream of small-town nirvana.*

ni•sei |nē'sā; 'nēsā| (also **Nisei**) • *n.* (pl. same or **niseis**) a person born in the US or Canada whose parents were immigrants from Japan. Cf. ISSEI, SANSEI.

ni•si |'nīsī| • *adj.* [postpositive] (of a legal decree, order, or rule) taking effect or having validity only after certain specified conditions are met: *a decree nisi.*

niv•e•ous |'nivēəs| • *adj.* snowy or resembling snow.

no•ble |'nōbəl| • *adj.* (**nobler, noblest**) **1** belonging to a hereditary class with high social or political status; aristocratic: *the Duchess of Kent and other noble ladies.* **2** having or showing fine personal qualities or high moral principles and ideals: *the promotion of human rights was a noble aspiration.*
■ of imposing or magnificent size or appearance: *the building with its noble arches and massive granite columns.* ■ of excellent or superior quality. • *n.* **1** (esp. in former times) a person of noble rank or birth. **2** a former English gold coin.
DERIVATIVES: **no•ble•ness** *n.* **no•bly** |-blē| *adv.*

no•blesse |nō'bles| • *n.* the nobility.
PHRASES: **noblesse oblige** |nō'bles ō 'blēzH| the inferred responsibility of privileged people to act with generosity and nobility toward those less privileged; (the idea that) privilege entails responsibility: *there was to being a celebrity a certain element of noblesse oblige.*

noc•tam•bu•list |näk'tæmbyəlist| • *n.* a sleepwalker.
DERIVATIVES: **noc•tam•bu•lism** |-ˌlizəm| *n.*

noc•tur•nal |näk'tərnəl| • *adj.* done, occurring, or active at night: *most owls are nocturnal.* Cf. DIURNAL, CREPUSCULAR.

DERIVATIVES: **noc•tur•nal•ly** *adv.*

noc•turne |'näktərn| • *n.* **1** a short musical composition of a romantic or dreamy character suggestive of night, typically for piano. **2** a painting of a night scene.

noc•u•ous |'näkyōōwəs| • *adj.* noxious, harmful, or poisonous.

no•dus |'nōdəs| • *n.* (pl. **nodi** |-dī|) a problem, difficulty, or complication.

no•et•ic |nō'etik| • *adj.* of or relating to mental activity or the intellect.

Noh |nō| (also **No** or **Nō**) • *n.* traditional Japanese masked drama with dance and song, evolved from Shinto rites.

noi•some |'noisəm| • *adj.* having an extremely offensive smell: *noisome vapors from smoldering waste.*
■ disagreeable; unpleasant: *involved in noisome scandals.* ■ harmful; noxious.
DERIVATIVES: **noi•some•ness** *n.*

no•lo con•ten•de•re |ˌnōlō kən'tendərē| • *n.* (also **nolo**) (in law) a plea by which a defendant in a criminal prosecution accepts conviction as though a guilty plea had been entered but does not admit guilt.

no•mad |'nō,mæd| • *n.* a member of a people having no permanent abode, and who travel from place to place to find fresh pasture for their livestock.
■ a person who does not stay long in the same place; a wanderer. • *adj.* relating to or characteristic of nomads.
DERIVATIVES: **no•mad•ic** |nō'mædik| *adj.* **no•mad•i•cal•ly** |nō'mædiklē| *adv.* **no•mad•ism** |'nōmæ,dizəm| *n.*

nom de guerre |ˌnäm də 'ger| • *n.* (pl. **noms de guerre** pronunc. same) an assumed name under which a person engages in combat or some other activity or enterprise.

nom de plume |ˌnäm də 'plōōm| • *n.* (pl. **noms de plume** pronunc. same) a name under which a person write; a pen name.

no•men•cla•ture |'nōmən,klāCHər| • *n.* the devising or choosing of names for things, esp. in a science or other discipline: *the Linnaean system of binomial nomenclature.*
■ the body or system of such names in a particular field: *the nomenclature of chemical compounds.* ■ the term or terms applied to someone or something: *"customers" was preferred to the original nomenclature "passengers."*
DERIVATIVES: **no•men•cla•tur•al** |ˌnōmən'klāCHərəl| *adj.*

nom•i•nal |'näminəl| • *adj.* **1** (of a role or status) existing in name only: *Thailand retained nominal independence under Japanese occupation.*
■ of, relating to, or consisting of names. ■ (in grammar) relating to, headed by, or having the function of a noun. **2** (of a price or amount of money) very small; far below the real value or cost: *some firms charge only a nominal fee for the service.* **3** (of a quantity or dimension, esp. of manufactured articles) stated or expressed but not necessarily corresponding exactly to the real value: *legislation allowed variation around the nominal weight (that printed on each packet).*

■ (in economics, of a rate or other figure) expressed in terms of a certain amount, without making allowance for changes in real value over time: *the nominal exchange rate.* **4** (chiefly in the context of space travel) functioning normally or acceptably.
DERIVATIVES: **nom•i•nal•ly** *adv.*

nom•i•nal•ism |'näminə,lizəm| • *n.* The philosophical doctrine that universals or general ideas are mere names without any corresponding reality, and that only particular objects exist; properties, numbers, and sets are thought of as merely features of the way of considering the things that exist. Important in medieval scholastic thought, nominalism is associated particularly with William of Occam (ca 1285–?1349). Cf. REALISM.
DERIVATIVES: **nom•i•nal•ist** *n.* **nom•i•nal•is•tic** |,nämənə'listik| *adj.*

nom•i•na•tive |'nämənətiv| • *adj.* **1** relating to or denoting a case of nouns, pronouns, and adjectives (as in Latin and other inflected languages) used for the subject of a verb. Cf. SUBJECTIVE. **2** |-,nātiv| of or appointed by nomination as distinct from election. • *n.* a word in the nominative case.
■ (**the nominative**) the nominative case.

non•age |'nänij; 'nō-| • *n.* [in sing.] the period of immaturity or youth.

nonce |näns| • *adj.* (of a word or expression) coined for or used on one occasion: *a nonce usage.*
PHRASES: **for the nonce** for the present; temporarily: *the room had been converted for the nonce into a nursery.*

non•cha•lant |,nänsHə'länt| • *adj.* (of a person or manner) feeling or appearing casually calm and relaxed; not displaying anxiety, interest, or enthusiasm: *she gave a nonchalant shrug.*
DERIVATIVES: **non•cha•lance** *n.* **non•cha•lant•ly** *adv.*

non•com•mis•sioned |,nankə'misHənd| • *adj.* (of an officer in the armed forces) ranking below warrant officer, as sergeant or petty officer, not holding a commision.
DERIVATIVES: **non•com** *n.* informal military term for a noncommissioned officer.

non•com•mit•tal |,nänkə'mitl| • *adj.* (of a person or a person's behavior or manner) not expressing or revealing commitment to a definite opinion or course of action: *her tone was noncommittal, and her face gave nothing away.*
DERIVATIVES: **non•com•mit•tal•ly** *adv.*

non com•pos men•tis |,nän 'kämpəs 'mentis| (also **non compos**) • *adj.* not sane or in one's right mind.

non•con•form•ist |,nänkən'fôrmist| • *n.* **1** a person whose behavior or views do not conform to prevailing ideas or practices. **2** (**Nonconformist**) a member of a Protestant church in England that dissents from the established Anglican Church. • *adj.* **1** of or characterized by behavior or views that do not conform to prevailing ideas or practices. **2** (**Nonconformist**) of or relating to Nonconformists or their principles and practices.

DERIVATIVES: **non•con•form•ism** |-,mizəm| *n.*

non•en•ti•ty |nän'entitē| • *n.* (pl. **-ies**) **1** a person or thing with no special or interesting qualities; an unimportant person or thing: *a political nonentity.* **2** the quality or state of not existing: *asserting the nonentity of evil.*

nones |nōnz| • *plural n.* **1** in the ancient Roman calendar, the ninth day before the ides by inclusive reckoning, i.e., the 7th day of March, May, July, and October, or the 5th of other months. **2** (also **none**) a service of the Western Christian church, traditionally said (or chanted) at the ninth hour of the day (3 p.m.)

none•such |'nən,səcH| (also **nonsuch**) • *n.* a person or thing that is regarded as perfect or unparalleled.

non•fea•sance |nän'fēzəns| • *n.* failure to perform an act that is required by law. Cf. MALFEASANCE.

non•pa•reil |,nänpə'rel| • *adj.* having no match or equal; unrivaled: *he is a nonpareil storyteller* | [postpositive] *a film critic nonpareil.* • *n.* an unrivaled or matchless person or thing.

non•plus |nän'pləs| • *v.* (**nonplussed, non-plussing**) [trans.] (usu. **be nonplussed**) surprise and confuse (someone) so much that they are unsure how to react: *Diane was nonplussed by such an odd question.* • *n.* a state of being surprised and confused in this way.

non•re•sis•tance |,nänri'zistəns| • *n.* the practice or principle of not resisting authority, even when it is unjustly exercised.
■ the practice or principle of not employing force to resist authority, even when it is exercised violently.

non se•qui•tur |,nän 'sekwitər| • *n.* a conclusion or statement that does not logically follow from the previous argument or statement.

Nor•dic |'nôrdik| • *adj.* of or relating to Scandinavia, Finland, Iceland, and the Faroe Islands.
■ relating to or denoting a physical type of northern European peoples characterized by tall stature, a bony frame, light coloring, and a dolichocephalic head. ■ relating to or denoting the disciplines of cross-country skiing or ski jumping, as distinguished from Alpine, or downhill, skiing. • *n.* a native of Scandinavia, Finland, or Iceland.

norm |nôrm| • *n.* **1** (**the norm**) something that is usual, typical, or standard: *this system has been the norm in Germany for decades.*
■ (usu. **norms**) a standard or pattern, esp. of social behavior, that is typical or expected of a group: *the norms of good behavior in the civil service.* ■ a required standard; a level to be complied with or reached: [with adj.] *the 7% pay norm had been breached again.* **2** (in mathematics) the product of a complex number and its conjugate, equal to the sum of the squares of its real and imaginary components, or the positive square root of this sum.
■ an analogous quantity used to represent the magnitude of a vector.

nor•ma•tive |'nôrmətiv| • *adj.* establishing, relating to, or deriving from a standard or norm, esp. of behavior.
DERIVATIVES: **nor•ma•tive•ly** *adv.* **nor•ma•tive•ness** *n.*

no•sol•o•gy |nō'säləjē| • *n.* the branch of medical science dealing with the classification of diseases.
DERIVATIVES: **nos•o•log•i•cal** |,näsə'läjikəl| *adj.* **no•sol•o•gist** |-jist| *n.*

nos•tal•gia |nä'stæljə; nə-| • *n.* a sentimental longing or wistful affection for the past, typically for a period or place with happy personal associations.
■ the evocation of these feelings or tendencies, esp. in commercialized form: *an evening of TV nostalgia.*
DERIVATIVES: **nos•tal•gic** |-jik| *adj.* **nos•tal•gi•cal•ly** |-jik(ə)lē| *adv.* **nos•tal•gist** |-jist| *n.*

nos•trum |'nästrəm| • *n.* a medicine, esp. one that is not considered effective, prepared by an unqualified person, e.g., a quack.
■ a pet scheme or favorite remedy, esp. one for bringing about some social or political reform or improvement.

no•tion•al |'nōsHənəl| • *adj.* **1** existing only in theory or as a suggestion or idea: *notional budgets for community health services.*
■ existing only in the imagination. **2** (in linguistics) denoting or relating to an approach to grammar that is dependent on the definition of terminology (e.g., "a verb is an action word") as opposed to identification of structures and processes. **3** (in language teaching) denoting or relating to a syllabus that aims to develop communicative competence.
DERIVATIVES: **no•tion•al•ly** *adv.*

no•to•ri•ous |nə'tôrēəs; nō'tôrēəs| • *adj.* famous or well known, typically for some bad quality or deed: *Los Angeles is notorious for its smog | a notorious drinker and womanizer.* Cf. INFAMOUS
DERIVATIVES: **no•to•ri•e•ty** |,nōtə'rīətē| *n.* **no•to•ri•ous•ly** *adv.*

nou•me•non |'nōōmə,nän| • *n.* (pl. **nou•mena** |-nə|) (in Kantian philosophy) a thing as it is in itself, as distinct from a thing as it is knowable by the senses through phenomenal attributes.
DERIVATIVES: **nou•me•nal** |-nəl| *adj.*

nous |nōōs; nows| • *n.* **1** (in philosophy) the mind or intellect. **2** *chiefly Brit.* common sense; practical intelligence.

nou•veau riche |'nōōvō 'rēsH| • *n.* [treated as pl.] (usu. **the nouveau riche**) people who have recently acquired wealth, typically those perceived as ostentatious or lacking in good taste. • *adj.* of, relating to, or characteristic of such people: *nouveau-riche social climbers.*

nou•velle cui•sine |nōō'vel kwi'zēn| • *n.* a modern style of cooking that avoids rich, heavy foods and emphasizes the freshness of the ingredients and the presentation of the dishes.

nov•el¹ |'nävəl| • *n.* a fictitious prose narrative of book length, typically representing

character and action with some degree of realism: *the novels of Jane Austen.*
■ a book containing such a narrative: *she was reading a paperback novel.* ■ **(the novel)** the literary genre represented or exemplified by such works: *the novel is the most adaptable of all literary forms.*

nov•el² • *adj.* new or unusual in an interesting way: *he hit on a novel idea to solve his financial problems.*
DERIVATIVES: **nov•el•ly** *adv.* **nov•el•ty** *n.*

no•vel•la |nō'velə| • *n.* a short novel or long short story.

nov•el•ty |'nävəltē| • *n.* (pl. **-ies**) **1** the quality of being new, original, or unusual: *the novelty of being a married woman wore off.*
■ a new or unfamiliar thing or experience: *in 1914 air travel was still a novelty.* ■ [as adj.] denoting something intended to be amusing as a result of its new or unusual quality: *a novelty teapot.* **2** a small and inexpensive toy or ornament: *he bought chocolate novelties to decorate the Christmas tree.*

no•ve•na |nō'vēnə| • *n.* (in the Roman Catholic Church) a form of worship consisting of special prayers or services on nine successive days.

nov•ice |'nävəs| • *n.* a person new to or inexperienced in a field or situation: *he was a complete novice in foreign affairs.*
■ a person who has entered a religious order and is under probation, before taking vows. ■ an animal, esp. a racehorse, that has not yet won a major prize or reached a level of performance to qualify for important events.

no•vi•ti•ate |nō'visH(ē)ət; nə-| (also **noviciate**) • *n.* the period or state of being a novice, esp. in a religious order.
■ a place housing religious novices. ■ a novice, esp. in a religious order.

nox•ious |'näksHəs| • *adj.* harmful, poisonous, or very unpleasant: *they were overcome by the noxious fumes.*
DERIVATIVES: **nox•ious•ly** *adv.* **nox•ious•ness** *n.*

no•yade |nwä'yäd| • *n.* an execution carried out by drowning.

nth |enTH| • *adj.* (in mathematics) denoting an unspecified member of a series of numbers or enumerated items: *systematic sampling by taking every nth name from the list.*
■ (in general use) denoting an unspecified item or instance in a series, typically the last or latest in a long series: *for the nth time that day they were forced to repeat the whole story.*
PHRASES: **to the nth degree** to the utmost: *the gullibility of the electorate was tested to the nth degree by such promises.*

nu•ance |'n(y)ōō,äns| • *n.* a subtle difference in or shade of meaning, expression, or sound: *the nuances of facial expression and body language.* • *v.* [trans.] (usu. **be nuanced**) give nuances to: *the effect of the music is nuanced by the social situation of listeners.*

nu•bile |'n(y)ōō,bīl; -bəl| • *adj.* (of a girl or young woman) sexually mature; suitable for marriage.
■ (of a girl or young woman) sexually attrac-

tive: *he employed a procession of nubile young secretaries.*

DERIVATIVES: **nu•bil•i•ty** |n(y)o͞o'bilitē| *n.*

nu•cle•ic ac•id |n(y)o͞o'klē-ik| • *n.* a complex organic substance present in living cells, esp. DNA or RNA, whose molecules consist of many nucleotides (compounds) linked in a long chain.

nu•cle•us |'n(y)o͞oklēəs| • *n.* (pl. **nuclei** |-klē ,ī|) the central and most important part of an object, movement, or group, forming the basis for its activity and growth: *the nucleus of a film-producing industry.*
■ (in physics) the positively charged central core of an atom, containing most of its mass. ■ (in biology) a dense organelle present in most eukaryotic cells, typically a single rounded structure bounded by a double membrane, containing the genetic material. ■ (in astronomy) the solid part of the head of a comet. ■ (in anatomy) a discrete mass of gray matter in the central nervous system.

nud•nik |'no͞od,nik| (also **nudnick**) • *n.* a pestering, nagging, or irritating person; a bore.

nu•ga•to•ry |'n(y)o͞ogə,tôrē| • *adj.* of no value or importance: *a nugatory and pointless observation.*
■ useless; futile.

nui•sance |'n(y)o͞osəns| • *n.* a person, thing, or circumstance causing inconvenience or annoyance.
■ (also **private nuisance**) (in law) an unlawful interference with the use and enjoyment of a person's land, which may become the subject of a lawsuit. ■ (also **public nuisance**) an act that interferes with the rights of the public generally, which may be prosecuted as a crime.

nuit blanche |,nwē 'blänSH| • *n.* (pl. **nuits blanches** pronunc. same) a sleepless night.

null |nəl| • *adj.* **1** [predic.] having no legal or binding force; invalid: *the establishment of a new interim government was declared **null and void**.* **2** having or associated with the value zero.
■ (in mathematics, of a set or matrix) having no elements, or only zeros as elements. ■ lacking distinctive qualities; having no positive substance or content: *his curiously null life.* • *n.* a zero.
■ a dummy letter in a cipher. ■ (in electronics) a condition of no signal. ■ a condition in which no electromagnetic radiation is detected or emitted. • *v.* [trans.] (in electronics) combine (a signal) with another in order to create a null; cancel out.

nul•li•fi•ca•tion |,nələfə'kāSHən| *n.* • **1** (in US history) the refusal of a state to allow federal law to be enforced within its boundaries. **2** (also **jury nullification**) the refusal of a jury to convict a defendant, disregarding its own findings of fact or the judge's instructions regarding the law.

nul•li•fid•i•an |,nələ'fidēən| • *n.* a person having no faith or religious belief. • *adj.* having no faith or religious belief.

nul•li•fy |'nələ,fī| • *v.* (**-ies, -ied**) [trans.] make legally null and void; invalidate: *judges were unwilling to nullify government decisions.*
■ make of no use or value; cancel out: *insulin can block the release of the hormone and thereby nullify the effects of training.*

DERIVATIVES: **nul•li•fi•er** *n.*

nul•li•ty |'nəlitē| • *n.* (pl. **-ies**) **1** an act or thing that is legally void: *the contract is a nullity.*
■ the state of being legally void; invalidity, esp. of a marriage. **2** a thing of no importance or worth.
■ nothingness.

nu•men |'n(y)o͞omən| • *n.* (pl. **numina** |-mə nə|) the spirit or divine power presiding over a thing or place.

nu•mer•ate |'n(y)o͞om(ə)rət| • *adj.* having a good basic knowledge of arithmetic; able to understand and work with numbers.

DERIVATIVES: **nu•mer•a•cy** *n.*

nu•mer•ol•o•gy |,n(y)o͞omə'räləjē| • *n.* the branch of knowledge that deals with the occult significance of numbers.

DERIVATIVES: **nu•mer•o•log•i•cal** |-rə 'läjikəl| *adj.* **nu•mer•ol•o•gist** |-jist| *n.*

nu•mi•nous |'n(y)o͞omənəs| • *adj.* having a strong religious or spiritual quality; indicating or suggesting the presence of a divinity (numen): *the strange, numinous beauty of this ancient landmark.*

nu•mis•mat•ics |,n(y)o͞oməz'mætiks; -məs-| • *plural n.* [usu. treated as sing.] the study or collection of coins, paper currency, and medals.

DERIVATIVES: **nu•mis•ma•tist** |n(y)o͞o 'mizmətist; -'mis-| *n.*

nun•ci•o |'nənsē,ō; 'no͞on-| • *n.* (pl. **-os**) (in the Roman Catholic Church) a papal ambassador to a foreign court or government.

nun•cu•pa•tive |'nənGkyə,pātiv| • *adj.* (of a will or testament) declared orally as opposed to in writing, esp. by a mortally wounded soldier or sailor.

nur•ture |'nərCHər| • *v.* [trans.] care for and encourage the growth or development of: *nurturing her brood | my father nurtured my love of art.*
■ cherish (a hope, belief, or ambition): *for a long time she had nurtured the dream of buying a shop.* • *n.* the process of caring for and encouraging the growth or development of someone or something: *the nurture of ethics and integrity.*
■ upbringing, education, and environment, esp as contrasted with inborn characteristics (nature) as an influence on or determinant of personality.

DERIVATIVES: **nur•tur•er** *n.*

nu•ta•tion |n(y)o͞o'tāSHən| • *n.* a periodic variation in the inclination of the axis of a rotating object.
■ (in astronomy) a periodic oscillation of the earth's axis that causes the precession of the poles to follow a wavy rather than a circular path. ■ (in botany) the circular swaying movement of the tip of a growing shoot.

nu•tri•ent |'n(y)o͞otrēənt| • *n.* a substance that provides nourishment essential for growth and the maintenance of life: *fish is a source of many important nutrients, including protein, vitamins, and minerals* | *leaf mold and other soil nutrients.*

nu•tri•ment |'n(y)o͞otrəmənt| • *n.* that which nourishes; sustenance.
DERIVATIVES: **nu•tri•men•tal** |ˌn(y)o͞otrə'mentl| *adj.*

nyc•ta•lo•pi•a |ˌniktə'lōpēə| • *n.* the inability to see in dim light or at night. (Also called **night blindness**.)

nymph |nimf| • *n.* **1** a mythological spirit of nature imagined as a beautiful maiden inhabiting rivers, woods, or other locations.
■ a beautiful young woman. **2** an immature form of an insect that does not change greatly as it grows, e.g., a dragonfly, mayfly, or locust. Cf. LARVA.

■ an artificial fly made to resemble the aquatic nymph of an insect, used in fishing.
DERIVATIVES: **nymph•al** |'nimfəl| *adj.* **nym•phe•an** |'nimfēən| *adj.* **nymph•like** |'nimfˌlīk| *adj.*

nym•phae•um |nim'fēəm| • *n.* (pl. **nym•phaea** |-'fēə|) a grotto or shrine dedicated to a nymph or nymphs.

nymph•et |nim'fet; 'nimfit| • *n.* an attractive and sexually mature young girl.

nym•pho•ma•ni•a |ˌnimfə'mānēə| • *n.* uncontrollable or excessive sexual desire in a woman.
DERIVATIVES: **nym•pho•ma•ni•ac** |-'mānē,æk| *n. & adj.* **nym•pho•ma•ni•a•cal** |-mə'nīəkəl| *adj.*

nys•tag•mus |nə'stægməs| • *n.* rapid involuntary movements of the eyes.
DERIVATIVES: **nys•tag•mic** |-mik| *adj.*

Oo

oath |ōTH| • *n.* (pl. **oaths** |ōTHs; ōTHz|) **1** a solemn promise, often invoking a divine witness, regarding one's future action or behavior: *they took an oath of allegiance to the state.*
■ a sworn declaration that one will tell the truth, esp. in a court of law. **2** a profane or offensive expression used to express anger or other strong emotions.

ob•bli•ga•to |ˌäblə'gätō| (also **obligato**) • *n.* (pl. **obbligatos** or **obbligati** |-'gätē|) [usu. with or as adj.] an instrumental part, typically distinctive in effect, that is integral to a piece of music and should not be omitted in performance.
■ such a part played to accompany another instrumental or vocal part. ■ notes played in accompaniment: *improvising obbligatos to the lead of Miles Davis.*

ob•du•rate |'äbd(y)ərit| • *adj.* stubbornly refusing to change one's opinion or course of action.
DERIVATIVES: **ob•du•ra•cy** |-rəsē| *n.* **ob•du•rate•ly** *adv.* **ob•du•rate•ness** *n.*

o•bei•sance |ō'bāsəns; ō'bē-| • *n.* deferential respect: *they **paid obeisance** to the sheikh.*
■ a gesture expressing deferential respect, such as a bow or curtsy: *she made a deep obeisance.*
DERIVATIVES: **o•bei•sant** |ō'bāsənt| *adj.*

ob•e•lisk |'äbə,lisk| • *n.* **1** a stone pillar, typically having a square or rectangular cross section and a pyramidal top, set up as a monument or landmark.
■ a mountain, tree, or other natural object of similar shape. **2** another term for OBELUS.

ob•e•lus |'äbələs| • *n.* (pl. **obeli** |-,lī|) **1** a symbol (†) used as a reference mark in printed matter, or to indicate that a person is deceased. (Also called **dagger**.) **2** a mark

(− or ÷) used in ancient texts to mark a word or passage as spurious, corrupt, or doubtful.

o•bese |ō'bēs| • *adj.* grossly fat or overweight.
DERIVATIVES: **o•be•si•ty** |-sitē| *n.* **o•bese•ness** *n.*

ob•fus•cate |'äbfə,skāt| • *v.* [trans.] render obscure, unclear, or unintelligible: *the spelling changes will obfuscate their etymological origins.*
■ bewilder (someone): *it is more likely to obfuscate people than enlighten them.*
DERIVATIVES: **ob•fus•ca•tion** |ˌäbfə'skāSHən| *n.* **ob•fus•ca•to•ry** |äb'fəskə,tôrē| *adj.*

ob•jec•ti•fy |əb'jektə,fī| • *v.* (**-ies, -ied**) [trans.] express (something abstract) in a concrete form: *good poetry objectifies feeling.*
■ degrade to the status of a mere object: *a sexist attitude that objectifies women.* Cf. REIFY
DERIVATIVES: **ob•jec•ti•fi•ca•tion** |əb,jektəfi'kāSHən| *n.*

ob•jec•tive |əb'jektiv| • *adj.* **1** (of a person or his or her judgment) not influenced by personal feelings or opinions in considering and representing facts.
■ not dependent on the mind for existence; actual: *a matter of objective fact.* **2** [attrib.] (in grammar) of, relating to, or denoting a case of nouns and pronouns used as the object of a transitive verb or a preposition. • *n.* **1** a thing aimed at or sought; a goal: *the system has achieved its objective.* **2** (**the objective**) (in grammar) the objective case. **3** (also **objective lens**) the lens in a telescope or microscope nearest to the object observed.
DERIVATIVES: **ob•jec•tive•ly** *adv.* **ob•jec•tive•ness** *n.* **ob•jec•tiv•i•ty** |,äbjek'tivitē| *n.* **ob•jec•ti•vi•za•tion** |əb,jektəvi'zāSHən| *n.* **ob•jec•tiv•ize** |-,vīz| *v.*

ob•jec•tiv•ism |əb'jektə,vizəm| • *n.* **1** the tendency to lay stress on what is external to or independent of the mind. **2** (in philosophy) the belief that certain things, esp. moral truths, exist independently of human knowledge or perception of them.
DERIVATIVES: **ob•jec•tiv•ist** *n.* & *adj.* **ob•jec•ti•vis•tic** |əb,jektə'vistik| *adj.*

ob•jet |ôb'zнɑ| • *n.* an object displayed or intended for display as an ornament.

ob•jet d'art |,ôbzнɑ 'där| • *n.* (pl. **objets d'art** pronunc. same) a small decorative or artistic object, typically when regarded as a collectible item.

ob•jur•gate |'äbjər,gāt| • *v.* [trans.] rebuke severely; scold.
DERIVATIVES: **ob•jur•ga•tion** |,äbjər'gā-sнən| *n.* **ob•jur•ga•tor** |-gā̤ər| *n.* **ob•jur•ga•to•ry** |əb'jərgə,tôrē| *adj.*

ob•late[1] |'äb,lāt| ,ō'blāt| • *n.* a person dedicated to monastic or religious life or work.

ob•late[2] • *adj.* (of a spheroid) flattened at the poles.

ob•la•tion |ə'blāsнən| • *n.* a thing presented or offered to God or a god.
■ the presentation of bread and wine to God in the Eucharist.
DERIVATIVES: **ob•la•tion•al** |-sнənl; -sнnəl| *adj.* **ob•la•to•ry** |'äblə,tôrē| *adj.*

ob•li•gate • *v.* |'äbli,gāt| **1** bind or compel (someone), esp. legally or morally: *the medical establishment is obligated to take action in the best interest of the public.* **2** [trans.] commit (assets) as security: *the money must be obligated within 30 days.* • *adj.* [attrib.] (in biology) restricted to a particular function or mode of life: *an obligate intracellular parasite.*
DERIVATIVES: **ob•li•ga•tor** |-,gā̤ər| *n.*

o•blig•a•to•ry |ə'bligə,tôrē| • *adj.* required by a legal, moral, or other rule; compulsory: *use of seat belts in cars is now obligatory.*
■ so customary or routine as to be expected of everyone or on every occasion: *after the obligatory remarks about the weather he got down to business.*
DERIVATIVES: **o•blig•a•to•ri•ly** |-,tôrəlē| *adv.*

o•blige |ə'blīj| • *v.* [with obj. and infinitive] make (someone) legally or morally bound to an action or course of action: *doctors are obliged by law to keep patients alive while there is a chance of recovery.*
■ [trans.] do as (someone) asks or desires in order to help or please them: *oblige me by not being sorry for yourself* | [intrans.] *tell me what you want to know and I'll see if I can oblige.* ■ (**be obliged**) be indebted or grateful: *if you can give me a few minutes of your time I'll be much obliged.* ■ [trans.] bind (someone) by an oath, promise, or contract.
DERIVATIVES: **o•blig•er** *n.*

o•blig•ing |ə'blījiNG| • *adj.* willing to do a service or kindness; helpful: *an obliging driver who dropped us at our door.*
DERIVATIVES: **o•blig•ing•ly** *adv.* **o•blig•ing•ness** *n.*

o•blique |ə'blēk; ō'blēk| • *adj.* **1** neither parallel nor at a right angle to a specified or implied line; slanting: *we sat on the settee oblique to the fireplace.*
■ not explicit or direct in addressing a point: *an oblique attack on the president.* ■ (of a line, plane figure, or surface) inclined at other than a right angle. ■ (of an angle) acute or obtuse. ■ (of a cone, cylinder, etc.) with an axis not perpendicular to the plane of its base.
■ (esp. of a muscle) neither parallel nor perpendicular to the long axis of a body or limb. **2** (in grammar) denoting any case other than the nominative or vocative. • *n.* a muscle neither parallel nor perpendicular to the long axis of a body or limb.
DERIVATIVES: **o•blique•ly** *adv.* **o•blique•ness** *n.* **o•bliq•ui•ty** |ə'blikwədē; -wədē| *n.*

ob•lit•er•ate |ə'blitə,rāt| • *v.* [trans.] destroy utterly; wipe out.
■ completely get rid of from the mind: *he obliterated the experience from his memory.* ■ cause to become invisible or indistinct; blot out.
DERIVATIVES: **ob•lit•er•a•tion** |ə,blitə'rā-sнən| *n.* **ob•lit•er•a•tive** |-,rā̤iv| *adj.* **o•blit•er•a•tor** |-,rā̤ər| *n.*

ob•liv•i•on |ə'blivēən| • *n.* the state of being unaware or unconscious of what is happening: *they drank themselves into oblivion.*
■ the state of being forgotten, esp. by the public: *his name will fade into oblivion.* ■ extinction: *only the levee stood between us and oblivion.*

ob•liv•i•ous |ə'blivēəs| • *adj.* not aware of or not concerned about what is happening around one: *she became absorbed, oblivious to the passage of time.*
DERIVATIVES: **ob•liv•i•ous•ly** *adv.* **ob•liv•i•ous•ness** *n.*

ob•lo•quy |'äbləkwē| • *n.* strong public criticism or verbal abuse: *endured years of contempt and obloquy.*
■ disgrace, esp. that brought about by public abuse: *conduct to which no more obloquy could reasonably attach.*
DERIVATIVES: **ob•lo•qui•al** |äb'lōkwēəl| *adj.* **ob•lo•qui•ous** |äb'lōkwēəs| *adj.*

ob•nox•ious |əb'näksнəs| • *adj.* extremely unpleasant.
DERIVATIVES: **ob•nox•ious•ly** *adv.* **ob•nox•ious•ness** *n.*

ob•scene |əb'sēn| • *adj.* (of the portrayal or description of sexual matters) offensive or disgusting by accepted standards of morality and decency: *obscene jokes* | *obscene literature.*
■ offensive to moral principles; repugnant: *using animals' skins for fur coats is obscene.*
DERIVATIVES: **ob•scene•ly** *adv.*

ob•scen•i•ty |əb'senitē| • *n.* (pl. **-ies**) the state or quality of being obscene; obscene behavior, language, or images: *the book was banned for obscenity.*
■ an extremely offensive word or expression: *the men scowled and muttered obscenities.* ■ something offensive to moral principles: *the ultimate obscenity is war.*

ob•se•quies |'äbsəkwēz| • *plural n.* funeral rites.

ob•se•qui•ous |əb'sēkwēəs| • *adj.* obedient or attentive to an excessive or servile degree: *they were served by obsequious waiters.*

DERIVATIVES: **ob•se•qui•ous•ly** *adv.* **ob•se•qui•ous•ness** *n.*

ob•ses•sion |əb'seSHən| • *n.* the state of having the mind filled continually with someone or something: *cared for him with a devotion bordering on obsession.*

■ an idea or thought that continually preoccupies or intrudes on a person's mind: *in the grip of an obsession he was powerless to resist.*

DERIVATIVES: **ob•ses•sion•al** |-SHənl| *adj.* **ob•ses•sion•al•ly** |-SHənl-ē| *adv.*

ob•so•les•cent |ˌäbsə'lesənt| • *adj.* becoming obsolete; going out of use: *the custom is now obsolescent.*

DERIVATIVES: **ob•so•lesce** *v.* *existing systems begin to obsolesce.* **ob•so•les•cence** *n.*

ob•so•lete |ˌäbsə'lēt| • *adj.* **1** no longer produced or used; out of date: *the disposal of obsolete machinery* | *the phrase was obsolete after 1625.* **2** (of a part or characteristic of an organism) less developed than formerly or in a related species; rudimentary; vestigial. • *v.* [trans.] cause (a product or idea) to be or become obsolete by replacing it with something new: *stimulating the business by obsoleting last year's designs.*

DERIVATIVES: **ob•so•lete•ly** *adv.* **ob•so•lete•ness** *n.* **ob•so•let•ism** |-'lē,tizəm| *n.*

ob•stet•rics |əb'stetriks; äb-| • *plural n.* [usu. treated as sing.] the branch of medicine and surgery concerned with childbirth and the care of women giving birth.

ob•sti•nate |'äbstənit| • *adj.* stubbornly refusing to change one's opinion or chosen course of action, despite attempts to persuade one to do so.

■ (of an unwelcome phenomenon or situation) very difficult to change or overcome: *the obstinate problem of unemployment.*

DERIVATIVES: **ob•sti•na•cy** |-nəsē| *n.* **ob•sti•nate•ly** *adv.*

ob•strep•er•ous |əb'strepərəs; äb-| • *adj.* noisy and difficult to control: *the boy is cocky and obstreperous.*

DERIVATIVES: **ob•strep•er•ous•ly** *adv.* **ob•strep•er•ous•ness** *n.*

ob•trude |əb'trōōd| • *v.* [intrans.] become noticeable in an unwelcome or intrusive way: *a sound from the reception hall obtruded into his thoughts.*

■ [trans.] impose or force (something) on someone in such a way: *I felt unable to obtrude my private sorrow upon anyone.*

DERIVATIVES: **ob•trud•er** *n.* **ob•tru•sion** |-'trōōzHən| *n.*

ob•tru•sive |əb'trōōsiv; äb-| • *adj.* noticeable or prominent in an unwelcome or intrusive way: *high-powered satellites can reach smaller and less obtrusive antennas.*

DERIVATIVES: **ob•tru•sive•ly** *adv.* **ob•tru•sive•ness** *n.*

ob•tuse |əb't(y)ōōs; äb-| • *adj.* **1** annoyingly insensitive or slow to understand: *he wondered if the doctor was being deliberately obtuse.*

■ difficult to understand: *some of the lyrics are*

a bit obtuse. **2** (of an angle) more than 90° and less than 180°.

■ not sharp-pointed or sharp-edged; blunt.

DERIVATIVES: **ob•tuse•ly** *adv.* **ob•tuse•ness** *n.* **ob•tu•si•ty** |-sitē| *n.*

ob•verse |'äb,vərs| • *n.* [usu. in sing.] **1** the side of a coin or medal bearing the head or principal design; the opposite of *reverse.*

■ the design or inscription on this side. **2** the opposite or counterpart of a fact or truth: *true solitude is the obverse of true society.* • *adj.* |əb'vərs; äb-| [attrib.] **1** of or denoting the obverse of a coin or medal. **2** corresponding to something else as its opposite or counterpart. **3** (in biology) narrower at the base or point of attachment than at the apex or top: *an obverse leaf.*

DERIVATIVES: **ob•verse•ly** |əb'vərslē; äb-| *adv.*

ob•vert |əb'vərt; äb-| • *v.* [trans.] (in logic) alter (a proposition) so as to infer another proposition with a contradictory predicate, e.g., *"no men are immortal"* to *"all men are mortal."*

DERIVATIVES: **ob•ver•sion** |əb'vərzHən; äb-| *n.*

ob•vi•ate |'äbvē,āt| • *v.* [trans.] remove (a need or difficulty): *the Venetian blinds obviated the need for curtains.*

■ avoid; prevent: *a parachute can be used to obviate disaster.*

DERIVATIVES: **ob•vi•a•tion** |äbvē'āsHən| *n.* **ob•vi•a•tor** |-,ātər| *n.*

Oc•ci•dent |'äksidənt; -,dent| • *n.* (the Occident) the countries of the West, esp. Europe and the Americas. Cf. ORIENT.

DERIVATIVES: **oc•ci•den•tal** *adj.*, *n.*

oc•clude |ə'klōōd| • *v.* **1** [trans.] stop, close up, or obstruct (an opening, orifice, or passage): *thick makeup can occlude the pores.*

■ shut (something) in: *they were occluding the waterfront with a wall of buildings.* ■ cover (an eye) to prevent its use: *it is placed at eye level with one eye occluded.* ■ (of a solid) absorb and retain (a gas or impurity). **2** [intrans.] (of a tooth) close on or come into contact with another tooth in the opposite jaw.

oc•cult |ə'kəlt| • *n.* (the occult) supernatural, mystical, or magical beliefs, practices, or phenomena: *a secret society dabbling in the occult.* • *adj.* **1** of, involving, or relating to supernatural, mystical, or magical powers or phenomena: *a follower of occult practices.*

■ beyond the range of ordinary knowledge or experience; mysterious: *an occult sensation of having experienced the identical situation before.*

■ communicated only to the initiated; esoteric: *the occult language of the community.* **2** (of a disease or process) not accompanied by readily discernible signs or symptoms.

■ (of blood) abnormally present, e.g., in feces, but detectable only chemically or microscopically. • *v.* [trans.] cut off from view by interposing something: *a wooden screen designed to occult the competitors.*

■ (of a celestial body) conceal (an apparently smaller body) from view by passing or being in front of it.

DERIVATIVES: **oc·cul·ta·tion** |ˌäkəl'tā-sHən| *n.* **oc·cult·ism** |-ˌtizəm| *n.* **oc·cult·ist** |-tist| *n.* **oc·cult·ly** *adv.* **oc·cult·ness** *n.*

o·cea·nog·ra·phy |ˌ ōsHə'nägrəfē| • *n.* the branch of science that deals with the physical and biological properties and phenomena of the sea. **Oceanology** deals more specifically with the technology and economics of human use of the sea.
DERIVATIVES: **o·cea·nog·ra·pher** |-fər| *n.* **o·cea·no·graph·ic** |ˌōsHənə'grafik| *adj.* **o·cea·no·graph·i·cal** |-nə'grafəkəl| *adj.*

och·loc·ra·cy |äk'läkrəsē| • *n.* government by a mob; mob rule.
DERIVATIVES: **och·lo·crat** |'äklə,krat| *n.* **och·lo·crat·ic** |ˌäklə'kraṯik| *adj.*

oc·tave |'äktəv; 'äk,tāv| • *n.* **1** (in music) a series of eight notes occupying the interval between (and including) two notes, one having twice or half the frequency of vibration of the other. ■ the interval between these two notes. ■ each of the two notes at the extremes of this interval. ■ these two notes sounding together. **2** a poem or stanza of eight lines; an octet. **3** the eighth day after a church festival, inclusive of the day of the festival. ■ a period of eight days beginning with the day of such a festival.

oc·u·list |'äkyələst| • *n.* (in earlier use) a person who specializes in the medical treatment of diseases or defects of the eye; an ophthalmologist. ■ an optometrist.

o·de·um |'ōdēəm| • *n.* (pl. **odeums** or **odea** |'ōdēə|) (also **odeon**) (esp. in ancient Greece or Rome) a building used for musical performances.

o·di·ous |'ōdēəs| • *adj.* extremely unpleasant; hateful; repulsive.
DERIVATIVES: **o·di·ous·ly** *adv.* **o·di·ous·ness** *n.*

o·di·um |'ōdēəm| • *n.* general or widespread hatred or disgust directed toward someone, often as a result of his or her actions. ■ disgrace over something hated or shameful; opprobrium.

o·dom·e·ter |ō'dämiṯər| • *n.* an instrument for measuring the distance traveled by a vehicle.

od·ys·sey a Greek epic poem traditionally ascribed to Homer, describing the travels of Odysseus (Roman, Ulysses) during his ten years of wandering after the fall of Troy. He eventually returned home to Ithaca and killed the suitors who had plagued his wife Penelope during his absence. ■ (**odyssey**) any long, adventurous journey. ■ an extended process of developement or change.
DERIVATIVES: **Od·ys·se·an** *adj.*

Oed·i·pus com·plex • *n.* (in Freudian psychoanalytic theory) the complex of emotions aroused in a young child, typically around the age of four, by an unconscious sexual desire for the parent of the opposite sex and a wish to exclude the parent of the same sex. (The term was originally applied to boys, the equivalent in girls being called the **Electra complex**.)
DERIVATIVES: **Oed·i·pal** |-pəl| *adj.*

oe·no·phile |'ēnə,fīl| • *n.* a connoisseur of wines.
DERIVATIVES: **oe·noph·i·list** |ē'näfəlist| *n.*

oeu·vre |'œvrə| • *n.* the works of a painter, composer, or author regarded collectively: *the complete oeuvre of Mozart.* ■ a work of art, music, or literature: *an early oeuvre.*

o·fay |'ō,fā| • *n.* an offensive term for a white person, used by black people: [as adj.] *ofay society.*

of·fal |'ôfəl; 'äfəl| • *n.* the entrails and internal organs of an animal used as food. ■ refuse or waste material. ■ decomposing animal flesh.

of·fer·to·ry |'ôfər,tôrē; 'äfər-| • *n.* (pl. **-ies**) **1** the offering of the bread and wine at the Christian Eucharist. ■ prayers or music accompanying this. **2** an offering or collection of money made at a religious service. ■ prayers or music accompanying this.

of·fi·cious |ə'fisHəs| • *adj.* assertive of authority in an annoyingly domineering way, esp. with regard to petty or trivial matters: *a policeman came to move them on, an officious, spiteful man.* ■ intrusively enthusiastic in offering help or advice; interfering: *an officious bystander.*
DERIVATIVES: **of·fi·cious·ly** *adv.* **of·fi·cious·ness** *n.*

off-price • *n.* a method of retailing in which brand-name goods (esp. clothing) are sold for less than the usual retail or discount price: [as adj.] *an off-price store.* • *adv.* using this method: *selling goods off-price.*
DERIVATIVES: **off-pricer** *n.*

off·shore |'ôf'sHôr; 'äf-| • *adj. & adv.* **1** situated at sea some distance from the shore: [as adj.] *this huge stretch of coastline is dominated by offshore barrier islands* | [as adv.] *we dropped anchor offshore.* ■ (of the wind) blowing toward the sea from the land. ■ of or relating to the business of extracting oil or gas from the seabed: *offshore drilling.* Cf. ONSHORE. **2** made, situated, or conducting business abroad, esp. in order to take advantage of lower costs or less stringent regulation: [as adj.] *huge deposits in offshore accounts.* ■ of, relating to, or derived from a foreign country: [as adj.] *offshore politics.*

o·gee |ō'jē| • *adj.* (in architecture) having a double continuous S-shaped curve. • *n.* an S-shaped line or molding.
DERIVATIVES: **o·geed** *adj.*

o·give |ō'jīv| • *n.* a pointed or Gothic arch. ■ one of the diagonal groins or ribs of a vault. ■ a thing having the profile of an ogive, esp. the head of a projectile or the nose cone of a rocket.
DERIVATIVES: **o·gi·val** |ō'jīvəl| *adj.*

o·gle |'ōgəl| • *v.* [trans.] stare at in a lecherous manner: *he was ogling her breasts* | [intrans.] *men* *who had turned up to ogle.* • *n.* a lecherous look.

DERIVATIVES: **o•gler** |'ōg(ə)lər| *n.*

oil•y |'oilē| • *adj.* (**oilier, oiliest**) **1** containing oil: *oily fish such as mackerel and sardines.*
■ covered or soaked with oil: *an oily rag.*
■ resembling oil in appearance or behavior: *the oily swell of the river.* **2** figurative (of a person or their behavior) unpleasantly smooth and ingratiating: *his oily smile.*

DERIVATIVES: **oil•i•ness** *n.*

Old Eng•lish • *n.* the language of the Anglo-Saxons (up to about 1150), a highly inflected language with a largely Germanic vocabulary, very different from modern English. Also called ANGLO-SAXON.

o•le•ag•i•nous |ˌōlē'æjənəs| • *adj.* rich in, covered with, or producing oil; oily or greasy.
■ exaggeratedly and distastefully complimentary; obsequious: *candidates made the usual oleaginous speeches.*

ol•fac•to•ry |äl'fækt(ə)rē; ōl-| • *adj.* of or relating to the sense of smell: *the olfactory organs.*

DERIVATIVES: **ol•fac•tion** *n.* the action or capacity of smelling.

ol•i•gar•chy |'äli,gärkē; 'ōl-| • *n.* (pl. **-ies**) a small group of people having control of a country, organization, or institution: *the ruling oligarchy of military men around the president.*
■ a state governed by such a group: *the English aristocratic oligarchy of the 19th century.* ■ government by such a group.

DERIVATIVES: **ol•i•gar•chic** |ˌäli'gärkik; ˌōli-| *adj.* **ol•i•gar•chi•cal** |ˌäli'gärkikəl; ˌōli-| *adj.* **ol•i•gar•chi•cal•ly** |ˌäli'gärkik(ə)lē; ˌōli-| *adv.*

USAGE: See **usage** at ARISTOCRACY.

ol•i•gop•o•ly |ˌäli'gäpəlē| • *n.* (pl. **-ies**) a state of limited competition, in which a market is shared by a small number of producers or sellers.

DERIVATIVES: **ol•i•gop•o•list** |-list| *n.* **ol•i•gop•o•lis•tic** |ˌäli,gäpə'listik| *adj.*

o•li•o |'ōlēō| (also **olla podrida**) • *n.* (pl. **-os**) a highly spiced stew of various meats and vegetables, of Spanish and Portuguese origin.
■ a miscellaneous collection of things. ■ a variety act or show.

om•buds•man |'ämbədzmən; -,bŏŏdz-| *n.* (pl. **-men**) an official appointed to investigate individuals' complaints against maladministration, esp. that of public authorities.

o•me•ga |ō'māgə; ō'mē-| • *n.* the twenty-fourth, and last, letter of the Greek alphabet (Ω, ω), transliterated as 'o' or 'ō.'
■ the last of a series; the final development: [as adj.] *the omega point.* See also **alpha and omega** at ALPHA.

o•men |'ōmən| • *n.* an event regarded as a portent of good or evil: *the ghost's appearance was an ill omen| a rise in imports might be an omen of recovery.*
■ prophetic significance: *the raven seemed a bird of evil omen.*

DERIVATIVES: **ominous** *adj.* **ominously** *adv.* **ominousness** *n.*

om•ni•bus |'ämnə,bəs| • *n.* **1** a volume containing several novels or other items previously published separately: *an omnibus of her first trilogy.* **2** formerly, a bus. • *adj.* comprising several items: *Congress passed an omnibus anti-crime package.*

om•ni•com•pe•tent |ˌämni'kämpitnt| • *adj.* able to deal with all matters or solve all problems.
■ (of a legislative body) having powers to legislate on all matters.

DERIVATIVES: **om•ni•com•pe•tence** *n.*

om•nip•o•tent |äm'nipətənt| • *adj.* (of a deity) having unlimited power; able to do anything.
■ having ultimate power and influence: *an omnipotent sovereign.* • *n.* (**the Omnipotent**) God.

DERIVATIVES: **om•nip•o•tence** *n.* **om•nip•o•tent•ly** *adv.*

om•nis•cient |äm'nisHənt| • *adj.* knowing everything: *the story is told by an omniscient narrator.*

DERIVATIVES: **om•nis•cience** *n.* **om•nis•cient•ly** *adv.*

om•niv•o•rous |äm'niv(ə)rəs| • *adj.* (of an animal or person) feeding on food of both plant and animal origin.
■ taking in or using whatever is available: *an omnivorous reader.*

DERIVATIVES: **om•ni•vore** *n.* **om•niv•o•rous•ly** *adv.* **om•niv•o•rous•ness** *n.*

om•pha•los |'ämfələs| • *n.* (pl. **omphaloi** |-loi|) the center or hub of something: *this was the omphalos of confusion and strife.*
■ a rounded stone (esp. that at Delphi) representing the navel of the earth in ancient Greek mythology.

o•nan•ism |'ōnə,nizəm| • *n.* **1** masturbation. **2** coitus interruptus.

DERIVATIVES: **o•nan•ist** *n.* **o•nan•is•tic** |ˌōnə'nistik| *adj.*

on•col•o•gy |än'käləjē; äNG-| • *n.* the study and treatment of tumors.

DERIVATIVES: **on•co•log•ic** *adj.* **on•co•log•i•cal** |-kə'läjikəl| *adj.* **on•col•o•gist** |-jist| *n.*

o•nei•ric |ō'nīrik| • *adj.* of or relating to dreams or dreaming.

o•nei•ro•man•cy |ō'nīrə,mænsē| • *n.* the interpretation of dreams in order to foretell the future.

on•er•ous |'ōnərəs; 'änərəs| • *adj.* (of a task, duty, or responsibility) involving an amount of effort and difficulty that is oppressively burdensome: *he found his duties increasingly onerous.*
■ (in law) involving excessively heavy obligations: *an onerous lease.*

DERIVATIVES: **on•er•ous•ly** *adv.* **on•er•ous•ness** *n.*

on•o•ma•si•ol•o•gy |ˌänə,māsē'äləjē; -,mä-zē-| • *n.* the branch of knowledge that deals with terminology, in particular contrasting terms for similar concepts. Compare with SEMASIOLOGY.

on•o•mat•o•poe•ia |ˌänə,mætə'pēə; -,mätə-| • *n.* the formation of a word from a sound associated with what is named (e.g., *cuckoo*, *sizzle*).

■ the use of such words for rhetorical effect.
on•shore |'än'sHôr; 'ôn-| • *adj. & adv.* situated or occurring on land : [as *adj.*] *an onshore oil field.*

■ (esp. of the direction of the wind) from the sea toward the land. Cf. OFFSHORE.

on•tic |'äntik| • *adj.* (in philosophy) of or relating to entities and the facts about them; relating to real as opposed to phenomenal existence.

on•tog•e•ny |än'täjənē| • *n.* the branch of biology that deals with ontogenesis (the development of an individual organism or anatomical or behavioral feature from the earliest stage to maturity). Cf. PHYLOGENY.
DERIVATIVES: **on•to•gen•ic** |,äntə'jenik| *adj.* **on•to•gen•i•cal•ly** |,äntə'jenik(ə)lē| *adv.*

on•tol•o•gy |än'täləjē| • *n.* the branch of metaphysics dealing with the nature of being.
DERIVATIVES: **on•to•log•i•cal** |,äntə'läjikəl| *adj.* **on•to•log•i•cal•ly** |,äntə'läjik(ə)lē| *adv.* **on•tol•o•gist** |-jist| *n.*

o•nus |'ōnəs| • *n.* (usu. as **the onus**) a burden; one's duty or responsibility: *the onus is on you to show that you have suffered loss.*

o•paque |ō'pāk| • *adj.* (**opaquer, opaquest**) not able to be seen through; not transparent: *the windows were opaque with steam.* Cf. TRANSLUCENT.

■ (esp. of language) hard or impossible to understand; unfathomable: *technical jargon that was opaque to her.*
DERIVATIVES: **o•pac•i•ty** *n.* **o•paque•ly** *adv.* **o•paque•ness** *n.*

op art (also **optical art**) • *n.* a form of abstract art that gives the illusion of movement by the precise use of pattern and color, or in which conflicting patterns emerge and overlap.

op•er•ant |'äpərənt| • *adj.* involving the modification of behavior by the reinforcing or inhibiting effect of its own consequences (instrumental conditioning). • *n.* an item of behavior that is initially spontaneous, rather than a response to a prior stimulus, but whose consequences may reinforce or inhibit recurrence of that behavior.

op•er•at•ic |,äpə'rætik| • *adj.* of, relating to, or characteristic of opera: *operatic arias.*

■ extravagantly theatrical; overly dramatic: *she wrung her hands in operatic despair.*
DERIVATIVES: **op•er•at•i•cal•ly** |-ik(ə)lē| *adv.*

op•er•ose |'äpə,rōs| • *adj.* involving or displaying much industry or effort.

oph•thal•mol•o•gist • *n.* a medical doctor who specializes in the study and treatment of disorders and diseases of the eye.
DERIVATIVES: **oph•thal•mo•log•i•cal** |-mə'läjikəl| *adj.* **oph•thal•mol•o•gy** *n.*

o•pi•ate • *adj.* |'ōpē-it| relating to, resembling, or containing opium: *the use of opiate drugs.*

■ causing drowsiness or a dulling of the senses. • *n.* a drug with morphinelike effects, derived from opium.

■ a thing that soothes or stupefies. • *v.* [trans.] [often as *adj.*] (**opiated**) impregnate with opium.
PHRASES: **the opiate of the masses** (or **people**) something regarded as inducing a false and unrealistic sense of contentment among people.

o•pine |ō'pīn| • *v.* [reporting verb] hold and state as one's opinion: [with direct speech] *"The man is a genius," he opined* | [with clause] *the critic opined that the most exciting musical moment occurred when the orchestra struck up the national anthem.*

o•pin•ion•at•ed |ə'pinyə,nātid| • *adj.* conceitedly assertive and dogmatic in one's opinons: *an arrogant and opinionated man.*

op•por•tune |,äpər't(y)oٝon| • *adj.* (of a time) well-chosen or particularly favorable or appropriate: *he couldn't have arrived at a less opportune moment.*

■ done or occurring at a favorable or useful time; well-timed: *the opportune use of humor to lower tension.*
DERIVATIVES: **op•por•tune•ly** *adv.* **op•por•tune•ness** *n.*

op•por•tun•ist |,äpər't(y)oٝonist| • *n.* a person who exploits circumstances to gain immediate advantage rather than being guided by consistent principles or plans: *most thefts are committed by casual opportunists.* • *adj.* opportunistic: *the calculating and opportunist politician.*
DERIVATIVES: **op•por•tun•ism** |-,nizəm| *n.*

op•por•tun•is•tic |,äpərt(y)oٝo'nistik| • *adj.* exploiting chances offered by immediate circumstances without reference to a general plan or moral principle: *the change was cynical and opportunistic.*

■ (of a plant or animal) able to spread quickly in a previously unexploited habitat. ■ (in medicine, of a microorganism or an infection caused by it) rarely affecting patients except in unusual circumstances, typically when the immune system is depressed.
DERIVATIVES: **op•por•tun•is•ti•cal•ly** |-ik-(ə)lē| *adv.*

op•press |ə'pres| • *v.* [trans.] (often **be oppressed**) keep (someone) in subservience and hardship, esp. by the unjust exercise of authority: *a system that oppressed working people* | [as *adj.*] (**oppressed**) *oppressed racial minorities.*

■ cause (someone) to feel distressed, anxious, or uncomfortable: *he was oppressed by some secret worry.* Cf. SUPPRESS, REPRESS.
DERIVATIVES: **op•pres•sor** |ə'presər| *n.*

op•pro•bri•ous |ə'prōbrēəs| • *adj.* (of language) expressing opprobrium.

■ disgraceful; shameful: *their opprobrious conduct.*
DERIVATIVES: **op•pro•bri•ous•ly** *adv.*

op•pro•bri•um |ə'prōbrēəm| • *n.* harsh criticism or censure: *his films and the critical opprobrium they have generated.*

■ the public disgrace arising from someone's shameful conduct: *the opprobrium of being closely associated with gangsters.* ■ an occasion or cause of reproach or disgrace.

op•ti•cian |äp'tisHən| • n. a person qualified to make and supply eyeglasses and contact lenses for correction of vision. Cf. OPHTHALMOLOGIST; OPTOMETRIST; OCULIST.
■ a person who makes or sells optical instruments.

op•ti•mal |'äptəməl| • adj. best or most favorable; optimum: *seeking the optimal solution.*
DERIVATIVES: **op•ti•mal•i•ty** |,äptə'mælitē| n. **op•ti•mal•ly** |-(ə)lē| adv.

op•ti•mism |'äptə,mizəm| • n. 1 hopefulness and confidence about the future or the successful outcome of something: *the talks had been amicable, and there were grounds for optimism.* 2 (in philosophy) the doctrine, esp. as set forth by G.W. Leibniz (1646–1716), that this world is the best of all possible worlds.
■ the belief that good must ultimately prevail over evil in the universe.
DERIVATIVES: **op•ti•mist** n.

op•ti•mum |'äptəməm| • adj. most conducive to a favorable outcome; best: *the optimum childbearing age.* • n. (pl. **optima** |-mə| or **optimums**) the most favorable conditions or level for growth, reproduction, or success.

op•tion•al |'äpsHənl| • adj. available to be chosen but not obligatory: *a wide range of optional excursions is offered.*
DERIVATIVES: **op•tion•al•i•ty** |,äpsHə'nælitē| n. **op•tion•al•ly** adv.

op•tom•e•trist |äp'tämitrist| • n. a person who practices **optometry,** the occupation of measuring eyesight, prescribing corrective lenses, and detecting eye disease.

op•u•lent |'äpyələnt| • adj. ostentatiously rich and luxurious or lavish: *the opulent comfort of a limousine.*
■ wealthy: *his more opulent tenants.*
DERIVATIVES: **op•u•lence** n. **op•u•lent•ly** adv.

o•pus |'ōpəs| • n. (pl. **opuses** or **opera** |'äp(ə)rə|) 1 (in music) a separate composition or set of compositions by a particular composer, usually ordered by date of publication: The Gambler *was Prokofiev's sixth opera, despite its early* **opus number.** 2 any artistic work, esp. one on a large scale.

or•a•cle |'ôrəkəl| • n. 1 a priest or priestess acting as a medium through whom advice or prophecy was sought from the gods in classical antiquity.
■ a place at which such advice or prophecy was sought. ■ a person or thing regarded as an infallible authority or guide on something. 2 a response or message given by an oracle, typically one that is ambiguous or obscure.

o•rac•u•lar |ô'rækyələr| • adj. of or relating to an oracle: *the oracular shrine.*
■ (of an utterance, advice, etc.) hard to interpret; enigmatic: *an ambiguous, oracular remark.* ■ holding or claiming the authority of an oracle: *he holds forth in oracular fashion.*
DERIVATIVES: **o•rac•u•lar•i•ty** |ô,rækyə'læritē; -'ler-| n. **o•rac•u•lar•ly** adv.

or•a•to•ri•o |,ôrə'tôrē,ō; ,är-| • n. (pl. **-os**) a large-scale musical work for orchestra and voices, typically a narrative on a religious

theme, performed without the use of costumes, scenery, or action.

or•a•to•ry[1] |'ôrə,tôrē; 'är-| • n. (pl. **-ies**) a small chapel, esp. for private worship.

or•a•to•ry[2] • n. the art or practice of formal speaking in public.
■ exaggerated, eloquent, or highly colored language: *learned discussions degenerated into pompous oratory.*
DERIVATIVES: **or•a•tor•i•cal** |,ôrə'tôrikəl| adj.

or•bic•u•lar |ôr'bikyələr| • adj. 1 having the shape of a flat ring or disk. 2 having a rounded convex or globular shape.
■ (of a rock) containing spheroidal igneous inclusions.
DERIVATIVES: **or•bic•u•lar•i•ty** |ôr,bikye'læritē; -'ler-| n. **or•bic•u•lar•ly** adv.

or•dain |ôr'dān| • v. [trans.] 1 make (someone) a priest or minister; confer holy orders on. 2 order or decree (something) officially: *equal punishment was ordained for the two crimes.*
■ (esp. of God or fate) prescribe; determine (something): *the path ordained by God.*
DERIVATIVES: **or•dain•er** n. **or•dain•ment** n.

or•der•ly |'ôrdərlē| • n. (pl. **-ies**) 1 an attendant in a hospital responsible for the nonmedical care of patients and the maintenance of order and cleanliness. 2 a soldier who carries out orders or performs minor tasks for an officer.
DERIVATIVES: **or•der•li•ness** n.

or•di•nal |'ôrdn-əl| • n. 1 (also **ordinal number**) any of the positive whole numbers defining a thing's position in a series (first, second, third, etc.). Cf. CARDINAL. 2 in the Christian Church, a service book, esp. one with the forms of service used at ordinations. • adj. of or relating to a thing's position in a series: *ordinal position of birth.*
■ of or relating to an ordinal number. ■ (in biology) of or relating to a taxonomic order.

or•di•nance |'ôrdn-əns| • n. 1 a piece of legislation enacted by a municipal authority: *a city ordinance.* 2 an authoritative order; a decree. 3 a prescribed religious rite: *Talmudic ordinances.*

or•di•nate |'ôrdnit| • n. (in a system of mathematical coordinates) the *y*-coordinate, representing the distance from a point to the horizontal or *x*-axis measured parallel to the vertical or *y*-axis.

or•di•na•tion |,ôrdn'āsHən| • n. 1 the action of ordaining or conferring holy orders on someone.
■ a ceremony in which someone is ordained. 2 the action of arranging in ranks or order; the condition of being ordered or arranged.
■ a statistical technique in which data from a large number of sites or populations are represented as points in a two- or three-dimensional coordinate frame.

ord•nance |'ôrdnəns| • n. 1 mounted guns; artillery.
■ military weapons, ammunition, and equipment used in connection with them. 2 a

branch of the armed forces dealing with the supply and storage of weapons, ammunition, and related equipment.

or•don•nance |ˈôrdn-əns; ˌôdōˈnäNs| • *n.* the systematic or orderly arrangement of parts, esp. in art and architecture.

or•dure |ˈôrjər| • *n.* excrement; dung.
■ something regarded as vile or abhorrent.

o•re•ad |ˈôrēˌæd| • *n.* (in Greek and Roman mythology) a nymph believed to inhabit mountains.

or•gan•elle |ˌôrgəˈnel| • *n.* (in biology) any of a number of organized or specialized structures within a living cell.

or•ga•non |ˈôrgəˌnän| • *n.* an instrument of thought, esp. a means of reasoning or a system of logic.

or•gasm |ˈôrˌgæzəm| • *n.* a climax of sexual excitement, characterized by feelings of pleasure centered in the genitals and (in men) experienced as an accompaniment to ejaculation of semen. • *v.* [intrans.] experience an orgasm.

or•gas•mic |ôrˈgæzmik| • *adj.* of or relating to orgasm.
■ (of a person) able to achieve orgasm. ■ very enjoyable or exciting: *the album is an orgasmic whirl of techno soundscapes.*
DERIVATIVES: **or•gas•mi•cal•ly** |-mik(ə)-lē| *adv.* **or•gas•tic** |-ˈgæstik| *adj.* **or•gas•ti•cal•ly** |-ˈgæstik(ə)lē| *adv.*

or•gy |ˈôrjē| • *n.* (pl. **-ies**) a wild party, esp. one involving excessive drinking and unrestrained sexual activity: *the college had a reputation for drunken orgies.*
■ excessive indulgence in a specified activity: *an orgy of buying.* ■ (usu. **orgies**) secret rites used in the worship of Bacchus, Dionysus, and other Greek and Roman deities, celebrated with dancing, drunkenness, and singing.
DERIVATIVES: **or•gi•ast** *n.* **or•gi•as•tic** *adj.*

o•ri•el |ˈôrēəl| • *n.* a projection from the wall of a building, typically supported from the ground or by corbels.
■ (also **oriel window**) a window in such a structure. ■ a projecting window, often on an upper story; a bay window.

o•ri•ent • *n.* |ˈôrēˌənt| **1** (**the Orient**) the countries of Asia, esp. eastern Asia. In earlier use, the countries of the eastern Mediterranean, including Asia Minor (modern Turkey), Arabia, and Egypt. Cf. OCCIDENT. **2** the special luster of a pearl of the finest quality.
■ a pearl with such a luster. • *adj.* situated in or belonging to the east; oriental.
■ (of the sun, daylight, etc.) rising. ■ (esp. of precious stones) lustrous (with reference to fine pearls from the East). • *v.* |ˈôrēˌent| **1** [with obj. and adverbial] (often **be oriented**) align or position (something) relative to the points of a compass or other specified positions: *the fires are oriented in direct line with the midsummer sunset.*
■ adjust or tailor (something) to specified circumstances or needs: *magazines oriented to the business community* | [as adj., in combination] (**-oriented**) *market-oriented economic reforms.*

■ guide (someone) physically in a specified direction. **2** (**orient oneself**) find one's position in relation to new and strange surroundings: *there are no street names that would enable her to orient herself.*

o•ri•en•tal |ˌôrēˈentl| (also **Oriental**) • *adj.*
1 of, from, or characteristic of the Far East (earlier, of all lands east of the Mediterranean): *oriental countries.*
■ of, from, or characteristic of the countries of Asia. **2** (of a pearl or other jewel) orient. • *n.* a person of East Asian (earler, of Asian, Arabian, or eastern Mediterranean) descent.
DERIVATIVES: **o•ri•en•tal•ize** |-īz| *v.* **o•ri•en•tal•ly** *adv.*

USAGE: The term **Oriental**, which has many associations with European imperialism in Asia, is regarded as offensive by many Asians, esp. Asian Americans. **Asian** or, if appropriate, **East Asian** is preferred.

O•ri•en•tal•ism |ˌôrēˈen(t)lˌizəm| • *n.* something considered characteristic of the peoples and cultures of Asia.
■ the knowledge and study of these languages and cultures.
DERIVATIVES: **O•ri•en•tal•ist** |ˌôrēˈen(t)l-əst| *n.*

o•ri•en•tate |ˈôrēənˌtāt| • *v.* another term for ORIENT.

o•ri•en•ta•tion |ˌôrēənˈtāSHən| • *n.* the determination of the relative position of something or someone (esp. oneself): *the child's surroundings provide clues to help in orientation.*
■ the relative physical position or direction of something: *two complex shapes, presented in different orientations.* ■ familiarization with something: *their training and orientation comes out of magazine and newspaper distribution.* ■ a program of introduction for students new to a school or college: *she attended freshman orientation.* ■ the direction of someone's interest or attitude, esp. political or sexual: *a common age of consent regardless of gender or sexual orientation.*
DERIVATIVES: **o•ri•en•ta•tion•al** *adj.*

o•ri•en•teer•ing |ˌôrēənˈtiriNG| • *n.* a competitive sport in which participants find their way to various checkpoints across rough country with the aid of a map and compass, the winner being the one with the lowest elapsed time.
DERIVATIVES: **o•ri•en•teer** *n., v.*

or•i•fice |ˈôrəfis| • *n.* an opening, as of a pipe or tube, or one in the body, such as a nostril or the anus.

o•rig•i•nal sin • *n.* (in Christian theology) the tendency to sin innate in all human beings, held to be inherited from Adam in consequence of the Fall. The concept of original sin was developed in the writings of St. Augustine (d. c.604).

or•i•son |ˈôrisən; -zən; ˈär-| • *n.* a prayer.

or•nate |ôrˈnāt| • *adj.* made in an intricate shape or decorated with complex patterns.
■ (of literary style) using unusual words and complex constructions: *ornate and metaphorical language.* ■ (of musical composition or

performance) using many ornaments such as grace notes and trills.
DERIVATIVES: **or•nate•ly** adv. **or•nate•ness** n.

or•ni•thol•o•gy |ˌôrnəˈTHäləjē| • n. the scientific study of birds.
DERIVATIVES: **or•ni•tho•log•i•cal** |ˌôrni-THəˈläjikəl| adj. **or•ni•tho•log•i•cal•ly** |ˌôr-niTHəˈläjik(ə)lē| adv. **or•ni•thol•o•gist** |-jist| n.

o•rog•e•ny |ôˈräjənē| • n. (in geology) a process in which a section of the earth's crust is folded and deformed by lateral compression to form a mountain range.
■ a period of mountain building
DERIVATIVES: **or•o•gen•e•sis** |ˌôrōˈjenəsis| n. **or•o•gen•ic** |ˌôrōˈjenik| adj.

o•rog•ra•phy |ôˈrägrəfē| • n. the branch of physical geography dealing with mountains.
DERIVATIVES: **or•o•graph•ic** adj. **or•o•graph•i•cal** adj. **or•o•graph•i•cal•ly** adv.

o•ro•tund |ˈôrəˌtənd| • adj. (of the voice or phrasing) full, round, and imposing.
■ (of writing, style, or expression) pompous; pretentious.
DERIVATIVES: **o•ro•tun•di•ty** |ˌôrəˈtəndi-tē| n.

Or•phism |ˈôrˌfizəm| • n. 1 a mystic religion of ancient Greece, originating in the 7th or 6th century BC and based on poems (now lost) attributed to Orpheus, emphasizing the necessity for individuals to rid themselves of the evil part of their nature by ritual and moral purification throughout a series of reincarnations. 2 a short-lived art movement (c.1912) within cubism, pioneered by a group of French painters (including Robert Delaunay, Sonia Delaunay-Terk, and Fernand Léger)and emphasizing the lyrical use of color rather than the austere intellectual cubism of Picasso, Braque, and Gris.

ort |ôrt| (usu. **orts**) • n. a scrap or remainder of food from a meal.
■ anything left over.

or•tho•don•tics |ˌôrTHəˈdäntiks| (also **or•thodontia** |-SH(ē)ə|) • plural n. [treated as sing.] the treatment of irregularities in the teeth (esp. of alignment and occlusion) and jaws, including the use of braces.
DERIVATIVES: **or•tho•don•tic** adj. **or•tho•don•ti•cal•ly** |-tik(ə)lē| adv. **or•tho•don•tist** |-tist| n.

or•tho•dox |ˈôrTHəˌdäks| • adj. 1 (of a person or personal views, esp. religious or political ones, or other beliefs or practices) conforming to what is generally or traditionally accepted as right or true; established and approved: *the orthodox economics of today* | *orthodox medical treatment* | *orthodox Hindus.*
■ (of a person) not independent-minded; conventional and unoriginal: *a relatively orthodox artist.* 2 (of a thing) of the ordinary or usual type; normal: *they avoided orthodox jazz venues.* 3 (usu. **Orthodox**) (of the Jews or Judaism) strictly keeping to traditional doctrine and ritual. 4 (usu. **Orthodox**) of or relating to the Orthodox (Eastern Christian) Church.
DERIVATIVES: **or•tho•dox•ly** adv.

or•tho•dox•y |ˈôrTHəˌdäksē| • n. (pl. **-ies**) 1 authorized or generally accepted theory, doctrine, or practice: *monetarist orthodoxy* | *he challenged many of the established orthodoxies.* Cf. FUNDAMENTALISM.
■ the quality of conforming to such theories, doctrines, or practices: *writings of unimpeachable orthodoxy.* 2 the whole community of Orthodox Jews or Orthodox Christians.

or•tho•pe•dics |ˌôrTHəˈpēdiks| (Brit. **ortho-paedics**) • plural n. [treated as sing.] the branch of medicine dealing with the correction of deformities of bones or muscles.
DERIVATIVES: **or•tho•pe•dic** adj. **or•tho•pe•di•cal•ly** |-ik(ə)lē| adv. **or•tho•pe•dist** |-dist| n.

or•thot•ics |ôrˈTHätiks| • plural n. [treated as sing.] the branch of medicine that deals with the provision and use of artificial devices such as splints and braces.
■ a treatment prescribing such a device, esp. for the foot.
■ (**orthotic** or **orthosis**, pl. **-ses**) a device used in such treatment.
DERIVATIVES: **or•thot•ic** adj. **or•thot•ist** n.

os•cil•late |ˈäsəˌlāt| • v. [intrans.] 1 move or swing back and forth at a regular speed: *a pendulum oscillates around its lowest point.*
■ [with adverbial] waver between extremes of opinion, action, or quality: *he was oscillating between fear and bravery.* 2 (in physics) vary in magnitude or position in a regular manner around a central point.
■ (of a circuit or device) cause the electric current or voltage running through it to behave in this way.
DERIVATIVES: **os•cil•la•tion** |ˌäsəˈlāSHən| n. **os•cil•la•to•ry** |əˈsiləˌtôrē| adj.

os•ci•ta•tion |ˌäsiˈtāSHən| (also **oscitancy**) • n. 1 yawning; drowsiness. 2 inattention; negligence.

os•cu•late |ˈäskyəˌlāt| • v. [trans.] 1 (of a curve or surface) touch (another curve or surface) so as to have a common tangent at the point of contact: [as adj.] (**osculating**) *the plots have been drawn using osculating orbital elements.* 2 kiss.
DERIVATIVES: **os•cu•lant** |-lənt| adj. **os•cu•la•tion** |ˌäskyəˈlāSHən| n. **os•cu•la•to•ry** |-ləˌtôrē| adj.

os•mic |ˈäzmik| • adj. relating to odors or the sense of smell.
DERIVATIVES: **os•mi•cal•ly** |-ik(ə)lē| adv.

os•mo•sis |äzˈmōsis; äs-| • n. a process by which molecules of a solvent tend to pass through a semipermeable membrane from a less concentrated solution into a more concentrated one, thus equalizing the concentrations on each side of the membrane.
■ the process of gradual or unconscious assimilation of ideas, knowledge, etc.: *living in Paris, she learned French through osmosis.*
DERIVATIVES: **os•mose** v. **os•mot•ic** |-mätik| adj. **os•mot•i•cal•ly** |-ˈmätik(ə)lē| adv.

os•se•ous |ˈäsēəs| • adj. consisting of or turned into bone; ossified.

os•si•fy | 'äsə‚fī | • v. (**-ies, -ied**) [intrans.] turn into bone or bony tissue: *these tracheal cartilages may ossify.*
■ [often as adj.] (**ossified**) cease developing; be stagnant or rigid: *ossified political institutions.*
DERIVATIVES: **os•si•fi•ca•tion** | ‚äsəfi'kā-sHən | n.

os•ten•si•ble | ä'stensəbəl; ə'sten- | • adj. [attrib.] stated or appearing to be true, but not necessarily so: *the delay may have a deeper cause than the ostensible reason.*
DERIVATIVES: **os•ten•si•bil•i•ty** | -‚stensə 'bilitē | n. **os•ten•si•bly** adv.

os•ten•ta•tious | ‚ästən'tāsHəs | • adj. characterized by vulgar or pretentious display; designed to impress or attract notice: *books that people buy and display ostentatiously but never actually read.*
DERIVATIVES: **os•ten•ta•tion** n. **os•ten•ta•tious•ly** adv. **os•ten•ta•tious•ness** n.

os•te•op•a•thy | ‚ästē'äpəᴛʜē | • n. a branch of medical practice that emphasizes the treatment of medical disorders through the manipulation and massage of the bones, joints, and muscles. Cf. CHIROPRACTIC.
DERIVATIVES: **os•te•o•path** | 'ästēə‚paᴛʜ | n. **os•te•o•path•ic** | ‚ästēə'paᴛʜik | adj. **os•te•o•path•i•cal•ly** | ‚ästēə'paᴛʜik(ə)lē | adv.

os•te•o•po•ro•sis | ‚ästēōpə'rōsis | • n. a medical condition in which the bones become brittle and fragile from loss of tissue, typically as a result of hormonal changes (esp. among older women), or deficiency of calcium or vitamin D.
DERIVATIVES: **os•te•o•po•rot•ic** | -'rätik | adj.

os•tra•cize | 'ästrə‚sīz | • v. [trans.] exclude (someone) from a society or group: *a group who have been ridiculed, ostracized, and persecuted for centuries.*
■ (in ancient Greece) banish (an unpopular or too powerful citizen) from a city for five or ten years by popular vote.
DERIVATIVES: **os•tra•cism** | -‚sizəm | n.

o•ti•ose | 'ōsHē‚ōs; 'ōtē‚ōs | • adj. serving no practical purpose or result: *he did fuss, uttering otiose explanations.*
■ indolent; idle.
DERIVATIVES: **o•ti•ose•ly** adv.

oust | owst | • v. [trans.] drive out or expel (someone) from a position or place: *he ousted the incumbent by only 500 votes.*
■ (in law) deprive (someone) of or exclude (someone) from possession of something.

ou•tré | ōō'trā | • adj. unusual and startling: *in 1975 the suggestion was considered outré—today it is orthodox.*

out•source | 'owt‚sôrs | • v. [trans.] obtain (goods or a service) from an outside supplier, esp. in place of an internal source: *outsourcing components from other countries* | [as n.] (**outsourcing**) *outsourcing can dramatically lower total costs, especially personnel costs.*
■ contract (work) out: *you may choose to outsource this function to another company or do it yourself.*

o•ver•arch•ing | ‚ōvər'ärcHiNG | • adj. [attrib.]
forming an arch over something: *the overarching mangroves.*
■ comprehensive; all-embracing: *a single overarching principle.*

o•ver•bear•ing | ‚ōvər'beriNG | • adj. unpleasantly or arrogantly domineering: *an overbearing, sometimes ruthless corporate director.*
DERIVATIVES: **o•ver•bear•ing•ly** adv. **o•ver•bear•ing•ness** n.

o•ver•blown | ‚ōvər'blōn | • adj. **1** excessively inflated or pretentious: *overblown dreams of glory and success.* **2** (of a flower) past its prime: *an overblown rose.*

o•ver•head • adj. | 'ōvər‚hed | [attrib.] (of a cost or expense) incurred in the general upkeep or running of a plant, commercial establishment, or business, and not attributable to specific products or items. • n. | 'ōvər‚hed | overhead cost or expense: *research conducted in space requires more overhead.*

o•ver•ride • v. | ‚ōvər'rīd | (past **-rode**; past part. **-ridden**) [trans.] **1** use one's authority to reject or cancel (a decision, view, etc.): *the legislature's ability to override budget vetoes.*
■ interrupt the action of (an automatic device), typically in order to take manual control: *you can override the cut-out by releasing the switch.* ■ be more important than: *this plan overrides all other considerations.* • n. | 'ōvər ‚rīd | **1** a device for suspending an automatic function on a machine. ■ the action or process of suspending an automatic function. **2** an excess or increase on a budget, salary, or cost. ■ a commission paid to a manager on sales made by a subordinate or representative. **3** a cancellation of a decision by exertion of authority or winning of votes: *the House vote in favor of the bill was 10 votes short of the number needed for an override.*

o•ver•shad•ow | ‚ōvər'sHædō | • v. [trans.] tower above and cast a shadow over.
■ cast a gloom over: *tragedy overshadows his story.* ■ appear much more prominent or important than: *his competitive nature often overshadows the other qualities.* ■ (often **be overshadowed**) be more impressive or successful than (another person).

o•vert | ō'vərt; 'ōvərt | • adj. done or shown openly; plainly or readily apparent, not secret or hidden: *an overt act of aggression.*
DERIVATIVES: **o•vert•ly** adv. **o•vert•ness** n.

o•ver•tone | 'ōvər‚tōn | • n. **1** a musical tone that is a part of the harmonic series above a fundamental note, and may be heard with it.
■ (in physics) a component of any oscillation whose frequency is an integral multiple of the fundamental frequency. **2** (often **overtones**) a subtle or subsidiary quality, implication, or connotation: *the decision may have political overtones.*

o•ver•ture | 'ōvər‚cHŏŏr; -‚cHər | • n. **1** an introduction to something more substantial: *the talks were no more than an overture to a long debate.*
■ (usu. **overtures**) an approach or proposal made to someone with the aim of opening

negotiations or establishing a relationship. **2** an orchestral piece at the beginning of an opera, suite, play, oratorio, or other extended composition.

■ an independent orchestral composition in one movement.

o•ver•ween•ing |ˈōvərˈwēniNG| • *adj.* showing excessive confidence or pride: *overweening ambition.*

DERIVATIVES: **o•ver•ween•ing•ly** *adv.*

o•ver•wrought |ˈōvəˈrôt| • *adj.* **1** in a state of nervous excitement or anxiety. **2** (of a piece of writing or a work of art) too elaborate or complicated in design or construction.

o•vine |ˈōˌvīn| • *adj.* of, relating to, or resembling sheep.

o•vip•a•rous |ōˈvipərəs| • *adj.* (of a bird, etc.) producing young by means of eggs that are hatched after they have been laid by the parent. Cf. VIVIPAROUS and OVOVIVIPAROUS.

DERIVATIVES: **o•vi•par•i•ty** |-ˈpærit̠ē; -ˈper-| *n.*

o•vo•vi•vip•a•rous |ōˌvōvīˈvip(ə)rəs| • *adj.* (of an animal) producing young by means of eggs that are hatched within the body of the parent, as in some snakes. Cf. OVIPAROUS and VIVIPAROUS.

DERIVATIVES: **o•vo•vi•vi•par•i•ty** |-ˌvīvəˈpærit̠ē; -ˈper-| *n.*

ov•u•late |ˈōvyəˌlāt; ˈäv-| • *v.* [intrans.] discharge ova (see OVUM) or ovules (the structure in a flowering plant that contains gamete and after fertilization becomes the seed) from the ovary.

DERIVATIVES: **ov•u•la•tion** |ˌōvyəˈlāsHən; -ˈläsHən| *n.* **ov•u•la•to•ry** |-ləˌtôrē| *adj.*

o•vum |ˈōvəm| • *n.* (pl. **ova** |ˈōvə|) a mature female reproductive cell, esp. of a human or other animal, that can divide to give rise to an embryo usually only after fertilization by a male cell.

ox•ide |ˈäkˌsīd| • *n.* (in chemistry) a binary compound of oxygen with another element or group: *iron oxide.*

ox•i•dize |ˈäksiˌdīz| • *v.* combine or become combined chemically with oxygen.

■ cover (metal) with a coating of oxide; rust.

■ (in chemistry) undergo or cause to undergo a reaction in which electrons are lost to another species.

DERIVATIVES: **ox•i•dant** *n.* **ox•i•diz•a•ble** *adj.* **ox•i•di•za•tion** |ˌäksidiˈzāsHən| *n.* **ox•i•diz•er** *n.*

ox•y•mo•ron |ˌäksəˈmôrˌän| • *n.* a figure of speech in which apparently contradictory terms appear in conjunction (e.g., *faith unfaithful kept him falsely true*).

DERIVATIVES: **ox•y•mo•ron•ic** |-məˈränik| *adj.*

o•zone |ˈōˌzōn| • *n.* a colorless unstable toxic gas with a pungent odor and powerful oxidizing properties, formed from oxygen by electrical discharges or ultraviolet light. It differs from normal oxygen (O_2) in having three atoms in its molecule (O_3).

■ (also **ozone layer**) a layer in the earth's stratosphere at an altitude of about 6.2 miles (10 km) containing a high concentration of ozone, which absorbs most of the ultraviolet radiation reaching the earth from the sun.

■ fresh invigorating air, esp. that blowing onto the shore from the sea.

DERIVATIVES: **o•zon•ic** |ōˈzänik| *adj.*

Pp

Pab•lum |ˈpæbləm| • *n.* (also **pabulum**) bland or insipid intellectual fare, entertainment, etc.; pap.

■ (**Pablum**) trademark a soft breakfast cereal for infants.

pace |ˈpāˌsē; ˈpäˌCHā| • *prep.* with due respect to (someone or an opinion), used to express polite disagreement or contradiction: *narrative history, pace some theorists, is not dead.*

pach•y•derm |ˈpækəˌdərm| • *n.* a very large mammal with thick skin, esp. an elephant, rhinoceros, or hippopotamus.

■ a thick-skinned person; someone relatively insensitive to taunts, criticism, or the like.

DERIVATIVES: **pach•y•der•mal** |ˌpækəˈdərməl| *adj.* **pach•y•der•ma•tous** |ˌpækəˈdərmətəs| *adj.* **pach•y•der•mous** *adj.* **pach•y•der•mic** |ˌpækəˈdərmik| *adj.*

pa•cif•ic |pəˈsifik| • *adj.* peaceful in character or intent: *a pacific gesture.*

DERIVATIVES: **pa•cif•i•cal•ly** |-(ə)lē| *adv.*

Pa•cif•ic Rim the countries and regions bordering the Pacific Ocean, esp. the small nations of eastern Asia.

pac•i•fism |ˈpæsəˌfizəm| • *n.* the belief that war and violence are unjustifiable under any circumstances, and that all disputes should be settled by peaceful means.

■ the refusal to participate in war or military service because of such a belief.

DERIVATIVES: **pac•i•fist** *n.* & *adj.* **pac•i•fis•tic** |ˌpæsəˈfistik| *adj.*

pac•i•fy |ˈpæsəˌfī| • *v.* (**-ies, -ied**) [trans.] quell the anger, agitation, or excitement of: *he had to pacify angry spectators.* | *I pacified the baby by singing.*

■ bring peace to (a country or warring factions), esp. by the use or threatened use of military force: *the general pacified northern Italy.*

DERIVATIVES: **pa•ci•fi•er** *n.* **pa•cif•i•ca•to•ry** |pəˈsifikəˌtôrē| *adj.*

pa•dre |'pädrā| • *n.* father; the title of a priest or chaplain in some regions.
■ a chaplain in any of the armed forces.

pa•dro•ne |pə'drōnā; pə'drōnē| • *n.* (pl. **padrones**) a patron or master, in particular: ■ a Mafia boss. ■ an employer, esp. one who exploits immigrant workers. ■ (in Italy) the proprietor of a hotel.

pae•an |'pēən| • *n.* a song of praise or triumph.
■ a thing that expresses enthusiastic praise: *his books are paeans to combat.*

pa•gan |'pāgən| • *n.* a person holding religious beliefs other than those of the main world religions.
■ a non-Christian. ■ an adherent of neopaganism, a modern religious movement that seeks to incorporate beliefs or ritual practices from traditions outside the main world religions, esp. those of pre-Christian Europe and North America. • *adj.* of or relating to such people or beliefs: *a pagan god.*
DERIVATIVES: **pa•gan•ish** *adj.* **pa•gan•ism** |-ˌnizəm| *n.* **pa•gan•ize** |-ˌnīz| *v.*

pal•a•din |'pælədin| • *n.* any of the twelve peers of Charlemagne's court, of whom the Count Palatine (a high official of the Holy Roman Empire) was the chief.
■ a knight renowned for heroism and chivalry.

pal•at•a•ble |'pælətəbəl| • *adj.* (of food or drink) pleasant to taste: *a very palatable local red wine.*
■ (of an action or proposal) acceptable or satisfactory: *a device that made increased taxation more palatable.*
DERIVATIVES: **pal•at•a•bil•i•ty** |ˌpælətə'bilətē| *n.* **pal•at•a•bly** |-blē| *adv.*

pal•a•tal |'pælətl| • *adj.* of or relating to the palate: *a palatal lesion.*

pal•ate |'pælit| • *n.* 1 the roof of the mouth, separating the cavities of the nose and the mouth in vertebrates. 2 a person's appreciation of taste and flavor, esp. when sophisticated and discriminating: *a fine range of drink for sophisticated palates.*
■ a person's taste or liking: *the suggestions may not suit everyone's palate.* ■ taste or flavor of wine or beer: *a wine with a zingy, peachy palate.*

pa•la•tial |pə'lāsHəl| • *adj.* resembling a palace in being spacious and splendid: *her palatial apartment in Chicago.*
DERIVATIVES: **pa•la•tial•ly** *adv.*

pa•lav•er |pə'lævər; -'läv-| • *n.* prolonged and idle discussion: *an hour of aimless palaver.*
■ a parley or improvised conference between two sides. • *v.* [intrans.] talk unnecessarily at length: *it's too hot to go on palavering.*

pal•ette |'pælit| • *n.* a thin board or slab on which an artist lays and mixes colors.
■ the range of colors used by a particular artist or in a particular picture: *I choose a palette of natural, earthy colors.* ■ the range or variety of tonal or instrumental color in a musical piece: *he commands the sort of tonal palette that this music needs.* ■ (in computer graph-

ics) the range of colors or shapes available to the user.

pal•imp•sest |'pælimpˌsest| • *n.* a manuscript or piece of writing material on which the original writing has been effaced to make room for later writing.
■ something reused or altered but still bearing visible traces of its earlier form.
DERIVATIVES: **pal•imp•ses•tic** |ˌpælimp 'sestik| *adj.*

pal•in•drome |'pælinˌdrōm| • *n.* a word, phrase, or sequence that reads the same backward as forward, e.g., *madam* or *nurses run.*
DERIVATIVES: **pal•in•drom•ic** |ˌpælin 'drämik| *adj.* **pa•lin•dro•mist** |pə'lindrəmist| *n.*

pal•in•gen•e•sis |ˌpælin'jenəsis| • *n.* 1 Biology the exact reproduction of ancestral characteristics during the developmental stages of a particular organism. 2 rebirth or regeneration.
DERIVATIVES: **pal•in•ge•net•ic** |ˌpælinjə 'netik| *adj.*

pal•i•sade |ˌpælə'sād| • *n.* a fence of wooden stakes or iron railings fixed in the ground, forming an enclosure or defense.
■ a strong pointed wooden stake fixed deeply in the ground with others in a close row, used as a defense. ■ (**palisades**) a line of high cliffs. • *v.* [trans.] [usu. as adj.] (**palisaded**) enclose or provide (a building or place) with a palisade.

pall¹ |pôl| • *n.* 1 a cloth spread over a coffin, hearse, or tomb.
■ a dark cloud or covering of smoke, dust, or similar matter: *a pall of black smoke hung over the quarry.* ■ something regarded as enveloping a situation with an air of gloom, heaviness, or fear: *the attacks have cast a pall of terror over the villages.* 2 an ecclesiastical pallium.

pall² • *v.* [intrans.] become less appealing or interesting through familiarity: *the novelty of the quiet life palled.*

pal•let • *n.* 1 a portable platform on which goods can be moved, stacked, and stored, esp. with the aid of a forklift. 2 a flat wooden blade with a handle, used to shape clay or plaster. 3 an artist's palette. 4 a projection on a machine part, serving to change the mode of motion of a wheel.

pal•li•ate |'pælēˌāt| • *v.* [trans.] make (a disease or its symptoms) less severe or unpleasant without removing the cause: *treatment works by palliating symptoms.*
■ allay or moderate (fears or suspicions): *this palliated the suspicions aroused by German unity.* ■ disguise the seriousness or gravity of (an offense): *there is no way to palliate his dirty deed.*
DERIVATIVES: **pal•li•a•tion** |ˌpælē'āsHən| *n.* **pal•li•a•tive** *n.* and *adj.* **pal•li•a•tor** |-ˌātər| *n.*

pal•lid |'pælid| • *adj.* (of a person's face) pale, typically because of poor health.
■ feeble or insipid: *an utterly pallid and charmless character.*
DERIVATIVES: **pal•lid•ly** *adv.* **pal•lid•ness** *n.*

pal•li•um |'pælēəm| • *n.* (pl. **pallia** |'pælēə| or **palliums**) **1** a woolen vestment conferred by the pope on an archbishop, consisting of a narrow, circular band placed around the shoulders with a short lappet hanging from front and back. **2** a man's large rectangular cloak, esp. as worn by Greek philosophical and religious teachers in antiquity.

pal•lor |'pælər| • *n.* [in sing.] an unhealthy pale appearance.

pal•pa•ble |'pælpəbəl| • *adj.* able to be touched or felt: *the palpable bump at the bridge of the nose.* ■ (esp. of a feeling or atmosphere) so intense as to be almost touched or felt: *a palpable sense of loss.* ■ clear to the mind or plain to see: *to talk of victory in the circumstances is palpable nonsense.*
DERIVATIVES: **pal•pa•bil•i•ty** |,pælpə'bil-itē| *n.* **pal•pa•bly** |-blē| *adv.*

pal•pate |'pæl,pāt| • *v.* [trans.] examine (a part of the body) by touch, esp. for medical purposes.
DERIVATIVES: **pal•pa•tion** |pæl'pāsHən| *n.*

pal•pi•tate |'pælpi,tāt| • *v.* [intrans.] [often as adj.] (**palpitating**) (of the heart) beat rapidly, strongly, or irregularly: *a palpitating heart.* ■ shake; tremble: *palpitating with terror.*
DERIVATIVES: **pal•pi•ta•tion** *n.*

pal•sy |'pôlzē| • *n.* (pl. **-ies**) paralysis, esp. that which is accompanied by involuntary tremors. ■ a condition of incapacity or helplessness. • *v.* (**-ies, -ied**) [trans.] (often **be palsied**) affect with paralysis and involuntary tremors: *the muscles on her face are palsied* | [as adj.] (**palsied**) *a palsied hand.*

pal•ter |'pôltər| • *v.* [intrans.] **1** equivocate or prevaricate in action or speech. **2** (**palter with**) trifle with: *this great work should not be paltered with.*
DERIVATIVES: **pal•ter•er** *n.*

pal•try |'pôltrē| • *adj.* (**paltrier, paltriest**) (of an amount) small or meager: *a paltry $33.* ■ petty; trivial: *naval glory struck him as paltry.*
DERIVATIVES: **pal•tri•ness** |-trēnis| *n.*

pa•lu•dal |pə'lood'l; 'pælyəd'l| • *adj.* (of a plant, animal, or soil) living or occurring in a marshy habitat.

pan•a•ce•a |,pænə'sēə| • *n.* a solution or remedy for all difficulties or diseases.
DERIVATIVES: **pan•a•ce•an** |-'sēən| *adj.*

pa•nache |pə'næsH; -'näsH| • *n.* **1** flamboyant confidence of style or manner: *he entertained with panache.* **2** a tuft or plume of feathers, esp. as a headdress or on a helmet.

pan•dect |'pæn,dekt| • *n.* a complete body of the laws of a country. ■ (usu. **the Pandects**) a compendium in 50 books of the Roman civil law made by order of Justinian in the 6th century.
DERIVATIVES: **pan•dect•ist** |pæn'dektist| *n.*

pan•dem•ic |pæn'demik| • *adj.* (of a disease) prevalent over a whole country or the world. • *n.* an outbreak of such a disease.

USAGE: On the difference between **pandemic, endemic,** and **epidemic,** see **usage** at EPIDEMIC.

pan•de•mo•ni•um |,pændə'mōnēəm| • *n.* wild and noisy disorder or confusion; uproar.

pan•der |'pændər| • *v.* [intrans.] (**pander to**) gratify or indulge (an immoral or distasteful desire, need, or habit or a person with such a desire, etc.): *candidates pander to interest groups.* • *n.* a pimp. ■ a person who assists the baser urges or evil designs of others: *the lowest panders of a venal press.*

Pan•do•ra's box • *n.* a process that generates many complicated problems as the result of unwise interference in something.

pan•e•gyr•ic |,pænə'jirik| • *n.* a public speech or published text in praise of someone or something: *Vera's panegyric on friendship.*
DERIVATIVES: **pan•e•gyr•i•cal** |-'jirikəl| *adj.* **pan•e•gyr•i•cal•ly** |-'jirik(ə)lē| *adv.*

pan•o•ply |'pænəplē| • *n.* a complete or impressive collection of things: *a deliciously inventive panoply of insults.* ■ a splendid display: *all the panoply of Western religious liturgy.* ■ a complete set of arms or suit of armor.
DERIVATIVES: **pan•o•plied** |-plēd| *adj.*

pan•the•ism |'pænTHē,izəm| • *n.* **1** a doctrine that identifies God with the universe, or regards the universe as a manifestation of God. **2** worship that admits or tolerates all gods.
DERIVATIVES: **pan•the•ist** *n.* **pan•the•is•tic** |,pænTHē'istik| *adj.* **pan•the•is•ti•cal** |,pænTHē'istikəl| *adj.* **pan•the•is•ti•cal•ly** |,pænTHē'istik(ə)lē| *adv.*

pan•the•on |'pænTHē,än; -THēən| • *n.* all the gods of a people or religion collectively: *the deities of the Hindu and Shinto pantheons.* ■ (esp. in ancient Greece and Rome) a temple dedicated to all the gods. ■ a building in which the distinguished dead of a nation are buried or honored. ■ a group of particularly respected, famous, or important people: *the pantheon of the all-time greats.*

pan•to•mime |'pæntə,mīm| • *n.* **1** a dramatic entertainment, originating in Roman mime, in which performers express meaning through gestures accompanied by music. ■ an absurdly exaggerated piece of behavior: *he made a pantomime of checking his watch.* ■ a ridiculous or confused situation or event: *the drive to town was a pantomime.* **2** Brit. a theatrical entertainment, mainly for children, that involves music, topical jokes, and slapstick comedy and is based on a fairy tale or nursery story, usually produced around Christmas. • *v.* [trans.] express or represent (something) by extravagant and exaggerated mime: *the clown candidates pantomimed different emotions.*
DERIVATIVES: **pan•to•mim•ic** |,pæntə'mimik| *adj.* **pan•to•mim•ist** *n.*

pa•pa•cy |'pāpəsē| • *n.* (pl. **-ies**) (usu. **the papacy**) the office or authority of the pope.

■ the tenure of office of a pope: *during the papacy of Pope John.*

pa•pal |'pāpəl| • *adj.* of or relating to a pope or to the papacy.
DERIVATIVES: **pa•pal•ly** *adv.*

pa•pa•raz•zo |ˌpäpəˈrätsō| • *n.* (pl. **paparazzi** |-sē|) (usu. **paparazzi**) a freelance photographer who pursues celebrities to get photographs of them.

pa•pier mâ•ché |ˌpāpər məˈsHā| • *n.* a moldable mixture of paper and glue, or paper, flour, and water, that becomes hard when dry: *George made a crocodile out of papier mâché.* | [as adj.] *a papier-mâché tree.*

pa•pist |'pāpist| • *n.* derogatory term for a Roman Catholic.
■ another term for *papalist,* a supporter of the papacy, esp. an advocate of papal supremacy. • *adj.* of, relating to, or associated with the Roman Catholic Church.
DERIVATIVES: **pa•pism** |'pāˌpizəm| *n.* **pa•pis•ti•cal** |pəˈpistəkəl| *adj.* **pa•pist•ry** |'pāpistrē| *n.*

par•a•ble |'pærəbəl| • *n.* a simple story used to illustrate a moral or spiritual lesson, such as those told by Jesus in the Gospels.

pa•rab•o•la |pəˈræbələ| • *n.* (pl. **parabolas** |pəˈræbələz| or **parabolae** |-lē|) a symmetrical open plane curve formed by the intersection of a cone with a plane parallel to its side. The path of a projectile under the influence of gravity follows a curve of this shape.
DERIVATIVES: **par•a•bol•ic** *adj.* **par•a•bol•i•cal•ly** *adv.*

pa•rach•ro•nism |peˈrækrəˌnizəm| • *n.* an error in chronology, esp. by assigning too late a date. Cf. ANACHRONISM.

par•a•digm |'pærəˌdīm| • *n.* **1** a typical example or pattern of something; a model: *there is a new paradigm for public art in this country.*
■ a worldview underlying the theories and methodology of a particular scientific subject: *the discovery of universal gravitation became the paradigm of successful science.* **2** a set of linguistic items that form mutually exclusive choices in particular syntactic roles: *English determiners form a paradigm: we can say "a book" or "his book" but not "a his book."*
■ (in the traditional grammar of Latin, Greek, and other inflected languages) a table of all the inflected forms of a particular verb, noun, or adjective, serving as a model for other words of the same conjugation or declension.
DERIVATIVES: **par•a•dig•mat•ic** *adj.*

par•a•dox |'pærəˌdäks| • *n.* a statement or proposition that, despite apparently sound reasoning from acceptable premises, leads to a conclusion that seems senseless, logically unacceptable, or self-contradictory: *a potentially serious conflict between quantum mechanics and the general theory of relativity known as the information paradox.*
■ a seemingly absurd or self-contradictory statement or proposition that when investigated or explained may prove to be well founded or true: *in a paradox, he has discovered that stepping back from his job has increased the rewards he gleans from it.* ■ a situation, per-

son, or thing that combines contradictory features or qualities: *a fascinating ecological paradox.*
DERIVATIVES: **par•a•dox•i•cal** *adj.* **par•a•dox•i•cal•ly** *adv.*

par•a•gon |'pærəˌgän; -gən| • *n.* a person or thing regarded as a perfect example of a particular quality: *it would have taken **a paragon** of virtue not to feel viciously jealous.*
■ a person or thing viewed as a model of excellence: *your cook is a paragon.* ■ a perfect diamond of 100 carats or more.

par•a•le•gal |ˌpærəˈlēgəl| • *n.* a person trained in subsidiary legal matters but not fully qualified as a lawyer, typically employed in a law firm. • *adj.* of or relating to auxiliary aspects of the law.

par•al•lax |'pærəˌlæks| • *n.* the effect whereby the position or direction of an object appears to differ when viewed from different positions, e.g., through the viewfinder and the lens of a camera.
■ the angular amount of this in a particular case, esp. that of a star viewed from different points in the earth's orbit.
DERIVATIVES: **par•al•lac•tic** |ˌpærəˈlæktik| *adj.*

par•al•lel•ism |'pærəlelˌizəm| • *n.* the state of being parallel or of corresponding in some way.
■ the use of successive verbal constructions in poetry or prose that correspond in grammatical structure, sound, meter, meaning, etc. ■ the use of parallel processing in computer systems.
DERIVATIVES: **par•al•lel•is•tic** |ˌpærələlˈistik| *adj.*

pa•ral•o•gism |pəˈræləˌjizəm| • *n.* a piece of illogical or fallacious reasoning, esp. one that appears superficially logical or that the reasoner believes to be logical.
DERIVATIVES: **pa•ral•o•gist** *n.*

pa•ram•e•ter |pəˈræmitər| • *n.* a numerical or other measurable factor forming one of a set that defines a system or sets the conditions of its operation: *the transmission will not let you downshift unless your speed is within the lower gear's parameters.*
■ a numerical quantity whose value is selected for the particular circumstances and in relation to which other variable quantities may be expressed. ■ a numerical characteristic of a population, as distinct from a statistic of a sample. ■ (in general use) a limit or boundary that defines the scope of a particular process or activity.

USAGE: Until recently, use of the word **parameter** was confined to mathematics and related technical fields. Since around the mid 20th century, however, it has been used in nontechnical fields as a technical-sounding word for 'a limit or boundary,' as in *they set the **parameters** of the debate.* This use, probably influenced by the word **perimeter,** has been criticized for being a weakening of the technical sense. Careful writers will leave **parameter** to specialists in mathematics, computer science, and other technical disciplines. As a loose synonym for *limit, boundary, guideline, framework,* it is a vogue word that blurs more than it clarifies. **Perimeter** is a different word, meaning 'border, outer boundary, or the length of such a boundary.'

par•a•mil•i•tar•y |ˌpærəˈmiləˌterē| • *adj.* (of an unofficial force) organized similarly to a military force: *the drug cartels and their paramilitary allies.* • *n.* (pl. **-ies**) a member of an unofficial paramilitary organization.

par•a•mour |ˈpærəˌmo͝or| • *n.* a lover, esp. the illicit partner of a married person.

par•a•noi•a |ˌpærəˈnoiə| • *n.* a mental condition characterized by delusions of persecution, unwarranted jealousy, or exaggerated self-importance, typically worked into an organized system. It may be an aspect of chronic personality disorder, of drug abuse, or of a serious condition such as schizophrenia in which the person loses touch with reality.
■ suspicion and mistrust of people or their actions without evidence or justification: *global paranoia about hackers and viruses.*
DERIVATIVES: **par•a•noi•ac** |-ˈnoiæk; -ˈnoi-ik| *adj. & n.* **par•a•noi•a•cal•ly** |-ˈnoi-ik(ə)lē| *adv.* **par•a•no•ic** |-ˈnoi-ik| *adj.* **par•a•no•i•cal•ly** |-ˈnoi-ik(ə)lē| *adv.* **par•a•noid** *adj.*

par•a•nor•mal |ˌpærəˈnôrməl| • *adj.* denoting events or phenomena such as telekinesis or clairvoyance that are beyond the scope of normal scientific understanding: *a mystic's paranormal powers* | [as n.] (**the paranormal**) *an investigator of the paranormal.*
DERIVATIVES: **par•a•nor•mal•ly** *adv.*

par•a•pet |ˈpærəpit| • *n.* a low, protective wall along the edge of a roof, bridge, or balcony.
■ a protective wall or earth defense along the top of a trench or other place of concealment for troops.
DERIVATIVES: **par•a•pet•ed** *adj.*

par•a•pher•na•lia |ˌpærəfə(r)ˈnālyə| • *n.* [treated as sing. or pl.] miscellaneous articles, esp. the equipment needed for a particular activity: *drills, saws, and other paraphernalia* | *drug paraphernalia.*
■ trappings associated with a particular institution or activity that are regarded as superfluous: *the rituals and paraphernalia of government.*

par•a•phil•i•a |ˌpærəˈfilēə| • *n.* (in psychiatry) a condition characterized by abnormal sexual desires, typically involving extreme or dangerous activities.
DERIVATIVES: **par•a•phil•i•ac** |-ˈfilēˌæk| *adj. & n.*

par•a•phrase |ˈpærəˌfrāz| • *v.* [trans.] express the meaning of (the writer or speaker or something written or spoken) using different words, esp. to achieve greater clarity: *you can either quote or paraphrase literary texts.* • *n.* (also **paraphrasis** prons) a rewording of something written or spoken by someone else. Cf. PERIPHRASIS

DERIVATIVES: **par•a•phras•a•ble** *adj.* **par•a•phras•er** **par•a•phra•sis** *n.* **par•a•phras•tic** |ˌpærəˈfræstik| *adj.*

par•a•ple•gi•a |ˌpærəˈplēj(ē)ə| • *n.* paralysis of the legs and lower body, typically caused by spinal injury or disease. Cf. QUADRIPLEGIA
DERIVATIVES: **par•a•ple•gic** |-jik| *adj. & n.*

par•a•psy•chol•o•gy |ˌpærəsīˈkäləjē| • *n.* the study of mental phenomena that are excluded from or inexplicable by orthodox scientific psychology (such as hypnosis, telepathy, clairvoyance, etc.).
DERIVATIVES: **par•a•psy•cho•log•i•cal** |-ˌsīkəˈläjikəl| *adj.* **par•a•psy•chol•o•gist** |-jist| *n.*

par•a•site |ˈpærəˌsīt| • *n.* an organism that lives in or on another organism (its host) and benefits by deriving nutrients at the host's expense. Cf. EPIPHYTE
■ a person who habitually relies on or exploits others and gives nothing in return.
DERIVATIVES: **par•a•sit•ic** *adj.* **par•a•sit•i•cal** *adj.* **par•a•sit•i•cal•ly** *adv.*

par•a•tax•is |ˌpærəˈtæksəs| • *n.* the placing of clauses or phrases one after another, without words to indicate coordination or subordination, as in *Tell me, how are you?* Contrasted with **hypotaxis**, the subordination of one clause to another.
DERIVATIVES: **par•a•tac•tic** |-ˈtæktik| *adj.* **par•a•tac•ti•cal•ly** |-ˈtæktik(ə)lē| *adv.*

pa•rens pa•tri•ae |ˌperənz ˈpætri-ē| • *n.* the government, or any other authority, regarded as the legal protector of citizens unable to protect themselves.
■ the principle that political authority carries with it the responsibility for such protection.

pa•ren•the•sis |pəˈrenтнəˌsis| • *n.* (pl. **parentheses** |-sēz|) a word, clause, or sentence inserted as an explanation or afterthought into a passage that is grammatically complete without it, in writing usually marked off by curved brackets, dashes, or commas.
■ (usu. **parentheses**) one or both of a pair of marks () used to include such a word, clause, or sentence. ■ an interlude or interval: *the three months of coalition government were a lamentable political parenthesis.*
DERIVATIVES: **par•en•thet•i•cal** *adj.* **par•en•thet•i•cal•ly** *adv.*

pa•ri•ah |pəˈrīə| • *n.* **1** an outcast: *they were treated as social pariahs.* **2** in former times, a member of a low caste or of no caste in southern India.

pa•ri•e•tal |pəˈrīətəl| • *adj.* **1** of, relating to, attached to, or denoting the wall of the body or of a body cavity or hollow structure.
■ of the parietal lobe of the brain: *the parietal cortex.* **2** relating to residence in a college or university dormitory and esp. to visits from members of the opposite sex: *parietal rules.* **3** denoting prehistoric art found on rock walls. • *n.* **1** a parietal structure, esp. the *parietal bone,* forming the central side and upper back part of each side of the skull. **2** (**pari-**

etals) dormitory rules governing visits from members of the opposite sex.

par•i•mu•tu•el |ˌpærə 'myo͞oCHəwəl| (also **parimutuel**) • n. [often as adj.] a form of betting in which those backing the first three places (called *win*, *place*, and *show*) divide the losers' stakes (less the operator's commission): *pari-mutuel betting*.
■ a booth for placing bets under such a system.

par•i•ty |'pæritē| • n. **1** the state or condition of being equal, esp. regarding status or pay: *parity of income between farmworkers and those in industrial occupations*.
■ the value of one currency in terms of another at an established exchange rate. ■ a system of providing farmers with consistent purchasing power by regulating prices of farm products, usually with government price supports. **2** (of a number) the fact of being even or odd.
■ (in computing) a function whose being even (or odd) provides a check on a set of binary values: [as adj.] *parity bits*.

par•lance |'pärləns| • n. a particular way of speaking or using words, esp. a way common to those with a particular job or interest: *medical parlance*.

par•lay |'pär,lā; -lē| • v. [trans.] (**parlay something into**) turn an initial stake or winnings from a previous bet into (a greater amount) by gambling: *it involved parlaying a small bankroll into big winnings*.
■ transform into (something greater or more valuable): *he parlayed an inheritance into an empire*. • n. a cumulative series of bets in which winnings accruing from each transaction are used as a stake for a further bet.

par•ley |'pärlē| • n. (pl. **-eys**) a conference between opposing sides in a dispute, esp. a discussion of terms for an armistice. • v. (**-eys**, **-eyed**) [intrans.] hold a conference with the opposing side to discuss terms: *they disagreed over whether to parley with the enemy*.

par•lous |'pärləs| • adj. full of danger or uncertainty; precarious: *the parlous state of the economy*. • adv. greatly or excessively: *she is parlous handsome*.
DERIVATIVES: **par•lous•ly** adv. **par•lous•ness** n.

Par•nas•si•an |pär'næsēən| • adj. **1** relating to poetry; poetic. **2** of or relating to a group of French poets of the late 19th century who emphasized strictness of form, named from the anthology *Le Parnasse contemporain* (1866). • n. a member of this group of French poets.

pa•ro•chi•al |pə'rōkēəl| • adj. of or relating to a church parish: *the parochial church council*.
■ denoting a school operated by a church, distinct from a public school or secular private school.
■ having a limited or narrow outlook or scope.
DERIVATIVES: **pa•ro•chi•al•ism** |-,izəm| n. **pa•ro•chi•al•i•ty** |-,rōkē'ælitē| n. **pa•ro•chi•al•ly** adv.

par•o•dy |'pærədē| • n. (pl. **-ies**) an imitation of the style of a particular writer, artist, or genre with deliberate exaggeration for comic effect.
■ an imitation or a version of something that falls far short of the real thing; a travesty: *he seems like a parody of a world leader*. • v. (**-ies, -ied**) [trans.] produce a humorously exaggerated imitation of (a writer, artist, or genre): *his specialty was parodying schoolgirl fiction*.
■ mimic humorously: *he parodied his friend's voice*.
DERIVATIVES: **pa•rod•ic** |pə'rädik| adj. **par•o•dist** |-dist| n.

pa•role |pə'rōl| • n. **1** the release of a prisoner temporarily (for a special purpose) or permanently before the completion of a sentence, on the promise of good behavior: *he committed a burglary while on parole*.
■ The period in which such an agreement is effective. ■ a promise or undertaking given by a prisoner of war not to escape or, if released, to return to custody under stated conditions. **2** The password used by a military officer or inspector of the guard. Cf. COUNTERSIGN. • v. [trans.] (usu. **be paroled**) release (a prisoner) on parole: *he was paroled after serving nine months*.
DERIVATIVES: **pa•rol•ee** |-,rō'lē| n.

par•o•no•ma•sia |ˌpærənō'māzHə| • n. a play on words; a pun.

par•o•nym |'pærənim| • n. a word that is a derivative of another and has a related meaning: *"wisdom" is a paronym of "wise."*
■ a word formed by adaptation of a foreign word: *"preface" is a paronym of Latin "prefatio."* Cf. HETERONYM.
DERIVATIVES: **par•o•nym•ic** |ˌpærə'nimik| adj. **pa•ron•y•mous** |pə'ränəməs| adj. **pa•ron•y•my** |pə'ränəmē| n.

par•ox•ysm |'pærək,sizəm| • n. a sudden attack or violent expression of a particular emotion or activity: *a paroxysm of weeping | a paroxysm of violence*.
■ a sudden recurrence or attack of a disease; a sudden worsening of symptoms.
DERIVATIVES: **par•ox•ys•mal** |ˌpærək'sizməl| adj.

par•quet |pär'kā| • n. **1** (also **parquet flooring**) flooring composed of wooden blocks arranged in a geometric pattern. **2** the ground floor of a theater or auditorium.

par•quet•ry |'pärkitrē| • n. inlaid work of blocks of various woods arranged in a geometric pattern, esp. for flooring or furniture.

par•ri•cide |'perə,sīd; 'pærə-| • n. the killing of a parent or other near relative.
■ a person who commits parricide.
DERIVATIVES: **par•ri•cid•al** |ˌperə'sīdl; ˌpærə-| adj.

parse |pärs| • v. [trans.] analyze (a sentence) into its component parts and describe their syntactic roles.
■ (in computing) analyze (captured or typed input) into logical components, typically in order to test conformability to a logical grammar or interpret instructions. ■ examine or analyze minutely: *he has always been quick to parse his own problems in public*. • n. an act of

or the result obtained by parsing computer input.

par•si•mo•ni•ous |ˌpärsəˈmōnēəs| • *adj.* unwilling to spend money or use resources; stingy or frugal: *so parsimonious she only bought dented canned goods.*
DERIVATIVES: **par•si•mo•ni•ous•ly** *adv.* **par•si•mo•ni•ous•ness** *n.*

par•si•mo•ny |ˈpärsəˌmōnē| • *n.* extreme unwillingness to spend money or use resources: *a great tradition of public design has been shattered by government parsimony.*
PHRASES: **principle** (or **law**) **of parsimony** the scientific principle that things are usually connected or behave in the simplest or most economical way, esp. with reference to alternative evolutionary pathways.

par•the•no•gen•e•sis |ˌpärTHənōˈjenəsis| • *n.* reproduction from an ovum without fertilization, esp. as a normal process in some invertebrates and lower plants.
DERIVATIVES: **par•the•no•ge•net•ic** |-jə'netik| *adj.* **par•the•no•ge•net•i•cal•ly** |-jə'netik(ə)lē| *adv.*

par•tial |ˈpärSHəl| • *adj.* **1** existing only in part; incomplete: *a question to which we have only partial answers.* **2** favoring one side in a dispute above the other; biased: *a distorted and partial view of the situation.*
■ [predic.] (**partial to**) having a liking for: *you know I'm partial to bacon and eggs.* • *n.* a component of a musical sound; an overtone or harmonic: *the upper partials of the string.*
DERIVATIVES: **par•ti•al•i•ty** *n.* **par•tial•ly** *adv.* [as submodifier] *a partially open door.* **par•tial•ness** *n.*

USAGE: In the sense 'to some extent, not entirely,' traditionalists prefer **partly** to **partially**: *The piece was written partly in poetry*; *What we decide will depend partly on the amount of the contract.* (Also, in certain contexts, the use of **partly** could prevent ambiguity: because *partial* can also mean 'biased, taking sides'; something written *partially in poetry* could be interpreted as biased verse.) The form **partial**, however, appears in many phrases as the adjectival form of **part**: *partial blindness, partial denture, partial paralysis, partial payment, partial shade, partial vacuum,* etc. **Partially** is therefore widely used, with the same sense as **partly**: *partially blind in one eye.*

par•ti•ci•ple |ˈpärtəˌsipəl| • *n.* a word formed from a verb (e.g., *going, gone, being, been*) and used as an adjective (e.g., *working woman, burned toast*) or a noun (e.g., *good breeding*). In English, participles are also used to make compound verb forms (e.g., *is going, has been*).
DERIVATIVES: **par•ti•cip•i•al** |ˌpärtə'sipēəl| *adj.* **par•ti•cip•i•al•ly** |ˌpärtə'sipēəlē| *adv.*

par•ti•cle |ˈpärtikəl| • *n.* **1** a minute portion of matter: *tiny particles of dust.*
■ (also **subatomic** or **elementary particle**) any of numerous subatomic constituents of the physical world that interact with each other, e.g., electrons, neutrinos, photons, and alpha particles. ■ [with negative] the least possible amount: *he agrees without hearing the least particle of evidence.* ■ (in mathematics) a hypothetical object having mass but no physical size. **2** (in grammar) a minor function word that has comparatively little meaning and is not inflected, in particular:
■ (in English) any of the class of words such as *in, up, off, over,* used with verbs to make phrasal verbs. ■ (in ancient Greek) any of the class of words such as *de* and *ge,* used for contrast and emphasis.

par•tic•u•late |pär'tikyəlit; -ˌlāt| • *adj.* of, relating to, or in the form of minute separate particles: *particulate pollution.* • *n.* (**particulates**) matter in such a form.

par•ti•san |ˈpärtəzən| • *n.* **1** a strong supporter of a party, cause, or person. **2** a member of an armed group formed to fight secretly against an occupying force, in particular one operating in enemy-occupied Yugoslavia, Italy, and parts of eastern Europe in World War II. • *adj.* prejudiced, or expressing prejudice, in favor of a particular cause: *newspapers have become increasingly partisan.*
DERIVATIVES: **par•ti•san•ship** |-ˌSHip| *n.*

par•tu•ri•ent |pär't(y)o͝orēənt| • *adj.* (of a woman or female mammal) about to give birth; in labor. • *n.* a parturient woman.

par•tu•ri•tion |ˌpärCHo͝o'riSHən| • *n.* the action of giving birth to young; childbirth.

par•ve•nu |ˈpärvəˌn(y)o͞o| • *n.* a person of obscure origin who has gained wealth, influence, or celebrity: *the social inexperience of a parvenu.* • *adj.* having recently achieved, or associated with someone who has recently achieved wealth, influence, or celebrity despite obscure origins: *he concealed the details of his parvenu lifestyle.* Cf. NOUVEAU RICHE

pas•chal |ˈpæskəl| • *adj.* **1** of or relating to Easter. **2** of or relating to the Jewish Passover.

pas•chal lamb • *n.* **1** a lamb sacrificed at Passover. **2** Christ.

pas de deux |ˌpä də 'do͞o| • *n.* (pl. same) a dance for two people, typically a man and a woman.
■ a relationship between two people that requires finesse or close cooperation.

pas•quin•ade |ˌpæskwə'nād| • *n.* a satire or lampoon, originally one displayed or delivered publicly in a public place.

pas•sé |pæ'sā| • *adj.* [predic.] no longer fashionable; out of date: *miniskirts are passé—the best skirts are knee-length.*
■ (esp. of a woman) past one's prime.

pas•ser•ine |ˈpæsərin; -ˌrīn| • *adj.* of, relating to, or denoting birds of a large order distinguished by feet that are adapted for perching, including all songbirds. • *n.* a passerine bird; a perching bird.

pas•sim |ˈpæsim| • *adv.* (of allusions or references in a published work) to be found at various places throughout the text.

Pas•sion |ˈpæSHən| • *n.* (**the Passion**) in Christianity, the suffering and death of Jesus.
■ a narrative of this from any of the Gospels.

■ a musical setting of any of these narratives: *Bach's St. Matthew Passion.*

pas•sive |'pæsiv| • *adj.* ■ (in grammar) denoting or relating to a voice of verbs in which the subject undergoes the action of the verb (e.g., *they were killed* as opposed to *he killed them*). The opposite of active. • *n.* a passive form of a verb. ■ **(the passive)** the passive voice. DERIVATIVES: **pas•sive•ly** *adv.* **pas•sive•ness** *n.* **pas•siv•i•ty** |pæ'sivitē| *n.*

Pass•o•ver |'pæs,ōvər| • *n.* the major Jewish spring festival that commemorates the liberation of the Israelites from Egyptian bondage, lasting seven or eight days from the 15th day of Nisan; pesach. ■ another term for PASCHAL LAMB.

pas•tiche |pæ'stēSH; pä-| • *n.* an artistic work in a style that imitates that of another work, artist, or period: *the operetta is a pastiche of 18th century styles.* ■ an artistic work consisting of a medley of pieces taken from various sources. ■ a confused mixture or jumble: *his speech is a pastiche of false starts and unfinished sentences.* • *v.* [trans.] imitate the style of (an artist or work): *Gauguin took himself to a Pacific island and pastiched the primitive art he found there.*

pas•to•ral |'pæstərəl; pæs'tôrəl| • *adj.* **1** (esp. of land or a farm) used for or related to the keeping or grazing of sheep or cattle: *scattered pastoral farms* | *society was then essentially pastoral.* ■ associated with country life: *the view was pastoral, with rolling fields and grazing sheep.* ■ (of a work of art) portraying or evoking country life, typically in a romanticized or idealized form: *decorated with pastorals featuring beautiful shepherdesses.* **2** (in the Christian Church) concerning or appropriate to the giving of spiritual guidance: *pastoral and doctrinal issues* | *clergy doing pastoral work.* • *n.* a work of literature portraying an idealized version of country life: *the story, though a pastoral, has an actual connection with the life of agricultural labor.* DERIVATIVES: **pas•to•ral•ism** |'pæstərə,lizəm| *n.* **pas•tor•al•ist** *n.* **pas•to•ral•ly** *adv.*

pas•to•rale |,pæstə'räl; -'ral| • *n.* (pl. **pas•torales** or **pastorali** |,pæstə'rälē|) **1** a slow instrumental composition, usually with drone notes in the bass. **2** a simple musical play with a rural subject.

pat•ent • *adj.* |'pātnt; 'pæt-| easily recognizable; obvious: *she smiled with patent insincerity.* DERIVATIVES: **pat•ent•ly** |'pætntlē; 'pā-| *adv.*

pa•ter•fa•mil•i•as |,pātərfə'milēəs; ,pä-| • *n.* (pl. **patresfamilias** |,pāt rēzfə-; ,pä-|) the male head of a family or household.

pa•ter•nal•ism |pə'tərnl,izəm| • *n.* the policy or practice on the part of people in positions of authority of restricting the freedom and responsibilities of those subordinate to them in their supposed best interest: *the arrogance and paternalism that underlies cradle-to-grave employment contracts.* DERIVATIVES: **pa•ter•nal•ist** *n.* & *adj.* **pa•**

ter•nal•is•tic |-,tərnl'istik| *adj.* **pa•ter•nal•is•ti•cal•ly** |-,tərnl'istik(ə)lē| *adv.*

pa•ter•nos•ter |'pätər,nästər; 'pætər-| • *n.* (in the Roman Catholic Church) the Lord's Prayer, esp. in Latin. ■ any of a number of special beads occurring at regular intervals in a rosary, indicating that the Lord's Prayer is to be recited.

pa•thet•ic |pə'THetik| • *adj.* **1** arousing pity, esp. through vulnerability or sadness: *she looked so pathetic that I bent down to comfort her.* ■ miserably inadequate: *their test scores in Chemistry were pathetic.* **2** relating to the emotions. DERIVATIVES: **pa•thet•i•cal•ly** |-(ə)lē| *adv.*

path•o•gen |'pæTHə,jen| • *n.* a bacterium, virus, or other microorganism that can cause disease. DERIVATIVES: **path•o•gen•ic** |,pæTHə'jenik| *adj.* **path•o•ge•nic•i•ty** |,pæTHəjə'nisitē| *n.* **pa•thog•e•nous** |pə'THäjənəs| *adj.*

path•o•log•i•cal |,pæTHə'läjikəl| (also **pathologic**) • *adj.* involving, caused by, or of the nature of a physical or mental disease. ■ compulsive; obsessive: *a pathological gambler.* DERIVATIVES: **path•o•log•i•cal•ly** *adv.*

pa•thol•o•gy |pə'THäləjē| • *n.* the science of the causes and effects of diseases, esp. the branch of medicine that deals with the laboratory examination of samples of body tissue for diagnostic or forensic purposes. ■ pathological features considered collectively; the typical behavior of a disease: *the pathology of Huntington's disease.* ■ a pathological condition: *the dominant pathology is multiple sclerosis.* ■ mental, social, or linguistic abnormality or malfunction: *the city's inability to cope with the pathology of a burgeoning underclass.* DERIVATIVES: **pa•thol•o•gist** |-jist| *n.*

pa•thos |'pā,THäs; -,THôs| • *n.* a quality that evokes pity or sadness.

pat•i•na |pə'tēnə| • *n.* a green or brown film on the surface of bronze or similar metals, produced by oxidation over a long period. ■ a gloss or sheen on wooden furniture produced by age and polishing. ■ an acquired change in the appearance of a surface: *plankton added a golden patina to the shallow, slowly moving water.* ■ an impression or appearance of something, esp. one deemed to be misleading: *the wedding ring gave her a patina of respectability.* DERIVATIVES: **pat•i•nat•ed** |'pætn,ātid| *adj.* **pat•i•na•tion** |,pætn'äSHən| *n.*

pa•tis•se•rie |pə'tisərē| • *n.* a shop where pastries and cakes are sold. ■ pastries and cakes collectively: *French patisserie.*

pat•ois |'pæ,twä; 'pä-| • *n.* (pl. same) the dialect of the common people of a region, differing in various respects from the standard language of the rest of the country. ■ the jargon or informal speech used by a particular social group: *the patois of inner-city kids.*

pa•tri•arch |'pātrē,ärk| • *n.* **1** the male head of a family or tribe. Cf. PATERFAMILIAS.

■ a man who is the oldest or most venerable of a group: *Hollywood's reigning patriarch.* ■ a man who behaves in a commanding manner. ■ a person or thing that is regarded as the founder of something: *the patriarch of all spin doctors.* **2** any of those biblical figures regarded as fathers of the human race, esp. Abraham, Isaac, and Jacob, their forefathers, or the sons of Jacob. **3** the title of a most senior Orthodox or Catholic bishop.

pa•tri•arch•y |ˈpātrēˌärkē| • *n.* (pl. **-ies**) a system of society or government in which the father or eldest male is head of the family and descent is traced through the male line.

■ a system of society or government in which men hold the power and women are largely excluded from it. ■ a society or community organized in this way.

pa•tri•ate |ˈpātrēˌāt| • *v.* [trans.] transfer control over (a constitution) from a mother country to its former dependency: *the Canadian government moved to patriate the constitution from Great Britain.*

pa•tri•cian |pəˈtriSHən| • *n.* an aristocrat or nobleman.

■ a member of a long-established wealthy family. ■ a member of a noble family or class in ancient Rome. • *adj.* belonging to or characteristic of the aristocracy: *a proud, patrician face.*

■ belonging to or characteristic of a long-established and wealthy family. ■ belonging to the nobility of ancient Rome.

pat•ri•cide |ˈpætrəˌsīd| • *n.* the killing of one's father.

■ a person who kills his or her father.

DERIVATIVES: **pat•ri•cid•al** |ˌpætrəˈsīdl| *adj.*

pat•ri•lin•e•al |ˌpætrəˈlinēəl| • *adj.* of, relating to, or based on relationship to the father or descent through the male line: *the inheritance of land was patrilineal.* Cf. MATRILINEAL.

pat•ri•mo•ny |ˈpætrəˌmōnē| • *n.* (pl. **-ies**) property inherited from one's father or male ancestor.

■ heritage: *our cultural patrimony.* ■ the estate or property belonging by ancient endowment or right to a church or other institution.

DERIVATIVES: **pat•ri•mo•ni•al** |ˌpætrəˈmōnēəl| *adj.*

pa•tron•ize |ˈpātrəˌnīz; ˈpæ-| • *v.* **1** [often as *adj.*] (**patronizing**) treat with an apparent kindness that betrays a feeling of superiority: *"She's a good-hearted girl," he said in a patronizing voice* | *she was determined not to be put down or patronized.* **2** frequent (a store, theater, restaurant, or other establishment) as a customer: *restaurants remaining open in the evening were well patronized.*

■ give encouragement and financial support to (a person, esp. an artist, or a cause): *local churches and voluntary organizations were patronized by the family.*

DERIVATIVES: **pa•tron•i•za•tion** |ˌpātrəni ˈzāSHən; ˌpæ-| *n.* **pa•tron•iz•ing•ly** |-ˌnīziNGlē| *adv.*

pat•ro•nym•ic |ˌpætrəˈnimik| • *n.* a name derived from the name of a father or ances-

tor, typically by the addition of a prefix or suffix, e.g., *Johnson, O'Brien, Ivanovich.*

pa•troon |pəˈtrōōn| • *n.* a person given land and granted certain manorial privileges under the former Dutch governments of New York and New Jersey.

DERIVATIVES: **pa•troon•ship** *n.*

pat•u•lous |ˈpæCHələs| • *adj.* (esp. of the branches of a tree) spreading.

DERIVATIVES: **pat•u•lous•ly** *adv.* **pat•u•lous•ness** *n.*

pau•ci•ty |ˈpôsitē| • *n.* [in sing.] the presence of something only in small or insufficient quantities or amounts; scarcity: *a paucity of information.*

pa•vane |pəˈvän| (also **pavan**) • *n.* a stately slow dance, popular in the 16th and 17th centuries and performed in elaborate clothing.

■ a piece of music for this dance.

pa•vé |pəˈvā; pæ-| • *n.* **1** a setting of precious stones placed so closely together that no metal shows: *a solid diamond pavé.* **2** a paved street, road, or path.

Pav•lov•i•an |pævˈlōvēən; -ˈläv-| • *adj.* of or relating to classical conditioning as described by Ivan P. Pavlov (1849–1936), Russian physiologist, esp. to the conditioned reflex, shown in his experiment in which a dog ('Pavlov's dog') could be trained to salivate at the sound of a bell it associated with food.

pay•o•la |pāˈōlə| • *n.* the practice of bribing someone to use his or her influence or position to promote a particular product or interest: *if a record company spends enough money on payola, it can make any record a hit.*

pec•ca•dil•lo |ˌpekəˈdilō| • *n.* (pl. **-oes** or **-os**) a small, relatively unimportant offense or sin.

pec•cant |ˈpekənt| • *adj.* **1** having committed a fault or sin; offending. **2** diseased or causing disease.

DERIVATIVES: **pec•can•cy** |ˈpekənsē| *n.*

peck•ish |ˈpekiSH| • *adj.* hungry: *we were both feeling a bit peckish and there was nothing to eat.*

pec•to•ral |ˈpektərəl| • *adj.* of or relating to the breast or chest: *pectoral development.*

■ worn on the chest: *a pectoral shield.* • *n.* (usu. **pectorals**) The four large muscles that cover the front of the ribcage.

■ (**pectorals**) the fins of a fish that correspond to the forelimbs of other vertebrates. ■ an ornamental breastplate, esp. one worn by a Jewish high priest.

pec•u•late |ˈpekyəˌlāt| • *v.* [trans.] embezzle or steal (money, esp. public funds).

DERIVATIVES: **pec•u•la•tion** |ˌpekyə ˈlāSHən| *n.* **pec•u•la•tor** |-ˌlātər| *n.*

pe•cu•ni•ar•y |pəˈkyōōnēˌerē| • *adj.* of, relating to, or consisting of money: *he admitted obtaining a pecuniary advantage by deception.* Cf. FISCAL.

DERIVATIVES: **pe•cu•ni•ar•i•ly** |pəˌkyōōnē ˈerəlē| *adv.*

ped•a•gog•ic |ˌpedəˈgäjik| • *adj.* of or relating to teaching: *they show great pedagogic skills.*

■ of or characteristic of a pedagogue.

DERIVATIVES: ped·a·gog·i·cal adj. **ped·a·gog·i·cal·ly** |-(ə)lē| adv.
ped·a·gogue |'pedə,gäg| • n. a teacher, esp. a strict or pedantic one.
ped·a·go·gy |'pedə,gäjē; -,gōjē| • n. (pl. **-ies**) the method and practice of teaching, esp. as an academic subject or theoretical concept.
DERIVATIVES: ped·a·gog·ics |,pedə'gäj·iks| n.
ped·ant |'pednt| • n. a person who is excessively concerned with minor details and rules or with displaying academic learning.
DERIVATIVES: pe·dan·tic adj. **pe·dan·ti·cal·ly** adv. **ped·ant·ry** |-trē| n.
ped·er·as·ty |'pedə,ræstē| • n. sexual activity involving a man and a boy.
DERIVATIVES: ped·er·ast n. a man who indulges in pederasty. **ped·er·as·tic** |,pedə'ræstik| adj.
pe·des·tri·an |pə'destrēən| • n. a person walking along a road or in a developed area. • adj. lacking inspiration or excitement; dull: disenchantment with their pedestrian lives.
DERIVATIVES: pe·des·tri·an·ly adv.
pe·dic·u·lar |pə'dikyələr| (also **pediculous**) • adj. of, relating to, or infested with lice.
DERIVATIVES: pe·dic·u·lo·sis |pə,dikyə'lōsəs| n.
ped·i·ment |'pedəmənt| • n. the triangular upper part of the front of a building in classical style, typically surmounting a portico of columns.
■ a similar feature surmounting a door, window, front, or other part of a building in another style. ■ a broad, gently sloping expanse of rock debris extending outward from the foot of a mountain slope, esp. in a desert. Cf. TALUS.
DERIVATIVES: ped·i·men·tal |,pedə'mentl| adj. **ped·i·ment·ed** adj.
pe·dol·o·gy |pə'däləjē| • n. the branch of science that deals with the formation, nature, and classification of soil; soil science.
DERIVATIVES: ped·o·log·i·cal |,pedə'läjikəl| adj. **pe·dol·o·gist** |-jist| n.
pe·dom·e·ter |pə'dämitər| • n. an instrument for estimating the distance traveled on foot by recording the number of steps taken.
pe·do·phile |'pedə,fīl| (Brit. **paedophile**) • n. a person, esp. a man, who is sexually attracted to children.
DERIVATIVES: pe·do·phil·i·a n. **pe·do·phil·ic** adj.
peer • n. **1** a member of the nobility in Britain or Ireland, comprising the ranks of duke, marquess, earl, viscount, and baron.

In the British peerage, earldoms and baronetcies were the earliest to be conferred; dukes were created from 1337, marquesses from the end of the 14th century, and viscounts from 1440. Such peerages are hereditary, although since 1958 there have also been nonhereditary life peerages. Peers are entitled to a seat in the House of Lords and exemption from jury service; they are debarred from election to the House of Commons.

2 a person of the same age, status, or ability as another specified person: he has incurred much criticism from his academic peers. • v. make or become equal with or of the same rank.
PHRASES: without peer unequaled; unrivaled: he is a goalkeeper without peer.
DERIVATIVES: peer·less adj. (in sense 2).
peer·age |'pirij| • n. the title and rank of peer or peeress: he was given a peerage.
■ **(the peerage)** peers as a class; those holding a hereditary or honorary title: elevated to the peerage. ■ a book containing a list of peers and peeresses, with their genealogy and history.
peeve |pēv| • v. [trans.] (usu. **be peeved**) annoy; irritate: he was peeved at being left out of the cabinet | [as adj.] (**peeved**) a somewhat peeved tone. • n. a cause of annoyance: his pet peeve is not having answers for questions from players.
peev·ish |'pēvish| • adj. easily irritated, esp. by unimportant things: all this makes Steve fretful and peevish.
■ querulous: a peevish, whining voice.
DERIVATIVES: peev·ish·ly adv. **peev·ish·ness** n.
peign·oir |,pān'wär| • n. a woman's light dressing gown or negligee.
pe·jo·ra·tive |pə'jôrətiv; 'pejə,rātiv| • adj. expressing contempt or disapproval: "permissiveness" is used almost universally as a pejorative term. • n. a word expressing contempt or disapproval.
DERIVATIVES: pe·jo·ra·tive·ly adv.
pe·la·gi·an |pə'lājēən| • adj. inhabiting the open sea. • n. an inhabitant of the open sea.
pe·lag·ic |pə'læjik| • adj. of or relating to the open sea.
■ (chiefly of fish) inhabiting the upper layers of the open sea.
pelf |pelf| • n. money, esp. when gained in a dishonest or dishonorable way.
pell-mell |'pel 'mel| • adv. in a confused, rushed, or disorderly manner: the contents were thrown pell-mell. • adj. recklessly hasty or disorganized; headlong: the pell-mell development of Europe. • n. [in sing.] a state of affairs or collection of things characterized by haste or confusion: the pell-mell of ascending gables and roof tiles.
pel·lu·cid |pə'lōōsid| • adj. translucent; clear: mountains reflected in the pellucid waters.
■ very lucid in style or meaning; easily understood: pellucid prose. ■ (of music or other sound) clear and pure in tone: a pellucid singing tone.
DERIVATIVES: pel·lu·cid·i·ty n. **pel·lu·cid·ness** n. **pel·lu·cid·ly** adv.
pem·mi·can |'pemikən| • n. dried and pounded meat mixed with melted fat and other ingredients, originally made by North American Indians and later adapted by Arctic explorers.
pe·nal |'pēnəl| • adj. of, relating to, or prescribing the punishment of offenders under the legal system:
■ used or designated as a place of punishment:

a *penal institution.* ■ (of an act or offense) punishable by law.
DERIVATIVES: **pe•nal•ly** *adv.*
pen•ance |'penəns| • *n.* **1** voluntary self-punishment inflicted as an outward expression of repentance for having done wrong: *he had done public penance for those hasty words.* **2** a Christian sacrament in which a member of the Church confesses sins to a priest and is given absolution.
■ a religious observance or other duty required of a person by a priest as part of this sacrament to indicate repentance. • *v.* [trans.] impose a penance on: *a hair shirt to penance him for his folly in offending.* Cf. PENITENT
pe•na•tes |pə'nätēz; -'nä-| • *plural n.* household gods worshiped in conjunction with Vesta and the lares by the ancient Romans.
pen•chant |'penCHənt| • *n.* [usu. in sing.] a strong or habitual liking for something or tendency to do something: *a penchant for adopting stray dogs.*
pend•ant |'pendənt| • *n.* **1** a piece of jewelry that hangs from a chain worn around the neck.
■ a necklace with such a piece of jewelry. ■ a light designed to hang from the ceiling. ■ the part of a pocket watch by which it is suspended. ■ **2** an artistic, literary, or musical composition intended to match or complement another: *the triptych's pendant will occupy the corresponding wall.* • *adj.* hanging downward; pendent: *pendant flowers on frail stems.*
pend•ent |'pendənt| • *adj.* **1** hanging down or overhanging: *pendent lichens.* **2** undecided; pending: *the use of jurisdiction to decide pendent claims.* **3** (esp. of a sentence) incomplete; not having a finite verb.
DERIVATIVES: **pen•den•cy** *n.*
pend•ing |'pendiNG| • *adj.* awaiting decision or settlement: *nine cases were still pending.*
■ (of a patent) having provisional status, and protected by law for one year, until a full patent is obtained. ■ about to happen; imminent: *the pending disaster.* • *prep.* until (something) happens or takes place: *they were released on bail pending an appeal.*
pen•du•lous |'penjələs; 'pendyə-| • *adj.* hanging down loosely: *pendulous branches.*
DERIVATIVES: **pen•du•lous•ly** *adv.*
pen•du•lum |'penjələm; 'pendyə-| • *n.* a weight hung from a fixed point so that it can swing freely backward and forward, esp. a rod with a weight at the end that regulates the mechanism of a clock.
■ used to refer to the tendency of a situation or state of affairs to oscillate regularly between one extreme and another: *the pendulum of fashion.*
DERIVATIVES: **pen•du•lar** |-lər| *adj.* .
pe•ne•plain |'pēnə,plān| (also **peneplane**) • *n.* a more or less level land surface produced by erosion over a long period, undisturbed by crustal movement.
pen•e•tra•li•a |,peni'trālēə| • *plural n.* the innermost parts of a building; a secret or hidden place.

pe•nile |'pēnəl; -nīl | • *adj.* [attrib.] of, relating to, or affecting the penis.
pen•i•tent |'penitnt| • *adj.* feeling or showing sorrow and regret for having done wrong; repentant: • *n.* a person who repents his or her sins or wrongdoings and (in the Christian Church) seeks forgiveness from God.
DERIVATIVES: **pen•i•tence** *n.* **pen•i•tent•ly** *adv.*
pen•i•ten•tia•ry |,penə'tensHərē| • *n.* (pl. **-ies**) **1** a prison for people convicted of serious crimes. **2** (in the Roman Catholic Church) a priest charged with certain aspects of the administration of the sacrament of penance.
■ an office in the papal court forming a tribunal for deciding on questions relating to penance, dispensations, and absolution.
pen•non |'penən| • *n.* a long triangular or swallow-tailed flag, esp. as the military ensign of lancer regiments.
DERIVATIVES: **pen•noned** *adj.*
pe•nol•o•gy |pē'näləjē| • *n.* the study of the punishment of crime and of prison management.
DERIVATIVES: **pe•no•log•i•cal** |,pēnə'läjikəl| *adj.* **pe•nol•o•gist** |-jist| *n.*
pen•sée |,pän'sā | • *n.* a thought or reflection put into literary form; an aphorism.
pen•sile |'pen,sīl; -sil | • *adj.* hanging down; pendulous: *pensile nests.*
pen•sive |'pensiv| • *adj.* engaged in, involving, or reflecting deep or serious thought: *a pensive mood.*
DERIVATIVES: **pen•sive•ly** *adv.* **pen•sive•ness** *n.*
pen•ta•cle |'pentəkəl| • *n.* a talisman or magical object, typically disk-shaped and inscribed with a pentagram or other figure, and used as a symbol of the element of earth.
pen•ta•gram |'pentə,græm| • *n.* a five-pointed star that is formed by drawing a continuous line in five straight segments, often used as a mystic and magical symbol.
pen•tan•gle |'pen,tæNGgəl| • *n.* another term for PENTAGRAM.
Pen•ta•teuch |'pentə,t(y)ōok| the first five books of the Hebrew Bible (Genesis, Exodus, Leviticus, Numbers, and Deuteronomy). Traditionally ascribed to Moses, it is now held by scholars to be a compilation from texts of the 9th to 5th centuries BC. Cf. TORAH.
DERIVATIVES: **Pen•ta•teuch•al** |-,t(y)ōokəl| *adj.*
Pen•te•cos•tal |,pentə'kôstl; -'kästl | • *adj.* **1** of or relating to the Christian festival commemorating the descent of the Holy Spirit on the disciples (the Pentecost). **2** of, relating to, or denoting any of a number of Christian sects and individuals emphasizing baptism in the Holy Spirit, evidenced by speaking in tongues, prophecy, healing, and exorcism. • *n.* a member of a Pentecostal sect.
DERIVATIVES: **Pen•te•cos•tal•ism** |-,izəm| *n.* **Pen•te•cos•tal•ist** |-ist| *adj. & n.*
pe•nul•ti•mate |pe'nəltəmit| • *adj.* [attrib.] second to last in a series of things: *the penultimate chapter of the book.*

pe•num•bra |pe'nəmbrə| • *n.* (pl. **penum-brae** |-,brē; -,brī| or **penumbras**) the partially shaded outer region of the shadow cast by an opaque object.
■ the shadow cast by the earth or moon over an area experiencing a partial eclipse. ■ the less dark outer part of a sunspot, surrounding the dark core. ■ any area of partial shade.
DERIVATIVES: **pe•num•bral** |-brəl| *adj.*
pen•u•ry |'penyərē| • *n.* extreme poverty; destitution.
DERIVATIVES: **pe•nu•ri•ous** *adj.*
pe•on |'pē,än; 'pēən| • *n.* **1** a Latin-American day laborer or unskilled farm worker.
■ a debtor held in servitude by a creditor, esp. formerly in the southern US and Mexico. ■ a person who does menial work; a drudge: **2** (in the Indian subcontinent and Southeast Asia) someone of low rank.
DERIVATIVES: **pe•on•age** |'pēənij| *n.*
pep•tic |'peptik| • *adj.* of or relating to digestion, esp. that which takes place in the stomach.
per•ad•ven•ture |,pərəd'venCHər; ,per-| • *adv.* perhaps: *peradventure I'm not as wealthy as he is.* • *n.* uncertainty or doubt as to whether something is the case: *that shows beyond peradventure the strength of the economy.*
per•am•bu•late |pə'ræmbyə,lāt| • *v.* [trans.] walk or travel through or around (a place or area), esp. for pleasure and in a leisurely way: *she perambulated the square.*
■ [intrans.] walk from place to place; walk about: *he grew weary of perambulating over rough countryside.*
DERIVATIVES: **per•am•bu•la•tion** |pə,ræmbyə'lāsHən| *n.* **per•am•bu•la•to•ry** |-lə,tôrē| *adj.*
per•cen•tile |pər'sen,tīl| • *n.* each of the 100 equal groups into which a population can be divided according to the distribution of values of a statistical variable.
per•cept |'pərsept| • *n.* an object of perception; something that is perceived.
■ a mental concept that is developed as a consequence of the process of perception.
per•chance |pər'CHæns| • *adv.* by some chance; perhaps.
per•cip•i•ent |pər'sipēənt| • *adj.* (of a person) having a good understanding; perceptive. • *n.* (esp. in philosophy or with reference to psychic phenomena) a person who is able to perceive things.
DERIVATIVES: **per•cip•i•ence** *n.* **per•cip•i•ent•ly** *adv.*
per•co•late |'pərkə,lāt| • *v.* (of a liquid or gas) filter gradually through a porous surface or substance: *the water percolating through the soil may leach out minerals.*
■ (of information or an idea or feeling) spread gradually through an area or group of people: *this idea soon percolated into the Christian Church.* ■ be or become full of lively activity or excitement: *the night was percolating with an expectant energy.*
DERIVATIVES: **per•co•la•tion** |,pərkə'lā-sHən| *n.*

per•di•tion |pər'disHən| • *n.* (in Christian theology) a state of eternal punishment and damnation into which a sinful and unpenitent person passes after death.
■ utter ruin or destruction.
per•dur•a•ble |pər'd(y)o͞orəbəl| • *adj.* enduring continuously; imperishable.
DERIVATIVES: **per•dur•a•bil•i•ty** |-,d(y)o͞o-rə'bilitē| *n.* **per•dur•a•bly** |-blē| *adv.*
per•dure |pər'd(y)o͞or| • *v.* [intrans.] remain in existence throughout a substantial period of time; endure: *bell music has perdured in Venice throughout five centuries.*
DERIVATIVES: **per•dur•ance** |-'d(y)o͞orəns| *n.*
père |per| • *n.* used after a surname to distinguish a father from a son of the same name: *Alexandre Dumas père.* Cf. FILS.
per•e•gri•nate |'perigrə,nāt| • *v.* [no obj., with adverbial] travel or wander around from place to place.
DERIVATIVES: **per•e•gri•na•tion** |,perigrə'nāsHən| *n.* **per•e•gri•na•tor** |-,nātər| *n.*
per•emp•to•ry |pə'remptərē| • *adj.* (esp. of a person's manner or actions) insisting on immediate attention or obedience, esp. in a brusquely imperious way: *"Just do it!" came the peremptory reply.*
■ not open to legal appeal or challenge; final.
DERIVATIVES: **per•emp•to•ri•ly** |-tərəlē| *adv.* **per•emp•to•ri•ness** |-rēnis| *n.*
USAGE: **Peremptory** and **preemptive** can be confused, as both involve stopping something. A **peremptory** act or statement is absolute; it cannot be denied: *He issued a peremptory order.* A **preemptive** action is one taken before an adversary can act: *Preemptive air strikes stopped the enemy from launching the new warship.*
per•en•ni•al |pə'renēəl| • *adj.* lasting or existing for a long or apparently infinite time; enduring: *his perennial distrust of the media.*
■ (of a plant) living for several years: *cow parsley is perennial.* Cf. ANNUAL, BIENNIAL. ■ (esp. of a problem or difficult situation) continually occurring: *perennial manifestations of urban crisis.* ■ [attrib.] (of a person) apparently permanently engaged in a specified role or way of life: *he's a perennial student.* ■ (of a stream or spring) flowing throughout the year. • *n.* a perennial plant.
DERIVATIVES: **per•en•ni•al•ly** *adv.*
pe•re•stroi•ka |,perə'stroikə| • *n.* (in the former Soviet Union) the policy or practice of restructuring or reforming the economic and political system. First proposed by Leonid Brezhnev in 1979 and actively promoted by Mikhail Gorbachev, perestroika originally referred to increased automation and labor efficiency, but came to entail greater awareness of economic markets and the ending of central planning.
per•fec•tion•ism |pər'feksHə,nizəm| • *n.* refusal to accept any standard short of perfection.
■ a philosophical doctrine holding that reli-

gious, moral, social, or political perfection is attainable, esp. the theory that human moral or spiritual perfection should be or has been attained.

DERIVATIVES: **per•fec•tion•ist** *n.* & *adj.* **per•fec•tion•is•tic** |-,feksHən'istik| *adj.*

per•fer•vid |pər'fərvid| • *adj.* intense and impassioned.

DERIVATIVES: **per•fer•vid•ly** *adv.*

per•fid•i•ous |pər'fidēəs| • *adj.* deceitful and untrustworthy; capable of treachery: *a perfidious lover.*

DERIVATIVES: **per•fid•i•ous•ly** *adv.* **per•fi•dy** *n.*

per•fo•rate • *v.* |'pərfə,rāt| [trans.] pierce and make a hole or holes in: *worms had perforated the pages* | [as adj.] (**perforated**) *a perforated appendix.*

■ make a row of small holes in (paper) so that a part may be torn off easily. • *adj.* |'pərfərit; -,rāt| perforated: *a perforate shell.*

DERIVATIVES: **per•fo•ra•tion** *n.* **per•fo•ra•tor** |-,rātər| *n.*

per•force |pər'fôrs| • *adv.* used to express necessity or inevitability: *amateurs, perforce, have to settle for less.*

per•for•ma•tive |pər'fôrmətiv| • *adj.* relating to or denoting an utterance by means of which the speaker performs a particular act (e.g., *I bet*, *I apologize*). • *n.* a performative verb, sentence, or utterance.

per•func•to•ry |pər'fəNGktərē| • *adj.* (of an action or gesture) carried out with a minimum of effort or reflection: *the investigation was merely perfunctory.*

DERIVATIVES: **per•func•to•ri•ly** |-'fəNGktərəlē| *adv.* **per•func•to•ri•ness** |-rēnis| *n.*

per•fuse |pər'fyo͞oz| • *v.* [trans.] permeate or suffuse (something) with a liquid, color, quality, etc.: *Glaser perfused the yellow light with white* | *such expression is perfused by rhetoric.*

■ supply (an organ, tissue, or body) with a fluid, typically blood or a blood substitute, by circulating it through blood vessels or other natural channels.

DERIVATIVES: **per•fu•sion** |-zHən| *n.* **per•fu•sion•ist** |-zHənist| *n.*

per•i•gee |'perijē| • *n.* the point in the orbit of the moon or a satellite at which it is nearest to the earth. The opposite of APOGEE.

pe•rim•e•ter |pə'rimitər| • *n.* the continuous line forming the boundary of a closed geometric figure.

■ the length of such a line: *the rectangle has a perimeter of 30 cm.* ■ the outermost parts or boundary of an area, concept, or object: *the perimeter of the garden* | *my presence on the perimeter of his life.* ■ a defended boundary of a military position or base. Cf. PERIPHERY. See **usage** at PARAMETER.

DERIVATIVES: **per•i•met•ric** |,perə'metrik| *adj.*

pe•ri•od•ic |,pirē'ädik| • *adj.* 1 appearing or occurring at intervals: *the periodic visits she made to her father.* 2 relating to the periodic table of elements or the pattern of chemical properties that underlies it. 3 of or relating to

a rhetorical period. 4 denoting a sentence that creates anticipation or suspense by ending with its main clause, esp. one containing several clauses.

pe•ri•od•i•cal |,pirē'ädikəl| • *n.* a magazine or newspaper published at regular intervals. • *adj.* [attrib.] occurring or appearing at intervals; occasional: *she took periodical gulps of her tea.*

■ (of a magazine or newspaper) published at regular intervals: *a periodical newsletter.*

DERIVATIVES: **pe•ri•od•i•cal•ly** *adv.*

per•i•pa•tet•ic |,peripə'tetik| • *adj.* 1 traveling from place to place, esp. working or based in various places for relatively short periods: *the peripatetic nature of military life.* 2 (**Peripatetic**) of or belonging to the philosophical school or Aristotle (384–322 BC); Aristotelian. • *n.* 1 a person who travels from place to place. 2 (**Peripatetic**) an Aristotelian philosopher.

DERIVATIVES: **per•i•pa•tet•i•cal•ly** |-ik-(ə)lē| *adv.* **per•i•pa•tet•i•cism** |-'teti,sizəm| *n.*

pe•riph•er•al |pə'rifərəl| • *adj.* of, relating to, or situated on the edge or periphery of something: *the peripheral areas of Europe.*

■ of secondary or minor importance; marginal: *she will see their problems as **peripheral to** her own.* ■ [attrib.] (of a device) able to be attached to and used with a computer, although not an integral part of it. ■ near the surface of the body, with special reference to the circulation and nervous system: *lymphocytes from peripheral blood.* • *n.* a device connected or connectable to a computer.

DERIVATIVES: **pe•riph•er•al•i•ty** |-'rælitē| *n.* **pe•riph•er•al•i•za•tion** |pə,rifərəli'zāsHən| *n.* **pe•riph•er•al•ize** |-,īz| *v.* **pe•riph•er•al•ly** *adv.*

pe•riph•er•y |pə'rifərē| • *n.* (pl. **-ies**) the outer limits or edge of an area or object: *new buildings on the periphery of the hospital site.*

■ a marginal or secondary position in, or part or aspect of, a group, subject, or sphere of activity: *a shift in power from the center to the periphery.* Cf. PERIMETER

pe•riph•ra•sis |pə'rifrəsis| • *n.* (pl. **periphrases** |-,sēz|) the use of indirect and circumlocutory speech or writing.

■ an indirect and circumlocutory phrase. ■ the use of separate words to express a grammatical relationship that is otherwise expressed by inflection, e.g., *did go* as opposed to *went* and *more intelligent* as opposed to *smarter.* Cf. PARAPHRASE

per•i•phras•tic |,perə'fræstik| • *adj.* (of speech or writing) indirect and circumlocutory: *the periphrastic nature of legal syntax.*

■ (of a case or tense) formed by a combination of words rather than by inflection (such as *did go* and *of the people* rather than *went* and *the people's*).

DERIVATIVES: **per•i•phras•ti•cal•ly** |-(ə)-lē| *adv.*

per•i•stal•sis |,perə'stôlsis| • *n.* the involuntary constriction and relaxation of the

muscles of the intestine or another canal, creating wavelike movements that push the contents of the canal along.
DERIVATIVES: **per•i•stal•tic** |-'stôltik| *adj.* **per•i•stal•ti•cal•ly** |-'stôltik(ə)lē| *adv.*

per•i•style |'peri,stīl| • *n.* a row of columns surrounding a space within a building such as a courtyard or internal garden or edging a veranda or porch.
▪ an architectural space such as a courtyard or porch that is surrounded or edged by such columns.

per•jure |'pərjər| • *v.* (**perjure oneself**) willfully tell a lie when giving evidence to a court; commit perjury.
DERIVATIVES: **per•jur•er** *n.*

per•ju•ry |'pərjərē| • *n.* (pl. **-ies**) (in law) the offense of willfully telling an untruth after having taken an oath or affirmation, in court or in a formal hering, etc.
▪ the action or an act of taking a vow one does not intend to keep.
DERIVATIVES: **per•ju•ri•ous** |pər'jo͝orēəs| *adj.* **perjuriously** *adv.*

per•lo•cu•tion |,pərlə'kyo͞osHən| • *n.* an act of speaking or writing that has an action as its aim but that in itself does not effect or constitute the action, for example persuading or convincing. Cf. ILLOCUTION.
DERIVATIVES: **per•lo•cu•tion•ar•y** |-,nerē| *adj.*

per•ma•frost |'pərmə,frôst; -,fräst| • *n.* a thick subsurface layer of soil that remains frozen throughout the year, occurring chiefly in polar regions.

per•me•a•ble |'pərmēəbəl| • *adj.* (of a material or membrane) allowing liquids or gases to pass through it: *a frog's skin is **permeable to** water.*

per•me•ate |'pərmē,āt| • *v.* [trans.] spread throughout (something); pervade: *the aroma of soup permeated the air* | [intrans.] *his personality has begun to **permeate through** the whole organization.*
DERIVATIVES: **per•me•a•tion** |,pərmē'āsHən| *n.*

per•mu•ta•tion |,pərmyo͞o'tāsHən| • *n.* a way, esp. one of several possible variations, in which a set or number of things can be ordered or arranged: *his thoughts raced ahead to fifty different permutations of what he must do.*
▪ the action of changing the arrangement, esp. the linear order, of a set of numbers or other items.
DERIVATIVES: **per•mu•ta•tion•al** |-'tā-sHənəl| *adj.*

per•ni•cious |pər'nisHəs| • *adj.* having a harmful effect, esp. in a gradual or subtle way: *the pernicious influences of the mass media.*
DERIVATIVES: **per•ni•cious•ly** *adv.* **per•ni•cious•ness** *n.*

per•o•rate |'perə,rāt| • *v.* [intrans.] speak at length: *in private he would perorate against his colleague.*
▪ sum up and conclude a speech: *the recapitulation with which she perorates.*

per•o•ra•tion |,perə'rāsHən| • *n.* the con-

cluding part of a speech, typically intended to inspire enthusiasm in the audience.

per•pe•trate |'pərpə,trāt| • *v.* [trans.] carry out or commit (a harmful, illegal, or immoral action): *a crime has been perpetrated against a sovereign state.*
DERIVATIVES: **per•pe•tra•tion** |,pərpə'trāsHən| *n.* **per•pe•tra•tor** |-,trātər| *n.*

USAGE: To **perpetrate** something is to commit it: *The gang perpetrated outrages against several citizens.* To **perpetuate** something is to cause it to continue or to keep happening: *The stories only serve to perpetuate the legend that the house is haunted.*

per•pet•u•al |pər'pecHəwəl| • *adj.* **1** never ending or changing: *deep caves in perpetual darkness.*
▪ [attrib.] denoting a position, job, or trophy held for life rather than a limited period, or the person holding it: *perpetual secretary of the society.* ▪ (of an investment) having no fixed maturity date; irredeemable: *a perpetual bond.* **2** occurring repeatedly; so frequent as to seem endless and uninterrupted: *their perpetual money worries.*
▪ (of a plant) blooming or fruiting several times in one season: *he grows perpetual carnations.* • *n.* a perpetual plant, esp. a hybrid rose.
DERIVATIVES: **per•pet•u•al•ly** *adv.*

per•pet•u•ate |pər'pecHə,wāt| • *v.* [trans.] make (something, typically an undesirable situation or an unfounded belief) continue indefinitely: *the law perpetuated the interests of the ruling class.*
▪ preserve (something valued) from oblivion or extinction: *how did these first humans survive to perpetuate the species?*
DERIVATIVES: **per•pet•u•ance** |-wəns| *n.* **per•pet•u•a•tion** |pər,pecHə'wāsHən| *n.* **per•pet•u•a•tor** |-,wātər| *n.*

USAGE: See **usage** at PERPETRATE.

per•pe•tu•i•ty |,pərpi't(y)o͞oitē| • *n.* (pl. **-ies**) **1** a thing that lasts forever or for an indefinite period, in particular:
▪ a bond or other security with no fixed maturity date. ▪ (in law) a restriction making an estate inalienable perpetually or for a period beyond certain limits fixed by law. ▪ an estate so restricted. **2** the state or quality of lasting forever: *he did not believe in the perpetuity of military rule.*
PHRASES: **in** (or **for**) **perpetuity** forever: *the Bonapartes were banished from France in perpetuity.*

per•plex•i•ty |pər'pleksitē| • *n.* (pl. **-ies**) inability to deal with or understand something complicated or unaccountable: *she paused in perplexity.*
▪ (usu. **perplexities**) a complicated or baffling situation, aspect, or thing: *the perplexities of international relations.*

per•qui•site |'pərkwəzit| • *n.* (also, informally **perk**) a benefit incidental to a particular job or position.
▪ a thing regarded as a special right or privi-

lege enjoyed as a result of one's position: *the wife of a president has all the perquisites of stardom.* ■ a thing that has served its primary use and is then given to a subordinate or employee as a customary right.

USAGE: **Perquisite** and **prerequisite** are sometimes confused. **Perquisite** usually means 'an extra allowance or privilege' (*he had all the perquisites of a movie star*). **Prerequisite** means `something required as a condition` (*passing the examination was one of the prerequisites for a teaching position*).

per•se•cute |ˈpərsəˌkyoōt| • v. [trans.] (often **be persecuted**) subject (someone) to hostility and ill-treatment, esp. because of their race or political or religious beliefs: *Jews who had been persecuted by the regime.*
■ harass or annoy (someone) persistently: *Hilda was persecuted by some of the other girls.*
DERIVATIVES: **per•se•cu•tion** |ˌpərsəˈkyoōSHən| n. **per•se•cu•tor** |-ˌkyoōt̩ər| n. **per•se•cu•to•ry** |-kyoōˌtôrē| adj.

USAGE: **Prosecute** means 'to take legal action against': *they prosecuted him for trespassing.* **Persecute** means 'to take hostile, generally nonlegal or illegal, action against': *they persecuted him for his religious views.*

per•sev•er•ate |pərˈsevəˌrāt| • v. [intrans.] repeat or prolong an action, thought, or utterance after the stimulus that prompted it has ceased.
DERIVATIVES: **per•sev•er•a•tion** |pərˌsevəˈrāSHən| n.
per•si•flage |ˈpərsəˌfläZH| • n. light mockery or banter.
per•snick•et•y |pərˈsnikətē| • adj. placing too much emphasis on trivial or minor details; fussy: *persnickety gardeners | she's **persnickety** about her food.*
■ requiring a particularly precise or careful approach: *the film is persnickety and difficult to use.*
per•so•na |pərˈsōnə| • n. (pl. **personas** or **personae** |-ˈsōnē|) the aspect of someone's character that is presented to or perceived by others: *her public persona.*
■ a role or character adopted by an author or an actor.
per•son•age |ˈpərsənij| • n. a person (often used to express his or her significance, importance, or elevated status): *it was no less a personage than the bishop.*
■ a character in a play or other work.
per•son•al•ty |ˈpərsənəltē| • n. personal property. The opposite of REALTY.
per•so•na non gra•ta |pərˈsōnə nän ˈgrätə| • n. (pl. **personae non gratae** |pərˈsōnē nän ˈgrätē|) an unacceptable or unwelcome person: *from now on, these scandal-seeking journalists can consider themselves personae non gratae.*
per•son•i•fy |pərˈsänəˌfī| • v. (**-ies, -ied**) [trans.] 1 represent (a quality or concept) by a figure in human form: *public pageants and dramas in which virtues and vices were personified.*
■ (usu. **be personified**) attribute a personal nature or human characteristics to (some-

thing nonhuman): *in the poem, the oak trees are personified.* ■ represent or embody (a quality, concept, or thing) in a physical form: *he fairly personifies trustworthiness.*
DERIVATIVES: **per•son•i•fi•ca•tion** n. **per•son•i•fi•er** |-ˌfī(ə)r| n.
per•spi•ca•cious |ˌpərspiˈkāSHəs| • adj. having a ready insight into and understanding of things: *it offers quite a few facts to the perspicacious reporter.*
DERIVATIVES: **per•spi•ca•cious•ly** adv. **per•spi•cac•i•ty** |-ˈkasitē| n.
per•spic•u•ous |pərˈspikyoōwəs| • adj. (of an account or representation) clearly expressed and easily understood; lucid: *it provides simpler and more perspicuous explanations than its rivals.*
■ (of a person) able to give an account or express an idea clearly.
DERIVATIVES: **per•spi•cu•i•ty** |ˌpərspiˈkyoōitē| n. **per•spic•u•ous•ly** adv.
pert |pərt| • adj. (of a girl or young woman) sexually attractive because lively or saucy: *a pert Belgian actress.*
■ (of a bodily feature or garment) attractive because neat and jaunty: *she had a pert nose and deep blue eyes.* ■ (of a young person or his or her speech or behavior) impudent: *no need to be pert, miss.* ■ another term for *peart* 'lively, cheerful.'
DERIVATIVES: **pert•ly** adv. **pert•ness** n.
per•ti•na•cious |ˌpərtnˈāSHəs| • adj. holding firmly to an opinion or a course of action: *he worked with a pertinacious resistance to interruptions.*
DERIVATIVES: **per•ti•na•cious•ly** adv. **per•ti•na•cious•ness** n. **per•ti•nac•i•ty** |-ˈasitē| n.
per•ti•nent |ˈpərtn-ənt| • adj. relevant or applicable to a particular matter; apposite: *very pertinent questions | not **pertinent to** the investigation.*
DERIVATIVES: **per•ti•nence** n. **per•ti•nen•cy** n. **per•ti•nent•ly** adv.
per•turb |pərˈtərb| • v. [trans.] 1 (often **be perturbed**) make (someone) anxious or unsettled: *they were perturbed by her capricious behavior.* 2 subject (a system, moving object, or process) to an influence tending to alter its normal or regular state or path: *nuclear weapons used to perturb the orbit of asteroids.*
DERIVATIVES: **per•turb•a•ble** adj. **per•tur•ba•tion** |ˌpərtərˌbā-tiv; pərˈtərbətiv| adj. (sense 2) **per•turb•ing•ly** adv.
pe•ruse |pəˈroōz| • v. [trans.] read thoroughly or carefully.
■ examine carefully or at length.
DERIVATIVES: **pe•rus•er** n. **pe•rus•al** n.

USAGE: The verb **peruse** means 'read thoroughly and carefully.' It is sometimes mistakenly taken to mean 'read through quickly; glance over,' as in *later documents will be **perused** rather than analyzed thoroughly.*

per•va•sive |pərˈvāsiv| • adj. (esp. of an unwelcome influence or physical effect) spreading widely throughout an area or a group of people: *ageism is pervasive and entrenched in our society.*

DERIVATIVES: **per•va•sive•ly** *adv.* **per•va•sive•ness** *n.*

per•verse |pər'vərs| • *adj.* (of a person or personal actions) showing a deliberate and obstinate desire to behave in a way that is unreasonable or unacceptable, often in spite of the consequences: *Kate's perverse decision not to cooperate.*
■ contrary to the accepted or expected standard or practice: *in two general elections the outcome was quite perverse.* ■ (of a verdict) against the weight of evidence or the direction of the judge on a point of law. ■ sexually perverted.
DERIVATIVES: **per•verse•ly** *adv.* **per•verse•ness** *n.* **per•ver•si•ty** |-'vərsitē| *n.* (pl. -ies) .

per•ver•sion |pər'vərZHən| • *n.* the alteration of something from its original course, meaning, or state to a distortion or corruption of what was first intended: *perversion of the law.*
■ sexual behavior or desire that is considered abnormal or unacceptable.

per•vert • *v.* |pər'vərt| [trans.] alter (something) from its original course, meaning, or state to a distortion or corruption of what was first intended: *charged with conspiring to pervert the course of justice.*
■ lead (someone) away from what is considered right, natural, or acceptable. • *n.* |'pərvərt| a person whose sexual behavior is regarded as abnormal and unacceptable.
DERIVATIVES: **per•vert•er** *n.*

per•vi•ous |'pərvēəs| • *adj.* (of a substance) allowing water to pass through; permeable: *pervious rocks.*
DERIVATIVES: **per•vi•ous•ness** *n.*

pes•si•mism |'pesə,mizəm| • *n.* a tendency to see the worst aspect of things or believe that the worst will happen; a lack of hope or confidence in the future.
■ (in philosophy) a belief that evil will ultimately prevail over good.
DERIVATIVES: **pes•si•mist** *n.*

pe•tard |pi'tärd| • *n.* a small bomb made of a metal or wooden box filled with powder, used to blast down a door or to make a hole in a wall.
■ a kind of firework that explodes with a sharp report.
PHRASES: **hoist with** (or **by**) **one's own petard** have one's plans to cause trouble for others backfire on one.

pet•it |'petē| • *adj.* (of a crime) petty; of lesser importance: *petit larceny.*

pet•it bour•geois |'petē boŏr'zHwä; pə'tē| • *adj.* of or characteristic of the lower middle class (the **petit bourgeoisie**), esp. with reference to a perceived conventionalism and conservatism: *the frail facade of petit bourgeois respectability.* • *n.* (pl. **petits bourgeois** pronunc. same) a member of the lower middle class, esp. when perceived as conventional and conservative.

pe•tit mal |'petē 'mäl| • *n.* a mild form of epilepsy characterized by brief spells of unconsciousness without loss of posture. Cf. GRAND MAL.
■ an epileptic seizure of this kind.

pet•ri•fy |'petrə,fī| • *v.* (**-ies, -ied**) [trans.] **1** make (someone) so frightened as to be unable to move or think: *his icy quietness petrified her* | [as adj.] (**petrified**) *the petrified child clung to her mother.* **2** change (organic matter) into stony material by encrusting or replacing its original substance with a calcareous or other mineral deposit.
■ [intrans.] (of organic matter) become converted into stony material in such a way. ■ deprive or become deprived of vitality or the capacity for change: [trans.] *death merely petrifies things for those who go on living* | [intrans.] *the inner life of the communist parties petrified.*
DERIVATIVES: **pet•ri•fac•tion** *n.* **pet•ri•fi•ca•tion** *n.*

pet•ro•glyph |'petrə,glif| • *n.* a rock carving or drawing, esp. a prehistoric one.

pet•ti•fog |'petē,fôg; 'petē,fäg| • *v.* (**pettifogged, pettifogging**) [intrans.] quibble about petty points.
■ practice legal deception or trickery.
DERIVATIVES: **pet•ti•fog•ger•y** |,petē'fôgərē; ,petē'fägərē| *n.*

pet•ty |'petē| • *adj.* (**pettier, pettiest**) **1** of little importance; trivial: *the petty divisions of party politics.*
■ (of behavior) characterized by an undue concern for trivial matters, esp. in a small-minded or spiteful way: *he was prone to petty revenge on friends and family.* **2** [attrib.] of secondary or lesser importance, rank, or scale; minor: *a petty official.*
■ (of a crime) of lesser importance (usu. in terms of money involved, as defined by statute): *petty larceny.*
DERIVATIVES: **pet•ti•ly** |'petəlē| *adv.* **pet•ti•ness** |'petēnəs| *n.*

pet•u•lant |'pecHələnt| • *adj.* (of a person or personal manner) childishly sulky or bad-tempered: *he was moody and petulant* | *a petulant shake of the head.*
DERIVATIVES: **pet•u•lance** *n.* **pet•u•lant•ly** *adv.*

pe•yo•te |pā'yōtē| • *n.* a small, soft, blue-green, spineless cactus (*Lophophora williamsii*), native to Mexico and the southern US. Also called **mescal**.
■ a hallucinogenic drug prepared from this cactus, containing mescaline.

pha•lanx |'fālæNGks; 'fæl-| • *n.* **1** (pl. **pha-lanxes**) a group of people or things of a similar type forming a compact body or brought together for a common purpose: *headed past the phalanx of waiting reporters.*
■ a body of troops or police officers, standing or moving in close formation: *six hundred marchers set off, led by a phalanx of police.* ■ (in ancient Greece) a body of Macedonian infantry drawn up in close order with shields touching and long spears overlapping. **2** (pl. **phalanges** |fə'lænjēz; fā'lænjēz|) a bone of the finger or toe.

phal•lic |'fælik| • *adj.* of, relating to, or

resembling a phallus or erect penis: *a phallic symbol.*

▪ of or denoting the genital phase in the Freudian view of psychosexual development, esp. in males.
DERIVATIVES: **phal•li•cal•ly** *adv.*

phal•lus |ˈfæləs| • *n.* (pl. **phalli** |ˈfælī| or **phalluses**) a penis, esp. when erect (typically used with reference to male potency or dominance).

▪ an image or representation of an erect penis, typically symbolizing fertility or potency.
DERIVATIVES: **phal•li•cism** |-ˌsizəm| *n.* **phal•lism** |ˈfælizəm| *n.*

phan•tasm |ˈfæntæzəm| • *n.* a figment of the imagination; an illusion or apparition.

▪ an illusory likeness of something: *every phantasm of a hope was quickly nullified.*
DERIVATIVES: **phan•tas•mal** |fænˈtæzməl| *adj.* **phan•tas•mic** |fænˈtæzmik| *adj.*

phan•tas•ma•go•ri•a |ˌfænˌtæzməˈgôrēə| • *n.* a sequence of real or imaginary images like that seen in a dream: *a phantasmagoria of horror and mystery.*
DERIVATIVES: **phan•tas•ma•gor•ic** |-gôrik| *adj.* **phan•tas•ma•gor•i•cal** |gôrikəl| *adj.*

Phar•i•see |ˈfærəˌsē| • *n.* a member of an ancient Jewish sect, distinguished by strict observance of the traditional and written law, and commonly held to have pretensions to superior sanctity.

▪ a self-righteous person; a hypocrite.
DERIVATIVES: **Phar•i•sa•ic** |ˌfærəˈsāik| *adj.* **Phar•i•sa•i•cal** |ˌfærəˈsāikəl| *adj.* **Phar•i•sa•ism** |-sāˌizəm| *n.*

phar•ma•co•poe•ia |ˌfärməkəˈpēə| (also **pharmacopeia**) • *n.* a book, esp. an official publication, containing a list of medicinal drugs with their effects and directions for their use.

▪ a stock of medicinal drugs.

Pha•ros |ˈferōs| a lighthouse, often considered one of the Seven Wonders of the World, erected by Ptolemy II (308–246 BC) in *c.*280 BC on the island of Pharos, off the coast of Alexandria, Egypt.

▪ [as n.] (**pharos**) a lighthouse or a beacon to guide sailors.

phe•nom•e•non |fəˈnäməˌnän; -nən| • *n.* (pl. **phenomena** |fəˈnämənə|) 1 a fact or situation that is observed to exist or happen, esp. one whose cause or explanation is in question: *glaciers are unique and interesting natural phenomena.*

▪ a remarkable person, thing, or event. 2 (in philosophy) the object of a person's perception; what the senses or the mind notice.

USAGE: The word **phenomenon** comes from Greek, and its plural form is **phenomena**, as in *these **phenomena** are not fully understood.* It is a mistake to treat **phenomena** as if it were a singular form, as in *this is a strange **phenomena***.

phe•no•type |ˈfēnəˌtīp| • *n.* (in biology) the set of observable characteristics of an individual resulting from the interaction of its genotype with the environment.

DERIVATIVES: **phe•no•typ•ic** |ˌfēnəˈtipik| *adj.* **phe•no•typ•i•cal** |ˌfēnəˈtipikəl| *adj.* **phe•no•typ•i•cal•ly** |ˌfēnəˈtipik(ə)lē| *adv.*

phi•lan•der |fəˈlændər| • *v.* [intrans.] (of a man) readily or frequently enter into casual sexual relationships with women.
DERIVATIVES: **phi•lan•der•er** *n.*

phi•lan•thro•pist |fəˈlænᴛʜrəpist| • *n.* a person who seeks to promote the welfare of others, esp. by the generous donation of money to good causes.

phi•lan•thro•py |fəˈlænᴛʜrəpē| • *n.* the desire to promote the welfare of others, expressed esp. by the generous donation of money to good causes.

▪ a charity.
DERIVATIVES: **phil•an•throp•ic** *adj.* **phi•lan•thro•pism** |-pizəm| *n.* **phi•lan•thro•pize** |-pīz| *v.*

phi•lat•e•ly |fəˈlætl-ē| • *n.* the collection and study of postage stamps.
DERIVATIVES: **phil•a•tel•ic** |ˌfiləˈtelik| *adj.* **phil•a•tel•i•cal•ly** |ˌfiləˈtelik(ə)lē| *adv.* **phi•lat•e•list** |fəˈlætl-ist| *n.*

phi•lip•pic |fəˈlipik| • *n.* a bitter attack or denunciation, esp. a verbal one.

Phil•is•tine |ˈfiləˌstēn; ˈfiləˌstīn| • *n.* 1 a member of a non-Semitic people of southern Palestine in ancient times, who came into conflict with the Israelites during the 12th and 11th centuries BC. 2 (usu. **philistine**) a person who is hostile or indifferent to culture and the arts, or who has no understanding of them: [as adj.] *a philistine government.*
DERIVATIVES: **phil•is•tin•ish** *adj.* **phil•is•tin•ism** |ˈfiləstēˌnizəm; fəˈlistə-| *n.*

phi•log•y•nist |fəˈläjənist| • *n.* a person who likes or admires women.
DERIVATIVES: **phi•log•y•ny** |-ˈläjənē| *n.*

phi•lol•o•gy |fəˈläləjē| • *n.* the branch of knowledge that deals with the structure, historical development, and relationships of a language or languages.

▪ literary or classical scholarship.
DERIVATIVES: **phil•o•lo•gi•an** |ˌfiləˈlōjēən| *n.* **phil•o•log•i•cal** |ˌfiləˈläjikəl| *adj.* **phil•o•log•i•cal•ly** |ˌfiləˈläjik(ə)lē| *adv.* **phi•lol•o•gist** *n.*

phil•ter |ˈfiltər| (Brit. **philtre**) • *n.* a drink supposed to excite sexual love in the drinker.

phlegm |flem| • *n.* the thick substance secreted by the mucous membranes of the respiratory passages, esp. when produced in excessive or abnormal quantities, e.g., when someone is suffering from a cold.

▪ (in medieval science and medicine) one of the four bodily humors, believed to be associated with a calm, stolid, or apathetic temperament. ▪ calmness of temperament.
DERIVATIVES: **phlegm•y** *adj.*

phleg•mat•ic |flegˈmætik| • *adj.* (of a person) having an unemotional and stolidly calm disposition.
DERIVATIVES: **phleg•mat•i•cal•ly** |-ək(ə)lē| *adv.*

phlo•em |ˈflōˌem| • *n.* the vascular tissue in plants that conducts sugars and other metabolic products downward from the leaves. Cf. XYLEM.

phlo•gis•ton |flō'jistän; -tən| • *n.* a substance supposed by 18th-century chemists to exist in all combustible bodies, and to be released in combustion.

pho•bi•a |'fōbēə| • *n.* an extreme or irrational fear of or aversion to something: *he had a phobia about being under water | a snake phobia.*
DERIVATIVES: **pho•bic** |'fōbik| *adj.* & *n.*

pho•neme |'fōnēm| • *n.* any of the perceptually distinct units of sound in a specified language that distinguish one word from another, for example *p, b, d,* and *t* in the English words *pad, pat, bad,* and *bat.*
DERIVATIVES: **pho•ne•mic** |fə'nēmik; fō-| *adj.* **pho•ne•mics** |fə'nēmiks; fō-| *n.* the branch of linguistics that deals with phonemes.

phon•ics |'fäniks| • *plural n.* [treated as sing.] a method of teaching people to read by correlating sounds with letters or groups of letters in an alphabetic writing system.

pho•nol•o•gy |fə'näləjē; fō-| • *n.* the branch of linguistics that deals with systems of sounds, esp. in a particular language.
■ the system of relationships among the speech sounds that constitute the fundamental components of a language.
DERIVATIVES: **pho•no•log•i•cal** |,fōnə'läjikəl| *adj.* **pho•no•log•i•cal•ly** |,fōnə'läjik(ə)lē| *adv.* **pho•nol•o•gist** |-əjist| *n.*

phos•pho•res•cence |,fäsfə'resəns| • *n.* light emitted by a substance without combustion or perceptible heat: *the stones overhead gleamed with phosphorescence.*
■ (in physics) the emission of radiation in a similar manner to fluorescence but on a longer timescale, so that emission continues after excitation ceases.
DERIVATIVES: **phos•pho•res•cent** *adj.*

pho•to•gen•ic |',fōṭə'jenik| • *adj.* **1** (esp. of a person) looking attractive in photographs or on film. **2** (of an organism or tissue) producing or emitting light.
DERIVATIVES: **pho•to•gen•i•cal•ly** |-(ə)lē| *adv.*

pho•to•re•al•ism |'fōṭō'rēə,lizəm| • *n.* **1** detailed and unidealized representation in art, esp. of banal, mundane, or sordid aspects of life. **2** detailed visual representation, like that obtained in a photograph, in a nonphotographic medium such as animation, painting, or computer graphics.
DERIVATIVES: **pho•to•re•al•ist** *n.* & *adj.* **pho•to•re•al•is•tic** |-istik| *adj.*

pho•to•sen•si•tive |,fōṭə'sensiṭiv| • *adj.* having a chemical, electrical, or other response to light: *photosensitive cells | photosensitive drugs.*
DERIVATIVES: **pho•to•sen•si•tiv•i•ty** |-,sensə'tivitē| *n.* **pho•to•sen•si•tize** *v.* **1** initiate (a chemical change) by absorbing light energy and transferring it to a reactant. **2** make photosensitive.

pho•to•syn•the•sis |,fōṭō'sinthəsis| • *n.* the process by which green plants and some other organisms use sunlight to synthesize foods from carbon dioxide and water. Photosynthesis in plants generally involves the green pigment chlorophyll and generates oxygen as a byproduct.
DERIVATIVES: **pho•to•syn•thet•ic** |-,sin THetik| *adj.* **pho•to•syn•thet•i•cal•ly** |-,sin 'THetik(ə)lē| *adv.*

phre•nol•o•gy |fre'näləjē| • *n.* the detailed study of the shape and size of the cranium as a supposed indication of character and mental abilities, popular in the 19th but largely discredited by the early 20th cent.
DERIVATIVES: **phre•no•log•i•cal** |,frenə'läjikəl| *adj.* **phre•nol•o•gist** |-jist| *n.*

phy•lac•ter•y |fi'læktərē| • *n.* (pl. **-ies**) a small leather box containing Hebrew texts, worn by Jewish men at morning prayer as a reminder to keep the law.

phy•log•e•ny |,fī'läjənē| • *n.* the branch of biology that deals with phylogenesis (the evolutionary development and diversification of a species or group of organisms, or of a particular feature of an organism).
DERIVATIVES: **phy•lo•ge•net•ic** *adj.* **phy•lo•gen•ic** |,fīlə'jenik| *adj.* **phy•lo•gen•i•cal•ly** |,fīlə'jeniklē| *adv.*

phy•lum |'fīləm| • *n.* (pl. **phyla** |'fīlə|) (in zoology) a principal taxonomic category that ranks above class and below kingdom.
■ (in linguistics) a group of languages related to each other less closely than those forming a family, esp. one in which the relationships are disputed or unclear.

phys•ics |'fiziks| • *plural n.* [treated as sing.] the branch of science concerned with the nature and properties of matter and energy. The subject matter of physics, distinguished from that of chemistry and biology, includes mechanics, heat, light and other radiation, sound, electricity, magnetism, and the structure of atoms.
■ the physical properties and phenomena of something: *the physics of plasmas.*
DERIVATIVES: **phys•i•cist** *n.*

phys•i•og•no•my |,fizē'ä(g)nəmē| • *n.* (pl. **-ies**) a person's facial features or expression, esp. when regarded as indicative of character or ethnic origin.
■ the supposed art of judging character from facial characteristics. ■ the general form or appearance of something: *the physiognomy of the landscape.*
DERIVATIVES: **phys•i•og•nom•ic** |,fizēə'nämik| *adj.* **phys•i•og•nom•i•cal** |,fizēə'nämikəl| *adj.* **phys•i•og•nom•i•cal•ly** |,fizēə'nämik(ə)lē| *adv.*

phys•i•ol•o•gy |,fizē'äləjē| • *n.* the branch of biology that deals with the normal functions of living organisms and their parts.
■ the way in which a living organism or bodily part functions: *the physiology of the brain.*
DERIVATIVES: **phys•i•o•log•ic** |,fizēə'läjik| *adj.* **phys•i•o•log•i•cal** |,fizēə'läjikəl| *adj.* **phys•i•o•log•i•cal•ly** |,fizēə'läjik(ə)lē| *adv.* **phys•i•ol•o•gist** |-jist| *n.*

pi•a•nis•si•mo |,pēə'nisi,mē| • *adv.* & *adj.* (esp. as a musical direction) very soft or softly. • *n.* (pl. **pianissimos** or **pianissimi** |-ˌmē|) a passage marked to be performed very softly.

pi•an•o•forte |pēˈˌænōˈfôrtā; pēˈænōˌfôrt| • *n.* formal term for a piano.

pi•az•za |pēˈätsə; pēˈæzə| • *n.* **1** |pēˈätsə| a public square or marketplace, esp. in an Italian town. **2** |pēˈæzə| the veranda of a house.

pic•a•resque |ˌpikəˈresk| • *adj.* of or relating to an episodic style of fiction dealing with the adventures of a rough and dishonest but appealing hero. • *n.* this style of fiction.

pic•a•yune |ˌpikiˈyo͞on| • *adj.* petty; worthless. • *n.* a small coin of little value, esp. a 5-cent piece.

■ an insignificant person or thing.

pic•tur•esque |ˌpikCHəˈresk| • *adj.* visually attractive, esp. in a quaint or pretty style: *the picturesque covered bridges of New England.*

■ (of language) unusual and vivid: *picturesque speech.*

DERIVATIVES: **pic•tur•esque•ly** *adv.* **pic•tur•esque•ness** *n.*

pidg•in |ˈpijen| • *n.* [often as adj.] a grammatically simplified form of a language, used for communication between people not sharing a common language. Pidgins have a limited vocabulary, some elements of which are taken from local languages, and are not native languages, but arise out of language contact between speakers of other languages. Cf. CREOLE.

pie•bald |ˈpīˌbôld| • *adj.* (of a horse) having irregular patches of two colors, typically black and white. • *n.* a piebald horse or other animal. Cf. SKEWBALD

pied |pīd| • *adj.* having two or more different colors: *pied dogs from the Pyrenees.*

pied•mont |ˈpēdmänt| • *n.* a gentle slope leading from the base of mountains to a region of flat land.

■ (**the Piedmont**) a hilly region of the eastern US, between the Appalachians and the coastal plain. ■ a region of NW Italy, in the foothills of the Alps.

pie•tà |ˌpēäˈtä| (often **Pietà**) • *n.* a picture or sculpture of the Virgin Mary holding the dead body of Christ on her lap or in her arms.

pi•e•tism |ˈpīiˌtizəm| • *n.* pious sentiment, esp. of an exaggerated or affected nature.

■ (usu. **Pietism**) a 17th-century movement for the revival of piety in the Lutheran Church.

DERIVATIVES: **pi•e•tist** *n.* **pi•e•tis•tic** |ˌpīə ˈtistik| *adj.* **pi•e•tis•ti•cal** |ˌpīəˈtistikəl| *adj.* **pi•e•tis•ti•cal•ly** |ˌpīəˈtistik(ə)lē| *adv.*

pi•e•ty |ˈpīi̯tē| • *n.* (pl. **-ies**) the quality of being religious or reverent: *acts of piety and charity.*

■ the quality of being dutiful: *filial piety.* ■ a belief or point of view that is accepted with unthinking conventional reverence: *the accepted pieties of our time.*

pi•las•ter |pəˈlæstər| • *n.* a rectangular column, esp. one projecting from a wall.

DERIVATIVES: **pi•las•tered** *adj.*

pil•grim |ˈpilgrəm| • *n.* a person who journeys to a sacred place for religious reasons.

■ (usu. **Pilgrim**) a member of a group of English Puritans fleeing religious persecution who sailed in the *Mayflower* and founded the colony of Plymouth, Massachusetts, in 1620.

■ a person who travels on long journeys. ■ a person whose life is compared to a journey. • *v.* (**pilgrimed, pilgriming**) [no obj., with adverbial of direction] archaic travel or wander like a pilgrim.

DERIVATIVES: **pil•grim•ize** |-ˌmīz| *v.* (archaic).

pil•lage |ˈpilij| • *v.* [trans.] rob (a place) using violence, esp. in wartime.

■ steal (something) using violence, esp. in wartime: *artworks pillaged from churches and museums.* • *n.* the action of pillaging a place or property, esp. in wartime.

DERIVATIVES: **pil•lag•er** *n.*

pil•lo•ry |ˈpilərē| • *n.* (pl. **-ies**) in former times, a wooden framework with holes for the head and hands, in which an offender was imprisoned and exposed to public abuse. The **stocks** were similar, but with holes for hands and feet, not for the head. • *v.* (**-ies, -ied**) [trans.] put (someone) in the pillory.

■ figurative attack or ridicule publicly: *he found himself pilloried by members of his own party.*

pi•lose |ˈpīlōs| (also **pilous**) • *adj.* covered with long soft hairs.

DERIVATIVES: **pi•los•i•ty** |pīˈläsiṯē| *n.*

pince-nez |ˈpænsˌnā; ˈpins| • *n.* [treated as sing. or pl.] a pair of eyeglasses with a nose clip instead of earpieces.

pin•ion • *n.* the outer part of a bird's wing including the flight feathers. • *v.* [trans.] **1** tie or hold the arms or legs of (someone): *he pinioned the limbs of his opponents.*

■ bind (the arms or legs) of someone. **2** cut off the pinion of (a wing or bird) to prevent flight.

pin•na•cle |ˈpinəkəl| • *n.* a high, pointed piece of rock.

■ a small pointed tower built as an ornament on a roof. ■ the most successful point; the culmination: *he had reached **the pinnacle of** his career.* • *v.* [trans.] set on or as if on a pinnacle: *a rustic cross was pinnacled upon the makeshift altar.*

■ form the culminating point or example of.

DERIVATIVES: **pin•na•cled** *adj.*

pin•nate |ˈpināt; -it| • *adj.* (of a compound leaf) having leaflets arranged on either side of the stem, typically in pairs opposite each other.

■ (esp. of an invertebrate animal) having branches, tentacles, etc., on each side of an axis.

DERIVATIVES: **pin•nat•ed** *adj.* **pin•nate•ly** *adv.* **pin•na•tion** |piˈnāSHən| *n.*

pi•ous |ˈpīəs| • *adj.* devoutly religious.

■ making a hypocritical display of virtue: *there'll be no pious words said over her.* ■ [attrib.] (of a hope) sincere but unlikely to be fulfilled.

■ (of a deception) with good or religious intentions, whether professed or real. ■ dutiful or loyal, esp. toward one's parents.

DERIVATIVES: **pi•ous•ly** adv. **pi•ous•ness** n.

pi•quant |'pēkənt; -känt| (also **piquante**) • adj. having a pleasantly sharp taste or appetizing flavor.

■ pleasantly stimulating or exciting to the mind.

DERIVATIVES: **pi•quan•cy** |-kənsē| n. **pi•quant•ly** adv.

pique |pēk| • n. a feeling of irritation or resentment resulting from a slight, esp. to one's pride: *he left in a fit of pique.* • v. (**piques** |pēks|, **piqued** |pēkt|, **piquing** |'pēkiNG|) **1** [trans.] stimulate (interest or curiosity): *you have piqued my curiosity about the man.* **2** (**be piqued**) feel irritated or resentful.

pir•ou•ette |ˌpiro͞o'wet| • n. an act of spinning on one foot, typically with the raised foot touching the knee of the supporting leg.

■ a movement performed in advanced dressage and classical riding, in which the horse makes a circle by pivoting on a hind leg while cantering. • v. [intrans.] perform a pirouette.

pis•ca•to•ri•al |ˌpiskə'tôrēəl| • adj. of or concerning fishermen or fishing.

pis•ci•cul•ture |'pisi,kəlCHər| • n. the controlled breeding and rearing of fish. Cf. AQUACULTURE; MARICULTURE.

DERIVATIVES: **pis•ci•cul•tur•al** |ˌpisi'kəlCHərəl| adj. **pis•ci•cul•tur•ist** |ˌpisi'kəlCHərist| n.

pis•ci•na |pi'sēnə; -'sīnə| • n. (pl. **piscinas** or **piscinae** |-'sēnē; -'sīnē|) **1** a stone basin near the altar in Catholic and pre-Reformation Christian churches for draining water used in the Mass. **2** (in ancient Roman architecture) a pool or pond for bathing or swimming.

pis•cine |'pīsēn; 'pisīn| • adj. of or concerning fish.

pis•til |'pistl| • n. the female organs of a flower, comprising the stigma, style, and ovary.

pit•e•ous |'pitēəs| • adj. deserving or arousing pity.

DERIVATIVES: **pit•e•ous•ly** adv. **pit•e•ous•ness** n.

pith |piTH| • n. **1** soft or spongy tissue in plants or animals, in particular:

■ spongy white tissue lining the rind of an orange, lemon, and other citrus fruits. ■ the spongy cellular tissue in the stems and branches of many higher plants. ■ spinal marrow. **2** the essence of something: *the pith and core of socialism.* **3** forceful and concise expression: *he writes with a combination of pith and exactitude.* • v. [trans.] **1** remove the pith from. **2** pierce or sever the spinal cord of (an animal) so as to kill or immobilize it.

DERIVATIVES: **pith•less** adj.

pith•y |'piTHē| • adj. (**pithier, pithiest**) (of language or style) concise and forcefully expressive.

DERIVATIVES: **pith•i•ly** |'piTHəlē| adv. **pith•i•ness** |-ēnis| n.

pit•i•a•ble |'pitēəbəl| • adj. deserving or arousing pity.

■ contemptibly poor or small.

DERIVATIVES: **pit•i•a•ble•ness** n. **pit•i•a•bly** |-əblē| adv.

pix•e•late |'piksə,lāt| (also **pixellate** or **pix-ilate**) • v. [trans.] divide (an electronic image) into pixels, typically for display or storage in a digital format.

■ display an image of (someone or something) on television as a small number of large pixels, typically in order to disguise someone's identity.

DERIVATIVES: **pix•e•la•tion** |ˌpiksə'lāsHən| n.

pix•i•lat•ed |'piksə,lātid| (Brit. also **pixil-lated**) • adj. crazy; confused; whimsical.

DERIVATIVES: **pix•i•la•tion** n.

pix•i•la•tion |ˌpiksə'lāsHən| (Brit. also **pixilla-tion**) • n. **1** a technique used in film whereby the movements of real people are made to appear like artificial animations. **2** the state of being crazy or confused (pixilated) **3** variant spelling of **pixelation** (see PIXELATE).

pla•cate |'plākāt| • v. [trans.] make (someone) less angry or hostile: *they attempted to placate the students with promises.*

DERIVATIVES: **pla•cat•er** n. **pla•cat•ing•ly** |plə'kādiNGlē| adv. **pla•ca•tion** |plā'kā-sHən| n. **pla•ca•to•ry** |-kə,tôrē; 'plækə-| adj.

pla•ce•bo |plə'sēbō| • n. (pl. **-os**) a harmless pill, medicine, or procedure prescribed more for the psychological benefit to the patient than for any physiological effect: [as adj.] *placebo drugs.*

■ a substance that has no therapeutic effect, used as a control in testing new drugs. ■ a measure designed merely to calm or please someone.

plac•id |'plæsid| • adj. (of a person or animal) not easily upset or excited: *this horse has a placid nature.*

■ (esp. of a place or stretch of water) calm and peaceful, with little movement or activity.

DERIVATIVES: **pla•cid•i•ty** |plə'sidiṭē| n. **plac•id•ly** adv.

pla•gia•rize |'plājə,rīz| • v. [trans.] take (the work or an idea of someone else) and pass it off as one's own.

■ copy from (someone) in such a way.

DERIVATIVES: **pla•gia•rism** n. **pla•gia•rist** n. **pla•gia•riz•er** n.

plague |plāg| • n. a contagious bacterial disease characterized by fever and delirium, typically with the formation of buboes (swollen inflamed lymph nodes in the groin or armpit, thus **bubonic plague**) and sometimes infection of the lungs (**pneumonic plague**): *an outbreak of plague* | *they died of **the plague**.*

■ a contagious disease that spreads rapidly and kills many people. Cf. EPIDEMIC; PANDEMIC. ■ an unusually large number of insects or animals infesting a place and causing damage: *a **plague of fleas**.* ■ [in sing.] a thing causing trouble or irritation: *staff theft is usually the **plague of restaurants**.* ■ a widespread affliction regarded as divine punishment: *the plagues of Egypt.* ■ [in sing.] used as a curse or an expression of despair or disgust: *a plague on all their houses!* • v. (**plagues, plagued**,

plaguing) [trans.] cause continual trouble or distress to: *the problems that plagued the company* | *has been plagued by ill health.*
■ pester or harass (someone) continually: *was plaguing her with questions.*

plain•song |'plān,sônG; -sänG| • *n.* unaccompanied church music sung in unison in medieval modes and in free rhythm corresponding to the accentuation of the words, which are taken from the liturgy.

plain•tive |'plāntiv| • *adj.* sounding sad and mournful: *a plaintive cry.*
DERIVATIVES: **plain•tive•ly** *adv.* **plain•tive•ness** *n.*

plan•gent |'plænjənt| • *adj.* (of a sound) loud, reverberating, and often melancholy.
DERIVATIVES: **plan•gen•cy** *n.* **plan•gent•ly** *adv.*

plan•tar |'plæntər| • *adj.* of or relating to the sole of the foot: *plantar warts.*

plan•ti•grade |'plænti,grād| • *adj.* (of a mammal) walking on the soles of the feet, like a human or a bear.

plaque |plæk| • *n.* **1** an ornamental tablet, typically of metal, porcelain, or wood, that is fixed to a wall or other surface in commemoration of a person or event. **2** a sticky deposit on teeth in which bacteria proliferate. Cf. TARTAR. **3** (in medicine) a small, distinct, typically raised patch or region resulting from local damage or deposition of material, such as a fatty deposit on an artery wall in atherosclerosis ('hardening of the arteries') or a site of localized damage or deposition of material, such as localized damage of brain tissue in Alzheimer's disease.
■ (in microbiology) a clear area in a cell culture caused by the inhibition of growth or destruction of cells by an agent such as a virus.

plas•ma |'plæzmə| (also **plasm** |'plæzəm|) • *n.* **1** the colorless fluid part of blood, lymph, or milk, in which corpuscles or fat globules are suspended.
■ this substance taken from donors or donated blood for administering in transfusions. **2** an ionized gas consisting of positive ions and free electrons in proportions resulting in little or no overall electric charge, typically at low pressures (as in the upper atmosphere and in fluorescent lamps) or at very high temperatures (as in stars and nuclear fusion reactors).
■ an analogous substance consisting of mobile charged particles (such as a molten salt or the electrons within a metal). **3** a dark green, translucent variety of quartz used in mosaic and for other decorative purposes. **4** (also called **cytoplasm**) the material within a living cell, excluding the nucleus. Cf. PROTOPLASM.
DERIVATIVES: **plas•mat•ic** |plæz'mætik| *adj.* **plas•mic** |-mik| *adj.*

plat |plæt| • *n.* a plot of land.
■ a map or plan of an area of land showing actual or proposed features. • *v.* [trans.] plan out or make a map of (an area of land, esp. a proposed site for construction): *the town was plated in 1815.*

plat•i•tude |'plæti,t(y)o͞od| • *n.* a remark or statement, esp. one with a moral content, that

has been used too often to be interesting or thoughtful: *she began uttering liberal platitudes.* Cf. BROMIDE.
■ the quality of being dull, ordinary, or trite: *educators willing to violate the bounds of platitude.*
DERIVATIVES: **plat•i•tu•di•nize** |,plæti't(y)o͞odn,īz| *v.* **plat•i•tu•di•nous** |,plæti't(y)o͞odn-əs| *adj.*

Pla•ton•ic |plə'tänik| • *adj.* of or associated with the Greek philosopher Plato (427–347 BC) or his ideas.
■ (**platonic**) (of love or friendship) intimate and affectionate but not sexual. ■ (**platonic**) confined to words, theories, or ideals, and not leading to practical action.
DERIVATIVES: **pla•ton•i•cal•ly** |-(ə)lē| *adv.*

plau•dits |'plôdits| • *plural n.* praise: *the network has received plaudits for its sports coverage.*
■ the applause of an audience: *the plaudits for the winner died down.*

plau•si•ble |'plôzəbəl| • *adj.* (of an argument or statement) seeming reasonable or probable: *a plausible explanation* | *it seems plausible that one of two things may happen.*
■ (of a person) skilled at producing persuasive arguments, esp. ones intended to deceive: *a plausible liar.*
DERIVATIVES: **plau•si•bil•i•ty** |,plôzə'bilitē| *n.* **plau•si•bly** |-əblē| *adv.*

plea |plē| • *n.* **1** a request made in an urgent and emotional manner: *she made a dramatic plea for disarmament.*
■ a claim that a circumstance means that one should not be blamed for or should not be forced to do something: *her plea of a headache was not entirely false.* **2** (in law) a formal statement by or on behalf of a defendant or prisoner, stating guilt or innocence in response to a charge, offering an allegation of fact, or claiming that a point of law should apply: *he changed his plea to not guilty.*

plead |plēd| • *v.* (past and past part. **pleaded** or **pled** |pled|) **1** [reporting verb] make an emotional appeal: [intrans.] *they pleaded with Carol to come home again* | [with direct speech] *"Don't go," she pleaded* | [with infinitive] *Anne pleaded to go with her.* **2** [trans.] present and argue for (a position), esp. in court or in another public context: *using cheap melodrama to plead the case for three prisoners.*
■ [intrans.] address a court as an advocate on behalf of a party. ■ [no obj., with complement] state formally in court whether one is guilty or not guilty of the offense with which one is charged: *he pleaded guilty to the drug charge.*
■ invoke (a reason or a point of law) as an accusation or defense: *on trial for attempted murder, she pleaded self-defense.* ■ offer or present as an excuse for doing or not doing something: *he pleaded family commitments as a reason for not attending.*
DERIVATIVES: **plead•er** *n.* **plead•ing•ly** *adv.*

USAGE: In a court of law a person can **plead guilty** or **plead not guilty** (see also

NOLO CONTENDERE). The phrase **plead inno-cent**, although commonly found in general use, is not a technical legal term. Note that one pleads *guilty to* (not *of*) an offense, and may be found *guilty of* an offense.

ple•be•ian |pli'bēən| • *n.* (in ancient Rome) a commoner.
■ a member of the lower social classes. • *adj.* of or belonging to the commoners of ancient Rome.
■ of or belonging to the lower social classes.
■ lacking in refinement: *he is a man of plebeian tastes.*

pleb•i•scite |'plebə,sīt| • *n.* 1 the direct vote of all the members of an electorate on an important public question such as a change in the constitution.
■ (in Roman history) a law enacted by the plebeians' assembly.
DERIVATIVES: **ple•bis•ci•tar•y** |plə'bisi,terē| *adj.*

plec•trum |'plektrəm| • *n.* (pl. **plectrums** or **plectra** |-trə|) a thin flat piece of plastic, tortoiseshell, or other slightly flexible material held by or worn on the fingers and used to pluck the strings of a musical instrument such as a guitar.
■ the corresponding mechanical part that plucks the strings of an instrument such as a harpsichord.

ple•iad |'plēəd| • *n.* an outstanding group of seven people or things.

Pleis•to•cene |'plīstə,sēn| • *adj.* (in geology) of, relating to, or denoting the first epoch of the Quaternary period, between the Pliocene and Holocene epochs.
■ [as n.] (**the Pleistocene**) the Pleistocene epoch or the system of deposits laid down during it.

The Pleistocene epoch lasted from 1,640,000 to about 10,000 years ago. It was marked by great fluctuations in temperature that caused the ice ages, with glacial periods followed by warmer interglacial periods. Several extinct forms of human, leading up to modern humans, appeared during this epoch.

ple•na•ry |'plenərē| • *adj.* 1 not deficient in any respect; full; unqualified; absolute: *crusaders were offered a plenary indulgence by the pope.* 2 (of a meeting) to be attended by all participants at a conference or assembly, who otherwise meet in smaller groups: *a plenary session of the European Parliament.* • *n.* a meeting or session of this type.

plen•i•po•ten•ti•ar•y |,plenəpə'tensHē,erē; -ə'tensHərē| • *n.* (pl. **-ies**) a person, esp. a diplomat, invested with the full power of independent action on behalf of his or her government, typically in a foreign country. • *adj.* having full power to take independent action: [postpositive] *he represented the Japanese government in Seoul as minister plenipotentiary.*
■ (of power) absolute.

plen•i•tude |'pleni,t(y)ōōd| • *n.* an abun-

dance: *the farm boasts a plenitude of animals and birds.*
■ the condition of being full or complete: *the plenitude of the pope's powers.*

ple•num |'plenəm; 'plēnəm| • *n.* 1 an assembly of all the members of a group or committee. 2 (in physics) a space completely filled with matter, or the whole of space so regarded.

ple•o•nasm |'plēə,nazəm| • *n.* the use of more words than are necessary to convey meaning (e.g., *see with one's eyes*), either as a fault of style or for emphasis.
DERIVATIVES: **ple•o•nas•tic** |,plēə'nastik| *adj.* **ple•o•nas•ti•cal•ly** |,plēə'nastik(ə)lē| *adv.*

pleth•o•ra |'pleTHərə| • *n.* (**a plethora of**) an excess of (something): *a plethora of committees and subcommittees.*
■ an excess of a bodily fluid, particularly blood.
DERIVATIVES: **ple•thor•ic** |'pleTHərik; plə'THôrik| *adj.*

plex•us |'pleksəs| • *n.* (pl. same or **plexuses**) a network of nerves or vessels in the body.
■ an intricate network or weblike formation.
DERIVATIVES: **plex•i•form** |'pleksə,fôrm| *adj.*

plight¹ |plīt| • *n.* a dangerous, difficult, or otherwise unfortunate situation: *the plight of children living in poverty.*

plight² • *v.* [trans.] pledge or promise solemnly (one's faith or loyalty).
■ (**be plighted to**) be engaged to be married to.

plinth |plinTH| • *n.* a heavy base supporting a statue or vase.
■ the lower square slab at the base of a column.

plo•sive |'plōsiv| • *adj.* denoting a consonant that is produced by stopping the airflow using the lips, teeth, or palate, followed by a sudden release of air. • *n.* a plosive speech sound. The basic plosives in English are *t*, *k*, and *p* (voiceless) and *d*, *g*, and *b* (voiced).
DERIVATIVES: **plo•sion** *n.*

plu•per•fect |,plōō'perfikt| • *adj. & n.* (in grammar) another term for *past perfect*, denoting an action completed before some past point of time specified or implied, formed in English by *had* and the past participle, as in *by three o'clock we had finished most of the recount.*
■ [as adj.] more than perfect: *they have one pluperfect daughter and are expecting an ideal little brother for her.*

plu•ral•ism |'plōōrə,lizəm| • *n.* 1 a condition or system in which two or more states, groups, principles, sources of authority, etc., coexist.
■ a form of society in which the members of minority groups maintain their independent cultural traditions. ■ a political theory or system of power-sharing among a number of political parties. ■ a theory or system of devolution and autonomy for individual bodies in preference to monolithic state control. ■ (in philosophy) a theory or system that recognizes more than one ultimate principle. 2 the

practice of holding more than one office or church benefice at a time.
DERIVATIVES: **plu•ral•ist** |-ləst| *n.* & *adj.* **plu•ral•is•tic** |-'listik| *adj.* **plu•ral•is•ti•cal•ly** |-'listək(ə)lē| *adv.*
plu•ral•i•ty |plŏŏ'ralitē| • *n.* (pl. **-ies**) **1** the fact or state of being plural: *some languages add an extra syllable to mark plurality.*
■ [in sing.] a large number of people or things: *a plurality of critical approaches.* **2** the number of votes cast for a candidate who receives more than any other but does not receive an absolute majority: *he won with a plurality of slightly over 46%; of the vote.*
■ the number by which this exceeds the number of votes cast for the candidate who placed second. **3** another term for PLURALISM (sense 2).
USAGE: On the difference between **plurality** and **majority**, see usage at MAJORITY.

plu•toc•ra•cy |plŏŏ'täkrəsē| • *n.* (pl. **-ies**) government by the wealthy.
■ a country or society governed in this way. ■ an elite or ruling class of people whose power derives from their wealth.
DERIVATIVES: **plu•to•crat•ic** |ˌplŏŏdə'kratik| *adj.* **plu•to•crat•i•cal•ly** |ˌplŏŏtə'kratiklē| *adv.*
USAGE: See usage at ARISTOCRACY.

plu•vi•al |'plŏŏvēəl| • *adj.* relating to or characterized by rainfall. • *n.* a period marked by increased rainfall.
pneu•mat•ic |n(y)ŏŏ'matik| • *adj.* **1** containing or operated by air or gas under pressure: *it's easier to work on cars if you've got a pneumatic lift.*
■ (chiefly of cavities in the bones of birds) containing air. ■ (of certain body parts, esp. a woman's breasts) large, as if inflated: *she's the one with the pneumatic lips and breasts.* ■ (of a woman) having large breasts. **2** of or relating to the spirit. • *n.* (usu. **pneumatics**) an item of pneumatic equipment.
DERIVATIVES: **pneu•mat•i•cal•ly** |n(y)ŏŏ'matik(ə)lē| *adv.* **pneu•ma•tic•i•ty** |ˌn(y)ŏŏmə'tisətē| *n.*
pneu•mo•nia |n(y)ŏŏ'mōnēə; n(y)ŏŏ'mōnyə| • *n.* lung inflammation caused by bacterial or viral infection, in which the air sacs fill with pus and may become solid. Inflammation may affect both lungs (**double pneumonia**) or only one (**single pneumonia**).
DERIVATIVES: **pneu•mon•ic** |n(y)ŏŏ'mänik| *adj.*
po•di•a•try |pə'dīətrē| • *n.* the treatment of the feet and their ailments.
DERIVATIVES: **po•di•a•trist** |-trəst| *n.*
po•di•um |'pōdēəm| • *n.* (pl. **podiums** or **podia** |-dēə|) a small platform on which a person may stand to be seen by an audience, as when making a speech or conducting an orchestra.
■ a lectern. ■ a continuous projecting base or pedestal under a building. ■ a raised platform surrounding the arena in an ancient amphitheater.

po•e•sy |'pōəzē; -sē| • *n.* poetry.
■ the art or composition of poetry.
po•et•as•ter |'pōəˌtæstər| • *n.* a person who writes inferior poetry.
po•et lau•re•ate |'lôrēət| • *n.* (pl. **poets laureate**) a poet appointed to, or regarded unofficially as holding, an honorary representative position in a particular country, region, or group: *the New York State poet laureate* | *the poet laureate of young America.*
poign•ant |'poinyənt| • *adj.* evoking a keen sense of sadness or regret: *a poignant reminder of the passing of time.*
■ keenly felt: *the sensation of being back at home was most poignant in the winter.* ■ sharp or pungent in taste or smell.
DERIVATIVES: **poign•ance** *n.* **poign•an•cy** |-yənsē| *n.* **poign•ant•ly** |-yəntlē| *adv.*
poin•til•lism |'pwæntēˌyizəm| • *n.* a technique of neo-Impressionist painting using tiny dots of various pure colors, which become blended in the viewer's eye.
DERIVATIVES: **poin•til•list** |ˌpwæntē'yēst; 'pointl-ist| *n.* & *adj.* **poin•til•list•ic** |ˌpwæntē'yistik; ˌpointl'istik| *adj.*
poise |poiz| • *n.* **1** graceful and elegant bearing in a person: *poise and good deportment can be cultivated.*
■ composure and dignity of manner: *at least he had a moment to think, to recover his poise.* **2** balance; equilibrium. • *v.* be or cause to be balanced or suspended: [intrans.] *he poised motionless on his toes* | [trans.] *the world was poised between peace and war.*
■ (**be poised**) (of a person or organization) be ready to do something:[with infinitive] *teachers are poised to resume their attack on government tests.*
po•lar |'pōlər| • *adj.* **1** of or relating to the North or South Pole: *the polar regions.*
■ (of an animal or plant) living in the north or south polar region. ■ of or relating to the poles of a celestial body. ■ of or relating to a celestial pole. ■ (in geometry) of or relating to the poles of a sphere. ■ (in biology) of or relating to the poles of a cell, organ, or part. **2** having electrical or magnetic polarity.
■ (of a liquid, esp. a solvent) consisting of molecules with a dipole moment. ■ (of a solid) ionic. **3** directly opposite in character or tendency: *depression and its polar opposite, mania.* • *n.* **1** (in geometry) the straight line joining the two points at which tangents from a fixed point touch a conic section. **2** a variable binary star that emits strongly polarized light, one component being a strongly magnetic white dwarf.
po•lar•i•ty |pə'lerətē; pō-| • *n.* (pl. **-ies**) the property of having poles or being polar: *it exhibits polarity when presented to a magnetic needle.*
■ the relative orientation of poles; the direction of a magnetic or electric field: *the magnetic field peaks in strength immediately after switching polarity.* ■ the state of having two opposite or contradictory tendencies, opinions, or aspects: *the polarity between male and female* | *the cold war's neat polarities can hardly be carried*

on. ■ the tendency of living organisms or parts to develop with distinct anterior and posterior (or uppermost and lowermost) ends, or to grow or orient in a particular direction.

po•lar•ize |'pōlə,rīz| • v. **1** [trans.] (in physics) restrict the vibrations of (a transverse wave, esp. light) wholly or partially to one direction:[as adj.] (**polarizing**) *a polarizing microscope*. **2** [trans.] cause (something) to acquire polarity: *the electrode is polarized in aqueous solution*. **3** divide or cause to divide into two sharply contrasting groups or sets of opinions or beliefs: [intrans.] *the cultural sphere has polarized into two competing ideological positions* | [trans.] *Vietnam polarized political opinion*.
DERIVATIVES: **po•lar•iz•a•bil•i•ty** |,pōlə ,rīzə'bilətē| *n*. **po•lar•iz•a•ble** *adj*. **po•lar•i•za•tion** |,pōlərə'zāsHən| *n*. **po•lar•iz•er** *n*.

pole•cat |'pōl,kæt| • *n*. a weasellike Eurasian mammal with mainly dark brown fur and a darker mask across the eyes, noted for its fetid smell. ■ another term for skunk. ■ a detested or immoral person.

po•lem•ic |pə'lemik| • *n*. a strong verbal or written attack on someone or something: *a polemic against the cultural relativism of the sixties* | *a writer of feminist polemic*. ■ (usu. **polemics**) the art or practice of engaging in controversial debate or dispute: *the history of science has become embroiled in religious polemics*. • *adj*. of the nature of controversy; controversial; polemical.
DERIVATIVES: **po•lem•i•cal** *adj*. **po•lem•i•cist** |pə'leməsəst| *n*. **po•lem•i•cize** |pə 'lemə,sīz| *v*.

pol•i•tesse |,pälə'tes| • *n*. formal politeness or etiquette.

pol•i•tic |'pälə,tik| • *adj*. (of an action) seeming sensible and judicious under the circumstances: [with infinitive] *I did not think it politic to express my reservations*. ■ (also **politick**) (of a person) prudent and sagacious. • *v*. (**politicked, politicking**) [intrans.] [often as n.] (**politicking**) engage in political activity: *news of this unseemly politicking invariably leaks into the press*.
DERIVATIVES: **pol•i•tic•ly** *adv*. (rare).

po•lit•i•cize |pə'litə,sīz| • *v*. [trans.] [often as adj.] (**politicized**) cause (an activity or event) to become political in character: *art was becoming politicized* | *attempts to politicize America's curricula*. ■ make (someone) politically aware, esp. by persuading him or her of the truth of views considered radical: *we successfully politicized a generation of women*. ■ [intrans.] engage in or talk about politics.
DERIVATIVES: **po•lit•i•ci•za•tion** |pə,litəsi 'zāsHən| *n*.

pol•i•ty |'pälətē| • *n*. (pl. **-ies**) a form or process of civil government or constitution. ■ an organized society; a state as a political entity.

pol•o•naise |,pälə'nāz; ,pō-| • *n*. a slow dance of Polish origin in triple time, consisting chiefly of an intricate march or procession.

■ a piece of music for this dance or in its rhythm.

pol•ter•geist |'pōltər,gīst| • *n*. a ghost or other supernatural being supposedly responsible for physical disturbances such as loud noises and objects flying.

pol•troon |päl'trōōn| • *n*. an utter coward.
DERIVATIVES: **pol•troon•er•y** |-'trōōnərē| *n*. **pol•troon•ish** *adj*.

pol•y•chrome |'päli,krōm| • *adj*. painted, printed, or decorated in several colors. • *n*. varied coloring. ■ a work of art in several colors, esp. a statue. • *v*. [trans.] [usu. as adj.] (**polychromed**) execute or decorate (a work of art) in several colors.

po•lyg•a•my |pə'ligəmē| • *n*. the practice or custom of having more than one wife (**polygyny**) or husband (**polyandry**)at the same time. ■ (in zoology) a pattern of mating in which an animal has more than one mate of the opposite sex.
DERIVATIVES: **po•lyg•a•mist** |-mist| *n*. **po•lyg•a•mous** *adj*.

pol•y•glot |'päli,glät| • *adj*. knowing or using several languages: *a polyglot diplomat*. ■ (of a book) having the text translated into several languages: *polyglot and bilingual technical dictionaries*. • *n*. a person who knows and is able to use several languages.
DERIVATIVES: **pol•y•glot•ism** |-,glät,izəm| *n*.

pol•y•graph |'päli,græf| • *n*. a machine designed to detect and record changes in physiological characteristics, such as a person's pulse and breathing rates, used esp. as a lie detector. ■ a lie-detector test carried out with a machine of this type.
DERIVATIVES: **pol•y•graph•ic** |,päli'græfik| *adj*.

pol•y•math |'päli,mæTH| • *n*. a person of wide-ranging knowledge or learning.
DERIVATIVES: **pol•y•math•ic** |,päli 'mæTHik| *adj*. **po•lym•a•thy** |pə'liməTHē; 'päli,mæTHē| *n*.

pol•y•mer |'päləmər| • *n*. a substance that has a molecular structure built up chiefly or completely from a large number of similar units bonded together, e.g., many synthetic organic materials used as plastics and resins.
DERIVATIVES: **pol•y•mer•ic** |,pälə'merik| *adj*.

pol•y•no•mi•al |,pälə'nōmēəl| • *adj*. consisting of several terms. ■ (in mathematics) of, relating to, or denoting a polynomial or polynomials. • *n*. (in mathematics) an expression of more than two algebraic terms, esp. the sum of several terms that contain different powers of the same variable(s). ■ (in biology) a Latin name with more than two parts.

pol•y•phon•ic |,päli'fänik| • *adj*. producing many sounds simultaneously; many-voiced: *a 64-voice polyphonic sound module*. ■ (esp. of vocal music) in two or more parts,

each having a melody of its own; contrapuntal. Cf. HOMOPHONIC. ■ (of a musical instrument) capable of producing more than one note at a time.
DERIVATIVES: **pol•y•phon•i•cal•ly** |-ik(ə)-lē| adv.

pol•y•syn•thet•ic |ˌpälisin'THeɹik| • adj. denoting or relating to a language characterized by complex words consisting of several morphemes, in which a single word may function as a whole sentence. Many American Indian languages are polysynthetic.

pol•y•un•sat•u•rat•ed |ˌpälēən'sæcHəˌraɹid| • adj. (of an organic compound, esp. a fat or oil molecule) containing several double or triple bonds between carbon atoms and therefore capable of further reaction. Polyunsaturated fats, which are usually of plant origin, are regarded as healthier in the diet than saturated fats.

pol•y•va•lent |ˌpäli'vālənt| • adj. (in chemistry) having a valence of three or more.
■ (in medicine) having the property of counteracting several related poisons or affording immunity against different strains of a microorganism. ■ (of an antigen or antibody) having several sites at which attachment to an antibody or antigen can occur. (Also called **multivalent**) . ■ having many different functions, forms, or facets: *as emotion, love is polyvalent.*
DERIVATIVES: **pol•y•va•lence** n.

pomp•ous |'pämpəs| • adj. affectedly and irritatingly grand, solemn, or self-important: *a pompous ass who pretends he knows everything.*
■ characterized by pomp or splendor: *there were many processions and other pompous shows.*
DERIVATIVES: **pom•pos•i•ty** |päm'päsəɹē| n. **pomp•ous•ly** adv. **pomp•ous•ness** n.

pon•der•ous |'pändərəs| • adj. slow and clumsy because of great weight: *her footsteps were heavy and ponderous.*
■ dull, laborious, or excessively solemn: *Liz could hardly restrain herself from finishing all his ponderous sentences.*
DERIVATIVES: **pon•der•os•i•ty** |ˌpändə'räsəɹē| n. **pon•der•ous•ly** adv. **pon•der•ous•ness** n.

pon•tiff |'päntəf| (also **sovereign** or **supreme pontiff**) • n. the pope.

pon•tif•i•cal |pän'tifikəl| • adj. 1 (in the Roman Catholic Church) of or relating to the pope: *a pontifical commission.* 2 characterized by a pompous and superior air of infallibility. • n. (in the Roman Catholic Church) an office book of the Western Church containing rites to be performed by the pope or bishops.
■ (**pontificals**) the vestments and insignia of a bishop, cardinal, or abbot: *a bishop in full pontificals.*
DERIVATIVES: **pon•tif•i•cal•ly** |-ik(ə)lē| adv.

pon•tif•i•cate • v. |pän'tifiˌkāt| [intrans.] 1 (in the Roman Catholic Church) officiate as bishop, esp. at Mass. 2 express one's opinions in a way considered annoyingly pompous and dogmatic: *pontificating about art and history.* • n. |-kət| (also **Pontificate**) (in the Roman

Catholic Church) the office of pope or bishop.
■ the period of such an office: *Pope Gregory VIII enjoyed only a ten-week pontificate.*
DERIVATIVES: **pon•tif•i•ca•tor** |-ˌkāɹər| n.

pop•in•jay |'päpənˌjā| • n. a vain or conceited person, esp. one who dresses or behaves extravagantly.

pop•u•list |'päpyələst| • n. a member or adherent of a political party seeking to represent the interests of ordinary people.
■ a person who holds, or who is concerned with, the views of ordinary people. ■ (**Populist**) a member of the Populist Party, a political party formed in 1891 that advocated the interests of labor and farmers, free coinage of silver, a graduated income tax, and government control of monopolies. • adj. of or relating to a populist or populists: *a populist leader.*
DERIVATIVES: **pop•u•lism** |-ˌlizəm| n. **pop•u•lis•tic** |ˌpäpyə'listik| adj.

por•cine |'pôrˌsīn| • adj. of, affecting, or resembling a pig or pigs: *his flushed, porcine features.*

por•ta•men•to |ˌpôrɹə'men,tō| • n. (pl. **portamentos** or **portamenti** |-'mentē|) 1 a slide from one note to another, esp. in singing or playing a bowed string instrument.
■ this as a technique or style. 2 piano playing in a manner intermediate between legato and staccato: [as adj.] *a portamento style.*

por•tent |'pôrˌtent| • n. 1 a sign or warning that something, esp. something momentous or calamitous, is likely to happen: *they believed that wild birds in the house were portents of death | JFK's political debut was a portent of the fame to come.*
■ future significance: *an omen of grave portent for the tribe.* 2 an exceptional or wonderful person or thing: *what portent can be greater than a pious notary?*

por•ten•tous |pôr'tentəs| • adj. of or like a portent: *the envelope with its portentous contents.*
■ done in a pompously or overly solemn manner so as to impress: *the author's portentous moralizings.*
DERIVATIVES: **por•ten•tous•ly** adv. **por•ten•tous•ness** n.

port•fo•li•o |pôrt'fōlē,ō| • n. (pl. **-os**) 1 a large, thin, flat case for loose sheets of paper such as drawings or maps.
■ a set of pieces of creative work collected by someone to display their skills, esp. to a potential employer. ■ a varied set of photographs of a model or actor intended to be shown to a potential employer. 2 a range of investments held by a person or organization: *better returns on its investment portfolio.*
■ a range of products or services offered by an organization, esp. when considered as a business asset: *an unrivaled portfolio of quality brands.* 3 the position and duties of a minister of state or a member of a cabinet: *he took on the Foreign Affairs portfolio.*

por•ti•co |'pôrɹi,kō| • n. (pl. **-oes** or **-os**) a structure consisting of a roof supported by columns at regular intervals, typically attached as a porch to a building.

port•man•teau |pôrt'mæntō| • *n.* (pl. **portmanteaus** |-tōz| or **portmanteaux** |-tōz|) a large trunk or suitcase, typically made of stiff leather and opening into two equal parts.
■ [as adj.] consisting of or combining two or more separable aspects or qualities: *a portmanteau movie composed of excerpts from his most famous films.*

port•man•teau word • *n.* a word blending the sounds and combining the meanings of two others, for example *motel* (from 'motor' and 'hotel') or *brunch* (from 'breakfast' and 'lunch').

po•seur |pō'zər| • *n.* (also **poser**) a person who poses for effect or adopts an affected style or demeanor.

posh |päSH| • *adj.* elegant or stylishly luxurious: *a posh Ensenada hotel.*
■ chiefly Brit. typical of or belonging to the upper class of society: *she had a posh accent.* • *adv.* Brit. in an upper-class way: *trying to talk posh.* • *n.* Brit. the quality or state of being elegant, stylish, or upper-class: *we finally bought a color TV, which seemed the height of posh.*
DERIVATIVES: **posh•ly** *adv.* **posh•ness** *n.*

pos•it |'päzit| • *v.* (**posited, positing**) 1 [trans.] assume as a fact; put forward as a basis of argument: *the Confucian view posits a perfectible human nature* | [with clause] *he posited that the world economy is a system with its own particular equilibrium.*
■ (**posit something on**) base something on the truth of (a particular assumption): *these plots are posited on a false premise about women's nature as inferior.* 2 [with obj. and adverbial] put in position; place: *the professor posits Cohen in his second category of poets.* • *n.* (in philosophy) a statement that is made on the assumption that it will prove to be true.

pos•i•tive |'päzətiv; 'päztiv| • *adj.* 1 consisting in or characterized by the presence or possession of features or qualities rather than their absence.
■ (of a statement or decision) expressing or implying affirmation, agreement, or permission: *the company received a positive response from investors.* ■ (of the results of a test or experiment) indicating the presence of something: *three players who had tested positive for cocaine use.* ■ constructive in intention or attitude: *there needs to be a positive approach to young offenders.* ■ showing optimism and confidence: *I hope you will be feeling very positive about your chances of success.* ■ showing pleasing progress, gain, or improvement: *the election result will have a positive effect because it will restore people's confidence.* 2 with no possibility of doubt; clear and definite: *he made a positive identification of a glossy ibis.*
■ convinced or confident in one's opinion; certain: *"You are sure it was the same man?" "Positive!"* | [with clause] *I am positive that he is not coming back.* ■ [attrib.] downright; complete (used for emphasis): *it's a positive delight to see you.* 3 of, containing, producing, or denoting an electric charge opposite to that carried by

electrons. 4 (of a photographic image) showing lights and shades or colors true to the original. 5 (of an adjective or adverb) expressing a quality in its basic, primary degree. Contrasted with *comparative* and *superlative* 6 dealing only with matters of fact and experience; not speculative or theoretical. Cf. POSITIVISM (sense 1). 7 (of a quantity) greater than zero. 8 (in astrology) of, relating to, or denoting any of the air or fire signs, considered active in nature. • *n.* 1 a good, affirmative, or constructive quality or attribute: *take your weaknesses and translate them into positives* | *to manage your way out of recession, accentuate the positive.* 2 a photographic image showing lights and shades or colors true to the original, esp. one printed from a negative. 3 a result of a test or experiment indicating the presence of something: *let us look at the distribution of those positives.* 4 the part of an electric circuit that is at a higher electrical potential than another point designated as having zero electrical potential. 5 an adjective or adverb in the positive degree. 6 a number greater than zero.
DERIVATIVES: **pos•i•tive•ness** *n.* **pos•i•tiv•i•ty** |ˌpäzə'tivətē| *n.*

pos•i•tive law • *n.* law created by a legislature, court, or other human institution and which can take whatever form the authors want.

pos•i•tiv•ism |'päzətiv,izəm; 'päztiv-| • *n.* 1 a philosophical system that holds that every rationally justifiable assertion can be scientifically verified or is capable of logical or mathematical proof, and that therefore rejects metaphysics and theism.
■ a humanistic religious system founded on this. 2 the theory that laws are to be understood as social rules, valid because they are enacted by authority or derive logically from existing decisions, and that ideal or moral considerations (e.g., that a rule is unjust) should not limit the scope or operation of the law. 3 the state or quality of being positive: *in this age of illogical positivism, no one wants to sound negative.*
DERIVATIVES: **pos•i•tiv•ist** *n.* & *adj.* **pos•i•tiv•is•tic** |ˌpäzətə'vistik| *adj.* **pos•i•tiv•is•ti•cal•ly** |ˌpäzətə'vistik(ə)lē| *adv.*

pos•se |'päsē| • *n.* a body of men, typically armed, summoned by a sheriff to enforce the law.
■ (also **posse comitatus** |ˌkämi'tätəs; -tā-təs|) the body of men in a county whom the sheriff could summon to enforce the law. ■ a group of people who have a common characteristic, occupation, or purpose: *he pompously led around a posse of medical students.* ■ a gang of youths involved in (usually drug-related) crime.

pos•te•ri•or |pä'stirēər; pō-| • *adj.* 1 farther back in position; of or nearer the rear or hind end, esp. of the body or a part of it: *the posterior part of the gut* | *a basal body situated just posterior to the nucleus.* The opposite of *anterior.*
■ relating to or denoting presentation of a fe-

tus in which the rear or caudal end is nearest the cervix and emerges first at birth: *a posterior labor.* **2** coming after in time or order; later: *a date posterior to the first Reform Bill.* • *n.* a person's buttocks.
DERIVATIVES: **pos•te•ri•or•i•ty** |pä‚stirē 'ôrətē; pō-| *n.* **pos•te•ri•or•ly** *adv.*

pos•ter•i•ty |pä'sterətē| • *n.* all future generations of people: *the victims' names are recorded for posterity.*
■ [in sing.] the descendants of a person: *God offered Abraham a posterity like the stars of heaven.*

pos•tern |'pōstərn; 'päs-| • *n.* a back or side entrance: [as adj.] *a small postern door.*

post•haste |'pōst'hāst| • *adv.* with great speed or immediacy: *she would go posthaste to England.*

post hoc |'pōst 'häk| • *adj. & adv.* occurring or done after the event: *a post hoc justification for the changes.*
■ referring to the logical fallacy **post hoc, ergo propter hoc** 'after this, therefore because of this': *a rank example of post hoc reasoning.*

post•hu•mous |'päsCHəməs; päst'(h)yŏŏ-məs| • *adj.* occurring, awarded, or appearing after the death of the originator: *he was awarded a posthumous Distinguished Service Medal* | *a posthumous collection of her articles.*
■ (of a child) born after the death of its father.
DERIVATIVES: **post•hu•mous•ly** *adv.*

post•mod•ern•ism |pōst'mädər‚nizəm| • *n.* a late 20th-century style and concept in the arts, architecture, and criticism that represents a departure from modernism and has at its heart a general distrust of grand theories and ideologies as well as a problematical relationship with any notion of "art."

Typical features include a deliberate mixing of different artistic styles and media, the self-conscious use of earlier styles and conventions, and often the incorporation of images relating to the consumerism and mass communication of late 20th-century postindustrial society.

DERIVATIVES: **post•mod•ern** *adj.* **post•mod•ern•ist** *n. & adj.* **post•mod•er•ni•ty** |‚pōstmə'dərnətē| *n.*

post•mor•tem |pōst'môrtəm| • *n.* (also **postmortem examination**) an examination of a body to determine the cause of death. Cf. AUTOPSY.
■ an analysis or discussion of an event held soon after it has occurred, esp. in order to determine why it was a failure: *an election postmortem on why the party lost.* • *adj.* [attrib.] of or relating to a postmortem: *a postmortem report.*
■ happening after death: *postmortem changes in the body* | [as adv.] *assessment of morphology in nerves taken postmortem.*

post•par•tum |pōst'pärtəm| • *adj.* following childbirth or the birth of young.

post•pone |pōst'pōn| • *v.* [trans.] cause or arrange for (something) to take place at a time later than that first scheduled: *the visit*

had to be postponed for some time | [with present participle] *the judge postponed sentencing a former government spokesman for fraud.* Cf. ADJOURN.
DERIVATIVES: **post•pon•a•ble** *adj.* **post•pone•ment** *n.* **post•pon•er** *n.*

post•pos•i•tive |‚pōst'päzətiv| • *adj.* (of a word) placed after or as a suffix on the word that it relates to. • *n.* a postpositive word.
DERIVATIVES: **post•pos•i•tive•ly** *adv.*

post•pran•di•al |pōst'prændēəl| • *adj.* during or relating to the period after dinner or lunch: *we were jolted from our postprandial torpor.*
■ (in medicine) occurring after a meal.

pos•tu•lant |'päsCHələnt| • *n.* a candidate, esp. one seeking admission into a religious order.

pos•tu•late • *v.* |'päsCHə‚lāt| [trans.] **1** suggest or assume the existence, fact, or truth of (something) as a basis for reasoning, discussion, or belief: *his theory postulated a rotatory movement for hurricanes* | [with clause] *he postulated that the environmentalists might have a case.* **2** (in ecclesiastical law) nominate or elect (someone) to an ecclesiastical office subject to the sanction of a higher authority. • *n.* |'päsCHələt| a thing suggested or assumed as true as the basis for reasoning, discussion, or belief: *perhaps the postulate of Babylonian influence on Greek astronomy is incorrect.*
■ an assumption used as a basis for mathematical reasoning.
DERIVATIVES: **pos•tu•la•tion** |‚päsCHə'lā-sHən| *n.*

po•ta•ble |'pōtəbəl| • *adj.* safe to drink; drinkable: *there is no supply of potable water available.*
DERIVATIVES: **po•ta•bil•i•ty** |‚pōtə'bilətē| *n.*

po•tage |pô'täzH| • *n.* thick soup.

po•ta•tion |pō'tāsHən| • *n.* a drink.
■ the action of drinking something, esp. alcohol: *I intend to abstain from potation.* ■ (often **potations**) a drinking bout: *the dreadful potations of his youth.*

po•ten•cy |'pōtnsē| • *n.* (pl. **-ies**) **1** power or influence: *a myth of enormous potency.*
■ the strength of an intoxicant, as measured by the amount needed to produce a certain response: *the unexpected potency of the rum punch.* ■ (in homeopathy) the number of times a remedy has been diluted and succussed (shaken vigorously), taken as a measure of the strength of the effect it will produce: *she was given a low potency twice daily.*
■ (in genetics) the extent of the contribution of an allele toward the production of a phenotypic characteristic. ■ (in biology) a capacity in embryonic tissue for developing into a particular specialized tissue or organ. **2** a male's ability to achieve an erection or to reach orgasm: *medications that diminish sexual potency.*

po•tent |'pōtnt| • *adj.* **1** having great power, influence, or effect: *thrones were potent symbols of authority* | *a potent drug* | *a potent argument.*

2 (of a male) able to achieve an erection or to reach an orgasm.
DERIVATIVES: **po•tence** *n.* **po•tent•ly** *adv.*
po•ten•tate |ˈpōtnˌtāt| • *n.* a monarch or ruler, esp. an autocratic one.
po•ten•tial |pəˈtenCHəl| • *n.* (in physics) the quantity determining the energy of mass in a gravitational field or of charge in an electric field.
po•ten•ti•ate |pəˈtenCHēˌāt| • *v.* [trans.] increase the power, effect, or likelihood of (something, esp. a drug or physiological reaction): *the glucose will potentiate intestinal absorption of sodium.*
pot•pour•ri |ˌpōpəˈrē; pō poōˈrē| • *n.* (pl. **potpourris**) a mixture of dried petals and spices placed in a bowl or small sack to perfume clothing or a room.
■ a mixture of things, esp. a musical or literary medley: *a potpourri of tunes from Gilbert and Sullivan.*
poul•tice |ˈpōltəs| • *n.* a soft, moist mass of material, typically of plant material or flour, applied to the body to relieve soreness and inflammation and kept in place with a cloth. • *v.* [trans.] apply a poultice to: *he poulticed the wound.*
prac•ti•ca•ble |ˈpræktikəbəl| • *adj.* able to be done or put into practice successfully: *the measures will be put into effect as soon as is reasonably practicable.*
■ able to be used; useful: *signal processing can let you transform a signal into a practicable form.*
DERIVATIVES: **prac•ti•ca•bil•i•ty** |ˌpræktikəˈbiləṯē| *n.* **prac•ti•ca•bly** |-blē| *adv.*
prac•ti•cal |ˈpræktikəl| • *adj.* **1** of or concerned with the actual doing or use of something rather than with theory and ideas: *there are two obvious practical applications of the research.*
■ (of an idea, plan, or method) likely to succeed or be effective in real circumstances; feasible: *neither of these strategies is practical for smaller businesses.* ■ suitable for a particular purpose: *a practical, stylish kitchen.* ■ (of a person) sensible and realistic in approaching a situation or problem: *I'm not unfeeling, just trying to be practical.* ■ (of a person) skilled at manual tasks: *Steve'll fix it—he's quite practical.* **2** so nearly the case that it can be regarded as so; virtual: *it was a practical certainty that he would quickly spend more money.*
prac•ti•cum |ˈpræktikəm| • *n.* (pl. **practicums**) a practical section of a course of study.
prag•mat•ic |prægˈmæṯik| • *adj.* dealing with things sensibly and realistically in a way that is based on practical rather than theoretical considerations: *a pragmatic approach to politics.*
■ relating to philosophical or political pragmatism. ■ (in linguistics) of or relating to pragmatics.
DERIVATIVES: **prag•mat•i•cal•ly** |-ik(ə)lē| *adv.*
prag•mat•ics |prægˈmædiks| • *plural n.* [usu. treated as sing.] the branch of linguistics deal-

ing with language in use and the contexts in which it is used.
prag•ma•tism |ˈprægməˌtizəm| • *n.* **1** a pragmatic attitude or policy: *ideology was tempered with pragmatism.* **2** (in philosophy) an approach that assesses the truth or meaning of theories or beliefs in terms of the success of their practical application.
DERIVATIVES: **prag•ma•tist** *n.* **prag•ma•tis•tic** |ˌprægməˈtistik| *adj.*
pran•di•al |ˈprændēəl| • *adj.* [attrib.] during or relating to dinner or lunch.
■ (in medicine) during or relating to the eating of food.
prate |prāt| • *v.* [intrans.] talk foolishly or at tedious length about something.
DERIVATIVES: **prat•er** *n.* (rare).
prat•fall |ˈprætˌfôl| • *n.* a fall on one's buttocks (prat): *he took a pratfall into the sand.*
■ a stupid and humiliating action: *the first political pratfalls of the new administration.*
prat•tle |ˈprædl| • *v.* [intrans.] talk at length in a foolish or inconsequential way: *she began to prattle on about her visit to the dentist.* • *n.* foolish or inconsequential talk: *do you intend to keep up this childish prattle?*
DERIVATIVES: **prat•tler** |ˈprædlər; ˈprædl-ər| *n.*
prax•is |ˈpræksəs| • *n.* practice, as distinguished from theory: *the divorce between theory and praxis of Marxism that ensued under Stalinism.*
■ accepted practice or custom.
pre•am•ble |ˈprēˌæmbəl| • *n.* a preliminary or preparatory statement; an introduction: *he could tell that what she said was by way of a preamble | I gave him the bad news without preamble.*
■ (in law) the introductory part of a statute, constitution, deed, etc., stating its purpose, aims, and justification. The preamble is not technically part of a law, but may be considered in determining the enactors' intent.
DERIVATIVES: **pre•am•bu•lar** |prēˈæmbyələr| *adj.*
Pre•cam•bri•an |prēˈkæmbrēən; -kām-| • *adj.* of, relating to, or denoting the earliest geologic eon, preceding the Cambrian period and the Phanerozoic eon. It is also called the Cryptozoic ('period of hidden life'), as its rocks contain few signs of organic matter.
■ [as n.] (**the Precambrian**) the Precambrian eon or the system of rocks deposited during it.

The Precambrian extended from the origin of the earth (believed to have been about 4,600 million years ago) to about 570 million years ago, representing nearly ninety percent of geological time. The oldest known Precambrian rocks are about 3,800 million years old, and the earliest living organisms date from the latter part of the eon. The Precambrian is now replaced in formal stratigraphic schemes by the Archean, Proterozoic, and (in some schemes) Priscoan eons.

pre•car•i•ous |priˈkerēəs| • *adj.* **1** not securely held or in position; dangerously likely

to fall or collapse: *a precarious ladder.* **2** dependent on chance; uncertain: *she made a precarious living by writing.*
DERIVATIVES: **pre•car•i•ous•ly** *adv.* **pre• car•i•ous•ness** *n.*
prec•a•to•ry | 'prekə,tôrē | • *adj.* of, relating to, or expressing a wish or request.
■ (in a will) expressing a wish or intention of the testator: *a trust can be left in precatory words.*
prec•e•dence | 'presədəns; pri'sēdns | • *n.* the condition of being considered more important than someone or something else; priority in importance, order, or rank: *his desire for power soon* **took precedence over** *any other consideration.*
■ the order to be ceremonially observed by people of different rank, according to an acknowledged or legally determined system: *quarrels over precedence among the Bonaparte family marred the coronation.*
prec•e•dent • *n.* | 'presədənt | an earlier event or action that is regarded as an example or guide to be considered in subsequent similar circumstances: *there are precedents for using interactive media in training.* • *adj.* | prē'sēdnt; 'prosədənt | preceding in time, order, or importance: *a precedent occurrence.*
pre•cept | 'prē,sept | • *n.* **1** a general rule intended to regulate behavior or thought: *moral precepts.* **2** a writ or warrant.
DERIVATIVES: **pre•cep•tive** | pri'septiv | *adj.*
pre•cep•tor | 'prē,septər; pri'septər | • *n.* a teacher or instructor.
DERIVATIVES: **pre•cep•to•ri•al** | pri,sep 'tôrēəl; 'prē- | *adj.* **pre•cep•tor•ship** | -,SHip | *n.*
pre•cinct | 'prē,siNGkt | • *n.* **1** a district of a city or town as defined for police purposes.
■ (also **precinct house**) the police station situated in such a subdivision. ■ an electoral district of a city or town served by a single polling place. **2** (usu. **precincts**) the area within the walls or perceived boundaries of a particular building or place: *all strata of society live within these precincts | beyond the precincts of my own family, I am quite inhibited.*
■ an enclosed or clearly defined area of ground around a cathedral, church, or college.
prec•i•pice | 'presəpəs | • *n.* a very steep rock face or cliff, typically a tall one.
■ a dangerous or hazardous situation: *the country was teetering on the precipice of anarchy.*
pre•cip•i•tate • *v.* | pri'sipə,tāt | [trans.] **1** cause (an event or situation, typically one that is bad or undesirable) to happen suddenly, unexpectedly, or prematurely: *the incident precipitated a political crisis.*
■ [with obj. and adverbial of direction] cause to move suddenly and with force: *suddenly the ladder broke, precipitating them down into a heap.*
■ (**precipitate someone/something into**) send someone or something suddenly into a particular state or condition: *they were precipitated into a conflict for which they were quite unprepared.* **2** (usu. **be precipitated**) (in chemistry) cause (a substance) to be deposited in solid form from a solution.

■ cause (drops of moisture or particles of dust) to be deposited from the atmosphere or from a vapor or suspension. • *adj.* | pri'sipətət | done, made, or acting suddenly or without careful consideration: *I must apologize for my staff—their actions were precipitate.*
■ (of an event or situation) occurring suddenly or abruptly: *a precipitate decline in cultural literacy.* • *n.* | pri'sipətət; -ə,tāt | (in chemistry) a substance precipitated from a solution.
DERIVATIVES: **pre•cip•i•ta•ble** | pri'sip ətəbəl | *adj.* **pre•cip•i•tate•ly** | pri'sipətətlē | *adv.* **pre•cip•i•tate•ness** | pri'sipətətnəs | *n.*
USAGE: The adjectives **precipitate** and **precipitous** are sometimes confused. **Precipitate** means 'sudden, hasty': *a precipitate decision; precipitate flight by the fugitive.* **Precipitous** means 'steep': *the precipitous slope of the moutain; a precipitous decline in stock prices.*
pre•cip•i•tous | pri'sipətəs | • *adj.* **1** dangerously high or steep: *the precipitous cliffs of the North Pacific coast.*
■ (of a change to a worse situation or condition) sudden and dramatic: *a precipitous decline in exports.* **2** (of an action) done suddenly and without careful consideration: *precipitous intervention.*
DERIVATIVES: **pre•cip•i•tous•ly** *adv.* **pre• cip•i•tous•ness** *n.*
pré•cis | prā'sē; 'prāsē | • *n.* (pl. same) a summary or abstract of a text or speech. • *v.* (**précises** | prā'sēz; 'prāsēz |, **précised** | prā 'sēd; 'prāsēd |, **précising** | prā'sēiNG; 'prāsē-iNG |) [trans.] make a précis of (a text or speech).
pre•clude | pri'klo͞od | • *v.* [trans.] prevent from happening; make impossible: *the secret nature of his work precluded official recognition.*
■ (**preclude someone from**) (of a situation or condition) prevent someone from doing something: *his difficulties preclude him from leading a normal life.*
DERIVATIVES: **pre•clu•sion** | -'klo͞oZHən | *n.* **pre•clu•sive** | -'klo͞osiv; -ziv | *adj.*
pre•co•cious | pri'kōSHəs | • *adj.* (of a child) having developed certain abilities or proclivities at an earlier age than usual: *he was a precocious, solitary boy.*
■ (of behavior or ability) indicative of such development: *a precocious talent for mathematics.*
■ (of a plant) flowering or fruiting earlier than usual.
DERIVATIVES: **pre•co•cious•ly** *adv.* **pre•co• cious•ness** *n.* **pre•coc•i•ty** | pri'käsətē | *n.*
pre•cog•ni•tion | ,prēkäg'nisHən | • *n.* foreknowledge of an event, esp. foreknowledge of a paranormal kind.
DERIVATIVES: **pre•cog•ni•tive** | prē'kägnə-tiv | *adj.*
pre-Co•lum•bi•an | kə'ləmbēən | • *adj.* of or relating to the history and cultures of the Americas before the arrival of Columbus in 1492.
pre•con•scious | prē'känCHəs | • *adj.* (in psychoanalysis) of or associated with a part of the mind below the level of immediate conscious awareness, from which memories and

emotions that have not been repressed can be recalled: *beliefs and values that are on a preconscious level.* • *n.* (**one's/the preconscious**) the part of the mind in which preconscious thoughts or memories reside.

DERIVATIVES: **pre•con•scious•ness** *n.*

pre•cur•sor | 'prē,kərsər; pri'kər- | • *n.* a person or thing that comes before another of the same kind; a forerunner: *a three-stringed precursor of the violin* | [as adj.] *precursor cells.* ■ (in biochemistry) a substance from which another is formed, esp. by metabolic reaction: *pepsinogen is the inactive precursor of pepsin.*

pre•da•cious | pri'dāsHəs | (also **predaceous**) • *adj.* (of an animal) predatory: *predacious insects.*

DERIVATIVES: **pre•da•cious•ness** *n.* **pre•dac•i•ty** | pri'dæsətē | *n.*

pred•a•to•ry | 'predə,tôrē | • *adj.* relating to or denoting an animal or animals preying naturally on others: *predatory birds.* ■ seeking to exploit or oppress others: *a life destroyed by predatory biographers and muckraking journalists.*

DERIVATIVES: **pred•a•to•ri•ly** | ,predə'tô-rəlē | *adv.* **pred•a•to•ri•ness** *n.*

pre•des•ti•na•tion | prē,destə'nāsHən | • *n.* (as a doctrine in Christian theology) the divine foreordaining of all that will happen, esp. with regard to the salvation of some and not others. It has been particularly associated with the teachings of St. Augustine of Hippo and of Calvin.

pred•i•cate • *n.* | 'predikət | the part of a sentence or clause containing a verb and stating something about the subject (e.g., *went home* in *John went home*): [as adj.] *predicate adjective.* ■ (in logic) something that is affirmed or denied concerning an argument of a proposition. • *v.* | 'predə,kāt | [trans.] **1** affirm (something) about the subject of a sentence or an argument of proposition: *a word that predicates something about its subject* | *aggression is predicated of those who act aggressively.* **2** (**predicate something on/upon**) found or base something on: *the theory of structure on which later chemistry was predicated.*

DERIVATIVES: **pred•i•ca•tion** | ,predə'kā-sHən | *n.*

pre•di•lec•tion | ,predl'eksHən; ,prēdl- | • *n.* a preference or special liking for something; a bias in favor of something: *my predilection for Asian food.*

pre•em•i•nent | prē'emənənt | • *adj.* surpassing all others; very distinguished in some way: *the world's preeminent expert on Australian varietal wines.*

DERIVATIVES: **pre•em•i•nence** *n.*

pre•empt | prē'empt | • *v.* [trans.] **1** take action in order to prevent (an anticipated event) from happening; forestall: *the government preempted a coup attempt.* ■ act in advance of (someone) in order to prevent him or her from doing something: *it looked as if she'd ask him more, but Parr preempted her.* ■ (of a broadcast) interrupt or replace (a scheduled program): *the violence preempted regular programming.* **2** acquire or appropriate (something) in advance: *many tables were already preempted by family parties.* • *n.* Bridge a preemptive bid.

DERIVATIVES: **pre•emp•tion** *n.* **pre•emp•tive** *adj.* **pre•emp•tor** | -tər | *n.*

pref•ace | 'prefəs | • *n.* an introduction to a book, typically stating its subject, scope, or aims. Cf. FOREWORD. ■ the introduction or preliminary part of a speech or event. ■ (in the Christian Church) the introduction to the central part of the Eucharist, historically forming the first part of the canon or prayer of consecration. • *v.* [trans.] provide (a book) with a preface: *the book is prefaced by a brief remembrance of Faulkner.* ■ (**preface something with/by**) introduce or begin (a speech or event) with or by doing something: *it is important to preface the debate with a general comment.*

DERIVATIVES: **pref•a•to•ry** | 'prefə,tôrē | *adj.*

pre•fect | 'prē,fekt | • *n.* **1** a chief officer, magistrate, or regional governor in certain countries: *the prefect of police.* ■ a senior magistrate or governor in the ancient Roman world: *Avitus was prefect of Gaul from AD 439.* **2** in some, esp. British, schools, a senior student authorized to enforce discipline.

DERIVATIVES: **pre•fec•tor•al** | prē'fektər-əl | *adj.* **pre•fec•to•ri•al** | ,prē,fek'tôrēəl | *adj.*

pre•fec•ture | 'prē,fekCHər | • *n.* a district under the government of a prefect. ■ a prefect's office or tenure. ■ the official residence or headquarters of a prefect.

DERIVATIVES: **pre•fec•tur•al** | prē'fek-CHərəl | *adj.*

pre•hen•sile | prē'hensəl; -,sīl | • *adj.* (chiefly of an animal's limb or tail) capable of grasping.

DERIVATIVES: **pre•hen•sil•i•ty** | prē,hen'silətē | *n.*

prel•ate | 'prelət | • *n.* a bishop or other high ecclesiastical dignitary.

DERIVATIVES: **prel•a•cy** *n.* **pre•lat•ic** | pri'lætik | *adj.* **pre•lat•i•cal** | pri'lætikəl | *adj.*

pre•lit•er•ate | prē'litərət | • *adj.* of, relating to, or denoting a society or culture that has not developed the use of writing. ■ (of a child) at a stage of development before acquiring literacy; pertaining to this stage. • *n.* a preliterate person.

prel•ude | 'prel,(y)o͞od; 'prā,l(y)o͞od | • *n.* **1** an action or event serving as an introduction to something more important: *education cannot simply be a prelude to a career.* **2** an introductory piece of music, most commonly an orchestral opening to an act of an opera, the first movement of a suite, or a piece preceding a fugue. ■ a short piece of music of a similar style, esp. for the piano. ■ the introductory part of a poem or other literary work. • *v.* [trans.] serve as a prelude or introduction to: *the bombardment preluded an all-out final attack.*

DERIVATIVES: **pre•lu•di•al** | pri'lo͞odēəl; prā- | *adj.*

pre•med•i•tate |pri'medə,tāt; prē-| • v. [trans.] [usu. as adj.] (**premeditated**) think out or plan (an action, esp. a crime) beforehand: *premeditated murder.*
DERIVATIVES: **pre•med•i•ta•tion** |-,medə 'tāshən| n.

pre•mier |prē'm(y)ir; 'prēmēər; 'prē,mir| • adj. [attrib.] first in importance, order, or position; leading: *Germany's premier rock band.*
■ of earliest creation: *the premier issue of the quarterly.* • n. a prime minister or other head of government.
■ (in Australia and Canada) the chief minister of a government of a state or province.

pre•miere |prē'myer; -'mir| • n. the first performance of a musical or theatrical work or the first showing of a movie. • v. [trans.] give the first performance of: *his first stage play was premiered at the Arena stage..*
■ [intrans.] (of a musical or theatrical work or a film) have its first performance: *the show premiered in New York this week.*

pre•mo•ni•tion |,prēmə'nishən; ,prem-| • n. a strong feeling that something is about to happen, esp. something unpleasant: *he had a premonition of imminent disaster.*
DERIVATIVES: **pre•mon•i•to•ry** |prē'mänə ,tôrē| adj.

pre•pon•der•ance |pri'pändərəns| • n. the quality or fact of being greater in number, quantity, or importance: *the preponderance of women among older people.*
DERIVATIVES: **pre•pon•der•ant** adj.

pre•pon•der•ate |pri'pändə,rāt| • v. [intrans.] be greater in number, influence, or importance: *the advantages preponderate over this apparent disadvantage.*

prep•o•si•tion |,prepə'zishən| • n. a word governing, and usually preceding, a noun or pronoun and expressing a relation to another word or element in the clause, as in "the man *on* the platform," "she arrived *after* dinner," "what did you do it *for?*"
DERIVATIVES: **prep•o•si•tion•al** |-shənl| adj. **prep•o•si•tion•al•ly** |-shənl-ē| adv.

USAGE: There is a traditional view, first set forth by the 17th-century poet and dramatist John Dryden, that it is incorrect to put a preposition at the end of a sentence, as in *where do you come from?* or *she's not a writer I've ever come across.* The rule was formulated on the basis that, since in Latin a preposition cannot come after the word it governs or is linked with, the same should be true in English. The problem is that English is not like Latin in this respect, and in many cases (particularly in questions and with phrasal verbs) the attempt to move the preposition produces awkward, unnatural-sounding results. Winston Churchill famously objected to the rule, saying '*This is the sort of English* **up with** *which I will not put.*' In standard English the placing of a preposition at the end of a sentence is widely accepted provided the use sounds natural and the meaning is clear.

pre•pos•sess•ing |,prēpə'zesiNG| • adj. [often with negative] attractive or appealing in appearance: *he was not a prepossessing sight.*
DERIVATIVES: **pre•pos•ses•sion** |-'zeshən| n.

pre•pos•ter•ous |pri'päst(ə)rəs| • adj. contrary to reason or common sense; utterly absurd or ridiculous: *a preposterous suggestion.*
DERIVATIVES: **pre•pos•ter•ous•ly** adv. **pre•pos•ter•ous•ness** n.

pre•pran•di•al |prē'prandēəl| • adj. done or taken before dinner: *a preprandial glass of sherry.*
■ (in medicine) before a main meal: *urine testing results in the preprandial state.*

pre•puce |'prē,pyōōs| • n. **1** technical term for the male FORESKIN. **2** the fold of skin surrounding the clitoris.
DERIVATIVES: **pre•pu•tial** |prē'pyōōshəl| adj.

Pre-Raph•a•el•ite |'rafēə,līt; -rāfē-; -'räfē-| • n. a member of a group of 19th-century artists, including Holman Hunt, John Everett Millais, and D. Gabriel Rossetti, who consciously sought to emulate the simplicity and sincerity of the work of Italian artists from before the time of Raphael (1483–1520). • adj. of or relating to the Pre-Raphaelites.
■ of a style or appearance associated with the later pre-Raphaelites or esp. with the women they frequently used as models, with long, thick, wavy auburn hair, pale skin, and a fey demeanor.
DERIVATIVES: **Pre-Raph•a•el•it•ism** |-,līt ,izəm| n.

pre•req•ui•site |prē'rekwəzət| • n. a thing that is required as a prior condition for something else to happen or exist: *sponsorship is not a prerequisite for any of our courses.* • adj. required as a prior condition: *the student must have the prerequisite skills.*

USAGE: See usage at PERQUISITE.

pre•rog•a•tive |pri'rägətiv; pə'räg-| • n. a right or privilege exclusive to a particular individual or class: *owning an automobile was still the prerogative of the rich.*
■ a faculty or property distinguishing a person or class: *it's not a female prerogative to feel insecure.* ■ (also **royal prerogative**) the right of a sovereign, which in British law is theoretically subject to no restriction.

pres•age |'presij; pri'sāj| • v. [trans.] (of an event) be a sign or warning that (something, typically something bad) will happen: *the outcome of the game presaged the coming year.*
■ (of a person) predict. • n. a sign or warning that something, typically something bad, will happen; an omen or portent: *the fever was a somber presage of his final illness.*
■ a feeling of presentiment or foreboding: *he had a strong presage that he had only a very short time to live.*
DERIVATIVES: **pres•ag•er** n. (archaic).

pres•by•o•pi•a |,prezbē'ōpēə; ,pres-| • n. farsightedness caused by loss of elasticity of the lens of the eye.
DERIVATIVES: **pres•by•op•ic** |-'äpik| adj.

pres•by•ter |'prezbətər; 'pres-| • *n.* an elder or minister of the early Christian Church. ■ (in presbyterian churches) an elder. ■ (in episcopal churches) a minister of the second order, under the authority of a bishop; a priest.

DERIVATIVES: **pres•byt•er•al** |prez'bitər-əl; pres-| *adj.* **pres•byt•er•ate** |prez'bitə,rāt; pres-| *n.* **pres•by•te•ri•al** |,prezbə'tirēəl; ,pres-| *adj.* **pres•by•ter•ship** |-,SHip| *n.*

Pres•by•te•ri•an•ism |,prezbə'tirēə,nizəm; ,pres-| • *n.* a form of Protestant Church government in which the Church is administered locally by the minister with a group of elected elders of equal rank, and regionally and nationally by representative courts of ministers and elders.

Presbyterianism was first introduced in Geneva in 1541 under John Calvin, in the belief that it best represented the pattern of the early church. There are now many Presbyterian Churches (often called Reformed Churches) worldwide, notably in the Netherlands and Scotland and in countries with which they have historic links (including the United States and Northern Ireland).

DERIVATIVES: **Pres•by•te•ri•an** *n.*, *adj.*

pres•by•ter•y |'prezbə,terē; 'pres-; -bətrē| • *n.* (pl. **-ies**) **1** [treated as sing. or pl.] a body of church elders and ministers, esp. (in Presbyterian churches) an administrative body (court) representing all the local congregations of a district.
■ a district represented by such a body of elders and ministers. **2** the house of a Roman Catholic parish priest. **3** the eastern part of a church chancel beyond the choir; the sanctuary.

pre•scient |'presH(ē)ənt; 'prē-| • *adj.* having or showing knowledge of events before they take place: *a prescient warning.*

DERIVATIVES: **pre•science** |-əns| *n.* **pre•scient•ly** *adv.*

pre•scind |pri'sind| • *v.* [intrans.] (**prescind from**) leave out of consideration: *we have prescinded from many vexing issues.*
■ [trans.] cut off or separate from something: *his is an idea entirely prescinded from all of the others.*

pre•scribe |pri'skrīb| • *v.* [trans.] (of a medical practitioner) advise and authorize the use of (a medicine or treatment) for someone, esp. in writing: *Dr. Greene prescribed magnesium sulfate* | [with two objs.] *he was prescribed a course of antibiotics.*
■ recommend (a substance or action) as something beneficial: *marriage is often prescribed as a universal remedy.* ■ state authoritatively or as a rule that (an action or procedure) should be carried out: *rules prescribing five acts for a play are purely arbitrary* | [as adj.] (**prescribed**) *doing things in the prescribed manner.*

DERIVATIVES: **pre•scrib•er** *n.*

USAGE: The verbs **prescribe** and **proscribe** do not have the same meaning. **Pre-**

scribe is a much commoner word than **proscribe** and means either 'issue a medical prescription' or 'recommend with authority,' as in *the doctor prescribed antibiotics.* **Proscribe**, on the other hand, is a formal word meaning 'condemn or forbid,' as in *gambling was strictly proscribed by the authorities.*

pre•scrip•tive |pri'skriptiv| • *adj.* **1** of or relating to the imposition or enforcement of a rule or method: *these guidelines are not intended to be prescriptive.*
■ attempting to impose rules of correct usage on the users of a language: *a prescriptive grammar book.* Often contrasted with *descriptive.* **2** (of a right, title, or institution) having become legally established or accepted by long usage or the passage of time: *a prescriptive right of way.*
■ established by long-standing custom or usage.

DERIVATIVES: **pre•scrip•tive•ly** *adv.* **pre•scrip•tive•ness** *n.* **pre•scrip•tiv•ism** |-'skriptə,vizəm| *n.* **pre•scrip•tiv•ist** |-vist| *n. & adj.*

pre•sid•i•um |pri'sidēəm; prī-; -'zid-| (also **praesidium**) • *n.* a standing executive committee in a communist country.
■ (**Presidium**) the committee of this type in the former USSR, which functioned as the legislative authority when the Supreme Soviet was not sitting.

pres•ti•dig•i•ta•tion |,prestə,dijə'tāsHən| • *n.* magic tricks performed as entertainment.

DERIVATIVES: **pres•ti•dig•i•tate** *v.* **pres•ti•dig•i•ta•tor** |-'dijə,tātər| *n.*

pre•sump•tive |pri'zəmptiv| • *adj.* of the nature of a presumption; presumed in the absence of further information: *a presumptive diagnosis.*
■ (in law) giving grounds for the inference of a fact or of the appropriate interpretation of the law. ■ another term for PRESUMPTUOUS.

DERIVATIVES: **pre•sump•tive•ly** *adv.*

pre•sump•tu•ous |pri'zəmpCH(əw)əs| • *adj.* (of a person or personal behavior) failing to observe the limits of what is permitted or appropriate: *I hope I won't be considered presumptuous if I offer some advice.*

DERIVATIVES: **pre•sump•tu•ous•ly** *adv.* **pre•sump•tu•ous•ness** *n.*

pre•tense |'prē,tens; pri'tens| (Brit. **pretence**) • *n.* **1** an attempt to make something that is not the case appear true: *his anger is masked by the pretense that all is well* | *they have finally abandoned their secrecy and pretense.*
■ a false display of feelings, attitudes, or intentions: *he asked me questions without any pretense at politeness.* ■ the practice of inventing imaginary situations in play: *before the age of two, children start to engage in pretense.* ■ affected and ostentatious speech and behavior. **2** (**pretense to**) a claim, esp. a false or ambitious one: *he was quick to disclaim any pretense to superiority.*

pre•ten•tious |pri'tenCHəs| • *adj.* attempting to impress by affecting greater importance,

talent, culture, etc., than is actually possessed: *a pretentious literary device.*
DERIVATIVES: **pre•ten•tious•ly** *adv.* **pre•ten•tious•ness** *n.*
pre•ter•nat•u•ral |ˌprētər'nætʃ(ə)rəl| • *adj.* beyond what is normal or natural: *autumn had arrived with preternatural speed.*
DERIVATIVES: **pre•ter•nat•u•ral•ism** |-'nætʃ(ə)rəˌlizəm| *n.* **pre•ter•nat•u•ral•ly** *adv.*
pre•text |'prēˌtekst| • *n.* a reason given in justification of a course of action that is not the real reason: *the rebels had the perfect pretext for making their move.*
PHRASES: **on** (or **under**) **the pretext** giving the specified reason as one's justification: *the police raided Grand River on the pretext of looking for moonshiners.*
pre•vail |pri'vāl| • *v.* [intrans.] prove more powerful than opposing forces; be victorious: *it is hard for logic to prevail over emotion.*
■ be widespread in a particular area at a particular time; be current: *an atmosphere of crisis prevails* | [as adj.] **(prevailing)** *the prevailing political culture.* ■ **(prevail on/upon)** persuade (someone) to do something: *she was prevailed upon to sing.*
DERIVATIVES: **pre•vail•ing•ly** *adv.*
prev•a•lent |'prevələnt| • *adj.* widespread in a particular area at a particular time: *the ills prevalent in society.*
■ predominant; powerful.
DERIVATIVES: **prev•a•lence** *n.* **prev•a•lent•ly** *adv.*
pre•var•i•cate |pri'verəˌkāt| • *v.* [intrans.] speak or act in an evasive way.
DERIVATIVES: **pre•var•i•ca•tion** |priˌverə'kāSHən| *n.* **pre•var•i•ca•tor** |-ˌkātər| *n.*
pri•ap•ic |prī'æpik; -āpik| (also **priapean**) • *adj.* of, relating to, or resembling a phallus: *priapic carvings.*
■ of or relating to male sexuality and sexual activity. ■ (of a male) having a persistently erect penis.
pri•a•pism |'prīəˌpizəm| • *n.* persistent and painful erection of the penis.
prig |prig| • *n.* a self-righteously moralistic person who behaves as if superior to others.
DERIVATIVES: **prig•ger•y** |'prigərē| *n.* **prig•gish** *adj.* **prig•gish•ly** *adv.* **prig•gish•ness** *n.*
pri•ma don•na |ˌprimə 'dänə; ˌprēmə| • *n.* the chief female singer in an opera or opera company.
■ a very temperamental person with an inflated view of their own talent or importance.
DERIVATIVES: **pri•ma don•na•ish** |-iSH| *adj.*
pri•ma fa•ci•e |ˌprimə 'fāSHə; 'fāSHē; 'fāSHēˌē| • *adj. & adv.* (in law) based on the first impression; accepted as correct until proved otherwise: [as adj.] *a prima facie case of professional misconduct* | [as adv.] *the original lessee prima facie remains liable for the payment of the rent.*
pri•mal |'priməl| • *adj.* of first imortance; essential; fundamental: *for me, writing is a primal urge.*

■ relating to an early stage in development; primeval: *primal hunting societies.* ■ (in psychology) of, relating to, or denoting the needs, fears, or behavior that are postulated to form the origins of emotional life: *he preys on people's primal fears.*
DERIVATIVES: **pri•mal•ly** *adv.*
pri•mate[1] |'prī,māt; prīmət| • *n.* (in Christianity) the chief bishop or archbishop of a province.
DERIVATIVES: **pri•ma•tial** |prī'māSHəl| *adj.*
pri•mate[2] |'prī,māt| • *n.* a mammal of an order (Primates) that includes the lemurs, bush babies, tarsiers, marmosets, monkeys, apes, and humans. They are distinguished by having hands, handlike feet, and forward-facing eyes, and, with the exception of humans, are typically agile tree-dwellers.
pri•me•val |prī'mēvəl| (Brit. also **primaeval**) • *adj.* of the earliest ages in the history of the world: *mile after mile of primeval forest.*
■ (of feelings or actions) based on primitive instinct; raw and elementary: *a primeval desire.*
DERIVATIVES: **pri•me•val•ly** *adv.*
prim•i•tiv•ism |'primətivˌizəm| • *n.* **1** a belief in the value of what is simple and unsophisticated, expressed as a philosophy of life or through art or literature. **2** unsophisticated behavior that is unaffected by objective reasoning.
DERIVATIVES: **prim•i•tiv•ist** *n. & adj.*
pri•mo•gen•i•ture |ˌprīmō'jenəˌCHər; -ˌCHŏŏr| • *n.* the state of being the firstborn child.
■ (also **right of primogeniture**) the right of succession belonging to the firstborn child, esp. the feudal rule by which the whole real estate of an intestate passed to the eldest son.
DERIVATIVES: **pri•mo•gen•i•tal** |-'jenət'l| *adj.* **pri•mo•gen•i•tar•y** |-'jenəˌterē| *adj.*
pri•mor•di•al |prī'môrdēəl| • *adj.* existing at or from the beginning of time; primeval: *the primordial oceans.*
■ (esp. of a state or quality) basic and fundamental: *the primordial needs of the masses.* ■ (of a cell, part, or tissue) in the earliest stage of development.
DERIVATIVES: **pri•mor•di•al•i•ty** |ˌprīˌmôrdē'ælətē| *n.* **pri•mor•di•al•ly** *adv.*
prin•ci•pal |'prinsəpəl| • *adj.* [attrib.] **1** first in order of importance; main: *the country's principal cities.* **2** (of money) denoting an original sum invested or lent: *the principal amount of your investment.* • *n.* **1** the person with the highest authority or most important position in an organization, institution, or group.
■ the head of a school, college, or other educational institution. ■ the leading performer in a concert, play, ballet, or opera. ■ the leading player in each section of an orchestra. **2** a sum of money lent or invested on which interest is paid. **3** a person for whom another acts as an agent or representative.
■ (in law) the person directly responsible for a crime. ■ each of the combatants in a duel (who are supported by *seconds*).
DERIVATIVES: **prin•ci•pal•ship** |-ˌSHip| *n.*

USAGE: **Principal** means 'most important' or 'person in charge': *my principal reason for coming tonight; the high school principal.* It also means 'a capital sum': *the principal would be repaid in five years.* **Principle** means 'rule, basis for conduct': *Her principles kept her from stealing despite her poverty.*

pri•or |ˈprī(ə)r| • *n.* a man who is head of a house or group of houses of certain religious orders, in particular:
■ the man next in rank below an abbot. ■ the head of a house of friars.
DERIVATIVES: **pri•or•ate** |ˈprīərət| *n.* **pri•or•ship** |-ˌSHip| *n.*

pri•or•ess |ˈprīərəs| • *n.* a woman who is head of a house of certain orders of nuns.
■ the woman next in rank below an abbess.

pri•o•ry |ˈprīərē| • *n.* (pl. **-ies**) a small monastery or nunnery that is governed by a prior or prioress.

pris•tine |ˈprisˌtēn; priˈstēn| • *adj.* in its original condition; unspoiled: *pristine copies of an early magazine.*
■ clean and fresh as if new; spotless.
DERIVATIVES: **pris•tine•ly** *adv.*

pri•va•teer |ˌprīvəˈtir| • *n.* an armed ship owned and officered by private individuals holding a government commission and authorized for use in war, esp. in the capture of enemy merchant shipping.
■ (also **privateersman**) a commander or crew member of such a ship, often regarded as a pirate. • *v.* [intrans.] engage in the activities of a privateer.
DERIVATIVES: **pri•va•teer•ing** *n.*

pri•va•tion |prīˈvāSHən| • *n.* a state in which things that are essential for well-being such as food and warmth are scarce or lacking: *years of rationing and privation* | *the privations of life at the front.*
■ the loss or absence of a quality or attribute that is normally present: *cold is the privation of heat.*

priv•i•lege |ˈpriv(ə)lij| • *n.* a special right, advantage, or immunity granted or available only to a particular person or group of people: *education is a right, not a privilege* | *he has been accustomed to wealth and privilege.*
■ something regarded as a rare opportunity and bringing particular pleasure: *I have the privilege of awarding you this grant.* ■ (also **absolute privilege**) (in a parliamentary context) the right to say or write something without the risk of incurring punishment or legal action for defamation. ■ the right of a lawyer or official to refuse to divulge confidential information: *the doctor-patient privilege.* ■ a grant to an individual, corporation, or place of special rights or immunities, esp. in the form of a franchise or monopoly. • *v.* [trans.] grant a privilege or privileges to: *English inheritance law privileged the eldest son.*
■ (usu. **be privileged from**) exempt (someone) from a liability or obligation to which others are subject.

priv•i•ty |ˈprivitē| • *n.* (pl. **-ies**) a relation between two parties that is recognized by law, such as that of blood, lease, or service: *the parties no longer have privity with each other.*

priv•y |ˈprivē| • *adj.* [predic.] (**privy to**) sharing in the knowledge of (something secret or private): *he was no longer privy to her innermost thoughts.*
■ hidden; secret: *a privy place.* • *n.* (pl. **-ies**) **1** a toilet located in a small shed outside a house or other building; outhouse. **2** (in law) a person having a part or interest in any action, matter, or thing.
DERIVATIVES: **priv•i•ly** |ˈprivəlē| *adv.*

prix fixe |ˈprē ˈfēks; ˈfiks| • *n.* a meal consisting of several courses, served at a fixed price.

pro•ac•tive |prōˈæktiv| • *adj.* (of a person, policy, or action) creating or controlling a situation by causing something to happen rather than responding to it after it has happened: *be proactive in identifying and preventing potential problems.*
DERIVATIVES: **pro•ac•tion** |prōˈækSHən| *n.* **pro•ac•tive•ly** *adv.* **pro•ac•tiv•i•ty** |ˌprō ˌæk'tivətē| *n.*

prob•a•bi•lis•tic |ˌpräbəbə'listik| • *adj.* based on or adapted to a theory of probability; subject to or involving chance variation: *the main approaches are either rule-based or probabilistic.*
DERIVATIVES: **prob•a•bi•lism** |ˈpräbəbəˌlizəm| *n.*

pro•bate |ˈprōˌbāt| • *n.* the official proving (establishing genuineness and validity) of a will: *the will was in probate* | [as adj.] *a probate court.*
■ a verified copy of a will with a certificate as handed to the executors. • *v.* [trans.] establish the validity of (a will).

pro•ba•tion |prōˈbāSHən| • *n.* (in law) the release of an offender from actual or potential detention, subject to a period of good behavior under supervision: *I went to court and was put on probation.*
■ the process or period of testing or observing the character or abilities of a person in a certain role, for example, a new employee: *for an initial period of probation, your manager will closely monitor your progress.*
DERIVATIVES: **pro•ba•tion•ar•y** |-ˌnerē| *adj.*

pro•bi•ty |ˈprōbitē| • *n.* the quality of having strong moral principles; honesty and decency.

prob•lem•at•ic |ˌpräblə'mætik| • *adj.* constituting or presenting a problem or difficulty: *the situation was problematic for teachers.* • *n.* a thing that constitutes a problem or difficulty: *the problematics of artificial intelligence.*
DERIVATIVES: **prob•lem•at•i•cal** *adj.* **prob•lem•at•i•cal•ly** |-ik(ə)lē| *adv.*

pro•bos•cis |prəˈbäsəs; -ˈbäskəs| • *n.* (pl. **proboscises**, **proboscides** |-ˈbäsəˌdēz|, or **probosces** |-ˈbäsēz|) the nose of a mammal, esp. when it is long and mobile, such as the trunk of an elephant or the snout of a tapir.
■ (in many insects) an elongated sucking mouthpart that is typically tubular and flexible. ■ (in some worms) an extensible tubular sucking organ.

pro•ce•dure |prə'sējər| • *n.* an established or official way of doing something: *the police are now reviewing procedures| rules of procedure.*
■ (in law) the formal steps to be taken in a legal action; the mode of conducting judicial precedings, as distinguished from the *law* involved.
■ a series of actions conducted in a certain order or manner: *the standard procedure for informing new employees about conditions of work.* ■ a surgical operation: *the procedure is carried out under general anesthesia.*
DERIVATIVES: **pro•ce•dur•al** |-jərəl| *adj.* **pro•ce•dur•al•ly** |-jərəlē| *adv.*

pro•ces•sion•al |prə'seSHənl| • *adj.* of, for, or used in a religious or ceremonial procession: *a processional cross.* • *n.* a book containing litanies and hymns for use in religious processions.
■ a hymn or other musical composition sung or played during a procession.

pro•cliv•i•ty |prō'klivətē; prə-| • *n.* (pl. **-ies**) a tendency to choose or do something regularly; an inclination or predisposition toward a particular thing: *a proclivity for hard work.*

pro•cras•ti•nate |prə'kræstə,nāt; prō-| • *v.* [intrans.] delay or postpone action; put off doing something: *it won't be this price for long, so don't procrastinate.*
DERIVATIVES: **pro•cras•ti•na•tion** |prə,kræstə'nāSHən; prō-| *n.* **pro•cras•ti•na•tor** |-,nātər; prō-| *n.* **pro•cras•ti•na•to•ry** |-nə,tôrē| *adj.*

pro•cre•ate |'prōkrē,āt| • *v.* [intrans.] (of people or animals) produce young; reproduce: *species that procreate by copulation.*
DERIVATIVES: **pro•cre•ant** |-krēənt| *adj.* **pro•cre•a•tion** |,prōkrē'āSHən| *n.* **pro•cre•a•tive** |-,ātiv| *adj.* **pro•cre•a•tor** |-,ātər| *n.*

pro•cure |prə'kyoŏr; prō-| • *v.* [trans.] **1** obtain (something), esp. with care or effort: *food procured for the rebels.*
■ obtain (someone) as a prostitute for another person: *he was charged with procuring a minor.* **2** [with obj. and infinitive] (in law) persuade or cause (someone) to do something: *he procured his wife to sign the agreement.*
DERIVATIVES: **pro•cur•a•ble** *adj.* **pro•cure•ment** *n.* **pro•cur•er** *n.*

prod•i•gal |'prädigəl| • *adj.* **1** spending money or resources freely and recklessly; wastefully extravagant: *prodigal habits die hard.* **2** having or giving something on a lavish scale: *the dessert was prodigal with whipped cream.* • *n.* a person who spends money in a recklessly extravagant way.
■ (also **prodigal son** or **daughter**) a person who leaves home and behaves in such a way, but later makes a repentant return.
DERIVATIVES: **prod•i•gal•i•ty** |,prädə'gælətē| *n.* **prod•i•gal•ly** |'prädig(ə)lē| *adv.*

pro•di•gious |prə'dijəs| • *adj.* **1** remarkably or impressively great in extent, size, or degree: *the stove consumed a prodigious amount of fuel.* **2** unnatural or abnormal: *rumors of prodigious happenings, such as monstrous births.*
DERIVATIVES: **pro•di•gious•ly** *adv.* **pro•di•gious•ness** *n.*

prod•i•gy |'prädəjē| • *n.* (pl. **-ies**) [often with adj.] a person, esp. a young one, endowed with exceptional qualities or abilities: *a pianist who was a child prodigy.*
■ an impressive or outstanding example of a particular quality: *Germany seemed a prodigy of industrial discipline.* ■ an amazing or unusual thing, esp. one out of the ordinary course of nature: *omens and prodigies abound in Livy's work.*

pro•em |'prō,em; -əm| • *n.* a preface or preamble to a book or speech.
DERIVATIVES: **pro•e•mi•al** |prō'emēəl; -'əmēəl| *adj.*

pro•fane |prə'fān; prō-| • *adj.* **1** not relating or devoted to that which is sacred or biblical; secular rather than religious: *a talk that tackled topics both sacred and profane.*
■ (of a person) not initiated into religious rites or any esoteric knowledge: *he was an agnostic, a profane man.* **2** (of a person or personal behavior) not respectful of orthodox religious practice; irreverent.
■ (of language) blasphemous or obscene. • *v.* [trans.] treat (something sacred) with irreverence or disrespect: *it was a serious matter to profane a tomb.*
DERIVATIVES: **prof•a•na•tion** |,präfə'nāSHən; ,prō-| *n.* **pro•fane•ly** *adv.* **pro•fane•ness** *n.* **pro•fan•er** *n.*

pro•fan•i•ty |prə'fænətē; prō-| • *n.* (pl. **-ies**) blasphemous language: *an outburst of profanity.*
■ obscene or vulgar language.
■ a swear word; an oath. ■ irreligious or irreverent behavior.

prof•fer |'präfər| • *v.* [trans.] hold out (something) to someone for acceptance; offer: *he proffered his resignation.* • *n.* an offer or proposal.

pro•fi•cient |prə'fiSHənt| • *adj.* competent or skilled in doing or using something: *I was proficient at my job | she felt reasonably proficient in Italian.* • *n.* a person who is proficient: *he became a proficient in Latin and Greek.*
DERIVATIVES: **pro•fi•cien•cy** *n.* **pro•fi•cient•ly** *adv.*

prof•it•eer |,präfə'tir| • *v.* [intrans.] make or seek to make an excessive or unfair profit, esp. illegally or in a black market: [as n.] (**profiteering**) *war profiteering.* • *n.* a person who profiteers.

prof•li•gate |'präfligət; -lə,gāt| • *adj.* recklessly extravagant or wasteful in the use of resources: *profligate consumers of energy.*
■ given to vice or indulgence; licentious; dissolute: *he succumbed to drink and a profligate lifestyle.* • *n.* a licentious, dissolute person.
DERIVATIVES: **prof•li•ga•cy** |'präfligəsē| *n.* **prof•li•gate•ly** *adv.*

pro for•ma |prō 'fôrmə| • *adv.* as a matter of form or politeness: *he nodded to him pro forma.* • *adj.* done or produced as a matter of form: *pro forma reports.*
■ [attrib.] denoting a standard document or form, esp. an invoice sent in advance of or with goods supplied. ■ [attrib.] (of a financial statement) showing potential or expected

income, costs, assets, or liabilities, esp. in relation to some planned or expected act or situation. • *n.* a standard document or form or financial statement of such a type.

pro•fun•di•ty |prə'fəndətē| • *n.* (pl. **-ies**) deep insight; great depth of knowledge or thought.
■ great depth or intensity of a state, quality, or emotion: *the profundity of her misery.* ■ a statement or idea that shows great knowledge or insight.

pro•fuse |prə'fyŏŏs; prō-| • *adj.* (esp. of something offered or discharged) exuberantly plentiful; abundant: *I offered my profuse apologies.*
■ (of a person) lavish; extravagant: *they are profuse in hospitality.*
DERIVATIVES: **pro•fuse•ly** *adv.* **pro•fuse•ness** *n.* **pro•fu•sion** *n.*

pro•gen•i•tive |prə'jenətiv; prō-| • *adj.* having the quality of producing offspring; having reproductive power.

pro•gen•i•tor |prə'jenətər; prō-| • *n.* a person or thing from which a person, animal, or plant is descended or originates; an ancestor or parent: *the progenitors of many of Scotland's leading noble families.*
■ a person who originates an artistic, political, or intellectual movement: *the progenitor of modern jazz.*
DERIVATIVES: **pro•gen•i•to•ri•al** |-,jenə'tôrēəl| *adj.*

prog•e•ny |'präjənē| • *n.* [treated as sing. or pl.] a descendant or the descendants of a person, animal, or plant; offspring: *the progeny of mixed marriages.*

prog•no•sis |präg'nōsəs| • *n.* (pl. **prognoses** |-,sēz|) the likely course of a disease or ailment: *the disease has a poor prognosis.* Cf. DIAGNOSIS.
■ a forecast of the likely course of a disease or ailment: *it is very difficult to make an accurate prognosis.* ■ a forecast of the likely outcome of a situation: *gloomy prognoses about overpopulation.*

prog•nos•ti•cate |präg'nästə,kāt| • *v.* [trans.] foretell or prophesy: *the economists were prognosticating financial Armageddon.*
DERIVATIVES: **prog•nos•ti•ca•tor** |-,kātər| *n.* **prog•nos•ti•ca•to•ry** |-kə,tôrē| *adj.*

pro•hib•i•tive |prə'hibitiv; prō-| • *adj.* **1** (of a price or charge) excessively high; difficult or impossible to pay: *the costs were prohibitive* | *prohibitive interest rates.* **2** (esp. of a law or rule) forbidding or restricting something: *prohibitive legislation.*
■ (of a condition or situation) preventing someone from doing something: *a wind over force 5 is prohibitive.*
DERIVATIVES: **pro•hib•i•tive•ly** *adv.* **pro•hib•i•tive•ness** *n.*

pro•jec•tile |prə'jektl; -,tīl| • *n.* a missile designed to be fired from a rocket or gun.
■ an object propelled through the air, esp. one thrown as a weapon: *they tried to shield John-son from the projectiles that were being thrown.* • *adj.* [attrib.] of or relating to such a missile or object: *a projectile weapon.*

■ impelled with great force.

pro•kar•y•ote |prō'kerē,ōt| (also **procary-ote**) • *n.* a microscopic single-celled organism that has neither a distinct nucleus with a membrane nor other specialized organelles, including the bacteria and cyanobacteria. Cf. EUKARYOTE.
DERIVATIVES: **pro•kar•y•ot•ic** |prō,kerē'ätik| *adj.*

pro•late |'prō,lāt| • *adj.* (in geometry, of a spheroid) lengthened in the direction of a polar diameter.

prole |prōl| • *n.* a member of the working class; a worker. • *adj.* working-class: *prole soldiers.*

pro•le•gom•e•non |,prōlə'gämə,nän; -nən| • *n.* (pl. **prolegomena** |-'gämənə|) a critical or discursive introduction to a book.
DERIVATIVES: **pro•le•gom•e•nous** |-nəs| *adj.*

pro•lep•sis |prō'lepsəs| • *n.* (pl. **prolepses** |-,sēz|) **1** the anticipation and answering of possible objections in rhetorical speech.
■ anticipation: *in the first of the novella's three parts Marlow gives a prolepsis of the climax.* **2** the representation of a thing as existing before it actually does or did so, as in *he was a dead man when he entered.*
DERIVATIVES: **pro•lep•tic** |-'leptik| *adj.* **pro•lep•ti•cal•ly** |-'leptik(ə)lē| *adv.*

pro•le•tar•i•at |,prōlə'terēət| • *n.* [treated as sing. or pl.] workers or working-class people, regarded collectively (often used with reference to Marxism): *the growth of the industrial proletariat.*
■ the lowest class of citizens in ancient Rome.
DERIVATIVES: **pro•le•tar•i•an** *adj.*

pro•lif•er•ate |prə'lifə,rāt| • *v.* [intrans.] increase rapidly in numbers; multiply: *the science-fiction magazines that proliferated in the 1920s.*
■ (of a cell, structure, or organism) reproduce rapidly: *the Mediterranean faces an ecological disaster if the seaweed continues to proliferate at its present rate.* ■ [trans.] cause (cells, tissue, structures, etc.) to reproduce rapidly: *electro-magnetic radiation can only proliferate cancers already present.* ■ [trans.] produce (something) in large or increasing quantities: *the promise of new technology proliferating options on every hand*
DERIVATIVES: **pro•lif•er•a•tive** |-,rātiv| *adj.* **pro•lif•er•a•tor** |-,rātər| *n.*

pro•lif•ic |prə'lifik| • *adj.* **1** (of a plant, animal, or person) producing much fruit or foliage or many offspring: *in captivity, tigers are prolific breeders.*
■ (of an artist, author, or composer) producing many works: *he was a prolific composer of operas.* ■ (of a sports player) doing or assisting in much scoring: *a prolific home-run hitter.* **2** present in large numbers or quantities; plentiful: *mahogany was once prolific in the tropical forests.*
■ (of a river, area, or season of the year) characterized by plentiful wildlife or produce: *the prolific rivers and lakes of Franklin County.*
DERIVATIVES: **pro•lif•i•ca•cy** |-ikəsē| *n.*

pro•lif•i•cal•ly |-ik(ə)lē| *adv.* **pro•lif•ic•ness** *n.*

pro•lix |prōˈliks| • *adj.* (of speech or writing) using or containing too many words; tediously lengthy: *he found the narrative prolix and discursive.*
DERIVATIVES: **pro•lix•i•ty** |-ˈliksətē| *n.* **pro•lix•ly** *adv.*

pro•lu•sion |prōˈlooZHən| • *n.* a preliminary action or event; a prelude.
■ a preliminary essay or article.

pro•mis•cu•ous |prəˈmiskyəwəs| • *adj.* **1** (of a person) having many sexual relationships, esp. transient ones: *she's a wild, promiscuous girl.*
■ (of sexual behavior or a society) characterized by such relationships: *they ran wild, indulging in promiscuous sex and experimenting with drugs.* **2** demonstrating or implying an undiscriminating or unselective approach; indiscriminate or casual: *the city fathers were promiscuous with their honors.*
■ consisting of a wide range of different things: *Americans are free to pick and choose from a promiscuous array of values and behavior.*
DERIVATIVES: **prom•is•cu•i•ty** |ˌprämə-ˈskyooətē; prəˌmisˈkyoo-| *n.* **prom•is•cu•ous•ly** *adv.* **prom•is•cu•ous•ness** *n.*

prom•is•so•ry |ˈpräməˌsôrē| • *adj.* (in law) conveying or implying a promise: *promissory words.*
■ indicative of something to come; full of promise: *the glow of evening is promissory of the days to come.*

prom•on•to•ry |ˈprämənˌtôrē| • *n.* (pl. **-ies**) a point of high land that juts out into the sea or a large lake; a headland: *a rocky promontory.*
■ a prominence or protuberance on an organ or other structure in the body.

prom•ul•gate |ˈpräməlˌgāt; prōˈməl-| • *v.* [trans.] promote or make widely known (an idea or cause): *these objectives have to be promulgated within the organization.*
■ put (a law or decree) into effect by official proclamation: *in 1852, the new constitution was promulgated.*
DERIVATIVES: **prom•ul•ga•tion** |ˌpräməl-ˈgāSHən; ˌprōməl-| *n.* **prom•ul•ga•tor** |-ˌgātər| *n.*

pro•nate |ˈprōˌnāt| • *v.* [trans.] put or hold (a hand, foot, or limb) with the palm or sole turned downward: [as adj.] **(pronated)** *a pronated foot.* The opposite of *supinate.*
DERIVATIVES: **pro•na•tion** |prōˈnāSHən| *n.* **pro•na•tor** *n.*

prone |prōn| • *adj.* **1** [predic.] **(prone to/prone to do something)** likely to or liable to suffer from, do, or experience something, typically something regrettable or unwelcome: *years of logging had left the mountains prone to mudslides* | *he is prone to jump to conclusions.* **2** lying flat, esp. face downward or on the stomach: *I was lying prone on a foam mattress* | *a prone position.*
■ denoting the position of the forearm with the palm of the hand facing downward. **3** with a downward slope or direction.
DERIVATIVES: **prone•ness** *n.*

pro•pae•deu•tic |ˌprōpiˈd(y)ootik| • *adj.* (of an area of study) serving as a preliminary instruction or as an introduction to further study.
DERIVATIVES: **pro•pae•deu•ti•cal** *adj.*

prop•a•gate |ˈpräpəˌgāt| • *v.* [trans.] **1** breed specimens of (a plant, animal, etc.) by natural processes from the parent stock: *propagating houseplants from cuttings.*
■ [intrans.] (of a plant, animal, etc.) reproduce in such a way. ■ cause (something) to increase in number or amount: *errors propagated during the process.* **2** spread and promote (an idea, theory, knowledge, etc.) widely: *the French propagated the idea that the English were violent and gluttonous drunkards.* **3** [with obj. and adverbial of direction] transmit (motion, light, sound, etc.) in a particular direction or through a medium: *electromagnetic effects can be propagated at a finite velocity only through material substances* | [as adj.] **(propagated)** *a propagated electrical signal.*
■ [intrans.] (of motion, light, sound, etc.) be transmitted or travel in such a way: *a hydraulic fracture is generally expected to propagate in a vertical plane.*
DERIVATIVES: **prop•a•ga•tion** |ˌpräpəˈgā-SHən| *n.* **prop•a•ga•tive** |-ˌgātiv| *adj.* **prop•a•ga•tor** |-ˌgātər| *n.*

pro•pel•lant |prəˈpelənt| • *n.* a thing or substance that causes something to move or be driven forward or outward, in particular:
■ an inert fluid, liquefied under pressure, in which the active contents of an aerosol are dispersed. ■ an explosive that fires bullets from a firearm. ■ a substance used as a reagent in a rocket engine to provide thrust.

pro•pen•si•ty |prəˈpensətē| • *n.* (pl. **-ies**) an inclination or natural tendency to behave in a particular way: *a propensity for violence* | [with infinitive] *their innate propensity to attack one another.*

pro•phy•lac•tic |ˌprōfəˈlaktik| • *adj.* intended to prevent disease: *prophylactic measures.* • *n.* a medicine or course of action used to prevent disease: *I took malaria prophylactics.*
■ a condom.
DERIVATIVES: **pro•phy•lac•ti•cal•ly** |-ik-(ə)lē| *adv.*

pro•phy•lax•is |ˌprōfəˈlaksəs| • *n.* action taken to prevent disease, esp. by specified means or against a specified disease: *the prophylaxis of angina pectoris.*

pro•pin•qui•ty |prəˈpiNGkwətē| • *n.* **1** the state of being close to someone or something; proximity: *he was afraid propinquity might lead him into temptation.* **2** close kinship.

pro•pi•ti•ate |prəˈpiSHēˌāt| • *v.* [trans.] win or regain the favor of (a god, spirit, or person) by doing something that pleases them: *propitiating the gods with sacrifices.*
DERIVATIVES: **pro•pi•ti•a•tion** *n.* **pro•pi•ti•a•tor** |-ˌātər| *n.* **pro•pi•ti•a•to•ry** |-ˈpi-SHēəˌtôrē| *adj.*

pro•pi•tious |prəˈpiSHəs| • *adj.* giving or indicating a good chance of success; favorable: *the timing for such a meeting seemed propitious.*

■ favorably disposed toward someone: *there were moments in which she did not seem propitious.*
DERIVATIVES: **pro•pi•tious•ly** *adv.* **pro•pi•tious•ness** *n.*

pro•po•nent |prə'pōnənt| • *n.* a person who advocates a theory, proposal, or project.

pro•pound |prə'pownd| • *v.* [trans.] put forward (an idea, theory, or point of view) for consideration by others: *he propounded the idea of a "social monarchy."*
DERIVATIVES: **pro•pound•er** *n.*

pro•pri•e•tar•y |p(r)ə'prīə,terē| • *adj.* of or relating to an owner or ownership: *the company has a proprietary right to the property.*

■ (of a product) marketed under and protected by a registered trade name: *proprietary brands of soap.* ■ behaving as if one were the owner of someone or something: *he looked about him with a proprietary air.* • *n.* an owner; proprietor.

■ a grantee or owner of a colony who has been granted, as an individual or as part of a group, the full rights of self-government: *the early proprietaries of Maryland.*

pro•pri•e•ty |p(r)ə'prīət̬ē| • *n.* (pl. **-ies**) the state or quality of conforming to conventional standards of behavior or morals: *always behaved with the utmost propriety.*

■ (**proprieties**) the details or rules of behavior conventionally considered to be correct: *she's a great one for the proprieties.* ■ the condition of being right, appropriate, or fitting: *they questioned the propriety of certain investments made by the township.*

pro•pri•o•cep•tive |,prōprēə'septiv| • *adj.* relating to stimuli that are produced and perceived within an organism, esp. those connected with the position and movement of the body.
DERIVATIVES: **pro•pri•o•cep•tion** |-'sep-sHən| *n.* **pro•pri•o•cep•tive•ly** *adv.* **pro•pri•o•cep•tor** *n.*

pro•rate |prō'rāt; 'prō,rāt| • *v.* [trans.] (usu. **be prorated**) allocate, distribute, or assess proportionally: *bonuses are prorated over the life of a player's contract.*
DERIVATIVES: **pro•ra•tion** |prō'rāSHən| *n.*

pro•rogue |p(r)ə'rōg| • *v.* (**-rogues, -rogued, -roguing**) [trans.] discontinue a session of (a parliament or other legislative assembly) without dissolving it: *James prorogued this Parliament, never to call another one.*

■ [intrans.] (of such an assembly) be discontinued in this way: *the House was all set to prorogue.*
DERIVATIVES: **pro•ro•ga•tion** |,prōrə'gā-SHən| *n.*

pro•sa•ic |prō'zāik| • *adj.* having the style or diction of prose; lacking poetic beauty: *prosaic language.*

■ commonplace; unromantic: *prosaic concerns.*
DERIVATIVES: **pro•sa•i•cal•ly** |-ik(ə)lē| *adv.* **pro•sa•ic•ness** *n.*

pro•sce•ni•um |prə'sēnēəm; prō-| • *n.* (pl.

prosceniums or **proscenia** |-nēə|) the part of a theater stage in front of the curtain.

■ (also **proscenium arch**) an arch framing the opening between the stage and the auditorium in some theaters. ■ the stage of an ancient theater.

pro•scribe |prō'skrīb| • *v.* [trans.] forbid, esp. by law: *strikes remained proscribed in the armed forces.*

■ denounce or condemn: *certain practices that the Catholic Church proscribed, such as polygyny.* ■ outlaw (someone).
DERIVATIVES: **pro•scrip•tion** |-'skrip-SHən| *n.* **pro•scrip•tive** |-'skriptiv| *adj.* **pro•scrip•tive•ly** *adv.*

USAGE: **Proscribe** does not have the same meaning as **prescribe**: see **usage** at PRESCRIBE.

pros•e•cute |'präsi,kyōōt| • *v.* [trans.] **1** institute legal proceedings against (a person or organization): *they were prosecuted for obstructing the highway.*

■ institute legal proceedings in respect of (a claim or offense): *this was a case worth prosecuting* | [intrans.] *the company didn't prosecute because of his age.* ■ [intrans.] (of a lawyer) conduct the case against the party being accused or sued in a lawsuit: *Mr. Ryan will be prosecuting this morning.* **2** continue with (a course of action) with a view to its completion: *the government's ability to prosecute the war.*

■ carry on (a trade or pursuit): *waiting for permission to prosecute my craft.*
DERIVATIVES: **pros•e•cut•a•ble** *adj.*

pros•e•lyte |'präsə,līt| • *n.* a person who has converted from one opinion, religion, or party to another, esp. recently.

■ a Gentile who has converted to Judaism. • *v.* another term for PROSELYTIZE.
DERIVATIVES: **pros•e•lyt•ism** |-lə,tizəm| *n.*

pros•e•lyt•ize |'präsələ,tīz| • *v.* [trans.] convert or attempt to convert (someone) from one religion, belief, or opinion to another: *the program did have a tremendous evangelical effect, proselytizing many* | [intrans.] *proselytizing for converts* | [as n.] (**proselytizing**) *no amount of proselytizing was going to change their minds.*

■ advocate or promote (a belief or course of action).
DERIVATIVES: **pros•e•lyt•iz•er** *n.*

pros•o•dy |'präsədē| • *n.* the patterns of rhythm and sound used in poetry.

■ the theory or study of these patterns, or the rules governing them. ■ the patterns of stress and intonation in a language: *early English prosodies.*
DERIVATIVES: **pro•sod•ic** |prə'sädik; -zädik| *or* **pro•sod•i•cal** *adj.* **pros•o•dist** |'präsədist; 'präz-| *n.*

pro•spec•tus |prə'spektəs| • *n.* (pl. **prospectuses**) a printed document that advertises or describes a school, commercial enterprise, forthcoming book, etc., in order to attract or inform clients, members, buyers, or investors.

pros•tate |'präs‚tāt| (also **prostate gland**) • *n.* a gland surrounding the neck of the bladder in male mammals and releasing a fluid component of semen.
DERIVATIVES: **pros•tat•ic** |prä'stætik| *adj.*
pros•the•sis |präs'THēsis| • *n.* (pl. **prostheses**) **1** an artificial body part, such as a leg, a heart, or a breast implant. **2** (also **prothesis**) the addition of a letter or syllable at the beginning of a word, as in Spanish *escribo* derived from Latin *scribo.*
DERIVATIVES: **pros•thet•ic** |-'THetik| *adj.* **pros•thet•i•cal•ly** |-'THetik(ə)lē| *adv.*
pros•trate • *adj.* |'präs‚trāt| lying stretched out on the ground with one's face downward. Cf. PRONE, SUPINE.
■ [predic.] completely overcome or helpless, esp. with distress or exhaustion: *his wife was* **prostrate with** *shock.* ■ (in botany) growing along the ground. • *v.* [trans.] (**prostrate oneself**) throw oneself flat on the ground so as to be lying face downward, esp. in reverence or submission: *she prostrated herself on the bare floor.*
■ (often **be prostrated**) (of distress, exhaustion, or illness) reduce (someone) to extreme physical weakness: *she was prostrated by a migraine.*
DERIVATIVES: **pros•tra•tion** |prä'strāsHən| *n.*
pro•tag•o•nist |prō'tægənist; prō-| • *n.* the leading character or one of the major characters in a drama, movie, novel, or other fictional text.
■ the main figure or one of the most prominent figures in a real situation: *in this colonial struggle, the main protagonists were Great Britain and France.* ■ an advocate or champion of a particular cause or idea: *a strenuous protagonist of the new agricultural policy.*

USAGE: The first sense of **protagonist**, as originally used in connection with ancient Greek drama, is 'the main character in a play.' In the early 20th century a new sense arose meaning 'a supporter of a cause,' as in *a strenuous* **protagonist** *of the new agricultural policy.* This new sense probably arose by analogy with **antagonist**, the **pro-** in **protagonist** being interpreted as meaning 'in favor of.' In fact, the **prot-** in **protagonist** derives from the Greek root meaning 'first.' **Protagonist** is best used in its original dramatic, theatrical sense, not as a synonym for *supporter* or *proponent.* Further, because of its basic meaning of 'leading character,' such usage as *the play's half-dozen protagonists were well cast* blurs the word's distinctiveness (equivalent to "too many chefs in the kitchen"); *characters,* instead of *protagonists,* would be more accurate and more widely understood.

pro•te•an |'prōtēən; prō'tēən| • *adj.* tending or able to change frequently or easily: *the ameba's protean shape.*
■ able to do many different things; versatile.
DERIVATIVES: **pro•te•an•ism** |-‚nizəm| *n.*
pro•té•gé |'prōtə‚ZHā; ‚prōtə'ZHā| (also **pro-**

tege) • *n.* a person who is guided and supported by an older and more experienced or influential person: *he was an aide and protégé of the former Tennessee senator.*
pro•tein |'prō‚tēn; 'prōtēən| • *n.* any of a class of nitrogenous organic compounds that have large molecules composed of one or more long chains of amino acids and are an essential part of all living organisms, esp. as structural components of body tissues such as muscle, hair, collagen, etc., and as enzymes and antibodies.
■ such substances collectively, esp. as a dietary component: *a diet high in protein.*
DERIVATIVES: **pro•tein•a•ceous** |‚prō‚tē 'nāsHəs; ‚prōtn'asHəs| *adj.*
pro tem |prō 'tem| • *adv. & adj.* for the time being: [as adv.] *a printer that Marisa could use pro tem* | [as adj.] *a pro tem committee* | [as postpositive adj.] *the president pro tem of the Senate.*
pro•to•col |'prōtə‚kôl; -‚käl| • *n.* **1** the official procedure or system of rules governing affairs of state or diplomatic occasions: *protocol forbids the prince from making any public statement in his defense.*
■ the accepted or established code of procedure or behavior in any group, organization, or situation: *what is the protocol for intoducing guest speakers?* ■ (in computing) a set of rules governing the exchange or transmission of data electronically between devices. **2** the original draft of a diplomatic document, esp. of the terms of a treaty agreed to in conference and signed by the parties.
■ an amendment or addition to a treaty or convention. **3** a formal or official record of scientific experimental observations.
■ a procedure for carrying out a scientific experiment or a course of medical treatment.
pro•to•plasm |'prōtə‚plæzəm| • *n.* the translucent material comprising the living part of a cell, including the cytoplasm, nucleus, and other organelles.
DERIVATIVES: **pro•to•plas•mic** |‚prōtə 'plæzmik| *adj.*
pro•to•type |'prōtə‚tīp| • *n.* a first or preliminary model of something, esp. a machine, from which other forms are developed or copied: *a prototype of a new weapon.*
■ a typical example of something: *the prototype of all careerists is Judas.* ■ the archetypal example of a class of living organisms, astronomical objects, or other items: *these objects are the prototypes of a category of rapidly spinning neutron stars.* ■ a building, vehicle, or other object that acts as a pattern for a full-scale model. • *v.* [trans.] make a prototype of (a product).
DERIVATIVES: **pro•to•typ•al** |‚prōtə'tīpəl| *adj.* **pro•to•typ•ic** |‚prōtə'tipik| *adj.* **pro•to•typ•i•cal** |‚prōtə'tipikəl| *adj.* **pro•to•typ•i•cal•ly** |‚prōtə'tipik(ə)lē| *adv.*
pro•tract |prə'trækt; prō-| • *v.* [trans.] **1** extend or prolong: *he had certainly protracted the process.* **2** extend a part of the body. **3** draw (a plan, etc.) to scale.
DERIVATIVES: **pro•trac•tile** *adj.* **pro•trac•tion** |prə'træksHən; prō-| *n.*

pro•trac•tor |ˈprōˌtræktər| • *n.* **1** an instrument for measuring angles, typically in the form of a flat semicircle marked with degrees along the curved edge. **2** (also **protractor muscle**) a muscle serving to extend a part of the body.

pro•trude |prəˈtro͞od; prō-| • *v.* [no obj., with adverbial of direction] extend beyond or above a surface: *something like a fin protruded from the water.*
■ [trans.] (of an animal) cause (a body part) to do this.
DERIVATIVES: **pro•tru•sion** |-ˈtro͞oZHən; prō-| *n.* **pro•tru•sive** |-ˈtro͞osiv; -ziv| *adj.*

pro•tu•ber•ant |prəˈt(y)o͞ob(ə)rənt; prō-| • *adj.* bulging or swelling out; protruding: *his protuberant eyes.*
DERIVATIVES: **pro•tu•ber•ance** *n.* **pro•tu•ber•ant•ly** *adv.*

prov•e•nance |ˈprävənəns| • *n.* the place of origin or earliest known history of something: *an orange rug of Iranian provenance.*
■ the beginning of something's existence; something's origin: *they try to understand the whole universe, its provenance and fate.* ■ a record of ownership of a work of art or an antique, used as a guide to authenticity or quality.

prov•en•der |ˈprävəndər| • *n.* food.
■ animal fodder.

pro•ve•ni•ence |prəˈvinyəns| • *n.* another term for PROVENANCE.

pro•ver•bi•al |prəˈvərbēəl| • *adj.* (of a word or phrase) referred to in a proverb or idiom: *I'm going to stick out like the proverbial sore thumb.*
■ well known, esp. so as to be stereotypical: *the Welsh people, whose hospitality is proverbial.*
DERIVATIVES: **pro•ver•bi•al•i•ty** |-ˌvərbē'ælət̬ē| *n.* **pro•ver•bi•al•ly** *adv.*

prov•i•dence |ˈprävədəns; -ˌdens| • *n.* the protective care of God or of nature as a spiritual power: *they found their trust in divine providence to be a source of comfort.*
■ (**Providence**) God or nature as providing such care: *I live out my life as Providence decrees.* ■ timely preparation for future eventualities: *it was considered a duty to encourage providence.*

prov•i•dent |ˈprävədənt; -ˌdent| • *adj.* making or indicative of timely preparation for the future: *she had learned to be provident.*
DERIVATIVES: **prov•i•dent•ly** *adv.*

prov•i•den•tial |ˌprävə'denCHəl| • *adj.* **1** occurring at a favorable time; opportune: *thanks to that providential snowstorm, the attack had been repulsed.* **2** involving divine foresight or intervention: *God's providential care for each of us.*
DERIVATIVES: **prov•i•den•tial•ly** *adv.*

prov•ince |ˈprävins| • *n.* **1** a principal administrative division of certain countries or empires: *the province of Manitoba.*
■ (**the provinces**) the whole of a country outside the capital, esp. when regarded as lacking in sophistication or culture: *I made my way home to the dreary provinces by train.* ■ an area of the world with respect to its flora, fauna, or physical characteristics: *the inaccessibility of underwater igneous provinces.* ■ (in certain Christian churches) a district under an archbishop or a metropolitan. ■ an historic territory outside Italy under a Roman governor. **2** (**one's province**) an area of special knowledge, interest, or responsibility: *she knew little about wine—that had been her father's province.*

pro•vin•cial |prəˈvinCHəl| • *adj.* **1** of or concerning a province of a country or empire: *provincial elections.*
■ of or pertaining to a style of architecture or furniture in fashion in the provinces of various European countries: *French Provincial furnishing.* **2** of or concerning the regions outside the capital city of a country: *scenes of violence were reported in provincial towns.*
■ unsophisticated or narrow-minded, esp. when considered as typical of such regions. • *n.* **1** an inhabitant of a province of a country or empire. **2** an inhabitant of the regions outside the capital city of a country, esp. when regarded as unsophisticated or narrow-minded. **3** (in the Christian Church) the head or chief of a province or of a religious order in a province.
DERIVATIVES: **pro•vin•ci•al•i•ty** |prəˌvinCHē'ælət̬ē| *n.* **pro•vin•cial•i•za•tion** |prəˌvinCHələ'zāSHən| *n.* **pro•vin•cial•ly** *adv.*

pro•vin•cial•ism |prəˈvinCHəˌlizəm| • *n.* **1** the way of life or mode of thought characteristic of the regions outside the capital city of a country, esp. when regarded as unsophisticated or narrow-minded.
■ narrow-mindedness, insularity, or lack of sophistication: *the myopic provincialism of their ideas.* **2** concern for one's own area or region at the expense of national or supranational unity. **3** a word or phrase peculiar to a local area.
DERIVATIVES: **pro•vin•ci•al•ist** *n.* & *adj.*

pro•vi•sion•al |prəˈviZHənl| • *adj.* arranged or existing for the present, possibly to be changed later: *a provisional government* | *a provisional construction permit.*
■ (of a postage stamp) put into circulation temporarily, usually owing to the unavailability of the definitive issue.

pro•vi•so |prəˈvīzō| • *n.* (pl. **-os**) a condition attached to an agreement: *he left his unborn grandchild a trust fund **with the proviso that** he be named after the old man.*
DERIVATIVES: **pro•vi•so•ry** *adj.*

pro•voc•a•tive |prəˈväkət̬iv| • *adj.* causing annoyance, anger, or another strong reaction, esp. deliberately: *a provocative article* | *his provocative remarks on race.*
■ arousing sexual desire or interest, esp. deliberately.
DERIVATIVES: **pro•voc•a•tive•ly** *adv.* **pro•voc•a•tive•ness** *n.*

pro•vost |ˈprōˌvōst| • *n.* **1** a senior administrative officer in certain colleges and universities.
■ Brit. the head of certain university colleges, esp. at Oxford or Cambridge, and public schools. **2** the head of a chapter in a cathedral.

■ the head of a Christian community.
DERIVATIVES: **pro•vost•ship** |-ˌsHip| *n.*

prox•e•mics |präk'sēmiks| • *plural n.* [treated as sing.] the branch of knowledge that deals with the amount of space that people feel it necessary to set between themselves and others.
DERIVATIVES: **prox•e•mic** *adj.*

prox•i•mal |'präksəməl| • *adj.* situated nearer to the center of the body or the point of attachment: *the proximal end of the forearm.*
■ relating to or denoting an area close to a center of a geological process such as sedimentation or volcanism.
DERIVATIVES: **prox•i•mal•ly** *adv.*

prox•i•mate |'präksəmət| • *adj.* **1** (esp. of a cause of something) closest in relationship; immediate: *that storm was the proximate cause of damage to the system.*
■ closest in space or time: *the failure of the proximate military power to lend assistance.* **2** nearly accurate; approximate: *he would try to change her speech into proximate ladylikeness.*
DERIVATIVES: **prox•i•mate•ly** *adv.* **prox•i•ma•tion** |ˌpräksə'māsHən| *n.*

prox•im•i•ty |präk'simətē| • *n.* nearness in space, time, or relationship: *do not operate microphones in close proximity to television sets.*

prox•i•mo |'präksəˌmō| • *adj.* [postpositive] of next month: *he must be in San Francisco on 1st proximo.*

prox•y |'präksē| • *n.* (pl. **-ies**) **1** the authority to represent someone else, esp. in voting: *they may register to vote **by proxy.***
■ a person authorized to act on behalf of another. ■ a document authorizing a person to vote on another's behalf. **2** a figure that can be used to represent the value of something in a calculation: *the use of a US wealth measure as a **proxy for** the true worldwide measure.*

prude |proōd| • *n.* a person who is or claims to be easily shocked by matters relating to sex or nudity.
DERIVATIVES: **prud•er•y** |'proōdərē| *n.* **prud•ish** *adj.* **prud•ish•ly** *adv.* **prud•ish•ness** *n.*

pru•dent |'proōdnt| • *adj.* acting with or showing care and thought for the future: *a prudent money manager.*
DERIVATIVES: **pru•dence** *n.* **pru•dent•ly** *adv.*

pru•den•tial |proō'denCHəl| • *adj.* involving or showing care and forethought, typically in business: *the prudential manager takes time for employee training.*
DERIVATIVES: **pru•den•tial•ly** *adv.*

pru•ri•ent |'proōrēənt| • *adj.* having or encouraging an excessive interest in sexual matters.
DERIVATIVES: **pru•ri•ence** *n.* **pru•ri•en•cy** *n.* **pru•ri•ent•ly** *adv.*

psal•ter |'sôltər| • *n.* (**the psalter** or **the Psalter**) the biblical Book of Psalms.

psal•ter•y |'sôltərē| • *n.* (pl. **-ies**) an ancient and medieval musical instrument like a dulcimer but played by plucking the strings with the fingers or a plectrum.

pse•phol•o•gy |sē'fäləjē| • *n.* the statistical study of elections and trends in voting.
DERIVATIVES: **pse•pho•log•i•cal** |ˌsēfə'läjikəl| *adj.* **pse•pho•log•i•cal•ly** |-ik(ə)lē| *adv.* **pse•phol•o•gist** |-jist| *n.*

pseud•e•pig•ra•pha |ˌsoōdə'pigrəfə| • *plural n.* spurious or pseudonymous writings, esp. Jewish writings ascribed to various biblical patriarchs and prophets but composed within approximately 200 years of the birth of Christ.
DERIVATIVES: **pseud•e•pig•ra•phal** *adj.* **pseud•e•pi•graph•ic** |ˌsoōd,epi'græfik| *adj.*

pseu•do•nym |'soōdn-im| • *n.* a fictitious name, esp. one used by an author.
DERIVATIVES: **pseu•do•nym•i•ty** |ˌsoōdn 'imətē| *n.*

psy•che |'sīkē| • *n.* the human soul, mind, or spirit: *I will never really fathom the female psyche.*

psy•che•del•ic |ˌsīkə'delik| • *adj.* relating to or denoting drugs (esp. LSD) that produce hallucinations and apparent expansion of consciousness.
■ relating to or denoting a style of rock music originating in the mid-1960s, characterized by musical experimentation and drug-related lyrics. ■ denoting or having an intense, vivid color or a swirling abstract pattern: *a psychedelic T-shirt.* • *n.* a psychedelic drug.
DERIVATIVES: **psy•che•del•i•cal•ly** |-ik(ə)-lē| *adv.*

psy•chi•a•try |sə'kīətrē; sī-| • *n.* the study and treatment of mental illness, emotional disturbance, and abnormal behavior.

psy•chic |'sīkik| • *adj.* **1** relating to or denoting faculties or phenomena that are apparently inexplicable by natural laws, esp. involving telepathy or clairvoyance: *psychic powers.*
■ (of a person) appearing or considered to have powers of telepathy or clairvoyance: *I could sense it—I must be psychic.* **2** of or relating to the soul or mind: *he dulled his psychic pain with gin.* • *n.* a person considered or claiming to have psychic powers; a medium.
■ (**psychics**) [treated as sing. or pl.] the study of psychic phenomena.
DERIVATIVES: **psy•chi•cal** |'sīkikəl| *adj.* (usu. in sense 1). **psy•chi•cal•ly** |'sīkik(ə)lē| *adv.* **psy•chism** |'sī,kizəm| *n.* (in sense 1).

psy•cho•ac•tive |ˌsīkō'æktiv| • *adj.* (chiefly of a drug) affecting the mind.

psy•cho•a•nal•y•sis |ˌsīkōə'næləsəs| • *n.* a system of psychological theory and therapy that aims to treat mental disorders by investigating the interaction of conscious and unconscious elements in the mind and bringing repressed fears and conflicts into the conscious mind by techniques such as dream interpretation and free association.
DERIVATIVES: **psy•cho•an•a•lyze** |ˌsīkō 'ænl,īz| (Brit. **psy•cho•an•a•lyse**) *v.* **psy•cho•an•a•lyt•ic** |ˌsīkō,ænl'itik| *adj.* **psy•cho•an•a•lyt•i•cal** |ˌsīkō,ænl'itikəl| *adj.* **psy•cho•an•a•lyt•i•cal•ly** |ˌsīkō,ænl'itik(ə)-lē| *adv.*

psy•cho•bi•ol•o•gy |ˌsīkō,bī'äləjē| • *n.* the branch of science that deals with the biological basis of behavior and mental phenomena.

DERIVATIVES: **psy·cho·bi·o·log·i·cal** |-,bī-ə'läjəkəl| *adj.* **psy·cho·bi·ol·o·gist** |-jist| *n.*

psy·cho·dra·ma |,sīkō'drämə; -'dræmə| • *n.*
1 a form of psychotherapy in which patients act out events from their past. **2** a play, movie, or novel in which psychological elements are the main interest.
▪ the genre to which such works belong.

DERIVATIVES: **psy·cho·dra·mat·ic** |-drə'mætik| *adj.*

psy·cho·gen·ic |,sīkō'jenik| • *adj.* having a psychological origin or cause rather than a physical one.

psy·chol·o·gy |sī'käləjē| • *n.* the scientific study of the human mind and its functions, esp. those affecting behavior in a given context.
▪ [in sing.] the mental characteristics or attitude of a person or group: *the psychology of Americans in the 1920s.* ▪ [in sing.] the mental and emotional factors governing a situation or activity: *the psychology of interpersonal relationships.*

psy·cho·met·rics |,sīkə'metriks| • *plural n.*
[treated as sing.] the science of measuring mental capacities and processes.

DERIVATIVES: **psy·chom·e·tri·cian** |-mə'trishən| *n.*

psy·chom·e·try |sī'kämətrē| • *n.* **1** the supposed ability to discover facts about an event or person by touching inanimate objects associated with them. **2** another term for PSYCHOMETRICS.

DERIVATIVES: **psy·chom·e·trist** |-trist| *n.*

psy·cho·path |'sīkə,pæTH| • *n.* a person suffering from chronic mental disorder with abnormal or violent social behavior. Cf. SOCIOPATH.

DERIVATIVES: **psy·cho·path·ic** |,sīkə'pæTHik| *adj.* **psy·cho·path·i·cal·ly** |,sīkə'pæTHik(ə)lē| *adv.*

psy·cho·sis |sī'kōsəs| • *n.* (pl. **psychoses** |-,sēz|) a severe mental disorder in which thought and emotions are so impaired that contact is lost with external reality. Cf. NEUROSIS.

DERIVATIVES: **psy·chot·ic** *adj.* **psy·chot·i·cal·ly** *adv.*

psy·cho·so·mat·ic |,sīkōsə'mætik| • *adj.* (of a physical illness or other condition) caused or aggravated by a mental factor such as internal conflict or stress.
▪ of or relating to the interaction of mind and body.

DERIVATIVES: **psy·cho·so·mat·i·cal·ly** |-ik(ə)lē| *adv.*

psy·cho·ther·a·py |,sīkō'THerəpē| • *n.* the treatment of mental disorder by psychological rather than medical means.

DERIVATIVES: **psy·cho·ther·a·peu·tic** |-,THerə'pyŏŏtik| *adj.* **psy·cho·ther·a·pist** |-'THerəpist| *n.*

psy·cho·tro·pic |,sīkə'trōpik; -'träpik| • *adj.* relating to or denoting drugs that affect a person's mental state. • *n.* a drug of this kind.

Ptol·e·ma·ic sys·tem • *n.* (in astronomy)

denoting or relating to the discredited theory that the earth is the stationary center of the universe, with the planets moving in epicyclic orbits within surrounding concentric spheres. Cf. COPERNICAN SYSTEM.

pto·maine |'tō,mān; tō'mān| • *n.* old name for any of a group of amine compounds of unpleasant taste and odor formed in putrefying animal and vegetable matter and formerly thought to cause food poisoning.

pu·bes |'pyŏŏbēz| • *n.* **1** (pl. same) the lower part of the abdomen at the front of the pelvis, covered with hair from puberty. **2** (pl. of **pubis**) either of two bones that form the lower and anterior part of the pelvis.

pu·bes·cent |pyŏŏ'besənt| • *adj.* **1** relating to or denoting a person at or approaching the age of puberty. **2** (in botany and zoology) covered with short soft hair; downy. • *n.* a person at or approaching the age of puberty.

pu·bic |'pyŏŏbik| • *adj.* [attrib.] of or relating to the pubes or pubis: *pubic hair.*

puce |pyŏŏs| • *adj.* of a dark red or purple-brown color. • *n.* a dark red or purple-brown color.

pu·den·dum |pyŏŏ'dendəm| • *n.* (pl. **pudenda** |-'dendə|) (often **pudenda**) a person's external genitals, esp. a woman's.

DERIVATIVES: **pu·den·dal** |-'dendəl| *adj.* **pu·dic** |'pyŏŏdik| *adj.*

pueb·lo |'pweblō; pŏŏ'eb-| • *n.* (pl. **-os**) **1** an American Indian settlement of the southwestern US, esp. one consisting of multistoried adobe houses built by the Pueblo people.
▪ (in Spanish-speaking regions) a town or village. **2** (**Pueblo**) (pl. same or **-os**) a member of any of various American Indian peoples, including the Hopi, occupying pueblo settlements chiefly in New Mexico and Arizona. • *adj.* (**Pueblo**) of, relating to, or denoting the Pueblo or their culture.

pu·er·ile |'pyŏŏ(ə)rəl; 'pyŏŏr,īl| • *adj.* childishly silly and trivial: *you're making puerile excuses.*

DERIVATIVES: **pu·er·ile·ly** *adv.* **pu·er·il·i·ty** |pyŏŏ(ə)'rilətē| *n.* (pl. **-ies**)

pu·er·pe·ri·um |,pyŏŏər'pirēəm| • *n.* the period of about six weeks after childbirth during which the mother's reproductive organs return to their original nonpregnant condition.

DERIVATIVES: **pu·er·per·al** |pyŏŏ'ərpər-əl| *adj.*

pu·gi·list |'pyŏŏjəlist| • *n.* a boxer, esp. a professional one.

DERIVATIVES: **pu·gi·lism** |-,lizəm| *n.* **pu·gi·lis·tic** |,pyŏŏjə'listik| *adj.*

pug·na·cious |pəg'nāshəs| • *adj.* eager or quick to argue, quarrel, or fight.
▪ having the appearance of a willing fighter: *the set of her pugnacious jaw.*

DERIVATIVES: **pug·na·cious·ly** *adv.* **pug·nac·i·ty** |,pəg'næsətē| *n.*

pu·is·sant |'pwisənt; 'pwēsənt; 'pyŏŏəsənt| • *adj.* having great power or influence.

DERIVATIVES: **pu·is·sance** *n.* **pu·is·sant·ly** *adv.*

pul•chri•tude |ˈpəlkrəˌt(y)o͞od| • *n.* beauty.
DERIVATIVES: **pul•chri•tu•di•nous** |ˌpəlkrəˈt(y)o͞odn-əs| *adj.*

pule |pyo͞ol| • *v.* [intrans.] [often as adj.] (**pul•ing**) cry querulously or weakly: *she's no puling infant.*

pul•lu•late |ˈpəlyəˌlāt| • *v.* [intrans.] [often as adj.] (**pullulating**) breed or spread so as to become extremely common: *the pullulating family.*
■ be very crowded; be full of life and activity: *the towers of our pullulating megalopolis.*
DERIVATIVES: **pul•lu•la•tion** |ˌpəlyəˈlāSHən| *n.*

pul•mo•nar•y |ˈpo͝olməˌnerē; ˈpəl-| • *adj.* [attrib.] of or relating to the lungs: *pulmonary blood flow.*

pul•sate |ˈpəlˌsāt| • *v.* [intrans.] expand and contract with strong regular movements: *blood vessels pulsate.*
■ [often as adj.] (**pulsating**) produce a regular throbbing sensation or sound: *a pulsating headache.* ■ [usu. as adj.] (**pulsating**) be very exciting: *victory in a pulsating semifinal.*
DERIVATIVES: **pul•sa•tion** |ˌpəlˈsāSHən| *n.* **pul•sa•tile** *adj.* **pul•sa•tor** |-ˌsātər| *n.* **pul•sa•to•ry** |-sə͟ˌtôrē| *adj.*

punc•til•i•o |ˌpəNGKˈtilēˌō| • *n.* (pl. **-os**) a fine or petty point of conduct or procedure.

punc•til•i•ous |ˌpəNGKˈtilēəs| • *adj.* showing great attention to detail or correct behavior: *he was punctilious in providing every amenity for his guests.*
DERIVATIVES: **punc•til•i•ous•ly** *adv.* **punc•til•i•ous•ness** *n.*

pun•dit |ˈpəndit| • *n.* **1** an expert in a particular subject or field who is frequently called on to give opinions about it to the public: *a globe-trotting financial pundit.* **2** (also **pandit**) a Hindu scholar; a wise man.
DERIVATIVES: **pun•dit•ry** |-trē| *n.* (in sense 1).

pun•gent |ˈpənjənt| • *adj.* having a sharply strong taste or smell: *the pungent smell of frying onions.*
■ (of comment, criticism, or humor) having a sharp and caustic quality.
DERIVATIVES: **pun•gen•cy** |ˈpənjənsē| *n.* **pun•gent•ly** *adv.*

pu•ni•tive |ˈpyo͞onətiv| • *adj.* inflicting or intended as punishment: *he called for punitive measures against the regime.*
■ (of a tax or other charge) extremely high: *a punitive interest rate of 31.3%.*
DERIVATIVES: **pu•ni•tive•ly** |ˈpyo͞onədivlē| *adv.* **pu•ni•tive•ness** *n.*

pu•ny |ˈpyo͞onē| • *adj.* (**punier, puniest**) small and weak: *skeletal, white-faced, puny children.*
■ poor in quality, amount, or size.
DERIVATIVES: **pu•ni•ly** |ˈpyo͞onl-ē| *adv.* **pu•ni•ness** *n.*

pu•pa |ˈpyo͞opə| • *n.* (pl. **pupae** |-ˌpē; -ˌpī|) an insect in its inactive immature form between larva and adult, e.g., a chrysalis.
DERIVATIVES: **pu•pal** *adj.*

pur•blind |ˈpərˌblīnd| • *adj.* having impaired or defective vision.

■ slow or unable to understand; dim-witted.
DERIVATIVES: **pur•blind•ness** |ˈpərˌblīn(d)nis| *n.*

pur•dah |ˈpərdə| • *n.* the custom under which women in certain Muslim and Hindu societies live in a separate room or behind a curtain, or dress in all-enveloping clothes, in order to stay out of the sight of men or strangers.
■ the state of living in such a place or dressing in this way: *she was supposed to be in purdah upstairs.*

pur•ga•tive |ˈpərgətiv| • *adj.* strongly laxative in effect.
■ having the effect of ridding someone of unwanted feelings or memories: *the purgative action of language.* • *n.* a laxative.
■ a thing that rids someone of unwanted feelings or memories: *confrontation would be a purgative.*

purge |pərj| • *v.* [trans.] rid (someone) of an unwanted feeling, memory, or condition, typically giving a sense of cathartic release: *She was now purged of the terrible guilt that had haunted her.*
■ remove (an unwanted feeling, memory, or condition) in such a way. ■ remove (a group of people considered undesirable) from an organization or place, typically in an abrupt or violent manner: *he purged all but 26 of the central committee members.* ■ remove someone from (an organization or place) in such a way: *an opportunity to purge the party of unsatisfactory members.* ■ (in law) atone for or wipe out (a charge of contempt of court). ■ physically remove (something) completely.
■ [intrans.] [often as n.] (**purging**) evacuate one's bowels, esp. as a result of taking a laxative. • *n.* an abrupt or violent removal of a group of people from an organization or place: *a purge of the ruling class.*
■ a laxative.
DERIVATIVES: **pur•ga•tion** *n.* **purg•er** *n.*

Pu•ri•tan |ˈpyoŏrətn| • *n.* a member of a group of English Protestants of the late 16th and 17th centuries who regarded the Reformation of the Church of England under Elizabeth as incomplete and sought to simplify and regulate forms of worship. Cf. PILGRIM.
■ (**puritan**) a person with censorious moral beliefs, esp. about pleasure and sex. • *adj.* of or relating to the Puritans.
■ (**puritan**) having or displaying censorious moral beliefs, esp. about pleasure and sex.
DERIVATIVES: **Pu•ri•tan•ism** |-ˌizəm| (also **pu•ri•tan•ism**) *n.*

pu•ri•tan•i•cal |ˌpyoŏrəˈtænikəl| • *adj.* practicing or affecting strict religious or moral behavior.
DERIVATIVES: **pu•ri•tan•i•cal•ly** |-ik(ə)lē| *adv.*

pur•lieu |ˈpərl(y)o͞o| • *n.* (pl. **purlieus** or **purlieux** |-l(y)o͞o(z)|) the area near or surrounding a place: *the middle-class purlieus of the Bronx.*
■ a person's usual haunts.

pur•loin |pərˈloin| • *v.* [trans.] steal (some-

thing): *he must have managed to purloin a copy of the key.*
DERIVATIVES: **pur•loin•er** *n.*

pur•port • *v.* |pər'pôrt| [with infinitive] appear or claim to be or do something, esp. falsely; profess: *she is not the democrat she purports to be.* • *n.* |'pər,pôrt| the meaning or substance of something, typically a document or speech: *I do not understand the purport of your remarks.*
■ the purpose of a person or thing.
DERIVATIVES: **pur•port•ed** *adj.* **pur•port•ed•ly** |pər'pôrtˌədlē| *adv.*

pur•pos•ive |'pərpəsiv; pər'pō-| • *adj.* having, serving, or done with a purpose: *teaching is a purposive activity.*
DERIVATIVES: **pur•pos•ive•ly** *adv.* **pur•pos•ive•ness** *n.*

pur•sui•vant |'pərs(w)ivənt| • *n.* a follower or attendant.

pu•ru•lent |'pyŏor(y)ələnt| • *adj.* consisting of, containing, or discharging pus.

pur•vey |pər'vā| • *v.* [trans.] provide or supply (food, drink, or other goods) as one's business.
DERIVATIVES: **pur•vey•or** |-'vāər| *n.*

pur•view |'pər,vyŏo| • *n.* [in sing.] the scope of the influence or concerns of something: *such a case might be within the purview of the legislation.* Cf. JURISDICTION.
■ a range of experience or thought: *little information was likely to come within the purview of women.*

pus |pəs| • *n.* a thick yellowish or greenish opaque liquid produced in infected tissue, consisting of dead white blood cells and bacteria with tissue debris and serum.

pu•sil•lan•i•mous |,pyŏosə'lænəməs| • *adj.* showing a lack of courage or determination; timid.
DERIVATIVES: **pu•sil•la•nim•i•ty** |-lə'nimətē| *n.* **pu•sil•lan•i•mous•ly** *adv.*

pus•tule |'pəsCHŏol; 'pəst(y)ŏol| • *n.* a small blister or pimple on the skin containing pus.
■ a small raised spot or rounded swelling, esp. one on a plant resulting from fungal infection.
DERIVATIVES: **pus•tu•lar** |'pəsCHələr; 'pəstyə-| *adj.*

pu•ta•tive |'pyŏotətiv| • *adj.* [attrib.] generally considered or reputed to be: *the putative father of a boy of two.*
DERIVATIVES: **pu•ta•tive•ly** *adv.*

pu•tre•fy |'pyŏotrə,fī| • *v.* (-ies, -ied) [intrans.] (of a body or other organic matter) decay or rot and produce a fetid smell.
DERIVATIVES: **pu•tre•fac•tion** *n.*

pu•tres•cent |pyŏo'tresənt| • *adj.* undergoing the process of decay; rotting: *the odor of putrescent flesh.*
DERIVATIVES: **pu•tres•cence** *n.*

putsch |pŏoCH| • *n.* a violent attempt to overthrow a government.

Pyg•my |'pigmē| (also **Pigmy**) • *n.* (pl. -ies)

a member of certain peoples of very short stature in equatorial Africa and parts of Southeast Asia.
■ **(pygmy)** a very small person, animal, or thing. ■ **(pygmy)** [usu. with adj.] an insignificant person, esp. one who is deficient in a particular respect: *he regarded them as intellectual pigmies.* • *adj.* [attrib.] of, relating to, or denoting the Pygmies: *centuries-old Pygmy chants from central Africa.*
■ **(pygmy)** (of a person or thing) very small.
■ **(pygmy)** used in names of animals and plants that are much smaller than more typical kinds, e.g., **pygmy hippopotamus, pygmy water lily.**
DERIVATIVES: **pyg•me•an** |'pigmēən; pig'mēən| *adj.*

py•lon |'pī,län; -lən| • *n.* an upright structure that is used for support or navigation, in particular:
■ (also **electricity pylon**) a tall towerlike structure used for carrying electricity cables high above the ground. ■ a pillarlike structure on the wing of an aircraft used for carrying an engine, weapon, fuel tank, or other load. ■ a tower or post marking a path for light aircraft, cars, or other vehicles, esp. in racing. ■ a monumental gateway to an ancient Egyptian temple formed by two truncated pyramidal towers.

pyr•a•mid |'pirə,mid| • *n.* an organization or system that is structured with fewer people or things at each level as one approaches the top: *the social pyramid.* ■ a system of financial growth achieved by a small initial investment, with subsequent investments being funded by using unrealized profits as collateral. • *v.* [trans.] heap or stack in the shape of a pyramid: *debt was pyramided on top of unrealistic debt.*
■ achieve a substantial return on (money or property) after making a small initial investment.
DERIVATIVES: **py•ram•i•dal** |pə'ræmədl; ,pirə'midl| *adj.* **py•ram•i•dal•ly** *adv.* **pyr•a•mid•i•cal** |,pirə'midikəl| *adj.* **pyr•a•mid•i•cal•ly** |,pirə'midik(ə)lē| *adv.* .

py•ro•ma•ni•a |,pīrō'mānēə| • *n.* an obsessive desire to set fire to things.
DERIVATIVES: **py•ro•ma•ni•ac** |-'mānē,æk| *n.* **py•ro•ma•ni•a•cal** |-mə'nīəkəl| *adj.* **py•ro•man•ic** |-'mænik| *adj.*

py•ro•tech•nics |,pīrə'tekniks| • *plural n.* a fireworks display.
■ [usu. with adj.] a brilliant performance or display, esp. of a specified skill: *he thrilled his audience with vocal pyrotechnics.* ■ [treated as sing.] the art of making or displaying fireworks.
DERIVATIVES: **py•ro•tech•ni•cal** *adj.* **py•ro•tech•nist** *n.*

pyr•rhic |'pirik| (also **pyrrhic**) • *adj.* [attrib.] (of a victory) won at too great a cost to have been worthwhile for the victor.

Qq

QED • *abbr.* See QUOD ERAT DEMONSTRANDUM.
qua |kwä| • *conj.* in the capacity of; as being: *the role of the teacher qua teacher.*
quad•rant |'kwädrənt| • *n.* each of four quarters of a circle.
■ each of four parts of a plane, sphere, space, or body divided by two lines or planes at right angles: *the right upper quadrant of the kidney.* ■ an instrument used for taking angular measurements of altitude in astronomy and navigation, typically consisting of a graduated quarter circle and a sighting mechanism. ■ a frame fixed to the head of a ship's rudder, to which the steering mechanism is attached.
■ a panel with slots through which a lever is moved to orient or otherwise control a mechanism.
DERIVATIVES: **quad•ran•tal** |kwä'dræn-(t)l| *adj.*
quad•rille |kwä'dril; k(w)ə-| • *n.* a square dance performed typically by four couples and containing five figures, each of which is a complete dance in itself.
■ a piece of music for this dance. ■ each of four groups of riders taking part in a tournament or carousel, distinguished by a special costume or colors. ■ a riding display.
quad•ri•ple•gi•a |ˌkwädrə'plēj(ē)ə| • *n.* paralysis of all four limbs; tetraplegia.
DERIVATIVES: **quad•ri•ple•gic** |-'plējik| *adj. & n.*
quad•roon |kwä'drōōn| • *n.* (esp. in 19th-cent. Louisiana) a person whose parents are a MULATTO and a white person and who is therefore one-quarter black by descent.
quag•mire |'kwægˌmīr| • *n.* a soft boggy area of land that gives way underfoot: *torrential rain turned the building site into a quagmire.*
■ an awkward, complex, or hazardous situation: *a legal quagmire.*
quail • *v.* [intrans.] feel or show fear or apprehension: *she quailed at his heartless words.*
quale |'kwālē| • *n.* (pl. **qualia** |'kwālēə|) (usu. **qualia**) (in philosophy) a quality or property as perceived or experienced by a person.
qual•i•ta•tive |'kwäləˌtāṭiv| • *adj.* relating to, measuring, or measured by the quality of something rather than its quantity: *a qualitative change in the schedule.*
■ (of an adjective) describing the quality of something in size, appearance, value, etc. Such adjectives can be submodified by words such as *very* and have comparative and superlative forms, unlike *classifying* adjectives like *American*, which describe the class something belongs to.
DERIVATIVES: **qual•i•ta•tive•ly** *adv.*
qual•i•ty |'kwäləṭē| • *n.* (pl. **-ies**) 1 the standard of something as measured against other things of a similar kind; the degree of excellence of something: *an improvement in product quality | people today] enjoy a better quality of life.*

■ general excellence of standard or level: *a masterpiece for connoisseurs of quality* | [as adj.] *a wide choice of quality beers.* ■ high social standing: *commanding the admiration of people of quality.* ■ [treated as pl.] people of high social standing: *he's dazed at being called on to speak before quality.* 2 a distinctive attribute or characteristic possessed by someone or something: *he shows strong leadership qualities | the plant's aphrodisiac qualities.*
■ the distinguishing characteristic or characteristics of a speech sound. ■ (in music) another term for TIMBRE. ■ (in logic) the property of a proposition of being affirmative or negative. ■ (in astrology) any of three properties (cardinal, fixed, or mutable), representing types of movement, that a zodiacal sign can possess.
qualm |kwä(l)m; kwô(l)m| • *n.* an uneasy feeling of doubt, worry, or fear, esp. about one's own conduct; a misgiving: *military regimes generally **have no qualms about** controlling the press.*
■ a momentary faint or sick feeling.
DERIVATIVES: **qualm•ish** *adj.*
quan•da•ry |'kwänd(ə)rē| • *n.* (pl. **-ies**) a state of perplexity or uncertainty over what to do in a difficult situation: *Kate is **in a quandary.***
■ a difficult situation; a practical dilemma: *a legal quandary.*
quan•ti•ta•tive |'kwäntəˌtāṭiv| • *adj.* relating to, measuring, or measured by the quantity of something rather than its quality: *quantitative analysis.*
■ denoting or relating to verse whose meter is based on the length of syllables, as in Latin, as opposed to the stress, as in English.
DERIVATIVES: **quan•ti•ta•tive•ly** *adv.*
quan•ti•ty |'kwäntəṭē| • *n.* (pl. **-ies**) 1 the amount or number of a material or immaterial thing not usually estimated by spatial measurement: *the quantity and quality of the fruit can be controlled | note down the sizes, colors, and quantities that you require.*
■ (in logic) the property of a proposition of being universal or particular.
■ a certain, usually specified, amount or number of something: *a small **quantity of** food | if taken in large quantities, the drug can result in liver failure.* ■ (often **quantities**) a considerable number or amount of something: *she was able to drink quantities of beer without degenerating into giggles | many people like to buy in quantity.* 2 the perceived length of a vowel sound or syllable. 3 (in mathematics and physics) a value or component that may be expressed in numbers.
■ the figure or symbol representing this.
quan•tum |'kwäntəm| • *n.* (pl. **quanta** |'kwäntə|) 1 (in physics) a discrete quantity of energy proportional in magnitude to the frequency of the radiation it represents.

■ an analogous discrete amount of any other physical quantity, such as momentum or electric charge. **2** a required or allowed amount, esp. an amount of money legally payable in damages.
■ a share or portion: *each man has only a quantum of compassion.*

quan•tum leap • *n.* a sudden large increase or advance: *a quantum leap in the quality of wines.*

quan•tum me•chan•ics • *plural n.* [treated as sing.] (in physics) the branch of mechanics that deals with the mathematical description of the motion and interaction of subatomic particles, incorporating the concepts of quantization of energy, wave-particle duality, the uncertainty principle, and the correspondence principle.
DERIVATIVES: **quan•tum-me•chan•i•cal** *adj.*

quan•tum me•ru•it |ˌkwäntəm ˈmerəwit| • *n.* [usu. as adj.] (in law) a reasonable sum of money to be paid for services rendered or work done when the amount due is not stipulated in a legally enforceable contract.

quar•an•tine |ˈkwôrənˌtēn| • *n.* a state, period, or place of isolation in which people or animals that have arrived from elsewhere or been exposed to infectious or contagious disease are placed: *many animals die in quarantine.*
■ any comparable period, instance, or state of isolation or detention, esp.a blockade. • *v.* [trans.] impose such isolation on (a person, animal, or place); put in quarantine.

quark |kwärk| • *n.* (in physics) any of a number of subatomic particles carrying a fractional electric charge, postulated as building blocks of larger subatomic particles. Quarks have not been directly observed, but theoretical predictions based on their existence have been confirmed experimentally.

quar•ry • *n.* (pl. **-ies**) an animal pursued by a hunter, hound, predatory mammal, or bird of prey.
■ a thing or person that is chased or sought: *crossed the border in pursuit of their quarry.*

quar•ter•deck |ˈkwôrtərˌdek| • *n.* the part of a ship's upper deck near the stern, traditionally reserved for officers. Cf. FORECASTLE.
■ the officers of a ship or the navy.

quar•tile |ˈkwôrˌtīl; ˈkwôrtl| • *n.* each of four equal groups into which a population can be divided according to the distribution of values of a particular variable.
■ each of the three values of the random variable that divide a population into four such groups.

qua•sar |ˈkwāˌzär| • *n.* a massive and extremely remote celestial object, emitting exceptionally large amounts of energy and typically having a starlike image in a telescope. It has been suggested that quasars contain massive black holes and may represent a stage in the evolution of some galaxies.

quash |kwôsh; kwäsh| • *v.* [trans.] reject as invalid, esp. by legal procedure: *the monetary award was quashed on appeal.*

■ put an end to; suppress: *a hospital executive quashed rumors that nursing staff will lose jobs.*

qua•si |ˈkwäˌzī; ˈkwäzē| • *adv.* that is to say; as it were (introducing an explanation, esp. of etymology): *The Earl of Wilbraham (quasi wild boar ham).*

quat•er•nar•y |ˈkwätərˌnerē| • *adj.* **1** fourth in order or rank; belonging to the fourth order. **2** (**Quaternary**) of, relating to, or denoting the most recent geologic period in the Cenozoic era, following the Tertiary period and comprising the Pleistocene and Holocene epochs. • *n.* (**the Quaternary**) the Quaternary period or the system of deposits laid down during it.

The Quaternary began about 1,640,000 years ago and is still current. Humans and other mammals evolved into their present forms and were strongly affected by the ice ages of the Pleistocene.

quat•tro•cen•to |ˌkwätrōˈCHentō| • *n.* (**the quattrocento**) the 15th century as a period of Italian art or architecture.

qua•ver |ˈkwāvər| • *v.* [intrans.] (of a person's voice) shake or tremble in speaking, typically through nervousness or emotion. • *n.* **1** a shake or tremble in a person's voice. **2** (in music) another term for eighth note
DERIVATIVES: **qua•ver•ing•ly** *adv.* **qua•ver•y** *adj.*

quean |kwēn| • *n.* old term for an impudent or badly behaved girl or woman.
■ a prostitute.

queen |kwēn| • *n.* **1** the female ruler of an independent state, esp. one who inherits the position by right of birth.
■ (also **queen consort**) a king's wife. ■ a woman or thing regarded as excellent or outstanding of its kind: *the queen of romance novelists* | *Venice: Queen of the Adriatic.* ■ a woman or girl chosen to hold the most important position in a festival or event: *football stars and homecoming queens.* **2** a reproductive female in a colony of social ants, bees, wasps, etc. **3** informal a male homosexual, typically one regarded as ostentatiously effeminate.
■ [with modifier] used as part of a figurative compound for a person obsessed, typically sexually, with a specified appetite. A 'drag queen' is a professional female impersonator or a male homosexual transvestite; a 'leather queen' is a male homosexual leather fetishist. • *v.* [trans.] (**queen it over**) (of a woman) behave in an unpleasant and superior way toward.
DERIVATIVES: **queen•dom** |-dəm| *n.* **queen•like** *adj.* **queen•ship** |-ˌSHip| *n.*

quell |kwel| • *v.* [trans.] put an end to (a rebellion or other disorder), typically by the use of force: *extra police were called to quell the disturbance.*
■ subdue or silence someone: *Connor quelled him with a look.* ■ suppress (a feeling, esp. an unpleasant one): *he spoke up again to quell any panic among the youngsters.*
DERIVATIVES: **quell•er** *n.*

que•rist |ˈkwirist| • n. a person who asks questions; a questioner.

quer•u•lous |ˈkwer(y)ələs| • adj. complaining in a petulant or whining manner: she became querulous and demanding.
DERIVATIVES: **quer•u•lous•ly** adv. **quer•u•lous•ness** n.

queue |kyo͞o| • n. **1** chiefly Brit. a line or sequence of people or vehicles awaiting their turn to be attended to or to proceed. **2** (in computing) a list of data items, commands, etc., stored so as to be retrievable in a definite order, usually the order of insertion. **3** a plait of hair worn at the back. • v. (**queues, queued, queuing** or **queueing**) **1** [intrans.] chiefly Brit. take one's place in a queue: in the war they had **queued for** food | [with infinitive] companies are **queuing up** to move to the bay. **2** [trans.] (in computing) arrange in a queue.

quid•di•ty |ˈkwidətē| • n. (pl. **-ies**) the inherent nature or essence of someone or something.
■ a distinctive feature; a peculiarity.

quid•nunc |ˈkwid,nəNGk| • n. an inquisitive and gossipy person.

quid pro quo |ˈkwid ˌprō ˈkwō| • n. (pl. **-os**) a favor or advantage granted in return for something: the pardon was a quid pro quo for their help in releasing hostages.

qui•es•cent |kwēˈesnt; kwī-| • adj. in a state or period of inactivity or dormancy.
DERIVATIVES: **qui•es•cence** n. **qui•es•cent•ly** adv.

qui•e•tus |ˈkwīətəs| • n. (pl. **quietuses**) death or something that causes death, regarded as a release from life.
■ something that has a calming or soothing effect.

quin•tes•sence |kwinˈtesəns| • n. the most perfect or typical example of a quality or class: the secretary is **the quintessence of** political professionalism.
■ the aspect of something regarded as the intrinsic and central constituent of its character: we were all brought up to believe that advertising is **the quintessence of** marketing. ■ a refined essence or extract of a substance. ■ (in classical and medieval philosophy) a fifth substance in addition to the four elements, thought to compose the heavenly bodies and to be latent in all things.

quire |kwīr| • n. four sheets of paper or parchment folded to form eight leaves, as in medieval manuscripts.
■ any collection of leaves one within another in a manuscript or book. ■ 25 (formerly 24) sheets of paper; one twentieth of a ream.

quirk |kwərk| • n. **1** a peculiar behavioral habit: his distaste for travel is an endearing quirk.
■ a strange chance occurrence: a quirk of fate had led her to Dallas that day. ■ a sudden twist, turn, or curve: wry humor put a slight quirk in his mouth. **2** (in architecture) an acute hollow between convex or other moldings. • v. [intrans.] (of a person's mouth or eyebrow) move or twist suddenly, esp. to express surprise or amusement.

■ [trans.] move or twist (one's mouth or eyebrow) in such a way.
DERIVATIVES: **quirk•ish** adj.

quit•claim |ˈkwit,klām| • n. (in law) a formal renunciation or relinquishing of a claim.
■ (**quitclaim deed**) a deed that passes to the grantee only the rights the grantor holds, without any WARRANTY as to their validity. • v. [trans.] renounce or relinquish a claim: Aikins quiclaimed his interest in the three parcels of real estate.

qui vive |ˌkē ˈvēv| • n. (in phrase **on the qui vive**) on the alert or lookout: on the qui vive for fascism.

quix•ot•ic |kwikˈsätik| • adj. exceedingly idealistic; unrealistic and impractical: a vast and perhaps quixotic project.
DERIVATIVES: **quix•ot•i•cal•ly** |-ik(ə)lē| adv. **quix•o•tism** |ˈkwiksə,tizəm| n. **quix•o•try** |ˈkwiksətrē| n.

quiz•zi•cal |ˈkwizəkəl| • adj. (of a person's expression or behavior) indicating mild or amused puzzlement: she gave me a quizzical look.
■ causing mild amusement because of its oddness or strangeness.
DERIVATIVES: **quiz•zi•cal•i•ty** |ˌkwiziˈkælətē| n. **quiz•zi•cal•ly** adv. **quiz•zi•calness** n.

quod e•rat de•mon•stran•dum |kwäd ˈerət ˌdemənˈsträndəm| (abbr.: **QED**) • used to convey that a fact or situation demonstrates the truth of one's theory or claim, esp. to mark the conclusion of a formal (mathematical, logical) proof.

quod•li•bet |ˈkwädli,bet| • n. **1** a topic for or exercise in philosophical or theological discussion. **2** a lighthearted medley of well-known tunes.
DERIVATIVES: **quod•li•be•tar•i•an** |ˌkwädləbəˈterēən| n.

quoin |k(w)oin| • n. **1** an external angle of a wall or building.
■ (also **quoin stone**) any of the stones or bricks forming such an angle; a cornerstone. **2** (in printing) a wedge or expanding mechanical device used for locking a letterpress form into a chase (metal frame). **3** a wedge for raising the level of a gun barrel or for keeping it from rolling. • v. [trans.] **1** provide (a wall) with quoins or corners. **2** (in printing) lock up (a form) with a quoin.

quon•dam |ˈkwändəm; -ˌdæm| • adj. [attrib.] that once was; former: quondam dissidents joined the establishment | its quondam popularity.

quo•rum |ˈkwôrəm| • n. (pl. **quorums**) the minimum number of members of an assembly, legislative body, or society that must be present at any of its meetings to make the proceedings of that meeting valid.

quota |ˈkwōtə| • n. a limited or fixed number or amount of people or things, in particular:
■ a limited quantity of a particular product that under official controls can be produced, exported, or imported: the country may be exceeding its OPEC quota of 1.1 million barrels of oil per day ■ a fixed share of something that

a person or group is entitled to take or receive from a total: *the salmon quota.* ■ a person's share of something that must be done: *a quota of arrests.* ■ a fixed minimum or maximum number of a particular group of people allowed to do something, as immigrants to enter a country, workers to undertake a job, or students to enroll for a course: *they demanded a quota for women on the committee.* ■ (in a system of proportional representation) the minimum number of votes required to elect a candidate. ■ a person's share of a particular thing, quality, or attribute: *a triple quota of charm.*

quo·tid·i·an |kwōˈtidēən| • *adj.* [attrib.] of or occurring every day; daily: *the quotidian traffic.*
■ ordinary or everyday, esp. when mundane: *his story is mired in quotidian details.*

quo·tient |ˈkwōSHənt| • *n.* **1** (in mathematics) a result obtained by dividing one quantity by another. **2** [usu. with adj.] a degree or amount of a specified quality or characteristic: *their cynicism quotient.*

Rr

rab·bi |ˈrabˌī| • *n.* (pl. **rabbis**) a Jewish scholar or teacher, esp. one who studies or teaches Jewish law.
■ a person appointed as a Jewish religious leader.
DERIVATIVES: **rab·bin·ate** |ˈrabənət; -ˌnāt| *n.*
rab·bin·i·cal |rəˈbinikəl; ra-| • *adj.* [attrib.] of or relating to rabbis or to Jewish law or teachings.
DERIVATIVES: **rab·bin·ic** |-ik| *adj.* **rab·bin·i·cal·ly** |-ik(ə)lē| *adv.*
rab·id |ˈrabəd; ˈrā-| • *adj.* **1** having or proceeding from an extreme or fanatical support of or belief in something: *a rabid feminist.* **2** (of an animal) affected with the viral disease rabies.
■ of or connected with rabies.
DERIVATIVES: **rab·id·i·ty** |rəˈbidətē; ra-; rā-| *n.* **rab·id·ly** *adv.* **rab·id·ness** *n.*
rack |rak| • *n.* **1** a framework, typically with rails, bars, hooks, or pegs, for holding or storing things: *a spice rack* | *a magazine rack.*
■ an overhead shelf on a bus, train, or plane for stowing luggage. ■ a vertically barred frame or wagon for holding animal fodder: *a hay rack.* ■ a lift used for elevating and repairing motor vehicles. ■ a set of antlers. ■ a bed. **2** a cogged or toothed bar or rail engaging with a wheel or pinion, or using pegs to adjust the position of something: *a steering rack.* **3** (**the rack**) an instrument of torture consisting of a frame on which the victim was stretched by turning rollers to which the wrists and ankles were tied. • *v.* [trans.] **1** (also **wrack**) (often **be racked**) cause extreme physical or mental pain to; subject to extreme stress: *he was racked with guilt.*
■ torture (someone) on the rack. **2** [with obj. and adverbial of place] place in or on a rack: *the shoes were racked neatly beneath the dresses.*
■ [trans.] put (pool balls) in a rack. **3** raise (rent) above a fair or normal amount.
PHRASES: **go to rack** (or **wrack**) **and ruin** gradually deteriorate in condition because of neglect: *fall into disrepair.* **off the rack** (of clothes) ready-made rather than made to order. **rack** (or **wrack**) **one's brains** (or **brain**) make a great effort to think of or remember something.
▸**rack something up** accumulate or achieve something, typically a score or amount: *Japan is racking up record trade surpluses with the United States.*

USAGE: The relationship between the forms **rack** and **wrack** is complicated. The most common noun sense of **rack** 'a framework for holding and storing things' is always spelled **rack**, never **wrack**. **Wrack** is often used where **rack** should be used, as in the senses denoting 'stretch, twist, torture, oppress, strain, stress,' as from the instrument of torture. **Wrack** is associated with wreckage, ruin, destruction. *Nerve-wracking*, correct, means 'nerve-stretching'; *nerve-wracking*, incorrect, would mean 'nerve-destroying.' In British English the common phrase is usually spelled *rack and ruin*; here **rack** is a variant spelling of **wrack** (Old English *wrǣc*), 'damage, destruction, disaster' (from which we get *wreck*—essentially two words for the same thing. The more common American spelling is *wrack and ruin*; both are correct.

rack·et·eer |ˌrakəˈtir| • *n.* a person who engages in dishonest and fraudulent business dealings, often involving extortion or forms of violence. • *v.* practice fraud, extortion, and other acts of a racketeer.
DERIVATIVES: **rack·et·eer·ing** *n.*
rac·on·teur |ˌrakˌänˈtər; -ən-| (fem. **raconteuse** |ˌrakˌäˈtə(r)z|) • *n.* a person who tells anecdotes in a skillful and amusing way.
ra·di·a·tion |ˌrādēˈāSHən| • *n.* **1** (in physics) the emission of energy as electromagnetic waves or as moving subatomic particles, esp. high-energy particles that cause ionization.
■ the energy transmitted in this way. **2** divergence out from a central point, in particular evolution from an ancestral animal or plant group into a variety of new forms.
DERIVATIVES: **ra·di·a·tion·al** |-ˈāSHənl| *adj.* **ra·di·a·tion·al·ly** |-ˈāSHənl-ē| *adv.*

ra•di•o•graph |ˈrādēō,graf| • *n.* an image produced on a sensitive plate or film by X-rays, gamma rays, or similar radiation, and typically used in medical examination. • *v.* [trans.] produce a radiograph of (something).
DERIVATIVES: **ra•di•og•ra•pher** |,rādēˈägrəfər| *n.* **ra•di•o•graph•ic** |,rādēōˈgrafik| *adj.* **ra•di•o•graph•i•cal•ly** |-ik(ə)lē| *adv.* **ra•di•og•ra•phy** |,rādēˈägrəfē| *n.*

ra•di•ol•o•gy |,rādēˈäləjē| • *n.* the science dealing with X-rays and other high-energy radiation, esp. the use of such radiation for the diagnosis and treatment of disease.
DERIVATIVES: **ra•di•o•log•ic** |,rādēəˈläjik| *adj.* **ra•di•o•log•i•cal** |ˈ,rādēəˈläjikəl| *adj.* **ra•di•o•log•i•cal•ly** |,rādēəˈläjik(ə)lē| *adv.* **ra•di•ol•o•gist** |-jist| *n.*

ra•di•om•e•ter |,rādēˈämitər| • *n.* an instrument for detecting, demonstrating, or measuring the intensity or force of radiation.
DERIVATIVES: **ra•di•o•met•ric** |-əˈmetrik| *adj.* **ra•di•o•met•ri•cal•ly** |-əˈmetrik(ə)lē| *adv.* **ra•di•om•e•try** |-trē| *n.*

ra•di•os•co•py |,rādēˈäskəpē| • *n.* the examination by X-rays or similar radiation of objects opaque to light.
DERIVATIVES: **ra•di•o•scop•ic** |,rādēə'skäpik| *adj.*

raff•ish |ˈrafiSH| • *adj.* unconventional and slightly disreputable, esp. in an attractive manner: *his raffish air.*
DERIVATIVES: **raff•ish•ly** *adv.* **raff•ish•ness** *n.*

ra•gout |raˈgo͞o| • *n.* a highly seasoned dish of meat cut into small pieces and stewed with vegetables. • *v.* [trans.] make a ragout of.

rail • *v.* [intrans.] (**rail against/at/about**) complain or protest strongly and persistently about: *he railed at human fickleness.*
DERIVATIVES: **rail•er** *n.*

rail•ler•y |ˈrālərē| • *n.* good-humored teasing.

rail•road |ˈrāl,rōd| • *n.* (Brit. and Canadian **railway**) **1** a track or set of tracks made of steel rails along which passenger and freight trains run:[as adj.] *a railroad line.* **2** a system of such tracks with the trains, organization, and personnel required for its working: • *v.* **1** [trans.] press (someone) into doing something by rushing or coercion: *she hesitated, unwilling to be railroaded into a decision.*
■ cause (a measure) to be passed or approved quickly by applying pressure: *the bill had been railroaded through the House.* ■ send (someone) to prison without a fair trial or by means of false evidence. **2** [intrans.] [usu. as *n.*] (**railroading**) travel or work on the railroads.

rai•ment |ˈrāmənt| • *n.* clothing: *ladies clothed in raiment bedecked with jewels.*

rai•son d'é•tat |rāˈzôN dāˈtä | • *n.* (pl. **raisons d'état** |rāˈzôN(z)|) a purely political reason for action on the part of a ruler or government, esp. where a departure from openness, justice, or honesty is involved.

rai•son d'ê•tre |rāˈzôN ˈdetr(ə) | • *n.* (pl. **raisons d'être** |rāˈzôN(z)| pronunc. same) the most important reason or purpose for some-

one or something's existence: *an institution whose raison d'être is public service broadcasting.*

Raj |räj| • *n.* (usu. **the Raj**) the former (before 1947) British sovereignty in India: *the last days of the Raj.*
■ (**raj**) (in India) rule; government.

ra•jah |ˈräjə; ˈräzHə| (also **raja**) • *n.* an Indian king or prince.

rake • *n.* a fashionable or wealthy man of dissolute or promiscuous habits.

rak•ish[1] |ˈrākiSH| • *adj.* having or displaying a dashing, jaunty, or slightly disreputable quality or appearance:
DERIVATIVES: **rak•ish•ly** *adv.* **rak•ish•ness** *n.*

rak•ish[2] • *adj.* (esp. of a boat or car) trim and fast-looking, with streamlined angles and curves.

rale |räl; ral| • *n.* (usu. **rales**) an abnormal rattling sound heard when examining unhealthy lungs with a stethoscope.

Ram•a•dan |ˈrämə,dän; ˈræmə,dæn| • *n.* the ninth month of the Muslim year, during which strict fasting is observed from sunrise to sunset.

ram•i•fi•ca•tion |,ræməfəˈkāSHən| • *n.* (usu. **ramifications**) a consequence of an action or event, esp. when complex or unwelcome: *legal ramifications.*
■ a subdivision of a complex structure or process perceived as comparable to a tree's branches: *an extended family with its ramifications of neighboring in-laws.* ■ the action or state of ramifying or being ramified.
DERIVATIVES: **ram•i•fy** *v.*

ram•pa•geous |ræmˈpājəs| • *adj.* boisterously or violently uncontrollable.

ramp•ant |ˈræmpənt| • *adj.* **1** (esp. of something unwelcome or unpleasant) flourishing or spreading unchecked: *political violence was rampant.*
■ (of a person or activity) violent or unrestrained in action or performance: *rampant sex.* ■ (of a plant) lush in growth; luxuriant. **2** [usu. postpositive] (in heraldry, of an animal) represented standing on one hind foot with its forefeet in the air (typically in profile, facing the dexter (right) side, with right hind foot and tail raised, unless otherwise specified): *two gold lions rampant.* **3** (of an arch) springing from a level of support at one height and resting on the other support at a higher level.
DERIVATIVES: **ramp•an•cy** |-pənsē| *n.* **ramp•ant•ly** *adv.*

ran•che•ri•a |,rænCHəˈrēə| • *n.* (in Spanish America and the western US, esp. California) a small Native American settlement.

ran•che•ro |rænˈCHerō| • *n.* (pl. **-os**) a person who farms or works on a ranch, esp. in the southwestern US and Mexico.

ran•cid |ˈrænsid| • *adj.* (of foods containing fat or oil) smelling or tasting unpleasant as a result of being old and stale.
DERIVATIVES: **ran•cid•i•ty** |rænˈsidətē| *n.*

ran•cor |ˈræNGkər| (Brit. **rancour**) • *n.* bitterness or resentfulness, esp. when longstanding: *he spoke without rancor.*

DERIVATIVES: **ran•cor•ous** |-rəs| *adj.*
ran•cor•ous•ly |-k(ə)rəslē| *adv.*

ran•kle |'raNGkəl| • *v.* [intrans.] **1** (of a wound or sore) continue to be painful; fester. **2** (of a comment, event, or fact) cause annoyance or resentment that persists: *the casual manner of his dismissal still rankles.*
■ [trans.] annoy or irritate (someone).

rant |rænt| • *v.* [intrans.] speak or shout at length in a wild, impassioned way. • *n.* a spell of ranting; a tirade: *his rants against organized religion.*
PHRASES: **rant and rave** shout and complain angrily and at length.
DERIVATIVES: **rant•er** **rant•ing•ly** *adv.*

rap |ræp| • *v.* (**rapped, rapping**) **1** [intrans.] talk or chat in an easy and familiar manner: *we could be here all night rapping about the finer points of spiritualism.* **2** [intrans.] perform rap music. • *n.* **1** a type of popular music of black origin in which words are recited rapidly and rhythmically over a prerecorded, typically electronic instrumental backing.
■ a piece of music performed in this style, or the words themselves. Cf. HIP-HOP. **2** informal a talk or discussion, esp. a lengthy or impromptu one: *dropping in after work for a rap over a beer* | [as adj.] *a rap session.* **3** [usu. with adj.] informal a criminal charge, esp. of a specified kind: *he's just been acquitted on a murder rap.*
■ a person or thing's reputation, typically a bad one: *there's no reason why drag queens should get a bad rap.*
PHRASES: **beat the rap** escape punishment for or be acquitted of a crime. **take the rap** informal be punished or blamed, esp. for something that is not one's fault or for which others are equally responsible.

ra•pa•cious |rə'pāSHəs| • *adj.* aggressively greedy or grasping: *rapacious landlords.*
DERIVATIVES: **ra•pa•cious•ly** *adv.* **ra•pa•cious•ness** *n.* **ra•pac•i•ty** |rə'pæsətē| *n.*

ra•pi•er |'rāpēər| • *n.* a thin, light, sharp-pointed sword used for thrusting.
■ [as adj.] (esp. of speech or intelligence) quick and incisive: *rapier wit.*

rap•port |ræ'pôr; rə-| • *n.* a close and harmonious relationship in which the people or groups concerned understand each other's feelings or ideas and communicate well: *there was little rapport between them.*

rap•por•teur |,ræ,pôr'tər| • *n.* a person appointed by an organization to report on the proceedings of its meetings: *the UN rapporteur.*

rap•proche•ment |,ræp,rōSH'mäN; -,rôSH-| • *n.* (esp. in international relations) an establishment or resumption of harmonious relations.

rap•scal•lion |ræp'skælyən| • *n.* a mischievous person.

rapt |ræpt| • *adj.* **1** completely fascinated by what one is seeing or hearing: *Andrew looked at her, rapt.*
■ indicating or characterized by such a state of fascination: *they listened with rapt attention.*
■ filled with an intense and pleasurable emo-

tion; enraptured. **2** having been carried away bodily or transported to heaven: *he was rapt on high.*
DERIVATIVES: **rapt•ly** *adv.* **rapt•ness** *n.*

rap•tor |'ræptər| • *n.* a bird of prey, e.g., an eagle, hawk, falcon, or owl.

rap•to•ri•al |ræp'tôrēəl| • *adj.* (of a bird or other animal) living by seizing prey; predatory.
■ (of a limb or other organ) adapted for seizing prey.
DERIVATIVES: **rap•to•ri•al•ly** *adv.*

rap•ture |'ræpCHər| • *n.* **1** a feeling of intense pleasure or joy: *Leonora listened with rapture.*
■ (**raptures**) expressions of intense pleasure or enthusiasm about something: *the critics went into raptures about her acting.* **2** (**the Rapture**) (according to some millenarian teaching) the transporting of believers to heaven at the second coming of Christ. • *v.* [trans.] (usu. **be raptured**) (according to some millenarian teaching) transport (a believer) from earth to heaven at the second coming of Christ.

ra•ra a•vis |,rerə 'āvis; ,rärə 'äwis| • *n.* (pl. **rarae aves**) another term for *rare bird.*; an exceptional person or thing; a rarity.

rar•e•fied |'rerə,fīd| (also **rarified**) • *adj.* (of air, esp. that at high altitudes) containing less oxygen than usual.
■ esoterically distant from the lives and concerns of ordinary people: *debates about the nature of knowledge can seem very rarefied.*

Ras•ta•far•i•an |,ræstə'ferēən| • *adj.* of or relating to a religious movement of Jamaican origin holding that blacks are the chosen people, that Emperor Haile Selassie (d. 1975) of Ethiopia was the Messiah, and that black people will eventually return to their Africa. • *n.* a member of the Rastafarian religious movement.
DERIVATIVES: **Ras•ta•far•i•an•ism** |-'ferēə,nizəm| *n.*

ratch•et |'ræCHit| • *n.* a device consisting of a bar or wheel with a set of angled teeth in which a pawl, cog, or tooth engages, allowing motion in one direction only.
■ a bar or wheel that has such a set of teeth. ■ a situation or process that is perceived to be deteriorating or changing steadily in a series of irreversible steps: *the best way to reverse the ratchet of socialism.* • *v.* (**ratcheted, ratcheting**) [trans.] operate by means of a ratchet.
■ (**ratchet something up/down**) cause something to rise (or fall) as a step in what is perceived as a steady and irreversible process: *the Bank of Japan ratcheted up interest rates again.* ■ [intrans.] make a sound like a ratchet.

Rathaus |'rät,hows| • *n.* (pl. **Rathäuser** |-,hoizər|) a town hall in a German-speaking country.

rathe |rāTH; ræTH| • *adj.* (of a person or personal actions) prompt and eager.
■ (of flowers or fruit) blooming or ripening early in the year.

raths•kel•ler |'rät,skelər; 'ræt-; 'ræTH-| • *n.* a beer hall or restaurant in a basement.

rat•i•fy |ˈraɾəˌfī| • v. (**-ies, -ied**) [trans.] sign or give formal consent to (a treaty, contract, or agreement), making it officially valid.
DERIVATIVES: **rat•i•fi•a•ble** |ˈraɾəˌfīəbəl| adj. **rat•i•fi•ca•tion** |ˌraɾəfəˈkāSHən| n. **rat•i•fi•er** n.

ra•tio |ˈrāSHŌ; ˈrāSHēˌō| • n. 1 (pl. **-os**) the quantitative relation between two amounts showing the number of times one value contains or is contained within the other: *the ratio of men's jobs to women's is 8 to 1.*
■ the relative value of silver and gold in bimetallic system of currency. 2 (in full, **ratio decidendi** pl. **rationes**) (in law) the principle forming the basis of a judicial decision.

ra•ti•oc•i•nate |ˌraɾēˈōsəˌnāt; ˌraSHē-| • v. [intrans.] form judgments by a process of logic; reason.
DERIVATIVES: **ra•ti•oc•i•na•tion** |-ˌōsəˈnāSHən| n. **ra•ti•oc•i•na•tor** |-ˈōsəˌnāɾər; -ˈäs-| n.

ra•tion•al |ˈraSHənl; ˈraSHnəl| • adj. 1 based on or in accordance with reason or logic: *I'm sure there's a perfectly rational explanation.*
■ (of a person) able to think clearly, sensibly, and logically: *Andrea's upset—she's not being very rational.* ■ endowed with the capacity to reason: *man is a rational being.* 2 (in mathematics, of a number, quantity, or expression) expressible, or containing quantities that are expressible, as a ratio of whole numbers. When expressed as a decimal, a rational number has a finite or recurring expansion. • n. a rational number.
DERIVATIVES: **ra•tion•al•i•ty** |ˌraSHəˈnaləɾē| n. **ra•tion•al•ly** |ˈraSHənl-ē; ˈraSHnəlē| adv.

ra•tion•ale |ˌraSHəˈnal| • n. a set of reasons or a logical basis for a course of action or a particular belief: *explained the rationale behind the change.*

ra•tion•al•ism |ˈraSHənlˌizəm; ˈraSHnəˌlizəm| • n. a belief or theory that opinions and actions should be based on reason and knowledge rather than on religious belief or emotional response.
■ the theory that reason rather than experience is the foundation of certainty in knowledge. ■ the practice of treating reason as the ultimate authority in religion.
DERIVATIVES: **ra•tion•al•ist** n. **ra•tion•al•is•tic** |ˌraSHənlˈistik; ˌraSHnəˈlistik| adj. **ra•tion•al•is•ti•cal•ly** |ˌraSHənlˈistik(ə)lē; ˌraSHnəˈlistik(ə)lē| adv.

ra•tion•al•ize |ˈraSHənlˌīz; ˈraSHnəˌlīz| • v. [trans.] 1 attempt to explain or justify (one's own or another's behavior or attitude) with logical, plausible reasons, even if these are not true or appropriate. 2 Brit. make (a company, process, or industry) more efficient by reorganizing it in such a way as to dispense with unnecessary personnel or equipment.
DERIVATIVES: **ra•tion•al•i•za•tion** |ˌraSHənl-əˈzāSHən; ˌraSHnələ-| n. **ra•tion•al•iz•er** n.

rav•age |ˈravij| • v. [trans.] cause severe and extensive damage to: *fears that a war could ravage their country.* • n. (**ravages**) the severely damaging or destructive effects of something: *his face had withstood the ravages of time.*
■ acts of destruction: *the ravages committed by man.*
DERIVATIVES: **rav•ag•er** n.

rav•el |ˈravəl| • v. (**raveled, raveling** ; Brit. **ravelled, ravelling**) [trans.] 1 (**ravel something out**) untangle or unravel something: *Davy had finished raveling out his herring net* | *sleep raveled out the tangles of his mind.* 2 confuse or complicate (a question or situation). • n. a tangle, cluster, or knot: *a lovely yellow ravel of sunflowers.*

rav•en |ˈravən| • v. [intrans.] (of a wild animal) hunt for prey.
■ [trans.] devour voraciously.
DERIVATIVES: **rav•en•ing** adj.

rav•en•ous |ˈravənəs| • adj. extremely hungry.
■ (of hunger or need) very great; voracious.
DERIVATIVES: **rav•en•ous•ly** adv. **rav•en•ous•ness** n.

rav•ish |ˈraviSH| • v. [trans.] 1 seize and carry off (someone) by force.
■ (of a man) force (a woman or girl) to have sexual intercourse against her will. 2 (often **be ravished**) fill (someone) with intense delight; enrapture.
DERIVATIVES: **rav•ish•er** n. **rav•ish•ment** n.

rav•ish•ing |ˈraviSHiNG| • adj. exciting delight; entrancing: *she looked ravishing.*
DERIVATIVES: **rav•ish•ing•ly** adv.

raze |rāz| • v. [trans.] (usu. **be razed**) completely destroy (a building, town, or other site):

re•act |rēˈakt| • v. [intrans.] respond or behave in a particular way in response to something: *Iraq reacted angrily to Jordan's shift in policy* | *the market reacted by falling a further 3.1%.*
■ (**react against**) respond with hostility, opposition, or a contrary course of action to: *they reacted against the elite art music of their time.* ■ (of a person) suffer from adverse physiological effects after ingesting, breathing, or touching a substance: *many babies react to soy-based formulas.* ■ interact and undergo a chemical or physical change: *the sulfur in the coal reacts with the limestone during combustion.* ■ [trans.] (in chemistry) cause (a substance) to undergo such a change by interacting with another substance. ■ (of stock prices) fall after rising.

re•ac•tance |rēˈaktəns| • n. (in physics) the nonresistive component of impedance in an AC circuit, arising from the effect of inductance or capacitance or both and causing the current to be out of phase with the electromotive force causing it.

re•ac•tion•ar•y |rēˈakSHəˌnerē| • adj. (of a person or a set of views) opposing political or social liberalization or reform. • n. (pl. **-ies**) a person who holds such views.

re•ac•tive |rēˈaktiv| • adj. showing a response to a stimulus: *pupils are reactive to light.*
■ acting in response to a situation rather than creating or controlling it: *a merely reactive ap-*

proach. ■ having a tendency to react chemically. ■ showing an immune response to a specific antigen. ■ (of a disease or illness) caused by a reaction to something: *reactive arthritis.* ■ (in physics) of or relating to reactance: *a reactive load.*

re•a•gent |rē'ajənt| • *n.* a substance or mixture for use in chemical analysis or other reactions.
■ (in earlier use) a substance used to test for the presence of another substance by means of the reaction it produced: *this compound is a very sensitive reagent for copper.*

re•al•ism |'rēə,lizəm; 'riə-| • *n.* **1** the attitude or practice of accepting a situation as it is and being prepared to deal with it accordingly. **2** the quality or fact of representing a person, thing, or situation accurately or in a way that is true to life: *the earthy realism of Raimu's characters.*
■ (in art and literature) the movement or style of representing familiar things as they actually are. **3** (in philosophy) the doctrine that universals or abstract concepts have an objective or absolute existence.
■ the doctrine that matter as the object of perception has real existence and is neither reducible to universal mind or spirit nor dependent on a perceiving agent. Cf. IDEALISM.
DERIVATIVES: **re•al•ist** |'rēəlist| *n.*

realm |relm| • *n.* a kingdom: *the peers of the realm* | *the defense of the realm.*
■ a field or domain of activity or interest: *the realm of applied chemistry* | *it is beyond the realms of possibility.* ■ a primary biogeographical division of the earth's surface.

re•al•po•li•tik |rā'äl,pôli,tēk| • *n.* a system of politics or principles based on practical rather than moral or ideological considerations, specifically, power politics.

real prop•er•ty • *n.* property consisting of land or buildings; realty.

re•al•tor |'rē(ə)ltər; -,tôr; 'rē(ə)lətər| • *n.* a person who acts as an agent for the sale and purchase of buildings and land; a real estate agent.

USAGE: **Realtor** is a legally registered service mark.

re•al•ty |'rē(ə)ltē| • *n.* (in law) a person's real property (land or immovables on or in the land). Cf. PERSONALITY.

re•ap•por•tion |,rēə'pôrsHən| • *v.* [trans.] assign or distribute (something, as representation in a legislature) again or in a different way.
DERIVATIVES: **re•ap•por•tion•ment** *n.*

reave |rēv| • *v.* (past and past part. **reft** |reft|) [intrans.] carry out raids in order to plunder.
■ [trans.] rob (a person or place) of something by force. ■ [trans.] steal (something).
DERIVATIVES: **reav•er** *n.*

re•bar•ba•tive |rə'bärbətiv| • *adj.* unattractive and objectionable: *rebarbative modern buildings.*

re•bate |'rē,bāt| • *n.* a partial refund to someone who has paid too much money for taxes, rent, or a utility.

■ a deduction or discount on a sum of money due. • *v.* |'rē,bāt; ri'bāt| [trans.] pay back (such a sum of money).
DERIVATIVES: **re•bat•a•ble** |'rē,bātəbəl; ri'bāt-| *adj.*

re•bel•lion |ri'belyən| • *n.* an act of violent or open resistance to an established government or ruler.
■ the action or process of resisting authority, control, or convention: *an act of teenage rebellion.*

re•bus |'rēbəs| • *n.* (pl. **rebuses**) a puzzle in which words are represented by combinations of pictures and individual letters; for instance, *apex* might be represented by a picture of an ape followed by a letter *X.*

re•but |ri'bət| • *v.* (**rebutted, rebutting**) [trans.] **1** claim or prove that (evidence or an accusation) is false: *he had to rebut charges of acting for the convenience of his political friends.* **2** drive back or repel (a person or attack).
DERIVATIVES: **re•but•ta•ble** *adj.*

re•but•tal |ri'bətl| • *n.* a refutation or contradiction.

re•cal•ci•trant |ri'kælsətrənt| • *adj.* having an obstinately uncooperative attitude toward authority or discipline: *a class of recalcitrant fifteen-year-olds.* • *n.* a person with such an attitude.
DERIVATIVES: **re•cal•ci•trance** *n.* **re•cal•ci•trant•ly** *adv.*

re•cant |ri'kænt| • *v.* [intrans.] say that one no longer holds an opinion or belief, esp. one considered heretical: *heretics were burned if they would not recant* | [trans.] *Galileo was forced to recant his assertion that the earth orbited the sun.*
DERIVATIVES: **re•can•ta•tion** |,rē,kæn'tā-sHən| *n.* **re•cant•er** *n.*

re•ca•pit•u•late |,rēkə'picHə,lāt| • *v.* [trans.] summarize and state again the main points of: *he began to recapitulate his argument with care.*
■ repeat (an evolutionary or other process) during development and growth.
DERIVATIVES: **re•ca•pit•u•la•to•ry** |-lə,tô-rē| *adj.*

re•cede |ri'sēd| • *v.* [intrans.] go or move back or further away from a previous position: *the flood waters had receded* | *his footsteps receded down the corridor.*
■ (of a quality, feeling, or possibility) gradually diminish: *the prospects of an early end to the war receded.* ■ (of a man's hair) cease to grow at the temples and above the forehead: *his dark hair was was receding a little* | [as adj.] (**receding**) *a receding hairline.* ■ (of a man) begin to go bald in such a way: *Fred was receding a bit.*
■ [usu. as adj.] (**receding**) (of a facial feature) slope backward: *a slightly receding chin.* ■ (**recede from**) withdraw from (an undertaking, promise, or agreement).

re•cen•sion |ri'sencHən| • *n.* a revised edition of a text; an act of making a revised edition of a text.

re•ces•sion |ri'sesHən| • *n.* **1** a period of temporary economic decline during which trade and industrial activity are reduced.

2 the action of receding; motion away from an observer.
DERIVATIVES: **re•ces•sion•ar•y** |-ˌnerē| *adj.*

re•ces•sive |riˈsesiv| • *adj.* **1** relating to or denoting heritable characteristics controlled by genes that are expressed in offspring only when inherited from both parents, i.e., when not masked by a dominant characteristic inherited from one parent. Cf. DOMINANT. **2** undergoing an economic recession: *the recessive housing market.* **3** (in phonetics) of the stress on a word or phrase) tending to fall on the first syllable. • *n.* a recessive trait or gene.
DERIVATIVES: **re•ces•sive•ly** *adv.* **re•ces•sive•ness** *n.* **re•ces•siv•i•ty** |ˌrēˌsesˈivətē| *n.*

re•cher•ché |rəˌSHerˈSHā rəˈSHerˌSHā| • *adj.* rare, exotic, or obscure: *terms a bit recherché for the average reader.*

re•cid•i•vist |riˈsidəvist| • *n.* a convicted criminal who commits further crimes, esp. repeatedly; repeat offender. • *adj.* denoting such a person: *recidivist addict prisoners.*
DERIVATIVES: **re•cid•i•vism** |-ˌvizəm| *n.* **re•cid•i•vis•tic** |riˌsidəˈvistik| *adj.*

re•cip•ro•cal |riˈsiprəkəl| • *adj.* **1** given, felt, or done in return: *she was hoping for some reciprocal gesture.* **2** (of an agreement or obligation) bearing on or binding each of two parties equally: *the treaty is a bilateral commitment with reciprocal rights and duties.*
■ (of a pronoun or verb) expressing mutual action or relationship. **3** (of a course or bearing) differing from a given course or bearing by 180 degrees. **4** (of a mathematical quantity or function) related to another so that their product is one. • *n.* **1** a mathematical expression or function so related to another that their product is one; the quantity obtained by dividing the number one by a given quantity. **2** a pronoun or verb expressing mutual action or relationship, e.g., *each other, fight.*
DERIVATIVES: **re•cip•ro•cal•i•ty** |riˌsiprəˈkalətē| *n.* **re•cip•ro•cal•ly** |-ik(ə)lē| *adv.*

re•cip•ro•cate |riˈsiprəˌkāt| • *v.* **1** [trans.] respond to (a gesture or action) by making a corresponding one: *the favor was reciprocated* | [intrans.] *perhaps I was expected to reciprocate with some remark of my own.*
■ experience the same (love, liking, or affection) for someone as that person does for oneself; requite: *her passion for him was not reciprocated.* **2** [intrans.] [usu. as adj.] (**reciprocating**) (of a part of a machine) move backward and forward in a straight line: *a reciprocating blade.*
DERIVATIVES: **re•cip•ro•ca•tion** |riˌsiprəˈkāSHən| *n.* **re•cip•ro•ca•tor** |-ˌkātər| *n.*

rec•i•ta•tive |ˌres(ə)təˈtēv| • *n.* musical declamation of the kind usual in the narrative and dialogue parts of opera and oratorio, sung in the rhythm of ordinary speech with many words on the same note.

rec•luse |ˈrəkˌlōōs; riˈklōōs; ˈrəkˌlōōz| • *n.* a person who lives a solitary life and tends to avoid other people. • *adj.* favoring a solitary life.

DERIVATIVES: **re•clu•sion** |riˈklōōzHən| *n.* **re•clu•sive** *adj.*

re•cog•ni•zance |riˈkägnəzəns; -ˈkänəzəns| • *n.* (in law) a bond by which a person undertakes before a court or magistrate to observe some condition, esp. to appear when summoned: *he was released on his own recognizance.*

rec•om•pense |ˈrekəmˌpens| • *v.* [trans.] make amends to (someone) for loss or harm suffered; compensate: *offenders should recompense their victims* | *he was recompensed for the wasted time.*
■ pay or reward (someone) for effort or work: *he was handsomely recompensed.* ■ make amends to or reward someone for (loss, harm, or effort): *he thought his loyalty had been inadequately recompensed.* ■ punish or reward (someone) appropriately for an action. • *n.* compensation or reward given for loss or harm suffered or effort made: *substantial damages were paid in recompense.*
■ restitution made or punishment inflicted for a wrong or injury.

rec•on•cile |ˈrekənˌsīl| • *v.* [trans.] (often be **reconciled**) restore friendly relations between: *she wanted to be reconciled with her father* | *the news reconciled us.*
■ cause to coexist in harmony; make or show to be compatible. ■ make (one account) consistent with another, esp. by allowing for transactions begun but not yet completed: *it is not necessary to reconcile the cost accounts to the financial accounts.* ■ settle (a disagreement): *advice on how to reconcile the conflict.*
■ (**reconcile someone to**) make someone accept (a disagreeable or unwelcome thing): *he could not reconcile himself to his mother's illness.*
DERIVATIVES: **rec•on•cil•a•bil•i•ty** |ˌrekənˌsīləˈbilətē| *n.* **rec•on•cil•a•ble** |ˌrekənˈsīləbəl| *adj.* **rec•on•cile•ment** *n.* **rec•on•cil•er** *n.* **rec•on•cil•i•a•tion** |ˌrekənˌsilēˈāSHən| *n.* **rec•on•cil•i•a•to•ry** |ˌrekənˈsilēəˌtôrē| *adj.*

rec•on•dite |ˈrekənˌdīt; riˈkän-| • *adj.* (of a subject or knowledge) little known; abstruse: *the book is full of recondite information.*

re•con•nais•sance |riˈkänəzəns; -səns| • *n.* military observation of a region to locate an enemy or ascertain strategic features: *an excellent aircraft for low-level reconnaissance* | [as adj.] *reconnaissance missions.*
■ preliminary surveying or research: *conducting client reconnaissance.*
DERIVATIVES: **re•con•noi•ter** *v.*

re•con•struc•tion |ˌrēkənˈstrəkSHən| • *n.* the action or process of reconstructing or being reconstructed: *the economic reconstruction of Russia* | [as adj.] *reconstruction work.*
■ a thing that has been rebuilt after being damaged or destroyed: *comparison between the original and the reconstruction.* ■ an impression, model, or reenactment of a past event formed from the available evidence: *a reconstruction of the accident would be staged to try to discover the cause.* ■ (**the Reconstruction**) the period 1865–77, following the Civil War,

during which the states of the Confederacy were controlled by federal government, and during which social legislation, including the granting of new rights to African-Americans, was introduced.
DERIVATIVES: **re•con•struc•tion•al** adj. **re•con•struc•tion•ar•y** adj. **re•con•struc• tion•ist** n., adj.

re•coup |riˈko͞op| • v. [trans.] regain (something lost): rains have helped recoup water levels. ■ regain (money spent or lost), esp. through subsequent profits: oil companies are keen to recoup their investment. ■ reimburse or compensate (someone) for money spent or lost. ■ (in law) deduct or keep back (part of a sum due). ■ regain (lost physical or mental resources): she needed to recoup her strength | [intrans.] he's recouping from the trial.
DERIVATIVES: **re•coup•a•ble** adj. **re•coup• ment** n.

re•course |ˈrēˌkôrs; riˈkôrs| • n. [in sing.] a source of help in a difficult situation: surgery may be the only recourse. ■ (**recourse to**) the use of someone or something as a source of help in a difficult situation: a means of solving disputes without recourse to courts of law. ■ the legal right to demand compensation or payment: the bank has recourse against the exporter for losses incurred.

rec•re•ant |ˈrekrēənt| • adj. 1 confessing oneself to be vanquished; cowardly. 2 unfaithful to a belief; apostate. • n. 1 a coward. 2 a person who is unfaithful to a belief; an apostate.
DERIVATIVES: **rec•re•an•cy** |-ənsē| n. **rec•re•ant•ly** adv.

re•crim•i•nate |riˈkriməˌnāt| • v. [intrans.] make counteraccusations: his party would never recriminate, never return evil for evil.
DERIVATIVES: **re•crim•i•na•tion** n. **re• crim•i•na•tive** adj. **re•crim•i•na•to•ry** adj.

re•cru•desce |ˌrēkro͞oˈdes| • v. [intrans.] break out again; recur.
DERIVATIVES: **re•cru•des•cence** |-ˈdesns| n. **re•cru•des•cent** |-ˈdesənt| adj.

rec•ti•fy |ˈrektəˌfī| • v. (-ies, -ied) [trans.] 1 put (something) right; correct: mistakes made now cannot be rectified later | efforts to rectify the situation. ■ [usu. as adj.] (**rectified**) purify or refine (a substance), esp. by repeated distillation: add 10 cc of rectified alcohol. 2 convert (alternating electrical current) to direct current: [as adj.] (**rectified**) rectified AC power systems. 3 find a straight line equal in length to (a curve).
DERIVATIVES: **rec•ti•fi•a•ble** adj. **rec•ti•fi• ca•tion** |ˌrektəfiˈkāSHən| n.

rec•ti•lin•e•ar |ˌrektəˈlinēər| (also **rectilineal** |-ēəl|) • adj. contained by, consisting of, or moving in a straight line or lines: a rectilinear waveform.
DERIVATIVES: **rec•ti•lin•e•ar•i•ty** |-ˌlinē ˈeritē| n. **rec•ti•lin•e•ar•ly** adv.

rec•ti•tude |ˈrektəˌt(y)o͞od| • n. morally correct behavior or thinking; righteousness: a model of rectitude.

rec•to |ˈrektō| • n. (pl. **-os**) a right-hand page of an open book, or the front of a loose document. Cf. VERSO.

rec•tor |ˈrektər| • n. 1 (in the Episcopal Church) a member of the clergy who has charge of a parish. ■ (in the Roman Catholic Church) a priest in charge of a church or of a religious institution. ■ (in the Church of England) the incumbent of a parish where all tithes formerly passed to the incumbent. Cf. VICAR. 2 the head of certain universities, colleges, and schools.
DERIVATIVES: **rec•tor•ate** |-rət| n. **rec•to• ri•al** |rekˈtôrēəl| adj. **rec•tor•ship** |-ˌSHip| n.

rec•to•ry |ˈrektərē| • n. (pl. **-ies**) a rector's house. 2 Brit. the benefice of a rector.

re•cum•bent |riˈkəmbənt| • adj. (esp. of a person or human figure) lying down: recumbent statues. ■ denoting a bicycle designed to be ridden lying almost flat on one's back. ■ (of a plant) growing close to the ground: recumbent shrubs.
DERIVATIVES: **re•cum•ben•cy** n. **re•cum• bent•ly** adv.

re•cu•per•ate |riˈko͞opəˌrāt| • v. 1 [intrans.] recover from illness or exertion: recuperating from a wound. 2 [trans.] recover or regain (something lost or taken): they will seek to recuperate the investment returns.
DERIVATIVES: **re•cu•per•a•ble** |-pərəbəl| adj.

re•cur |riˈkər| • v. (**recurred, recurring**) [intrans.] occur again, periodically or repeatedly: the symptoms recurred | [as adj.] (**recurring**) a recurring theme. ■ (of a thought, image, or memory) come back to one's mind: Steve's words kept recurring to him. ■ (**recur to**) go back to (something) in thought or speech: the book remained a favorite and she constantly recurred to it.
DERIVATIVES: **re•cur•rence** |riˈkərəns| n.

re•cur•rent |riˈkərənt| • adj. 1 occurring often or repeatedly, esp. (of a disease or symptom) recurring after apparent cure or remission: a recurrent fever. 2 (of a nerve or blood vessel) turning back so as to reverse direction.
DERIVATIVES: **re•cur•rent•ly** adv.

re•cur•sive |riˈkərsiv| • adj. characterized by recurrence or repetition, in particular: ■ relating to or involving the repeated application of a rule, definition, or procedure to successive results. ■ relating to or involving a computer program or routine of which a part requires the application of the whole, so that its explicit interpretation requires in general many successive executions.
DERIVATIVES: **re•cur•sive•ly** adv.

re•curve |rēˈkərv| • v. [intrans.] bend backward: [as adj.] (**recurved**) large recurved tusks. • n. (in archery) a bow that curves forward at the ends, which straighten out under tension when the bow is drawn.
DERIVATIVES: **re•cur•va•ture** |-vəCHər| n.

rec•u•sant |ˈrekyəzənt; riˈkyo͞ozənt| • n. a

person who refuses to submit to an authority or to comply with a regulation.
DERIVATIVES: **rec•u•sance** n. **rec•u•san•cy** |-zənsē| n.
re•cuse |ri'kyōōz| • v. [trans.] challenge (a judge, prosecutor, or juror) as unqualified to perform legal duties because of a possible conflict of interest or lack of impartiality: *a motion to recuse the prosecutor.*
■ (**recuse oneself**) (of a judge) excuse oneself from a case because of a possible conflict of interest or lack of impartiality.
DERIVATIVES: **re•cus•al** |-zəl| n.
re•dact |ri'dækt| • v. [trans.] edit (text) for publication.
DERIVATIVES: **re•dac•tor** |-tər| n.
re•deem |ri'dēm| • v. [trans.] **1** compensate for the faults or bad aspects of (something): *a disappointing debate redeemed only by an outstanding speech* | [as adj.] (**redeeming**) *the splendid views are the one redeeming feature of the center.*
■ (**redeem oneself**) do something that compensates for poor past performance or behavior: *they redeemed themselves in the playoffs by pushing the Red Wings to a seventh game.* ■ (of a person) atone or make amends for (error or evil): *the thief on the cross who by a single act redeemed a life of evil.* ■ save (someone) from sin, error, or evil: *he was a sinner, redeemed by the grace of God.* **2** gain or regain possession of (something) in exchange for payment: *his best suit had been redeemed from the pawnbrokers.*
■ repay (a stock, bond, or other instrument) at the maturity date. ■ exchange (a coupon, voucher, or trading stamp) for merchandise, a discount, or money. ■ pay the necessary money to clear (a debt): *owners were unable to redeem their mortgages.* ■ exchange (paper money) for gold or silver. ■ fulfill or carry out (a pledge or promise): *the party prepared to redeem the pledges of the past three years.* ■ buy the freedom of.
DERIVATIVES: **re•deem•a•ble** adj.
re•demp•tion |ri'dempsHən| • n. **1** the action of saving or being saved from sin, error, or evil: *God's plans for the redemption of his world.*
■ [in sing.] a thing that saves someone from error or evil: *his marginalization by Hollywood proved to be his redemption.* **2** the action of regaining or gaining possession of something in exchange for payment, or clearing a debt.
■ the action of buying one's freedom.
red•in•te•grate |ri'dintə,grāt| • v. [trans.] restore (something) to a state of wholeness, unity, or perfection.
DERIVATIVES: **red•in•te•gra•tion** |ri,dintə 'grāsHən| n. **red•in•te•gra•tive** |-,grāṭiv| adj.
re•di•rect |,rēdə'rekt; ,rē,dī'rekt| • v. [trans.] direct (something) to a new or different place or purpose: *get the post office to redirect your mail* | *resources were redirected to a major project.* • n. (in law) (also **redirect examination**) examination of a witness a second time by the party who introduced him or her, following cross-examination.

DERIVATIVES: **re•di•rec•tion** |-'reksHən| n.
red•i•vi•vus |,redə'vīvəs; -'vēvəs| • adj. [postpositive] brought back to life; reborn: *a sort of Poe redivivus.*
red•neck |'red,nek| • n. offensive a working-class white person, esp. a politically reactionary one from a rural area.
red•o•lent |'redl-ənt| • adj. **1** [predic.] (**redolent of/with**) strongly reminiscent or suggestive of (something): *names redolent of history and tradition.*
■ strongly smelling of something: *the church was old, dark, and redolent of incense.* **2** fragrant or sweet-smelling: *a rich, inky, redolent wine.*
DERIVATIVES: **red•o•lence** n. **red•o•lent•ly** adv.
re•dou•ble |rē'dəbəl| • v. [trans.] make much greater, more intense, or more numerous: *we will redouble our efforts to reform agricultural policy.*
■ [intrans.] become greater or more intense or numerous: *pressure to solve the problem has redoubled.* ■ [intrans.] (in bridge) double a bid already doubled by an opponent. • n. (in bridge) a call that doubles a bid already doubled by an opponent.
re•doubt |ri'dowt| • n. a temporary or supplementary fortification, typically square or polygonal and without flanking defenses.
■ an entrenched stronghold or refuge.
re•doubt•a•ble |ri'dowṭəbəl| • adj. (of a person) formidable, esp. as an opponent: *he was a redoubtable debater.*
DERIVATIVES: **re•doubt•a•bly** |-blē| adv.
re•dound |ri'downd| • v. [intrans.] **1** (**redound to**) contribute greatly to (a person's credit or honor): *his latest diplomatic effort will redound to his credit.* **2** (**redound upon**) come back upon; rebound on: *may his sin redound upon his head!*
re•dress |ri'dres; 'rē,dres| • v. [trans.] remedy or set right (an undesirable or unfair situation): *the power to redress the grievances of our citizens.*
■ set upright again: *some ambitious architect being called to redress a leaning wall.* • n. remedy or compensation for a wrong or grievance: *those seeking redress for an infringement of rights.*
DERIVATIVES: **re•dress•a•ble** adj. **re•dress•al** |-əl| n. **re•dress•er** n.
re•duce |ri'd(y)ōōs| • v. [trans.] **1** (in cooking) boil (a sauce or other liquid) so that it becomes thicker and more concentrated. **2** (in older military use) conquer (a place), in particular besiege and capture (a town or fortress). **3** (in photography) make (a negative or print) less dense. **4** articulate (a speech sound) in a way requiring less muscular effort. In vowels, this gives rise to a more central articulatory position. **5** (**reduce something to**) change a substance to (a different or more basic form): *it is difficult to understand how lava could have been reduced to dust.*
■ present a problem or subject in (a simplified form): *he reduces unimaginable statistics to manageable proportions.* ■ convert a fraction to (the form with the lowest terms). **6** (in chem-

istry) cause to combine chemically with hydrogen. ■ undergo or cause to undergo a reaction in which electrons are gained from another substance or molecule. Cf. OXIDIZE. **7** restore (a dislocated part) to its proper position by manipulation or surgery. ■ remedy (a dislocation) in such a way.

DERIVATIVES: **re•duc•er** n.

re•dun•dant |ri'dəndənt| • adj. no longer needed or useful; superfluous: a new use for a redundant church. ■ (of words or data) able to be omitted without loss of meaning or function. ■ (in engineering, of a component) not strictly necessary to functioning but included in case of failure in another component. ■ Brit. (of a person) no longer in employment because there is no more work available: eight permanent staff were made redundant.

DERIVATIVES: **re•dun•dan•cy** n. **re•dun•dant•ly** adv.

re•dux |rē'dəks; 'rē'dəks| • adj. [postpositive] brought back; revived: the '80s were more than just the '50s redux.

reeve[1] |rēv| • n. Canadian the president of a village or town council. ■ a local official, in particular the chief magistrate of a town or district in Anglo-Saxon England.

reeve[2] |rēv| • v. (past and past part. **rove** |rōv| or **reeved**) [trans.] (in nautical use) thread (a rope or rod) through a ring or other aperture, esp. in a block: one end of the new rope was reeved through the chain. ■ fasten (a rope or block) in this way.

re•fec•tion |ri'fekSHən| • n. refreshment by food or drink. ■ a meal, esp. a light one. ■ the eating of partly digested fecal pellets, as practiced by rabbits.

re•fec•to•ry |ri'fekt(ə)rē| • n. (pl. **-ies**) a room used for communal meals, esp. in an educational or religious institution.

ref•er•en•dum |,refə'rendəm| • n. (pl. **referendums** or **referenda** |-də|) a general vote by the electorate on a single political question that has been referred to them for a direct decision. Cf. INITIATIVE. ■ the process of referring a political question to the electorate for this purpose.

ref•er•ent |'ref(ə)rənt| • n. the thing that a word or phrase denotes or stands for: "the Morning Star" and "the Evening Star" have the same referent (the planet Venus).

re•flec•tive |ri'flektiv| • adj. **1** providing a reflection; capable of reflecting light or other radiation: reflective glass | reflective clothing. ■ produced by reflection: a colorful reflective glow. **2** relating to or characterized by deep thought; thoughtful: a quiet, reflective, astute man.

DERIVATIVES: **re•flec•tive•ly** adv. **re•flec•tive•ness** n.

re•flex |'rē,fleks| • n. **1** an action that is performed without conscious thought as a response to a stimulus: a newborn baby is equipped with basic reflexes. ■ (**reflexes**) a person's ability to perform such

actions, esp. quickly: he was saved by his superb reflexes. ■ (in reflexology) a response in a part of the body to stimulation of a corresponding point on the feet, hands, or head: [as adj.] reflex points. **2** a thing that is determined by and reproduces the essential features or qualities of something else: politics was no more than a reflex of economics. ■ a word formed by development from an earlier stage of a language. ■ a reflected source of light: the reflex from the window lit his face. • adj. **1** (of an action) performed without conscious thought as an automatic response to a stimulus: sneezing is a reflex action. **2** (of an angle) exceeding 180°. ■ (of light) reflected. ■ bent or turned backward. ■ (of a thought) directed or turned back upon the mind itself; introspective.

DERIVATIVES: **re•flex•ly** |'rē,flekslē; ri 'flekslē| adv.

re•flex•ive |ri'fleksiv| • adj. **1** denoting a pronoun that refers back to the subject of the clause in which it is used, e.g., myself, themselves. ■ (of a verb or clause) having a reflexive pronoun as its object, e.g., wash oneself. **2** (of an action) performed as a reflex, without conscious thought: at concerts like this one, standing ovations have become reflexive. **3** (in logic, of a relation) always holding between a term and itself. **4** (of a method or theory in the social sciences) taking account of itself or of the effect of the personality or presence of the researcher on what is being investigated. • n. a reflexive word or form, esp. a pronoun.

DERIVATIVES: **re•flex•ive•ly** adv. **re•flex•ive•ness** n. **re•flex•iv•i•ty** |ri,flek'sivətē; ,rē flek-| n.

re•flex•ol•o•gy |,rēflek'säləjē| • n. **1** a system of massage used to relieve tension and treat illness, based on the theory that there are reflex points on the feet, hands, and head linked to every part of the body. **2** the scientific study of reflex action as it affects behavior.

DERIVATIVES: **re•flex•ol•o•gist** |-jist| n. (usu. in sense 1).

re•flux |'rē,fləks| • n. (in chemistry) the process of boiling a liquid so that any vapor is liquefied and returned to the stock. ■ the flowing back of a liquid, esp. that of a fluid in the body. • v. [intrans.] (in chemistry) boil or cause to boil in circumstances such that the vapor returns to the stock of liquid after condensing. ■ [no obj., with adverbial of direction] (of a liquid, esp. a bodily fluid) flow back.

re•fract |ri'frakt| • v. [trans.] (usu. be refracted) (of water, air, or glass) make (a ray of light) change direction when it enters at an angle: the rays of light are refracted by the material of the lens. ■ measure the focusing characteristics of (an eye) or of the eyes of (someone).

DERIVATIVES: **re•frac•tion** n.

re•frac•to•ry |ri'fraktərē| • adj. **1** stubborn or unmanageable: a refractory pony. **2** resistant to a process or stimulus: *some granules are* **refractory to** *secretory stimuli.* ■ (of a person, illness, or diseased tissue) not yielding to treatment: *healing of previously refractory ulcers.* ■ (of a person or animal) resistant to infection. ■ (of a substance) resistant to heat; hard to melt or fuse. • *n.* (pl. **-ies**) a substance that is resistant to heat.

DERIVATIVES: **re•frac•to•ri•ness** *n.*

reft |reft| past and past participle of REAVE.

re•ful•gent |ri'fo͞oljənt; -'fəljənt| • *adj.* shining brightly: *refulgent blue eyes.*

DERIVATIVES: **re•ful•gence** *n.* **re•ful•gent•ly** *adv.*

re•fur•bish |ri'fərbiSH| • *v.* [trans.] (usu. **be refurbished**) renovate and redecorate (something, esp. a building).

DERIVATIVES: **re•fur•bish•ment** *n.*

re•fute |ri'fyo͞ot| • *v.* [trans.] prove (a statement or theory) to be wrong or false; disprove: *these claims have not been convincingly refuted.*

■ prove that (someone) is wrong. ■ deny or contradict (a statement or accusation): *a spokesman totally refuted the allegation of bias.*

DERIVATIVES: **re•fut•a•ble** *adj.* **re•fut•al** |-'fyo͞otl| *n.* (rare) **ref•u•ta•tion** |ˌrefyo͞o'tāSHən| *n.* **re•fut•er** *n.*

USAGE: **Refute** and **repudiate** are sometimes confused. To **refute** is to actually prove something or someone to be false or erroneous (*attempts to refute Einstein's theory*), whereas to **repudiate** is 'to reject as baseless, disown, refuse to acknowledge.' One could **repudiate** by silently turning one's back; to **refute** would require disproving by argument. In the second half of the 20th century, a more general sense developed from the core one, meaning simply 'deny,' as in *I absolutely refute the charges made against me.* Traditionalists object to the second use on the grounds that it is an unacceptable degradation of the language.

re•gale |ri'gāl| • *v.* [trans.] entertain or amuse (someone) with talk: *he regaled her with a colorful account of that afternoon's meeting.*

■ lavishly supply (someone) with food or drink: *he was regaled with excellent home cooking.*

re•ga•li•a |ri'gālyə| • *plural n.* [treated as sing. or pl.] the emblems or insignia of royalty, esp. the crown, scepter, and other ornaments used at a coronation.

■ the distinctive clothing worn and ornaments carried at formal occasions as an indication of status: *a Bishop in full regalia.* ■ distinctive, elaborate clothing: *young men, a few in gang regalia.*

USAGE: The word **regalia** comes from Latin and is, technically speaking, the plural of *regalis.* However, in the way the word is used in English today it behaves as a collective noun, similar to words like **staff** or **government.** This means that it can be used with either a singular or plural verb (*the regalia of Russian czardom is now displayed in the Kremlin* or *the regalia of Russian czardom are now displayed in the Kremlin*), but it has no other singular form.

re•gat•ta |ri'gätə; ri'gætə| • *n.* a sporting event consisting of a series of boat or yacht races.

re•gen•cy |'rējənsē| • *n.* (pl. **-ies**) the office or period of government by a regent.

■ a commission acting as regent. ■ (**the Regency**) the particular period of a regency, esp. (in Britain) from 1811 to 1820 and (in France) from 1715 to 1723. • *adj.* (**Regency**) relating to or denoting British architecture, clothing, and furniture of the Regency or, more widely, of the late 18th and early 19th centuries. Regency style was contemporary with the Empire style and shares many of its features: elaborate and ornate, it is generally neoclassical, with a generous borrowing of Greek and Egyptian motifs.

re•gen•er•ate • *v.* |ri'jenəˌrāt| [trans.] (of a living organism) regrow (new tissue) to replace lost or injured tissue: *a crab in the process of regenerating a claw.*

■ [intrans.] (of an organ or tissue) regrow. ■ bring into renewed existence; generate again. ■ bring new and more vigorous life to (an area or institution), esp. in economic terms; revive: *regenerating the inner cities.* ■ (esp. in Christian use) give a new and higher spiritual nature to. • *adj.* |ri'jenərət| reformed or reborn, esp. in a spiritual or moral sense.

DERIVATIVES: **re•gen•er•a•tor** |-ˌrātər| *n.*

re•gent |'rējənt| • *n.* **1** a person appointed to administer a country because the monarch is a minor or is absent or incapacitated. **2** a member of the governing body of a university or other academic institution. • *adj.* [postpositive] acting as regent for a monarch: *the queen regent of Portugal.*

reg•i•cide |'rejəˌsīd| • *n.* the action of killing a king.

■ a person who kills or takes part in killing a king.

DERIVATIVES: **reg•i•cid•al** |ˌrejə'sīdl| *adj.*

re•gime |rā'ZHēm; ri-| (also **régime**) • *n.* **1** a government, esp. an authoritarian one. **2** a system or planned way of doing things, esp. one imposed from above: *detention centers with a very tough physical regime.*

■ a coordinated program for the promotion or restoration of health; a regimen: *a low-calorie, low-fat regime.* ■ the conditions under which a scientific or industrial process occurs.

reg•i•men |'rejəmən; 'rezH-| • *n.* **1** a prescribed course of medical treatment, way of life, or diet for the promotion or restoration of health. **2** a system of government.

re•gis•seur |ˌrāzHē'sər| • *n.* a person who stages a theatrical production, esp. a ballet.

reg•nant |'regnənt| • *adj.* **1** [often postpositive] reigning; ruling: *a queen regnant.* **2** currently having the greatest influence; dominant: *the regnant belief.*

reg•o•lith |'regəˌliTH| • *n.* the layer of unconsolidated solid material covering the bedrock of a planet.

re•gret•ful |ri'gretfəl| • *adj.* feeling or showing regret.
DERIVATIVES: **re•gret•ful•ness** *n.*

re•gret•ta•ble |ri'gretəbəl| • *adj.* (of conduct or an event) giving rise to regret; undesirable; unwelcome.

re•ha•bil•i•tate |ˌrē(h)ə'bilə,tāt| • *v.* [trans.] restore (someone) to health or normal life by training and therapy after imprisonment, addiction, or illness.
■ restore (someone) to former privileges or reputation after a period of critical or official disfavor: *with the fall of the government many former dissidents were rehabilitated.* ■ return (something, esp. an environmental feature) to its former condition.
DERIVATIVES: **re•ha•bil•i•ta•tion** |-,bilə'tāsHən| *n.* **re•ha•bil•i•ta•tive** |-,tātiv| *adj.*

re•i•fy |'rēə,fī| • *v.* (**-ies, -ied**) [trans.] make (something abstract) more concrete or real; convert (a concept) mentally into a thing: *these instincts are, in humans, reified as verbal constructs.*
DERIVATIVES: **re•i•fi•ca•tion** |ˌrēəfə'kā-sHən| *n.* **re•if•i•ca•to•ry** |rē'ifəkə,tôrē; rā-| *adj.*

re•im•burse |ˌrēim'bərs| • *v.* [trans.] (often **be reimbursed**) repay (a person who has spent or lost money): *the investors should be reimbursed for their losses.*
■ repay (a sum of money that has been spent or lost): *thousands of dollars that are not reimbursed.*
DERIVATIVES: **re•im•burs•a•ble** *adj.* **re•im•burse•ment** *n.*

re•in•car•na•tion |ˌrē,in,kär'nāsHən| • *n.* the rebirth of a soul in a new body.
■ a person or animal in whom a particular soul is believed to have been reborn: *he is said to be a reincarnation of the Hindu godVishnu.* Cf. AVATAR. ■ a new version or close match of something from the past: *the latest reincarnation of the hippie look.*

re•it•er•ate |rē'itə,rāt| • *v.* say something again or a number of times, typically for emphasis or clarity.
DERIVATIVES: **re•it•er•a•tion** |rē,itə'rā-sHən| *n.* **re•it•er•a•tive** |-,rātiv; -rətiv| *adj.*

re•join |ri'join| • *v.* [reporting verb] say something in answer to a remark, typically rudely or in a discouraging manner: *Joe said he longed for soft towels, to which Sue rejoined that he was a big baby.*

re•join•der |ri'joindər| • *n.* a reply, esp. a sharp or witty one.

re•ju•ve•nate |ri'jōōvə,nāt| • *v.* [trans.] make (someone or something) look or feel younger, fresher, or more lively: *a bid to rejuvenate the town center* [as adj.] (**rejuvenating**) *the rejuvenating effects of therapeutic clay.*
■ [often as adj.] (**rejuvenated**) restore (a river or stream) to a condition characteristic of a younger landscape.
DERIVATIVES: **re•ju•ve•na•tion** |ri,jōōvə'nāsHən| *n.* **re•ju•ve•na•tor** |-,nātər| *n.*

re•lapse |ri'læps; 'rē,læps| • *v.* [intrans.] (of

someone suffering from a disease) suffer deterioration after a period of improvement.
■ (**relapse into**) return to (a less active or a worse state): *he relapsed into silence.* • *n.* |'rē,læps| a deterioration in someone's state of health after a temporary improvement: *he suffered a relapse of schizophrenia after a car crash.*
DERIVATIVES: **re•laps•er** |ri'læpsər; 'rē,læpsər| *n.*

rel•a•tive hu•mid•i•ty • *n.* the amount of water vapor present in air expressed as a percentage of the amount needed for saturation at the same temperature.

rel•a•tiv•ism |'relətə,vizəm| • *n.* the doctrine that knowledge, truth, and morality exist in relation to culture, society, or historical context, and are not absolute.
DERIVATIVES: **rel•a•tiv•ist** *n.*

rel•a•tiv•i•ty |ˌrelə'tivətē| • *n.* **1** the absence of standards of absolute and universal application: *moral relativity.* **2** the dependence of various physical phenomena on relative motion of the observer and the observed objects, esp. regarding the nature and behavior of light, space, time, and gravity.

rel•e•gate |'relə,gāt| • *v.* [trans.] consign or dismiss to an inferior rank or position: *they aim to prevent women from being relegated to a secondary role.*
DERIVATIVES: **rel•e•ga•tion** |ˌrelə'gāsHən| *n.*

re•lent |ri'lent| • *v.* [intrans.] abandon or mitigate a harsh intention or cruel treatment: *she was going to refuse his request, but relented.*
■ (esp. of bad weather) become less severe or intense: *by evening the rain relented.*

rel•e•vant |'reləvənt| • *adj.* closely connected or appropriate to the matter at hand: *the candidate's experience is relevant to the job.*
■ (in law) bearing on the matter at issue; pertinent.
DERIVATIVES: **rel•e•vance** *n.* **rel•e•van•cy** |-vənsē| *n.* **rel•e•vant•ly** *adv.*

rel•ic |'relik| • *n.* an object surviving from an earlier time, esp. one of historical or sentimental interest.
■ a part of a deceased holy person's body or belongings kept as an object of reverence.
■ an object, custom, or belief that has survived from an earlier time but is now outmoded: *individualized computer programming and time-sharing would become expensive relics.*
■ (**relics**) all that is left of something: *relics of a lost civilization.*

rel•ict |'relikt| • *n.* **1** a thing that has survived from an earlier period or in a primitive form.
■ an animal or plant that has survived while others of its group have become extinct, e.g., the coelacanth or ginkgo. ■ a species or community that formerly had a wider distribution but now survives in only a few localities. **2** a widow.

re•lief |ri'lēf| • *n.* (in art) the state of being clearly visible or obvious due to being accentuated in some way: *the setting sun throws the snow-covered peaks into relief.*
■ a method of molding, carving, or stamping in which the design stands out from the sur-

face, to a greater (**high relief**) or lesser (**bas-relief**) extent. ■ a piece of sculpture in relief.
■ a representation of relief given by an arrangement of line or color or shading. ■ (in physical geography) difference in height from the surrounding terrain.
PHRASES: **in relief** carved, molded, or stamped so as to stand out from the surface.
re•li•gi•ose |riˈlijēˌōs| • adj. excessively religious.
DERIVATIVES: **re•li•gi•os•i•ty** |riˌlijēˈäsə-tē| n.
re•li•gious |riˈlijəs| • adj. **1** believing in and worshiping a superhuman controlling power or powers, esp. a personal God or gods.
■ (of a belief or practice) forming part of someone's thought about or worship of a divine being: *has strong religious convictions.* ■ of or relating to the worship of or a doctrine concerning a divine being or beings: *religious music.* ■ belonging or relating to a monastic order or other group of people who are united by their practice of religion. ■ treated or regarded with a devotion and scrupulousness appropriate to worship: *I have a religious aversion to reading manuals.* • n. (pl. same) a person bound by monastic vows.
DERIVATIVES: **re•li•gious•ly** adv. **re•li•gious•ness** n.
re•lin•quish |riˈliNGkwiSH| • v. [trans.] voluntarily cease to keep or claim; give up: *he relinquished his title.*
DERIVATIVES: **re•lin•quish•ment** n.
re•liq•ui•ae |rəˈlikwēˌī; -wēˌē| • plural n. remains.
■ (in geology) fossil remains of animals or plants.
rel•ish |ˈreliSH| • n. **1** great enjoyment: *she drank the wine with relish.*
■ liking for or pleasurable anticipation of something: *an assignment for which I had little relish.* **2** a condiment eaten with plain food to add flavor.
■ chopped sweet pickles used as such a condiment. **3** an appetizing flavor.
■ a distinctive taste or tinge: *the relish of wine.*
■ an attractive quality. • v. [trans.] **1** enjoy greatly: *relishing his moment of glory.*
■ be pleased by or about: *I don't relish the long ride.* **2** make pleasant to the taste; add relish to.
re•main•der |riˈmāndər| • n. **1** a part, number, or quantity that is left over: *leave a few mushrooms for garnish and slice the remainder.*
■ a part that is still to come: *the remainder of the year.* ■ the number that is left over in a division in which one quantity does not exactly divide another: *23 divided by 3 is 7, remainder 2.* ■ a copy of a book left unsold when demand has fallen. **2** (in law) an interest in an estate that becomes effective in possession only when a prior interest (devised at the same time) ends. • v. [trans.] (often **be remaindered**) dispose of (a book left unsold) at a reduced price: *titles are being remaindered increasingly quickly to save on overheads.*
re•mand |riˈmænd| • v. [trans.] (in law) place (a defendant) on bail or in custody, esp. when

a trial is adjourned: *I had a seventeen-year-old son remanded to a drug-addiction program.*
■ return (a case) to a lower court for reconsideration: *the Supreme Court vacated the opinion and remanded the matter back to the California court.* • n. a committal to custody.
rem•a•nent |ˈremənənt| • adj. remaining; residual.
■ (of magnetism) remaining after the magnetizing field has been removed.
DERIVATIVES: **rem•a•nence** n.
re•me•di•al |riˈmēdēəl| • adj. giving or intended as a remedy or cure: *remedial surgery.*
■ provided or intended for students who are experiencing learning difficulties: *remedial education.*
DERIVATIVES: **re•me•di•al•ly** adv.
rem•e•dy |ˈremədē| • n. (pl. **-ies**) **1** a medicine or treatment for a disease or injury: *herbal remedies for aches and pains.*
■ a means of counteracting or eliminating something undesirable: *shopping became a remedy for personal problems.* ■ a means of legal reparation: *the doctrine took away their only remedy against merchants who refused to honor their contracts.* **2** the margin within which coins as minted may differ from the standard fineness and weight. • v. (**-ies, -ied**) [trans.] set right (an undesirable situation): *by the time a problem becomes patently obvious, it may be almost too late to remedy it.*
DERIVATIVES: **re•me•di•a•ble** |riˈmēdēə-bəl| adj. **rem•e•di•less** adj.
rem•i•nis•cence |reməˈnisəns| • n. a story told about a past event remembered by the narrator: *his reminiscences of his early days in Washington.*
■ the enjoyable recollection of past events: *his story made me smile in reminiscence.* ■ (**reminiscences**) a collection in literary form of incidents and experiences that someone remembers. ■ a characteristic of one thing reminding or suggestive of another: *his first works are too full of reminiscences of earlier poetry.*
DERIVATIVES: **rem•i•nisce** v. **rem•i•nis•cent** adj.
re•mon•strate |riˈmänˌstrāt; ˈremən-| • v. [intrans.] make a forcefully reproachful protest: *he turned angrily to remonstrate with Tommy* | [with direct speech] *"You don't mean that," she remonstrated.*
DERIVATIVES: **re•mon•stra•tion** |riˌmän-ˈstrāSHən; ˌremən-| n. **re•mon•stra•tive** |-strətiv| adj. **re•mon•stra•tor** |-ˌstrātər; ˈremən-| n.
re•mu•ner•ate |riˈmyōōnəˌrāt| • v. [trans.] pay (someone) for services rendered or work done: *they should be remunerated fairly for their work.*
DERIVATIVES: **re•mu•ner•a•tive** |-rətiv; -ˌrātiv| adj.
Ren•ais•sance |ˈrenəˌsäns; -ˌzäns| • the revival of European art and literature under the influence of classical models in the 14th–16th centuries.
■ the culture and style of art and architecture developed during this era. ■ [as n.] (**a renais-**

sance) a revival of or renewed interest in something: *rail travel is enjoying a renaissance.*

re•nal |'rēnl| • *adj.* of or relating to the kidneys.

re•nas•cent |ri'næsənt; -'nāsənt| • *adj.* becoming active or popular again: *renascent fascism.*

ren•e•gade |'reni,gād| • *n.* a person who deserts and betrays an organization, country, or set of principles.

■ a person who behaves in a rebelliously unconventional manner. ■ a person who abandons religion; an apostate. • *adj.* having treacherously changed allegiance: *a renegade bodyguard.*

■ having abandoned one's religious beliefs: *a renegade monk.*

re•nege |ri'neg; -'nig| • *v.* [intrans.] go back on a promise, undertaking, or contract: *the administration had reneged on election promises.*

■ another term for REVOKE (in card games). ■ [trans.] renounce or abandon (someone or something).

DERIVATIVES: **re•neg•er** *n.*

ren•net |'renit| • *n.* curdled milk from the stomach of an unweaned calf, containing rennin and used in curdling milk for cheese.

■ any preparation containing rennin.

ren•nin |'renin| • *n.* an enzyme secreted into the stomach of unweaned mammals causing the curdling of milk.

re•nounce |ri'nowns| • *v.* [trans.] formally declare one's abandonment of (a claim, right, or possession): *Isabella offered to renounce her son's claim to the French crown.*

■ refuse to recognize or abide by any longer: *these agreements were renounced after the fall of the regime.* ■ declare that one will no longer engage in or support: *they renounced the armed struggle.* ■ reject and stop using or consuming: *he renounced drugs and alcohol completely.* ■ [intrans.] (in law) refuse or resign a right or position, esp. one as an heir or trustee: *there will be forms enabling the allottee to renounce.*

DERIVATIVES: **re•nounce•a•ble** *adj.* **re•nounce•ment** *n.* **re•nounc•er** *n.*

ren•o•vate |'renə,vāt| • *v.* [trans.] restore (something old, esp. a building) to a good state of repair.

■ refresh; reinvigorate: *a little warm nourishment renovated him for a short time.*

DERIVATIVES: **ren•o•va•tion** |,renə'vāSHən| *n.* **ren•o•va•tor** |-,vātər| *n.*

re•nown |ri'nown| • *n.* the condition of being known or talked about by many people; fame: *authors of great renown.*

DERIVATIVES: **re•nowned** *adj.*

ren•tier |rän'tyā| • *n.* a person living on income from property or investments.

re•nun•ci•a•tion |ri,nənsē'āSHən| • *n.* the formal renouncing or rejection of something, typically a belief, claim, or course of action: *a renunciation of violence.*

■ a legal document expressing renunciation.

DERIVATIVES: **re•nun•ci•ant** |ri'nənsē-ənt| *n. & adj.*

rep•a•ra•tion |,repə'rāSHən| • *n.* 1 the making of amends for a wrong one has done, by

paying money to or otherwise helping those who have been wronged: *the courts required a convicted offender to make financial reparation to his victim.*

■ (**reparations**) the compensation for war damage paid by a defeated state. 2 the action of repairing something: *the old hall was pulled down to avoid the cost of reparation.*

DERIVATIVES: **re•par•a•tive** |ri'perətiv| *adj.*

rep•ar•tee |,repər'tē; ,rep,är'tē; -'tā| • *n.* conversation or speech characterized by quick, witty comments or replies.

re•pa•tri•ate |rē'pātrē,āt; rē'pæ-| • *v.* [trans.] send (someone) back to his or her own country: *the government sought to repatriate thousands of Albanian refugees.*

■ send or bring (money) back to one's own country: *foreign firms would be permitted to repatriate all profits.* • *n.* a person who has been repatriated.

DERIVATIVES: **re•pa•tri•a•tion** |,rē,pātrē'āSHən; ,rē,pæ-| *n.*

re•peal |ri'pēl| • *v.* [trans.] revoke or annul (a law or congressional act): *the legislation was repealed five months later.* • *n.* the action of revoking or annulling a law or congressional act: *the House voted in favor of repeal.*

DERIVATIVES: **re•peal•a•ble** *adj.*

re•pe•chage |,repə'SHäzH| (also **repechage**) • *n.* (in rowing and other sports) a contest in which the runners-up in the eliminating heats compete for a place in the final.

re•pel•lent |ri'pelənt| (also **repellant**) • *adj.* 1 [often in combination] able to repel a particular thing; impervious to a particular substance: *water-repellent nylon.* 2 causing disgust or distaste: *the idea of eating snails was repellent to her.* • *n.* 1 a substance that dissuades particular insects or other pests from approaching or settling: *a flea repellent.* 2 a substance used to treat something, esp. fabric or stone, so as to make it impervious to water: *treat brick with a silicone water repellent.*

DERIVATIVES: **re•pel•lence** *n.* **re•pel•len•cy** *n.* **re•pel•lent•ly** *adv.*

USAGE: **Repellent** and **repulsive** are very close in meaning, but the latter, perhaps because of its sound, is felt to express stronger feeling.

re•per•cus•sion |,rēpər'kəSHən; ,rep-| • *n.* 1 (usu. **repercussions**) an unintended consequence occurring some time after an event or action, esp. an unwelcome one: *the move would have grave repercussions for the entire region.* 2 the recoil of something after impact. 3 an echo or reverberation.

DERIVATIVES: **re•per•cus•sive** |-'kəsiv| *adj.*

rep•er•toire |'repə(r),twär| • *n.* a stock of plays, dances, or pieces that a company or a performer knows or is prepared to perform.

■ the whole body of items that are regularly performed: *the mainstream concert repertoire.*

■ a stock of skills or types of behavior that a person habitually uses: *his repertoire of threats, stares, and dismissive gestures.*

rep•er•to•ry |'repə(r),tôrē| • *n.* (pl. **-ies**)
1 the performance of various plays, operas, or ballets by a company at regular short intervals: [as adj.] *a repertory actor.* ■ repertory theaters regarded collectively. ■ a repertory company. **2** another term for REPERTOIRE.
■ a repository or collection, esp. of information or retrievable examples.
DERIVATIVES: **rep•er•to•ri•al** |,repə(r)'tôrēəl| *adj.*

re•pine |ri'pīn| • *v.* [intrans.] feel or express discontent; fret; complain.

re•plen•ish |ri'plenisн| • *v.* [trans.] fill (something) up again: *he replenished Justin's glass with mineral water.* ■ restore (a stock or supply of something) to the former level or condition: *all creatures need sleep to replenish their energies.*
DERIVATIVES: **re•plen•ish•er** *n.* **re•plen•ish•ment** *n.*

re•plete |ri'plēt| • *adj.* [predic.] filled or well-supplied with something: *sensational popular fiction, **replete with** adultery and sudden death.* ■ very full of or sated by food: *I went out into the sun-drenched streets again, replete and relaxed.*
DERIVATIVES: **re•ple•tion** |ri'plēsнən| *n.*

re•plev•in |ri'plevən| • *n.* (in law) a procedure whereby seized goods may be provisionally restored to their owner pending the outcome of an action to determine the rights of the parties concerned.
■ an action arising from such a process.

rep•li•ca |'replikə| • *n.* an exact copy or model of something, esp. one on a smaller scale: *a replica of the Empire State Building.* ■ a duplicate of an original artistic work.

rep•li•cate • *v.* |'repli,kāt| [trans.] make an exact copy of; reproduce: *it might be impractical to replicate eastern culture in the west.* ■ (**replicate itself**) (of genetic material or a living organism) reproduce or give rise to a copy of itself: *interleukin-16 prevents the virus from replicating itself* | [intrans.] *an enzyme that HIV needs in order to replicate.* ■ repeat (a scientific experiment or trial) to obtain a consistent result. • *adj.* |'repli,kit| [attrib.] of the nature of a copy: *a replicate Earth.* ■ of the nature of a repetition of a scientific experiment or trial: *the variation of replicate measurements.* • *n.* |'repli,kit| **1** a close or exact copy; a replica. ■ a repetition of an experimental test or procedure. **2** a musical tone one or more octaves above or below the given tone.
DERIVATIVES: **rep•li•ca•bil•i•ty** |,replikə'bilətē| *n.* **rep•li•ca•ble** |'replikəbəl| *adj.* **rep•li•ca•tive** *adj.*

re•port•age |rə'pôrtij; ,repôr'täzн| • *n.* the reporting of news, for the press and the broadcast media: *extensive reportage of elections.*
■ factual presentation in a book or other text, esp. when this adopts a journalistic style.

re•pose |ri'pōz| • *n.* temporary rest from activity, excitement, or exertion, esp. sleep or the rest given by sleep: *in repose her face looked relaxed.*
■ a state of peace: *the repose of the soul of the dead man.* ■ composure: *he had lost none of his grace or his repose.* ■ (in art) harmonious arrangement of colors and forms, providing a restful visual effect. ■ **angle of repose** the greatest angle between two planes that is consistent with stability. • *v.* [no obj., with adverbial of place] be lying, situated, or kept in a particular place: *the diamond now reposes in the Louvre.*
■ lie down in rest: *how sweetly he would repose in the four-poster bed.* ■ [trans.] (**repose something on/in**) lay something to rest in or on (something): *I'll go to him, and repose our distresses on his friendly bosom.* ■ [trans.] give rest to: *he halted to repose his wayworn soldiers.*
DERIVATIVES: **re•pose•ful** |-fəl| *adj.* **re•pose•ful•ly** |-fəlē| *adv.*

re•pous•sé |rə,pōō'sā| • *adj.* (of metalwork) hammered into (raised) relief from the reverse side. • *n.* ornamental metalwork fashioned in this way.

rep•re•hend |,repri'hend| • *v.* [trans.] find fault with; blame or reprimand: *a recklessness that cannot be too severely reprehended.*
DERIVATIVES: **rep•re•hen•sion** |-'hencнən| *n.*

rep•re•sen•ta•tion |,repri,zen'tāsнən; -zən-| • *n.* **1** the action of speaking or acting on behalf of someone or the state of being so represented: *asylum-seekers should be guaranteed good legal advice and representation.* **2** the description or portrayal of someone or something in a particular way or as being of a certain nature: *the representation of women in newspapers.*
■ the depiction of someone or something in a picture or other work of art: *Picasso is striving for some absolute representation of reality.* ■ a thing, esp. a picture or model, that depicts a likeness or reproduction of someone or something: *a striking representation of a vase of flowers.* ■ (in some theories of perception) a mental state or concept regarded as corresponding to a thing perceived. **3** (**representations**) formal statements made to a higher authority, esp. so as to communicate an opinion or register a protest: *certain church groups are making strong representations to the government.*
■ a statement or allegation: *relying on a representation that the tapes were genuine.*

rep•re•sen•ta•tive |,repri'zentətiv| • *adj.*
1 typical of a class, group, or body of opinion: *these courses are representative of those taken by most Harvard undergraduates.*
■ containing typical examples of many or all types: *a representative sample of young people in the South.* **2** (of a legislative or deliberative assembly) consisting of people chosen to act and speak on behalf of a wider group.
■ (of a government or political system) based on representation of the people by such deputies: *free elections and representative democracy.* Cf. DIRECT. **3** serving as a portrayal or symbol of something: *the show would be more **representative of** how women really are.*

■ (of art) representational: *the bust involves a high degree of representative abstraction.* **4** (in philosophy) of or relating to mental representation. • *n.* **1** a person chosen or appointed to act or speak for another or others, in particular:
■ an agent of a firm who travels to potential clients to sell its products. ■ an employee of a travel company who looks after the needs of its vacationing clients. ■ a person chosen or elected to speak and act on behalf of others in a legislative assembly or deliberative body. ■ a delegate who attends a conference, negotiations, legal hearing, etc., so as to represent the interests of another person or group. ■ a person who takes the place of another on a ceremonial or official occasion. **2** an example of a class or group: *fossil representatives of lampreys and hagfishes.*
DERIVATIVES: **rep•re•sent•a•tive•ly** *adv.* **rep•re•sent•a•tive•ness** *n.*

re•press |ri'pres| • *v.* [trans.] subdue (someone or something) by force: *the uprisings were repressed.* Cf. OPPRESS, SUPPRESS.
■ restrain or prevent (the expression of a feeling). ■ hold back (a thought, feeling, or desire) within oneself so that it becomes or remains unconscious: *the thought that he had killed his brother was so terrible that he repressed it.* ■ inhibit the natural development or self-expression of (someone or something): *too much bureaucracy represses creativity.* ■ (in biology) prevent the transcription of (a gene).
DERIVATIVES: **re•press•er** *n.* **re•press•i•ble** |-əbəl| *adj.* **re•pres•sion** |ri'preSHən| *n.* **re•pres•sive** *adj.*

re•prieve |ri'prēv| • *v.* [trans.] cancel or postpone the punishment of (someone, esp. someone condemned to death).
■ abandon or postpone plans to close or put an end to (something): *the threatened mines could be reprieved.* • *n.* a cancellation or postponement of a punishment.
■ a temporary escape from an undesirable fate or unpleasant situation.

rep•ri•mand |'reprə,mænd| • *n.* a rebuke, esp. an official one. • *v.* [trans.] rebuke (someone), esp. officially: *officials were dismissed or reprimanded for poor work.*

re•pris•al |ri'prīzəl| • *n.* an act of retaliation: *the threat of reprisal.*
■ the forcible seizure of a foreign subject or their goods as an act of retaliation.

re•prise |ri'prēz| • *n.* a repeated passage in music.
■ a repetition or further performance of something: *many Syrians fear a reprise of the showdown 12 years ago.* • *v.* [trans.] repeat (a piece of music or a performance).

re•proach |ri'prōCH| • *v.* [trans.] address (someone) in such a way as to express disapproval or disappointment: *critics of the administration* **reproached** *the president* **for** *his failure to tackle the deficit.* | [with direct speech] *"You know that isn't true," he reproached her.*
■ (**reproach someone with**) accuse someone of: *his wife reproached him with cowardice.*
■ censure or rebuke (an offense). • *n.* the ex-

pression of disapproval or disappointment: *he gave her a look of reproach.*
■ (**a reproach to**) a thing that makes the failings of someone or something else more apparent: *his elegance is a living reproach to our slovenly habits.*
DERIVATIVES: **re•proach•a•ble** *adj.* **re•proach•er** *n.* **re•proach•ing•ly** *adv.*

rep•ro•bate |'reprə,bāt| • *n.* an unprincipled person (often used humorously or affectionately): *you old reprobate, you!*
■ (in Christian theology, esp. in Calvinism) a sinner who is not of the elect and is predestined to damnation. • *adj.* unprincipled (often used as a humorous or affectionate reproach): *a long-missed old reprobate drinking comrade.*
■ (in Calvinism) predestined to damnation. • *v.* [trans.] express or feel disapproval of: *his neighbors reprobated his method of proceeding.*
DERIVATIVES: **rep•ro•ba•tion** |,reprə'bāSHən| *n.*

re•prove |ri'prōōv| • *v.* [trans.] reprimand or censure someone: *he was reproved for obscenity* | [with direct speech] *"Don't be childish, Kate," he reproved mildly* | [as adj.] (**reproving**) *a reproving glance.*
DERIVATIVES: **re•proof** *n.* **re•prov•a•ble** *adj.* **re•prov•er** *n.* **re•prov•ing•ly** *adv.*

re•pub•li•can |ri'pəblikən| • *adj.* (of a form of government, constitution, etc.) belonging to, or characteristic of, a republic.
■ advocating or supporting republican government: *the republican movement.* • *n.* **1** a person advocating or supporting republican government. **2** (**Republican**) a member or supporter of the Republican Party; one who advocates or supports Republican positions, e.g. reduction of federal action in economic matters.
DERIVATIVES: **re•pub•li•can•ism** |-,nizəm| *n.*

re•pu•di•ate |ri'pyōōdē,āt| • *v.* [trans.] refuse to accept or be associated with: *she has repudiated policies associated with previous party leaders.*
■ deny the truth or validity of: *the minister repudiated allegations of human rights abuses.* ■ refuse to fulfill or discharge (an agreement, obligation, or debt).
DERIVATIVES: **re•pu•di•a•tion** |ri,pyōōdē 'āSHən| *n.* **re•pu•di•a•tor** |-,ātər| *n.*

re•pug•nant |ri'pəgnənt| • *adj.* **1** extremely distasteful; unacceptable. **2** [predic.] (**repugnant to**) in conflict with; incompatible with: *a bylaw must not be repugnant to state law.*
■ given to stubborn resistance.
DERIVATIVES: **re•pug•nance** *n.* **re•pug•nant•ly** *adv.*

re•pulse |ri'pəls| • *v.* [trans.] **1** drive back (an attack or attacking enemy) by force: *rioters tried to storm government buildings but were repulsed by police.*
■ fail to welcome (friendly advances or the person making them); rebuff: *she left, feeling hurt because she had been repulsed.* ■ refuse to accept (an offer): *his bid for the company was repulsed.* **2** (usu. **be repulsed**) cause (some-

one) to feel intense distaste and aversion: *audiences at early screenings of the film were repulsed by its brutality.* • *n.* the action of driving back an attacking force or of being driven back: *the repulse of the invaders.*
■ a discouraging response to friendly advances: *her evasion of his plan had been another repulse.*

re•pul•sion |ri'pəlsHən| • *n.* **1** a feeling of intense distaste or disgust: *people talk about the case with a mixture of fascination and repulsion.* **2** (in physics) a force under the influence of which objects tend to move away from each other, e.g., through having the same magnetic polarity or electric charge.
DERIVATIVES: **re•pul•sive** |ri'pəlsiv| • *adj.* **1** arousing intense distaste or disgust: *a repulsive smell.*
■ lacking friendliness or sympathy. **2** of or relating to repulsion between physical objects.
DERIVATIVES: **re•pul•sive•ly** *adv.* **re•pul•sive•ness** *n.*

USAGE: **Repulsive** and **repellent** are very close in meaning, but the former, perhaps because of its sound, is felt to express stronger feeling.

rep•u•ta•ble |'repyətəbəl| • *adj.* having a good reputation: *a reputable company.*
DERIVATIVES: **rep•u•ta•bly** |-blē| *adv.*
rep•u•ta•tion |,repyə'tāsHən| • *n.* the beliefs or opinions that are generally held about someone or something: *his reputation was tarnished by allegations that he had taken bribes.*
■ a widespread belief that someone or something has a particular habit or characteristic: *his knowledge of his subject earned him a reputation as an expert.*
re•pute |ri'pyo͞ot| • *n.* the opinion generally held of someone or something; the state of being generally regarded in a particular way: *pollution could bring the authority's name into bad repute.*
■ the state of being highly thought of; fame: *chefs of international repute.* • *v.* (**be reputed**) be generally said or believed to do something or to have particular characteristics: *he was reputed to have a fabulous house.*
■ [usu. as adj.] (**reputed**) be generally said or believed to exist or be of a particular type, despite not being so: *this area gave the lie to the reputed flatness of the country.* ■ [usu. as adj.] (**reputed**) be widely known and well thought of: *intensive training with reputed coaches.*
DERIVATIVES: **re•put•ed•ly** *adv.*
req•ui•em |'rekwēəm; 'rā-| • *n.* (also **requiem mass**) (esp. in the Roman Catholic Church) a mass for the repose of the souls of the dead.
■ a musical composition setting parts of such a mass, or of a similar character. ■ an act or token of remembrance: *he designed the epic as a requiem for his wife.*
req•ui•site |'rekwəzət| • *adj.* made necessary by particular circumstances or regulations: *the application will not be processed until the requisite fee is paid.* • *n.* a thing that is necessary

for the achievement of a specified end: *she believed privacy to be a requisite for a peaceful life.*
DERIVATIVES: **req•ui•site•ly** *adv.*
req•ui•si•tion |,rekwə'zisHən| • *n.* an official order laying claim to the use of property or materials.
■ a formal written demand that some duty should be performed or something be put into operation. ■ the appropriation of goods, esp. for military or public use. • *v.* [trans.] demand the use or supply of, esp. by official order and for military or public use.
■ demand the performance or occurrence of: *one of the investors has requisitioned a special meeting.*
DERIVATIVES: **req•ui•si•tion•er** *n.*
re•quite |ri'kwīt| • *v.* [trans.] make appropriate return for (a favor or service); reward: *they are quick to requite a kindness.*
■ avenge or retaliate for (an injury or wrong). ■ return a favor to (someone): *to win enough to requite my friends.* ■ respond to (love or affection); return: *she did not requite his love.*
DERIVATIVES: **re•quit•al** |-'kwītl| *n.*
re•scind |ri'sind| • *v.* [trans.] revoke, cancel, or repeal (a law, order, or agreement): *the government eventually rescinded the directive.*
DERIVATIVES: **re•scind•a•ble** *adj.* **re•scis•sion** *n.*
ré•seau |rā'zō ri-| • *n.* (pl. **réseaux** |-'zōz|) a network or grid.
■ a plain net ground used in lacemaking. ■ a reference marking pattern on a photograph, used in astronomy and surveying. ■ a spy or intelligence network, esp. in the French resistance movement during the German occupation in World War II.
re•sect |ri'sekt| • *v.* [trans.] [often as adj.] (**resected**) cut out (tissue or part of an organ).
DERIVATIVES: **re•sec•tion** |ri'seksHən| *n.* **re•sec•tion•al** |ri'seksHənl| *adj.*
res•er•va•tion |,rezər'vāsHən| • *n.* **1** the action of reserving something: *the reservation of positions for non-Americans.*
■ an arrangement whereby something, esp. a seat or room, is booked or reserved for a particular person. ■ an area of land set aside for occupation by North American Indians or Australian Aboriginals. In Canada called a **reserve**. ■ (in law) a right or interest retained in an estate being conveyed. **2** a qualification to an expression of agreement or approval; a doubt: *some generals voiced reservations about air strikes. I say this without reservation.*
re•side |ri'zīd| • *v.* [no obj., with adverbial of place] have one's permanent home in a particular place: *people who work in the city actually reside in neighboring towns.*
■ be situated: *the paintings now reside on the walls of a restaurant.* ■ (of power or a right) belong by right to a person or body: *legislative powers reside in the stata assembly.* ■ (of a quality) be present or inherent in something: *the meaning of an utterance does not wholly reside in the semantic meaning.*

res•i•dence |'rez(ə)dəns; 'rezə,dens| • *n.* a person's house, esp. a large and impressive one.

■ the official house of a government minister or other public and official figure. ■ the fact of living in a particular place: *Rome was his main place of residence.* Cf. DOMICILE.

PHRASES: ■ (—— **in residence**) a person with a particular occupation (esp. an artist or writer) paid to work in a college or other institution.

res•i•den•cy |'rez(ə)dənsē; 'rezə,densē| • *n.* (pl. -ies) **1** the fact of living in a place: *a government ruling confirmed the returning refugees' right to residency.*

■ a residential post held by a writer, musician, or artist, typically for teaching purposes. **2** formerly, the official residence of the British governor general's representative or other government agent, esp. at the court of an Indian state.

■ a group or organization of intelligence agents in a foreign country. **3** a period of specialized medical training in a hospital; the position of a resident.

res•i•dent |'rez(ə)dənt; 'rezə,dent| • *n.* **1** a person who lives somewhere permanently or on a long-term basis. Cf. CITIZEN.

■ a bird, butterfly, or other animal of a species that does not migrate. ■ a person who boards at a boarding school or college. ■ formerly, a British government agent in any semi-independent state, esp. the governor general's agent at the court of an Indian state. **2** a medical graduate engaged in specialized practice under supervision in a hospital. Cf. INTERN. • *adj.* living somewhere on a long-term basis: *she has been **resident in** Brazil for a long time.*

■ having quarters on the premises of one's work: *resident farm workers.* ■ attached to and working regularly for a particular institution: *the film studio needed a resident historian.* ■ (of a bird, butterfly, or other animal) nonmigratory; remaining in an area throughout the year. ■ (of a computer program, file, etc.) immediately available in computer memory, rather than having to be loaded from elsewhere.

DERIVATIVES: **res•i•dent•ship** |-,SHip| *n.* (historical).

re•sid•u•al |ri'zijəwəl| • *adj.* remaining after the greater part or quantity has gone: *the withdrawal of residual occupying forces.*

■ (of a quantity) left after other things have been subtracted: *residual income after tax and mortgage payments.* ■ (of a physical state or property) remaining after the removal of or present in the absence of a causative agent: *residual stenosis.* ■ (of an experimental or arithmetical error) not accounted for or eliminated. ■ (of a soil or other deposit) formed in situ by weathering. • *n.* a quantity remaining after other things have been subtracted or allowed for.

■ a difference between a value measured in a scientific experiment and the theoretical or true value. ■ a royalty paid to a performer,

writer, etc., for a repeat of a play, television show, etc. ■ a portion of rocky or high ground remaining after erosion. ■ the resale value of a new car or other item at a specified time after purchase, expressed as a percentage of its purchase price.

DERIVATIVES: **re•sid•u•al•ly** |-(ə)wəlē| *adv.*

res•i•due |'rezə,d(y)o͞o| • *n.* a small amount of something that remains after the main part has gone or been taken or used.

■ (in law) the part of an estate that is left after the payment of charges, debts, and bequests. ■ a substance that remains after a process such as combustion or evaporation.

re•sid•u•um |ri'zijəwəm| • *n.* (pl. **residua** |-əwə|) a substance or thing that remains or is left behind, in particular, a chemical residue.

re•sil•i•ent |ri'zilyənt| • *adj.* (of a substance or object) able to recoil or spring back into shape after bending, stretching, or being compressed.

■ (of a person or animal) able to withstand or recover quickly from difficult conditions: *the fish are **resilient to** most infections.*

DERIVATIVES: **re•sil•ience** *n.* **re•sil•ien•cy** *n.* **re•sil•ient•ly** *adv.*

res•in |'rezən| • *n.* a sticky flammable organic substance, insoluble in water, exuded by some trees and other plants (notably fir and pine).

■ (also **synthetic resin**) a solid or liquid synthetic organic polymer used as the basis of plastics, adhesives, varnishes, or other products. • *v.* (**resined, resining**) [trans.] [usu. as adj.] (**resined**) rub or treat with resin: *resined canvas.*

DERIVATIVES: **res•in•ous** |'rezənəs| *adj.*

re•sist•ance |ri'zistəns| • *n.* **1** the refusal to accept or comply with something; the attempt to prevent something by action or argument: *she **put up** no **resistance to** being led away.*

■ (in psychoanalysis) opposition, frequently unconscious, to the emergence of repressed memories or desires.

■ armed or violent opposition: *government forces were unable to crush guerrilla-style resistance.* Cf. NONRESISTANCE. ■ (also **resistance movement**) [in sing.] a secret organization resisting authority, esp. in an occupied country. ■ (**the Resistance**) the underground movement formed in France during World War II to fight the German occupying forces and the Vichy government. (Also called **maquis**.) ■ the impeding, slowing, or stopping effect exerted by one material thing on another: *air resistance would need to be reduced by streamlining.* **2** the ability not to be affected by something, esp. adversely: *some of us have a lower resistance to cold than others.*

■ lack of sensitivity or vulnerability to a drug, insecticide, etc., esp. as a result of continued exposure or genetic change. **3** the degree to which a substance or device opposes the passage of an electric current, causing energy dissipation. By Ohm's law resistance (measured in ohms) is equal to the voltage divided by the current.

■ a resistor or other circuit component that opposes the passage of an electric current. PHRASES: **the line** (or **path**) **of least resistance** an option avoiding difficulty or unpleasantness; the easiest course of action. DERIVATIVES: **re•sist•ant** adj., n.

res•o•lute |'rezə‚lo͞ot; -lət| • adj. admirably purposeful, determined, and unwavering. DERIVATIVES: **res•o•lute•ly** adv. **res•o•lute•ness** n.

res•o•lu•tion |‚rezə'lo͞oSHən| • n. 1 a firm decision to do or not to do something.

■ a formal expression of opinion or intention agreed on by a legislative body, committee, or other formal meeting, typically after taking a vote: *the conference passed two resolutions.* ■ the quality of being determined or resolute: *they handled the last missions of the war with resolution.* 2 the action of solving a problem, dispute, or contentious matter: *the peaceful resolution of all disputes.*

■ (in music) the passing of a discord into a concord during the course of changing harmony. ■ (in medicine) the disappearance of inflammation, or of any symptom or condition. 3 (in chemistry) the process of reducing or separating something into constituent parts or components.

■ (in physics) the replacing of a single force or other vector quantity by two or more jointly equivalent to it. ■ the conversion of something abstract into another form. ■ (in prosody) the substitution of two short syllables for one long one. 4 the smallest interval measurable by a scientific (esp. optical) instrument; the resolving power.

■ the degree of detail visible in a photographic or television image.

re•solve |ri'zälv; -'zôlv| • v. 1 [trans.] settle or find a solution to (a problem, dispute, or contentious matter): *the firm aims to resolve problems within 30 days.*

■ [trans.] (in medicine) cause (a symptom or condition) to disperse, subside, or heal: *endoscopic biliary drainage can rapidly resolve jaundice.* ■ [intrans.] (of a symptom or condition) disperse, subside, or heal: *symptoms resolved after a median of four weeks.* ■ [intrans.] (of a musical discord) lead into a concord during the course of harmonic change. ■ [trans.] Music cause (a discord) to pass into a concord. 2 [intrans.] decide firmly on a course of action: [with infinitive] *she resolved to call Dana as soon as she got home.*

■ [with clause] (of a legislative body, committee, or other formal meeting) make a decision by a formal vote: *the committee resolved that teachers should make their recommendations without knowledge of test scores* | [with infinitive] *the conference resolved to support an alliance.* 3 separate or cause to be separated into constituent parts or components.

■ [trans.] (**resolve something into**) reduce a subject, statement, etc., by mental analysis into (separate elements or a more elementary

form): *the ability to resolve facts into their legal categories.* ■ [intrans.] (of something seen at a distance) turn into a different form when seen more clearly: *the orange glow resolved itself into four lanterns.* ■ [trans.] (of optical or photographic equipment) separate or distinguish between (closely adjacent objects): *Hubble was able to resolve six variable stars in M31.* ■ [trans.] separately distinguish (peaks in a graph or spectrum). ■ [trans.] (in physics) analyze (a force or velocity) into components acting in particular directions. • n. firm determination to do something: *she received information that strengthened her resolve* | *she intended to stick to her initial resolve.*

■ a formal resolution by a legislative body or public meeting. DERIVATIVES: **re•solv•a•bil•i•ty** |ri‚zälvə'bilə‚tē; -'zôlvə-| n. **re•solv•a•ble** adj. **re•solv•er** n.

res•o•nant |'rezənənt| • adj. (of sound) deep, clear, and continuing to sound or ring.

■ of, relating to, or bringing about resonance in a circuit, atom, or other object. ■ (of a room, musical instrument, or hollow body) tending to reinforce or prolong sounds, esp. by synchronous vibration. ■ (of a color) enhancing or enriching another color or colors by contrast. ■ [predic.] (**resonant with**) (of a place) filled or resounding with (the sound of something): *alpine valleys resonant with the sound of church bells.* ■ having the ability to evoke or suggest enduring images, memories, or emotions: *the prints are resonant with traditions of Russian folk art.* DERIVATIVES: **res•o•nant•ly** adv.

res•o•nate |'rezn‚āt| • v. [intrans.] produce or be filled with a deep, full, reverberating sound: *the sound of the siren resonated across the harbor.*

■ evoke or suggest images, memories, and emotions: *the words resonate with so many different meanings.* ■ (of an idea or action) meet with someone's agreement: *the judge's ruling resonated among many of the women.* ■ produce electrical or mechanical resonance: *the crystal resonates at 16 MHz.*

res•pi•ra•tion |‚respə'rāSHən| • n. the action of breathing: *opiates affect respiration.*

■ a single breath. ■ a process in living organisms involving the production of energy, typically with the intake of oxygen and the release of carbon dioxide from the oxidation of complex organic substances.

re•spire |ri'spīr| • v. [intrans.] breathe; inhale or exhale.

■ (of a plant) carry out respiration, esp. at night when photosynthesis has ceased.

res•pite |'respət; ri'spīt| • n. a short period of rest or relief from something difficult or unpleasant.

■ a short delay permitted before an unpleasant obligation is met or a punishment is carried out. • v. [trans.] postpone (a sentence, obligation, etc.): *the execution was only respited a few months.*

■ grant a delay or extension of time to; reprieve from death or execution.

re·splend·ent |ri'splendənt| • *adj.* attractive and impressive through being richly colorful or sumptuous: *she was resplendent in a sea-green dress.*
DERIVATIVES: **re·splend·ence** *n.* **re·splend·en·cy** *n.* **re·splend·ent·ly** *adv.*

re·spond·ent |ri'spändənt| • *n.* **1** a defendant in a lawsuit, esp. one in an appeals or divorce case.
■ the party in a lawsuit or trial who responds to a motion, defends a prior outcome against an appeal, etc. **2** a person who replies to something, esp. one supplying information for a survey or questionnaire or responding to an advertisement. • *adj.* [attrib.] **1** in the position of defendant in a lawsuit: *the respondent defendant.* **2** replying to something, esp. a survey or questionnaire: *the respondent firms in the survey.* **3** (in psychology) involving or denoting a response, esp. a conditioned reflex, to a specific stimulus.

res pu·bli·ca |räs 'pŏŏbli,kä; 'pəblikə| • *n.* the state, republic, or commonwealth.

res·sen·ti·ment |rə,sänte'mäN| • *n.* a psychological state arising from suppressed feelings of envy and hatred that cannot be acted upon, frequently resulting in some form of self-abasement.

res·ti·tu·tion |,restə't(y)ŏŏsHən| • *n.* **1** the restoration of something lost or stolen to its proper owner. **2** recompense for injury or loss: *he was ordered to pay $6,000 in restitution.* **3** the restoration of something to its original state.
■ (in physics) the resumption of an object's original shape or position through elastic recoil.
DERIVATIVES: **res·ti·tu·tive** | 'restə,t(y)ŏŏtiv| *adj.*

res·tive | 'restiv| • *adj.* (of a person) unable to keep still or silent and becoming increasingly difficult to control, esp. because of impatience, dissatisfaction, or boredom.
■ (of a horse) refusing to advance, stubbornly standing still or moving backward or sideways.
DERIVATIVES: **res·tive·ly** *adv.* **res·tive·ness** *n.*

re·strain |ri'strān| • *v.* [trans.] prevent (someone or something) from doing something; keep under control or within limits: *he had to be restrained from walking out of the meeting* | [as adj.] (**restraining**) *Cara put a restraining hand on his arm.*
■ prevent oneself from displaying or giving way to (a strong urge or emotion: *Amiss had to restrain his impatience.* ■ deprive (someone) of freedom of movement or personal liberty: *leg cuffs are used for restraining and transporting violent and dangerous criminals.* ■ (of a seat belt) hold (a person or part of the body) down and back while in a vehicle seat.
DERIVATIVES: **re·strain·a·ble** *adj.* **re·strain·er** *n.*

re·straint |ri'strānt| • *n.* **1** (often **restraints**) a measure or condition that keeps someone or something under control or within limits.
■ the action of keeping someone or something

under control. ■ deprivation or restriction of personal liberty or freedom of movement. ■ a device that limits or prevents freedom of movement: *car safety restraints.* **2** unemotional, dispassionate, or moderate behavior; self-control: *he urged the protestors to exercise restraint.*
■ understatement, esp. of artistic expression: *all restraint vanished in the cadenza.*

ré·su·mé | 'rezə,mā ,rezə'mā| (also **resumé** or **resume**) • *n.* **1** a brief account of a person's education, qualifications, and previous occupations, typically sent with a job application. Also called CURRICULUM VITAE. **2** a summary: *I gave him a quick résumé of events.*

re·sur·gent |ri'sərjənt| • *adj.* increasing or reviving after a period of little activity, popularity, or occurrence: *resurgent nationalism.*
DERIVATIVES: **re·sur·gence** *n.*

res·ur·rect |,rezə'rekt| • *v.* [trans.] restore (a dead person) to life.
■ revive the practice, use, or memory of (something); bring new vigor to.
DERIVATIVES: **res·ur·rec·tion** *n.*

re·sus·ci·tate |ri'səsə,tāt| • *v.* [trans.] revive (someone) from unconsciousness or apparent death.
■ make (something such as an idea or enterprise) active or vigorous again.
DERIVATIVES: **re·sus·ci·ta·tion** |ri,səsə 'tāsHən| *n.* **re·sus·ci·ta·tive** |-,tātiv| *adj.* **re·sus·ci·ta·tor** |-,tātər| *n.*

re·ta·ble |'rē,tābəl; 'retəbəl| (also **retablo** |ri 'täblō|) • *n.* (pl. **retables** or **retablos**) a frame or shelf enclosing decorated panels or revered objects above and behind an altar.
■ a painting or other image in such a position.

re·tain |ri'tān| • *v.* continue to have (something); keep possession of: *built in 1830, the house retains many of its original features.*
■ not abolish, discard, or alter: *the rights of defendants must be retained.* ■ keep in one's memory: *I retained a few French words and phrases.* ■ absorb and continue to hold (a substance): *limestone is known to retain water.* ■ [often as adj.] (**retaining**) keep (something) in place; hold fixed: *remove the retaining bar.* ■ keep (someone) engaged in one's service: *he has been retained as a secretary.* ■ secure the services of (a person, esp. an attorney) with a preliminary payment: *retain an attorney to handle the client's business.*
DERIVATIVES: **re·tain·a·bil·i·ty** |ri,tānə 'bilətē| *n.* **re·tain·a·ble** *adj.* **re·tain·ment** *n.* **re·ten·tion** *n.*

re·tain·er |ri'tānər| • *n.* **1** a thing that holds something in place: *a guitar string retainer.*
■ an appliance for keeping a loose tooth or orthodontic prosthesis in place. **2** a fee paid in advance to someone, esp. an attorney, in order to secure or keep their services when required. **3** a servant or follower of a noble or wealthy person, esp. who has worked for a person or family for a long time.

re·tal·i·ate |ri'tælē,āt| • *v.* [intrans.] make an attack or assault in return for a similar attack: *the blow stung and she retaliated immediately.*

■ [trans.] repay (an injury or insult) in kind: *they used their abilities to retaliate the injury.*
DERIVATIVES: **re·tal·i·a·tion** |ri,tælē'ā-sHən| *n.* **re·tal·i·a·tive** |ri'tælē,āt̬iv; -ēət̬iv| *adj.* **re·tal·i·a·tor** |-,āt̬ər| *n.* **re·tal·i·a·to·ry** |ri'tælēə,tôrē| *adj.*
retch |reCH| • *v.* [intrans.] make the sound and movement of vomiting.
■ vomit. • *n.* a movement or sound of vomiting.
re·ten·tive |ri'tentiv| • *adj.* **1** (of a person's memory) having the ability to remember facts and impressions easily. **2** (of a substance) able to absorb and hold moisture.
■ serving to keep something in place.
DERIVATIVES: **re·ten·tive·ly** *adv.* **re·ten·tive·ness** *n.*
ret·i·cent |'ret̬əsənt| • *adj.* not revealing one's thoughts or feelings readily: *she was extremely reticent about her personal affairs.*
DERIVATIVES: **ret·i·cence** *n.* **ret·i·cent·ly** *adv.*
re·tic·u·late • *v.* |ri'tikyə,lāt| [trans.] divide or mark (something) in such a way as to resemble a net or network: *the numerous canals and branches of the river reticulate the flat alluvial plain.* • *adj.* |-lət; -,lāt| (also, **reticulated**) **1** (in botany) having a conspicuous network of veins. **2** (of evolution) characterized by repeated hybridization between related lineages.
ret·i·cule |'ret̬i,kyōōl| • *n.* a woman's small handbag, originally netted and typically having a drawstring and decorated with embroidery or beading.
ret·i·nue |'retn,(y)ōō| • *n.* a group of advisers, assistants, or others accompanying an important person.
re·tort¹ |ri'tôrt| • *v.* **1** say something in answer to a remark or accusation, typically in a sharp, angry, or wittily incisive manner: [with direct speech] *"No need to be rude," retorted Isabel* | [with clause] *he retorted that this was nonsense* | [intrans.] *I resisted the urge to retort.* **2** [trans.] repay (an insult or injury): *it was now his time to retort the humiliation.*
■ turn (an insult or accusation) back on the person who has issued it: *he was resolute to retort the charge of treason on his foes.* ■ use (an opponent's argument) against them: *the answer they make to us may very easily be retorted.* • *n.* a sharp, angry, or wittily incisive reply to a remark: *she opened her mouth to make a suitably cutting retort.*
re·tort² • *n.* **1** a container or furnace for carrying out a chemical process on a large or industrial scale. **2** a glass container with a long neck, used in distilling liquids and other chemical operations. • *v.* [trans.] heat in a retort in order to separate or purify: *the raw shale is retorted at four crude oil works.*
re·tract |ri'trækt| • *v.* [trans.] draw or pull (something) back or back in: *she retracted her hand as if she'd been burned.*
■ withdraw (a statement or accusation) as untrue or unjustified. ■ withdraw or go back on (an undertaking or promise). ■ (of an animal) draw (a part of itself) back into its body:

the cat retracted its claws. ■ draw (the undercarriage or the wheels) up into the body of an aircraft.
DERIVATIVES: **re·tract·a·ble** *adj.* **re·trac·tion** |ri'træksHən| *n.* **re·trac·tive** |-tiv| *adj.*
re·trac·tile |ri'træktəl; -tīl| • *adj.* capable of being retracted: *an insect with a long retractile proboscis.*
DERIVATIVES: **re·trac·til·i·ty** |,rē,træk'tilət̬ē| *n.*
re·trench |ri'trenCH| • *v.* [intrans.] (of a company, government, or individual) reduce costs or spending in response to economic difficulty.
■ [trans.] reduce or diminish (something) in extent or quantity.
DERIVATIVES: **re·trench·ment** *n.*
ret·ri·bu·tion |,retrə'byōōsHən| • *n.* punishment that is considered to be morally right and fully deserved.
DERIVATIVES: **re·trib·u·tive** |ri'tribyət̬iv| *adj.* **re·trib·u·to·ry** |ri'tribyə,tôrē| *adj.*
ret·ro |'retrō| • *adj.* imitative of a style, fashion, or design from the recent past: *retro 60s fashions.* • *n.* clothes or music whose style or design is imitative of those of the recent past: *a look that mixes Italian casual wear and American retro.*
ret·ro·ac·tive |,retrō'æktiv| • *adj.* (esp. of legislation) taking effect from a date in the past: *a big retroactive tax increase.*
DERIVATIVES: **ret·ro·ac·tion** |-'æksHən| *n.* **ret·ro·ac·tive·ly** *adv.* **ret·ro·ac·tiv·i·ty** |-,æk'tivət̬ē| *n.*
ret·ro·cede |,retrə'sēd| • *v.* [trans.] cede (territory) back again: *the British colony of Hong Kong, retroceded to China.*
DERIVATIVES: **ret·ro·ces·sion** |-'sesHən| *n.*
ret·ro·fit |,retrō'fit| • *v.* (**retrofitted, retrofitting**) [trans.] add (a component or accessory) to something that did not have it when manufactured: *drivers who retrofit catalysts to older cars.*
■ provide (something) with a component or accessory not fitted to it during manufacture: *buses have been retrofitted with easy-access features.* • *n.* an act of adding a component or accessory to something that did not have it when manufactured.
■ a component or accessory added to something after manufacture.
ret·ro·grade |'retrə,grād| • *adj.* **1** directed or moving backward: *a retrograde flow.*
■ reverting to an earlier and inferior condition: *to go back on the progress that has been made would be a retrograde step.* ■ (of the order of something) reversed; inverse: *the retrograde form of these inscriptions.* ■ (of amnesia) involving the period immediately preceding the causal event. ■ (in geology, of a metamorphic change) resulting from a decrease in temperature or pressure. ■ (of the apparent motion of a planet) in a reverse direction from normal (from east to west), resulting from the relative orbital progress of the earth and the planet. The opposite of *prograde* ■ (of the orbit or rotation of a planet or planetary

satellite) in a reverse direction from that normal in the solar system. • *n.* a degenerate person. • *v.* [intrans.] **1** go back in position or time: *our history must retrograde for the space of a few pages.*

■ revert to an earlier and usually inferior condition: *people cannot habitually trample on law and justice without retrograding toward barbarism.* **2** show retrogradation: *all the planets will at some time appear to retrograde.*
DERIVATIVES: **ret•ro•gra•da•tion** *n.* **ret•ro•grade•ly** *adv.* (rare).

ret•ro•gress |ˌretrəˈgres| • *v.* [intrans.] go back to an earlier state, typically a worse one: *she retrogressed to the starting point of her rehabilitation.*

ret•ro•spect |ˈretrəˌspekt| • *n.* a survey or review of a past course of events or period of time.
PHRASES: **in retrospect** when looking back on a past event or situation; with hindsight.
DERIVATIVES: **ret•ro•spec•tion** *n.*

ret•ro•spec•tive |ˌretrəˈspektiv| • *adj.* looking back on or dealing with past events or situations: *our survey was retrospective.*
■ (of an exhibition or compilation) showing the development of an artist's work over a period of time. ■ (of a statute or legal decision) taking effect from a date in the past; retroactive: *retrospective pay awards.* • *n.* an exhibition or compilation showing the development of the work of a particular artist over a period of time: *a Georgia O'Keeffe retrospective.*
DERIVATIVES: **ret•ro•spec•tive•ly** *adv.*

re•vamp |rēˈvæmp| • *v.* [trans.] give new and improved form, structure, or appearance to: *an attempt to revamp the museum's image* | [as adj.] (**revamped**) *a revamped magazine.* • *n.* [usu. in sing.] an act of improving the form, structure, or appearance of something.
■ a new and improved version: *the show was a revamp of an old idea.*

rev•e•nant |ˈrevəˌnän; -nənt| • *n.* a person who has returned, esp. supposedly from the dead.

re•ver•ber•ate |riˈvərbəˌrāt| • *v.* [no obj., usu. with adverbial] (of a loud noise) be repeated several times as an echo: *her deep booming laugh reverberated around the room.*
■ (of a place) appear to vibrate or be disturbed because of a loud noise: *the hall reverberated with gaiety.* ■ [trans.] return or reecho (a sound). ■ have continuing and serious effects: *the statements by the professor reverberated through the capitol.*
DERIVATIVES: **re•ver•ber•ant** |-rənt| *adj.* **re•ver•ber•ant•ly** |-rəntlē| *adv.* **re•ver•ber•a•tion** |riˌvərbəˈrāSHən| *n.* **re•ver•ber•a•tive** |-rətiv| *adj.* **re•ver•ber•a•tor** |-ˌrātər| *n.* **re•ver•ber•a•to•ry** |-rə,tôrē| *adj.*

re•vere |riˈvir| • *v.* [trans.] (often **be revered**) feel deep respect or admiration for (something): *Cézanne's still lifes were revered by his contemporaries*

rev•er•ence |ˈrev(ə)rəns| • *n.* deep respect for someone or something: *rituals showed honor and reverence for the dead.*
■ a gesture indicative of such respect; a bow or

curtsy: *the messenger made his reverence.*
■ (**His/Your Reverence**) a title given to a member of the clergy, or used in addressing them. • *v.* [trans.] regard or treat with deep respect: *the many divine beings reverenced by Hindu tradition.*

rev•er•ent |ˈrev(ə)rənt; ˈrevərnt| • *adj.* feeling or showing deep and solemn respect: *a reverent silence.*
DERIVATIVES: **rev•er•ent•ly** *adv.*

rev•er•en•tial |ˌrevəˈrenCHəl| • *adj.* of the nature of, due to, or characterized by deep and solemn respect: *their names are always mentioned in reverential tones.*
DERIVATIVES: **rev•er•en•tial•ly** *adv.*

rev•er•ie |ˈrevərē| • *n.* a state of being pleasantly lost in one's thoughts; a daydream: *a knock on the door broke her reverie* | *I slipped into reverie.*
■ an instrumental musical piece suggesting a dreamy or musing state. ■ a fanciful or impractical idea or theory.

re•ver•sion |riˈvərzHən| • *n.* **1** a return to a previous state, practice, or belief: *there was some reversion to polytheism* | [in sing.] *a reversion to the two-party system.*
■ (in biology) the action of reverting to a former or ancestral type. **2** (in law) the right, esp. of the original owner or his or her heirs, to possess or succeed to property on the death of the present possessor or at the end of a lease: *the reversion of property.*
■ a property to which someone has such a right. ■ the right of succession to an office or post after the death or retirement of the holder: *he was given a promise of the reversion of Boraston's job.*
DERIVATIVES: **re•ver•sion•ar•y** |-ˌnerē| *adj.*

re•vert |riˈvərt| • *v.* [intrans.] (**revert to**) return to (a previous state, condition, practice, etc.): *he reverted to his native language.*
■ return to (a previous topic): *he ignored her words by reverting to the former subject.* ■ (in biology) return to (a former or ancestral type): *it is impossible that a fishlike mammal will actually revert to being a true fish.* ■ (in law, of property) return or pass to (the original owner) by reversion. ■ [trans.] turn (one's eyes or steps) back: *on reverting our eyes, every step presented some new and admirable scene.*
DERIVATIVES: **re•vert•er** *n.* (Law).

re•vet |riˈvet| • *v.* (**revetted, revetting**) [trans.] [usu. as adj.] (**revetted**) face (a rampart, wall, etc.) with masonry, esp. in fortification: *sandbagged and revetted trenches.*
DERIVATIVES: **re•vet•ment** *n.*

re•vile |riˈvīl| • *v.* [trans.] (usu. **be reviled**) criticize in an abusive or angrily insulting manner: *he was now reviled by the party he had helped to lead.*
DERIVATIVES: **re•vile•ment** *n.* **re•vil•er** *n.*

re•vise |riˈvīz| • *v.* [trans.] reconsider and alter (something) in the light of further evidence: *he had cause to revise his opinion a moment after expressing it.*
■ reexamine and make alterations to (written

or printed matter): *the book was published in 1960 and revised in 1968* | [as adj.] (**revised**) *a revised edition.* ■ alter so as to make more efficient or realistic: [as adj.] (**revised**) *the revised finance and administrative departments.* • *n.* (in printing) a proof including corrections made in an earlier proof.
DERIVATIVES: **re•vis•a•ble** *adj.* **re•vis•al** |-'vīzəl| *n.* **re•vis•er** *n.* **re•vi•sion** *n.* **re•vi•so•ry** |-'vīzərē| *adj.*

re•vi•sion•ism |ri'vizHə,nizəm| • *n.* a policy of revision or modification, esp. of Marxism on evolutionary socialist (rather than revolutionary) or pluralist principles.
■ the theory or practice of revising one's attitude to a previously accepted situation or point of view.
DERIVATIVES: **re•vi•sion•ist** *n.* & *adj.*

re•viv•al |ri'vīvəl| • *n.* an improvement in the condition or strength of something: *an economic revival.*
■ an instance of something becoming popular, active, or important again: *cross-country skiing is enjoying a revival.* ■ a new production of an old play or similar work. ■ a reawakening of religious fervor, esp. by means of a series of evangelistic meetings. ■ such a meeting or series of meetings. ■ a restoration to bodily or mental vigor, to life or consciousness, or to sporting success: *his revival in the third round was unexpected.*

re•viv•al•ism |ri'vīvə,lizəm| • *n.* belief in or the promotion of a revival of religious fervor.
■ a tendency or desire to revive a former custom or practice: *French rococo revivalism.*
DERIVATIVES: **re•viv•al•ist** *n.* & *adj.* **re•viv•al•is•tic** |-,vīvə'listik| *adj.*

re•vive |ri'vīv| • *v.* [trans.] restore to life or consciousness: *both men collapsed, but were revived.*
■ [intrans.] regain life, consciousness, or strength: *she was beginning to revive from her faint.* ■ give new strength or energy to: *the cool, refreshing water revived us all.* ■ restore interest in or the popularity of: *many pagan traditions continue or are being revived.* ■ improve the position or condition of: *the paper made panicky attempts to revive falling sales.*
DERIVATIVES: **re•viv•a•ble** *adj.* **re•viv•er** *n.*

re•voke |ri'vōk| • *v.* **1** [trans.] put an end to the validity or operation of (a decree, decision, or promise): *following a public outcry, the sentence was revoked.* **2** [intrans.] (in bridge, whist, and other card games) fail to follow suit despite being able to do so.
DERIVATIVES: **rev•o•ca•ble** *adj.* **rev•o•ca•tion** |,revə'kāSHən; ri,vō-| *n.* **rev•o•ca•to•ry** |'revəkə,tôrē; ri'vōkə-| *adj.* **re•vok•er** *n.*

rev•o•lu•tion |,revə'lōōSHən| • *n.* **1** a forcible overthrow of a government or social order in favor of a new system.
■ a dramatic and wide-reaching change in the way something works or is organized or in people's ideas about it: *marketing underwent a revolution.* **2** an instance of revolving: *one revolution a second.*
■ motion in orbit or a circular course around

an axis or center. ■ the single completion of an orbit or rotation.
DERIVATIVES: **rev•o•lu•tion•ism** |-,nizəm| *n.* **rev•o•lu•tion•ist** |-nist| *n.*

re•vue |ri'vyōō| • *n.* a light theatrical entertainment consisting of a series of short sketches, songs, and dances, typically dealing satirically with topical issues.

re•vul•sion |ri'vəlsHən| • *n.* **1** a sense of disgust and loathing. **2** (in older medicine) the drawing of disease or blood congestion from one part of the body to another, e.g., by counterirritation.

rhap•so•dize |'ræpsə,dīz| • *v.* [intrans.] speak or write about someone or something with great enthusiasm and delight.

rhap•so•dy |'ræpsədē| • *n.* (pl. **-ies**) **1** an effusively enthusiastic or ecstatic expression of feeling: *rhapsodies of praise.*
■ (in music) a free instrumental composition in one extended movement, typically one that is emotional or exuberant in character. **2** (in ancient Greece) an epic poem, or part of it, of a suitable length for recitation at one time.
DERIVATIVES: **rhap•sod•ic** |ræp'sädik| *adj.*

rhet•o•ric |'retərik| • *n.* the art or study of effective or persuasive speaking or writing, esp. the use of figures of speech and other compositional techniques.
■ the body of rules to be observed by a speaker or writer in order to achieve effective or eloquent expression.
■ language designed to have a persuasive or impressive effect on its audience, but often regarded as lacking in sincerity or meaningful content: *all we have from the opposition is empty rhetoric.*
DERIVATIVES: **rhet•o•ri•cian** *n.*

rhe•tor•i•cal |rə'tôrikəl| • *adj.* of, relating to, or concerned with the art of rhetoric: *repetition is a common rhetorical device.*
■ expressed in terms intended to persuade or impress: *the rhetorical commitment of the government to give priority to primary education.*
DERIVATIVES: **rhe•tor•i•cal•ly** |-ik(ə)lē| *adv.*

rhe•tor•i•cal ques•tion • *n.* a question asked not for information but to produce an effect, e.g., *who cares?* for *nobody cares.*

rheum |rōōm| • *n.* a watery fluid that collects in or drips from the nose or eyes.

rheu•ma•tism |'rōōmə,tizəm| • *n.* any disease marked by inflammation and pain in the joints, muscles, or fibrous tissue, esp. rheumatoid arthritis.
DERIVATIVES: **rheu•mat•ic** *adj.*

rhythm |'riTHəm| • *n.* a strong, regular, repeated pattern of movement or sound.
■ the systematic arrangement of musical sounds, principally according to duration and periodic stress. Cf. METER. ■ a particular type of pattern formed by such arrangement: *guitar melodies with deep African rhythms.* ■ a person's natural feeling for such arrangement: *they've got no rhythm.* ■ the measured flow of words and phrases in verse or prose as determined by the relation of long and short

or stressed and unstressed syllables. ■ a regularly recurring sequence of events, actions, or processes: *the twice daily rhythms of the tides.* ■ (in art) a harmonious sequence or correlation of colors or elements.
DERIVATIVES: **rhyth•mic** *adj.* **rhyth•mi•cal** *adj.* **rhythm•less** *adj.*

rib•ald |ˈribəld; ˈribˌôld; ˈrīˌbôld| • *adj.* referring to sexual matters in an amusingly rude or irreverent way: *a ribald comment.*

rib•ald•ry |ˈribəldrē; ˈrī-| • *n.* ribald talk or behavior.

ric•tus |ˈriktəs| • *n.* a fixed grimace or grin: *Ned's smile had become a rictus of repulsion.*
DERIVATIVES: **ric•tal** |ˈriktəl| *adj.*

rife |rīf| • *adj.* [predic.] (esp. of something undesirable or harmful) of common occurrence; widespread: *male chauvinism was rife in medicine in those days.* ■ (**rife with**) full of: *the streets were rife with rumor.* • *adv.* in an unchecked or widespread manner: *speculation ran rife that he was an arms dealer.*
DERIVATIVES: **rife•ness** *n.*

riff |rif| • *n.* (in popular music and jazz) a short repeated phrase, frequently played over changing chords or harmonies or used as a background to a solo improvisation: *a brilliant guitar riff.* • *v.* [intrans.] play such phrases: *the other horns would be riffing behind him.*

rift |rift| • *n.* a crack, split, or break in something: *the wind had torn open a rift in the clouds.* ■ a major geological fault separating blocks of the earth's surface; a rift valley. ■ a serious break in friendly relations: *the killings caused a **rift between** the two nations.* • *v.* [intrans.] form fissures, cracks, or breaks, esp. through large-scale faulting; move apart: *a fragment of continental crust that rifted away from eastern Australia* | [as n.] (**rifting**) *active rifting in southwestern Mexico.* ■ [trans.] [usu. as adj.] (**rifted**) tear or force (something) apart: *the nascent rifted margins of the Red Sea.*

right |rīt| • *adj.* (in politics) of or relating to a person or party or grouping favoring conservative views. • *n.* (often **the Right**) [treated as sing. or pl.] a grouping or political party favoring conservative views and supporting capitalist economic principles. ■ the section of a group or political party adhering particularly strongly to such views.
DERIVATIVES: **right•ist** *n.*

right•eous |ˈrīCHəs| • *adj.* 1 (of a person or conduct) morally right or justifiable; virtuous. 2 perfectly wonderful; fine and genuine; of the preferred type: *righteous bread pudding.*
DERIVATIVES: **right•eous•ly** *adv.* **right•eous•ness** *n.*

right wing • *n.* (**the right wing**) the conservative or reactionary section of a political party or system.
DERIVATIVES: **right-wing•er** *n.*

rig•or |ˈrigər| • *n.* 1 the quality of being extremely thorough, exhaustive, or accurate: *his analysis is lacking in rigor.* ■ severity or strictness: *the full rigor of the law.* ■ (**rigors**) demanding, difficult, or extreme conditions: *the rigors of a harsh winter.* 2 a sudden feeling of cold with shivering accompanied by a rise in temperature, often with copious sweating, esp. at the onset or height of a fever. ■ short for *rigor mortis,* stiffening of the joints and muscles a few hours after death, usually lasting from one to four days.

rig•or•ism |ˈrigəˌrizəm| • *n.* extreme strictness in interpreting or enforcing a law, precept, or principle.
DERIVATIVES: **rig•or•ist** *n.* & *adj.*

rile |rīl| • *v.* [trans.] 1 make (someone) annoyed or irritated: *it was his air of knowing all the answers that riled her* | *he's getting you all **riled up.*** 2 make (water) turbulent or muddy.

rill |ril| • *n.* a small stream. ■ a shallow channel cut in the surface of soil or rocks by running water. ■ variant spelling of RILLE. • *v.* [intrans.] (of water) flow in or as in a rill: *the springwater rilled over our cold hands.* ■ [as adj.] (**rilled**) indented with small grooves: *blocks of butter pounded into artful shapes with rilled paddles.*

rille |ˈrilə| (also **rill**) • *n.* a fissure or narrow channel on the moon's surface.

rime |rīm| • *n.* (also **rime ice**) frost formed on cold objects by the rapid freezing of water vapor in cloud or fog. ■ poetic term for HOARFROST. • *v.* [trans.] cover (an object) with rime.

ri•par•i•an |rəˈpe(ə)rēən; rī-| • *adj.* of, relating to, or situated on the banks of a river: *all the riparian states must sign an agreement.* ■ of or relating to wetlands adjacent to rivers and streams.

rip-off |ˈripˌôf| • *n.* a fraud or swindle, esp. something that is grossly overpriced. ■ an inferior imitation of something: *rip-offs of all the latest styles.* Cf. KNOCKOFF.

ri•poste |riˈpōst| • *n.* 1 a quick clever reply to an insult or criticism. 2 (in fencing) a quick return thrust following a parry. • *v.* 1 [with direct speech] make a quick clever reply to an insult or criticism: *"You've got a strange sense of honor," Grant riposted.* 2 [intrans.] make a quick return thrust in fencing.

ris•i•ble |ˈrizəbəl| • *adj.* such as to provoke laughter: *a risible scene of lovemaking in a tent.* ■ (of a person) having the faculty or power of laughing; inclined to laugh.
DERIVATIVES: **ris•i•bil•i•ty** |ˌrizəˈbilətē| *n.* **ris•i•bly** |-blē| *adv.*

ris•qué |riˈskā| • *adj.* slightly indecent or liable to shock, esp. by being sexually suggestive: *risqué humor.*

rite |rīt| • *n.* a religious or other solemn ceremony or act: *the rite of communion* | *fertility rites.* Cf. RITUAL. ■ a body of customary observances characteristic of a church or a part of it: *the Byzantine rite.* ■ a social custom, practice, or conventional act: *the family Christmas rite.*
PHRASES: **rite of passage** a ceremony or event marking an important stage in someone's life, esp. birth, puberty, marriage, and

death: *a novel that depicts the rites of passage that lead to adulthood.*

rit·u·al |ˈrichəwəl| • *n.* a religious or solemn ceremony consisting of a series of actions performed according to a prescribed order: *the role of ritual in religion.*
■ a prescribed order of performing such a ceremony, esp. one characteristic of a particular religion or church. ■ a series of actions or type of behavior regularly and invariably followed by someone: *her visits to Joy became a ritual.* • *adj.* [attrib.] of, relating to, or done as a religious or solemn rite: *ritual burial.*
■ (of an action) arising from convention or habit: *the players gathered for the ritual pregame huddle.*
DERIVATIVES: **rit·u·al·ly** *adv.*

rit·u·al·ism |ˈrichəwəˌlizəm| • *n.* the regular observance or practice of ritual, esp. when excessive or without regard to its function.
DERIVATIVES: **rit·u·al·ist** |-list| *n.* **rit·u·al·is·tic** |ˌrichəwəˈlistik| *adj.* **rit·u·al·is·ti·cal·ly** |ˈˌrich(əw)əˈlistik(ə)lē| *adv.*

rit·u·al·ize |ˈrichəwəˌlīz| • *v.* [trans.] [usu. as adj.] (**ritualized**) make (something) into a ritual by following a pattern of actions or behavior: *hooliganism as a ritualized expression of aggression.*
■ (in zoology) cause (an action or behavior pattern) to undergo *ritualization,* the evolutionary process by which an action or behavior pattern loses its ostensible function but is retained for its role in social interaction. In psychology, *ritualization* is the formalization of certain actions expressing a particular emotion or state of mind.

ritz·y |ˈritsē| • *adj.* (**ritzier, ritziest**) expensively stylish: *the ritzy Plaza Hotel.*
DERIVATIVES: **ritz·i·ly** |ˈritsilē| *adv.* **ritz·i·ness** *n.*

rive |rīv| • *v.* (past **rived** |rīvd|; past part. **riven** |ˈrivən|) (usu. **be riven**) split or tear apart violently: *the party was riven by disagreements over abortion.*
■ split or crack (wood or stone): *the wood was riven with deep cracks.* ■ [intrans.] (of wood or stone) split or crack.

riv·et |ˈrivit| • *n.* a short metal pin or bolt for holding together two plates of metal, its headless end being beaten out or pressed down when in place.
■ a similar device for holding seams of clothing together. • *v.* (**riveted** |ˈrividid|, **riveting**) [trans.] join or fasten (plates of metal or other material) with a rivet or rivets.
■ hold (someone or something) fast so as to make them incapable of movement: *the grip on her arm was firm enough to rivet her to the spot.* ■ attract and completely engross (someone): *he was riveted by the reports shown on television* | [as adj.] (**riveting**) *a riveting story.* ■ (usu. **be riveted**) direct (one's eyes or attention) intently: *all eyes were riveted on him.*
DERIVATIVES: **riv·et·er** *n.* **riv·et·ing·ly** *adv.*

riv·u·let |ˈriv(y)ələt| • *n.* a very small stream: *a rivulet that started near the hilltop.*

RNA • *n.* ribonucleic acid, a nucleic acid present in all living cells. Its principal role is to act as a messenger carrying instructions from DNA for controlling the synthesis of proteins, although in some viruses RNA rather than DNA carries the genetic information.

ro·bot |ˈrōˌbät; ˈrōbət| • *n.* a machine capable of carrying out a complex series of actions automatically, esp. one programmable by a computer.
■ (esp. in science fiction) a machine resembling a human being and able to replicate certain human movements and functions automatically. ■ used to refer to a person who behaves in a mechanical or unemotional manner.
DERIVATIVES: **ro·bot·ic** *adj.* **ro·bot·i·cal·ly** *adv.*

ro·bot·ics |rōˈbätiks| • *plural n.* [treated as sing.] the branch of technology that deals with the design, construction, operation, and application of robots.
DERIVATIVES: **ro·bot·i·cist** |-ˈbätəsist| *n.*

ro·bust |rōˈbəst; ˈrōˌbəst| • *adj.* (**robuster, robustest**) (of a person, animal, or plant) strong and healthy; vigorous: *the Kaplans are a robust, healthy lot.*
■ (of an object) sturdy in construction: *a robust desk.* ■ (of a process or system, esp. an economic one) able to withstand or overcome adverse conditions: *California's robust property market.* ■ (of an intellectual approach or the person taking or expressing it) not perturbed by or attending to subtleties or difficulties; uncompromising and forceful: *he took quite a robust view of my case.* ■ (of action) involving physical force or energy: *a robust game of rugby.* ■ (of wine or food) strong and rich in flavor or smell.
DERIVATIVES: **ro·bust·ly** *adv.* **ro·bust·ness** *n.*

ro·caille |rōˈkī; rä-| • *n.* **1** an 18th-century artistic or architectural style of decoration characterized by elaborate ornamentation with pebbles and shells, typical of grottos and fountains. **2** (**rocailles**) tiny beads.

ro·co·co |rəˈkōkō; ˌrōkəˈkō| • *adj.* (of furniture or architecture) of or characterized by an elaborately ornamental late baroque style of decoration prevalent in 18th-century Continental Europe, with asymmetrical patterns involving motifs and scrollwork.
■ extravagantly or excessively ornate, esp. (of music or literature) highly ornamented and florid. • *n.* the rococo style of art, decoration, or architecture.

rod·o·mon·tade |ˌrädəmənˈtād; ˌrōd-; -ˈtäd| • *n.* boastful or inflated talk or behavior. • *v.* [intrans.] talk boastfully.

rogue |rōg| • *n.* **1** a dishonest or unprincipled man.
■ a person whose behavior one disapproves of but who is nonetheless likable or attractive (often used as a playful term of reproof): *Cenzo, you old rogue!* **2** [usu. as adj.] an elephant or other large wild animal driven away or living apart from the herd and having sav-

age or destructive tendencies: *a rogue elephant.*
■ a person or thing that behaves in an aberrant, faulty, or unpredictable way: [as adj.] *he hacked into data and ran rogue programs.* ■ an inferior or defective specimen among many satisfactory ones, esp. a seedling or plant deviating from the standard variety. • *v.* [trans.] remove inferior or defective plants or seedlings from (a crop).

roil |roil| • *v.* **1** [trans.] make (a liquid) turbid or muddy by disturbing the sediment: *winds roil these waters.*
■ [intrans.] (esp. of a liquid) move in a turbulent, swirling manner: *the sea roiled below her.* **2** another term for RILE (sense 1).

roist•er |ˈroistər| • *v.* [intrans.] enjoy oneself or celebrate in a noisy or boisterous way.
DERIVATIVES: **roist•er•er** *n.* **roist•er•ous** |ˈroist(ə)rəs| *adj.*

roll•o•ver • *n.* **1** the extension or transfer of a debt or other financial arrangement.
■ (in a lottery) the accumulative carryover of prize money to the following drawing. **2** the overturning of a vehicle. **3** a facility on an electronic keyboard enabling one or several keystrokes to be registered correctly while another key is depressed.

ro•man à clef |rō͵män ä ˈklä| (also **roman-à-clef**) • *n.* (pl. **romans à clef** pronunc. same) a novel in which real people or events appear with invented names.

Ro•mance |rōˈmæns; ˈrō͵mæns| • *n.* the group of Indo-European languages descended from Latin, principally French, Spanish, Portuguese, Italian, Catalan, Provençal, and Romanian. • *adj.* of, relating to, or denoting this group of languages: *the Romance languages.*

Ro•man•esque |͵rōməˈnesk| • *adj.* of or relating to a style of architecture that prevailed in Europe *c.*900–1200, although sometimes dated back to the end of the Roman Empire (5th century). • *n.* Romanesque architecture.

Romanesque architecture is characterized by round arches and massive vaulting, and by heavy piers, columns, and walls with small windows. Although disseminated throughout western Europe, the style reached its fullest development in central and northern France; the equivalent style in England is usually called Norman. In America, it enjoyed a 19th-cent. revival, notably in the work of Henry Hobson Richardson (1838–86).

ro•man-fleuve |rō͵män ˈflœv| • *n.* (pl. **romans-fleuves** pronunc. same) a novel featuring the leisurely description of the lives of closely-related people.
■ a sequence of related, self-contained novels.

Ro•man hol•i•day • *n.* an occasion on which enjoyment or profit is derived from others' suffering or discomfort.

Ro•man•ist |ˈrōmənist| • *n.* **1** an expert in or student of Roman antiquities or law, or of the Romance languages. **2** a member or supporter of the Roman Catholic Church. • *adj.* belonging or adhering to the Roman Catholic Church.

ro•man•ize |ˈrōmə͵nīz| (also **Romanize**) • *v.* [trans.] **1** bring (something, esp. a region or people) under Roman influence or authority. **2** make Roman Catholic in character. **3** put (text) into the Roman alphabet or into Roman type: *Atatürk's decision to romanize written Turkish.*
DERIVATIVES: **ro•man•i•za•tion** |͵rōmənəˈzāsHən| *n.*

ro•man•tic |rōˈmæntik; rə-| • *adj.* **1** inclined toward or suggestive of the feeling of excitement and mystery associated with love: *a romantic candlelit dinner.*
■ relating to love, esp. in a sentimental or idealized way: *a romantic comedy.* **2** of, characterized by, or suggestive of an idealized view of reality: *a romantic attitude toward the past.* **3** (usu. **Romantic**) of, relating to, or denoting the artistic and literary movement of Romanticism: *the Romantic tradition.* • *n.* a person with romantic beliefs or attitudes.
■ (usu. **Romantic**) a writer or artist of the Romantic movement.
DERIVATIVES: **ro•man•ti•cal•ly** |-ik(ə)lē| *adv.*

ro•man•ti•cism |rōˈmæntə͵sizəm; rə-| • *n.* **1** (often **Romanticism**) a movement in the arts and literature that originated in the late 18th century, emphasizing inspiration, subjectivity, and the primacy of the individual. **2** the state or quality of being romantic.

Rom•a•ny |ˈrämənē; ˈrō-| (also **Romani**) • *n.* (pl. **-ies**) **1** the Indic language of the gypsies, spoken in many dialects. **2** a gypsy. • *adj.* of or relating to gypsies or their language.

ronde |ˈränd| • *n.* a dance in which the dancers move in a circle.
■ a round or course of talk, activity, etc.; a treadmill.

ron•deau |ˈrändō; ränˈdō| • *n.* (pl. **rondeaux** |-dōz; ˈdōz|) a thirteen-line poem, divided into three stanzas of 5, 3, and 5 lines, with only two rhymes throughout and with the opening words of the first line used as a refrain at the end of the second and third stanzas.

ron•del |ˈrändəl; ränˈdel| • *n.* **1** a rondeau, esp. one of three stanzas of thirteen or fourteen lines, with the first two lines of the opening quatrain recurring at the end of the second quatrain and the concluding sestet. **2** a circular object: *at the point where these paths join there is a rondel with a fountain.*

ron•do |ˈrändō; ränˈdō| • *n.* (pl. **-os**) a musical form with a recurring leading theme, often found in the final movement of a sonata or concerto.

rood |rood| • *n.* **1** a crucifix, esp. one positioned above the *rood screen* (separating the nave and chancel) of a church or on a beam over the entrance to the chancel. **2** chiefly Brit. a measure of land area equal to a quarter of an acre.

rook•er•y |ˈrook̵ərē| • *n.* (pl. **-ies**) a breeding colony of rooks (Eurasian crows), typically

seen as a collection of nests high in a clump of trees.
- a breeding colony of seabirds (esp. penguins), seals, or turtles. ■ a dense collection of housing, esp. in a slum area.

ro•se•ate |'rōzēət; -ˌāt| • adj. **1** rose-colored.
- used in names of birds with partly pink plumage, e.g., roseate tern, roseate spoonbill. **2** optimistic; promising good fortune: *his letters home give a somewhat too roseate idea of how he lived.*

Ro•set•ta Stone |rō'zetə| an inscribed stone found near Rosetta on the western mouth of the Nile in 1799. Its text is written in three scripts: hieroglyphic, demotic, and Greek. The deciphering of the hieroglyphs by Jean-François Champollion in 1822 led to the interpretation of many other early records of Egyptian civilization.

Ro•si•cru•cian |ˌrōzə'krōōsHən; -'krōōsHən| • n. a member of a secretive 17th- and 18th-century society devoted to the study of metaphysical, mystical, and alchemical lore. An anonymous pamphlet of 1614 about a mythical 15th-century knight called Christian Rosenkreuz is said to have launched the movement.
- a member of any of a number of later organizations deriving from this. • adj. of or relating to the Rosicrucians.
DERIVATIVES: **Ro•si•cru•cian•ism** |-ˌnizəm| n.

ros•in |'räzən| • n. resin, esp. the solid amber residue obtained after the distillation of crude turpentine oleoresin, or of naphtha extract from pine stumps. It is used in adhesives, varnishes, and inks and for treating the bows of stringed instruments. • v. (**rosined, rosining**) [trans.] rub (something, esp. the bow of a stringed instrument) with rosin.
DERIVATIVES: **ros•in•y** adj.

ros•ter |'rästər; 'rô-| • n. a list or plan showing turns of duty or leave for individuals or groups in an organization: *next week's duty roster.*
- a list of members of a team or organization, in particular of athletes available to play.

ros•trum |'rästrəm; 'rô-| • n. (pl. **rostra** |'rästrə; 'rô-| or **rostrums**) **1** a raised platform on which a person stands to make a public speech, receive an award or medal, play music, or conduct an orchestra.
- a similar platform for supporting a movie or television camera. **2** a beaklike projection, esp. a stiff snout or anterior prolongation of the head in an insect, crustacean, or cetacean.
DERIVATIVES: **ros•trate** |'räsˌtrāt; 'rô ˌstrāt| adj. (in sense 2).

ro•ta•ry |'rōtərē| • adj. (of motion) revolving around a center or axis; rotational: *a rotary motion.*
- (of a thing) acting by means of rotation, esp. (of a machine) operating through the rotation of some part: *a rotary mower.* • n. (pl. **-ies**) **1** a rotary machine, engine, or device. **2** a traffic circle.

rote |rōt| • n. mechanical or habitual repetition of something to be learned: *a poem learned by rote.*

ro•to•gra•vure |ˌrōtəgrə'vyo͝or| • n. a printing system using a rotary press with intaglio cylinders, typically running at high speed and used for long print runs of magazines and stamps.
- a sheet or magazine printed with this system, esp. the color magazine of a Sunday newspaper.

ro•tund |rō'tənd; 'rōˌtənd| • adj. (of a person) plump.
- round or spherical: *huge stoves held great rotund cauldrons.* ■ (of speech or literary style) indulging in grandiloquent expression; orotund.
DERIVATIVES: **ro•tun•di•ty** |-'təndətē| n. **ro•tund•ly** adv.

rou•é |rōō'ā| • n. a debauched man, esp. an elderly one.

rou•lade |rōō'läd| • n. **1** a dish cooked or served in the form of a roll, typically made from a flat piece of meat, fish, or sponge cake, spread with a soft filling and rolled up into a spiral. **2** a florid passage of runs in classical music for a solo virtuoso, esp. one sung to one syllable.

round |rownd| • n. (in music) a song for three or more unaccompanied voices or parts, each singing the same theme but starting one after another, at the same pitch or in octaves; a simple canon.
PHRASES: **in the round 1** (of sculpture) standing free with all sides shown, rather than carved in relief against a ground. ■ treated fully and thoroughly; with all aspects shown or considered: *to understand social phenomena one must see them in the round.* **2** (of a theatrical performance) with the audience placed on at least three sides of the stage.

roun•del |'rowndl| • n. **1** a small disk, esp. a decorative medallion.
- a picture or pattern contained in a circle. ■ (in heraldry) a plain filled circle as a charge (often with a special name according to color). ■ Brit. a circular identifying mark painted on military aircraft. **2** a short poem consisting of three stanzas of three lines each, rhyming alternately, with the opening words repeated as a refrain after the first and third stanzas. The form, a variant of the *rondeau,* was developed by A.C. Swinburne.

roun•de•lay |'rowndəˌlā; 'rän-| • n. a short simple song with a refrain.
- a circle dance.

round rob•in • n. **1** [often as adj.] a tournament in which each competitor plays in turn against every other. **2** a petition, esp. one with signatures written in a circle to conceal the order of writing (so as to protect the originator).
- a letter written by several people in turn, each person adding text before passing the letter on to someone else: [as adj.] *a round-robin letter.* **3** a series or sequence: *a round robin of talks.*

roust•a•bout |'rowstəˌbowt| • n. an unskilled or casual laborer.

■ a laborer on an oil rig. ■ a dock laborer or deckhand. ■ a circus laborer.

row•el |'row(ə)l| • *n.* a spiked revolving disk at the end of a spur. • *v.* (**roweled, roweling**; Brit. **rowelled, rowelling**) [trans.] use a rowel to urge on (a horse): *he* **roweled** *his horse on as fast as he could.*

ru•ba•to |rōō'bätō| • *n.* (pl. **rubatos** or **rubati** |-'bätē|) (also **tempo rubato**) (in music) the temporary disregarding of strict tempo to allow an expressive quickening or slackening, usually without altering the overall pace. • *adj.* performed in this way.

ru•bes•cent |rōō'besənt| • *adj.* reddening; blushing.

Ru•bi•con |'rōōbə,kän, -kün| a stream in northeastern Italy that marked the ancient boundary between Italy and Cisalpine Gaul. Julius Caesar led his army across it into Italy in 49 BC, breaking the law forbidding a general to lead an army out of his province, and so committing himself to war against the Senate and Pompey. The ensuing civil war resulted in victory for Caesar after three years.
■ [as n.] a point of no return: *on the way to political union we are now* **crossing the Rubicon.**

ru•bi•cund |'rōōbə,kənd| • *adj.* (esp. of someone's face) having a ruddy complexion; high-colored.
DERIVATIVES: **ru•bi•cun•di•ty** |,rōōbə'kəndətē| *n.*

ru•big•i•nous |rōō'bijənəs| • *adj.* rust-colored.

ru•bric |'rōōbrik| • *n.* a heading on a document.
■ a direction in a liturgical book as to how a church service should be conducted. ■ a statement of purpose or function: *art of a purpose, not for its own sake, was its rubric.* ■ a category: *party policies on matters falling* **under the rubric of** *law and order.*
DERIVATIVES: **ru•bri•cal** *adj.*

ru•bri•cate |'rōōbri,kāt| • *v.* add elaborate, typically red, capital letters or other decorations to (a manuscript).
■ provide (a text) with a rubric or rubrics.
DERIVATIVES: **ru•bri•ca•tion** |-'kāsHən| *n.* **ru•bri•ca•tor** |-,kātər| *n.*

ruck |rək| • *n.* a tightly packed crowd of people.
■ (**the ruck**) the mass of ordinary people or things: *education was the key to success, a way out of the ruck.*

ruc•tion |'rəksHən| • *n.* a disturbance or quarrel.

rud•dy |'rədē| • *adj.* (**ruddier, ruddiest**) (of a person's face) having a healthy red color: *a cheerful man of ruddy complexion.*
■ having a reddish color: *the ruddy evening light.* • *v.* (**-ies, -ied**) [trans.] make ruddy in color.
DERIVATIVES: **rud•di•ly** |'rədl-ē| *adv.* **rud•di•ness** *n.*

ru•di•ment |'rōōdəmənt| • *n.* **1** (**the rudiments of**) the first principles of a subject: *she taught the girls the rudiments of reading and writing.*

■ an elementary or primitive form of something: *the rudiments of a hot-water system.* **2** an undeveloped or immature part or organ, esp. a structure in an embryo or larva that will develop into an organ, limb, etc.: *the fetal lung rudiment.* **3** a basic pattern used by drummers, such as the roll or paradiddle.
DERIVATIVES: **ru•di•men•ta•ry** *adj.*

rue |rōō| • *v.* (**rues, rued, ruing** or **rueing**) [trans.] bitterly regret (something one has done or allowed to happen) and wish it undone: *Ferguson will* **rue the day** *he turned down that offer.* • *n.* repentance; regret: *with rue my heart is laden.*
■ compassion; pity: *tears of pitying rue.*

rue•ful |'rōōfəl| • *adj.* expressing sorrow or regret, esp. when in a slightly humorous way: *she gave a rueful grin.*
DERIVATIVES: **rue•ful•ly** *adv.* **rue•ful•ness** *n.*

ru•fes•cent |rōō'fesənt| • *adj.* tinged with red or rufous.
DERIVATIVES: **ru•fes•cence** *n.*

ru•fous |'rōōfəs| • *adj.* reddish brown in color. • *n.* a reddish-brown color.

ru•gose |'rōō,gōs| • *adj.* wrinkled; corrugated: *rugose corals.*
DERIVATIVES: **ru•gos•i•ty** |rōō'gäsətē| *n.*

rum•bus•tious |,rəm'bəscHəs| • *adj.* boisterous or unruly.
DERIVATIVES: **rum•bus•tious•ly** *adv.* **rum•bus•tious•ness** *n.*

ru•mi•nant |'rōōmənənt| • *n.* **1** an even-toed ungulate mammal that chews the cud regurgitated from its first stomach (rumen). The ruminants comprise the cattle, sheep, antelopes, deer, giraffes, and their relatives. **2** a contemplative person; a person given to meditation. • *adj.* of or belonging to ruminants.

ru•mi•nate |'rōōmə,nāt| • *v.* [intrans.] **1** think deeply about something: *we sat* **ruminating on** *the nature of existence.* **2** (of a ruminant) chew the cud.
DERIVATIVES: **ru•mi•na•tion** |,rōōmə'nāsHən| *n.* **ru•mi•na•tive** |-,nātiv| *adj.* **ru•mi•na•tive•ly** |-,nātivlē| *adv.* **ru•mi•na•tor** |-,nātər| *n.*

rum•mage |'rəmij| • *v.* [intrans.] search unsystematically and untidily through a mass or receptacle: *she rummaged in her purse for the keys.* | [trans.] *he rummaged the drawer for his false teeth.*
■ [trans.] find (something) by searching in this way: *Mick* **rummaged up** *his skateboard.* ■ [trans.] (of a customs officer) make a thorough search of (a vessel): *our brief was to rummage as many of the vessels as possible.* • *n.* an unsystematic and untidy search through a mass or receptacle.
■ a thorough search of a vessel by a customs officer.
■ miscellaneous articles: [as adj.] *a rummage sale.*
DERIVATIVES: **rum•mag•er** *n.*

rump |rəmp| • *n.* **1** (**the** rump) the hind part of the body of a mammal or the lower back of a bird.
■ a person's buttocks. **2** a small or unimportant remnant of something originally larger:

once the profitable enterprises have been sold the unprofitable rump will be left.

rune |rōōn| • *n.* a letter of an ancient Germanic alphabet, related to the Roman alphabet.
■ a similar mark of mysterious or magic significance. ■ (**runes**) small stones, pieces of bone, etc., bearing such marks, and used as divinatory symbols: *the casting of the runes.* ■ a spell or incantation. ■ a section of the Kalevala or of an ancient Scandinavian poem.

Runes were used by Scandinavians and Anglo-Saxons from about the 3rd century. They were formed mainly by modifying Roman or Greek characters to suit carving, and were used both in writing and in divination.

DERIVATIVES: **ru·nic** |ˈrōōnik| *adj.*
run·nel |ˈrənl| • *n.* a narrow channel in the ground for liquid to flow through.
■ a brook or rill. ■ a small stream of a particular liquid: *a runnel of sweat.*
run·ning dog • *n.* a servile follower, esp. of a political system: *the running dogs of capitalism.*
ruse |rōōz; rōōs| • *n.* an action intended to deceive someone; a trick: *Eleanor tried to think of a ruse to get Paul out of the house.*
rus·set |ˈrəsət| • *adj.* **1** reddish brown in color: *gardens of russet and gold chrysanthemums.* **2** rustic; homely. • *n.* **1** a reddish-brown color: *the woods in autumn are a riot of russet and gold.* **2** a dessert apple of a variety with a slightly rough greenish-brown skin. **3** a coarse homespun reddish-brown or gray cloth used for simple clothing.
DERIVATIVES: **rus·set·y** *adj.*

rus·tic |ˈrəstik| • *adj.* **1** having a simplicity and charm that is considered typical of the countryside.
■ lacking the sophistication of the city; backward and provincial: *a rustic boor.* **2** constructed or made in a plain and simple fashion, in particular:
■ made of untrimmed branches or rough timber: *a rustic oak bench.* ■ with rough-hewn or roughened surface or with deeply sunk joints: *a rustic bridge.* ■ denoting freely formed lettering, esp. a relatively informal style of handwritten Roman capital letter. • *n.* an unsophisticated country person.
DERIVATIVES: **rus·ti·cal·ly** |-ik(ə)lē| *adv.* **rus·tic·i·ty** |rəˈstisətē| *n.*
rus·ti·cate |ˈrəstiˌkāt| • *v.* **1** [intrans.] go to, live in, or spend time in the country. **2** [trans.] fashion (masonry) in large blocks with sunk joints and a roughened surface: [as adj.] (**rusticated**) *the stable block was built of rusticated stone.* **3** [trans.] suspend (a student) from a school or university as a punishment.
DERIVATIVES: **rus·ti·ca·tion** |ˌrəstiˈkāSHən| *n.*
rut • *n.* (**the rut**) an annual period of sexual activity in deer and some other mammals, during which the males fight each other for access to the females. • *v.* (**rutted, rutting**) [intrans.] [often as adj.] (**rutting**) engage in such activity: *a rutting stag.*
ruth·less |ˈrōōTHlis| • *adj.* having or showing no pity or compassion for others: *a ruthless manipulator.*
DERIVATIVES: **ruth·less·ly** *adv.* **ruth·less·ness** *n.*

Ss

sab·bat·i·cal |səˈbætikəl| • *n.* a period of paid leave granted to a university teacher for study or travel, traditionally every seventh year: *she's away on sabbatical.* • *adj.* **1** of or relating to a sabbatical. **2** of or appropriate to the sabbath.
sab·o·tage |ˈsæbəˌtäzH| • *v.* [trans.] deliberately destroy, damage, or obstruct (something), esp. for political or military advantage. • *n.* the action of sabotaging something.
sa·bra |ˈsäbrə| • *n.* a Jew born in Israel (or before 1948 in Palestine).
sac·cha·rine |ˈsæk(ə)rin; -rēn; -rīn| • *adj.* [attrib.] **1** excessively sweet or sentimental. **2** relating to or containing sugar; sugary. • *n.* another term for the artificial sweetener saccharin.
sac·er·do·tal |ˌsæsərˈdōtl; ˌsækər-| • *adj.* relating to priests or the priesthood; priestly.
■ relating to or denoting a doctrine that ascribes sacrificial functions and spiritual or supernatural powers to ordained priests.
DERIVATIVES: **sac·er·do·tal·ism** |-ˌizəm| *n.*
sa·chem |ˈsāCHəm| • *n.* (among some American Indian peoples) a chief or leader.
■ a boss or leader, as, formerly, a leader in New York City's Tammany political machine.
sa·cral |ˈsækrəl; ˈsā-| • *adj.* [attrib.] **1** of or relating to the sacrum. **2** of, for, or relating to sacred rites or symbols: *sacral horns of a Minoan type.*
DERIVATIVES: **sa·cral·i·ty** |sāˈkralətē; sə-| *n.* (in sense 2).
sac·ra·ment |ˈsækrəmənt| • *n.* a religious ceremony or act of the Christian Church that is regarded as an outward and visible sign of inward and spiritual divine grace, in particular:
■ (in the Roman Catholic and many Orthodox Churches) the seven rites of baptism, confirmation, the Eucharist, penance, anointing of the sick, ordination, and matrimony.
■ (among Protestants) baptism and the Eu-

charist. ■ (also **the Blessed Sacrament** or **the Holy Sacrament**) (in Roman Catholic use) the consecrated elements of the Eucharist, esp. the Host: *he heard Mass and received the sacrament.* ■ a thing of mysterious and sacred significance; a religious symbol.

sac•ra•men•tal |ˌsækrəˈmentl| • *adj.* relating to or constituting a sacrament or the sacraments: *the sacramental wine was poured into a golden chalice.*
■ attaching great importance to sacraments. • *n.* an observance analogous to but not reckoned among the sacraments, such as the use of holy water or the sign of the cross.
DERIVATIVES: **sac•ra•men•tal•ism** |-ˌizəm| *n.* **sac•ra•men•tal•i•ty** |ˌsækrəmənˈtælitē; ˌsækrˌmenˈtælədē| *n.* **sac•ra•men•tal•ize** |-ˌīz| *v.* **sac•ra•men•tal•ly** *adv.*

sa•crar•i•um |səˈkrerēəm| • *n.* (pl. **sacraria** |-ˈkrerēə|) the sanctuary of a church.
■ (in the Roman Catholic Church) a piscina (a stone basin near the altar, for draining water used in the mass). ■ (in the ancient Roman world) a shrine, in particular the room in a house containing the penates.

sa•cred |ˈsākrid| • *adj.* connected with God (or the gods) or dedicated to a religious purpose and so deserving veneration: *sacred rites| the site at Eleusis is* **sacred to** *Demeter.*
■ religious rather than secular: *sacred music.* ■ (of writing or text) embodying the laws or doctrines of a religion: *a sacred Hindu text.* ■ regarded with great respect and reverence by a particular religion, group, or individual: *an animal* **sacred to** *Mexican culture.* ■ sacrosanct: *to a police officer nothing is sacred.*
DERIVATIVES: **sa•cred•ly** *adv.* **sa•cred•ness** *n.*

sac•ri•lege |ˈsækrəlij| • *n.* violation or misuse of what is regarded as sacred: *putting ecclesiastical vestments to secular use was considered sacrilege.*
DERIVATIVES: **sac•ri•le•gious** |ˌsækrəˈlijəs| *adj.* **sac•ri•le•gious•ly** |ˌsækrəˈlijəslē| *adv.*

sac•ris•tan |ˈsækristən| (also **sacrist** |ˈsākrist; ˈsæk-|) • *n.* **1** a person in charge of a sacristy and its contents. **2** (in earlier use) the sexton of a parish church.

sac•ris•ty |ˈsækristē| • *n.* (pl. **-ies**) a room in a church where a priest prepares for a service, and where vestments and other things used in worship are kept.

sac•ro•il•i•ac |ˌsækrōˈilēˌæk| • *adj.* relating to the sacrum and the ilium.
■ denoting the rigid joint at the back of the pelvis between the sacrum and the ilium.

sac•ro•sanct |ˈsækrōˌsæNG(k)t| • *adj.* (esp. of a principle, place, or routine) regarded as too important or valuable to be interfered with: *the individual's right to work has been upheld as sacrosanct.*
DERIVATIVES: **sac•ro•sanc•ti•ty** |ˌsækrō ˈsæNG(k)titē| *n.*

sac•rum |ˈsākrəm; ˈsā-| • *n.* (pl. **sacra** |-krə| or **sacrums**) a triangular bone in the lower back formed from fused vertebrae and situated between the two hipbones of the pelvis.

Sad•du•cee |ˈsæjəˌsē; ˈsædyə-| • *n.* a member of a Jewish sect or party of the time of Christ that denied the resurrection of the dead, the existence of spirits, and the obligation of oral tradition, emphasizing acceptance of the written Law alone. Cf. PHARISEE.
DERIVATIVES: **Sad•du•ce•an** |ˌsæjəˈsēən; ˌsædyə-| *adj.*

sa•dism |ˈsāˌdizəm| • *n.* the tendency to derive pleasure, esp. sexual gratification, from inflicting pain, suffering, or humiliation on others.
■ (in general use) deliberate cruelty.
DERIVATIVES: **sa•dist** *n.* **sa•dis•tic** |səˈdistik| *adj.* **sa•dis•ti•cal•ly** |səˈdistik(ə)lē| *adv.*

sa•do•mas•o•chism |ˌsādōˈmæsəˌkizəm; ˌsædō-| • *n.* psychological tendency or sexual practice characterized by both sadism and masochism.
DERIVATIVES: **sa•do•mas•o•chist** *n.* **sa•do•mas•o•chis•tic** |ˌsādō,mæsəˈkistik; ˌsædō-| *adj.*

sa•ga |ˈsägə| • *n.* a long story of heroic achievement, esp. a medieval prose narrative in Old Norse or Old Icelandic: *a figure straight out of a Viking saga.*
■ a long, involved story, account, or series of incidents: *the saga of her engagement.*

sa•ga•cious |səˈgāSHəs| • *adj.* having or showing keen mental discernment and good judgment; shrewd: *they were sagacious enough to avoid any outright confrontation.*
DERIVATIVES: **sa•ga•cious•ly** *adv.*

sag•a•more |ˈsægəˌmôr| • *n.* (among some American Indian peoples) a chief; a sachem.

sage • *n.* a profoundly wise man, esp. one who features in ancient history or legend. • *adj.* having, showing, or indicating profound wisdom: *they nodded in agreement with these sage remarks.*
DERIVATIVES: **sage•ly** *adv.* **sage•ness** *n.*

sa•la•cious |səˈlāSHəs| • *adj.* (of writing, pictures, or talk) treating sexual matters in an indecent way and typically conveying undue interest in or enjoyment of the subject: *salacious stories.*
■ lustful; lecherous: *his salacious grin faltered.*
DERIVATIVES: **sa•la•cious•ly** *adv.* **sa•la•cious•ness** *n.*

sa•li•ent |ˈsālyənt; -lēənt| • *adj.* **1** most noticeable or important: *it succinctly covered all the salient points of the case.*
■ prominent; conspicuous: *a salient ridge on the horizon.* ■ (of an angle) pointing outward. **2** [*postpositive*] (of a heraldic animal) standing on its hind legs with the forepaws raised, as if leaping. • *n.* a piece of land or section of fortification that juts out to form an angle.
■ an outward bulge in a line of military attack or defense.
DERIVATIVES: **sa•li•ence** *n.* **sa•li•en•cy** *n.* **sa•li•ent•ly** *adv.*

sa•line |ˈsāˌlēn; -ˌlīn| • *adj.* containing or impregnated with salt: *saline alluvial soils.*
■ relating to chemical salts. ■ (of a solution used medicinally) containing sodium chloride and/or a salt or salts of magnesium or an-

other alkali metal. • *n.* a solution of salt in water.

■ a saline solution used in medicine.
DERIVATIVES: **sa•lin•i•ty** |sə'linitē| *n.* **sal•i•ni•za•tion** |ˌsæləni'zāSHən| *n.* **sal•i•nize** |'sælə,nīz| *v.*

sal•i•vate |'sælə,vāt| • *v.* [intrans.] secrete saliva, esp. in anticipation of food.

■ display great relish at the sight or prospect of something: *I was salivating at the prospect of a $10 million loan.* ■ [trans.] cause (a person or animal) to produce an unusually copious secretion of saliva.
DERIVATIVES: **sal•i•va•tion** |ˌsælə'vāSHən| *n.*

sal•low |'sælō| • *adj.* (**sallower, sallowest**) (of a person's face or complexion) of an unhealthy yellow or pale brown color. • *v.* [trans.] make sallow.
DERIVATIVES: **sal•low•ish** *adj.* **sal•low•ness** *n.*

sal•ma•gun•di |ˌsælmə'gəndē| • *n.* (pl. **salmagundis**) a dish of chopped meat, anchovies, eggs, onions, and seasoning.

■ a general mixture; a miscellaneous collection.

sal•mo•nel•la |ˌsælmə'nelə| • *n.* (pl. **salmonellae** |-'nelē|) a bacterium that occurs mainly in the intestine, esp. a strain causing food poisoning.

■ food poisoning caused by infection with such a bacterium: *an outbreak of salmonella.*
DERIVATIVES: **sal•mo•nel•lo•sis** |-,ne'lōsis| *n.*

sa•lon |sə'län; sæ'lôN| • *n.* **1** an establishment where a hairdresser, beautician, or couturier conducts business. **2** a reception room in a large house.

■ a regular social gathering of eminent people (esp. writers and artists) at the house of a woman prominent in high society. ■ a meeting of intellectuals or other eminent people at the invitation of a celebrity or socialite. **3** (**Salon**) an annual exhibition of the work of living artists held by the Royal Academy of Painting and Sculpture in Paris, originally in the Salon d'Apollon in the Louvre in 1667.

sal•sa |'sälsə| • *n.* **1** a type of Latin American dance music incorporating elements of jazz and rock.

■ a dance performed to this music. **2** (esp. in Latin American cooking) a spicy sauce of chopped vegetables, usually including tomatoes or chilies.

sal•ta•tion |ˌsôl'tāSHən| • *n.* **1** abrupt evolutionary change; sudden large-scale mutation. **2** (in geology) the movement of hard particles over an uneven surface in a turbulent flow of air or water. **3** the action of leaping or dancing.
DERIVATIVES: **sal•ta•to•ry** |'sæltə,tôrē; 'sôl-| *adj.*

sa•lu•bri•ous |sə'lōōbrēəs| • *adj.* health-giving; healthy: *salubrious weather.*

■ (of a place) pleasant; not run-down.
DERIVATIVES: **sa•lu•bri•ous•ly** *adv.* **sa•lu•bri•ous•ness** *n.* **sa•lu•bri•ty** |-britē| *n.*

sal•u•tar•y |'sælyə,terē| • *adj.* producing good effects; beneficial: *a salutary reminder of where we came from.*

■ health-giving: *the salutary Atlantic air.*

sal•u•ta•tion |ˌsælyə'tāSHən| • *n.* a gesture or utterance made as a greeting or acknowledgment of another's arrival or departure.

■ a standard formula of words used in a letter to address the person being written to.
DERIVATIVES: **sal•u•ta•tion•al** |-SHənl| *adj.*

sa•lu•ta•to•ry |sə'lōōtə,tôrē| • *adj.* (esp. of an address) relating to or of the nature of a salutation. • *n.* (pl. **-ies**) an address of welcome, esp. one given as an oration by the student ranking second highest in a graduating class at a high school or college (the salutatorian). Cf. VALEDICTORIAN.

sal•vage |'sælvij| • *v.* [trans.] rescue (a wrecked or disabled ship or its cargo) from loss at sea: *an emerald and gold cross was salvaged from the wreck.*

■ retrieve or preserve (something) from potential loss or adverse circumstances: *it was the only crumb of comfort he could salvage from the ordeal.* • *n.* the rescue of a wrecked or disabled ship or its cargo from loss at sea: [as adj.] *a salvage operation.*

■ the cargo saved from a wrecked or sunken ship: *salvage taken from a ship that had sunk in the river.* ■ the rescue of property or material from potential loss or destruction. ■ (in law) payment made or due to a person who has saved a ship or its cargo.
DERIVATIVES: **sal•vage•a•ble** *adj.* **sal•vag•er** *n.*

sal•va•tion |sæl'vāSHən| • *n.* deliverance from sin and its consequences, believed by Christians to be brought about by faith in Christ.

■ preservation or deliverance from harm, ruin, or loss: *they try to sell it to us as economic salvation.* ■ (**one's salvation**) a source or means of being saved in this way: *his only salvation was to outfly the enemy.*

salve |sæv; säv| • *n.* an ointment used to promote healing of the skin or as protection.

■ something that is soothing or consoling for wounded feelings or an uneasy conscience: *the idea provided him with a salve for his guilt.* • *v.* [trans.] apply salve to.

■ soothe (wounded pride or one's conscience): *charity salves our conscience.*

sal•ver |'sælvər| • *n.* a tray, typically one made of silver and used on formal occasions.

sam•iz•dat |'sämiz,dät; səmyiz'dät| • *n.* the clandestine copying and distribution of literature banned by the state, esp. formerly in the communist countries of eastern Europe.

sam•sa•ra |səm'särə| • *n.* (in Hinduism and Buddhism) the cycle of death and rebirth to which life in the material world is bound, pending the attainment of NIRVANA.

■ the material world.
DERIVATIVES: **sam•sa•ric** |-'särik| *adj.*

sam•u•rai |'sæmə,rī| • *n.* (pl. same) a member of a powerful military caste in feudal Japan, esp. a member of the class of military retainers of the daimyos (see DAIMYO).

san•a•tive |ˈsænətiv| • adj. conducive to physical or spiritual health and well-being; healing.

san•a•to•ri•um |ˌsænəˈtôrēəm| • n. (pl. **sanatoriums** or **sanatoria** |-rēə|) another term for SANITARIUM.

sanc•ti•fy |ˈsæNG(k)təˌfī| • v. (-ies, -ied) [trans.] set apart as or declare holy; consecrate. ■ (often **be sanctified**) make legitimate or binding by religious sanction: *they see their love sanctified by the sacrament of marriage.* ■ free from sin; purify. ■ (often **be sanctified**) give the appearance of being right or good; legitimize: *they looked to royalty to sanctify their cause.*
DERIVATIVES: **sanc•ti•fi•ca•tion** |-fiˈkā-sHən| n. **sanc•ti•fi•er** n.

sanc•ti•mo•ni•ous |ˌsæNG(k)təˈmōnēəs| • adj. making a show of being morally superior to other people: *what happened to all the sanctimonious talk about putting his family first?*
DERIVATIVES: **sanc•ti•mo•ni•ous•ly** adv. **sanc•ti•mo•ni•ous•ness** n. **sanc•ti•mo•ny** |ˈsæNG(k)təˌmōnē| n.

sanc•tion |ˈsæNG(k)sHən| • n. **1** a threatened penalty for disobeying a law or rule: *a range of sanctions aimed at deterring insider abuse.* ■ (**sanctions**) measures taken by a nation to coerce another to conform to an international agreement or norms of conduct, typically in the form of restrictions on trade or on participation in official sporting events. ■ a consideration operating to enforce obedience to any rule of conduct. **2** official permission or approval for an action: *he appealed to the bishop for his sanction.* ■ official confirmation or ratification of a law. ■ a law or decree, esp. an ecclesiastical decree. • v. [trans.] **1** (often **be sanctioned**) give official permission or approval for (an action): *only two treatments have been sanctioned by the FDA.* **2** impose a sanction or penalty on.
DERIVATIVES: **sanc•tion•a•ble** adj.

USAGE: **Sanction** is confusing because it has two meanings that are almost opposite. In most domestic contexts, **sanction** means 'approval; permission': *Voters gave the measure their sanction.* In foreign affairs, **sanction** means 'penalty; deterrent': *International sanctions against the republic go into effect in January.*

sanc•tu•ar•y |ˈsæNG(k)CHəˌwerē| • n. (pl. -ies) **1** a place of refuge or safety: *seeking a sanctuary in time of trouble* | *his sons took sanctuary in the church.* ■ immunity from arrest: *he has been given sanctuary in the US Embassy in Beijing.* **2** [usu. with adj.] a nature reserve: *a bird sanctuary.* **3** a holy place; a temple or church. ■ the inmost recess or holiest part of a temple or church. ■ the part of the chancel of a church containing the high altar.

sanc•tum |ˈsæNG(k)təm| • n. (pl. **sanctums**) a sacred place, esp. a shrine within a temple or church.

■ a private place from which most people are excluded.

sang•froid |säNGˈfrwä| (also **sang-froid**) • n. composure or coolness as shown in danger or under trying circumstances.

san•gui•nar•y |ˈsæNGgwəˌnerē| • adj. involving or causing much bloodshed: *sanguinary battles.*

san•guine |ˈsæNGgwin| • adj. **1** cheerfully optimistic. ■ (in medieval science and medicine) of or having the constitution associated with the predominance of blood among the bodily humors, supposedly marked by a ruddy complexion and an optimistic disposition. ■ (of the complexion) florid; ruddy. ■ bloody or bloodthirsty. **2** (in heraldry) blood-red. • n. a blood-red color. ■ a deep red-brown crayon or pencil containing iron oxide. ■ a blood-red stain used in heraldic blazoning.
DERIVATIVES: **san•guine•ly** adv. **san•guine•ness** n.

san•guin•e•ous |sæNGˈgwinēəs| • adj. Medicine, & archaic of or relating to blood. ■ sanguinary. ■ blood red. ■ full-blooded; plethoric.

san•i•tar•i•um |ˌsænəˈterēəm| • n. (pl. **sanitariums** or **sanitaria** |-ˈterēə|) an establishment for the medical treatment of people who are convalescing or have a chronic illness.

sans-cu•lotte |ˌsænz k(y)o͞oˈlät| • n. a lower-class Parisian republican in the French Revolution. ■ an extreme republican or revolutionary.
DERIVATIVES: **sans-cu•lot•tism** |k(y)əˈlätizəm| n.

san•sei |ˈsänsā| • n. (pl. same) a person born in the US or Canada whose grandparents were immigrants from Japan. Cf. NISEI, ISSEI.

sans ser•if |ˌsæn(z) ˈserəf| • n. (in printing, engraving, etc.) a style of type without serifs. • adj. without serifs.

sap•id |ˈsæpid| • adj. having a strong, pleasant taste. ■ (of talk or writing) pleasant or interesting.
DERIVATIVES: **sa•pid•i•ty** |səˈpidité| n.

sa•pi•ent |ˈsāpēənt| • adj. **1** wise, or attempting to appear wise. ■ (chiefly in science fiction) intelligent: *sapient life forms.* **2** of or relating to the human species (Homo sapiens): *our sapient ancestors of 40,000 years ago.* • n. a human of the species Homo sapiens.
DERIVATIVES: **sa•pi•ence** n. **sa•pi•ent•ly** adv.

sap•o•na•ceous |ˌsæpəˈnāsHəs| • adj. of, like, or containing soap; soapy.

sa•pon•i•fy |səˈpänəˌfī| • v. (-ies, -ied) [trans.] turn (fat or oil) into soap by reaction with an alkali: [as adj.] (**saponified**) *saponified vegetable oils.* ■ convert (any ester) into an alcohol and a metal salt by treatment with an alkaline solution.
DERIVATIVES: **sa•pon•i•fi•a•ble** adj. **sa•pon•i•fi•ca•tion** |səˌpänəfiˈkāsHən| n.

sap•phic |'sæfik| • adj. 1 of or relating to lesbians or lesbianism: sapphic lovers. 2 (**Sapphic**) of or relating to the Greek lyric poet Sappho (7th cent. BC) or her poetry. • plural n. (**sapphics**) verse in a meter associated with Sappho.
DERIVATIVES: **sap•phism** n.
sap•ro•phyte |'sæprə‚fīt| • n. a plant, fungus, or microorganism that lives on dead or decaying organic matter.
DERIVATIVES: **sap•ro•phyt•ic** |‚sæprə'fi-ṭik| adj. **sap•ro•phyt•i•cal•ly** |‚sæprə'fi-ṭik(ə)lē| adv.
sar•casm |'sär‚kæzəm| • n. the use of irony to mock or convey contempt: his voice, hardened by sarcasm, could not hide his resentment.
DERIVATIVES: **sar•cas•tic** adj. **sar•cas•ti•cal•ly** adj.
sar•coid |'sär‚koid| • adj. [attrib.] resembling flesh.
sar•coph•a•gus |sär'käfəgəs| • n. (pl. **sar•cophagi** |-‚jī|) a stone coffin, typically adorned with a sculpture or inscription and associated with the ancient civilizations of Egypt, Rome, and Greece.
sar•don•ic |sär'dänik| • adj. grimly mocking or cynical: Starkey attempted a sardonic smile.
DERIVATIVES: **sar•don•i•cal•ly** |-ik(ə)lē| adv. **sar•don•i•cism** |-'dänə‚sizəm| n.
sar•to•ri•al |sär'tôrēəl| • adj. [attrib.] of or relating to tailoring, clothes, or style of dress: sartorial elegance.
DERIVATIVES: **sar•to•ri•al•ly** adv.
sa•shay |sæ'SHā| • v. [intrans.] 1 [with adverbial of direction] walk in an ostentatious yet casual manner, typically with exaggerated movements of the hips and shoulders: Louise was sashaying along in a long black satin dress. 2 perform the sashay. • n. (in square dancing) a figure in which partners circle each other by taking sideways steps.
Sa•tan |'sātn| (in Christianity) the supreme evil spirit; the Devil; Lucifer.
Sa•tan•ism |'sātn‚izəm| • n. the worship of Satan, typically involving a travesty of Christian symbols and practices, such as placing a cross upside down.
■ evil practice; wickedness.
DERIVATIVES: **sa•tan•ist** n. & adj. **sa•tan•is•tic** adj.
sate |sāt| • v. [trans.] satisfy (a desire or an appetite) to the full: sate your appetite at the resort's restaurant.
■ supply (someone) with as much as or more of something than is desired or can be managed: afterward, sated and happy, they both slept.
DERIVATIVES: **sate•less** adj.
sa•teen |sæ'tēn| • n. a cotton fabric woven like satin with a glossy surface.
sat•el•lite |'sæṭl‚īt| • n. 1 (also **artificial satellite**) an artificial body placed in orbit around the earth or another planet in order to collect information or for communication.
■ [as adj.] transmitted by satellite; using or relating to satellite technology: satellite broadcasting. ■ satellite television: a news service on satellite. 2 Astronomy a celestial body orbiting the earth or another planet. 3 [usu. as adj.]

something that is separated from or on the periphery of something else but is nevertheless less dependent on or controlled by it: satellite offices.
■ a small country or state politically or economically dependent on another. 4 a portion of the DNA of a genome with repeating base sequences and of different density from the main sequence.
sa•ti•ate |'sāSHē‚āt| • v. another term for SATE. • adj. satisfied to the full; satiated.
DERIVATIVES: **sa•tia•ble** |-SHəbəl| adj. **sa•ti•a•tion** |‚sāSHē'āSHən| n.
sa•ti•e•ty |sə'tīəṭē| • n. the feeling or state of being sated.
sat•ire |'sæ‚tīr| • n. the use of humor, irony, exaggeration, or ridicule to expose and criticize people's stupidity or vices, particularly in the context of contemporary politics and other topical issues.
■ a play, novel, film, or other work that uses satire: a stinging satire on American politics. ■ a genre of literature characterized by the use of satire. ■ (in Latin literature) a literary miscellany, esp. a poem ridiculing prevalent vices or follies.
DERIVATIVES: **sa•tir•i•cal** adj. **sat•i•rist** |'sæṭərist| n. **sat•i•ri•za•tion** n. **sat•i•rize** v.
sa•to•ri |sə'tôrē| • n. (in Zen Buddhism) sudden enlightenment: the road that leads to satori.
sa•trap |'sā‚træp; 'sæ-| • n. a provincial governor in the ancient Persian empire.
■ any subordinate or local ruler.
sat•u•rate • v. |'sæCHə‚rāt| [trans.] (usu. **be saturated**) cause (something) to become thoroughly soaked with liquid so that no more can be absorbed: the soil is saturated.
■ cause (a substance) to combine with, dissolve, or hold the greatest possible quantity of another substance: the groundwater is saturated with calcium hydroxide. ■ (usu. **be saturated with**) fill (something or someone) with something until no more can be held or absorbed: thoroughly saturated with powerful and seductive messages from the media. ■ supply (a market) beyond the point at which the demand for a product is satisfied: Japan's electronics industry began to saturate the world markets. ■ overwhelm (an enemy target area) by concentrated bombing. • n. |-rət| (usu. **saturates**) a saturated fat. • adj. |-rət| saturated with moisture.
DERIVATIVES: **sat•u•ra•ble** |-rəbəl| adj.
sat•u•rat•ed |'sæCHə‚rāṭid| • adj. 1 holding as much water or moisture as can be absorbed; thoroughly soaked.
■ (in chemistry, of a solution) containing the largest possible amount of a particular solute. ■ [often in combination] having or holding as much as can be absorbed of something: the glitzy, media-saturated plasticity of Los Angeles. 2 (of an organic molecule) containing the greatest possible number of hydrogen atoms, without carbon–carbon double or triple bonds.
■ denoting fats containing a high proportion of fatty acid molecules without double

bonds, considered to be less healthy in the diet than unsaturated fats. **3** (of color) very bright, full, and free from an admixture of white: *intense and saturated color.*

Sat•ur•na•li•a |ˌsætərˈnālēə; -nālyə| • *n.* [treated as sing. or pl.] the ancient Roman festival of Saturn in December, which was a period of general merrymaking and was the predecessor of Christmas.
■ **(saturnalia)** an occasion of wild revelry.
DERIVATIVES: **sat•ur•na•li•an** *adj.*

sat•ur•nine |ˈsætərˌnīn| • *adj.* (of a person or personal manner) slow and gloomy: *a saturnine temperament.*
■ (of a person or personal features) dark in coloring and moody or mysterious: *his saturnine face and dark, watchful eyes.* ■ (of a place or an occasion) gloomy.
DERIVATIVES: **sat•ur•nine•ly** *adv.*

sat•ya•gra•ha |səˈtyägrəhə; ˈsətyə,grəhə| • *n.* a policy of passive political resistance, esp. that advocated by Mahatma Gandhi against British rule in India.

sa•tyr |ˈsætər; ˈsātər| • *n.* one of a class of lustful, drunken woodland gods. In Greek art they were represented as a man with a horse's ears and tail, but in Roman representations as a man with a goat's ears, tail, legs, and horns.
■ a man who has strong sexual desires.
DERIVATIVES: **sa•tyr•ic** |səˈtirik| *adj.*

sa•ty•ri•a•sis |ˌsætəˈrīəsis; ˌsā-| • *n.* uncontrollable or excessive sexual desire in a man. Cf. NYMPHOMANIA.

sau•dade |sow'dädə| • *n.* a feeling of longing, melancholy, or nostalgia that is supposedly characteristic of the Portuguese or Brazilian temperament.

saun•ter |ˈsôntər| • *v.* [no obj., with adverbial of direction] walk in a slow, relaxed manner, without hurry or effort. • *n.* a leisurely stroll: *a quiet saunter down the road.*
DERIVATIVES: **saun•ter•er** *n.*

sa•van•na |səˈvænə| (also **savannah**) • *n.* a grassy plain in tropical and subtropical regions, with few trees.

sa•vant |sæˈvänt; sə-| • *n.* a learned person, esp. a distinguished scientist. See also IDIOT SAVANT.

sav•oir faire |ˌsævwär 'fer| (also **savoir-faire**) • *n.* the ability to act or speak appropriately in social situations.

sa•vor |ˈsāvər| (Brit. **savour**) • *v.* **1** [trans.] taste (good food or drink) and enjoy it to the full: *gourmets will savor our game specialties.*
■ enjoy or appreciate (something pleasant) to the full, esp. by dwelling on it: *I wanted to savor every moment.* **2** [intrans.] **(savor of)** have a suggestion or trace of (something, esp. something bad): *their genuflections savored of superstition and popery.* • *n.* a characteristic taste, flavor, or smell, esp. a pleasant one: *the subtle savor of wood smoke.*
■ a suggestion or trace, esp. of something bad.
DERIVATIVES: **sa•vor•less** *adj.*

sa•vor•y |ˈsāvərē| (Brit. **savoury**) • *adj.* **1** (of food) belonging to the category that is salty or spicy rather than sweet. **2** [usu. with negative] morally wholesome or acceptable: *everyone knew*

it was a front for less savory operations. • *n.* (pl. **-ies**) chiefly Brit. a savory dish, esp. a snack or an appetizer.
DERIVATIVES: **sa•vor•i•ly** |-rəlē| *adv.* **sa•vor•i•ness** *n.*

Sa•voy•ard |səˈvoi| **1** an inhabitant of Savoy, an area of SE France that borders on NW Italy, a former duchy ruled by the counts of Savoy from the 11th century. **2** a member of the D'Oyly Carte company that originally presented Gilbert and Sullivan operas at the Savoy Theatre in London.
■ a devotee of these operas.

sa•yo•na•ra |ˌsīəˈnärə| • *exclam.* goodbye.

sc. • *abbr.* scilicent; that is to say (used to introduce a word to be supplied or an explanation of an ambiguity).

scab |skæb| • *n.* **1** a dry, rough protective crust that forms over a cut or wound during healing.
■ mange or a similar skin disease in animals. ■ [usu. with adj.] any of a number of fungal diseases of plants in which rough patches develop, esp. on apples and potatoes. **2** a person or thing regarded with dislike and disgust.
■ a person who refuses to strike or to join a labor union or who takes over the job responsibilites of a striking worker. • *v.* **(scabbed, scabbing)** [intrans.] **1** [usu. as adj.] **(scabbed)** become encrusted or covered with a scab or scabs: *she rested her scabbed fingers on his arm.* **2** act or work as a scab.
DERIVATIVES: **scab•like** |-ˌlīk| *adj.*

scab•lands |ˈskæb,lændz| • *plural n.* flat elevated land deeply scarred by channels of glacial origin and with poor soil and little vegetation, esp. in the Columbia Plateau of Washington State.

scab•rous |ˈskæbrəs| • *adj.* **1** rough and covered with, or as if with, scabs. **2** indecent; salacious: *scabrous publications.*
DERIVATIVES: **scab•rous•ly** *adv.* **scab•rous•ness** *n.*

sca•lar |ˈskālər| • *adj.* (of a quantity) having only magnitude, not direction. • *n.* a scalar quantity. Cf. VECTOR (sense 1).

scal•a•wag |ˈskælə,wæg| (also **scallywag** |ˈskælē-|) • *n.* a person who behaves badly but in an amusingly mischievous rather than harmful way; a rascal.
■ a white Southerner who collaborated with northern Republicans during Reconstruction (1865–77), often for personal profit. The term was used derisively by white Southern Democrats who opposed Reconstruction legislation.

scalp |skælp| • *n.* **1** the skin covering the head, excluding the face.
■ the scalp with the hair belonging to it cut or torn away from an enemy's head as a battle trophy, esp. by an American Indian. • *v.* [trans.] take the scalp of (an enemy).
■ punish severely: *if I ever heard anybody doing that, I'd scalp them.* ■ sell (a ticket) for a popular event at a price higher than the official one: *tickets were scalped for forty times their face value.*
DERIVATIVES: **scalp•er** *n.*

scan |skæn| • *v.* (**scanned, scanning**) [trans.] **1** look at all parts of (something) carefully in order to detect some feature: *he raised his binoculars to scan the coast.*
■ look quickly but not very thoroughly through (a document or other text) in order to identify relevant information: *we scan the papers for news from the trouble spots* | [intrans.] *I* **scanned through** *the reference materials.*
■ cause (a surface, object, or part of the body) to be traversed by a detector or an electromagnetic beam: *their brains are scanned so that researchers can monitor the progress of the disease.* ■ [with obj. and adverbial] cause (a beam) to traverse across a surface or object: *we scanned the beam over a sector of 120°.* ■ resolve (a picture) into its elements of light and shade in a prearranged pattern for the purposes of television transmission. ■ convert (a document or picture) into digital form for storage or processing on a computer: *text and pictures can be* **scanned into** *the computer.* **2** analyze the meter of (a line of verse) by reading with the emphasis on its rhythm or by examining the pattern of feet or syllables.
■ [intrans.] (of verse) conform to metrical principles. • *n.* an act of scanning someone or something: *a quick scan of the sports page.*
■ a medical examination using a scanner: *a brain scan.* ■ an image obtained by scanning or with a scanner: *we can't predict anything until we have seen the scan.*
DERIVATIVES: **scan•na•ble** *adj.*

scan•dent |'skændənt| • *adj.* (esp. of a plant) having a climbing habit.

scant |skænt| • *adj.* barely sufficient or adequate: *companies with scant regard for the safety of future generations.*
■ [attrib.] barely amounting to a specified number or quantity: *she weighed a scant two pounds.* • *v.* [trans.] provide grudgingly or in insufficient amounts: *he does not scant his attention to the later writings.*
■ deal with inadequately; neglect: *the press regularly scants a host of issues relating to safety and health.*
DERIVATIVES: **scant•ly** *adv.* **scant•ness** *n.*

scant•y |'skæntē| • *adj.* (**scantier, scantiest**) small or insufficient in quantity or amount: *scanty wages.*
■ (of clothing) revealing; skimpy: *the women looked cold in their scanty gowns.*
DERIVATIVES: **scant•i•ly** |'skæntəlē; 'skæntḻ-ē| *adv.* **scant•i•ness** *n.*

scape•goat |'skāp,gōt| • *n.* (in the Bible) a goat sent into the wilderness after the Jewish chief priest had symbolically laid the sins of the people upon it (Lev. 16).
■ a person who is blamed for the wrongdoings, mistakes, or faults of others, esp. for reasons of expediency. • *v.* [trans.] make a scapegoat of.
DERIVATIVES: **scape•goat•er** *n.* **scape•goat•ing** *n.* **scape•goat•ism** |-,izəm| *n.*

scape•grace |'skāp,grās| • *n.* a mischievous or wayward person, esp. a young person or child; a rascal.

scap•u•lar |'skæpyələr| • *adj.* of or relating to

the shoulder or shoulder blade (*scapula*). • *n.* **1** a short monastic cloak covering the shoulders.
■ a symbol of affiliation to an ecclesiastical order, consisting of two strips of cloth hanging down the breast and back and joined across the shoulders. **2** a bandage passing over and around the shoulders. **3** a feather above the point where the wing joins the body.

scar•ab |'skærəb; 'sker-| • *n.* (also **scarab beetle** or **sacred scarab**) a large dung beetle *Scarabaeus sacer* of the eastern Mediterranean area, regarded as sacred in ancient Egypt.
■ an ancient Egyptian gem cut in the form of this beetle, sometimes depicted with the wings spread, and engraved with hieroglyphs on the flat underside.

scar•a•mouch |'skærə,mōōSH; -,mōōCH; 'sker-| • *n.* a boastful but cowardly person.

scar•i•fy[1] |'skærə,fī; 'sker-| • *v.* (**-ies, -ied**) [trans.] make cuts or scratches in (the surface of something), in particular:
■ break up the surface of (soil or a road or pavement). ■ make shallow incisions in (the skin), esp. as a medical procedure or traditional cosmetic practice: *she scarified the snakebite with a paring knife.* ■ criticize severely and hurtfully.
DERIVATIVES: **scar•i•fi•ca•tion** |-fi'kā-SHən| *n.*

scar•i•fy[2] • *v.* (**-ies, -ied**) [trans.] [usu. as adj.] (**scarifying**) frighten: *a scarifying mix of extreme violence and absurdist humor.*

scarp |skärp| • *n.* a very steep bank or slope; an escarpment.
■ the inner wall of a ditch in a fortification. • *v.* [trans.] cut or erode (a slope or hillside) so that it becomes steep, perpendicular, or precipitous.
■ provide (a ditch in a fortification) with a steep scarp (inner wall) and counterscarp (outer wall).

scathe |skāT͟H| • *v.* [with obj. and usu. with negative] (usu. **be scathed**) harm; injure: *he was barely scathed.*
■ damage or destroy by fire or lightning. • *n.* harm; injury.

scath•ing |'skāT͟HiNG| • *adj.* witheringly scornful; severely critical: *a scathing attack on the governor.*
DERIVATIVES: **scath•ing•ly** *adv.*

sca•tol•o•gy |skə'täləjē| • *n.* an interest in or preoccupation with excrement and excretion.
■ obscene literature that is concerned with excrement and excretion.
DERIVATIVES: **scat•o•log•i•cal** |'skætḻ'äjikəl| *adj.*

scav•eng•er |'skævənjər| • *n.* an animal that feeds on carrion, dead plant material, or refuse.
■ a person who searches for and collects discarded items. ■ (in chemistry) a substance or microorganism that reacts with and removes particular molecules, radicals, etc.

sce•nar•i•o |sə'nerē,ō| • *n.* (pl. **-os**) a written outline of a movie, piece of writing, or stage work giving details of the plot and individual scenes. ■ a postulated sequence or development of events: *a possible scenario is that he was attacked after opening the front door.* ■ a setting, in particular for a work of art or literature: *the scenario is World War II.*

USAGE: The proper meaning of this word is 'an outline of a plot' or 'a postulated sequence of events' (*the worst-case scenario*). It should not be used loosely to mean 'situation,' e.g., *a nightmare scenario.*

scep•ter |ˈseptər| (Brit. **sceptre**) • *n.* an ornamented staff carried by rulers on ceremonial occasions as a symbol of sovereignty. ■ the authority symbolized by a scepter.
DERIVATIVES: **scep•tered** *adj.*

sche•ma |ˈskēmə| • *n.* (pl. **schemata** |-mə-tə| or **schemas**) a representation of a plan or theory in the form of an outline or model: *a schema of scientific reasoning.* ■ (in logic) a syllogistic figure. ■ (in Kantian philosophy) a conception of what is common to all members of a class; a general or essential type or form.
DERIVATIVES: **sche•ma•ti•za•tion** *n.* **sche•ma•tize** *v.*

sche•mat•ic |skəˈmætik; skē-| • *adj.* (of a diagram or other representation) symbolic and simplified. ■ (of thought, ideas, etc.) simplistic or formulaic in character, usually to an extent inappropriate to the complexities of the subject matter: *a highly schematic reading of the play.* • *n.* (in technical contexts) a schematic diagram, in particular of an electric or electronic circuit.
DERIVATIVES: **sche•mat•i•cal•ly** |-ik(ə)-lē| *adv.*

scher•zo |ˈskertsō| • *n.* (pl. **scherzos** or **scherzi** |-sē|) a vigorous, light, or playful musical composition, typically comprising a movement in a symphony or sonata.

schism |ˈs(k)izəm| • *n.* a split or division between strongly opposed sections or parties, caused by differences in opinion or belief. ■ the formal separation of a church into two churches or the secession of a group owing to doctrinal and other differences.

schis•mat•ic |s(k)izˈmætik| • *adj.* of, characterized by, or favoring schism. • *n.* (esp. in the Christian Church) a person who promotes schism; an adherent of a schismatic group.
DERIVATIVES: **schis•mat•i•cal•ly** |-ik(ə)-lē| *adv.*

schiz•oid |ˈskitˌsoid| • *adj.* denoting or having a personality type characterized by emotional aloofness and solitary habits. ■ (in general use) resembling schizophrenia in having inconsistent or contradictory elements; mad or crazy: *it's a frenzied, schizoid place.* • *n.* a schizoid person.

schiz•o•phre•ni•a |ˌskitsəˈfrēnēə; -ˈfrenēə| • *n.* a long-term mental disorder involving a breakdown in the relation between thought, emotion, and behavior, leading to faulty perception, inappropriate actions and feelings, withdrawal from reality and personal relationships into fantasy and delusion, and a sense of mental fragmentation. ■ (in general use) a mentality or approach characterized by inconsistent or contradictory elements.
DERIVATIVES: **schiz•o•phren•ic** |-ˈfrenik| *adj. & n.*

schle•miel |SHləˈmēl| (also **shlemiel**) • *n.* a stupid, awkward, or unlucky person.

schlep |SHlep| (also **schlepp** or **shlep**) • *v.* (**schlepped, schlepping**) [trans.] haul or carry (something heavy or awkward): *she schlepped her groceries home.* ■ [no obj., with adverbial of direction] (of a person) go or move reluctantly or with effort: *I would have preferred not to schlep all the way over there to run an errand.* • *n.* **1** a tedious or difficult journey. **2** (also **schlepper**) a person of little worth; a fool; a pauper, beggar, or hanger-on.

schlock |SHläk| (also **shlock**) • *n.* cheap or inferior goods or material; trash: *they peddle their schlock to willing tourists* | [as adj.] *schlock journalism.* Cf. kitsch.
DERIVATIVES: **schlock•y** *adj.*

schmaltz |SHmälts; SHmôlts| (also **schmalz**) • *n.* excessive sentimentality, esp. in music or movies.
DERIVATIVES: **schmaltz•y** *adj.* (**schmaltz•i•er, schmaltz•i•est**).

schmear |SHmir| (also **schmeer, shmeer,** or **shmear**) • *n.* **1** a corrupt or underhanded inducement; a bribe. **2** a smear or spread: *the bagel so perfect with a schmear of low-fat cream cheese.* • *v.* [trans.] flatter or ingratiate oneself with (someone): *he was constantly buying us drinks and schmearing us up.*
PHRASES: **the whole schmear** everything possible or available; every aspect of the situation: *I'm going for the whole schmear.*

schmo |SHmō| (also **shmo**) • *n.* (pl. **-oes**) informal a fool or a bore.

schmooze |SHmo͞oz| (also **shmooze**) • *v.* talk intimately and cozily; gossip. ■ talk in such a way to (someone), typically in order to manipulate, flatter, or impress them: *schmooze with prospective clients.* • *n.* a long and intimate conversation.
DERIVATIVES: **schmooz•er** *n.* **schmooz•y** *adj.*

schmuck |SHmək| (also **shmuck**) • *n.* a foolish or contemptible person.

schnapps |SHnäps; SHnæps| • *n.* a strong alcoholic drink resembling gin and often flavored with fruit: *peach schnapps.*

schnook |SHno͝ok| (also **shnook**) • *n.* a person easily duped; a fool.

schnor•rer |ˈSHnôrər| (also **shnorrer**) • *n.* a beggar or scrounger; a layabout.

scho•las•tic |skəˈlæstik| • *adj.* **1** of or concerning schools and education: *scholastic achievement.* ■ of or relating to secondary schools. **2** of, relating to, or characteristic of medieval scholasticism. ■ typical of scholasticism in being pedantic or overly subtle. • *n.* **1** historical an adherent of

scholasticism; a schoolman. **2** (in the Roman Catholic Church) a member of a religious order, esp. the Society of Jesus, who is between the novitiate and the priesthood.
DERIVATIVES: **scho•las•ti•cal•ly** |-ik(ə)lē| adv.

schuss |SHo͞os; SHo͞os| • n. a straight downhill run on skis. • v. [intrans.] make a straight downhill run on skis.

schwa |SHwä| • n. the unstressed central vowel (as in a moment ago), represented by the symbol (ə) in the International Phonetic Alphabet.

sci•at•ic |sīˈætik| • adj. of or relating to the hip. ■ of or affecting the sciatic nerve. ■ suffering from or liable to sciatica.
DERIVATIVES: **sci•at•i•cal•ly** |-ik(ə)lē| adv.

sci•at•i•ca |sīˈætikə| • n. pain affecting the back, hip, and outer side of the leg, caused by compression of a spinal nerve root in the lower back, often owing to degeneration of an intervertebral disk.

sci•ence |ˈsīəns| • n. the intellectual and practical activity encompassing the systematic study of the structure and behavior of the physical and natural world through observation and experiment: the world of science and technology. ■ a particular area of this: veterinary science | the agricultural sciences. ■ a systematically organized body of knowledge on a particular subject: the science of criminology. ■ knowledge of any kind.

sci•i•cet |ˈsīlə,set| (abbr. **sc**) • adv. that is to say; namely (introducing a word to be supplied or an explanation of an ambiguity).

scin•til•la |sinˈtilə| • n. [in sing.] a tiny trace or spark of a specified quality or feeling: a scintilla of doubt.

scin•til•late |ˈsin(t)l,āt| • v. [intrans.] emit flashes of light; sparkle. ■ fluoresce momentarily when struck by a charged particle or photon. ■ talk or write cleverly or wittily: [as adj.] scintillating repartee.
DERIVATIVES: **scin•til•la•tion** n. **scin•til•lant** |-ənt| adj. & n.

sci•o•list |ˈsīəlist| • n. a person who pretends to be knowledgeable and well informed.
DERIVATIVES: **sci•o•lism** |-,lizəm| n. **sci•o•lis•tic** |,sīəˈlistik| adj.

sci•on |ˈsīən| • n. **1** (also **cion**) a young shoot or twig of a plant, esp. one cut for grafting or rooting. **2** a descendant of a notable family or one with a long lineage: he was the scion of a wealthy family.

scis•sion |ˈsizHən; ˈsisH-| • n. the action or state of cutting or being cut, in particular: ■ breakage of a chemical bond, esp. one in a long chain molecule so that two smaller chains result. ■ a division or split between people or parties; a schism.

scle•ro•sis |skləˈrōsis| • n. abnormal hardening of body tissue. ■ excessive resistance to change: the challenge was to avoid institutional sclerosis.
DERIVATIVES: **scle•rot•ic** adj.

sco•li•o•sis |,skōlēˈōsis| • n. abnormal lateral curvature of the spine.
DERIVATIVES: **sco•li•ot•ic** |-ˈätik| adj.

sconce[1] |skäns| • n. **1** a candle holder, or a holder of another light source, that is attached to a wall with an ornamental bracket. **2** a flaming torch or candle secured in such a holder.

sconce[2] • n. a small fort or earthwork defending a ford, pass, or castle gate. ■ a shelter or screen serving as protection from fire or the weather.

sco•ri•a |ˈskôrēə| • n. (pl. **scoriae** |ˈskôrē-ē|) basaltic lava ejected as fragments from a volcano, typically with a frothy texture. ■ slag separated from molten metal during smelting.
DERIVATIVES: **sco•ri•a•ceous** |,skôrē ˈäsHəs| adj.

scot-free • adv. without suffering any punishment or injury: the people who kidnapped you will get off scot-free.

sco•top•ic |skəˈtōpik; -ˈtäpik| • adj. relating to or denoting vision in dim light, believed to involve chiefly the rods of the retina.

Scots |skäts| • adj. another term for Scottish: a Scots accent. • n. the form of English used in Scotland.

scour[1] |skowr| • v. [trans.] **1** clean or brighten the surface of (something) by rubbing it hard, typically with an abrasive or detergent: he scoured the bathtub. ■ remove (dirt or unwanted matter) by rubbing in such a way: use an electric toothbrush to scour off plaque | [intrans.] I've spent all day mopping and scouring. ■ (of water or a watercourse) make (a channel or pool) by flowing quickly over something and removing soil or rock: a stream came crashing through a narrow cavern to scour out a round pool below. **2** administer a strong purgative to. • n. **1** the action or an act of scouring or the state of being scoured, esp. by swift-flowing water. **2** (also **scours**) diarrhea in livestock, esp. cattle and pigs.
DERIVATIVES: **scour•er** n.

scour[2] • v. [trans.] subject (a place, text, etc.) to a thorough search in order to locate something: David scoured each newspaper for an article on the murder. ■ [no obj., with adverbial of direction] move rapidly in a particular direction, esp. in search or pursuit of someone or something: he scoured up the ladder.

scourge |skərj| • n. **1** a whip used formerly as an instrument of punishment. **2** a person or thing that causes great trouble or suffering: the scourge of mass unemployment. • v. [trans.] **1** whip (someone) as a punishment. **2** cause great suffering to: political methods used to scourge and oppress workers.
DERIVATIVES: **scourg•er** n.

scree |skrē| • n. a mass of small loose stones that form or cover a slope on a mountain. ■ a slope covered with such stones. Cf. TALUS.

screed |skrēd| • n. **1** a long speech or piece of writing, typically one regarded as tedious.

2 a leveled layer of material (e.g., concrete) applied to a floor or other surface. ■ a strip of plaster or other material placed on a surface as a guide to thickness.

scribe |skrīb| • *n.* **1** a person who copies out documents, esp. one employed to do this before printing was invented. ■ a writer, esp. a journalist. **2** (also **Scribe**) an ancient Jewish record-keeper or, later, a professional theologian and jurist. **3** (also **scriber, scribe awl**) a pointed tool for marking wood, stone, metal, etc., to guide a saw, or in sign-writing. • *v.* [trans.] **1** write: *he scribed a note that he passed to Dan.* **2** mark with a scribe.
DERIVATIVES: **scrib•al** |-bəl| *adj.*

scrim |skrim| • *n.* strong, coarse fabric, chiefly used for heavy-duty lining or upholstery. ■ a piece of gauze cloth that appears opaque until lit from behind, used as a theatrical screen or backdrop. ■ a similar heatproof cloth put over film or television lamps to diffuse the light. ■ a thing that conceals or obscures something: *a thin scrim of fog.*

scrim•mage |ˈskrimij| • *n.* **1** a confused struggle or fight. **2** (in football) the beginning of each down of play, with the ball placed on the ground with its longest axis at right angles to the goal line. Cf. SCRUM. ■ offensive plays begun in this way: *none of their 10 points was scored from scrimmage.* ■ a session in which teams practice by playing a simulated game. • *v.* [intrans.] (chiefly football) engage in a practice scrimmage.
DERIVATIVES: **scrim•mag•er** *n.*

scrim•shaw |ˈskrim,shô| (also **scrimshander**) • *v.* [trans.] adorn (whalebone, ivory, shells, or other materials) with carved or colored designs. • *n.* a piece of work done in such a way. ■ the art or technique of producing such work.
DERIVATIVES: **scrim•shand•er** *n.*

scrip |skrip| • *n.* **1** a provisional certificate of money subscribed to a bank or company, entitling the holder to a formal certificate and dividends. ■ such certificates collectively. ■ (also **scrip issue** or **dividend**) an issue of additional shares to shareholders in proportion to the shares already held. **2** (also **land scrip**) a certificate entitling the holder to acquire possession of certain portions of public land. **3** paper money in small amounts.

script[1] |skript| • *n.* **1** handwriting as distinct from print; written characters: *her neat, tidy script.* ■ printed type imitating handwriting. ■ [with adj.] writing using a particular alphabet: *Russian script.* **2** the written text of a play, movie, or broadcast. ■ an automated series of instructions to a computer carried out in a specific order. ■ the social role or behavior appropriate to particular situations that an individual absorbs through cultural influences and association with others. • *v.* [trans.] write a script for (a play, movie, or broadcast).

■ arrange or devise (something): *his farewell dinner was carefully scripted.*

script[2] • *n.* a doctor's prescription.

scrip•to•ri•um |ˌskrip'tôrēəm| • *n.* (pl. **scriptoria** |-'tôrēə| or **scriptoriums**) a room set apart for writing, esp. one in a monastery where manuscripts were copied.

scrive•ner |ˈskriv(ə)nər| • *n.* a clerk, scribe, or notary.

scrof•u•la |ˈskrôfyələ| • *n.* a disease with glandular swellings, probably a form of tuberculosis.
DERIVATIVES: **scrof•u•lous** |-ləs| *adj.*

scrum |skrəm| • *n.* (in rugby) an ordered formation of players, used to restart play, in which the forwards of a team form up with arms interlocked and heads down, and push forward against a similar group from the opposing side. The ball is thrown into the scrum and the players try to gain possession of it by kicking it backward toward their own side. ■ chiefly Brit. a disorderly crowd of people or things: *there was quite a scrum of people at the bar.* • *v.* (**scrummed, scrumming**) [intrans.] form or take part in a scrum.

scru•ple |ˈskro͞opəl| • *n.* **1** (usu. **scruples**) a feeling of doubt or hesitation with regard to the morality or propriety of a course of action: *I had no scruples about eavesdropping | without scruple, these politicians use fear as a persuasion weapon.* **2** a unit of weight equal to 20 grains, formerly used by apothecaries. ■ a very small amount of something, esp. a quality. • *v.* [no obj., with infinitive] [usu. with negative] hesitate or be reluctant to do something that one thinks may be wrong: *she doesn't scruple to ask her parents for money.*

scru•pu•lous |ˈskro͞opyələs| • *adj.* (of a person or process) diligent, thorough, and extremely attentive to details: *the research has been carried out with scrupulous attention to detail.* ■ very concerned to avoid doing wrong: *she's too scrupulous to have an affair with a married man.*
DERIVATIVES: **scru•pu•los•i•ty** |ˌskro͞opyə'läsitē| *n.* **scru•pu•lous•ly** *adv.* **scru•pu•lous•ness** *n.*

scru•ti•nize |ˈskro͞otn,īz| • *v.* [trans.] examine or inspect closely and thoroughly: *customers were warned to scrutinize the small print.*
DERIVATIVES: **scru•ti•ni•za•tion** |ˌskro͞otn-i'zāsHən| *n.* **scru•ti•niz•er** *n.* **scru•ti•ny** *n.*

scud |skəd| • *v.* (**scudded, scudding**) [no obj., with adverbial of direction] move fast in a straight line because or as if driven by the wind: *we lie watching the clouds scudding across the sky | three small ships were scudding before a brisk breeze.* • *n.* a formation of vapory clouds driven fast by the wind. ■ a mass of windblown spray. ■ a driving shower of rain or snow; a gust. ■ the action of moving fast in a straight line when driven by the wind: *the scud of the clouds before the wind.*

scull |skəl| • *n.* each of a pair of small oars used by a single rower.

■ an oar placed over the stern of a boat to propel it by a side-to-side motion, reversing the blade at each turn. ■ a light, narrow boat propelled with a scull or a pair of sculls. ■ (**sculls**) a race between boats in which each participant uses a pair of oars. • v. [intrans.] propel a boat with sculls.
■ [with obj. and adverbial of direction] transport (someone) in a boat propelled with sculls. ■ [no obj., with adverbial of direction] (of an aquatic animal) propel itself with fins or flippers.

scul•ler•y |ˈskəl(ə)rē| • n. (pl. **-ies**) a small kitchen or room at the back of a house used for washing dishes and other dirty household work.

scul•lion |ˈskəlyən| • n. a servant assigned the most menial kitchen tasks.

scum•ble |ˈskəmbəl| • v. [trans.] modify (a painting or color) by applying a very thin coat of opaque paint to give a softer or duller effect.
■ modify (a drawing) in a similar way with light shading in pencil or charcoal. • n. a thin, opaque coat of paint or layer of shading applied to give a softer or duller effect. ■ the effect produced by adding such a coat or layer.

scup•per[1] |ˈskəpər| • n. (usu. **scuppers**) a hole in a ship's side to carry water overboard from the deck.
■ an outlet in the side of a building for draining water.

scup•per[2] • v. [trans.] sink (a ship or its crew) deliberately.
■ prevent from working or succeeding; thwart: *plans for a casino were scuppered by a public inquiry.*

scur•ril•ous |ˈskərələs| • adj. making or spreading scandalous claims about someone with the intention of damaging his or her reputation: *a scurrilous attack on his integrity.*
■ humorously insulting: *scurrilous writings.*
DERIVATIVES: **scur•ril•i•ty** |skəˈrilitē| n. (pl. **-ies**) **scur•ril•ous•ly** adv. **scur•ril•ous•ness** n.

scu•tage |ˈsk(y)o͞otij| • n. (in a feudal society) money paid by a vassal to his lord in lieu of military service.

scut•tle[1] • v. [no obj., with adverbial of direction] run hurriedly or furtively with short quick steps: *a mouse scuttled across the floor.* • n. [in sing.] an act or sound of scuttling: *I heard the scuttle of rats.*

scut•tle[2] • v. [trans.] sink (one's own ship) deliberately by holing it or opening its seacocks (valves) to let water in.
■ deliberately cause (a scheme) to fail: *some of the stockholders are threatening to scuttle the deal.* • n. an opening with a lid in a ship's deck or side.

scut•tle•butt |ˈskətl̩ˌbət| • n. rumor; gossip: *the scuttlebutt has it that he was a spy.* | *the court cautioned against relying on scuttlebutt.*

se•ance |ˈsāˌäns| • n. a meeting at which people attempt to make contact with the dead, esp. through the agency of a medium.

sea•son•a•ble |ˈsēznəbəl| • adj. **1** usual for or appropriate to a particular season of the year: *seasonable temperatures.* **2** coming at the right time or meeting the needs of the occasion; opportune.
DERIVATIVES: **sea•son•a•bil•i•ty** |ˌsēzənəˈbilitē| n. **sea•son•a•ble•ness** n. **sea•son•a•bly** |-blē| adv.

USAGE: **Seasonable** means 'usual or suitable for the season' or 'opportune,' e.g., *Although seasonable, the weather was not warm enough for a picnic.* **Seasonal** means 'of, depending on, or varying with the season,' e.g., *Seasonal changes in labor requirements draw migrant workers to the area in spring and fall.*

sec • adj. (of wine) dry.

sec•co |ˈsekō| (also **fresco secco**) • n. the technique of painting on dry plaster with pigments mixed in water.

se•ces•sion |səˈseSHən| • n. the action of withdrawing formally (*seceding*) from membership of a federation or body, esp. a political state: *the republics want secession from the union.*
■ (**the Secession**) the withdrawal of eleven Southern states from the Union in 1860–61, leading to the Civil War. ■ (also **Sezession**) a radical movement in art that began in Vienna and was contemporaneous with and related to ART NOUVEAU.
DERIVATIVES: **se•cede** v. **se•ces•sion•al** |-SHənl| adj. **se•ces•sion•ism** |-ˌnizəm| n. **se•ces•sion•ist** |-ist| n.

se•clude |siˈklo͞od| • v. [trans.] keep (someone) away from other people: *I secluded myself up here for a life of study and meditation.*

se•clu•sion |siˈklo͞oZHən| • n. the state of being private and away from other people: *they enjoyed ten days of peace and seclusion.*
■ a sheltered or private place.
DERIVATIVES: **se•clu•sive** |-siv| adj.

sec•re•tar•i•at |ˌsekrəˈterēət| • n. a permanent administrative office or department, esp. a governmental one.
■ [treated as sing. or pl.] the staff working in such an office.

se•crete[1] |siˈkrēt| • v. [trans.] (of a cell, gland, or organ) produce and discharge (a substance): *insulin is secreted in response to rising levels of glucose in the blood.*
DERIVATIVES: **se•cre•tor** |-tər| n. **se•cre•to•ry** |-tərē| adj.

se•crete[2] • v. [trans.] conceal; hide: *the assets had been secreted in Swiss bank accounts.*

se•cre•tion |siˈkrēSHən| • n. a process by which substances are produced and discharged from a cell, gland, or organ for a particular function in the organism or for excretion.
■ a substance discharged in such a way.

sect |sekt| • n. a group of people with somewhat different religious beliefs (typically regarded as heretical) from those of a larger group to which they belong.
■ a group that has separated from an established church. ■ a philosophical or political group, esp. one regarded as extreme or dangerous.

sec•tar•i•an |sek'terēən| • *adj.* denoting or concerning a sect or sects: *among the sectarian offshoots of Ismailism were the Druze of Lebanon.*
■ (of an action) carried out on the grounds of membership of a sect, denomination, or other group: *the recent sectarian killings of Catholics.* ■ rigidly following the doctrines of a sect or other group: *the sectarian Bolshevism advocated by Moscow.* • *n.* a member of a sect. ■ a person who rigidly follows the doctrines of a sect or other group.
DERIVATIVES: **sec•tar•i•an•ism** |-ˌnizəm| *n.* **sec•tar•i•an•ize** |-ˌnīz| *v.*
sec•ta•ry |'sektərē| • *n.* (pl. **-ies**) a member of a religious or political sect.
sec•tion•al•ism |'seksHənlˌizəm| • *n.* restriction of interest to a narrow sphere; undue concern with local interests or petty distinctions at the expense of general well-being. ■ regionalism.
DERIVATIVES: **sec•tion•al•ist** *n.* & *adj.*
sec•tor |'sektər| • *n.* **1** an area or portion that is distinct from others.
■ a distinct part or branch of a nation's economy or society or of a sphere of activity such as education: *the industrial and commercial sector.* ■ a division of a larger area, esp. one with particular characteristics: *the Muslim sector of the village.* ■ a subdivision of an area for military operations. ■ a subdivision of a track on a magnetic storage device. **2** the plane figure enclosed by two radii of a circle or ellipse and the arc between them. **3** a mathematical instrument consisting of two arms hinged at one end and marked with sines, tangents, etc., for making diagrams.
DERIVATIVES: **sec•tor•al** |-rəl| *adj.*
sec•u•lar |'sekyələr| • *adj.* **1** denoting attitudes, activities, or other things that have no religious or spiritual basis: *secular buildings | secular moral theory.* **2** (of Christian clergy) not subject to or bound by religious rule; not belonging to or living in a monastic or other order. **3** (of an economic fluctuation or trend) occurring or persisting over an indefinitely long period: *there is evidence that the slump is not cyclical but secular.* • *n.* a secular priest.
DERIVATIVES: **sec•u•lar•ism** |-ˌrizəm| *n.* **sec•u•lar•ist** |-rist| *n.* **sec•u•lar•i•ty** |ˌsekyə'laritē; -'ler-| *n.* **sec•u•lar•i•za•tion** |ˌsekyələri'zāsHən| *n.* **sec•u•lar•ize** |-ˌrīz| *v.* **sec•u•lar•ly** *adv.*
se•dan |si'dæn| • *n.* **1** (also **sedan chair**) an enclosed chair for conveying one person, carried between horizontal poles by two porters. **2** an automobile for four or more people. Cf. COUPE[1].
se•date[1] |si'dāt| • *adj.* calm, dignified, and unhurried: *in the old days, business was carried on at a more sedate pace.*
■ quiet and rather dull: *sedate suburban domesticity.*
se•date[2] • *v.* [trans.] calm (someone) or make them sleep by administering a sedative drug: *she was heavily sedated.*

sed•a•tive |'sedətiv| • *adj.* promoting calm or inducing sleep: *the seeds have a sedative effect.* • *n.* a drug taken for its calming or sleep-inducing effect.
sed•en•tar•y |'sednˌterē| • *adj.* (of a person) tending to spend much time seated; somewhat inactive.
■ (of work or a way of life) characterized by much sitting and little physical exercise. ■ (of a position) sitting; seated. ■ inhabiting the same locality throughout life; not migratory or nomadic. ■ (of an animal) sessile.
DERIVATIVES: **sed•en•tar•i•ly** |-ˌterəlē| *adv.* **sed•en•tar•i•ness** *n.*
Se•der |'sādər| • *n.* a Jewish ritual service and ceremonial dinner for the first night or first two nights of Passover.
sed•i•ment |'sedəmənt| • *n.* matter that settles to the bottom of a liquid; dregs. Cf. LEES.
■ particulate matter that is carried by water or wind and deposited on the surface of the land or the seabed, and may in time become consolidated into rock. • *v.* [intrans.] settle as sediment.
■ (of a liquid) deposit a sediment. ■ [trans.] deposit (something) as a sediment: *the DNA was sedimented by centrifugation* | [as adj.] (**sedimented**) *sedimented waste.*
DERIVATIVES: **sed•i•men•ta•tion** |ˌsedəmən'tāsHən| *n.*
sed•i•men•ta•ry |ˌsedə'mentərē| • *adj.* of or relating to sediment.
■ (of rock) that has formed from sediment deposited by water or air. Cf. IGNEOUS; METAMORPHIC.
se•di•tion |si'disHən| • *n.* conduct or speech inciting people to rebel against the authority of a state or monarch.
se•duce |si'd(y)o͞os| • *v.* [trans.] attract (someone) to a belief or into a course of action that is inadvisable or foolhardy: *they should not be **seduced into** thinking that their success ruled out the possibility of a relapse.*
■ entice into sexual activity. ■ attract powerfully: *the melody seduces the ear with warm string tones.*
DERIVATIVES: **se•duc•er** *n.* **se•duc•i•ble** *adj.* **se•duc•tion** *n.*
sed•u•lous |'sejələs| • *adj.* (of a person or action) showing dedication and diligence: *he watched himself with the most sedulous care.*
DERIVATIVES: **se•du•li•ty** |sə'jo͞olitē| *n.* **sed•u•lous•ly** *adv.* **sed•u•lous•ness** *n.*
see • *n.* (in some Christian churches) the place in which a cathedral church stands, identified as the seat of authority of a bishop or archbishop.
■ (also, **the Holy See**) the office or jurisdiction of the pope; papacy.
seed•y |'sēdē| • *adj.* (**seedier**, **seediest**) **1** sordid and disreputable: *his seedy affair with a soft-porn starlet.*
■ shabby and squalid: *an increasingly seedy and dilapidated property.* **2** unwell: *she felt weak and seedy.*
DERIVATIVES: **seed•i•ly** |'sēdl-ē| *adv.* **seed•i•ness** *n.*

seem•ly |'sēmlē| • *adj.* **1** conforming to accepted notions of propriety or good taste; decorous: *I felt it was not seemly to observe too closely.* **2** pleasing and attractive; handsome.
DERIVATIVES: **seem•li•ness** *n.*

seer |'sēər; sir| • *n.* **1** a person of supposed supernatural insight who sees visions of the future.
■ an expert who provides forecasts of the economic or political future: *our seers have grown gloomier about prospects for growth.* **2** [usu. in combination] a person who sees something specified: *a seer of the future* | *ghost-seers.*

seethe |sēTH| • *v.* [intrans.] (of a liquid) bubble up as a result of being boiled: *the brew foamed and seethed.*
■ [trans.] cook (food) by boiling it in a liquid: *cut into joints and seethed in cauldrons.* ■ (of a river or the sea) foam as if it were boiling; be turbulent: *the gray ocean seethed.* ■ [intrans.] (of a person) be filled with intense but unexpressed anger: *inwardly he was seething at the slight to his authority.* ■ (of a place) be crowded with people or things moving about in a rapid or hectic way: *the entire cellar was* **seething with** *spiders* | *the village* **seethed with** *life.* | [as adj.] (**seething**) *the seething mass of commuters.*

seg•men•tal |seg'men(t)l| • *adj.* **1** composed of separate parts or sections. **2** denoting or of the form of an arch the curved part of which forms a shallow arc of a circle, less than a semicircle.
DERIVATIVES: **seg•men•tal•i•za•tion** |-,men(t)li'zāsHən| *n.* **seg•men•tal•ize** |-,īz| *v.* **seg•men•tal•ly** *adv.*

seg•re•gate |'segri,gāt| • *v.* [trans.] (usu. be **segregated**) set apart from the rest or from each other; isolate or divide: *handicapped people should not be segregated from the rest of society.*
■ separate or divide (people, activities, or institutions) along racial, sexual, or religious lines: *blacks were segregated in churches, schools, and colleges* | [as adj.] (**segregated**) *segregated education systems.* ■ [intrans.] (in genetics, of pairs of alleles) be separated at meiosis and transmitted independently via separate gametes.
DERIVATIVES: **seg•re•ga•ble** |-gəbəl| *adj.* **seg•re•ga•tive** |-,gātiv| *adj.*

se•gue |'segwā; 'sā-| • *v.* (**segues, segued** |'segwād; 'sā-|, **segueing** |'segwā-iNG; 'sā-|) [no obj., with adverbial] (in music and film) move without interruption from one song, melody, or scene to another: *allowing one song to segue into the next.*
■ make an uninterrupted and seemingly natural transition. • *n.* an uninterrupted transition from one subject to another, esp. in music or film.

sei•cen•to |sā'CHen,tō| • *n.* [often as adj.] the style of Italian art and literature of the 17th century.
DERIVATIVES: **sei•cen•tist** |-tist| *n.*

seine |sān| • *n.* (also **seine net**) a fishing net that hangs vertically in the water with floats at the top and weights at the bottom edge, the ends being drawn together to encircle the fish. • *v.* [trans.] fish (an area) with a seine: *the fishermen then seine the weir.*
■ catch (fish) with a seine: *they seine whitefish and salmon.*
DERIVATIVES: **sein•er** *n.*

seis•mic |'sīzmik| • *adj.* of or relating to earthquakes or other vibrations of the earth and its crust.
■ relating to or denoting geological surveying methods involving vibrations produced artificially by explosions. ■ of enormous proportions or effect: *there are seismic pressures threatening American society.*
DERIVATIVES: **seis•mi•cal** *adj.* **seis•mi•cal•ly** |-ik(ə)lē| *adv.* **seis•mo•graph** *n.* **seis•mog•ra•pher** *n.*

seize |sēz| • *v.* **1** [trans.] (of the police or another authority) take possession of (something) by warrant or legal right; confiscate; impound: *police have seized 726 lb of cocaine.* **2** (**be seized of**) (in older legal use) be in legal possession of: *the court is currently seized of custody applications.*
■ have or receive freehold possession of (property): *any person who is seized of land has a protected interest in that land.* ■ be aware or informed of: *the judge was fully seized of the point.*
DERIVATIVES: **seiz•a•ble** *adj.* **seiz•er** *n.*

sei•zure |'sēzHər| • *n.* **1** the action of capturing someone or something using force: *the seizure of the Assembly building* | *the Nazi seizure of power.*
■ the action of confiscating or impounding property by warrant or legal right. **2** a sudden attack of illness, esp. a stroke or an epileptic fit: *the patient* **had a seizure.**
■ the seizing-up, jamming, or failure of a machine.

self•less |'selfləs| • *adj.* concerned more with the needs and wishes of others than with one's own; unselfish: *an act of selfless devotion.*
DERIVATIVES: **self•less•ly** *adv.* **self•less•ness** *n.*

sel•vage |'selvij| • *n.* an edge produced on woven fabric during manufacture that prevents it from unraveling.
■ a zone of altered rock, esp. volcanic glass, at the edge of a rock mass.

se•man•tic |sə'mæntik| • *adj.* relating to meaning in language or logic. Cf. SYNTACTIC.
DERIVATIVES: **se•man•ti•cal•ly** |-ik(ə)lē| *adv.*

se•man•tics |sə'mæn'tiks| • *plural n.* [usu. treated as sing.] the branch of linguistics and logic concerned with meaning. There are a number of branches and subbranches of semantics, including **formal semantics**, which studies the logical aspects of meaning, such as sense, reference, implication, and logical form, **lexical semantics**, which studies word meanings and word relations, and **conceptual semantics**, which studies the cognitive structure of meaning.
■ the meaning of a word, phrase, sentence, or text: *such quibbling over semantics may seem petty stuff.*

DERIVATIVES: **se•man•ti•cian** |ˌsēmæn
'tiSHən| *n.* **se•man•ti•cist** *n.*

se•ma•si•ol•o•gy |səˌmāsē'äləjē; -zē-| • *n.*
the branch of knowledge that deals with concepts and the terms that represent them. Cf.
ONOMASIOLOGY.

DERIVATIVES: **se•ma•si•o•log•i•cal** |-ə'läj-
ikəl| *adj.*

sem•bla•ble |'sembləbəl| • *n.* a counterpart
or equal to someone: *this person is our brother,
our semblable, our very self.*

sem•blance |'sembləns| • *n.* the outward ap-
pearance or apparent form of something, esp.
when the reality is different: *she tried to force
her thoughts back into some semblance of
order.*

■ resemblance; similarity: *it bears some semblance to the thing I have in mind.*

se•mes•ter |sə'mestər| • *n.* a half-year term
in a school or university, typically lasting for
fifteen to eighteen weeks.

sem•i•con•duc•tor |'semēkən,dəktər; ˌsem
ˌī-| • *n.* a solid substance that has a conduc-
tivity between that of an insulator and that of
most metals, either due to the addition of an
impurity or because of temperature effects.
Devices made of semiconductors, notably silicon, are essential components of most electronic circuits.

sem•i•nal |'semənl| • *adj.* **1** (of a work,
event, moment, or figure) strongly influenc-
ing later developments: *his seminal work on
chaos theory.* **2** of, relating to, or denoting
semen.

■ of, relating to, or derived from the seed of a
plant.

DERIVATIVES: **sem•i•nal•ly** *adv.*

sem•i•nar•y |'semə,nerē| • *n.* (pl. **-ies**) a col-
lege that prepares students to be priests, ministers, or rabbis.

■ a place or thing in which something is developed or cultivated: *a seminary of sedition.* ■ a
private school or college, esp. one for young
women.

DERIVATIVES: **sem•i•nar•i•an** |ˌsemə
'nerēən| *n.* **sem•i•na•rist** |-nərist| *n.*

se•mi•ol•o•gy |ˌsēmē'äləjē; ˌsemē-; ˌsem,ī-|
• *n.* another term for SEMIOTICS.

DERIVATIVES: **se•mi•o•log•i•cal** |-ə'läji-
kəl| *adj.* **se•mi•ol•o•gist** |-jist| *n.*

se•mi•ot•ics |ˌsēmē'ätiks; ˌsemē-; ˌsem,ī-|
• *plural n.* [treated as sing.] the study of signs
and symbols and their use or interpretation.

DERIVATIVES: **se•mi•ot•ic** *adj.* **se•mi•ot•i•**
cal•ly |-ik(ə)lē| *adv.* **se•mi•o•ti•cian** |ˌse
mēə'tiSHən; ˌsemēə-| *n.*

Sem•ite |'semīt| • *n.* a member of any of the
peoples of SW Asian origin who speak or
spoke a Semitic language, including in particular the Jews and Arabs.

Se•mit•ic |sə'mitik| • *adj.* **1** relating to or
denoting a family of languages that includes
Hebrew, Arabic, and Aramaic and certain ancient languages such as Phoenician and
Akkadian, constituting the main subgroup of
the Afro-Asiatic family. **2** of or relating to the
peoples who speak these languages, esp. Hebrew and Arabic.

sem•pi•ter•nal |ˌsempə'tərnl| • *adj.* eternal
and unchanging; everlasting: *his writings have
the sempiternal youth of poetry.*

DERIVATIVES: **sem•pi•ter•nal•ly** *adv.*
sem•pi•ter•ni•ty |-'tərnitē| *n.*

se•nes•cence |sə'nesəns| • *n.* the condition
or process of deterioration with age.

■ loss of a cell's power of division and growth.

DERIVATIVES: **se•nes•cent** *adj.*

se•nile |'sē,nīl; 'sen-| • *adj.* (of a person) hav-
ing or showing the weaknesses or diseases of
old age, esp. a loss of mental faculties: *she
couldn't cope with her senile husband.*

■ (of a condition) characteristic of or caused
by old age: *senile decay.* • *n.* a senile person:
*you never know where you stand with these so-
called seniles.*

DERIVATIVES: **se•nil•i•ty** |si'nilitē| *n.*

sen•sate |'sen,sāt| • *adj.* able to perceive
with the senses; sensing: *the infant stretches,
sensate, wakening.*

■ perceived by the senses: *you are immersed in
an illusionary, yet sensate, world.*

sen•so•ri•um |sen'sôrēəm| • *n.* (pl. **sensoria**
|-'sôrēə| or **sensoriums**) the sensory appa-
ratus or faculties considered as a whole: *virtual reality technology directed at recreating the
human sensorium.*

DERIVATIVES: **sen•so•ri•al** |-'sôrēəl| *adj.*
sen•so•ri•al•ly |-'sôrēəlē| *adv.*

sen•su•al |'sensHəwəl| • *adj.* of or arousing
gratification of the senses and physical, esp.
sexual, pleasure: *the dancing is sensual and passionate.*

DERIVATIVES: **sen•su•al•ism** |-,lizəm| *n.*
sen•su•al•ist |-ist| *n.* **sen•su•al•ize** |-,līz|
v. **sen•su•al•ly** *adv.*

USAGE: The words **sensual** and **sensuous**
are frequently used interchangeably to mean
'gratifying the senses,' esp. in a sexual sense.
Strictly speaking, this goes against a traditional distinction, by which **sensuous** is a
more neutral term, meaning 'relating to the
senses rather than the intellect,' as in *swimming is a beautiful, **sensuous** experience,*
while **sensual** relates to gratification of the
senses, esp. sexually, as in *a **sensual** mas-
sage.* In fact the word **sensuous** is thought
to have been invented by John Milton (1641)
in a deliberate attempt to avoid the sexual
overtones of **sensual**. In practice the connotations are such that it is difficult to use
sensuous in this sense. While traditionalists
struggle to maintain a distinction, the evidence suggests that the 'neutral' use of **sensuous** is rare in modern English. If a neutral
use is intended, it is advisable to use alternative wording.

sen•su•ous |'sensHəwəs| • *adj.* **1** relating to
or affecting the senses rather than the intellect: *the work showed a deliberate disregard of the
more sensuous and immediately appealing
aspects of painting.* **2** attractive or gratifying
physically, esp. sexually: *her voice was rather
deep but very sensuous.*

DERIVATIVES: **sen•su•ous•ly** *adv.* **sen•su•**
ous•ness *n.*

sen•ten•tious |sen'tenCHəs| • *adj.* given to moralizing in a pompous or affected manner: *he tried to encourage his men with sententious rhetoric.*
DERIVATIVES: **sen•ten•tious•ly** *adv.* **sen•ten•tious•ness** *n.*

sen•tient |'senCH(ē)ənt| • *adj.* able to perceive or feel things: *she had been instructed from birth in the equality of all sentient life forms.*
DERIVATIVES: **sen•tience** *n.* **sen•tient•ly** *adv.*

sen•ti•men•tal•ism |,sen(t)ə'men(t)l,izəm| • *n.* the excessive expression of feelings of tenderness, sadness, or nostalgia in behavior, writing, or speech: *the author blends realism with surrealism, journalism with sentimentalism.*
■ a sentimental idea or expression.
DERIVATIVES: **sen•ti•men•tal•ist** *n.*

sen•ti•men•tal•ize |,sen(t)ə'men(t)l,īz| • *v.* [trans.] treat (someone or something) with exaggerated and self-indulgent feelings of tenderness, sadness, or nostalgia: [as adj.] (**sentimentalized**) *the impossibly sentimentalized and saintly ideal of the Virgin Mother.*
■ [intrans.] indulge in sentimental thoughts or behavior.
DERIVATIVES: **sen•ti•men•tal•i•za•tion** |-,men(t)li'zāsHən| *n.*

se•pal |'sēpəl| • *n.* each of the parts of the calyx of a flower, enclosing the petals and typically green and leaflike.

sep•pu•ku |'sepoō,koō; sə'poōkoō| • *n.* another term for HARA-KIRI.

sep•tic |'septik| • *adj.* **1** (chiefly of a wound or a part of the body) infected with bacteria; suffering *sepsis.* **2** [attrib.] denoting a drainage system incorporating a septic tank, which collects sewage and allows it to decompose through bacterial action. • *n.* a drainage system incorporating a septic tank.
DERIVATIVES: **sep•ti•cal•ly** |-ik(ə)lē| *adv.* **sep•tic•i•ty** |sep'tisitē|

sep•ul•cher |'sepəlkər| (Brit. **sepulchre**) • *n.* a small room or monument, cut in rock or built of stone, in which a dead person is laid or buried. • *v.* [trans.] lay or bury in or as if in a sepulcher: *tomes are soon out of print and sepulchered in the dust of libraries.*
■ serve as a burial place for: *when ocean shrouds and sepulchers our dead.*

se•pul•chral |sə'pəlkrəl| • *adj.* of or relating to a tomb or interment: *sepulchral monuments.*
■ gloomy; dismal: *a speech delivered in sepulchral tones.*
DERIVATIVES: **se•pul•chral•ly** *adv.*

sep•ul•ture |'sepəlCHər| • *n.* burial; interment: *the rites of sepulture.*

se•qua•cious |si'kwāsHəs| • *adj.* (of a person) lacking independence or originality of thought.
DERIVATIVES: **se•qua•cious•ly** *adv.* **se•quac•i•ty** |-'kwæsitē| *n.*

se•que•la |si'kwelə| • *n.* (pl. **sequelae** |-'kwelē; -'kwelī|) (usu. **sequelae**) a condition that is the consequence of a previous disease or injury: *the long-term sequelae of infection.*

se•quent |'sēkwənt| • *adj.* following in a se-

quence or as a logical conclusion; consequential.
DERIVATIVES: **se•quent•ly** *adv.*

se•ques•ter |sə'kwestər| • *v.* [trans.] **1** isolate or hide away (someone or something): *Tiberius was sequestered on an island* | *the artist* **sequestered himself** *in his studio for two years.*
■ isolate (a jury) from outside influences during a trial: *the jurors had been sequestered since Monday.* **2** another term for SEQUESTRATE.

se•ques•trate |'sēkwi,strāt; 'sek-; sə'kwes,trāt| • *v.* [trans.] take legal possession of (assets) until a debt has been paid or other claims have been met: *the power of courts to sequestrate the assets of unions.*
■ take forcible possession of (something); confiscate: *compensation for Jewish property sequestrated by the Libyan regime.* ■ legally place (the property of a bankrupt) in the hands of a trustee for division among the creditors: [as adj.] (**sequestrated**) *a trustee in a sequestrated estate.* ■ chiefly Brit. declare (someone) bankrupt: *two more poll tax rebels were sequestrated.*
DERIVATIVES: **se•ques•tra•ble** |si'kwestrəbəl| *adj.* **se•ques•tra•tor** |'sēkwi,strātər; 'sek-; si'kwes,trātər| *n.*

se•ragl•io |sə'rälyō| • *n.* (pl. **-os**) **1** the women's apartments (harem) in a Muslim palace.
■ another term for HAREM (sense 2). **2** (**the Seraglio**) a Turkish palace, esp. the Ottoman Sultan's court and government offices at Constantinople.

ser•aph |'serəf| • *n.* (pl. **seraphim** |-,fim| or **seraphs**) an angelic being, regarded in traditional Christian angelology as belonging to the highest order of the ninefold celestial hierarchy, associated with light, ardor, and purity.
DERIVATIVES: **se•raph•ic** *adj.*

sere[1] |sir| • *adj.* dried up; withered.

sere[2] • *n.* (in ecology) a natural succession of plant (or animal) communities, esp. a full series from uncolonized habitat to the appropriate climax vegetation.

ser•en•dip•i•ty |,serən'dipitē| • *n.* the occurrence and development of events by chance in a happy or beneficial way: *a fortunate stroke of serendipity.*
DERIVATIVES: **ser•en•dip•i•tous** |-'dipitəs| *adj.* **ser•en•dip•i•tous•ly** |-'dipətəslē| *adv.*

se•rene |sə'rēn| • *adj.* **1** calm, peaceful, and untroubled; tranquil: *her eyes were closed and she looked very serene* | *serene certainty.* Cf. PLACID. **2** (**Serene**) (in a title) used as a term of respect for members of some European royal families: *His Serene Highness.* • *n.* (usu. **the serene**) an expanse of clear sky or calm sea: *not a cloud obscured the deep serene.*
DERIVATIVES: **se•rene•ly** *adv.*

serf |sərf| • *n.* an agricultural laborer bound under the feudal system to work on his lord's estate.
DERIVATIVES: **serf•age** |-fij| *n.* **serf•dom** |-dəm| *n.*

se•ri•al |'sirēəl| • adj. **1** consisting of, forming part of, or taking place in a series: *a serial publication.*
■ (in music) using transformations of a fixed series of notes. ■ (in computing, of a device) involving the transfer of data as a single sequence of bits. ■ (in computing, of a processor) running only a single task, as opposed to multitasking. ■ (of verbs) used in sequence to form a construction, as in *they wanted, needed, longed for peace.* **2** [attrib.] (of a criminal) repeatedly committing the same offense and typically following a characteristic, predictable behavior pattern: *police have arrested a suspected serial rapist.*
■ (of a person) repeatedly following the same behavior pattern: *a serial adulterer.* ■ denoting an action or behavior pattern that is committed or followed repeatedly: *serial killings | serial monogamy.* • n. a story or play appearing in regular installments on television or radio or in a magazine or newspaper: *a new three-part drama serial.*
■ (usu. **serials**) (in a library) a periodical.
DERIVATIVES: **se•ri•al•i•ty** |,sirē'ælitē| n. **se•ri•al•ly** adv.
se•ri•al•ism |'sirēə,lizəm| • n. a technique of musical composition in which a fixed series of notes, esp. the twelve notes of the chromatic scale, are used to generate the harmonic and melodic basis of a piece and are subject to change only in specific ways.
DERIVATIVES: **se•ri•al•ist** adj. & n.
se•ri•al•ize |'sirēə,liz| • v. [trans.] **1** publish or broadcast (a story or play) in regular installments: *sections of the book were serialized in the* New Yorker. **2** arrange (something) in a series.
■ compose according to the techniques of serialism.
DERIVATIVES: **se•ri•al•i•za•tion** |,sirēəli'zāSHən| n.
se•ri•a•tim |,sirē'ātəm; -'ætəm| • adv. taking one subject after another in regular order; point by point: *it is proposed to deal with these matters seriatim.*
ser•i•cul•ture |'seri,kəlCHər| • n. the production of silk and the rearing of silkworms for this purpose.
DERIVATIVES: **ser•i•cul•tur•al** |,seri'kəl-CHərəl| adj. **ser•i•cul•tur•ist** |,seri'kəlCHərist| n.
ser•if |'serəf| • n. (in printing, calligraphy, engraving, etc.) a slight projection finishing off a stroke of a letter, as in T contrasted with T. Cf. SANS SERIF.
DERIVATIVES: **ser•iffed** adj.
ser•i•graph |'seri,græf| • n. a printed design produced by means of a silkscreen.
DERIVATIVES: **se•rig•ra•pher** |sə'rigrəfər| n. **se•rig•ra•phy** |sə'rigrəfē| n.
se•rol•o•gy |si'räləjē| • n. the scientific study or diagnostic examination of blood serum, esp. with regard to the response of the immune system to pathogens or introduced substances.
DERIVATIVES: **se•ro•log•ic** |,sirə'läjik| adj. **se•ro•log•i•cal** |,sirə'läjikəl| adj. **se•ro•log•**

i•cal•ly |,sirə'läjik(ə)lē| adv. **se•rol•o•gist** |-jist| n.
ser•pen•tine |'sərpən,tēn; -,tīn| • adj. of or like a serpent or snake: *serpentine coils.*
■ winding and twisting like a snake: *serpentine country lanes.* ■ complex, cunning, or treacherous: *his charm was too subtle and serpentine for me.* • n. **1** a dark green mineral that is sometimes mottled or spotted like a snake's skin, used in architecture and jewelry. **2** a thing in the shape of a winding curve or line, in particular:
■ a riding exercise consisting of a series of half-circles made alternately to right and left. **3** a kind of cannon, used esp. in the 15th and 16th centuries. • v. [no obj., with adverbial of direction] move or lie in a winding path or line: *fresh tire tracks serpentined back toward the shed.*
ser•rat•ed |'serātid; sə'rātid| (also, esp. in botany, **serrate** |'serāt; –it|) • adj. having or denoting a jagged edge; sawlike: *a knife with a serrated edge.*
ser•ried |'serēd| • adj. [attrib.] (of rows of people or things) standing close together: *serried ranks of soldiers | the serried rows of vines.*
se•rum |'sirəm| • n. (pl. **sera** |'sɛrə| or **serums**) an amber-colored, protein-rich liquid that separates out when blood coagulates.
■ the blood serum of an animal, used esp. to provide immunity to a pathogen or toxin by inoculation or as a diagnostic agent.
serv•ice•a•ble |'sərvəsəbəl| • adj. fulfilling its function adequately; usable: *an aging but still serviceable water supply system.*
■ functional and durable rather than attractive. ■ in working order: *twelve aircraft were fully serviceable.*
DERIVATIVES: **serv•ice•a•bil•i•ty** |,sərvəsə'bilitē| n. **serv•ice•a•bly** |-blē| adv.
ser•vile |'sərvəl; -,vīl| • adj. **1** having or showing an excessive willingness to serve or please others: *bowing his head in a servile manner.* **2** of or characteristic of a slave or slaves.
DERIVATIVES: **ser•vile•ly** adv. **ser•vil•i•ty** |sər'vilitē| n.
ses•qui•pe•da•li•an |,seskwəpə'dālyən| • adj. (of a word) polysyllabic; long: *sesquipedalian surnames.*
■ characterized by long words; long-winded: *the sesquipedalian prose of scientific journals.*
ses•sile |'sesəl; -,īl| • adj. (of an organism, e.g., a barnacle) fixed in one place; immobile.
■ (of a plant or animal structure) attached directly by its base without a stalk or stem: *sporangia may be stalked or sessile.*
ses•tet |ses'tet| • n. the last six lines of a sonnet.
ses•ti•na |se'stēnə| • n. a poem with six stanzas of six lines and a final triplet, all stanzas having the same six words at the line-ends in six different sequences that follow a fixed pattern, and with all six words appearing in the closing three-line envoi.
se•ta•ceous |si'tāSHəs| • adj. having the form or character of a bristle.
■ covered in bristles; bristly.
DERIVATIVES: **se•ta•ceous•ly** |si'tāSHəslē| adv.

set•tlor |'setl-ər; 'setlər| • *n.* a person who makes a legal settlement (the act of passing something along), esp. of a property.

sev•en dead•ly sins • *plural n.* (**the seven deadly sins**) (in Christian tradition) the sins of pride, covetousness, lust, anger, gluttony, envy, and sloth.

sev•er•al |'sev(ə)rəl| • *adj. & pron.* more than two but not many: [as adj.] *the author of several books* | [as pron.] *Van Gogh was just one of several artists who gathered at Auvers* | *several of his friends attended.* • *adj.* separate or respective: *the two levels of government sort out their several responsibilities.*
■ (in law) applied or regarded separately.
DERIVATIVES: **sev•er•al•ly** *adv.*

sev•er•al•ty |'sev(ə)rəltē| • *n.* **1** (legal use) the condition of being separate. **2** The condition of land held absolutely by an individual, not jointly.
■ The land so held.

sev•er•ance |'sev(ə)rəns| • *n.* the action of ending a connection or relationship: *the severance and disestablishment of the Irish Church* | *a complete severance of links with the Republic.*
■ the state of being separated or cut off: *she works on the feeling of severance, of being deprived of her mother.* ■ dismissal or discharge from employment: [as adj.] *employees were offered severance terms.* ■ (also **severance pay**) money paid to an employee on the early termination of a contract.

se•vere |sə'vir| • *adj.* **1** (of something bad or undesirable) very great; intense: *a severe shortage of technicians* | *a severe attack of asthma* | *damage is not too severe.*
■ demanding great ability, skill, or resilience: *a severe test of stamina.* **2** strict or harsh: *the charges would have warranted a severe sentence* | *he is unusually severe on what he regards as tendentious pseudo-learning.* **3** very plain in style or appearance: *she wore another severe suit, gray this time.*
DERIVATIVES: **se•vere•ly** *adv.* **se•ver•i•ty** |-'veritē| *n.*

sex•ism |'sek,sizəm| • *n.* prejudice, stereotyping, or discrimination, typically against women, on the basis of sex: *sexism in the workplace hasn't disappeared yet.*
DERIVATIVES: **sex•ist** *adj. & n.*

sex•less |'seksləs| • *adj.* **1** lacking in sexual desire, interest, activity, or attractiveness: *I've no patience with pious, sexless females.* **2** neither male nor female: *the stylized and sexless falsetto.*
DERIVATIVES: **sex•less•ly** *adv.* **sex•less•ness** *n.*

sex•ol•o•gy |sek'säləjē| • *n.* the study of human sexual life or relationships.
DERIVATIVES: **sex•o•log•i•cal** |ˌseksə'läjikəl| *adj.* **sex•ol•o•gist** |-jist| *n.*

sex•tant |'sekstənt| • *n.* an instrument with a graduated arc of 60° and a sighting mechanism, used for measuring the angular distances between objects and esp. for taking altitudes in navigation and surveying.

sex•ton |'sekstən| • *n.* a person who looks

after a church and churchyard, typically acting as bell-ringer and gravedigger.

sfor•zan•do |sfôrt'sändō| (also **sforzato**) • *adv. & adj.* (esp. as a musical direction) with sudden emphasis. • *n.* (pl. **sforzandos** or **sforzandi** |-dē|) a sudden or marked emphasis.

sgraf•fi•to |zgrä'fētō; skrä-| • *n.* (pl. **sgraffiti** |-tē|) a form of decoration made by scratching through a surface to reveal a lower layer of a contrasting color, typically done in plaster or stucco on walls, or in a clay solution on ceramics before firing. Cf. GRAFFITI.

shack•le |'sнækəl| • *n.* **1** (**shackles**) a pair of fetters connected together by a chain, used to fasten a prisoner's wrists or ankles together.
■ used in reference to something that restrains or impedes: *society is going to throw off the shackles of racism and colonialism.* **2** a metal link, typically U-shaped, closed by a bolt, used to secure a chain or rope to something.
■ a pivoted link connecting a spring in a vehicle's suspension to the body of the vehicle. • *v.* [trans.] chain with shackles.
■ restrain; limit: *they seek to shackle the oil and gas companies by imposing new controls.*

shad•ow•y |'sнædəwē| • *adj.* (**shadowier**, **shadowiest**) full of shadows: *the shadowy back streets of Stringtown.*
■ of uncertain identity or nature: *a shadowy figure appeared through the mist* | *the shadowy world of covert operations.* ■ insubstantial; unreal: *they were attacked by a swarm of shadowy, ethereal forms.*
DERIVATIVES: **shad•ow•i•ness** *n.*

shad•y |'sнādē| • *adj.* (**shadier**, **shadiest**) situated in or full of shade: *shady woods.*
■ giving shade from sunlight: *they sprawled under a shady carob tree.* ■ of doubtful honesty or legality: *he was involved in his grandmother's shady deals.*
DERIVATIVES: **shad•i•ly** *adv.* **shad•i•ness** *n.*

Shak•er |'sнākər| • *n.* a member of an American religious sect, the United Society of Believers in Christ's Second Coming, established in England c. 1750 and living simply in celibate mixed communities.
■ [as adj.] denoting a style of elegantly functional furniture traditionally produced by Shaker communities.
DERIVATIVES: **Shak•er•ism** |-ˌrizəm| *n.*

shal•lop |'sнæləp| • *n.* a light sailboat used mainly for coastal fishing or as a tender.
■ a large heavy sailing vessel with one or more masts and sometimes equipped with guns.

sham |sнæm| • *n.* a thing that is not what it is purported to be: *the proposed legislation is a farce and a sham.*
■ pretense: *it all turned out to be sham and hypocrisy.* ■ a person who pretends to be someone or something they are not: *he was a sham, totally unqualified for his job as a senior doctor.* • *adj.* bogus; false: *a clergyman who arranged a sham marriage.* • *v.* (**shammed**, **shamming**) [intrans.] falsely present something as the truth: *was he ill or was he shamming?*

■ [trans.] pretend to be or to be experiencing: *she shams indifference.*
DERIVATIVES: **sham•mer** *n.*

sha•man |ˈSHämən; ˈSHā-| • *n.* (pl. **shamans**) a person regarded as having access to, and influence in, the world of good and evil spirits, esp. among some peoples of northern Asia and North America. Typically shamans enter a trance state during a ritual, and practice divination and healing.
DERIVATIVES: **sha•man•ic** |SHəˈmænik| *adj.* **sha•man•ism** |-ˌnizəm| *n.* **sha•man•ist** |-nist| *n. & adj.* **sha•man•is•tic** |ˌSHämə ˈnistik; ˌSHā-| *adj.* **sha•man•ize** |-ˌnīz| *v.*

sham•ble |ˈSHæmbəl| • *v.* [no obj., with adverbial of direction] (of a person) move with a slow, shuffling, awkward gait: *he shambled off down the corridor* | [as adj.] (**shambling**) *a big, shambling, shy man.* • *n.* [in sing.] a slow, shuffling, awkward gait.

Shan•gri-La |ˈSHæNGgri ˈlä| a Tibetan utopia in James Hilton's novel *Lost Horizon* (1933).
■ [as n.] (**a Shangri-La**) a place regarded as an earthly paradise, esp. when involving a retreat from the pressures of modern civilization.

shan•ty[1] |ˈSHæn(t)ē| • *n.* (pl. **-ies**) a small, crudely built shack.

shan•ty[2] • *n.* (pl. **-ies**) variant spelling of CHANTEY.

sheikh |SHēk; SHāk| (also **sheik, shaikh,** or **shaykh**) • *n.* **1** an Arab leader, in particular the chief or head of an Arab tribe, family, or village.
■ a strong, romantic, or dashing male lover. **2** a leader in a Muslim community or organization.
DERIVATIVES: **sheikh•dom** |-dəm| *n.*

Shi•a |ˈSHē,ä| (also **Shi'a**) • *n.* (pl. same or **Shias**) one of the two main branches of Islam, followed esp. in Iran, that rejects the first three Sunni caliphs and regards Ali, as Muhammad's first true successor. Cf. SUNNI.
■ a Muslim who adheres to this branch of Islam. (Also called **Shiite**.)

shib•bo•leth |ˈSHibəliTH; -ˌleTH| • *n.* a custom, principle, or belief distinguishing a particular class or group of people, esp. a long-standing one regarded as outmoded or no longer important: *the party began to break with the shibboleths of the left.*

Shi•ite |ˈSHē,īt| (also **Shi'ite**) • *n.* an adherent of the Shia branch of Islam. • *adj.* of or relating to Shia.
DERIVATIVES: **Shi•ism** |ˈSHē,izəm| (also **Shi'ism**) *n.*

shik•sa |ˈSHiksə| • *n.* (used esp. by Jews) a gentile girl or woman.

shil•le•lagh |SHəˈlālē| • *n.* a thick stick of blackthorn or oak used in Ireland, typically as a weapon.

shil•ly-shal•ly |ˈSHilē ˌSHælē| • *v.* (**-ies, -ied**) [intrans.] fail to act resolutely or decisively: *the government shilly-shallied about the matter.* • *n.* indecisive behavior.
DERIVATIVES: **shil•ly-shal•ly•er** |ˌSHælē ər| (also **-shal•li•er**) *n.*

shim |SHim| • *n.* a washer or thin strip of material used to align parts, make them fit, or reduce wear. • *v.* (**shimmed, shimming**) [trans.] wedge (something) or fill up (a space) with a shim.

shim•mer |ˈSHimər| • *v.* [intrans.] shine with a soft tremulous light: *the sea shimmered in the sunlight.* • *n.* [in sing.] a light with such qualities: *a pale shimmer of moonlight.*
DERIVATIVES: **shim•mer•ing•ly** *adv.* **shim•mer•y** *adj.*

shim•my |ˈSHimē| • *n.* (pl. **-ies**) a kind of ragtime dance in which the whole body shakes or sways.
■ shaking, esp. abnormal vibration of the wheels of a motor vehicle: *steering stabilizers reduce shimmy even from oversized tires.* • *v.* (**-ies, -ied**) [intrans.] dance the shimmy.
■ shake or vibrate abnormally: *he braked hard and felt the car shimmy dangerously.* ■ move with a graceful swaying motion: *her hair swung in waves as she shimmied down the catwalk.* ■ [with adverbial of direction] move swiftly and effortlessly: *he shimmied right across the downed tree.*

shin•dy |ˈSHindē| • *n.* (pl. **-ies**) a noisy disturbance or quarrel: *there were plenty of gulls kicking up a shindy.*
■ a large, lively party.

shin•gles |ˈSHiNGgəlz| • *plural n.* [treated as sing.] an acute, painful inflammation of the nerve ganglia, with a skin eruption often forming a girdle around the middle of the body. It is caused by the same virus as chicken pox. Also called **herpes zoster**.

shin•ny |ˈSHinē| (also **shin**) • *v.* (**-ies, -ied**) climb something by clasping it with the arms and legs and hauling oneself up: *he loved to shinny up that tree.*

Shin•to |ˈSHin,tō| • *n.* a Japanese religion dating from the early 8th century and incorporating the worship of ancestors and nature spirits and a belief in sacred power (**kami**) in both animate and inanimate things. In much modified form, it was the state religion of Japan until 1945.
DERIVATIVES: **Shin•to•ism** |-izəm| *n.* **Shin•to•ist** |-ist| *n.*

shire |ˈSHīr| • *n.* a county, esp. in England.
■ (**the Shires**) used in reference to parts of England regarded as strongholds of traditional rural culture, esp. the rural Midlands.

shiv |SHiv| • *n.* a knife or razor used as a weapon.

Shi•va |ˈSHēvə| (also **Siva**) (in Indian religion) a god associated with the powers of reproduction and dissolution.

Shiva is regarded by some as the supreme being and by others as forming a triad with Brahma and Vishnu. He is worshiped in many aspects: as destroyer, ascetic, lord of the cosmic dance, and lord of beasts, and through the symbolic lingam. His wife is Parvati.

shi•va |ˈSHivə| (also **shivah**) • *n.* (in Judaism) a period of seven days' formal mourning for the dead, beginning immediately after the funeral: *she went to her sister's funeral and sat shiva.*

shiv•a•ree • *n.* variant spelling of CHARIVARI.

shmear |SHmir| (also **shmeer**) • *n.* & *v.* variant spelling of SCHMEAR.

shoal[1] |SHŌl| • *n.* a large number of fish swimming together: *a shoal of bream.*
■ a large number of people: *a rock star's entrance, preceded by his shoal of attendants.* • *v.* [intrans.] (of fish) form shoals.

shoal[2] • *n.* an area of shallow water, esp. as a navigational hazard.
■ a submerged sandbank visible at low water.
■ (usu. **shoals**) a hidden danger or difficulty: *he alone could safely guide them through Hollywood's treacherous shoals.* • *v.* [intrans.] (of water) become shallower. • *adj.* (of water) shallow.
DERIVATIVES: **shoal•y** *adj.*

shock |SHäk| • *n.* (in medicine) an acute condition associated with a fall in blood pressure, caused by such events as loss of blood, severe burns, bacterial infection, allergic reaction, or sudden emotional stress, and marked by cold, pallid skin, irregular breathing, rapid pulse, and dilated pupils: *he died of shock due to massive abdominal hemorrhage.*
■ short for *electric shock*, a sudden discharge of electricity through a part of the body. • *v.* [trans.] (usu. **be shocked**) affect with physiological shock, or with an electric shock.
DERIVATIVES: **shock•a•bil•i•ty** |-ə'bilit̲ē| *n.* **shock•a•ble** *adj.*

shod•dy |'SHädē| • *adj.* (**shoddier, shoddiest**) badly made or done: *we're not paying good money for shoddy goods.*
■ lacking moral principle; sordid: *a shoddy misuse of the honor system.* • *n.* an inferior quality yarn or fabric made from the shredded fiber of waste woolen cloth or clippings.
DERIVATIVES: **shod•di•ly** |-əlē| *adv.* **shod•di•ness** *n.*

sho•far |'SHōfər; SHō'fär| • *n.* (pl. **shofars** or **shofroth** |SHō'frōt; -'frōs|) a ram's-horn trumpet used by Jews in religious ceremonies and as an ancient battle signal.

sho•gun |'SHōgən| • *n.* a hereditary commander in chief in feudal Japan. Because of the military power concentrated in his hands and the consequent weakness of the nominal head of state (the *mikado* or emperor), the shogun was generally the real ruler of the country until feudalism was abolished in 1867. Cf. DAIMYO.
DERIVATIVES: **sho•gun•ate** |-gənit; -gə ˌnāt| *n.*

short shrift • *n.* rapid and unsympathetic dismissal; curt treatment: *the judge gave short shrift to an argument based on the right to free speech.*
■ little time between condemnation and execution or other punishment.

shrewd |SHro͞od| • *adj.* **1** having or showing sharp powers of judgment; astute: *she was shrewd enough to guess the motive behind his gesture* | *a shrewd career move.* **2** (esp. of weather) piercingly cold: *a shrewd east wind.*

■ (of a blow) severe; *a bayonet's shrewd thrust.*
■ mischievous; malicious.
DERIVATIVES: **shrewd•ly** *adv.* **shrewd• ness** *n.*

shrift |SHrift| • *n.* confession, esp. to a priest: *go to shrift.* See also SHORT SHRIFT.
■ absolution by a priest.

shrive |SHrīv| • *v.* (past **shrove** |SHrōv| ; past part. **shriven** |'SHrivən|) [trans.] (of a priest) hear the confession of, assign penance to, and absolve (someone).
■ (**shrive oneself**) present oneself to a priest for confession, penance, and absolution.

shtick |SHtik| • *n.* an attention-getting or theatrical routine, gimmick, or talent that is characteristic of an entertainer.

shuck |SHək| • *n.* **1** an outer covering such as a husk or pod, esp. the husk of an ear of corn.
■ the shell of an oyster or clam. ■ the integument of certain insect pupae or larvae. **2** a person or thing regarded as worthless or contemptible: *William didn't dig the idea at all and said it was a shuck.* • *exclam.* (**shucks**) used to express surprise, regret, irritation, or, in response to praise, self-deprecation: *"Thank you for getting it." "Oh, shucks, it was nothing."* • *v.* [trans.] **1** remove the shucks from corn or shellfish: *shuck and drain the oysters.*
■ take off (a garment): *she shucked off her robe and started dressing.* ■ abandon; get rid of: *the regime's ability to shuck off its totalitarian characteristics.* **2** cause (someone) to believe something that is not true; fool or tease.
■ [intrans.] put on a show of knowledge, mastery, etc.: *keep on shucking and jiving—no one buys it.*
DERIVATIVES: **shuck•er** *n.*

shul |SHo͞ol; SHo͝ol| • *n.* a synagogue.

shy[1] |SHī| • *v.* (**-ies, -ied**) [intrans.] (esp. of a horse) start suddenly aside in fright at an object, noise, or movement.
■ (**shy from**) avoid doing or becoming involved in (something) owing to nervousness or a lack of confidence: *don't shy away from saying what you think.*
DERIVATIVES: **shy•er** |'SHī(ə)r| *n.*

shy[2] • *v.* (**-ies, -ied**) [trans.] fling or throw (something) at a target: *he picked up the magazines and shied them at her.* • *n.* (pl. **-ies**) an act of flinging or throwing something at a target.
PHRASES: **have a shy at** try to hit something, esp. with a ball or stone. ■ attempt to do or obtain something. ■ jeer at: *you are always having a shy at Lady Ann and her relations.*

Shy•lock |'SHī,läk| a Jewish moneylender in Shakespeare's *Merchant of Venice*, who lends money to Antonio but demands in return a pound of Antonio's own flesh should the debt not be repaid on time.
■ [as n.] (**a Shylock**) a moneylender who charges extremely high rates of interest.

shy•ster |'SHīstər| • *n.* a person, esp. a lawyer, who uses unscrupulous, fraudulent, or deceptive methods in business.

sib•i•lant |'sibələnt| • *adj.* (of a speech sound) sounded with a hissing effect, for example *s, sh.*

■ making or characterized by a hissing sound: *his sibilant whisper.* • *n.* a sibilant speech sound.

DERIVATIVES: **sib•i•lance** *n.*

sib•i•late | 'sibə,lāt | • *v.* [trans.] utter with a hissing sound.

DERIVATIVES: **sib•i•la•tion** | ˌsibəˈlāSHən | *n.*

sib•ling | 'sibliNG | • *n.* each of two or more children or offspring having one or both parents in common; a brother or sister.

sic[1] | sik | • *adv.* used in brackets after a copied or quoted word that appears odd or erroneous to show that the word is quoted exactly as it stands in the original, as in *a story must hold a child's interest and "enrich his [sic] life."*

sic[2] (also **sick**) • *v.* (**sicced, siccing** or **sicked, sicking**) [trans.] (**sic something on**) order a dog or other animal to attack (someone or something): *the plan was to surprise the hell out of the grizzly by sicking the dog on him.*
■ (**sic someone on**) set someone to pursue, keep watch on, or accompany (another).

side•bar | 'sīd,bär | • *n.* a short article in a newspaper or magazine, typically boxed, placed alongside a main article, and containing additional or explanatory material.
■ a secondary, additional, or incidental thing; a side issue. ■ (also **sidebar conference**) (in a court of law) a discussion between the lawyers and the judge held out of hearing of the jury.

si•de•re•al • *adj.* (of time) reckoned from the motion of the earth (or a planet) relative to the distant stars (rather than with respect to the sun): *a sidereal clock.*

si•dle | 'sīdl | • *v.* [no obj., with adverbial of direction] walk in a furtive, unobtrusive, or timid manner, esp. sideways or obliquely: *I sidled up to her.* • *n.* [in sing.] an instance of walking in this way.

si•er•ra | sēˈerə | • *n.* a long jagged mountain chain.

sight-read • *v.* [trans.] read and perform (music) at sight, without preparation.

DERIVATIVES: **sight-read•er** *n.* **sight-read•ing** *n.*

sig•il | 'sijəl | • *n.* an inscribed or painted symbol considered to have magical power.
■ a seal: *the supply wagons bore the High King's sigil.* ■ a sign or symbol.

sig•nal•ize | 'signə,līz | • *v.* [trans.] **1** mark or indicate (something), esp. in a striking or conspicuous manner: *signalize a change in status.*
■ make (something) noteworthy or remarkable: *a little flower with not much to signalize it.* **2** provide (an intersection) with traffic signals.

sig•net | 'signit | • *n.* a small seal, esp. one set in a ring, formerly used instead of or with a signature to give authentication to an official document.

sig•nif•i•cant oth•er • *n.* a person with whom someone has an established romantic or sexual relationship.

Si•le•nus | sīˈlēnəs | an aged woodland deity of Greek mythology, one of the *sileni*, who was

entrusted with the education of Dionysus. He is depicted either as dignified and musical, or as an old drunkard.
■ [as n.] (**a silenus**) (pl. **sileni** | sīˈlē,nī |) a woodland spirit, usually depicted in art as old and having ears like those of a horse.

sil•i•con | 'silə,kän; -kən | • *n.* the chemical element of atomic number 14, a nonmetal with semiconducting properties, used in making electronic circuits. Pure silicon exists in a shiny dark gray crystalline form and as an amorphous powder. (Symbol: **Si**)

sil•i•cone | 'silə,kōn | • *n.* any of a class of synthetic materials that are polymers with a chemical structure based on chains of alternate silicon and oxygen atoms, with organic groups attached to the silicon atoms. Such compounds are typically resistant to chemical attack and insensitive to temperature changes and are used to make rubber and plastics and in polishes and lubricants. • *v.* [trans.] (usu. **be siliconed**) join or otherwise treat (something) with a silicone.

silk•screen | 'silk,skrēn | (also **silk screen**) • *n.* a screen of fine mesh used in screen-printing (the process of forcing ink on to a surface through a screen prepared so as to create a picture or pattern).
■ a print made by screen-printing • *v.* [trans.] print, decorate, or reproduce using a silkscreen.

sill | sil | • *n.* (in geology) a tabular sheet of igneous rock intruded between and parallel with the existing strata.
■ an underwater ridge or rock ledge extending across the bed of a body of water.

sil•vi•cul•ture | 'silvi,kəlCHər | • *n.* the growing and cultivation of forest trees. Cf. ARBORICULTURE.

DERIVATIVES: **sil•vi•cul•tur•al** | ˌsilviˈkəlCHərəl | *adj.* **sil•vi•cul•tur•ist** | ˌsilviˈkəlCHərist | *n.*

sim•i•le | 'siməlē | • *n.* a figure of speech involving the comparison of one thing with another thing of a different kind, used to make a description more emphatic or vivid (e.g., *as brave as a lion*). Cf. METAPHOR.
■ the use of such a method of comparison.

si•mil•i•tude | siˈmilə,t(y) o͞od | • *n.* the quality or state of being similar to something.
■ a comparison between two things. ■ a person or thing resembling someone or something else.

si•mo•ny | 'sīmənē; 'si- | • *n.* the buying or selling of ecclesiastical privileges, for example pardons or benefices.
■ preferential treatment of members of a church or religious organization by its clerics.

DERIVATIVES: **si•mo•ni•ac** | sīˈmōnē,æk; si- | *adj.* & *n.* **si•mo•ni•a•cal** | ˌsīməˈnīəkəl; si- | *adj.*

sim•pa•ti•co | simˈpæti,kō | • *adj.* (of a person) likable and easy to get along with.
■ having or characterized by shared attributes or interests; compatible: *a simpatico relationship.*

sim•per | 'simpər | • *v.* [intrans.] smile or gesture in an affectedly coquettish, coy, or ingra-

tiating manner: *she simpered, looking pleased with herself.* • *n.* [usu. in sing.] an affectedly coquettish, coy, or ingratiating smile or gesture: *an exaggerated simper.*
DERIVATIVES: **sim•per•ing•ly** *adv.*

sim•plism |'simplizəm| • *n.* the oversimplification of an issue.

sim•plis•tic |sim'plistik| • *adj.* treating complex issues and problems as if they were much simpler than they really are: *simplistic solutions.*
DERIVATIVES: **sim•plis•ti•cal•ly** *adv.*

sim•u•la•crum |,simyə'lākrəm; -'læk-| • *n.* (pl. **simulacra** |-'lākrə; -'lækrə| or **simulacrums**) an image or representation of someone or something.
■ an unsatisfactory imitation or substitute.

sim•u•late |'simyə,lāt| • *v.* [trans.] imitate the appearance or character of: *red ocher intended to simulate blood* | [as adj.] (**simulated**) *a simulated leather handbag.*
■ pretend to have or feel (an emotion): *it was impossible to force a smile, to simulate pleasure.*
■ produce a computer model of: *future population changes were simulated by computer.* Cf. EMULATE.
DERIVATIVES: **sim•u•la•tion** |,simyə'lāsHən| *n.* **sim•u•la•tive** |'simyə,lātiv| *adj.*

si•ne•cure |'sīnə,kyŏor; 'si-| • *n.* a position requiring little or no work but giving the holder status or financial benefit.
DERIVATIVES: **si•ne•cur•ism** |'sīnəkyŏor-izəm; si-| *n.* **si•ne•cur•ist** |'sīnə,kyŏorist; si-| *n.*

si•ne di•e |'sīnə 'dīē; 'senā 'dēä| • *adv.* (with reference to business or proceedings that have been adjourned) with no appointed date for resumption: *the case was adjourned sine die.*

si•ne qua non |,sini ,kwä 'nōn; ,sini ,kwä 'nän| • *n.* an essential condition; a thing that is absolutely necessary: *grammar is the sine qua non of language teaching.*

sin•ew |'sinyŏo| • *n.* a piece of tough fibrous tissue uniting muscle to bone or bone to bone; a tendon or ligament.
■ (usu. **sinews**) the parts of a structure, system, or thing that give it strength or bind it together: *the sinews of government.* • *v.* [trans.] [usu. as adj.] (**sinewed**) strengthen with or as if with sinews: *the sinewed shape of his back.*
DERIVATIVES: **sin•ew•less** |-lis| *adj.* **sin•ew•y** |-wē| *adj.*

sin•fo•ni•a |,sinfə'nēə| • *n.* a symphony.
■ (in the 17th and 18th centuries) an orchestral piece used as an introduction, interlude, or postlude to an opera, oratorio, cantata, or suite. ■ a small symphony orchestra.

sin•fo•niet•ta |,sinfən'yeṭə| • *n.* a short or simple symphony.
■ a small symphony orchestra.

sing•spiel |'siNG,spēl| • *n.* (pl. **singspiele** |-lə|) a form of German light opera, typically with spoken dialogue, popular esp. in the late 18th century.

sin•is•ter |'sinistər| • *adj.* **1** giving the impression that something harmful or evil is happening or will happen: *there was something sinister about that murmuring voice.*

■ wicked or criminal. **2** [attrib.] of, on, or toward the left-hand side (in a coat of arms, from the bearer's point of view, i.e., the right as it is depicted). The opposite of DEXTER.
DERIVATIVES: **sin•is•ter•ly** *adv.* **sin•is•ter•ness** *n.*

sin•is•tral |'sinəstrəl| • *adj.* of, on, or moving to the left side or the left hand (the opposite of DEXTRAL), in particular:
■ left-handed.
DERIVATIVES: **sin•is•tral•i•ty** |,sinə'strælitē| *n.* **sin•is•tral•ly** *adv.*

sin•ter |'sin(t)ər| • *n.* **1** a hard siliceous or calcareous deposit precipitated from mineral springs. **2** solid material that has been sintered, esp. a mixture of iron ore and other materials prepared for smelting. • *v.* [trans.] make (a powdered material) coalesce into a solid or porous mass by heating it (and usually also compressing it) without liquefaction.
■ [intrans.] coalesce in this way.

sin•u•ous |'sinyəwəs| • *adj.* having many curves and turns: *the river follows a sinuous trail through the forest.*
■ lithe and supple: *the sinuous grace of a cat.*
DERIVATIVES: **sin•u•ous•ly** *adv.* **sin•u•ous•ness** *n.*

Sioux |sŏo| • *n.* (pl. same) another term for the Dakota people or their language. The Dakota inhabited the northern Mississippi valley and surrounding plains. The **Lakota** of western South Dakota are a subgroup, also called the Teton Sioux. • *adj.* of or relating to this people or their language, part of the larger *Siouan* language group.

si•ren |'sīrən| • *n.* (in Greek mythology) each of a number of women or winged creatures whose singing lured unwary sailors onto rocks.
■ a woman who is considered to be alluring or fascinating but also dangerous in some way.

si•roc•co |sə'räkō| (also **scirocco** |sHə'rä-kō; sə-|) • *n.* (pl. **-os**) a hot wind, often dusty or rainy, blowing from North Africa across the Mediterranean to southern Europe.

Sis•y•phe•an |,sisə'fēən| • *adj.* (of a task) such that it can never be completed.

sit•u•a•tion•ism |,siCHə'wāsHə,nizəm| • *n.* the theory that human behavior is determined by surrounding circumstances rather than by personal qualities.
DERIVATIVES: **sit•u•a•tion•ist** *n.* & *adj.*

si•tus |'sīṭəs; 'sē-| • *n.* situation or position, esp. the normal position of an organ or other part of a living thing.
■ the place to which, for purposes of legal jurisdiction or taxation, a property belongs.

skald |skôld; skäld| (also **scald**) • *n.* (in ancient Scandinavia) a composer and reciter of poems honoring heroes and their deeds.
DERIVATIVES: **skald•ic** |-ik| *adj.*

skein |skān| • *n.* a length of thread or yarn, loosely coiled and knotted.
■ a tangled or complicated arrangement, state, or situation: ***the skeins of** her long hair* | *a **skein of** lies.* ■ a flock of wild geese or swans in flight, typically in a V-shaped formation.

skep•tic |'skeptik| (Brit. **sceptic**) • *n.* **1** a person inclined to question or doubt all accepted opinions.

■ a person who doubts the truth of Christianity and other religions; an agnostic or nonbeliever. **2** an ancient or modern philosopher who denies the possibility of knowledge, or even rational belief, in some sphere.

The leading ancient skeptic was Pyrrho, whose followers at the Academy vigorously opposed Stoicism. Modern skeptics have held diverse views: the most extreme have doubted whether any knowledge at all of the external world is possible (see SOLIPSISM), while others have questioned the existence of objects beyond our experience of them.

DERIVATIVES: **skep•ti•cal** *adj.* **skep•ti•cism** |'skeptə,sizəm| *n.*

skew |skyoo| • *adj.* **1** neither parallel nor at right angles to a specified or implied line; askew; crooked: *his hat looked slightly skew* | *a skew angle.*

■ (of a statistical distribution) not symmetrical. **2** (of a pair of lines) neither parallel nor intersecting.

■ (of a curve) not lying in a plane. • *n.* an oblique angle; a slant.

■ a bias toward one particular group or subject: *the paper had a working-class skew.* ■ the state of not being statistically symmetrical. • *v.* [no obj., with adverbial] suddenly change direction or position: *the car had skewed across the track.*

■ twist or turn or cause to do this: *he skewed around in his saddle* | [trans.] *his leg was skewed in and pushed against the other one.* ■ [trans.] make biased or distorted in a way that is regarded as inaccurate, unfair, or misleading: *the curriculum is skewed toward the practical subjects.* ■ [trans.] cause (a statistical distribution) to be asymmetrical.

DERIVATIVES: **skew•ness** *n.*

skew•bald |'skyoo,bôld| • *adj.* (of an animal) with irregular patches of white and another color (properly not black). Cf. PIEBALD. • *n.* a skewbald animal, esp. a horse.

skid row |'rō| • *n.* a run-down part of a town frequented by vagrants, alcoholics, and drug addicts.

■ a desperately unfortunate or difficult situation: *I don't want to end up on skid row.*

skin•flint |'skin,flint| • *n.* a person who spends as little money as possible; a miser.

skin game • *n.* a rigged gambling game; a swindle.

skin•head |'skin,hed| • *n.* a young person with close-cropped hair, often perceived as aggressive, violent, and racist.

skin-pop • *v.* [trans.] inject (a drug, typically a narcotic) under the skin (rather than into a vein). • *n.* an under-the-skin injection of a drug, typically a narcotic.

DERIVATIVES: **skin-pop•per** *n.*

skit•ter |'skitər| • *v.* [intrans.] **1** [no obj., with adverbial of direction] move lightly and quickly or hurriedly: *the girls skittered up the stairs* | *her mind skittered back to that day at the office.*

2 [trans.] draw (bait) jerkily across the surface of the water as a technique in fishing.

skit•tish |'skitiSH| • *adj.* lively and unpredictable; playful: *my skittish and immature mother.*

■ (esp. of a horse) nervous; inclined to shy.

DERIVATIVES: **skit•tish•ly** *adv.* **skit•tish•ness** *n.*

skoal |skōl| (also **skol**) • *exclam.* used to express friendly feelings toward one's companions before drinking.

skul•dug•ger•y |skəl'dəgərē| (also **skullduggery**) • *n.* underhanded or unscrupulous behavior; trickery: *a firm that investigates commercial skulduggery.*

skulk |skəlk| • *v.* [intrans.] keep out of sight, typically with a sinister or cowardly motive: *don't skulk outside the door like a spy!*

■ [with adverbial of direction] move stealthily or furtively: *he spent most of his time skulking around in the corridors.* ■ shirk duty.

DERIVATIVES: **skulk•er** *n.*

sky•hook |'skī,ho͝ok| (also **sky hook** or **sky-hook**) • *n.* **1** an imaginary or fanciful device by which something could be suspended in the air.

■ a false hope, or a premise or argument which has no logical grounds. **2** a small flattened hook, with an eye for attaching a rope, fixed temporarily into a rock face while climbing. **3** a very high-arcing hook shot in basketball. **4** a helicopter equipped with a steel line and hook for hoisting and transporting heavy objects.

■ this apparatus attached to a helicopter.

slack•er |'slækər| • *n.* a person who avoids work or effort.

■ a person who evades military service. ■ a young person (esp. in the 1990s) of a subculture characterized by apathy and aimlessness.

slag |slæg| • *n.* **1** stony waste matter separated from metals during the smelting or refining of ore.

■ similar material produced by a volcano; scoria. **2** Brit. a promiscuous woman. • *v.* (**slagged**, **slagging**) [intrans.] [usu. as n.] (**slagging**) produce deposits of slag.

DERIVATIVES: **slag•gy** *adj.* (**slag•gi•er**, **slag•gi•est**) .

slake |slāk| • *v.* [trans.] quench or satisfy (one's thirst): *slake your thirst with some lemonade.*

■ satisfy (desires): *restaurants worked to slake the Italian obsession with food.*

slan•der |'slændər| • *n.* the action or crime of making a false spoken statement damaging to a person's reputation: *he is suing the TV network for slander.* Cf. LIBEL, DEFAMATION.

■ a false and malicious spoken statement: *I've had just about all I can stomach of your slanders.* • *v.* [trans.] make false and damaging statements about (someone): *they were accused of slandering the head of state.*

DERIVATIVES: **slan•der•er** *n.* **slan•der•ous** |-rəs| *adj.* **slan•der•ous•ly** |-rəslē| *adv.*

slap•stick |'slæp,stik| • *n.* comedy based on deliberately clumsy actions and humorously embarrassing events: [as adj.] *slapstick humor.*

■ a device consisting of two flexible pieces of wood joined together at one end, used by clowns and in pantomime to produce a loud slapping noise.

slat•tern |'slæt̬ərn| • *n.* a dirty, untidy woman.
DERIVATIVES: **slat•tern•li•ness** *n.* **slat•tern•ly** *adj.*

slav•ish |'slāvisн| • *adj.* relating to or characteristic of a slave, typically by behaving in a servile or submissive way: *he noted the slavish, feudal respect they had for her.*
■ showing no attempt at originality, constructive interpretation, or development: *a slavish adherence to protocol.*
DERIVATIVES: **slav•ish•ly** *adv.* **slav•ish•ness** *n.*

slea•zy |'slēzē| • *adj.* (**sleazier, sleaziest**) **1** (of a person or situation) sordid, corrupt, or immoral.
■ (of a place) squalid and seedy: *a sleazy all-night cafe.* **2** (of textiles and clothing) flimsy.
DERIVATIVES: **sleaze** *n.* **slea•zi•ly** |'slēzəlē| *adv.* **slea•zi•ness** *n.*

sledge |slej| • *n.* a vehicle on runners for conveying loads or passengers esp. over snow or ice, often pulled by draft animals.
■ British term for sled. • *v.* [with obj., with adverbial of direction] carry (a load or passengers) on a sledge: *the task of sledging lifeboats across tundra.*

sleight |slīt| • *n.* the use of dexterity or cunning, esp. so as to deceive: *except by **sleight of logic,** the two positions cannot be harmonized.*
PHRASES: **sleight of hand** manual dexterity, typically in performing tricks: *a nifty bit of sleight of hand got the ashtray into the correct position.* ■ skillful deception: *this is financial sleight of hand of the worst sort.*

sleuth |slōoтн| • *n.* a detective. • *v.* [intrans.] [often as n.] (**sleuthing**) carry out a search or investigation in the manner of a detective: *scientists began their genetic sleuthing for honey mushrooms four years ago.*
■ [trans.] investigate (someone or something).

slew[1] |slōo| (also **slue**) • *v.* **1** [no obj., with adverbial of direction] (of a vehicle or person) turn or slide violently or uncontrollably in a particular direction: *the Chevy slewed from side to side in the snow.*
■ [trans.] turn or slide (something, esp. a vehicle) in such a way: *he managed to slew the aircraft around before it settled on the runway.* **2** [intrans.] (of an electronic device) undergo slewing. • *n.* [in sing.] a violent or uncontrollable sliding movement: *I was assaulted by the thump and slew of the van.*

slew[2] • *n.* a large number or quantity of something: *he asked me **a slew of** questions.*

slink |slинGk| • *v.* (past and past part. **slunk** |sləнGk|) [no obj., with adverbial of direction] move smoothly and quietly with gliding steps, in a stealthy or sensuous manner: *the fox came slinking through the woods.*
■ come or go unobtrusively or furtively: *all his so-called friends have **slunk off.** • *n.* [in sing.] an act of moving in this way: *she moved with a sensuous slink.*

slink•y |'slинGkē| • *adj.* (**slinkier, slinkiest**) graceful and sinuous in movement, line, or figure: *a slinky black evening dress.*
DERIVATIVES: **slink•i•ly** |'slинGkəlē| *adv.* **slink•i•ness** *n.*

slip•page |'slipij| • *n.* the action or process of something slipping or subsiding; the amount or extent of this: *$16 million has been spent on cracks and slippage.*
■ failure to meet a standard or deadline: the extent of this: *slippage on any job will entail slippage on the overall project.*

slip•shod |'slip,sнäd| • *adj.* (typically of a person or method of work) characterized by a lack of care, thought, or organization: *he'd caused many problems with his slipshod management.*
■ (of shoes) worn down at the heel.

slip•stream |'slip,strēm| • *n.* a current of air or water driven back by a revolving propeller or jet engine.
■ the partial vacuum created in the wake of a moving vehicle, often used by other vehicles in a race to assist in passing. ■ an assisting force regarded as drawing something along behind something else: *when the US economy booms, the rest of the world is pulled along in the slipstream.* • *v.* [intrans.] (esp. in auto racing) follow closely behind another vehicle, traveling in its slipstream and awaiting an opportunity to pass; draft.
■ [trans.] travel in the slipstream of (someone), esp. in order to overtake them; draft (another vehicle).

slith•er |'slithər| • *v.* [no obj., with adverbial of direction] move smoothly over a surface with a twisting or oscillating motion: *I spied an adder slithering away.*
■ slide or slip unsteadily on a loose or slippery surface: *we slithered down a snowy mountain track.* • *n.* [in sing.] a movement in such a manner: *a snakelike slither across the grass.*
DERIVATIVES: **slith•er•y** *adj.*

sloe-eyed • *adj.* having attractive dark, typically almond-shaped eyes.

sloth |slôтн; slätн; slōтн| • *n.* **1** reluctance to work or make an effort; laziness: *he should overcome his natural sloth and complacency.* **2** any of several slow-moving tropical American mammals that hang upside down from the branches of trees using their long limbs and hooked claws.
DERIVATIVES: **sloth•ful** *adj.* **sloth•ful•ly** *adv.* **sloth•ful•ness** *n.*

slough[1] |slow; slōo| • *n.* a piece of soft miry ground; swamp.
■ a situation characterized by lack of progress or activity: *the economic slough of the interwar years.* ■ a muddy side channel or inlet.
DERIVATIVES: **slough•y** *adj.*

slough[2] |sləf| • *v.* [trans.] (of an animal, esp. a snake, or a person) cast off or shed (an old skin or dead skin): *a snake **sloughs off** its old skin* | *he is concerned to **slough off** the country's bad environmental image.*
■ [intrans.] (**slough off**) (of dead skin) drop off; be shed. ■ [intrans.] (**slough away/down**) (of soil or rock) collapse or slide into a hole or

depression. • *n.* the dropping off of dead tissue from living flesh: *the drugs can cause blistering and slough.*

DERIVATIVES: **slough•y** *adj.*

slov•en | 'sləvən | • *n.* a person who is habitually messy or careless.

slov•en•ly | 'sləvənlē; 'slä- | • *adj.* (esp. of a person or personal appearance) messy and dirty: *he was upbraided for his slovenly appearance.* ■ (esp. of a person or action) careless; excessively casual: *slovenly speech.*

DERIVATIVES: **slov•en•li•ness** *n.*

slug•gard | 'sləgərd | • *n.* a lazy, sluggish person.

DERIVATIVES: **slug•gard•li•ness** *n.* **slug•gard•ly** *adj.*

sluice | sloōs | • *n.* **1** (also **sluice gate**) a sliding gate or other device for controlling the flow of water, esp. one in a lock gate. ■ (also **sluiceway**) an artificial water channel for carrying off overflow or surplus water. ■ (in gold mining) a channel or trough constructed with grooves into which a current of water is directed in order to separate gold from the sand or gravel containing it. **2** an act of rinsing or showering with water: *a sluice with cold water.* • *v.* [trans.] wash or rinse freely with a stream or shower of water: *she sluiced her face in cold water* | *crews sluiced down the decks of their ship.* ■ [no obj., with adverbial of direction] (of water) pour, flow, or shower freely: *the waves sluiced over them.*

smarm•y | 'smärmē | • *adj.* (**smarmier, smarmiest**) ingratiating and wheedling in a way that is perceived as insincere or excessive: *a smarmy, unctuous reply.*

DERIVATIVES: **smarm•i•ly** | -məlē | *adv.* **smarm•i•ness** *n.*

smat•ter•ing | 'smætəriNG | (also **smatter**) • *n.* a slight superficial knowledge of a language or subject: *Edward had only a smattering of Spanish.* ■ a small amount of something: *a smattering of snow.*

smeg•ma | 'smegmə | • *n.* a sebaceous secretion in the folds of the skin, esp. under a man's foreskin.

smelt | smelt | • *v.* [trans.] [often as *n.*] (**smelting**) extract (metal) from its ore by a process involving heating and melting: *tin smelting.* ■ extract a metal from (ore) in this way.

smirch | smərCH | • *v.* [trans.] make (something) dirty; soil: *the window was smirched by heat and smoke.* ■ discredit (a person or reputation); taint: *I am not accustomed to having my honor smirched.* • *n.* a dirty mark or stain. ■ a blot on someone's character; a flaw.

smirk | smərk | • *v.* [intrans.] smile in an irritatingly smug, conceited, or silly way: *Dr. Ali smirked in triumph.* • *n.* a smug, conceited, or silly smile: *Gloria pursed her mouth in a self-satisfied smirk.*

DERIVATIVES: **smirk•er** *n.* **smirk•i•ly** | -kəlē | *adv.* **smirk•ing•ly** *adv.* **smirk•y** *adj.*

smite | smīt | • *v.* (past **smote** | smōt | ; past part. **smitten** | 'smitn |) [trans.] strike with a firm blow: *he smites the water with his sword.* ■ defeat or conquer (a people or land): *he may smite our enemies.* ■ (usu. **be smitten**) (esp. of disease) attack or affect severely: *various people had been smitten with untimely summer flu.* ■ (**be smitten**) be strongly attracted to someone or something: *she was so smitten with the boy.* • *n.* a heavy blow or stroke with a weapon or the hand.

DERIVATIVES: **smit•er** *n.*

smith•y | 'smiTHē | • *n.* (pl. **-ies**) a blacksmith's workshop; a forge. ■ a blacksmith.

smol•der | 'smōldər | • *v.* [intrans.] burn slowly with smoke but no flame: *the bonfire still smoldered.* ■ show or feel barely suppressed anger, hatred, or another powerful emotion: *Anna smoldered with indignation* | [as adj.] (**smoldering**) *he met her smoldering eyes.* ■ exist in a suppressed or concealed state: *the controversy smoldered on for several years* | [as adj.] (**smoldering**) *smoldering rage.* • *n.* smoke coming from a fire that is burning slowly without a flame: *the last acrid smolder of his cigarette.*

DERIVATIVES: **smol•der•ing•ly** *adv.*

snick•er | 'snikər | • *v.* [intrans.] give a smothered or half-suppressed laugh; snigger. ■ (of a horse) whinny. • *n.* a smothered laugh; a snigger. ■ a whinny.

DERIVATIVES: **snick•er•ing•ly** *adv.*

snide | snīd | • *adj.* **1** derogatory or mocking in a sneering, usu. indirect way: *snide remarks about my mother.* ■ (of a person) devious and underhanded: *a snide divorce lawyer.* **2** chiefly Brit. counterfeit; inferior: *snide Rolex watches.* • *n.* an unpleasant or underhanded person or remark.

DERIVATIVES: **snide•ly** *adv.* **snide•ness** *n.* **snide•y** *adj.*

snif•ter | 'sniftər | • *n.* a footed glass that is wide at the bottom and tapers to the top, used for brandy and other drinks. ■ a small quantity of an alcoholic drink: *care to join me for a snifter?*

snig•ger | 'snigər | • *n.* a smothered or half-suppressed laugh. • *v.* [intrans.] give such a laugh: *the boys at school were sure to snigger at him behind his back* | [with direct speech] *"Doesn't he look like a fool?" they sniggered.*

DERIVATIVES: **snig•ger•er** *n.* **snig•ger•ing•ly** *adv.*

snit | snit | • *n.* a fit of irritation; a sulk: *the ambassador and delegation had withdrawn in a snit.*

sniv•el | 'snivəl | • *v.* (**sniveled, sniveling**; Brit. **snivelled, snivelling**) [intrans.] cry and sniffle: *Kate started to snivel, looking sad and stunned.* ■ complain in a whining or tearful way: *he shouldn't snivel about his punishment* | [as adj.] (**sniveling**) *you sniveling little brat!* • *n.* a slight sniff indicating suppressed emotion or crying: *the boy's torrent of howls weakened to a snivel.*

DERIVATIVES: **sniv•el•er** *n.* **sniv•el•ing•ly** *adv.*

snoot•y |'sno͞otē| • *adj.* (**snootier, snootiest**) showing disapproval or contempt toward others, esp. those considered to belong to a lower social class: *snooty neighbors.*
DERIVATIVES: **snoot•i•ly** |-t̬əlē| *adv.* **snoot•i•ness** *n.*

snot•ty |'snät̬ē| • *adj.* (**snottier, snottiest**) **1** full of or covered with nasal mucus (snot): *a snotty nose.* **2** having or showing a superior or conceited attitude: *a snotty letter.*
DERIVATIVES: **snot•ti•ly** |-t̬əlē| *adv.* **snot•ti•ness** *n.*

snuf•fle |'snəfəl| • *v.* [intrans.] breathe noisily through the nose due to a cold or crying: *Alice was weeping quietly, snuffling a little.*
■ (esp. of an animal) make repeated sniffing sounds as though smelling at something: *the collie snuffled around his boots* | [as n.] (**snuffling**) *she heard a strange, persistent snuffling.* • *n.* a sniff or sniffing sound: *a silence broken only by the faint snuffles of the dogs.*
DERIVATIVES: **snuf•fler** *n.* **snuf•fly** *adj.*

so•bri•e•ty |sə'brīət̬ē; sō-| • *n.* the state of being sober: *the price of beer compelled me to maintain a certain level of sobriety.*
■ the quality of being staid or solemn.

so•bri•quet |'sōbrə‚kā; -‚ket| (also **soubriquet**) • *n.* a person's nickname.

so•cial |'sōsHəl| • *adj.* **1** [attrib.] of or relating to society or its organization: *alcoholism is recognized as a major social problem* | *traditional Japanese social structure.*
■ of or relating to rank and status in society: *a recent analysis of social class in Mexico* | *her mother is a lady of the highest social standing.* ■ needing companionship and therefore best suited to living in communities: *we are social beings as well as individuals.* ■ relating to or designed for activities in which people meet each other for pleasure: *Guy led a full social life.* **2** (of birds) gregarious; breeding or nesting in colonies.
■ (of insects) living together in organized communities, typically with different castes, as ants, bees, wasps, and termites do. ■ (of mammals) living together in groups, typically in a hierarchical system with complex communication. • *n.* an informal social gathering, esp. one organized by the members of a particular club or group: *a church social.*
DERIVATIVES: **so•cial•i•ty** |‚sōsHē'ælədē| *n.* **so•cial•ly** |'sōsHəlē| *adv.* : *families who are socially disadvantaged.*

so•cial•ism |'sōsHə‚lizəm| • *n.* a political and economic theory of social organization that advocates that the means of production, distribution, and exchange should be owned or regulated by the community as a whole.
■ policy or practice based on this theory. ■ (in Marxist theory) a transitional social state between the overthrow of capitalism and the realization of communism.
DERIVATIVES: **so•cial•ist** *n.* & *adj.* **so•cial•is•tic** |‚sōsHə'listik| *adj.* **so•cial•is•ti•cal•ly** |‚sōsHə'listik(ə)lē| *adv.*

so•cial•ite |'sōsHə‚līt| • *n.* a person who is well known in fashionable society and is fond of social activities and entertainment.

so•ci•o•bi•ol•o•gy |‚sōsēō‚bī'äləjē| • *n.* the scientific study of the biological (esp. ecological and evolutionary) aspects of social behavior in animals and humans.
DERIVATIVES: **so•ci•o•bi•o•log•i•cal** |-‚bīə'läjikəl| *adj.* **so•ci•o•bi•o•log•i•cal•ly** |-‚bīə'läjik(ə)lē| *adv.* **so•ci•o•bi•ol•o•gist** |-jist| *n.*

so•ci•om•e•try |‚sōsē'ämətrē| • *n.* the quantitative study and measurement of relationships within a group of people.
DERIVATIVES: **so•ci•o•met•ric** |‚sōsēō'metrik| *adj.* **so•ci•o•met•ri•cal•ly** |‚sōsēō'metrik(ə)lē| *adv.* **so•ci•om•e•trist** |-trist| *n.*

so•ci•o•path |'sōsēō‚pæTH| • *n.* a person with a personality disorder manifesting itself in extreme antisocial attitudes and behavior and a lack of conscience.
DERIVATIVES: **so•ci•o•path•ic** |‚sōsēō'pæTHik| *adj.* **so•ci•op•a•thy** |‚sōsē'äpəTHē| *n.*

So•crat•ic i•ro•ny • *n.* a pose of ignorance assumed in order to entice others into making statements that can then be challenged.

so•dal•i•ty |sō'dælət̬ē| • *n.* (pl. **-ies**) a confraternity or association, esp. a Roman Catholic religious guild or brotherhood.
■ fraternity; friendship.

sod•den |'sädn| • *adj.* saturated with liquid, esp. water; soaked through: *his clothes were sodden.*
■ [in combination] having drunk an excessive amount of a particular alcoholic drink: *a whiskey-sodden criminal.* • *v.* [trans.] saturate (something) with water.
DERIVATIVES: **sod•den•ly** *adv.* **sod•den•ness** *n.*

sod•om•y |'sädəmē| • *n.* sexual intercourse involving anal or oral copulation.
DERIVATIVES: **sod•om•ite** *n.* **sod•om•ize** |'sädə‚mīz| *v.*

sof•fit |'säfit| • *n.* the underside of an architectural structure, such as an arch, a balcony, or overhanging eaves.

soi-di•sant |‚swä dē'zän(t)| • *adj.* self-styled; so-called: *a soi-disant novelist.*

soi•gné |swän'yā| • *adj.* (fem. **soignée** pronunc. same) dressed very elegantly; well groomed: *she was dark, petite, and soignée.*

soi•rée |swä'rā| • *n.* an evening party or gathering, typically in a private house, for conversation or music.

so•journ |'sōjərn| • *n.* a temporary stay: *her sojourn in Rome.* • *v.* [no obj., with adverbial of place] stay somewhere temporarily: *she had sojourned once in Egypt.*
DERIVATIVES: **so•journ•er** *n.*

sol•ace |'sälis| • *n.* comfort or consolation in a time of distress or sadness: *she sought solace in her religion.* • *v.* [trans.] give solace to.

so•lar•i•um |sə'lerēəm; sō-| • *n.* (pl. **solariums** or **solaria** |-rēə|) a room fitted with extensive areas of glass to admit sunlight.
■ a room equipped with sunlamps or tanning

beds that can be used to acquire an artificial suntan.

so•lar plex•us |'pleksəs| • n. a complex of ganglia and radiating nerves of the sympathetic system at the pit of the stomach.

■ the area of the body near the base of the sternum: *she felt as if someone had punched her in the solar plexus.*

sol•dier |'sōljər| • v. [intrans.] serve as a soldier: [as n.] (**soldiering**) *soldiering was what the colonel understood.*

■ (**soldier on**) carry on doggedly; persevere: *Gary wasn't enjoying this, but he soldiered on.*

■ work more slowly than one's capacity; loaf or malinger: *is it the reason you've been soldiering on the job?*

sol•e•cism |'sälə,sizəm; 'sō-| • n. a grammatical mistake in speech or writing.

■ a breach of good manners; a piece of incorrect behavior.

DERIVATIVES: **sol•e•cis•tic** |,sälə'sistik; ,sō-| adj.

so•lem•ni•ty |sə'lemnitē| • n. (pl. **-ies**) the state or quality of being serious and dignified: *his ashes were laid to rest with great solemnity.*

■ (usu. **solemnities**) a formal, dignified rite or ceremony: *the ritual of the church was observed in all its solemnities.*

sol•em•nize |'säləm,nīz| • v. [trans.] duly perform (a ceremony, esp. that of marriage).

■ mark with a formal ceremony.

DERIVATIVES: **sol•em•ni•za•tion** |,säləmni'zāsHən| n.

so•lic•it |sə'lisit| • v. (**solicited, soliciting**) [trans.] ask for or try to obtain (something) from someone: *he called a meeting to solicit their views.*

■ ask (someone) for something: *historians and critics are solicited for opinions by the auction houses.* ■ [intrans.] accost someone and offer one's or someone else's services as a prostitute: [as n.] (**soliciting**) *although prostitution was not itself an offense, soliciting was.*

DERIVATIVES: **so•lic•i•ta•tion** |sə,lisə'tā-sHən| n.

so•lic•i•tor |sə'lisitər| • n. 1 a person who tries to obtain business orders, advertising, etc.; a canvasser. 2 the chief law officer of a city, town, or government department. The **solicitor general** is the second-ranking official in the US Justice Department, after the attorney general.

■ Brit. a member of the legal profession qualified to deal with conveyancing (drawing up documents for land transfers), the drawing up of wills, and other legal matters. Cf. BAR-RISTER.

so•lic•i•tous |sə'lisitəs| • adj. characterized by or showing interest or concern: *she was always solicitous about the welfare of her students | a solicitous inquiry.*

■ eager or anxious to do something: *he was solicitous to cultivate her mamma's good opinion.*

DERIVATIVES: **so•lic•i•tous•ly** adv. **so•lic•i•tous•ness** n.

sol•id state • n. the state of matter in which materials are not fluid but retain their boundaries without support, the atoms or mole-

cules occupying fixed positions with respect to each other and unable to move freely.

• adj. (**solid-state**) (of a device) making use of the electronic properties of solid semiconductors (as opposed to valves).

sol•i•dus |'sälidəs| • n. (pl. **solidi** |'säli,dī|) 1 another term for slash, an oblique (/) formerly written to separate shillings from pence, and now used in writing fractions, to separate figures and letters, or to denote alternatives or ratios. 2 a gold coin of the later Roman Empire.

so•lil•o•quy |sə'liləkwē| • n. (pl. **-ies**) an act of speaking one's thoughts aloud when by oneself or regardless of any hearers, esp. by a character in a play.

■ a part of a play involving such an act.

DERIVATIVES: **so•lil•o•quist** |-kwist| n. **so•lil•o•quize** |-,kwīz| v.

sol•ip•sism |'sälip,sizəm| • n. the view or theory that the self is all that can be known to exist.

DERIVATIVES: **sol•ip•sist** n. **sol•ip•sis•tic** |,sälip'sistik| adj. **sol•ip•sis•ti•cal•ly** |,sälip 'sistik(ə)lē| adv.

sol•mi•za•tion |,sälmi'zāsHən; ,sōl-| • n. a system of associating each note of a musical scale with a syllable, esp. to teach singing.

so•lon |'sōlən; 'sō,län| a sage; a wise statesman.

■ a legislator, esp. a member of Congress.

DERIVATIVES: **So•lo•ni•an** adj. **So•lon•ic** adj.

sol•stice |'sōlstis| • n. either of the two times in the year, the **summer solstice** (about June 21 in the Northern Hemisphere) and the **winter solstice** (about Dec. 22), when the sun reaches its highest or lowest point in the sky at noon, marked by the longest and shortest days.

DERIVATIVES: **sol•sti•tial** |sōl'stisHəl| adj.

sol•u•ble |'sälyəbəl| • adj. 1 (of a substance) able to be dissolved, esp. in water: *the poison is soluble in alcohol.* 2 (of a problem) able to be solved.

DERIVATIVES: **sol•u•bil•i•ty** |,sälyə'bilitē| n.

sol•ute |'säl,yŏŏt| • n. the minor component in a solution, dissolved in the solvent.

so•lu•tion |sə'lōōsHən| • n. 1 a means of solving a problem or dealing with a difficult situation: *there are no easy solutions to financial and marital problems.*

■ the correct answer to a puzzle: *the solution to this month's crossword.* 2 a liquid mixture in which the minor component (the solute) is uniformly distributed within the major component (the solvent).

■ the process or state of being dissolved in a solvent. 3 the action of separating or breaking down; dissolution: *the solution of British supremacy in South Africa.*

sol•vent |'sälvənt| • adj. 1 having assets in excess of liabilities; able to pay one's debts: *interest rate rises have severe effects on normally solvent companies.* 2 [attrib.] able to dissolve other substances: *osmotic, chemical, or solvent action.* • n. the liquid in which a solute is dissolved to form a solution.

■ a liquid, typically one other than water, used

for dissolving other substances. ■ something that acts to weaken or dispel a particular attitude or situation: *an unrivaled solvent of social prejudices.*
DERIVATIVES: **sol•ven•cy** *n.* (sense 1 of the adjective).
so•ma[1] |ˈsōmə| • *n.* [usu. in sing.] (in biology) the parts of an organism other than the reproductive cells.
■ the body as distinct from the soul, mind, or psyche.
so•ma[2] • *n.* (in Hinduism) an intoxicating drink prepared from a plant and used in Vedic ritual, believed to be the drink of the gods.
■ (also **soma plant**) the plant from which this drink is prepared.
so•mat•ic |səˈmætik; sō-| • *adj.* of or relating to the body, esp. as distinct from the mind.
■ (in biology) of or relating to the soma. ■ (in anatomy) of or relating to the outer wall of the body, as opposed to the viscera.
DERIVATIVES: **so•mat•i•cal•ly** *adv.*
so•mat•o•type |səˈmætəˌtip; ˌsōmə-| • *n.* a category to which people are assigned according to the extent to which their bodily physique conforms to a basic type (usually endomorphic, mesomorphic, or ectomorphic).
DERIVATIVES: **so•mat•o•typ•ing** *n.*
som•ber |ˈsämbər| (Brit. also **sombre**) • *adj.* dark or dull in color or tone; gloomy.
■ oppressively solemn or sober in mood; grave: *he looked at her with a somber expression.*
DERIVATIVES: **som•ber•ly** *adv.* **som•ber•ness** *n.*
som•me•lier |ˌsəməlˈyā| • *n.* a wine waiter.
som•nam•bu•lism |sämˈnæmbyəˌlizəm| • *n.* sleepwalking.
DERIVATIVES: **som•nam•bu•lant** |-lənt| *adj.* **som•nam•bu•lant•ly** |-ləntlē| *adv.* **som•nam•bu•list** *n.* **som•nam•bu•lis•tic** |-ˌnæmbyəˈlistik| *adj.* **som•nam•bu•lis•ti•cal•ly** |-ˌnæmbyəˈlistik(ə)lē| *adv.*
som•nif•er•ous |sämˈnifərəs| • *adj.* tending to induce sleep; soporific.
som•no•lent |ˈsämnələnt| • *adj.* sleepy; drowsy.
■ causing or suggestive of drowsiness: *a somnolent summer day.* ■ abnormally drowsy.
DERIVATIVES: **som•no•lence** *n.* **som•no•len•cy** *n.* **som•no•lent•ly** *adv.*
so•nant |ˈsōnənt| Phonetics • *adj.* (of a sound) voiced and syllabic. • *n.* a voiced sound forming a syllable, a vowel, or any of the consonants *l, m, n* pronounced as a syllable.
so•na•ta |səˈnätə| • *n.* a classical musical composition for an instrumental soloist, often with a piano accompaniment. It is typically in several movements with one (esp. the first) or more in sonata form.
son et lu•mière |ˈsôN ā lōomˈyer| • *n.* an entertainment held by night at a historic monument or building, telling its history by the use of lighting effects and recorded sound.
son•ic |ˈsänik| • *adj.* relating to or using sound waves.
■ denoting or having a speed equal to that of

sound. Lower speeds are **subsonic**, higher speeds **supersonic**. Cf. HYPERSONIC.
DERIVATIVES: **son•i•cal•ly** *adv.*
son•ics |ˈsäniks| • *plural n.* musical sounds artificially produced or reproduced.
so•no•rous |ˈsänərəs| • *adj.* (of a person's voice or other sound) imposingly deep and full.
■ capable of producing a deep or ringing sound: *the alloy is sonorous and useful in making bells.* ■ (of a speech or style) using imposing language: *they had expected the lawyers to deliver sonorous lamentations.* ■ having a pleasing sound: *she used the misleadingly sonorous name "melanoma" to describe it.*
DERIVATIVES: **so•no•rous•ly** *adv.* **so•no•rous•ness** *n.*
sooth•say•er |ˈsōōTHˌsāər| • *n.* a person supposed to be able to foresee the future.
DERIVATIVES: **sooth•say•ing** *n.*
soph•ism |ˈsäfizəm| • *n.* a fallacious argument, esp. one used deliberately to deceive.
soph•ist |ˈsäfist| • *n.* a paid teacher of philosophy and rhetoric in ancient Greece, associated in popular thought with moral skepticism and specious reasoning.
■ a person who reasons with clever but fallacious arguments.
DERIVATIVES: **so•phis•tic** |səˈfistik| *adj.* **so•phis•ti•cal** |səˈfistikəl| *adj.* **so•phis•ti•cal•ly** |səˈfistik(ə)lē| *adv.*
so•phis•ti•cate • *v.* |səˈfistəˌkāt| [trans.] cause (a person or his or her thoughts, attitudes, and expectations) to become less simple or straightforward through education or experience: *readers who have been sophisticated by modern literary practice.*
■ develop (something such as a piece of equipment or a technique) into a more complex form: *a function that many other software applications have sophisticated.* ■ [intrans.] talk or reason in an impressively complex and educated manner. ■ mislead or corrupt (a person, an argument, the mind, etc.) by sophistry: *books of casuistry, which sophisticate the understanding and defile the heart.* • *adj.* |səˈfistə,kāt; -kit| sophisticated. • *n.* |səˈfistə,kāt; -kit| a person with much worldly experience and knowledge of fashion and culture: *he is still the butt of jokes made by New York sophisticates.*
DERIVATIVES: **so•phis•ti•ca•tion** |sə,fisti ˈkāSHən| *n.*
so•phis•ti•cat•ed |səˈfisti,kātid| • *adj.* (of a machine, system, or technique) developed to a high degree of complexity: *highly sophisticated computer systems.*
■ (of a person or his or her thoughts, reactions, and understanding) aware of and able to interpret complex issues; subtle: *discussion and reflection are necessary for a sophisticated response to a text.* ■ having, revealing, or proceeding from a great deal of worldly experience and knowledge of fashion and culture: *a chic, sophisticated woman | a young man with sophisticated tastes.* ■ appealing to people with such knowledge of experience: *a sophisticated restaurant.*
DERIVATIVES: **so•phis•ti•cat•ed•ly** *adv.*

soph•ist•ry |'säfəstrē| • *n.* (pl. **-ies**) the use of fallacious arguments, esp. with the intention of deceiving.

■ a fallacious argument.

soph•o•mor•ic |ˌsäf(ə)'môrik| • *adj.* of, relating to, or characteristic of a sophomore (second-year student in a college or school): *my sophomoric year.*

■ pretentious or juvenile: *sophomoric double entendres.*

DERIVATIVES: **soph•o•mor•i•cal•ly** *adv.*

sop•o•rif•ic |ˌsäpə'rifik| • *adj.* (also **soporif-erous**)tending to induce drowsiness or sleep: *the motion of the train had a soporific effect.*

■ sleepy or drowsy: *the medicine made her soporific.* ■ tediously boring or monotonous: *a libel trial is in large parts intensely soporific.* • *n.* drug or other agent of this kind.

DERIVATIVES: **sop•o•rif•i•cal•ly** *adv.*

so•pra•ni•no |ˌsäprə'nēnō| • *n.* Music (pl. **-os**) an instrument, esp. a recorder or saxophone, higher than soprano.

so•pran•o |sə'pranō| • *n.* (pl. **-os**) the highest of the four standard singing voices: *a piece composed for soprano, flute, and continuo* | [as adj.] *a good soprano voice.*

■ a female or boy singer with such a voice. ■ a part written for such a voice. ■ [usu. as adj.] an instrument of a high or the highest pitch in its family: *a soprano saxophone.* Cf. SOPRANINO.

sor•did |'sôrdid| • *adj.* involving ignoble actions and motives; arousing moral distaste and contempt: *the story paints a sordid picture of bribes and scams.*

■ dirty or squalid: *housing conditions were sordid.*

DERIVATIVES: **sor•did•ly** *adv.* **sor•did•ness** *n.*

so•ro•ral |sə'rôrəl| • *adj.* of or like a sister or sisters.

sort•ie |ˌsôr'tē; 'sôrtē| • *n.* an attack made by troops coming out from a position of defense.

■ an operational flight by a single military aircraft. ■ a short trip or journey: *I went on a shopping sortie.* • *v.* (**sorties, sortied, sortieing**) [intrans.] come out from a defensive position to make an attack.

sor•ti•lege |'sôrdl-ij| • *n.* the practice of foretelling the future from a card or other item drawn at random from a collection.

■ a person who practices sortilege.

sos•te•nu•to |ˌsästə'noōotō| Music • *adj.* (of a passage of music) to be played in a sustained or prolonged manner. • *n.* (pl. **-os**) a passage to be played in a sustained and prolonged manner.

■ performance in this manner.

so•te•ri•ol•o•gy |səˌtirē'äləjē| • *n.* the theological doctrine of salvation.

DERIVATIVES: **so•te•ri•o•log•i•cal** |-rēə 'läjikəl| *adj.*

sot•to vo•ce |ˌsätō 'vōchē| • *adv.* & *adj.* (of singing or a spoken remark) in a quiet voice, as if not to be overheard: [as adv.] *"It won't be cheap," he added sotto voce* | [as adj.] *a sotto voce remark.*

sou•brette |soō'bret| • *n.* a minor female role in a comedy, typically that of a pert maidservant.

sough |səf; sow| • *v.* [intrans.] (of the wind in trees, the sea, etc.) make a moaning, whistling, or rushing sound. • *n.* [in sing.] a sound of this type.

sound bite • *n.* a short extract from a recorded interview, chosen for its pungency or appropriateness.

soup•çon |soōp'sôN| • *n.* [in sing.] a very small quantity of something: *a soupçon of mustard.*

sov•er•eign |'säv(ə)rən| • *n.* **1** a supreme ruler, esp. a monarch. **2** a former British gold coin worth one pound sterling, now only minted for commemorative purposes. • *adj.* possessing supreme or ultimate power: *in modern democracies the people's will is in theory sovereign.*

■ [attrib.] (of a nation or state) fully independent and determining its own affairs: *a sovereign, democratic republic.* ■ [attrib.] (of affairs) subject to a specified state's control without outside interference: *criticism was seen as interference in China's sovereign affairs.* ■ [attrib.] possessing royal power and status: *our most sovereign lord the King.* ■ [attrib.] very good or effective: *a sovereign remedy for all ills.*

■ pertaining to the sovereign or state **Sovereign immunity** a government from lawsuits unless it chooses to waive immunity.

DERIVATIVES: **sov•er•eign•ly** *adv.*

sov•er•eign•ty |'säv(ə)rəntē| • *n.* (pl. **-ies**) supreme power or authority.

■ the authority of a state to govern itself or another state: *national sovereignty.* ■ a self-governing state.

so•vi•et |'sōvēit; -ˌet| • *n.* **1** an elected local, district, or national council in the former Soviet Union.

■ a revolutionary council of workers or peasants in Russia before 1917. **2** (**Soviet**) a citizen of the former Soviet Union. • *adj.* (**Soviet**) of or concerning the former Soviet Union: *the Soviet leader.*

DERIVATIVES: **So•vi•et•i•za•tion** |ˌsōvēiti 'zāsHən| *n.* **So•vi•et•ize** |-ˌtīz| *v.*

sparge |spärj| • *v.* [trans.] moisten by sprinkling, esp. with water in brewing. • *n.* the action of sprinkling or splashing.

■ a spray of hot water, esp. water sprinkled over malt when brewing.

DERIVATIVES: **sparg•er** *n.*

spar•ing |'speriNG| • *adj.* moderate; economical: *physicians advised sparing use of the ointment.*

DERIVATIVES: **spar•ing•ly** *adv.* **spar•ing•ness** *n.*

Spar•tan |'spärtn| • *adj.* of or relating to Sparta in ancient Greece.

■ (also **spartan**) showing the indifference to comfort or luxury traditionally associated with ancient Sparta: *Spartan but adequate rooms.* ■ a citizen of Sparta.

spas•mod•ic |spaz'mädik| • *adj.* occurring or done in brief, irregular bursts: *spasmodic fighting continued.*

■ caused by, subject to, or in the nature of a spasm or spasms: *a spasmodic cough.*
DERIVATIVES: **spas•mod•i•cal•ly** *adv.*

spas•tic |ˈspæstik| • *adj.* relating to or affected by muscle spasm.

■ relating to or denoting a form of muscular weakness (**spastic paralysis**) typical of cerebral palsy, caused by damage to the brain or spinal cord and involving reflex resistance to passive movement of the limbs and difficulty in initiating and controlling muscular movement. ■ (of a person) suffering from cerebral palsy. ■incompetent or uncoordinated. • *n.* a person suffering from cerebral palsy.
■ an incompetent or uncoordinated person.
DERIVATIVES: **spas•ti•cal•ly** *adv.* **spas•tic•i•ty** |spæˈstisiṯē| *n.*

USAGE: **Spastic,** usually used as an adjective, has been used in medical senses since the 18th century and is still a neutral term for conditions like *spastic colon* or *spastic paraplegia.* In the latter part of the 20th cent., **spastic,** usually used as a noun, became a term of abuse and was directed toward anyone regarded as incompetent or physically uncoordinated. Nowadays, this latter use of **spastic,** whether as a noun or as an adjective, is likely to cause offense, and even in medical use it is preferable to use phrasing such as *person with **cerebral palsy*** instead of the noun *spastic.*

spate |spāt| • *n.* **1** [usu. in sing.] a large number of similar things or events appearing or occurring in quick succession: *a spate of attacks on travelers.* **2** a sudden flood in a river, esp. one caused by heavy rains or melting snow.
PHRASES: **in (full) spate** (of a river) overflowing due to a sudden flood. ■ (of a person or action) at the height of activity: *work was in full spate.*

spav•in |ˈspævin| • *n.* a disorder of a horse's hock.
DERIVATIVES: **spav•ined** *adj.*

spawn |spôn| • *v.* [intrans.] (of a fish, frog, mollusk, crustacean, etc.) release or deposit eggs: *the fish spawn among fine-leaved plants* | [trans.] *a large brood is spawned.*
■ (**be spawned**) (of a fish, frog, etc.) be laid as eggs. ■ [trans.] (of a person) produce (offspring, typically offspring regarded as undesirable): *why had she married a man who could spawn a boy like that?* ■ [trans.] produce or generate, esp. in large numbers: *the decade spawned a variety of books on the subject.* • *n.* the eggs of fish, frogs, etc.: *the fish covers its spawn with gravel.*
■ the process of producing such eggs. ■ the product or offspring of a person or place (used to express distaste or disgust): *the spawn of chaos: demons and sorcerers.* ■ the mycelium (vegetative part) of a fungus, esp. a cultivated mushroom.
DERIVATIVES: **spawn•er** *n.*

spe•cie |ˈspēsHē,-sē| • *n.* money in the form of coins rather than bills.

PHRASES: **in specie 1** in coin. **2** (in law) in the real, precise, or actual form specified: *the plaintiff could not be sure of recovering his goods in specie.*

spe•cies |ˈspēsēz; -sHēz| • *n.* (pl. same) **1** (abbr.: **sp., spp.**) (in biology) a group of living organisms consisting of similar individuals capable of exchanging genes or interbreeding. The species is the principal natural taxonomic unit, ranking below a genus and denoted by a Latin binomial, e.g., *Homo sapiens.*
■ (in logic) a group subordinate to a genus and containing individuals agreeing in some common attributes and called by a common name. ■ a kind or sort: *a species of invective at once tough and suave.* ■ used humorously to refer to people who share a characteristic or occupation: *a political species that is becoming more common, the environmental statesman.*
■ (in chemistry and physics) a particular kind of atom, molecule, ion, or particle: *a new molecular species.* **2** (in the Christian Church) the visible form of each of the elements of consecrated bread and wine in the Eucharist.

spe•cies•ism |ˈspēsHē,zizəm; spēsē-| • *n.* the assumption of human superiority leading to the exploitation of animals.
DERIVATIVES: **spe•cies•ist** *adj. & n.*

spe•cious |ˈspēsHəs| • *adj.* superficially plausible, but actually wrong: *a specious argument.*
■ misleading in appearance, esp. misleadingly attractive: *the music trade gives Golden Oldies a specious appearance of novelty.*
DERIVATIVES: **spe•cious•ly** *adv.* **spe•cious•ness** *n.*

spec•ter |ˈspektər| (Brit. **spectre**) • *n.* a ghost.
■ something widely feared as a possible unpleasant or dangerous occurrence: ***the specter of** nuclear holocaust.*

spec•tral |ˈspektrəl| • *adj.* **1** of or like a ghost. **2** of or concerning spectra or the spectrum.
DERIVATIVES: **spec•tral•ly** *adv.*

spec•trum |ˈspektrəm| • *n.* (pl. **spectra** |-trə|) **1** a band of colors, as seen in a rainbow, produced by separation of the components of light by their different degrees of refraction according to wavelength.
■ (**the spectrum**) the entire range of wavelengths of electromagnetic radiation. ■ an image or distribution of components of any electromagnetic radiation arranged in a progressive series according to wavelength. ■ a similar image or distribution of components of sound, particles, etc., arranged according to such characteristics as frequency, charge, and energy. **2** used to classify something, or suggest that it can be classified, in terms of its position on a scale between two extreme or opposite points: *the left or the right of the political spectrum.*
■ a wide range: *self-help books are covering a broader and broader spectrum.*

spec•u•lar |ˈspekyələr| • *adj.* of, relating to, or having the properties of a mirror.

spec·u·lum |'spekyələm| • *n.* (pl. **specula** |'spekyələ|) **1** a metal or plastic instrument that is used to dilate an orifice or canal in the body to allow inspection. **2** a bright patch of plumage on the wings of certain birds, esp. a strip of metallic sheen on the secondary flight feathers of many ducks. **3** a mirror or reflector of glass or metal, esp. (formerly) a metallic mirror in a reflecting telescope.

spe·le·ol·o·gy |ˌspēlē'äləjē| • *n.* the study or exploration of caves.
DERIVATIVES: **spe·le·o·log·i·cal** |ˌspēlēə'läjikəl| *adj.* **spe·le·ol·o·gist** |-jist| *n.*

spe·lunk·ing |spi'ləNGkiNG| • *n.* the exploration of caves, esp. as a hobby.
DERIVATIVES: **spe·lunk·er** |-kər| *n.*

spend·thrift |'spen(d)ˌTHrift| • *n.* a person who spends money in an extravagant, irresponsible way.

sper·ma·cet·i |ˌspərmə'setē| • *n.* a white waxy substance produced by the sperm whale, formerly used in candles and ointments. It is present in a rounded organ in the head, where it focuses acoustic signals and aids in the control of buoyancy.

sphinc·ter |'sfiNGktər| • *n.* a ring of muscle surrounding and serving to guard or close an opening or tube, such as the anus or the openings of the stomach.
DERIVATIVES: **sphinc·ter·al** |-rəl| *adj.* **sphinc·ter·ic** |ˌsfiNGk'terik| *adj.*

sphinx |sfiNGks| • *n.* (**Sphinx**) a winged monster of Thebes, having a woman's head and a lion's body. It propounded a riddle about the three ages of man, killing those who failed to solve it, until Oedipus was successful, whereupon the Sphinx committed suicide.
■ an ancient Egyptian stone figure having a lion's body and a human or animal head, esp. the huge statue near the Pyramids at Giza.
■ an enigmatic or inscrutable person.
DERIVATIVES: **sphinx·like** *adj.*

spiel |spēl; SHpēl| • *n.* a long or fast speech or story, typically one intended as a means of persuasion or as an excuse but regarded with skepticism or contempt by those who hear it: *he delivers a breathless and effortless spiel in promotion of his new novel.* • *v.* [trans.] reel off; recite: *he solemnly spieled all he knew.*
■ [intrans.] speak glibly or at length.

spin doc·tor • *n.* a spokesperson employed to give a favorable interpretation of events (*spin* them) to the media, esp. on behalf of a political party.

spin·drift |'spinˌdrift| • *n.* spray blown from the crests of waves by the wind.
■ driving snow or sand.

spin·et |'spinit| • *n.* **1** a small harpsichord with the strings set obliquely to the keyboard, popular in the 18th century. **2** a type of small upright piano.

spin·ster |'spinstər| • *n.* an unmarried woman, typically an older woman beyond the usual age for marriage.
DERIVATIVES: **spin·ster·hood** |-ˌho͝od| *n.* **spin·ster·ish** *adj.*

USAGE: The development of the word **spinster** is a good example of the way in which a word acquires strong connotations to the extent that it can no longer be used in a neutral sense. From the 17th century the word was appended to names as the official legal description of an unmarried woman: *Elizabeth Harris of London, Spinster*; this type of use survives today in some legal and religious contexts. In modern everyday English, however, **spinster** cannot be used to mean simply 'unmarried woman'; it is now a derogatory term, referring or alluding to a stereotype of an older woman who is unmarried, childless, prissy, and repressed.

spir·it·u·al |'spiriCHəwəl| • *adj.* **1** of, relating to, or affecting the human spirit or soul as opposed to material or physical things: *I'm responsible for his spiritual welfare* | *the spiritual values of life.*
■ (of a person) not concerned with material values or pursuits. **2** of or relating to religion or religious belief: *Iran's spiritual leader.* • *n.* (also **Negro spiritual**) a religious song of a kind associated with black Christians of the southern US, and thought to derive from the combination of European hymns and African musical elements by black slaves. Cf. GOSPEL.
PHRASES: **one's spiritual home** a place in which one feels a profound sense of belonging: *I had always thought of Italy as my spiritual home.*
DERIVATIVES: **spir·it·u·al·i·ty** |ˌspiriCHə'wælətē| *n.* **spir·it·u·al·ly** *adv.*

spir·it·u·al·ism |'spiriCHəwəˌlizəm| • *n.* **1** a system of belief or religious practice based on supposed communication with the spirits of the dead, esp. through mediums. **2** (in philosophy) the doctrine that the spirit exists as distinct from matter, or that spirit is the only reality.
DERIVATIVES: **spir·it·u·al·ist** *n.* **spir·it·u·al·is·tic** |ˌspiriCHəwə'listik| *adj.*

splay |splā| • *v.* [trans.] thrust or spread (things, esp. limbs or fingers) out and apart: *her hands were splayed across his broad shoulders* | *he stood with his legs and arms splayed out.*
■ [intrans.] (esp. of limbs or fingers) be thrust or spread out and apart: *his legs splayed out in front of him.* ■ [intrans.] (of a thing) diverge in shape or position; become wider or more separated: *the river splayed out, becoming an estuary.* ■ [usu. as adj.] (**splayed**) construct (a window, doorway, or aperture) so that it diverges or is wider at one side of the wall than the other: *the walls are pierced by splayed window openings.* • *n.* **1** a widening or outward tapering of something, in particular:
■ a tapered widening of a road at an intersection to increase visibility. ■ a splayed window aperture or other opening. **2** a surface making an oblique angle with another, such as the splayed side of a window or embrasure.
■ the degree of bevel or slant of a surface.
• *adj.* [usu. in combination] turned outward or widened: *the girls were sitting splay-legged.*

spleen |splēn| • *n.* **1** an abdominal organ involved in the production and removal of blood cells in most vertebrates and forming part of the immune system. **2** bad temper; spite: *he could* ***vent his spleen*** *on the institutions that had duped him.*
DERIVATIVES: **spleen•ful** |-fəl| *adj.* (in sense 2).
splen•dent |'splendənt| • *adj.* shining brightly.
■ illustrious; great.
sple•net•ic |splə'neṯik| • *adj.* bad-tempered; spiteful: *a splenetic outburst.*
DERIVATIVES: **sple•net•i•cal•ly** *adv.*
spline |splīn| • *n.* **1** a rectangular key fitting into grooves in the hub and shaft of a wheel, esp. one formed integrally with the shaft that allows movement of the wheel on the shaft.
■ a corresponding groove in a hub along which the key may slide. **2** a slat.
■ a flexible wood or rubber strip used esp. in drawing large curves. **3** (also **spline curve**) (in mathematics) a continuous curve constructed so as to pass through a given set of points and have a certain number of continuous derivatives. • *v.* [trans.] secure (a part) by means of a spline.
■ [usu. as adj.] (**splined**) fit with a spline: *splined freewheels.*
split in•fin•i•tive • *n.* a construction consisting of an infinitive with an adverb or other word inserted between *to* and the verb, e.g., *she seems to really like it.*

USAGE: *You have* **to** *really* **watch** *him;* **to** *boldly* **go** *where no one has gone before.* It is still widely held that splitting infinitives—separating the infinitive marker **to** from the verb, as in the examples above—is wrong. Writers who insisted that English could be modeled on Latin long ago created the "rule" that the English infinitive must not be split: *to clearly state* was wrong; one must say *to state clearly.* But the Latin infinitive is one word, e.g., *amare,* 'to love,' and cannot be split, so the "rule" is not firmly grounded, and treating two English words as one can lead to awkward, stilted sentences. In particular, the placing of an adverb in English is extremely important in giving the appropriate emphasis: *you really have* **to watch** *him* and **to go** *boldly where no one has gone before,* examples where the infinitive is not split, convey a different emphasis or sound awkward. Some traditionalists may continue to hold up the split infinitive as an error, but in standard English the principle of allowing split infinitives is broadly accepted as both normal and useful.

spoil•er |'spoilər| • *n.* **1** a person or thing that spoils.
■ (esp. in political and sporting context) someone who, while having no chance of winning a contest, obstructs or prevents an opponent's success. ■ an electronic device for preventing unauthorized copying of sound recordings by means of a disruptive signal inaudible on the original. **2** a flap on an air-

craft or glider that can be projected from the surface of a wing in order to create drag and so reduce speed.
■ a similar device on a motor vehicle intended to prevent it from being lifted off the road when traveling at very high speeds.
spo•li•a•tion |ˌspōlē'asHən| • *n.* **1** the action of ruining or destroying something: *spoliation of the countryside.* **2** the action of taking goods or property from somewhere by illegal or unethical means: *the spoliation of country churches.*
DERIVATIVES: **spo•li•a•tor** |'spōlē,āṯər| *n.*
spon•dee |'spändē| • *n.* a prosodic foot consisting of two long (or stressed) syllables.
DERIVATIVES: **spon•da•ic** *adj.*
spoon•er•ism |'spoonə,rizəm| • *n.* a verbal error in which a speaker accidentally transposes the initial sounds or letters of two or more words, often to humorous effect, as in the sentence *you have hissed the mystery lecture,* accidentally spoken instead of the intended sentence *you have missed the history lecture.*
spoor |spoor; spô(ə)r| • *n.* the track or scent of an animal: *they searched around the hut for a spoor | the trail is marked by wolf spoor.* • *v.* [trans.] follow the track or scent of (an animal or person): *taking the spear, he set off to spoor the man.*
DERIVATIVES: **spoor•er** *n.*
spo•rad•ic |spə'rædik| • *adj.* occurring at irregular intervals or only in a few places; scattered or isolated: *sporadic fighting broke out.*
DERIVATIVES: **spo•rad•i•cal•ly** |-ik(ə)lē| *adv.*
spore |spôr| • *n.* a minute, typically one-celled, reproductive unit capable of giving rise to a new individual without sexual fusion, characteristic of lower plants, fungi, and protozoans.
spous•al |'spowzəl| • *adj.* [attrib.] (in law) of or relating to marriage or to a husband or wife: *the spousal benefits of married couples.*
sprain |sprān| • *v.* [trans.] wrench or twist the ligaments of (an ankle, wrist, or other joint) violently so as to cause pain and swelling but not dislocation: *he left in a wheelchair after spraining an ankle.* • *n.* the result of such a wrench or twist of a joint.
spread-ea•gle • *v.* [trans.] (usu. **be spread-eagled**) stretch (someone) out with their arms and legs extended: *he lay spread-eagled in the road.* • *n.* (**spread eagle**) an emblematic representation of an eagle with its legs and wings extended. • *adj.* **1** stretched out with one's arms and legs extended: *prisoners are chained to their beds, spread-eagle, for days at a time.* **2** loudly or aggressively patriotic about the United States: *spread-eagle oratory.*
Sprech•ge•sang |'sHprekgə,zäNG| (also **sprechgesang**) • *n.* a style of dramatic vocalization intermediate between speech and song.
springe |sprinj| • *n.* a noose or snare for catching small game.
sprite |sprīt| • *n.* **1** an elf or fairy.
■ a small, dainty person, esp. a child. **2** a com-

puter graphic that may be moved on-screen and otherwise manipulated as a single entity. **3** a faint flash, typically red, sometimes emitted in the upper atmosphere over a thunderstorm owing to the collision of high-energy electrons with air molecules.

spritz |ˈsprits| • v. [trans.] squirt or spray something at or onto (something) in quick short bursts: *she spritzed her neck with cologne.* • n. an act or an instance of squirting or spraying in quick short bursts.

spry |sprī| • adj. (**spryer**, **spryest** or **sprier**, **spriest**) (esp. of an old person) active; lively: *he continued to look spry and active well into his eighties.*
DERIVATIVES: **spry•ly** adv. **spry•ness** n.

spume |spyo͞om| • n. froth or foam, esp. that found on waves. • v. [intrans.] form or produce a mass of froth or foam: *water was spuming under the mill.*
DERIVATIVES: **spu•mous** |-məs| adj. **spum•y** adj.

spu•ri•ous |ˈspyo͝orēəs| • adj. not being what it purports to be; false or fake: *separating authentic and spurious claims.* Cf. SPECIOUS.
■ (of a line of reasoning) apparently but not actually valid: *this spurious reasoning results in nonsense.* ■ (of offspring) illegitimate.
DERIVATIVES: **spu•ri•ous•ly** adv. **spu•ri•ous•ness** n.

spurn |spərn| • v. [trans.] reject with disdain or contempt: *he spoke gruffly, as if afraid that his invitation would be spurned.*
■ strike, tread, or push away with the foot: *with one touch of my feet, I spurn the solid Earth.* • n. an act of spurning.
DERIVATIVES: **spurn•er** n.

squal•id |ˈskwälid| • adj. (of a place) extremely dirty and unpleasant, esp. as a result of poverty or neglect: *the squalid, overcrowded tenements.*
■ showing or involving a contemptible lack of moral standards: *a squalid attempt to save themselves from electoral embarrassment.*
DERIVATIVES: **squal•id•ly** adv. **squal•id•ness** n. **squal•or** n.

squa•mous |ˈskwāməs| (also **squamose**) • adj. covered with or characterized by scales: *a squamous black hide.*
■ relating to, consisting of, or denoting a layer of epithelium that consists of very thin flattened cells: *squamous cell carcinoma.* ■ [attrib.] denoting the flat portion of the temporal bone that forms part of the side of the skull.

squan•der |ˈskwändər| • v. [trans.] waste (something, esp. money or time) in a reckless and foolish manner: *entrepreneurs squander their profits on expensive cars.*
■ allow (an opportunity) to pass or be lost: *the team squandered several good scoring chances.*
DERIVATIVES: **squand•er•er** n.

square one • n. the point or place from which one starts (e.g., in pursuit of a goal).

squelch |skwelCH| • v. [intrans.] make a soft sucking sound such as that made by walking heavily through mud: *bedraggled guests squelched across the lawn to seek shelter.*
■ forcefully silence or suppress: *property devel-*

opers tried to squelch public protest. • n. a soft sucking sound made when pressure is applied to liquid or mud: *the squelch of their feet.*
DERIVATIVES: **squelch•er** n. **squelch•y** adj.

squib |skwib| • n. **1** a small firework that burns with a hissing sound before exploding.
■ a short piece of satirical writing. ■ a short news item or filler in a newspaper. **2** a small, slight, or weak person, esp. a child. **3** (in football) a short kick on a kickoff.
■ (in baseball) (also **squibber**) a blooper or infield grounder that becomes a base hit. • v. (**squibbed**, **squibbing**) **1** [trans.] (in football) kick (the ball) a comparatively short distance on a kickoff; execute (a kick) in this way.
■ (in baseball) hit (the ball) with little force, usually with the end of the bat, the typical result being a blooper or infield grounder. **2** [intrans.] utter, write, or publish a satirical or sarcastic attack.
■ [trans.] lampoon; satirize: *the mendicant parson, whom I am so fond of squibbing.*

squire |ˈskwīr| • n. **1** a man of high social standing who owns and lives on an estate in a rural area, esp. the chief landowner in such an area: *the squire of Radbourne Hall* | [as title] *Squire Hughes.*
■ Brit. used by a man as a friendly or humorous form of address to another man. ■ a title given to a magistrate, lawyer, or judge in some rural districts. **2** a young nobleman acting as an attendant to a knight before becoming a knight himself. • v. [trans.] (of a man) accompany or escort (a woman): *she was squired around Rome by a reporter.*
■ (of a man) have a romantic relationship with (a woman).
DERIVATIVES: **squire•dom** |-dəm| n. **squire•ship** |-ˌSHip| n.

sta•bile |ˈstāˌbēl| • n. a freestanding abstract sculpture or structure, typically of wire or sheet metal, in the style of a mobile but rigid and stationary.

stac•ca•to |stəˈkäto| • adv. & adj. (in music) with each sound or note sharply detached or separated from the others: [as adj.] *a staccato rhythm.* Cf. LEGATO. • n. (pl. **-os**) performance in this manner.
■ a noise or speech resembling a series of short, detached musical notes: *her heels made a rapid staccato on the polished boards.*

stag•fla•tion |ˌstagˈflāSHən| • n. persistent high inflation combined with high unemployment and stagnant demand in a country's economy.

stag•nant |ˈstagnənt| • adj. (of a body of water or the atmosphere of a confined space) having no current or flow and often having an unpleasant smell as a consequence: *a stagnant ditch.*
■ showing no activity; dull and sluggish: *a stagnant economy.*
DERIVATIVES: **stag•nan•cy** |-nənsē| n. **stag•nant•ly** adv.

staid |stād| • adj. sedate, respectable, and unadventurous: *staid law firms.*
DERIVATIVES: **staid•ly** adv. **staid•ness** n.

sta•lac•tite |stə'læk͵tīt| • *n.* a tapering structure hanging like an icicle from the roof of a cave, formed of calcium salts deposited by dripping water. Cf. STALAGMITE.
DERIVATIVES: **sta•lac•tit•ic** |͵stælək'titik| *adj.*

Sta•lag |'stä͵läg| • *n.* (in World War II) a German prison camp, esp. for noncommissioned officers and privates.

sta•lag•mite |stə'læg͵mīt| • *n.* a mound or tapering column rising from the floor of a cave, formed of calcium salts deposited by dripping water and often uniting with a stalactite.
DERIVATIVES: **stal•ag•mit•ic** |͵stæləg'mitik| *adj.*

stale•mate |'stāl͵māt| • *n.* (in chess) a position counting as a draw, in which a player is not in check but cannot move except into check.
■ a situation in which further action or progress by opposing or competing parties seems impossible: *the war had again reached stalemate.* • *v.* [trans.] bring to or cause to reach stalemate: [as adj.] (**stalemated**) *the currently stalemated peace talks.*

Sta•lin•ism |'stälə͵nizəm| • *n.* the ideology and policies adopted by Soviet leader Joseph Stalin (General Secretary of the Communist Party of the USSR 1922–53), based on centralization, totalitarianism, and the pursuit of communism.
■ any rigid centralized authoritarian form of communism.
DERIVATIVES: **Sta•lin•ist** *n.* & *adj.*

stal•wart |'stôlwərt| • *adj.* loyal, reliable, and hardworking: *he remained a stalwart supporter of the cause.*
■ strongly built and sturdy: *he was of stalwart build.* • *n.* a loyal, reliable, and hardworking supporter or participant in an organization or team: *the stalwarts of the Ladies' Auxiliary.*
DERIVATIVES: **stal•wart•ly** *adv.* **stal•wart• ness** *n.*

sta•men |'stāmin| • *n.* the male fertilizing organ of a flower, typically consisting of a pollen-containing anther and a filament.

stam•i•na |'stæmənə| • *n.* the ability to sustain prolonged physical or mental effort: *their secret is stamina rather than speed.*

stam•mer |'stæmər| • *v.* [intrans.] speak with sudden involuntary pauses and a tendency to repeat the initial letters of words. Cf. STUTTER.
■ [trans.] utter (words) in such a way: *I stammered out my history* | [with direct speech] *"I . . . I can't," Isabel stammered.* • *n.* [in sing.] a tendency to stammer: *as a young man, he had a dreadful stammer.*
DERIVATIVES: **stam•mer•er** *n.* **stam•mer• ing•ly** *adv.*

stanch |stônCH; stänCH| (also **staunch**) • *v.* [trans.] stop or restrict (as, a flow of blood) from a wound: *colleagues may have saved her life by stanching the flow* | *the company did nothing to stanch the tide of rumors.*
■ stop the flow of blood from (a wound).

stan•chion |'stænCHən| • *n.* an upright bar, post, or frame forming a support or barrier.
DERIVATIVES: **stan•chioned** *adj.*

stan•za |'stænzə| • *n.* a group of lines forming the basic recurring metrical unit in a poem; a verse.
■ a group of four lines in some Greek and Latin meters.
DERIVATIVES: **stan•zaed** (also **stan•za'd**) *adj.* **stan•za•ic** |stæn'zā-ik| *adj.*

starch•y |'stärCHē| • *adj.* (**starchier, starchiest**) (of a person or personal behavior) very stiff, formal, or prim in manner or character: *the manager is usually a bit starchy.*
DERIVATIVES: **starch•i•ly** |-CHəlē| *adv.* **starch•i•ness** *n.*

star•dust |'stär͵dəst| • *n.* (esp. in the context of success in the world of entertainment or sports) a magical or charismatic quality or feeling: *a gang of Hollywood stars anointing us with sparkling stardust.*
■ a romantic, sentimentalized quality.

starve•ling |'stärvliNG| • *n.* an undernourished or emaciated person or animal. • *adj.* (of a person or animal) lacking enough food; emaciated: *a starveling child.*

sta•sis |'stāsis| • *n.* a period or state of inactivity or equilibrium.
■ a stoppage of flow of a body fluid.

state•craft |'stāt͵kræft| • *n.* the skillful management of state affairs; statesmanship.

stat•ic |'stætik| • *adj.* **1** lacking in movement, action, or change, esp. in a way viewed as undesirable or uninteresting: *demand has grown in what was a fairly static market* | *the whole ballet appeared too static.*
■ (of a process or variable in computing) not able to be changed during a set period, for example while a program is running. **2** (in physics) concerned with bodies at rest or forces in equilibrium. Cf. DYNAMIC.
■ (of an electric charge) having gathered on or in an object that cannot conduct a current.
■ acting as weight but not moving. ■ of statics. **3** (of a memory or store in computing) not needing to be periodically refreshed by an applied voltage. • *n.* crackling or hissing noises on a telephone, radio, or other telecommunications system.
■ short for STATIC ELECTRICITY. ■ angry or critical talk or behavior: *the reception was going sour, breaking up into static.*
DERIVATIVES: **stat•i•cal•ly** |-ik(ə)lē| *adv.* **stat•ick•y** |-ikē| *adj.*

stat•ic e•lec•tric•i•ty • *n.* a stationary electric charge, typically produced by friction, that causes sparks or crackling or the attraction of dust or hair.

stat•ics |'stætiks| • *plural n.* [usu. treated as sing.] the branch of mechanics concerned with bodies at rest and forces in equilibrium. Cf. DYNAMICS.

sta•tion•ar•y |'stāSHə͵nerē| • *adj.* not moving or not intended to be moved: *a car collided with a stationary vehicle* | *a stationary cold front.*
■ (of a planet) having no apparent motion in longitude. ■ not changing in quantity or condition: *a stationary population.*

USAGE: Be careful to distinguish **stationary** ('not moving, fixed') from **stationery** ('writing paper and other supplies').

stat•ism |'stāt‚izəm| • *n.* any political system in which the state has substantial centralized control over social and economic affairs: *the rise of authoritarian statism.*
DERIVATIVES: **stat•ist** *n.* & *adj.*

sta•tive |'stātiv| • *adj.* (of a verb) expressing a state or condition rather than an activity or event, such as *be* or *know*, as opposed to *run* or *grow.* Cf. DYNAMIC. • *n.* a stative verb.

stat•ute |'stæCHo͝ot| • *n.* a written law passed by a legislative body: *violation of the hate crimes statute* | *the tax is not specifically disallowed by statute.*
■ a rule of an organization or institution: *the appointment will be subject to the statutes of the university.* ■ (in biblical use) a law or decree made by a sovereign, or by God.

stat•u•to•ry |'stæCHə‚tôrē| • *adj.* required, permitted, or enacted by statute: *the courts did award statutory damages to each of the plaintiffs.*
■ (of a criminal offense) carrying a penalty prescribed by statute: *statutory theft.* **Statutory rape** is sexual intercourse with a person (esp. a girl) under a defined age of consent. ■ of or relating to statutes: *constitutional and statutory interpretation.*
DERIVATIVES: **stat•u•to•ri•ly** |-‚tôrəlē| *adv.*

staunch |stônCH; stänCH| • *adj.* **1** loyal and committed in attitude: *a staunch supporter of the antinuclear lobby* | *a staunch Catholic.* **2** (of a wall) of strong or firm construction.
■ (also **stanch**) (of a ship) watertight.
DERIVATIVES: **staunch•ly** *adv.* **staunch•ness** *n.*

stead•y state • *n.* an unvarying condition in a physical process, esp. as in the theory that the universe is eternal and maintained by constant creation of matter.
DERIVATIVES: **steady-state** *adj.*

stealth |stelTH| • *adj.* (chiefly of aircraft) designed in accordance with technology that makes detection by radar or sonar difficult: *a stealth bomber.*

steer•age |'stirij| • *n.* **1** the part of a ship providing accommodations for passengers with the cheapest tickets: *poor emigrants in steerage.* **2** the action of steering a boat.

steer•age-way • *n.* (of a vessel) the minimum speed required for proper response to the helm.

ste•la |'stēlə| • *n.* (also **stele**) (pl. **stelae** |-‚lē|) an upright stone slab or column typically bearing a commemorative inscription or relief design, often serving as a gravestone.

stem•ma |'stemə| • *n.* (pl. **stemmata**) a recorded genealogy of a family; a family tree.
■ a diagram showing the relationship between a text and its various manuscript versions.

stem•ma•tics |stem'ætiks| • *plural n.* [treated as sing.] the branch of study concerned with analyzing the relationship of surviving variant versions of a text to each other, esp. so as to reconstruct a lost original.

stem-wind•er |‚wīndər| (also **stemwinder**) • *n.* **1** an entertaining and rousing speech: *the speech was a classic stem-winder in the best southern tradition.* **2** a watch wound by turning a knob on the end of a stem.

ste•no•sis |stə'nōsis| • *n.* (pl. **stenoses** |-‚sēz|) (in medicine) the abnormal narrowing of a passage in the body.
DERIVATIVES: **ste•nosed** |stə'nōst; -nōzd| *adj.* **ste•no•sing** |-'nōsiNG; -'nōz-| *adj.* **ste•not•ic** |stə'nätik| *adj.*

stent |stent| • *n.* a tubular support placed temporarily inside a blood vessel, canal, or duct to aid healing or relieve an obstruction.
■ an impression or cast of a part or body cavity, used to maintain pressure so as to promote healing, esp. of a skin graft.

sten•tor |'sten‚tôr; 'stentər| • *n.* a person with a powerful voice.

sten•to•ri•an |sten'tôrēən| • *adj.* (of a person's voice) loud and powerful: *he introduced me to the staff with a stentorian announcement.*

ster•e•og•ra•phy |‚sterē'ägrəfē; ‚stir-| • *n.* the depiction or representation of three-dimensional things by projection onto a two-dimensional surface, e.g., in cartography.
DERIVATIVES: **ster•e•o•graph** |'sterēə‚græf; 'stir-| *n.* **ster•e•o•graph•ic** |‚sterēə'græfik; ‚stir-| *adj.*

ster•e•op•ti•con |‚sterē'äpti‚kän; ‚stir-| • *n.* a slide projector that combines two images to create a three-dimensional effect, or makes one image dissolve into another.

ster•e•o•scope |'sterēə‚skōp; 'stir-| • *n.* a device by which two photographs of the same object taken at slightly different angles are viewed together, creating an impression of depth and solidity.
DERIVATIVES: **ster•e•o•scop•ic** |‚sterēə'skäpik; ‚stir-| *adj.* **ster•e•o•scop•i•cal•ly** |‚sterēə'skäpik(ə)lē; ‚stir-| *adv.* **ster•e•os•co•py** |‚sterē'äskəpē| *n.*

ster•e•o•type |'sterēə‚tīp; 'stir-| • *n.* **1** a widely held but fixed and oversimplified image or idea of a particular type of person or thing: *the stereotype of the woman as the caregiver* | *sexual and racial stereotypes.*
■ a person or thing that conforms to such an image: *don't treat anyone as a stereotype.* **2** a relief printing plate cast in a mold made from composed type or an original plate. • *v.* [trans.] view or represent as a stereotype: *the city is too easily stereotyped as an industrial wasteland* | [as adj.] (**stereotyped**) *the film is weakened by its stereotyped characters.*
DERIVATIVES: **ster•e•o•typ•ic** |‚sterēə'tipik| *adj.* **ster•e•o•typ•i•cal** |‚sterēə'tipikəl| *adj.* **ster•e•o•typ•i•cal•ly** |‚sterēə'tipik(ə)lē| *adv.*

ster•ile |'sterəl| • *adj.* **1** not able to produce or procreate children or young: *the disease had made him sterile.*
■ (of a plant) not able to produce fruit or seeds. ■ (of land or soil) too poor in quality to produce crops. ■ lacking in imagination, creativity, or excitement; uninspiring or unproductive: *he found the fraternity's teachings sterile.* **2** free from bacteria or other living

microorganisms; totally clean: *a sterile needle and syringes.*

DERIVATIVES: **ster•ile•ly** | ˈsterə(l)lē | *adv.* **ste•ril•i•ty** | stəˈrilitē | *n.*

ster•ling | ˈstərliNG | • *n.* British money: *prices in sterling are shown* | [as adj.] *issues of sterling bonds.*

■ short for sterling silver (silver of 92.25% purity): [as adj.] *a sterling spoon.* • *adj.* (of a person or work, efforts, or qualities) excellent or valuable: *this organization does sterling work for youngsters.*

ster•nu•ta•tion | ˌstərnyəˈtāSHən | • *n.* the action of sneezing.

ster•to•rous | ˈstərtərəs | • *adj.* (of breathing) noisy and labored.

DERIVATIVES: **ster•to•rous•ly** *adv.*

stet | stet | • *v.* (**stetted, stetting**) [no obj., in imperative] let it stand (used as an instruction on a printed proof to indicate that a correction or alteration should be ignored).

■ [trans.] write such an instruction against (something corrected or deleted). • *n.* such an instruction made on a printed proof.

ste•ve•dore | ˈstēvəˌdôr | • *n.* a person employed, or a contractor engaged, at a dock to load and unload cargo from ships.

sthen•ic | ˈsTHenik | • *adj.* of or having a high or excessive level of strength and energy.

stig•ma | ˈstigmə | • *n.* (pl. **stigmas** or esp. in sense 2 **stigmata** | stigˈmätə; ˈstigmətə |) **1** a mark of disgrace associated with a particular circumstance, quality, or person: *the stigma of mental disorder | to be a nonreader carries a social stigma.* **2** (**stigmata**) (in Christian tradition) marks corresponding to those left on Jesus' body by the Crucifixion, said to have been impressed by divine favor on the bodies of St. Francis of Assisi and others. **3** a visible sign or characteristic of a disease.

■ a mark or spot on the skin. **4** (in a flower) the part of a pistil that receives the pollen during pollination.

stig•ma•tize | ˈstigməˌtīz | • *v.* [trans.] **1** (usu. **be stigmatized**) describe or regard as worthy of disgrace or great disapproval: *the institution was stigmatized as a last resort for the destitute.* **2** mark with stigmata.

DERIVATIVES: **stig•ma•ti•za•tion** | ˌstigmətiˈzāSHən | *n.*

stile | stīl | • *n.* an arrangement of steps that allows people but not animals to climb over a fence or wall.

still•birth | ˈstilˌbərTH | • *n.* the birth of an infant that has died in the womb (strictly, after having survived through at least the first 28 weeks of pregnancy, earlier instances being regarded as abortion or miscarriage).

stilt•ed | ˈstiltid | • *adj.* **1** (of a manner of talking or writing) stiff and self-conscious or unnatural: *we made stilted conversation.* **2** standing on stilts: *villages of stilted houses.*

DERIVATIVES: **stilt•ed•ly** *adv.* **stilt•ed•ness** *n.*

sting | stiNG | • *n.* (in law enforcement) a carefully planned and swiftly executed theft; a swindle; a confidence trick.

■ a police undercover operation to trap a crim-

inal: *five blackmailers were jailed last week after they were snared in a police sting.* • *v.* (past and past part. **stung** | stəNG |) [trans.] swindle or exorbitantly overcharge (someone): *an elaborate fraud that stung a bank for thousands.*

stint | stint | • *v.* [trans.] [often with negative] supply an ungenerous or inadequate amount of (something): *stowage room hasn't been stinted.*

■ [intrans.] be economical or frugal about spending or providing something: *he doesn't stint on wining and dining.* ■ restrict (someone) in the amount of something (esp. money) given or permitted: *to avoid having to stint yourself, budget in advance.* • *n.* **1** a person's fixed or allotted period of work: *his varied career included a stint as a magician.* **2** limitation of supply or effort: *a collector with an eye for quality and the means to indulge it **without stint**.*

sti•pend | ˈstīˌpend; -pənd | • *n.* a fixed regular sum paid as a salary or allowance.

stip•ple | ˈstipəl | • *v.* [trans.] (in drawing, painting, and engraving) mark (a surface) with numerous small dots or specks: [as n.] (**stippling**) *the miniaturist's use of stippling.*

■ produce a decorative effect on (paint or other material) by roughening its surface when it is wet. • *n.* the process or technique of stippling a surface, or the effect so created.

DERIVATIVES: **stip•pler** | ˈstip(ə)lər | *n.*

stip•u•late | ˈstipyəˌlāt | • *v.* [trans.] demand or specify (a requirement), typically as part of a bargain or agreement: *he stipulated certain conditions before their marriage* | [as adj.] (**stipulated**) *the stipulated time has elapsed.*

DERIVATIVES: **stip•u•la•tion** | ˌstipyəˈlāSHən | *n.* **stip•u•la•tor** | -ˌlātər | *n.*

sto•a | ˈstōə | • *n.* a classical portico or roofed colonnade.

■ (**the Stoa**) the great hall in Athens in which the ancient Greek philosopher Zeno (fl. c.300 BC)gave the founding lectures of the Stoic school of philosophy.

sto•chas•tic | stəˈkæstik | • *adj.* randomly determined; having a random probability distribution or pattern that may be analyzed statistically but may not be predicted precisely.

DERIVATIVES: **sto•chas•ti•cal•ly** | -ik(ə)lē | *adv.*

sto•ic | ˈstō-ik | • *n.* **1** a person who can endure pain or hardship without showing his or her feelings or complaining. **2** (**Stoic**) a member of the ancient philosophical school of Stoicism, which was characterized by austere ethical doctrines. • *adj.* **1** (also **stoical**) enduring pain or hardship without showing feelings or complaining. **2** (**Stoic**) of or belonging to the Stoics or their school of philosophy.

stoke | stōk | • *v.* [trans.] add coal or other solid fuel to (a fire, furnace, or boiler).

■ encourage or incite (a strong emotion or tendency): *his composure had the effect of stoking her anger.* ■ [often as adj.] (**stoked**) excite or thrill: *when they told me I was on the team, I was stoked.* ■ [intrans.] consume a large quantity of food or drink to give one energy: *Carol was at the coffee machine, **stoking up** for the day.*

stol•id | 'stälid | • *adj.* (of a person) calm, dependable, and showing little emotion or animation.
DERIVATIVES: **sto•lid•i•ty** | stə'lidit̪ē | *n.* **stol•id•ly** adv. **stol•id•ness** *n.*

stoup | stoōp | • *n.* a basin for holy water, esp. on the wall near the door of a Roman Catholic church for worshipers to dip their fingers in before crossing themselves.
■ a flagon or beaker for drink.

stra•bis•mus | strə'bizməs | • *n.* abnormal alignment of the eyes; the condition of having a squint.
DERIVATIVES: **stra•bis•mic** | -mik | *adj.*

strait | strāt | • *n.* **1** (also **straits**) a narrow passage of water connecting two seas or two large areas of water: [in place names] *the Strait of Gibraltar.* **2** (**straits**) used in reference to a situation characterized by a specified degree of trouble or difficulty: *the economy is **in dire straits** | a crippling disease could leave anyone in serious financial straits.* • *adj.* (of a place) of limited spatial capacity; narrow or cramped: *the road was so strait that a handful of men might have defended it.*
■ close, strict, or rigorous: *my captivity was strait as ever.*
DERIVATIVES: **strait•ly** adv. **strait•ness** *n.*

strap•pa•do | strə'pädō; -'pä- | • *n.* (pl. **-os**) (usu. **the strappado**) a form of punishment or torture in which the victim was secured to a rope and made to fall from a height almost to the ground before being stopped with an abrupt jerk.
■ the instrument used for inflicting this punishment or torture.

strat•a•gem | 'strætəjəm | • *n.* a plan or scheme, esp. one used to outwit an opponent or achieve an end: *a series of devious stratagems.*
■ skill in devising such plans or schemes; cunning.

stra•te•gic | strə'tējik | • *adj.* relating to the identification of long-term or overall aims and interests and the means of achieving them: *the company should take strategic actions to cope with fundamental changes in the environment | strategic planning for the organization is the responsibility of top management.*
■ carefully designed or planned to serve a particular purpose or advantage: *alarms are positioned at strategic points around the prison.*
■ relating to the gaining of overall or long-term military advantage: *New Orleans was of strategic importance | a hazard to our strategic and commercial interests.* ■ (of human or material resources) essential in fighting a war: *the strategic forces on Russian territory.* ■ (of bombing or weapons) done or for use against industrial areas and communication centers of enemy territory as a long-term military objective: *strategic nuclear missiles.*
DERIVATIVES: **stra•te•gi•cal** adj. **stra•te•gi•cal•ly** | -ik(ə)lē | adv. [as submodifier] *a strategically placed mirror.*

strat•i•fy | 'strætə‚fī | • *v.* (**-ies, -ied**) [trans.] [usu. as adj.] (**stratified**) form or arrange into strata: *socially stratified cities* | [intrans.] *the residues have begun to stratify.*
■ arrange or classify: *stratifying patients into well-defined risk groups.* ■ place (seeds) close together in layers in moist sand or peat to preserve them or to help them germinate. ■ [intrans.] (of seeds) be germinated by this method.
DERIVATIVES: **strat•i•fi•ca•tion** | ‚strætəfi'kāSHən | *n.*

stra•tig•ra•phy | strə'tigrəfē | • *n.* the branch of geology concerned with the order and relative position of strata and their relationship to the geological time scale.
■ the analysis of the order and position of layers of archaeological remains. ■ the structure of a particular set of strata.
DERIVATIVES: **stra•tig•ra•pher** | -fər | *n.* **strat•i•graph•ic** | ‚strætə'græfik | adj. **strat•i•graph•i•cal** | ‚strætə'græfikəl | adj.

stra•toc•ra•cy | strə'täkrəsē | • *n.* (pl. **-ies**) government by military forces.
■ a military government.

stra•tum | 'strātəm; 'stræ- | • *n.* (pl. **strata** | 'strāt̪ə; 'stræ-|) **1** a layer or a series of layers of rock in the ground: *a stratum of flint.*
■ a thin layer within any structure: *thin strata of air.* **2** a level or class to which people are assigned according to their social status, education, or income: *members of other social strata.*
■ (in statistics) a group into which members of a population are divided in stratified sampling.

USAGE: In Latin, the word **stratum** is singular and its plural form is **strata**. In English, this distinction is maintained. It is therefore incorrect to use **strata** as a singular or to create the form **stratas** as the plural: *a series of overlying **strata**, not a series of overlying **stratas**, and a new **stratum** was uncovered, not a new **strata** was uncovered.*

stream of con•scious•ness • *n.* a person's thoughts and conscious reactions to events, perceived as a continuous flow. The term was introduced by William James in his *Principles of Psychology* (1890).
■ a literary style in which a character's thoughts, feelings, and reactions are depicted in a continuous flow uninterrupted by objective description or conventional dialogue.

stri•a | 'strīə | • *n.* (pl. **striae** | 'strī-ē |) a linear mark, slight ridge, or groove on a surface, often one of a number of similar parallel features.
■ any of a number of longitudinal collections of nerve fibers in the brain.

stri•ate technical • *adj.* | 'strī‚āt | marked with striae: *the striate cortex.* • *v.* [trans.] [usu. as adj.] (**striated**) mark with striae: *striated bark.*
DERIVATIVES: **stri•a•tion** | strī'āSHən | *n.*

strict con•struc•tion • *n.* a literal interpretation of a statute or document (e.g., the US Constitution) by a court.
DERIVATIVES: **strict con•struc•tion•ist** *n.*

stric•ture |ˈstrik(t)SHər| • n. **1** a restriction on a person or activity: *religious strictures on everyday life.* **2** a sternly critical or censorious remark or instruction: *his strictures on their lack of civic virtue.* **3** Medicine abnormal narrowing of a canal or duct in the body: *a colonic stricture* | *jaundice caused by bile duct stricture.*
DERIVATIVES: **stric•tured** adj.

stri•dent |ˈstrīdnt| • adj. loud and harsh; grating: *his voice had become increasingly sharp, almost strident.*
■ presenting a point of view, esp. a controversial one, in an excessively and unpleasantly forceful way: *public pronouncements on the crisis became less strident.* ■ (in phonetics) another term for SIBILANT.
DERIVATIVES: **stri•den•cy** n. **stri•dent•ly** adv.

stri•dor |ˈstrīdər| • n. a harsh or grating sound: *the engines' stridor increased.*
■ a harsh vibrating noise when breathing, caused by obstruction of the windpipe or larynx.

strid•u•late |ˈstrijə,lāt| • v. [intrans.] (of an insect, esp. a male cricket or grasshopper) make a shrill sound by rubbing the legs, wings, or other parts of the body together.
DERIVATIVES: **strid•u•lant** |-lənt| adj. **strid•u•la•tion** |,strijəˈlāSHən| n. **strid•u•la•to•ry** |-lə,tôrē| adj.

strin•gent |ˈstrinjənt| • adj. (of regulations, requirements, or conditions) strict, precise, and exacting: *California's air pollution guidelines are stringent.*
DERIVATIVES: **strin•gen•cy** n. **strin•gent•ly** adv.

stro•phe |ˈstrōfē| • n. the first section of an ancient Greek choral ode or of one division of it.
■ a structural division of a poem containing stanzas of varying line-length, especially an ode or free verse poem.
DERIVATIVES: **stroph•ic** |-fik; ˈsträ-| adj.

struc•tur•al•ism |ˈstrəkCHərə,lizəm| • n. a method of interpretation and analysis of aspects of human cognition, behavior, culture, and experience that focuses on relationships of contrast between elements in a conceptual system that reflect patterns underlying a superficial diversity.
■ the doctrine that structure is more important than function.
DERIVATIVES: **struc•tur•al•ist** n. & adj.

strum•pet |ˈstrəmpət| • n. a female prostitute or a promiscuous woman.

strut |strət| • n. **1** a rod or bar forming part of a framework and designed to resist compression. **2** [in sing.] a stiff, erect, and apparently arrogant or conceited gait: *that old confident strut and swagger have returned.* • v. (**strutted, strutting**) **1** [no obj., with adverbial] walk with a stiff, erect, and apparently arrogant or conceited gait: *peacocks strut through the grounds.* **2** [trans.] brace (something) with a strut or struts: *the holes were close-boarded and strutted.*
DERIVATIVES: **strut•ter** n. **strut•ting•ly** adv.

stul•ti•fy |ˈstəltə,fī| • v. (**-ies, -ied**) [trans.] **1** [usu. as adj.] (**stultifying**) cause to lose enthusiasm and initiative, esp. as a result of a tedious or restrictive routine: *the mentally stultifying effects of a disadvantaged home.* **2** cause (someone) to appear foolish or absurd: *Counsel is not expected to stultify himself in an attempt to advance his client's interests.*
DERIVATIVES: **stul•ti•fi•ca•tion** |,stəltəfiˈkāSHən| n. **stul•ti•fi•er** n.

stu•pe•fy |ˈst(y)ōōpə,fī| • v. (**-ies, -ied**) [trans.] make (someone) unable to think or feel properly: *the offense of administering drugs to a woman with intent to stupefy her.*
■ astonish and shock: *the amount they spend on clothes would appall their parents and stupefy their grandparents.*
DERIVATIVES: **stu•pe•fac•tion** |,st(y)ōōpəˈfakSHən| n. **stu•pe•fi•er** n. **stu•pe•fy•ing** adj. **stu•pe•fy•ing•ly** adv. [as submodifier] *a stupefyingly tedious task.*

stu•por |ˈst(y)ōōpər| • n. [in sing.] a state of near-unconsciousness or insensibility: *a drunken stupor.*
DERIVATIVES: **stu•por•ous** |-rəs| adj.

Sturm und Drang |ˈSHtōōrm ōōn(d) ˈdräNG| • n. a literary and artistic movement in Germany in the late 18th century, influenced by Jean-Jacques Rousseau and characterized by the expression of emotional unrest and a rejection of neoclassical literary norms.

stut•ter |ˈstətər| • v. [intrans.] talk with continued involuntary repetition of sounds, esp. initial consonants: *the child was stuttering in fright.* Cf. STAMMER.
■ [trans.] utter in such a way: *he shyly stuttered out an invitation to the movies* | [with direct speech] *"W-what's happened?" she stuttered.*
■ (of a machine or gun) produce a series of short, sharp sounds: *she flinched as a machine gun stuttered nearby.* • n. a tendency to stutter while speaking.
■ a series of short, sharp sounds produced by a machine or gun.
DERIVATIVES: **stut•ter•er** n. **stut•ter•ing•ly** adv.

style |stīl| • n. **1** (in business) an official or legal title: *the partnership traded under the style of Storr and Mortimer.* **2** a rodlike object or part, in particular:
■ archaic term for STYLUS (sense 2). ■ (in a flower) a narrow, typically elongated extension of the ovary, bearing the stigma. ■ (in an invertebrate animal) a small slender pointed appendage; a stylet. ■ the gnomon of a sundial.

sty•lis•tics |stīˈlistiks| • plural n. [treated as sing.] the study of the distinctive styles found in particular literary genres and in the works of individual writers.

sty•lus |ˈstīləs| • n. (pl. **styli** |-,lī| or **styluses**) **1** a hard point, typically of diamond or sapphire, following a groove in a phonograph record and transmitting the recorded sound for reproduction.
■ a similar point producing such a groove when recording sound. **2** an ancient writing implement, consisting of a small rod with a

pointed end for scratching letters on wax-covered tablets, and a blunt end for obliterating them.
■ an implement of similar shape used esp. for engraving and tracing. ■ a penlike device used to input handwritten text or drawings directly into a computer.

sty•mie |'stīmē| • v. (**stymies, stymied, stymying** |'stīmēiNG| or **stymieing** |'stīmēiNG|) [trans.] prevent or hinder the progress of: *the changes must not be allowed to stymie new medical treatments.*

styp•tic |'stiptik| • adj. (of a substance) capable of causing bleeding to stop when it is applied to a wound. • n. a substance of this kind.

sua•sion |'swāzHən| • n. persuasion as opposed to force or compulsion.
DERIVATIVES: **sua•sive** adj.

suave |swäv| • adj. (**suaver, suavest**) (esp. of a man) charming, confident, and elegant: *all the waiters were suave and deferential.*
DERIVATIVES: **suave•ly** adv. **suave•ness** n. **suav•i•ty** |-itē| n. (pl. **-ies**) .

sub•con•scious |səb'känsHəs| • adj. of or concerning the part of the mind of which one is not fully aware but which influences one's actions and feelings: *my subconscious fear.* • n. (**one's/the subconscious**) this part of the mind (not in technical use in psychoanalysis, where *unconscious* is preferred). Cf. CONSCIOUS, PRECONSCIOUS.
DERIVATIVES: **sub•con•scious•ly** adv. **sub•con•scious•ness** n.

sub•cul•ture |'səb,kəlCHər| • n. a cultural group within a larger culture, often having beliefs or interests at variance with those of the larger culture: *the hip subculture.*
DERIVATIVES: **sub•cul•tur•al** |,səb'kəlCHərəl| adj.

sub•duc•tion |səb'dəksHən| • n. the sideways and downward movement of the edge of a plate of the earth's crust into the mantle beneath another plate.
DERIVATIVES: **sub•duct** |-'dəkt| v.

sub•ja•cent |səb'jāsənt| • adj. situated below something else: *the building requires subjacent support.*
DERIVATIVES: **sub•ja•cen•cy** n.

sub•ject • n. |'səbjəkt| **1** a person or thing that is being discussed, described, or dealt with: *I've said all there is to be said on the subject* | *he's the subject of a major new biography.* ■ a person or circumstance giving rise to a specified feeling, response, or action: *the incident was the subject of international condemnation.* ■ (in grammar) a noun or noun phrase functioning as one of the main components of a clause, being the element about which the rest of the clause is predicated. ■ (in logic) the part of a proposition about which a statement is made. ■ a theme of a fugue or of a piece of music in sonata form; a leading phrase or motif. ■ a person who is the focus of scientific or medical attention or experiment. **2** a branch of knowledge studied or taught in a school, college, or university. **3** a member of a state other than its supreme

ruler. Cf. CITIZEN. **4** (in philosophy) a thinking or feeling entity; the conscious mind; the ego, esp. as opposed to anything external to the mind.
■ the central substance or core of a thing as opposed to its attributes. • adj. |'səbjəkt| [predic.] (**subject to**) **1** likely or prone to be affected by (a particular condition or occurrence, typically an unwelcome or unpleasant one): *he was subject to bouts of manic depression.* **2** dependent or conditional upon: *the proposed merger is subject to the approval of the shareholders.* **3** under the authority of: *legislation making Congress subject to the laws it passes.*
■ [attrib.] under the control or domination of (another ruler, country, or government): *the Greeks were the first subject people to break free from Ottoman rule.* • adv. |'səbjəkt| (**subject to**) conditionally upon: *subject to bankruptcy court approval, the company expects to begin liquidation of its inventory.* • v. |səb'jekt| [trans.] **1** (**subject someone/something to**) cause or force to undergo (a particular experience of form of treatment): *he'd subjected her to a terrifying ordeal.* **2** bring (a person or country) under one's control or jurisdiction, typically by using force:
DERIVATIVES: **sub•jec•tion** |səb'jeksHən| n. **sub•ject•less** |'səbjək(t)ləs| adj.

sub•jec•tive |səb'jektiv| • adj. **1** based on or influenced by personal feelings, tastes, or opinions: *his views are highly subjective* | *there is always the danger of making a subjective judgment.* Cf. OBJECTIVE.
■ dependent on the mind or on an individual's perception for its existence. **2** (in grammar) of, relating to, or denoting a case of nouns and pronouns used for the subject of a sentence. • n. (**the subjective**) (in grammar) the subjective case.
DERIVATIVES: **sub•jec•tive•ly** adv. **sub•jec•tive•ness** n. **sub•jec•tiv•i•ty** |,səbjek 'tivitē| n.

sub•ju•gate |'səbjə,gāt| • v. [trans.] bring under domination or control, esp. by conquest: *the invaders had soon subjugated most of the native population.*
■ (**subjugate someone/something to**) make someone or something subordinate to: *the new ruler firmly subjugated the Church to the state.*
DERIVATIVES: **sub•ju•ga•tion** |,səbjə'gā-sHən| n. **sub•ju•ga•tor** |-,gātər| n.

sub•junc•tive |səb'jəNG(k)tiv| Grammar • adj. relating to or denoting a mood of verbs expressing what is imagined or wished or possible. Cf. INDICATIVE. • n. a verb in the subjunctive mood.
■ (**the subjunctive**) the subjunctive mood.
DERIVATIVES: **sub•junc•tive•ly** adv.

USAGE: *... if I were you; the report recommends that he face the tribunal; it is important that they be aware of the provisions of the act.* These sentences all contain a verb in the **subjunctive mood**. The subjunctive is used to express situations that are hypothetical or not yet realized and is typically used for what is imagined, hoped for, demanded, or expected. In English the subjunctive mood is fairly uncommon (esp. in comparison with other languages such as French and Spanish), mainly because most of the functions of the subjunctive are covered by modal verbs such as **might, could,** and **should.** In fact, in English the subjunctive is often indistinguishable from the ordinary **indicative mood** since its form in most contexts is identical. It is distinctive only in the third person singular, where the normal indicative **-s** ending is absent (he **face** rather than he **faces** in the example above), and in the verb 'to be' (I **were** rather than I **was** and they **be** rather than they **are** in the examples above). In modern English the subjunctive mood still exists but is regarded in many contexts as optional. Use of the subjunctive tends to convey a more formal tone, but there are few people who would regard its absence as actually wrong. Today it survives mostly in fixed expressions, as in be **that as it may;** if I **were** you; **far be it from me; as it were; lest we forget; God help** you; **perish** the thought; and **come** what may.

sub•li•mate |ˈsəbləˌmāt| • v. **1** [trans.] (esp. in psychoanalytic theory) divert or modify (an instinctual impulse) into a culturally higher or socially more acceptable activity: people who will **sublimate** sexuality **into** activities that help to build up and preserve civilization | he sublimates his hurt and anger into humor. **2** (in chemistry) another term for SUBLIME. • n. |-ˌmit; -ˌmāt| (in chemistry) a solid deposit of a substance that has sublimed.
DERIVATIVES: **sub•li•ma•tion** |ˌsəbləˈmāSHən| n.

sub•lime |səˈblīm| • adj. (**sublimer, sublimest**) of such excellence, grandeur, or beauty as to inspire great admiration or awe: Mozart's sublime piano concertos | [as n.] (**the sublime**) experiences that ranged **from the sublime to the ridiculous.**
■ used to denote the extreme or unparalleled nature of a person's attitude or behavior: he had the sublime confidence of youth. • v. **1** [intrans.] (of a solid substance) change directly into vapor rather than liquid when heated, typically forming a solid deposit again on cooling.
■ [trans.] cause (a substance) to do this: these crystals could be sublimed under a vacuum. **2** [trans.] elevate to a high degree of moral or spiritual purity or excellence.
DERIVATIVES: **sub•lime•ly** adv. **sub•lim•i•ty** |-ˈblimitē| n.

sub•lim•i•nal |səˈbliminl| • adj. (of a stimulus or mental process) below the threshold of sensation or consciousness; perceived by or affecting someone's mind without their being aware of it.
DERIVATIVES: **sub•lim•i•nal•ly** adv.

sub•lu•nar•y |səbˈloōnərē| • adj. belonging to this world as contrasted with a better or more spiritual one: the concept was irrational to sublunary minds.

sub•or•di•nate • adj. |səˈbôrdnit| lower in rank or position: his subordinate officers.
■ of less or secondary importance: in adventure stories, character must be **subordinate to** action. • n. a person under the authority or control of another within an organization. • v. |-ˌāt| [trans.] treat or regard as of lesser importance than something else: practical considerations were **subordinated to** political expediency.
■ make subservient to or dependent on something else.
DERIVATIVES: **sub•or•di•nate•ly** adv. **sub•or•di•na•tion** |-ˌbôrdnˈāSHən| n. **sub•or•di•na•tive** |-ətiv| adj.

sub•or•di•nate clause • n. (in grammar) a clause, typically introduced by a conjunction, that forms part of and is dependent on a main clause (e.g., "when it rang" in "she answered the phone when it rang").

sub•orn |səˈbôrn| • v. [trans.] bribe or otherwise induce (someone) to commit an unlawful act such as perjury: he was accused of conspiring to suborn witnesses.
■ procure the performance of (an unlawful act): accused of suborning perjury.
DERIVATIVES: **sub•or•na•tion** |ˌsəbôrˈnāSHən| n. **sub•orn•er** n.

sub•ro•ga•tion |ˌsəbrəˈgāSHən| • n. (in law) the substitution of one person or group by another in respect of a debt or insurance claim, accompanied by the transfer of any associated rights and duties.
DERIVATIVES: **sub•ro•gate** |ˈsəbrəˌgāt| v.

sub ro•sa |ˌsəb ˈrōzə| • adj. & adv. happening or done in secret: [as adv.] the committee operates sub rosa | [as adj.] sub rosa inspections.

sub•se•quent |ˈsəbsəkwənt| • adj. coming after something in time; following: the theory was developed **subsequent to** the earthquake of 1906. Cf. CONSEQUENT.
■ (of a stream or valley) having a direction or character determined by the resistance to erosion of the underlying rock, and typically following the strike (horizontal or compass direction) of the strata.
DERIVATIVES: **sub•se•quent•ly** adv.

sub•ser•vi•ent |səbˈsərvēənt| • adj. prepared to obey others unquestioningly: she was **subservient to** her parents.
■ less important; subordinate: Marxism makes freedom **subservient to** control. ■ serving as a means to an end: the whole narration is **subservient to** the moral plan of exemplifying twelve virtues in twelve knights.
DERIVATIVES: **sub•ser•vi•ence** n. **sub•ser•vi•en•cy** n. **sub•ser•vi•ent•ly** adv.

sub•side |səbˈsīd| • v. [intrans.] **1** become less intense, violent, or severe: I'll wait a few minutes until the storm subsides.
■ lapse into silence or inactivity: Fred opened his mouth to protest again, then subsided. **2** (of water) go down to a lower or the normal level: the floods subside almost as quickly as they arise.
■ (of the ground) cave in; sink: the island is subsiding. ■ (of a swelling) reduce until gone: it

took seven days for the swelling to subside completely.
DERIVATIVES: **sub•sid•ence** n.
sub•sid•i•ar•y |səb'sidē,erē| • adj. less important than but related or supplementary to: | *many environmentalists argue that the cause of animal rights is subsidiary to that of protecting the environment.*
■ [attrib.] (of a company) controlled by a holding or parent company. • n. (pl. **-ies**) a company controlled by a holding or parent company.
■ a thing that is of lesser importance than but related to something else.
DERIVATIVES: **sub•sid•i•ar•i•ly** |-,sidē'erəlē| adv. (rare).
sub•si•dy |'səbsidē| • n. (pl. **-ies**) 1 a sum of money granted by the state or a public body to assist an industry or business so that the price of a commodity or service may remain low or competitive: *a farm subsidy | they disdain government subsidy.*
■ a sum of money granted to support an arts organization or other undertaking held to be in the public interest. ■ a sum of money paid by one state to another for the preservation of neutrality, the promotion of war, or to repay military aid. ■ a grant or contribution of money. 2 a parliamentary grant to a sovereign for state needs.
■ a tax levied on a particular occasion.
sub•sist |səb'sist| • v. [intrans.] 1 maintain or support oneself, esp. at a minimal level: *thousands of refugees subsist on international handouts.*
■ [trans.] provide sustenance for: *the problem of subsisting the poor in a period of high bread prices.* 2 (in law) remain in being, force, or effect.
■ (**subsist in**) be attributable to: *the effect of genetic maldevelopment may subsist in chromosomal mutation.*
DERIVATIVES: **sub•sist•ence** n. **sub•sist•ent** |-ənt| adj.
sub•stan•ti•ate |səb'stænCHē,āt| • v. [trans.] provide evidence to support or prove the truth of: *they had found nothing to substantiate the allegations.*
DERIVATIVES: **sub•stan•ti•a•tion** |-,stænCHē'āSHən| n.
sub•stan•tive |'səbstəntiv| • adj. 1 having a firm basis in reality and therefore important, meaningful, or considerable: *there is no substantive evidence for the efficacy of these drugs.* 2 having a separate and independent existence.
■ (of a dye) not needing a mordant. 3 (of law) defining rights and duties as opposed to giving the rules by which such things are established. • n. a noun.
DERIVATIVES: **sub•stan•ti•val** |,səbstən'tivəl| adj. **sub•stan•tive•ly** adv.
sub•strate |'səb,strāt| • n. a substance or layer that underlies something, or on which some process occurs, in particular:
■ the surface or material on or from which an organism lives, grows, or obtains its nourishment. ■ the substance on which an enzyme

acts. ■ a material that provides the surface on which something is deposited or inscribed, for example the silicon wafer used to manufacture integrated circuits.
sub•sume |səb'soōm| • v. [trans.] (often be **subsumed**) include or absorb (something) in something else: *most of these phenomena can be subsumed under two broad categories.*
DERIVATIVES: **sub•sum•a•ble** adj. **sub•sump•tion** |-'səm(p)SHən| n.
sub•tend |səb'tend| • v. [trans.] 1 (of a line, arc, or figure) form (an angle) at a particular point when straight lines from its extremities are joined at that point.
■ (of an angle or chord) have bounding lines or points that meet or coincide with those of (a line or arc). 2 (of a bract) extend under (a flower) so as to support or enfold it.
sub•ter•fuge |'səbtər,fyooj| • n. deceit used in order to achieve one's goal.
■ a statement or action resorted to in order to deceive.
sub•text |'səb,tekst| • n. an underlying and often distinct theme in a piece of writing or conversation.
DERIVATIVES: **sub•tex•tu•al** adj.
sub•tle |'sətl| • adj. (**subtler, subtlest**) (esp. of a change or distinction) so delicate or precise as to be difficult to analyze or describe: *his language expresses rich and subtle meanings.*
■ (of a mixture or effect) delicately complex and understated: *subtle lighting.* ■ making use of clever and indirect methods to achieve something: *he tried a more subtle approach.* ■ capable of making fine distinctions: *a subtle mind.* ■ arranged in an ingenious and elaborate way. ■ crafty; cunning.
DERIVATIVES: **sub•tle•ness** n. **sub•tle•ty** n. **sub•tly** adv.
sub•vent |səb'vent| • v. [trans.] support or assist by the payment of a grant or subsidy (a *subvention*).
DERIVATIVES: **sub•ven•tion** n.
sub•vert |səb'vərt| • v. [trans.] undermine the power and authority of (an established system or institution): *an attempt to subvert democratic government.*
DERIVATIVES: **sub•ver•sion** |-'vərzHən; -SHən| n. **sub•ver•sive** adj., n. **sub•vert•er** n.
suc•ceed |sək'sēd| • v. 1 [intrans.] achieve what one aims or wants to: *he succeeded in winning a pardon.*
■ (of a plan, request, or undertaking) lead to the desired result: *a mission which could not possibly succeed.* 2 [trans.] take over a throne, inheritance, office, or other position from: *he would succeed Reno as attorney general.*
■ [intrans.] become the new rightful holder of an inheritance, office, title, or property: *he succeeded to his father's kingdom.* ■ come after and take the place of: *her embarrassment was succeeded by fear.*
DERIVATIVES: **suc•ceed•er** n. (archaic).
suc•ces•sion |sək'seSHən| • n. 1 a number of people or things sharing a specified characteristic and following one after the other:

she had been secretary to a succession of board directors. ■ (in geology) a group of strata representing a single chronological sequence. **2** the action or process of inheriting a title, office, property, etc.: *the new king was already elderly at the time of his succession.* ■ the right or sequence of inheriting a position, title, etc.: *the succession to the Crown was disputed.* ■ the process by which a plant or animal community successively gives way to another until a stable climax is reached.
DERIVATIVES: **suc•ces•sion•al** |-SHənl| *adj.*

suc•cinct |sə(k)ˈsiNG(k)t| • *adj.* (esp. of something written or spoken) briefly and clearly expressed: *use short, succinct sentences.*
DERIVATIVES: **suc•cinct•ly** *adv.* **suc•cinct•ness** *n.*

suc•cor |ˈsəkər| (Brit. **succour**) • *n.* assistance and support in times of hardship and distress. ■ (**succors**) reinforcements of troops. • *v.* [trans.] give assistance or aid to: *prisoners of war were liberated and succored.*
DERIVATIVES: **suc•cor•less** *adj.*

suc•cu•bus |ˈsəkyəbəs| • *n.* (pl. **succubi** |-ˌbī|) a female demon believed to have sexual intercourse with sleeping men. Cf. INCUBUS.

suc•cu•lent |ˈsəkyələnt| • *adj.* (of food) tender, juicy, and tasty. ■ (of a plant, esp. a xerophyte) having thick fleshy leaves or stems adapted to storing water. • *n.* a succulent plant.
DERIVATIVES: **suc•cu•lence** *n.* **suc•cu•lent•ly** *adv.*

suc•cumb |səˈkəm| • *v.* [intrans.] fail to resist (pressure, temptation, or some other negative force): *he has become the latest to succumb to the strain.* ■ die from the effect of a disease or injury. ■ fail to succeed in a contest: *after a strong first half, the Lions succumbed 20–17.*

su•dor•if•ic |ˌsoōdəˈrifik| • *adj.* relating to or causing sweating. • *n.* a drug that induces sweating.

suf•fer |ˈsəfər| • *v.* [trans.] **1** experience or be subjected to (something bad or unpleasant): *he'd suffered intense pain* | [intrans.] *he'd suffered a great deal since his arrest* | [as n.] (**suffering**) *weapons that cause unnecessary suffering.* ■ [intrans.] (**suffer from**) be affected by or subject to (an illness or ailment): *his daughter suffered from agoraphobia.* ■ [intrans.] become or appear worse in quality: *his relationship with Anne did suffer.* ■ [intrans.] undergo martyrdom or execution: *to suffer for the faith.* **2** tolerate: *France will no longer suffer the existing government.* ■ [with obj. and infinitive] allow (someone) to do something: *my conscience would not suffer me to accept any more.*
PHRASES: **not suffer fools gladly** be impatient or intolerant toward people one regards as foolish or unintelligent.
DERIVATIVES: **suf•fer•a•ble** |ˈsəf(ə)rəbəl| *adj.* **suf•fer•er** |ˈsəf(ə)rər| *n.* (in sense 1).

suf•fer•ance |ˈsəf(ə)rəns| • *n.* **1** absence of objection rather than genuine approval; toleration: *Charles was only here on sufferance.* ■ (in law) the condition of the holder of an estate who continues to hold it after the title has ceased, without the express permission of the owner: *an estate at sufferance.* ■ patient endurance. **2** the suffering or undergoing of something bad or unpleasant.

suf•fice |səˈfīs| • *v.* [intrans.] be enough or adequate: *a quick look should suffice* | [with infinitive] *two examples should suffice to prove the contention.* ■ [trans.] meet the needs of: *simple mediocrity cannot suffice them.*
DERIVATIVES: **suf•fi•cient** *adj.* **suf•fi•cien•cy** *n.* **suf•fi•cient•ly** *adj.*

suf•frage |ˈsəfrij| • *n.* **1** the right to vote in political elections. Cf. FRANCHISE. ■ a vote given in assent to a proposal or in favor of the election of a particular person. **2** (usu. **suffrages**) a series of intercessory prayers or petitions.

suf•fra•gist |ˈsəfrəjist| • *n.* a person advocating the extension of suffrage, esp. to women.
DERIVATIVES: **suf•fra•gism** |-ˌjizəm| *n.*

USAGE: The term **suffragist** dates from the early 19th cent. The early-20th-cent. term **suffragette**, applied to women then agitating for the vote for women, is so often regarded as derogatory, in part because of its seemingly diminutive ending.

suf•fuse |səˈfyoōz| • *v.* [trans.] gradually spread through or over: *her cheeks were suffused with color* | *the first half of the poem is suffused with idealism.* Cf. INFUSE.
DERIVATIVES: **suf•fu•sion** |-ˈfyoōZHən| *n.* **suf•fu•sive** |-ˈfyoōsiv| *adj.*

Su•fi |ˈsoōfē| • *n.* (pl. **Sufis**) a Muslim ascetic and mystic.
DERIVATIVES: **Su•fic** |-fik| *adj.*

sug•ges•tive |sə(g)ˈjestiv| • *adj.* tending to suggest an idea: *there were various suggestive pieces of evidence.* ■ indicative or evocative: *flavors suggestive of coffee and blackberry.* ■ making someone think of sex and sexual relationships: *a suggestive remark.*
DERIVATIVES: **sug•ges•tive•ly** *adv.* **sug•ges•tive•ness** *n.*

su•i ge•ne•ris |ˌsoō,ī ˈjenərəs; ˌsoōē| • *adj.* unique: *the sui generis nature of animals.*

suite |swēt| • *n.* **1** a set of things belonging together, in particular: ■ a set of rooms designated for one person's or family's use or for a particular purpose. ■ a set of furniture of the same design. ■ a set of instrumental musical compositions, originally in dance style, to be played in succession. ■ a set of selected pieces from an opera or musical, arranged to be played as one instrumental work. ■ (in computing) a set of programs with a uniform design and the ability to share data. ■ (in geology) a group of minerals, rocks, or fossils occurring together and characteristic of a location or period. **2** a group of people in attendance on a monarch or other person of high rank.

sul•len |'sələn| • *adj.* bad-tempered and sulky; gloomy: *a sullen pout* | *a sullen sunless sky.*
■ (esp. of water) slow-moving: *rivers in sullen, perpetual flood.* • *n.* (**the sullens**) a sulky or depressed mood.
DERIVATIVES: **sul•len•ly** *adv.* **sul•len•ness** *n.*

sul•ly |'səlē| • *v.* (**-ies, -ied**) [trans.] damage the purity or integrity of; defile: *they were outraged that anyone should sully their good name.*

sul•try |'səltrē| • *adj.* (**sultrier, sultriest**) **1** (of the air or weather) hot and humid. **2** (of a person, esp. a woman) attractive in a way that suggests a passionate nature.
DERIVATIVES: **sul•tri•ly** |-trəlē| *adv.* **sul•tri•ness** *n.*

sum•ma•ry |'səmərē| • *n.* (pl. **-ies**) a brief statement or account of the main points of something: *a summary of Chapter Three.* • *adj.* **1** dispensing with needless details or formalities; brief: *summary financial statements.* **2** (of a judicial process) conducted without the customary legal formalities: *summary proceedings.*
■ (of a conviction) made by a judge or magistrate without a jury. ■ (of an offence) that can only be tried summarily. ■ (of a judgement) that may be granted by the court when one party at trial moves for it, on the grounds that there is no issue of fact, and that as a matter of law that party is entitled to prevail: *when the prosecution rested its case, the defense moved for summary judgement.*
DERIVATIVES: **sum•mar•i•ly** |sə'merəlē; 'səmərəlē| *adv.* **sum•mar•i•ness** |sə'merēnis| *n.*

sum•ma•tion |sə'māsHən| • *n.* **1** the process of adding things together: *the summation of numbers of small pieces of evidence.*
■ a sum total of things added together. **2** the process of summing something up: *these will need summation in a single document.*
■ a summary. ■ an attorney's speech at the conclusion of the giving of evidence; closing argument.
DERIVATIVES: **sum•ma•tion•al** |-SHənl| *adj.* **sum•ma•tive** |'səmətiv| *adj.*

sump•tu•ary |'səm(p)CHə,werē| • *adj.* [attrib.] relating to or denoting laws that limit private expenditure on food and personal items.

sump•tu•ous |'səm(p)CHəwəs| • *adj.* splendid and expensive-looking: *the banquet was a sumptuous, luxurious meal.*
DERIVATIVES: **sump•tu•os•i•ty** |,səm(p)-CHə'wäsət̯ē| *n.* **sump•tu•ous•ly** *adv.* **sump•tu•ous•ness** *n.*

sun•der |'səndər| • *v.* [trans.] split apart: *the crunch of bone when it is sundered.*
PHRASES: **in sunder** apart or into pieces: *hew their bones in sunder!*

sun•dry |'səndrē| • *adj.* [attrib.] of various kinds; several: *lemon rind and sundry herbs.* • *n.* (pl. **-ies**) (**sundries**) various items not important enough to be mentioned individu-

ally: *a drugstore selling magazines, newspapers, and sundries.*

Sun•ni |'soŏnē| • *n.* (pl. same or **Sunnis**) one of the two main branches of Islam, commonly described as orthodox, and differing from Shia in its understanding of the Sunna (portion of Muslim law based on Muhammad's words or acts) and in its acceptance of the first three caliphs. Cf. SHIA.
■ a Muslim who adheres to this branch of Islam.
DERIVATIVES: **Sun•nite** |soŏnīt| *adj.* & *n*;

su•per•an•nu•ate |,soŏpər'ænyə,wāt| • *v.* [trans.] (usu. **be superannuated**) retire (someone) with a pension: *his pilot's license was withdrawn and he was superannuated.*
■ [as adj.] (**superannuated**) (of a post or employee) belonging to a superannuation scheme: *she is not superannuated and has no paid vacation.* ■ [usu. as adj.] (**superannuated**) cause to become obsolete through age or new technological or intellectual developments: *superannuated computing equipment.*
DERIVATIVES: **su•per•an•nu•a•ble** |-'æn-yəwəbəl| *adj.* **su•per•an•nu•a•tion** *n.*

su•per•cil•i•ous |,soŏpər'silēəs| • *adj.* behaving or looking as though one thinks one is superior to others: *a supercilious lady's maid.*
DERIVATIVES: **su•per•cil•i•ous•ly** *adv.* **su•per•cil•i•ous•ness** *n.*

su•per•con•duc•tiv•i•ty |,soŏpər,kändək'ti-vit̯ē| • *n.* (in physics) the property of zero electrical resistance in some substances at very low temperatures.
DERIVATIVES: **su•per•con•duct** |-kən'dəkt| *v.* **su•per•con•duct•ing** |-kən'dəkt-iNG| *adj.* **su•per•con•duc•tive** |-kən'dək-tiv| *adj.*

su•per•con•duc•tor |'soŏpərkən,dəktər| • *n.* a substance capable of becoming superconducting at sufficiently low temperatures.
■ a substance in the superconducting state.

su•per•e•go |,soŏpər'ēgō| • *n.* (pl. **-os**) (in psychoanalysis) the part of a person's mind that acts as a self-critical conscience, reflecting social standards learned from parents and teachers. Cf. EGO and ID.

su•per•er•o•ga•tion |,soŏpər,erə'gāshən| • *n.* the performance of more work than duty requires.
DERIVATIVES: **su•per•e•rog•a•to•ry** |-ə'rägə,tôrē| *adj.*

su•per•fi•cial |,soŏpər'fishəl| • *adj.* existing or occurring at or on the surface: *the building suffered only superficial damage.*
■ situated or occurring on the skin or immediately beneath it: *the superficial muscle groups.* ■ appearing to be true or real only until examined more closely: *the resemblance between the breeds is superficial.* ■ not thorough, deep, or complete; cursory: *he had only the most superficial knowledge of foreign countries.* ■ not having or showing any depth of character or understanding: *perhaps I was a superficial person.*
DERIVATIVES: **su•per•fi•ci•al•i•ty** |-,fisHē'ælit̯ē| *n.* (pl. **-ies**) **su•per•fi•cial•ly** *adv.* **su•per•fi•cial•ness** *n.*

su•per•fi•ci•es |ˌso͞opər'fisHēz; -'fisHē-ēz| • *n.* (pl. same) a surface: *the superficies of a sphere.*
■ an outward part or appearance: *the superficies of life.*

su•per•flu•i•ty |ˌso͞opər'flo͞o-itē| • *n.* (pl. **-ies**) [in sing.] an unnecessarily or excessively large amount or number of something: *a super-fluity of unoccupied time.*
■ an unnecessary thing: *they thought the garrison a superfluity.* ■ the state of being superfluous: *servants who had nothing to do but to display their own superfluity.*

su•per•flu•ous |so͞o'pərfləwəs| • *adj.* unnecessary, esp. through being more than enough: *the purchaser should avoid asking for superfluous information.*
DERIVATIVES: **su•per•flu•ous•ly** *adv.* **su•per•flu•ous•ness** *n.*

su•per•la•tive |sə'pərlətiv| • *adj.* **1** of the highest quality or degree: *a superlative piece of craftsmanship.* **2** (of an adjective or adverb) expressing the highest or a very high degree of a quality (e.g., *bravest, most fiercely*). Cf. POSITIVE, COMPARATIVE. • *n.* **1** a superlative adjective or adverb.
■ (**the superlative**) the highest degree of comparison. **2** (usu. **superlatives**) an exaggerated or hyperbolical expression of praise: *the critics ran out of superlatives to describe him.* **3** something or someone embodying excellence.
DERIVATIVES: **su•per•la•tive•ly** *adv.* **su•per•la•tive•ness** *n.*

su•per•lu•na•ry |ˌso͞opər'lo͞onərē| • *adj.* belonging to a higher world; celestial.
■ extravagant; fantastic. Cf. SUBLUNARY.

su•per•nal |sə'pərnl| • *adj.* of or relating to the sky or the heavens; celestial.
■ of exceptional quality or extent: *he is the supernal poet of our age* | *supernal erudition.*
DERIVATIVES: **su•per•nal•ly** *adv.*

su•per•nat•u•ral |ˌso͞opər'næCH(ə)rəl| • *adj.* (of a manifestation or event) attributed to some force beyond scientific understanding or the laws of nature: *a supernatural being.* Cf. PRETERNATURAL.
■ unnaturally or extraordinarily great: *a woman of supernatural beauty.* • *n.* (**the supernatural**) manifestations or events considered to be of supernatural origin, such as ghosts.
DERIVATIVES: **su•per•nat•u•ral•ism** |-ˌlizəm| *n.* **su•per•nat•u•ral•ist** *n.* **su•per•nat•u•ral•ly** *adv.*

su•per•nu•mer•ar•y |ˌso͞opər'n(y)o͞oməˌrerē| • *adj.* present in excess of the normal or requisite number, in particular:
■ (of a person) not belonging to a regular staff but engaged for extra work. ■ not wanted or needed; redundant: *books were obviously supernumerary, and he began jettisoning them.* ■ (in botany and zoology) denoting a structure or organ occurring in addition to the normal ones: *a pair of supernumerary teats.* ■ (of an actor) appearing on stage but not speaking. • *n.* (pl. **-ies**) a supernumerary person or thing.

su•per•or•di•nate |ˌso͞opər'ôrdn-ət| • *n.* a thing that represents a superior order or category within a system of classification: *a pair of compatibles must have a common superordinate.*
■ a person who has authority over or control of another within an organization. ■ a word whose meaning includes the meaning of one or more other words: *"bird" is the superordinate of "canary."* • *adj.* superior in status: *the principal's superordinate position.*

su•per•script |'so͞opərˌskript| • *adj.* (of a letter, figure, or symbol) written or printed above the line, e.g. the ^{2}; in $e=mc^2$. • *n.* a superscript letter, figure, or symbol.

su•per•sede |ˌso͞opər'sēd| • *v.* [trans.] take the place of (a person or thing previously in authority or use); supplant: *the older models have now been superseded.*
DERIVATIVES: **su•per•ses•sion** |-'seSHən| *n.*

su•per•struc•ture |'so͞opərˌstrəkCHər| • *n.* a structure built on top of something else.
■ the parts of a ship, other than masts and rigging, built above its hull and main deck. ■ the part of a building above its foundations. ■ a concept or idea based on others. ■ (in Marxist theory) the institutions and culture considered to result from or reflect the economic system underlying a society.
DERIVATIVES: **su•per•struc•tur•al** |ˌso͞opər'strəkCHərəl| *adj.*

su•per•vene |ˌso͞opər'vēn| • *v.* [intrans.] occur later than a specified or implied event or action, typically in such a way as to change the situation: [as adj.] (**supervening**) *any plan that is made is liable to be disrupted by supervening events.*
■ (in philosophy, of a fact or property), be entailed by or consequent on the existence or establishment of another: *the view that mental events supervene upon physical ones.*
DERIVATIVES: **su•per•ven•ient** |-'vēnyənt| *adj.* **su•per•ven•tion** |-'venCHən| *n.*

su•pine |'so͞oˌpīn| • *adj.* **1** (of a person) lying face upward.
■ having the front or ventral part upward. ■ (of the hand) with the palm upward. Cf. PRONE. **2** failing to act or protest as a result of moral weakness or indolence: *the government was supine in the face of racial injustice.*
DERIVATIVES: **su•pine•ly** *adv.* **su•pine•ness** *n.*

sup•plant |sə'plænt| • *v.* [trans.] supersede and replace: *the socialist society that Marx believed would eventually supplant capitalism.*
DERIVATIVES: **sup•plant•er** *n.*

sup•ple |'səpəl| • *adj.* (**suppler, supplest**) bending and moving easily and gracefully; flexible: *her supple fingers* | *my mind is becoming more supple.*
■ not stiff or hard; easily manipulated: *this body oil leaves your skin feeling deliciously supple.* • *v.* [trans.] make more flexible.
DERIVATIVES: **sup•ple•ly** |'səp(ə)lē| (also **supply**) *adv.* **sup•ple•ness** *n.*

sup•pli•ant |'səplēənt| • *n.* a person making a humble plea to someone in power or authority. • adj. making or expressing a plea, esp. to someone in power or authority: *their faces were suppliant.*

DERIVATIVES: **sup•pli•ant•ly** adv.

sup•pli•cate |'səpli‚kāt| • v. [intrans.] ask or beg for something earnestly or humbly:[with infinitive] *they supplicated to be made peers.*

■ [trans.] ask or beg (someone) for something: *he supplicated them earnestly.* ■ [trans.] ask or beg (something) from someone.

DERIVATIVES: **sup•pli•cant** |-kənt| adj. & n. **sup•pli•ca•tion** |‚səpli'kāsHən| n. **sup•pli•ca•to•ry** |-kə‚tōrē| adj.

sup•po•si•tion |‚səpə'zisHən| • n. an uncertain belief: *working on the supposition that his death was murder.*

DERIVATIVES: **sup•po•si•tion•al** |-SHənl| adj.

sup•po•si•tious |‚səpə'zisHəs| • adj. **1** based on assumption rather than fact: *most of the evidence is purely suppositious.* **2** supposititious.

DERIVATIVES: **sup•po•si•tious•ly** adv. **sup•po•si•tious•ness** n.

sup•pos•i•ti•tious |sə‚päzə'tisHəs| • adj. **1** substituted for the real thing; not genuine: *the supposititious heir to the throne.* **2** suppositious.

DERIVATIVES: **sup•pos•i•ti•tious•ly** adv. **sup•pos•i•ti•tious•ness** n.

sup•press |sə'pres| • v. [trans.] forcibly put an end to: *the uprising was savagely suppressed.*

■ prevent the development, action, or expression of (a feeling, impulse, idea, etc.); restrain: *she could not suppress a rising panic.* ■ prevent the dissemination of (information): *the report had been suppressed.* ■ prevent or inhibit (a process or reaction): *use of the drug suppressed the immune response.* ■ partly or wholly eliminate (electrical interference). ■ consciously inhibit (an unpleasant idea or memory) to avoid considering it. Cf. OPPRESS, REPRESS.

DERIVATIVES: **sup•press•i•ble** adj. **sup•pres•sion** n. **sup•pres•sive** |-siv| adj. **sup•pres•sor** |-sər| n.

sup•pu•rate |'səpyə‚rāt| • v. [intrans.] undergo the formation of pus; fester.

DERIVATIVES: **sup•pu•ra•tion** |‚səpyə'rāsHən| n. **sup•pu•ra•tive** |-‚rātiv| adj.

su•ra |'soŏrə| (also **surah**) • n. a chapter or section of the Koran.

su•ral |'soŏrəl| • adj. of or relating to the calf of the leg.

sur•cease |sər'sēs| • n. the action or act of bringing something to an end; cessation: *he teased us without surcease.*

■ relief or consolation: *drugs are taken to provide surcease from intolerable psychic pain.* • v. [intrans.] cease.

surd |sərd| • adj. **1** (in mathematics, of a number) irrational. **2** (of a speech sound) uttered with the breath and not the voice (e.g., *f, k, p, s, t*). • n. **1** a surd number, esp. the irrational root of an integer (e.g., 2). **2** a surd consonant.

sure•ty |'sHoŏritē| • n. (pl. **-ies**) a person who takes responsibility for another's performance of an undertaking, for example their

appearing in court or paying of a debt; a guarantor.

■ money given to support an undertaking that someone will perform a duty, pay debts, etc.; a guarantee: *the judge granted bail with a surety of $500.* ■ the state of being sure or certain of something: *I was enmeshed in the surety of my impending fatherhood.*

DERIVATIVES: **sur•e•ty•ship** |-‚sHip| n.

sur•feit |'sərfət| • n. [usu. in sing.] an excessive amount of something: *a surfeit of food and drink.*

■ an illness caused or regarded as being caused by excessive eating or drinking: *he died of a surfeit.* • v. (**surfeited, surfeiting**) [trans.] (usu. **be surfeited with**) cause (someone) to desire no more of something as a result of having consumed or done it to excess: *I am surfeited with shopping.* ■ [intrans.] consume too much of something: *he never surfeited on rich wine.*

sur•fi•cial |sər'fisHəl| • adj. of or relating to the earth's surface: *surficial deposits.*

DERIVATIVES: **sur•fi•cial•ly** adv.

sur•mise |sər'mīz| • v. [intrans.] [usu. with clause] suppose that something is true without having evidence to confirm it: *he surmised that something must be wrong* | [with direct speech] *"I don't think they're locals," she surmised.* • n. |sər'mīz; 'sər‚mīz| a supposition that something may be true, even though there is no evidence to confirm it: *Charles was glad to have his surmise confirmed* | *all these observations remain surmise.*

sur•mount |sər'mownt| • v. [trans.] **1** overcome (a difficulty or obstacle): *all manner of cultural differences were surmounted.* **2** (usu. **be surmounted**) stand or be placed on top of: *the tomb was surmounted by a sculptured angel.*

DERIVATIVES: **sur•mount•a•ble** adj.

sur•pass |sər'pæs| • v. [trans.] exceed; be greater than: *prewar levels of production were surpassed in 1956.*

■ be better than: *he continued to surpass me at all games.* ■ (**surpass oneself**) do or be better than ever before: *the organist was surpassing himself.* ■ [as adj.] (**surpassing**) incomparable or outstanding: *a picture of surpassing beauty.*

DERIVATIVES: **sur•pass•a•ble** adj. **sur•pass•ing•ly** adv.

sur•plice |'sərplis| • n. a loose white linen vestment varying from hip-length to calf-length, worn over a cassock by clergy, acolytes, and choristers at Christian church services.

sur•re•al |sə'rēəl| • adj. having the qualities of surrealism; bizarre: *a surreal mix of fact and fantasy.*

DERIVATIVES: **sur•re•al•i•ty** |‚sərē'ælitē| n. **sur•re•al•ly** adv.

sur•re•al•ism |sə'rēə‚lizəm| • n. a 20th-century avant-garde movement in art and literature that sought to release the creative potential of the unconscious mind, for example by the irrational juxtaposition of images and the creation of mysterious symbols.

DERIVATIVES: **sur•re•al•ist** n. & adj. **sur•**

re•al•is•tic |sə,rēə'listik| *adj.* **sur•re•al•is•ti•cal•ly** |sə,rēə'listik(ə)lē| *adv.*

sur•rep•ti•tious |,sərəp'tisHəs| • *adj.* kept secret, esp. because it would not be approved of: *they carried on a surreptitious affair.*
DERIVATIVES: **sur•rep•ti•tious•ly** *adv.* **sur•rep•ti•tious•ness** *n.*

sur•ro•gate |'sərəgit; -,gāt| • *n.* a substitute, esp. a person deputizing for another in a specific role or office: *she was regarded as the surrogate for the governor during his final illness.*
■ (in the Christian Church) a bishop's deputy who grants marriage licenses. ■ a judge in charge of probate, inheritance, and guardianship.

sur•tax |'sər,tæks| • *n.* an additional tax on something already taxed, esp. a higher rate of tax on incomes above a certain level.

sur•veil•lance |sər'vāləns| • *n.* close observation, esp. of a suspected spy or criminal: *he found himself put **under surveillance** by military intelligence.*

sus•cep•ti•ble |sə'septəbəl| • *adj.* **1** likely or liable to be influenced or harmed by a particular thing: *patients with liver disease may be **susceptible to** infection.*
■ (of a person) easily influenced by feelings or emotions; sensitive: *they only do it to tease him—he's too susceptible.* **2** [predic.] (**susceptible of**) capable or admitting of: *the problem is not susceptible of a simple solution.*
DERIVATIVES: **sus•cep•ti•bly** |-blē| *adv.*

sus•pen•sion |sə'spensHən| • *n.* **1** the action of suspending someone or something or the condition of being suspended, in particular:
■ the temporary prevention of something from continuing or being in force or effect: *the suspension of military action.* ■ the official prohibition of someone from holding their usual post or carrying out their usual role for a particular length of time: *the investigation led to the suspension of several officers | a four-game suspension.* ■ (in music) a discord made by prolonging a note of a chord into the following chord. **2** the system of springs and shock absorbers by which a vehicle is supported on its wheels: *the car's rear suspension.* **3** a mixture in which particles are dispersed throughout the bulk of a fluid: *a suspension of corn starch in peanut oil.* Cf. COLLOID.
■ the state of being dispersed in such a way: *the agitator in the vat keeps the slurry **in suspension**.*

sus•pire |sə'spīr| • *v.* [intrans.] breathe, esp. out.
■ [intrans.] sigh.
DERIVATIVES: **sus•pi•ra•tion** |,səspə'rā-sHən| *n.*

sus•tain |sə'stān| • *v.* [trans.] **1** strengthen or support physically or mentally: *this thought had sustained him throughout the years | [as adj.] (sustaining) a sustaining breakfast of bacon and eggs.*
■ cause to continue or be prolonged for an extended period or without interruption: *he cannot sustain a normal conversation | [as adj.] (sustained) several years of sustained economic growth.* ■ (of a performer) represent (a part or character) convincingly: *he sustained the role with burly resilience.* ■ bear (the weight of an object) without breaking or falling: *he sagged against her so that she could barely sustain his weight | his health will no longer enable him to sustain the heavy burdens of office.* **2** undergo or suffer (something unpleasant, esp. an injury): *he died after sustaining severe head injuries.* **3** uphold, affirm, or confirm the justice or validity of: *the allegations of discrimination were sustained. the judge sustained the objection.* • *n.* an effect or facility on a keyboard or electronic musical instrument whereby a note can be sustained after the key is released.
DERIVATIVES: **sus•tain•ed•ly** |-nidlē| *adv.* **sus•tain•er** *n.* **sus•tain•ment** *n.*

sus•te•nance |'səstənəns| • *n.* food and drink regarded as a source of strength; nourishment: *poor rural economies turned to potatoes for sustenance.*
■ the maintaining of someone or something in life or existence: *he kept two or three cows for the sustenance of his family | the sustenance of democracy.*

su•sur•rus |soo'sərəs| (also **susurration** |,soosə'rāsHən|) • *n.* whispering, murmuring, or rustling: *the susurrus of the stream.*
DERIVATIVES: **su•sur•rant** |soo'sərənt| *adj.* **su•sur•rate** |'soosə,rāt; soo'sər,āt| *v.* **su•sur•rous** |soo'sərəs| *adj.*

sut•tee |sə'tē; 'soo,tē| (also **sati**) • *n.* (pl. **suttees** or **satis** |sə'tēz; 'sə,tēz|) the former Hindu practice of a widow immolating herself on her husband's funeral pyre.
■ a widow who committed such an act.

su•ze•rain |'soozərən; -,rān| • *n.* a sovereign or state having some control over another state that is internally autonomous.
■ a feudal overlord.
DERIVATIVES: **su•ze•rain•ty** |-rəntē; -,rān-tē| *n.*

svelte |svelt; sfelt| • *adj.* (of a person) slender and elegant.

Sven•ga•li |sven'gälē; sfen-| a musician in George du Maurier's novel *Trilby* (1894) who trains Trilby's voice and controls her stage singing hypnotically.
■ [as n.] (**a Svengali**) a person who exercises a controlling or mesmeric influence on another, esp. for a sinister purpose.

swain |swān| • *n.* a country youth.
■ a young lover or suitor.

swale |swāl| • *n.* a low or hollow place, esp. a marshy depression between ridges.

swa•mi |'swämē| • *n.* (pl. **swamis**) a Hindu male religious teacher: [as title] *Swami Satchidananda.*

swank |swæNGk| • *v.* [intrans.] display one's wealth, knowledge, or achievements in a way that is intended to impress others: *swanking about, playing the dashing young master spy.* • *n.* behavior, talk, or display intended to impress others: *a little money will buy you a good deal of swank.* • *adj.* (also **swanky**) imposing, stylish, or posh: *coming out of some swank nightclub.*

swan song • *n.* a person's final public perfor-

mance or professional activity before retirement: *he has decided to make this tour his swan song.*
■ any final effort, as before death, etc.
sward |swôrd| • *n.* an expanse of short grass.
■ the upper layer of soil, esp. when covered with grass.
DERIVATIVES: **sward•ed** *adj.*
swarth•y |ˈswôrᴛHē| • *adj.* (**swarthier, swarthiest**) (also **swart**) dark-skinned: *she looked frail standing next to her strong and swarthy brother.*
DERIVATIVES: **swarth•i•ly** |-ᴛHəlē| *adv.* **swarth•i•ness** *n.*
swathe |swäᴛH; swäᴛH| • *v.* [trans.] (usu. **be swathed in**) wrap in several layers of fabric: *his hands were swathed in bandages.* • *n.* a piece or strip of material in which something is wrapped.
swel•ter |ˈsweltər| • *v.* [intrans.] (of a person or the atmosphere at a particular time or place) be uncomfortably hot: *Barney sweltered in his doorman's uniform* | [as adj.] (**sweltering**) *the sweltering afternoon heat.* • *n.* [in sing.] an uncomfortably hot atmosphere: *the swelter of an August day.*
DERIVATIVES: **swel•ter•ing•ly** *adv.*
swinge |swinj| • *v.* (**swingeing** |ˈswinjiNG|) [trans.] strike hard; beat.
swiv•et |ˈswivit| • *n.* [in sing.] a fluster or panic: *the incomprehensible did not throw him into a swivet.*
syb•a•rite |ˈsibəˌrīt| • *n.* a person who is self-indulgent in his or her fondness for sensuous luxury.
DERIVATIVES: **syb•a•rit•ic** *adj.* **syb•a•rit•ism** |-rīˌtizəm| *n.*
syc•o•phant |ˈsikəfənt; -ˌfænt| • *n.* a person who acts obsequiously toward someone in order to gain advantage; a servile flatterer.
DERIVATIVES: **syc•o•phan•cy** |-fənsē; -ˌfænsē| *n.* **syc•o•phan•tic** |ˌsikəˈfæn(t)ik| *adj.* **syc•o•phan•ti•cal•ly** |ˌsikəˈfæn(t)-ik(ə)lē| *adv.*
syl•la•bar•y |ˈsiləˌberē| • *n.* (pl. **-ies**) a set of written characters representing syllables and (in some languages or stages of writing) serving the purpose of an alphabet.
syl•lab•ic |səˈlæbik| • *adj.* of, relating to, or based on syllables: *a system of syllabic symbols.*
■ (in prosody) based on the number of syllables in a line, etc.: *the recreation of classical syllabic verse.* ■ (of a consonant, esp. a nasal or other continuant) constituting a whole syllable, such as the *m* in *Mbabane* or the *l* in *bottle.* ■ articulated in syllables: *syllabic singing.* • *n.* a written character that represents a syllable: *Inuit syllabics.*
DERIVATIVES: **syl•lab•i•cal•ly** |-ik(ə)lē| *adv.* **syl•la•bic•i•ty** |ˌsiləˈbisitē| *n.*
syl•la•bus |ˈsiləbəs| • *n.* (pl. **syllabuses** or **syllabi** |-ˌbī|) an outline of the subjects in a course of study or teaching: *there isn't time to cover the syllabus* | *the history syllabus.*
syl•lep•sis |səˈlepsis| • *n.* (pl. **syllepses** |-sēz|) a figure of speech in which a word is applied to two others in different senses (e.g.,

caught the train and a bad cold) or to two others of which it grammatically suits only one (e.g., *neither they nor it is working*). Cf. ZEUGMA.
DERIVATIVES: **syl•lep•tic** |-tik| *adj.*
syl•lo•gism |ˈsiləˌjizəm| • *n.* an instance of a form of reasoning in which a conclusion is drawn (whether validly or not) from two given or assumed propositions (premises) that each share a term with the conclusion, and that share a common or middle term not present in the conclusion (e.g., *all dogs are animals; all animals have four legs; therefore all dogs have four legs*).
■ deductive reasoning as distinct from induction: *logic is rules or syllogism.*
DERIVATIVES: **syl•lo•gis•tic** |ˌsiləˈjistik| *adj.* **syl•lo•gis•ti•cal•ly** |ˌsiləˈjistik(ə)lē| *adv.*
sylph |silf| • *n.* an imaginary spirit of the air.
■ a slender woman or girl.
syl•van |ˈsilvən| (also **silvan**) • *adj.* consisting of or associated with woods; wooded: *trees and contours all add to a sylvan setting.*
■ pleasantly rural or pastoral: *vistas of sylvan charm.*
sym•bi•o•sis |ˌsimbēˈōsis; -bī-| • *n.* (pl. **symbioses** |-ˌsēz|) (in biology) interaction between two different organisms living in close physical association, typically to the advantage of both; distinguished from *antibiosis,* in which one organism is harmed.
■ a mutually beneficial relationship between different people or groups: *a perfect mother and daughter symbiosis.*
DERIVATIVES: **sym•bi•ot•ic** |-ˈätik| *adj.* **sym•bi•ot•i•cal•ly** |-ˈätik(ə)lē| *adv.*
sym•bol•ism |ˈsimbəˌlizəm| • *n.* the use of symbols to represent ideas or qualities: *in China, symbolism in gardens achieved great subtlety.*
■ symbolic meaning attributed to natural objects or facts: *the symbolism of flowers.*
■ (also **Symbolism**) an artistic and poetic movement or style using symbolic images and indirect suggestion to express mystical ideas, emotions, and states of mind.
DERIVATIVES: **sym•bol•ist** *n.* & *adj.*
sym•bol•o•gy |simˈbäləjē| • *n.* the study or use of symbols.
■ symbols collectively: *the use of religious symbology.*
sym•me•try |ˈsimitrē| • *n.* (pl. **-ies**) the quality of being made up of exactly similar parts facing each other or around an axis: *this series has a line of symmetry through its center* | *a crystal structure with hexagonal symmetry.*
■ correct or pleasing proportion of the parts of a thing: *an overall symmetry making the poem pleasant to the ear.* ■ similarity or exact correspondence between different things: *a lack of symmetry between men and women* | *history sometimes exhibits weird symmetries between events.* ■ (in physics and mathematics) a law or operation where a physical property or process has an equivalence in two or more directions.
DERIVATIVES: **sym•me•trize** |-ˌtrīz| *v.*
sym•pa•thet•ic |ˌsimpəˈᴛHeṯik| • *adj.* **1** feeling, showing, or expressing sympathy: *he was*

sympathetic toward staff with family problems | *he spoke in a sympathetic tone.*
■ [predic.] showing approval of or favor toward an idea or action: *he was* **sympathetic to** *evolutionary ideas.* **2** pleasant or agreeable, in particular: ■ (of a person) attracting the liking of others: *Audrey develops as a sympathetic character.* ■ (of a structure) designed in a sensitive or fitting way: *buildings that were* **sympathetic to** *their surroundings.* **3** relating to or denoting the part of the autonomic nervous system consisting of nerves arising from ganglia near the middle part of the spinal cord, supplying the internal organs, blood vessels, and glands, and balancing the action of the parasympathetic nerves. **4** relating to, producing, or denoting an effect that arises in response to a similar action elsewhere: *the deep bell set off sympathetic vibrations throughout the room.*
DERIVATIVES: **sym•pa•thet•i•cal•ly** |-ik-(ə)lē| *adv.*

sym•pa•thy |'simpəTHē| • *n.* (pl. **-ies**) **1** feelings of pity and sorrow for someone else's misfortune: *they had great* **sympathy for** *the flood victims.* Cf. EMPATHY.
■ (**one's sympathies**) formal expression of such feelings; condolences: *all Tony's friends joined in sending their sympathies to his widow Jean.* **2** understanding between people; common feeling: *the special sympathy between the two boys was obvious to all.*
■ (**sympathies**) support in the form of shared feelings or opinions: *his sympathies lay with his constituents.* ■ agreement with or approval of an opinion or aim; a favorable attitude: *I have some* **sympathy for** *this view.* ■ (**in sympathy**) relating harmoniously to something else; in keeping: *repairs had to be in* **sympathy with** *the original structure.* ■ the state or fact of responding in a way similar or corresponding to an action elsewhere: *the magnetic field oscillates* **in sympathy.**

sym•po•si•um |sim'pōzēəm| • *n.* (pl. **symposia** |-zēə| or **symposiums**) a conference or meeting to discuss a particular subject.
■ a collection of essays or papers on a particular subject by a number of contributors. ■ a drinking party or convivial discussion, esp. as held in ancient Greece after a banquet (and notable as the title of a work by Plato).

syn•apse |'sin,æps| • *n.* a junction between two nerve cells, consisting of a minute gap across which impulses pass by diffusion of a (chemical) neurotransmitter.

syn•chron•ic |siNG'kränik| • *adj.* concerned with something, esp. a language, as it exists at one point in time: *synchronic linguistics.*
DERIVATIVES: **syn•chron•i•cal•ly** |-ik(ə)-lē| *adv.*

syn•chro•nic•i•ty |,siNGkrə'nisitē| • *n.* **1** the simultaneous occurrence of events that appear significantly related but have no discernible causal connection: *the death of the old lord and the birth of his heir on the same day demonstrated a striking synchronicity.* **2** another term for SYNCHRONY (sense 1).

syn•chro•nize |'siNGkrə,nīz| • *v.* [trans.] cause to occur or operate at the same time or rate: *soldiers used watches to synchronize movements* | *synchronize your hand gestures with your main points.*
■ [intrans.] occur at the same time or rate: *sometimes converging swells will synchronize to produce a peak.* ■ adjust (a clock or watch) to show the same time as another: *It is now 5:48. Synchronize watches.* ■ [intrans.] tally; agree: *their version failed to synchronize with the police view.* ■ coordinate; combine: *both media* **synchronize** *national interests* **with** *multinational scope.*
DERIVATIVES: **syn•chro•ni•za•tion** |,siNGkrənə'zāSHən| *n.* **syn•chro•niz•er** *n.*

syn•chro•nous |'siNGkrənəs| • *adj.* **1** existing or occurring at the same time: *glaciations were approximately synchronous in both hemispheres.* **2** (of a satellite or its orbit) making or denoting an orbit around the earth or another celestial body in which one revolution is completed in the period taken for the body to rotate about its axis.
DERIVATIVES: **syn•chro•nous•ly** *adv.*

syn•chro•ny |'siNGkrənē| • *n.* **1** simultaneous action, development, or occurrence.
■ the state of operating or developing according to the same time scale as something else: *some individuals do not remain in synchrony with the twenty-four-hour day.* **2** synchronic treatment or study: *the structuralist distinction between synchrony and diachrony.*

syn•co•pate |'siNGkə,pāt| • *v.* [trans.] **1** (usu. as adj.) (**syncopated**) displace the beats or accents in (music or a rhythm) so that strong beats become weak and vice versa: *syncopated dance music.* **2** shorten (a word) by dropping sounds or letters in the middle, as in *symbology* for *symbolology,* or *Gloster* for *Gloucester.*
DERIVATIVES: **syn•co•pa•tion** |,siNGkə'pāSHən| *n.* **syn•co•pa•tor** |-,pātər| *n.*

syn•co•pe |'siNGkəpē| • *n.* **1** temporary loss of consciousness caused by a fall in blood pressure. **2** the omission of sounds or letters from within a word, e.g., when *library* is pronounced .
DERIVATIVES: **syn•co•pal** |-pəl| *adj.*

syn•cre•tism |'siNGkrə,tizəm| • *n.* **1** the amalgamation or attempted amalgamation of different religions, cultures, or schools of thought. **2** (in linguistics) the merging of different inflectional varieties of a word during the development of a language.
DERIVATIVES: **syn•cret•ic** |siNG'kretik| *adj.* **syn•cre•tist** *n. & adj.* **syn•cre•tis•tic** |,siNGkrə'tistik| *adj.*

syn•di•cate • *n.* |'sindikit| a group of individuals or organizations combined to promote some common interest: *large-scale buyouts involving a syndicate of financial institutions* | *a crime syndicate.*
■ an association or agency supplying material simultaneously to a number of newspapers or periodicals. ■ a committee of syndics. • *v.* |'sində,kāt| [trans.] (usu. **be syndicated**) control or manage by a syndicate: *the loans are syndicated to a group of banks.*
■ publish or broadcast (material) simultane-

ously in a number of newspapers, television stations, etc.: *his reports were syndicated to 200 other papers.* ■ sell (a horse) to a syndicate: *the stallion was syndicated for a record $5.4 million.* DERIVATIVES: **syn•di•ca•tion** |ˌsindiˈkā-SHən| *n.* **syn•di•ca•tor** |-ˌkātər| *n.*

syn•drome |ˈsinˌdrōm| • *n.* a group of symptoms that consistently occur together, or a condition characterized by a set of associated symptoms: *a rare syndrome in which the production of white blood cells is damaged.*
■ a characteristic combination of opinions, emotions, or behavior: *the "Not In My Back Yard" syndrome.* DERIVATIVES: **syn•drom•ic** |sinˈdrämik| *adj.*

syn•ec•do•che |səˈnekdəkē| • *n.* a figure of speech in which a part is made to represent the whole or vice versa, as in *Cleveland won by six runs* (meaning "Cleveland's baseball team"). DERIVATIVES: **syn•ec•doch•ic** |ˌsiˈnekˈdäkik| *adj.* **syn•ec•doch•i•cal** |ˌsinekˈdäkikəl| *adj.* **syn•ec•doch•i•cal•ly** |ˌsinekˈdäkik(ə)lē| *adv.*

syn•er•gy |ˈsinərjē| (also **synergism** |-ˌjizəm|) • *n.* the interaction or cooperation of two or more organizations, substances, or other agents to produce a combined effect greater than the sum of their separate effects: *the synergy between artist and record company.* DERIVATIVES: **syn•er•get•ic** |ˌsinərˈjetik| *adj.* **syn•er•gic** |səˈnərjik| *adj.* **syn•er•gis•tic** *adj.*

syn•od |ˈsinəd| • *n.* **1** an assembly of the clergy and sometimes also the laity in a diocese or other division of a particular Christian church. **2** a Presbyterian ecclesiastical court above the presbyteries and subject to the General Assembly. DERIVATIVES: **syn•od•al** *adj.* **syn•od•ic** *adj.* **syn•od•i•cal•ly** *adv.*

syn•o•nym |ˈsinəˌnim| • *n.* a word or phrase that means exactly or nearly the same as another word or phrase in the same language, for example *shut* is a synonym of *close.*
■ a person or thing so closely associated with a particular quality or idea that the mention of its name calls it to mind: *the Victorian age is a synonym for sexual puritanism.* ■ a taxonomic name that has the same application as another, esp. one that has been superseded and is no longer valid. DERIVATIVES: **syn•o•nym•ic** |ˌsinəˈnimik| *adj.* **syn•o•nym•i•ty** |ˌsinəˈnimitē| *n.* **syn•on•y•mous** *adj.* **syn•on•y•my** *n.*

syn•op•sis |səˈnäpsis| • *n.* (pl. **synopses** |-ˌsēz|) a brief summary or general survey of something: *a synopsis of the accident.*
■ an outline of the plot of a play, film, or book. DERIVATIVES: **syn•op•size** |-ˌsīz| *v.*

syn•op•tic |səˈnäptik| • *adj.* **1** of or forming a general summary or synopsis: *a synoptic outline of the contents.*
■ taking or involving a comprehensive mental view: *a synoptic model of higher education.* **2** of or relating to the Synoptic Gospels (the first three Gospels, Matthew, Mark, and Luke,

which give more or less similar accounts). • *n.* (**Synoptics**) the Synoptic Gospels. DERIVATIVES: **syn•op•ti•cal** *adj.* **syn•op•ti•cal•ly** |-ik(ə)lē| *adv.*

syn•tac•tic |sinˈtaktik| • *adj.* of or according to syntax: *syntactic analysis.* DERIVATIVES: **syn•tac•ti•cal** *adj.* **syn•tac•ti•cal•ly** |-ik(ə)lē| *adv.*

syn•tax |ˈsinˌtaks| • *n.* the arrangement of words and phrases to create well-formed sentences in a language: *the syntax of English.*
■ a set of rules for or an analysis of this: *generative syntax.* ■ the branch of linguistics that deals with this.

syn•the•sis |ˈsinTHəsis| • *n.* (pl. **syntheses** |-ˌsēz|) combination or composition, in particular:
■ the combination of ideas to form a theory or system: *the synthesis of intellect and emotion in his work | the ideology represented a synthesis of certain ideas.* Often contrasted with ANALYSIS.
■ the production of chemical compounds by reaction from simpler materials: *the synthesis of methanol from carbon monoxide and hydrogen.* ■ (in Hegelian philosophy) the final stage in the process of dialectical reasoning, in which a new idea resolves the conflict between THESIS and ANTITHESIS. ■ the process of making compound and derivative words. ■ the use of inflected forms rather than word order to express grammatical structure. DERIVATIVES: **syn•the•sist** *n.*

syn•thet•ic |sinˈTHetik| • *adj.* relating to or using synthesis.
■ (of a substance) made by chemical synthesis, esp. to imitate a natural product: *synthetic rubber.* ■ (of an emotion or action) not genuine; insincere: *their tears are a bit synthetic.* ■ (of a proposition in logic) having truth or falsity determinable by recourse to experience. Cf. ANALYTIC. ■ (of a language) characterized by the use of inflections rather than word order to express grammatical structure. Cf. ANALYTIC. • *n.* (usu. **synthetics**) a synthetic material or chemical, esp. a textile fiber. DERIVATIVES: **syn•thet•i•cal** *adj.* **syn•thet•i•cal•ly** |-ik(ə)lē| *adv.*

sys•tem•ic |səˈstemik| • *adj.* **1** of or relating to a system, esp. as opposed to a particular part: *the disease is localized rather than systemic.*
■ (of an insecticide, fungicide, or similar substance) entering the plant via the roots or shoots and passing through the tissues. **2** denoting the part of the circulatory system concerned with the transportation of oxygen to and carbon dioxide from the body in general, esp. as distinct from the pulmonary part concerned with the transportation of oxygen from and carbon dioxide to the lungs. DERIVATIVES: **sys•tem•i•cal•ly** |-ik(ə)lē| *adv.*

syz•y•gy |ˈsizijē| • *n.* (pl. **-ies**) (in astronomy) a conjunction or opposition, esp. of the moon with the sun: *the planets were aligned in syzygy.*
■ a pair of connected or corresponding things: *animus and anima represent a supreme pair of opposites, the syzygy.* DERIVATIVES: **sy•zyg•i•al** *adj.*

Tt

tab•er•nac•le |ˈtæbərˌnækəl| • *n.* **1** (in biblical use) a fixed or movable habitation, typically of light construction. ■ a tent used as a sanctuary for the Ark of the Covenant by the Israelites during the Exodus and until the building of the Temple. **2** a meeting place for worship used by some Protestants or Mormons. **3** an ornamented receptacle or cabinet in which a pyx or ciborium containing the reserved sacrament may be placed in Catholic churches, usually on or above an altar. ■ a canopied niche or recess in the wall of a church.
DERIVATIVES: **tab•er•nac•led** *adj.*

ta•bes•cent |təˈbesənt| • *adj.* wasting away.

tab•la•ture |ˈtæbləCHər| • *n.* a form of musical notation indicating fingering rather than the pitch of notes, written on lines corresponding to, for example, the strings of a lute or the holes on a flute.

tab•leau |ˌtæˈblō| • *n.* (pl. **tableaux** |-ˈblōz|) a group of models or motionless figures representing a scene from a story or from history; a tableau vivant. ■ more generally, a picture; a picturesque presentation or description.

tab•leau vi•vant |täˈblō vēˈväN; -ˈvänt| • *n.* (pl. **tableaux vivants** |täˈblō vēˈväN; -ˈvänt| pronunc. same) a silent and motionless group of people arranged to represent a scene or incident.

tab•u•lar |ˈtæbyələr| • *adj.* **1** (of data) consisting of or presented in columns or tables: *a tabular presentation of running costs.* **2** broad and flat like the top of a table: *a huge tabular iceberg.* ■ (of a crystal) relatively broad and thin, with two well-developed parallel faces.
DERIVATIVES: **tab•u•lar•ly** *adv.*

ta•bu•la ra•sa |ˈtäbyo͞olə ˈräsə; ˈräzə| • *n.* (pl. **tabulae rasae**) an absence of preconceived ideas or predetermined goals; a clean slate: *the team did not have complete freedom and a tabula rasa on which to work.* ■ the human mind, esp. at birth, viewed as having no innate ideas.

tab•u•late |ˈtæbyəˌlāt| • *v.* [trans.] arrange (data) in the form of a table; draw up a table: [as adj.] (**tabulated**) *tabulated results.*
DERIVATIVES: **tab•u•la•tion** |ˌtæbyəˈlāSHən| *n.*

ta•cet |ˈtāsit; ˈtæs-; ˈtäket| • *v.* [intrans.] (as a musical direction) indicating that a voice or instrument is silent.

ta•chom•e•ter |taˈkämitər; tə-| • *n.* an instrument that measures the working speed of an engine (esp. in a road vehicle), typically in revolutions per minute (RPM).

tac•it |ˈtæsit| • *adj.* understood or implied without being stated: *your silence may be taken as tacit agreement.*
DERIVATIVES: **tac•it•ly** *adv.*

tac•i•turn |ˈtæsiˌtərn| • *adj.* (of a person) reserved or uncommunicative in speech; saying little.
DERIVATIVES: **tac•i•tur•ni•ty** |ˌtæsəˈtərnitē| *n.* **tac•i•turn•ly** *adv.*

tack |tæk| • *n.* (in sailing) an act of changing course by turning a vessel's head into and through the wind, so as to bring the wind on the opposite side. ■ a boat's course relative to the direction of the wind: *the brig bowled past **on the** opposite **tack.*** ■ a distance sailed between such changes of course. ■ a method of dealing with a situation or problem; a course of action or policy: *as she could not stop him from going she tried another tack and insisted on going with him.* • *v.* [intrans.] change course by turning a boat's head into and through the wind. Cf. JIBE. ■ [trans.] alter the course of (a boat) in such a way. ■ [with adverbial of direction] make a series of such changes of course while sailing: *she spent the entire night tacking back and forth.* ■ make a change in one's conduct, policy, or direction of attention: *he answered, but she had tacked and was off in a new direction.*
DERIVATIVES: **tack•er** *n.*

tack•y[1] |ˈtækē| • *adj.* (**tackier, tackiest**) (of glue, paint, or other substances) retaining a slightly sticky feel; not fully dry: *the paint was still tacky.*
DERIVATIVES: **tack•i•ness** *n.*

tack•y[2] • *adj.* (**tackier, tackiest**) showing poor taste and quality: *even in her faintly tacky costumes, she won our hearts.*
DERIVATIVES: **tack•i•ly** |ˈtækəlē| *adv.* **tack•i•ness** *n.*

tact |tækt| • *n.* adroitness and sensitivity in dealing with others or with difficult issues: *the inspector broke the news to me with tact and consideration.*

tac•tic |ˈtæktik| • *n.* an action or strategy carefully planned to achieve a specific end. ■ (**tactics**) [also treated as sing.] the art of disposing armed forces in order of battle and of organizing operations, esp. during contact with an enemy.
DERIVATIVES: **tac•ti•cian** |tækˈtiSHən| *n.*

tac•ti•cal |ˈtæktikəl| • *adj.* of, relating to, or constituting actions carefully planned to gain a specific military end: *as a tactical officer in the field he had no equal.* ■ (of bombing or weapons) done or for use in immediate support of military or naval operations. Cf. STRATEGIC. ■ (of a person or his or her actions) showing adroit planning; aiming at an end beyond the immediate action: *in a tactical retreat, she moved into a hotel with her daughters.*
DERIVATIVES: **tac•ti•cal•ly** |-ik(ə)lē| *adv.*

tac•tile |ˈtæktl; ˈtækˌtīl| • *adj.* of or connected with the sense of touch: *vocal and visual signals become less important as tactile signals intensify.*

■ perceptible by touch or apparently so; tangible: *she had a distinct, almost tactile memory.* ■ designed to be perceived by touch: *tactile exhibitions help blind people enjoy the magic of sculpture.* ■ (of a person) given to touching others, esp. as an unselfconscious expression of sympathy or affection.
DERIVATIVES: **tac•til•i•ty** |tæk'tilitē| *n.*

taint |tānt| • *n.* a trace of a bad or undesirable quality or substance: *the taint of corruption.*
■ a thing whose influence or effect is perceived as contaminating or undesirable: *the taint that threatens to stain most of the company's other partners.* ■ an unpleasant smell: *the lingering taint of creosote.* • *v.* [trans.] (often **be tainted**) contaminate or pollute (something): *the air was tainted by fumes from the cars.*
■ affect with a bad or undesirable quality: *his administration was often tainted by scandal.* ■ [intrans.] (of food or water) become contaminated or polluted.
DERIVATIVES: **taint•less** *adj.*

take•o•ver |'tāk,ōvər| • *n.* an act of assuming control of something, esp. the buying out of one company by another.
■ a (usually forcible) assumption of government or military power; coup.

tal•is•man |'tælismən; -iz-| • *n.* (pl. **talismans** |'tæləsmənz|) an object, typically an inscribed ring or stone, that is thought to have magic powers and to bring good luck.
DERIVATIVES: **tal•is•man•ic** |ˌtæliz'mænik| *adj.*

Tal•mud |'täl,mŏod; 'tælməd| • *n.* (**the Talmud**) the body of Jewish civil and ceremonial law, debates, commentaries, and legend comprising the Mishnah (the 'Oral Law') and the Gemara. There are two versions of the Talmud: the Babylonian Talmud (which dates from the 5th century AD but includes earlier material) and the earlier Palestinian or Jerusalem Talmud.
DERIVATIVES: **Tal•mud•ic** |tæl'm(y)ŏodik; -'mŏodik| *adj.* **Tal•mud•i•cal** |tæl'm(y)ŏodikəl; -'mŏod-| *adj.* **Tal•mud•ist** |'tälmŏokhdist; 'tælməd-| *n.*

tal•on |'tælən| • *n.* **1** a claw, esp. one belonging to a bird of prey. **2** the shoulder of a bolt against which the key presses to slide it in a lock. **3** (in various card games) the cards remaining undealt.
DERIVATIVES: **tal•oned** *adj.*

ta•lus • *n.* (pl. **taluses**) a sloping mass of rock fragments at the foot of a cliff.
■ the sloping side of an earthwork, or of a wall that tapers to the top.

tam•bour |'tæm,bŏor| • *n.* **1** a small drum. **2** something resembling a drum in shape or construction, in particular:
■ a circular frame for holding fabric taut while it is being embroidered. ■ a wall of circular plan, such as one supporting a dome or surrounded by a colonnade. ■ each of a sequence of cylindrical stones forming the shaft of a column. ■ [usu. as adj.] a sliding flexible shutter or door on a piece of furniture, made of strips of wood attached to a backing of canvas: *a desk with a tambour door.* • *v.* [trans.] [often as adj.] (**tamboured**) decorate or embroider on a tambour: *a tamboured waistcoat.*

tan•dem |'tændəm| • *n.* (also **tandem bicycle**) a bicycle with seats and pedals for two riders, one behind the other.
■ a carriage driven by two animals harnessed one in front of the other. ■ a group of two people or machines working together. ■ a truck with two rear drive axles.
■ (also **tandem trailer**) a combination truck whose tractor hauls two trailers, one after the other. • *adv.* with two or more horses harnessed one behind another: *I rode tandem to Paris.*
■ alongside each other; together. • *adj.* having two things arranged one in front of the other: *satisfactory steering angles can be maintained with tandem buses.*
PHRASES: **in tandem** alongside each other; together: *a tight fiscal policy working in tandem with a tight foreign exchange policy.* ■ one behind another.

tan•gent |'tænjənt| • *n.* **1** a straight line or plane that touches a curve or curved surface at a point, but if extended does not cross it at that point.
■ a completely different line of thought or action: *she went off on a tangent about how she and her husband had driven past a department store window.* **2** the trigonometric function that is equal to the ratio of the sides (other than the hypotenuse) opposite and adjacent to an angle in a right triangle. • *adj.* (of a line or plane) touching, but not intersecting, a curve or curved surface.
DERIVATIVES: **tan•gen•cy** |-jənsē| *n.*

tan•gen•tial |tæn'jenCHəl| • *adj.* of, relating to, or along a tangent: *a tangential line.*
■ diverging from a previous course or line; erratic: *tangential thoughts.* ■ hardly touching a matter; peripheral: *the reforms were tangential to efforts to maintain a basic standard of life.*
DERIVATIVES: **tan•gen•tial•ly** *adv.*

tan•gi•ble |'tænjəbəl| • *adj.* perceptible by touch: *the atmosphere of neglect and abandonment was almost tangible.*
■ clear and definite; real: *the emphasis is now on tangible results.* • *n.* (usu. **tangibles**) a thing that is perceptible by touch.
DERIVATIVES: **tan•gi•bil•i•ty** |ˌtænjə'bilitē| *n.* **tan•gi•ble•ness** *n.* **tan•gi•bly** |-blē| *adv.*

tan•ta•lize |'tæn(t)l,īz| • *v.* [trans.] torment or tease (someone) with the sight or promise of something that is unobtainable: *such ambitious questions have long tantalized the world's best thinkers.*
■ excite the senses or desires of (someone): *she still tantalized him* | [as adj.] (**tantalizing**) *the tantalizing fragrance of fried bacon.*
DERIVATIVES: **tan•ta•li•za•tion** |ˌtæn(t)li'zāSHən| *n.* **tan•ta•liz•er** *n.* **tan•ta•liz•ing•ly** *adv.*

tan•ta•mount |'tæn(t)ə,mownt| • *adj.* [predic.] (**tantamount to**) equivalent in seriousness to; virtually the same as: *the resignations were tantamount to an admission of guilt.*

Tao |dow; tow| • *n.* (in Chinese philosophy) the absolute principle underlying the universe, combining within itself the principles of yin and yang and signifying the way, or code of behavior, that is in harmony with the natural order. The interpretation of Tao in the Tao-te-Ching developed into the philosophical religion of Taoism.

tare[1] |ter| • *n.* **1** a vetch, esp. the common vetch (a scrambling plant of the pea family). **2** (**tares**) (in biblical use) an injurious weed resembling wheat when young (Matt. 13:24–30).

tare[2] • *n.* an allowance made for the weight of the packaging in order to determine the net weight of goods.
■ the weight of a motor vehicle, railroad car, or aircraft without its fuel or load.

tar•iff |ˈtærəf; ˈter-| • *n.* a tax or duty to be paid on a particular class of imports or exports.
■ a list of these taxes. ■ a table of the fixed charges made by a business, esp. in a hotel or restaurant. • *v.* [trans.] fix the price of (something) according to a tariff: *these services are tariffed by volume.*

tar•tar |ˈtärtər| • *n.* a hard calcified deposit that forms on the teeth and contributes to their decay.
■ a deposit of impure potassium hydrogen tartrate formed during the fermentation of wine. A byproduct of fermentation, *cream of tartar*, is used in baking powder. DERIVATIVES: **tar•tar•ic** |tärˈtærik; -ˈter-| *adj.*

tat•too |tæˈto͞o| • *n.* (pl. **tattoos**) an evening drum or bugle signal recalling soldiers to their quarters.
■ an entertainment consisting of music, marching, and the performance of displays and exercises by military personnel. ■ a rhythmic tapping or drumming.

tau•rine |ˈtô,rīn| • *adj.* of or like a bull.
■ of or relating to bullfighting: *taurine skill.*

tau•rom•a•chy |tôˈräməkē| • *n.* (pl. **-ies**) bullfighting.
■ a bullfight. DERIVATIVES: **tau•ro•ma•chi•an** |ˌtôrəˈmākēən| *adj.* **tau•ro•mach•ic** |ˌtôrəˈmækik| *adj.* .

taut |tôt| • *adj.* stretched or pulled tight; not slack: *the fabric stays taut without adhesive.*
■ (esp. of muscles or nerves) tense; not relaxed. ■ (of writing, music, etc.) concise and controlled: *a taut text of only a hundred and twenty pages.* ■ (of a ship) having a disciplined and efficient crew. DERIVATIVES: **taut•en** |ˈtôtn| *v.* **taut•ly** *adv.* **taut•ness** *n.*

tau•tol•o•gy |tôˈtäləjē| • *n.* (pl. **-ies**) the saying of the same thing twice in different words, generally considered to be a fault of style (e.g., *they arrived one after the other in succession*).
■ a phrase or expression in which the same thing is said twice in different words. ■ (in logic) a statement that is true by necessity or by virtue of its logical form.

DERIVATIVES: **tau•to•log•i•cal** |ˌtôtlˈäjikəl| *adj.* **tau•to•log•i•cal•ly** |ˌtôtlˈäjik(ə)lē| *adv.* **tau•tol•o•gist** |-jist| *n.* **tau•tol•o•gize** |-ˌjīz| *v.* **tau•tol•o•gous** |-gəs| *adj.*

taw•dry |ˈtôdrē| • *adj.* (**tawdrier, tawdriest**) showy but cheap and of poor quality: *tawdry jewelry.*
■ sordid or unpleasant: *the tawdry business of politics.* • *n.* cheap and gaudy finery. DERIVATIVES: **taw•dri•ly** |-drəlē| *adv.* **taw•dri•ness** *n.*

tax•on•o•my |tækˈsänəmē| • *n.* the branch of science concerned with classification, esp. of organisms; systematics.
■ the classification of something, esp. organisms: *the taxonomy of these fossils has been arduous.* ■ a scheme of classification: *a taxonomy of smells.* DERIVATIVES: **tax•o•nom•ic** |ˌtæksəˈnämik| *adj.* **tax•o•nom•i•cal** |ˌtæksəˈnämikəl| *adj.* **tax•o•nom•i•cal•ly** |ˌtæksəˈnämik(ə)lē| *adv.* **tax•on•o•mist** |-mist| *n.* **tax•on•o•mize** *v.*

tech•ni•cal |ˈteknikəl| • *adj.* **1** of or relating to a particular subject, art, or craft, or its techniques: *technical terms* | *a test of an artist's technical skill.*
■ (esp. of a book or article) requiring special knowledge to be understood: *a technical report.* **2** of, involving, or concerned with applied and industrial sciences: *an important technical achievement.* **3** resulting from mechanical failure: *a technical fault.* **4** according to a strict application or interpretation of the law or rules: *the shipment was a technical violation of the treaty.*

tech•noc•ra•cy |tekˈnäkrəsē| • *n.* (pl. **-ies**) the government or control of society or industry by an elite of technical experts.
■ an instance or application of this. ■ an elite of technical experts. DERIVATIVES: **tech•no•crat** *n.*

tec•ton•ic |tekˈtänik| • *adj.* **1** of or relating to the structure of the earth's crust and the large-scale processes that take place within it. **2** of or relating to building or construction. DERIVATIVES: **tec•ton•i•cal•ly** |-ik(ə)lē| *adv.*

tec•ton•ics |tekˈtäniks| • *plural n.* [treated as sing. or pl.] large-scale processes affecting the structure of the earth's crust.

te•di•ous |ˈtēdēəs| • *adj.* too long, slow, or dull: tiresome or monotonous: *a tedious journey.* DERIVATIVES: **te•di•ous•ly** *adv.* **te•di•ous•ness** *n.*

tee•to•tal |ˈtē,tōtl| • *adj.* choosing or characterized by abstinence from alcohol: *a teetotal lifestyle.* DERIVATIVES: **tee•to•tal•er** *n.* **tee•to•tal•ism** |-,izəm| *n.*

tel•e•com•mute |ˈteləkəˌmyo͞ot| • *v.* [intrans.] [usu. as n.] (**telecommuting**) work from home, communicating with the workplace using equipment such as telephones, fax machines, and modems. DERIVATIVES: **tel•e•com•mut•er** *n.*

tel•e•ki•ne•sis |ˌteləkiˈnēsis| • *n.* the supposed ability to move objects at a distance by mental power or other nonphysical means.
DERIVATIVES: **tel•e•ki•net•ic** |-ˈnetik| *adj.*

te•lep•a•thy |təˈlepəTHē| • *n.* the supposed communication of thoughts or ideas by means other than the known senses.
DERIVATIVES: **tel•e•path•ic** |ˌteləˈpæTHik| *adj.* **tel•e•path•i•cal•ly** |ˌteləˈpæTHik(ə)lē| *adv.* **te•lep•a•thist** |-THist| *n.*

tel•ex |ˈteleks| • *n.* an international system of telegraphy with printed messages transmitted and received by teleprinters using the public telecommunications network.
■ a device used for this. ■ a message sent by this system. • *v.* [trans.] communicate with (someone) by telex.
■ send (a message) by telex.

tel•ic |ˈtelik; ˈtē-| • *adj.* (of an action or attitude) directed or tending to a definite end.
■ (of a verb, conjunction, or clause) expressing goal, result, or purpose.
DERIVATIVES: **te•lic•i•ty** |təˈlisitē| *n.*

tel•lu•ri•an |təˈloŏrēən| • *adj.* of or inhabiting the earth. • *n.* an inhabitant of the earth.

tel•lu•ric |təˈloŏrik| • *adj.* of the earth as a planet.
■ of the soil.

te•mer•i•ty |təˈmeritē| • *n.* excessive confidence or boldness; audacity: *no one had the temerity to question his conclusions.*

tem•per•a |ˈtempərə| • *n.* a method of painting with pigments dispersed in an emulsion miscible with water, typically egg yolk. The method was used in Europe for fine painting, mainly on wood panels, from the 12th or early 13th century until the 15th, when it began to give way to oils.
■ emulsion used in this method of painting.

tem•per•ance |ˈtemp(ə)rəns| • *n.* rational self-restraint, esp. moderation in eating and drinking; total or partial abstinence from alcoholic drink: [as adj.] *the temperance movement.*

tem•per•ate |ˈtemp(ə)rət| • *adj.* **1** of, relating to, or denoting a region or climate characterized by mild temperatures. **2** showing moderation or self-restraint: *Charles was temperate in his consumption of both food and drink.*
DERIVATIVES: **tem•per•ate•ly** *adv.* **tem•per•ate•ness** *n.*

tem•pes•tu•ous |temˈpesCHəwəs| • *adj.* **1** characterized by strong and turbulent or conflicting emotion: *he had a reckless and tempestuous streak.* **2** very stormy: *a tempestuous wind.*
DERIVATIVES: **tem•pes•tu•ous•ly** *adv.* **tem•pes•tu•ous•ness** *n.*

tem•po |ˈtempō| • *n.* (pl. **tempos** or **tempi** |-pē|) **1** the speed at which a passage of music is or should be played. **2** the rate or speed of motion or activity; pace: *the tempo of life dictated by a heavy workload.*

tem•po•ral |ˈtemp(ə)rəl| • *adj.* **1** relating to worldly as opposed to spiritual affairs; secular. **2** of or relating to time.
■ (in grammar) relating to or denoting time or tense.

DERIVATIVES: **tem•po•ral•ly** *adv.*

tem•po•rize |ˈtempəˌrīz| • *v.* **1** [intrans.] avoid making a decision or committing oneself in order to gain time: *the opportunity was missed because the mayor temporized.* **2** temporarily adopt a particular course in order to conform to the circumstances: *their unwillingness to temporize had driven their country straight into conflict with France.*
DERIVATIVES: **tem•po•ri•za•tion** |ˌtempəriˈzāSHən| *n.* **tem•po•riz•er** *n.*

ten•a•ble |ˈtenəbəl| • *adj.* **1** able to be maintained or defended against attack or objection: *such a simplistic approach is no longer tenable.* **2** (of an office, position, scholarship, etc.) able to be held or used: *the post is tenable for three years.*
DERIVATIVES: **ten•a•bil•i•ty** |ˌtenəˈbilitē| *n.*

te•na•cious |təˈnāSHəs| • *adj.* not readily letting go of, giving up, or separated from an object that one holds, a position, or a principle: *a tenacious grip* | *the most tenacious politician in South Korea.*
■ not easily dispelled or discouraged; persisting in existence or in a course of action: *a tenacious local legend* | *you're tenacious and you get at the truth.*
DERIVATIVES: **te•na•cious•ly** *adv.* **te•na•cious•ness** *n.* **te•nac•i•ty** |-ˈnæsitē| *n.*

ten•ant |ˈtenənt| • *n.* a person who occupies land or property rented from a landlord.
■ (in law) a person holding real property by private ownership. • *v.* [trans.] (usu. **be tenanted**) occupy (property) as a tenant.
DERIVATIVES: **ten•an•cy** *n.* **ten•ant•a•ble** *adj.* (formal) **ten•ant•less** *adj.*

ten•den•tious |tenˈdenSHəs| • *adj.* expressing or intending to promote a particular cause or point of view, esp. a controversial one: *a tendentious reading of history.*
DERIVATIVES: **ten•den•tious•ly** *adv.* **ten•den•tious•ness** *n.*

ten•e•brous |ˈtenəbrəs| • *adj.* dark; shadowy or obscure.

ten•e•ment |ˈtenəmənt| • *n.* **1** a room or a set of rooms forming a separate residence within a house or block of apartments.
■ (also **tenement house**) a house divided into and rented in such separate residences, esp. one that is run-down and overcrowded. **2** a piece of land held by an owner.
■ (in law) any kind of permanent property, e.g., lands or rents, held from a superior.

ten•et |ˈtenit| • *n.* a principle or belief, esp. one of the main tenets of a religion or philosophy: *the tenets of classical liberalism.* Cf. CREED, DOGMA.

ten•on |ˈtenən| • *n.* a projecting piece of wood made for insertion into a mortise in another piece. • *v.* [trans.] (usu. **be tenoned**) join by means of a tenon.
■ cut as a tenon.
DERIVATIVES: **ten•on•er** *n.*

ten•sile |ˈtensəl; -ˌsīl| • *adj.* **1** of or relating to tension. **2** capable of being drawn out or stretched.
DERIVATIVES: **ten•sil•i•ty** |tenˈsilitē| *n.*

ten•sive | 'tensiv | • *adj.* causing or expressing tension.

ten•ta•tive | 'ten(t)ətiv | • *adj.* not certain or fixed; provisional: *a tentative conclusion.*
■ done without confidence; hesitant: *he tried a few tentative steps around his hospital room.*
DERIVATIVES: **ten•ta•tive•ly** *adv.* **ten•ta•tive•ness** *n.*

ten•u•ous | 'tenyəwəs | • *adj.* very weak or slight: *the tenuous link between interest rates and investment.*
■ very slender or fine; insubstantial: *a tenuous cloud.*
DERIVATIVES: **ten•u•ous•ly** *adv.* **ten•u•ous•ness** *n.*

ten•ure | 'tenyər; -ˌyoŏr | • *n.* **1** the conditions under which land or buildings are held or occupied. **2** the holding of an office: *his tenure as EPA head would be threatened.*
■ a period for which an office is held. **3** guaranteed permanent employment, esp. as a teacher or professor, after a probationary period. • *v.* [trans.] give (someone) a permanent post, esp. as a teacher or professor: *I had recently been tenured and then promoted to full professor.*
■ [as adj.] (**tenured**) having or denoting such a post: *a tenured faculty member.*

tep•id | 'tepid | • *adj.* (esp. of a liquid) only slightly warm; lukewarm.
■ showing little enthusiasm: *the applause was tepid.*
DERIVATIVES: **te•pid•i•ty** | tə'pidiṭē | *n.* **tep•id•ly** *adv.* **tep•id•ness** *n.*

ter•a•tol•o•gy | ˌterə'täləjē | • *n.* **1** the scientific study of congenital abnormalities and abnormal formations. **2** mythology relating to fantastic creatures and monsters.
DERIVATIVES: **ter•a•to•log•i•cal** | ˌterətə'läjikəl | *adj.* **ter•a•tol•o•gist** | -jist | *n.*

ter•cet | 'tersət | • *n.* a set or group of three lines of verse rhyming together or connected by rhyme with an adjacent tercet.

ter•gi•ver•sate | 'tərjivər,sāt | • *v.* [intrans.] **1** make conflicting or evasive statements; equivocate: *the more she tergiversated, the greater grew the demands of the reporters for an interview.* **2** change one's loyalties; be apostate.
DERIVATIVES: **ter•gi•ver•sa•tion** | ˌtərjivər'sāsʜən | *n.* **ter•gi•ver•sa•tor** | -ˌsāṭər | *n.*

ter•ma•gant | 'tərməgənt | • *n.* a harsh-tempered or overbearing woman.

ter•mi•nal | 'tərmənl | • *adj.* **1** [attrib.] of, forming, or situated at the end or extremity of something: *a terminal date* | *the terminal tip of the probe.*
■ of or forming a transportation terminal: *terminal platforms.* ■ situated at, forming, or denoting the end of a part or series of parts furthest from the center of the body. ■ (of a flower, inflorescence, etc.) borne at the end of a stem or branch. Often contrasted with *axillary* (growing from an *axil*, the upper angle between a stalk or branch and the stem or trunk from which it is growing). **2** (of a disease) predicted to lead to death, esp. slowly; incurable: *terminal cancer.*

■ [attrib.] suffering from or relating to such a disease: *a hospice for terminal cases.* ■ [attrib.] (of a condition) forming the last stage of such a disease. ■ extreme and usually beyond cure or alteration (used to emphasize the extent of something regarded as bad or unfortunate): *you're making a terminal ass of yourself.* • *n.* **1** an end or extremity of something, in particular:
■ the end of a railroad or other transport route, or a station at such a point. ■ a departure and arrival building for air passengers at an airport. ■ an installation where oil or gas is stored at the end of a pipeline or at a port. **2** a point of connection for closing an electric circuit. **3** a device at which a user enters data or commands for a computer system and that displays the received output. **4** (also **terminal figure**) another term for TERMINUS 'boundary marker.'
DERIVATIVES: **ter•mi•nal•ly** *adv.* (in sense 2 of the adjective) [as submodifier] *a terminally ill woman.*

ter•mi•nate | 'tərmə,nāt | • *v.* [trans.] bring to an end: *he was advised to terminate the contract.*
■ [intrans.] (**terminate in**) (of a thing) have its end at (a specified place) or of (a specified form): *the chain terminated in an iron ball covered with spikes.* ■ [intrans.] (of a train, bus, or boat service) end its journey: *the train will terminate at New Orleans.* ■ end (a pregnancy) before term by artificial means.
■ end the employment of (someone); dismiss: *They're putting pressure on me to terminate you.* ■ assassinate (someone, esp. an intelligence agent): *he was terminated by persons unknown.* ■ form the physical end or extremity of (an area).

ter•mi•nol•o•gy | ˌtərmə'näləjē | • *n.* (pl. **-ies**) the body of terms used with a particular technical application in a subject of study, theory, profession, etc.: *the terminology of semiotics* | *specialized terminologies for higher education.*
DERIVATIVES: **ter•mi•no•log•i•cal** | -nə'läjikəl | *adj.* **ter•mi•no•log•i•cal•ly** | -nə'läjik(ə)lē | *adv.* **ter•mi•nol•o•gist** | -jist | *n.*

ter•mi•nus | 'tərmənəs | • *n.* (pl. **termini** | -nī | or **terminuses**) **1** a final point in space or time; an end or extremity: *the exhibition's terminus is 1962.* **2** the end of a railway or other transportation route, or a station at such a point; a terminal.
■ an oil or gas terminal. **3** a figure of a human bust or an animal ending in a square pillar from which it appears to spring, originally used as a boundary marker in ancient Rome.

ter•na•ry | 'tərnərē | • *adj.* composed of three parts.
■ (in mathematics) using three as a base.

Terp•sich•o•re | ˌtərp'sikərē | (in Greek and Roman mythology) the Muse of lyric poetry and dance.
DERIVATIVES: **Terp•sich•o•re•an** *adj.*

ter•ra cot•ta | 'terə 'kätə | (also **terracotta**) • *n.* unglazed, typically brownish-red earthenware, used chiefly as an ornamental building material and in modeling.
■ a statuette or other object made of such

earthenware. ■ a strong brownish-red or brownish-orange color.

ter•rane |təˈrān; ˈterān| (also **terrain**) • *n.* (in geology) a fault-bounded area or region with a distinctive stratigraphy, structure, and geological history.

ter•res•tri•al |təˈrestrēəl; -ˈresCHəl| • *adj.* **1** of, on, or relating to the earth: *increased ultraviolet radiation may disrupt terrestrial ecosystems.* ■ denoting television broadcast using equipment situated on the ground rather than by satellite: *terrestrial and cable technology.* ■ of or on dry land: *a submarine eruption will be much more explosive than its terrestrial counterpart.* ■ (of an animal) living on or in the ground; not aquatic, arboreal, or aerial. ■ (of a plant) growing on land or in the soil; not aquatic or epiphytic. ■ (of a planet) similar in size or composition to the earth, esp. being one of the four inner planets. ■ of or relating to the earth as opposed to heaven. • *n.* an inhabitant of the earth.
DERIVATIVES: **ter•res•tri•al•ly** *adv.*

ter•ror•ism |ˈterəˌrizəm| • *n.* the use of violence and intimidation in the pursuit of political aims.
DERIVATIVES: **ter•ror•ist** *n., adj.* **ter•ror•is•tic** *adj.*

USAGE: **Terrorism**, in precise usage, means the use of violence to instill terror in a population, administration, etc. In looser recent use, it has come to refer to various forms of unconventional warfare, although purists would argue that it is not possible to commit a terrorist act against, e.g., on-duty soldiers.

terse |tərs| • *adj.* (**terser, tersest**) sparing in the use of words; abrupt: *a terse statement.*
DERIVATIVES: **terse•ly** *adv.* **terse•ness** *n.*

ter•ti•ar•y |ˈtərsHē,erē; -sHərē| • *adj.* **1** third in order or level: *most of the enterprises were of tertiary importance* | *the tertiary stage of the disease.* ■ chiefly Brit. relating to or denoting education at a level beyond that provided by schools, esp. that provided by a college or university. ■ relating to or denoting the medical treatment provided at a specialist institution. **2** (**Tertiary**) of, relating to, or denoting the first geologic period of the Cenozoic era, between the Cretaceous and Quaternary periods, and comprising the Paleogene and Neogene subperiods. **3** (of an organic compound) having its functional group located on a carbon atom that is itself bonded to three other carbon atoms. ■ (chiefly of amines) derived from ammonia by replacement of three hydrogen atoms by organic groups. • *n.* **1** (**the Tertiary**) the Tertiary period or the system of rocks deposited during it.

The Tertiary lasted from about 65 million to 1.6 million years ago. The mammals diversified following the demise of the dinosaurs and became dominant, as did the flowering plants.

2 a lay associate of certain Christian monastic organizations: *a Franciscan tertiary.*

tes•sel•late |ˈtesə,lāt| (also **tesselate**) • *v.* [trans.] decorate (a floor) with mosaics. ■ (in mathematics) cover (a plane surface) by repeated use of a single shape, without gaps or overlapping.
DERIVATIVES: **tes•sel•la•tion** |,tesəˈlāsHən| (also **tes•se•la•tion**)

tes•ser•a |ˈtesərə| • *n.* (pl. **tesserae** |-rē|) a small block of stone, tile, glass, or other material used in the construction of a mosaic. ■ (in ancient Greece and Rome) a small tablet of wood or bone used as a token.
DERIVATIVES: **tes•ser•al** |-rəl| *adj.*

tes•si•tu•ra |,tesiˈtŏŏrə| • *n.* (in music) the range within which most notes of a vocal part fall.

tes•tate |ˈtes,tāt| • *adj.* [predic.] having made a valid will before one dies. • *n.* a person who has died leaving such a will.

tes•ta•tor |ˈtestātər| (fem. **testatrix**) • *n.* (in law) a person who has made a will or given a legacy.

tes•ti•cle |ˈtestikəl| • *n.* either of the two oval organs that produce sperm in men and other male mammals, enclosed in the scrotum behind the penis.
DERIVATIVES: **tes•tic•u•lar** |teˈstikyələr| *adj.*

tes•ty |ˈtestē| • *adj.* easily irritated; impatient and somewhat bad-tempered.
DERIVATIVES: **tes•ti•ly** |ˈtestəlē| *adv.* **tes•ti•ness** *n.*

tête-à-tête |ˈtat ə ˈtāt; ˈtet ə ˈtet| • *n.* a private conversation between two people. • *adj. & adv.* involving or happening between two people in private: [as adj.] *a tête-à-tête meal* | [as adv.] *his business was conducted tête-à-tête.*

tha•las•sic |THəˈlæsik| • *adj.* of or relating to the sea.

than•a•tol•o•gy |,THænəˈtäləjē| • *n.* the scientific study of death and the practices associated with it, including the study of the needs of the terminally ill and their families.
DERIVATIVES: **than•a•to•log•i•cal** |-ətəˈläjikəl| *adj.* **than•a•tol•o•gist** |-jist| *n.*

thane |THān| • *n.* (in Anglo-Saxon England) a man who held land granted by the king or by a military nobleman, ranking between an ordinary freeman and a hereditary noble. ■ (in Scotland) a man, often the chief of a clan, who held land from a Scottish king and ranked with an earl's son.
DERIVATIVES: **thane•dom** |-dəm| *n.*

thau•ma•turge |ˈTHômə,tərj| • *n.* a worker of wonders and performer of miracles; a magician.
DERIVATIVES: **thau•ma•tur•gic** |,THômə'tərjik| *adj.* **thau•ma•tur•gi•cal** |,THômə'tərjikəl| *adj.* **thau•ma•tur•gist** |-jist| *n.* **thau•ma•tur•gy** |-,tərjē| *n.*

the•an•throp•ic |,THēən'THräpik| • *adj.* embodying deity in a human form; both divine and human.

the•ar•chy |ˈTHē,ärkē| • *n.* (pl. **-ies**) rule by a god or gods.

the•ism |ˈTHēˌizəm| • n. belief in the existence of a god or gods, esp. belief in one god as creator of the universe, intervening in it and sustaining a personal relation to his creatures. Cf. DEISM.
DERIVATIVES: **the•ist** n. **the•is•tic** |-ˈistik| adj.

the•o•cen•tric |ˌTHēōˈsentrik| • adj. having God as a central focus: a theocentric civilization.

the•oc•ra•cy |THēˈäkrəsē| • n. (pl. -ies) a system of government in which priests rule in the name of God or a god.
■ (the Theocracy) the commonwealth of Israel from the time of Moses until the election of Saul as king.
DERIVATIVES: **the•o•crat** |ˈTHēəˌkræt| n. **the•o•crat•ic** |THēəˈkrætik| adj. **the•o•crat•i•cal•ly** |THēəˈkrætik(ə)lē| adv.

the•o•rem |ˈTHēərəm; ˈTHir-| • n. (in physics and mathematics) a general proposition not self-evident but proved by a chain of reasoning; a truth established by means of accepted truths.
■ a rule in algebra or other branches of mathematics expressed by symbols or formulae.
DERIVATIVES: **the•o•re•mat•ic** |ˌTHēərəˈmætik; ˌTHirə-| adj.

the•o•ry |ˈTHiərē; ˈTHirē| • n. (pl. -ies) a supposition or a system of ideas intended to explain something, esp. one based on general principles independent of the thing to be explained: Darwin's theory of evolution.
■ a set of principles on which the practice of an activity is based: a theory of education | music theory. ■ an idea used to account for a situation or justify a course of action: my theory is that the place has been seriously mismanaged. ■ (in mathematics) a collection of propositions to illustrate the principles of a subject.

the•os•o•phy |THēˈäsəfē| • n. any of a number of philosophies maintaining that a knowledge of God may be achieved through spiritual ecstasy, direct intuition, or special individual relations.
DERIVATIVES: **the•os•o•pher** |-fər| n. **the•o•soph•ic** |ˌTHēəˈsäfik| adj. **the•o•soph•i•cal** |ˌTHēəˈsäfikəl| adj. **the•o•soph•i•cal•ly** |ˌTHēəˈsäfik(ə)lē| adv. **the•os•o•phist** |-fist| n.

ther•a•peu•tic |ˌTHerəˈpyo͞otik| • adj. of or relating to the healing of disease: diagnostic and therapeutic facilities.
■ administered or applied for reasons of health: a therapeutic shampoo. ■ having a good effect on the body or mind; contributing to a sense of well-being: a therapeutic silence.
DERIVATIVES: **ther•a•peu•ti•cal** adj. **ther•a•peu•ti•cal•ly** |-ik(ə)lē| adv.

ther•a•peu•tics |ˌTHerəˈpyo͞otiks| • plural n. [treated as sing.] the branch of medicine concerned with the treatment of disease and the action of remedial agents.

Ther•a•va•da |ˌTHerəˈvädə| (also **Theravada Buddhism**) • n. the more conservative of the two major traditions of Buddhism (the other being Mahayana), and a school of Hinayana Buddhism. It is practiced mainly in Sri Lanka, Myanmar (Burma), Thailand, Cambodia, and Laos.

the•ri•an•throp•ic |ˌTHirē,ənˈTHräpik| • adj. (esp. of a deity) combining the form of an animal with that of a man.

the•ri•o•mor•phic |ˌTHirēəˈmôrfik| • adj. (esp. of a deity) having an animal form.

ther•mal |ˈTHərməl| • adj. of or relating to heat.
■ another term for GEOTHERMAL. ■ (of a garment) made of a fabric that provides exceptional insulation to keep the body warm: thermal underwear. • n. 1 an upward current of warm air, used by gliders, balloons, and birds to gain height. 2 (usu. **thermals**) a thermal garment, esp. underwear.
DERIVATIVES: **ther•mal•ly** adv.

ther•mo•dy•nam•ics |ˌTHərmōdīˈnæmiks| • plural n. [treated as sing.] the branch of physical science that deals with the relations between heat and other forms of energy (such as mechanical, electrical, or chemical energy), and, by extension, of the relationships and interconvertibility of all forms of energy.
DERIVATIVES: **ther•mo•dy•nam•ic** adj. **ther•mo•dy•nam•i•cal** |-ikəl| adj. **ther•mo•dy•nam•i•cal•ly** |-ik(ə)lē| adv. **ther•mo•dy•nam•i•cist** |-,dīˈnæmisist| n.

ther•mo•nu•cle•ar |ˌTHərmō'n(y)o͞okli(ə)r; -ˈn(y)o͞okyələr| • adj. relating to or using nuclear reactions that occur only at very high temperatures such as those inside stars, esp. as fusion of hydrogen or other light nuclei.
■ of, relating to, or involving weapons in which explosive force is produced by thermonuclear reactions (e.g., the hydrogen bomb).

the•sau•rus |THəˈsôrəs| • n. (pl. **thesauri** |-ˈsôrī| or **thesauruses**) a book that lists words in groups of synonyms and related concepts.
■ old term for a dictionary or encyclopedia.

the•sis |ˈTHēsis| • n. (pl. **theses** |-ˌsēz|) 1 a statement or theory that is put forward as a premise to be maintained or proved: his central thesis is that psychological life is not part of the material world. 2 a long essay or dissertation involving personal research, written by a candidate for a university degree: a master's thesis. Cf. DISSERTATION. 3 an unstressed syllable or part of a metrical foot in Greek or Latin verse.

thes•pi•an |ˈTHespēən| • adj. of or relating to drama and the theater: thespian talents. • n. an actor or actress.

the•ur•gy |ˈTHēərjē| • n. the operation or effect of a supernatural or divine agency in human affairs.
■ a system of white (beneficial) magic practiced by the early Neoplatonists.
DERIVATIVES: **the•ur•gic** |THēˈərjik| adj. **the•ur•gi•cal** |THēˈərjikəl| adj. **the•ur•gist** |-jist| n.

thew |TH(y)o͞o| • n. muscular strength.
■ (**thews**) muscles and tendons perceived as generating such strength.
DERIVATIVES: **thew•y** adj. **thew•less** adj.

Third World • *n.* (usu. **the Third World**) the developing countries of Asia, Africa, and Latin America.

thrall |THrôl| • *n.* the state of being in someone's power or having great power over someone: *she was in thrall to her abusive husband.*
■ a slave, servant, or captive.
DERIVATIVES: **thrall•dom** |-dəm| (also **thral•dom**) *n.*

thread•y |'THredē| • *adj.* (**threadier, threadiest**) (of a sound, esp. the voice) scarcely audible: *he managed a thready whisper.*
■ (of a person's pulse) scarcely perceptible.

thren•o•dy |'THrenədē| • *n.* (pl. **-ies**) a lament, esp. for the dead; a dirge.
DERIVATIVES: **thre•no•di•al** |THrə'nōdē-əl| *adj.* **thre•nod•ic** |THrə'nädik| *adj.* **thren•o•dist** |-dist| *n.*

thresh |THresH| • *v.* [trans.] **1** separate grain from (a plant), typically with a flail or by the action of a revolving mechanism: *machinery that can reap and thresh corn in the same process* | [as n.] (**threshing**) *farm workers started the afternoon's threshing.* **2** variant spelling of *thrash* (in the sense of violent movement).

thrift•y |'THriftē| • *adj.* (**thriftier, thriftiest**) **1** (of a person or behavior) using money and other resources carefully and not wastefully. **2** (of livestock or plants) strong and healthy.
■ prosperous.
DERIVATIVES: **thrift•i•ly** |-lē| *adv.* **thrift•i•ness** *n.*

throes |THrōz| • *plural n.* intense or violent pain and struggle, esp. accompanying birth, death, or great change: *he convulsed in his death throes.*

throm•bo•sis |THräm'bōsis| • *n.* (pl. **thromboses** |-,sēz|) local coagulation or clotting of the blood in a part of the circulatory system.
■ congestion in general.
DERIVATIVES: **throm•bot•ic** |-'bätik| *adj.*

thwart |THwôrt| • *v.* [trans.] prevent (someone) from accomplishing something: *he never did anything to thwart his father* | *she was thwarted in her desire to punish them.*
■ oppose (a plan, attempt, or ambition) successfully: *the government had been able to thwart all attempts by opposition leaders to form new parties.* • *n.* a structural crosspiece forming a seat for a rower in a boat. • *prep. & adv.* from one side to another side of; across: [as prep.] *a pink-tinged cloud spread thwart the shore.*

tic |tik| • *n.* a habitual spasmodic contraction of the muscles, most often in the face.
■ a characteristic or recurrent behavioral trait; idiosyncrasy: *one of my tics as a writer.*

til•de |'tildə| • *n.* an accent (˜) placed over Spanish *n* when pronounced *ny* (as in *señor*) or Portuguese *a* or *o* when nasalized (as in *São Paulo*), or over a vowel in phonetic transcription, indicating nasalization.
■ a similar symbol used in mathematics to indicate similarity, and in logic to indicate negation.

tim•bre |'tæmbər; 'täNbrə| • *n.* the character or quality of a musical sound or voice as distinct from its pitch and intensity: *trumpet mutes with different timbres.*

ti•moc•ra•cy |tə'mäkrəsē| • *n.* (pl. **-ies**) **1** a form of government in which possession of property is required in order to hold office. **2** a form of government in which rulers are motivated by ambition or love of honor.
DERIVATIVES: **ti•mo•crat•ic** |,timə'kræt-ik| *adj.*

tim•or•ous |'timərəs| • *adj.* showing or suffering from nervousness, fear, or a lack of confidence: *a timorous voice.*
DERIVATIVES: **tim•or•ous•ly** *adv.* **tim•or•ous•ness** *n.*

tinc•ture |'tiNG(k)CHər| • *n.* **1** a medicine made by dissolving a drug in alcohol. **2** a slight trace of something: *she could not keep a tincture of bitterness out of her voice.* **3** (in heraldry) any of the conventional colors used in coats of arms. • *v.* (**be tinctured**) be tinged, flavored, or imbued with a slight amount of: *Arthur's affability was tinctured with faint sarcasm.*

tin•ni•tus |'tinitəs; ti'nī-| • *n.* ringing or buzzing in the ears.

tin•tin•nab•u•la•tion |,tintə,næbyə'lāsHən| • *n.* a ringing or tinkling sound.

ti•rade |'tī,rād; ,tī'rād| • *n.* a long, angry speech of criticism or accusation: *a tirade of abuse.*

tithe |tīTH| • *n.* one tenth of annual produce or earnings, formerly taken as a tax for the support of the church and clergy.
■ (in certain religious denominations) a tenth of an individual's income pledged to the church. ■ [in sing.] a tenth of a specified thing: *he hadn't said a tithe of the prayers he knew.* • *v.* [trans.] pay or give as a tithe: *he tithes 10 percent of his income to the church.*
■ subject to a tax of one tenth of income or produce.
DERIVATIVES: **tith•a•ble** *adj.*

tit•il•late |'titl,āt| • *v.* [trans.] stimulate or excite (someone), esp. in a sexual way: *these journalists are paid to titillate the public* | [as adj.] (**titillating**) *she let slip titillating details about her clients.*
■ lightly touch; tickle.
DERIVATIVES: **tit•il•lat•ing•ly** *adv.* **tit•il•la•tion** |,titl'āsHən| *n.*

tit•i•vate |'titə,vāt| • *v.* [trans.] make small enhancing alterations to (something): *she titivated her hair.*
■ (**titivate oneself**) make oneself look attractive.
DERIVATIVES: **tit•i•va•tion** |,titə'vāsHən| *n.*

tit•u•lar |'tiCHələr| • *adj.* **1** holding or constituting a purely formal position or title without any real authority: *the queen is titular head of the Church of England.*
■ [attrib.] (of a cleric) nominally appointed to serve a diocese, abbey, or other foundation no longer in existence, and typically in fact having authority in another capacity. **2** denoting a person or thing from whom or which the name of an artistic work or similar is taken: *the work's titular song.*

■ [attrib.] denoting any of the parish churches in Rome to which cardinals are formally appointed and from which their titles are derived: *the priests of the titular churches.*

tme•sis |tə'mēsis| • *n.* (pl. **tmeses**) the separation of parts of a compound word by an intervening word or words, heard mainly in informal speech (e.g., *a whole nother story*; *shove it back any-old-where in the pile*).

toc•sin |'täksən| • *n.* an alarm bell or signal.

toile |twäl| • *n.* **1** an early version of a finished garment made up in cheap material so that the design can be tested and perfected. **2** a translucent linen or cotton fabric, used for making clothes.

tol•er•ance |'täl(ə)rəns| • *n.* **1** the ability or willingness to tolerate something, in particular the existence of opinions or behavior that one does not necessarily agree with: *the tolerance of corruption* | *an advocate of religious tolerance.*
■ the capacity to endure continued subjection to something, esp. a drug, transplant, antigen, or environmental conditions, without adverse reaction: *the desert camel shows the greatest tolerance to dehydration*| *species were grouped according to pollution tolerance* | *various species of diatoms display different tolerances to acid.* ■ diminution in the body's response to a drug after continued use. **2** an allowable amount of variation of a specified quantity, esp. in the dimensions of a machine or part: *250 parts in his cars were made to tolerances of one thousandth of an inch.*

tome |tōm| • *n.* a book, esp. a large, heavy, scholarly one: *a weighty tome.*

ton•al |'tōnl| • *adj.* of or relating to the tone of music, color, or writing: *his ear for tonal color* | *the poem's tonal lapses.*
■ of or relating to music written using conventional keys and harmony. ■ (of a language) expressing semantic differences by varying the intonation given to words or syllables of a similar sound.
DERIVATIVES: **ton•al•ly** *adv.*

ton•ic |'tänik| • *n.* **1** a medicinal substance taken to give a feeling of vigor or well-being.
■ something with an invigorating effect: *being needed is a tonic for someone at my age.* **2** the first note in a scale that, in conventional harmony, provides the keynote of a piece of music. • *adj.* **1** giving a feeling of vigor or well-being; invigorating. **2** relating to or denoting the first degree of a musical scale. **3** (in phonetics) denoting or relating to the syllable within a tone group that has greatest prominence, because it carries the main change of pitch. **4** relating to or restoring normal tone to muscles or other organs.
■ relating to, denoting, or producing continuous muscular contraction.
DERIVATIVES: **ton•i•cal•ly** |-ik(ə)lē| *adv.*

ton•so•ri•al |tän'sôrēəl| • *adj.* of or relating to hairdressing.

ton•sure |'tänsHər| • *n.* a part of a monk's or priest's head left bare on top by shaving off the hair.
■ [in sing.] an act of shaving the top of a monk's

or priest's head as a preparation for entering a religious order. • *v.* [trans.] [often as adj.] (**tonsured**) shave the hair on the crown of.

ton•tine |'tän,tēn; tän'tēn| • *n.* an annuity shared by subscribers to a loan or common fund, the shares increasing as subscribers die until the last survivor enjoys the whole income.

tooth•some |'tōoTHsəm| • *adj.* (of food) temptingly tasty: *a toothsome morsel.*
■ (of a person) good-looking; attractive.
DERIVATIVES: **tooth•some•ly** *adv.* **tooth•some•ness** *n.*

tope |tōp| • *v.* [intrans.] drink alcohol to excess, esp. on a regular basis.
DERIVATIVES: **top•er** *n.*

to•pi•ar•y |'tōpē,erē| • *n.* (pl. **-ies**) the art or practice of clipping shrubs or trees into ornamental shapes.
■ shrubs or trees clipped into ornamental shapes in such a way: *a cottage surrounded by topiary.*
DERIVATIVES: **to•pi•ar•i•an** |,tōpē'erēən| *adj.* **to•pi•a•rist** |-ərist| *n.*

to•pog•ra•phy |tə'pägrəfē| • *n.* the arrangement of the natural and artificial physical features of an area: *the topography of the island.*
■ a detailed description or representation on a map of such features. ■ the distribution of parts or features on the surface of or within an organ or organism.
DERIVATIVES: **to•pog•ra•pher** |-fər| *n.*

to•pol•o•gy |tə'päləjē| • *n.* **1** (in mathematics) the study of geometric properties and spatial relations unaffected by the continuous change of shape or size of figures.
■ a family of open subsets of an abstract space such that the union and the intersection of any two of them are members of the family, and that includes the space itself and the empty set. **2** the way in which constituent parts are interrelated or arranged: *the topology of a computer network.*
DERIVATIVES: **top•o•log•i•cal** |,täpə'läjikəl| *adj.* **top•o•log•i•cal•ly** |,täpə'läjik(ə)lē| *adv.* **to•pol•o•gist** |-jist| *n.*

top•o•nym |'täpə,nim| • *n.* a place name, esp. one derived from a topographical feature.
DERIVATIVES: **top•o•nym•ic** *adj.*

tor |tôr| • *n.* a hill or rocky peak.

To•rah |'tōrə; 'tô-; tô'rä| • *n.* (usu. **the Torah**) (in Judaism) the law of God as revealed to Moses and recorded in the first five books of the Hebrew scriptures (the Pentateuch).
■ a scroll containing this.

to•reu•tics |tə'rōotiks| • *plural n.* [treated as sing.] the art of making designs in relief or intaglio, esp. by chasing, carving, and embossing in metal.
DERIVATIVES: **to•reu•tic** *adj.*

tor•pid |'tôrpid| • *adj.* mentally or physically inactive; lethargic: *we sat around in a torpid state.*
■ (of an animal) dormant, esp. during hibernation.
DERIVATIVES: **tor•pid•i•ty** |tôr'piditē| *n.* **tor•pid•ly** *adv.*

tor•por |ˈtôrpər| • *n.* a state of physical or mental inactivity; lethargy: *they veered between apathetic torpor and hysterical fanaticism.*

torque |tôrk| • *n.* a twisting force that tends to cause rotation. • *v.* [trans.] apply torque or a twisting force to (an object): *he gently torqued the hip joint.*
DERIVATIVES: **tor•quey** *adj.*

tor•rid |ˈtôrəd; ˈtär–| • *adj.* very hot and dry: *the torrid heat of the afternoon.*
■ full of passionate or highly charged emotions arising from sexual love: *a torrid love affair.*
■ full of difficulty or tribulation: *Wall Street is in for a torrid time in the next few weeks.*
DERIVATIVES: **tor•rid•i•ty** |təˈridiṯē| *n.* **tor•rid•ly** *adv.*

tor•sion |ˈtôrSHən| • *n.* the action of twisting or the state of being twisted, esp. of one end of an object relative to the other.
■ (in mathematics) the extent to which a curve departs from being planar.
DERIVATIVES: **tor•sion•al** |–SHənl| *adj.* **tor•sion•al•ly** |–SHənl-ē| *adv.* **tor•sion•less** *adj.*

tor•so |ˈtôrsō| • *n.* (pl. **torsos** or **torsi** |–sē|) the trunk of the human body.
■ the trunk of a statue without, or considered independently of, the head and limbs. ■ an unfinished or mutilated thing, esp. a work of art or literature: *the Requiem torso was preceded by the cantata.*

tort |tôrt| • *n.* (in law) a wrongful act or an infringement of a right (other than one acquired under contract), not a crime but leading to legal liability and giving cause for a lawsuit.
DERIVATIVES: **tor•tious** *adj.* **tort•fea•sor** *n.* a person who commits a tort.

torte |tôrt| • *n.* (pl. **tortes** or German **torten** |ˈtôrtn|) a sweet cake or tart.

tor•tu•ous |ˈtôrCHwəs| • *adj.* full of twists and turns: *the route is remote and tortuous.*
■ excessively lengthy and complex: *a tortuous argument.*
DERIVATIVES: **tor•tu•os•i•ty** |ˌtôrCHə'wäsiṯē| *n.* (pl. **-ies**) **tor•tu•ous•ly** *adv.* **tor•tu•ous•ness** *n.*

USAGE: **Tortuous** and **torturous** have different core meanings. **Tortuous** means 'full of twists and turns' or 'devious; circuitous,' e.g., *Both paths were tortuous and strewn with boulders.* **Torturous** is derived from *torture* and means 'involving torture; excruciating,' e.g., *I found the concert torturous because of the music's volume.* **Torturous** should be reserved for agonized suffering; it is not a fancy word for 'painful' or 'discomforting.'

tor•tur•ous |ˈtôrCHərəs| • *adj.* characterized by, involving, or causing extreme pain or suffering: *a torturous eight weeks of boot camp.*
DERIVATIVES: **tor•tur•ous•ly** *adv.*

To•ry |ˈtôrē| • *n.* (pl. **-ies**) **1** an American colonist who supported the British side during the Revolutionary War. Cf. LOYALIST. **2** (in the UK) a member or supporter of the Conservative Party.
■ a member of the English political party

opposing the exclusion of James II from the succession. It remained the name for members of the English, later British, parliamentary party supporting the established religious and political order until the emergence of the Conservative Party in the 1830s. Cf. WHIG.. • *adj.* of or relating to the British Conservative Party or its supporters: *Tory voters.*
DERIVATIVES: **To•ry•ism** |–,izəm| *n.*

to•tal•i•tar•i•an |tō,tælə'terēən| • *adj.* of or relating to a system of government that is centralized and dictatorial and requires complete subservience to the state: *a totalitarian regime.* • *n.* a person advocating or acting as part of such a system of government.
DERIVATIVES: **to•tal•i•tar•i•an•ism** |–,nizəm| *n.*

to•tem |ˈtōṯəm| • *n.* a natural object or animal believed by a particular society to have spiritual significance and adopted by it as an emblem.
DERIVATIVES: **to•tem•ic** |tō'temik| *adj.* **to•tem•ism** |–,mizəm| *n.* **to•tem•ist** |–mist| *n.* **to•tem•is•tic** |,tōdə'mistik| *adj.*

tout |towt| • *v.* **1** [trans.] attempt to sell (something), typically by pestering people in an aggressive or bold manner: *Stephen was touting his wares.*
■ (often **be touted**) attempt to persuade people of the merits of (someone or something): *the headquarters facility was **touted as** the best in the country.* ■ Brit. scalp (a ticket). **2** [intrans.] offer racing tips for a share of any resulting winnings.
■ [trans.] chiefly Brit. observe the movements and condition of (a racehorse in training) in order to gain information to be used when betting. • *n.* **1** a person soliciting customers or business, typically in an aggressive or bold manner.
■ Brit. a person who buys tickets for an event to resell them at a profit; a scalper. **2** a person who offers racing tips for a share of any resulting winnings.
DERIVATIVES: **tout•er** *n.*

tout² |tŏŏ| • *adj.* (often **le tout**) used before the name of a city to refer to its high society or people of importance: *le tout Washington adored him.*

tout de suite |,tŏŏt 'swēt| • *adv.* immediately; at once: *she left tout de suite.*

town•ship |ˈtown,SHip| • *n.* **1** a division of a county with some corporate powers (sometimes also called a *town*).
■ a district six miles square. **2** (in South Africa) a suburb or city of predominantly black occupation, formerly officially designated for black occupation by apartheid legislation. **3** a manor or parish as a territorial division.
■ a small town or village forming part of a large parish.

tox•ic |ˈtäksik| • *adj.* poisonous: *the dumping of toxic waste* | *alcohol is toxic to several organs.*
■ of or relating to poison: *toxic hazards.*
■ caused by poison: *toxic liver injury.* • *n.* (**toxics**) poisonous substances.

DERIVATIVES: **tox•i•cal•ly** |-sik(ə)lē| adv. **tox•ic•i•ty** |täk'sisitē| n.

tox•i•col•o•gy |ˌtäksi'käləjē| • n. the branch of science concerned with the nature, effects, and detection of poisons. DERIVATIVES: **tox•i•co•log•ic** |-kə'läjik| adj. **tox•i•co•log•i•cal** |-kə'läjikəl| adj. **tox•i•co•log•i•cal•ly** |-kə'läjik(ə)lē| adv. **tox•i•col•o•gist** |-jist| n.

tox•in |'täksin| • n. an antigenic poison or venom of plant or animal origin, esp. one produced by or derived from microorganisms and causing disease when present at low concentration in the body.

tract[1] |trækt| • n. **1** an area of indefinite extent, typically a large one: *large tracts of natural forest.* ▪ an indefinitely large extent of something: *the vast tracts of time.* **2** a major passage in the body, large bundle of nerve fibers, or other continuous elongated anatomical structure or region: *the digestive tract.*

tract[2] • n. a short treatise in pamphlet form, typically on a religious or political subject.

tract[3] • n. (in the Roman Catholic Church) an anthem of scriptural verses formerly replacing the alleluia in certain penitential and requiem Masses.

trac•ta•ble |'træktəbəl| • adj. (of a person or animal) easy to control or influence: *tractable dogs.* ▪ (of a situation or problem) easy to deal with: *trying to make the mathematics tractable.* DERIVATIVES: **trac•ta•bil•i•ty** |ˌtræktə'bilitē| n. **trac•ta•bly** |-blē| adv.

tra•di•tion |trə'disHən| • n. **1** the transmission of customs or beliefs from generation to generation, or the fact of being passed on in this way: *every shade of color is fixed by tradition and governed by religious laws.* ▪ a long-established custom or belief that has been passed on in this way: *Japan's unique cultural traditions.* ▪ [in sing.] an artistic or literary method or style established by an artist, writer, or movement, and subsequently followed by others: *visionary works in the tradition of William Blake.* **2** (in theology) a doctrine believed to have divine authority though not in the scriptures, in particular: ▪ (in Christianity) doctrine not explicit in the Bible but held to derive from the oral teaching of Jesus and the Apostles. ▪ (in Judaism) an ordinance of the oral law not in the Torah but held to have been given by God to Moses. ▪ (in Islam) a saying or act ascribed to the Prophet but not recorded in the Koran. DERIVATIVES: **tra•di•tion•ar•y** |-ˌnerē| adj. **tra•di•tion•ist** |-nist| n. **tra•di•tion•less** adj.

tra•di•tion•al |trə'disHənl| • adj. existing in or as part of a tradition; long-established: *traditional festivities of the church year.* ▪ produced, done, or used in accordance with tradition: *a traditional fish soup.* ▪ habitually done, used, or found: *the traditional drinks in the clubhouse.* ▪ (of a person or group) adhering to tradition, or to a particular tradition:

traditional Elgarians. ▪ (of jazz) in the style of the early 20th century. DERIVATIVES: **tra•di•tion•al•ly** adv.

tra•duce |trə'd(y)ōōs| • v. [trans.] speak badly of or tell lies about (someone) so as to damage their reputation. DERIVATIVES: **tra•duce•ment** n. **tra•duc•er** n.

trag•e•dy |'træjidē| • n. (pl. **-ies**) (in literature and the arts) a play dealing with tragic events and having an unhappy ending, esp. one concerning the downfall of the main (originally powerful or important) character. ▪ the dramatic genre represented by such plays: *Greek tragedy.*

trag•ic |'træjik| • adj. causing or characterized by extreme distress or sorrow: *the shooting was a tragic accident.* ▪ suffering extreme distress or sorrow: *the tragic parents reached the end of their tether.* ▪ of or relating to tragedy in a literary work. In classic tragedy, the hero's HAMARTIA, or tragic flaw, brings about his or her *tragic fall.* The audience may be aware of the *tragic irony* in the hero's wonds or actions, although the fatal significance in unknown to the character himself or herself. DERIVATIVES: **trag•i•cal** adj. **trag•i•cal•ly** |-ik(ə)lē| adv.

trag•i•com•e•dy |ˌtræjə'kämidē| • n. (pl. **-ies**) a play or novel containing elements of both comedy and tragedy. ▪ such works as a genre. DERIVATIVES: **trag•i•com•ic** |-'kämik| adj. **trag•i•com•i•cal•ly** |-'kämik(ə)lē| adv.

tra•jec•to•ry |trə'jektərē| • n. (pl. **-ies**) **1** the path described by a projectile flying or an object moving under the action of given forces. **2** (in geometry) a curve or surface cutting a family of curves or surfaces at a constant angle.

tram•mel |'træməl| • n. **1** (usu. **trammels**) a restriction or impediment to someone's freedom of action: *we will forge our own future, free from the trammels of materialism.* **2** (also **trammel net**) a dragnet consisting of three layers of netting, designed so that a fish entering through one of the large-meshed outer sections will push part of the finer-meshed central section through the large meshes on the further side, forming a pocket in which the fish is trapped. • v. (**trammeled, trammeling**; Brit. **trammelled, trammelling**) [trans.] deprive of freedom of action: *those less trammeled by convention than himself.*

tra•mon•tane |trə'mänˌtān; 'træmən| (also **transmontane**) • adj. traveling to, situated on, coming from (as, a wind), or living on the other side of mountains. ▪ (esp. from the Italian point of view) foreign; barbarous. • n. a person who lives on the other side of mountains (used in particular by Italians to refer to people beyond the Alps).

tran•quil |'træNGkwəl| • adj. free from disturbance; calm: *her tranquil gaze* | *the sea was tranquil.* DERIVATIVES: **tran•quil•i•ty** |ˌtræNG'kwilitē| (also **tran•quil•li•ty**) n. **tran•quil•ly** adv.

tran•scend |trænˈsend| • v. [trans.] be or go beyond the range or limits of (something abstract, typically a conceptual field or division): *this was an issue transcending party politics.*
■ surpass (a person or an achievement).

tran•scend•ent |trænˈsendənt| • adj. beyond or above the range of normal or merely physical human experience: *the search for a transcendent level of knowledge.*
■ surpassing the ordinary; exceptional: *the conductor was described as a "transcendent genius."* ■ (of God) existing apart from and not subject to the limitations of the material universe. Often contrasted with IMMANENT. ■ (in scholastic philosophy) higher than or not included in any of Aristotle's ten categories. ■ (in Kantian philosophy) not realizable in experience.
DERIVATIVES: **tran•scend•ence** n. **tran•scend•en•cy** n. **tran•scend•ent•ly** adv.

tran•scen•den•tal |ˌtrænsenˈdentl| • adj. 1 of or relating to a spiritual or nonphysical realm: *the transcendental importance of each person's soul.*
■ (in Kantian philosophy) presupposed in and necessary to experience; a priori. ■ relating to or denoting Transcendentalism. 2 (of a number, e.g., *e* or π) real but not a root of an algebraic equation with rational roots.
■ (of a function) not capable of being produced by the algebraic operations of addition, multiplication, and involution, or the inverse operations.
DERIVATIVES: **tran•scen•den•tal•ize** |-ˌīz| v. **tran•scen•den•tal•ly** adv.

tran•scen•den•tal•ism |ˌtrænˌsenˈdentl͵izəm| • n. 1 (**Transcendentalism**) an idealistic philosophical and social movement that developed in New England around 1836 in reaction to rationalism. Influenced by romanticism, Platonism, and Kantian philosophy, it taught that divinity pervades all nature and humanity, and its members held socially progressive views. 2 a system developed by Immanuel Kant, based on the idea that, in order to understand the nature of reality, one must first examine and analyze the reasoning process that governs the nature of experience.
DERIVATIVES: **tran•scen•den•tal•ist** (also **Tran•scen•den•tal•ist**) n. & adj.

tran•scribe |trænˈskrīb| • v. [trans.] put (thoughts, speech, or data) into written or printed form: *each interview was taped and transcribed.*
■ transliterate (foreign characters) or write or type out (shorthand, notes, or other abbreviated forms) into ordinary characters or full sentences. ■ arrange (a piece of music) for a different instrument, voice, or group of these: *his largest early work was **transcribed for organ**.* ■ synthesize (a nucleic acid, typically RNA) using an existing nucleic acid, typically DNA, as a template, so that the genetic information in the latter is copied.
DERIVATIVES: **tran•scrib•er** n.

tran•script |ˈtrænˌskript| • n. a written or printed version of material originally presented in another medium.

■ (in biochemistry) a length of RNA or DNA that has been transcribed respectively from a DNA or RNA template. ■ an official record of a student's work, showing courses taken and grades achieved.
DERIVATIVES: **tran•scrip•tive** |ˌtrænˈskriptiv| adj.

tran•scrip•tion |trænˈskripsʜən| • n. a written or printed representation of something.
■ the action or process of transcribing something: *the funding covers transcription of nearly illegible photocopies.* ■ an arrangement of a piece of music for a different instrument, voice, or number of these: *a transcription for voice and lute.* ■ a form in which a speech sound or a foreign character is represented. ■ the process by which genetic information represented by a sequence of DNA nucleotides is copied into newly synthesized molecules of RNA, with the DNA serving as a template.
DERIVATIVES: **tran•scrip•tion•al** |-sʜənl| adj. **tran•scrip•tion•al•ly** |-sʜənl-ē| adv. **tran•scrip•tion•ist** |-nist| n.

tran•sept |ˈtrænˌsept| • n. (in a cross-shaped church) either of the two parts forming the arms of the cross shape, projecting at right angles from the nave: *the north transept.*
DERIVATIVES: **tran•sep•tal** |trænˈseptl| adj.

trans•fig•u•ra•tion |ˌtrænsˌfigyəˈrāsʜən| • n. a complete change of form or appearance into a more beautiful or spiritual state: *in this light the junk undergoes a transfiguration; it shines.*
■ (**the Transfiguration**) Christ's appearance in radiant glory to three of his disciples (Matthew 17:2, Mark 9:2–3, Luke 9:28–36). ■ the church festival commemorating this, held on August 6.

trans•fig•ure |trænsˈfigyər| • v. [trans.] (usu. **be transfigured**) transform into something more beautiful or elevated: *the world is made luminous and is transfigured.*

trans•fix |trænsˈfiks| • v. [trans.] 1 (usu. **be transfixed**) cause (someone) to become motionless with horror, wonder, or astonishment: *he was transfixed by the pain in her face | she stared at him, transfixed.* 2 pierce with a sharp implement or weapon: *a field mouse transfixed by the curved talons of an owl.*
DERIVATIVES: **trans•fix•ion** |-ˈfiksʜən| n.

trans•fuse |trænsˈfyo͞oz| • v. [trans.] 1 transfer (blood or its components) from one person or animal to another.
■ inject (liquid) into a blood vessel to replace lost fluid. 2 cause (something or someone) to be permeated or infused by something: *transfused by a radiance of joy.*

tran•sient |ˈtrænsʜənt; -zʜənt; -zēənt| • adj. lasting only for a short time; impermanent: *a transient cold spell.*
■ staying or working in a place for only a short time: *the transient nature of the labor force in catering.* • n. 1 a person who is staying or working in a place for only a short time. 2 a momentary variation in current, voltage, or frequency.

DERIVATIVES: **tran•sience** n. **tran•sien•cy** n. **tran•sient•ly** adv.

tran•si•tion |træn'zisHən| • n. the process or a period of changing from one state or condition to another: *students in transition from one program to another*| *a transition to multiparty democracy.*
■ a passage in a piece of writing that smoothly connects two topics or sections to each other. ■ (in music) a momentary modulation from one key to another. ■ (in physics) a change of an atom, nucleus, electron, etc., from one quantum state to another, with emission or absorption of radiation.
DERIVATIVES: **tran•si•tion•al** |-SHənl| adj. **tran•si•tion•a•ry** |-,nerē| adj.

tran•si•tive |'trænsitiv; 'trænz-| • adj. 1 (of a verb or a sense or use of a verb) able to take a direct object (expressed or implied), e.g., *saw* in *he saw the donkey.* 2 (of a relation in logic and mathematics) such that, if it applies between successive members of a sequence, it must also apply between any two members taken in order. For instance, if A is larger than B, and B is larger than C, then A is larger than C. • n. a transitive verb.
DERIVATIVES: **tran•si•tive•ly** adv. **tran•si•tive•ness** n. **tran•si•tiv•i•ty** |,trænsə'tivitē; -zə-| n.

tran•si•to•ry |'trænsi,tôrē; 'trænzi-| • adj. not permanent: *transitory periods of medieval greatness.*
DERIVATIVES: **tran•si•to•ri•ly** |-rəlē| adv. **tran•si•to•ri•ness** n.

trans•late |træns'lāt; trænz-| • v. [trans.] 1 express the sense of (words or text) in another language: *the German original has been translated into English.*
■ [intrans.] be expressed or be capable of being expressed in another language: *shiatsu literally translates as "finger pressure."* ■ (**translate something into/translate into**) convert or be converted into (another form or medium): [trans.] *few of Shakespeare's other works have been translated into ballets.* 2 move from one place or condition to another: *she had been translated from familiar surroundings to a foreign court.*
■ move (a bishop) to another see or pastoral charge. ■ remove (a saint's relics) to another place. ■ convey (someone, typically still alive) to heaven. ■ convert (a sequence of nucleotides in messenger RNA) to an amino-acid sequence in a protein or polypeptide during synthesis. 3 (in physics) cause (a body) to move so that all its parts travel in the same direction, without rotation or change of shape.
■ transform (a geometric figure) in an analogous way.
DERIVATIVES: **trans•lat•a•bil•i•ty** |,træns ,lātə'bilədē; ,trænz-| n. **trans•lat•a•ble** adj.

trans•lit•er•ate |træns'litə,rāt; trænz-| • v. [trans.] (usu. **be transliterated**) write or print (a letter or word) using the closest corresponding letters of a different alphabet or language: *names from Russian transliterated into the roman alphabet.*

DERIVATIVES: **trans•lit•er•a•tion** |træns ,litə'rāsHən; trænz-| n. **trans•lit•er•a•tor** |-,rātər| n.

trans•lu•cent |træns'lōōsnt; trænz-| • adj. (of a substance) allowing light, but not detailed shapes, to pass through; semitransparent: *fry until the onions become translucent.* Cf. OPAQUE.
DERIVATIVES: **trans•lu•cence** n. **trans•lu•cen•cy** n. **trans•lu•cent•ly** adv.

trans•mi•grate |træns'mī,grāt; trænz-| • v. [intrans.] 1 (of the soul) pass into a different body after death. 2 migrate.
DERIVATIVES: **trans•mi•gra•tion** |,træns ,mī'grāsHən; ,trænz-| n. **trans•mi•gra•tor** |-,grātər| n. **trans•mi•gra•to•ry** |-grə,tôrē| adj.

trans•mog•ri•fy |træns'mägrə,fī; trænz-| • v. (**-ies, -ied**) [trans.] (often **be transmogrified**) transform, esp. in a surprising or magical manner: *the cucumbers were transmogrified into pickles.*
DERIVATIVES: **trans•mog•ri•fi•ca•tion** |-,mägrəfi'kāsHən| n.

trans•mute |træns'myōōt; trænz-| • v. change in form, nature, or substance: [trans.] *the raw material of his experience was transmuted into stories* | [intrans.] *the discovery that elements can transmute by radioactivity.*
■ [trans.] subject (base metals) to alchemical transmutation: *the quest to transmute lead into gold.*
DERIVATIVES: **trans•mut•a•bil•i•ty** |-,myōōtə'bilitē| n. **trans•mut•a•ble** adj. **trans•mut•a•tive** |-'myōōtətiv| adj. **trans•mut•er** n.

tran•som |'trænsəm| • n. the flat surface forming the stern of a vessel.
■ a horizontal beam reinforcing the stern of a vessel. ■ a strengthening crossbar, in particular one set above a window or door. Cf. MULLION. ■ short for *transom window*, a window set above the transom of a door or larger window; e.g., a fanlight.
PHRASES: **over the transom** offered or sent without prior agreement; unsolicited: *the editors receive about ten manuscripts a week over the transom.*
DERIVATIVES: **tran•somed** adj.

trans•par•ent |træn'sperənt; -'spær-| • adj. (of a material or article) allowing light to pass through so that objects behind can be distinctly seen: *transparent blue water.* Cf. TRANSLUCENT.
■ easy to perceive or detect: *residents will see through any transparent attempt to buy their votes* | *the meaning of the paragraph is by no means transparent.* ■ having thoughts, feelings, or motives that are easily perceived: *you'd be no good at poker—you're too transparent.* ■ (in physics) transmitting heat or other electromagnetic rays without distortion. ■ (of a computing process or interface) functioning without the user being aware of its presence.
DERIVATIVES: **trans•par•en•cy** n. **trans•par•ent•ly** adv. [as submodifier] *a transparently feeble argument.*

tran•spire |træn'spīr| • v. [intrans.] **1** occur; happen: *I'm going to find out exactly what transpired.*
■ prove to be the case: *as it transpired, he was right.* ■ [with clause] (usu. **it transpires**) (of a secret or something unknown) come to be known; be revealed: *Lennon, it transpired, had been under FBI surveillance for some time.* **2** (of a plant or leaf) give off water vapor through the stomata.
DERIVATIVES: **tran•spi•ra•tion** |-spə'rā-SHən| *n.* (in sense 2).

trans•port • v. |træns'pôrt| [trans.] take or carry (people or goods) from one place to another by means of a vehicle, aircraft, or ship: *the bulk of freight traffic was transported by truck.*
■ cause (someone) to feel that he or she is in another place or time: *for a moment she was transported to a warm summer garden on the night of a ball.* ■ (usu. **be transported**) overwhelm (someone) with a strong emotion, esp. joy: *she was transported with pleasure.*
■ send (a convict) to a penal colony. • n. |'træns,pôrt| **1** a system or means of conveying people or goods from place to place by means of a vehicle, aircraft, or ship: *many possess their own forms of transport| air transport.*
■ the action of transporting something or the state of being transported: *the transport of crude oil.* ■ a large vehicle, ship, or aircraft used to carry troops or stores. ■ a convict who was transported to a penal colony. **2** (usu. **transports**) an overwhelmingly strong emotion: *art can send people into **transports of delight**.*

trans•pose |træns'pōz| • v. [trans.] **1** cause (two or more things) to change places with each other: *the captions describing the two state flowers were accidentally transposed.* **2** transfer to a different place or context: *the problems of civilization are transposed into a rustic setting.*
■ write or play (music) in a different key from the original: *the basses are transposed down an octave.* ■ transfer (a mathematical term), with its sign changed, to the other side of an equation. ■ change into a new form: *he transposed a gaffe by the mayor into a public-relations advantage.* • n. (in mathematics) a matrix obtained from a given matrix by interchanging each row and the corresponding column.
DERIVATIVES: **trans•pos•a•ble** *adj.* **trans•pos•al** |-'spōzəl| *n.* **trans•pos•er** *n.*

trans•sex•u•al |træn(s)'sekSHəwəl| • n. a person born with the physical characteristics of one sex who emotionally and psychologically indentifies with the opposite sex.
■ a person who has undergone surgery and hormone treatment in order to acquire the physical characteristics of the opposite sex. Cf. TRANSVESTITE. • adj. of or relating to such a person.
DERIVATIVES: **trans•sex•u•al•ism** |-,lizəm| *n.* **trans•sex•u•al•i•ty** |-,sekSHə'wælite| *n.*

trans•ves•tite |træns'ves,tīt; trænz-| • n. a person, typically a man, who derives pleasure from dressing in clothes appropriate to the opposite sex; a cross-dresser. Cf. TRANSSEXUAL.
DERIVATIVES: **trans•ves•tism** |-,tizəm| *n.* **trans•ves•ti•tism** |-ti,tizəm| *n.*

trau•ma |'trowmə; 'trô-| • n. (pl. **traumas** or **traumata** |-mətə|) a deeply distressing or disturbing experience: *they were reluctant to talk about the traumas of the revolution.*
■ emotional shock following a stressful event or a physical injury, which may be associated with physical shock and sometimes leads to long-term neurosis. ■ physical injury.

trau•mat•ic |trə'mætik; trow-; trô-| • adj. emotionally disturbing or distressing: *she was going through a traumatic divorce.*
■ relating to or causing psychological trauma. ■ relating to or denoting physical injury.
DERIVATIVES: **trau•mat•i•cal•ly** |-ik(ə)lē| *adv.* **trau•ma•tize** *v.*

tra•vail |trə'vāl; 'træv,āl| • n. (also **travails**) painful or laborious effort: *advice for those who wish to save great sorrow and travail.*
■ labor pains: *a woman in travail.* • v. [intrans.] engage in painful or laborious effort.
■ (of a woman) be in labor.

trav•erse |trə'vərs| • v. [trans.] **1** travel across or through: *he traversed the forest.*
■ extend across or through: *a moving catwalk that traversed a vast, cavernous space.* ■ [no obj., with adverbial of direction] cross a hill or mountain by means of a series of sideways movements: *I often use this route, eventually traversing around the headwall.* ■ ski diagonally across (a slope), with only a slight descent.
■ consider or discuss the whole extent of (a subject): *he would traverse a number of subjects and disciplines.* **2** [with obj. and adverbial of direction] move (something) back and forth or sideways: *a probe is traversed along the tunnel.*
■ turn (a large gun or other device on a pivot) to face a different direction. ■ [intrans.] (of such a gun or device) be turned in this way. **3** (in law) deny (an allegation) in pleading.
■ oppose or thwart (a plan). • n. **1** an act of traversing something.
■ a sideways movement, or a series of such movements, across a rock face from one line of ascent or descent to another. ■ a place where a movement of this type is necessary: *a narrow traverse made lethal by snow and ice.* ■ a movement following a diagonal course made by a skier descending a slope. ■ a zigzag course followed by a ship because winds or currents prevent it from sailing directly toward its destination. **2** a part of a structure that extends or is fixed across something.
■ a gallery extending from side to side of a church or other building. **3** a mechanism enabling a large gun to be turned to face a different direction.
■ the sideways movement of a part in a machine. **4** a single line of survey, usually plotted from compass bearings and chained or paced distances between angular points.
■ a tract surveyed in this way. **5** a pair of right-angled bends incorporated in a military trench to avoid enfilading fire. • adj. (of a

curtain rod) allowing the curtain to be opened and closed by sliding it along the rod.
DERIVATIVES: **tra•vers•a•ble** *adj.* **tra•vers•al** |-səl| *n.* **tra•vers•er** *n.*

trav•es•ty |'trævistē| • *n.* (pl. **-ies**) a false, absurd, or distorted representation of something: *the absurdly lenient sentence is a travesty of justice.* • *v.* (**-ies, -ied**) [trans.] represent in such a way: *Michael has betrayed the family by travestying them in his plays.*

treach•er•y |'treCHərē| • *n.* (pl. **-ies**) betrayal of trust; deceptive action or nature: *his resignation was perceived as an act of treachery* | *the treachery of language.*

trea•cle |'trēkəl| • *n.* British term for *molasses.*

■ cloying sentimentality or flattery: *enough of this treacle—let's get back to business.*
DERIVATIVES: **trea•cly** |'trēk(ə)lē| *adj.*

trea•tise |'trētis| • *n.* a written work dealing formally and systematically with a subject: *a comprehensive **treatise on** electricity and magnetism.*

tre•ble[1] |'trebəl| • *adj.* [attrib.] consisting of three parts; threefold: *the fish were caught with treble hooks.*

■ multiplied or occurring three times: *the plaintiff was awarded treble damages.* • *predeterminer* three times as much or as many: *the tip was at least treble what she would normally have given.* • *n.* a threefold quantity or thing, in particular:

■ (in show jumping) a fence consisting of three elements. ■ a crochet stitch made with three loops of wool on the hook at a time. ■ a drink of liquor of three times the standard measure. • *pron.* a number or amount that is three times as large as a contrasting or usual number or amount: *by virtue of having paid treble, he had a double room to himself.* • *v.* make or become three times as large or numerous: [trans.] *rents were trebled* | [intrans.] *his salary has trebled.*

tre•ble[2] • *n.* a high-pitched voice, esp. a boy's singing voice.

■ a boy or girl with such a singing voice. ■ a part written for a high voice or an instrument of a high pitch. ■ [as adj.] denoting a relatively high-pitched member of a family of similar instruments: *a treble viol.* ■ (also **treble bell**) the smallest and highest-pitched bell of a set. ■ the high-frequency output of an audio system or radio, corresponding to the treble in music.

tre•cen•to |trā'CHentō| • *n.* (**the trecento**) the 14th century as a period of Italian art, architecture, or literature.

trek |trek| • *n.* a long arduous journey, esp. one made on foot: *a trek to the South Pole.* • *v.* (**trekked, trekking**) [no obj., with adverbial of direction] go on a long arduous journey, typically on foot: *we trekked through the jungle.*
DERIVATIVES: **trek•ker** *n.*

trem•or |'tremər| • *n.* an involuntary quivering movement: *a disorder that causes tremors and muscle rigidity.*

■ (also **earth tremor**) a slight earthquake. ■ a sudden feeling of fear or excitement: *a tremor*

of unease. ■ a tremble or quaver in a person's voice.

trem•u•lous |'tremyələs| • *adj.* shaking or quivering slightly: *Barbara's voice was tremulous.*

■ timid; nervous: *he gave a tremulous smile.*
DERIVATIVES: **trem•u•lous•ly** *adv.* **trem•u•lous•ness** *n.*

trench•ant |'trenCHənt| • *adj.* **1** vigorous or incisive in expression or style: *she heard their trenchant voices.* **2** (of a weapon or tool) having a sharp edge: *a trenchant blade.*
DERIVATIVES: **trench•an•cy** |-CHənsē| *n.* (in sense 1). **trench•ant•ly** *adv.* (in sense 1).

trep•i•da•tion |,trepi'dāSHən| • *n.* **1** a feeling of fear or agitation about something that may happen: *the men set off in fear and trepidation.* **2** trembling motion.

très |trā| • *adv.* (usually with reference to a fashionable quality) very: *très macho, très chic.*

tri•ad |'trī,æd| • *n.* **1** a group or set of three connected people or things: *the triad of medication, diet, and exercise are necessary in diabetes care.* Cf. MONAD; DYAD.

■ a chord of three musical notes, consisting of a given note with the third and fifth above it. ■ a Welsh form of literary composition with an arrangement of subjects or statements in groups of three. **2** (also **Triad**) a secret society originating in China, typically involved in organized crime.

■ a member of such a society.
DERIVATIVES: **tri•ad•ic** |trī'ædik| *adj.* (in sense 1).

tri•age |trē'äzH; 'trē,äzH| • *n.* **1** the action of sorting according to quality. **2** (in medical use) the assignment of degrees of urgency to wounds or illnesses to decide the order of treatment of a large number of patients or casualties. • *v.* [trans.] assign degrees of urgency to (wounded or ill patients).

trib•al•ism |'trībə,lizəm| • *n.* the state or fact of being organized in a tribe or tribes.

■ the behavior and attitudes that stem from strong loyalty to one's own tribe or social group: *the tribalism of British soccer fans.*

trib•u•la•tion |,trībyə'lāSHən| • *n.* (usu. **tribulations**) a cause of great trouble or suffering: *the tribulations of being a megastar.*

■ a state of great trouble or suffering.

trib•une[1] |'tribyo͞on| • *n.* (also **tribune of the people**) an official in ancient Rome chosen by the plebeians to protect their interests.

■ (also **military tribune**) a Roman legionary officer. ■ a popular leader; a champion of the people. ■ used in names of newspapers: *the Chicago Tribune.*
DERIVATIVES: **trib•u•nate** |'tribyənit; trī'byo͞onit; -,nāt| *n.* **trib•une•ship** |-,SHip| *n.*

trib•une[2] • *n.* **1** an apse in a basilica. **2** a dais or rostrum, esp. in a church.

■ a raised area or gallery with seats, esp. in a church.

trib•ute |'tribyo͞ot| • *n.* **1** an act, statement, or gift that is intended to show gratitude, respect, or admiration: *the video is a tribute to the musicals of the '40s* | *a symposium organized to **pay tribute to** Darwin.*

■ [in sing.] something resulting from something else and indicating its worth: *his victory in the championship was a tribute to his persistence.* **2** payment made periodically by one state or ruler to another, esp. as a sign of dependence: *the king had at his disposal plunder and tribute amassed through warfare.* **3** a proportion of ore or its equivalent, paid to a miner for his work, or to the owner or lessor of a mine.

trick•le-down • *adj.* (of an economic system) in which the poorest gradually benefit as a result of the increasing wealth of the richest.

tri•en•ni•al |trī'enēəl| • *adj.* recurring every three years: *the triennial meeting of the association.*
■ lasting for or relating to a period of three years.
DERIVATIVES: **tri•en•ni•al•ly** *adv.*

tri•fling |'trīf(ə)liNG| • *adj.* unimportant or trivial: *a trifling sum.*
DERIVATIVES: **tri•fling•ly** *adv.*

tril•o•gy |'triləjē| • *n.* (pl. **-ies**) a group of three related novels, plays, films, operas, or albums.
■ (in ancient Greece) a series of three tragedies performed one after the other. ■ a group or series of three related things: *a trilogy of cases reflected this development.*

tri•mes•ter |trī'mestər; 'trī,mes-| • *n.* a period of three months, esp. as a division of the duration of pregnancy.
■ each of the three terms in an academic year.
DERIVATIVES: **tri•mes•tral** |trī'mestrəl| *adj.* **tri•mes•tri•al** |trī'mestrēə| *adj.*

tri•par•tite |trī'pär,tīt| • *adj.* consisting of three parts: *a tripartite classification.*
■ shared by or involving three parties: *a tripartite coalition government.*
DERIVATIVES: **tri•par•tite•ly** *adv.* **tri•par•ti•tion** |,trīpär'tisHən| *n.*

tripe |trīp| • *n.* **1** the first or second stomach of a cow or other ruminant used as food. **2** nonsense; rubbish: *you do talk tripe sometimes.*

tris•kai•dek•a•pho•bi•a |,triskī,dekə'fōbēə; ,triskə-| • *n.* extreme superstition regarding the number thirteen.

tri•um•vi•rate |trī'əmvərit; -,rāt| • *n.* **1** (in ancient Rome) a group of three men (triumvers) holding power, in particular (**the First Triumvirate**) the unofficial coalition of Julius Caesar, Pompey, and Crassus in 60 BC and (**the Second Triumvirate**) a coalition formed by Antony, Lepidus, and Octavian in 43 BC.
■ a group of three powerful or notable people or things existing in relation to each other: *a triumvirate of three former executive vice presidents.* **2** the office of triumvir in ancient Rome.

tri•une |'trī,(y)ōon| • *adj.* consisting of three in one (used esp. with reference to the Trinity): *the triune Godhead.*
DERIVATIVES: **tri•u•ni•ty** |trī'yōonitē| *n.* (pl. **-ies**) .

triv•i•a |'trivēə| • *plural n.* details, considerations, or pieces of information of little impor-

tance or value: *we fill our days with meaningless trivia* | [as *adj.*] *trivia games are popular in our family.*
DERIVATIVES: **triv•i•al** *adj.* **triv•i•al•i•ty** *n.* **triv•i•al•ly** *adv.*

triv•i•um |'trivēəm| • *n.* an introductory course at a medieval university involving the study of grammar, rhetoric, and logic.

tro•chee |'trōkē| • *n.* a prosodic foot consisting of one long or stressed syllable followed by one short or unstressed syllable.
DERIVATIVES: **tro•cha•ic** *adj.*

trog•lo•dyte |'träglə,dīt| • *n.* (esp. in prehistoric times) a person who lived in a cave.
■ a hermit. ■ a person who is regarded as being deliberately ignorant or old-fashioned.
DERIVATIVES: **trog•lo•dyt•ic** |,träglə'di-tik| *adj.* **trog•lo•dyt•ism** |-dī,tizəm| *n.*

troi•ka |'troikə| • *n.* **1** a Russian vehicle pulled by a team of three horses abreast.
■ a team of three horses for such a vehicle. **2** a group of three people working together, esp. in an administrative or managerial capacity.

trol•lop |'träləp| • *n.* a woman perceived as sexually disreputable or promiscuous.

trompe l'oeil |,trômp 'loi | • *n.* (pl. **trompe l'œils** pronunc. same) visual illusion in art, esp. as used to trick the eye into perceiving a painted detail as a three-dimensional object.
■ a painting or design intended to create such an illusion.

trope |trōp| • *n.* a figurative or metaphorical use of a word or expression: *he used the two-Americas trope to explain how a nation free and democratic at home could act wantonly abroad.*
■ a conventional idea or phrase: *her suspicion of ambiguity was more a trope than a fact.* • *v.* [intrans.] create a trope.

troph•ic |'trōfik; 'träf-| • *adj.* of or relating to feeding and nutrition.
■ (of a hormone or its effect) stimulating the activity of another endocrine gland.

tro•pism |'trō,pizəm| • *n.* the turning of all or part of an organism in a particular direction in response to an external stimulus, such as sunlight.

trop•o•sphere |'träpə,sfir; 'trō-| • *n.* the lowest region of the atmosphere, extending from the earth's surface to a height of about 6–10 km (the lower boundary of the stratosphere).
DERIVATIVES: **trop•o•spher•ic** |,träpə 'sfirik; -'sferik; ,trō-| *adj.*

troth |trôTH; trōTH| • *n.* **1** faith or loyalty when pledged in a solemn agreement or undertaking: *a pledge of troth.* **2** truth.
PHRASES: **pledge** (or **plight**) **one's troth** make a solemn pledge of commitment or loyalty, esp. in marriage.

Trot•sky•ism |'trätskē,izəm| • *n.* the political or economic principles of Leon Trotsky, esp. the theory that socialism should be established throughout the world by continuing revolution. Trotskyism has generally included elements of anarchism and syndicalism, but the term has come to be used indiscriminately to describe a great many forms of radical socialism.

DERIVATIVES: **Trot•sky•ist** *n.* & *adj.* **Trot• sky•ite** |-,īt| *n.* & *adj.*

trou•ba•dour |'trōōbə,dôr; -,dŏŏr| • *n.* a French medieval lyric poet composing and singing in Provençal in the 11th to 13th centuries, esp. on the theme of courtly love.
■ a poet who writes verse to music.

troup•er |'trōōpər| • *n.* an actor or other entertainer, typically one with long experience (originally with a *troupe*, a group of traveling entertainers).
■ a reliable and uncomplaining person: *a real trouper, Ma concealed her troubles.*

truck•le • *v.* [intrans.] submit or behave obsequiously: *she despised her husband, who truckled to her.*
DERIVATIVES: **truck•ler** |'trək(ə)lər| *n.*

truc•u•lent |'trəkyələnt| • *adj.* eager or quick to argue or fight; aggressively defiant: *his days of truculent defiance were over.*
DERIVATIVES: **truc•u•lence** *n.* **truc•u• lent•ly** *adv.*

tru•ism |'trōō,izəm| • *n.* a statement that is obviously true and says nothing new or interesting: *the oft-repeated truism that you get what you pay for.*
■ (in logic) a proposition that states nothing beyond what is implied by any of its terms.
DERIVATIVES: **tru•is•tic** |trōō'istik| *adj.*

trump•er•y |'trəmpərē| archaic • *n.* (pl. **-ies**) attractive articles of little value or use.
■ practices or beliefs that are superficially or visually appealing but have little real value or worth. • *adj.* showy but worthless: *trumpery jewelry.*
■ delusive or shallow: *that trumpery hope which lets us dupe ourselves.*

trun•cate • *v.* |'trəNG,kāt| [trans.] [often as adj.] (**truncated**) shorten (something) by cutting off the top or the end: *a truncated cone shape | discussion was truncated by the arrival of tea.* • *adj.* (of a leaf, feather, or other part) ending abruptly as if cut off across the base or tip.
DERIVATIVES: **trun•ca•tion** |,trəNG'kā- SHən| *n.*

trun•cheon |'trənCHən| • *n.* chiefly Brit. a short, thick stick carried as a weapon by a police officer.
■ a staff or baton acting as a symbol of authority.

trust•ee |trə'stē| • *n.* (in law) an individual person or member of a board given control or powers of administration of property in trust with a legal obligation to administer it solely for the purposes specified. Cf. FIDUCIARY.
■ a state made responsible for the government of an area by the United Nations.
DERIVATIVES: **trust•ee•ship** |-,SHip| *n.*

tryst |trist| • *n.* a private, romantic rendezvous between lovers: *a moonlight tryst.* • *v.* [intrans.] keep a rendezvous of this kind: [as n.] (**trysting**) *a trysting place.*
DERIVATIVES: **trys•ter** *n.*

tsar, etc. • *n.* variant spelling of CZAR, etc.

tsu•na•mi |(t)sōō'nämē| • *n.* (pl. same or **tsu- namis**) a long high sea wave caused by an earthquake or other disturbance.

tulle |tōōl| • *n.* a soft, fine silk, cotton, or nylon material like net, used for making veils and dresses.

tu•mes•cent |t(y)ōō'mesənt| • *adj.* swollen or becoming swollen, esp. as a response to sexual arousal.
■ (esp. of language or literary style) pompous or pretentious; tumid: *his prose is tumescent, full of orotund language.*
DERIVATIVES: **tu•mes•cence** *n.* **tu•mes• cent•ly** *adv.*

tu•mid |'t(y)ōōmid| • *adj.* (esp. of a part of the body) swollen: *a tumid belly.*
■ (esp. of language or literary style) pompous or bombastic: *tumid oratory.*
DERIVATIVES: **tu•mid•i•ty** |t(y)ōō'miditē| *n.* **tu•mid•ly** *adv.*

tu•mul•tu•ous |t(y)ōō'məlCHəwəs; tə-| • *adj.* making a loud, confused noise; uproarious: *tumultuous applause.*
■ excited, confused, or disorderly: *a tumultuous crowd | a tumultuous personal life.*
DERIVATIVES: **tu•mul•tu•ous•ly** *adv.* **tu• mul•tu•ous•ness** *n.*

tu•mu•lus |'t(y)ōōmyə,ləs| • *n.* (pl. **tumuli** |-,lī|) an ancient burial mound; a barrow.

tun |tən| • *n.* **1** a large beer or wine cask.
■ a brewer's fermenting vat. **2** an imperial measure of capacity, equal to 4 hogsheads.
• *v.* (**tunned, tunning**) [trans.] store (wine or other alcoholic drinks) in a tun.

tun•dra |'təndrə| • *n.* a vast, flat, treeless Arctic region of Europe, Asia, and North America in which the subsoil is permanently frozen.

tur•bid |'tərbid| • *adj.* (of a liquid) cloudy, opaque, or thick with suspended matter: *the turbid estuary.*
■ characterized by or producing confusion or obscurity of thought, feeling, etc; unclear: *a turbid piece of cinéma vérité.*
DERIVATIVES: **tur•bid•i•ty** |tər'biditē| *n.* **tur•bid•ly** *adv.* **tur•bid•ness** *n.*

USAGE: **Turbid** is used of a liquid or color to mean 'muddy, not clear,' or of literary style, etc., to mean 'confused,' for example, *the turbid utterances and twisted language of Carlyle.* **Turgid** means 'swollen, inflated, enlarged.' When used of literary style it means 'pompous, bombastic': *Communications from headquarters were largely turgid exercises in self-congratulation.*

tur•bine |'tər,bīn; -bin| • *n.* a machine for producing continuous power in which a wheel or rotor, typically fitted with vanes, is made to revolve by a fast-moving flow of water, steam, gas, air, or other fluid.

tur•bu•lence |'tərbyələns| • *n.* violent or unsteady movement of air or water, or of some other fluid: *the plane shuddered as it entered some turbulence.*
■ conflict; confusion: *a time of political turbulence.*
DERIVATIVES: **tur•bu•lent** *adj.* **tur•bu• lent•ly** *adv.*

tur•ges•cent |tər'jesənt| • *adj.* becoming or seeming swollen or distended.
DERIVATIVES: **tur•ges•cence** *n.*

tur•gid |'tərjid| • *adj.* swollen and distended or congested: *a turgid and fast-moving river.*
■ (of language or style) tediously pompous or bombastic: *some turgid verses on the death of Prince Albert.*
DERIVATIVES: **tur•gid•i•ty** |tər'jidité| *n.* **tur•gid•ly** *adv.*

USAGE: On the differences in use between **turgid** and **turbid**, see usage at TURBID.

tur•pi•tude |'tərpi,t(y)ōōd| • *n.* the quality of being disgraceful; depravity; wickedness: *acts of moral turpitude.*

tu•te•lage |'t(y)ōōtlij| • *n.* protection of or authority over someone or something; guardianship: *the organizations remained under firm government tutelage.*
■ instruction; tuition: *he felt privileged to be under the tutelage of an experienced actor.*

tu•te•lar•y |'t(y)ōōtl,erē| (also **tutelar** |-ər|) • *adj.* serving as a protector, guardian, or patron: *the tutelary spirits of these regions.*
■ of or relating to protection or a guardian: *the state maintained a tutelary relation with the security police.*

tweed•y |'twēdē| • *adj.* (**tweedier, tweediest**) (of a garment) made of tweed cloth: *a tweedy suit.*
■ (of a person) habitually wearing tweed clothes: *a stout, tweedy woman.* ■ of a refined, traditional, upscale character: *the tweedy world of books.*
DERIVATIVES: **tweed•i•ly** |-dilē| *adv.* **tweed•i•ness** *n.*

ty•chism |'tī,kizəm| • *n.* (in philosophy) the doctrine that account must be taken of the element of chance in reasoning or explanation of the universe.

ty•coon |tī'kōōn| • *n.* a wealthy, powerful person in business or industry: *a newspaper tycoon.*
DERIVATIVES: **ty•coon•er•y**

tym•pa•num |'timpənəm| • *n.* (pl. **tympanums** or **tympana** |-nə|) **1** the tympanic membrane or eardrum.
■ a membrane covering the hearing organ on the leg or body of some insects, sometimes adapted (as in cicadas) for producing sound.
■ a drum. **2** (in architecture) a vertical recessed triangular space forming the center of a pediment, typically decorated.
■ a similar space over a door between the lintel and the arch.

ty•pol•o•gy |tī'päləjē| • *n.* (pl. **-ies**) **1** a classification according to general type, esp. in archaeology, psychology, or the social sciences: *a typology of Anasazi pottery.*
■ study or analysis using such classification. **2** the study and interpretation of types and symbols, originally esp. in the Bible.
DERIVATIVES: **ty•po•log•i•cal** |,tīpə'läjikəl| *adj.* **ty•pol•o•gist** |-jist| *n.*

ty•ran•ni•cide |tə'ræni,sīd| • *n.* the killing of a tyrant.
■ the killer of a tyrant.
DERIVATIVES: **ty•ran•ni•cid•al** |tə,ræni'sīdl| *adj.*

tyr•an•ny |'tirənē| • *n.* (pl. **-ies**) cruel and oppressive government or rule: *refugees who managed to escape Nazi tyranny* | *the removal of the regime may be the end of a tyranny.*
■ a nation under such cruel and oppressive government. ■ cruel, unreasonable, or arbitrary use of power or control: *she resented his rages and his tyranny* | *the tyranny of the nine-to-five day* | *his father's tyrannies.* ■ (esp. in ancient Greece) rule by one who has absolute power without legal right.
DERIVATIVES: **tyr•an•nous** |-nəs| *adj.* **tyr•an•nous•ly** |-nəslē| *adv.*

ty•rant |'tīrənt| • *n.* a cruel and oppressive ruler: *the tyrant was deposed by popular demonstrations.*
■ a person exercising power or control in a cruel, unreasonable, or arbitrary way: *her father was a tyrant and a bully.* ■ (esp. in ancient Greece) a ruler who seized power without legal right.

ty•ro |'tīrō| (also **tiro**) • *n.* (pl. **-os**) a beginner or novice.

Uu

Ü•ber•mensch |'ōōbər,men(t)SH| • *n.* (pl. **Übermenschen** |'ōōbər,men(t)SHən|) the ideal superior man of the future who could rise above conventional Christian morality to create and impose his own values, originally described by Fredrich Nietzsche in *Thus Spake Zarathustra* (1883–85). Also called **superman** and **overman**.

u•bi•e•ty |yōō'bīətē| • *n.* poetic/literary the condition of being in a definite place.

u•bi•qui•tar•i•an |yōō,bikwə'terēən| • *n.* a person, typically a Lutheran, who believes that Christ is present everywhere at all times.
• *adj.* relating to or believing in such a doctrine.
DERIVATIVES: **u•biq•ui•tar•i•an•ism** |-,nizəm| *n.*

u•biq•ui•tous |yōō'bikwətəs| • *adj.* present, appearing, or found everywhere: *his ubiquitous influence was felt by all the family* | *cowboy hats are ubiquitous among the singers.*
DERIVATIVES: **u•biq•ui•tous•ly** *adv.* **u•biq•ui•tous•ness** *n.* **u•biq•ui•ty** |-wətē| *n.*

u•kase |yōō'kās; -'kāz| • *n.* an edict of the

Russian government: *Czar Alexander I issued his famous ukase decreeing the North Pacific Coast Russian territory.*
■ an arbitrary command: *defying the publisher in the very building from which he had issued his ukase.*

u•ki•yo-e |ˌo͞okēyō '(y)ā| • *n.* a school of Japanese art depicting subjects from everyday life, dominant in the 17th–19th centuries in paintings and woodblock prints.

ul•lage |'əlij| • *n.* the amount by which a container falls short of being full.
■ loss of liquid by evaporation or leakage.

ul•te•ri•or |əl'tirēər| • *adj.* existing beyond what is obvious or admitted; intentionally hidden: *could there be an ulterior motive behind his request?*
■ beyond what is immediate or present; coming in the future: *ulterior pay promised to the mariners.*

ul•ti•mate |'əltəmit| • *adj.* being or happening at the end of a process; final: *their ultimate aim was to force his resignation.*
■ being the best or most extreme example of its kind: *the ultimate accolade.* ■ basic or fundamental: *the ultimate constituents of anything that exists are atoms.* ■ (in physics) denoting the maximum possible strength or resistance beyond which an object breaks. • *n.* **1** (**the ultimate**) the best achievable or imaginable of its kind: *the ultimate in decorative luxury.* **2** a final or fundamental fact or principle.
DERIVATIVES: **ul•ti•ma•cy** |-məsē| *n.* (pl. **-ies**). **ul•ti•mate•ly** *adv.*

ul•ti•ma•tum |ˌəltə'mātəm; -'mät-| • *n.* (pl. **ultimatums** or **ultimata** |-'mätə; -'mätə|) a final demand or statement of terms, the rejection of which will result in retaliation or a breakdown in relations: *the UN Security Council ultimatum demanding Iraq's withdrawal from Kuwait* | *a "Marry me or else" ultimatum.*

ul•ti•mo |'əltə,mō| (abbr.: **ult.** or **ulto**) • *adj.* [postpositive] of last month: *the 3rd ultimo.* Used in formal letters. Cf. INSTANT; PROXIMO.

ul•tra•mon•tane |ˌəltrə,män'tān; -'män,tān| • *adj.* **1** advocating supreme papal authority in matters of faith and discipline. **2** situated on the other side of the Alps from the point of view of the speaker. • *n.* a person advocating supreme papal authority.
DERIVATIVES: **ul•tra•mon•ta•nism** |-'mäntə,nizəm| *n.* **ul•tra•mon•ta•nist** *n.*

ul•tra•son•ic |ˌəltrə'sänik| • *adj.* of or involving sound waves with a frequency above the upper limit of human hearing.
DERIVATIVES: **ul•tra•son•i•cal•ly** |-ik(ə)lē| *adv.*

ul•u•late |'əlyə,lāt; 'yo͞ol-| • *v.* [intrans.] howl or wail as an expression of strong emotion, typically grief; make a high wavering sound with the voice and tongue: *women were ululating as the body was laid out.*
DERIVATIVES: **ul•u•lant** |-lənt| *adj.* **ul•u•la•tion** |ˌəlyə'lāshən; ˌyo͞ol-| *n.*

um•brage |'əmbrij| • *n.* **1** offense or annoyance: *she took umbrage at his remarks.* **2** shade or shadow, esp. as cast by trees.

DERIVATIVES: **um•bra•geous** |ˌəm'brājəs| *adj.*

um•brif•er•ous |ˌəm'brif(ə)rəs| • *adj.* poetic/literary providing shade.

un•as•sum•ing |ˌənə'so͞omiNG| • *adj.* not pretentious or arrogant; modest: *he was an unassuming and modest man.*
DERIVATIVES: **un•as•sum•ing•ly** *adv.* **un•as•sum•ing•ness** *n.*

un•can•ny |ˌən'kænē| • *adj.* (**uncannier**, **uncanniest**) strange or mysterious, esp. in an unsettling way: *an uncanny feeling that he was being watched.*
DERIVATIVES: **un•can•ni•ly** |-'kænəl-ē| *adv.* **un•can•ni•ness** *n.*

un•ci•al |'ənshəl; -sēəl| • *adj.* **1** of or written in a majuscule script with rounded unjoined letters that is found in European manuscripts of the 4th–8th centuries and from which modern capital letters are derived. **2** of or relating to an inch or an ounce. • *n.* an uncial letter or script.
■ a manuscript in uncial script.

un•con•scion•a•ble |ˌən'känsh(ə)nəbəl| • *adj.* not right or reasonable: *the unconscionable conduct of his son.*
■ unreasonably excessive: *shareholders have had to wait an unconscionable time for the facts to be established.*
DERIVATIVES: **un•con•scion•a•bly** |-blē| *adv.*

un•con•scious |ˌən'känshəs| • *n.* (**the unconscious**) the part of the mind that is inaccessible to the conscious mind but that affects behavior and emotions.

unc•tion |'əNG(k)shən| • *n.* **1** the action of anointing someone with oil or ointment as a religious rite or as a symbol of investiture as a monarch.
■ the oil or ointment so used. **2** treatment with a medicinal oil or ointment.
■ an ointment: *mercury in the form of unctions.* **3** a manner of expression arising or apparently arising from deep emotion, esp. as intended to flatter: *he spoke the last two words with exaggerated unction.*

unc•tu•ous |'əNG(k)CHo͞oəs; -sho͞oəs; -CHəs| • *adj.* **1** (of a person) excessively or ingratiatingly flattering; oily: *he seemed anxious to please but not in an unctuous way.* **2** (chiefly of minerals) having a greasy or soapy feel.
DERIVATIVES: **unc•tu•ous•ly** *adv.* **unc•tu•ous•ness** *n.*

un•der•class |'əndər,klæs| • *n.* the lowest social stratum in a country or community, consisting of the poor and unemployed.

un•der•mine |ˌəndər'mīn; 'əndər,mīn| • *v.* [trans.] erode the base or foundation of (mass of rock).
■ dig or excavate beneath (a building or fortification) so as to make it collapse. ■ damage or weaken (someone or something), esp. gradually or insidiously: *this could undermine years of hard work.*
DERIVATIVES: **un•der•min•er** *n.*

un•der•priv•i•leged |ˌəndər'priv(ə)lijd| • *adj.* (of a person) not enjoying the same standard of living or rights as the majority of people in a society.

un•der•tone |ˈəndərˌtōn| • *n.* a subdued or muted tone of sound or color: *they were talking in undertones* | *a pallid undertone to her tanned skin.*
■ an underlying quality or feeling: *the sexual undertones of most advertising.*

un•der•whelm |ˌəndərˈ(h)welm| • *v.* [trans.] (usu. **be underwhelmed**) fail to impress or make a positive impact on (someone); disappoint: *American voters seem underwhelmed by the choices for president.*

un•dine |ˌənˈdēn; ˈənˌdēn| • *n.* a female spirit or nymph imagined as inhabiting water.

un•du•late • *v.* |ˈənjəˌlāt; ˈəndyə-| [intrans.] move with a smooth wavelike motion: *her body undulated to the thumping rhythm of the music.*
■ [usu. adj.] (**undulating**) have a wavy form or outline: *delightful views over undulating countryside.* • *adj.* |-lit; -ˌlāt| (esp. of a leaf) having a wavy surface or edge.
DERIVATIVES: **un•du•late•ly** |-litlē| *adv.* **un•du•la•tion** |ˌənjəˈlāsHən; ˌəndyə-| *n.* **un•du•la•to•ry** |ˈənjələˌtôrē; ˈəndyə-| *adj.*

un•earth |ˌənˈərTH| • *v.* [trans.] find (something) in the ground by digging.
■ discover (something hidden, lost, or kept secret) by investigation or searching: *they have done all they can to unearth the truth.*

un•earth•ly |ˌənˈərTHlē| • *adj.* **1** unnatural or mysterious, esp. in a disturbing way: *unearthly quiet.* **2** unreasonably early or inconvenient: *a job that involves getting up at an unearthly hour.*
DERIVATIVES: **un•earth•li•ness** *n.*

un•e•quiv•o•cal |ˌəniˈkwivəkəl| • *adj.* leaving no doubt; unambiguous: *an unequivocal answer* | *he was unequivocal in condemning the violence.*
DERIVATIVES: **un•e•quiv•o•cal•ly** |-ik(ə)-lē| *adv.* **un•e•quiv•o•cal•ness** *n.*

un•gain•ly |ˌənˈgānlē| • *adj.* (of a person or movement) awkward; clumsy: *an ungainly walk.*
DERIVATIVES: **un•gain•li•ness** *n.*

un•glued |ˌənˈglo͞od| • *adj.* not or no longer stuck or cohesive: *grease particles come unglued from the plate.* | *it was only a matter of time before the whole operation came unglued.*
■ (of a person or state of mind) confused and emotionally strained: *it had been a long day, and tempers were becoming unglued.*

un•guent |ˈəNGgwənt| • *n.* a soft greasy or viscous substance used as an ointment or for lubrication.

un•gu•late |ˈəNGgyələt; -ˌlāt| • *n.* a hoofed mammal.

un•hinge |ˌənˈhinj| • *v.* [trans.] [usu. as adj.] (**unhinged**) make (someone) mentally unbalanced: *I thought she must be unhinged by grief.*
■ deprive of stability or fixity; throw into disorder.

un•ho•ly |ˌənˈhōlē| • *adj.* (**unholier, unholiest**) sinful; wicked.
■ not holy; unconsecrated: *an unholy marriage.*

■ denoting an alliance with potentially harmful implications between two or more parties that are not natural allies: *an unholy alliance between economic and political power.* ■ awful; dreadful (used for emphasis): *she was making an unholy racket.*
DERIVATIVES: **un•ho•li•ness** *n.*

u•ni•cam•er•al |ˌyo͞onəˈkæm(ə)rəl| • *adj.* (of a legislative body) having a single legislative chamber.

u•ni•form•i•tar•i•an•ism |ˌyo͞onəˌfôrməˈterēəˌnizəm| • *n.* the theory that changes in the earth's crust during geological history have resulted from the action of continuous and uniform processes. Cf. CATASTROPHISM.
DERIVATIVES: **u•ni•form•i•tar•i•an** *adj.* & *n.*

u•ni•form•i•ty |ˌyo͞onəˈfôrmətē| • *n.* (pl. **-ies**) the quality or state of being uniform: *an attempt to impose administrative uniformity.*
■ lack of variety or diversity; sameness; monotony.

u•ni•lat•er•al |ˌyo͞onəˈlætərəl; -ˈlætrəl| • *adj.* **1** (of an action or decision) performed by or affecting only one person, group, or country involved in a particular situation, without the agreement of another or the others: *unilateral nuclear disarmament.* **2** relating to, occurring on, or affecting only one side of an organ or structure, or of the body.
DERIVATIVES: **u•ni•lat•er•al•ly** *adv.*

un•in•i•ti•at•ed |ˌənəˈnisHēˌātid| • *adj.* without special knowledge or experience: [as plural n.] (**the uninitiated**) *the discussion wasn't easy to follow for the uninitiated.*

u•nique |yo͞oˈnēk| • *adj.* being the only one of its kind; unlike anything else: *the situation was unique in modern politics* | *original and unique designs.*
■ particularly remarkable, special, or unusual: *a unique opportunity to see the spectacular Bolshoi Ballet.* ■ [predic.] (**unique to**) belonging or connected to (one particular person, group, or place): *a style of architecture unique to Portugal.* • *n.* a unique person or thing.
DERIVATIVES: **u•nique•ly** *adv.* **u•nique•ness** *n.*

USAGE: There is a set of adjectives—including **unique, complete, equal, infinite,** and **perfect**—whose core meaning embraces an absolute concept and which therefore, according to a traditional argument, cannot be modified by adverbs such as **really, quite,** or **very.** For example, since the core meaning of **unique** (from Latin 'one') is 'being only one of its kind,' it is logically impossible, the argument goes, to submodify it: it is either 'unique' or it is not, and there are no stages in between. In practice the situation in the language is more complex than this. Words like **unique** have a core sense but they often also have a secondary, less precise (nonabsolute) sense of 'very remarkable or unusual,' as in *a really unique opportunity.* It is advisable, however, to use **unique** sparingly and not to modify it with *very, quite, really,* etc.

U•ni•tar•i•an |ˌyōōnəˈterēən| • *n.* a person, esp. a Christian, who asserts the unity of God and rejects the doctrine of the Trinity.
■ a member of a church or religious body maintaining this belief and typically rejecting formal dogma in favor of a rationalist and inclusivist approach to belief. • *adj.* of or relating to the Unitarians.
DERIVATIVES: **U•ni•tar•i•an•ism** |-ˌnizəm| *n.*

u•ni•ver•sal |ˌyōōnəˈvərsəl| • *adj.* of, affecting, or done by all people or things in the world or in a particular group; applicable to all cases: *universal adult suffrage* | *the incidents caused universal concern.*
■ denoting a logical proposition in which something is asserted of all of a class. Contrasted with *particular.* ■ denoting or relating to a grammatical rule, set of rules, or other linguistic feature that is found in all languages. ■ (of a tool or machine) adjustable to or appropriate for all requirements; not restricted to a single purpose or position. • *n.* a person or thing having universal effect, currency, or application, in particular:
■ (in logic) a universal proposition. ■ (in philosophy) a term or concept of general application. ■ (in philosophy) a nature or essence signified by a general term. ■ a universal grammatical rule or linguistic feature.
DERIVATIVES: **u•ni•ver•sal•i•ty** |-vərˈsæl-ətē| *n.* **u•ni•ver•sal•ly** *adv.*

u•ni•ver•sal•ist |ˌyōōnəˈvərsəlist| • *n.* **1** (in Christian theology) a person who believes that all humankind will eventually be saved.
■ (usu. **Universalist**) a member of an organized body of Christians who hold such beliefs. **2** a person advocating loyalty to and concern for others without regard to national or other allegiances. • *adj.* **1** (in Christian theology) of or relating to universalists. **2** universal in scope or character.
DERIVATIVES: **u•ni•ver•sal•ism** |-ˌlizəm| *n.* **u•ni•ver•sal•is•tic** |-ˌvərsəˈlistik| *adj.*

u•ni•verse |ˈyōōnəˌvərs| • *n.* (**the universe**) all existing matter and space considered as a whole; the cosmos. The universe is believed to be at least 10 billion light years in diameter and contains a vast number of galaxies; it has, according to current theory, been expanding since its creation in the big bang about 13 billion years ago.
■ a particular sphere of activity, interest, or experience: *the front parlor was the hub of her universe.*

u•ni•ver•si•ty |ˌyōōnəˈvərsətē| • *n.* (pl. **-ies**) an educational institution designed for instruction, examination, or both, of students in many branches of advanced learning, conferring degrees in various faculties, and often embodying colleges and similar institutions: [in names] *Oxford University* | *the University of California* | [as adj.] *the university buildings* | *a university professor.*
■ the members of this collectively. ■ the grounds and buildings of such an institution.

un•kempt |ˌənˈkem(p)t| • *adj.* (esp. of a per-

son) having an untidy or disheveled appearance: *they were unwashed and unkempt.*
DERIVATIVES: **un•kempt•ly** *adv.* **un•kempt•ness** *n.*

un•lim•ber |ˌənˈlimbər| • *v.* [trans.] detach (a gun) from its limber (carriage) so that it can be used.
■ unpack or unfasten (something) ready for use: *we had to unlimber some of the gear.* ■ [intrans.] get ready for some activity.

un•man |ˌənˈmæn| • *v.* (**unmanned, unmanning**) [trans.] deprive of qualities traditionally associated with men, such as self-control or courage: *awaiting a sentence will unman the stoutest heart.*

un•mit•i•gat•ed |ˌənˈmitəˌgātid| • *adj.* [attrib.] absolute; unqualified: *the tour had been an unmitigated disaster.*
DERIVATIVES: **un•mit•i•gat•ed•ly** *adv.*

un•nerve |ˌənˈnərv| • *v.* [trans.] make (someone) lose courage or confidence: [as adj.] (**unnerving**) *an unnerving experience.*
DERIVATIVES: **un•nerv•ing•ly** *adv.*

un•prec•e•dent•ed |ˌənˈpresəˌdəntəd| • *adj.* never done or known before: *the government took the unprecedented step of releasing confidential correspondence.*
DERIVATIVES: **un•prec•e•dent•ed•ly** *adv.*

un•rav•el |ˌənˈrævəl| • *v.* (**unraveled, unraveling**; Brit. **unravelled, unravelling**) [trans.] **1** undo (twisted, knitted, or woven threads).
■ [intrans.] (of twisted, knitted, or woven threads) become undone: *part of the crew neck had unraveled.* ■ unwind (something wrapped around another object): *he unraveled the cellophane from a small cigar.* **2** investigate and solve or explain (something complicated or puzzling): *they were attempting to unravel the cause of death.*
■ [intrans.] begin to fail or collapse: *his painstaking diplomacy of the last eight months could quickly unravel.*

un•re•quit•ed |ˌənriˈkwītid| • *adj.* (of a feeling, esp. love) not returned or rewarded.
DERIVATIVES: **un•re•quit•ed•ly** *adv.* **un•re•quit•ed•ness** *n.*

un•ru•ly |ˌənˈrōōlē| • *adj.* (**unrulier, unruliest**) disorderly and disruptive and not amenable to discipline or control: *complaints about unruly behavior.*
■ (of hair) difficult to keep neat and tidy.
DERIVATIVES: **un•ru•li•ness** *n.*

un•sa•vor•y |ˌənˈsāv(ə)rē| (Brit. **unsavoury**) • *adj.* disagreeable to taste, smell, or look at.
■ disagreeable and unpleasant because morally disreputable: *an unsavory reputation.*
DERIVATIVES: **un•sa•vor•i•ly** |-rəlē| *adv.* **un•sa•vor•i•ness** *n.*

un•scathed |ˌənˈskāᴛʜd| • *adj.* [predic.] without suffering any injury, damage, or harm: *I came through all those perils unscathed.*

un•seem•ly |ˌənˈsēmlē| • *adj.* (of behavior or actions) not proper or appropriate: *an unseemly squabble.*
DERIVATIVES: **un•seem•li•ness** *n.*

un•string |ˌənˈstriNG| • *v.* (past and past part. **unstrung** |-ˈstrəNG|) [trans.] **1** [usu. as adj.]

(**unstrung**) (of a person) unnerve: *a mind unstrung by loneliness.*

un•touch•a•ble |ˌənˈtəCHəbəl| • *adj.* **1** not able or allowing to be touched or affected: *the receptionist looked gorgeous and untouchable.*
■ unable to be matched or rivaled: *we took the silver medal behind the untouchable US team.* **2** of or belonging to the lowest-caste Hindu group or the people outside the caste system. • *n.* a member of the lowest-caste Hindu group or a person outside the caste system. Contact with untouchables is traditionally held to defile members of higher castes.
DERIVATIVES: **un•touch•a•bil•i•ty** |-ˌtəCHə ˈbilitē| *n.*

USAGE: In senses relating to the traditional Hindu caste system, the term **untouchable** and the social restrictions accompanying it were declared illegal in the constitution of India in 1949 and of Pakistan in 1953. The official term today is **scheduled caste**.

un•to•ward |ˌənˈtôrd; -t(ə)ˈwôrd| • *adj.* unexpected and inappropriate or inconvenient: *both tried to behave as if nothing untoward had happened* | *untoward jokes and racial remarks.*
DERIVATIVES: **un•to•ward•ly** *adv.* **un•to•ward•ness** *n.*

un•tried |ˌənˈtrīd| • *adj.* **1** not yet tested to discover quality or reliability; inexperienced: *he chose two untried actors for leading roles.* **2** (of an accused person) not yet subjected to a trial in court.

un•wield•y |ˌənˈwēldē| • *adj.* (**unwieldier, unwieldiest**) difficult to carry or move because of its size, shape, or weight: *the first mechanical clocks were large and unwieldy.*
■ (of a system or bureaucracy) too big or badly organized to function efficiently.
DERIVATIVES: **un•wield•i•ly** |-ˈwēldəlē| *adv.* **un•wield•i•ness** *n.*

un•wit•ting |ˌənˈwitiNG| • *adj.* (of a person) not aware of the full facts: *an unwitting accomplice.*
■ not done on purpose; unintentional: *we are anxious to rectify the unwitting mistakes made in the past.*
DERIVATIVES: **un•wit•ting•ly** *adv.* [sentence adverb] *quite unwittingly you played right into my hands that night.* **un•wit•ting•ness** *n.*

up•braid |ˌəpˈbrād| • *v.* [trans.] find fault with (someone); scold: *he was upbraided for his slovenly appearance.*

up•mar•ket |ˌəpˈmärkit; ˈəpˌmär-| (also **upmarket**) • *adj. & adv.* of or toward the more expensive end of the market; upscale.

up•pish |ˈəpiSH| • *adj.* arrogantly self-assertive.
DERIVATIVES: **up•pish•ly** *adv.* **up•pish•ness** *n.*

up•shot |ˈəpˌSHät| • *n.* [in sing.] the final or eventual outcome or conclusion of a discussion, action, or series of events: *the upshot of the meeting was that he was on the next plane to New York.*

up•stage |ˌəpˈstāj| • *adv. & adj.* at or toward the back of a theater stage: [as adv.] *Hamlet turns to face upstage* | [as adj.] *an upstage exit.*
■ [as adj.] superior; aloof. • *v.* [trans.] divert attention from (someone) toward oneself; outshine: *they were totally upstaged by two newcomers in the film.*
■ (of an actor) move toward the back of a stage to make (another actor) face away from the audience.

u•ra•nog•ra•phy |ˌyo͝orəˈnägrəfē| • *n.* the branch of astronomy concerned with describing and mapping the stars.
DERIVATIVES: **u•ra•nog•ra•pher** |-fər| *n.* **u•ra•no•graph•ic** |-nəˈgrafik| *adj.*

ur•bane |ˌərˈbān| • *adj.* (of a person, esp. a man) suave, courteous, and refined in manner.
DERIVATIVES: **ur•bane•ly** *adv.*

ur•chin |ˈərCHin| • *n.* **1** a mischievous young child, esp. one who is poorly or raggedly dressed. Cf. GAMINE.
■ old term for a goblin. **2** short for sea *urchin*, a marine echinoderm.

ur•sine |ˈərˌsīn; -ˌsēn| • *adj.* of, relating to, or resembling bears.

ur•text |ˈo͝orˌtekst| • *n.* (pl. **urtexte** |-ˌtekstə|) an original or the earliest surviving version of a text, to which later versions can be compared.

ur•ti•cate |ˈərtəˌkāt| • *v.* [intrans.] cause a stinging or prickling sensation like that given by a nettle: [as adj.] (**urticating**) *the urticating hairs.*
DERIVATIVES: **ur•ti•ca•tion** |ˌərtəˈkāSHən| *n.*

u•surp |yo͞oˈsərp| • *v.* [trans.] take (a position of power or importance) illegally or by force: *Richard usurped the throne.*
■ take the place of (someone in a position of power) illegally; supplant: *the Hanoverian dynasty had usurped the Stuarts.* [intrans.] (**usurp on/upon**) encroach or infringe upon (someone's rights): *the Church had usurped upon the domain of the state.*
DERIVATIVES: **u•sur•pa•tion** |ˌyo͞osər ˈpāSHən| *n.* **u•surp•er** *n.*

u•su•ry |ˈyo͞oZH(ə)rē| • *n.* the action or practice of lending money at excessive rates of interest, variously defined in criminal laws.
■ interest at such rates.
DERIVATIVES: **u•sur•er** *n.* **u•su•ri•ous** *adj.*

u•tile |ˈyo͞oˌtl; yo͞oˌtīl| • *adj.* advantageous.

U•to•pi•a |yo͞oˈtōpēə| (also **utopia**) • *n.* an imagined place or state of things in which everything is perfect.
DERIVATIVES: **U•to•pi•an** (also **u•to•pi•an**) *adj., n.*

ux•o•ri•al |ˌək'sôrēəl; əgˈzôr-| • *adj.* of or relating to a wife.

ux•o•ri•ous |ˌəkˈsôrēəs; ˌəgˈzôr-| • *adj.* having or showing an excessive or submissive fondness for one's wife.
DERIVATIVES: **ux•o•ri•ous•ly** *adv.* **ux•o•ri•ous•ness** *n.*

Vv

vac•ci•nate | 'væksə,nāt | • v. [trans.] treat with a vaccine to produce immunity against a disease: *all the children were vaccinated against diphtheria.* Cf. INOCULATE.
DERIVATIVES: **vac•ci•na•tion** | ,væksə'nāsHən | n. **vac•ci•na•tor** | -,nātər | n.

vac•cine | væk'sēn | • n. a substance used to stimulate the production of antibodies and provide immunity against one or several diseases, prepared from the causative agent of a disease, its products, or a synthetic substitute, treated to act as an antigen without inducing the disease: *there is no vaccine against HIV infection.*
■ a program designed to detect computer viruses, and prevent them from operating.
DERIVATIVES: **vac•ci•nate** v. **vac•ci•na•tion** n.

vac•il•late | 'væsə,lāt | • v. [intrans.] alternate or waver between different opinions or actions; be indecisive: *I had for a time vacillated between teaching and journalism.*
DERIVATIVES: **vac•il•la•tion** | ,væsə'lā-SHən | n. **vac•il•la•tor** | -,lātər | n.

vac•u•ous | 'vækyəwəs | • adj. having or showing a lack of thought or intelligence; mindless: *a vacuous smile | vacuous slogans.*
■ empty.
DERIVATIVES: **va•cu•i•ty** | væ'kyōōətē; və- | n. **vac•u•ous•ly** adv. **vac•u•ous•ness** n.

vac•u•um | 'væk,yōōm; -yə(wə)m | • n. (pl. **vacuums** or **vacua** | -yəwə |) **1** a space entirely devoid of matter.
■ a space or container from which the air has been completely or partly removed. ■ [usu. in sing.] a gap left by the loss, death, or departure of someone or something formerly playing a significant part in a situation or activity: *the political vacuum left by the death of Lincoln.*
2 (pl. **vacuums**) a vacuum cleaner. • v. [trans.] clean with a vacuum cleaner: *the room needs to be vacuumed.*
PHRASES: **in a vacuum** (of an activity or a problem to be considered) isolated from the context normal to it and in which it can best be understood or assessed.

va•de me•cum | ,vädē 'mākəm; ,vādē 'mē- | • n. a handbook or guide that is kept constantly at hand for consultation.

vag•a•bond | 'vægə,bänd | • n. a person who wanders from place to place without a home or job.
■ a rascal; a rogue. • adj. [attrib.] having no settled home. • v. [intrans.] wander about as or like a vagabond.

va•gar•y | 'vāgərē | • n. (pl. **-ies**) (usu. **vagaries**) an unexpected and inexplicable change in a situation or in someone's behavior: *the vagaries of the weather.*

va•grant | 'vāgrənt | • n. a person without a settled home or regular work who wanders from place to place and lives by begging.
■ a wanderer. ■ a bird that has strayed or been blown from its usual range or migratory route. • adj. [attrib.] characteristic of, relating to, or living the life of a vagrant: *vagrant beggars.*
■ moving from place to place; wandering: *vagrant whales.* ■ moving or occurring unpredictably; inconstant: *the vagrant heart of my mother.*
DERIVATIVES: **va•gran•cy** | -grənsē | n. **va•grant•ly** adv.

vail | vāl | • v. [trans.] take off or lower (one's hat or crown) as a token of respect or submission.
■ [intrans.] take off one's hat or otherwise show respect or submission to someone.

vain•glo•ry | 'vān,glôrē; ,vān'glôrē | • n. inordinate pride in oneself or one's achievements; excessive vanity.
DERIVATIVES: **vain•glo•ri•ous** | ,vān'glôr-ēəs | adj. **vain•glo•ri•ous•ly** | ,vān'glôrēəs-lē | adv. **vain•glo•ri•ous•ness** | ,vān'glôrēəs-nəs | n.

val•ance | 'væləns; 'vāləns | • n. a length of decorative drapery attached to the canopy or frame of a bed in order to screen the structure or the space beneath it.
■ a length of decorative drapery hung above a window to screen the curtain fittings. ■ a dust ruffle.
DERIVATIVES: **val•anced** adj.

vale[1] | vāl | • n. a valley (used in place names or as a poetic term): *the Vale of Avoca.*
PHRASES: **vale of tears** the world regarded as a scene of trouble or sorrow.

vale[2] | 'vālā | archaic • exclam. farewell. • n. a written or spoken farewell.

val•e•dic•to•ri•an | ,vælə,dik'tôrēən | • n. a student, typically having the highest academic achievements of the class, who delivers the valedictory at a graduation ceremony. Cf. **salutatorian** at SALUTATORY.

val•e•dic•to•ry | ,vælə'dikt(ə)rē | • adj. serving as a farewell: *a valedictory wave.* • n. (pl. **-ies**) a farewell address.

va•lence | 'vāləns | • n. (in chemistry) the combining power of an element, esp. as measured by the number of hydrogen atoms it can displace or combine with: *carbon always has a valence of 4.*
■ [as adj.] relating to or denoting electrons involved in or available for chemical bond formation: *molecules with unpaired valence electrons.* ■ (in linguistics) the number of grammatical elements with which a particular word, esp. a verb, combines in a sentence.

val•e•tu•di•nar•i•an | ,vælə,t(y)ōōdn'erēən | • n. a person who is unduly anxious about their health.
■ a person suffering from poor health. • adj. showing undue concern about one's health.
■ suffering from poor health.
DERIVATIVES: **val•e•tu•di•nar•i•an•ism** | -,nizəm | n.

Val•hal•la |væl'hælə; väl'hälə| (in Scandinavian mythology) a hall in which heroes killed in battle were believed to feast with Odin for eternity. ■ a place or sphere assigned to a person or thing worthy of special honor. ■ paradise.

val•i•date |'vælə,dāt| • v. [trans.] check or prove the validity or accuracy of (something): *these estimates have been validated by periodic surveys.* ■ demonstrate or support the truth or value of: *in a healthy family a child's feelings are validated.* ■ make or declare legally valid. DERIVATIVES: **val•i•da•tion** |,vælə'dā-SHən| n.

val•or |'vælər| (Brit.**valour**) • n. great courage in the face of danger, esp. in battle: *acts of valor.* DERIVATIVES: **val•or•ous** |-ərəs| adj.

val•ue-add•ed tax (abbr.: **VAT**) • n. a tax on the amount by which the value of an article has been increased at each stage of its production or distribution.

vamp¹ |væmp| • n. **1** the upper front part of a boot or shoe. **2** (in jazz and popular music) a short, simple introductory passage, usually repeated several times until otherwise instructed. • v. **1** [intrans.] repeat a short, simple passage of music: *the band was vamping gently behind his busy lead guitar.* **2** [trans.] attach a new upper to (a boot or shoe). ■ **(vamp something up)** repair or improve something: *the production values have been vamped up.*

vamp² • n. a woman who uses sexual attraction to exploit men. • v. [trans.] blatantly set out to attract: *she had not vamped him like some wicked Jezebel.* DERIVATIVES: **vamp•ish** adj. **vamp•ish•ly** adv. **vamp•y** adj.

Van•dyke beard • n. a neat pointed beard.

van•guard |'væn,gärd| • n. a group of people leading the way in new developments or ideas: *the experimental spirit of the modernist vanguard.* ■ a place or position at the forefront of new developments or ideas: *the prototype was in the vanguard of technical development.* ■ the foremost part of an advancing army or naval force. DERIVATIVES: **van•guard•ism** n. **van•guard•ist** n.

vap•id |'væpəd| • adj. offering nothing that is stimulating or challenging: *tuneful but vapid musical comedies.* DERIVATIVES: **va•pid•i•ty** |væ'pidətē| n. **vap•id•ly** adv.

var•i•a•ble |'verēəbəl| • adj. **1** not consistent or having a fixed pattern; liable to change: *the quality of hospital food is highly variable | awards can be for variable amounts.* ■ (of a wind) tending to change direction. ■ (of a quantity) able to assume different numerical values. ■ (of a species) liable to deviate from the typical color or form, or to occur in different colors or forms. **2** able to be changed or adapted: *the drill has variable speed.*

■ (of a gear) designed to give varying ratios or speeds. • n. an element, feature, or factor that is liable to vary or change: *there are too many variables involved to make any meaningful predictions.* ■ a quantity that during a calculation is assumed to vary or be capable of varying in value. ■ (in computing) a data item that may take on more than one value during or between programs. ■ short for **variable star**, a star whose brightness changes, either regularly or irregularly. ■ **(variables)** the region of light, variable winds between the trade winds and the westerlies, esp. in the southern hemisphere. DERIVATIVES: **var•i•a•bil•i•ty** |,verēə'bilə-tē| n. **var•i•a•ble•ness** n. **var•i•a•bly** |-blē| adv.

var•i•ance |'verēəns| • n. the fact or quality of being different, divergent, or inconsistent: *her light tone was at variance with her sudden trembling.* ■ the state or fact of disagreeing or quarreling: *they were at variance with all their previous allies.* ■ (in law) a discrepancy between two statements or documents. ■ an official dispensation from a rule or regulation, typically a building regulation. ■ a quantity equal to the square of the standard deviation. ■ (in accounting) the difference between expected and actual costs, profits, output, etc., in a statistical analysis.

var•i•cose |'værə,kōs; 'ver-| • adj. [attrib.] affected by a condition causing the tortuous enlargement lengthening of veins, most often in the legs: *varicose veins.* DERIVATIVES: **var•i•cosed** adj. **var•i•cos•i•ty** |,værə'käsətē; ,ver-| n.

var•i•e•gat•ed |'ver(ē)ə,gātid| • adj. exhibiting different colors, esp. as irregular patches or streaks: *variegated yellow bricks.* ■ (of a plant or foliage) having or consisting of leaves that are edged or patterned in a second color, esp. white as well as green. ■ marked by variety: *his variegated and amusing observations.* DERIVATIVES: **var•i•e•ga•tion** |,ver(ē)ə'gāSHən| n.

va•ri•e•tal |və'rīətl| • adj. **1** (of a wine or grape) made from or belonging to a single specified variety of grape. **2** of, relating to, characteristic of, or forming a variety: *varietal names.* • n. a varietal wine. DERIVATIVES: **va•ri•e•tal•ly** adv.

va•ri•e•ty |və'rīətē| • n. (pl. **-ies**) **1** the quality or state of being different or diverse; the absence of uniformity, sameness, or monotony: *it's the variety that makes my job so enjoyable.* ■ **(a variety of)** a number or range of things of the same general class that are different or distinct in character or quality: *the center offers a variety of leisure activities.* ■ a thing that differs in some way from others of the same general class or sort; a type: *fifty varieties of fresh and frozen pasta.* ■ a form of television or theater entertainment consisting of a series of different types of acts, such as singing, danc-

ing, and comedy:[as adj.] *a variety show*. **2** a taxonomic category that ranks below subspecies (where present) or species, its members differing from others of the same subspecies or species in minor but permanent or heritable characteristics. Varieties are more often recognized in botany, in which they are designated in the style *Apium graveolens* var. *dulce*.
■ a cultivated form of a plant. See CULTIVAR. ■ a plant or animal that varies in some trivial respect from its immediate parent or type.
var•let |ˈvärlət| • *n*. a man or boy acting as an attendant or servant.
■ a knight's page. ■ an unprincipled rogue or rascal.
DERIVATIVES: **var•let•ry** |-lətrē| *n*.
var•mint |ˈvärmənt| • *n*. a troublesome wild animal, esp. a fox.
■ a troublesome and mischievous person, esp. a child.
vas•cu•lar |ˈvæskyələr| • *adj*. of, relating to, affecting, or consisting of a vessel or vessels, esp. those that carry blood: *vascular disease* | *the vascular system*.
■ relating to or denoting the plant tissues (xylem and phloem) that conduct water, and nutrients in flowering plants, ferns, and their relatives.
DERIVATIVES: **vas•cu•lar•i•ty** |ˌvæskyəˈlærətē; -ˈler-| *n*.
vas•ec•to•my |vəˈsektəmē; væ-| • *n*. (pl. **-ies**) the surgical cutting and sealing of part of each vas deferens (the duct that conveys a male's sperm from the testicle to the urethra), typically as a means of sterilization.
DERIVATIVES: **va•sec•to•mize** |-ˌmīz| *v*.
vas•sal |ˈvæsəl| • *n*. a holder of land by feudal tenure on conditions of homage and allegiance.
■ a person or country in a subordinate position to another: [as adj.] *a vassal state of the Chinese empire*.
DERIVATIVES: **vas•sal•age** |-əlij| *n*.
vat•ic |ˈvætik| • *adj*. describing or predicting what will happen in the future: *vatic utterances*.
va•tic•i•nate |vəˈtisəˌnāt| • *v*. [intrans.] foretell the future.
DERIVATIVES: **va•tic•i•nal** |-ənl| *adj*. **va•tic•i•na•tion** |-ˌtisəˈnāsHən| *n*. **va•tic•i•na•tor** |-ˌnātər| *n*. **va•tic•i•na•to•ry** |-ənəˌtôrē| *adj*.
vaunt |vônt; vänt| • *v*. [trans.] [usu. as adj.] (**vaunted**) boast about or praise (something), esp. excessively: *the much vaunted information superhighway*. • *n*. a boast.
DERIVATIVES: **vaunt•er** *n*. **vaunt•ing•ly** *adv*.
vec•tor |ˈvektər| • *n*. **1** a quantity having direction as well as magnitude, esp. as determining the position of one point in space relative to another. Cf. SCALAR.
■ a matrix with one row or one column. ■ a course to be taken by an aircraft. ■ [as adj.] (in computing) denoting a type of graphical representation using lines to construct the outlines of objects. **2** an organism, typically a bit-

ing insect or tick, that transmits a disease or parasite from one animal or plant to another.
■ (in genetics) a bacteriophage or plasmid that transfers genetic material into a cell, as from one bacterium to another. • *v*. [with obj. and adverbial of direction] (often **be vectored**) direct (an aircraft in flight) to a desired point.
DERIVATIVES: **vec•to•ri•al** |vekˈtôrēəl| *adj*. (in sense 1 of the noun). **vec•to•ri•al•ly** |vekˈtôrēəlē| *adv*. (in sense 1 of the noun). **vec•tor•i•za•tion** |ˌvektərəˈzāsHən| *n*. **vec•tor•ize** |-ˌrīz| *v*. (in sense 1 of the noun).
Ve•da |ˈvādə; ˈvēdə| • *n*. [treated as sing. or pl.] the most ancient Hindu scriptures, written in early Sanskrit and containing hymns, philosophy, and guidance on ritual for the priests of Vedic religion.
DERIVATIVES: **Ve•dic** *adj*.
ve•dette |vəˈdet| • *n*. **1** a mounted sentry positioned beyond an army's outposts to observe the movements of the enemy. **2** a leading star of stage, screen, or television.
veg•an |ˈvēgən; ˈvejən| • *n*. a person who does not eat or use animal products:[as adj.] *a vegan diet*.
veg•e•tal |ˈvejətl| • *adj*. **1** of or relating to plants: *a vegetal aroma*.
■ characterized by the faculty of growth but not of sensation or reason.
veg•e•tate |ˈvejəˌtāt| • *v*. [intrans.] **1** live or spend a period of time in a dull, inactive, unchallenging way: *he'd sit in front of the television set and vegetate*. **2** (of a plant or seed) grow; sprout.
■ [trans.] cause plants to grow in or cover (a place). **3** (of an abnormal growth) increase in size.
veg•e•ta•tive |ˈvejəˌtātiv| • *adj*. **1** (in biology) of, relating to, or denoting reproduction or propagation achieved by asexual means, either naturally (budding, rhizomes, runners, bulbs, etc.) or artificially (grafting, layering, or taking cuttings): *vegetative spores* | *a vegetative replicating phase*.
■ of, relating to, or concerned with growth rather than sexual reproduction: *environmental factors trigger the switch from vegetative to floral development*. **2** of or relating to vegetation or plant life: *diverse vegetative types*. **3** (in medicine, of a person) alive but comatose and without apparent brain activity or responsiveness. In a **persistent vegetative state**, a patient is kept alive by such means as artificial respiration.
DERIVATIVES: **veg•e•ta•tive•ly** *adv*. **veg•e•ta•tive•ness** *n*.
ve•he•ment |ˈvēəmənt| • *adj*. showing strong feeling; forceful, passionate, or intense: *her voice was low but vehement* | *vehement criticism*.
DERIVATIVES: **ve•he•mence** *n*. **ve•he•ment•ly** *adv*.
vel•le•i•ty |vəˈlēədē; ve-| • *n*. (pl. **-ies**) a wish or inclination not strong enough to lead to action: *the notion intrigued me, but remained a velleity*.
■ the least degree of volition, unaccompanied by any effort or advance toward action or realization.

vel•lum |'veləm| • *n.* **1** fine parchment made originally from the skin of a calf. **2** smooth writing paper imitating vellum.

ve•loc•i•ty |və'läsəte| • *n.* (pl. **-ies**) the speed of something in a given direction: *the velocities of the emitted particles.*
■ (in general use) speed: *the tank shot backward at an incredible velocity.*

ve•lo•drome |'velə,drōm; 'vēlə-| • *n.* a cycle-racing track, typically with steeply banked curves.
■ a stadium containing such a track.

ve•lu•ti•nous |və'lōōtn-əs| • *adj.* covered with soft fine hairs.

ve•nal |'vēnl| • *adj.* showing or motivated by susceptibility to bribery: *why should these venal politicians care how they are rated?* | *their generosity had been at least partly venal.*
DERIVATIVES: **ve•nal•i•ty** |vē'nælətē; və-| *n.* **ve•nal•ly** *adv.*

USAGE: **Venal** and **venial** are sometimes confused. **Venal** means 'corrupt, able to be bribed, or involving bribery,' for example, *Local customs officials are notoriously venal, and smuggling thrives.* **Venial** is used among Christians to describe a certain type of sin and means 'pardonable, excusable, not mortal,' for example, *Purgatory, to Catholics, was an intermediate stage in which those who had committed venial sins might earn their way into heaven.*

ve•na•tion |vē'nāsHən| • *n.* the arrangement of veins in a leaf or in an insect's wing.
■ the system of venous blood vessels in an animal.
DERIVATIVES: **ve•na•tion•al** |-sHənl| *adj.*

ven•det•ta |ven'detə| • *n.* a blood feud in which the family of a murdered person seeks vengeance on the murderer or the murderer's family.
■ a prolonged bitter quarrel with or campaign against someone: *he has accused the British media of pursuing a vendetta against him.*

ve•neer |və'nir| • *n.* a thin decorative covering of fine wood applied to a coarser wood or other material.
■ a layer of wood used to make plywood. ■ [in sing.] an attractive appearance that covers or disguises someone or something's true nature or feelings: *her veneer of composure cracked a little.* • *v.* [trans.] (usu. as adj.) (**veneered**) cover (something) with a decorative layer of fine wood.
■ cover or disguise (someone or something's true nature) with an attractive appearance.

ven•er•a•ble |'venərəbəl; 'venrə-| • *adj.* accorded a great deal of respect, esp. because of age, wisdom, or character: *a venerable statesman.*
■ (in the Anglican Church) a title given to an archdeacon. ■ (in the Roman Catholic Church) a title given to a deceased person who has attained a certain degree of sanctity but has not been fully beatified or canonized.
DERIVATIVES: **ven•er•a•bil•i•ty** |,venərə'bilətē| *n.* **ven•er•a•ble•ness** *n.* **ven•er•a•bly** |-blē| *adv.*

ven•er•ate |'venə,rāt| • *v.* [trans.] (often **be venerated**) regard with great respect; revere: *Mother Teresa is venerated as a saint.*
DERIVATIVES: **ven•er•a•tion** |,venə'rāsHən| *n.* **ven•er•a•tor** |-,rātər| *n.*

ve•ne•re•al |və'nirēəl| • *adj.* of or relating to sexual desire or sexual intercourse.
■ of or relating to venereal disease.
DERIVATIVES: **ve•ne•re•al•ly** *adv.*

ven•er•y[1] |'venərē| • *n.* sexual indulgence.

ven•er•y[2] • *n.* hunting.

ve•ni•al |'vēnēəl; 'vēnyəl| • *adj.* (in Christian theology) denoting a sin that is not regarded as depriving the soul of divine grace.
■ (of a fault or offense) slight and pardonable.
DERIVATIVES: **ve•ni•al•i•ty** |,vēnē'ælətē| *n.* **ve•ni•al•ly** *adv.*

USAGE: See usage at VENAL.

ven•om•ous |'venəməs| • *adj.* (of animals, esp. snakes, or their parts) secreting venom; capable of injecting venom by means of a bite or sting.
■ (of a person or personal behavior) full of malice or spite: *she replied with a venomous glance.*
DERIVATIVES: **ven•om•ous•ly** *adv.* **ven•om•ous•ness** *n.*

ve•nous |'vēnəs| • *adj.* of or relating to a vein or the veins. ■ of or relating to the dark red, oxygen-poor blood in the veins and pulmonary artery.
DERIVATIVES: **ve•nos•i•ty** |vi'näsətē| *n.* **ve•nous•ly** *adv.*

ven•tral |'ventrəl| • *adj.* of, on, or relating to the underside of an animal or plant; abdominal: *a ventral nerve cord* | *the ventral part of the head.* Cf. DORSAL.
DERIVATIVES: **ven•tral•ly** *adv.*

ven•ue |'ven,yōō| • *n.* the place where something happens, esp. an organized event such as a concert, conference, or sports event: *the river could soon be the venue for a powerboat world championship event.*
■ (in law) the county or district within which a criminal or civil case must be heard.

ve•ra•cious |və'rāsHəs| • *adj.* speaking or representing the truth: *the veracious child admitted her misbehavior.*
DERIVATIVES: **ve•ra•cious•ly** *adv.* **ve•ra•cious•ness** *n.*

ve•rac•i•ty |və'rasətē| • *n.* conformity to facts; accuracy: *officials expressed doubts concerning the veracity of the story.*
■ habitual truthfulness: *voters should be concerned about his veracity and character.*

ver•bal•ism |'vərbə,lizəm| • *n.* concentration on forms of expression rather than content.
■ a verbal expression. ■ excessive or empty use of language.
DERIVATIVES: **ver•bal•ist** *n.* **ver•bal•is•tic** |,vərbə'listik| *adj.*

ver•bal•ize |'vərbə,līz| • *v.* **1** [trans.] express (ideas or feelings) in words, esp. by speaking out loud: *they are unable to verbalize their real feelings.* **2** [intrans.] speak, esp. at excessive length and with little real content: *the dangers*

of verbalizing about art. **3** [trans.] make (a word, esp. a noun) into a verb.
DERIVATIVES: **ver•bal•iz•a•ble** *adj.* **ver•bal•i•za•tion** |ˌvərbələˈzāsHən; -ˌlīˈzā-| *n.* **ver•bal•iz•er** *n.*

ver•ba•tim |vərˈbātəm| • *adv. & adj.* in exactly the same words as were used originally: [as adv.] *subjects were instructed to recall the passage verbatim* | [as adj.] *your quotations must be verbatim.*

ver•bi•age |ˈvərbē-ij| • *n.* speech or writing that uses too many words or excessively technical expressions.
■ diction; wording; verbal expression.

ver•bose |vərˈbōs| • *adj.* using or expressed in more words than are needed: *much academic language is obscure and verbose.*
DERIVATIVES: **ver•bose•ly** *adv.* **ver•bos•i•ty** |-ˈbäsətē| *n.*

ver•bo•ten |fərˈbōtn; vər-| • *adj.* forbidden, esp. by an authority.

ver•dant |ˈvərdnt| • *adj.* (of countryside) green with grass or other rich vegetation.
■ of the bright green color of lush grass: *a deep, verdant green.*
DERIVATIVES: **ver•dan•cy** |ˈvərdn-sē| *n.* **ver•dant•ly** *adv.*

ver•di•gris |ˈvərdəˌgrēs; -ˌgris; -ˌgrē| • *n.* a bright bluish-green encrustation or patina formed on copper or brass by atmospheric oxidation, consisting of basic copper carbonate.

ver•dure |ˈvərjər| • *n.* lush green vegetation.
■ the fresh green color of such vegetation. ■ a condition of freshness.
DERIVATIVES: **ver•dured** *adj.* **ver•dur•ous** |-jərəs| *adj.*

verge |vərj| • *n.* an edge or border: *they came down to the verge of the lake.*
■ an extreme limit beyond which something specified will happen: *I was on the verge of tears.* ■ Brit. a grass edging such as that by the side of a road or path. ■ an edge of tiles projecting over a gable. • *v.* [intrans.] (**verge on**) approach (something) closely; be close or similar to (something): *despair verging on the suicidal.*

ve•rid•i•cal |vəˈridikəl| • *adj.* truthful.
■ coinciding with reality: *such memories are not necessarily veridical.*
DERIVATIVES: **ve•rid•i•cal•i•ty** |-ˌridə ˈkalətē| *n.* **ve•rid•i•cal•ly** |-ik(ə)lē| *adv.*

ver•i•fy |ˈverəˌfī| • *v.* (**-ies, -ied**) [trans.] (often **be verified**) make sure or demonstrate that (something) is true, accurate, or justified: *his conclusions have been verified by later experiments* | [with clause] *"Can you verify that the guns are licensed?"*
■ (in law) swear to or support (a statement) by affidavit.
DERIVATIVES: **ver•i•fi•a•ble** |ˈverəˌfīəbəl; ˌverəˈfī-| *adj.* **ver•i•fi•a•bly** |ˈverəˌfīəblē; ˌverəˈfī-| *adv.* **ver•i•fi•er** *n.*

ver•i•si•mil•i•tude |ˌverəsəˈmiləˌt(y)o͞od| • *n.* the appearance of being true or real: *the detail gives the novel some verisimilitude.*
DERIVATIVES: **ver•i•sim•i•lar** |-ˈsimələr| *adj.*

ve•ris•mo |vəˈrizmō; ve-| • *n.* realism in the arts, esp. with reference to late 19th-century Italian opera.
■ this genre of opera, as composed principally by Puccini, Mascagni, and Leoncavallo.

ve•ris•tic |vəˈristik| • *adj.* (of art or literature) extremely or strictly naturalistic.
DERIVATIVES: **ver•ism** |ˈverˌizəm| *n.* **ver•ist** |ˈverist| *n. & adj.*

ver•i•ta•ble |ˈverətəbəl| • *adj.* [attrib.] used as an intensifier, often to qualify a metaphor: *the early 1970s witnessed a veritable price explosion.*
DERIVATIVES: **ver•i•ta•bly** |-blē| *adv.*

vé•ri•té |ˌveriˈtā| • *n.* a genre of film, television, and radio programs emphasizing realism and naturalism.

ver•i•ty |ˈverətē| • *n.* (pl. **-ies**) a true principle or belief, esp. one of fundamental importance: *the eternal verities.*
■ truth: *irrefutable, objective verity.*

ver•nac•u•lar |vərˈnakyələr| • *n.* **1** (usu. **the vernacular**) the language or dialect spoken by the ordinary people in a particular country or region: *he wrote in the vernacular to reach a larger audience.*
■ [with adj.] the terminology used by people belonging to a specified group or engaging in a specialized activity: *gardening vernacular.* **2** architecture concerned with domestic and functional rather than monumental buildings: *buildings in which Gothic merged into farmhouse vernacular.* • *adj.* **1** (of language) spoken as one's mother tongue; not learned or imposed as a second language.
■ (of speech or written works) using such a language: *vernacular literature.* **2** (of architecture) concerned with domestic and functional rather than monumental buildings.
DERIVATIVES: **ver•nac•u•lar•ism** |-ˌrizəm| *n.* **ver•nac•u•lar•i•ty** |-ˌnakyəˈlærətē; -ˈler-| *n.* **ver•nac•u•lar•ize** |-ˌrīz| *v.* **ver•nac•u•lar•ly** *adv.*

ver•nal |ˈvərnl| • *adj.* of, in, or appropriate to spring: *the vernal freshness of the land.*
DERIVATIVES: **ver•nal•ly** *adv.*

ver•sa•tile |ˈvərsətl| • *adj.* able to adapt or be adapted to many different functions or activities: *a versatile sewing machine* | *he was versatile enough to play either position.* **2** changeable; inconstant.
DERIVATIVES: **ver•sa•tile•ly** *adv.* **ver•sa•til•i•ty** |ˌvərsəˈtilətē| *n.*

ver•so |ˈvərsō| • *n.* (pl. **-os**) **1** a left-hand page of an open book, or the back of a loose document. Cf. RECTO. **2** the reverse of something such as a coin or painting.

ver•te•brate |ˈvərtəbrət; -ˌbrāt| • *n.* an animal of a large group (Subphylum Vertebrata, phylum Chordata: seven classes.) distinguished by the possession of a backbone or spinal column, including mammals, birds, reptiles, amphibians, and fishes. Cf. INVERTEBRATE. • *adj.* of or relating to the vertebrates.

ver•tex |ˈvərˌteks| • *n.* (pl. **vertices** |-tə,sēz| or **vertexes**) **1** the highest point; the top or apex.
■ the crown of the head. **2** each angular point of a polygon, polyhedron, or other figure.

■ a meeting point of two lines that form an angle. ■ the point at which an axis meets a curve or surface.

ver•tig•i•nous |vər'tijənəs| • *adj.* causing vertigo, esp. by being extremely high or steep: *vertiginous drops to the valleys below.*
■ relating to or affected by vertigo.
DERIVATIVES: **ver•tig•i•nous•ly** *adv.*

ver•ti•go |'vərtəgō| • *n.* a sensation of whirling and loss of balance, associated particularly with looking down from a great height, or caused by disease affecting the inner ear or the vestibular nerve; giddiness.

verve |vərv| • *n.* vigor and spirit or enthusiasm: *Kollo sings with supreme verve and flexibility.*

ve•si•cle |'vesikəl| • *n.* a fluid- or air-filled cavity or sac, in particular:
■ a small fluid-filled bladder, sac, cyst, or vacuole within the human or animal body. ■ an air-filled swelling in a plant, esp. a seaweed. ■ a small cavity in volcanic rock, produced by gas bubbles. ■ (in medicine) a small blister full of clear fluid.
DERIVATIVES: **ve•sic•u•lar** |və'sikyələr| *adj.* **ve•sic•u•lat•ed** |və'sikyə,lātid| *adj.* **ve•sic•u•la•tion** |və,sikyə'lāSHən| *n.*

ves•pers |'vespərz| • *n.* a service of evening prayer in the Divine Office of the Western Christian Church (sometimes said earlier in the day).
■ a service of evening prayer in other churches.

ves•per•tine |'vespər,tīn; -,tēn| • *adj.* of, relating to, occurring, or active in the evening.
■ (of a flower) opening in the evening.
■ (of an animal) active in the evening. Cf. CREPUSCULAR.

ves•pine |'ves,pīn; -pin| • *adj.* of or relating to wasps.

vest |vest| • *v.* **1** [trans.] (usu. **be vested in**) confer or bestow (power, authority, property, etc.) on someone: *executive power is vested in the President.*
■ (usu. **be vested with**) give (someone) the legal right to power, property, etc.: *the socialists came to be vested with the power of legislation.* ■ [intrans.] (**vest in**) (of power, property, etc.) come into the possession of: *the bankrupt's property vests in his trustee.* **2** [intrans.] (of a chorister or member of the clergy) put on vestments.
■ [trans.] dress (someone): *the Speaker vested him with a rich purple robe.*

ves•tal |'vestl| • *adj.* of or relating to the Roman goddess Vesta: *a vestal temple.*
■ chaste; pure. • *n.* a vestal virgin, one of the virgin priestesses of the goddess Vesta, vowed to chastity, who had the duty of keeping the sacred fire burning on the goddess's altar.
■ a chaste woman, esp. a nun.

ves•ti•ar•y |'vestē,erē| • *adj.* of or relating to clothes or dress. • *n.* (pl. **-ies**) a room or building in a monastery or other large establishment in which clothes are kept.

ves•ti•bule |'vestə,byōōl| • *n.* **1** an antechamber, hall, or lobby next to the outer door of a building.

■ an enclosed entrance compartment in a railroad car. **2** (in anatomy) a chamber or channel communicating with or opening into another, in particular:
■ the central cavity of the labyrinth of the inner ear. ■ the part of the mouth outside the teeth. ■ the space in the vulva into which both the urethra and vagina open.
DERIVATIVES: **ves•tib•u•lar** *adj.* **ves•ti•buled** *adj.*

ves•tige |'vestij| • *n.* a trace of something that is disappearing or no longer exists: *the last vestiges of colonialism.*
■ [usu. with negative] the smallest amount (used to emphasize the absence of something): *he waited patiently, but without a vestige of sympathy.* ■ a part or organ of an organism that has become reduced or functionless in the course of evolution.

ves•tig•i•al |ve'stij(ē)əl| • *adj.* forming a very small remnant of something that was once much larger or more noticeable: *he felt a vestigial flicker of anger from last night.*
■ (of an organ or part of the body) degenerate, rudimentary, or atrophied, having become functionless in the course of evolution: *the vestigial wings of kiwis are entirely hidden.*
DERIVATIVES: **ves•tig•i•al•ly** *adv.*

vest•ment |'ves(t)mənt| • *n.* (usu. **vestments**) a chasuble or other robe worn by the clergy or choristers during religious services.
■ a garment, esp. a ceremonial or official robe.

ves•try |'vestrē| • *n.* (pl. **-ies**) a room of, or building attached to a church, used as an office and for changing into vestments.
■ a meeting of parishioners, originally in a vestry, for the conduct of parochial business. ■ a body of such parishioners.

vet |vet| • *v.* (**vetted, vetting**) [trans.] make a careful and critical examination of (something): *proposals for vetting large takeover bids.*
■ (often **be vetted**) Brit. investigate (someone) thoroughly, esp. in order to ensure that they are suitable for a job requiring secrecy, loyalty, or trustworthiness: *each applicant will be vetted by police.*

ve•to |'vētō| • *n.* (pl. **-oes**) a constitutional right to reject a decision or proposal made by a law-making body: *the president may exercise his veto if the final bill contains the controversial provision.* [as adj.] veto power. A **pocket veto** is exercised by an executive who refuses to sign a bill near the end of a legislative session, allowing a period during which it must be signed in order to take effect to lapse, with the now out-of-session legislature unable to override an actual veto. A **line-item veto** is the power to reject part of a bill, esp. a particular provision of a finance measure.
■ such a rejection. ■ a prohibition: *his veto on our drinking after the meal was annoying.* • *v.* (**-oes, -oed**) [trans.] exercise a veto against (a decision or proposal made by a law-making body): *the president vetoed the bill.*
■ refuse to accept or allow: *the film star often has a right to veto the pictures used for publicity.*
DERIVATIVES: **ve•to•er** *n.*

vex•il•lol•o•gy |ˌveksə'läləjē| • n. the study of flags.
DERIVATIVES: **vex•il•lol•log•i•cal** |-lə'läji-kəl| adj. **vex•il•lol•o•gist** |-jist| n.

vi•a•ble |'vīəbəl| • adj. capable of working successfully; feasible: the proposed investment was economically viable. ■ (of a seed or spore) able to germinate. ■ (of a plant, animal, or cell) capable of surviving or living successfully, esp. under particular environmental conditions. ■ (of a fetus or unborn child) able to live after birth.
DERIVATIVES: **vi•a•bil•i•ty** |ˌvīə'bilətē| n. **vi•a•bly** |-blē| adv.

vi•a•duct |'vīəˌdəkt| • n. a long bridgelike structure, typically a series of arches, carrying a road or railroad across a valley or other low ground. Cf. AQUEDUCT.

vic•ar |'vikər| • n. (in the Church of England) an incumbent of a parish where tithes formerly passed to a chapter or religious house or layman. ■ (in other Anglican Churches) a member of the clergy deputizing for another. ■ (in the Roman Catholic Church) a representative or deputy of a bishop. ■ (in the Episcopal Church) a clergyman in charge of a chapel. ■ a cleric or choir member appointed to sing certain parts of a cathedral service.
DERIVATIVES: **vic•ar•ship** |-ˌSHip| n.

vi•car•i•ous |vī'kerēəs, və-| • adj. experienced in the imagination through the feelings or actions of another person: I could glean vicarious pleasure from the struggles of my imaginary film friends. ■ acting or done for another: a vicarious atonement. ■ of or pertaining to the performance by one organ of the functions normally discharged by another.
DERIVATIVES: **vi•car•i•ous•ly** adv. **vi•car•i•ous•ness** n.

vice•roy |'vīsˌroi| • n. 1 a ruler exercising authority in a colony on behalf of a sovereign.
DERIVATIVES: **vice•roy•al** |ˌvīs'roi-əl| adj. **vice•roy•ship** |-ˌSHip| n.

vic•i•nage |'visənij| • n. another term for vicinity.

vic•i•nal |'visənl| • adj. neighboring; adjacent. ■ (in chemistry) relating to or denoting substituents attached to adjacent atoms in a ring or chain.

vi•cious |'visHəs| • adj. 1 deliberately cruel or violent: a vicious assault. ■ (of an animal) wild and dangerous to people. ■ serious or dangerous: a vicious flu bug. ■ immoral: every soul on earth, virtuous or vicious, shall perish. 2 (of language or a line of reasoning) imperfect; defective.
DERIVATIVES: **vi•cious•ly** adv. **vi•cious•ness** n.

vi•cious cir•cle (also **vicious cycle**) • n. 1 a sequence of reciprocal cause and effect in which two or more elements intensify and aggravate each other, leading inexorably to a worsening of the situation. 2 (in logic) a definition or statement that begs the question.

vi•cis•si•tude |və'sisəˌt(y)o͞od| • n. (usu. vicissitudes) a change of circumstances or fortune, typically one that is unwelcome or unpleasant: her husband's sharp vicissitudes of fortune. ■ alternation between opposite or contrasting things: the vicissitude of the seasons.
DERIVATIVES: **vi•cis•si•tu•di•nous** |-ˌsisə't(y)o͞odn-əs; -'t(y)o͞odnəs| adj.

vic•tim•ize |'viktəˌmīz| • v. [trans.] single (someone) out for cruel or unjust treatment: scam artists who victimize senior citizens.
DERIVATIVES: **vic•tim•i•za•tion** |ˌviktəmə'zāsHən| n. **vic•tim•iz•er** n.

vict•ual |'vitl| dated • n. (victuals; sometimes in informal contexts, **vittles**) food or provisions, esp. as prepared for consumption. • v. (**victualed, victualing**; Brit. **victualled, victualling**) [trans.] provide with food or other stores: the ship wasn't even properly victualed. ■ [intrans.] obtain or lay in food or other stores: a voyage of such length, that no ship could victual for. ■ [intrans.] eat: victual with me next Saturday.

vi•de |'vēdē; 'vēˌdā; 'vīdē| • v. [with obj., in imperative] see; consult (used as an instruction in a text to refer the reader to a specified passage, book, author, etc., for fuller or further information): vide note 6 on p. 225.

vi•de•li•cet |və'deləˌset; -set; -'dāləˌket| • adv. more formal term for VIZ.

vie |vī| • v. (**vying**) [intrans.] compete eagerly with someone in order to do or achieve something: rival mobs **vying for** control of the liquor business.

vig•i•lance |'vijələns| • n. the action or state of keeping careful watch for possible danger or difficulties.
DERIVATIVES: **vig•i•lant** adj. **vig•i•lant•ly** adv.

vig•i•lan•te |ˌvijə'læntē| • n. a member of a self-appointed group of citizens who undertake law enforcement in their community without legal authority, typically because the legal agencies are thought to be inadequate.
DERIVATIVES: **vig•i•lan•tism** |-ˌtizəm| n.

vi•gnette |vin'yet| • n. 1 a brief evocative description, account, or episode. 2 a small illustration or portrait photograph that fades into its background without a definite border. ■ a small ornamental design filling a space in a book or carving, typically based on foliage. • v. [trans.] portray (someone) in the style of a vignette. ■ produce (a photograph) in the style of a vignette by softening or shading away the edges of the subject.
DERIVATIVES: **vi•gnet•tist** |-'yetist| n.

vig•or |'vigər| (Brit. **vigour**) • n. 1 physical strength and good health. ■ effort, energy, and enthusiasm: they set about the new task with vigor. ■ strong, healthy growth of a plant. 2 (in law) legal or binding force; validity.
DERIVATIVES: **vig•or•less** |'vigərləs| adj.

vil•i•fy |'viləˌfī| • v. (-ies, -ied) [trans.] speak or write about in an abusively disparaging manner: he has been vilified in the press.

DERIVATIVES: vil•i•fi•ca•tion |ˌviləfi′kā-sHən| *n.* **vil•i•fi•er** *n.*

vil•lein |′vilən; -ˌān| • *n.* (in medieval England) a feudal tenant entirely subject to a lord or manor to whom he paid dues and services in return for land.
DERIVATIVES: vil•lein•age *n.*

vim |vim| • *n.* energy; enthusiasm: *in his youth he was full of vim and vigor.*

vin•di•cate |′vindəˌkāt| • *v.* [trans.] clear (someone) of blame or suspicion: *hospital staff were vindicated by the inquest.*
■ show or prove to be right, reasonable, or justified: *more sober views were vindicated by events.*
DERIVATIVES: vin•di•ca•ble |-kəbəl| *adj.* **vin•di•ca•tion** |ˌvində′kāsHən| *n.* **vin•di•ca•tor** |-ˌkātər| *n.* **vin•di•ca•to•ry** |-kə ˌtôrē| *adj.*

vin•dic•tive |vin′diktiv| • *adj.* having or showing a strong or unreasoning desire for revenge: *the criticism was both vindictive and personalized.*
DERIVATIVES: vin•dic•tive•ly *adv.* **vin•dic•tive•ness** *n.*

vin•i•cul•ture |′vinəˌkəlcHər| • *n.* the cultivation of grapevines for winemaking.
DERIVATIVES: vin•i•cul•tur•al |ˌvinə′kəl-CH(ə)rəl| *adj.* **vin•i•cul•tur•ist** |ˌvinə′kəl-CHərist| *n.*

vi•nous |′vīnəs| • *adj.* of, resembling, or associated with wine: *a vinous smell.*
■ fond of or influenced by drinking wine: *his vinous companion.* ■ of the reddish color of wine.
DERIVATIVES: vi•nos•i•ty |vi′näsətē| *n.* **vi•nous•ly** *adv.*

vi•ol |′vīəl| • *n.* a musical instrument of the Renaissance and baroque periods, typically six-stringed, held vertically and played with a bow.

vi•per |′vīpər| • *n.* **1** a venomous snake (family Viperidae) with large hinged fangs, typically having a broad head and stout body, with dark patterns on a lighter background.
■ a spiteful or treacherous person. **2** a smoker of marijuana or opium; a heroin addict.
DERIVATIVES: vi•per•ine |′vīpəˌrīn; -rin| *adj.* **vi•per•ish** *adj.* **vi•per•ous** |′vīp(ə)rəs| *adj.*

vi•ra•go |və′rägō; -′rā-| • *n.* (pl. **-os** or **-oes**) a domineering, violent, or bad-tempered woman.
■ a woman of masculine strength or spirit; a female warrior.

vi•res•cent |və′resənt; vī-| • *adj.* greenish.
DERIVATIVES: vi•res•cence *n.* **vi•res•cent•ly** *adv.*

vir•gin |′vərjən| • *n.* a person, typically a woman, who has never had sexual intercourse.
■ a naive, innocent, or inexperienced person, esp. in a particular context: *a political virgin.*
■ (**the Virgin**) the mother of Jesus; the Virgin Mary. ■ a woman who has taken a vow to remain a virgin. ■ (**the Virgin**) the zodiacal sign or constellation Virgo. ■ a female insect that produces eggs without being fertilized.

• *adj.* **1** [attrib.] being, relating to, or appropriate for a virgin: *his virgin bride.* Cf. CELIBATE; CHASTE. **2** not yet touched, used or exploited: *acres of virgin forests | virgin snow.*
■ (of clay) not yet fired. ■ (of wool) not yet, or only once, spun or woven. ■ (of olive oil) obtained from the first pressing of olives. ■ (of metal) made from ore by smelting.

vir•gule |′vərˌgyo͞ol| • *n.* a slanting or upright line used esp. in medieval manuscripts to mark a caesura, or as a punctuation mark equivilent to a comma.

vir•i•des•cent |ˌvirə′desənt| • *adj.* greenish or becoming green.
DERIVATIVES: vir•i•des•cence *n.*

vir•id•i•ty |və′ridətē| • *n.* poetic/literary the quality or state of being green; verdancy.
■ figurative innocence; freshness; inexperience.

vir•ile |′virəl| • *adj.* (of a man) having strength, energy, and a strong sex drive.
■ having or characterized by strength and energy: *a strong, virile performance of the symphony.*
DERIVATIVES: vi•ril•i•ty |və′rilətē| *n.*

vir•tu |vər′to͞o| (also **vertu**) • *n.* **1** knowledge of or expertise in the fine arts.
■ curios or objets d'art collectively. **2** the good qualities inherent in a person or thing.

vir•tu•al |′vərCHəwəl| • *adj.* almost or nearly as described, but not completely or according to strict definition: *the virtual absence of border controls.*
■ (in computing) not physically existing as such but made by software to appear to do so: *a virtual computer.* See also VIRTUAL REALITY.
■ (in optics) relating to the points at which rays would meet if produced backward. ■ (in physics) denoting particles or interactions with extremely short lifetimes and (owing to the uncertainty principle) indefinitely great energies, postulated as intermediates in some processes.
DERIVATIVES: vir•tu•al•i•ty |ˌvərCHə′wæl-ətē| *n.*

vir•tu•al re•al•i•ty • *n.* the computer-generated simulation of a three-dimensional image or environment that can be interacted with in a seemingly real or physical way by a person using special electronic equipment, such as a helmet with a screen inside or gloves fitted with sensors.

vir•tue |′vərCHo͞o| • *n.* **1** behavior showing high moral standards: *paragons of virtue.*
■ a quality considered morally good or desirable in a person: *patience is a virtue.* ■ a good or useful quality of a thing: *Mike was extolling the virtues of the car | there's no virtue in suffering in silence.* ■ virginity or chastity, esp. of a woman. **2** (**virtues**) (in traditional Christian angelology) the seventh highest order of the ninefold celestial hierarchy.
DERIVATIVES: vir•tue•less *adj.* **vir•tu•ous** *adj.*

vir•tu•o•so |ˌvərCHə′wōsō; -zō| • *n.* (pl. **vir•tuo•si** |-sē; -zē| or **virtuosos**) a person highly skilled in music or another artistic pursuit: *a celebrated clarinet virtuoso | [as adj.] virtuoso guitar playing.*

■ a person with a special knowledge of or interest in works of art or curios.
DERIVATIVES: **vir•tu•os•ic** |-'wäsik; -'wō-| adj. **vir•tu•os•i•ty** |-'wäsətē| n.
vir•u•lent |'vir(y)ələnt| • adj. 1 (of a disease or poison) extremely severe or harmful in its effects.
■ (of a pathogen, esp. a virus) highly infective. 2 bitterly hostile: a virulent attack on liberalism.
DERIVATIVES: **vir•u•lence** n. **vir•u•lent•ly** adv.
vis•age |'vizij| • n. [usu. in sing.] a person's face, with reference to the form or proportions of the features: an elegant, angular visage.
■ a person's facial expression: there was something hidden behind his visage of cheerfulness.
■ the surface of an object presented to view: the moonlit visage of the port's whitewashed buildings.
DERIVATIVES: **vis•aged** adj. [in combination] a stern-visaged old man.
vis-à-vis |'vēz ə 've | • prep. in relation to; with regard to: many agencies now have a unit to deal with women's needs vis-à-vis employment.
■ as compared with; as opposed to: the advantage for US exports is the value of the dollar vis-à-vis other currencies. • adv. in a position facing a specified or implied subject: he was there vis-à-vis with Miss Arundel. • n. (pl. same) 1 a person or group occupying a corresponding position to that of another person or group in a different area or domain; a counterpart: his admiration for the US armed services extends to their vis-à-vis, the Russian military. 2 a face-to-face meeting: the dreaded vis-à-vis with his boss.

USAGE: This expression means 'face to face.' Avoid using it to mean 'about, concerning,' for example, He wanted to talk to me vis-à-vis next weekend. In the sense 'in contrast, comparison, or relation to,' however, **vis-à-vis** is generally acceptable: Let us consider government regulations vis-à-vis employment rates.

vis•cer•a |'visərə| • plural n. (sing. **viscus** |'viskəs|) the internal organs in the main cavities of the body, esp. those in the abdomen, e.g., the intestines.
vis•cer•al |'vis(ə)rəl| • adj. of or relating to the viscera: the visceral nervous system.
■ relating to deep inward feelings rather than to the intellect: the voters' visceral fear of change.
DERIVATIVES: **vis•cer•al•ly** adv.
vis•cid |'visid| • adj. glutinous; sticky: the viscid mucus lining of the intestine.
DERIVATIVES: **vis•cid•i•ty** |və'sidətē| n.
vis•cos•i•ty |,vi'skäsitē| • n. (pl. **-ies**) the state of being thick, sticky, and semifluid in consistency, due to internal friction.
■ a quantity expressing the magnitude of such friction, as measured by the force per unit area resisting a flow in which parallel layers unit distance apart have unit speed relative to one another.

vis•cous |'viskəs| • adj. having a thick, sticky consistency between solid and liquid; having a high viscosity: viscous lava.
DERIVATIVES: **vis•cous•ly** adv. **vis•cous•ness** n.
vi•sion•ar•y |'vizHə,nerē| • adj. 1 (esp. of a person) thinking about or planning the future with imagination or wisdom: a visionary leader.
■ (of a scheme or idea) not practical. 2 of, relating to, or able to see visions in a dream or trance, or as a supernatural apparition: a visionary experience.
■ existing only in a vision or in the imagination.
■ connected with or pertaining to a vision or visions: visionary art. • n. (pl. **-ies**) a person with original ideas about what the future will or could be like.
■ a visionary artist.
DERIVATIVES: **vi•sion•ar•i•ness** n.
vis•it•ant |'vizətənt| • n. a supernatural being or agency; an apparition.
■ a visitor or guest. ■ a migratory bird that frequents a certain locality only at particular times of the year; a visitor. • adj. paying a visit: the housekeeper was abrupt with the poor visitant niece.
vi•tal•ism |'vītl,izəm| • n. the theory that the origin and phenomena of life are dependent on a force or principle distinct from purely chemical or physical forces.
DERIVATIVES: **vi•tal•ist** n. & adj. **vi•tal•is•tic** |,vītl'istik| adj.
vi•tal signs |'vītl sīnz| • plural n. clinical measurements, specifically pulse rate, temperature, respiration rate, and blood pressure, that indicate the state of a patient's essential body functions.
vi•tal sta•tis•tics |'vītl stə'tistiks| • plural n. 1 quantitative data concerning a population, such as the number of births, marriages, and deaths. 2 the measurements of a woman's bust, waist, and hips.
vi•ti•ate |'visHē,āt| • v. [trans.] spoil or impair the quality or efficiency of: development programs have been vitiated by the rise in population.
■ destroy or impair the legal validity of.
DERIVATIVES: **vi•ti•a•tion** |,visHē'āsHən| n. **vi•ti•a•tor** |-,ātər| n.
vit•i•cul•ture |'vitə,kəlcHər| • n. the cultivation of grapevines.
■ the study of grape cultivation. Cf. VINICULTURE.
DERIVATIVES: **vit•i•cul•tur•al** |,vitiˈkəl-cH(ə)rəl| adj. **vit•i•cul•tur•ist** |-rist| n.
vit•re•ous |'vitrēəs| • adj. like glass in appearance or physical properties.
■ (of a substance) derived from or containing glass: toilet and bidet are made of vitreous china.
DERIVATIVES: **vit•re•ous•ness** n.
vit•ri•fy |'vitrə,fī| • v. (**-ies, -ied**) [trans.] (often **be vitrified**) convert (something) into glass or a glasslike substance, typically by exposure to heat.
DERIVATIVES: **vit•ri•fac•tion** |,vitrə'fæk-sHən| n. **vit•ri•fi•a•ble** |'vitrə,fīəbəl; ,vitrə

'fī-| *adj.* **vit•ri•fi•ca•tion** |ˌvitrəfi'kāsHən| *n.*

vit•ri•ol |'vitrēəl; -ˌôl| • *n.* sulfuric acid.
■ cruel and bitter criticism: *her mother's sudden gush of fury and vitriol.*
DERIVATIVES: **vit•ri•ol•ic** |ˌvitrē'älik| *adj.*

vi•tu•per•ate |və't(y) o͞opəˌrāt; vī-| • *v.* [trans.] blame or insult (someone) in strong or violent language.
DERIVATIVES: **vi•tu•per•a•tive** *adj.* **vi•tu•per•a•tor** |-ˌrātər| *n.*

vi•va•cious |və'vāsHəs; vī-| • *adj.* (esp. of a woman) attractively lively and animated.
DERIVATIVES: **vi•va•cious•ly** *adv.* **vi•va•cious•ness** *n.* **vi•vac•i•ty** |və'væsitē; vī-| *n.*

vi•va vo•ce |ˌvēvə 'vōcHā; ˌvīvə 'vōsē| • *adj.* (esp. of an examination) oral rather than written. • *adv.* orally rather than in writing. • *n.* (also **viva**) Brit. an oral examination, typically for an academic qualification.

viv•i•fy |'vivəˌfī| • *v.* (**-ies, -ied**) [trans.] enliven or animate: *outings vivify learning for children.*
DERIVATIVES: **viv•i•fi•ca•tion** |ˌvivəfi'kāsHən| *n.*

vi•vip•a•rous |vī'vip(ə)rəs; və-| • *adj.* (of an animal) bringing forth live young that have developed inside the body of the parent.
■ (of a plant) reproducing from buds that form plantlets while still attached to the parent plant, or from seeds that germinate within the fruit.
DERIVATIVES: **viv•i•par•i•ty** |ˌvivə'pærətē; ˌvīvə-; -'per-| *n.* **vi•vip•a•rous•ly** *adv.*

viv•i•sec•tion |ˌvivə'seksHən| • *n.* the practice of performing operations on live animals for the purpose of experimentation or scientific research (used chiefly by *antiviviesction-ists,* people who are opposed to such work).
■ ruthlessly sharp and detailed criticism or analysis: *the vivisection of America's seamy underbelly.*
DERIVATIVES: **viv•i•sect** *v.* **viv•i•sec•tor** *n.* **viv•i•sec•tion•ist** |-ist| *n. & adj.*

vix•en |'viksən| • *n.* a female fox.
■ a spiteful or quarrelsome woman.
DERIVATIVES: **vix•en•ish** *adj.*

viz. • *adv.* namely; in other words (used esp. to introduce a gloss or explanation): *the first music reproducing media, viz., the music box and the player piano.*

viz•ard |'vizərd| • *n.* a mask or disguise.

vi•zier |və'zir| • *n.* a high official in some Muslim countries, esp. in Turkey under Ottoman rule.
DERIVATIVES: **vi•zier•ate** |-'zirət; -'zirˌāt| *n.* **vi•zier•i•al** |-'zirēəl| *adj.* **vi•zier•ship** |-ˌsHip| *n.*

vo•ca•tion |vō'kāsHən| • *n.* a strong feeling of suitability for a particular career or occupation: *not all of us have a vocation to be nurses or doctors.*
■ a person's employment or main occupation, esp. regarded as particularly worthy and requiring great dedication: *her vocation as a poet.* ■ a trade or profession. Cf. AVOCATION.

voc•a•tive |'väkətiv| • *adj.* relating to or denoting a case of nouns, pronouns, and adjectives in Latin and other languages, used in addressing or invoking a person or thing.
• *n.* a word in the vocative case.
■ **(the vocative)** the vocative case.

vo•cif•er•ate |və'sifəˌrāt; vō-| • *v.* [intrans.] shout, complain, or argue loudly or vehemently: *he then began to vociferate pretty loudly* | [trans.] *he entered, vociferating curses.*
DERIVATIVES: **vo•cif•er•ant** |-rənt| *adj.* **vo•cif•er•a•tion** |-ˌsifə'rāsHən| *n.*

vo•cif•er•ous |və'sifərəs; vō-| • *adj.* (esp. of a person or speech) vehement or clamorous: *he was a vociferous opponent of the takeover.*
DERIVATIVES: **vo•cif•er•ous•ly** *adv.* **vo•cif•er•ous•ness** *n.*

vogue |vōg| • *n.* [usu. in sing.] the prevailing fashion or style at a particular time: *the vogue is to make realistic films.*
■ general acceptance or favor; popularity: *the 1920s and 30s, when art deco was much in vogue.* • *adj.* [attrib.] popular; fashionable: *"citizenship" was to be the government's vogue word.*
DERIVATIVES: **vogu•ish** *adj.*

voile |voil| • *n.* a thin, plain-weave, semitransparent fabric of cotton, wool, or silk.

vo•lant |'vōlənt| • *adj.* (of an animal) able to fly or glide: *newly volant young.*
■ of, relating to, or characterized by flight: *volant ways of life.* ■ [usu. postpositive] (in heraldry) represented as flying: *a falcon volant.*
■ moving rapidly or lightly: *her sails caught a volant wind.*

vol•a•tile |'välətl| • *adj.* **1** (of a substance) easily evaporated at normal temperatures. **2** liable to change rapidly and unpredictably, esp. for the worse: *the political situation was becoming more volatile.*
■ (of a person) liable to display rapid changes of emotion. ■ (of a computer's memory) retaining data only as long as there is a power supply connected. • *n.* (usu. **volatiles**) a volatile substance.
DERIVATIVES: **vol•a•til•i•ty** |ˌvälə'tilitē| *n.*

vol•can•ism |'välkəˌnizəm; 'vôl-| (also **vulcanism**) • *n.* volcanic activity or phenomena.

vol•i•tant |'välətənt| • *adj.* volant.

vo•li•tion |və'lisHən; vō-| • *n.* the faculty or power of using one's will: *without conscious volition she backed into her office.*
DERIVATIVES: **vo•li•tion•al** |-sHənl| *adj.* **vo•li•tion•al•ly** |-sHənl-ē| *adv.* **vol•i•tive** |'välətiv| *adj.*

vol•u•ble |'välyəbəl| • *adj.* speaking or spoken incessantly and fluently: *she was as voluble as her husband.*
DERIVATIVES: **vol•u•bil•i•ty** |ˌvälyə'bilitē| *n.* **vol•u•ble•ness** *n.* **vol•u•bly** |-blē| *adv.*

vo•lu•mi•nous |və'lo͞omənəs| • *adj.* occupying or containing much space; large in volume, in particular:
■ (of clothing or drapery) loose and ample. ■ (of writing) very lengthy and full. ■ (of a writer) producing many books.
DERIVATIVES: **vo•lu•mi•nous•ly** *adv.* **vo•lu•mi•nous•ness** *n.*

vol•un•ta•rism |'väləntəˌrizəm| • *n.* **1** the principle of relying on voluntary action (used

esp. with reference to the involvement of voluntary organizations in social welfare).
■ (esp. in the 19th century) the principle that churches or schools should be independent of the state and supported by voluntary contributions. **2** (in philosophy) the doctrine that the will is a fundamental or dominant factor in the individual or the universe.
DERIVATIVES: **vol·un·ta·rist** *n.* & *adj.* **vol·un·ta·ris·tic** *adj.*

vol·un·tar·y |'välən,terē| • *adj.* done, given, or acting of one's own free will: *we are funded by voluntary contributions.*
■ working, done, or maintained without payment: *a voluntary helper.* ■ supported by contributions rather than taxes or fees: *voluntary hospitals.* ■ under the conscious control of the brain. ■ (of a legal conveyance or disposition) made without return in money or other consideration. • *n.* (pl. **-ies**) an organ solo played before, during, or after a church service.
■ a piece of music performed extempore, esp. as a prelude to other music, or composed in a free style.
DERIVATIVES: **vol·un·tar·i·ly** |,välən'terəlē; 'välən,ter-| *adv.* **vol·un·tar·i·ness** *n.*

vol·un·teer·ism |,välən'tir,izəm| • *n.* the use or involvement of volunteer labor, esp. in community services; voluntarism.

vo·lup·tu·ous |və'ləpCHəwəs| • *adj.* of, relating to, or characterized by luxury or sensual pleasure: *long curtains in voluptuous crimson velvet.*
■ (of a woman) curvaceous and sexually attractive.
DERIVATIVES: **vo·lup·tu·ous·ly** *adv.* **vo·lup·tu·ous·ness** *n.*

vo·lute |və'lōōt| • *n.* **1** a spiral scroll characteristic of Ionic capitals and also used in Corinthian and composite capitals. **2** a deepwater marine mollusk (family Volutidae) with a thick spiral shell that is colorful and prized by collectors. • *adj.* forming a spiral curve or curves: *spoked wheels with outside volute springs.*
DERIVATIVES: **vo·lut·ed** *adj.*

vo·lu·tion |və'lōōSHən| • *n.* **1** a rolling or revolving motion. **2** a single turn of a spiral or coil.

vo·ra·cious |və'rāSHəs| • *adj.* wanting or devouring great quantities of food: *he had a voracious appetite.*
■ having a very eager approach to an activity: *his voracious reading of literature.*
DERIVATIVES: **vo·ra·cious·ly** *adv.* **vo·ra·cious·ness** *n.* **vo·rac·i·ty** |-'ræsitē| *n.*

vor·tex |'vôr,teks| • *n.* (pl. **vortexes** or **vortices** |'vôrtə,sēz|) a mass of whirling fluid or air, esp. a whirlpool or whirlwind.
■ something regarded as a whirling mass: *the vortex of existence.*
DERIVATIVES: **vor·ti·cal** |'vôrtikəl| *adj.* **vor·ti·cal·ly** |'vôrtik(ə)lē| *adv.* **vor·tic·i·ty** |vôr'tisitē| *n.* **vor·ti·cose** |'vôrtə,kōs| *adj.* **vor·tic·u·lar** |vôr'tikyələr| *adj.*

vo·ta·ry |'vōtərē| • *n.* (pl. **-ies**) a person, such as a monk or nun, who has made vows of dedication to religious service.

■ a devoted follower, adherent, or advocate of someone or something: *he was a votary of Keats.*
DERIVATIVES: **vo·ta·rist** |-rist| *n.*

vo·tive |'vōtiv| • *adj.* offered or consecrated in fulfillment of a vow: *votive offerings.* • *n.* an object offered in this way, such as a candle used as a vigil light.

vouch·er |'vowCHər| • *n.* a small printed piece of paper that entitles the holder to a discount or that may be exchanged for goods or services.
■ a receipt.

vouch·safe |vowCH'sāf; 'vowCH,sāf| • *v.* [with two objs.] (often **be vouchsafed**) give or grant (something) to (someone) in a gracious or condescending manner: *it is a blessing vouchsafed him by heaven.*
■ [trans.] reveal or disclose (information): *you never vouchsafed that interesting tidbit before.*

vous·soir |vōō'swär| • *n.* a wedge-shaped or tapered stone used to construct an arch.

vox po·pu·li |'väks 'päpyə,lī; -,lē| • *n.* [in sing.] the opinions or beliefs of the majority.
■ popular opinion; general attitudes.

vo·ya·geur |,vwäyə'zHər; ,voi-ə-| • *n.* (in Canada and the northern US) a woodsman employed by fur companies in transporting goods and passengers to and from trading posts on the lakes and rivers.

vo·yeur |voi'yər; vwä-| • *n.* a person who gains sexual pleasure from watching others when they are naked or engaged in sexual activity.
■ a person who enjoys seeing the pain or distress of others.
DERIVATIVES: **vo·yeur·ism** |'voiyə,rizəm; voi'yər,izəm; vwä'yər-| *n.* **voy·eur·is·tic** |,voiyə'ristik; ,vwäyə-| *adj.* **voy·eur·is·ti·cal·ly** |,voiyə'ristik(ə)lē; ,vwäyə-| *adv.*

vul·can·ize |'vəlkə,nīz| • *v.* [trans.] harden (rubber or rubberlike material) by treating it with sulfur at a high temperature.
DERIVATIVES: **vul·can·iz·a·ble** *adj.* **vul·can·i·za·tion** |,vəlkənə'zāSHən| *n.* **vul·can·iz·er** *n.*

vul·gar |'vəlgər| • *adj.* lacking sophistication or good taste; unrefined: *the vulgar trappings of wealth.*
■ making explicit and offensive reference to sex or bodily functions; coarse and rude: *a vulgar joke.* ■ characteristic of or belonging to the masses.
DERIVATIVES: **vul·gar·i·ty** |,vəl'gæritē; -'ger-| *n.* (pl. **-ies**) **vul·gar·ly** *adv.*

vul·gar·i·an |,vəl'gerēən| • *n.* an unrefined person, esp. one with newly acquired power or wealth.

vul·gar·ism |'vəlgə,rizəm| • *n.* a word or expression that is considered inelegant, esp. one that makes explicit and offensive reference to sex or bodily functions.
■ an instance of rude or offensive behavior.

Vul·gate |'vəl,gāt; -gət| • *n.* **1** the principal Latin version of the Bible, prepared mainly by St. Jerome in the late 4th century, and (as revised in 1592) adopted as the official text for the Roman Catholic Church. **2** (**vulgate**) [in sing.] common or colloquial speech: *I required a new, formal language in which to address him, not the vulgate.* **2** (**vulgate**) the traditionally accepted text of any author.

vul•pine | ˈvəlˌpīn | • *adj.* of or relating to a fox or foxes: *the vulpine habit of retreating to their dens.*

■ crafty; cunning: *Karl gave a vulpine smile.*

vul•va | ˈvəlvə | • *n.* the female external genitals.

■ the external opening of the vagina or reproductive tract in a female mammal or nematode.

DERIVATIVES: **vul•val** *adj.* **vul•var** *adj.*

Ww

wa•di | ˈwädē | • *n.* (pl. **wadis** |-ēz| or **wadies** |-ēz|) (in certain Arabic-speaking countries) a valley, ravine, or channel that is dry except in the rainy season.

waft | wäft; wæft | • *v.* pass or cause to pass easily or gently through or as if through the air: [no obj., with adverbial of direction] *the smell of stale fat wafted out from the café* | [with obj. and adverbial of direction] *each breeze would waft pollen around the house.* • *n.* a gentle movement of air.

■ a scent or odor carried on such a movement of air.

Wag•ne•ri•an | vägˈnerēən | • *adj.* of, relating to, or characteristic of the operas of German composer Richard Wagner (1813–83).

■ having the enormous dramatic scale and intensity of a Wagner opera: *a strategic predicament of positively Wagnerian proportions.* ■ (of a woman) large-bosomed and imposing, as a soprano in a Wagner opera is said typically to be. • *n.* an admirer of Wagner or his music.

wag•on-lit | ˈvägôN ˈlē | • *n.* (pl. **wagons-lits** pronunc. same) a sleeping car on a European train.

waif | wāf | • *n.* **1** a homeless and helpless person, esp. a neglected or abandoned child: *she is foster-mother to various waifs and strays.*

■ an abandoned pet animal. **2** a piece of property thrown away by a fleeing thief and held by the state in trust for the owner to claim.

DERIVATIVES: **waif•ish** *adj.*

waive | wāv | • *v.* [trans.] refrain from insisting on or using (a right or claim); relinquish: *he will waive all rights to the money.*

■ refrain from applying or enforcing (a rule, restriction, or fee): *her tuition fees would be waived.*

USAGE: **Waive**, meaning 'surrender,' and the related noun, **waiver**, should not be confused with **wave**, 'a back-and-forth or up-and-down motion,' or with **waver**, 'to go back and forth, vacillate': *He waived potential rights in the case by signing the waiver*; *She waved the papers at her friends across the room*; *Just as we were all ready to go, he wavered and said he wasn't sure whether he should go.*

waiv•er | ˈwāvər | • *n.* an act or instance of waiving a right or claim.

■ a document recording such waiving of a right or claim.

wal•low | ˈwälō | • *v.* [intrans.] **1** (chiefly of large mammals) roll about or lie relaxed in mud or water, esp. to keep cool, avoid biting insects, or spread scent: *watering places where buffalo liked to wallow.*

■ (of a boat or aircraft) roll from side to side: *the small jet wallowed in the sky.* **2** (**wallow in**) (of a person) indulge in an unrestrained way in (something that creates a pleasurable sensation): *I was wallowing in the luxury of the hotel* | *he had been wallowing in self-pity.* • *n.* **1** an act of wallowing: *a wallow in nostalgia.* **2** an area of mud or shallow water where mammals go to wallow, typically developing into a depression in the ground over long use.

DERIVATIVES: **wal•low•er** *n.*

wam•pum | ˈwämpəm | • *n.* a quantity of small cylindrical beads made by North American Indians from quahog shells, strung together and worn as a decorative belt or other decoration or used as money.

wan | wän | • *adj.* (of a person's complexion or appearance) pale and giving the impression of illness or exhaustion: *she was looking wan and bleary-eyed.*

■ (of light) pale; weak: *the wan dawn light.* ■ (of a smile) weak; strained. ■ (of the sea) without luster; dark and gloomy.

DERIVATIVES: **wan•ly** *adv.* **wan•ness** *n.*

wane | wān | • *v.* [intrans.] (of the moon between full and new) have a progressively smaller part of its visible surface illuminated, so that it appears to decrease in size.

■ (esp. of a condition or feeling) decrease in vigor, power, or extent; become weaker: *confidence in the dollar waned.*

PHRASES: **on the wane** becoming weaker, less vigorous, or less extensive: *the epidemic was on the wane.*

wan•na•be | ˈwänəbē; ˈwô- | • *n.* a person who tries to be like someone else or to fit in with a particular group of people: *a star-struck wannabe.*

wan•ton | ˈwäntn | • *adj.* **1** (of a cruel or violent action) deliberate and unprovoked: *sheer wanton vandalism.* **2** (esp. of a woman) sexually immodest or promiscuous.

growing profusely; luxuriant: *where wanton ivy twines.* ■ lively; playful: *a wanton fawn.* • *n.* a sexually immodest or promiscuous woman. • *v.* [intrans.] archaic **1** play; frolic. **2** behave in a sexually immodest or promiscuous way.

DERIVATIVES: **wan•ton•ly** *adv.* **wan•ton•ness** *n.*

war•lock |'wôr,läk| • *n.* a man who practices witchcraft; a sorcerer.

warp |wôrp| • *v.* **1** become or cause to become bent or twisted out of shape, typically as a result of the effects of heat or dampness: [intrans.] *wood has a tendency to warp* | [trans.] *moisture had warped the box.*
■ [trans.] cause to become abnormal or strange; have a distorting effect on: *your judgment has been warped by your obvious dislike of him* | [as adj.] (**warped**) *a warped sense of humor.* **2** [with obj. and adverbial of direction] move (a boat) along by hauling on a rope attached to a stationary object on shore.
■ [no obj., with adverbial of direction] (of a boat) move in such a way. **3** [trans.] (in weaving) arrange (yarn) so as to form the warp of a piece of cloth. **4** [trans.] cover (land) with a deposit of alluvial soil by natural or artificial flooding. • *n.* **1** a twist or distortion in the shape or form of something: *the head of the racket had a curious warp.*
■ an abnormality or perversion in a person's character. ■ [as adj.] relating to or denoting (fictional or hypothetical) space travel by means of distorting space-time: *the craft possessed warp drive* | *warp speed.* **2** [in sing.] (in weaving) the threads on a loom over and under which other threads (the weft) are passed to make cloth: *the warp and weft are the basic constituents of all textiles.*
■ (**warp and weft**) the basic structure, or essence, of something: *rugby is woven into the warp and weft of South African society.* **3** a rope attached at one end to a fixed point and used for moving or mooring a boat. **4** alluvial sediment; silt.

DERIVATIVES: **warp•age** |'wôrpij| *n.* (in sense 1 of the verb). **warp•er** *n.* (in sense 3 of the verb).

war•rant |'wôrənt; 'wä-| • *n.* **1** a document issued by a legal or government official authorizing the police or some other body to make an arrest, search premises, or carry out some other action relating to the administration of justice: *magistrates issued a warrant for his arrest* | *an extradition warrant.*
■ a document that entitles the holder to receive goods, money, or services: *we'll issue you a travel warrant.* ■ a negotiable security allowing the holder to buy shares at a specified price at or before some future date. ■ [usu. with negative] justification or authority for an action, belief, or feeling: *there is* **no warrant** *for this assumption.* **2** an official certificate of appointment issued to an officer of lower rank than a commissioned officer. • *v.* [trans.] justify or necessitate (a certain course of action): *that offense is serious enough to warrant a court marshal.*

■ officially affirm or guarantee: *the vendor warrants the accuracy of the report.*

DERIVATIVES: **war•rant•er** *n.*

war•ran•ty |'wôrəntē; 'wä-| • *n.* (pl. **-ies**) a written guarantee, issued to the purchaser of an article by its manufacturer, promising to repair or replace it if necessary within a specified period of time: *the car comes with a three-year warranty* | *as your machine is under warranty, I suggest getting it checked.*
■ (in contract law) a promise that something in furtherance of the contract is guaranteed by one of the contractors, esp. the seller's promise that the thing being sold is as promised or represented. ■ (in an insurance contract) an engagement by the insured party that certain statements are true or that certain conditions shall be fulfilled, the breach of it invalidating the policy. ■ (in property law) a covenant by which the seller and his or her heirs are bound to secure to the buyer the estate conveyed in the deed. ■ (in contract law) a term or promise in a contract, breach of which entitles the innocent party to damages but not to treat the contract as discharged by breach. ■ [usu. with negative] justification or grounds for an action or belief: *you have no warranty for such an audacious doctrine.*

USAGE: See **usage** at GUARANTEE.

war•y |'werē| • *adj.* (**warier, wariest**) feeling or showing caution about possible dangers or problems: *dogs that have been mistreated often remain very* **wary** *of strangers* | *a wary look.*

DERIVATIVES: **war•i•ly** |-rəlē| *adv.* **war•i•ness** *n.*

Wasp |wäsp| (also **WASP**) • *n.* an upper- or middle-class American white Protestant, considered to be a member of the most powerful group in society.

DERIVATIVES: **Wasp•ish** *adj.* **Wasp•y** *adj.*

wasp•ish |'wäspiSH| • *adj.* readily expressing anger or irritation: *he had a waspish tongue.*

DERIVATIVES: **wasp•ish•ly** *adv.* **wasp•ish•ness** *n.*

was•sail |'wäsəl; -,sāl| • *n.* spiced ale or mulled wine drunk during celebrations for Twelfth Night and Christmas Eve.
■ lively and noisy festivities involving the drinking of plentiful amounts of alcohol; revelry. • *v.* **1** [intrans.] drink plentiful amounts of alcohol and enjoy oneself with others in a noisy, lively way. **2** go from house to house at Christmas singing carols: *here we go a-wassailing.*

DERIVATIVES: **was•sail•er** *n.*

was•trel |'wāstrəl| • *n.* **1** a wasteful or good-for-nothing person. **2** a waif; a neglected child.

wa•ter•shed |'wôtər,SHed; 'wä-| • *n.* a height of land that separates waters flowing to different rivers, basins, or seas.
■ an area or region drained by a river, river system, or other body of water. ■ an event or period marking a turning point in a course of action or state of affairs: *these works mark a watershed in the history of music.*

wax • v. [intrans.] (of the moon between new and full) have a progressively larger part of its visible surface illuminated, increasing its apparent size.

■ become larger or stronger: *his anger waxed.*
■ [with complement] begin to speak or write about something in the specified manner: *they* **waxed lyrical** *about the old days.*
PHRASES: **wax and wane** undergo alternate increases and decreases: *companies whose fortunes wax and wane with the economic cycle.*

way•far•er | 'wā,ferər | • n. a person who travels on foot.
DERIVATIVES: **way•far•ing** n. and adj.

way•lay | 'wā,lā | • v. (past and past part. **waylaid** | -,lād |) [trans.] stop or interrupt (someone) and detain them in conversation or trouble them in some other way: *he waylaid me on the stairs.*
■ lie in wait and ambush (someone).
DERIVATIVES: **way•lay•er** n.

way•ward | 'wāwərd | • adj. difficult to control or predict because of unusual or perverse behavior: *her wayward, difficult sister* | *his wayward emotions.*
DERIVATIVES: **way•ward•ly** adv. **way•ward•ness** n.

weal[1] | wēl | (also **wheal**) • n. a red, swollen mark left on flesh by a blow or pressure.
■ an area of the skin that is temporarily raised, typically reddened, and usually accompanied by itching.

weal[2] • n. that which is best for someone or something: *I am holding this trial behind closed doors in the public weal.*

wean | wēn | • v. [trans.] accustom (an infant or other young mammal) to food other than its mother's milk.
■ accustom (someone) to managing without something on which they have become dependent or of which they have become excessively fond: *the doctor tried to* **wean** *her off the sleeping pills.* ■ (**be weaned on**) be strongly influenced by (something), esp. from an early age: *I was weaned on a regular diet of Hollywood fantasy.*

weed•y | 'wēdē | • adj. (**weedier, weediest**) 2 (of a person) thin and physically weak in appearance.
DERIVATIVES: **weed•i•ness** n.

weft | weft | (also **woof**) • n. [in sing.] (in weaving) the crosswise threads on a loom over and under which other threads (the warp) are passed to make cloth.

weir | wir | • n. a low dam built across a river to raise the level of water upstream or regulate its flow.
■ an enclosure of stakes set in a stream as a trap for fish.

weird | wird | • adj. suggesting something supernatural; uncanny: *the weird crying of a seal.*
■ very strange; bizarre: *a weird coincidence* | *all sorts of* **weird** *and* **wonderful** *characters.*
■ connected with fate. • v. [trans.] (**weird someone out**) induce a sense of disbelief or alienation in someone.
DERIVATIVES: **weird•ly** adv. **weird•ness** n.

wen | wen | • n. a boil or other swelling or growth on the skin, esp. a sebaceous cyst.
■ an outstandingly large or overcrowded city: *the great wen of London.*

wend | wend | • v. [no obj., with adverbial] (**wend one's way**) go in a specified direction, typically slowly or by an indirect route: *they wended their way across the city.*

were•wolf | 'wer,wŏŏlf | • n. (pl. **werewolves** | -,wŏŏlvz |) (in myth or fiction) a person who changes for periods of time into a wolf, typically when there is a full moon. See also LYCANTHROPY.

west | west | • n. (usu. **the West**) Europe and its culture seen in contrast to other civilizations.
■ (usu. **the West**) the non-Communist states of Europe and North America, contrasted with the former Communist states of eastern Europe. ■ (usu. **the West**) the western part of the United States, esp. the states from the Great Plains to the Pacific.

west•er•ly | 'westərlē | • adj. & adv. (of a wind) blowing from the west: [as adj.] *a stiff westerly breeze.* • n. (often **westerlies**) a wind blowing from the west.
■ (**westerlies**) the belt of prevailing westerly winds in medium latitudes, esp. well developed in the southern hemisphere.

whee•dle | '(h)wēdl | • v. [intrans.] employ endearments or flattery to persuade someone to do something or give one something: *you can contrive to* **wheedle your way** *into the job.* | [with direct speech] *"Please, for my sake," he wheedled.*
■ [trans.] (**wheedle someone into doing something**) coax or persuade someone to do something. ■ [trans.] (**wheedle something out of**) coax or persuade (someone) to say or give something.
DERIVATIVES: **whee•dler** n. **whee•dling•ly** adv.

whelm | (h)welm | archaic • v. [trans.] engulf, submerge, or bury (someone or something): *a swimmer whelmed in a raging storm.*
■ [no obj., with adverbial of direction] flow or heap up abundantly: *the brook whelmed up from its source.* • n. an act or instance of flowing or heaping up abundantly; a surge: *the whelm of the tide.*

whelp | (h)welp | • n. a puppy.
■ a cub. ■ a boy or young man (often as a disparaging form of address). • v. [trans.] (of a female dog) give birth to (a puppy): *Copper whelped seven puppies* | [intrans.] *a bitch due to whelp.*
PHRASES: **in whelp** (of a female dog) pregnant.

wher•ry | '(h)werē | • n. (pl. **-ies**) a light rowing boat used chiefly for carrying passengers.
■ Brit. a large light barge.
DERIVATIVES: **wher•ry•man** | '(h)werēmən | n. (pl. **-men**)

whet | (h)wet | • v. (**whetted, whetting**) [trans.] sharpen the blade of (a tool or weapon): *he's whetting his knife in preparation for the Thanksgiving turkey.*
■ excite or stimulate (someone's desire, inter-

est, or appetite): *here's a sample chapter to whet your appetite.* • *n.* a thing that stimulates appetite or desire: *he swallowed his two dozen oysters as a whet.*

DERIVATIVES: **whet•ter** *n.* (rare).

whey |(h)wā| • *n.* the watery part of milk that remains after the formation of curds.

Whig |(h)wig| • *n.* **1** a member of the British reforming and constitutional party that sought the supremacy of Parliament and was eventually succeeded in the 19th century by the Liberal Party. **2** an American colonist who supported the American Revolution.

■ a member of an American political party in the 19th century, succeeded by the Republicans. **3** a 17th-century Scottish Presbyterian. **4** [as adj.] denoting a historian who interprets history as the continuing and inevitable victory of progress over reaction.

DERIVATIVES: **Whig•ger•y** |-ərē| *n.* **Whig•gish** *adj.* **Whig•gism** |-,izəm| *n.*

whi•lom |'(h)wīləm| archaic • *adv.* formerly; in the past: *the wistful eyes which whilom glanced down upon the fields.* • *adj.* former; erstwhile: *a whilom circus acrobat.*

whim•si•cal |'(h)wimzikəl| • *adj.* **1** playfully quaint or fanciful, esp. in an appealing and amusing way: *a whimsical sense of humor.* **2** acting or behaving in a capricious manner: *the whimsical arbitrariness of autocracy.*

DERIVATIVES: **whim•si•cal•i•ty** |,(h)wim-zi'kælɪte| *n.* **whim•si•cal•ly** |-ik(ə)lē| *adv.*

whim•sy |'(h)wimzē| (also **whimsey**) • *n.* (pl. **-ies** or **-eys**) playfully quaint or fanciful behavior or humor: *the film is an awkward blend of whimsy and moralizing.*

■ a whim. ■ a thing that is fanciful or odd: *the stone carvings and whimsies.*

whinge |(h)winj| Brit. • *v.* (**whingeing**) [intrans.] complain persistently and in a peevish or irritating way: *stop whingeing and get on with it!* • *n.* an act of complaining in such a way.

DERIVATIVES: **whinge•ing•ly** *adv.* **whing•er** *n.* **whing•y** |-jē| *adj.*

whip•per•snap•per |'(h)wipər,snæpər| • *n.* a young and inexperienced person considered to be presumptuous or overconfident.

whirl•i•gig |'(h)wərlē,gig| • *n.* **1** a toy that spins around, for example a top or windmill.

■ a merry-go-round. **2** [in sing.] a thing regarded as hectic or constantly changing: *the whirligig of time.*

whis•key |'(h)wiskē| • *n.* (pl. **whiskeys**) (also **whisky** (pl. **-ies**)) a spirit distilled from malted grain, esp. barley or rye.

USAGE: Note that the British and Canadian spelling is without the *e*, so that properly one would write of *Scotch whisky* or *Canadian whisky,* but *Kentucky bourbon whiskey.*

white lie • *n.* a harmless or trivial lie, esp. one told to avoid hurting someone's feelings.

white noise • *n.* (in physics) noise containing many frequencies with equal intensities.

■ artificially produced sound designed to block out other noises, thus allowing sleep, concentration on work, etc.

white•out • *n.* **1** a blizzard, esp. in polar regions.

■ a weather condition in which the features and horizon of snow-covered country are indistinguishable due to uniform light diffusion. **2** a loss of color vision due to rapid acceleration, often before a loss of consciousness.

white tie • *n.* a white bow tie worn by men as part of full evening dress.

■ full evening dress with a white bow tie: *he was wearing immaculate white tie and tails.* Cf. BLACK TIE. • *adj.* (of an event) requiring full evening dress to be worn, including a white bow tie.

who•lism |'hōlizəm| • *n.* variant spelling of HOLISM.

DERIVATIVES: **who•lis•tic** *adj.* **who•lis•ti•cal•ly** *adv.*

whorl |(h)wôrl| • *n.* a coil or ring, in particular:

■ each of the turns or convolutions in the shell of a gastropod or ammonoid mollusk. ■ a set of leaves, flowers, or branches springing from the stem at the same level and encircling it. ■ (in a flower) each of the sets of organs, esp. the petals and sepals, arranged concentrically around the receptacle. ■ a complete circle in a fingerprint. • *v.* [intrans.] spiral or move in a twisted and convoluted fashion: *the dances are kinetic kaleidoscopes where steps whorl into wildness.*

DERIVATIVES: **whorled** *adj.*

Wic•ca |'wikə| • *n.* the religious cult of modern witchcraft, esp. an initiatory tradition founded in England in the mid 20th century and claiming its origins in pre-Christian pagan religions.

DERIVATIVES: **Wic•can** *adj.* & *n.*

wid•der•shins |'widər,sHinz| (also **withershins**) • *adv.* chiefly Scottish in a direction contrary to the sun's course, considered as unlucky; counterclockwise.

widg•et |'wijit| • *n.* a small gadget or mechanical device, esp. one whose name is unknown or unspecified.

■ (in computing) a component of a user interface that operates in a particular way.

wield•y |'wēldē| • *adj.* (**wieldier, wieldiest**) easily controlled or handled: *the overloaded SUV is far from wieldy.*

wild•cat |'wīld,kæt| • *adj.* [attrib.] (of a strike) sudden and unofficial; not called by labor leadership: *legislation to curb wildcat strikes.*

■ commercially unsound or risky. • *v.* [intrans.] prospect for oil.

wild•cat•ter |'wīld,kæṭər| • *n.* a prospector who sinks exploratory oil wells.

■ a risky investor.

wild•ing[1] |'wīldiNG| • *n.* the activity by a gang of youths of going on a protracted and violent rampage in a public place, attacking at random.

wild•ing[2] (also **wildling** |-liNG|) • *n.* a wild plant, esp. an apple tree descended from cultivated varieties, or its fruit.

wile |wīl| • *n.* (**wiles**) devious or cunning stratagems employed in manipulating or

persuading someone to do what one wants.
• *v.* [trans.] **1** lure; entice: *she could be neither driven nor wiled into the parish kirk.* **2** (**wile away the time**) another way of saying **while away (pass) the time.**

will•ful |'wilfəl| (also **wilful**) • *adj.* (of an immoral or illegal act or omission) intentional; deliberate: *willful acts of damage.*
■ having or showing a stubborn and determined intention to do as one wants, regardless of the consequences or effects: *the peevish, willful side of him.*
DERIVATIVES: **will•ful•ly** |'wilfəlē| *adv.* **will•ful•ness** |'wilfəlnəs| *n.*

wil•li•waw |'wilē,wô| • *n.* a sudden violent squall blowing offshore from a mountainous coast.

will-o'-the-wisp |'wil ə ᴛнə 'wisp| • *n.* an **ignis fatuus.**
■ a person or thing that is difficult or impossible to find, reach, understan, or catch.

wil•low•y |'wilōē| • *adj.* (of a person) tall, slim, and lithe.

wil•y |'wīlē| • *adj.* (**wilier, wiliest**) skilled at gaining an advantage, esp. deceitfully; employing wiles: *his wily opponents.*
DERIVATIVES: **wil•i•ly** |'wīləlē| *adv.* **wil•i•ness** *n.*

wimp |wimp| • *n.* a weak and cowardly or unadventurous person. • *v.* [intrans.] (**wimp out**) withdraw from a course of action or a stated position in a way that is seen as feeble or cowardly.
DERIVATIVES: **wimp•ish** *adj.* **wimp•ish•ly** *adv.* **wimp•ish•ness** *n.* **wimp•y** *adj.*

wim•ple |'wimpəl| • *n.* a cloth headdress covering the head, the neck, and the sides of the face, formerly worn by women and still worn by some nuns.
DERIVATIVES: **wim•pled** *adj.*

wind•fall |'wind,fôl| • *n.* an apple or other fruit blown down from a tree or bush by the wind.
■ a piece of unexpected good fortune, typically one that involves receiving a large amount of money: [as adj.] *windfall profits.*

win•di•go |'windi,gō| (also **wendigo**) • *n.* (pl. **-os** or **-oes**) (in the folklore of northern Algonquian peoples) a cannibalistic giant; a person who has been transformed into a monster by the consumption of human flesh.

wind•ward |'windwərd| • *adj.* & *adv.* facing the wind or on the side facing the wind: [as adj.] *the windward side of the boat.* Cf. LEEWARD.
• *n.* the side or direction from which the wind is blowing: *the ships drifted west, leaving the island quite a distance to windward.*
PHRASES: **to windward of** in an advantageous position in relation to: *I happen to have got to windward of the young woman.*

win•now |'winō| • *v.* **1** [trans.] blow a current of air through (grain) in order to remove the chaff.
■ remove (chaff) from grain: *women winnow the chaff from piles of unhusked rice.* ■ reduce the number in a set of (people or things) gradually until only the best ones are left: *the contenders had been winnowed to five.* ■ find or

identify (a valuable or useful part of something): *among these confusing signals, it's difficult to winnow out the truth.* ■ identify and remove (the least valuable or useful people or things): *guidelines that would help winnow out those not fit to be soldiers.* **2** [intrans.] (of the wind) blow: *the autumn wind winnowing its way through the grass.*
■ [trans.] (of a bird) fan (the air) with wings.
DERIVATIVES: **win•now•er** *n.*

win•some |'winsəm| • *adj.* attractive or appealing in appearance or character: *a winsome smile.*
DERIVATIVES: **win•some•ly** *adv.* **win•some•ness** *n.*

wise•a•cre |'wīz,ākər| • *n.* a person with an affectation of wisdom or knowledge, regarded with scorn or irritation by others; a know-it-all; a wise guy.

wis•en•heim•er |'wīzən,hīmər| • *n.* a person who behaves in an irritatingly smug or arrogant fashion, typically by making clever remarks and displaying his or her knowledge.

wist•ful |'wistfəl| • *adj.* having or showing a feeling of vague or regretful longing: *a wistful smile.*
DERIVATIVES: **wist•ful•ly** *adv.* **wist•ful•ness** *n.*

witch-hunt • *n.* a search for and subsequent persecution of a supposed witch.
■ a campaign directed against a person or group holding unorthodox or unpopular views.
DERIVATIVES: **witch-hunt•ing** *n.*

with•ers |'wiᴛнərz| • *plural n.* the highest part of a horse's back, lying at the base of the neck above the shoulders. The height of a horse is measured to the withers.

with•y |'wiᴛнē; 'wiᴛнē| (also **withe** |wiᴛн; wiᴛн; wīᴛн|) • *n.* (pl. **withies** or **withes**) a tough flexible branch of an osier or other willow, used for tying, binding, or basketry.

wit•less |'witlis| • *adj.* foolish; stupid: *a witless retort.*
■ [as complement] to such an extent that one cannot think clearly or rationally: *I was scared witless.*
DERIVATIVES: **wit•less•ly** *adv.* **wit•less•ness** *n.*

wit•ti•cism |'witi,sizəm| • *n.* a witty remark.

wiz•ard |'wizərd| • *n.* **1** a man who has magical powers, esp. in legends and fairy tales.
■ a person who is very skilled in a particular field or activity: *a financial wizard.* **2** (in computing) a help feature of a software package that automates complex tasks by asking the user a series of easy-to-answer questions.
• *adj.* Brit. wonderful; excellent.
DERIVATIVES: **wiz•ard•ly** *adj.* (in sense 1 of the noun).

wiz•ard•ry |'wizərdrē| • *n.* the art or practice of magic: *Merlin used his powers of wizardry for good.*
■ great skill in a particular area of activity: *his wizardry with leftovers.* ■ the product of such skill: *the car is full of hi-tech wizardry.*

wiz•ened |'wizənd; 'wē-| • *adj.* shriveled or wrinkled with age: *a wizened, weather-beaten old man.*

woe•be•gone |'wōbi,gôn; -,gän| • *adj.* sad or miserable in appearance: *don't look so woebegone, Joanna.*

wonk |wäNGk| • *n.* a studious or hardworking person: *any kid with an interest in science was a wonk.*

■ a person who takes an excessive interest in minor details of political policy: *he is a **policy wonk** in tune with a younger generation of voters.*

wont |wônt; wōnt| • *adj.* [predic., with infinitive] (of a person) in the habit of doing something; accustomed: *he was wont to arise at 5:30 every morning.* • *n.* (**one's wont**) one's customary behavior in a particular situation: *Constance, as was her wont, had paid her little attention.*

woof |wŏŏf; wōŏf| • *n.* another term for WEFT.

wool•gath•er•ing • *n.* indulgence in aimless thought or dreamy imagining; absentmindedness: *he wanted to be free to indulge his woolgathering.*

DERIVATIVES: **wool•gath•er** *v.*

work•fare |'wərk,fer| • *n.* a welfare system that requires those receiving benefits to perform some work or to participate in job training.

world•ling |'wərldliNG| • *n.* a cosmopolitan and sophisticated person.

world•ly |'wərldlē| • *adj.* (**worldlier, worldliest**) of or concerned with material values or ordinary life rather than a spiritual existence: *ambitions for worldly success.*

■ (of a person) experienced and sophisticated. PHRASES: **worldly goods** (or **possessions** or **wealth**) everything that one owns. DERIVATIVES: **world•li•ness** *n.*

worm•wood |'wərm,wŏŏd| • *n.* **1** a woody shrub (genus *Artemisia*)with a bitter aromatic taste, formerly used as an ingredient of vermouth and absinthe and in medicine. **2** a state or source of bitterness or grief.

wrack |ræk| • *v.* variant spelling of RACK.

wraith |rāTH| • *n.* a ghost or ghostlike image of someone, esp. one seen shortly before or after their death.

■ a pale, thin, or insubstantial person or thing: *heart attacks had reduced his mother to a wraith.* ■ a wisp or faint trace of something: *a sea breeze was sending a gray **wraith of** smoke up the slopes.*

DERIVATIVES: **wraith•like** |-,līk| *adj.*

wrath |ræTH| • *n.* extreme anger: *he hid his pipe for fear of incurring his father's wrath.*

wreak |rēk| • *v.* [trans.] cause (a large amount of damage or harm): *torrential rainstorms **wreaked havoc** yesterday* | *the environmental damage wreaked by ninety years of phosphate mining.*

■ inflict (vengeance): *he was determined to **wreak** his revenge **on** the girl who had rejected him.* ■ avenge (someone who has been

wronged): *grant me some knight to wreak me for my son.*

DERIVATIVES: **wreak•er** *n.*

USAGE: In the phrase **wrought havoc,** as in *they **wrought havoc** on the countryside,* **wrought** is an archaic past tense of **work** and also an archaic past participle of **work** (as in *wrought iron*). It is not, as is sometimes assumed, a past tense of **wreak.**

wrest |rest| • *v.* [trans.] forcibly pull (something) from a person's grasp: *Leila tried to wrest her arm from his hold.*

■ take (something, esp. power or control) from someone or something else after considerable effort or difficulty: *they wanted to allow people to wrest control of their lives from impersonal bureaucracies.* ■ distort the meaning or interpretation of (something) to suit one's own interests or views: *you appear convinced of my guilt, and wrest every reply I have made.* • *n.* a key for tuning a harp or piano.

wright |rīt| • *n.* a maker or builder.

writ[1] |rit| • *n.* a form of written command in the name of a court or other legal authority to act, or abstain from acting, in some way.

■ (**one's writ**) one's power to enforce compliance or submission; one's authority: *you have business here which is out of my writ and competence.*

writ[2] • *v.* archaic past participle of **write.**

PHRASES: **writ large** clear and obvious: *the unspoken question writ large upon Rose's face.* ■ in a stark or exaggerated form: *bribing people by way of tax allowances is the paternalistic state writ large.*

writhe |rīTH| • *v.* [intrans.] make continual twisting, squirming movements or contortions of the body: *he writhed in agony on the ground.*

■ [trans.] cause to move in such a way: *a snake writhing its body in a sinuous movement.* ■ (**writhe in/with/at**) respond with great emotional or physical discomfort to (a violent or unpleasant feeling or thought): *she bit her lip, writhing in suppressed fury.* • *n.* a twisting, squirming movement.

wroth |rôTH| • *adj.* intensely angry; incensed.

wry |rī| • *adj.* (**wryer, wryest** or **wrier, wriest**) **1** using or expressing dry, esp. mocking, humor: *a wry smile* | *wry comments.* **2** (of a person's face or features) twisted into an expression of disgust, disappointment, or annoyance.

■ (of the neck or features) distorted or turned to one side: *a remedy for wry necks.*

DERIVATIVES: **wry•ly** *adv.* **wry•ness** *n.*

wun•der•kind |'wŏŏndər,kind,| • *n.* (pl. **wunderkinds** or **wunderkinder**) a person who achieves great success relatively young.

wuss |wŏŏs| • *n.* a weak or ineffectual person (often used as a general term of abuse).

DERIVATIVES: **wuss•y** |-sē| *n.* (pl. **-ies**) & *adj.*

Xx

Xan•thip•pe |zæn'tipē; -'THipē| (also **Xan-tippe** |-'tipē|) (5th century BC), wife of Socrates. Her allegedly bad-tempered behavior toward her husband made her proverbial as a shrew.
■ a shrewish, scolding, or ill-tempered woman or wife.

xen•o•pho•bi•a |‚zēnə'fōbēə; ‚zenə-| • n. intense or irrational dislike or fear of people from other countries: *racism and xenophobia are steadily growing in Europe.*
DERIVATIVES: **xen•o•phobe** |'zēnə‚fōb; 'zenə-| n. **xen•o•pho•bic** |-'fōbik| adj.

xe•ric |'zirik; 'zer-| • adj. (of an environment or habitat) containing little moisture; very dry.

xe•rog•ra•phy |zi'rägrəfē| • n. a dry copying process in which black or colored powder adheres to parts of a surface remaining electrically charged after being exposed to light from an image of the document to be copied.
DERIVATIVES: **xe•ro•graph•ic** |‚zirə'græfik| adj. **xe•ro•graph•i•cal•ly** |‚zirə'græfik(ə)lē| adv.

xe•ro•phyte |'zirə‚fīt| • n. a plant that needs very little water. Cf. SUCCULENT.
DERIVATIVES: **xe•ro•phyt•ic** |‚zirəfitik| adj.

Xe•rox |'zir‚äks; 'zē‚räks| • n. trademark a xerographic copying process.
■ a copy made using such a process. ■ a machine for copying by xerography. • v. (**xerox**) [trans.] copy (a document) by such a process.

xy•lem |'zīləm| • n. the vascular tissue in plants that conducts water and dissolved nutrients upward from the root and also helps to form the woody element in the stem. Cf. PHLOEM.

Yy

ya•hoo |'yä‚hoo; yä'hoo| • n. a rude, noisy, or violent person.
■ a boorish, xenophobic person.

yam•mer |'yæmər| • n. loud and sustained or repetitive noise: *the yammer of their animated conversation* | *the yammer of enemy fire.* • v. [intrans.] make a loud repetitive noise.
■ talk volubly.
DERIVATIVES: **yam•mer•er** n.

yang |yæNG; yäNG| • n. (in Chinese philosophy) the active male principle of the universe, characterized as male and creative and associated with heaven, heat, and light. Cf. YIN.

yare |yer; yär| • adj. (of a ship) moving lightly and easily; easily manageable.

yar•mul•ke |'yämə(l)kə| (also **yarmulka**) • n. a skullcap worn in public by Orthodox Jewish men or during prayer by other Jewish men.

yaw |yô| • v. [intrans.] (of a moving ship or aircraft) twist or oscillate about a vertical axis: [with adverbial of direction] *the jet yawed sharply to the right.* • n. a twisting or oscillation of a moving ship or aircraft about a vertical axis.

yawl |yôl| • n. a two-masted fore-and-aft-rigged sailboat with the mizzenmast stepped far aft so that its boom overhangs the stern. Cf. KETCH.

y•clept |i'klept| • adj. [predic.] by the name of: *a lady yclept Eleanora.*

year•ling |'yirliNG| • n. an animal (esp. a sheep, calf, or foal) a year old, or in its second year.
■ a racehorse in the calendar year after the year it was born.

yegg |yeg| • n. a burglar or safecracker.

yel•low dog • n. a contemptible or cowardly person or thing. • 1 adj. (of a party-line voter, esp. a Democrat) inclined to support any candidate affiliated with one's chosen party, regardless of the candidate's personal qualities or political qualifications: *a self-proclaimed yellow-dog Democrat.* 2 (of a labor contract) in which a worker agrees, in order to obtain the job, to leave or not join a union.

yen informal • n. [in sing.] a longing or yearning: [with infinitive] *she always had a yen to be a writer.* • v. (**yenned, yenning**) [intrans.] feel a longing or yearning: *it's no use yenning for the old simplicities.*

yen•ta |'yentə| • n. 1 a woman who is a gossip or busybody. 2 a vulgar person.

yeo•man |'yōmən| • n. (pl. **-men**) 1 a man holding and cultivating a small landed estate; a freeholder.
■ a person qualified for certain duties and rights, such as to serve on juries and vote for local officials, by virtue of possessing free land of a specified value. 2 a servant in a royal or noble household, ranking between a sergeant and a groom or a squire and a page. 3 a petty officer in the US Navy performing clerical duties on board ship.
PHRASES: **yeoman service** efficient or useful help in time of need. **a yeoman job** a solid piece of work.
DERIVATIVES: **yeo•man•ly** adj.

yeo•man•ry |'yōmənrē| • n. [treated as sing. or pl.] a group of men who held and cultivated small landed estates.

■ (in Britain) a volunteer cavalry force raised from such a group (1794–1908).

yet•i |ˈyetē; ˈyātē| • *n.* a large hairy creature resembling a human or bear, said to live in the highest part of the Himalayas; abominable snowman.

yin |yin| • *n.* (in Chinese philosophy) the passive female principle of the universe, characterized as female and sustaining and associated with earth, dark, and cold. Cf. YANG.

yo•ga |ˈyōgə| • *n.* a Hindu spiritual and ascetic discipline, a part of which, including breath control, simple meditation, and the adoption of specific bodily postures, is widely practiced for health and relaxation.
DERIVATIVES: **yo•gic** |-gik| *adj.*

yo•gi |ˈyōgē| • *n.* (pl. **yogis**) a person who is proficient in yoga.

yoke |yōk| • *n.* **1** a wooden crosspiece that is fastened over the necks of two animals and attached to the plow or cart that they are to pull.
■ (pl. same or **yokes**) a pair of animals coupled together in such a way: *a yoke of oxen.* ■ the amount of land that one pair of oxen could plow in a day. ■ a frame fitting over the neck and shoulders of a person, used for carrying pails or baskets. ■ used of something that is regarded as oppressive or burdensome: *the yoke of imperialism.* ■ used of something that represents a bond between two parties: *the yoke of marriage.* **2** something resembling or likened to such a crosspiece, in particular: ■ a part of a garment that fits over the shoulders and to which the main part of the garment is attached, typically in gathers or pleats. ■ the crossbar of a rudder, to whose ends ropes are fastened. ■ a bar of soft iron between the poles of an electromagnet. ■ (in ancient Rome) an arch of three spears under which a defeated army was made to march. ■ a control lever in an aircraft. • *v.* [trans.] put a yoke on (a pair of animals); couple or attach with or to a yoke, or in a similar manner: *a plow drawn by a camel and donkey yoked together* | *Hong Kong's dollar has been yoked to America's.*

yup•pie |ˈyəpē| (also **yuppy**) • *n.* (pl. **-ies**) a well-paid young middle-class professional who has a relatively luxurious lifestyle.
DERIVATIVES: **yup•pie•dom** |-dəm| *n.*

yup•pi•fy |ˈyəpə,fī| • *v.* (**-ies, -ied**) [trans.] make more affluent and upmarket in keeping with the taste and lifestyle of yuppies: *Williamsburg is slowly being yuppified with tony little eating places.*
DERIVATIVES: **yup•pi•fi•ca•tion** |,yəpəfiˈkāSHən| *n.*

Zz

zaf•tig |ˈzäftig; -tik| (also **zoftig**) • *adj.* (of a woman) having a full, rounded figure; plump.

za•ny |ˈzānē| • *adj.* (**zanier, zaniest**) amusingly unconventional and idiosyncratic: *zany humor.* • *n.* an erratic or eccentric person: ■ formerly, a comic performer partnering a clown, whom he imitated in an amusing way.
DERIVATIVES: **za•ni•ly** |-nəlē| *adv.* **za•ni•ness** *n.*

zeal•ot |ˈzelət| • *n.* a person who is fanatical and uncompromising in pursuit of religious, political, or other ideals.
■ (**Zealot**) a member of an ancient Jewish sect aiming at a Jewish theocracy and resisting the Romans until AD 70.
DERIVATIVES: **zeal•ot•ry** |-ətrē| *n.*

zed |zed| • *n.* Brit. the letter Z.

zeit•geist |ˈtsīt,gīst; ˈzīt-| • *n.* [in sing.] the defining spirit or mood of a particular period of history as shown by the ideas and beliefs of the time: *the story captured the zeitgeist of the late 1960s.*

Zen |zen| (also **Zen Buddhism**) • *n.* a Japanese school of Buddhism emphasizing the value of meditation and intuition.

Zen Buddhism was introduced to Japan from China in the 12th century and has had a profound cultural influence. It has many correspondences with Taoism. The aim of Zen is to achieve sudden enlightenment (satori), esp. through meditation in a seated posture (zazen), usually under the guidance of a teacher and often using paradoxical statements (koans) to transcend rational thought.

DERIVATIVES: **Zen Bud•dhist** *n.*

ze•nith |ˈzēniTH| • *n.* [in sing.] the highest point reached by a celestial or other object: *the sun was well past the zenith* | *the missile reached its zenith and fell.*
■ the point in the sky or celestial sphere directly above an observer. The opposite of NADIR. ■ the time at which something is most powerful or successful: *under Justinian, the Byzantine Empire reached its zenith of influence.*
DERIVATIVES: **ze•nith•al** |-nəTHəl| *adj.*

zeph•yr |ˈzefər| • *n.* a soft gentle breeze.

ze•ro-sum • *adj.* [attrib.] (of a game or situation) in which whatever is gained by one side is lost by the other.

zeug•ma |ˈzoōgmə| • *n.* a figure of speech in which a word applies to two others in different senses (e.g., *John and his license expired last week*) or to two others of which it semantically suits only one (e.g., *with weeping eyes and hearts*). Cf. SYLLEPSIS.
DERIVATIVES: **zeug•mat•ic** |zoōgˈmætik| *adj.*

zig•gu•rat |'zigə,ræt| • *n.* (in ancient Mesopotamia) a rectangular stepped tower, sometimes surmounted by a temple. Ziggurats are first attested in the late 3rd millennium BC and probably inspired the biblical story of the Tower of Babel (Gen. 11:1–9).

zing•er |'ziNGər| • *n.* a striking or amusing remark: *open a speech with a zinger.*
■ an outstanding person or thing: *a zinger of a shot.*

Zi•on•ism |'zīə,nizəm| • *n.* a movement for (originally in 1897) the reestablishment and (now) the development and protection of a Jewish nation in what is now Israel.
DERIVATIVES: **Zi•on•ist** *n.* & *adj.*

zo•di•ac |'zōdē,æk| • *n.* a belt of the heavens within about 8° either side of the ecliptic, including all apparent positions of the sun, moon, and most familiar planets. It is divided into twelve equal divisions or signs (Aries, Taurus, Gemini, Cancer, Leo, Virgo, Libra, Scorpio, Sagittarius, Capricorn, Aquarius, Pisces).
■ a representation of the signs of the zodiac or of a similar astrological system.

The supposed significance of the movements of the sun, moon, and planets within the zodiacal band forms the basis of astrology. However, the modern constellations do not represent equal divisions of the zodiac, and the ecliptic now passes through a thirteenth (Ophiuchus). Also, owing to precession, the signs of the zodiac now roughly correspond to the constellations that bear the names of the *preceding* signs.

DERIVATIVES: **zo•di•a•cal** |zō'dīəkəl| *adj.*

zom•bie |'zämbē| • *n.* **1** a snake-deity of or deriving from West Africa and Haiti. **2** a soulless corpse said to be revived by witchcraft, esp. in certain African and Caribbean religions.
■ a person who is or appears lifeless, apathetic, or completely unresponsive to his or her surroundings.
DERIVATIVES: **zom•bie•like** |-,līk| *adj.*

zo•o•mor•phic |,zōə'môrfik| • *adj.* having or representing animal forms or gods of animal form: *pottery decorated with anthropomorphic and zoomorphic designs.*
DERIVATIVES: **zo•o•mor•phism** |-'môr ,fizəm| *n.*

zo•o•phyte |'zōə,fīt| • *n.* a plantlike animal, esp. a coral, sea anemone, sponge, or sea lily.

zuc•chet•to |(t)soo'ketō; zoo-| • *n.* (pl. **-os**) a Roman Catholic cleric's skullcap: black for a priest, purple for a bishop, red for a cardinal, and white for the pope.

zy•de•co |'zīdə,kō| • *n.* a kind of black American dance music originally from southern Louisiana, typically featuring accordion and guitar.

zy•mur•gy |'zī,mərjē| • *n.* the study or practice of fermentation in brewing, winemaking, or distilling.